Beginning Java 2

Ivor Horton

Wrox Press Ltd. ®

Beginning Java 2

Published by Wrox Press Ltd,
Arden House, 1102 Warwick Road, Acocks Green,
Birmingham, B27 6BH, UK
Printed in the United States
ISBN 1-861005-69-5

Trademark Acknowledgements

Wrox has endeavored to provide trademark information about all the companies and products mentioned in this book by the appropriate use of capitals. However, Wrox cannot guarantee the accuracy of this information.

Credits

Author
Ivor Horton

Technical Editors
Mankee Cheng
Shivanand Nadkarni
Girish Sharangpani
Roberts Shaw
Andrew Tracey

Commissioning Editors
Louay Fatoohi
Chanoch Wiggers

Index
John Collins
Andrew Criddle

Project Manager
Emma Batch

Proof Readers
Lisa Stephenson
Fiona Berryman
Agnes Wiggers
Keith Westmooreland

Technical Reviewers
Steve Baker
Robert Chang
Phil Powers De George
Justin Foley
David Hudson
Jim MacIntosh
Craig McQueen
Karen Ritchie
Gavin Smyth
John Timney
David Whitney

Production Coordinator
Natalie O'Donnell

Illustrations
Pippa Wonson
Rachel Taylor

Cover Design
Chris Morris

Cover photograph by John Wright Photography, Warwick

A Note from the Author

In all my *Beginning...* books, my objective is to minimize what, in my judgment, are the three main hurdles the aspiring programmer must face: getting to grips with the jargon that pervades every programming language and environment, understanding the *use* of the language elements (as opposed to what they are), and appreciating how the language is applied in a practical context.

Jargon is an invaluable and virtually indispensable means of communication for the competent amateur as well as the expert professional, so it can't be avoided. My approach is to ensure that the beginner understands what the jargon means and gets comfortable with using it in context. In that way, they can use the documentation that comes along with most programming products more effectively, and can also feel competent to read and learn from the literature that surrounds most programming languages.

Comprehending the syntax and effects of the language elements are obviously essential to learning a language, but I believe illustrating *how* the language features work and *how* they are used are equally important. Rather than just use code fragments, I always try to provide the reader with practical working examples that show the relationship of each language feature to specific problems. These can then be a basis for experimentation, to see at first hand the effects of changing the code in various ways.

The practical context needs to go beyond the mechanics of applying individual language elements. To help the beginner gain the competence and confidence to develop their own applications, I aim to provide them with an insight into how things work in combination and on a larger scale than a simple example with a few lines of code. That's why I like to have at least one working example that builds over several chapters. In that way it's possible to show something of the approach to managing code as well as how language features can be applied together.

Finally, I know the prospect of working through a book of doorstop proportions can be quite daunting. For that reason it's important for the beginner to realize three things that are true for most programming languages. First, there *is* a lot to it, but this means there will be a greater sense of satisfaction when you've succeeded. Second, it's great fun, so you really will enjoy it. Third, it's a lot easier than you think, so you positively *will* make it.

Ivor Horton

Table of Contents

Table of Contents

Table of Contents

Table of Contents

Table of Contents

Table of Contents

Introduction

Welcome

Welcome to the third edition of *Beginning Java 2*, a comprehensive and easy-to-use tutorial guide to learning the Java language and the Java 2 platform API. This book provides you with the essential know-how for developing programs using the SDK 1.3 or later.

In this book, as well as teaching you Java, we introduce you to the wide variety of topics that will be relevant to you as a Java programmer. We've structured the book so that you learn Java programming in a carefully designed and logical way, and at each stage you will be building on what you have learned at the previous stage.

Who is this Book For?

Java programming is a huge and rapidly expanding area. Since its release, the growth of Java as *the* object-oriented language of choice for Internet programming and teaching has been phenomenal. The Java 2 platform is a significant maturing in the level of support offered to you, especially for application development. It is the language of choice of many programmers for major application development, offering advantages in ease of development and maintenance compared to other languages, as well as built-in capability to run on a variety of computers and operating systems without code changes. With it you can do a lot more, more quickly, and more easily.

In this book we aim to provide you with a comprehensive understanding of the language, plus suitable experience of Java application contexts to give you a solid base in each of these core areas. Every aspect of Java that is covered in the book is illustrated by fully working program examples that you can and should create and run for yourself. With an understanding of the topics in this book, you can start to write fully featured and effective Java programs.

The word *Beginning* in the title refers more to the style of the book's teaching than to your skill level. It could equally well be called *Straight into Java,* because the tutorial structure is designed so that, whether you're a seasoned programmer from another language or a newcomer to programming in general, this book takes you straight to your floor.

We assume, as a minimum, that you know something about programming, in that you understand at least the fundamental concepts of how programs work. However, you don't need to have significant prior programming experience to use the book successfully. The pace of the book is fairly rapid, but without stinting on any of the necessary explanations of how Java works.

What's Covered in this Book

The book aims to teach you Java programming following a logical format:

❑ First, it covers some of the main terms and concepts that underpin programming in Java. Without these we'll get nowhere fast.

❑ Second, it provides you with a clear explanation of the features of the Java language – the basic data types, the control structures that manipulate data, the object-oriented features of the language, the way runtime errors are handled, and how threads are used. The book doesn't just explain what the language elements do, but also how you can apply them in practice.

❑ Third, it gives you an extensive introduction to the key packages in the Java class library – amongst others, the `io`, `nio`, `util`, `awt`, `awt.event`, `applet`, `javax.swing`, and `javax.xml` packages are all covered and illustrated with full working examples. These packages cover file handling, helper objects, Graphical User Interfaces, Applets, and XML.

❑ Fourth, it guides you through the process of building a substantial application, `Sketcher`, in which you apply the Java language capabilities and the Java class library in a realistic context. Our sketching application will have menus, toolbars, and a status panel, as well as the ability to draw and manipulate a number of elements, handle text, print, and save sketches – including saving sketches in XML. This will give you a much better understanding of how you apply Java in practical projects of your own, something that's hard to appreciate from any number of more trivial examples.

❑ Lastly, it shows how you can use the various tools that come with the JDK 1.3.

As we progress through these topics, we introduce you to the theory, and then illustrate it with an appropriate example and a clear explanation. You can learn quickly on a first read, and look back over things to brush up on all the essential elements when you need to. The small examples in each chapter are designed mainly to illustrate a class and its methods, or some new piece of theory in action. They focus specifically on showing you how the particular language feature or method works.

To get the most from the chapters, we strongly recommend that you try out the examples as you read. Type them in yourself, even if you have downloaded the example source code. It really does make a difference. The examples also provide a good base for experimentation and will hopefully inspire you to create programs of your own. It's important to try things out – you will learn as much (if not more) from your mistakes as you will from the things that work first time.

The source code for all of the example programs in the book is available at http://www.wrox.com.

What You Need to Use this Book

This book has been tested against the SDK 1.4 release code so you should ideally be using SDK 1.4 or later. Other requirements for most of the chapters are fairly minimal: a copy of a text editor and a command line window from which to run the Java tools. Details of the requirements for the book and how to acquire and install them are provided in Chapter 1.

Conventions

To help you get the most from the text and keep track of what's happening, we've used a number of conventions throughout the book.

For instance, when discussing code, we have two conventions:

> *Background is used to hold asides on programming code.*

while:

> **These boxes hold important, not-to-be-forgotten information which is directly relevant to the surrounding text.**

When we introduce important words, we **highlight** them. We show keyboard strokes as *Ctrl-A*.

The command line and terminal output is shown as:

```
C:\> java ShowStyle
When the command line is shown - this will be for you to enter - it's in the above
style, whereas terminal output is in this style.
```

while text for windowed applications, such as on buttons, is shown as OK and Cancel. Filenames are shown as MyFile.java.

We present code in four different ways. Firstly, variables, Java keywords, methods, and classes are referenced in the text using a code style.

Definitions of Java methods and structures are shown in definition boxes. For example:

```
if(life==aimless) {
  DoSomething;          // Italics show that words should be replaced
  DoSomethingElse;      // with something more meaningful
}
```

```
Lastly in our code examples, the code foreground style shows new, important,
  pertinent code;
while code background shows code that's less important in the present context,
  or has been seen before.
```

We'll presage example code with a Try It Out, which is used to split the code up where that's helpful, to highlight the component parts and to show the progression of the application. When it's important, we also follow the code with a How It Works to explain any salient points of the code in relation to previous theory. We find these two conventions help break up the more formidable code listings into more palatable morsels.

Tell Us What You Think

We've worked hard to make this book as useful to you as possible, so we'd like to get a feel for what it is you want and need to know, and what you think about how we've presented things to you. The positive feedback we received about the first edition of this book has helped make this new and revised edition an even better book.

Return the reply card in the back of the book, and you'll register this copy of Beginning Java 2 with Wrox Press, and be put on our mailing list for information on the latest Wrox products.

If you've anything to say, let us know on:

feedback@wrox.com

or at:

http://www.wrox.com

Errata & Updates

We've made every effort to make sure there are no errors in the text or the code. However, to err is human and as such we recognize the need to keep you informed of any mistakes as they're spotted and amended.

While you're visiting our web site, please make use of our *Errata* page that's dedicated to fixing any small errors in the book or offering new ways around a problem and its solution. Errata sheets are available for all our books – please download them, or take part in the continuous improvement of our tutorials and upload a 'fix'.

p2p.wrox.com

This book introduces a totally comprehensive and unique support system. Wrox now has a commitment to supporting you not just while you read the book, but once you start developing applications as well. We provide you with a forum where you can put your questions to the authors, reviewers, and fellow industry professionals. You have the choice of how to receive this information; either you can enroll onto one of several mailing lists, or you can just browse the online forums and newsgroups for an answer.

Go to http://p2p.wrox.com. Here you'll find a link to the **Beg_Java** forum. If you find something wrong with this book, or you just think something has been badly explained or is misleading in some way, then leave your message here. You'll still receive our customary quick reply, but you'll also have the advantage that every author will be able to see your problem at once and help deal with it.

Enroll now; it's all part of our free support system. For more instructions on how to enroll, please see Appendix F at the back of this book.

Introducing Java

This chapter will give you an appreciation of what the Java language is all about. Understanding the details of what we'll discuss in this chapter is not important at this stage; you will see all of them again in greater depth in later chapters of the book. The intent of this chapter is to introduce you to the general ideas that underpin what we'll be covering through the rest of the book, as well as the major contexts in which Java programs can be used and the kind of program that is applicable in each context.

In this chapter you will learn:

- ❏   The basic characteristics of the Java language.
- ❏   How Java programs work on your computer.
- ❏   Why Java programs are portable between different computers.
- ❏   The basic ideas behind object-oriented programming.
- ❏   How a simple Java program looks and how you can run it using the Java Development Kit.
- ❏   What HTML is and how it is used to include a Java program in a web page.

What is Java All About?

Java is an innovative programming language that has become the language of choice for programs that need to run on a variety of different computer systems. First of all Java enables you to write small programs called **applets.** These are programs that you can embed in Internet web pages to provide some intelligence. Being able to embed executable code in a web page introduces a vast range of exciting possibilities. Instead of being a passive presentation of text and graphics, a web page can be interactive in any way that you want. You can include animations, games, interactive transaction processing – the possibilities are almost unlimited.

Of course, embedding program code in a web page creates special security requirements. As an Internet user accessing a page with embedded Java code, you need to be confident that it will not do anything that might interfere with the operation of your computer, or damage the data you have on your system. This implies that execution of the embedded code must be controlled in such a way that it will prevent accidental damage to your computer environment, as well as ensure that any Java code that was created with malicious intent is effectively inhibited. Java implicitly incorporates measures to minimize the possibility of such occurrences arising with a Java applet.

Java also allows you to write large-scale application programs that you can run unchanged on any computer with an operating system environment in which the language is supported. This applies to the majority of computers in use today. You can even write programs that will work both as ordinary applications and as applets.

Java has matured immensely in recent years, particularly with the introduction of Java 2. The breadth of function provided by the standard core Java has grown incredibly. Java provides you with comprehensive facilities for building application with an interactive GUI, extensive image processing and graphics programming facilities, as well as support for accessing relational databases and communicating with remote computers over a network. Release 1.4 of Java added a very important additional capability, the ability to read and write XML. Just about any kind of application can now be programmed effectively in Java, with the implicit plus of complete portability.

Features of the Java Language

The most important characteristic of Java is that it was designed from the outset to be machine independent. Java programs can run unchanged on any operating system that supports Java. Of course there is still the slim possibility of the odd glitch as you are ultimately dependent on the implementation of Java on any particular machine, but Java programs are intrinsically more portable than programs written in other languages. An application written in Java will only require a single set of sourcecode, regardless of the number of different computer platforms on which it is run. In any other programming language, the application will frequently require the sourcecode to be tailored to accommodate different computer environments, particularly if there is an extensive graphical user interface involved. Java offers substantial savings in time and resources in developing, supporting, and maintaining major applications on several different hardware platforms and operating systems.

Possibly the next most important characteristic of Java is that it is **object oriented**. The object-oriented approach to programming is also an implicit feature of all Java programs, so we will be looking at what this implies later in this chapter. Object-oriented programs are easier to understand, and less time-consuming to maintain and extend than programs that have been written without the benefit of using objects.

Not only is Java object oriented, but it also manages to avoid many of the difficulties and complications that are inherent in some other object-oriented languages, making it easy to learn and very straightforward to use. It lacks the traps and 'gotchas' that arise in some other programming languages. This makes the learning cycle shorter and you need less real-world coding experience to gain competence and confidence. It also makes Java code easier to test.

Java has a built-in ability to support national character sets. You can write Java programs as easily for Greece or Japan, as you can for English speaking countries always assuming you are familiar with the national languages involved, of course. You can even build programs from the outset to support several different national languages with automatic adaptation to the environment in which the code executes.

Learning Java

Java is not difficult, but there is a great deal to it. The language itself is fairly compact, but very powerful. To be able to program effectively in Java, however, you also need to understand the libraries that go with the language, and these are very extensive. In this book, the sequence in which you learn how the language works, and how you apply it, has been carefully structured so that you can gain expertise and confidence with programming in Java through a relatively easy and painless process. As far as possible, each chapter avoids the use of things you haven't learned about already. A consequence, though, is that you won't be writing Java applications with a graphical user interface right away. While it may be an appealing idea, this would be a bit like learning to swim by jumping in the pool at the deep end. Generally speaking, there is good evidence that by starting in the shallow end of the pool and learning how to float before you try to swim, the chance of drowning is minimized, and there is a high expectation that you will end up a competent swimmer.

Java Programs

As we have already noted, there are two kinds of programs you can write in Java. Programs that are to be embedded in a web page are called Java **applets**, and normal standalone programs are called Java **applications**. You can further subdivide Java applications into **console applications,** which only support character output to your computer screen (to the command line on a PC under Windows, for example), and **windowed Java applications** that can create and manage multiple windows. The latter use the typical graphical user interface (GUI) mechanisms of window-based programs – menus, toolbars, dialogs and so on.

While we are learning the Java language basics, we will be using console applications as examples to illustrate how things work. These are application that use simple command line input and output. With this approach we can concentrate on understanding the specifics of the language, without worrying about any of the complexity involved in creating and managing windows. Once we are comfortable with using all the features of the Java language, we'll move on to windowed applications and applet examples.

Learning Java – the Road Ahead

Before starting out, it is always helpful to have an idea of where you are heading and what route you should take, so let's take a look at a brief road map of where you will be going with Java. There are five broad stages you will progress through in learning Java using this book:

1. The first stage is this chapter. It sets out some fundamental ideas about the structure of Java programs and how they work. This includes such things as what object-oriented programming is all about, and how an executable program is created from a Java source file. Getting these concepts straight at the outset will make learning to write Java programs that much easier for you.

2. Next you will learn how statements are put together, what facilities you have for storing basic data in a program, how you perform calculations and how you make decisions based on the results of them. These are the nuts and bolts you need for the next stages.

3. In the third stage you will learn about **classes** – how you define them and how you can use them. This is where you learn the object-oriented characteristics of the language. By the time you are through this stage you will have learned all the basics of how the Java language works so you will be ready to progress further into how you can use it.

4. In the fourth stage, you will learn how you can segment the activities that your programs carry out into separate tasks that can execute concurrently. This is particularly important for when you want to include several applets in a web page, and you don't want one applet to have to wait for another to finish executing before it can start. You may want a fancy animation to continue running while you play a game, for example, with both programs sitting in the same web page.

5. In the fifth stage you will learn in detail how you implement an application or an applet with a graphical user interface, and how you handle interactions with the user in this context. This amounts to applying the capabilities provided by the Java class libraries. When you finish this stage you will be equipped to write your own fully-fledged applications and applets in Java. At the end of the book, you should be a knowledgeable Java programmer. The rest is down to experience.

Throughout this book we will be using complete examples to explore how Java works. You should create and run all of the examples, even the simplest, preferably by typing them in yourself. Don't be afraid to experiment with them. If there is anything you are not quite clear on, try changing an example around to see what happens, or better still – write an example of your own. If you are uncertain how some aspect of Java that you have already covered works, don't look it up right away – try it out. Making mistakes is a great way to learn.

The Java Environment

You can run Java programs on a wide variety of computers using a range of operating systems. Your Java programs will run just as well on a PC running Windows 95/98/NT/2000/XP as it will on Linux or a Sun Solaris workstation. This is possible because a Java program does not execute directly on your computer. It runs on a standardized hypothetical computer that is called the **Java virtual machine** or **JVM,** which is emulated inside your computer by a program.

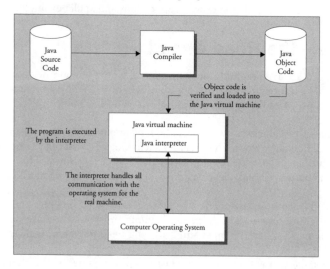

A **Java compiler** converts the Java sourcecode that you write into a binary program consisting of **byte codes**. Byte codes are machine instructions for the Java virtual machine. When you execute a Java program, a program called the **Java interpreter** inspects and deciphers the byte codes for it, checks it out to ensure that it has not been tampered with and is safe to execute, and then executes the actions that the byte codes specify within the Java virtual machine. A Java interpreter can run standalone, or it can be part of a web browser such as Netscape Navigator or Microsoft Internet Explorer where it can be invoked automatically to run applets in a web page.

Because your Java program consists of byte codes rather than native machine instructions, it is completely insulated from the particular hardware on which it is run. Any computer that has the Java environment implemented will handle your program as well as any other, and because the Java interpreter sits between your program and the physical machine, it can prevent unauthorized actions in the program from being executed.

In the past there has been a penalty for all this flexibility and protection in the speed of execution of your Java programs. An interpreted Java program would typically run at only one tenth of the speed of an equivalent program using native machine instructions. With present Java machine implementations, much of the performance penalty has been eliminated, and in programs that are not computation intensive – which is usually the case with the sort of program you would want to include in a web page, for example – you really wouldn't notice this anyway. With the JVM that is supplied with the current Java 2 System Development Kit (SDK) available from the Sun web site, there are very few circumstances where you will notice any appreciable degradation in performance compared to a program compiled to native machine code.

Java Program Development

There are a number of excellent professional Java program development environments available, including products from Sun, Borland and Symantec. These all provide very friendly environments for creating and editing your sourcecode, and compiling and debugging your programs. These are powerful tools for the experienced programmer, but for learning Java using this book, I recommend that you resist the temptation to use any of these, especially if you are relatively new to programming. Instead, stick to using the Java 2 SDK from Sun together with a suitable simple editor for creating your sourcecode. The professional development systems tend to hide a lot of things you need to understand, and also introduce complexity that you really are better off without while you are learning. These products are intended primarily for knowledgeable and experienced programmers, so start with one when you get to the end of the book.

You can download the SDK from Sun for a variety of hardware platforms and operating systems, either directly from the Sun Java web site at http://java.sun.com (for Windows, Solaris, and Linux operating systems), or from sites that you can link to from there. The SDK we are going to use is available from http://java.sun.com/j2se/1.4. For instance a version of the SDK for Mac OS is available from http://devworld.apple.com/java/.

There is one aspect of terminology that sometimes causes confusion – the SDK used to be known as the JDK – the Java Development kit. If you see JDK this generally means the same as SDK. When you install the Java 2 SDK, you will see the old terminology survives in the name of the root directory where the SDK is installed, currently /jdk1.4.

I would urge you to install the SDK even if you do use one or other of the interactive development environments that are available. The SDK provides an excellent reference environment that you can use to check out problems that may arise. Not only that, your programs will only consist of the code that you write plus the classes from the Java libraries that you use. Virtually all commercial Java development systems provide pre-built facilities of their own to speed development. While this is very helpful for production program development, it really does get in the way when you are trying to learn Java.

A further consideration is that the version of Java supported by a commercial Java product is not always the most recent. This means that some features of the latest version of Java just won't work. If you really do prefer to work with a commercial Java development system for whatever reason, and you have problems with running a particular example from the book, try it out with the SDK. The chances are it will work OK.

To make use of the SDK you will need a plain text editor. Any editor will do as long as it does not introduce formatting codes into the contents of a file. There are quite a number of shareware and freeware editors around that are suitable, some of which are specific to Java, and you should have no trouble locating one. I find the JCreator editor is particularly good. There's a free version and a fee version with more functionality but the free version is perfectly adequate for learning. You can download a free copy from `http://www.jcreator.com`. A good place to start looking if you want to explore what is available is the `http://www.download.com` web site.

Installing the SDK

You can obtain detailed instructions on how to install the SDK for your particular operating system from the Sun web site, so I won't go into all the variations for different systems here. However, there are a few things to watch out for that may not leap out from the pages of the installation documentation.

First of all, the SDK and the documentation are separate and you install them separately. The SDK for Windows is distributed as a `.exe` file that you just execute to start installation. The documentation for the SDK consists of a large number of HTML files structured in a hierarchy that are distributed in a ZIP archive. You will find it easier to install the SDK first, followed by the documentation. If you install the SDK to drive `C:` under Windows, the directory structure shown in the diagram will be created.

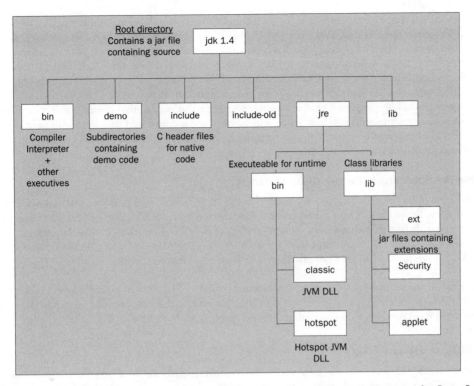

The jdk1.4 directory in the diagram is sometimes referred to as the **root directory** for Java. In some contexts it is also referred to as the **Java home directory**. If you want the documentation installed in the hierarchy shown above, then you should now extract the documentation from the archive to the jdk1.4 directory. This corresponds to C:\jdk1.4 if you installed the SDK to your C: drive. This will create a new subdirectory, docs, to the jdk1.4 root directory, and install the documentation files in that. To look at the documentation you just open the index.html file that is in the docs subdirectory.

You don't need to worry about the contents of most of these directories, at least not when you get started, but you should add the path for the jdk1.4\bin directory to the paths defined in your PATH environment variable. That way you will be able to run the compiler and the interpreter from anywhere without having to specify supplying the path to it. If you installed the SDK to C:, then you need to add the path C:\jdk1.4\bin. A word of warning – if you have previously installed a commercial Java development product, check that it has not modified your PATH environment variable to include the path to its own Java executables.

If it has, when you try to run the Java compiler or interpreter, you are likely to get the versions supplied with the commercial product rather that those that came with the SDK. One way to fix this is to remove the path or paths that cause the problem. If you don't want to remove the paths that were inserted for the commercial product, you will have to use the full path specification when you want to run the compiler or interpreter from the SDK. The jre directory contains the Java Runtime facilities that are used when you execute a Java program. The classes in the Java libraries are stored in the jre\lib directory. They don't appear individually though. They are all packaged up in the archive, rt.jar. Leave this alone. The Java Runtime takes care of retrieving what it needs from the archive when your program executes.

The CLASSPATH environment variable is a frequent source of problems and confusion to newcomers to Java. The current SDK does **NOT** require CLASSPATH to be defined, and if it has been defined by some other Java version or system, it is likely to cause problems. Commercial Java development systems and versions of the Java Development Kit prior to 1.2 may well define the CLASSPATH environment variable, so check to see whether CLASSPATH has been defined on your system. If it has and you no longer have whatever defined it installed, you should delete it. If you have to keep the CLASSPATH environment variable – maybe because you want to keep the system that defined it or you share the machine with someone who needs it – you will have to use a command line option to define CLASSPATH temporarily whenever you compile or execute your Java code. We will see how to do this a little later in this chapter.

Extracting the Sourcecode for the Class Libraries

The sourcecode for the class libraries is included in the archive `src.zip` that you will find in the `jdk1.4` root directory. Browsing this source can be very educational, and it can also be helpful when you are more experienced with Java in giving a better understanding of how things works – or when they don't, why they don't. You can extract the source files from the archive using the `Winzip` utility or any other utility that will unpack `.zip` archives – but be warned – there's a lot of it and it takes a while!

Extracting the contents of `src.zip` to the root directory `\jdk1.4` will create a new subdirectory, `src`, and install the sourcecode in subdirectories to this. To look at the sourcecode, just open the `.java` file that you are interested in, using any plain text editor.

Compiling a Java Program

Java sourcecode is always stored in files with the extension `.java`. Once you have created the sourcecode for a program and saved it in a `.java` file, you need to process the source using a Java compiler. Using the compiler that comes with the JDK, you would make the directory that contains your Java source file the current directory, and then enter the following command:

```
javac -source 1.4 MyProgram.java
```

Here, `javac` is the name of the Java compiler, and `MyProgram.java` is the name of the program source file. This command assumes that the current directory contains your source file. If it doesn't the compiler won't be able to find your source file. The `-source` command line option with the value `1.4` here tells the compiler that you want the code compiled with the SDK 1.4 language facilities. This causes the compiler to support a facility called **assertions**, and we will see what these are later on. If you leave this option out, the compiler will compile the code with SDK 1.3 capabilities so if the code uses assertions, these will be flagged as errors.

If you need to override an existing definition of the **CLASSPATH** environment variable – perhaps because it has been set by a Java development system you have installed, the command would be:

```
javac -source 1.4 -classpath . MyProgram.java
```

The value of **CLASSPATH** follows the **-classpath** specification and is just a period. This defines just the path to the current directory, whatever that happens to be. This means that the compiler will look for your source file or files in the current directory. If you forget to include the period, the compiler will not be able to find your source files in the current directory. If you include the **-classpath .** command line option in any event, it will do no harm.

Note that you should avoid storing your source files within the directory structure that was created for the SDK, as this can cause problems. Set up a separate directory of your own to hold the sourcecode for a program and keep the code for each program in its own directory.

Assuming your program contains no errors, the compiler generates a byte code program that is the equivalent of your source code. The compiler stores the byte code program in a file with the same name as the source file, but with the extension `.class`. Java executable modules are always stored in a file with the extension `.class`. By default, the `.class` file will be stored in the same directory as the source file.

The command line options we have introduced here are by no means all the options you have available for the compiler. You will be able to compile all of the examples in the book just knowing about the options we have discussed. There is a comprehensive description of all the options within the documentation for the SDK. You can also specify the **-help** command line option to get a summary of the standard options you can use.

If you are using some other product to develop your Java programs, you will probably be using a much more user-friendly, graphical interface for compiling your programs that won't involve entering commands such as that shown above. The file name extensions for your source file and the object file that results from it will be just the same however.

Executing a Java Application

To execute the byte code program in the `.class` file with the Java interpreter in the SDK, you make the directory containing the .class file current, and enter the command:

```
java -enableassertions MyProgram
```

Note that we use **MyProgram** to identify the program, *NOT* MyProgram.class. It is a common beginner's mistake to use the latter by analogy with the compile operation. If you put a `.class` file extension on MyProgram, your program won't execute and you will get an error message:

```
Exception in thread "main" java.lang.NoClassDefFoundError: MyProgram/class
```

While the compiler expects to find the name of your source file, the java interpreter expects the name of a class, which is **MyProgram** in this case, not the name of a file. The MyProgram.class file contains the **MyProgram** class. We will explain what a class is shortly.

The **-enableassertions** option is necessary for SDK1.4 programs that use assertions, but since we will be using assertions once we have learned about them it's a good idea to get into the habit of always using this option. You can abbreviate the **-enableassertions** option to **-ea** if you wish.

If you want to override an existing **CLASSPATH** definition, the option is the same as with the compiler. You can also abbreviate **-classpath** to **-cp** with the Java interpreter, but strangely, this abbreviation does not apply to the compiler. Here's how the command would look:

```
java -ea -cp . MyProgram
```

To execute your program, the Java interpreter analyzes and then executes the byte code instructions. The Java virtual machine is identical in all computer environments supporting Java, so you can be sure your program is completely portable. As we already said, your program will run just as well on a Unix Java implementation as it will on that for Windows 95/98/NT/2000/XP, for Solaris, Linux, OS/2, or any other operating system that supports Java. (Beware of variations in the level of Java supported though. Some environments, such as the Macintosh, tend to lag a little, so implementations for Java 2 will typically be available later than under Windows or Solaris.)

Executing an Applet

Note that the Java compiler in the SDK will compile both applications and applets. However, an applet is not executed in the same way as an application. You must embed an applet in a web page before it can be run. You can then execute it either within a Java 2-enabled web browser, or by using the `appletviewer`, a bare-bones browser provided as part of the SDK. It is a good idea to use the `appletviewer` to run applets while you are learning. This ensures that if your applet doesn't work, it is almost certainly your code that is the problem, rather than some problem in integration with the browser.

If you have compiled an applet and you have included it in a web page stored as `MyApplet.html` in the current directory on your computer, you can execute it by entering the command:

```
appletviewer MyApplet.html
```

So how do you put an applet in a web page?

The Hypertext Markup Language

The HyperText Markup Language, or **HTML** as it is commonly known, is used to define a web page. If you want a good, compact, reference guide to HTML, I recommend the book *Instant HTML Programmer's Reference* (Wrox Press, ISBN 1-861001-56-8). Here we will gather just enough on HTML so that you can run a Java applet.

When you define a web page as an HTML document, it is stored in a file with the extension `.html`. An HTML document consists of a number of elements, and each element is identified by **tags**. The document will begin with `<html>` and end with `</html>`. These delimiters, `<html>` and `</html>`, are tags, and each element in an HTML document will be enclosed between a similar pair of tags between angle brackets. All element tags are case insensitive, so you can use uppercase or lowercase, or even a mixture of the two, but by convention they are capitalized so they stand out from the text. Here is an example of an HTML document consisting of a title and some other text:

```
<html>
  <head>
    <title>This is the title of the document</title>
  </head>
  <body>
    You can put whatever text you like here. The body of a document can contain
    all kinds of other HTML elements, including <B>Java applets</B>. Note how each
    element always begins with a start tag identifying the element, and ends with
    an end tag that is the same as the start tag but with a slash added. The pair
    of tags around 'Java applets' in the previous sentence will display the text
    as bold.
```

```
    </body>
  </html>
```

There are two elements that can appear directly within the `<html>` element, a `<head>` element and a `<body>` element, as in the example above. The `<head>` element provides information about the document, and is not strictly part of it. The text enclosed by the `<title>` element tags that appears here within the `<head>` element, will be displayed as the window title when the page is viewed.

Other element tags can appear within the `<body>` element, and they include tags for headings, lists, tables, links to other pages and Java applets. There are some elements that do not require an end tag because they are considered to be empty. An example of this kind of element tag is `<hr/>`, which specifies a horizontal rule, a line across the full width of the page. You can use the `<hr/>` tag to divide up a page and separate one type of element from another. You will find a comprehensive list of available HTML tags in the book I mentioned earlier.

Adding an Applet to an HTML Document

For many element tag pairs, you can specify an **element attribute** in the starting tag that defines additional or qualifying data about the element. This is how a Java applet is identified in an `<applet>` tag. Here is an example of how you might include a Java applet in an HTML document:

```
<html>
  <head>
    <title> A Simple Program </title>
  </head>
  <body>
    <hr/>
    <applet code = "MyFirstApplet.class"  width = 300  height = 200 >
    </applet>
    <hr/>
  </body>
</html>
```

The two shaded lines between tags for horizontal lines specify that the byte codes for the applet are contained in the file `MyFirstApplet.class`. The name of the file containing the byte codes for the applet is specified as the value for the `code` attribute in the `<applet>` tag. The other two attributes, `width` and `height`, define the width and height of the region on the screen that will be used by the applet when it executes. These always have to be specified to run an applet. There are lots of other things you can optionally specify, as we will see. Here is the Java sourcecode for a simple applet:

```
import javax.swing.JApplet;
import java.awt.Graphics;

public class MyFirstApplet extends JApplet {

  public void paint(Graphics g) {
    g.drawString("To climb a ladder, start at the bottom rung", 20, 90);
  }
}
```

Note that Java is case sensitive. You can't enter `public` with a capital P – if you do the program won't compile. This applet will just display a message when you run it. The mechanics of how the message gets displayed are irrelevant here – the example is just to illustrate how an applet goes into an HTML page. If you compile this code and save the previous HTML page specification in the file `MyFirstApplet.html` in the same directory as the Java applet code, you can run the applet using `appletviewer` from the JDK with the command:

```
appletviewer MyFirstApplet.html
```

This will display a window something like that shown below:

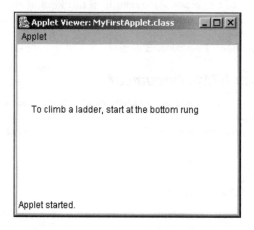

In this particular case, the window is produced under Windows 95/98/NT/2000. Under other operating systems it is likely to look a little different since Java 'takes on' the style of the platform on which it is running. Since the height and width of the window for the applet is specified in pixels, the physical dimensions of the window will depend on the resolution and size of your monitor.

This example won't work with Internet Explorer or Netscape Navigator as neither of these supports Java 2 directly. Let's see what can be done about that.

Making Applets Run in Any Browser

The key to making all your Java applets work with any browser is to make sure the Java 2 Plug-in is installed for each browser that views any of your web pages that contain applets. Making sure that each browser that runs your applet has a Java 2 Plug-in installed is not as hard as you might imagine because you can arrange for it to be automatically downloaded when required – assuming that the computer is online to the Web at the time of course.

The Java Plug-in is a module that can be integrated with Internet Explorer (version 4.0 or later) or Netscape Navigator (version 6.0 or later) to provide full support for Java 2 applets. It supports the use of the `<applet>` tag on any version of Windows from Windows 95 to Windows XP, as well as Linux and Unix.

To enable automatic download of the Java 2 Plug-in with your applets, you need to add some HTML to your web page that invokes a Visual Basic script that handles the download and installation process for the plug-in. To modify our HTML to do this we just need to add one extra tag:

```
<html>
 <head>
  <title> A Simple Program </title>
  <SCRIPT language="VBSCRIPT"
          src="http://java.sun.com/products/plugin/1.4/autodl/autodownload.vbs">
  </SCRIPT>
 </head>
 <body>
  <hr/>
   <applet code = "MyFirstApplet.class"  width = 300  height = 200 >
   </applet>
  <hr/>
 </body>
</html>
```

This makes use of a script that is downloaded from the Sun Java web site. If you want, you can download a copy of the script to your local machine and run it from there. In this case you will need to amend the URL for the src attribute in the <SCRIPT> to reflect where you have stored the .vbs file.

Object-Oriented Programming in Java

As we said at the beginning of this chapter, Java is an object-oriented language. When you use a programming language that is not object oriented, you must express the solution to every problem essentially in terms of numbers and characters – the basic kinds of data that you can manipulate in the language. In an object-oriented language like Java, things are different. Of course, you still have numbers and characters to work with – these are referred to as the **basic data types** – but you can define other kinds of entities that are relevant to your particular problem. You solve your problem in terms of the entities or objects that occur in the context of the problem. This not only affects how a program is structured, but also the terms in which the solution to your problem is expressed. If your problem concerns baseball players, your Java program is likely to have BaseballPlayer objects in it; if you are producing a program dealing with fruit production in California, it may well have objects that are Oranges in it. Apart from seeming to be inherently sensible, object-oriented programs are usually easier to understand.

In Java almost everything is an object. If you haven't delved into object-oriented programming before, or maybe because you have, you may feel this is a bit daunting. But fear not. Objects in Java are particularly easy. So easy, in fact, that we are going to start out by understanding some of the ideas behind Java objects right now. In that way you will be on the right track from the outset.

This doesn't mean we are going to jump in with all the precise nitty-gritty of Java that you need for describing and using objects. We are just going to get the concepts straight at this point. We will do this by taking a stroll through the basics using the odd bit of Java code where it helps the ideas along. All the code that we use here will be fully explained in later chapters. Concentrate on understanding the notion of objects first. Then we can ease into the specific practical details as we go along.

So What Are Objects?

Anything can be thought of as an object. Objects are all around you. You can consider `Tree` to be a particular class of objects: trees in general; although it is a rather abstract class as you would be hard pushed to find an actual occurrence of a totally generic tree. Hence the Oak tree in my yard which I call `myOak`, the Ash tree in your yard which you call `thatDarnedTree`, and a `generalSherman`, the well-known redwood, are actual instances of specific types of tree, subclasses of `Tree` that in this case happen to be `Oak`, `Ash`, and `Redwood`. Note how we drop into the jargon here – **class** is a term that describes a specification for a collection of objects with common properties.

A class is a specification, or template – expressed as a piece of program code – which defines what goes to make up a particular sort of object. A subclass is a class that inherits all the properties of the parent class, but that also includes extra specialization. Of course, you will define a class specification to fit what you want to do. There are no absolutes here. For my trivial problem, the specification of a `Tree` class might just consist of its species and its height. If you are an arboriculturalist, then your problem with trees may require a much more complex class, or more likely a set of classes, that involve a mass of arboreal characteristics.

Every object that your program will use will have a corresponding class definition somewhere for objects of that type. This is true in Java as well as in other object-oriented languages. The basic idea of a class in programming parallels that of classifying things in the real world. It is a convenient and well-defined way to group things together.

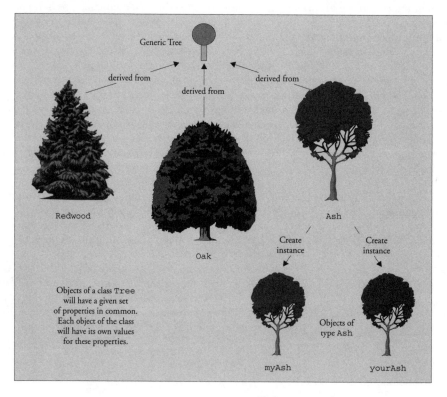

An **instance** of a class is a technical term for an existing object of that class. Ash is a specification for a type of object and yourAsh is an object constructed to that specification, so yourAsh would be an instance of the class Ash. Once you have a class defined, then you can come up with objects, or instances of that class. This raises the question of what differentiates an object of a given class, an Ash class object say, from a Redwood object. In other words, what sort of information defines a class?

What Defines a Class of Objects?

You may have already guessed the answer. A class definition lists all the parameters that you need to define an object of that particular class, at least, so far as your needs go. Someone else might choose a larger or smaller set of parameters to define the same sort of object – it all depends on what you want to do with the class. You will decide what aspects of the objects you need to include to define that particular class of object, and you will choose them depending on the kinds of problems that you want to address using the objects of the class. Let's think about a specific class of objects.

For a class Hat for example, you might use just two parameters in the definition. You could include the type of hat as a string of characters such as "Fedora" or "Baseball cap", and its size as a numeric value. These parameters that define an object of a class are referred to as **instance variables** or **attributes** of a class, or class **fields**. The instance variables can be basic types of data such as numbers, but they could also be other class objects. For example, the name of a Hat object could be of type String – the class String defines objects that are strings of characters.

Of course there are lots of other things you could include to define a Hat if you wanted to, color for instance, which might be another string of characters such as "Blue". To specify a class you just decide what set of attributes suit your needs, and those are what you use. This is called **data abstraction** in the parlance of the object-oriented aficionado, because you just abstract the attributes you want to use from the myriad possibilities for a typical object.

In Java the definition of the class Hat would look something like:

```
class Hat {
    // Stuff defining the class in detail goes here.
    // This could specify the name of the hat, the size,
    // maybe the color, and whatever else you felt was necessary.
}
```

The name of the class follows the word class, and the details of the definition appear between the curly braces.

> Because the word **class** has this special role in Java it is called a keyword, **and it is reserved for use only in this context. There are lots of other keywords in Java that you will pick up as we go along. You just need to remember that you must not use any of them for any other purposes.**

We won't go into the detail of how the class `Hat` is defined, since we don't need it at this point. The lines appearing between the braces above are not code; they are actually **program comments**, since they begin with two successive forwarded slashes. The compiler will ignore anything on a line that follows two successive forward slashes in your Java programs, so you will use this to add explanations to your programs. Generally the more useful comments you can add to your programs, the better. We will see in Chapter 2 that there are other ways you can write comments in Java.

Each object of your class will have a particular set of values defined that characterize that particular object. You could have an object of type `CowboyHat`, which might be defined by values such as `"Stetson"` for the name of the hat, `"White"` for the color, and the size as 7.

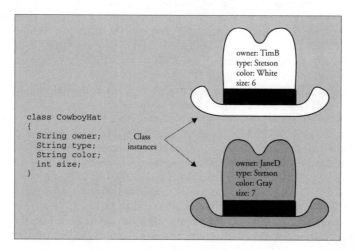

The parameters defining an object are not necessarily fixed values though. You would expect the `name` and `size` attributes for a particular `CowboyHat` object to stay fixed since hats don't usually change their size, but you could have other attributes. You might have `state` for example, which could indicate whether the hat was on or off the owner's head, or even `owner`, which would record the owner's name, so the value stored as the attribute `owner` could be changed when the hat was sold or otherwise transferred to someone else.

Operating on Objects

A class object is not just a collection of various items of data though. The fundamental difference between a class and the complex data types that you find in some other languages is that a class includes more than just data. A class specifies what you can do with an object of the class – that is, it defines the operations that are possible on objects of the class. Clearly for objects to be of any use in a program, you need to decide what you can do with them. This will depend on what sort of objects you are talking about, the attributes they contain, and how you intend to use them.

To take a very simple example, if your objects were numbers, of type `Integer` for example, it would be reasonable to plan for the usual arithmetic operations; add, subtract, multiply and divide, and probably a few others you can come up with. On the other hand it would not make sense to have operations for calculating the area of an `Integer`, boiling an `Integer` or for putting an `Integer` object on. There are lots of classes where these operations would make sense, but not those dealing with integers.

Coming back to our CowboyHat class, you might want to have operations that you could refer to as putHatOn and takeHatOff, which would have meanings that are fairly obvious from their names, and do make sense for CowboyHat objects. However, these operations would only be effective if a CowboyHat object also had another defining value that recorded whether it was on or off. Then these operations on a particular CowboyHat object could set this value for the object. To determine whether your CowboyHat was on or off, you would just need to look at this value. Conceivably you might also have an operation changeOwner by which you could set the instance variable recording the current owner's name to a new value. The illustration shows two operations applied in succession to a CowboyHat object.

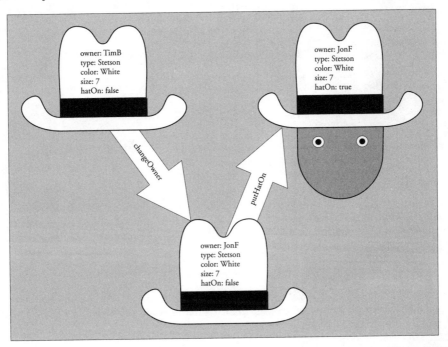

Of course, you can have any operation for each type of object that makes sense for you. If you want to have a shootHoleIn operation for Hat objects, that's no problem. You just have to define what that operation does to an object.

You are probably wondering at this point how an operation for a class is defined. As we shall see in detail a bit later, it boils down to a self-contained block of program code called a **method** that is identified by the name you give to it. You can pass data items – which can be integers, floating point numbers, character strings or class objects – to a method, and these will be processed by the code in the method. A method may also return a data item as a result. Performing an operation on an object amounts to 'executing' the method that defines that operation for the object.

> Of course, the only operations you can perform on an instance of a particular class are those defined within the class, so the usefulness and flexibility of a class is going to depend on the thought that you give to its definition. We will be looking into these considerations more in Chapter 5.

Let's take a look at an example of a complete class definition. The code for the class `CowboyHat` we have been talking about might look like the following:

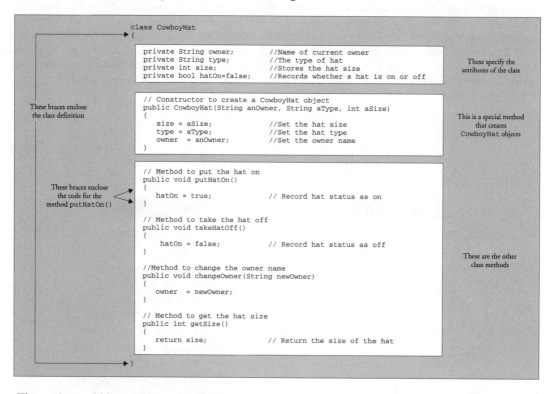

```
                              class CowboyHat
                              {
                                  private String owner;        //Name of current owner
                                  private String type;         //The type of hat
                                  private int size;            //Stores the hat size
                                  private bool hatOn=false;    //Records whether a hat is on or off

                                  // Constructor to create a CowboyHat object
                                  public CowboyHat(String anOwner, String aType, int aSize)
                                  {
                                      size = aSize;            //Set the hat size
                                      type = aType;            //Set the hat type
                                      owner = anOwner;         //Set the owner name
                                  }

                                  // Method to put the hat on
                                  public void putHatOn()
                                  {
                                      hatOn = true;            // Record hat status as on
                                  }

                                  // Method to take the hat off
                                  public void takeHatOff()
                                  {
                                      hatOn = false;           // Record hat status as off
                                  }

                                  //Method to change the owner name
                                  public void changeOwner(String newOwner)
                                  {
                                      owner = newOwner;
                                  }

                                  // Method to get the hat size
                                  public int getSize()
                                  {
                                      return size;             // Return the size of the hat
                                  }
                              }
```

These braces enclose the class definition

These braces enclose the code for the method putHatOn()

These specify the attributes of the class

This is a special method that creates CowboyHat objects

These are the other class methods

This code would be saved in a file with the name `CowboyHat.java`. The name of a file that contains the definition of a class is always the same as the class name, and the extension will be `.java` to identify that the file contains Java sourcecode.

The code for the class definition appears between the braces following the identification for the class, as shown in the illustration. The code for each of the methods in the class also appears between braces. The class has three instance variables, `owner`, `size`, and `hatOn`, and this last variable is always initialized as `false`. Each object that is created according to this class specification will have its own independent copy of each of these variables, so each object will have its own unique values for the owner, the hat size, and whether the hat is on or off.

The keyword `private`, which has been applied to each instance variable, ensures that only code within the methods of the class can access or change the values of these directly. Methods of a class can also be specified as `private`. Being able to prevent access to some members of a class from outside is an important facility. It protects the internals of the class from being changed or used incorrectly. Someone using your class in another program can only get access to the bits to which you want them to have access. This means that you can change how the class works internally without affecting other programs that may use it. You can change any of the things inside the class that you have designated as `private`, and you can even change the code inside any of the public methods, as long as the method name and the number and types of values passed to it or returned from it remain the same.

Our `CowboyHat` class also has five methods, so you can do five different things with a `CowboyHat` object. One of these is a special method called a **constructor**, which creates a `CowboyHat` object – this is the method with the name, `CowboyHat`, that is the same as the class name. The items between the parentheses that follow the name of the constructor specify data that is to be passed to the method when it is executed – that is, when a `CowboyHat` object is created.

> In practice you might need to define a few other methods for the class to be useful; you might want to compare `CowboyHat` objects for example, to see if one was larger than another. However, at the moment you just need to get an idea of how the code looks. The details are of no importance here, as we will return to all this in Chapter 5.

Java Program Statements

As you saw in the `CowboyHat` class example, the code for each method in the class appears between braces, and it consists of **program statements**. A semicolon terminates each program statement. A statement in Java can spread over several lines if necessary, since the end of each statement is determined by the semicolon, not by the end of a line. Here is a Java program statement:

```
hatOn = false;
```

If you wanted to, you could also write this as:

```
hatOn =
            false;
```

You can generally include spaces and tabs, and spread your statements over multiple lines to enhance readability if it is a particularly long statement, but sensible constraints apply. You can't put a space in the middle of a name for instance. If you write `hat On`, for example, the compiler will read this as two words.

Encapsulation

At this point we can introduce another bit of jargon you can use to impress or bore your friends – **encapsulation**. Encapsulation refers to the hiding of items of data and methods within an object. This is achieved by specifying them as `private` in the definition of the class. In the `CowboyHat` class, the instance variables, `owner`, `type`, `size`, and `hatOn` were encapsulated. They were only accessible through the methods defined for the class. Therefore the only way to alter the values they contain is to call a method that does that. Being able to encapsulate members of a class in this way is important for the security and integrity of class objects. You may have a class with data members that can only take on particular values. By hiding the data members and forcing the use of a method to set or change the values, you can ensure that only legal values are set.

We mentioned earlier another major advantage of encapsulation – the ability to hide the implementation of a class. By only allowing limited access to the members of a class, you have the freedom to change the internals of the class without necessitating changes to programs that use the class. As long as the external characteristics of the methods that can be called from outside the class remain unchanged, the internal code can be changed in any way that you, the programmer, want.

A particular object, an instance of `CowboyHat`, will incorporate, or encapsulate, the `owner`, the `size` of the object, and the status of the hat in the instance variable `hatOn`. Only the constructor, and the `putHatOn()`, `takeHatOff()`, `changeOwner()`, and `getSize()` methods can be accessed externally.

> **Whenever we are referring to a method in the text, we will add a pair of parentheses after the method name to distinguish it from other things that have names. Some examples of this appear in the paragraph above. A method always has parentheses in its definition and in its use in a program, as we shall see, so it makes sense to represent it in this way in the text.**

Classes and Data Types

Programming is concerned with specifying how data of various kinds is to be processed, massaged, manipulated or transformed. Since classes define the types of objects that a program will work with, you can consider defining a class to be the same as defining a data type. Thus `Hat` is a type of data, as is `Tree`, and any other class you care to define. Java also contains a library of standard classes that provide you with a whole range of programming tools and facilities. For the most part then, your Java program will process, massage, manipulate or transform class objects.

There are some basic types of data in Java that are not classes, and these are called **primitive types**. We will go into these in detail in the next chapter, but they are essentially data types for numeric values such as 99 or 3.75, for single characters such as 'A' or '?', and for logical values that can be `true` or `false`. Java also has classes that correspond to each of the primitive data types for reasons that we will see later on so there is an `Integer` class that defines objects that encapsulate integers for instance. Every entity in your Java program that is not of a primitive data type will be an object of a class – either a class that you define yourself, a class supplied as part of the Java environment, or a class that you obtain from somewhere else, such as from a specialized support package.

Classes and Subclasses

Many sets of objects that you might define in a class can be subdivided into more specialized subsets that can also be represented by classes, and Java provides you with the ability to define one class as a more specialized version of another. This reflects the nature of reality. There are always lots of ways of dividing a cake – or a forest. `Conifer` for example could be a subclass of the class `Tree`. The `Conifer` class would have all the instance variables and methods of the `Tree` class, plus some additional instance variables and/or methods that make it a `Conifer` in particular. You refer to the `Conifer` class as a **subclass** of the class `Tree`, and the class `Tree` as a **superclass** of the class `Conifer`.

When you define a class such as `Conifer` using another class such as `Tree` as a starting point, the class `Conifer` is said to be **derived** from the class `Tree`, and the class `Conifer` **inherits** all the attributes of the class `Tree`.

Advantages of Using Objects

As we said at the outset, object-oriented programs are written using objects that are specific to the problem being solved. Your pinball machine simulator may well define and use objects of type `Table`, `Ball`, `Flipper`, and `Bumper`. This has tremendous advantages, not only in terms of easing the development process, but also in any future expansion of such a program. Java provides a whole range of standard classes to help you in the development of your program, and you can develop your own generic classes to provide a basis for developing programs that are of particular interest to you.

Because an object includes the methods that can operate on it as well as the data that defines it, programming using objects is much less prone to error. Your object-oriented Java programs should be more robust than the equivalent in a procedural programming language. Object-oriented programs take a little longer to design than programs that do not use objects since you must take care in the design of the classes that you will need, but the time required to write and test the code is sometimes substantially less than that for procedural programs. Object-oriented programs are also much easier to maintain and extend.

Java Program Structure

Let's summarize the general nature of how a Java program is structured :

- ❑   A Java program always consists of one or more classes.

- ❑   You typically put the program code for each class in a separate file, and you must give each file the same name as that of the class that is defined within it.

- ❑   A Java source file must also have the extension `.java`.

Thus your file containing the class `Hat` will be called `Hat.java` and your file containing the class `BaseballPlayer` must have the file name `BaseballPlayer.java`.

A typical program will consist of several files as illustrated in the following diagram.

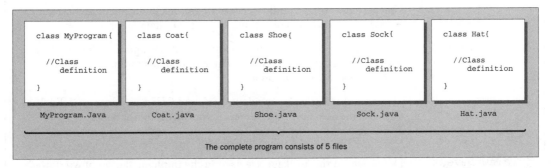

This program clearly majors on apparel with four of the five classes representing clothing. Each source file will contain a class definition, and all of the files that go to make up the program will be stored in the same directory. The source files for your program will contain all the code that you wrote, but this is not everything that is ultimately included in the program. There will also be code from the **Java standard class library**, so let's take a peek at what that can do.

Java's Class Library

A library in Java is a collection of classes – usually providing related facilities – which you can use in your programs. The Java class library provides you with a whole range of goodies, some of which are essential for your programs to work at all, and some of which make writing your Java programs easier. To say that the standard class library covers a lot of ground would be something of an understatement so we won't be going into it in detail here, but we will be looking into how to apply many of the facilities it provides throughout the book.

Since the class library is a set of classes, it is stored in sets of files where each file contains a class definition. The classes are grouped together into related sets that are called **packages**, and each package is stored in a separate directory. A class in a package can access any of the other classes in the package. A class in another package may or may not be accessible. We will learn more about this in Chapter 5.

The package name is based on the path to the directory in which the classes belonging to the package are stored. Classes in the package `java.lang` for example are stored in the directory path `java\lang` (or `java/lang` under Unix). This path is relative to a particular directory that is automatically known by the Java runtime environment that executes your code. You can also create your own packages that will contain classes of your own that you want to reuse in different contexts, and that are related in some way.

The SDK includes a growing number of standard packages – well over 100 the last time I counted. Some of the packages you will meet most frequently are:

Package Name	Description
`java.lang`	These classes support the basic language features and the handling of arrays and strings. Classes in this package are always available directly in your programs by default because this package is always automatically loaded with your program.
`java.io`	Classes for data input and output operations.
`java.util`	This package contains utility classes of various kinds, including classes for managing data within collections or groups of data items.
`javax.swing`	These classes provide easy-to-use and flexible components for building graphical user interfaces (GUIs). The components in this package are referred to as Swing components.
`java.awt`	Classes in this package provide the original GUI components (JDK1.1) as well as some basic support necessary for Swing components.
`java.awt.geom`	These classes define 2-dimensional geometric shapes.
`java.awt.event`	The classes in this package are used in the implementation of windowed application to handle events in your program. Events are things like moving the mouse, pressing the left mouse button, or clicking on a menu item.

As noted above, you can use any of the classes from the `java.lang` package in your programs by default. To use classes from the other packages, you will typically use `import` statements to identify the names of the classes that you need from each package. This will allow you to reference the classes by the simple class name. Without an `import` statement you would need to specify the fully qualified name of each class from a package each time you refer to it. As we will see in a moment, the fully qualified name for a class includes the package name as well as the basic class name. Using fully qualified class names would make your program code rather cumbersome, and certainly less readable. It would also make them a lot more tedious to type in.

You can use an `import` statement to import the name of a single class from a package into your program, or all the class names. The two `import` statements at the beginning of the code for the applet you saw earlier in this chapter are examples of importing a single class name. The first was:

```
import javax.swing.JApplet;
```

This statement imports the `JApplet` class name that is defined in the `javax.swing` package. Formally, the name of the `JApplet` class is not really `JApplet` – it is the fully qualified name `javax.swing.JApplet`. You can only use the unqualified name when you import the class or the complete package containing it into your program. You can still reference a class from a package even if you don't import it though – you just need to use the full class name, `javax.swing.JApplet`. You could try this out with the applet you saw earlier if you like. Just delete the two import statements from the file and use the full class names in the program. Then recompile it. It should work the same as before. Thus the fully qualified name for a class is the name of the package in which it is defined, followed by a period, followed by the name given to the class in its definition.

You could import the names of all the classes in the `javax.swing` package with the statement:

```
import javax.swing.*;
```

The asterisk specifies that all the class names are to be imported. Importing just the class names that your sourcecode uses makes compilation more efficient, but when you are using a lot of classes from a package you may find it more convenient to import all the names. This saves typing reams of import statements for one thing. We will do this with examples of Java code in the book to keep the number of lines to a minimum. However, there are risks associated with importing all the names in a package. There may be classes with names that are identical to names you have given to your own classes, which would obviously create some confusion when you compile your code.

> You will see more on how to use **import** statements in Chapter 5, as well as more about how packages are created and used, and you will be exploring the use of classes from the standard packages in considerable depth throughout the book.

As we indicated earlier, the standard classes do not appear as files or directories on your hard disk. They are packaged up in a single compressed file, `rt.jar`, that is stored in the `jre/lib` directory. This directory is created when you install the JDK on your computer. A `.jar` file is a Java **ar**chive – a compressed archive of Java classes. The standard classes that your executable program requires are loaded automatically from `rt.jar`, so you don't have to be concerned with it directly at all.

Java Applications

Every Java application contains a class that defines a method called main(). The name of this class is the name that you use as the argument to the Java interpreter when you run the application. You can call the class whatever you want, but the method which is executed first in an application is always called main(). When you run your Java application the method main() will typically cause methods belonging to other classes to be executed, but the simplest possible Java application program consists of one class containing just the method main(). As we shall see below, the main() method has a particular fixed form, and if it is not of the required form, it will not be recognized by the Java interpreter as the method where execution starts.

We'll see how this works by taking a look at just such a Java program. You need to enter the program code using your favorite plain text editor, or if you have a Java development system with an editor, you can enter the code for the example using that. When you have entered the code, save the file with the same name as that used for the class and the extension .java. For this example the file name will be OurFirstProgram.java. The code for the program is:

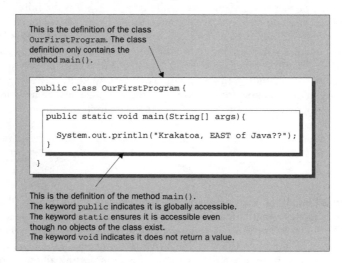

The program consists of a definition for a class we have called OurFirstProgram. The class definition only contains one method, the method main(). The first line of the definition for the method main() is always of the form:

```
public static void main(String[] args)
```

The code for the method appears between the pair of curly braces. Our version of the method has only one executable statement:

```
System.out.println("Krakatoa, EAST of Java??");
```

So what does this statement do? Let's work through it from left to right:

❏   `System` is the name of a standard class that contains objects that encapsulate the standard I/O devices for your system – the keyboard for command line input and command line output to the display. It is contained in the package `java.lang` so it is always accessible just by using the simple class name, `System`.

❏   The object `out` represents the standard output stream – the command line on your display screen, and is a data member of the class `System`. The member, `out`, is a special kind of member of the `System` class. Like the method `main()` in our `OurFirstProgram` class, it is `static`. This means that `out` exists even though there are no objects of type `System` (more on this in forthcoming chapters). Using the class name, `System`, separated from the member name out by a period – `System.out`, references the `out` member.

❏   The bit at the rightmost end of the statement, `println("Krakatoa, EAST of Java??")`, calls the `println()` method that belongs to the object `out`, and that outputs the text string that appears between the parentheses to your display. This demonstrates one way in which you can call a class method – by using the object name followed by the method name, with a period separating them. The stuff between the parentheses following the name of a method is information that is passed to the method when it is executed. As we said, for `println()` it is the text we want to output to the command line.

For completeness, the keywords `public`, `static`, *and* `void`, *that appear in the method definition are explained briefly in the annotations to the program code, but you need not be concerned if these still seem a bit obscure at this point. We will be coming back to them in much more detail later on.*

You can compile this program using the JDK compiler with the command,

```
javac -source 1.4 OurFirstProgram.java
```

Or with the `-classpath` option specified:

```
javac -source 1.4 -classpath . OurFirstProgram.java
```

If it didn't compile, there's something wrong somewhere. Here's a checklist of possible sources of the problem:

❏   You forgot to include the path to the **jdk1.4\bin** directory in your **PATH**, or maybe you did not specify the path correctly. This will result in your operating system not being able to find the `javac` compiler that is in that directory.

❏   You made an error typing in the program code. Remember Java is case sensitive so `OurfirstProgram` is not the same as `OurFirstProgram`, and of course, there must be no spaces in the class name. If the compiler discovers an error it will usually identify the line number in the code where the error was found. In general, watch out for confusing zero, 0, with a small letter, o, or the digit one, 1, with the small letter l. All characters such as periods, commas, and semicolons in the code are essential, and must be in the right place. Parentheses, (), curly braces, {}, and square brackets, [], always come in matching pairs and are not interchangeable.

❏   The source file name must match the class name exactly. The slightest difference will result in an error. It must have the extension `.java`.

Once you have compiled the program successfully, you can execute it with the command:

```
java -ea OurFirstProgram
```

The -ea option is not strictly necessary since this program does not use assertions but if you get used to putting it in, you won't forget it when it is necessary. If you need the -classpath option specified:

```
java -ea -classpath . OurFirstProgram
```

Assuming the source file compiled correctly, and the jdk1.4\bin directory is defined in your path, the most common reason for the program failing to execute is a typographical error in the class name, OurFirstProgram. The second most common reason is writing the file name, OurFirstProgram.class, in the command, whereas it should be just the class name, OurFirstProgram.

When you run the program, it will display the text:

```
Krakatoa, EAST of Java??
```

Java and Unicode

Programming to support languages that use anything other than the Latin character set has always been a major problem. There are a variety of 8-bit character sets defined for many national languages, but if you want to combine the Latin character set and Cyrillic in the same context, for example, things can get difficult. If you want to handle Japanese as well, it becomes impossible with an 8-bit character set because with 8 bits you only have 256 different codes so there just aren't enough character codes to go round. Unicode is a standard character set that was developed to allow the characters necessary for almost all languages to be encoded. It uses a 16-bit code to represent a character (so each character occupies two bytes), and with 16 bits up to 65,535 non-zero character codes can be distinguished. With so many character codes available, there is enough to allocate each major national character set its own set of codes, including character sets such as Kanji which is used for Japanese, and which requires thousand of character codes. It doesn't end there though. Unicode supports three encoding forms that allow up to a million additional characters to be represented.

As we shall see in Chapter 2, Java sourcecode is in Unicode characters. Comments, identifiers (names – see Chapter 2), and character and string literals can all use any characters in the Unicode set that represent letters. Java also supports Unicode internally to represent characters and strings, so the framework is there for a comprehensive international language capability in a program. The normal ASCII set that you are probably familiar with corresponds to the first 128 characters of the Unicode set. Apart from being aware that each character occupies two bytes, you can ignore the fact that you are handling Unicode characters in the main, unless of course you are building an application that supports multiple languages from the outset.

Summary

In this chapter we have looked at the basic characteristics of Java, and how portability between different computers is achieved. We have also introduced the elements of object-oriented programming. There are bound to be some aspects of what we have discussed that you don't feel are completely clear to you. Don't worry about it. Everything we have discussed here we will be revisiting again in more detail later on in the book.

The essential points we have covered in this chapter are:

❏ Java applets are programs that are designed to be embedded in an HTML document. Java applications are standalone programs. Java applications can be console programs that only support text output to the screen, or they can be windowed applications with a GUI.

❏ Java programs are intrinsically object-oriented.

❏ Java sourcecode is stored in files with the extension `.java`.

❏ Java programs are compiled to byte codes, which are instructions for the Java Virtual Machine. The Java Virtual Machine is the same on all the computers on which it is implemented, thus ensuring the portability of Java programs.

❏ Java object code is stored in files with the extension `.class`.

❏ Java programs are executed by the Java interpreter, which analyses the byte codes and carries out the operations they specify.

❏ The Java System Development Kit (the SDK) supports the compilation and execution of Java applications and applets.

❏ Experience is what you get when you are expecting something else.

Resources

You can download the sourcecode for the examples in the book from any of:

❏ http://www.wrox.com

❏ ftp://www.wrox.com

❏ ftp://www.wrox.co.uk

The sourcecode download also includes ancillary files, such as `.gif` files containing icons for instance, where they are used in the examples.

If you have any questions on the fine formal detail of Java, the reference works we've used are:

❏ *The Java Language Specification, Second Edition (The Java Series)* James Gosling et al., Addison-Wesley, ISBN 0-201-31008-2

❏ *The Java Virtual Machine Specification Second Edition* Tim Lindholm and Frank Yellin, Addison-Wesley, ISBN 0-201-43294-3,

Other sites of interest are:

- http://www.wrox.com for support for this book and information on forthcoming Java books.
- http://p2p.wrox.com for lists where you can get answers to your Java problems.
- http://java.sun.com/docs/books/tutorial/index.html for the JavaSoft tutorials. Follow that Java trail.

and for online magazine reading and opinion, check out:

- http://www.javaworld.com/javasoft.index.html
- http://www.javareport.com/
- http://www.sys-con.com/java/

We also like the Java Developer Connection, subscribe to it at http://java.sun.com/jdc

Programs, Data, Variables, and Calculation

In this chapter we will look at the entities in Java that are not objects – numbers and characters. This will give you all the elements of the language you need to perform numerical calculations, and we will apply these in a few working examples.

By the end of this chapter you will have learnt:

- ❑ How to declare and define variables of the basic integer and floating point types
- ❑ How to write an assignment statement
- ❑ How integer and floating point expressions are evaluated
- ❑ How to output data from a console program
- ❑ How mixed integer and floating point expressions are evaluated
- ❑ What casting is and when you must use it
- ❑ What `boolean` variables are
- ❑ What determines the sequence in which operators in an expression are executed
- ❑ How to include comments in your programs

Data and Variables

A variable is a named piece of memory that you use to store information in your Java program – a piece of data of some description. Each named piece of memory that you define in your program will only be able to store data of one particular type. If you define a variable to store integers, for example, you cannot use it to store a value that is a decimal fraction, such as 0.75. If you have defined a variable that you will use to refer to a `Hat` object, you can only use it to reference an object of type `Hat` (or any of its subclasses, as we saw in Chapter 1). Since the type of data that each variable can store is fixed, whenever you use a variable in your program the compiler is able to check that it is not being used in a manner or a context that is inappropriate to its type. If a method in your program is supposed to process integers, the compiler will be able to detect when you inadvertently try to use the method with some other kind of data, for example, a string or a numerical value that is not integral.

Explicit data values that appear in your program are called literals. Each literal will also be of a particular type: 25, for instance, is an integer value of type `int`. We will go into the characteristics of the various types of literals that you can use as we discuss each variable type.

Before you can use a variable you must specify its name and type in a declaration statement. Before we look at how you write a declaration for a variable, we should consider what flexibility you have in choosing a name.

Variable Names

The name that you choose for a variable, or indeed the name that you choose for anything in Java, is called an identifier. An identifier can be any length, but it must start with a letter, an underscore (_), or a dollar sign ($). The rest of an identifier can include any characters except those used as operators in Java (such as +, –, or *), but you will be generally better off if you stick to letters, digits, and the underscore character.

Java is case sensitive so the names `republican` and `Republican` are not the same. You must not include blanks or tabs in the middle of a name, so `Betty May` is out, but you could have `BettyMay` or even `Betty_May`. Note that you can't have `10Up` as a name since you cannot start a name with a numeric digit. Of course, you could use `tenUp` as an alternative.

Subject to the restrictions we have mentioned, you can name a variable almost anything you like, except for two additional restraints – you can't use keywords in Java as a name for something, and a name can't be anything that is a constant value. Keywords are words that are an essential part of the Java language. We saw some keywords in the previous chapter and we will learn a few more in this chapter. If you want to know what they all are, a complete list appears in Appendix A. The restriction on constant values is there because, although it is obvious why a name can't be `1234` or `37.5`, constants can also be alphabetic, such as `true` and `false` for example. We will see how we specify constant values later in this chapter. Of course, the basic reason for these rules is that the compiler has to be able to distinguish between your variables and other things that can appear in a program. If you try to use a name for a variable that makes this impossible, then it's not a legal name.

Clearly, it makes sense to choose names for your variables that give a good indication of the sort of data they hold. If you want to record the size of a hat, for example, `hatSize` is not a bad choice for a variable name whereas qqq would be a bad choice. It is a common convention in Java to start variable names with a lower case letter and, where you have a name that combines several words, to capitalize the first letter of each word, as in `hatSize` or `moneyWellSpent`. You are in no way obliged to follow this convention but since almost all the Java world does, it helps to do so.

If you feel you need more guidance in naming conventions (and coding conventions in general) take a look at http://www.javasoft.com/docs/codeconv/.

Variable Names and Unicode

Even though you are likely to be entering your Java programs in an environment that stores ASCII, all Java source code is in Unicode (subject to the reservations we noted in Chapter 1). Although the original source that you create is ASCII, it is converted to Unicode characters internally, before it is compiled. While you only ever need ASCII to write any Java language statement, the fact that Java supports Unicode provides you with immense flexibility. It means that the identifiers that you use in your source program can use any national language character set that is defined within the Unicode character set, so your programs can use French, Greek, or Cyrillic variable names, for example, or even names in several different languages, as long as you have the means to enter them in the first place. The same applies to character data that your program defines.

Variables and Types

As we mentioned earlier, each variable that you declare can store values of a type determined by the data type of that variable. You specify the type of a particular variable by using a type name in the variable declaration. For instance, here's a statement that declares a variable that can store integers:

```
int numberOfCats;
```

The data type in this case is `int`, the variable name is `numberOfCats`, and the semicolon marks the end of the statement. The variable, `numberOfCats`, can only store values of type `int`.

Many of your variables will be used to reference objects, but let's leave those on one side for the moment as they have some special properties. The only things in Java that are not objects are variables that correspond to one of eight basic data types, defined within the language. These fundamental types, also called primitive types, allow you to define variables for storing data that fall into one of three categories:

- ❑ Numeric values, which can be either integer or floating point
- ❑ Variables which store a single Unicode character
- ❑ Logical variables that can assume the values `true` or `false`

All of the type names for the basic variable types are keywords in Java so you must not use them for other purposes. Let's take a closer look at each of the basic data types and get a feel for how we can use them.

Integer Data Types

There are four types of variables that you can use to store integer data. All of these are signed, that is, they can store both negative and positive values. The four integer types differ in the range of values they can store, so the choice of type for a variable depends on the range of data values you are likely to need.

The four integer types in Java are:

Data Type	Description
byte	Variables of this type can have values from -128 to +127 and occupy 1 byte (8 bits) in memory
short	Variables of this type can have values from -32768 to 32767 and occupy 2 bytes (16 bits) in memory
int	Variables of this type can have values from -2147483648 to 2147483647 and occupy 4 bytes (32 bits) in memory
long	Variables of this type can have values from -9223372036854775808 to 9223372036854775807 and occupy 8 bytes (64 bits) in memory

Let's take a look at declarations of variables of each of these types:

```
byte smallerValue;
short pageCount;
int wordCount;
long bigValue;
```

Each of these statements declares a variable of the type specified.

The range of values that can be stored by each integer type in Java, as shown in the table above, is always the same, regardless of what kind of computer you are using. This is also true of the other basic types that we will see later in this chapter, and has the rather useful effect that your program will execute in the same way on computers that may be quite different. This is not necessarily the case with other programming languages.

Of course, although we have expressed the range of possible values for each type as decimal values, integers are stored internally as binary numbers, and it is the number of bits available to store each type that determines the maximum and minimum values, as shown on the next page.

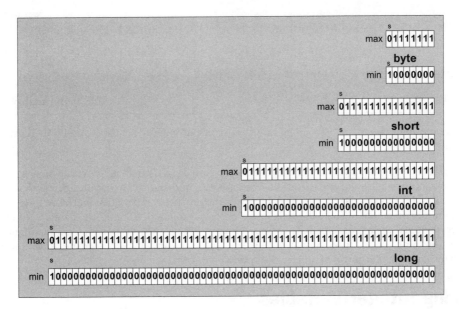

For each of the binary numbers shown here, the leftmost bit is the sign bit, marked with an 's'. When the sign bit is 0 the number is positive, and when it is 1 the number is negative. Binary negative numbers are represented in what is called 2's complement form. If you are not familiar with this, you will find an explanation of how it works in Appendix B.

Integer Values

An integer variable stores an integer value, so before we get to use integer variables we need to investigate how we write various integer values. As we said earlier, a value of any kind in Java is referred to as a literal. So 1, 10.5, and "This is text" are all examples of literals.

Any integer literal that you specify is of type int by default. Thus 1, -9999, and 123456789 are all literals of type int. If you want to define an integer of type long, and the value that you assign to the variable is bigger than an int, you need to append an L to the value. The values 1L, -9999L, and 123456789L are all of type long. You can also use a lower case letter l, but don't – it is too easily confused with the digit 1.

You are perhaps wondering how you specify literals of type byte or short. Because of the way integer arithmetic works in Java, they just aren't necessary in the main. We will see a couple of instances where an integer literal may be interpreted by the compiler as type byte or short later in this chapter, but these situations are the exception.

Integer literals can also be specified to base 16, in other words, as hexadecimal numbers. Hexadecimal literals in Java have 0x or 0X in front of them and follow the usual convention of using the letters A to F (or a to f) to represent digits with values 10 to 15 respectively. In case you are a little rusty on hexadecimal values, here are some examples:

`0x100`	$1*16^2 + 0*16^1 + 0*16^0$	which is 256 in decimal
`0x1234`	$1*16^3 + 2*16^2 + 3*16^1 + 4*16^0$	which is 4660 in decimal
`0xDEAF`	$13*16^3 + 14*16^2 + 10*16^1 + 15*16^0$	which is 57007 in decimal
`0xCAB`	$12*16^2 + 10*16^1 + 11*16^0$	which is 3243 in decimal

If you are not familiar with hexadecimal numbers, you can find an explanation of how these work in Appendix B.

There is a further possibility for integer constants – you can also define them as octal, which is to base 8. Octal numbers have a leading zero so 035 and 067 are examples of octal numbers. Each octal digit defines three bits, so this number base was used a lot more frequently in the days when machines used a multiple of three bits to store a number. You will rarely find it necessary to use octal numbers these days, but you should take care not to use them by accident. If you put a leading zero at the start of an integer literal, the Java compiler will think you are specifying an octal value. Unless one of the digits is greater than 7, which will result in the compiler flagging it as an error, you won't know that you have done this.

Declaring Integer Variables

As you saw earlier, we can declare a variable of type `long` with the statement:

```
long bigOne;
```

This statement is a declaration for the variable `bigOne`. This specifies that the variable `bigOne` will store a value of type `long`. When this statement is compiled, 8 bytes of memory will be allocated for the variable `bigOne`. Java does not automatically initialize a variable such as this. If you want your variables to have an initial value rather than a junk value left over from when the memory was last used, you must specify your own value in the declaration. To declare and initialize the variable `bigOne` to 2999999999, you just write:

```
long bigOne = 2999999999L;
```

The variable will be set to the value following the equal sign. It is good practice to always initialize your variables when you declare them. Note that if you try to use a variable in a calculation that has not had a value assigned to it, your program will not compile. There are also circumstances where the compiler cannot determine whether or not a variable has been initialized before it is used if you don't initialize it when you declare it, even though it may be obvious to you that it has been. This will also be flagged as an error but getting into the habit of always initializing variables when you declare them will avoid all of these problems.

You can declare a variable just about anywhere in your program, but you must declare a variable before you use it in a calculation. The placement of the declaration therefore has an effect on whether a particular variable is accessible at a given point in a program, and we will look deeper into the significance of this in the next chapter. Broadly, you should group related variable declarations together, before the block of code that uses them.

You can declare and define multiple variables in a single statement. For example:

```
long bigOne = 999999999L, largeOne = 100000000L;
```

Here we have declared two variables of type `long`. A comma separates each variable from the next. You can declare as many variables as you like in a single statement, although it is usually better to stick to declaring one variable in each statement as it helps to make your programs easier to read. A possible exception occurs with variables that are closely related – an (x,y) coordinate pair representing a point, for example, which you might reasonably declare as:

```
int xCoord = 0, yCoord = 0;          // Point coordinates
```

On the same line as the declaration of these two variables, we have a comment following the double slash, explaining what they are about. The compiler ignores everything from the double slash until the end of the line. Explaining in comments what your variables are for is a good habit to get into, as it can be quite surprising how something that was as clear as crystal when you wrote it transmogrifies into something as clear as mud a few weeks later. There are other ways in which you can add comments to your programs that we will see a little later in this chapter.

You can also spread a single declaration over several lines if you want. This also can help to make your program more readable. For example:

```
int miles    = 0,      // One mile is 8 furlongs
    furlongs = 0,       // One furlong is 220 yards
    yards    = 0,       // One yard is 3 feet
    feet     = 0;
```

Naturally, you must be sure that an initializing value for a variable is within the range of the type concerned, otherwise the compiler will complain. Your compiler is intelligent enough to recognize that you can't get a quart into a pint pot, or, alternatively, a `long` constant into a variable of type `int`, `short`, or `byte`.

To complete the set we can declare and initialize a variable of type `byte` and one of type `short` with the following two statements:

```
byte luckyNumber = 7;
short smallNumber = 1234;
```

Here the compiler can deduce that the integer literals are to be of type `byte` and `short` respectively and convert the literals to the appropriate type. It is your responsibility to make sure the initial value will fit within the range of the variable that you are initializing. If it doesn't the compiler will throw it out with an error message.

Most of the time you will find that variables of type `int` will cover your needs for dealing with integers, with `long` ones being necessary now and again when you have some really big integer values to deal with. Variables of type `byte` and `short` do save a little memory, but unless you have a lot of values of these types to store, that is, values with a very limited range, they won't save enough to be worth worrying about. They also introduce complications when you use them in calculations, as we shall see shortly, so generally you should not use them unless it is absolutely necessary. Of course, when you are reading data from some external source, a disk file for instance, you will need to make the type of variable for each data value correspond to what you expect to read.

Floating Point Data Types

Numeric values that are not integral are stored as floating point numbers. A floating point number has a fixed number of digits of accuracy but with a very wide range of values. You get a wide range of values, even though the number of digits is fixed, because the decimal point can "float". For example the values 0.000005, 500.0, and 5000000000000.0 can be written as 5×10^{-6}, 5×10^{2}, and 5×10^{12} respectively – we have just one digit '5' but we move the decimal point around.

There are two basic floating point types in Java, `float` and `double`. These give you a choice in the number of digits precision available to represent your data values, and in the range of values that can be accommodated:

Data Type	Description
float	Variables of this type can have values from -3.4E38 (-3.4×10^{38}) to +3.4E38 ($+3.4\times10^{38}$) and occupy 4 bytes in memory. Values are represented with approximately 7 digits accuracy.
double	Variables of this type can have values from -1.7E308 (-1.7×10^{308}) to +1.7E308 ($+1.7\times10^{308}$) and occupy 8 bytes in memory. Values are represented with approximately 17 digits accuracy. The smallest non-zero value that you can have is roughly $\pm4.9\times10^{-324}$.

> All floating point operations and the definitions for values of type `float` and type `double` in Java conform to the IEEE 754 standard.

As with integer calculations, floating point calculations in Java will produce the same results on any computer.

Floating Point Values

When you are specifying floating point literals they are of type `double` by default, so 1.0 and 345.678 are both of type `double`. When you want to specify a value of type `float`, you just append an f, or an F, to the value, so `1.0f` and `345.678F` are both constants of type `float`. If you are new to programming it is important to note that you must not include commas as separators when specifying numerical values in your program code. Where you might normally write a value as 99,786.5, in your code you must write it without the comma, as 99786.5.

When you need to write very large or very small floating point values, you will usually want to write them with an exponent – that is, as a decimal value multiplied by a power of 10. You can do this in Java by writing the number as a decimal value followed by an E, or an e, preceding the power of 10 that you require. For example, the distance from the Earth to the Sun is approximately 149,600,000 kilometers, more conveniently written as 1.496E8. Since the E (or e) indicates that what follows is the exponent, this is equivalent to 1.496×10^{8}. At the opposite end of the scale, the mass of an electron is around 0.00000000000000000000000000009 grams. This is much more convenient, not to say more readable, when it is written as 9.0E-28 grams.

Declaring Floating Point Variables

You declare floating point variables in a similar way to that we've already used for integers. We can declare and initialize a variable of type `double` with the statement:

```
double sunDistance = 1.496E8;
```

Declaring a variable of type `float` is much the same. For example:

```
float electronMass = 9E-28F;
```

You can of course declare more than one variable of a given type in a single statement:

```
float hisWeight = 185.2F, herWeight = 108.5F;
```

Note that you must put the `F` or `f` for literals of type `float`. If you leave it out, the literal will be of type `double`, and the compiler won't convert it automatically to type `float`.

Now that we know how to declare and initialize variables of the basic types, we are nearly ready to write a program. We just need to look at how to calculate and store the results of a calculation.

Arithmetic Calculations

You store the result of a calculation in a variable by using an assignment statement. An assignment statement consists of a variable name followed by an assignment operator, followed by an arithmetic expression, followed by a semicolon. Here is a simple example of an assignment statement:

```
numFruit = numApples + numOranges;      // Calculate the total fruit
```

Here, the assignment operator is the = sign. The value of the expression to the right of the = sign is calculated and stored in the variable that appears to the left of the = sign. In this case, the values in the variables `numApples` and `numOranges` are added together and the result is stored in the variable `numFruit`. Of course, we would have to declare all three variables before this statement.

Incrementing a variable by a given amount is a common requirement in programming. Look at the following assignment statement:

```
numApples = numApples + 1;
```

The result of evaluating the expression on the right of the = is one more than the value of `numApples`. This result is stored back in the variable `numApples`, so the overall effect of executing the statement is to increment the value in `numApples` by 1. We will see an alternative, more concise, way of producing the same effect shortly.

You can write multiple assignments in a single statement. Suppose you have three variables a, b, and c, of type `int`, and you want to set all three to 777. You can do this with the statement:

```
a = b = c = 777;
```

Note that an assignment is different from initialization in a declaration. Initialization causes a variable to have the value of the constant that you specify when it is created. An assignment involves copying data from one place in memory to another. For the assignment statement above, the compiler will have allocated some memory (4 bytes) to store the constant 777 as type int. This value will then be copied to the variable c. The value in c will be extracted and copied to b. Finally the value in b will be copied to a. (However, strictly speaking, the compiler may optimize these assignments when it compiles the code to reduce the inefficiency of performing successive assignments of the same value in the way I have described.)

With simple assignments of a constant value to a variable of type short or byte, the constant will be stored as the type of the variable on the left of the =, rather than type int. For example:

```
short value = 0;
value = 10;
```

This declaration, when compiled and run, will allocate space for the variable value, and arrange for its initial value to be 0. The assignment operation needs to have 10 available as an integer literal of type short, occupying 2 bytes, because value is of type short. The value 10 will then be copied to the variable value.

Now let's look in more detail at how we can perform calculations with integers.

Integer Calculations

The basic operators you can use on integers are +, -, *, and /, which have the usual meanings – add, subtract, multiply, and divide, respectively. Each of these is a binary operator; that is, they combine two operands to produce a result, 2 + 3 for example. An operand is a value to which an operator is applied. The priority or precedence that applies when an expression using these operators is evaluated is the same as you learnt at school. Multiplication and division are executed before any addition or subtraction operations, so the expression:

```
20 - 3*3 - 9/3
```

will produce the value 8, since it is equivalent to 20 - 9 - 3.

As you will also have learnt in school, you can use parentheses in arithmetic calculations to change the sequence of operations. Expressions within parentheses are always evaluated first, starting with the innermost when they are nested. Therefore the expression:

```
(20 - 3)*(3 - 9)/3
```

is equivalent to 17*(-6)/3 which results in -34.

Of course, you use these operators with variables that store integer values as well as integer literals. You could calculate a value for area of type int from values stored in the variables length and breadth, also of type int, by writing:

```
area = length * breadth;
```

The arithmetic operators we have described so far are binary operators, so called because they require two operands. There are also unary versions of the + and – operators that apply to a single operand to the right of the operator. Note that the unary – operator is not just a sign, as in a literal such as –345, it is an operator that has an effect. When applied to a variable it results in a value that has the opposite sign to that of the value stored in the variable. For example, if the variable count has the value -10, the expression –count has the value +10. Of course, applying the unary + operator to the value of a variable results in the same value.

Let's try out some simple arithmetic in a working console application.

Try It Out – Apples and Oranges (or Console Yourself)

Key in this example and save it in a file Fruit.java. You will remember from the last chapter that each file will contain a class, and that the name of the file will be the same as that of the class with the extension .java. Store the file in a directory that is separate from the hierarchy containing the SDK. You can give the directory any name that you want, even the name Fruit if that helps to identify the program that it contains.

```
public class Fruit {
  public static void main(String[] args) {
    // Declare and initialize three variables
    int numOranges = 5;                    // Count of oranges
    int numApples = 10;                    // Count of apples
    int numFruit = 0;                      // Count of fruit

    numFruit = numOranges + numApples;     // Calculate the total fruit count
    // Display the result
    System.out.println("A totally fruity program");
    System.out.println("Total fruit is " + numFruit);
  }
}
```

Just to remind you, to compile this program using the SDK, first make sure that the current directory is the one containing your source file, and execute the command:

```
javac Fruit.java
```

As we noted in the previous chapter, you may need to use the -classpath option if the CLASSPATH environment variable has been defined. If there are no errors, this will generate a file, Fruit.class, in the same directory, and this file contains the byte codes for the program. To execute the program you then invoke the Java interpreter with the class name for your application program:

```
java Fruit
```

In some Java development environments, the output may not be displayed long enough for you to see it. If this is the case, you can add a few lines of code to get the program to wait until you press *Enter* before it ends. The additional lines to do this are shown shaded in the following listing:

```
import java.io.IOException;  // For code that delays ending the program

public class Fruit {
  public static void main(String[] args) {
    // Declare and initialize three variables
    int numOranges = 5;                // Count of oranges
    int numApples = 10;                // Count of apples
    int numFruit = 0;                  // Count of fruit

    numFruit = numOranges + numApples;  // Calculate the total fruit count

    // Display the result
    System.out.println("A totally fruity program");
    System.out.println("Total fruit is " + numFruit);
    // Code to delay ending the program
    System.out.println("(press Enter to exit)");

    try {
      System.in.read();                // Read some input from the keyboard

    } catch (IOException e) {           // Catch the input exception
      return;                          // and just return
    }
  }
}
```

We won't go into this extra code here. If you need to, just put it in for the moment. You will understand exactly how it works later in the book.

The stuff between parentheses following main – that is String[] args – provides a means of accessing data that passed to the program from the command line when you run it. We will be going into this in detail later on so you can just ignore it for now, though you must always include it in the first line of main().

All that additional code in the body of the main() method just waits until you press **Enter** before ending the program. If necessary, you can include this in all of your console programs to make sure they don't disappear before you can read the output. It won't make any difference to how the rest of the program works. We will defer discussing in detail what is happening in the bit of code that we have added until we get to exceptions in Chapter 7.

If you run this program with the additional code, the output will be similar to the following window:

The basic elements in the original version of the program are shown below:

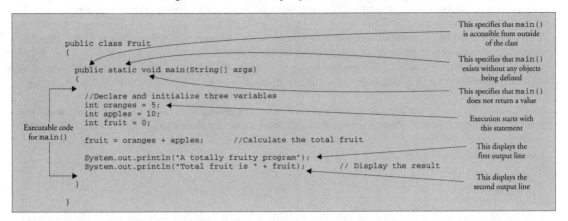

Our program consists of just one class, Fruit, and just one method, main(). Execution of an application always starts at the first executable statement in the method main(). There are no objects of our class Fruit defined, but the method main() can still be executed because we have specified it as static. The method main() is always specified as public and static and with the return type void. We can summarize the effects of these on the method as:

public	Specifies that the method is accessible from outside the Fruit class.
static	Specifies that the method is a class method that is to be executable, even though no class objects have been created. (Methods that are not static can only be executed for a particular object of the class, as we will see in Chapter 5.)
void	Specifies that the method does not return a value.

Don't worry if these are not completely clear to you at this point – you will meet them all again later.

The first three statements in main() declare the variables numOranges, numApples, and numFruit to be of type int and initialize them to the values 5, 10, and 0 respectively. The next statement adds the values stored in numOranges and numApples, and stores the result, 15, in the variable numFruit. We then generate some output from the program.

Producing Output

The next two statements use the method println() which displays text output. The statement looks a bit complicated but it breaks down quite simply:

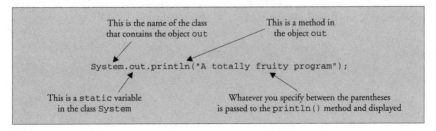

The text between double quotes, `"A totally fruity program"`, is a character string. Whenever you need a string constant, you just put the sequence of characters between double quotes.

You can see from the annotations above how you execute methods that belong to an object. Here we execute the method `println()` which belongs to the object `out`, which, in turn, is a `static` variable of the class `System`. Because the object `out` is `static`, it will exist even if there are no objects of type `System` in existence. This is analogous to the use of the keyword `static` for the method `main()`.

Most objects in a program are not static members of a class though, so calling a method for an object typically just involves the object name and the method name. For instance, if you guessed from the last example that to call the `putHatOn()` method for an object `cowboyHat`, of type `Hat` introduced in Chapter 1, you would write:

```
cowboyHat.putHatOn();
```

you would be right. Don't worry if you didn't though. We will be going into this again when we get to look at classes in detail. For the moment, any time we want to output something as text to the console, we will just write,

```
System.out.println( whateverWeWantToDisplay );
```

with whatever data we want to display plugged in between the parentheses.

Thus the second statement in our example:

```
System.out.println("Total fruit is " + numFruit);
```

outputs the character string `"Total fruit is "` followed by the value of `numFruit` converted to characters, that is 15. So what's the + doing here – it's obviously not arithmetic we are doing, is it? No, but the plus has a special effect when used with character strings – it joins them together. But `numFruit` is not a string, is it? No, but `"Total fruit is "` is, and this causes the compiler to decide that the whole thing is an expression working on character strings. It therefore converts `numFruit` to a character string to be compatible with the string `"Total fruit is "` and tacks it on the end. The composite string is then passed to the `println()` method. Dashed clever, these compilers.

If you wanted to output the value of `numOranges` as well, you could write:

```
System.out.println("Total fruit is " + numFruit
                   + " and oranges = " + numOranges);
```

Try it out if you like. You should get the output:

```
Total fruit is 15 and oranges = 5
```

Integer Division and Remainders

When you divide one integer by another and the result is not exact, any remainder is discarded, so the final result is always an integer. The division 3/2, for example, produces the result 1, and 11/3 produces the result 3. This makes it easy to divide a given quantity equally amongst a given number of recipients. To divide numFruit equally between four children, you could write:

```
int numFruitEach = 0;              // Number of fruit for each child
numFruitEach = numFruit/4;
```

Of course, there are circumstances where you may want the remainder and on these occasions you can calculate the remainder using the modulus operator, %. If you wanted to know how many fruit were left after dividing the total by 4, you could write:

```
int remainder = 0;
remainder = numFruit % 4;    // Calculate the remainder after division by 4
```

You could add this to the program too if you want to see the modulus operator in action. The modulus operator has the same precedence as multiplication and division, and is therefore executed in a more complex expression before any add or subtract operations.

The Increment and Decrement Operators

If you want to increment an integer variable by one, instead of using an assignment you can use the increment operator, which is written as two successive plus signs, ++. For example, if you have an integer variable count declared as:

```
int count = 10;
```

you can then write the statement:

```
++count;      // Add 1 to count
```

which will increase the value of count to 11. If you want to decrease the value of count by 1 you can use the decrement operator, --:

```
--count;      // Subtract 1 from count
```

At first sight, apart from reducing the typing a little, this does not seem to have much of an advantage over writing:

```
count = count - 1;     // Subtract 1 from count
```

One big advantage of the increment and decrement operators is that you can use them in an expression. Try changing the arithmetic statement calculating the sum of numApples and numOranges in the previous example:

```
public class Fruit {
  public static void main(String[] args)    {
```

```
            // Declare and initialize three variables
            int numOranges = 5;
            int numApples = 10;
            int numFruit = 0;

            // Increment oranges and calculate the total fruit
            numFruit = ++numOranges + numApples;

            System.out.println("A totally fruity program");
            // Display the result
            System.out.println("Value of oranges is " + numOranges);
            System.out.println("Total fruit is " + numFruit);
        }
    }
```

The lines that have been altered or added have been highlighted. In addition to the change to the numFruit calculation, an extra statement has been added to output the final value of numOranges. The value of numOranges will be increased to 6 before the value of numApples is added, so the value of fruit will be 16. You could try the decrement operation in the example as well.

A further property of the increment and decrement operators is that they work differently in an expression depending on whether you put the operator in front of the variable, or following it. When you put the operator in front of a variable, as in the example we have just seen, it's called the prefix form. The converse case, with the operator following the variable, is called the postfix form. If you change the statement in the example to:

```
    numFruit = numOranges++ + numApples;
```

and run it again, you will find that numOranges still ends up with the value 6, but the total stored in numFruit has remained 15. This is because the effect of the postfix increment operator is to change the value of numOranges to 6 *after* the original value, 5, has been used in the expression to supply the value of numFruit. The postfix decrement operator works similarly, and both operators can be applied to any type of integer variable.

As you see, no parentheses are necessary in the expression numOranges++ + numApples. You could even write it as numOranges+++numApples and it will still mean the same thing but it is certainly a lot less obvious what *you* mean. You could write it as (numOranges++) + numApples if you want to make it absolutely clear where the ++ operator belongs. It is a good idea to add parentheses to clarify things when there is some possibility of confusion.

Computation with Shorter Integer Types

All the previous examples have quite deliberately been with variables of type int. Computations with variables of the shorter integer types introduce some complications. With arithmetic expressions using variables of type byte or short, all the values of the variables are first converted to type int and the calculation is carried out in the same way as with type int – using 32-bit arithmetic. The result will therefore be type int – a 32-bit integer. As a consequence, if you change the types of the variables numOranges, numApples, and numFruit in the original version of the program to short, for example:

```
short numOranges = 5;
short numApples = 10;
short numFruit = 0;
```

then the program will no longer compile. The problem is with the statement:

```
numFruit = numOranges + numApples;
```

Since the expression numOranges + numApples produces a 32-bit result, the compiler cannot store this value in numFruit, as the variable numFruit is only 16-bits long. You must modify the code to convert the result of the addition back to a 16-bit number. You do this by changing the statement to:

```
numFruit = (short)(numOranges + numApples);
```

The statement now calculates the sum of numOranges and numApples and then converts or casts it to the type short before storing it in numFruit. This is called an explicit cast, and the conversion process is referred to as casting. The cast to type short is the expression (short), and the cast applies to whatever is immediately to the right of (short) so the parentheses around the expression numOranges + numApples are necessary. Without them the cast would only apply to the variable numOranges, which is a short anyway, and the code would still not compile. Similarly, if the variables here were of type byte, you would need to cast the result of the addition to the type byte.

The effect of the cast to short is just to take the least significant 16 bits of the result, discarding the *most significant* 16 bits. The least significant bits are those at the right hand end of the number because the bits in a binary number in Java increase in value from right to left. Thus the most significant bits are those at the left hand end. For the cast to type byte only the least significant 8 bits are kept. This means that if the magnitude of the result is such that more than 16 bits are necessary to represent it (or 8 bits in the case of a cast to byte), your answer will be wrong. You will get no indication from the compiler that this has occurred because it was you, after all, that expressly specified the cast and the compiler assumes that you know what you are doing. You should therefore avoid explicit casts in your programs unless they are absolutely essential.

An integer arithmetic operation involving a value of type long will always be carried using 64-bit values. If the other number in such an operation is not of type long, it will be cast to long before the operation is executed. For example:

```
long result = 0;
long factor = 10L;
int number = 5;
result = factor*number;
```

To execute the last statement, because the variable, factor, is of type long, the multiplication will be carried out using long values. The value stored in the variable, number, will be converted to type long, and that will be multiplied by the value of factor.

All other integer arithmetic operations involving types other than long are carried out with 32-bit values. Thus, you only really need to consider two kinds of integer literals:

❑ The type `long` for operations with 64-bit values where the value has an `L` appended

❑ The type `int` for operations with 32-bit values for all other cases where there is no `L` at the end of the number

Errors in Integer Arithmetic

If you divide an integer value by zero, no sensible result can be produced so an exception will be thrown. An exception is the way of signaling errors in Java that we will discuss in detail in Chapter 7. Using the `%` operator with a variable or expression for the right hand operand that has a zero value will also cause an exception to be thrown.

Note that if an integer expression results in a value that is outside the range of the type of the result, the result will be truncated to the number of bits for the type you are using and therefore will be incorrect, but this will not be indicated in any way. It is up to you to make sure that the integer types that you are using in your program are always able to accommodate any value that might be produced by your calculations. Problems can arise with intermediate results in some situations. Even when the ultimate result of an expression is within the legal range, if any intermediate calculation is outside the range it will be truncated causing an incorrect result to be produced. To take a trivial example – if you multiply 1000000 by 2000000 and divide by 500000 using type `int`, you will not obtain the correct result if the multiplication is executed first, because the result of the multiplication exceeds the maximum that can be stored as type `int`. Obviously where you know this sort of problem can occur, you may be able to circumvent it by using parentheses to make sure the division takes place first – but you need to remember that integer division produces an integer result, so a different sequence of execution can produce a different answer.

Floating Point Calculations

The four basic arithmetic operators, +, -, *, /, are also available for use in floating point expressions. We can try some of these out in another version of the `Fruit` program which we'll call `AverageFruit`.

Try It Out – Average Fruit

Make the following changes to the `Fruit.java` file, and save this as `AverageFruit.java`. If necessary, you can add in the code we used earlier to make the program wait for the *Enter* key to be pressed before finishing.

```
public class AverageFruit {
  public static void main(String[] args) {
    // Declare and initialize three variables
    double numOranges = 50.0E-1;        // Initial value is 5.0
    double numApples = 1.0E1;           // Initial value is 10.0
    double averageFruit = 0.0;

    averageFruit = (numOranges + numApples) / 2.0;

    System.out.println("A totally fruity program");
    System.out.println("Average fruit is " + averageFruit);
  }
}
```

This will produce the output:

```
A totally fruity program
Average fruit is 7.5
```

The program just computes the average number of fruits by dividing the total by 2.0.

> As you can see, we have used various representations for the initializing values for the variables in the program, which are now of type **double**. It's not the ideal way to write 5.0 but at least it demonstrates that you can write a negative exponent value.

Other Floating Point Operators

You can use ++ and -- with floating point variables, and they have the same effect as with integer variables, incrementing or decrementing the floating point variable to which they are applied by 1.0. You can use them in prefix or postfix form, and their operation in each case is the same as with integer variables.

You can apply the modulus operator, %, to floating point values too. For the operation.

```
floatOperand1 % floatOperand2
```

the result will be the floating point remainder after dividing floatOperand2 into floatOperand1 an integral number of times. For example, the expression 12.6 % 5.1 will give the result 2.4.

Error Conditions in Floating Point Arithmetic

There are two error conditions that are signaled by a special result value being generated. One occurs when a calculation produces a value which is outside the range that can be represented, and the other arises when the result is mathematically indeterminate, such as when your calculation is effectively dividing zero by zero.

To illustrate the first kind of error we could use a variable to specify the number of types of fruit. We could define the variable:

```
double fruitTypes = 2.0;
```

and then rewrite the calculation as:

```
averageFruit = (numOranges + numApples) / fruitTypes;
```

This in itself is not particularly interesting, but if we happened to set fruitTypes to 0.0, the output from the program would be:

```
A totally fruity program
Average fruit is Infinity
```

The value `Infinity` indicates a positive but effectively infinite result, in that it is greater than the largest number that can be represented as type `double`. A negative infinite result would be output as `-Infinity`. You don't actually need to divide by zero to produce this effect; any calculation, that generates a value that exceeds the maximum value that can be represented as type `double` will have the same effect. For example, repeatedly dividing by a very small number, such as 1.0E-300, will yield an out-of-range result.

If you want to see what an indeterminate result looks like, you can replace the statement to calculate `averageFruit` with:

```
averageFruit = (numOranges - 5.0)/(numApples - 10.0);
```

This statement doesn't make much sense but it will produce an indeterminate result. The value of `averageFruit` will be output as `NaN`. This value is referred to as Not-a-Number, indicating an indeterminate value. A variable with an indeterminate value will contaminate any subsequent expression in which it is used, producing the same result of `NaN`.

A value that is `Infinity` or `-Infinity` will be unchanged when you add, subtract, or multiply by finite values, but if you divide any finite value by `Infinity` or `-Infinity` the result will be zero.

Mixed Arithmetic Expressions

You can mix values of the basic types together in a single expression. The way mixed expressions are treated is governed by some simple rules that apply to each operator in such an expression. The rules, in the sequence in which they are checked, are:

❑ If either operand is of type `double`, the other is converted to `double` before the operation is carried out.

❑ If either operand is of type `float`, the other is converted to `float` before the operation is carried out.

❑ If either operand is of type `long`, the other is converted to `long` before the operation is carried out.

The first rule in the sequence that applies to a given operation is the one that is carried out. If neither operand is `double`, `float`, or `long`, they must be `int`, `short`, or `byte`, so they use 32-bit arithmetic as we saw earlier.

Explicit Casting

It may well be that the default treatment of mixed expressions listed above is not what you want. For example, if you have a `double` variable `result`, and you compute its value using two `int` variables `three` and `two` with the values 3 and 2 respectively, with the statement:

```
result = 1.5 + three/two;
```

the value stored will be 2.5, since `three/two` will be executed as an integer operation and will produce the result 1. You may have wanted the term `three/two` to produce the value 1.5 so the overall result would be 3.0. You could do this using an explicit cast:

```
result = 1.5 + (double)three/two;
```

This causes the value stored in `three` to be converted to `double` before the divide operation takes place. Then rule 1 applies for the divide operation, and the operand `two` is also converted to `double` before the divide is executed. Hence the value of `result` will be 3.0.

> You can cast any of the basic types to any other, but you need to take care that you don't lose information when you do so. Obviously casting from a larger integer type to a smaller has the potential for losing information, as does casting any floating point value to an integer. Casting from **double** to **float** can also produce effective infinity when the original value is greater than the maximum value for a **float**.

Casting in Assignments

When the type of the result of an expression on the right of an assignment statement differs from the type of the variable on the left, an automatic cast will be applied as long as there is no possibility of losing information. If you think of the basic types that we have seen so far as being in the sequence:

byte → short → int → long → float → double

then an automatic conversion will be made as long as it is upwards through the sequence, that is, from left to right. If you want to go in the opposite direction, from `double` to `float` or `long`, for example, then you must use an explicit cast.

The op= Operators

The `op=` operators are used in statements of the form:

```
lhs op= rhs;
```

where op can be any of the operators +, -, *, /, %, plus some others you haven't seen yet. The above is basically a shorthand representation of the statement:

```
lhs = lhs op (rhs);
```

The right hand side is in brackets because it is worked out first – then the result is combined with the left hand side using the operation, op. Let's look at a few examples of this to make sure it's clear. To increment an `int` variable `count` by 5 you can write:

```
count += 5;
```

57

This has the same effect as the statement:

```
count = count + 5;
```

Of course, the expression to the right of the op= operator can be anything that is legal in the context, so the statement:

```
result /= a % b/(a + b);
```

is equivalent to:

```
result = result/(a % b/(a + b));
```

> You should note that if the type of the result of the rhs expression is different from the type of lhs, the compiler will automatically insert a cast. In the last example, the statement would work with **result** being of type **int** and **a** and **b** being of type **double**, for instance. This is quite different from the way the normal assignment operation is treated. A statement using the **op=** operator is really equivalent to: **lhs = (type_of_lhs)(lhs op (rhs));** Of course, this can result in information being lost due to the cast, and you will get no indication that it has occurred.

The complete set of op= operators appears in the precedence table later in this chapter.

Mathematical Functions and Constants

Sooner or later you are likely to need mathematical functions in your programs, even if it's only obtaining an absolute value or calculating a square root. Java provides a range of methods that support such functions as part of the standard library stored in the package java.lang, and all these are available in your program automatically.

The methods that support various additional mathematical functions are implemented in the class Math as static methods, so to reference a particular function you can just write Math and a period in front of the name of the method you wish to use. For example, to use sqrt(), which calculates the square root of whatever you place between the parentheses, you would write Math.sqrt(aNumber) to produce the square root of the floating point value in the variable aNumber.

The class Math includes a range of methods for standard trigonometric functions. These are:

Method	Function	Argument Type	Result Type
sin(arg)	sine of the argument	double in radians	double
cos(arg)	cosine of the argument	double in radians	double

Method	Function	Argument Type	Result Type
`tan(arg)`	tangent of the argument	`double` in radians	`double`
`asin(arg)`	sin⁻¹ (arc sine) of the argument	`double`	`double` in radians with values from $-\pi/2$ to $\pi/2$.
`acos(arg)`	cos⁻¹ (arc cosine) of the argument	`double`	`double` in radians, with values from 0.0 to π.
`atan(arg)`	tan⁻¹ (arc tangent) of the argument	`double`	`double` in radians with values from $-\pi/2$ to $\pi/2$.
`atan2 (arg1,arg2)`	tan⁻¹ (arc tangent) of `arg1/arg2`	Both `double`	`double` in radians with values from $-\pi$ to π.

As with all methods, the arguments that you put between the parentheses following the method name can be any expression that produces a value of the required type. If you are not familiar with these trigonometric operations you can safely ignore them.

You also have a range of useful numerical functions that are implemented in the class `Math`. These are:

Method	Function	Argument type	Result type
`abs(arg)`	Calculates the absolute value of the argument	`int`, `long`, `float`, or `double`	The same type as the argument
`max (arg1,arg2)`	Returns the larger of the two arguments, both of the same type	`int`, `long`, `float`, or `double`	The same type as the argument
`min (arg1,arg2)`	Returns the smaller of the two arguments, both of the same type	`int`, `long`, `float`, or `double`	The same type as the argument
`ceil(arg)`	Returns the smallest integer that is greater than or equal to the argument	`double`	`double`
`floor(arg)`	Returns the largest integer that is less than or equal to the argument	`double`	`double`

Method	Function	Argument Type	Result Type
round(arg)	Calculates the nearest integer to the argument value	float or double	Of type int for a float argument, of type long for a double argument
rint(arg)	Calculates the nearest integer to the argument value	double	double
IEEEremainder (arg1,arg2)	Calculates the remainder when arg1 is divided by arg2	Both of type double	Of type double

The IEEEremainder() method produces the remainder from arg1 after dividing arg2 into arg1 the integral number of times that is closest to the exact value of arg1/arg2. This is somewhat different from the remainder operator. The operation arg1 % arg2 produces the remainder after dividing arg2 into arg1 the integral number of times that does not exceed the absolute value of arg1. In some situations this can result in markedly different results. For example, executing the expression 9.0 % 5.0 results in 4.0, whereas the expression Math.IEEEremainder(9.0,5.0) results in -1.0. You can pick one approach to calculating the remainder or the other, to suit your requirements.

Where more than one type of argument is noted in the table, there are actually several methods, one for each type of argument, but all have the same name. We will see how this is possible in Java when we look at implementing class methods in Chapter 5.

The mathematical functions available in the class Math are:

Method	Function	Argument Type	Result Type
sqrt(arg)	Calculates the square root of the argument	double	double
pow (arg1,arg2)	Calculates the first argument raised to the power of the second argument $arg1^{arg2}$	Both double	double
exp(arg)	Calculates e raised to the power of the argument e^{arg}	double	double
log(arg)	Calculates the natural logarithm (base e) of the argument	double	double
random()	Returns a pseudo-random number greater than or equal to 0.0 and less than 1.0	None	double

The toRadians() method in the class Math will convert a double argument that is an angular measurement in degrees to radians. There is a complementary method, toDegrees(), to convert in the opposite direction. The Math class also defines double values for e and π, which you can access as Math.E and Math.PI respectively.

Let's try out a sample of the contents of the class `Math` in an example to make sure we know how they are used.

Try It Out – The Math Class

The following program will calculate the radius of a circle in feet and inches, given that it has an area of 100 square feet:

```
public class MathCalc {
  public static void main(String[] args) {
    // Calculate the radius of a circle
    // which has an area of 100 square feet
    double radius = 0.0;
    double circleArea = 100.0;
    int feet = 0;
    int inches = 0;
    radius = Math.sqrt(circleArea/Math.PI);
    feet = (int)Math.floor(radius); // Get the whole feet and nothing but the feet
    inches = (int)Math.round(12.0*(radius - feet));
    System.out.println("The radius of a circle with area " + circleArea +
                       " square feet is\n " +
                       feet + " feet " + inches + " inches");
  }
}
```

Save the program as `MathCalc.java`. When you compile and run it, you should get:

```
The radius of a circle with area 100.0 square feet is
 5 feet 8 inches
```

How It Works

The first calculation, after defining the variables we need, uses the `sqrt()` method to calculate the radius. Since the area of a circle with radius r is given by the formula πr^2, the radius must be $\sqrt{(area/\pi)}$, and we specify the argument to the `sqrt()` method as the expression `circleArea/Math.PI`, where `Math.PI` references the value of π. The result is in feet as a `double` value. To get the number of whole feet we use the `floor()` method. Note that the cast to `int` is essential in this statement otherwise you will get an error message from the compiler. The value returned from the `floor()` method is type `double`, and the compiler will not cast this to `int` for you automatically because the process potentially loses information.

Finally, we get the number of inches by subtracting the value for whole feet from the original radius, multiplying the fraction of a foot by 12 to get the equivalent inches, and then rounding the result to the nearest integer using the `round()` method.

Note how we output the result. We specify the combination (or concatenation) of strings and variables as an argument to the `println()` method. The statement is spread over two lines for convenience here. The `\n` in the output specifies a newline character, so the output will be on two lines. Any time you want the next bit of output to begin a new line, just add `\n` to the output string. You can't enter a newline character just by typing it because when you do that the cursor just moves to the next line. That's why it's specified as `\n`. There are other characters like this that we'll look into now.

Storing Characters

Variables of the type char store a single character. They each occupy 16 bits, two bytes, in memory because all characters in Java are stored as Unicode. To declare and initialize a character variable myCharacter you would use the statement:

```
char myCharacter = 'X';
```

This initializes the variable with the Unicode character representation of the letter 'X'. You must put single quotes around a character in a statement – 'X'. This is necessary to enable the compiler to distinguish between the character 'X' and a variable with the name X. Note that you can't use double quotes here as they are used to delimit a character string. A character string such as "X" is quite different from the literal of type char, 'X'.

Character Escape Sequences

If you are using an ASCII text editor you will only be able to enter characters directly that are defined within ASCII. You can define Unicode characters by specifying the hexadecimal representation of the character codes in an escape sequence. An escape sequence is simply an alternative means of specifying a character, often by its code. A backslash indicates the start of an escape sequence, and you create an escape sequence for a Unicode character by preceding the four hexadecimal digits of the character by \u. Since the Unicode coding for the letter X is 0x0058 (the low order byte is the same as the ASCII code), you could also declare and define myCharacter with the statement:

```
char myCharacter = '\u0058';
```

You can enter any Unicode character in this way, although it is not exactly user-friendly for entering a lot of characters.

> You can get more information on the full Unicode character set on the Internet by visiting http://www.unicode.org/.

As you have seen, we can write a character string (a String literal as we will see in Chapter 4) enclosed between double quotes. Because the backslash indicates the beginning of an escape sequence in a character string, you must use an escape sequence to specify a backslash character itself in text strings, \\. Since a single quote is used to delimit characters, and we use a double quote to delimit a text string, we also need escape sequences for these. You can define a single quote with the escape sequence \', and a double quote with \". For example, to produce the output:

```
"It's freezing in here", he said coldly.
```

you could write:

```
System.out.println("\"It\'s freezing in here\", he said coldly.");
```

In fact, it's not strictly necessary to use an escape sequence to specify a single quote within a string, but obviously it will be when you want to specify it as a single character. Of course, it is always necessary to specify a double quote within a string using an escape sequence otherwise it would be interpreted as the end of the string.

There are other escape characters you can use to define control characters:

\b	Backspace
\f	Form feed
\n	New line
\r	Carriage return
\t	Tab

Character Arithmetic

You can perform arithmetic on char variables. With myCharacter containing the character 'X', the statement:

```
myCharacter += 1;     // Increment to next character
```

will result in the value of myCharacter being changed to 'Y'. This is because the Unicode code for 'Y' is one more than the code for 'X'. You could use the increment operator ++ to increase the code stored in myCharacter by just writing:

```
++myCharacter;        // Increment to next character
```

You can use variables of type char in an arithmetic expression, and their values will be converted to type int to carry out the calculation. It doesn't necessarily make a whole lot of sense, but you could write,

```
char aChar = 0;
char bChar = '\u0028';
aChar = (char)(2*bChar + 8);
```

which will leave aChar holding the code for X – which is 0x0058.

Bitwise Operations

As you already know, all these integer variables we have been talking about are represented internally as binary numbers. A value of type int consists of 32 **binary digits**, known to us computer fans as bits. You can operate on the bit values of integers using the bitwise operators, of which there are four available:

&	AND
|	OR
^	Exclusive OR
~	Complement

Each of these operators works with individual bits as follows:

❑ The bitwise AND operator, &, combines corresponding bits in its two operands such that if the first bit *AND* the second bit are 1, the result is 1 – otherwise the result is 0.

❑ The bitwise OR operator, |, combines corresponding bits such that if either one bit *OR* the other is 1, then the result is 1. Only if both bits are 0 is the result 0.

❑ The bitwise exclusive OR (XOR) operator, ^, combines corresponding bits such that if both bits are the same the result is 0, otherwise the result is 1.

❑ The complement operator, ~ , takes a single operand in which it inverts all the bits, so that each 1 bit becomes 0, and each 0 bit becomes 1.

You can see the effect of these operators in the following examples.

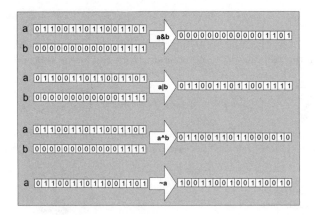

The illustration shows the binary digits that make up the operands and the results. Each of the three binary operations applies to corresponding individual pairs of bits from the operands separately. The complement operator flips the state of each bit in the operand.

Since you are concerned with individual bits with bitwise operations, writing a constant as a normal decimal value is not going to be particularly convenient. A much better way of writing binary values in this case is to express them as hexadecimal numbers, because you can convert from binary to hexadecimal, and vice versa, very quickly. There's more on this in Appendix B.

Converting from binary to hexadecimal is easy. Each group of four binary digits from the right corresponds to one hexadecimal digit. You just work out what the value of each four bits is and write the appropriate hexadecimal digit. For example, the value of a from the illustration is:

Binary	0110	0110	1100	1101
Decimal value	6	6	12	13
Hexadecimal	6	6	C	D

So the value of the variable a in hexadecimal is `0x66CD`, where the `0x` prefix indicates that this is a hexadecimal value. The variable b in the illustration has the hexadecimal value `0x000F`. If you think of the variable b as a mask applied to a, you can view the & operator as keeping bits unchanged where the mask is 1 and setting the rest to 0. Mask is a term used to refer to a particular configuration of bits designed to select out specific bits when it is combined with a variable using a bitwise operator. So if you want to select a particular bit out of an integer variable, just **AND** it with a mask that has that bit set to 1 and all the others as 0.

You can also look at what the & operator does from another perspective – it forces a bit to 0, if the corresponding mask bit is 0. Similarly, the | operator forces a bit to be 1 when the mask bit is 1.

The & and | operators are the most frequently used, mainly for dealing with variables where the individual bits are used as state indicators of some kind for things that can be either true or false, or on or off. You could use a single bit as a state indicator determining whether something should be displayed, with the bit as 1, or not displayed, with the bit as 0. A single bit can be selected using the & operator – for example, to select the third bit in the int variable indicators, you can write:

```
thirdBit = indicators & 0x4;      // Select the 3rd bit
```

We can illustrate how this works if we assume the variable indicators contains the hexadecimal value `0xFF07`:

	Hexadecimal	Binary			
indicators	0xFF07	1111	1111	0000	0111
mask value	0x4	0000	0000	0000	0100
indicators & 0x4	0x4	0000	0000	0000	0100

All these values should have 32 bits and we are only showing 16 bits here, but you see all you need to know how it works. The mask value sets all the bits in indicators to zero except for the third bit. Here, the result of the expression is non-zero because the third bit in indicators is 1.

On the other hand, if the variable indicators contained the value `0xFF09` the result would be different:

	Hexadecimal	Binary			
indicators	0xFF09	1111	1111	0000	1001
mask value	0x4	0000	0000	0000	0100
indicators & 0x4	0x0004	0000	0000	0000	0000

The result of the expression is now zero because the third bit of `indicators` is zero.

To set a particular bit on, you can use the | operator, so to set the third bit in `indicators` on, you can write:

```
indicators = indicators | 0x4;    // Set the 3rd bit on
```

We can see how this applies to the last value we had for indicators:

	Hexadecimal	Binary			
indicators	0xFF09	1111	1111	0000	1001
mask value	0x4	0000	0000	0000	0100
indicators | 0x4	0xFF0D	1111	1111	0000	1101

As you can see, the effect is just to switch the third bit of indicators on. All the others are unchanged. Of course, if the bit were already on, it would stay on.

The bitwise operators can also be used in the `op=` form. Setting the third bit in the variable `indicators` is usually written as:

```
indicators |= 0x4;
```

Although there is nothing wrong with the original statement we wrote, the one above is just a bit more concise.

To set a bit off you need to use the & operator again, with a mask that has 0 for the bit you want as 0, and 1 for all the others. To set the third bit of `indicators` off you could write:

```
indicators &= ~0x4;              // Set the 3rd bit off
```

With `indicators` having the value `0xFF07`, this would work as follows:

	Hexadecimal	Binary			
indicators	0xFF07	1111	1111	0000	0111
mask value	0x4	0000	0000	0000	0100
~0x4	0xFFFB	1111	1111	1111	1011
indicators & ~0x4	0xFF03	1111	1111	0000	0011

The ^ operator has the slightly surprising ability to interchange two values without moving either value somewhere else. The need for this turns up most frequently in tricky examination questions. If you execute the three statements:

```
a ^= b;
b ^= a;
a ^= b;
```

the values of a and b will be interchanged, but remember this only works for integers. We can try this out with a couple of arbitrary values for a and b, 0xD00F and 0xABAD respectively – again we will just look at 16 bits for each variable. The first statement will change a to a new value:

a ^= b	Hexadecimal	Binary			
a	0xD00F	1101	0000	0000	1111
b	0xABAD	1010	1011	1010	1101
a from a^b	0x7BA2	0111	1011	1010	0010

Now the next statement, which calculates a new value of b using the new value of a:

b ^= a	Hexadecimal	Binary			
a	0x7BA2	0111	1011	1010	0010
b	0xABAD	1010	1011	1010	1101
b from b^a	0xD00F	1101	0000	0000	1111

So b now has a value that looks remarkably like the value that a started out with. Let's look at the last step, which calculates a new value for a using the new value of b:

a ^= b	Hexadecimal	Binary			
a	0x7BA2	0111	1011	1010	0010
b	0xD00F	1101	0000	0000	1111
a from a^b	0xABAD	1010	1011	1010	1101

Lo and behold, the value of a is now the original value of b. In the old days when all programmers wore lab coats, when computers were driven by steam, and when memory was measured in bytes rather than megabytes, this mechanism could be quite useful since you could interchange two values in memory without having to have extra memory locations available. So if antique computers are your things, this may turn out to be a valuable technique. In fact it's more useful than that. When we get to do some graphics programming you will see that this is very relevant.

Don't forget – all of these bitwise operators can only be applied to integers. They don't work with any other type of value. As with the arithmetic expressions, the bitwise operations are carried out with 32 bits for integers of type short and of type byte, so a cast to the appropriate type is necessary for the result of the expression on the right of the assignment operator. One note of caution – special care is needed when initializing variables of type byte and type short with hexadecimal values to avoid being caught out. For example, you might be tempted to initialize a variable of type byte to binary 1111 1111 with the statement:

```
byte allBitsOne = 0xFF;      // Wrong!!
```

In fact this results in a compiler error message. The literal `0xFF` is 1111 1111, so what's the beef here? The beef is that `0xFF` is *not* 1111 1111 at all. The literal `0xFF` is type int, so it is the binary value 0000 0000 0000 0000 1111 1111. This happens to be equivalent to the decimal value 128, which is outside the range of type byte. The byte value we are looking for, 1111 1111, is equivalent to the decimal value -1 so the correct way to initialize `allBitsOne` to 1s is to write:

```
byte allBitsOne = 0xFFFFFFFF;      // Correct - well done!!
```

Now the compiler will happily chop off the high order bits to produce the result we are looking for.

Shift Operations

Another mechanism that you have for working with integer variables at the bit level is shifting. You can shift the bits in an integer to the right or the left. Shifting binary digits right or left can be envisaged as dividing or multiplying by powers of two. Shifting the binary value of 3, which is 0011, to the left one bit multiplies it by two. It becomes binary 0110, which is decimal 6. Shifting it to the right by one bit divides it by 2. It becomes binary 0001, which is 1.

Java has three shift operators:

<<	Shift left, filling with zeros from the right
>>	Shift right, propagating the sign bit from the left
>>>	Shift right, filling with zeros from the left

The effect of the operators is shown in the following illustration:

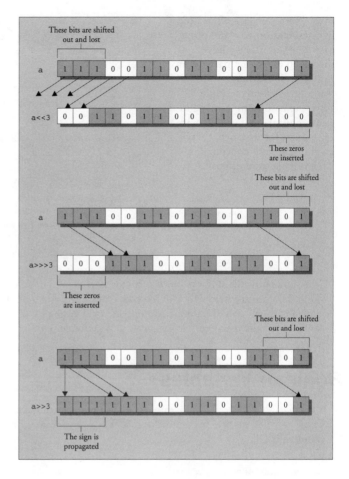

Of course, if the high order bit in the >> operation in the illustration was zero, there would be three zeros at the leftmost end of the result.

Shift operations are often used in combination with the other bitwise operators we have discussed to extract parts of an integer value. In many operating systems a single 32-bit value is sometimes used to store multiple values – two 16-bit values, for instance, that might be screen coordinates. This is illustrated opposite.

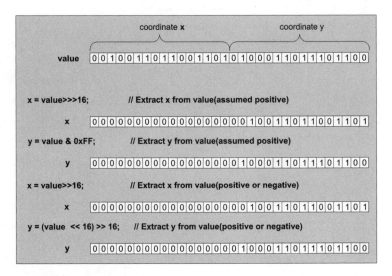

This shows how the shift operations can be used to extract either the left or the right 16 bits from the variable value. You can see here why you have an extra shift right operation that propagates the leftmost bit. It is related to the notion of a shift as multiplying or dividing by a power of 2, and the implications of that in the context of negative integers represented in 2's complement form (see Appendix B).

Boolean Variables

Variables that can only have one of two values, `true` or `false`, are of type `boolean`, and the values `true` and `false` are `boolean` literals. You can define a `boolean` variable, called `state`, with the statement:

```
boolean state = true;
```

This statement also initializes the variable `state` with the value `true`. You can also set a `boolean` variable in an assignment statement. For example, the statement:

```
state = false;
```

sets the value of the variable `state` to `false`.

At this point we can't do much with a `boolean` variable, other than to set its value to `true` or `false`, but, as you will see in the next chapter, Boolean variables become much more useful in the context of decision making in a program, particularly when we can use expressions that produce a `boolean` result.

There are several operators that combine Boolean values including operators for Boolean AND, Boolean OR, and Boolean negation (these are &&, ||, and !, respectively), as well as comparison operators that produce a Boolean result. Rather than go into these here in the abstract, we will defer discussion until the next chapter where we will also look at how we can apply them in practice to alter the sequence of execution in a program.

One point you should note is that `boolean` **variables differ from the other primitive data types in that they cannot be cast to any other basic type, and the other primitive types cannot be cast to** `boolean`.

Operator Precedence

We have already introduced the idea of a pecking order for operators, which determines the sequence in which they are executed in a statement. A simple arithmetic expression such as 3 + 4*5 results in the value 23 because the multiply operation is executed first – it takes precedence over the addition operation. We can now formalize the position by classifying all the operators present in Java. Each operator in Java has a set priority or precedence in relation to the others, as shown in the following table. Operators with a higher precedence are executed before those of a lower precedence. Precedence is highest for operators in the top line in the table, down through to the operators in the bottom line, which have the lowest precedence:

Operator Precedence Group	Associativity
(), [], . postfix ++, postfix --	left
unary +, unary -, prefix ++, prefix --, ~, !	right
(type), new	left
*, /, %	left
+, -	left
<<, >>, >>>	left
< , <= , > , >=, instanceof	left
==, !=	left
&	left
^	left
|	left
&&	left
||	left
?:	left
=, +=, -=, *=, /=, %=, <<=, >>=, >>>=, &=, |=, ^=	right

Most of the operators that appear in the table you have not seen yet, but you will meet them all in this book eventually, and it is handy to have them all gathered together in a single precedence table that you can refer to when necessary.

By definition, the postfix ++ operator is executed after the other operators in the expression in which it appears, despite its high precedence. In this case, precedence determines what it applies to, in other words, the postfix ++ only acts on the variable that appears immediately before it. For this reason the expression `oranges+++apples` that we saw earlier is evaluated as (`oranges++`) + `apples` rather than `oranges` + (++`apples`).

The sequence of execution of operators with equal precedence in a statement is determined by a property called `associativity`. Each group of operators appearing on the same line in the table above are either `left associative` or `right associative`. A left associative operator attaches to its immediate left operand. This results in an expression involving several left associative operators with the same precedence in the same expression being executed in sequence starting with the leftmost and ending with the rightmost. Right associative operators of equal precedence in an expression bind to their right operand and consequently are executed from right to left. For example, if you write the statement:

```
a = b + c + 10;
```

the left associativity of the group to which the + operator belongs implies that this is effectively:

```
a = (b + c) + 10;
```

On the other hand, = and op= are right associative, so if you have `int` variables a, b, c, and d each initialized to 1, the statement:

```
a += b = c += d = 10;
```

sets a to 12, b and c to 11, and d to 10. The statement is equivalent to:

```
a += (b = (c += (d = 10)));
```

Note that these statements are intended to illustrate how associativity works, and are not a recommended approach to coding.

You will probably find that you will learn the precedence and associativity of the operators in Java by just using them in your programs. You may need to refer back to the table from time to time, but as you gain experience you will gain a feel for where the operators sit and eventually you will automatically know when you need parentheses and when not.

Program Comments

We have been adding comments in all our examples so far, so you already know that // plus everything following in a line is ignored by the compiler (except when the // appears in a character string between double quotes of course). Another use for // is to comment out lines of code. If you want to remove some code from a program temporarily, you just need to add // at the beginning of each line you want to eliminate.

It is often convenient to include multiple lines of comment in a program, for example, at the beginning of a method to explain what it does. An alternative to using // at the beginning of each line in a block of comments is to put /* at the beginning of the first comment line and */ at the end of the last comment line. Everything between the /* and the next */ will be ignored. By this means you can annotate your programs, like this for example:

```
/****************************************
 *    This is a long explanation of     *
 *    some particularly important       *
 *    aspect of program operation.      *
 ****************************************/
```

Of course, you can frame blocks like this in any way that you like, or even not at all, just so long as there is /* at the beginning and */ at the end.

Documentation Comments

You can also include comments in a program that are intended to produce separate documentation for the program. These are called documentation comments. All the documentation that you get with the JDK is produced in this way. A program called javadoc, which contains the documentation comments, produces the documentation once it is processed.

The documentation that is generated is in the form of HTML web pages that can be viewed using a browser such as Netscape Navigator or Internet Explorer. A full discussion of documentation comments is outside the scope of this book – not because they are difficult, they aren't, but it would need a lot of pages to cover them properly. We will just describe them sufficiently so that you will recognize documentation comments when you see them.

A documentation comment begins with /** and ends with */. An example of a simple documentation comment is:

```
/**
 * This is a documentation comment.
 */
```

Any asterisks at the beginning of each line in a documentation comment are ignored, as are any spaces preceding the first *.

A documentation comment can also include HTML tags, as well as special tags beginning with @ that are used to document methods and classes in a standard form. The @ is followed by a keyword that defines the purpose of the tag. Here are some of the keywords that you can use:

@author	Used to define the author of the code.
@deprecated	Used in the documentation of library classes and methods to indicate that they have been superseded and generally should not be used in new applications.
@exception	Used to document exceptions that the code can throw and the circumstance which can cause this to occur.
{@link}	Generates a link to another part of the documentation within the documentation that is produced. The curly brackets are used to separate it from the rest of the in-line text.
@param	Used to describe the parameters for a method.
@return	Used to document the value returned from a method.
@see	Used to specify cross references to some other part of the code such as another class or a method. It can also reference a URL.
@throws	A synonym for @exception.
@version	Used to describe the current version of the code.

You can use any HTML tags within a documentation comment except for header tags. The HTML tags you insert are used to structure and format the documentation appropriately when it is viewed, and javadoc will add HTML tags to format the comments that include the special @ tags that we mentioned above.

The few comments I have made here really don't do justice to the power and scope of javadoc. For that you need to look into it in detail. The JDK comes with the javadoc program and documentation. Javadoc also has its own home page on the Javasoft web site at http://java.sun.com/products/jdk/javadoc/.

Summary

In this chapter you have seen all of the basic types of variables available in Java. The discussion of `boolean` variables will be more meaningful in the context of the next chapter since their primary use is in decision making and modifying the execution sequence in a program.

The important points you have learned in this chapter are:

❑   The integer types are `byte`, `short`, `int`, and `long`, occupying 1, 2, 4, and 8 bytes respectively.

❑   Variables of type `char` occupy 2 bytes and can store a single Unicode character code.

❑   Integer expressions are evaluated using 64-bit operations for variables of type `long`, and using 32-bit operations for all other integer types. You must therefore add a cast for all assignment operations storing a result of `type byte`, `short`, or `char`.

❑   A cast will be automatically supplied where necessary for `op=` assignment operations.

❑   The floating-point types are `float` and `double`, occupying 4 and 8 bytes respectively.

❑   Values that are outside the range of a floating-point type are represented by a special value that is displayed as either `Infinity` or `-Infinity`.

❑   Where the result of a floating point calculation is indeterminate, the value is displayed as `NaN`. Such values are referred to as not-a-number.

❑   Variables of type `boolean` can only have either the value true or the value false.

❑   The order of execution of operators in an expression is determined by their precedence. Where operators are of equal precedence, the order of execution is determined by their associativity.

Exercises

1.   Write a console program to define and initialize a variable of type `byte` to 1, and then successively multiply it by 2 and display its value 8 times. Explain the reason for the last result.

2.   Write a console program to declare and initialize a `double` variable with some value such as 1234.5678. Then retrieve the integral part of the value and store it in a variable of type `long`, and the first four digits of the fractional part and store them in an integer of type `short`. Display the value of the `double` variable by outputting the two values stored as integers.

3. Write a program that defines a floating point variable initialized with a dollar value for your income and a second floating point variable initialized with a value corresponding to a tax rate of 35 percent. Calculate and output the amount of tax you must pay with the dollars and cents stored as separate integer values (use two variables of type `int` to hold the tax, perhaps `taxDollars` and `taxCents`).

4. The diameter of the Sun is approximately 865,000 miles. The diameter of the Earth is approximately 7600 miles. Use the methods in the class `Math` to calculate:

❑ the volume of the Earth in cubic miles

❑ the volume of the Sun in cubic miles

❑ the ratio of the volume of the Sun to the volume of the Earth

Loops and Logic

In this chapter we'll look at how you make decisions and choices in your Java programs. You will also learn how to make your programs repeat a set of actions until a specific condition is met. We will cover:

- ❏ How you compare data values

- ❏ How you can define logical expressions

- ❏ How you can use logical expressions to alter the sequence in which program statements are executed

- ❏ How you can select different expressions depending on the value of a logical expression

- ❏ How to choose between options in a fixed set of alternatives

- ❏ How long your variables last

- ❏ How you can repeat a block of code a given number of times

- ❏ How you can repeat a block of code as long as a given logical expression is true

- ❏ How you can break out of loops and statement blocks

- ❏ What assertions are and how you use them

All your programs of any consequence will use at least some, and often most, of the language capabilities and programming techniques we will cover in this chapter, so make sure you have a good grasp of them.

But first, how do we make decisions in code, and so affect the way the program runs?

Making Decisions

Making choices will be a fundamental element in all your programs. You need to be able to make decisions like, "If the bank balance is large, buy the car with the go-faster stripes, else renew the monthly bus ticket". In programming terms this requires the ability to make comparisons between variables, constants, and the values of expressions, then executing one group of statements or another, depending on the result of a given comparison. The first step to making decisions in a program is to look at how we make comparisons.

Making Comparisons

Java provides you with six relational operators for comparing two data values. Either of the data values you are comparing can be variables, constants or expressions drawn from Java's primitive data types – `byte`, `short`, `int`, `long`, `char`, `float` or `double`.

Relational Operators	Description
>	Produces the value `true` if the left operand is greater than the right operand, and `false` otherwise.
>=	Produces the value `true` if the left operand is greater than or equal to the right operand, and `false` otherwise.
==	Produces the value `true` if the left operand is equal to the right operand, and `false` otherwise.
!=	Produces the value `true` if the left operand is not equal to the right operand, and `false` otherwise.
<=	Produces the value `true` if the left operand is less than or equal to the right operand, and `false` otherwise.
<	Produces the value `true` if the left operand is less than the right operand, and `false` otherwise.

As you see, each operator produces either the value `true`, or the value `false`, and so is eminently suited to the business of making decisions.

If you wish to store the result of a comparison, you use a boolean variable. We saw how to declare these in the previous chapter. For example you can define a boolean variable `state` and you can set its value in an assignment as follows:

```
boolean state = false;
state = x - y < a + b;
```

The value of the variable `state` will be set to `true` in the assignment if `x-y` is less than `a+b`, and to `false` otherwise.

To understand how the expression above is evaluated, take a look back at the precedence table for operators that we introduced in the last chapter. You will see that the comparison operators are all of lower precedence than the arithmetic operators, so arithmetic operations will always be completed before any comparisons are made, unless of course there are parentheses saying otherwise. The expression,

```
x - y == a + b
```

will produce the result `true` if `x-y` is equal to `a+b`, since these arithmetic sub-expressions will be evaluated first, and the values that result will be the operands for the `==` operator. Of course, it is helpful to put the parentheses in, even though they are not strictly necessary. It leaves no doubt as to what is happening if you write:

```
(x - y) == (a + b)
```

Note that if the left and right operands of a relational operator are of differing types, values will be promoted in the same way as we saw in the last chapter for mixed arithmetic expressions. So if `aDouble` is of type `double`, and `number` is of type `int`, in the following expression:

```
aDouble < number + 1
```

the value produced by `number + 1` will be calculated as type `int`, and this value will be promoted to type `double` before comparing it with the value of `aDouble`.

The if Statement

The first statement we will look at that can make use of the result of a comparison is the `if` statement. The `if` statement, in its simplest configuration, is of the form:

```
if(expression)
    statement;
```

where `expression` can be any expression that produces a value `true` or `false`. You can see a graphical representation of this logic in the following diagram:

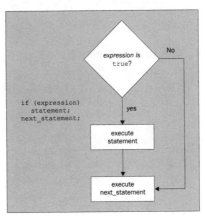

If the value of expression is true, the statement that follows the if is executed, otherwise it isn't. A practical example of this is as follows:

```
if(number%2 != 0)         // Test if number is odd
  ++number;               // If so make it even
```

The if tests whether the value of number is odd by comparing the remainder, after dividing by 2, with 0. If the remainder isn't equal to 0, the value of number is odd, so we add 1 to make it even. If the value of number is even, the statement incrementing number will not be executed.

> **Note how the statement is indented. This is to show that it is subject to the if condition. You should always indent statements in your Java programs as cues to the program structure. We will gather more guidelines on the use of statement indenting as we work with more complicated examples.**

You may sometimes see a simple if written on a single line. The previous example could have been written:

```
if(number%2 != 0) ++number;   // If number is odd, make it even
```

This is perfectly legal. The compiler ignores excess spaces and newline characters – the semi-colon acts as the delimiter for a statement. Writing an if in this way saves a little space, and occasionally it can be an aid to clarity, when you have a succession of such comparisons for instance, but generally it is better to write the action statement on a separate line to the condition being tested.

Statement Blocks

In general, wherever you can have one executable statement in Java, you can replace it with a block of statements enclosed between braces instead. So a statement block between braces can also be nested in another statement block to any depth. This means that we can use a statement block within the basic if statement that we just saw. The if statement can equally well be of the form:

```
if(expression) {
  statement 1;
  statement 2;
  ...
  statement n;
}
```

Now if the value of expression is true, all the statements enclosed in the following block will be executed. Of course, without the braces to enclose the block, the code no longer has a statement block:

```
if(expression)
  statement 1;
  statement 2;
  ...
  statement n;
```

Here, only the first statement, statement 1, will be omitted when the if expression is false; the remaining statements will always be executed regardless of the value of expression. You can see from this that indenting is just a visual cue to the logic. It has no effect on how the program code executes. This looks as though the sequence of statements belongs to the if, but only the first one does because there are no braces. The indenting is incorrect here.

> **In this book, we will adopt the convention of having the opening brace on the same line as the statement. The closing brace will then be aligned with the statement. We will indent all the statements within the block from the braces so that they are easily identified as belonging to the block. There are other conventions that you can use if you prefer, the most important consideration being that you are consistent.**

As a practical example of an if statement that includes a statement block, we could write:

```
if(number%2 != 0) {          // Test if number is odd
   // If so make it even and output a message
   ++number;
   System.out.println("Number was forced to be even and is now " + number);
}
```

Now both statements between the braces are executed if the if expression is true, and neither of them is executed if the if expression is false.

It is a good practice to always have opening and closing braces even when there is only a single action statement, this helps clarify the code and will stop confusion of its logic.

Statement blocks are more than just a convenient way of grouping statements together – they affect the life and accessibility of variables. We will learn more about statement blocks when we discuss variable scope later in this chapter. In the meantime let's look a little deeper into what we can do with the if statement.

The else Clause

We can extend the basic if statement by adding an else clause. This provides a second choice of statement, or statement block, that is executed when the expression in the if statement is false. You can see the syntax of this clause, and how the program's control flow works, in this diagram:

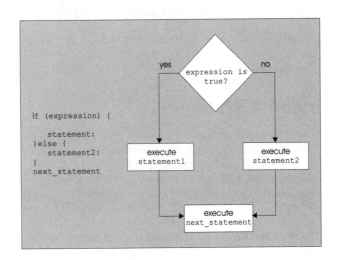

This provides an explicit choice between two courses of action – one for when the `if` expression is `true` and another for when it is `false`.

We can apply this in a console program and try out the `random()` method from the `Math` class at the same time.

Try It Out – if-else

When you have entered the program text, save it in a file called `NumberCheck.java`. Compile it and then run it a few times to see what results you get.

```java
public class NumberCheck {
  public static void main(String[] args) {
    int number = 0;
    number = 1+(int)(100*Math.random());  // Get a random integer between 1 & 100
    if(number%2 == 0) {                    // Test if it is even
      System.out.println("You have got an even number, " + number); // It is even

    } else {
      System.out.println("You have got an odd number, " + number);  // It is odd
    }
  }
}
```

How It Works

We saw the method `random()` in the standard class `Math` in the previous chapter. It returns a random value of type `double` between 0.0 and 1.0, but the result is always less than 1.0, so the largest number you will get is 0.9999... (with the number of recurring digits being limited to the maximum number that the type `double` will allow, of course). Consequently, when we multiply the value returned by 100.0 and convert this value to type `int` with the explicit cast, we discard any fractional part of the number and produce a random integer between 0 and 99. Adding 1 to this will result in a random integer between 1 and 100, which we store in the variable `number`. We then generate the program output in the `if` statement. If the value of `number` is even, the first `println()` call is executed, otherwise the second `println()` call in the `else` clause is executed.

Note the use of indentation here. It is evident that `main()` is within the class definition, and the code for `main()` is clearly distinguished. You can also see immediately which statement is executed when the `if` expression is `true`, and which applies when it is `false`.

Nested if Statements

The statement that is executed when an `if` expression is `true` can be another `if`, as can the statement in an `else` clause. This will enable you to express such convoluted logic as "if my bank balance is healthy then I will buy the car if I have my check book with me, else I will buy the car if I can get a loan from the bank". An `if` statement that is nested inside another can also itself contain a nested `if`. You can continue nesting `if`s one inside the other like this for as long as you still know what you are doing – or even beyond if you enjoy confusion.

To illustrate the nested `if` statement, we can modify the `if` from the previous example:

```
if(number%2 == 0) {                       // Test if it is even
  if(number < 50) {                       // Output a message if number is < 50
    System.out.println("You have got an even number < 50, " + number);
  }

} else {
  System.out.println("You have got an odd number, " + number); // It is odd
}
```

Now the message for an even value is only displayed if the value of number is also less than 50.

The braces around the nested if are necessary here because of the else clause. The braces constrain the nested if in the sense that if it had an else clause, it would have to appear between the braces enclosing the nested if. If the braces were not there, the program would still compile and run but the logic would be different. Let's see how.

With nested ifs, the question of to which if statement a particular else clause belongs often arises. If we remove the braces from the code above, we have:

```
if(number%2 == 0)                         // Test if it is even
  if(number < 50 )                        // Output a message if number is < 50
    System.out.println("You have got an even number < 50, " + number);
else
  System.out.println("You have got an odd number, " + number); // It is odd
```

This has substantially changed the logic from what we had before. The else clause now belongs to the nested if that tests whether number is less than 50, so the second println() call is only executed for **even** numbers that are greater than or equal to 50. This is clearly not what we wanted since it makes nonsense of the output in this case, but it does illustrate the rule for connecting elses to ifs, which is:

An **else** always belongs to the nearest preceding **if** that is not in a separate block, and is not already spoken for by another **else**.

You need to take care that the indenting of statements with nested ifs is correct. It is easy to convince yourself that the logic is as indicated by the indentation, even when this is completely wrong.

Let's try the if-else combination in another program:

Try It Out – Deciphering Characters the Hard Way

Create the class LetterCheck, and code its main() method as follows:

```
public class LetterCheck {
  public static void main(String[] args) {
    char symbol = 'A';
    symbol = (char)(128.0*Math.random());      // Generate a random character

    if(symbol >= 'A') {                         // Is it A or greater?
```

```
          if(symbol <= 'Z') {                              // yes, and is it Z or less?
          // Then it is a capital letter
          System.out.println("You have the capital letter " + symbol);

       } else {                                  // It is not Z or less
          if(symbol >= 'a') {                    // So is it a or greater?
             if(symbol <= 'z') {                 // Yes, so is it z or less?
             // Then it is a small letter
             System.out.println("You have the small letter " + symbol);

             } else {                            // It is not less than z
             System.out.println(
             "The code is greater than a but it's not a letter");
             }

          } else {
             System.out.println(
                     "The code is less than a and it's not a letter");
          }
       }

    } else {
       System.out.println("The code is less than A so it's not a letter");
    }
  }
}
```

How It Works

This program figures out whether the character stored in the variable `symbol` is an uppercase letter, a lowercase letter, or some other character. The program first generates a random character with a numeric code between 0 and 127, which corresponds to the characters in the basic 7-bit ASCII (ISO 646) character set. The Unicode coding for the ASCII characters is numerically the same as the ASCII code values. Within this character set, the letters 'A' to 'Z' are represented by a contiguous group of ASCII codes with decimal values from 65 to 90. The lowercase letters are represented by another contiguous group with ASCII code values that have decimal values from 97 to 122. So to convert any capital letter to a lowercase letter, you just need to add 32 to the character code.

The `if` statements are a bit convoluted so let's look at a diagram of the logic.

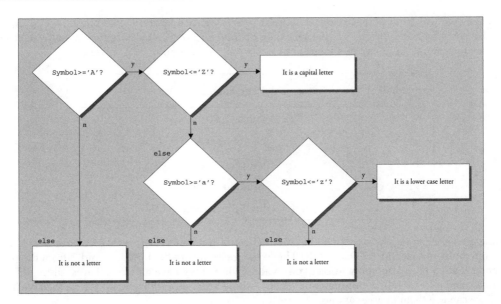

We have four if statements altogether. The first if tests whether symbol is 'A' or greater. If it is, it could be a capital letter, a small letter, or possibly something else. But if it isn't, it is not a letter at all, so the else for this if statement (towards the end of the program) produces a message to that effect.

The nested if statement, which is executed if symbol is 'A' or greater, tests whether it is 'Z' or less. If it is, then symbol definitely contains a capital letter and the appropriate message is displayed. If it isn't then it may be a small letter, so another if statement is nested within the else clause of the first nested if, to test for this possibility.

The if statement in the else clause tests for symbol being greater than 'a'. If it isn't, we know that symbol is not a letter and a message is displayed. If it is, another if checks whether symbol is 'z' or less. If it is we have a small letter, and if not we don't have a letter at all.

You will have to run the example a few times to get all the possible messages to come up. They all will – eventually.

Having carefully crafted our convoluted and cumbersome condition checking, now's the time to reveal that there is a much easier way to achieve the same result.

Logical Operators

The tests we have put in the if expressions have been relatively simple so far, except perhaps for the last one. Real life is typically more complicated. You will often want to combine a number of conditions so that you execute a particular course, for example, if they are all true simultaneously. You can ride the roller coaster if you are over 12 years old, over four feet tall, *and* less than six feet six. Failure on any count and it's no go. Sometimes, though, you may need to test for any one of a number of conditions being true, for example, you get a lower price entry ticket if you are under 16, or over 65.

You can deal with both of these cases, and more, using **logical operators** to combine several expressions that have a value `true` or `false`. Because they operate on `boolean` values they are also referred to as **boolean operators**. There are five logical operators that operate on `boolean` values:

Symbol	Long name
&	logical AND
&&	conditional AND
|	logical OR
||	conditional OR
!	logical negation (NOT)

These are very simple, the only point of potential confusion being the fact that we have the choice of two operators for each of AND and OR. The extra operators are the bitwise & and | from the previous chapter that you can also apply to `boolean` values where they have an effect that is subtly different from && and ||. We'll first consider what each of these are used for in general terms, then we'll look at how we can use them in an example.

Boolean AND Operations

You can use either AND operator, && or &, where you have two logical expressions that must both be `true` for the result to be `true` – that is, you want to be rich *and* healthy. Either operator will produce the same result from the logical expression. We will come back to how they are different in a moment. First, let's explore how they are used. All of the following discussion applies equally well to & as well as &&.

Let's see how logical operators can simplify the last example. You could use the && operator if you were testing a variable of type `char` to determine whether it contained an uppercase letter or not. The value being tested must be both greater than or equal to 'A' AND less than or equal to 'Z'. Both conditions must be `true` for the value to be a capital letter. Taking the example from our previous program, with a value stored in a `char` variable `symbol`, we could implement the test for an uppercase letter in a single `if` by using the && operator:

```
if(symbol >= 'A' && symbol <= 'Z')
   System.out.println("You have the capital letter " + symbol);
```

If you take a look at the precedence table back in Chapter 2, you will see that the relational operators will be executed before the && operator, so no parentheses are necessary. Here, the output statement will be executed only if both of the conditions combined by the operator && are `true`. However, as we have said before, it is a good idea to add parentheses if they make the code easier to read. It also helps to avoid mistakes.

In fact, the result of an && operation is very simple. It is `true` only if both operands are `true`, otherwise the result is `false`.

We can now rewrite the set of `if`s from the last example.

Try It Out – Deciphering Characters the Easy Way

Replace the outer `if-else` loop and its contents in `LetterCheck.java` with the following:

```
if(symbol >= 'A' && symbol <= 'Z') {        // Is it a capital letter
  System.out.println("You have the capital letter " + symbol);

} else {
  if(symbol >= 'a' && symbol <= 'z') {      // or is it a small letter?
    System.out.println("You have the small letter " + symbol);

  } else {                                  // It is not less than z
    System.out.println("The code is not a letter");
  }
}
```

How It Works

Using the `&&` operator has condensed the example down quite a bit. We now can do the job with two `if`s, and it's certainly easier to follow what's happening.

You might want to note that when the statement in an `else` clause is another `if`, the `if` is sometimes written on the same line as the `else`, as in:

```
if(symbol >= 'A' && symbol <= 'Z') {            // Is it a capital letter
  System.out.println("You have the capital letter " + symbol);

} else if(symbol >= 'a' && symbol <= 'z') {   // or is it a small letter?
  System.out.println("You have the small letter " + symbol);

} else {                                        // It is not less than z
  System.out.println("The code is not a letter");
}
```

I think the original is clearer, so I prefer not to do this.

&& versus &

So what distinguishes `&&` from `&` ? The difference between them is that the conditional `&&` will not bother to evaluate the right-hand operand if the left-hand operand is `false`, since the result is already determined in this case to be `false`. This can make the code a bit faster when the left-hand operand is `false`.

For example, consider the following statements:

```
int number = 50;
if(number<40 && (3*number - 27)>100) {
  System.out.println("number = " + number);
}
```

Here the expression `(3*number - 27)>100` will never be executed since the expression `number<40` is always `false`. On the other hand, if you write the statements as:

87

```
int number = 50;
if(number<40 & (3*number - 27)>100) {
  System.out.println("number = " + number);
}
```

the effect is different. The whole logical expression is always evaluated, so even though the left-hand operand of the & operator is false and the result is a forgone conclusion once that is known, the right hand operand ((3*number - 27)>100) will still be evaluated. So, we can just use && all the time to make our programs a bit faster and forget about &, right? Wrong – it all depends on what you are doing. Most of the time you can use &&, but there are occasions when you will want to be sure that the right-hand operand is evaluated – and equally, there are instances where you want to be certain the right-hand operand won't be evaluated if the left operand is false.

The first situation can arise for instance when the right hand expression involves modifying a variable – and you want the variable to be modified in any event. An example of a statement like this is:

```
if(++value%2 == 0 & ++count < limit) {
  // Do something
}
```

Here, the variable count will be incremented in any event. If you use && instead of &, count will only be incremented if the left operand of the AND operator is true. You get a different result depending on which operator is used.

We can illustrate the second situation with the following statement:

```
if(count > 0 && total/count > 5) {
  // Do something...
}
```

In this case the right operand for the && operation will only be executed if the left operand is True – that is, when count is positive. Clearly, if we were to use & here, and count happened to be zero, we will be attempting to divide the value of total by 0, which in the absence of code to prevent it, will terminate the program.

Boolean OR Operations

The OR operators, | and ||, apply when you want a true result if either or both of the operands are true. The conditional OR, ||, has a similar effect to the conditional AND, in that it omits the evaluation of the right-hand operand when the left-hand operand is true. Obviously if the left operand is true, the result will be True regardless of whether the right operand is true or false.

Let's take an example. A reduced entry ticket price is issued to under 16 year olds and to those aged 65 or over; this could be tested using the following if:

```
if(age < 16 || age>= 65) {
  ticketPrice *= 0.9;          // Reduce ticket price by 10%
}
```

The effect here is to reduce ticketPrice by ten percent if either condition is true. Clearly in this case both conditions cannot be true.

With an | or an || operation, you only get a `false` result if both operands are `false`. If either or both operands are `true`, the result is `true`.

Boolean NOT Operations

The third type of logical operator, `!`, takes one boolean operand and inverts its value. So if the value of a `boolean` variable, `state`, is `true`, then the expression `!state` has the value `false`, and if it is `false` then `!state` becomes `true`. To see how the operator is used with an expression, we could rewrite the code fragment we used to provide discounted ticket price as:

```
if(!(age >= 16 && age < 65)) {
   ticketPrice *= 0.9;          // Reduce ticket price by 10%
}
```

The expression `(age >= 16 && age < 65)` is `true` if age is from 16 to 64. People of this age do not qualify for the discount, so the discount should only be applied when this expression is `false`. Applying the `!` operator to the result of the expression does what we want.

We could also apply the `!` operator in an expression that was a favorite of Charles Dickens:

```
!(Income>Expenditure)
```

If this expression is `true`, the result is misery, at least as soon as the bank starts bouncing your checks.

Of course, you can use any of the logical operators in combination if necessary. If the theme park decides to give a discount on the price of entry to anyone who is under 12 years old and under 48 inches tall, or someone who is over 65 and over 72 inches tall, you could apply the discount with the test:

```
if((age < 12 && height < 48) || (age > 65 && height > 72)) {
   ticketPrice *= 0.8;              // 20% discount on the ticket price
}
```

The parentheses are not strictly necessary here, as `&&` has a higher precedence than `||`, but adding the parentheses makes it clearer how the comparisons combine and makes it a little more readable.

> Don't confuse the bitwise operators `&`, `|`, and `!`, with the logical operators that look the same. Which type of operator you are using in any particular instance is determined by the type of operand with which you use it. The bitwise operators apply to integer types and produce an integer result. The logical operators apply to operands that have `boolean` values and produce a result of type `boolean` – `true` or `false`. You can use both bitwise and logical operators in an expression if it is convenient to do so.

Character Testing Using Standard Library Methods

While testing characters using logical operators is a useful way of demonstrating how these operators work, in practice there is an easier way. The standard Java packages provide a range of standard methods to do the sort of testing for particular sets of characters such as letters or digits that we have been doing with `if` statements. They are all available within the class `Character`, which is automatically available in your programs. For example, we could have written the `if` statement in our `LetterCheck` program as shown in the following example.

Try It Out – Deciphering Characters Trivially

Replace the code body of the `LetterCheck` class with the following code:

```
if(Character.isUpperCase(symbol)) {
    System.out.println("You have the capital letter " + symbol);

} else {
    if(Character.isLowerCase(symbol)) {
       System.out.println("You have the small letter " + symbol);

    } else {
       System.out.println("The code is not a letter");
    }
}
```

How It Works

The `isUpperCase()` method returns `true` if the `char` value passed to it is uppercase, and `false` if it is not. Similarly, the `isLowerCase()` method returns `true` if the `char` value passed to it is lowercase.

The following table shows some of the other methods included in the class `Character` that you may find useful for testing characters. In each case the argument to be tested is of type `char`, and is placed between the parentheses following the method name:

Method	Description
isDigit()	Returns the value `true` if the argument is a digit (0 to 9) and `false` otherwise.
isLetter()	Returns the value `true` if the argument is a letter, and `false` otherwise.
isLetterOrDigit()	Returns the value `true` if the argument is a letter or a digit, and `false` otherwise.
isWhitespace()	Returns the value `true` if the argument is whitespace, which is any one of the characters: space (' '), tab ('\t'), newline ('\n'), carriage return ('\r'), form feed ('\f') The method returns `false` otherwise.

You will find information on other methods in the class `Character` in the documentation for the class that is part of the Java Development Kit.

The Conditional Operator

The **conditional operator** is sometimes called a **ternary operator** because it involves three operands. It is best understood by looking at an example. Suppose we have two variables of type `int`, `yourAge` and `myAge`, and we want to assign the greater of the values stored in `yourAge` and `myAge` to a third variable also of type `int`, `older`. We can do this with the statement:

```
older = yourAge > myAge ? yourAge : myAge;
```

The conditional operator has a logical expression as its first argument, in this case `yourAge>myAge`. If this expression is `true`, the operand which follows the `?` symbol – in this case `yourAge` – is selected as the value resulting from the operation. If the expression `yourAge>myAge` is `false`, the operand which comes after the colon – in this case `myAge` – is selected as the value. Thus, the result of this conditional expression is `yourAge`, if `yourAge` is greater than `myAge`, and `myAge` otherwise. This value is then stored in the variable, `older`. The use of the conditional operator in this assignment statement is equivalent to the `if` statement:

```
if(yourAge > myAge) {
  older = yourAge;

} else {
  older = myAge;
}
```

Remember, though, the conditional operator is an operator and not a statement, so it can be used in a more complex expression involving other operators.

The conditional operator can be written generally as:

```
logical_expression ? expression1 : expression2
```

If the `logical_expression` evaluates as `true`, the result of the operation is the value of `expression1`, and if `logical_expression` evaluates to `false`, the result is the value of `expression2`. Note that if `expression1` is evaluated because `logical_expression` is `true`, then `expression2` will not be, and vice versa.

There are lots of circumstances where the conditional operator can be used, and one common application of it is to control output, depending on the result of an expression or the value of a variable. You can vary a message by selecting one text string or another depending on the condition specified.

Try It Out – Conditional Plurals

Type in the following code which will add the correct ending to `'hat'` depending on how many hats you have:

```
public class ConditionalOp {
```

```
    public static void main(String[] args) {
      int nHats = 1;         // Number of hats
      System.out.println("I have " + nHats + " hat" + (nHats == 1 ? "." : "s."));

      nHats++;               // Increment number of hats
      System.out.println("I have " + nHats + " hat" + (nHats == 1 ? "." : "s."));
    }
}
```

The output from this program will be:

```
I have 1 hat.
I have 2 hats.
```

How It Works

The result of the conditional operator is a string containing just a period when the value of `nHats` is 1, and a string containing an `s` followed by a period in all other cases. The effect of this is to cause the output statement to automatically adjust the output between singular and plural. You can use the same technique in other situations such as where you need to choose "he" or "she" for example, as long as you are able to specify a logical expression to differentiate the situation where you should use one rather than the other.

The switch Statement

The `switch` statement enables you to select from multiple choices based on a set of fixed values for a given expression. The expression must produce a result of type `char`, `byte`, `short` or `int`, but not `long`, otherwise the statement will not compile. In normal use it operates rather like a rotary switch in that you can select one of a fixed number of choices. For example, on some makes of washing machine you choose between the various possible machine settings in this way, with positions for cotton, wool, synthetic fiber and so on, which you select by turning the knob to point to the option that you want.

A `switch` statement reflecting this logic would be:

```
switch(wash) {
  case 1:                          // wash is 1 for Cotton
    System.out.println("Cotton selected");
    break;
  case 2:                          // wash is 2 for Linen
    System.out.println("Linen selected");
    break;
  case 3:                          // wash is 3 for Wool
    System.out.println("Wool selected");
    break;
  default:                         // Not a valid value for wash
    System.out.println("Selection error");
    break;
}
```

In the `switch` statement, the selection is determined by the value of an expression that you specify, which is enclosed between the parentheses after the keyword `switch`. In this case it's the variable `wash` that would need to be previously declared as of type `char`, `byte`, `short` or `int`. You define the possible switch positions by one or more **case values**, also called **case labels**, which are defined using the keyword `case`. All the case labels for a `switch` are enclosed between the braces for the `switch` statement and they can appear in any order. We have used three case values in the example above. A particular case value is selected if the value of the `switch` expression is the same as that of the particular case value.

When a particular case is selected, the statements which follow that case label are executed. So if `wash` has the value 2, the statements that follow:

```
case 2:                          // wash is 2 for Linen
```

are executed. In this case, these are:

```
System.out.println("Linen selected");
break;
```

When a `break` statement is executed here, it causes execution to continue with the statement following the closing brace for the `switch`. The break is not mandatory, but if you don't put a `break` statement at the end of the statements for a case, the statements for the next case in sequence will be executed as well, through to whenever another `break` is found or the end of the switch block is reached. This is not usually what you want. The `break` after the `default` statements in our example is not strictly necessary, but it does protect against the situation when you might add another case label at the end of the `switch` statement block, and overlook the need for the `break` at the end of the last case.

There is a case label for each handled choice in the `switch`, and they must all be unique. The `default` case we have in the example above is, in general, optional. It is selected when the value of the expression for the `switch` does not correspond with any of the case values that have been defined. If you don't specify a `default` case and the value of the `switch` expression does not match any of the case labels, execution continues at the statement following the closing brace of the `switch` statement.

We can illustrate the logic of the general `switch` statement in a flow chart.

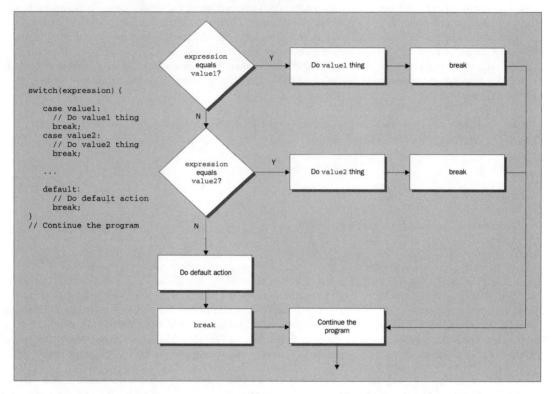

Each `case` value is notionally compared with the value of an expression. If one matches then the code for that case is executed and the `break` branches to the first statement after the switch. As we said earlier, if you don't include the `break` statements, the logic is quite different, as shown next.

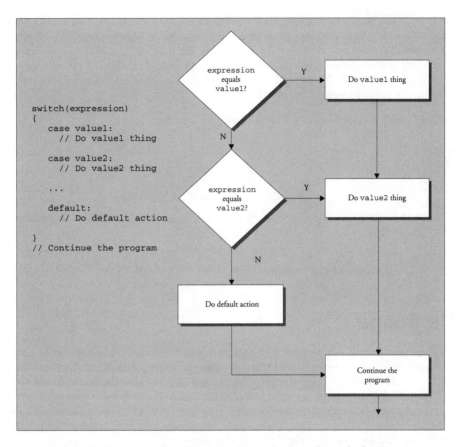

Now when a case label value is equal to the `switch` expression, the code for that case is executed, and we fall through to execute all the other cases that follow, including that for the default case if that follows. This is not usually what you want, so make sure you don't forget the `break` statements.

You can arrange to execute the same statements for several different case labels, as in the following `switch` statement:

```
char yesNo = 'N';
// more program logic...

switch(yesNo) {
  case 'n':
  case 'N':
      System.out.println("No selected");
      break;
  case 'y':
  case 'Y':
      System.out.println("Yes selected");
      break;
}
```

Here the variable yesNo receives a character from the keyboard somehow. You want a different action depending on whether the user enters 'Y' or 'N' but you want to be able to accept either uppercase or lowercase entries. This switch does just this by putting the case labels together. Note that there is no default case here. If yesNo contains a character other than those identified in the case statements, the switch statement has no effect. You might add a default case in this kind of situation to output a message to indicate that the value in yesNo is not valid.

Of course, you could also implement this logic using if statements:

```
if(yesNo=='n' || yesNo=='N') {
  System.out.println("No selected");

} else {
  if(yesNo=='y' || yesNo=='Y') {
    System.out.println("Yes selected");
  }
}
```

I prefer the switch statement as I think it's easier to follow, but you decide for yourself.

Variable Scope

The **scope** of a variable is the part of the program over which the variable name can be referenced – in other words, where you can use the variable in the program. Every variable that we have declared so far in program examples has been defined within the context of a method, the method main(). Variables that are declared within a method are called **local variables**, as they are only accessible within the confines of the method in which they are declared. However, they are not necessarily accessible everywhere in the code for the method in which they are declared. Look at the example in the illustration below that shows nested blocks inside a method.

```
{
    int a = 1;                          // Declare and define a

    // Reference to a is OK here
    // Reference to b here is an error
    {

        // Reference to a here is OK
        // Reference to b here is still an error

        int b = 2;                      // Declare and define b

        // References to a and b are OK here - b exists now

    }
    // Reference to b is an error here - it doesn't exist
    // Reference to a is still OK though
}
```

A variable does not exist before its declaration; you can only refer to it after it has been declared. It continues to exist until the end of the block in which it is defined, and that includes any blocks nested within the block containing its declaration. The variable b only exists within the inner block. After the brace at the end of the inner block, b no longer exists so you can't refer to it. The variable a is still around though since it survives until the last brace.

So, the rule for accessibility of local variables is simple. They are only accessible from the point in the program where they are declared to the end of the block that contains the declaration. At the end of the block in which they are declared they cease to exist. We can demonstrate this with an example:

Try It Out – Scoping

We will define our method `main()` to illustrate how variable scope works. First we declare and initialize the variable `outer`, then start an inner block. Within that block, we will define another variable `inner`. When the block closes we have to redeclare `inner` to use it once more.

```
public class Scope {
  public static void main(String[] args) {
    int outer = 1;                               // Exists throughout the method

    {
      // You cannot refer to a variable before its declaration
      // System.out.println("inner = " + inner);  // Uncomment this for an error

      int inner = 2;
      System.out.println("inner = " + inner);    // Now it is OK
      System.out.println("outer = " + outer);    // and outer is still here

      // All variable defined in the enclosing outer block still exist,
      // so you cannot redefine them here
      // int outer = 5;                           // Uncomment this for an error
    }

    // Any variables declared in the previous inner block no longer exist
    // so you cannot refer to them
    // System.out.println("inner = " + inner);    // Uncomment this for an error

    // The previous variable, inner, does not exist so you can define a new one
    int inner = 3;
    System.out.println("inner = " + inner);      // ... and output its value
    System.out.println("outer = " + outer);      // outer is still around
  }
}
```

As it stands, this program will produce the output:

```
inner = 2
outer = 1
inner = 3
outer = 1
```

If you uncomment any or all of the three statements as suggested, it won't compile:

```
javac Scope.java
Scope.java:11: Undefined variable: inner
        System.out.println("inner = " + inner);   // Uncomment this for an error
                                        ^
1 error
```

```
javac Scope.java
Scope.java:19: Variable 'outer' is already defined in this method.
      int outer = 5;                              // Uncomment this for an error
          ^
1 error
```

```
javac Scope.java
Scope.java:23: Undefined variable: inner
      System.out.println("inner = " + inner);    // Uncomment this for an error
                                       ^
1 error
```

How It Works

The method `main()` in this program has one block nested inside the block containing the code for the method. The variable `outer` is defined right at the start, so you can refer to this anywhere within the method `main()`, including inside any nested blocks. You are not allowed to re-declare a variable, so the commented statement that re-declares `outer` within the inner block will cause a compiler error, if you remove the double slash at the beginning of the line.

The variable `inner` is defined inside the nested block with the initial value 2, and you can refer to it anywhere from its declaration to the end of the inner block. After the closing brace of the inner block, the variable `inner` no longer exists, so the commented output statement that refers to `inner` is illegal. However, since the variable `inner` has expired, we can declare another one with the same name and with the initial value 3.

Note that all this is just to demonstrate the lifetime of local variables. It is not good practice to redefine variables that have expired, because of the potential for confusion. Also, although we have just used variables of type `int` in the example above, scoping rules apply to variables of any type.

> There are other variables called class variables which have much longer lifetimes when they are declared in a particular way. The variables **PI** and **E** in the standard library class **Math** are examples of these. They hang around as long as your program is executing. There are also variables that form part of a class object called instance variables. We will learn more about these in Chapter 5.

Loops

A loop allows you to execute a statement or block of statements repeatedly. The need to repeat a block of code arises in almost every program. If you did the first exercise at the end of the last chapter, based on what you had learned up to that point you would have come up with a program along the lines of:

```
public class TryExample1_1 {
  public static void main(String[] args) {
    byte value = 1;
    value *= 2;
    System.out.println("Value is now "+value);
    value *= 2;
```

```
      System.out.println("Value is now "+value);
      value *= 2;
      System.out.println("Value is now "+value);
      value *= 2;
      System.out.println("Value is now "+value);
      value *= 2;
      System.out.println("Value is now "+value);
      value *= 2;
      System.out.println("Value is now "+value);
      value *= 2;
      System.out.println("Value is now "+value);
      value *= 2;
      System.out.println("Value is now "+value);
      value *= 2;
      System.out.println("Value is now "+value);
    }
  }
```

The same pair of statements has been entered eight times. This is a rather tedious way of doing things. If the program for the company payroll had to include separate statements for each employee, it would never get written. A loop removes this sort of the difficulty. We could write the method main() to do the same as the code above as:

```
public static void main(String[] args) {
  byte value = 1;
  for (int i=0; i<8 ; i++) {
    value *= 2;
    System.out.println("Value is now " + value);
  }
}
```

The for loop statement causes the statements in the following block to be repeated eight times. The number of times it is to be repeated is determined by the stuff between parentheses following the keyword for – we will see how in a moment. The point is you could, in theory, repeat the same block of statements as many times as you want – a thousand or a million – it is just as easy and it doesn't require any more lines of code. The primary purpose of the for loop is to execute a block of statements a given number of times.

There are three kinds of loop statements you can use, so let's look at these in general terms first:

1. The for loop:

```
for (initialization_expression ; loop_condition ; increment_expression) {
  // statements
}
```

The control of the for loop appears in parentheses following the keyword for. It has three parts separated by semi-colons.

The first part, the initialization_expression, is executed before execution of the loop starts. This is typically used to initialize a counter for the number of loop iterations – for example i = 0. With a loop controlled by a counter, you can count up or down using an integer or a floating point variable.

Execution of the loop continues as long as the condition you have specified in the second part, the `loop_condition`, is `true`. This expression is checked at the beginning of each loop iteration, and when it is `false`, execution continues with the statement following the loop block. A simple example of what the `loop_condition` expression might be is `i<10`, so the loop would continue in this case as long as the variable `i` has a value less than 10.

The third part of the control information between the parentheses, the `increment_expression`, is usually used to increment the loop counter. This is executed at the end of each loop iteration. This could be `i++`, which would increment the loop counter, `i`, by one. Of course, you might want to increment the loop counter in steps other than 1. For instance, you might write `i += 2` as the `increment_expression` to go in steps of 2, or even something more complicated such as `i = 2*i+1`.

2. The `while` loop:

```
while (expression) {
  // statements
}
```

This loop executes as long as the given logical expression between parentheses is `true`. When `expression` is `false`, execution continues with the statement following the loop block. The expression is tested at the beginning of the loop, so if it is initially `false`, the loop statement block will not be executed at all. An example of a `while` loop condition might be, `yesNo=='Y' ||
yesNo=='y'`. This expression would be `true` if the variable `yesNo` contained 'y' or 'Y', so `yesNo` might hold a character entered from the keyboard in this instance.

3. The `do while` loop

```
do {
  // statements
} while (expression);
```

This loop is similar to the `while` loop, except that the expression controlling the loop is tested at the end of the loop block. This means that the loop block is executed at least once, even if the expression is always `false`.

We can contrast the basic logic of the three kinds of loop in a diagram.

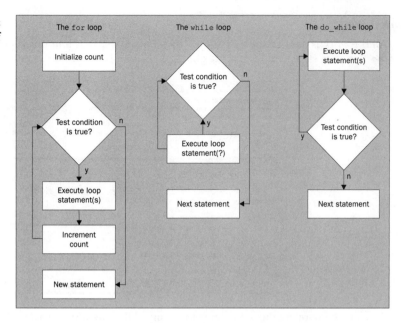

This shows quite clearly that the only difference between the while loop and the do while loop is where the test is carried out.

Let's explore each of these in turn and see how they work in a practical context.

Try It Out – The for Loop

Let's start with a very simple example. Suppose you want to calculate the sum of the integers from 1 to a given value. You can do this using the for loop as in the following example:

```
public class ForLoop {
  public static void main(String[] args) {
    int limit = 20;                      // Sum from 1 to this value
    int sum = 0;                         // Accumulate sum in this variable

    // Loop from 1 to the value of limit, adding 1 each cycle
    for(int i = 1; i <= limit; i++) {
      sum += i;                          // Add the current value of i to sum
    }
    System.out.println("sum = " + sum);
  }
}
```

This program will produce the output,

```
sum = 210
```

but you can try it out with different values for limit.

How It Works

All the work is done in the `for` loop. The loop counter is `i`, and this is declared and initialized within the `for` loop statement. The syntax of the `for` loop is shown in the following diagram:

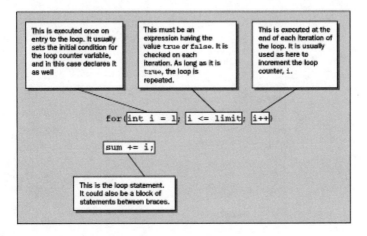

As you see, there are three elements that control the operation of a `for` loop, and they appear between the parentheses that follow the keyword `for`. In sequence their purpose is to:

❑ Set the initial conditions for the loop, particularly the loop counter

❑ Specify the condition for the loop to continue

❑ Increment the loop counter

They are always separated by semi-colons.

The first control element is executed when the loop is first entered. Here we declare and initialize the loop counter `i`. Because it is declared within the loop, it will not exist outside it. If you try to output the value of `i` after the loop with a statement such as,

```
System.out.println("Final value of i = " + i);  // Will not work outside the loop
```

you will find that the program will not compile. If you need to initialize and/or declare other variables for the loop, you can do it here by separating the declarations by commas. For example, we could write:

```
for (int i = 1, j = 0; i <= limit; i++) {
  sum += i * j++;                    // Add the current value of i*j to sum
}
```

We initialize an additional variable `j`, and, to make the loop vaguely sensible, we have modified the value to add the sum to `i*j++` which is the equivalent of `i*(i-1)` in this case. Note that `j` will be incremented after the product `i*j` has been calculated. You could declare other variables here, but note that it would not make sense to declare `sum` at this point. If you can't figure out why, delete the original declaration of `sum` and, put it in the `for` loop instead to see what happens. The program won't compile – right? After the loop ends the variable `sum` no longer exists, so you can't reference it.

The second control element in a `for` loop is a logical expression which is checked at the beginning of each iteration through the loop. If the expression is `true`, the loop continues, and as soon as it is `false` the loop is finished. In our program the loop ends when `i` is greater than the value of `limit`.

The third control element in a `for` loop typically increments the loop variable, as we have in our example. You can also put multiple expressions here too, so we could rewrite the above code fragment, which added `j` to the loop, as:

```
for (int i = 1, int j = 0; i <= limit; i++, j++) {
  sum+=i*j;                          // Add the current value of i*j to sum
}
```

Again, there can be several expressions here, and they do not need to relate directly to the control of the loop. We could even rewrite the original loop for summing integers so that the summation occurs in the loop control element:

```
for (int i = 1; i <= limit; sum += i, i++) {
  ;
}
```

Now the loop statement is empty – you still need the semi-colon to terminate it though. It doesn't really improve things though and there are hazards in writing the loop this way. If you forget the semi-colon the next statement will be used as the loop statement, which is likely to cause chaos. Another potential problem arises if you happen to reverse the sequence of adding to `sum` and incrementing `i`, as follows:

```
for (int i = 1; i <= limit; i++, sum += i) {   // Wrong!!!
  ;
}
```

Now you will generate the wrong answer. This is because the expression `i++` will be executed before `sum += i`, so the wrong value of `i` is used.

You can omit any or all of the elements that control the `for` loop, but you must include the semi-colons. It is up to you to make sure that the loop does what you want. We could write the loop in our program as:

```
for(int i = 1; i <= limit; ) {
  sum += i++;                          // Add the current value of i to sum
}
```

We have simply transferred the incrementing of `i` from the `for` loop control to the loop statement. The `for` loop works just as before. However, this is not a good way to write the loop, as it makes it much less obvious how the loop counter is incremented.

Counting Using Floating Point Values

You can use a floating point variable as the loop counter if you need to. This may be needed when you are calculating the value of a function for a range of fractional values. Suppose you wanted to calculate the area of a circle with values for the radius from 1 to 2 in steps of 0.2. You could write this as:

```
for(double radius = 1.0; radius <= 2.0; radius += 0.2) {
    System.out.println("radius = " + radius + " area = " + Math.PI*radius*radius);
}
```

This will produce the output:

```
radius = 1.0 area = 3.141592653589793
radius = 1.2 area = 4.523893421169302
radius = 1.4 area = 6.157521601035994
radius = 1.5999999999999999 area = 8.04247719318987
radius = 1.7999999999999998 area = 10.178760197630927
radius = 1.9999999999999998 area = 12.566370614359169
```

The area has been calculated using the formula πr^2 with the standard value PI defined in the Math class, which is 3.14159265358979323846. Although we intended the values of radius to increment from 1.0 to 2.0 in steps of 0.2, they don't quite make it. The value of radius is never exactly 2.0 or any of the other intermediate values because 0.2 cannot be represented exactly as a binary floating point value. If you doubt this, and you are prepared to deal with an infinite loop, change the loop to:

```
// BE WARNED - THIS LOOP DOES NOT END
for(double radius = 1.0; radius != 2.0; radius += 0.2) {
    System.out.println("radius = " + radius + " area = " + Math.PI*radius*radius);
}
```

If the value of radius reaches 2.0, the condition radius ! =2.0 will be false and the loop will end, but unfortunately it doesn't. Its last value before 2 will be approximately 1.999... and the next value will be something like 2.1999... and so it will never be 2.0. From this we can deduce a golden rule:

> **Never use tests that depend on an exact value for a floating point variable to control a loop.**

Try It Out – The while Loop

We can write the program for summing integers again using the while loop, so you can see how the loop mechanism differs from the for loop.

```
public class WhileLoop {
    public static void main(String[] args) {
        int limit = 20;                    // Sum from 1 to this value
        int sum = 0;                       // Accumulate sum in this variable
        int i = 1;                         // Loop counter

        // Loop from 1 to the value of limit, adding 1 each cycle
        while(i <= limit) {
            sum += i++;                    // Add the current value of i to sum
        }
        System.out.println("sum = " + sum);
    }
}
```

You should get the result:

```
sum = 210
```

How It Works

The `while` loop is controlled wholly by the logical expression that appears between the parentheses that follow the keyword `while`. The loop continues as long as this expression has the value `true`, and how it ever manages to arrive at the value `false` to end the loop is up to you. You need to be sure that the statements within the loop will eventually result in this expression being `false`. Otherwise you have an infinite loop.

How the loop ends in our example is clear. We have a simple count as before, and we increment `i` in the loop statement that accumulates the sum of the integers. Sooner or later `i` will exceed the value of `limit` and the `while` loop will end.

You don't always need to use the testing of a count limit as the loop condition. You can use any logical condition you want.

And last, but not least, we have the `do while` loop.

Try It Out – The do while Loop

As we said at the beginning of this topic, the `do while` loop is much the same as the `while` loop, except for the fact that the continuation condition is checked at the end of the loop. We can write an integer summing program with this kind of loop too:

```
public class DoWhileLoop {
  public static void main(String[] args) {
    int limit = 20;                    // Sum from 1 to this value
    int sum = 0;                       // Accumulate sum in this variable
    int i = 1;                         // Loop counter

    // Loop from 1 to the value of limit, adding 1 each cycle
    do {
      sum += i;                        // Add the current value of i to sum
      i++;
    } while(i <= limit);

    System.out.println("sum = " + sum);
  }
}
```

How It Works

The statements within the loop are always executed at least once because the condition determining whether the loop should continue is tested at the end of each iteration. Within the loop we add the value of `i` to `sum`, and then increment it. When `i` exceeds the value of `limit`, the loop ends, at which point `sum` will contain the sum of all the integers from 1 to `limit`.

The loop statement here has braces around the block of code that is within the loop. We could rewrite the loop so that only one statement was within the loop, in which case the braces are not required. For instance:

```
      do
        sum += i;                       // Add the current value of i to sum
      while(++i <= limit);
```

Of course, you could still put the braces in if you want. I advise that you always use brackets in your loops even when they are only a single statement. There are often several ways of writing the code to produce a given result, and this is true here – we could also move the incrementing of the variable i back inside the loop and write it as:

```
      do
        sum += i++;                     // Add the current value of i to sum
      while (i <= limit);
```

Note the semi-colon after the `while` condition is present in each version of the loop. This is part of the loop statement so you must not forget to put it in. The primary reason for using this loop over the `while` loop would be if you want to be sure that the loop code always executes at least once.

Nested Loops

You can nest loops of any kind one inside another to any depth. Let's look at an example where we can use nested loops.

A **factorial** of an integer, *n*, is the product of all the integers from 1 to *n*. It is written as *n*!. It may seem a little strange if you haven't come across it before, but it can be a very useful value. For instance, *n*! is the number of ways you can arrange *n* different things in sequence, so a deck of cards can be arranged in 52! different sequences. Let's try calculating some factorial values.

Try It Out – Calculating Factorials

Our example will calculate the factorial of every integer from 1 up to a given limit. Enter the following code with the two `for` loops:

```
public class Factorial {
  public static void main(String[] args) {
    long limit = 20;          // to calculate factorial of integers up to this value
    long factorial = 1;       // factorial will be calculated in this variable

    // Loop from 1 to the value of limit
    for (int i = 1; i <= limit; i++) {
      factorial = 1;          // Initialize factorial

      for (int factor = 2; factor <= i; factor++) {
        factorial *= factor;
      }
      System.out.println(i + "!" + " is " + factorial);
    }
  }
}
```

This program will produce the output:

```
1! is 1
2! is 2
3! is 6
4! is 24
5! is 120
6! is 720
7! is 5040
8! is 40320
9! is 362880
10! is 3628800
11! is 39916800
12! is 479001600
13! is 6227020800
14! is 87178291200
15! is 1307674368000
16! is 20922789888000
17! is 355687428096000
18! is 6402373705728000
19! is 121645100408832000
20! is 2432902008176640000
```

How It Works

The outer loop, controlled by i, walks through all the integers from 1 to the value of limit. In each iteration of the outer loop, the variable `factorial` is initialized to 1 and the nested loop calculates the factorial of the current value of i using `factor` as the control counter that runs from 2 to the current value of i. The resulting value of `factorial` is then displayed, before going to the next iteration of the outer loop.

Although we have nested a `for` loop inside another `for` loop here, as we said at the outset, you can nest any kind of loop inside any other. We could have written the nested loop as:

```
for (int i = 1; i <= limit; i++) {
  factorial = 1;         // Initialize factorial
  int factor = 2;
  while (factor <= i) {
    factorial *= factor++;
  }
  System.out.println(i + "!" + " is " + factorial);
}
```

Now we have a `while` loop nested in a `for` loop. It works just as well, but it is rather more natural coded as two nested `for` loops because they are both controlled by a counter.

> If you have been concentrating, you may well have noticed that you don't really need nested loops to display the factorial of successive integers. You can do it with a single loop that multiplies the current factorial value by the loop counter. However, this would be a very poor demonstration of a nested loop.

The continue Statement

There are situations where you may want to skip all or part of a loop iteration. Suppose we want to sum the values of the integers from 1 to some limit, except that we don't want to include integers that are multiples of three. We can do this using an `if` and a `continue` statement:

```
for(int i = 1; i <= limit; i++) {
  if(i % 3 == 0) {
    continue;                        // Skip the rest of this iteration
  }
  sum += i;                          // Add the current value of i to sum
}
```

The `continue` statement is executed in this example when `i` is an exact multiple of 3, causing the rest of the current loop iteration to be skipped. Program execution continues with the next iteration if there is one, and if not, with the statement following the end of the loop block. The `continue` statement can appear anywhere within a block of loop statements. You may even have more than one `continue` in a loop.

The Labeled continue Statement

Where you have nested loops, there is a special form of the `continue` statement that enables you to stop executing the inner loop – not just the current iteration of the inner loop – and continue at the beginning of the next iteration of the outer loop that immediately encloses the current loop. This is called the **labeled continue statement**.

To use the labeled continue statement, you need to identify the loop statement for the enclosing outer loop with a **statement label**. A statement label is simply an identifier that is used to reference a particular statement. When you need to reference a particular statement, you write the statement label at the beginning of the statement in question, and separated from the statement by a colon. Let's look at an example:

Try It Out – Labeled continue

We could add a labeled `continue` statement to omit the calculation of factorials of odd numbers greater than 10. This is not the best way to do this, but it does demonstrate how the labeled `continue` statement works:

```
public class Factorial {
  public static void main(String[] args) {
    long limit = 20;        // to calculate factorial of integers up to this value
    long factorial = 1;     // factorial will be calculated in this variable

    // Loop from 1 to the value of limit
    OuterLoop:
    for(int i = 1; i <= limit; i++) {
      factorial = 1;                   // Initialize factorial
      for(int j = 2; j <= i; j++) {
        if(i > 10 && i % 2 == 1) {
          continue OuterLoop;          // Transfer to the outer loop
        }
        factorial *= j;
      }
```

```
                System.out.println(i + "!" + " is " + factorial);
            }
        }
    }
```

If you run this it will produce the output:

```
1! is 1
2! is 2
3! is 6
4! is 24
5! is 120
6! is 720
7! is 5040
8! is 40320
9! is 362880
10! is 3628800
12! is 479001600
14! is 87178291200
16! is 20922789888000
18! is 6402373705728000
20! is 2432902008176640000
```

How It Works

The outer loop has the label `OuterLoop`. In the inner loop, when the condition in the `if` statement is true, the labeled `continue` is executed causing an immediate transfer to the beginning of the next iteration of the outer loop.

In general, you can use the labeled `continue` to exit from an inner loop to any enclosing outer loop, not just the one immediately enclosing the loop containing the labeled `continue` statement.

Using the break Statement in a Loop

We have seen how to use the `break` statement in a `switch` block. Its effect is to exit the `switch` block and continue execution with the first statement after the switch. You can also use the `break` statement to break out from a loop when you need. When break is executed within a loop, the loop ends immediately and execution continues with the first statement following the loop. To demonstrate this we will write a program to find prime numbers. In case you have forgotten, a prime number is an integer that is not exactly divisible by any number less than itself, other than 1 of course.

Try It Out – Calculating Primes I

Start with the `main()` method in the class `Primes`, and declare `nValues` and `isPrime`. Then start a `for` loop that will loop through all integers from 2 to `nValues`.

```
public class Primes {
  public static void main(String[] args) {
    int nValues = 50;            // The maximum value to be checked
    boolean isPrime = true;      // Is true if we find a prime
```

109

```
            // Check all values from 2 to nValues
            for(int i = 2; i <= nValues; i++) {
```

Then we try dividing i by all integers less than its value.

```
        isPrime=true;                          // Assume the current i is prime

        // Try dividing by all integers from 2 to i-1
        for(int j = 2; j < i; j++) {
          if(i % j == 0) {          // This is true if j divides exactly
            isPrime = false;     // If we got here, it was an exact division
            break;               // so exit the loop
          }
        }
```

The final section prints out any primes.

```
        // We can get here through the break, or through completing the loop
        if(isPrime)                    // So is it prime?
          System.out.println(i);     // Yes, so output the value
        }
      }
    }
  }
```

You should get the output:

```
2
3
5
7
11
13
17
19
23
29
31
37
41
43
47
```

How It Works

There are much more efficient ways to calculate primes, but this does demonstrate the break statement in action. The basic idea of the program is to go through the integers from 2 to the value of nValues, and check each one to see if it has an integer divisor less than the number being checked. The outer loop is indexed by i stepping through the possible values that need to be checked. The inner loop is indexed by j, the value of j being a trial divisor. This determines whether any integer less than the value being tested for primality is an exact divisor.

The checking is done in the `if` statement in the inner loop. If `j` divides `i` exactly `i%j` will be 0, so `isPrime` will be set to `false`. In this case the `break` will be executed to exit the inner loop – there is no point in continuing as we now know that the value being tested is not prime. The next statement to be executed will be the `if` statement after the closing brace of the inner loop block. You can also reach this point by a normal exit from the loop which occurs when the value is prime, so it is necessary to check the value of `isPrime` to see whether we do have a prime or not.

This example could be simplified if we used the labeled `continue` instead of the `break` statement:

Try It Out – Calculating Primes II

Try the following changes to the code in the `Primes` class.

```
public class Primes {
  public static void main(String[] args) {
    int nValues = 50;                    // The maximum value to be checked

    // Check all values from 2 to nValues
    OuterLoop:
    for(int i = 2; i <= nValues; i++) {
      // Try dividing by all integers from 2 to i-1
      for(int j = 2; j < i; j++) {
        if(i%j == 0) {                   // This is true if j divides exactly
          continue OuterLoop;            // so exit the loop
        }
      }
      // We only get here if we have a prime
      System.out.println(i);             // so output the value
    }
  }
}
```

How It Works

We no longer need the `isPrime` variable to indicate whether we have a prime or not, as we can only reach the output statement through a normal exit from the inner loop. When this occurs it means we have a prime. If we get an exact divisor, implying the current value of `i` is not prime, the labeled `continue` transfers immediately to the next iteration of the outer loop. The output from this version of the program is the same as before.

Breaking Indefinite Loops

You will find that sometimes you will need to use a loop where you don't know in advance how many iterations are required. This can arise when you are processing external data items that you might be reading in from the keyboard for example, and you do not know in advance how many there are. You can often use a `while` loop in these circumstances with the loop condition determining when the loop should end, but sometimes it can be convenient to use an indefinite loop instead, with a `break` statement to end the loop.

Try It Out – Calculating Primes III

Suppose we want our `Primes` program to generate a given number of primes, rather than check up to a given integer value. In this case we don't know how many numbers we need to check to generate the required number of primes. This is a case where an indefinite loop is useful. We can code this as follows:

```
public class FindPrimes {
  public static void main(String[] args) {
    int nPrimes = 50;                      // The maximum number of primes required

    OuterLoop:
    for(int i = 2; ; i++) {                // This loop runs forever

      // Try dividing by all integers from 2 to i-1
      for(int j = 2; j < i; j++) {
        if(i % j == 0) {                   // This is true if j divides exactly
          continue OuterLoop;              // so exit the loop
        }
      }
      // We only get here if we have a prime
      System.out.println(i);               // so output the value
      if(--nPrimes == 0) {                 // Decrement the prime count
        break;                             // It is zero so we have them all
      }
    }
  }
}
```

How It Works

This program is very similar to the previous version. The principal differences are that `nPrimes` contains the number of primes required, so the program will produce the first 50 primes, instead of finding the primes between 2 and 50. The outer loop, controlled by `i`, has the loop condition omitted, so the loop has no direct mechanism for ending it. The loop must be terminated by the code within the loop, otherwise it will continue to execute indefinitely.

Here the termination of the outer loop is controlled by the `if` statement following the output statement. As we find each prime, the value is displayed, after which the value of `nPrimes` is decremented in the `if` statement:

```
if(--nPrimes == 0) {     // Decrement the prime count
  break;                 // It is zero so we have them all
}
```

The `break` statement will be executed when `nPrimes` has been decremented to zero, and this will exit the outer loop.

The Labeled break Statement

Java also makes a labeled `break` statement available to you. This enables you to jump immediately to the statement following the end of any enclosing statement block or loop that is identified by the label in the labeled `break` statement. This mechanism is illustrated in the following diagram:

```
Block1: {

  Block2: {

  ...
    OuterLoop:
    for(...) {

      break Block1;
      while(...) {

      ...
        break Block2;
      ...
        break OuterLoop;
      }
      ...
    }
    ...
  } // end of Block2
  ...
} // end of Block1
...
```

breaks out beyond Block1

breaks out beyond Block2

breaks out beyond OuterLoop

The labeled break enables you to break out to the statement following an enclosing block or loop that has a label regardless of how many levels there are. You might have several loops nested one within the other, and using the labeled break you could exit from the innermost loop (or indeed any of them) to the statement following the outermost loop. You just need to add a label to the beginning of the relevant block or loop that you want to break out of, and use that label in the break statement.

Just to see it working we can alter the previous example to use a labeled break statement:

```java
public class FindPrimes {
  public static void main(String[] args) {
    int nPrimes = 50;                       // The maximum number of primes required

    // Check all values from 2 to nValues
    OuterLoop:
    for(int i = 2; ; i++) {                 // This loop runs forever

      // Try dividing by all integers from 2 to i-1
      for(int j = 2; j < i; j++) {
        if(i % j == 0) {                    // This is true if j divides exactly
          continue OuterLoop;               // so exit the loop
        }
      }
      // We only get here if we have a prime
      System.out.println(i);                // so output the value
      if(--nPrimes == 0) {                  // Decrement the prime count
        break OuterLoop;                    // It is zero so we have them all
      }
    }
    // break OuterLoop goes to here
  }
}
```

The program works in exactly the same way as before. The labeled break ends the loop operation beginning with the label OuterLoop, and so effectively branches to the point indicated by the comment.

Of course, in this instance its effect is no different from that of an unlabeled break. However, in general this would work wherever the labeled break statement was within OuterLoop. For instance, it could be nested inside another inner loop, and its effect would be just the same – control would be transferred to the statement following the end of OuterLoop. The following code fragment illustrates this sort of situation. Our label this time is Outside:

```
Outside:
for(int i = 0 ; i< count1 ; i++) {
  ...
  for(int j = 0 ; j< count2 ; j++) {
    ...
    for(int k = 0 ; k< count3 ; k++) {
      ...
      break Outside;
      ...
    }
  }
}
// The labeled break transfers to here...
```

The labeled break is not needed very often, but when you need to break out of a deeply nested set of loops it can be invaluable since it makes it a simple operation.

Assertions

Every so often you will find that the logic in your code leads to some logical condition that should always be true. If you test an integer and establish that it is odd, it is certainly true that it cannot be even for instance. You may also find yourself writing a statement or statements that, although they could be executed in theory, in practice they never really should be. I don't mean by this the usual sorts of errors that occur such as some incorrect data has been read in somehow. This should be handled ordinarily by the normal code. I mean circumstances where if the statements were to be executed, it would imply that something was very seriously wrong with the program or its environment. These are precisely the circumstances to which assertions apply.

A simple assertion is a statement of the form:

```
assert logical_expression;
```

Here, assert is a keyword and logical_expression is any expression that results in a value of true or false. When this statement executes, if logical_expression evaluates to true, then the program continues normally. If logical_expression evaluates to false, the program will be terminated with an error message starting with:

```
java.lang.AssertionError
```

This will be followed by more information about where the error occurred in the code. When this occurs, the program is said to *assert*.

Let's consider an example. Suppose we have a variable of type `int` that stores the number of days in the current month. We might use it like this:

```
if(daysInMonth == 30) {
  System.out.println("Month is April, June, September, or November");

} else if(daysInMonth == 31) {
  System.out.println(
           "Month is January, March, May, July, August, October, or December.");
} else {
  assert daysInMonth == 28 || daysInMonth == 29;
  System.out.println("Month is February.");
}
```

We are presuming that `daysInMonth` is valid – that is, it has one of the values 28, 29, 30 or 31. Maybe it came from a file that is supposed to be accurate so we should not need to check it, but if it turns out not to be valid, the assertion will check it.

We could have written this slightly differently:

```
if(daysInMonth == 30) {
  System.out.println("Month is April, June, September, or November");

} else if(daysInMonth == 31) {
  System.out.println(
           "Month is January, March, May, July, August, October, or December.");

} else if(daysInMonth == 28 || daysInMonth == 29) {
  System.out.println("Month is February.");

} else {
  assert false;
}
```

Here, if `daysInMonth` is valid, the program should never execute the last else clause. An assertion with the logical expression as `false` will always assert, and terminate the program.

If you include assertions in your code you must compile the code with the command line option `-source 1.4` specified. This is necessary for backwards compatibility reasons. It is possible that Java programs that predate the assertion facility may have used the word assert as a name somewhere. Without the `-source 1.4` option specified for the compiler, such programs can execute normally. For assertions to have an effect when you run your program, you must specify the `-enableassertions` option, or its abbreviated form `-ea`. If you don't specify this option, assertions will be ignored.

There is a slightly more complex form of assertions that have this form:

```
assert logical_expression : string_expression;
```

Here, `logical_expression` must evaluate to a `boolean` value, either True or False. If `logical_expression` is False then the program will terminate with an error message including the string that results from `string_expression`.

For example, we could have written the assertion in the last code fragment as:

```
assert false : "daysInMonth has the value" + daysInMonth;
```

Now if the program asserts, the output will include information about the value of daysInMonth.

Let's see how it works in practice.

Try It Out – A Working Assertion

Here's some code that is guaranteed to assert – if you compile and execute it right:

```
public class TryAssertions {
  public static void main(String args[]) {
    int daysInMonth = 32;
    if(daysInMonth == 30) {
      System.out.println("Month is April, June, September, or November");

    } else if(daysInMonth == 31) {
      System.out.println(
            "Month is January, March, May, July, August, October, or December.");

    } else if(daysInMonth == 28 || daysInMonth == 29) {
      System.out.println("Month is February.");

    } else {
      assert false;
    }
  }
}
```

Don't forget, you must compile this with the -source 1.4 option specified:

```
javac -source 1.4 TryAssertions.java
```

You must also execute it with the command:

```
java -enableassertions TryAssertions
```

You should then get the output:

```
java.lang.AssertionError
    at TryAssertions.main(TryAssertions.java:1)
Exception in thread "main"
```

How It Works

Since we have set daysInMonth to an invalid value, the assertion statement is executed, and that results in the error message. You could try the other form of the assertion:

```
assert false : "daysInMonth has the value " + daysInMonth;
```

Now you should see that the output includes the string resulting from the second expression in the assertion statement:

```
java.lang.AssertionError: daysInMonth has the value 32
    at TryAssertions.main(TryAssertions.java:1)
Exception in thread "main"
```

We will use assertions from time to time in the examples in subsequent chapters.

Summary

In this chapter you have learned about all of the essential mechanisms for making decisions in Java. You have also learned all of the looping facilities that you have available when programming. The essential points we have covered are:

- ❑ You can use **relational operators** to compare values, and such comparisons result in values of either `true` or `false`.

- ❑ You can combine basic comparisons and logical variables in more complex logical expressions by using **logical operators**.

- ❑ The `if` statement is a basic decision making tool in Java. It enables you to choose to execute a block of statements if a given logical expression has the value `true`. You can optionally execute another block of statements if the logical expression is `false` by using the `else` keyword.

- ❑ You can use the **conditional operator** to choose between two expressions depending on the value of a logical expression.

- ❑ You can use the `switch` statement to choose from a fixed number of alternatives.

- ❑ The variables in a method come into existence at the point at which you declare them, and cease to exist after the end of the block that immediately encloses their declaration. The program extent where the variable is accessible is the **scope** of the variable.

- ❑ You have three options for repeating a block of statements, a `for` loop, a `while` loop or a `do while` loop.

- ❑ The `continue` statement enables you to skip to the next iteration in the loop containing the `continue` statement.

- ❑ The labeled `continue` statement enables you to skip to the next iteration in a loop enclosing the labeled `continue` that is identified by the label. The labeled loop need not be that immediately enclosing the labeled `continue`.

- ❑ The `break` statement enables you to break out of a loop or block of statements in which it appears.

- ❑ The labeled `break` statement enables you to break out of a loop or block of statements that encloses it that is identified by the label. This is not necessarily the block that encloses it directly.

- ❑ You use an assertion statement to verify logical conditions that should always be `true`, or as code in parts of a program that should not be reached, but theoretically can be.

❏   Horse sense is the thing a horse has which keeps it from betting on people.

Exercises

1.   Write a program to display a random choice from a set of six choices for breakfast (you could use any set, for example, scrambled eggs, waffles, fruit, cereal, toast or yogurt).

2.   When testing whether an integer is a prime, it is sufficient to try to divide by integers up to the square root of the number being tested. Rewrite the program example from this chapter to use this approach.

3.   A lottery requires that you select six different numbers from the integers 1 to 49. Write a program to do this for you and generate five sets of entries.

4.   Write a program to generate a random sequence of capital letters that does not include vowels.

Arrays and Strings

In this chapter you will start to use Java objects. You will first be introduced to arrays, which enable you to deal with a number of variables of the same type through a single variable name, and then you will look at how to handle character strings. By the end of this chapter you will have learned:

- ❑   What arrays are and how you declare and initialize them.
- ❑   How you access individual elements of an array.
- ❑   How you can use individual elements of an array.
- ❑   How to declare arrays of arrays.
- ❑   How you can create arrays of arrays with different lengths.
- ❑   How to create `String` objects.
- ❑   How to create and use arrays of `String` objects.
- ❑   What operations are available for `String` objects.
- ❑   What `StringBuffer` objects are and how they relate to operations on `String` objects.
- ❑   What operations are available for `StringBuffer` objects.

Some of what we discuss in this chapter relates to objects, and as we have not yet covered in detail how a class (or object definition) is defined we will have to skate over some points, but all will be revealed in Chapter 5.

Arrays

With the basic built-in Java data types we have seen in the previous chapters, each identifier corresponds to a single variable. But when you want to handle sets of values of the same type – the first 1000 primes for example – you really don't want to have to name them individually. What you need is an **array**.

An array is a named set of variables of the same type. Each variable in the array is called an **array element**. To reference a particular element in an array you use the array name combined with an integer value of type int, called an **index**. The index for an array element is the offset of that particular element from the beginning of the array. The first element will have an index of 0, the second will have an index of 1, the third an index of 2, and so on. The index value does not need to be an integer literal. It can be any expression that results in a value of type int equal to or greater than zero. Obviously a for loop control variable is going to be very useful for processing array elements – which is why you had to wait until now to hear about arrays.

Array Variables

You are not obliged to create the array itself when you declare the array variable. The array variable is distinct from the array itself. You could declare the integer array variable primes with the statement:

```
int[] primes;            // Declare an integer array variable
```

The variable primes is now a place holder for an integer array that you have yet to define. No memory is allocated to hold the array itself at this point. We will see in a moment that to create the array itself we must specify its type and how many elements it is to contain. The square brackets following the type in the previous statement indicates that the variable is for referencing an array of int values, and not for storing a single value of type int.

You may come across an alternative notation for declaring an array variable:

```
int primes[];            // Declare an integer array variable
```

Here the square brackets appear after the variable name, rather than after the type name. This is exactly equivalent to the previous statement so you can use either notation. Many programmers prefer the original notation, as int[] tends to indicate more clearly that the type is an int array.

Defining an Array

Once you have declared an array variable, you can define an array that it will reference:

```
primes = new int[10];    // Define an array of 10 integers
```

This statement creates an array that will store 10 values of type int, and records a **reference** to the array in the variable primes. The reference is simply where the array is in memory. You could also declare the array variable and define the array of type int to hold 10 prime numbers with a single statement, as shown in the following illustration:

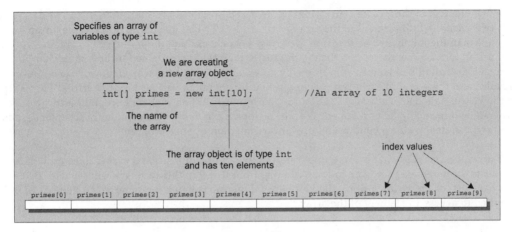

The first part of the definition specifies the type of the array. The type name, int in this case, is followed by an empty pair of square brackets to indicate you are declaring an array rather than a single variable of type int. The part following the equal sign defines the array. The keyword new indicates that you are allocating new memory for the array, and int[10] specifies you want capacity for 10 variables of type int in the array. Since each element in the primes array is an int variable requiring 4 bytes, the whole array will occupy 40 bytes, plus 4 bytes to store the reference to the array. When an array is created like this, all the array elements are initialized to a default value automatically. The initial value is zero in the case of an array of numerical values, false for boolean arrays, '\u0000' for arrays storing type char, and null for an array of a class type.

Before we go any further, let's clarify a bit of terminology we have been using in this discussion. A **declaration** for an array just defines the variable name. So the statement:

```
double[] myArray;
```

is a declaration for the array name, myArray. No memory has been allocated to store the array itself and the number of elements has not been defined.

The statement:

```
double[] myArray = new double[100];
```

is a declaration of the array variable myArray and a **definition** of the array, since the array size is specified. The variable myArray will refer to an array of 100 values of type double and each element will have the value 0.0 assigned by default.

Accessing Array Elements

You refer to an element of an array by using the array name followed by the element's index value enclosed between square brackets. You can specify an index value by any expression that produces zero or a positive result of type int. If you use a value of type long as an index, you will get an error message from the compiler; if your calculation of an index uses long variables you will need to cast it to type int. You will no doubt recall from Chapter 2 that expressions involving values of type short and type byte produce a result of type int, so you can use those in an index expression.

The first element of the `primes` array that we declared previously is referred to as `primes[0]`, and you reference the fifth element in the array as `primes[4]`. The maximum index value for an array is one less than the number of elements in the array. Java checks that the index values you use are valid. If you use an index value that is less than 0, or greater than the index value for the last element in the array, an **exception** will be thrown – throwing an exception is just the way errors at execution time are signaled and there are different types of exceptions for signaling various kinds of errors. The exception in this case is called an `IndexOutOfBoundsException`. When such an exception is thrown, your program will normally be terminated. We will be looking in detail at exceptions in Chapter 7, including how you can deal with exceptions and prevent termination of your program.

The array, `primes`, is what is sometimes referred to as a **one-dimensional array**, since each of its elements is referenced using one index – running from 0 to 9 in this case. We will see later that arrays can have two or more dimensions, the number of dimensions being the same as the number of indexes required to access an element of the array.

Reusing Array Variables

The array variable is separate from the array itself. Rather like the way an ordinary variable can refer to different values at different times, you can use an array variable to reference different arrays at different points in your program. Suppose you have declared and defined the variable `primes` as before:

```
int[] primes = new int[10];    // Allocate an array of 10 integer elements
```

This produces an array of 10 elements of type `int`. Perhaps a bit later in your program you want the array variable `primes` to refer to a larger array, with 50 elements say. You would simply write:

```
primes = new int[50];          // Allocate an array of 50 integer elements
```

Now the variable `primes` refers to a new array of values of type `int` that is entirely separate from the original. When this statement is executed, the previous array of 10 elements is discarded, along with all the data values you may have stored in it. The variable `primes` can now only be used to reference elements of the new array. This is illustrated in the next diagram.

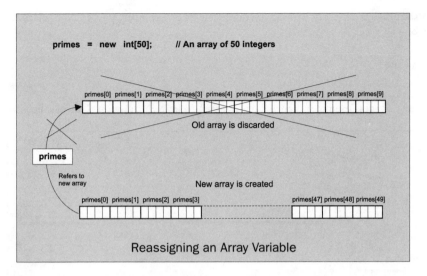

```
primes  =  new  int[50];        // An array of 50 integers
```

primes[0] primes[1] primes[2] primes[3] primes[4] primes[5] primes[6] primes[7] primes[8] primes[9]

Old array is discarded

primes

Refers to
new array

New array is created

primes[0] primes[1] primes[2] primes[3]   primes[47] primes[48] primes[49]

Reassigning an Array Variable

After executing the statement shown in the diagram, the array variable `primes` now points to a new integer array of 50 elements, with index values running from 0 to 49. Although you can change the array that an array variable references, you can't alter the type of value that an element stores. All the arrays referenced by a given variable must correspond to the original type specified when the array variable was declared. The variable `primes`, for example, can only reference arrays of type `int`. We have used an `int` array in the illustration, but everything applies equally well to `long` or `double` or to any of the basic types. More than that, you can create arrays of any other type of object, including the classes that you will be defining yourself in Chapter 5.

Initializing Arrays

You can initialize an array with your own values when you declare it, and at the same time determine how many elements it will have. Following the declaration of the array variable, simply add an equal sign followed by the list of element values enclosed between braces. For example, if you write:

```
int[] primes = {2, 3, 5, 7, 11, 13, 17};    // An array of 7 elements
```

the array is created with sufficient elements to store all of the initializing values that appear between the braces, seven in this case. The array size is determined by the number of initial values so no other information is necessary to define the array. If you specify initializing values for an array, you must include values for *all* the elements. If you only want to set some of the array elements to values explicitly, you should use an assignment statement for each element. For example:

```
int[] primes = new int[100];
primes[0] = 2;
primes[1] = 3;
```

The first statement declares and defines an integer array of 100 elements, all of which will be initialized to zero. The two assignment statements then set values for the first two array elements.

You can also initialize an array with an existing array. For example, you could declare the following array variables:

```
long[] even = {2L, 4L, 6L, 8L, 10L};
long[] value = even;
```

where the array even is used to initialize the array value in its declaration. This has the effect shown below.

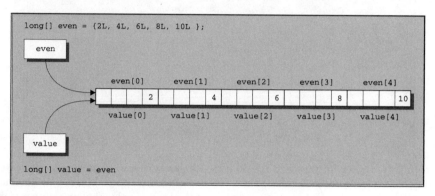

You have created two array variables, but you only have one array. Both arrays refer to the same set of elements and you can access the elements of the array through either variable name – for example, even[2] refers to the same variable as value[2]. One use for this is when you want to switch the arrays referenced by two variables. If you were sorting an array by repeatedly transferring elements from one array to another, by flipping the array you were copying from with the array you were copying to, you could use the same code. For example, if we declared array variables as:

```
double[] inputArray = new double[100];    // Array to be sorted
double[] outputArray = new double[100];   // Reordered array
double[] temp;                             // Temporary array reference
```

when we want to switch the array referenced by outputArray to be the new input array, we could write:

```
temp = inputArray;          // Save reference to inputArray in temp
inputArray = outputArray;   // Set inputArray to refer to outputArray
outputArray = temp;         // Set outputArray to refer to what was inputArray
```

None of the array elements are moved here. Just the addresses of where the arrays are located in memory are swapped, so this is a very fast process. Of course, if you want to replicate an array, you have to define a new array of the same size and type, and then copy each element of the array individually to your new array.

Using Arrays

You can use array elements in expressions in exactly the same way as you might use a single variable of the same data type. For example, if you declare an array samples, you can fill it with random values between 0.0 and 100.0 with the following code:

```
double[] samples = new double[50];    // An array of 50 double values
for(int i = 0; i < 50; i++)
samples[i] = 100.0*Math.random();     // Generate random values
```

To show that array elements can be used in exactly the same way as ordinary variables, you could write:

```
double result = (samples[10]*samples[0] -
                              Math.sqrt(samples[49]))/samples[29];
```

This is a totally arbitrary calculation of course. More sensibly, to compute the average of the values stored in the `samples` array, you could write:

```
double average = 0.0;          // Variable to hold the average

for(int i = 0; i < 50; i++)
  average += samples[i];       // Sum all the elements

average /= 50;                 // Divide by the total number of elements
```

Within the loop we accumulate the sum of all the elements of the array `samples` in the variable `average`. We then divide this sum by the number of elements.

Notice how we use the length of the array, 50, all over the place. It appears in the `for` loop, and in floating point form as a divisor to calculate the average. When you use arrays you will often find that references to the length of the array are strewn all through your code. And if you later want to change the program, to handle 100 elements for instance, you need to be able to decide whether any particular value of 50 in the code is actually the number of elements, and therefore should be changed to 100, or if it is a value that just happens to be the same and should be left alone. Java helps you avoid this problem, as we will now see.

Array Length

You can refer to the length of the array using `length`, a data member of the `array` object. For our array `samples`, we can refer to its length as `samples.length`. We could use this to write the calculation of the average as:

```
double average = 0.0;          // Variable to hold the average
for(int i = 0; i < samples.length; i++)
average += samples[i];         // Sum all the elements
average /= samples.length;     // Divide by the total number of elements
```

Now the code is independent of the number of array elements. If you change the number of elements in the array, the code will automatically deal with that. You will also see in Chapter 6 that being able to obtain the length of an array in this way is very convenient in the context of coding your own class methods that process arrays. You should always use this approach when you need to refer to the length of an array – never use explicit values.

Let's try out an array in an improved program to calculate prime numbers:

Try It Out – Even More Primes

Try out the following code derived, in part, from the code we used in Chapter 2.

```
public class MorePrimes {
  public static void main(String[] args) {
    long[] primes = new long[20];        // Array to store primes
    primes[0] = 2;                       // Seed the first prime
    primes[1] = 3;                       // and the second
    int count = 2;                       // Count of primes found - up to now,
                                         // which is also the array index
    long number = 5;                     // Next integer to be tested

    outer:
    for( ; count < primes.length; number += 2) {
      // The maximum divisor we need to try is square root of number
      long limit = (long)Math.ceil(Math.sqrt((double)number));

      // Divide by all the primes we have up to limit
      for(int i = 1; i < count && primes[i] <= limit; i++) {
        if(number%primes[i] == 0) {              // Is it an exact divisor?
          continue outer;                        // Yes, try the next number
        }
      }
      primes[count++] = number;                  // We got one!
    }

    for(int i=0; i < primes.length; i++)
      System.out.println(primes[i]);             // Output all the primes
  }
}
```

This program computes as many prime numbers as the capacity of the array `primes` will allow.

How It Works

Any number that is not a prime must be a product of prime factors, so we only need to divide a prime number candidate by prime numbers that are less than or equal to the square root of the candidate to test for whether it is prime. This is fairly obvious if you think about it. For every factor a number has that is greater than the square root of the number, the result of division by this factor is another factor that is less than the square root. You perhaps can see this more easily with a specific example. The number 24 has a square root that is a bit less than 5. You can factorize it as 2x12, 3x8, 4x6, then we come to cases where the first factor is greater than the square root so the second is less, 6x4, 8x3 etc., and so we are repeating the pairs of factors we already have.

We first declare the array `primes` to be of type `long`, and define it as having 20 elements. We set the first two elements of the `primes` array to 2 and 3 respectively to start the process off, as we will use the primes we have in the array as divisors when testing a new candidate. The variable, `count`, is the total number of primes we have found, so this starts out as 2. Note that we use `count` as the `for` loop counter, so we omit the first expression between parentheses in the loop statement as `count` has already been set.

The candidate to be tested is stored in `number`, with the first value set as 5. The `for` loop statement labeled `outer` is slightly unusual. First of all, the variable `count` that determines when the loop ends is not incremented in the `for` loop statement, but in the body of the loop. We use the third expression between the `for` loop parentheses to increment `number` in steps of two, since we don't want to check even numbers. The `for` loop ends when `count` is equal to the length of the array. We test the value in `number` in the inner `for` loop by dividing `number` by all of the prime numbers we have in the `primes` array that are less than, or equal to, the square root of the candidate. If we get an exact division the value in `number` is not prime, so we go immediately to the next iteration of the `outer` loop via the `continue` statement.

We calculate the limit for divisors we need to try with the statement:

```
long limit = (long)Math.ceil(Math.sqrt((double)number));
```

The `Math.sqrt()` method produces the square root of number as a `double` value, so if number has the value 7, for instance, a value of about 2.64575 will be returned. This is passed to the `ceil()` method that is also a member of the `Math` class. The `ceil()` method returns a value of type `double` that is the minimum whole number that is not less than the value passed to it. With `number` as 7, this will return 3.0, the smallest integral value not less than the square root of 7. We want to use this number as the limit for our integer divisors, so we cast it to type `long` and store the result in `limit`.

If we get no exact division, we exit normally from the inner loop and execute the statement:

```
primes[count++] = number;      // We got one!
```

Because `count` is the number of values we have stored, it also corresponds to the index for the next free element in the `primes` array. Thus we use `count` as the index to the array element in which we want to store the value of `number`, and then increment `count`.

When we have filled the `primes` array, the `outer` loop will end and we will output all the values in the array. Note that, because we have used the `length` member of the `primes` object whenever we need the number of elements in the array, changing the number of elements in the definition of the array to generate a larger or smaller number of primes is simple.

We can express the logical process of the program with an algorithm as follows:

1. Take the **number** in question and determine its square root.

2. Set the **limit** for divisors to be the smallest integer that is greater than this square root value.

3. Test to see if the **number** can be divided exactly (without remainder) by any of the **primes** already in the `primes` **array** that are less than the **limit** for divisors.

4. If it can, discard the existing **number** and start a new iteration of the loop with the next candidate **number**. If it can't, it is a prime, so enter the existing **number** in the first available empty slot in the array and then move to the next iteration for a new candidate **number**.

5. If the **array** of primes is full, do no more iterations, and print out all the prime number values in the array.

Arrays of Arrays

We have only worked with one-dimensional arrays up to now, that is, arrays that use a single index. Why would you ever need the complications of using more indexes to access the elements of an array?

Suppose that you have a fanatical interest in the weather, and you are intent on recording the temperature each day at 10 separate geographical locations throughout the year 2002. Once you have sorted out the logistics of actually collecting this information, you can use an array of 10 elements corresponding to the number of locations, where each of these elements is an array of 365 elements to store the temperature values. You would declare this array with the statement:

```
float[][] temperature = new float[10][365];
```

This is called a **two-dimensional array**, since it has two dimensions – one with index values running from 0 to 9, and the other with index values from 0 to 364. The first index will relate to a geographical location, and the second index corresponds to the day of the year. That's much handier than a one-dimensional array with 3650 elements, isn't it?

The organization of the two-dimensional array is shown in the following diagram.

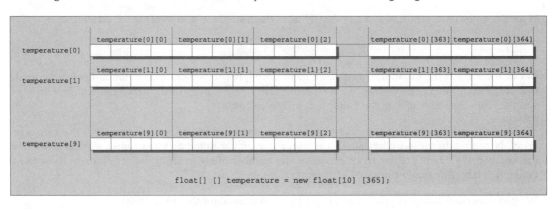

There are 10 arrays, each having 365 elements. In referring to an element, the first square brackets enclose the index for a particular array, and the second pair of square brackets enclose the index value for an element within that array. So to refer to the temperature for day 100 for the sixth location, you would use `temperature[5][99]`. Since each `float` variable occupies 4 bytes, the total space required to store the elements in this two-dimensional array is 10x365x4 bytes, which is a total of 14,600 bytes.

For a fixed second index value in a two-dimensional array, varying the first index direction is often referred to as accessing a **column** of the array. Similarly, fixing the first index value and varying the second, you access a **row** of the array. The reason for this terminology is apparent from the last diagram.

You could just as well have used two statements to create the last array, one to declare the array variable, and the other to define the array:

```
float [][] temperature;              // Declare the array variable
temperature = new float[10][365];    // Create the array
```

The first statement declares the array variable `temperature` for two-dimensional arrays of type `float`. The second statement creates the array with ten elements, each of which is an array of 365 elements.

Let's exercise this two-dimensional array in a program to calculate the average annual temperature for each location.

Try It Out – The Weather Fanatic

In the absence of real samples, we will generate the temperatures as random values between -10° and 35°. This assumes we are recording temperatures in degrees Celsius. If you prefer Fahrenheit you could use 14° to 95° to cover the same range.

```java
public class WeatherFan {
    public static void main(String[] args) {
        float[][] temperature = new float[10][365]; // Temperature array

        // Generate random temperatures
        for(int i = 0; i < temperature.length; i++) {
            for(int j = 0; j < temperature[i].length; j++)
                temperature[i][j] = (float)(45.0*Math.random() - 10.0);
        }

        // Calculate the average per location
        for(int i = 0; i < temperature.length; i++) {
            float average = 0.0f;      // Place to store the average

            for(int j = 0; j < temperature[0].length; j++)
                average += temperature[i][j];

            // Output the average temperature for the current location
            System.out.println("Average temperature at location "
                    + (i+1) + " = " + average/(float)temperature[i].length);
        }
    }
}
```

How It Works

After declaring the array `temperature` we fill it with random values using nested `for` loops. Note how `temperature.length` used in the outer loop refers to the length of the first dimension, 10 in this case. In the inner loop we use `temperature[i].length` to refer to the length of the second dimension, 365. We could use any index value here; `temperature[0].length` would have been just as good for all the elements, since the lengths of the rows of the array are all the same in this case.

The `Math.random()` method generates a value of type `double` from 0.0 up to, but excluding, 1.0. This value is multiplied by 45.0 in the expression for the temperature, which results in values between 0.0 and 45.0. Subtracting 10.0 from this value gives us the range we require, -10.0 to 35.0.

We then use another pair of nested `for` loops, controlled in the same way as the first, to calculate the averages of the stored temperatures. The outer loop iterates over the locations and the inner loop sums all the temperature values for a given location. Before the execution of the inner loop, the variable `average` is declared and initialized, and this is used to accumulate the sum of the temperatures for a location in the inner loop. After the inner loop has been executed, we output the average temperature for each location, identifying the locations by numbers 1 to 10, one more than the index value for each location. Note that the parentheses around `(i+1)` here are essential. To get the average we divide the variable `average` by the number of samples, which is `temperature[i].length`, the length of the array holding temperatures for the current location. Again, we could use any index value here since, as we have seen, they all return the same value, 365.

Arrays of Arrays of Varying Length

When you create an array of arrays, the arrays in the array do not need to be all the same length. You could declare an array variable `samples` with the statement:

```
float[][] samples;          // Declare an array of arrays
```

This declares the array object `samples` to be of type `float[][]`. You can then define the number of elements in the first dimension with the statement:

```
samples = new float[6][];       // Define 6 elements, each is an array
```

The variable `samples` now references an array with six elements, each of which can hold a reference to a one-dimensional array. You can define these arrays individually if you want:

```
samples[2] = new float[6];    // The 3rd array has 6 elements
samples[5] = new float[101];  // The 6th array has 101 elements
```

This defines two of the arrays. Obviously you cannot use an array until it has been defined, but you could conceivably use these two and define the others later – not a likely approach though!

If you wanted the array `samples` to have a triangular shape, with one element in the first row, two elements in the second row, three in the third row, and so on, you could define the arrays in a loop:

```
for(int i = 0; i < samples.length; i++)
   samples[i] = new float[i+1];       // Allocate each array
```

The effect of this is to produce an array layout that is shown in the diagram below.

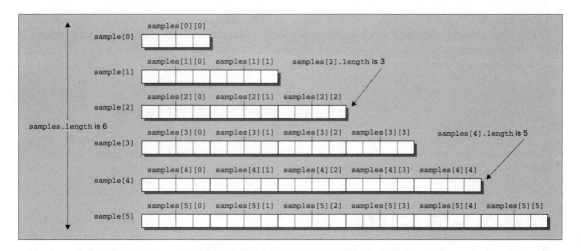

The 21 elements in the array will occupy 84 bytes. When you need a two-dimensional array with rows of varying length, allocating them to fit the requirement can save a considerable amount of memory compared to just using rectangular arrays where the row lengths are all the same.

To check out that the array is as shown, you could implement this in a program, and display the length member for each of these arrays.

Multi-dimensional Arrays

You are not limited to two-dimensional arrays either. If you are an international Java Bean grower with multiple farms across several countries, you could arrange to store the results of your bean counting in the array declared and defined in the statement:

```
long[][][] beans = new long[5][10][30];
```

The array, beans, has three dimensions. It provides for holding bean counts for each of up to 30 fields per farm, with 10 farms per country in each of 5 countries.

You can envisage this as just a three-dimensional array, but remember that beans is an array of five elements, each of which holds a two-dimensional array, and each of these two-dimensional arrays can be different. For example if you really want to go to town, you can declare the array beans with the statement:

```
long[][][] beans = new long[3][][];  // Three two-dimensional arrays
```

Each of the three elements in the first dimension of beans can hold a different two-dimensional array, so you could specify the first dimension of each explicitly with the statements:

```
beans[0] = new long[4][];
beans[1] = new long[2][];
beans[2] = new long[5][];
```

These three arrays have elements that each hold a one-dimensional array, and you can also specify the sizes of these independently. Note how the empty square brackets indicate there is still a dimension undefined. You could give the arrays in each of these elements random dimensions between 1 and 7 with the following code:

```
for(int i = 0; i < beans.length; i++)          // Vary over 1st dimension
    for(int j = 0; j < beans[i].length; j++)   // Vary over 2nd dimension
        beans[i][j] = new long[(int)(1.0 + 6.0*Math.random())];
```

If you can find a sensible reason for doing so, or if you are just a glutton for punishment, you can extend this to four, or more, dimensions.

Arrays of Characters

All our arrays have been numeric so far. You can also have arrays of characters. For example, we can declare an array variable of type char[] to hold 50 characters with the statement:

```
char[] message = new char[50];
```

We could also define an array of type char[] by the characters it holds:

```
char[] vowels = { 'a', 'e', 'i', 'o', 'u'};
```

This defines an array of five elements, initialized with the characters appearing between the braces. This is fine for things like vowels, but what about proper messages?

Using an array of type char, you can write statements such as:

```
char[] sign = {'F', 'l', 'u', 'e', 'n', 't', ' ',
               'G', 'i', 'b', 'b', 'e', 'r', 'i', 's', 'h', ' ',
               's', 'p', 'o', 'k', 'e', 'n', ' ',
               'h', 'e', 'r', 'e'};
```

Well, you get the message – just – but it's not a very friendly way to deal with it. It looks like a collection of characters, which is what it is. What we really need is something that is a bit more integrated – something that looks like a message, but still gives us the ability to get at the individual characters if we want. What we need is a String.

Strings

You will need to use character strings in most of your programs – headings, names, addresses, product descriptions... – the list is endless. In Java, strings are objects of the class String. The String class is a standard class that comes with Java, and it is specifically designed for creating and processing strings.

String Literals

You have already made extensive use of string literals for output. Just about every time the `println()` method was used in an example, we used a string literal as the argument. A **string literal** is a sequence of characters between double quotes:

```
"This is a string literal!"
```

This is actually a `String` literal with a capital `S` – in other words, a constant object of the class `String` that the compiler creates for use in your program.

Some characters can't be entered explicitly from the keyboard for inclusion in a string literal. You can't include a double quote character as it is, for example, as this is used to indicate where a string literal begins and ends. You can't include a newline character by pressing the *Enter* key since this will move the cursor to a new line. As we saw back in Chapter 2, all of these characters are provided in the same way as `char` constants – you use an escape sequence. All the escape sequences you saw when we looked at `char` constants apply to strings. The statement:

```
System.out.println("This is \na string constant!");
```

will produce the output:

```
This is
a string constant!
```

since `\n` is used for a newline character. Like values of type `char`, strings are stored internally as Unicode characters. You can also include Unicode character codes in a string as escape sequences of the form `\Unnnn` where nnnn are the four hexadecimal digits of the Unicode coding for a particular character. The `U` can be upper or lower case. The Greek letter, π, for example, is `\U03C0`.

You will recall from our preliminary discussion of classes and objects in Chapter 1 that a class usually contains data and methods and, naturally, this is true of the `String` class. The sequence of characters included in the string is the class data, and the methods in the class `String` enable you to process the data in a variety of ways. We will go into the detail of how the class is defined in Chapter 5, but in this chapter we will concentrate on how we can create and use objects of the class `String`. You know how to define a `String` literal. The next step is to learn how a `String` variable is declared and how `String` objects are created.

Creating String Objects

Just to make sure there is no confusion in your mind, a `String` variable is simply an object of the class `String`. You declare a `String` variable in much the same way as you define a variable of one of the basic types. You can also initialize it in the declaration, which is generally a good idea:

```
String myString = "My inaugural string";
```

This declares the variable `myString` as type `String`, and initializes it with the value `"My inaugural string"`. You can store a reference to another string in a `String` variable, once you have declared it, by using an assignment. For example, we can change the value of our `String` variable `myString` to the statement:

```
myString = "Strings can be knotty";
```

The effect of this is illustrated below:

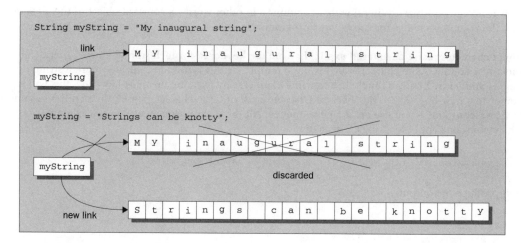

The string itself is distinct from the variable you use to refer to it. In the same way as we saw with array objects, the variable `myString` stores a reference to a `String` object, in other words, it keeps track of where the string object is in memory. When we declare and initialize `myString`, it links to the initializing string value. When we execute the assignment statement, the original link is severed, the old string is discarded, and the variable `myString` stores a reference to the new string value. This means that you cannot extend the string that is referred to in a variable of type `String`. `String` objects are said to be **immutable** – which just means that they cannot be changed. To change the string referenced by a `String` variable you throw away the reference to the old string and replace it with a reference to a new one. The distinction between a `String` variable and the string it references is not apparent most of the time, but we will see situations later in this chapter where it is important to understand this, so keep it in mind.

You should also keep in mind that characters in a string are Unicode characters, so each one occupies two bytes. This is also not something you need worry about most of the time, but there are occasions where you need to be conscious of that too.

Of course, if you declare a variable of type `String` in a method without initializing it:

```
String anyString;          // Uninitialized String variable
```

then it does not refer to anything. However, if you try to compile a program containing this statement you will get an error. If you don't want it to refer to anything at the outset, for instance, if you may or may not assign a `String` object to it before you use the variable, then you must initialize it to a special `null` value:

```
String anyString = null;     // String variable that doesn't reference a string
```

The actual value it stores in this situation is referred to as `null`, so you can test whether a `String` variable refers to anything or not by a statement such as:

```
if(anyString == null)
   System.out.println("anyString does not refer to anything!");
```

The variable `anyString` will continue to be `null` until you use an assignment to make it reference a particular string. Attempting to use a variable that has not been initialized is an error. When you declare a `String` variable, or any other variable that is not an array, in a block of code without initializing it, the compiler can detect any attempts to use the variable before it has a value assigned, and will flag it as an error. As a rule, you should always initialize variables as you declare them.

Arrays of Strings

Since `String` variables are objects, you can create arrays of strings. You declare an array of `String` objects with the same mechanism that we used to declare arrays of elements for the basic types. You just use the type `String` in the declaration. For example, to declare an array of five `String` objects, you could use the statement:

```
String[] names = new String[5];
```

It should now be apparent that the argument to the method `main()` is an array of `String` objects.

We can try out arrays of strings with a small example.

Try It Out – Twinkle, Twinkle, Lucky Star

Let's create a console program to generate your lucky star for the day.

```
public class LuckyStars {
  public static void main(String[] args) {
    String[] stars = {
                     "Robert Redford"   , "Marilyn Monroe",
                     "Boris Karloff"    , "Lassie",
                     "Hopalong Cassidy", "Trigger"
                   };
    System.out.println("Your lucky star for today is "
                      + stars[(int)(stars.length*Math.random())]);

  }
}
```

How It Works

This program creates the array `stars`, of type `String`. The array length will be set to however many initializing values appear between the braces in the declaration statement, six in this case.

We select a random element from the array by creating a random index value within the output statement with the expression `(int)(stars.length*Math.random())`. Multiplying the random number produced using the method `Math.random()` by the length of the array, we will get a value between 0.0 and 6.0 since the value returned by `random()` will be between 0.0 and 1.0. The result won't ever be 6.0 because the value returned by the `random()` method is strictly less than 1.0, which is just as well as this would be an illegal index value. The result is then cast to an `int`, making it a valid array index value.

Thus the program selects a random string from the array and displays it.

Operations on Strings

There are many kinds of operations that can be performed on strings, but we can start with one you have used already, joining strings together, often called **string concatenation**.

Joining Strings

To join two `String` objects to form a single string you use the + operator, just as you have been doing with the argument to the `println()` method in the program examples thus far. The simplest use of this is to join two strings together:

```
myString = "The quick brown fox" + " jumps over the lazy dog";
```

This will join the two strings on the right of the assignment, and store the result in the `String` variable `myString`. The + operation generates a completely new `String` object that is separate from the original `String` objects that are the operands, and this new object is stored in `myString`.

Note that you can also use the += operator to concatenate strings. For example:

```
String phrase = "Too many";
phrase += " cooks spoil the broth";
```

After executing these statements the variable `phrase` will refer to the string "Too many cooks spoil the broth". Note that this does not modify the string "Too many". The string that is referenced by `phrase` after this statement has been executed is a completely new `String` object. This is illustrated on the following page.

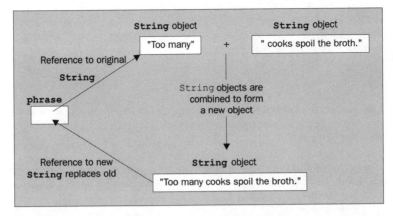

Let's see how some variations on the use of the + operator with `String` objects work in an example.

Try It Out – String Concatenation

Enter the following code for the class `JoinStrings`:

```java
public class JoinStrings {
    public static void main(String[] args) {

        String firstString = "Many ";
        String secondString = "hands ";
        String thirdString = "make light work";

        String myString;          // Variable to store results

        // Join three strings and store the result
        myString = firstString + secondString + thirdString;
        System.out.println(myString);

        // Convert an integer to String and join with two other strings
        int numHands = 99;
        myString = numHands + " " + secondString + thirdString;
        System.out.println(myString);

        // Combining a string and integers
        myString = "fifty five is " + 5 + 5;
        System.out.println(myString);

        // Combining integers and a string
        myString = 5 + 5 + " is ten";
        System.out.println(myString);
    }
}
```

If you run this example, it will produce some interesting results:

```
Many hands make light work
99 hands make light work
fifty five is 55
10 is ten
```

How It Works

The first line of output is quite straightforward. It simply joins the three string values stored in the String variables firstString, secondString, and thirdString into a single string, and stores this in the variable myString.

The second line of output is a use of the + operator we have used regularly with the println() method, but clearly something a little more complicated is happening here. This is illustrated below:

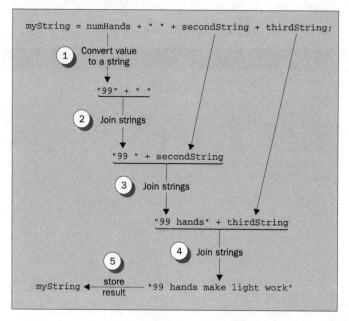

Behind the scenes, the value of the variable numHands is being converted to a string that represents this value as a decimal number. This is prompted by the fact that it is combined with the string literal, " ". Dissimilar types in a binary operation cannot be operated on, so one operand must be converted to the type of the other if the operation is to be possible. Here the compiler arranges that the numerical value stored in numHands is converted to type String to match the type of the right operand of the + operator. If you look back at the table of operator precedences, you will see that the associativity of the operator + is from left to right, so the strings are combined in pairs starting from the left, as shown in the diagram.

The left-to-right associativity of the + operator is important in understanding the next two lines of output. The two statements involved in creating these strings look very similar. Why does "5 + 5" result in 55 in one statement, and 10 in the other? The reason is illustrated below.

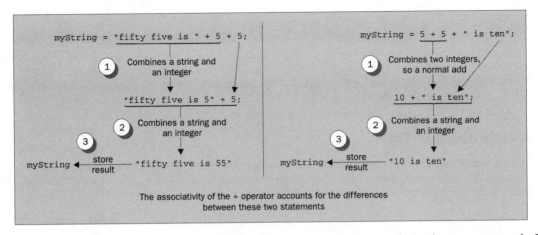

The associativity of the + operator accounts for the differences between these two statements

The essential difference between the two is that the first statement always has at least one operand of type String, so the operation is one of string concatenation, whereas in the second statement the first operation is an arithmetic add, as both operands are integers. In the first statement each of the integers is converted to type String individually. In the second, the numerical values are added, and the result, 10, is converted to a string representation to allow the literal " is ten" to be concatenated.

You don't need to know about this at this point, but in case you were wondering, the conversion of values of the basic types to type String is actually accomplished by using a static method, toString(), of a standard class that corresponds to the basic type. Each of the basic types has an equivalent class defined, so for the types we have discussed earlier there are the following classes:

Basic Type	Wrapper Class
byte	Byte
short	Short
int	Integer
long	Long
float	Float
double	Double
boolean	Boolean
character	Character

A value of one of the basic types is passed to the toString() method of the corresponding class as an argument, and that returns the String equivalent. All of this happens automatically when you are concatenating strings using the + operator. As we shall see, not only these classes have a toString() method – all classes do. We won't go into the further significance of these classes now, as we'll be covering these in more detail in Chapter 5.

The String class also defines a method, valueOf(), that will create a String object from a value of any of the basic types. You just pass the value you want converted to a string as the argument to the method, for instance:

141

```
String doubleString = String.valueOf(3.14159);
```

You call the `valueOf()` method using the name of the class, `String`, as shown above. This is because the method is a `static` member of the `String` class. You will learn what this means in Chapter 5. A literal or variable of any of the basic types can be passed to the `valueOf()` method, and it will return a `String` representation of the value.

Comparing Strings

Here is where the difference between the `String` variable and the string it references will become apparent. To compare variables of the basic types for equality you use the `==` operator. This does **not** apply to `String` objects (or any other objects). The expression:

```
string1 == string2
```

will check whether the two `String` variables refer to the same string. If they reference separate strings, this expression will have the value `false`, regardless of whether or not the strings happen to be identical. In other words, the expression above does not compare the strings themselves, it compares the references to the strings, so the result will be true only if `string1` and `string2` both refer to one and the same string. We can demonstrate this with a little example.

Try It Out – Two Strings, Identical but not the Same

In the following code, we test to see whether `string1` and `string3` refer to the same string.

```java
public class MatchStrings {
  public static void main(String[] args) {

    String string1 = "Too many ";
    String string2 = "cooks";
    String string3 = "Too many cooks";

  // Make string1 and string3 refer to separate strings that are identical
    string1 += string2;

    // Display the contents of the strings
    System.out.println("Test 1");
    System.out.println("string3 is now: " + string3);
    System.out.println("string1 is now: " + string1);

    if(string1 == string3)                          // Now test for identity
      System.out.println("string1 == string3 is true." +
                         " string1 and string3 point to the same string");
    else
      System.out.println("string1 == string3 is false." +
                  " string1 and string3 do not point to the same string");

    // Now make string1 and string3 refer to the same string
    string3 = string1;
```

```
        // Display the contents of the strings
        System.out.println("\n\nTest 2");
        System.out.println("string3 is now: " + string3);
        System.out.println("string1 is now: " + string1);

        if(string1 == string3)      // Now test for identity
            System.out.println("string1 == string3 is true." +
                              " string1 and string3 point to the same string");
        else
            System.out.println("string1 == string3 is false." +
                         " string1 and string3 do not point to the same string");
    }
}
```

We have created two scenarios. In the first, the variables `string1` and `string3` refer to separate strings that happen to be identical. In the second, they both reference the same string. This will produce the output:

```
Test 1
string3 is now: Too many cooks
string1 is now: Too many cooks
string1==string3 is false. string1 and string3 do not point to the same string

Test 2
string3 is now: Too many cooks
string1 is now: Too many cooks
string1==string3 is true. string1 and string3 point to the same string
```

How It Works

The three variables `string1`, `string2`, and `string3` are initialized with the string literals you see. After executing the assignment statement, the string referenced by `string1` will be identical to that referenced by `string3`, but as you see from the output, the comparison for equality in the `if` statement returns `false` because the variables refer to two separate strings.

Next we change the value of `string3` so that it refers to the same string as `string1`. The output demonstrates that the `if` expression has the value `true`, and that the `string1` and `string3` objects do indeed refer to the same string. This clearly shows that the comparison is not between the strings themselves, but between the references to the strings. So how do we compare the strings?

Comparing Strings for Equality

To compare two `String` variables, that is, to decide whether the strings they reference are equal or not, you must use the method `equals()`, which is defined in the `String` class. This method does a case sensitive comparison. Two strings are equal if they are the same length, that is, have the same number of characters, and each character in one string is identical to the corresponding character in the other.

To check for equality between two strings ignoring the case of the string characters, you use the method `equalsIgnoreCase()`. Let's put these in the context of an example to see how they work.

Try It Out – String Identity

Make the following changes to the `MatchStrings.java` file of the previous example:

```java
public class MatchStrings {
  public static void main(String[] args) {

    String string1 = "Too many ";
    String string2 = "cooks";
    String string3 = "Too many cooks";

  // Make string1 and string3 refer to separate strings that are identical
    string1 += string2;

    // Display the contents of the strings
    System.out.println("Test 1");
    System.out.println("string3 is now: " + string3);
    System.out.println("string1 is now: " + string1);

    if(string1.equals(string3))                    // Now test for equality
      System.out.println("string1.equals(string3) is true." +
                                " so strings are equal.");
    else
      System.out.println("string1.equals(string3) is false." +
                            " so strings are not equal.");

    // Now make string1 and string3 refer to strings differing in case
    string3 = "TOO many cooks";
    // Display the contents of the strings
    System.out.println("\n\nTest 2");
    System.out.println("string3 is now: " + string3);
    System.out.println("string1 is now: " + string1);

    if(string1.equals(string3))                    // Compare for equality
      System.out.println("string1.equals(string3) is true " +
                                " so strings are equal.");
    else
      System.out.println("string1.equals(string3) is false" +
                            " so strings are not equal.");

    if(string1.equalsIgnoreCase(string3))         // Compare, ignoring case
      System.out.println("string1.equalsIgnoreCase(string3) is true" +
                                " so strings are equal ignoring case.");
    else
      System.out.println("string1.equalsIgnoreCase(string3) is false" +
                                " so strings are different.");
  }
}
```

If you run this example, you should get the output:

```
Test 1
string3 is now: Too many cooks
```

```
string1 is now: Too many cooks
string1.equals(string3) is true. so strings are equal.


Test 2
string3 is now: TOO many cooks
string1 is now: Too many cooks
string1.equals(string3) is false so strings are not equal.
string1.equalsIgnoreCase(string3) is true so strings are equal ignoring case.
```

How It Works

Before we look in detail at how the program works, let's first take some time to look at how the method calls that pepper the code are put together.

In the `if` expression, we've called the method `equals()` of the object `string1` to test for equality with `string3`. This is the syntax we have been using to call the method `println()` in the object `out`. In general, to call a method belonging to an object you write the object name, then a period, then the name of the method. The parentheses following the method name enclose the information to be passed to the method – `string3` in this case. The general form for calling a method for an object is shown below.

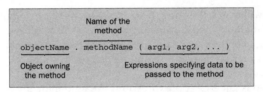

> We will learn more about this in Chapter 5, when we look at how to define our own classes. For the moment, just note that you don't necessarily need to pass any arguments to a method. On the other hand there can be several. It all depends on how the method was defined in the class.

The `equals()` method requires one argument that you put between the parentheses. This must be the `String` object that is to be compared with the original object. The method returns `true` if the value passed to it (`string3` in our example) is identical to the string pointed to by the `String` object that owns the method, in this case `string1`. As you may have already guessed, we could just as well call the `equals()` method for the object `string3`, and pass `string1` as the argument to compare the two strings. In this case, the expression to call the method would be:

```
string3.equals(string1)
```

and we would get exactly the same result.

Looking at the program code, after outputting the values of `string3` and `string1`, the next line shows that calling the `equals()` method for `string1` with `string3` as the argument returns `true`. After the `if`, we make `string3` reference a new string. We then compare the values of `string1` and `string3` once more, and, of course, the result of the comparison is now `false`.

Finally we compare `string1` with `string3` using the `equalsIgnoreCase()` method. Here the result is `true` since the strings only differ in the case of the first three characters.

String Interning

Having convinced you of the necessity for using the `equals` method for comparing strings, we can now reveal that there is a way to make comparing strings with the `==` operator effective. The mechanism to make this possible is called **string interning**. String interning ensures that no two `String` objects encapsulate the same string so all `String` objects encapsulates unique strings. This means that if two `String` variables reference strings that are identical, the references must be identical too. To put it another way, if two `String` variables contain references that are not equal, they must refer to strings that are not equal. So how do we arrange that all `String` objects encapsulate unique strings? You just call the `intern()` method for every new `String` object that you create. For instance, let's amend a bit of an earlier example:

```
String string1 = "Too many ";
String string2 = "cooks";
String string3 = "Too many cooks";

// Make string1 and string3 refer to separate strings that are identical
string1 += string2;
string1 = string1.intern();            // Intern string1
```

The `intern()` method will check the string referenced by `string1` against all the `String` objects currently in existence. If it already exists, the current object will be discarded and `string1` will contain a reference to the existing object encapsulating the same string. As a result, the expression `string1 ==` `string3` will evaluate to `true`, whereas without the call to `intern()` it evaluated to `false`.

All string constants and constant `String` expressions are automatically interned. Thus if you add another variable to the code fragment above:

```
String string4 = "Too " +"many ";
```

the reference stored in `string4` will be automatically the same as the reference stored in `string1`. Only `String` expressions involving variables need to be interned. We could have written the statement that created the combined string to be stored in `string1` with the statement:

```
string1 = (string1 + string2).intern();
```

This now interns the result of the expression `(string1 + string2)`, ensuring that the reference stored in `string1` will be unique.

String interning has two benefits. First, it reduces the amount of memory required for storing `String` objects in your program. If your program generates a lot of duplicate strings then this will be significant. Second, it allows the use of `==` instead of the `equals()` method when you want to compare strings for equality. Since the `==` operator just compares two references, it will be much faster than the `equals()` method, which involves a sequence of character by character comparisons. This implies that you *may* make your program run much faster, but only in certain cases. Keep in mind that the `intern()` method has to use the `equals()` method to determine whether a string already exists. More than that, it will compare the current string against a succession of, and possibly all, existing strings in order to determine whether the current string is unique. Realistically you should stick to using the `equals()` method in the majority of situations and only use interning when you are sure that the benefits outweigh the cost.

Checking the Start and End of a String

It can be useful to be able to check just part of a string. You can test whether a string starts with a particular character sequence by using the method `startsWith()`. If `string1` has been defined as `"Too many cooks"`, the expression `string1.startsWith("Too")` will have the value `true`. So would the expression `string1.startsWith("Too man")`. The comparison is case sensitive so the expression `string1.startsWith("tOO")` will be `false`.

A complementary method `endsWith()` checks for what appears at the end of a string, so the expression `string1.endsWith("cooks")` will have the value `true`. The test is case sensitive here, too.

Sequencing Strings

You will often need to place strings in order, for example, when you have a collection of names. Testing for equality doesn't help – what you need is the method `compareTo()` in the class `String`. This method compares the `String` object from which it is called with the argument passed to it, and returns an integer which is negative if the `String` object is less than the argument passed, zero if the `String` object is equal to the argument, and positive if the `String` object is greater than the argument. It is not that obvious what the terms 'less than', 'equal to', and 'greater than' mean when applied to strings, so let's define that a bit more precisely.

Two strings are compared in the `compareTo()` method by comparing successive corresponding characters, starting with the first character in each string. The process continues until a pair of corresponding characters are found to be different, or the last character in the shortest string is reached. Individual characters are compared by comparing their Unicode representations – so two characters are equal if the numeric values of their Unicode representations are equal. One character is greater than another if the numerical value of its Unicode representation is greater than that of the other.

One string is greater than another if it has a character greater than the corresponding character in the other string, and all the previous characters were equal. So if `string1` has the value `"mad dog"`, and `string2` has the value `"mad cat"`, then the expression:

```
string1.compareTo(string2)
```

will return a positive value as a result of comparing the fifth characters in the strings: the 'd' in `string1` with the 'c' in `string2`.

What if the corresponding characters in both strings are equal up to the end of the shorter string, but the other string has more characters? In this case the longer string is greater than the shorter string, so `"catamaran"` is greater than `"cat"`.

One string is less than another string if it has a character less than the corresponding character in the other string, and all the preceding characters are equal. Thus the following expression will return a negative value:

```
string2.compareTo(string1)
```

Two strings are equal if they contain the same number of characters and corresponding characters are identical. In this case the `compareTo()` method returns 0.

We can exercise the `compareTo()` method in a simple example.

Try It Out – Ordering Strings

We will just create three strings that we can compare using the `compareTo()` method. Enter the following code:

```java
public class SequenceStrings {
  public static void main(String[] args) {

    // Strings to be compared
    String string1 = "A";
    String string2 = "To";
    String string3 = "Z";

    // Strings for use in output
    String string1Out = "\"" + string1 + "\"";       // string1 with quotes
    String string2Out = "\"" + string2 + "\"";       // string2 with quotes
    String string3Out = "\"" + string3 + "\"";       // string3 with quotes

    // Compare string1 with string3
    if(string1.compareTo(string3) < 0) {
      System.out.println(string1Out + " is less than " + string3Out);

    } else {
      if(string1.compareTo(string3) > 0)
        System.out.println(string1Out + " is greater than " + string3Out);
      else
        System.out.println(string1Out + " is equal to " + string3Out);
    }

    // Compare string2 with string1
    if(string2.compareTo(string1) < 0) {
      System.out.println(string2Out + " is less than " + string1Out);

    } else {
      if(string2.compareTo(string1) > 0)
        System.out.println(string2Out + " is greater than " + string1Out);
      else
        System.out.println(string2Out + " is equal to " + string1Out);
    }
  }
}
```

The example will produce the output:

```
"A" is less than "Z"
"To" is greater than "A"
```

How It Works

You should have no trouble with this example. It declares and initializes three `String` variables, `string1`, `string2`, and `string3`. We then create three further `String` variables that correspond to the first three strings with double quote characters at the beginning and the end. This is just to simplify the output statements. We then have an `if` with a nested `if` to compare `string1` with `string3`. We compare `string2` with `string1` in the same way.

As with the `equals()` method, the argument to the method `compareTo()` can be any expression that results in a `String` object.

Accessing String Characters

When you are processing strings, sooner or later you will need to access individual characters in a `String` object. To refer to a character at a particular position in a string you use an index of type `int` that is the offset of the character position from the beginning of the string. This is exactly the same principle as we used for referencing an array element. The first character in a string is at position 0, the second is at position 1, the third is at position 2, and so on. However, although the principle is the same, the practice is not. You can't use square brackets to access characters in a string – you must use a method.

Extracting String Characters

You can extract a character from a `String` object by using the method `charAt()`. This accepts an argument that is the offset of the character position from the beginning of the string – in other words, an index. If you attempt to use an index that is less than 0 or greater than the index for the last position in the string, you will cause an **exception** to be thrown, which will cause your program to be terminated. We will discuss exactly what exceptions are, and how you should deal with them, in Chapter 7. For the moment, just note that the specific type of exception thrown in this case is called `StringIndexOutOfBoundsException`. It's rather a mouthful, but quite explanatory.

To avoid unnecessary errors of this kind, you obviously need to be able to determine the length of a `String` object. To obtain the length of a string, you just need to call its `length()` method. Note that this is different from the way you got the length of an array. Here you are calling a method, `length()`, in the class `String`, whereas with an array you were accessing a data member, `length`. We can explore the use of the `charAt()` and `length()` methods in the `String` class with another example.

Try It Out – Getting at Characters in a String

In the following code the soliloquy is analyzed character-by-character to determine the vowels, spaces, and letters used.

```
public class StringCharacters {
  public static void main(String[] args) {
    // Text string to be analyzed
    String text = "To be or not to be, that is the question;"
                +"Whether 'tis nobler in the mind to suffer"
                +" the slings and arrows of outrageous fortune,"
                +" or to take arms against a sea of troubles,"
                +" and by opposing end them?";
```

```
      int spaces  = 0,                            // Count of spaces
          vowels  = 0,                            // Count of vowels
          letters = 0;                            // Count of letters

      // Analyze all the characters in the string
      int textLength = text.length();             // Get string length

      for(int i = 0; i < textLength; i++) {
        // Check for vowels
        char ch = Character.toLowerCase(text.charAt(i));
        if(ch == 'a' || ch == 'e' || ch == 'i' || ch == 'o' || ch == 'u')
          vowels++;

        //Check for letters
        if(Character.isLetter(ch))
          letters++;

        // Check for spaces
        if(Character.isWhitespace(ch))
          spaces++;
      }

      System.out.println("The text contained vowels:     " + vowels + "\n" +
                 "              consonants: " + (letters-vowels) + "\n"+
                 "              spaces:     " + spaces);
    }
  }
```

Running the example, you'll see:

```
The text contained vowels:     60
                   consonants: 93
                   spaces:     37
```

How It Works

The String variable text is initialized with the quotation you see. All the counting of letter characters is done in the for loop, which is controlled by the index i. The loop continues as long as i is less than the length of the string, which is returned by the method text.length() and which we saved in the variable textLength.

Starting with the first character, which has the index value 0, each character is retrieved from the string by calling its charAt() method. The loop index i is used as the index to the character position string. The method returns the character at index position i as a value of type char, and we convert this to lower case, where necessary, by calling the static method toLowerCase() in the class Character. The character to be converted is passed as an argument and the method returns either the original character or, if it is upper case, the lower case equivalent. This enables us to deal with the string in just one case.

There is an alternative to using the toLowerCase() method in the Character class. The String class also contains a method toLowerCase() that will convert a whole string and return the converted string. You could convert the string text to lower case with the statement:

```
text = text.toLowerCase();    // Convert string to lower case
```

This statement replaces the original string with the lower case equivalent. If you wanted to retain the original, you could store the lower case string in another variable of type `String`. For converting strings to upper case, the class `String` also has a method `toUpperCase()` which is used in the same way.

The `if` expression checks for any of the vowels by ORing the comparisons for the five vowels together. If the expression is `true` we increment the `vowels` count. To check for a letter of any kind we use the `isLetter()` method in the class `Character`, and accumulate the total letter count in the variable `letters`. This will enable us to calculate the number of consonants by subtracting the number of vowels from the total number of letters. Finally, the loop code checks for a space by using the `isWhitespace()` method in the class `Character`. This method returns `true` if the character passed as an argument is a Unicode whitespace character. As well as spaces, whitespace in Unicode also includes horizontal and vertical tab, newline, carriage return, and form-feed characters. If you just wanted to count the blanks in the text, you could compare for a blank character. After the `for` loop ends, we just output the results.

Searching Strings for Characters

There are two methods, available to you in the class `String`, that will search a string, `indexOf()` and `lastIndexOf()`. Both of these come in four different flavors to provide a range of search possibilities. The basic choice is whether you want to search for a single character, or for a substring; so let's look first at the options for searching a string for a given character.

To search a string `text` for a single character, `'a'` for example, you could write:

```
int index = 0;              // Position of character in the string
index = text.indexOf('a'); // Find first index position containing 'a'
```

The method `indexOf()` will search the contents of the string `text` forwards from the beginning, and return the index position of the first occurrence of `'a'`. If `'a'` is not found, the method will return the value -1.

> **This is characteristic of both the search methods in the class `String`. They always return either the index position of what is sought or -1 if the search objective is not found. It is important that you check the index value returned for -1 before you use it to index a string, otherwise you will get an error when you don't find what you are looking for.**

If you wanted to find the last occurrence of `'a'` in the `String` variable `text`, you just use the method `lastIndexOf()`:

```
index = text.lastIndexOf('a');  // Find last index position containing 'a'
```

The method searches the string backwards, starting with the last character in the string. The variable `index` will therefore contain the index position of the last occurrence of `'a'`, or -1 if it is not found.

We can find the first and last occurrences of a character, but what about the ones in the middle? Well, there's a variation of each of the above methods that has a second argument to specify a 'from position', from which to start the search. To search forwards from a given position, `startIndex`, you would write:

```
index = text.indexOf('a', startIndex);
```

This version of the method `indexOf()` searches the string for the character specified by the first argument starting with the position specified by the second argument. You could use this to find the first 'b' that comes after the first 'a' in a string with the statements:

```
int aIndex = -1;                        // Position of 1st 'a'
int bIndex = -1;                        // Position of 1st 'b' after 'a'
aIndex = text.indexOf('a');             // Find first 'a'
if(aIndex >= 0)
    bIndex = text.indexOf('b', ++aIndex); // Find 1st 'b' after 1st 'a'
```

Once we have the index value from the initial search for 'a', we need to check that 'a' was really found by verifying that aIndex is not negative. We can then search for 'b' from the position following 'a'. As you can see, the second argument of this version of the method `indexOf()` is separated from the first argument by a comma. Since the second argument is the index position from which the search is to start, and aIndex is the position at which 'a' was found, we should increment aIndex to the position following 'a' before using it in the search for 'b' to avoid checking for 'b' in the position we already know contains 'a'.

If 'a' happened to be the last character in the string, it wouldn't matter, since the `indexOf()` method just returns −1 if the index value is beyond the last character in the string. If you somehow supplied a negative index value to the method, it would simply search the whole string from the beginning.

Searching for Substrings

The methods `indexOf()` and `lastIndexOf()` also come in versions that accept a string as the first argument, which will search for this string rather than a single character. In all other respects they work in the same way as the character searching methods we have just seen. The complete set of `indexOf()` methods is:

Method	Description
indexOf(int ch)	Returns the index position of the first occurrence of the character ch in the String for which the method is called. If the character ch does not occur, -1 is returned.
indexOf(int ch, int index)	Same as the method above, but with the search starting at position index. If the value of index is outside the legal limits for the String object, -1 is returned.
indexOf(String str)	Returns the index position of the first occurrence of the substring str in the String object for which the method is called. If the substring str does not occur, -1 is returned.
indexOf(String str, int index)	Same as the method above, but with the search starting at position index. If the value of index is outside the legal limits for the String object, -1 is returned.

The four flavors of the `lastIndexOf()` method have the same parameters as the four versions of the `indexOf()` method. The difference is that the last occurrence of the character or substring that is sought is returned by the `lastIndexOf()` method.

The method `startsWith()` that we mentioned earlier also comes in a version that accepts an additional argument that is an offset from the beginning of the string being checked. The check for the matching character sequence then begins at that offset position. If you have defined a string as:

```
String string1 = "The Ides of March";
```

then the expression `String1.startsWith("Ides", 4)` will have the value `true`.
We can show the `indexOf()` and `lastIndexOf()` methods at work with substrings in an example.

Try It Out – Exciting Concordance Entries

We'll use the `indexOf()` method to search the quotation we used in the last example for "and" and the `lastIndexOf()` method to search for "the".

```java
public class FindCharacters {
  public static void main(String[] args) {
    // Text string to be analyzed
    String text = "To be or not to be, that is the question;"
                + " Whether 'tis nobler in the mind to suffer"
                + " the slings and arrows of outrageous fortune,"
                + " or to take arms against a sea of troubles,"
                + " and by opposing end them?";

    int andCount = 0;              // Number of ands
    int theCount = 0;              // Number of thes

    int index = -1;                // Current index position

    String andStr = "and";         // Search substring
    String theStr = "the";         // Search substring

    // Search forwards for "and"
    index = text.indexOf(andStr);  // Find first 'and'
    while(index >= 0) {
      ++andCount;
      index += andStr.length();    // Step to position after last 'and'
      index = text.indexOf(andStr, index);
    }

    // Search backwards for "the"
    index = text.lastIndexOf(theStr);   // Find last 'the'
    while(index >= 0) {
      ++theCount;
      index -= theStr.length();         // Step to position before last 'the'
      index = text.lastIndexOf(theStr, index);
    }
```

```
        System.out.println("The text contains " + andCount + " ands\n"
                        + "The text contains " + theCount + " thes");
    }
}
```

The program will produce the output:

```
The text contains 2 ands
The text contains 5 thes
```

> If you were expecting the "`the`" count to be 3, note that there is one instance in "`whether`" and another in "`them`". If you want to find three, you need to refine your program to eliminate such pseudo-occurrences by checking the characters either side of the "`the`" substring.

How It Works

We define the `String` variable, `text`, as before, and set up two counters, `andCount` and `theCount`, for the two words. The variable `index` will keep track of the current position in the string. We then have `String` variables `andStr` and `theStr` holding the substrings we will be searching for.

To find the instances of "and", we first find the index position of the first occurrence of "and" in the string `text`. If this index is negative, `text` does not contain "and", and the `while` loop will not execute as the condition is false on the first iteration. Assuming there is at least one "and", the `while` loop block is executed and `andCount` is incremented for the instance of "and" we have just found. The method `indexOf()` returns the index position of the first character of the substring, so we have to move the index forward to the character following the last character of the substring we have just found. This is done by adding the length of the substring, as shown in the following diagram:

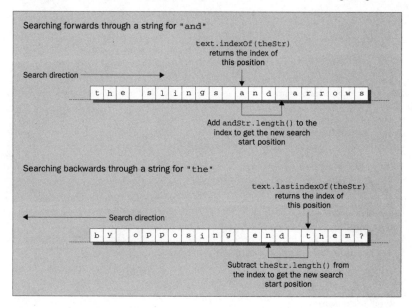

We can then search for the next occurrence of the substring by passing the new value of index to the method indexOf(). The loop continues as long as the index value returned is not -1.

To count the occurrences of the substring "the" the program searches the string text backwards, by using the method lastIndexOf() instead of indexOf(). This works in much the same way, the only significant difference being that we decrement the value of index, instead of incrementing it. This is because the next occurrence of the substring has to be at least that many characters back from the first character of the substring we have just found. If the string "the" happened to occur at the beginning of the string we are searching, the lastIndexOf() method would be called with a negative value for index. This would not cause any problem – it would just result in -1 being returned in any event.

Extracting Substrings

The String class includes a method, substring(), that will extract a substring from a string. There are two versions of this method. The first version will extract a substring consisting of all the characters from a given index position to the end of the string. This works as illustrated in the following code fragment:

```
String place = "Palm Springs";
String lastWord = place.substring(5);
```

After executing these statements, lastWord will contain the string Springs. The substring is copied from the original to form a new string. This is useful when a string has basically two constituent substrings, but a more common requirement is to extract several substrings from a string where each substring is separated from the next by a special character such as a comma, a slash, or even just a space. The second version of substring() will help with this.

You can extract a substring from a string by specifying the index positions of the first character in the substring and one beyond the last character of the substring as arguments to the method substring(). With the variable place being defined as before, the following statement will result in the variable segment being set to the string "ring":

```
String segment = place.substring(7, 11);
```

> The substring() **method is not like the** indexOf() **method when it comes to illegal index values. With either version of the method** substring(), **if you specify an index that is outside the bounds of the string, you will get an error. As with the** charAt() **method,** substring() **will throw a** StringIndexOutOfBoundsException **exception.**

We can see how substring() works with a more substantial example.

Try It Out – Word for Word

We can use the indexOf() method in combination with the substring() method to extract a sequence of substrings that are separated by spaces from a single string:

```
public class ExtractSubstring {
  public static void main(String[] args) {
    String text = "To be or not to be";      // String to be segmented
    int count = 0;                            // Number of substrings
    char separator = ' ';                     // Substring separator

    // Determine the number of substrings
    int index = 0;
    do {
      ++count;                                // Increment count of substrings
      ++index;                                // Move past last position
      index = text.indexOf(separator, index);
    } while (index != -1);

    // Extract the substring into an array
    String[] subStr = new String[count];      // Allocate for substrings
    index = 0;                                // Substring start index
    int endIndex = 0;                         // Substring end index
    for(int i = 0; i < count; i++) {
      endIndex = text.indexOf(separator,index);  // Find next separator

      if(endIndex == -1)                      // If it is not found
        subStr[i] = text.substring(index);    // extract to the end
      else                                    // otherwise
        subStr[i] = text.substring(index, endIndex);  // to end index

      index = endIndex + 1;                   // Set start for next cycle
    }

    // Display the substrings
    for(int i = 0; i < subStr.length; i++)
      System.out.println(subStr[i]);
  }
}
```

When you run this example, you should get the output:

```
To
be
or
not
to
be
```

How It Works

After setting up the string `text` to be segmented into substrings, a `count` variable to hold the number of substrings, and the separator character, `separator`, the program has three distinct phases.

The first phase counts the number of substrings by using the `indexOf()` method to find separators. The number of separators is always one less than the number of substrings. By using the `do-while` loop, we ensure that the value of `count` will be one more than the number of separators.

The second phase extracts the substrings in sequence from the beginning of the string, and stores them in an array of String variables that has count elements. Following each substring from the first to the penultimate is a separator, so we use the version of the substring() method that accepts two index arguments for these. The last substring is signaled by a failure to find the separator character when index will be -1. In this case we use the substring() method with a single argument to extract the substring through to the end of the string text.

The third phase simply outputs the contents of the array by displaying each element in turn, using a for loop.

What we have been doing here is breaking a string up into **tokens** – substrings in other words – that are separated by **delimiters** – characters that separate one token from the next. This is a sufficiently frequent requirement that Java provides you with an easier way to do this – using the StringTokenizer class.

Using a String Tokenizer

We can use an object of the StringTokenizer class to do what we did in the previous example. You can construct a StringTokenizer that can process a given string like this:

```
String text = "To be or not to be";          // String to be segmented
StringTokenizer st = new StringTokenizer(text);   // Create a tokenizer for it
```

The tokenizer object st that we have created here will assume that a delimiter can be a space, a tab, a newline character, a carriage return, or a form-feed character. It is also possible to specify your own set of delimiters when you create the tokenizer object. For example, if we only wanted a comma or a space to be considered as a delimiter we could create the tokenizer with the statement:

```
StringTokenizer st = new StringTokenizer(text, " ,"); // Tokenize using , or space
```

The second argument is a string containing all the characters that are to be considered as delimiters in the string text.

First of all, you can call the countTokens() method for the StringTokenizer object to determine how many tokens the string contains. This is handy when you want to store the tokens away in an array as it gives you the means to create the array ahead of time, like this:

```
String[] subStr = new String[st.countTokens()];
```

The countTokens() method returns an int value that is the number of tokens in the string – assuming you haven't extracted any in the way we will see next. If you have extracted tokens, the value returned will be the number remaining in the string. Now we have an array that is just large enough to accommodate all the tokens in the string text. All we have to do is extract them.

You can use the StringTokenizer object to pass once through the string to extract each of the tokens in turn. Calling the nextToken() method for the StringTokenizer object will return a reference to a String object that is the next token in the string being processed. We could therefore extract all the tokens like this:

```
for (int i = 0 ; i< subStr.length ; i++)
  subStr[i] = st.nextToken();
```

The `StringTokenizer` object also has a method `hasMoreTokens()` that returns `true` if the string contains more tokens and `false` when there are none left. We could therefore also extract all the tokens from our string like this:

```
int i = 0;
while(st.hasMoreTokens() && i<subStr.length)
  subStr[i++] = st.nextToken();
```

The loop will continue to extract tokens from the string as long as there are still tokens left, and as long as we have not filled the array, `subStr`. Of course, we should never fill the array since we created it to accommodate all the tokens but it does no harm here to verify that we don't. It is also a reminder of how you can use the `&&` operator.

Try It Out – Using a Tokenizer

Based on what we have just discussed, the whole program to do what the previous example did is as follows:

```
import java.util.StringTokenizer;                    // Import the tokenizer class

public class TokenizeAString {
  public static void main(String[] args) {
    String text = "To be or not to be";             // String to be segmented
    StringTokenizer st = new StringTokenizer(text); // Create a tokenizer for it
    String[] subStr = new String[st.countTokens()];  // Array to hold the tokens

    // Extract the tokens
    for (int i = 0 ; i< subStr.length ; i++) {
      subStr[i] = st.nextToken();
    }

    // Display the substrings
    for(int i = 0; i < subStr.length; i++) {
      System.out.println(subStr[i]);
    }
  }
}
```

The `import` statement is necessary because the `StringTokenizer` class is not in the `java.lang` package whose classes are imported by default, but in the `java.util` package. The program should produce output that is identical to that of the previous example. It's a lot simpler though; isn't it?

Modified Versions of String Objects

There are a couple of methods that you can use to create a new `String` object that is a modified version of an existing `String` object. They don't change the original string, of course – as we said, `String` objects are immutable. To replace one specific character with another throughout a string, you can use the `replace()` method. For example, to replace each space in our string `text` with a slash, you could write:

```
String newText = text.replace(' ', '/');      // Modify the string text
```

The first argument of the `replace()` method specifies the character to be replaced, and the second argument specifies the character that is to be substituted in its place. We have stored the result in a new variable `newText` here, but you could save it back in the original `String` variable, `text`, if you wanted.

To remove whitespace from the beginning and end of a string (but not the interior) you can use the `trim()` method. You could apply this to a string as follows:

```
String sample = "   This is a string   ";
String result = sample.trim();
```

after which the `String` variable `result` will contain the string `"This is a string"`. This can be useful when you are segmenting a string into substrings and the substrings may contain leading or trailing blanks. For example, this might arise if you were analyzing an input string that contained values separated by one or more spaces.

Creating Character Arrays from String Objects

You can create an array of variables of type `char` from a `String` variable by using the `toCharArray()` method in the class `String`. Because this method returns an array of type `char`, you only need to declare the array variable of type `char[]` – you don't need to allocate the array. For example:

```
String text = "To be or not to be";
char[] textArray = text.toCharArray();      // Create the array from the string
```

The `toCharArray()` method will return an array containing the characters of the `String` variable `text`, one per element, so `textArray[0]` will contain `'T'`, `textArray[1]` will contain `'o'`, `textArray[2]` will contain `' '`, and so on.

You can also extract a substring as an array of characters using the method `getChars()`, but in this case you do need to create an array that is large enough to hold the characters. This enables you to reuse a single array to store characters when you want to extract a succession of substrings, and thus saves the need to repeatedly create new arrays. Of course, the array must be large enough to accommodate the longest substring. The method `getChars()` has four parameters. In sequence, these are:

❑   Index position of the first character to be extracted (type `int`)

❑   Index position following the last character to be extracted (type `int`)

❑   The name of the array to hold the characters extracted (type `char[]`)

❑   The index of the array element to hold the first character (type `int`)

You could copy a substring from `text` into an array with the statements:

```
String text = "To be or not to be";
char[] textArray = new char[3];
text.getChars(9, 12, textArray, 0);
```

This will copy characters from `text` at index positions 9 to 11 inclusive, so `textArray[0]` will be 'n', `textArray[1]` will be 'o', and `textArray[2]` will be 't'.

You can also extract characters into a `byte` array using the `getBytes()` method in the class `String`. This converts the original string characters into the character encoding used by the underlying operating system – which is usually ASCII. For example:

```
String text = "To be or not to be";      // Define a string
byte[] textArray = text.getBytes();      // Get equivalent byte array
```

The `byte` array `textArray` will contain the same characters as in the `String` object, but stored as 8-bit characters. The conversion of characters from Unicode to 8-bit bytes will be in accordance with the default encoding for your system. This will typically mean that the upper byte of the Unicode character is discarded resulting in the ASCII equivalent.

Creating String Objects from Character Arrays

The `String` class also has a static method, `copyValueOf()`, to create a `String` object from an array of type `char[]`. You will recall that a static method of a class can be used even if no objects of the class exist.

Suppose you have an array defined as:

```
char[] textArray = {'T', 'o', ' ', 'b', 'e', ' ', 'o', 'r', ' ',
                    'n', 'o', 't', ' ', 't', 'o', ' ', 'b', 'e' };
```

You can then create a `String` object with the statement:

```
String text = String.copyValueOf(textArray);
```

This will result in the object `text` referencing the string `To be or not to be`.
Another version of the `copyValueOf()` method can create a string from a subset of the array elements. It requires two additional arguments to specify the index of the first character in the array to be extracted and the count of the number of characters to be extracted. With the array defined as previously, the statement:

```
String text = String.copyValueOf(textArray, 9, 3);
```

extracts three characters starting with `textArray[9]`, so `text` will contain the string `not` after this operation.

StringBuffer Objects

`String` objects cannot be changed, but we have been creating strings that are combinations and modifications of existing `String` objects, so how is this done? Java has another standard class for defining strings, `StringBuffer`, and a `StringBuffer` object can be altered directly. Strings that can be changed are often referred to as **mutable strings** whereas a `String` object is an **immutable string**. Java uses objects of the class `StringBuffer` internally to perform many of the operations on `String` objects. You can use a `StringBuffer` object whenever you need a string that you can change directly.

So when do you use `StringBuffer` objects rather than `String` objects? `StringBuffer` objects come into their own when you are transforming strings – adding, deleting, or replacing substrings in a string. Operations will be faster and easier using `StringBuffer` objects. If you have static strings, which you occasionally need to concatenate, then `String` objects will be the best choice. Of course, if you want to you can mix the use of both in the same program.

Creating StringBuffer Objects

You can create a `StringBuffer` object that contains a given string with the statement:

```
StringBuffer aString = new StringBuffer("A stitch in time");
```

This declares a `StringBuffer` object, `aString`, and initializes it with the string `A stitch in time`. When you are initializing a `StringBuffer` object, you must use this syntax, with the keyword `new`, the `StringBuffer` class name, and the initializing value between parentheses. You cannot just use the string as the initializing value as we did with `String` objects. This is because there is rather more to a `StringBuffer` object than just the string that it contains initially, and, of course, a string literal is a `String` object by definition.

You can just create the `StringBuffer` variable, in much the same way as you created a `String` variable:

```
StringBuffer myString = null;
```

This variable does not refer to anything until you initialize it with a defined `StringBuffer` object. For example, you could write:

```
myString = new StringBuffer("Many a mickle makes a muckle");
```

which will initialize it with the string specified. You can also initialize a `StringBuffer` variable with an existing `StringBuffer` object:

```
myString = aString;
```

Both `myString` and `aString` will now refer to a single `StringBuffer` object.

The Capacity of a StringBuffer Object

The `String` objects that we have been using each contain a fixed string, and memory is allocated to accommodate however many Unicode characters are in the string. Everything is fixed so memory usage is not a problem. A `StringBuffer` object is a little different. It contains a block of memory called a **buffer**, which may or may not contain a `String`, and if it does, the string need not occupy all of the buffer. Thus the length of a string in a string object can be different from the length of the buffer. The length of the buffer is referred to as the **capacity** of the `StringBuffer` object.

Once you have created a `StringBuffer` object, you can find the length of the string it contains, by using the `length()` method for the object:

```
StringBuffer aString = new StringBuffer("A stitch in time");
int theLength = aString.length();
```

If the object `aString` was defined as in the declaration above, the variable `theLength` will have the value 16. However, the capacity of the object is larger, as illustrated in the diagram.

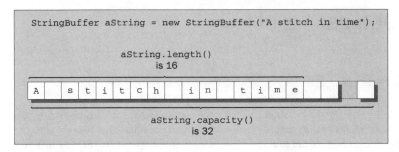

When you create a `StringBuffer` object from an existing string, the capacity will be the length of the string plus 16. Both the capacity and the length are in units of Unicode characters, so twice as many bytes will be occupied in memory.

The capacity of a `StringBuffer` object is not fixed though. For instance, you can create a `StringBuffer` object with a given capacity by specifying the capacity when you declare it:

```
StringBuffer newString = new StringBuffer(50);
```

This will create an object, `newString`, with the capacity to store 50 characters. If you omitted the capacity value in this declaration, the object would have a default capacity of 16 characters. A `String` object is always a fixed string, so capacity is irrelevant – it is always just enough to hold the characters in the string. A `StringBuffer` object is a container in which you can store any string and therefore has a capacity – a potential for storing strings up to a given size. Although you can set it, the capacity is unimportant in the sense that it is just a measure of how much memory is available to store Unicode characters at this particular point in time. You can get by without worrying about the capacity of a `StringBuffer` object since the capacity required to cope with what your program is doing will always be provided automatically. It just gets increased as necessary.

On the other hand, the capacity of a `StringBuffer` object is important in the sense that it affects the amount of overhead involved in storing and modifying a string. If the initial capacity is small, and you store a string that is long, or you add to an existing string significantly, extra memory will need to be allocated, which will take time. It is more efficient to make the capacity of a `StringBuffer` sufficient for the needs of your program.

To find out what the capacity of a `StringBuffer` object is at any given time, you use the `capacity()` method for the object:

```
int theCapacity = aString.capacity();
```

This method will return the number of Unicode characters the object can currently hold. For `aString` defined as shown, this will be 32. When you create a `StringBuffer` object containing a string, its capacity will be 16 characters greater than the minimum necessary to hold the string.

The `ensureCapacity()` method enables you to change the default capacity of a `StringBuffer` object. You specify the minimum capacity you need as the argument to the method, for example:

```
aString.ensureCapacity(40);
```

If the current capacity of the `aString` object is less than 40, this will increase the capacity of `aString` by allocating a new larger buffer, but not necessarily with a capacity of 40. The capacity will be the larger of either the value you specify, 40 in this case, or twice the current capacity plus 2, which is 66, given that `aString` is defined as before.

Changing the Length for a StringBuffer Object

You can change the length of the string contained in a `StringBuffer` object with the method `setLength()`. Note that the length is a property of the string the object holds, as opposed to the capacity, which is a property of the string buffer. When you increase the length for a `StringBuffer` object, the extra characters will contain `'\u0000'`. A more common use of this method would be to decrease the length, in which case the string will be truncated. If `aString` contains `"A stitch in time"`, the statement:

```
aString.setLength(8);
```

will result in `aString` containing the string `"A stitch"`, and the value returned by the `length()` method will be 8. The characters that were cut from the end of the string by this operation are lost.

To increase the length to what it was before, you could write:

```
aString.setLength(16);
```

Now `aString` will contain:
`"A stitch\u0000\u0000\u0000\u0000\u0000\u0000\u0000\u0000"`

The `setLength()` method does not affect the capacity of the object unless you set the length to be greater than the capacity. In this case the capacity will be increased to accommodate the new string length to a value that is twice the original capacity plus two if the length you set is less than this value. If you specify a length that is greater than twice the original capacity plus two, the new capacity will be the same as the length you set. If the capacity of `aString` is 66, executing the statement.

```
aString.setLength(100);
```

will set the capacity of the object, `aString`, to 134. If you supplied a value for the length of 150, then the new capacity would be 150. You must not specify a negative length here. If you do a `StringIndexOutOfBoundsException` exception will be thrown.

Adding to a StringBuffer Object

The `append()` method enables you to add a string to the end of the existing string stored in a `StringBuffer` object. This method comes in quite a few flavors, but perhaps the simplest adds a `String` constant to a `StringBuffer` object.

If we have defined a `StringBuffer` object with the statement:

```
StringBuffer aString = new StringBuffer("A stitch in time");
```

we can add to it with the statement:

```
aString.append(" saves nine");
```

after which `aString` will contain "A stitch in time saves nine". The length of the string contained in the `StringBuffer` object will be increased by the length of the string that you add. You don't need to worry about running out of space though. If necessary, the capacity will be increased automatically to accommodate the longer string.

The `append()` method returns the extended `StringBuffer` object, so you could also assign it to another `StringBuffer` object. Instead of the previous statement, you could have written:

```
StringBuffer bString = aString.append(" saves nine");
```

Now both `aString` and `bString` point to the same `StringBuffer` object.

If you take a look at the operator precedence table back in Chapter 2, you will see that the '.' operator (sometimes called the member selection operator) that we use to execute a particular method for an object has left-to-right associativity. You could therefore write:

```
StringBuffer proverb = new StringBuffer();              // Capacity is 16
proverb.append("Many").append(" hands").append(" make").
                     append(" light").append(" work.");
```

The second statement is executed from left to right, so that the string contained in the object `proverb` is progressively extended until it contains the complete string.

Appending a Substring

Another version of the `append()` method will add part of a `String` object to a `StringBuffer` object. This version of `append()` requires you to specify two additional arguments: the index position of the first character to be appended, and the total number of characters to be appended. This operation is shown in the following diagram.

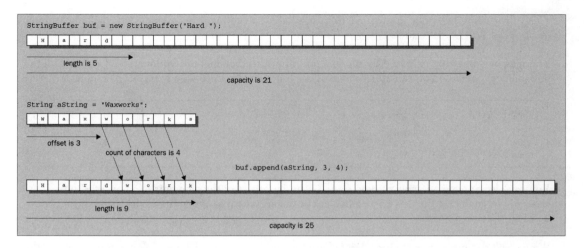

```
StringBuffer buf = new StringBuffer("Hard ");
```

length is 5

capacity is 21

```
String aString = "Waxworks";
```

offset is 3

count of characters is 4

```
buf.append(aString, 3, 4);
```

length is 9

capacity is 25

This operation appends a substring of `aString` consisting of four characters starting at index position 3 to the `StringBuffer` object, `buf`. The capacity of `buf` is automatically increased by the length of the appended substring, if necessary.

Appending Basic Types

You have a set of versions of the `append()` method that will enable you to `append()` any of the basic types to a `StringBuffer` object. These will accept arguments of any of the following types: `boolean`, `char`, `byte`, `short`, `int`, `long`, `float`, or `double`. In each case, the value is converted to a string equivalent of the value, which is appended to the object, so a `boolean` variable will be appended as either `"true"` or `"false"`, and for numeric types the string will be a decimal representation of the value. For example:

```
StringBuffer buf = new StringBuffer("The number is ");
long number = 999;
buf.append(number);
```

will result in `buf` containing the string `"The number is 999"`.

There is nothing to prevent you from appending constants to a `StringBuffer` object. For example, if you now execute the statement:

```
buf.append(12.34);
```

the object `buf` will contain `"The number is 99912.34"`.

There is also a version of the `append()` method which accepts an array of type `char` as an argument. The contents of the array are appended to the `StringBuffer` object as a string. A further variation on this enables you to append a subset of the elements from an array of type `char` by using two additional arguments: one to specify the index of the first element to be appended, and another to specify the total number of elements to be appended. An example of how you might use this is as follows;

```
char[] text = { 'i', 's', ' ', 'e', 'x', 'a', 'c', 't', 'l', 'y'};
buf.append(text, 2, 8);
```

165

This will append the string "exactly" to buf, so after executing this statement buf will contain "The number is 99912.34 exactly".

You may be somewhat bemused by the plethora of append() method options, so let's collect all the possibilities together. You can append any of the following types to a StringBuffer object:

boolean	char	String	Object
int	long	float	double
byte	short		

You can also append an array of type char[], and a subset of the elements of an array of type char[]. In each case the String equivalent of the argument is appended to the string in the StringBuffer object.

We haven't discussed type Object – it is here for the sake of completeness. You will learn about this type of object in Chapter 6.

Inserting Strings

To insert a string into a StringBuffer object, you use the insert() method of the object. The first argument specifies the index of the position in the object where the first character is to be inserted. For example, if buf contains the string "Many hands make light work", the statement:

```
buf.insert(4, " old");
```

will insert the string "old" starting at index position 4, so buf will contain the string "Many old hands make light work" after executing this statement.

There are many versions of the insert() method that will accept a second argument of any of the same range of types that apply to the append() method, so you can use any of the following with the insert() method:

boolean	char	String	Object
int	long	float	double
byte	short		

In each case the string equivalent of the second argument is inserted starting at the index position specified by the first argument. You can also insert an array of type char[], and if you need to insert a subset of an array of type char[] into a StringBuffer object, you can call the version of insert() that accepts four arguments:

Method	Description

`insert(int index,`
`        char[] str,`
`        int offset,`
`        int length)`
	Inserts a substring into the `StringBuffer` object starting at position `index`. The substring is the `String` representation of `length` characters from the `str[]` array, starting at position `offset`.

If the value of `index` is outside the range of the string in the `StringBuffer` object, or the `offset` or `length` values result in illegal indexes for the array, `str`, then an exception of type `StringIndexOutOfBoundsException` will be thrown.

Extracting Characters from a StringBuffer Object

The `StringBuffer` includes the `charAt()` and `getChars()` methods, both of which work in the same way as the methods of the same name in the class `String` which we've already seen. The `charAt()` method extracts the character at a given index position, and the `getChars()` method extracts a range of characters and stores them in an array of type `char` starting at a specified index position. You should note that there is no equivalent to the `getBytes()` method for `StringBuffer` objects.

Other StringBuffer Operations

You can change a single character in a `StringBuffer` object by using the `setCharAt()` method. The first argument indicates the index position of the character to be changed, and the second argument specifies the replacement character. For example, the statement:

```
buf.setCharAt(3, 'Z');
```

will set the fourth character in the string to `'Z'`.

You can completely reverse the sequence of characters in a `StringBuffer` object with the `reverse()` method. For example, if you define the object with the declaration:

```
StringBuffer palindrome = new StringBuffer("so many dynamos");
```

you can then transform it with the statement:

```
palindrome.reverse();
```

which will result in `palindrome` containing the useful phrase `"somanyd ynam os"`.

Creating a String Object from a StringBuffer Object

You can produce a `String` object from a `StringBuffer` object by using the `toString()` method of the `StringBuffer` class. This method creates a new `String` object and initializes it with the string contained in the `StringBuffer` object. For example, to produce a `String` object containing the proverb that we created in the previous section, you could write:

```
String saying = proverb.toString();
```

The object `saying` will contain "Many hands make light work".

The `toString()` method is used extensively by the compiler together with the `append()` method to implement the concatenation of `String` objects. When you write a statement such as:

```
String saying = "Many" + " hands" + " make" + " light" + " work";
```

the compiler will implement this as:

```
String saying = new StringBuffer().append("Many").append(" hands").
                                   append(" make").append(" light").
                                   append(" work").toString();
```

The expression to the right of the = sign is executed from left to right, so the segments of the string are appended to the `StringBuffer` object that is created until finally the `toString()` method is invoked to convert it to a `String` object. `String` objects can't be modified, so any alteration or extension of a `String` object will involve the use of a `StringBuffer` object, which can be changed.

Summary

You should now be thoroughly familiar with how to create and use arrays. Most people have little trouble dealing with one-dimensional arrays, but arrays of arrays are a bit more tricky so try to practice using these.

You have also acquired a good knowledge of what you can do with `String` and `StringBuffer` objects. Most operations with these objects are very straightforward and easy to understand. Being able to decide which methods you should apply to the solution of specific problems is a skill that will come with a bit of practice.

The essential points that we have discussed in this chapter are:

❑   You use an array to hold multiple values of the same type, identified through a single variable name.

❑   You reference an individual element of an array by using an index value of type `int`. The index value for an array element is the offset of that element from the first element in the array.

❑   An array element can be used in the same way as a single variable of the same type.

❑   You can obtain the number of elements in an array by using the `length` member of the array object.

❑   An array element can also contain an array, so you can define arrays of arrays, or arrays of arrays of arrays...

❑   A `String` object stores a fixed character string that cannot be changed. However, you can assign a given `String` variable to a different `String` object.

❑   You can obtain the number of characters stored in a `String` object by using the `length()` method for the object.

❏ The String class provides methods for joining, searching, and modifying strings – the modifications being achieved by creating a new String object.

❏ A StringBuffer object can store a string of characters that can be modified.

❏ You can get the number of characters stored in a StringBuffer object by calling its length() method, and you can find out the current maximum number of characters it can store by using its capacity() method.

❏ You can change both the length and the capacity for a StringBuffer object.

❏ The StringBuffer class contains a variety of methods for modifying StringBuffer objects.

❏ You can create a String object from a StringBuffer object by using the toString() method of the StringBuffer object.

Exercises

1. Create an array of String variables and initialize the array with the names of the months from January to December. Create an array containing 12 random decimal values between 0.0 and 100.0. Display the names of each month along with the corresponding decimal value. Calculate and display the average of the 12 decimal values.

2. Write a program to create a rectangular array containing a multiplication table from 1x1 up to 12x12. Output the table as 13 columns with the numeric values right aligned in columns. (The first line of output will be the column headings, the first column with no heading, then the numbers 1 to 12 for the remaining columns. The first item in each of the succeeding lines is the row heading, which ranges from 1 to 12.)

3. Write a program that sets up a String variable containing a paragraph of text of your choice. Extract the words from the text and sort them into alphabetical order. Display the sorted list of words. You could use a simple sorting method called the bubble sort. To sort an array into ascending order the process is as follows:

Starting with the first element in the array compare successive elements (0 and 1, 1 and 2, 2 and 3, and so on).

If the first element of any pair is greater than the second, interchange the two elements.

Repeat the process for the whole array until no interchanges are necessary. The array elements will now be in ascending order.

4. Define an array of ten String elements each containing an arbitrary string of the form "month/day/year", for example,"10/29/99" or "12/5/01". Analyze each element in the array and output the date represented in the form 29th October 1999.

5. Write a program that will reverse the sequence of letters in each word of your chosen paragraph from Exercise 3. For instance, "To be or not to be." would become "oT eb ro ton ot eb."

Defining Classes

In this chapter we will explore the heart of the Java language – classes. Classes specify the objects you use in object-oriented programming. These form the basic building blocks of any Java program, as we saw in Chapter 1. Every program in Java involves classes, since the code for a program can only appear within a class definition.

We will now explore the details of how a class definition is put together, how to create your own classes and how to use classes to solve your own computing problems. And in the next chapter we'll extend this to look at how object-oriented programming helps us work with related classes.

By the end of this chapter you will have learned:

❑   What a class is, and how you define one.

❑   How to implement class constructors.

❑   How to define class methods.

❑   What method overloading is.

❑   What a recursive method is and how it works.

❑   How to create objects of a class.

❑   What packages are and how you can create and use them.

❑   What access attributes are and how you should use them in your class definitions.

❑   When you should add the `finalize()` method to a class.

❑   What native methods are.

What is a Class?

As you saw in Chapter 1, a class is a prescription for a particular kind of object – it defines a new **type**. We can use the class definition to create objects of that class type, that is, to create objects that incorporate all the components specified as belonging to that class.

> *In case that's too abstract, look back to the last chapter, where we used the* String *class. This is a comprehensive definition for a string object, with all the operations you are likely to need built in. This makes* String *objects indispensable and string handling within a program easy.*

The String class lies towards one end of a spectrum in terms of complexity in a class. The String class is intended to be usable in any program. It includes facilities and capabilities for operating on String objects to cover virtually all circumstances in which you are likely to use strings. In most cases your own classes won't need to be this elaborate. You will typically be defining a class to suit your particular application. A very simple class for instance, a Plane or a Person, may well represent objects that can potentially be very complicated, if that fulfils your needs. A Person object might just contain a name, address, and phone number for example if you are just implementing an address book. In another context, in a payroll program perhaps, you might need to represent a Person with a whole host of properties, such as age, marital status, length of service, job code, pay rate, and so on. It all depends on what you intend to do with objects of your class.

In essence a class definition is very simple. There are just two kinds of things that you can include in a class definition:

❑ **Fields**
These are variables that store data items that typically differentiate one object of the class from another. They are also referred to as **data members** of a class.

❑ **Methods**
These define the operations you can perform for the class – so they determine what you can do to, or with, objects of the class. Methods typically operate on the fields – the variables of the class.

The fields in a class definition can be of any of the basic types, or they can be references to objects of any class type, including the one that you are defining.

The methods in a class definition are named, self-contained blocks of code that typically operate on the variables that appear in the class definition. Note though, that this doesn't necessarily have to be the case, as you might have guessed from the main() methods we have written in all our examples up to now.

Variables in a Class Definition

An object of a class is also referred to as an **instance** of that class. When you create an object, the object will contain all the variables that were included in the class definition. However, the variables in a class definition are not all the same – there are two kinds.

One kind of variable in a class is associated with each object uniquely – each instance of the class will have its own copy of each of these variables, with its own value assigned. These differentiate one object from another, giving an object its individuality – the particular name, address, and telephone number in a given Person object for instance. These are referred to as **instance variables**.

The other kind of class variable is associated with the class, and is shared by all objects of the class. There is only one copy of each of these kinds of variables no matter how many class objects are created, and they exist even if no objects of the class have been created. This kind of variable is referred to as a **class variable** because the variable belongs to the class, not to any particular object, although as we have said, all objects of the class will share it. These variables are also referred to as **static fields** because, as we will see, you use the keyword `static` when you declare them.

Because this is extremely important to understand, let's summarize the two kinds of variables that you can include in your classes:

❑ **Instance variables**

Each object of the class will have its own copy of each of the instance variables that appear in the class definition. Each object will have its own values for each instance variable. The name 'instance variable' originates from the fact that an object is an 'instance' or an occurrence of a class and the values stored in the instance variables for the object differentiate the object from others of the same class type. An instance variable is declared within the class definition in the usual way, with a type name and a variable name, and can have an initial value specified.

❑ **Class variables**

A given class will only have one copy of each of its class variables, and these will be shared between all the objects of the class. The class variables exist even if no objects of the class have been created. They belong to the class, and they can be referenced by any object or class, not just instances of that class. If the value of a class variable is changed, the new value is available in all the objects of the class. This is quite different from instance variables where changing a value for one object does not affect the values in other objects. A class variable must be declared using the keyword `static` preceding the type name.

Look at the following diagram, which illustrates the difference between the two:

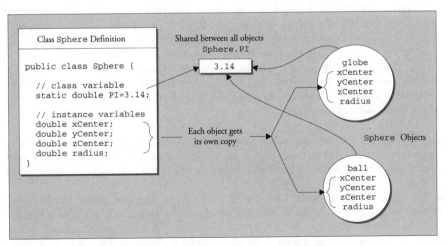

This shows a schematic of a class `Sphere` with one class variable `PI`, and four instance variables, `radius`, `xCenter`, `yCenter`, and `zCenter`. Each of the objects, `globe` and `ball`, will have their own variables, `radius`, `xCenter`, `yCenter`, and `zCenter`, but both will share a single copy of the class variable `PI`.

Why would you need two kinds of variables in a class definition? The instance variables are clearly necessary since they are the parameters that distinguish a particular object. The radius and the coordinates of the center of the sphere are fundamental to determining how big a particular `Sphere` object is, and where it is in space. However, although the variable `PI` is a fundamental parameter for a sphere – to calculate the volume for example – it would be wasteful to store a value for `PI` in every object, since it is always the same. Incidentally, it is also available from the standard class `Math` so it is somewhat superfluous in this case, but you get the general idea. So one use for class variables is to hold constant values such as π that are common to all objects of the class.

Another use for class variables is to track data values that are common to all objects of a class, and that need to be available even when no objects have been defined. For example, if you wanted to keep a count of how many objects of a class have been created in your program, you would define the variable storing the count as a class variable. It would be essential to use a class variable, because you would still want to be able to use your `count` variable even when no objects have been declared.

Methods in a Class Definition

The methods that you define for a class provide the actions that can be carried out using the variables specified in the class definition.

Analogous to the variables in a class definition, there are two varieties of methods – **instance methods** and **class methods**. You can execute class methods even when no objects of a class exist, whereas instance methods can only be executed in relation to a particular object, so if no objects exist, there are no instance methods to be executed. Again, like class variables, class methods are declared using the keyword `static` so they are sometimes referred to as **static methods**. We saw in the previous chapter that the `valueOf()` method is a static member of the `String` class.

Since class methods can be executed when there are no objects in existence, they cannot refer to instance variables. This is quite sensible if you think about it – trying to operate with variables that might not exist is bound to cause trouble. In fact the Java compiler won't let you try. If you reference an instance variable in the code for a class method, it won't compile – you'll just get an error message. The method `main()`, where execution of a Java application starts, must always be declared as static, as you have seen. The reason for this should be apparent by now. Before an application starts execution, no objects exist, so in order to start execution, you need a method that is executable even though there are no objects – a static method therefore.

The class `Sphere` might well have an instance method `volume()` to calculate the volume of a particular object. It might also have a class method `objectCount()` to return the current count of how many objects of type `Sphere` have been created. If no objects exist, you could still call this method and get the count 0.

> *Note that, although instance methods are specific to objects of a class, there is only ever one copy of an instance method in memory that is shared by all objects of the class, as it would be extremely expensive to replicate all the instance methods for each object. There is a special mechanism that ensures that, each time you call a method the codes executes in a manner that is specific to an object, but we will defer exploring this until a little later in this chapter.*

Apart from making the method `main()`, perhaps the most common use for class methods is when a class is just used to contain a bunch of utility methods, rather than as a specification for objects. All executable code in Java has to be within a class, but there are lots of general-purpose functions that you need that don't necessarily have an object association – calculating a square root, for instance, or generating a random number. For example, the mathematical functions that are implemented as class methods in the standard class `Math`, don't relate to class objects at all – they operate on values of the basic types. You don't need objects of type `Math`, you just want to use the methods from time to time, and you can do this as we saw in Chapter 2. The class `Math` also contains some class variables containing useful mathematical constants such as e and π.

Accessing Variables and Methods

You will often want to access variables and methods, defined within a class, from outside it. We will see later that it is possible to declare class members with restrictions on accessing them from outside, but let's cover the principles that apply where the members are accessible. We need to consider accessing static members and instance members separately.

You can access a static member of a class using the class name, followed by a period, followed by the member name. With a class method you will also need to supply the parentheses enclosing any arguments to the method after the method name. The period here is called the dot operator. So, if you wanted to calculate the square root of π you could access the class method `sqrt()` and the class variable `PI` that are defined in the `Math` class as follows:

```
double rootPi = Math.sqrt(Math.PI);
```

This shows how you call a static method – you just prefix it with the class name and put the dot operator between them. We also reference the static data member, `PI`, in the same way – as `Math.PI`. If you have a reference to an object of a class type available, then you can also use that to access a static member of a class method. You just use the variable name, followed by the dot operator, followed by the member name.

Instance variables and methods can only be called using an object reference, as by definition they relate to a particular object. The syntax is exactly the same as we have outlined for static members. You put the name of the variable referencing the object followed by a period, followed by the member name. To use a method `volume()` that has been declared as an instance method in the `Sphere` class, you might write:

```
double ballVolume = ball.volume();
```

Here the variable `ball` is of type `Sphere` and it contains a reference to an object of this type. We call its `volume()` method that calculates the volume of the `ball` object, and the result that is returned is stored in the variable, `ballVolume`.

Defining Classes

To define a class you use the keyword `class` followed by the name of the class, followed by a pair of braces enclosing the details of the definition. Let's consider a concrete example to see how this works in practice. The definition of the `Sphere` class we mentioned earlier could be:

```
class Sphere {
   static final double PI = 3.14;    // Class variable that has a fixed value
   static int count = 0;             // Class variable to count objects

   // Instance variables
   double radius;                    // Radius of a sphere

   double xCenter;                   // 3D coordinates
   double yCenter;                   // of the center
   double zCenter;                   // of a sphere

   // Plus the rest of the class definition...
}
```

You name a class using an identifier of the same sort you've been using for variables. By convention though, class names in Java begin with a capital letter so our class name is `Sphere` with a capital S. If you adopt this approach, you will be consistent with most of the code you come across. You could enter this sourcecode and save it as the file `Sphere.java`. We will be building on this class, and using it in a working example, a little later in this chapter.

The keyword `static` in the first line of the definition specifies the variable `PI` as a class variable rather than an instance variable. The variable `PI` is also initialized with the value 3.14. The keyword `final` tells the compiler that you do not want the value of this variable to be changed, so the compiler will check that this variable is not modified anywhere in your program. Obviously this is a very poor value for π. You would normally use `Math.PI` – which is defined to twenty decimal places, close enough for most purposes.

> Whenever you want to fix the value stored in a variable, that is, make it a constant, you just need to declare the variable with the keyword **final** and specify its initial value. By convention, constants have names in capital letters.

The next variable, `count`, is also declared with the keyword `static`. All objects of the `Sphere` class will share one copy of `count`, and one of `PI`. We have initialized the variable count to 0, but since it is not declared with the keyword `final`, we can change its value.

The next four variables in the class definition are instance variables, as they don't have the keyword `static` applied to them. Each object of the class will have its own separate set of these variables storing the radius and the coordinates of the center of the sphere. Although we haven't put initial values for these variables here, we could do so if we wanted. If you don't specify an initial value, a default value will be assigned automatically when the object is created. Fields that are of numeric types will be initialized with zero, fields of type char will be initialized with `'\u000'`, and fields that store class references or references to arrays will be initialized with `null`.

There has to be something missing from the definition of the `Sphere` class – there is no way to set the value of `radius` and the other instance variables once a particular `Sphere` object is created. There is nothing to update the value of `count` either. Adding these things to the class definition involves using methods, so we now need to look at how a method is put together.

Defining Methods

We have been producing versions of the method `main()` since Chapter 1, so you already have an idea of how a method is constructed. Nonetheless, we will go through from the beginning to make sure everything is clear.

We'll start with the fundamental concepts. A method is a self-contained block of code that has a name, and has the property that it is reusable – the same method can be executed from as many different points in a program as you require. Methods also serve to break up large and complex calculations that might involve many lines of code into more manageable chunks. A method is executed by calling its name, as we will see, and the method may or may not return a value. Methods that do not return a value are called in a statement that just does the call. Methods that do return a value are usually called from within an expression, and the value that is returned by such a method is used in the evaluation of the expression.

The basic structure of a method is shown below.

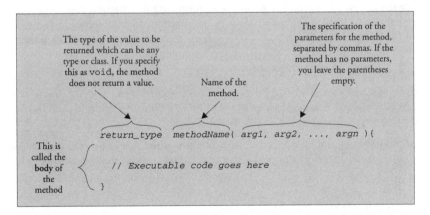

When you specify the return type for a method, you are defining the type for the value that will be returned by the method when you execute it. The method must always return a value of this type. To define a method that does not return a value, you specify the return type as `void`. Something called an **access attribute** can optionally precede the return type in a method definition, but we will defer looking into this until later in this chapter.

The parameters to a method appear in its definition between parentheses following the method name. These specify what information is to be passed to the method when you execute it. Your methods do not have to have parameters specified. A method that does not require any information to be passed to it when it is executed has an empty pair of parentheses after the name.

Running from a Method

To return a value from a method when its execution is complete you use a `return` statement, for example:

```
return return_value;    // Return a value from a method
```

After executing the `return` statement, the program continues from the point where the method was called. The value, `return_value`, that is returned by the method can be any expression that produces a value of the type specified for the return value in the declaration of the method. Methods that return a value – that is methods declared with a return type other than `void` – must always finish by executing a `return` statement that returns a value of the appropriate type. Note, though, that you can put several `return` statements within a method if the logic requires this. If a method does not return a value, you can just use the keyword `return` by itself to end execution of the method:

```
return;     // Return from a method
```

Note that, for methods that do not return a value, falling through the closing brace enclosing the body of the method is equivalent to executing a `return` statement.

The Parameter List

The **parameter list** appears between the parentheses following the method name. This specifies the type of each value that can be passed as an argument to the method, and the variable name that is to be used in the body of the method to refer to each value passed. The difference between a **parameter** and an **argument** is sometimes confusing because people often, incorrectly, use them interchangeably. We will try to differentiate them consistently, as follows:

❑ A parameter has a name and appears in the parameter list in the definition of a method. A parameter defines the type of value that can be passed to the method, and the name that is used to reference it within the code for the method.

❑ An argument is a value that is passed to a method when it is executed, and the value of the argument is referenced by the parameter name during execution of the method.

This is illustrated in the following diagram.

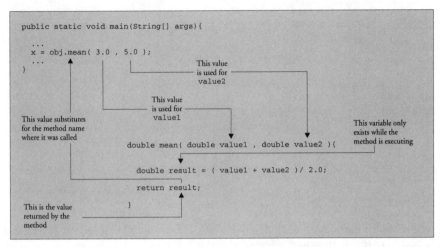

Here we have the definition of a method `mean()`. This can only appear within the definition of a class, but the rest of the class definition has been omitted so as not to clutter up the diagram. You can see that the method has two parameters, `value1`, and `value2`, both of which are of type `double`, that are used to refer to the arguments `3.0` and `5.0` respectively within the body of the method. Since this method has not been defined as `static`, you can only call it for an object of the class. We call `mean()` in our example for the object, `obj`.

When you call the method from another method (from `main()` in this case, but it could be from some other method), the values of the arguments passed are the initial values assigned to the corresponding parameters. You can use any expression you like for an argument when you call a method, as long as the value it produces is of the same type as the corresponding parameter in the definition of the method. With our method `mean()`, both parameters are of type `double`, so both argument values must always be of type `double`.

The method `mean()` declares the variable `result`, which only exists within the body of the method. The variable is created each time you execute the method and it is destroyed when execution of the method ends. All the variables that you declare within the body of a method are local to the method, and are only around while the method is being executed. Variables declared within a method are called **local variables** because they are local to the method. The scope of a local variable is as we discussed in Chapter 2, and local variables are not initialized automatically. If you want your local variables to have initial values you must supply the initial value when you declare them.

How Argument Values Are Passed to a Method

You need to be clear about how your argument values are passed to a method, otherwise you may run into problems. In Java, all argument values that belong to one of the basic types are transferred to a method using what is called the **pass-by-value** mechanism. How this works is illustrated below.

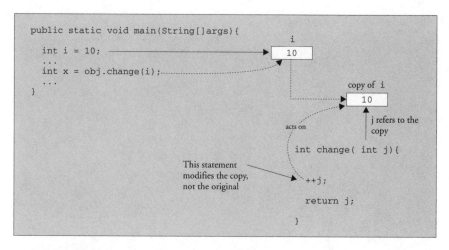

This just means that for each argument value that you pass to a method, a copy is made, and it is the copy that is passed to the method and referenced through the parameter name, not the original value. This implies that if you use a variable of any of the basic types as an argument, the method cannot modify the value of this variable in the calling program. In the example shown, the method `change()` will modify the copy of i that is created automatically, so the value of j that is returned will be 11 and this will be stored in x. However, the original value of i will remain at 10.

> While the pass-by-value mechanism applies to all types of arguments, the effect for objects is different from that for variables of the basic types. You can change an object, as we shall see a little later in this chapter, because a copy of a reference to the object is passed to the method, not a copy of the object itself.

Final Parameters

You can specify any method parameter as `final`. This has the effect of preventing modification of any argument value that is substituted for the parameter when you call the method. The compiler will check that your code in the body of the method does not attempt to change any final parameters. Since the pass-by-value mechanism makes copies of values of the basic types, `final` really only makes sense when it is applied to parameters that are references to class objects, as we will see later on.

Specifying a parameter of a class as `final` is of limited value. It does prevent accidental modification of the object reference that is passed to the method, but it does not prevent modification of the object itself.

Defining Class Methods

You define a class method by adding the keyword `static` to its definition. For example, the class `Sphere` could have a class method to return the value stored in the static variable, `count`:

```
class Sphere {
  // Class definition as before...
```

```
  // Static method to report the number of objects created
  static int getCount() {
    return count;                         // Return current object count
  }
}
```

This method needs to be a class method because we want to be able to get at the count of the number of objects even when it is zero. You can amend the `Sphere.java` file to include the definition of `getCount()`.

> Note that you cannot directly refer to any of the instance variables in the class within a **static** method. This is because your **static** method may be executed when no objects of the class have been created, and therefore no instance variables exist.

Accessing Class Data Members in a Method

An instance method can access any of the data members of the class, just by using the appropriate name. Let's extend the class `Sphere` a little further by adding a method to calculate the volume of a `Sphere` object:

```
class Sphere {
  static final double PI = 3.14; // Class variable that has a fixed value
  static int count = 0;          // Class variable to count objects

  // Instance variables
  double radius;                 // Radius of a sphere

  double xCenter;                // 3D coordinates
  double yCenter;                // of the center
  double zCenter;                // of a sphere

  // Static method to report the number of objects created
  static int getCount(){
    return count;                // Return current object count
  }

  // Instance method to calculate volume
  double volume() {
    return 4.0/3.0*PI*radius*radius*radius;
  }

  // Plus the rest of the class definition...
}
```

You can see that the method `volume()` is an instance method because it is not declared as static. It has no parameters but it does return a value of type `double` – the required volume. The method uses the class variable `PI` and the instance variable `radius` in the volume calculation – this is the expression `4.0/3.0*PI*radius*radius*radius` $(4/3)\pi r^3$ in the return statement. The value that results from this expression will be returned to the point where the method is called for a `Sphere` object.

We know that each object of the class will have its own separate set of instance variables, so how is an instance variable for a particular object selected in a method? How does our `volume()` method pick up the radius for a particular `Sphere` object?

The Variable this

Every instance method has a variable with the name, `this`, which refers to the current object for which the method is being called. The compiler uses this implicitly when your method refers to an instance variable of the class. For example, when the method `volume()` refers to the instance variable `radius`, the compiler will insert the `this` object reference, so that the reference will be equivalent to `this.radius`. The return statement in the definition of the `volume()` method is actually:

```
return 4.0/3.0*PI*this.radius*this.radius*this.radius;
```

In general, every reference to an instance variable is in reality prefixed with `this`. You could put it in yourself, but there's no need, the compiler does it for you. In fact, it is not good practice to clutter up your code with `this` unnecessarily. However, there are occasions where you have to include it, as we shall see.

When you execute a statement such as:

```
double ballVolume = ball.volume();
```

where `ball` is an object of the class `Sphere`, the variable `this` in the method `volume()` will refer to the object `ball`, so the instance variable `radius` for this particular object will be used in the calculation.

> We mentioned earlier that only one copy of each instance method for a class exists in memory, even though there may be many different objects. You can see that the variable **this** allows the same instance method to work for different class objects. Each time an instance method is called, the **this** variable is set to reference the particular class object to which it is being applied. The code in the method will then relate to the specific data members of the object referred to by **this**.

We have seen that there are four different potential sources of data available to you when you write the code for a method:

❑ Arguments passed to the method, which you refer to by using the parameter names.

❑ Data members, both instance variables and class variables, which you refer to by their variable names.

❑ Local variables declared in the body of the method.

❑ Values that are returned by other methods that are called from within the method.

The names of variables that are declared within a method are local to the method. You can use a name for a local variable or a parameter in a method that is the same as that of a class data member. If you find it necessary to do this then you must use the name `this` when you refer to the data member of the class from within the method. The variable name by itself will always refer to the variable that is local to the method, not the instance variable.

For example, let us suppose we wanted to add a method to change the radius of a `Sphere` object to a new radius value that is passed as an argument. We could code this as:

```
void changeRadius(double radius) {
  // Change the instance variable to the argument value
  this.radius = radius;
}
```

In the body of the `changeRadius()` method, `this.radius` refers to the instance variable, and `radius` by itself refers to the parameter. There is no confusion in the duplication of names here. It is clear that we are receiving a radius value as a parameter and storing it in the `radius` variable for the class object.

Initializing Data Members

We have seen how we were able to supply an initial value for the static members `PI` and `count` in the `Sphere` class with the declaration:

```
class Sphere {
  static final double PI = 3.14;    // Class variable that has a fixed value
  static int count = 0;             // Class variable to count objects

  // Rest of the class...
}
```

We can also initialize ordinary non-static data members in the same way. For example:

```
class Sphere {
  static final double PI = 3.14;    // Class variable that has a fixed value
  static int count = 0;             // Class variable to count objects

  // Instance variables
  double radius = 5.0;              // Radius of a sphere

  double xCenter = 10.0;            // 3D coordinates
  double yCenter = 10.0;            // of the center
  double zCenter = 10.0;            // of a sphere

  // Rest of the class...
}
```

Now every object of type `Sphere` will start out with a radius of 5.0 and have the center at the point 10.0, 10.0, 10.0.

There are some things that can't be initialized with a single expression. If you had a large array as a data member for example, that you wanted to initialize, with a range of values that required some kind of calculation, this would be a job for an **initialization block**.

Using Initialization Blocks

An initialization block is a block of code between braces that is executed before an object of the class is created. There are two kinds of initialization blocks. A **static initialization block** is a block defined using the keyword, `static`, and that is executed once when the class is loaded and can only initialize static data members of the class. A **non-static initialization block** is executed for each object that is created and thus can initialize instance variables in a class. This is easiest to understand by considering specific code.

Try It Out – Using an Initialization Block

Let's define a simple class with a static initialization block first of all:

```
class TryInitialization {
  static int[] values = new int[10];                   // Static array  member

  // Initialization block
  static {
    System.out.println("Running initialization block.");
    for(int i=0; i<values.length; i++)
      values[i] = (int)(100.0*Math.random());
  }

  // List values in the array for an object
  void listValues() {
    System.out.println();                              // Start a new line
    for(int i=0; i<values.length; i++)
      System.out.print(" " + values[i]);               // Display values

    System.out.println();                              // Start a new line
  }

  public static void main(String[] args) {
    TryInitialization example = new TryInitialization();
    System.out.println("\nFirst object:");
    example.listValues();

    example = new TryInitialization();
    System.out.println("\nSecond object:");
    example.listValues();
  }
}
```

When you compile and run this you will get identical sets of values for the two objects – as might be expected since the `values` array is static:

```
Running initialization block.

First object:

 40 97 88 63 58 48 84 5 32 67

Second object:

 40 97 88 63 58 48 84 5 32 67
```

How It Works

The `TryInitialization` class has a static member, `values`, that is an array of 10 integers. The static initialization block is the code:

```
static {
  System.out.println("Running initialization block.");
  for(int i=0; i<values.length; i++)
    values[i] = (int)(100.0*Math.random());
}
```

This initializes the `values` array with pseudo-random integer values generated in the `for` loop. The output statement in the block is there just to record when the initialization block executes. Because this initialization block is static, it is only ever executed once during program execution, when the class is loaded.

The `listValues()` method provides us with a means of outputting the values in the array. The `print()` method we are using in the `listValues()` method works just like `println()`, but without starting a new line before displaying the output, so we get all the values on the same line.

In `main()`, we generate an object of type `TryInitialization`, and then call its `listValues()` method. We then create a second object and call the `listValues()` method for that. The output demonstrates that the initialization block only executes once, and that the values reported for both objects are the same.

If you delete the modifier `static` from before the initialization block, and recompile and run the program again, you will get the output along the lines of:

```
Running initialization block.

First object:

 66 17 98 59 99 18 40 96 40 21

Running initialization block.

Second object:

 57 86 79 31 75 99 51 5 31 44
```

Now we have a non-static initialization block. You can see from the output that the values are different for the second object because the non-static initialization block is executed each time an object is created. In fact, the `values` array is static, so the array is shared between all objects of the class. You could demonstrate this by amending `main()` to store each object separately, and calling `listValues()` for the first object after the second object has been created. Amend the `main()` method in the program to read as follows:

```
public static void main(String[] args) {
  TryInitialization example = new TryInitialization();
  System.out.println("\nFirst object:");
  example.listValues();
```

```
        TryInitialization nextexample = new TryInitialization();
        System.out.println("\nSecond object:");
        nextexample.listValues();

        example.listValues();
   }
```

While we have demonstrated that this is possible, you will not normally want to initialize static variables with a non-static initialization block.

As we said at the outset, a non-static initialization block can initialize instance variables too. If you want to demonstrate this too, you just need to remove the static modifier from the declaration of values and compile and run the program once more.

You can have multiple initialization blocks in a class, in which case they execute in the sequence in which they appear. The static blocks execute when the class is loaded and the non-static blocks execute when each object is created. Initialization blocks are useful, but you need more than that to create objects properly.

Constructors

When you create an object of a class, a special kind of method called a **constructor** is always invoked. If you don't define any constructors for your class, the compiler will supply a **default constructor** in the class that does nothing. The primary purpose of a constructor is to provide you with the means of initializing the instance variables uniquely for the object that is being created. If you are creating a Person object with the name John Doe, then you want to be able to initialize the member holding the person's name to "John Doe". This is precisely what a constructor can do. Any initialization blocks that you have defined in a class are always executed before a constructor.

A constructor has two special characteristics that differentiate it from other class methods:

❑   A constructor never returns a value and you must not specify a return type – not even of type void.

❑   A constructor always has the same name as the class.

To see a practical example we could add a constructor to our Sphere class definition:

```
class Sphere {
  static final double PI = 3.14; // Class variable that has a fixed value
  static int count = 0;          // Class variable to count objects

  // Instance variables
  double radius;                 // Radius of a sphere

  double xCenter;                // 3D coordinates
  double yCenter;                // of the center
  double zCenter;                // of a sphere
```

```
      // Class constructor
      Sphere(double theRadius, double x, double y, double z) {
        radius = theRadius;            // Set the radius

        // Set the coordinates of the center
        xCenter = x;
        yCenter = y;
        zCenter = z;
        ++count;                       // Update object count
      }

      // Static method to report the number of objects created
      static int getCount() {
        return count;                  // Return current object count
      }

      // Instance method to calculate volume
      double volume() {
        return 4.0/3.0*PI*radius*radius*radius;
      }
    }
```

The definition of the constructor is shaded above. We are accumulating quite a lot of code to define the `Sphere` class, but as it's just an assembly of the pieces we have been adding, you should find it all quite straightforward.

As you can see, the constructor has the same name as the class and has no return type specified. A constructor can have any number of parameters, including none. The default constructor has no parameters. In our case we have four parameters, and each of the instance variables is initialized with the value of the appropriate parameter. Here is a situation where we might have used the name `radius` for the parameter, in which case we would need to use the keyword `this` to refer to the instance variable of the same name. The last action of our constructor is to increment the class variable, `count`, by 1, so that `count` accumulates the total number of objects created.

The Default Constructor

If you don't define any constructors for a class, the compiler will supply a default constructor that has no parameters and does nothing. Before we defined a constructor for our Sphere class, the compiler would have supplied one defined like this:

```
Sphere() {
}
```

It has no parameters and has no statements in its body so it does nothing – except enable you to create an object of type `Sphere` of course. The object created by the default constructor will have fields with their default values set.

Note that if you define a constructor of any kind for a class, the compiler will not supply a default constructor. If you need one – and there are occasions when you do – you must define it explicitly.

Creating Objects of a Class

When you declare a variable of type `Sphere` with the statement:

```
Sphere ball;      // Declare a variable
```

no constructor is called and no object is created. All you have created at this point is the variable `ball`, which can store a reference to an object of type `Sphere`, if and when you create one.

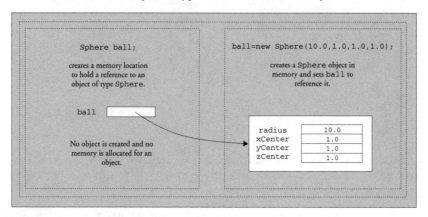

You will recall from our discussion of `String` objects and arrays that the variable and the object it references are distinct entities. To create an object of a class you must use the keyword `new` followed by a call to a constructor. To initialize `ball` with an object, you could write:

```
ball = new Sphere(10.0, 1.0, 1.0, 1.0);   // Create a sphere
```

Now we have a `Sphere` object with a radius of 10.0 located at the coordinates (1.0, 1,0, 1.0). The object is created in memory and will occupy a sufficient number of bytes to accommodate all the data necessary to define the object. The variable `ball` will record where in memory the object is – it acts as a reference to the object.

Of course, you can do the whole thing in one step, with the statement:

```
Sphere ball = new Sphere(10.0, 1.0, 1.0, 1.0);   // Create a sphere
```

This declares the variable `ball` and defines the `Sphere` object to which it refers.

You can create another variable that refers to the same object as `ball`:

```
Sphere myBall = ball;
```

Now the variable `myBall` refers to the same object as `ball`. We have only one object still, but we have two different variables that reference it. You could have as many variables as you like referring to the same object.

The separation of the variable and the object has an important effect on how objects are passed to a method, so we need to look at that.

Passing Objects to a Method

When you pass an object as an argument to a method, the mechanism that applies is called **pass-by-reference**, because a copy of the reference contained in the variable is transferred to the method, not the object itself. The effect of this is shown in the following diagram.

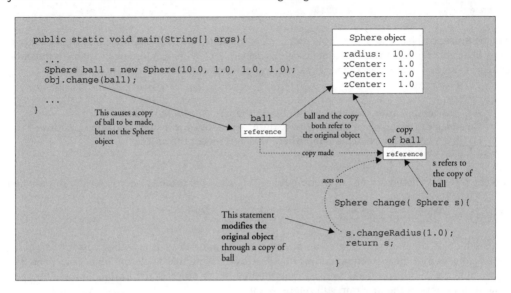

This illustration presumes we have defined a method, changeRadius(), in the class Sphere that will alter the radius value for an object, and that we have a method change() in some other class that calls changeRadius(). When the variable ball is used as an argument to the method change(), the pass-by-reference mechanism causes a copy of ball to be made and stored in s. The variable ball just stores a reference to the Sphere object, and the copy contains that same reference and therefore refers to the same object. No copying of the actual object occurs. This is a major plus in term s of efficiency when passing arguments to a method. Objects can be very complex involving a lot of instance variables. If objects themselves were always copied when passed as arguments, it could be very time consuming and make the code very slow.

Since the copy of ball refers to the same object as the original, when the changeRadius() method is called the original object will be changed. You need to keep this in mind when writing methods that have objects as parameters because this is not always what you want.

In the example shown, the method change() returns the modified object. In practice you would probably want this to be a distinct object, in which case you would need to create a new object from s. You will see how you can write a constructor to do this a little later in this chapter.

> Remember that this only applies to objects. If you pass a variable of type **int** or **double** to a method for example, a copy of the value is passed. You can modify the value passed as much as you want in the method, but it won't affect the original value.

The Lifetime of an Object

The lifetime of an object is determined by the variable that holds the reference to it – assuming there is only one. If we have the declaration:

```
Sphere ball = new Sphere(10.0, 1.0, 1.0, 1.0);    // Create a sphere
```

then the `Sphere` object that the variable `ball` refers to will die when the variable `ball` goes out of scope. This will be at the end of the block containing this declaration. Where an instance variable is the only one referencing an object, the object survives as long as the instance variable owning the object survives.

> **A slight complication can arise with objects though. As you have seen, several variables can reference a single object. In this case the object survives as long as there is still a variable in existence somewhere that references the object.**

You can reset a variable to refer to nothing by setting its value to `null`. If you write the statement:

```
ball = null;
```

the variable `ball` no longer refers to an object, and assuming there is no other object referencing it, the `Sphere` object it originally referenced will be destroyed. Note that while the object has been discarded, the variable `ball` still continues to exist. The lifetime of the object is determined by whether any variable anywhere in the program still references it.

The process of disposing of dead objects is called **garbage collection**. Garbage collection is automatic in Java, but this doesn't necessarily mean that objects disappear from memory straight away. It can be some time after the object becomes inaccessible to your program. This won't affect your program directly in any way. It just means you can't rely on memory occupied by an object that is done with being available immediately. For the most part it doesn't matter; the only circumstances where it might would be if your objects were very large, millions of bytes say, or you were creating and getting rid of very large numbers of objects. In this case you can call the static `gc()` method defined in the `System` class to encourage the JVM to do some garbage collecting and recover the memory that the objects occupy:

```
System.gc();
```

This is a best efforts deal on the part of the JVM. When the `gc()` method returns, the JVM will have tried to reclaim the space occupied by discarded objects, but there's no guarantee that it will all be recovered.

Defining and Using a Class

To put what we know about classes to use, we can use our `Sphere` class in an example.

You will be creating two source files. The first is the file `CreateSpheres.java`, which will contain the definition of the `CreateSpheres` class that will have the method `main()` defined as a static method. As usual, this is where execution of the program starts. The second file will be the file `Sphere.java` that contains the definition of the class `Sphere` that we have been assembling.

Both files will need to be in the same directory or folder – I suggest you name the directory CreateSpheres. Then copy or move the last version of Sphere.java to this directory.

Try It Out – Using the Sphere Class

Enter the following code for the file CreateSpheres.java:

```
class CreateSpheres {
  public static void main(String[] args) {
    System.out.println("Number of objects = " + Sphere.getCount());

    Sphere ball = new Sphere(4.0, 0.0, 0.0, 0.0);      // Create a sphere
    System.out.println("Number of objects = " + ball.getCount());

    Sphere globe = new Sphere(12.0, 1.0, 1.0, 1.0);    // Create a sphere
    System.out.println("Number of objects = " + Sphere.getCount());

    // Output the volume of each sphere
    System.out.println("ball volume = " + ball.volume());
    System.out.println("globe volume = " + globe.volume());
  }
}
```

Compile the source files and then run CreateSpheres, and you should get the output:

```
Number of objects = 0
Number of objects = 1
Number of objects = 2
ball volume = 267.94666666666666
globe volume = 7234.559999999999
```

This is the first time we have run a program involving two source files. If you are using the JDK compiler, then compile CreateSpheres.java with the current directory as CreateSpheres using the command:

```
javac CreateSpheres.java
```

The compiler will find and compile the Sphere.java source file automatically. If all the source files for a program are in the current directory, then compiling the file containing a definition of main() will compile all the source files for the program.

Note that by default, the .class files generated by the compiler will be stored in the current directory, that is, the directory containing your sourcecode. If you want the .class files stored in a different directory, then you can use the -d option with the Java compiler to specify where they should go. For example, to store the class files in a directory called C:\classes you would type:

```
javac -d C:/classes CreateSpheres.java
```

How It Works

The `Sphere` class definition includes a constructor and the method `volume()` to calculate the volume of a particular sphere. It also contains the `static` method, `getCount()`, we saw earlier, which returns the current value of the class variable `count`. We need to define this method as `static` since we want to able to call it regardless of how many objects have been created, including the situation when there are none.

The method `main()` in the `CreateSpheres` class puts the class `Sphere` through its paces. When the program is compiled, the compiler will look for a file `Sphere.java` to provide the definition of the class `Sphere`. As long as this file is in the current directory the compiler will be able to find it.

The first thing the program does is to call the `static` method `getCount()`. Because no objects exist, you must use the class name to call it at this point. We then create the object `ball`, which is a `Sphere` object, with a radius of 4.0 and its center at the origin point, (0.0, 0.0, 0.0). The method `getCount()` is called again, this time using the object name to demonstrate that you can call a `static` method through an object. Another `Sphere` object, `globe`, is created with a radius of 12.0. The `getCount()` method is called again, this time using the class name. Static methods are usually called using the class name because in most situations, where you would use such a method, you cannot be sure that any objects exist. After all, the reason for calling this particular method would be to find out how many objects exist. A further reason to use the class name when calling a static method is that it makes it quite clear in the sourcecode that it *is* a static method that is being called. You can't call a non-static method using the class name.

Our program finally outputs the volume of both objects by calling the `volume()` method for each, from within the expressions, specifying the arguments to the `println()` method calls.

Method Overloading

Java allows you to define several methods in a class with the same name, as long as each method has a set of parameters that is unique. This is called **method overloading**.

The name of a method together with the type and sequence of the parameters form the **signature** of the method – the signature of each method in a class must be distinct to allow the compiler to determine exactly which method you are calling at any particular point.

Note that the return type has no effect on the signature of a method. You cannot differentiate between two methods just by the return type. This is because the return type is not necessarily apparent when you call a method. For example, suppose you write a statement such as:

```
Math.round(value);
```

Although the statement above is pointless since we discard the value that the `round()` method produces, it does illustrate why the return type cannot be part of the signature for a method. There is no way for the compiler to know from this statement what the return type of the method `round()` is supposed to be. Thus, if there were several different versions of the method `round()`, and the return type was the only distinguishing aspect of the method signature, the compiler would be unable to determine which version of `round()` you wanted to use.

There are many circumstances where it is convenient to use method overloading. You have already seen that the standard class Math contains two versions of the method round(), one that accepts an argument of type float, and the other that accepts an argument of type double. You can see now that method overloading makes this possible. It would be rather tedious to have to use a different name for each version of round() when they both do essentially the same thing. The valueOf() method in the String class is another example. There is a version of this method for each of the basic types. One context in which you will regularly need to use overloading is when you write constructors for your classes, which we'll look at now.

Multiple Constructors

Constructors are methods that can be overloaded, just like any other method in a class. In most situations, you will need to generate objects of a class from different sets of initial defining data. If we just consider our class Sphere, we could conceive of a need to define a Sphere object in a variety of ways. You might well want a constructor that accepted just the (x, y, z) coordinates of a point, and have a Sphere object created with a default radius of 1.0. Another possibility is that you may want to create a default Sphere with a radius of 1.0 positioned at the origin, so no arguments would be specified at all. This requires two constructors in addition to the one we have already written.

Try It Out – Multiple Constructors for the Sphere Class

The code for the extra constructors is:

```
class Sphere {
  // First Constructor and variable declarations
  ...
  // Construct a unit sphere at a point
  Sphere(double x, double y, double z) {
    xCenter = x;
    yCenter = y;
    zCenter = z;
    radius = 1.0;
    ++count;                      // Update object count
  }

  // Construct a unit sphere at the origin
  Sphere() {
    xCenter = 0.0;
    yCenter = 0.0;
    zCenter = 0.0;
    radius = 1.0;
    ++count;                      // Update object count
  }

  // The rest of the class as before...
}
```

The statements in the default constructor that set three data members to zero are not really necessary, as the data members would be set to zero by default. They are there just to emphasize that the primary purpose of a constructor is to enable you to set initial values for the data members.

If you add the following statements to the CreateSpheres class, you can test out the new constructors:

```
public class CreateSpheres {
  public static void main(String[] args) {
    System.out.println("Number of objects = " + Sphere.getCount());

    Sphere ball = new Sphere(4.0, 0.0, 0.0, 0.0);          // Create a sphere
    System.out.println("Number of objects = " + ball.getCount());

    Sphere globe = new Sphere(12.0, 1.0, 1.0, 1.0);        // Create a sphere
    System.out.println("Number of objects = " + Sphere.getCount());

    Sphere eightBall = new Sphere(10.0, 10.0, 0.0);
    Sphere oddBall = new Sphere();
    System.out.println("Number of objects = " + Sphere.getCount());

    // Output the volume of each sphere
    System.out.println("ball volume = " + ball.volume());
    System.out.println("globe volume = " + globe.volume());
    System.out.println("eightBall volume = " + eightBall.volume());
    System.out.println("oddBall volume = " + oddBall.volume());
  }
}
```

Now the program should produce the output:

```
Number of objects = 0
Number of objects = 1
Number of objects = 2
Number of objects = 4
ball volume = 267.94666666666666
globe volume = 7234.559999999999
eightBall volume = 4.1866666666666665
oddBall volume = 4.1866666666666665
```

How It Works

When you create a Sphere object, the compiler will select the constructor to use based on the types of the arguments you have specified. So, the first of the new constructors is applied in the first statement that we added to main(), as its signature fits with the argument types used. The second statement that we added clearly selects the last constructor as no arguments are specified. The other additional statements are there just to generate some output corresponding to the new objects. You can see from the volumes of eightBall and oddBall that they both are of radius 1.

It is the number and types of the parameters that affect the signature of a method, not the parameter names. If you wanted a constructor that defined a Sphere object at a point, by specifying the diameter rather than the radius, you have a problem. You might try to write it as:

```
// Illegal constructor!!!
// This WON'T WORK because it has the same signature as the original!!!
Sphere(double diameter, double x, double y, double z) {
  xCenter = x;
  yCenter = y;
  zCenter = z;
  radius = diameter/2.0;
}
```

If you try adding this to the `Sphere` class and recompile, you'll get a compile-time error. This constructor has four arguments of type `double`, so its signature is identical to the first constructor that we wrote for the class. This is not permitted – hence the compile-time error. When the number of parameters is the same in two overloaded methods, at least one pair of corresponding parameters must be of different types.

Calling a Constructor from a Constructor

One class constructor can call another constructor in the same class in its first executable statement. This can often save duplicating a lot of code. To refer to another constructor in the same class, you use `this` as the name, followed by the appropriate arguments between parentheses. In our `Sphere` class, we could have defined the constructors as:

```
class Sphere {
  // Construct a unit sphere at the origin
  Sphere() {
    radius = 1.0;
    // Other data members will be zero by default
    ++count;                    // Update object count
  }

// Construct a unit sphere at a point
  Sphere(double x, double y, double z)
  {
    this();                     // Call the constructor with no arguments
    xCenter = x;
    yCenter = y;
    zCenter = z;
  }

  Sphere(double theRadius, double x, double y, double z) {
    this(x, y, z);              // Call the 3 argument constructor
    radius = theRadius;         // Set the radius
  }
  // The rest of the class as before...
}
```

In the constructor that accepts the point coordinates as argument, we call the default constructor to set the radius and increment the count of the number of objects. In the constructor that sets the radius, as well as the coordinates, the constructor with three arguments is called to set the coordinates, which in turn will call the constructor that requires no arguments.

Duplicating Objects Using a Constructor

When we were looking at how objects were passed to a method, we came up with a requirement for duplicating an object. The need to produce an identical copy of an object occurs surprisingly often.

> Java provides a `clone()` method, but the details of using it must wait for the next chapter.

Suppose you declare a `Sphere` object with the following statement:

```
Sphere eightBall = new Sphere(10.0, 10.0, 0.0);
```

Later in your program you want to create a new object `newBall`, which is identical to the object `eightBall`. If you write:

```
Sphere newBall = eightBall;
```

this will compile OK but it won't do what you want. You will remember from our earlier discussion that the variable `newBall` will reference the same object as `eightBall`. You will not have a distinct object. The variable `newBall`, of type `Sphere`, is created but no constructor is called, so no new object is created.

Of course, you could create `newBall` by specifying the same arguments to the constructor as you used to create `eightBall`. In general, however, it may be that `eightBall` has been modified in some way during execution of the program, so you don't know that its instance variables have the same values – for example, the position might have changed. This presumes that we have some other class methods that alter the instance variables. You could fix this by adding a constructor to the class that will accept an existing `Sphere` object as an argument:

```
// Create a sphere from an existing object
Sphere(final Sphere oldSphere) {
    radius = oldSphere.radius;
    xCenter = oldSphere.xCenter;
    yCenter = oldSphere.yCenter;
    zCenter = oldSphere.yCenter;
}
```

This works by copying the values of the instance variables of the `Sphere` object, passed as an argument, to the corresponding instance variables of the new object.

Now you can create `newBall` as a distinct object by writing:

```
Sphere newBall = new Sphere(eightBall);  // Create a copy of eightBall
```

Let's recap what we have learned about methods and constructors with another example.

Using Objects

Let's create an example to do some simple 2D geometry. This will give us an opportunity to use more than one class. We will define two classes, a class of point objects and a class of line objects – we then use these to find the point at which the lines intersect. We will call the example `TryGeometry`, so this will be the name of the directory or folder in which you should save the program files. Quite a few lines of code are involved so we will put it together piecemeal, and try to understand how each piece works as we go.

We first define a basic class for point objects:

```
class Point {
  // Coordinates of the point
  double x;
  double y;

  // Create a point from coordinates
  Point(double xVal, double yVal) {
    x = xVal;
    y = yVal;
  }

  // Create a point from another Point object
  Point(final Point oldPoint) {
    x = oldPoint.x;     // Copy x coordinate
    y = oldPoint.y;     // Copy y coordinate
  }

  // Move a point
  void move(double xDelta, double yDelta) {
    // Parameter values are increments to the current coordinates
    x += xDelta;
    y += yDelta;
  }

  // Calculate the distance to another point
  double distance(final Point aPoint) {
    return Math.sqrt(
      (x - aPoint.x)*(x - aPoint.x) + (y - aPoint.y)*(y - aPoint.y) );
  }

  // Convert a point to a string
  public String toString() {
    return Double.toString(x) + ", " + y;     // As "x, y"
  }
}
```

You should save this as `Point.java` in the directory `TryGeometry`.

How It Works

This is a simple class that has just two instance variables, x and y, which are the coordinates of the Point object. At the moment we have two constructors. One will create a point from a coordinate pair passed as arguments, and the other will create a new Point object from an existing one.

There are three methods included in the class. First we have the move() method that moves a Point to another position by adding an increment to each of the coordinates. We also have the distance() method that calculates the distance from the current Point object to the Point object passed as an argument. This uses the Pythagorean theorem to compute the distance as shown below.

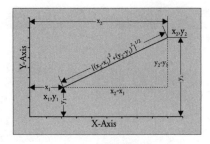

Finally we have a method `toString()` that returns a string representation of the coordinates of the current point. If a class defines the `toString()` method, an object of that class can be used as an operand of the string concatenation operator +, so you can implement this in any of your classes to allow objects to be used in this way. The compiler will automatically insert a call to `toString()` when necessary. For example, suppose `thePoint` is an object of type `Point`, and we write the statement:

```
System.out.println("The point is at " + thePoint);
```

The `toString()` method will be automatically invoked to convert `thePoint` to a `String`, and the result will be appended to the `String` literal. We have specified the `toString()` method as `public`, as this is essential here for the class to compile. We will defer explanations as to why this is so until later in this chapter.

Note how we use the static `toString()` method defined in the class `Double` to convert the x value to a `String`. The compiler will insert a call to the same method automatically for the y value as the left operand of the + operation is a `String` object. Note that we could equally well have used the `valueOf()` method in the `String` class. In this case the statement would be written like this:

```
        return String.valueOf(x) + ", " + y;    // As "x, y"
```

Try It Out – The Line Class

We can use `Point` objects in the definition of the class `Line`:

```
class Line {
   Point start;    // Start point of line
   Point end;      // End point of line

   // Create a line from two points
   Line(final Point start, final Point end) {
     this.start = new Point(start);
     this.end = new Point(end);
   }

   // Create a line from two coordinate pairs
   Line(double xStart, double yStart, double xEnd, double yEnd) {
     start = new Point(xStart, yStart);    // Create the start point
     end = new Point(xEnd, yEnd);          // Create the end point
   }
```

```
    // Calculate the length of a line
    double length() {
       return start.distance(end);   // Use the method from the Point class
    }

    // Convert a line to a string
    public String toString() {
       return "(" + start+ "):(" + end + ")";     // As "(start):(end)"
    }                                              // that is, "(x1, y1):(x2, y2)"
}
```

You should save this as `Line.java` in the directory `TryGeometry`.

How It Works

You shouldn't have any difficulty with this class definition, as it is very straightforward. The class `Line` stores two `Point` objects as instance variables. There are two constructors for `Line` objects, one accepting two `Point` objects as arguments, the other accepting the (x, y) coordinates of the start and end points. You can see how we use the variable `this` to differentiate the class instance variables, `start` and `end`, from the parameter names in the constructor.

Note how the constructor that accepts `Point` objects works:

```
    // Create a line from two points
    Line(final Point start, final Point end) {
      this.start = new Point(start);
      this.end = new Point(end);
    }
```

With this implementation of the constructor, two new `Point` objects are created which will be identical to, but independent of, the objects passed to the constructor. If you don't think about what happens you might be tempted to write it as:

```
    // Create a line from two points
    Line(final Point start, final Point end) {
      this.start = start;                // Dependent on external object!!!
      this.end = end;                    // Dependent on external object!!!
    }
```

The important thing you should notice here, is that the way the constructor is implemented could cause problems that might be hard to track down. It's the same problem of an object variable being separate from the object to which it refers. In this version of the constructor no new points are created. The `start` and `end` members of the object refer to the `Point` objects passed as arguments. The `Line` object will be implicitly dependent on the `Point` objects that are used to define it. If these were changed outside the `Line` class, by using the `move()` method for example, this would 'silently' modify the `Line` object. You might consciously decide that this is what you want, so the `Line` object continues to be dependent on its associated `Point` objects, for instance in a drawing package. But, in general, you should avoid implicit dependencies between objects.

199

In the `toString()` method for the `Line` class, we are able to use the `Point` objects directly in the formation of the `String` representation of a `Line` object. This works because the `Point` class also defines a `toString()` method.

We've now defined two classes. In these class definitions, we've included the basic data that defines an object of each class. We've also defined some methods which we think will be useful, and added constructors for a variety of input parameters. Note how the `Point` class is used in the definition of the `Line` class. It is quite natural to define a line in terms of two `Point` objects, and the `Line` class is much simpler and more understandable than if it was defined entirely in terms of the individual x and y coordinates. To further demonstrate how classes can interact, and how you can solve problems directly, in terms of the objects involved, let's devise a method to calculate the intersection of two `Line` objects.

Creating a Point from Two Lines

We could add this method to the `Line` class. The diagram below illustrates how the mathematics works out.

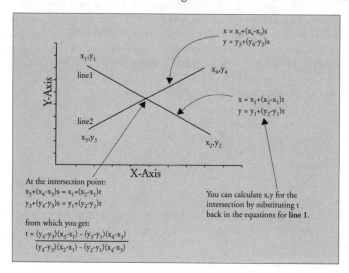

You can ignore the mathematics if you want to, as it is not the most important aspect of the example. If you are willing to take the code in the new constructor on trust, then skip to the *Try It Out* section below. On the other hand you shouldn't find it too difficult if you can still remember what you did in high school.

One way to get the intersection of two lines is to use equations like those shown. These are called parametric equations because they use a parameter value (s or t) as the variable for determining points on each line. The parameters s and t vary between 0 and 1 to give points on the lines between the defined start and end points. When a parameter s or t is 0 the equations give the coordinates of the start point of each line, and when the parameter value is 1 you get the end point of the line.

*Where the lines intersect, the equations for the lines must produce the same (x, y) values, so, at this point, the right-hand sides of the equations for x for the two lines must be equal, and the same goes for the equations for y. This will give you two equations in s and t, and with a bit of algebraic juggling you can eliminate s to get the equation shown for t. You can then replace t in the equations defining **line 1** to get x and y for the intersection point.*

Try It Out – Calculating the Intersection of Two Lines

We can use these results to write the additional method we need for the `Line` class. Add the following code to the definition in `Line.java`:

```
// Return a point as the intersection of two lines -- called from a Line object
Point intersects(final Line line1) {
  Point localPoint = new Point(0, 0);

  double num = (this.end.y - this.start.y)*(this.start.x - line1.start.x) -
               (this.end.x - this.start.x)*(this.start.y - line1.start.y);

  double denom = (this.end.y - this.start.y)*(line1.end.x - line1.start.x) -
                 (this.end.x - this.start.x)*(line1.end.y - line1.start.y);

  localPoint.x = line1.start.x + (line1.end.x - line1.start.x)*num/denom;
  localPoint.y = line1.start.y + (line1.end.y - line1.start.y)*num/denom;

  return localPoint;
}
```

Since the `Line` class definition refers to the `Point` class, the `Line` class can't be compiled without the other being available. When you compile the `Line` class the compiler will compile the other class too.

How It Works

The `intersects()` method is called from one `Line` object, and takes another `Line` object as an argument. In the code, the local variables `num` and `denom` are the numerator and denominator in the expression for `t` in the diagram. We then use these values to calculate the `x` and `y` coordinates for the intersection.

> If the lines are parallel, the denominator in the equation for `t` will be zero, something you should really check for in the code. For the moment, we will ignore it and end up with coordinates that are `Infinity` if it occurs.

Note how we get at the values of the coordinates for the `Point` objects defining the lines. The dot notation for referring to a member of an object is just repeated when you want to reference a member of a member. For example, for the object `line1`, the expression `line1.start` refers to the `Point` object at the beginning of the line. Therefore `line1.start.x` refers to its x coordinate, and `line1.start.y` accesses its y coordinate.

Now we have a `Line` class, which we can use to calculate the intersection point of two `Line` objects. We need a program to test the code out.

Try It Out – The TryGeometry Class

We can demonstrate the two classes we have defined, with the following code in the method `main()`:

```
public class TryGeometry {
  public static void main(String[] args) {
    // Create two points and display them
    Point start = new Point(0.0, 1.0);
```

```
        Point end = new Point(5.0, 6.0);
        System.out.println("Points created are " + start + " and " + end);


        // Create two lines and display them
        Line line1 = new Line(start, end);
        Line line2 = new Line(0.0, 3.0, 3.0, 0.0);
        System.out.println("Lines created are " + line1 + " and " + line2);

        // Display the intersection
        System.out.println("Intersection is " + line2.intersects(line1));

        // Now move the end point of line1 and show the new intersection
        end.move(1.0, -5.0);
        System.out.println("Intersection is " + line1.intersects(line2));
    }
}
```

The program will produce the output:

```
Points created are 0.0, 1.0 and 5.0, 6.0
Lines created are (0.0, 1.0):(5.0, 6.0) and (0.0, 3.0):(3.0, 0.0)
Intersection is 1.0, 2.0
Intersection is 1.0, 2.0
```

How It Works

We first create two `Point` objects, which we will use later in the creation of the object `line1`. We then display the points using the `println()` method. The `toString()` method that we defined in the `Point` class is used automatically to generate the `String` representation for each `Point` object.

After creating `line1` from our two points, we use the other constructor in the `Line` class to create `line2` from two pairs of coordinates. We then display the two lines. The `toString()` member of the `Line` class is invoked here to create the `String` representation of each `Line` object, and this in turn uses the `toString()` method in the `Point` class.

The next statement calls the `intersects()` method from the `line2` object and returns the `Point` object at the intersection of the two lines, `line1` and `line2`, as part of the argument to the `println()` method that outputs the point. As you see, we are not obliged to save an object when we create it. Here we just use it to create the string to be displayed.

We use the `move()` method in the class `Point` to modify the coordinates of the object, `end`, that we used to create `line1`. We then get the intersection of the two lines again, this time calling the `intersects()` method from `line1`. The output result demonstrates that `line1` is independent of the object `end`, as moving the point has made no difference to the intersection.

If you change the constructor in the `Line` class, to the version we saw earlier that does not create new `Point` objects to define the line, you can run the example again to see the effect. The output will be:

```
Points created are 0.0, 1.0 and 5.0, 6.0
Lines created are (0.0, 1.0):(5.0, 6.0) and (0.0, 3.0):(3.0, 0.0)
Intersection is 1.0, 2.0
Intersection is 2.0, 1.0
```

Changing the end object now alters the line, so we get a different intersection point for the two lines after we move the point end. This is because the Line object, line1, contains references to the Point objects defined in main(), not independent Point objects.

Recursion

The methods you have seen so far have been called from within other methods, but a method can also call itself – something referred to as **recursion**. Clearly you must include some logic in a recursive method so that it will eventually stop calling itself. We can see how this might be done with a simple example.

We can write a method that will calculate integer powers of a variable, in other words, evaluate xn, or x*x...*x where x is multiplied by itself **n** times. We can use the fact that we can obtain xn by multiplying xn-1 by x. To put this in terms of a specific example, we can calculate 2^4 as 2^3 multiplied by 2, and we can get 2^3 by multiplying 2^2 by 2, and 2^2 is produced by multiplying 2^1, which is 2 of course, by 2.

Try It Out – Calculating Powers

Here is the complete program including the recursive method, power():

```
public class PowerCalc {
  public static void main(String[] args) {
    double x = 5.0;
    System.out.println(x + " to the power 4 is " + power(x,4));
    System.out.println("7.5 to the power 5 is " + power(7.5,5));
    System.out.println("7.5 to the power 0 is " + power(7.5,0));
    System.out.println("10 to the power -2 is " + power(10,-2));
  }

  // Raise x to the power n
  static double power(double x, int n) {
    if(n > 1)
      return x*power(x, n-1);     // Recursive call
    else if(n < 0)
      return 1.0/power(x, -n);    // Negative power of x
    else
      return n == 0 ? 1.0 : x;    // When n is 0 return 1, otherwise x
  }
}
```

This program will produce the output:

```
5.0 to the power 4 is 625.0
7.5 to the power 5 is 23730.46875
7.5 to the power 0 is 1.0
10 to the power -2 is 0.01
```

How It Works

The method `power()` has two parameters, the value x and the power n. The method performs four different actions, depending on the value of n:

$n > 1$	A recursive call to **power()** is made with n reduced by 1, and the value returned is multiplied by **x**. This is effectively calculating x^n as x times x^{n-1}.
$n < 0$	x-n is equivalent to $1/xn$ so this is the expression for the return value. This involves a recursive call to `power()` with the sign of n reversed.
$n = 0$	x0 is defined as 1, so this is the value returned.
$n = 1$	x1 is x, so x is returned.

Just to make sure the process is clear we can work through the sequence of events as they occur in the calculation of 5^4.

Level	Description	Relevant Code

1	The first call of the `power()` method passes 5.0 and 4 as arguments. Since the second argument, n, is greater than 1, the `power()` method is called again in the return statement, with the second argument reduced by 1.	```Power(5.0, 4) {
		  if(n > 1)
		    return 5.0*power(5.0, 4-1);
		  ...
		}```

2	The second call of the `power()` method passes 5.0 and 3 as arguments. Since the second argument, n, is still greater than 1, the `power()` method is called again in the return statement with the second argument reduced by 1.	```Power(5.0, 3) {
		  if(n > 1)
		    return 5.0*power(5.0, 3-1);
		  ...
		}```

3	The third call of the `power()` method passes 5.0 and 2 as arguments. Since the second argument, n, is still greater than 1, the `power()` method is called again, with the second argument again reduced by 1.	```Power(5.0, 2) {
		  if(n > 1)
		    return 5.0*power(5.0, 2-1);
		  ...
		}```

4	The fourth call of the `power()` method passes 5.0 and 1 as arguments. Since the second argument, n, is not greater than 1, the value of the first argument, 5.0, is returned to level **3**.	```Power(5.0, 1) {
		  if(n > 1)
		    ...
		  else
		    return 5.0;
		}```

Level	Description	Relevant Code
3	Back at level **3**, the value returned, 5.0, is multiplied by the first argument, 5.0, and returned to level **2**.	```Power(5.0, 2) {` ` if(n>1)` ` ...` ` else` ` return 5.0*5.0;` `}```
2	Back at level **2**, the value returned, 25.0, is multiplied by the first argument, 5.0, and returned to level **1**.	```Power(5.0, 3) {` ` if(n > 1)` ` ...` ` else` ` return 5.0*25.0;` `}```
1	Back at level **1**, the value returned, 125.0, is multiplied by the first argument, 5.0, and 625.0 is returned as the result of calling the method in the first instance.	```Power(5.0, 4) {` ` if(n > 1)` ` ...` ` else` ` return 5.0*125.0;` `}```

You can see from this that the method `power()` is called four times in all. The calls cascade down through four levels until the value of n is such that it allows a value to be returned. The return values ripple up through the levels until we are eventually back at the top, and 625.0 is returned to the original calling point.

As a rule, you should only use recursion where there are evident advantages in the approach, as there is quite of lot of overhead in recursive method calls. This particular example could be more easily programmed as a loop and it would execute much more efficiently. One example of where recursion can be applied very effectively is in the handling of data structures such as trees. Unfortunately these don't make convenient illustrations of how recursion works at this stage of the learning curve, because of their complexity.

Before we can dig deeper into classes, we need to take an apparent detour to understand what a package is in Java.

Understanding Packages

> Packages are fundamental to Java programs so make sure you understand this section.

Packages are implicit in the organization of the standard classes as well as your own programs, and they influence the names you can use for classes and the variables and methods they contain. Essentially, a **package** is a unique named collection of classes. The purpose of grouping classes in a package with a unique name is to make it easy to add any or all of the classes in a package into your program code. One aspect of this is that the names used for classes in one package will not interfere with the names of classes in another package, or your program, because the class names in a package are qualified by the package name.

Every class in Java is contained in a package, including all those we have defined in our examples. You haven't seen many references to package names so far because we have been implicitly using the **default package** to hold our classes, and this doesn't have a name.

All of the standard classes in Java are contained within packages. The package that contains most of the standard classes that we have used so far is called java.lang. You haven't seen any explicit reference to this in your code either, because this package is automatically available to your programs. Things are arranged this way because some of the classes in java.lang, such as String, are used in every program. There are other packages containing standard classes that you will need to include explicitly when you use them, as we did in the previous chapter with the StringTokenizer class.

Packaging Up Your Classes

Putting one of your classes in a package is very simple. You just add a package statement as the first statement in the source file containing the class definition. Note that it must always be the first statement. Only comments or blank lines are allowed to precede the package statement. A **package statement** consists of the keyword, package, followed by the package name, and is terminated by a semi-colon. If you want the classes in a package to be accessible outside the package, you must declare the class using the keyword public in the first line of your class definition. Class definitions that aren't preceded by the keyword public are only accessible from methods in classes that belong to the same package.

For example, to include the class Sphere in a package called Geometry, the contents of the file Sphere.java would need to be:

```
package Geometry;

public class Sphere {
  // Details of the class definition
}
```

Each class that you want to include in the package Geometry must contain the same package statement at the beginning, and you should save all the files for the classes in the package in a directory with the same name as the package, that is, Geometry. Note the use of the public keyword in the definition of the Sphere class. This is to make the class usable generally.

Note that you would also need to declare the constructors and methods in the class as public if you want them to be accessible from outside of the package. We will return to this in more detail a little later in this chapter.

Packages and the Directory Structure

Packages are actually a little more complicated than they appear at first sight, because a package is intimately related to the directory structure in which it is stored. You already know that the definition of a class with the name ClassName must be stored in a file with the name ClassName.java, and that all the files for classes within a package, PackageName, must be included in a directory with the name PackageName. You can compile the source for a class within a package and have the .class file that is generated stored in a different directory, but the directory name must still be the same as the package name.

A package need not have a single name. You can specify a package name as a sequence of names separated by periods. For example, you might have developed several collections of classes dealing with geometry, one dealing with 2D shapes and another with 3D shapes. In this case you might include the class Sphere in a package with the statement:

```
package Geometry.Shapes3D;
```

and the class for circles in a package using the statement:

```
package Geometry.Shapes2D;
```

In this situation, the packages are expected to be in the directories Shapes3D and Shapes2D, and both of these must be sub-directories of Geometry. In general, you can have as many names as you like separated by periods to identify a package, but the name must reflect the directory structure where the package is stored.

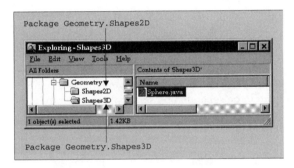

Compiling a Package

Compiling the classes in a package can be a bit tricky unless you are clear on how you go about it. We will illustrate what you need to do assuming you are using the JDK under Microsoft Windows. The path to the package directory has to be explicitly made known to the compiler, even when the current directory is the one containing the package. If we have stored the Geometry package source files in the directory with the path C:\Beg Java Stuff\Geometry, then the path to the Geometry directory is C:\Beg Java Stuff. You can tell the compiler about this path using the -classpath option on the command line. Assuming that the current directory is the Geometry directory, we could compile the Line.java source file with the command:

```
C:\JavaStuff\Geometry>javac -classpath "C:\Beg Java Stuff" Line.java
```

This will result in both the Line.java and Point.java files being compiled, since Line.java refers to the other class. Since the directory in the path contains spaces, we have to enclose the path between double quotes.

Accessing a Package

How you access a package, when you are compiling a program that uses the package, depends on where you have put it. There are a couple of options here. The first, but not the best, is to leave the .class files for the classes in the package in the directory with the package name.

Let's look at that before we go on to the second possibility.

With the .class files in the original package directory, either the path to your package must appear in the string set for the CLASSPATH environment variable, or you must use the -classpath option on the command line when you invoke the compiler or the interpreter. This overrides the CLASSPATH environment variable if it happens to be set. Note that it is up to you to make sure the classes in your package are in the right directory. Java will not prevent you from saving a file in a directory that is quite different from that appearing in the package statement. Of the two options here, using the -classpath option on the command line is preferable, because it sets the classpaths transiently each time, and can't interfere with anything you do subsequently. In any event we will look at both possibilities.

If you elect to use the CLASSPATH environment variable, it only needs to contain the paths to your packages. The standard packages supplied with Java do not need to be considered as the compiler and the interpreter can always find them. For example, you might set it under Windows 95 or 98 by adding the command,

```
set CLASSPATH=.;C:\MySource;C:\MyPackages
```

to your autoexec.bat file. Now the compiler and the interpreter will look for the directories containing your packages in the current directory, as specified by the period, and the directories C:\MySource and C:\MyPackages. Of course, you may have as many paths as you want defined in CLASSPATH. They just need to be separated by semi-colons under Windows.

Under Unix, the equivalent to this might be:

```
CLASSPATH=.:/usr/local/mysource:/usr/local/mypackages
```

If you are using the Sun Java Development Kit, you also specify where your packages can be found by using the -classpath option when you execute the Java compiler or the interpreter. This has the advantage that it only applies for the current compilation or execution so you can easily set it to suit each run. The command to compile MyProgram.java defining the classpath as in the environment variable above would be:

```
javac -classpath ".;C:\MySource;C:\MyPackages" MyProgram.java
```

If you don't set the classpath in one of these ways, or you set it incorrectly, Java will not be able to find the classes in any new packages you might create.

A new feature introduced with Java 2 provides you with a second way to make your packages available once you have compiled them. This provides a way of adding **extensions** to the set of standard packages.

Using Extensions

Extensions are .jar files stored within the ext directory that is created when you install the JDK. For more information on the use of the JAR tool to create .jar archives, see Appendix A. The default directory structure that is created is shown below.

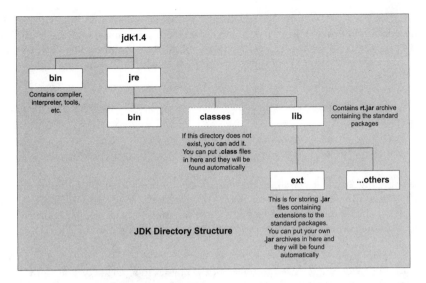

The classes and packages in the `.jar` archives that you place in the `ext` directory will automatically be accessible when you compile or run your Java programs, without the need to set the CLASSPATH environment variable, or to use the `-classpath` command line option. When you create a `.jar` file for a package, you need to make sure that you add the `.class` files with the directory structure corresponding to the package name – you can't just add the `.class` files to the archive. For example, suppose we want to store our `Geometry` package in an archive. Assuming we have already compiled the package and the current directory contains the package directory, the following command can be used to create the archive:

```
C:\JavaStuff>jar cvf Geometry.jar Geometry\*.class
```

This will create the archive `Geometry.jar`, and add all the `.class` files that are in the `Geometry` directory to it. All you now need to do, to make the package available to any program that needs it is to copy it, to the `ext` directory in the JDK directory hierarchy.

The diagram above also shows the `classes` directory, which may not be created by default. You can put `.class` files in this directory and they will be found automatically when a program uses the classes they contain.

Adding Classes from a Package to Your Program

Assuming they have been defined with the `public` keyword, you can add all or any of the classes in a package to the code in your program by using an **import statement**. You can reference the classes that you make available to your program using the import statement just by using the class names. For example, to make available all the classes in the package `Geometry.Shapes3D` to a source file, you just need to add the following import statement to the beginning of the file:

```
import Geometry.Shapes3D.*;    // Include all classes from this package
```

The keyword `import` is followed by the specification of what you want to import. The wildcard *, following the period after the package name, selects all the classes in the package, rather like selecting all the files in a directory. Now you can refer to any public class in the package just by using the class name. Again, the names of other classes in your program must be different from the names of the classes in the package.

If you want to add a particular class rather than an entire package, you specify its name explicitly in the `import` statement:

```
import Geometry.Shapes3D.Sphere;   // Include the class Sphere
```

This includes only the `Sphere` class into the source file. By using a separate import statement for each individual class from the package, you can ensure that your source file only includes the classes that you need. This reduces the likelihood of name conflicts with your own classes, particularly if you are not fully familiar with the contents of the package and it contains a large number of classes.

> Note that the * can only be used to select all the classes in a package. You can't use
> `Geometry.*` to select all the packages in the directory `Geometry`.

Packages and Names in Your Programs

A package creates a self-contained environment for naming your classes. This is the primary reason for having packages in Java. You can specify the names for classes in one package without worrying about whether the same names have been used elsewhere. Java makes this possible by treating the package name as part of the class name – actually as a prefix. This means that the class `Sphere` in the package `Geometry.Shapes3D` has the full name `Geometry.Shapes3D.Sphere`. If you don't use an import statement to incorporate the class in your program, you can still make use of the class by referring to it using its full class name. If you needed to do this with the class `Sphere`, you might declare a variable with the statement:

```
Geometry.Shapes3D.Sphere ball = new Geometry.Shapes3D.Sphere(10.0, 1.0, 1.0, 1.0);
```

While this is rather verbose, and certainly doesn't help the readability of the program, it does ensure there will be no conflict between this class and any other `Sphere` class that might be part of your program. You can usually contrive that your class names do not conflict with those in the commonly used standard Java packages, but in cases where you can't manage this, you can always fall back on using fully qualified class names. Indeed, there are occasions when you have to do this. This is necessary when you are using two different classes from different packages that share the same basic class name.

Standard Packages

All of the standard classes that are provided with Java are stored in standard packages. There is a substantial (more than 130 in SDK1.4) and growing list of standard packages but some of the ones you may hear about quite frequently are:

`java.lang`	Contains classes that are fundamental to Java (e.g. the **Math** class) and all of these are available in your programs automatically. You do not need an **import** statement to include them.
`java.io`	Contains classes supporting stream input/output operations.
`java.nio`	Contains classes supporting new input/output operations in JDK1.4 – especially with files.
`java.nio.channels`	Contains more classes supporting new input/output operations in JDK1.4 – the ones that actually read and write files.
`java.awt`	Contains classes that support Java's Graphical User Interface (GUI). While you can use these classes for GUI programming, it is almost always easier and better to use the alternative Swing classes.
`javax.swing`	Provides classes supporting the 'Swing' GUI components. These are not only more flexible and easier to use than the `java.awt` equivalents, but they are also implemented largely in Java with minimal dependency on native code.
`javax.swing.border`	Classes to support generating borders around Swing components.
`javax.swing.event`	Classes supporting event handling for Swing components.
`java.awt.event`	Contains classes that support event handling.
`java.awt.geom`	Contains classes for drawing and operating with 2D geometric entities.
`java.awt.image`	Contains classes to support image processing.
`java.applet`	This contains classes that enable you to write applets – programs that are embedded in a web page.
`java.util`	This contains classes that support a range of standard operations for managing collections of data, accessing date and time information, and analyzing strings.

The standard packages and the classes they contain cover an enormous amount of ground, so even in a book of this size it is impossible to cover them all exhaustively. There are now many more classes in the standard packages with JDK1.4 than there are pages in this book. However, we will be applying some classes from all of the packages in the table above, plus one or two others besides, in later chapters of the book.

Standard Classes Encapsulating the Basic Data Types

You saw in the previous chapter that we have classes available that allow you to define objects that encapsulate each of the basic data types in Java. These classes are:

Boolean	Character	Byte
Short	Integer	Long
Float	Double	

These are all contained in the package `java.lang` along with quite a few other classes such as the `String` and `StringBuffer` classes that we saw in Chapter 4, and the `Math` class. Each of these classes encapsulates the corresponding basic type, and includes methods for manipulating and interrogating objects of the class, as well as a number of static methods that provide utility functions for the underlying basic types. Each of the classes corresponding to a numeric type provides a static `toString()` method to convert to a `String` object, as we saw in the last chapter. There is also a non-static `toString()` method in all of these classes that returns a `String` representation of a class object.

The classes encapsulating the numeric basic types each contain the `static final` constants `MAX_VALUE` and `MIN_VALUE` that define the maximum and minimum values that can be represented. The floating-point classes also define the constants `POSITIVE_INFINITY`, `NEGATIVE_INFINITY`, and NaN (stands for **N**ot **a** **N**umber as it is the result of 0/0), so you can use these in comparisons. Alternatively, you can test floating point values with the static methods `isInfinite()` and `isNaN()` – you pass your variable as an argument, and the methods return `true` for an infinite value or the NaN value respectively. Remember that an infinite value can arise without necessarily dividing by zero. Any computation that results in an exponent that is too large to be represented will produce either `POSITIVE_INFINITY` or `NEGATIVE_INFINITY`.

Conversely there are methods to convert from a `String` to a basic type. For example, the static `parseInt()` member of the class `Integer` accepts a `String` representation of an integer as an argument, and returns the equivalent value as type `int`. An alternative version of this method accepts a second argument of type `int` that specifies the radix to be used. If the `String` object cannot be parsed for any reason, if it contains invalid characters for instance, the method will throw an exception of type `NumberFormatException`. All the standard classes define methods to parse strings – `parseShort()`, `parseByte()`, and `parseLong()`.

There are many other operations supported by these classes so it is well worth browsing the JDK documentation for them.

Controlling Access to Class Members

We have not yet discussed in any detail how accessible class members are outside a class. You know that from inside a static class method you can refer to any of the static members of the class, and a non-static method can refer to any member of the class. The degree to which variables and methods within one class are accessible from other classes is more complicated. It depends on what **access attributes** you have specified for the members of a class, and whether the classes are in the same package. This is why we had to understand packages first.

Using Access Attributes

Let's start by considering classes in the same package. Within a given package, any class has direct access to any other class name – for declaring variables or specifying method parameter types, for example – but the variables and methods that are members of that other class are not necessarily accessible. The accessibility of these is controlled by **access attributes**. You have four possibilities when specifying an access attribute for a class member, including what we have used in our examples so far – that is, not to specify anything at all – and each possibility has a different effect overall. The options you have for specifying the accessibility of a variable or a method in a class are:

Attribute	Permitted access
No access attribute	From methods in any class in the same package.
public	From methods in any class anywhere.
private	Only accessible from methods inside the class. No access from outside the class at all.
protected	From methods in any class in the same package and from any sub-class anywhere.

The table shows you how the access attributes you set for a class member determine the parts of the Java environment from which you can access it. We will discuss sub-classes in the next chapter, so don't worry about these for the moment. We will be coming back to how and when you use the `protected` attribute then. Note that `public`, `private`, and `protected` are all keywords. Specifying a member as `public` makes it completely accessible, and at the other extreme, making it `private` restricts access to members of the same class.

This may sound more complicated than it actually is. Look at the next diagram, which shows the access allowed between classes within the same package.

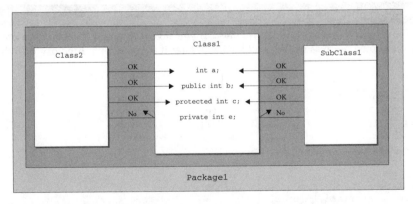

Within a package such as `package1`, only the `private` members of the class `Class1` can't be directly accessed by a method in another class in the same package. Declaring a class member to be `private` limits its availability solely to methods in the same class.

We saw earlier that a class definition must have an access attribute of `public` if it is to be accessible from outside the package. The next diagram shows the situation where the classes, seeking access to the members of a public class, are in different packages.

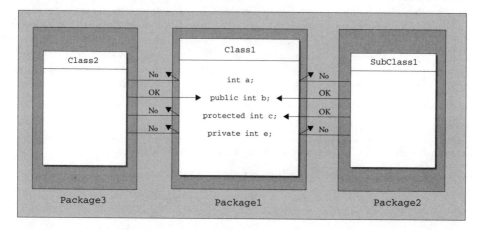

Here access is more restricted. The only members of `Class1` that can be accessed from an ordinary class, `Class2`, in another package are those specified as `public`. Keep in mind that the class, `Class1`, must also have been defined with the attribute `public`. From a sub-class of `Class1` that is in another package, the members of `Class1`, without an access attribute, cannot be reached, and neither can the `private` members – these can never be accessed externally under any circumstances.

Specifying Access Attributes

As you probably gathered from the diagrams that we just looked at, to specify an access attribute for a class member, you just add the keyword to the beginning of the declaration. Here is the `Point` class you saw earlier, but now with access attributes defined for its members:

Try It Out – Accessing the Point Class

Make the following changes to your `Point` class. If you save it in a new directory, do make sure `Line.java` is copied there as well. It will be useful later if they are in a directory with the name `Geometry`.

```
public class Point {
  // Create a point from its coordinates
  public Point(double xVal, double yVal) {
    x = xVal;
    y = yVal;
  }

  // Create a Point from an existing Point object
  public Point(final Point aPoint) {
    x = aPoint.x;
    y = aPoint.y;
  }
```

```
          // Move a point
      public void move(double xDelta, double yDelta) {
          // Parameter values are increments to the current coordinates
          x += xDelta;
          y += yDelta;
      }

      // Calculate the distance to another point
      public double distance(final Point aPoint) {
          return Math.sqrt((x - aPoint.x)*(x - aPoint.x)+(y - aPoint.y)*(y - aPoint.y));
      }

      // Convert a point to a string
      public String toString() {
          return Double.toString(x) + ", " + y;      // As "x, y"
      }

      // Coordinates of the point
      private double x;
      private double y;
  }
```

The members have been re-sequenced within the class with the `private` members appearing last. You should maintain a consistent ordering of class members according to their access attributes, as it makes the code easier to follow. The ordering adopted most frequently is for the most accessible members to appear first, and the least accessible last, but a consistent order is more important than the particular order you choose.

How It Works

Now the instance variables x and y cannot be accessed or modified from outside the class as they are private. The only way these can be set or modified is through methods within the class, either with constructors, or the move() method. If it is necessary to obtain the values of x and y from outside the class, as it might well be in this case, a simple function would do the trick. For example:

```
public double getX() {
   return x;
}
```

Couldn't be easier really, could it? This makes x freely available, but prevents modification of its value from outside the class. In general, such methods are referred to as **accessor** methods, and usually have the form getXXX(). Methods that allow a private data member to be changed are called **mutator** methods, and are typically of the form setXXX() where a new value is passed as an argument. For example:

```
public void setX(double inputX) {
   x = inputX;
}
```

It may seem odd to use a method to alter the value of a `private` data member when you could just make it `public`. The main advantage of using a method in this way is that you can apply validity checks on the new value that is to be set.

Choosing Access Attributes

As you can see from the table of access attributes, all the classes we have defined so far have had members that are freely accessible within the same package. This applies both to the methods and the variables that were defined in the classes. This is not good object-oriented programming practice. As we said in Chapter 1, one of the ideas behind objects is to keep the data members encapsulated so they cannot be modified by all and sundry, even from other classes within the same package. On the other hand, the methods in your classes generally need to be accessible. They provide the outside interface to the class and define the set of operations that are possible with objects of the class. Therefore in the majority of situations with simple classes (i.e. no sub-classes), you should be explicitly specifying your class members as either `public` or `private`, rather than omitting the access attributes.

Broadly, unless you have good reasons for declaring them otherwise, the variables in a public class should be `private` and the methods that will be called from outside the class should be `public`. Even where access to the values of the variables from outside a class is necessary, you don't need to make them `public` or leave them without an access attribute. As we've just seen, you can provide access quite easily by adding a simple `public` method to return the value of a data member.

Of course, there are always exceptions:

❑   For classes in a package that are not public, and therefore not accessible outside the package, it may sometimes be convenient to allow other classes in the package direct access to the data members.

❑   If you have data members that have been specified as `final` so that their values are fixed, and they are likely to be useful outside the class, you might as well declare them to be `public`.

❑   You may well have methods in a class that are only intended to be used internally by other methods in the class. In this case you should specify these as `private`.

❑   In a class like the standard class, `Math`, which is just a convenient container for utility functions and standard data values, you will want to make everything `public`.

All of this applies to simple classes. We will see in the next chapter, when we will be looking at sub-classes, that there are some further aspects of class structure that you must take into account.

Using a Package and Access Attributes

Let's put together an example that uses a package that we will create. We could put the `Point` and `Line` classes that we defined earlier in a package we could call `Geometry`. We can then write a program that will import these classes and test them.

Try It Out – Packaging Up the Line and Point Classes

The source and `.class` files for each class in the package must be in a directory with the name `Geometry`. Remember that you need to ensure the path to the directory (or directories if you are storing `.class` files separately) `Geometry` appears in the `CLASSPATH` environment variable setting before you try compile or use either of these two classes. You can do this by specifying the `-classpath` option when you run the compiler or the interpreter.

To include the class `Point` in the package, the code in `Point.java` will be:

```
package Geometry;

public class Point {

  // Create a point from its coordinates
  public Point(double xVal, double yVal) {
    x = xVal;
    y = yVal;
  }

  // Create a Point from an existing Point object
  public Point(final Point aPoint) {
    x = aPoint.x;
    y = aPoint.y;
  }

    // Move a point
  public void move(double xDelta, double yDelta) {
    // Parameter values are increments to the current coordinates
    x += xDelta;
    y += yDelta;
  }

  // Calculate the distance to another point
  public double distance(final Point aPoint) {
    return Math.sqrt((x - aPoint.x)*(x - aPoint.x)+(y - aPoint.y)*(y - aPoint.y));
  }

  // Convert a point to a string
  public String toString() {
    return Double.toString(x) + ", " + y;     // As "x, y"
  }

  // Retrieve the x coordinate
  public double getX() {
    return x;
  }

  // Retrieve the y coordinate
  public double getY() {
    return y;
  }

  // Set the x coordinate
  public void setX(double inputX) {
    x = inputX;
  }

  // Set the y coordinate
  public void setY(double inputY) {
    y = inputY;
  }

  // Coordinates of the point
  private double x;
  private double y;
}
```

Note that we have added the getX(), getY(), setX() and setY() methods to the class to make the private data members accessible.

The Line class also needs to be amended to make the methods public and to declare the class as public. We also need to change its intersects() method so that it can access the private data members of Point objects using the set...() and get...() methods in the Point class. The code in Line.java, with changes highlighted, will be:

```java
package Geometry;

public class Line {

  // Create a line from two points
  public Line(final Point start, final Point end) {
    this.start = new Point(start);
    this.end = new Point(end);
  }

  // Create a line from two coordinate pairs
  public Line(double xStart, double yStart, double xEnd, double yEnd) {
    start = new Point(xStart, yStart);           // Create the start point
    end = new Point(xEnd, yEnd);                 // Create the end point
  }

  // Calculate the length of a line
  public double length() {
    return start.distance(end);                  // Use the method from the Point class
  }

  // Return a point as the intersection of two lines -- called from a Line object
  public Point intersects(final Line line1) {

    Point localPoint = new Point(0, 0);

    double num =(this.end.getY() - this.start.getY())
            * (this.start.getX()-line1.start.getX())
            - (this.end.getX() - this.start.getX())
            * (this.start.getY() - line1.start.getY());

    double denom = (this.end.getY() - this.start.getY())
            * (line1.end.getX() - line1.start.getX())
            - (this.end.getX() - this.start.getX())
            * (line1.end.getY() - line1.start.getY());

    localPoint.setX(line1.start.getX() + (line1.end.getX() -
                              line1.start.getX())*num/denom);
    localPoint.setY(line1.start.getY() + (line1.end.getY() -
                              line1.start.getY())*num/denom);

    return localPoint;
  }

  // Convert a line to a string
  public String toString() {
    return "(" + start+ "):(" + end + ")";       // As "(start):(end)"
  }                                              // that is, "(x1, y1):(x2, y2)"

  // Data members
```

```
      Point start;                        // Start point of line
      Point end;                          // End point of line
}
```

Here we have left the data members without an access attribute, so they are accessible from the Point class, but not from classes outside the Geometry package.

How It Works

The package statement at the beginning of each source file defines the package to which the class belongs. Remember, you still have to save it in the correct directory, Geometry. Without the public attribute, the classes would not be available to classes outside the Geometry package.

Since we have declared the data members in the class Point as private, they will not be accessible directly. We have added the methods getX(), getY(), setX(), and setY() to the Point class to make the values accessible to any class that needs them.

The Line class hasn't been updated since our first example, so we first have to sort out the access attributes. The two instance variables are declared as before, without any access attribute, so they can be accessed from within the package but not from classes outside the package. This is an instance where exposing the data members within the package is very convenient, and we can do it without exposing the data members to any classes using the package. And we have updated the intersects() method to reflect the changes in accessibility made to the members of the Point class.

We can now write the program that is going to import and use the package that we have just created.

Try It Out – Testing the Geometry Package

We can create a succession of points, and a line joining each pair of successive points in the sequence, and then calculate the total line length.

```java
import Geometry.*;     // Import the Point and Line classes

public class TryPackage {
  public static void main(String[] args) {
    double[][] coords = { {1.0, 0.0}, {6.0, 0.0}, {6.0, 10.0},
                          {10.0,10.0}, {10.0, -14.0}, {8.0, -14.0}};
    // Create an array of points and fill it with Point objects
    Point[] points = new Point[coords.length];
    for(int i = 0; i < coords.length; i++)
      points[i] = new Point(coords[i][0],coords[i][1]);

    // Create an array of lines and fill it using Point pairs
    Line[] lines = new Line[points.length - 1];
    double totalLength = 0.0;             // Store total line length here
    for(int i = 0; i < points.length - 1; i++) {
      lines[i] = new Line(points[i], points[i+1]); // Create a Line
      totalLength += lines[i].length();            // Add its length
      System.out.println("Line "+(i+1)+' ' +lines[i] +
                         " Length is " + lines[i].length());
    }
```

```
   // Output the total length
   System.out.println("\nTotal line length = " + totalLength);
  }
 }
```

You should save this as `TryPackage.java` in the directory `TryPackage`. If the path to your `Geometry` directory on a PC running Windows is `C:\Packages\Geometry`, you can compile this with the command:

```
javac -classpath ".;C:\Packages" TryPackage.java
```

This assumes the current directory contains the `TryPackage.java` file. The **-classpath** option specifies two paths separated by a semi-colon. The first path, specified by a period, is the current directory. This is necessary to enable the `TryPackage.java` source file to be found. The second path is `C:\Packages`, which is the directory containing our `Geometry` package. Without this the compiler will not be able to find the classes in the `Geometry` package and the compilation will fail.

Once you have a successful compilation, you can execute the program with the command:

```
java -classpath ".;C:\Packages" TryPackage
```

When the program executes, you should see the following output:

```
Line 1 (1.0, 0.0):(6.0, 0.0)    Length is 5.0
Line 2 (6.0, 0.0):(6.0, 10.0)    Length is 10.0
Line 3 (6.0, 10.0):(10.0, 10.0)    Length is 4.0
Line 4 (10.0, 10.0):(10.0, -14.0)    Length is 24.0
Line 5 (10.0, -14.0):(8.0, -14.0)    Length is 2.0

Total line length = 45.0
```

How It Works

This example is a handy review of how you can define arrays, and also shows that you can declare an array of objects in the same way as you declare an array of one of the basic types. The dimensions of the array of arrays, `coords`, are determined by the initial values that are specified between the braces. The number of values within the outer braces determines the first dimension. Each of the elements in the array is itself an array of length two, with each pair of element values being enclosed within their own braces.

Since there are six sets of these, we have an array of six elements, each of which is itself an array of two elements. Each of these elements correspond to the (x, y) coordinates of a point.

You can see from this that, if necessary, you can create an array of arrays with each row having a different number of elements. The number of initializing values that appear, so they could all be different in the most general case, determines the length of each row.

We declare an array of `Point` objects with the same length as the number of (x, y) pairs in the `coords` array. This array is filled with `Point` objects in the `for` loop, which we created using the pairs of coordinate values from the `coords` array.

Since each pair of `Point` objects will define a `Line` object, we need one less element in the array `lines` than we have in the `points` array. We create the elements of the lines array in the second `for` loop using successive `Point` objects, and accumulate the total length of all the line segments by adding the length of each `Line` object to `totalLength` as it is created. On each iteration of the `for` loop, we output the details of the current line. Finally, we output the value of `totalLength`, which in this case is 45.

Note that the `import` statement adds the classes from the package `Geometry` to our program. These classes can be added to any application using the same `import` statement. You might like to try putting the classes in the `Geometry` package in a JAR file and try it out as an extension. Let's look at one other aspect of generating your own packages – compiling just the classes in the package without any program that makes use of them. We can demonstrate how this can be done on our `Geometry` package if you delete the `Line.class` and `Point.class` files from the package directory.

First make the directory, `C:\TryPackage`, that contains the package directory, current. Now you can compile just the classes in the `Geometry` package with the command:

```
javac -classpath "C:\TryPackage" Geometry/*.java
```

This will compile both the `Line` and `Point` classes so you should see the `.class` files restored in the `Geometry` directory. The files to be compiled are specified relative to the current directory as **Geometry/*.java.** Under Microsoft Windows this could equally well be **Geometry*.java.** This specifies all files in the `Geometry` subdirectory to the current directory. The classpath must contain the path to the package directory, otherwise the compiler will not be able to find the package. We have defined it here using the **-classpath** option. We have not specified the current directory in classpath since we do not have any files there that need to be compiled. If we had included it in classpath it would not have made any difference – the classes in the `Geometry` package would compile just the same.

Nested Classes

All the classes we have defined so far have been separate from each other – each stored away in its own file. Not all classes have to be defined like this. You can put the definition of one class inside the definition of another class. The inside class is called a **nested class**. A nested class can itself have another class nested inside it, if need be.

When you define a nested class, it is a member of the enclosing class in much the same way as other members. A nested class can have an access attribute just like other class members, and the accessibility from outside the enclosing class is determined by the attributes in the same way.

```
public class Outside {

  // Nested class
  public class Inside {
    // Details of Inside class...
  }

  // More members of Outside class...
}
```

Here the class `Inside` is nested inside the class `Outside`. The `Inside` class is declared as a public member of `Outside`, so it is accessible from outside `Outside`. Obviously a nested class should have some specific association with the enclosing class. Arbitrarily nesting one class inside another would not be sensible. The enclosing class here is referred to as a **top-level class**. A top-level class is a class that contains a nested class but is not itself a nested class.

Our nested class here only has meaning in the context of an object of type `Outside`. This is because `Inside` is not declared as a static member of the class `Outside`. Until an object of type `Outside` has been created, you can't create any `Inside` objects. However, when you declare an object of a class containing a nested class, no objects of the nested class are necessarily created – unless of course the enclosing class's constructor creates them. For example, suppose we create an object with the following statement:

```
Outside outer = new Outside();
```

No objects of the nested class, `Inside`, are created. If you now wish to create an object of the type of the nested class you must refer to the nested class type using the name of the enclosing class as a qualifier. For instance, having declared an object of type `Outside`, we can create an object of type `Inside` as follows:

```
Outside.Inside inner = outer.new Inside();    // Define a nested class object
```

Here we have created an object of the nested class type that is associated with the object, `outer`, created earlier. We are creating an object of type `Inside` in the context of the object `outer`. Within non-static methods that are members of `Outside`, you can use the class name `Inside` without any qualification as it will be automatically qualified by the compiler with the `this` variable. So we could create a new `Inside` object from within the method of the object `Outside`:

```
Inside inner = new Inside();    // Define a nested class object
```

which is equivalent to:

```
this.Inside inner = this.new Inside();    // Define a nested class object
```

All this implies that a static method cannot create objects of a non-static nested class type. Because the `Inside` class is not a static member of the `Outside` class, such a member could refer to an object which does not exist – an error, if there are no `Inside` objects extant in the context of an `Outside` object. And as `Inside` is not a static data member of the `Outside` class, if a static method in the `Outside` class tried to create an object of type `Inside` directly, without first invoking an object of type `Outside`, it would be trying to create an object outside of that object's legitimate scope – an illegal maneuver.

Further, because the class `Inside` is not a static member of the `Outside` class, it cannot in turn contain any static data members itself. Since `Inside` is not static, it cannot act as a freestanding class with static members – this would be a logical contradiction.

Nested classes are typically used to define objects that at least have a strong association with objects of the enclosing class type, and often there is a tight coupling between the two. A further use for nested classes is for grouping a set of related classes under the umbrella of an enclosing class. We will be using this approach in examples later on in the book.

Static Nested Classes

To make objects of a nested class type independent of objects of the enclosing class, you can declare the nested class as `static`. For example,

```
public class Outside {
  public static class Skinside {
    // Details of Skinside
  }

  // Nested class
  public class Inside {
    // Details of Inside class...
  }
  // More members of Outside class...
}
```

Now with `Skinside` inside `Outside` declared as `static`, we can declare objects of this nested class, independent from objects of `Outside`, and regardless of whether we have created any `Outside` objects or not. For example:

```
Outside.Skinside example = new Outside.Skinside();
```

This is significantly different from what we needed to do for a non-static nested class. Now we must use the nested class name qualified by the enclosing class name as the type for creating the object. Note that a static nested class can have static members, whereas a non-static nested class cannot.

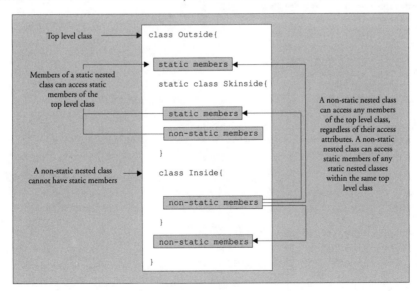

Let's see how a nested class works in practice with a simple example. We will create a class `MagicHat` that will define an object containing a variable number of rabbits. We will put the definition for the class `Rabbit` inside the definition of the class `MagicHat`. The basic structure of `MagicHat.java` will be:

```
public class MagicHat {
  // Definition of the MagicHat class...

  // Nested class to define a rabbit
  static class Rabbit {
    // Definition of the Rabbit class...
  }
}
```

Here the nested class is defined as static because we want to be able to have static members of this class. We will see a little later how it might work with a non-static nested class.

Try It Out – Rabbits Out of Hats

Let's add the detail of the MagicHat class definition:

```
import java.util.Random;                    // Import Random class

public class MagicHat {
  static int maxRabbits = 5;                 // Maximum rabbits in a hat
  static Random select = new Random();       // Random number generator

  // Constructor for a hat
  public MagicHat(String hatName) {
    this.hatName = hatName;                  // Store the hat name
    rabbits = new Rabbit[1+select.nextInt(maxRabbits)]; // Random rabbits

    for(int i = 0; i < rabbits.length; i++)
      rabbits[i] = new Rabbit();             // Create the rabbits
  }

  // String representation of a hat
  public String toString() {
    // Hat name first...
    String hatString = "\n" + hatName + " contains:\n";

    for(int i = 0; i < rabbits.length; i++)
      hatString += "\t" + rabbits[i] + " ";  // Add the rabbits strings
    return hatString;
  }

  private String hatName;                     // Name of the hat
  private Rabbit rabbits[];                    // Rabbits in the hat

  // Nested class to define a rabbit
  static class Rabbit {
    // Definition of the Rabbit class...
  }
}
```

Instead of the old `Math.random()` method that we have been using up to now to generate pseudo-random values, we are using an object of the class `Random` that is defined in the package `java.util`. An object of type `Random` has a variety of methods to generate pseudo-random values of different types, and with different ranges. The method `nextInt()` that we are using here returns an integer that is zero or greater, but less than the integer value you pass as an argument. Thus if you pass the length of an array to it, it will generate a random index value that will always be legal for the array size.

We can now add the definition of the `Rabbit` class. When we create a `Rabbit` object, we want it to have a unique name so we can distinguish one `Rabbit` from another. We can generate unique names by selecting one from a limited set of fixed names, and then appending an integer that is different each time the base name is used. Here's what we need to add for the `Rabbit` class definition:

```
public class MagicHat {

   // Definition of the MagicHat class - as before...

   // Nested class to define a rabbit
   static class Rabbit {
      // A name is a rabbit name from rabbitNames followed by an integer
      static private String[] rabbitNames = {"Floppsy", "Moppsy",
                                             "Gnasher", "Thumper"};
      static private int[] rabbitNamesCount = new int[rabbitNames.length];
      private String name;                         // Name of the rabbit

      // Constructor for a rabbit
      public Rabbit() {
         int index = select.nextInt(rabbitNames.length);   // Get random name index
         name = rabbitNames[index] + (++rabbitNamesCount[index]);
      }

      // String representation of a rabbit
      public String toString() {
         return name;
      }
   }
}
```

Note that the constructor in the `Rabbit` class can access the `select` member of the enclosing class `MagicHat`, without qualification. This is only possible with static members of the enclosing class – you can't refer to non-static members of the enclosing class here because there is no object of type `MagicHat` associated with it.

We can use the following application class to try out our nested class:

```
public class TryNestedClass {
   static public void main(String[] args) {
      // Create three magic hats and output them
      System.out.println(new MagicHat("Gray Topper"));
      System.out.println(new MagicHat("Black Topper"));
      System.out.println(new MagicHat("Baseball Cap"));
   }
}
```

When I ran the program, I got the output:

```
Gray Topper contains:
     Moppsy1      Moppsy2      Floppsy1

Black Topper contains:
     Thumper1     Moppsy3      Thumper2     Gnasher1

Baseball Cap contains:
     Moppsy4      Moppsy5      Thumper3
```

You are likely to get something different.

How It Works

Each `MagicHat` object will contain a random number of `Rabbit` objects. The constructor for a `MagicHat` object stores the name of the hat in its private member `hatName`, and generates a `Rabbit` array with at least one, and up to `maxRabbits` elements. This is done with the expression `1+select.nextInt(maxRabbits)`. Calling `nextInt()` with the argument `maxRabbits` will return a value that is from 0 to `maxRabbits-1` inclusive. Adding 1 to this will result in a value from 1 to `maxRabbits` inclusive. The array so created is then filled with `Rabbit` objects.

The `MagicHat` class also has a method `toString()` method which returns a `String` object containing the name of the hat and the names of all the rabbits in the hat. This assumes that the `Rabbit` class also has a `toString()` method defined. We will be able to use the `toString()` implicitly in an output statement when we come to create and display `MagicHat` class objects.

The base names that we use to generate rabbit names are defined in the `static` array `rabbitNames[]` in the `Rabbit` class. The count for each base name, which we will append to the base name to produce a unique name for a rabbit, is stored in the `static` array `rabbitNamesCount[]`. This has the same number of elements as the `rabbitNames` array, and each element stores a value to be appended to the corresponding name in the `rabbitNames` array. The `Rabbit` class has the data member, `name`, to store a name that is initialized in the constructor. A random base name is selected from the `rabbitNames[]` array using an index value from 0 up to one less than the length of this array. We then append the current count for the name incremented by 1, so successive uses of any base name such as `Gnasher`, for example, will produce names `Gnasher1`, `Gnasher2`, and so on. The `toString()` method for the class returns the name for the `Rabbit` object.

The method `main()` in `TryNestedClass` creates three `MagicHat` objects and outputs the string representation of each of them. Putting the object as an argument to the `println()` method will call the `toString()` method for the object automatically, and the `String` object that is returned will be output to the screen.

Using a Non-Static Nested Class

In our previous example, we could define the `Rabbit` class as non-static by deleting the keyword `static`. However, if you try that, the program will no longer compile and run. The problem is the static data members' `rabbitNames` and `rabbitNamesCount` in the `Rabbit` class. We saw earlier that a non-static nested class cannot have static members, so we must seek an alternative way of dealing with names.

We could consider making these arrays non-static. This has several disadvantages. First, each `Rabbit` object would have its own copy of these arrays – an unnecessary duplication of data. A more serious problem is that our naming process would not work. Because each object has its own copy of the `rabbitNamesCount` array, the names generated are not going to be unique.

The answer is to keep `rabbitNames` and `rabbitNamesCount` as static, but put them in the `MagicHat` class instead. Let's see that working.

Try It Out – Accessing the Top Level Class Members

We need to modify the class definition to:

```
public class MagicHat {
  static int maxRabbits = 5;                       // Maximuum rabbits in a hat
  static Random select = new Random();             // Random number generator
  static private String[] rabbitNames = {"Floppsy", "Moppsy",
                                          "Gnasher", "Thumper"};
  static private int[] rabbitNamesCount = new int[rabbitNames.length];

  // Constructor for a hat
  public MagicHat(final String hatName) {
    this.hatName = hatName;                         // Store the hat name
    rabbits = new Rabbit[1+select.nextInt(maxRabbits)]; // Random rabbits

    for(int i = 0; i < rabbits.length; i++)
      rabbits[i] = new Rabbit();                     // Create the rabbits
  }

  // String representation of a hat
  public String toString() {
    // Hat name first...
    String hatString = "\n" + hatName + " contains:\n";

    for(int i = 0; i < rabbits.length; i++)
      hatString += "\t" + rabbits[i] + " ";  // Add the rabbits strings
    return hatString;
  }
  private String hatName;        // Name of the hat
  private Rabbit rabbits[];       // Rabbits in the hat

  // Nested class to define a rabbit
  class Rabbit {
    private String name;                          // Name of the rabbit

    // Constructor for a rabbit
    public Rabbit() {
      int index = select.nextInt(rabbitNames.length);  // Get random name index
      name = rabbitNames[index] + (++rabbitNamesCount[index]);
    }

    // String representation of a rabbit
    public String toString() {
```

```
            return name;
        }
    }
}
```

The only changes are the deletion of the static keyword in the definition of the `Rabbit` class – the data members relating to rabbit names have been moved to the `MagicHat` class. You can run this with the same version of `TryNestedClass` and it should produce output much the same as before.

How It Works

Although the output is much the same, what is happening is distinctly different. The `Rabbit` objects that are created in the `MagicHat` constructor are now associated with the current `MagicHat` object that is being constructed. The `Rabbit()` constructor call is actually `this.Rabbit()`.

Using a Nested Class outside the Top-Level Class

You can create objects of an inner class outside the top-level class containing the inner class. As we discussed, how you do this depends on whether the nested class is a static member of the enclosing class. With the first version of our `MagicHat` class, with a static `Rabbit` class, you could create an independent rabbit by adding the following statement to the end of `main()`:

```
System.out.println("An independent rabbit: " + new MagicHat.Rabbit());
```

This `Rabbit` object is completely free – there is no `MagicHat` object to restrain it. In the case of a non-static `Rabbit` class, things are different. Let's try this using a modified version of the previous program.

Try It Out – Free Range Rabbits (Almost)

We can see how this works by modifying the method `main()` in `TryNestedClass` to create another `MagicHat` object, and then create a `Rabbit` object for it:

```
static public void main(String[] args) {
  // Create three magic hats and output them
  System.out.println(new MagicHat("Gray Topper"));
  System.out.println(new MagicHat("Black Topper"));
  System.out.println(new MagicHat("Baseball Cap"));

  MagicHat oldHat = new MagicHat("Old hat");        // New hat object
  MagicHat.Rabbit rabbit = oldHat.new Rabbit();     // Create rabbit object
  System.out.println(oldHat);                       // Show the hat
  System.out.println("\nNew rabbit is: " + rabbit); // Display the rabbit
}
```

The output produced is:

```
Gray Topper contains:
    Thumper1

Black Topper contains:
    Moppsy1     Thumper2     Thumper3
```

```
Baseball Cap contains:
     Floppsy1    Floppsy2      Thumper4

Old hat contains:
     Floppsy3    Thumper5    Thumper6  Thumper7      Thumper8

New rabbit is: Thumper9
```

How It Works

The new code first creates a `MagicHat` object, `oldHat`. This will have its own rabbits. We then use this object to create an object of the class `MagicHat.Rabbit`. This is how a nested class type is referenced – with the top-level class name as a qualifier. You can only call the constructor for the nested class in this case by qualifying it with a `MagicHat` object name. This is because a non-static nested class can refer to members of the top-level class – including instance members. Therefore, an instance of the top-level class must exist for this to be possible.

Note how the top-level object is used in the constructor call. The object name qualifier goes before the keyword `new` which precedes the constructor call for the inner class. This creates an object, `rabbit`, in the context of the object `oldHat`. This doesn't mean `oldHat` has `rabbit` as a member. It means that, if top-level members are used in the inner class, they will be the members for `oldHat`. You can see from the example that the name of the new rabbit is not part of the `oldHat` object, although it is associated with `oldHat`. You could demonstrate this by modifying the `toString()` method in the `Rabbit` class to:

```
public String toString() {
  return name + " parent: "+hatName;
}
```

If you run the program again, you will see that when each `Rabbit` object is displayed, it will also show its parent hat.

Local Nested Classes

You can define a class inside a method – where it is called a **local nested class**. It is also referred to as a **local inner class**, since a non-static nested class is often referred to as an **inner class**. You can only create objects of a local inner class locally – that is, within the method in which the class definition appears. This is useful when the computation in a method requires the use of a specialized class that is not required or used elsewhere.

A local inner class can refer to variables declared in the method in which the definition appears, but only if they are `final`.

The finalize() Method

You have the option of including a method `finalize()` in a class definition. This method is called automatically by Java before an object is finally destroyed and the space it occupies in memory is released. Please note that this may be some time after the object is inaccessible in your program. When an object goes out of scope, it is dead as far as your program is concerned, but the Java Virtual Machine may not get around to disposing of the remains until later. When it does, it calls the `finalize()` method for the object. The form of the `finalize()` method is:

```
protected void finalize() {
    // Your clean-up code...
}
```

This method is useful if your class objects use resources that require some special action when they are destroyed. Typically these are resources that are not within the Java environment and not guaranteed to be released by the object itself. This means such things as graphics resources – fonts or other drawing related resources that are supplied by the host operating system, or external files on the hard disk. Leaving these around after an object is destroyed wastes system resources and, in some circumstances (with graphics resources under Windows 95 for instance) if you waste enough of them, your program, and possibly other programs the system is supporting, may stop working. For most classes this is not necessary, but if an object opened a disk file for example, but did not guarantee its closure, you would want to make sure that the file was closed when the object was destroyed. You can implement the `finalize()` method to take care of this.

Another use for the `finalize()` method is to record the fact that the object has been destroyed. We could implement the `finalize()` method for the `Sphere` class to decrement the value of the static member, `count`, for instance. This would make `count` a measure of how many `Sphere` objects were around, rather than how many had been created. It would, however, not be an accurate measure for reasons that we will come to in a moment.

You cannot rely on an object being destroyed when it is no longer available to your program code. Unless your program calls the `System.gc()` method, the Java Virtual Machine will only get rid of unwanted objects and free the memory they occupy if it runs out of memory, or if there is no activity within your program – for example when waiting for input. As a result objects may not get destroyed until execution of your program ends. You also have no guarantee as to when a `finalize()` method will be called. All you are assured is that it will be called before the memory that the object occupied is freed. Nothing time-sensitive should be left to the `finalize()` method.

One consequence of this is that there are circumstances where this can cause problems – when you don't allow for the possibility of your objects hanging around. For example, suppose you create an object in a method that opens a file, and rely on the `finalize()` method to close it. If you then call this method in a loop, you may end up with a large number of files open at one time, since the object that is created in each call of the method will not necessarily be destroyed immediately on return from the method. This introduces the possibility of your program attempting to have more files open simultaneously than the host operating system allows. In this situation, you should make sure a file is closed when you have finished with it, by including an object method to close it explicitly – for example `close()`.

The System class also provides another possible approach. You can suggest to the JVM that the `finalize()` methods for all discarded objects should be run, if they haven't been already. You just call the `runFinalization()` method:

```
System.runFinalization();
```

This is another of those 'best efforts' deals on the part of the JVM. It will do its very best to run finalize() for any dead objects that are laying around before return from the `runFinalization()` method, but like with a lot of things in this life, there are no guarantees.

Native Methods

It is possible to include a method in a class that is implemented in some other programming language, such as C or C++, external to the Java Virtual Machine. To specify such a method within a class definition you use the keyword `native` in the declaration of the method. For example:

```
public native long getData();      // Declare a method that is not in Java
```

Of course the method will have no body in Java since it is defined elsewhere, where all the work is done, so the declaration ends with a semi-colon. The implementation of a native method will need to use an interface to the Java environment. The standard API for implementing native methods in C for example, is called JNI – the **J**ava **N**ative **I**nterface.

The major drawback to using native methods in Java is that your program will no longer be portable. Security requirements for applets embedded in Web pages require that the code must all be written in Java – using native methods in an applet is simply not possible. Since the primary reasons for using Java are the portability of the code and the ability to produce applets, the need for you to add native methods to your Java programs will be minimal. We will, therefore, not delve any deeper into this topic.

Summary

In this chapter you have learned all the essentials of defining your own classes. You can now create your own class types to fit the context of the problems you are dealing with. We will build on this in the next chapter to enable you to add more flexibility to the operations on your class objects by showing you how to realize polymorphism.

The important points covered in this chapter are:

❑ A class definition specifies the variables and methods that are members of the class.

❑ Each class must be saved in a file with the same name as the class, and with the extension `.java`.

❑ Class variables are declared using the keyword `static`, and one instance of each class variable is shared amongst all objects of a class.

❑ Each object of a class will have its own instance variables – these are variables declared without using the keyword `static`.

❑ Methods that are specified as `static` can be called even if no class objects exist, but a `static` method cannot refer to instance variables.

❑ Methods that are not specified as `static` can access any of the variables in the class directly.

❑ Recursive methods are methods that call themselves.

❑ Access to members of a class is determined by the access attributes that are specified for each of them. These can be `public`, `private`, `protected`, package `private`, or nothing at all.

❑ Classes can be grouped into a package. If a class in a package is to be accessible from outside the package the class must be declared using the keyword `public`.

❑ To designate that a class is a member of a package you use a `package` statement at the beginning of the file containing the class definition.

❑ To add classes from a package to a file you use an `import` statement immediately following any package statement in the file.

❑ A native method is a method implemented in a language other than Java. Java programs containing native methods cannot be applets and are no longer portable.

❑ A field does not get ploughed by turning it over in your mind.

Exercises

1. Define a class for rectangle objects defined by two points, the top-left and bottom-right corners of the rectangle. Include a constructor to copy a rectangle, a method to return a rectangle object, that encloses the current object and the rectangle passed as an argument, and a method to display the defining points of a rectangle. Test the class by creating four rectangles, and combining these cumulatively, to end up with a rectangle enclosing them all. Output the defining points of all the rectangles you create.

2. Define a class, `mcmLength`, to represent a length measured in meters, centimeters, and millimeters, each stored as integers. Include methods to add and subtract objects, to multiply and divide an object by an integer value, to calculate an area resulting from the product of two objects, and to compare objects. Include constructors that accept: three arguments – meters, centimeters, and millimeters; one integer argument in millimeters; one `double` argument in centimeters and no arguments, which creates an object with the length set to zero. Check the class by creating some objects and testing the class operations.

3. Define a class, `tkgWeight`, to represent a weight in tons, kilograms, and grams, and include a similar range of methods and constructors as the previous example. Demonstrate this class by creating and combining some class objects.

4. Put both the previous classes in a package called `Measures`. Import this package into a program that will calculate and display the total weight of the following: 200 carpets – size: 4 meters by 2 meters 9 centimeters, that weigh 1.25 kilograms per square meter; and 60 carpets – size: 3 meters 57 centimeters by 5 meters, that weigh 1.05 kilograms per square meter.

Extending Classes and Inheritance

A very important part of object-oriented programming allows you to create a new class based on a class that has already been defined. The class that you use as the base for your new class can be either one you have defined, a standard class in Java, or a class defined by someone else – perhaps from a package supporting a specialized application area.

This chapter focuses on how you can reuse existing classes by creating new classes based on the ones you have, and explores the ramifications of using this facility, and the additional capabilities it provides. We will also delve into an important related topic – **interfaces** – and how you can use them.

In this chapter you will learn:

❑   How to reuse classes by defining a new class based on an existing class.

❑   What polymorphism is and how to define your classes to take advantage of it.

❑   What an abstract method is.

❑   What an abstract class is.

❑   What an interface is and how you can define your own interfaces.

❑   How to use interfaces in your classes.

❑   How interfaces can help you implement polymorphic classes.

Using Existing Classes

Let's start by understanding the jargon. Defining a new class based on an existing class is called **derivation**. The new class, or **derived class**, is referred to as a **direct subclass** of the class from which it is derived. The original class is called a **base class** because it forms the base for the definition of the derived class. The original class is also referred to as a **superclass** of the derived class. You can also derive a new class from a derived class, which in turn was derived from some other derived class, and so on. This is illustrated in the following diagram:

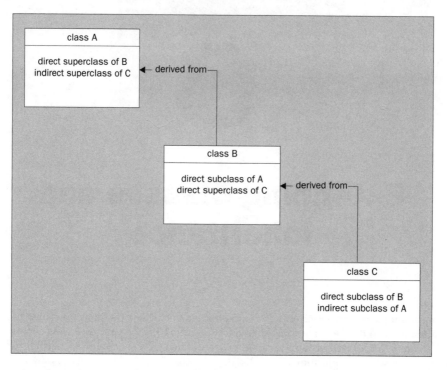

This shows just three classes in a hierarchy, but there can be as many as you like.

Let's consider a more concrete example. We could define a class Dog that could represent a dog of any kind.

```
class Dog {
   // Members of the Dog class...
}
```

This might contain a data member identifying the name of a particular dog such as "Lassie" or "Poochy" and another data member to identify the breed, such as "Border Collie" or "Pyrenean Mountain Dog". From the Dog class, we could derive a Spaniel class that represented dogs that were spaniels:

```
class Spaniel extends Dog {
   // Members of the Spaniel class...
}
```

The extends keyword that we use here identifies that Dog is a base class for Spaniel, so an object of type Spaniel will have members that are inherited from the Dog class, in addition to the members of the Spaniel class that appear in its definition. The breed would be "spaniel" for all instances of the class Spaniel although in general the name for each spaniel would be different. The Spaniel class might have some additional data members that characterize the specifics of what it means to be a spaniel. We will see in a moment how we can arrange for the base class data members to be set appropriately.

236

A `Spaniel` object is a specialized instance of a `Dog` object. This reflects real life. A spaniel is obviously a dog and will have all the properties of a basic dog, but it has some unique characteristics of its own which distinguish it from all the dogs that are not spaniels. The inheritance mechanism that adds all the properties of the base class – `Dog` in this instance – to those in the derived class, is a good model for the real world. The members of the derived class define the properties that differentiate it from the base type, so when you derive one class from another, you can think of your derived class as a specification for objects that are specializations of the base class object.

Class Inheritance

In summary, when you derive a new class from a base class, the process is additive in terms of what makes up a class definition. The additional members that you define in the new class establish what makes a derived class object different from a base class object. Any members that you define in the new class are in addition to those that are already members of the base class. For our `Spaniel` class, derived from `Dog`, the data members to hold the name and the breed, that are defined for the class `Dog`, would automatically be in the class `Spaniel`. A `Spaniel` object will always have a complete `Dog` object inside it – with all its data members and methods. This does not mean that all the members defined in the `Dog` class are available to methods that are specific to the `Spaniel` class. Some are and some aren't. The inclusion of members of a base class in a derived class so that they are accessible in that derived class is called **class inheritance**. An **inherited member** of a base class is one that is *accessible* within the derived class. If a base class member is not accessible in a derived class, then it is not an inherited member of the derived class, but base class members that are not inherited still form part of a derived class object.

An inherited member of a derived class is a full member of that class and is freely accessible to any method in the class. Objects of the derived class type will contain all the inherited members of the base class – both fields and methods, as well as the members that are specific to the derived class. Note that a derived class object always contains a complete base class object within it, including all the fields and methods that are not inherited. We need to take a closer look at how inheritance works, and how the access attribute of a base class member affects its visibility in a derived class.

We need to consider several aspects of defining and using a derived class. First of all we need to know which members of the base class are inherited in the derived class. We will look at what this implies for data members and methods separately – there are some subtleties here we should be quite clear on. We will also look at what happens when you create an object of the derived class. There are some wrinkles in this context that require closer consideration. Let's start by looking at the data members that are inherited from a base class.

Inheriting Data Members

The next diagram shows which access attributes permit a class member to be inherited in a subclass. It shows what happens when the subclass is defined in either the same package or a different package from that containing the base class. Remember that inheritance implies accessibility of the member in a derived class, not just presence.

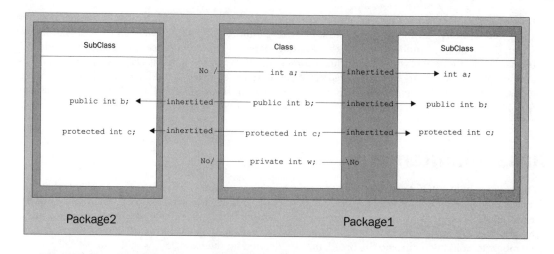

Note that a class itself can be specified as `public`. This makes the class accessible from any package anywhere. A class that is not declared as `public` can only be accessed from classes within the same package. This means for instance that you cannot define objects of a non-`public` class type within classes in other packages. It also means that to derive a new class in a package that does not contain the base class, the base class must be declared as `public`. If the base class is not declared as `public`, it cannot be reached directly from outside the package.

As you can see, a subclass that you define in the same package as its base inherits everything except for `private` data members of the base. If you define a subclass outside the package containing the base class, the `private` data members are not inherited, and neither are any data members in the base class that you have declared without access attributes. Members defined as `private` in the base class are never inherited under any circumstances.

You should also be able to see where the explicit access specifiers now sit in relation to one another. The `public` specifier is the least restrictive on class members since a public member is available everywhere, `protected` comes next, and prevents access from classes outside of a package, but does not limit inheritance – provided the class itself is `public`. Putting no access specifier on a class member limits access to classes within the same package, and prevents inheritance in subclasses that are defined in a different package. The most restrictive is `private` since access is constrained to the same class.

The inheritance rules apply to class variables – variables that you have declared as `static` – as well as instance variables. You will recall that only one occurrence of each `static` variable exists, and is shared by all objects of the class, whereas each object has its own set of instance variables. So for example, a variable that you declare as `private` and `static` in the base class is not inherited in a derived class, whereas a variable that you declare as `protected` and `static` will be inherited, and will be shared between all objects of a derived class type, as well as objects of the base class type.

Hiding Data Members

You can define a data member in a derived class with the same name as a data member in the base class. This is not a recommended approach to class design generally, but it is possible that it can arise unintentionally. When it occurs, the base class data member may still be inherited, but will be hidden by the derived class member with the same name. The hiding mechanism applies regardless of whether the respective types or access attributes are the same or not – the base class member will be hidden in the derived class if the names are the same.

Any use of the derived class member name will always refer to the member defined as part of the derived class. To refer to the inherited base class member, you must qualify it with the keyword super to indicate it is the member of the superclass that you want. Suppose you have a data member, value, as a member of the base class, and a data member with the same name in the derived class. In the derived class, the name value references the derived class member, and the name super.value refers to the member inherited from the base class. Note that you cannot use super.super.something to refer to a member name hidden in the base class of a base class.

In most situations you won't need to refer to inherited data members in this way as you would not deliberately set out to use duplicate names. The situation can commonly arise if you are using a class as a base that is subsequently modified by adding data members – it could be a Java library class for instance, or some other class in a package designed and maintained by someone else. Since your code did not presume the existence of the base class member, with the same name as your derived class data member, hiding the inherited member is precisely what you want. It allows the base class to be altered without breaking your code.

Inherited Methods

Ordinary methods in a base class, by which I mean methods that are not constructors, are inherited in a derived class in the same way as the data members of the base class. Those methods declared as private in a base class are not inherited, and those that you declare without an access attribute are only inherited if you define the derived class in the same package as the base class. The rest are all inherited.

Constructors are different from ordinary methods. Constructors in the base class are never inherited, regardless of their attributes. We can look into the intricacies of constructors in a class hierarchy by considering how derived class objects are created.

Objects of a Derived Class

We said at the beginning of this chapter that a derived class extends a base class. This is not just jargon – it really does do this. As we have said several times, inheritance is about what members of the base class are *accessible* in a derived class, not what members of the base class *exist* in a derived class object. An object of a subclass will contain **all** the members of the original base class, plus any new members defined in the derived class (see following diagram).

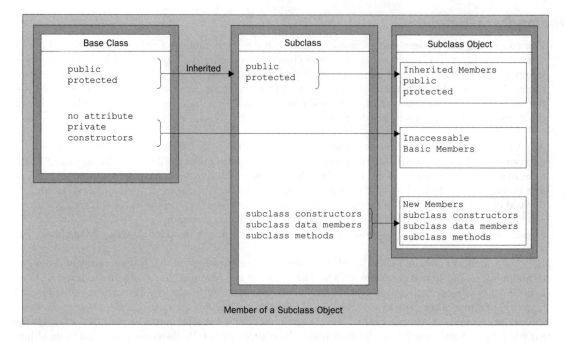

Member of a Subclass Object

The base members are all there in a derived class object – you just can't access some of them in the methods that you have defined for the derived class. The fact that you can't access some of the base class members does not mean that they are just excess baggage – they are essential members of your derived class objects. A Spaniel object needs all the Dog attributes that make it a Dog object, even though some of these may not be accessible to the Spaniel methods. Of course, the base class methods that are inherited in a derived class can access all the base class members, including those that are not inherited.

Though the base class constructors are not inherited in your derived class, you can still call them to initialize the base class members. More than that, if you don't call a base class constructor from your derived class constructor, the compiler will try to arrange to do it for you. The reasoning behind this is that since a derived class object has a base class object inside it, a good way to initialize the base part of a derived class object is using a base class constructor.

To understand this better, let's take a look at how it works in practice.

Deriving a Class

Let's take a simple example. Suppose we have defined a class to represent an animal as follows:

```
public class Animal {
  public Animal(String aType) {
    type = new String(aType);
  }

  public String toString() {
    return "This is a " + type;
  }
```

```
        private String type;
}
```

This has a member, type, to identify the type of animal, and its value is set by the constructor. We also have a toString() method for the class to generate a string representation of an object of the class.

We can now define another class, based on the class Animal, to define dogs. We can do this immediately, without affecting the definition of the class Animal. We could write the basic definition of the class Dog as:

```
public class Dog extends Animal {
  // constructors for a Dog object

    private String name;                    // Name of a Dog
    private String breed;                   // Dog breed
}
```

We use the keyword extends in the definition of a subclass to identify the name of the superclass. The class Dog will only inherit the method toString() from the class Animal, since the private data member and the constructor cannot be inherited. Of course, a Dog object will have a type data member that needs to be set to "Dog", it just can't be accessed by methods that we define in the Dog class. We have added two new instance variables in the derived class. The name member holds the name of the particular dog, and the breed member records the kind of dog it is. All we need to add is the means of creating Dog class objects.

Derived Class Constructors

We can define two constructors for the subclass Dog, one that just accepts an argument for the name of a dog, and the other accepts both a name and the breed of the Dog object. For any derived class object, we need to make sure that the private base class member, type, is properly initialized. We do this by calling a base class constructor from the derived class constructor:

```
public class Dog extends Animal {
  public Dog(String aName) {
    super("Dog");                          // Call the base constructor
    name = aName;                          // Supplied name
    breed = "Unknown";                     // Default breed value
  }

  public Dog(String aName, String aBreed) {
    super("Dog");                          // Call the base constructor
    name = aName;                          // Supplied name
    breed = aBreed;                        // Supplied breed
  }

    private String name;                    // Name of a Dog
    private String breed;                   // Dog breed
}
```

The statement in the derived class constructors that calls the base class constructor is:

```
super("Dog");                              // Call the base constructor
```

The use of the `super` keyword here as the method name calls the constructor in the superclass – the direct base class of the class `Dog`, which is the class `Animal`. This will initialize the `private` member type to `"Dog"` since this is the argument passed to the base constructor. The superclass constructor is always called in this way, in the subclass, using the name `super` rather than the constructor name `Animal`. The keyword `super` has other uses in a derived class. We have already seen that we can access a hidden member of the base class by qualifying the member name with `super`.

Calling the Base Class Constructor

You should always call an appropriate base class constructor from the constructors in your derived class. The base class constructor call must be the first statement in the body of the derived class constructor. If the first statement in a derived class constructor is not a call to a base class constructor, the compiler will insert a call to the default base class constructor for you:

```
super();                         // Call the default base constructor
```

Unfortunately, this can result in a compiler error, even though the offending statement was inserted automatically. How does this come about?

When you define your own constructor in a class, as is the case for our class `Animal`, no default constructor is created by the compiler. It assumes you are taking care of all the details of object construction, including any requirement for a default constructor. If you have not defined your own default constructor in a base class – that is, a constructor that has no parameters – when the compiler inserts a call to the default constructor from your derived class contructor, you will get a message saying that the constructor is not there.

Try It Out – Testing a Derived Class

We can try out our class `Dog` with the following code:

```
public class TestDerived {
  public static void main(String[] args) {
    Dog aDog = new Dog("Fido", "Chihuahua");     // Create a dog
    Dog starDog = new Dog("Lassie");             // Create a Hollywood dog
    System.out.println(aDog);                    // Let's hear about it
    System.out.println(starDog);                 // and the star
  }
}
```

Of course, the files containing the `Dog` and `Animal` class definition must be in the same directory as `TestDerived.java`. The example produces the rather uninformative output:

```
This is a Dog
This is a Dog
```

How It Works

Here, we create two `Dog` objects, and then output information about them using the `println()` method. This will implicitly call the `toString()` method for each. You could try commenting out the call to `super()` in the constructors of the derived class to see the effect of the compiler's efforts to call the default base class constructor.

We have called the inherited method `toString()` successfully, but this only knows about the base class data members. At least we know that the `private` member, `type`, is being set up properly. What we really need though, is a version of `toString()` for the derived class.

Overriding a Base Class Method

You can define a method in a derived class that has the same signature as a method in the base class. The access attribute for the method in the derived class can be the same as that in the base class or less restrictive, but it cannot be more restrictive. This means that if a method is declared as `public`, in the base class for example, any derived class definition of the method must also be declared as `public`. You cannot omit the access attribute in the derived class in this case, or specify it as `private` or `protected`.

When you define a new version of a base class method in this way, the derived class method will be called for a derived class object, not the method inherited from the base class. The method in the derived class **overrides** the method in the base class. The base class method is still there though, and it is still possible to call it in a derived class. Let's see an overriding method in a derived class in action.

Try It Out – Overriding a Base Class Method

We can add the definition of a new version of `toString()` to the definition of the derived class, `Dog`:

```
// Present a dog's details as a string
public String toString() {
   return "It's " + name + " the " + breed;
}
```

With this change to the example, the output will now be:

```
It's Fido the Chihuahua
It's Lassie the Unknown
```

How It Works

This method **overrides** the base class method because it has the same signature. You will recall from the last chapter that the signature of a method is determined by its name and the parameter list. So, now whenever you use the `toString()` method for a `Dog` object either explicitly or implicitly, this method will be called – not the base class method.

> Note that you are obliged to declare the `toString()` method as `public`. **When you override a base class method, you cannot change the access attributes of the new version of the method to be more stringent than that of the base class method that it overrides. Since** `public` **is the least stringent access attribute, you have no other choice.**

Of course, ideally we would like to output the member, type, of the base class, but we can't reference this in the derived class, because it is not inherited. However, we can still call the base class version of toString(). It's another job for the super keyword.

Try It Out – Calling a Base Class Method from a Derived Class

We can rewrite the derived class version of toString() to call the base method:

```
// Present a dog's details as a string
public String toString() {
   return super.toString() + "\nIt's " + name + " the " + breed;
}
```

Running the example again will produce the output:

```
This is a Dog
It's Fido the Chihuahua
This is a Dog
It's Lassie the Unknown
```

How It Works

The keyword super is used to identify the base class version of toString() that is hidden by the derived class version. We used the same notation to refer to superclass data members that were hidden by derived class data members with the same name. Calling the base class version of toString() returns the String object for the base part of the object. We then append extra information to this about the derived part of the object to produce a String object specific to the derived class.

Choosing Base Class Access Attributes

You now know the options available to you in defining the access attributes for classes you expect to use to define subclasses. You know what effect the attributes have on class inheritance, but how do you decide which you should use?

There are no hard and fast rules – what you choose will depend on what you want to do with your classes in the future, but there are some guidelines you should consider. They follow from basic object oriented principles:

❑ The methods that make up the external interface to a class should be declared as public. As long as there are no overriding methods defined in a derived class, public base class methods will be inherited and fully available as part of the external interface to the derived class. You should not normally make data members public unless they are constants intended for general use.

❑ If you expect other people will use your classes as base classes, your classes will be more secure if you keep data members private, and provide public methods for accessing and manipulating them. In this way you control how a derived class object can affect the base class data members.

❏ Making base class members `protected` allows them to be accessed from other classes in the same package, but prevents direct access from a class in another package. Base class members that are `protected` are inherited in a subclass and can, therefore, be used in the implementation of a derived class. You can use the `protected` option when you have a package of classes in which you want uninhibited access to the data members of any class within the same package, because they operate in a closely coupled way, for instance, but you want free access to be limited to subclasses in other packages.

❏ Omitting the access attribute for a class member makes it directly available to other classes in the same package, while preventing it from being inherited in a subclass that is not in the same package – it is effectively `private` when viewed from another package.

Polymorphism

Class inheritance is not just about reusing classes that you have already defined as a basis for defining a new class. It also adds enormous flexibility to the way in which you can program your applications, with a mechanism called **polymorphism**. So what is polymorphism?

The word 'polymorphism' generally means the ability to assume several different forms or shapes. In programming terms it means the ability of a single variable of a given type to be used to reference objects of different types, and to automatically call the method that is specific to the type of object the variable references. This enables a single method call to behave differently, depending on the type of the object to which the call applies.

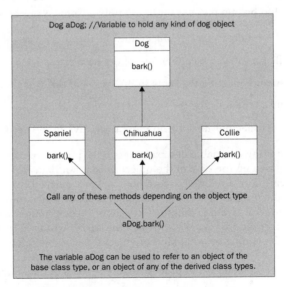

There are a few requirements that need to be fulfilled to get polymorphic behavior, so let's step through them.

First of all, polymorphism works with derived class objects. It also depends on a new capability that is possible within a class hierarchy that we haven't met before. Up to now, we have always been using a variable of a given type to reference objects of the same type. Derived classes introduce some new flexibility in this. Of course, we can store a reference to a derived class object in a variable of the derived class type, but we can also store it in a variable of any direct or indirect base class type. More than that, a reference to a derived class object *must* be stored in a variable of a direct or indirect class type for polymorphism to work. For instance, as shown in the previous diagram, a variable of type Dog can be used to store a reference to an object of any type derived from Dog. If the Dog class was derived from the Animal class here, a variable of type Animal could also be used to reference Spaniel, Chihuahua, or Collie objects.

Polymorphism means that the actual type of the object involved in a method call determines which method is called, rather than the type of the variable being used to store the reference to the object. In the previous diagram, if aDog contains a reference to a Spaniel object, the bark() method for that object will be called. If it contains a reference to a Collie object, the bark() method in the Collie class will be called. To get polymorphic operation when calling a method, the method must be a member of the base class – the class type of the variable you are using – as well that of the class type of the object involved. So in our example, the Dog class must contain a bark() method, as must each of the derived classes. You cannot call a method for a derived class object using a variable of a base class type if the method is not a member of the base class. Any definition of the method in a derived class must have the same signature and the same return type as in the base class, and must have an access specifier that is no more restrictive. Indeed, if you define a method in a derived class with the same signature as a method in a base class, any attempt to specify a different return type, or a more restrictive access specifier, will be flagged as an error by the compiler.

The conditions that need to be met if you want to use polymorphism can be summarized as:

❑ The method call for a derived class object must be through a variable of a base class type.

❑ The method called must also be a member of the base class.

❑ The method signature must be the same in the base and derived classes.

❑ The method return type must be the same in the base and derived classes.

❑ The method access specifier must be no more restrictive in the derived class than in the base.

When you call a method using a variable of a base class type, polymorphism results in the method that is called being selected based on the type of the object stored, not the type of the variable. Because a variable of a base type can store a reference to an object of any derived type, the kind of object stored will not be known until the program executes. Thus the choice of which method to execute has to be made dynamically when the program is running – it cannot be determined when the program is compiled. The bark() method that is called through the variable of type Dog in the earlier illustration, may do different things depending on what kind of object the variable references. As we will see, this introduces a whole new level of capability in programming using objects. It implies that your programs can adapt at runtime to accommodate and process different kinds of data quite automatically.

Note that polymorphism only applies to methods. It does not apply to data members. When you access a data member of a class object, the variable type always determines the class to which the data member belongs. This implies that a variable of type Dog can only be used to access data members of the Dog class. Even when it references an object of type Spaniel, for instance, you can only use it to access data members of the Dog part of a Spaniel object.

Using Polymorphism

As we have seen, polymorphism relies on the fact that you can assign an object of a subclass type to a variable that you have declared as being of a superclass type. Suppose you declare the variable:

```
Animal theAnimal;      // Declare a variable of type Animal
```

You can quite happily make this refer to an object of any of the subclasses of the class Animal. For example, you could use it to reference an object of type Dog:

```
theAnimal = new Dog("Rover");
```

As you might expect, you could also initialize the variable theAnimal when you declare it:

```
Animal theAnimal = new Dog("Rover");
```

This principle applies quite generally. You can use a variable of a base class type to store a reference to an object of any class type that you have derived, directly or indirectly, from the base. We can see what magic can be wrought with this in practice by extending our previous example. We can add a new method to the class Dog that will display the sound a Dog makes. We can add a couple of new subclasses that represent some other kinds of animals.

Try It Out – Enhancing the Dog Class

First of all we will enhance the class Dog by adding a method to display the sound that a dog makes:

```
public class Dog extends Animal {
  // A barking method
  public void sound() {
    System.out.println("Woof    Woof");
  }

  // Rest of the class as before...
}
```

We can also derive a class Cat from the class Animal:

```
public class Cat extends Animal {
  public Cat(String aName) {
    super("Cat");          // Call the base constructor
    name = aName;          // Supplied name
    breed = "Unknown";     // Default breed value
  }

  public Cat(String aName, String aBreed) {
    super("Cat");          // Call the base constructor
    name = aName;          // Supplied name
    breed = aBreed;        // Supplied breed
  }
```

```
    // Return a String full of a cat's details
    public String toString() {
      return super.toString() + "\nIt's " + name + " the " + breed;
    }

    // A miaowing method
    public void sound() {
      System.out.println("Miiaooww");
    }

    private String name;      // Name of a cat
    private String breed;     // Cat breed
}
```

Just to make it a crowd, we can derive another class – of ducks:

```
public class Duck extends Animal {
  public Duck(String aName) {
    super("Duck");           // Call the base constructor
    name = aName;            // Supplied name
    breed = "Unknown";       // Default breed value
  }

  public Duck(String aName, String aBreed) {
    super("Duck");           // Call the base constructor
    name = aName;            // Supplied name
    breed = aBreed;          // Supplied breed
  }

  // Return a String full of a duck's details
  public String toString() {
    return super.toString() + "\nIt's " + name + " the " + breed;
  }

  // A quacking method
  public void sound() {
    System.out.println("Quack quackquack");
  }

  private String name;       // Duck name
  private String breed;      // Duck breed
}
```

You can fill the whole farmyard, if you need the practice, but three kinds of animal are sufficient to show you how polymorphism works.

We need to make one change to the class Animal. To select the method sound() dynamically for derived class objects, it needs to be a member of the base class. We can add a content-free version of sound() to the class Animal:

```
class Animal {
```

```
    // Rest of the class as before...

    // Dummy method to be implemented in the derived classes
    public void sound(){}
  }
```

We need a program that will use these classes. To give the classes a workout, we can create an array of type `Animal` and populate its elements with different subclass objects. We can then select an object random from the array, so that there is no possibility that the type of the object selected is known ahead of time. Here's the code to do that:

```
import java.util.Random;

public class TryPolymorphism {
  public static void main(String[] args) {
    // Create an array of three different animals
    Animal[] theAnimals = {
                      new Dog("Rover", "Poodle"),
                      new Cat("Max", "Abyssinian"),
                      new Duck("Daffy","Aylesbury")
                   };

    Animal petChoice;                          // Choice of pet

    Random select = new Random();              // Random number generator
    // Make five random choices of pet
    for(int i = 0; i < 5; i++) {
      // Choose a random animal as a pet
      petChoice = theAnimals[select.nextInt(theAnimals.length)];

      System.out.println("\nYour choice:\n" + petChoice);
      petChoice.sound();                       // Get the pet's reaction
    }
  }
}
```

When I ran this I got the output:

```
Your choice:
This is a Duck
It's Daffy the Aylesbury
Quack quackquack
Your choice:
This is a Cat
It's Max the Abyssinian
Miiaooww

Your choice:
This is a Duck
It's Daffy the Aylesbury
Quack quackquack
```

Your choice:
This is a Duck
It's Daffy the Aylesbury
Quack quackquack

Your choice:
This is a Cat
It's Max the Abyssinian
Miiaooww

The chances are that you will get a different set from this, and a different set again when you re-run the example. The output from the example clearly shows that the methods are being selected at runtime, depending on which object happens to get stored in the variable petChoice.

How It Works

The definition of the sound() method in the Animal class has no statements in the body, so it will do nothing if it is executed. We will see a little later in this chapter how we can avoid including the empty definition for the method, but still get polymorphic behavior in the derived classes.

We need the import statement because we use a Random class object in our example to produce pseudo-random index values in the way we have seen before. The array theAnimals of type Animal contains a Dog object, a Cat object and a Duck object. We select objects randomly from this array in the for loop using the Random object, select, and store the selection in petChoice. We can then call the toString() and sound() methods using the object reference stored. The effect is that the appropriate method is selected automatically to suit the object stored, so our program operates differently depending on what type of object is referenced by petChoice.

Of course, we call the toString() method implicitly in the argument to println(). The compiler will insert a call to this method to produce a String representation of the petChoice object. The particular toString() method will automatically be selected to correspond with the type of object referenced by petChoice. This would still work even if we had not included the toString() method in the base class. We will see a little later in this chapter there is a toString() method in every class that you define, regardless of whether you define one or not.

Polymorphism is a fundamental part of object-oriented programming. We will be making extensive use of polymorphism in many of the examples we will develop later in the book, you will find that you will use it often in your own applications and applets. But this is not all there is to polymorphism in Java, and we will come back to it again later in this chapter.

Multiple Levels of Inheritance

As we indicated at the beginning of the chapter, there is nothing to prevent a derived class being used as a base class. For example, we could derive a class Spaniel from the class Dog without any problem:

Start the `Spaniel` class off with this minimal code:

```
class Spaniel extends Dog {
  public Spaniel(String aName) {
    super(aName, "Spaniel");
  }
}
```

To try this out you can add a `Spaniel` object to the array `theAnimals` in the previous example, by changing the statement to:

```
Animal[] theAnimals = {
                    new Dog("Rover", "Poodle"),
                    new Cat("Max", "Abyssinian"),
                    new Duck("Daffy","Aylesbury"),
                    new Spaniel("Fido")
                  };
```

Don't forget to add in the comma after the `Duck`. Try running the example again.

How It Works

The class `Spaniel` will inherit members from the class `Dog`, including the members of `Dog` that are inherited from the class `Animal`. The class `Dog` is a direct superclass, and the class `Animal` is an indirect superclass of the class `Spaniel`. The only additional member of `Spaniel` is the constructor. This calls the `Dog` class constructor using the keyword `super` and passes the value of aName and the `String` object "Spaniel" to it.

If you run the `TryPolymorphism` class once more, you should get a choice of the `Spaniel` object from time to time. Thus the class `Spaniel` is also participating in the polymorphic selection of the methods `toString()` and `sound()`, which in this case are inherited from the parent class, `Dog`. The inherited `toString()` method works perfectly well with the `Spaniel` object, but if you wanted to provide a unique version, you could add it to the `Spaniel` class definition. This would then be automatically selected for a `Spaniel` object rather than the method inherited from the `Dog` class.

Abstract Classes

In the class `Animal`, we introduced a version of the method `sound()` that did nothing because we wanted to call the `sound()` method in the subclass objects dynamically. The method `sound()` has no meaning in the context of the generic class `Animal`, so implementing it does not make much sense. This situation often arises in object-oriented programming. You will often find yourself creating a superclass from which you will derive a number of subclasses, just to take advantage of polymorphism.

To cater for this, Java has **abstract classes**. An abstract class is a class in which one or more methods are declared, but not defined. The bodies of these methods are omitted, because, as in the case of the method `sound()` in our class `Animal`, implementing the methods does not make sense. Since they have no definition and cannot be executed, they are called **abstract methods**. The declaration for an abstract method ends with a semi-colon and you specify the method with the keyword `abstract` to identify it as such. To define an abstract class you use the keyword `abstract` in front of the class name.

We could have defined the class `Animal` as an abstract class by amending it as follows:

```
public abstract class Animal {
  public abstract void sound();    // Abstract method

  public Animal(String aType) {
    type = new String(aType);
  }

  public String toString() {
    return "This is a " + type;
  }

  private String type;
}
```

The previous program will work just as well with these changes. It doesn't matter whether you prefix the class name with `public abstract` or `abstract public`, they are equivalent, but you should be consistent in your usage. The sequence `public abstract` is typically preferred. The same goes for the declaration of an abstract method, but both `public` and `abstract` must precede the return type specification, which is `void` in this case.

An `abstract` method cannot be `private` since a `private` method cannot be inherited, and therefore cannot be redefined in a subclass.

You cannot instantiate an object of an abstract class, but you can declare a variable of an abstract class type. With our new abstract version of the class `Animal`, we can still write:

```
Animal thePet;    // Declare a variable of type Animal
```

just as we did in the `TryPolymorphism` class. We can then use this variable to store objects of the subclasses, `Dog`, `Spaniel`, `Duck` and `Cat`.

When you derive a class from an abstract base class, you don't have to define all the abstract methods in the subclass. In this case the subclass will also be abstract and you won't be able to instantiate any objects of the subclass either. If a class is abstract, you must use the `abstract` keyword when you define it, even if it only inherits an abstract method from its superclass. Sooner or later you must have a subclass that contains no abstract methods. You can then create objects of this class.

The Universal Superclass

I must now reveal something I have been keeping from you. *All* the classes that you define are subclasses by default – whether you like it or not. All your classes have a standard class, Object, as a base, so Object is a superclass of every class. You never need to specify the class Object as a base in the definition of your classes – it happens automatically.

There are some interesting consequences of having Object as a universal superclass. For one thing, a variable of type Object can hold an object of any class type. This is useful when you want to write a method that needs to handle objects of unknown type. You can use a variable of type Object as a parameter to a method, to receive an object, and then include code in the method that figures out what kind of object it actually is (we will see something of the tools that will enable you to do this a little later in this chapter).

Of course, your classes will inherit members from the class Object. These all happen to be methods, of which seven are public, and two are protected. The seven public methods are:

Method	Purpose
toString()	This method returns a String object that describes the current object. In the inherited version of the method, this will be the name of the class, followed by '@' and the hexadecimal representation for the object. This method is called automatically when you concatenate objects with String variables using +. You can override this method in your classes to return your own String object for your class.
equals()	This compares the object passed as an argument with the current object, and returns true if they are the same object (not just equal – they must be one and the same object). It returns false if they are different objects, even if the objects have identical values for their data members.
getClass()	This method returns an object of type Class that identifies the class of the current object. We will see a little more about this later in this chapter.
hashCode()	This method calculates a hash code value for an object and returns it as type int. Hash code values are used in classes defined in the package java.util for storing objects in hash tables. We will see more about this in Chapter 12.
notify()	This is used to wake up a thread associated with the current object. We will discuss in Chapter 14 how threads work.
notifyAll()	This is used to wake up all threads associated with the current object. We will also discuss this in Chapter 14.
wait()	This method causes a thread to wait for a change in the current object. We will discuss this method in Chapter 14.

Note that getClass(), notify(), notifyAll(), and wait() cannot be overridden in your own class definitions – they are 'fixed' with the keyword final in the class definition for Object (see the section on the final modifier later in this chapter).

It should be clear now why we could get polymorphic behavior with `toString()` in our derived classes when our base class did not define the method. There is always a `toString()` method in all your classes that is inherited from `Object`.

The two `protected` methods your classes inherit from `Object` are:

Method	Purpose
`clone()`	This will create an object that is a copy of the current object regardless of type. This can be of any type as an `Object` variable can refer to an object of any class. Note that this does not work with all class objects and does not always do precisely what you want, as we will see later in this section.
`finalize()`	This is the method that is called to clean up as an object is destroyed. As you have seen in the last chapter you can override this to add your own clean-up code.

Since all your classes will inherit the methods defined in the `Object` class we should look at them in a little more detail.

The toString() Method

We have already made extensive use of the `toString()` method and you know that it is used by the compiler to obtain a `String` representation of an object when necessary. It is obvious now why we must always declare the `toString()` method as `public` in a class. It is declared as such in the `Object` class and you can't declare it as anything else.

You can see what the `toString()` method, that is inherited from class `Object`, will output for an object of one of your classes by commenting out the `toString()` method in `Animal` class in the previous example. A typical sample of the output for an object is:

```
Your choice:
Spaniel@b75778b2
It's Fido the Spaniel
Woof    Woof
```

The second line here is generated by the `toString()` method implemented in the `Object` class. This will be inherited in the `Animal` class, and it is called because we no longer override it. The hexadecimal digits following the @ in the output are the hash code of the object.

Determining the Type of an Object

The `getClass()` method, that all your classes inherit from `Object`, will return an object of type `Class` that identifies the class of an object. Suppose you have a variable `pet`, of type `Animal`, that might refer to an object of type `Dog`, `Cat`, `Duck`, or even `Spaniel`. To figure out what sort of thing it really is, you could write the following statements:

```
Class objectType = pet.getClass();            // Get the class type
System.out.println(objectType.getName());     // Output the class name
```

The method `getName()` is a member of the class `Class` which returns the fully qualified name of the class as a `String` object – the second statement will output the name of the class for the `pet` object. If `pet` referred to a `Duck` object this would output:

Duck

This is the fully qualified name in this case as the class is in the default package, which has no name. For a class defined in a named package the class name would be prefixed with the package name. If you just wanted to output the class identity you need not explicitly store the `Class` object. You can combine both statements into one:

```
System.out.println(pet.getClass().getName());   // Output the class name
```

This will produce the same output as before.

Members of the Class class

When your program is executing there are instances of the class `Class` representing each of the classes and interfaces in your program. The Java Virtual Machine generates these when your program is loaded. Since `Class` is intended for use by the Java Virtual Machine, it has no public constructors, so you can't create objects of type `Class` yourself.

`Class` defines a lot of methods, but most of them are not relevant in normal programs. The primary use you will have for `Class` is obtaining the class of an object by calling the `getClass()` method for the object as we have just discussed. However, you also get a number of other useful methods with an object of class `Class`:

Method	Purpose
forName()	You can get the `Class` object for a known class type with this method. You pass the name of the class as a `String` object to this method, and it returns a `Class` object for the class that has the name you have supplied. If no class of the type you specify exists, a `ClassNotFoundException` exception will be thrown. You can use this method to test whether an object is of a particular class type.
newInstance()	This method will call the default constructor for the class, represented by the current `Class` object, and will return the object created as type `Object`. Unless you want to store the result in a variable of type `Object`, you must cast the object to the appropriate type. When things don't work as they should, this method can throw two exceptions – `InstantiationException` or `IllegalAccessException`.
	If you use this method and don't provide for handling the exceptions, your program will not compile. We'll learn how to deal with this in the next chapter.

Table continued on following page

Method	Purpose
getSuperclass()	This method returns a `Class` object for the superclass of the class for the current `Class` object. For example, for the `Class` object `objectType` for the variable `pet` we just defined, this would return a `Class` object for the class `Animal`. You could output the name of the superclass with the statement: `System.out.println(pet.getClass().getSuperclass().getName());` Where your class is not a derived class, the method will return a `Class` object for the class `Object`.
isInterface()	This method returns `true` if the current `Class` object represents an interface. We will discuss interfaces a little later in this chapter.
getInterface()	This method will return an array of `Class` objects that represent the interfaces implemented by the class. We will investigate interfaces later in this chapter.
toString()	This method returns a `String` object representing the current `Class` object. For example, the `Class` object, `objectType`, corresponding to the `pet` variable we created would output: `class Duck`

This is not an exhaustive list. There are a number of other methods defined in the class `Class` that enable you to find out details of the contents of a class – the fields or data members in other words, the public methods defined in the class, even the classes defined in the class. If you need this kind of capability you can find out more by browsing the API documentation that comes with the JDK.

Although you can use the `forName()` method in the table above to get the `Class` object corresponding to a particular class type, there is a more direct way. If you append `.class` to the name of any class, you have a reference to the `Class` object for that class. For example, `String.class` references the `Class` object for the `String` class and `Duck.class` references the `Class` object for our `Duck` class. This may not seem particularly relevant at this point, but keep it in mind. We will need to use this later on when we get to explore the capabilities of the Java Sound API. Because there is only one `Class` object for each class or interface type, you could test for the class of an object programmatically. Given a variable, pet, of type `Animal`, we could check whether the object referenced was of type `Duck` with the statement:

```
if(pet.getClass()==Duck.class)
   System.out.println("By George - it is a duck!");
```

This tests whether the object referenced by `pet` is of type `Duck`. Because each `Class` object is unique, this is a precise test. If `pet` contained a reference to an object that was a subclass of `Duck`, the result of the comparison in the `if` would be `false`. We will see a little later in this chapter that we have an operator in Java, `instanceof`, that does almost the same thing – but not quite.

Copying Objects

As you saw in the summary at the beginning of this section, the `protected` method, `clone()`, that is inherited from the `Object` class will create a new object that is a copy of the current object. It will only do this if the class of the object to be cloned indicates that cloning is acceptable. This is the case if the class implements the `Cloneable` interface. Don't worry about what an interface is at this point – we will look into this a little later in this chapter.

The `clone()` method that is inherited from `Object` clones an object by creating a new object of the same type as the current object, and setting each of the fields in the new object to the same value as the corresponding fields in the current object. When the data members of the original object refer to class objects, the objects referred to are not duplicated when the clone is created – only the references are copied from the fields in the old object to the fields in the cloned object. This is not typically what you want to happen – both the old and the new class objects can now be modifying a single shared object that is referenced through their corresponding data members, and not recognizing that this is occurring.

If objects are to be cloned, the class must implement the `Cloneable` interface. We will discuss interfaces later in this chapter where we will see that implementing an interface typically involves implementing a specific set of methods. All that is required to make a class implement this interface is to declare it in the first line of the class definition. This is done using the `implements` keyword – for example:

```
class Dog implements Cloneable {
   // Details of the definition of the class...
}
```

This makes `Dog` objects cloneable since we have declared that the class implements the interface.

We can understand the implications of the inherited `clone()` method more clearly if we take a simple specific instance. Let's suppose we define a class `Flea` that has a method that allows the name to be changed:

```
public class Flea extends Animal implements Cloneable {
   // Constructor
   public Flea(String aName, String aSpecies) {
      super("Flea");                        // Pass the type to the base
      name = aName;                         // Supplied name
      species = aSpecies;                   // Supplied species
   }

   // Change the flea's name
   public void setName(String aName) {
      name = aName;                         // Change to the new name
   }

   // Return the flea's name
   public String getName() {
      return name;
   }

   // Return the species
   public String getSpecies() {
```

```
      return species;
    }

    public void sound() {
      System.out.println("Psst");
    }

    // Present a flea's details as a String
    public String toString() {
      return super.toString() + "\nIt's " + name + " the " + species;
    }

    // Override inherited clone() to make it public
    public Object clone() throws CloneNotSupportedException {
      return super.clone();
    }

    private String name;                      // Name of flea!
    private String species;                    // Flea species
}
```

We have defined accessor methods for the name and the species. We don't need them now but they will be useful later. By implementing the `Cloneable` interface we are indicating that we are happy to clone objects of this class. Since we have said that `Flea` is cloneable, we must implement the `Cloneable` interface in the base class, so the class `Animal` needs to be changed to:

```
public class Animal implements Cloneable {
  // Details of the class as before...
}
```

No other changes are necessary to the `Animal` class here. We can now define a class `PetDog` that contains a `Flea` object as a member that is also cloneable:

```
public class PetDog extends Animal implements Cloneable {
  // Constructor
  public PetDog(String name, String breed) {
    super("Dog");
    petFlea = new Flea("Max","circus flea");        // Initialize petFlea
    this.name = name;
    this.breed = breed;
  }

  // Rename the dog
  public void setName(String name) {
    this.name = name;
  }

  // Return the dog's name
  public String getName() {
    return name;
  }
```

```
  // Return the breed
  public String getBreed() {
    return breed;
  }

  // Return the flea
  public Flea getFlea() {
    return petFlea;
  }

  public void sound() {
    System.out.println("Woof");
  }

  // Return a String for the pet dog
  public String toString() {
    return super.toString() + "\nIt's " + name + " the "
          + breed + " & \n" + petFlea;
  }

  // Override inherited clone() to make it public
  public Object clone() throws CloneNotSupportedException {
    return super.clone();
  }

  private Flea petFlea;                  // The pet flea
  private String name;                   // Dog's name
  private String breed;                  // Dog's breed
}
```

To make it possible to clone a `PetDog` object, we override the inherited `clone()` method with a `public` version that calls the base class version. Note that the inherited method throws the `CloneNotSupportedException` so we must declare the method as shown – otherwise it won't compile. We will be looking into what exceptions are in the next chapter.

We can now create a `PetDog` object with the statement:

```
PetDog myPet = new PetDog("Fang", "Chihuahua");
```

After seeing my pet, you want one just like it, so we can clone him:

```
PetDog yourPet = (PetDog)myPet.clone();
```

Now we have individual `PetDog` objects that regrettably contain references to the same `Flea` object. The `clone()` method will create the new `PetDog` object, `yourPet`, and copy the reference to the `Flea` object from the `thePet` data member in `myPet` to the member with the same name in `yourPet`. If you decide that you prefer the name "Gnasher" for `yourPet`, we can change the name of your pet with the statement:

```
yourPet.setName("Gnasher");
```

Your dog will probably like a personalized flea too, so we can change the name of its flea with the statement:

```
yourPet.getFlea().setName("Atlas");
```

Unfortunately Fang's flea will also be given the name Atlas because, under the covers, Fang and Gnasher both share a common Flea. If you want to demonstrate this, you can put all the classes together in an example, with the following class:

```java
// Test cloning
public class TestFlea {
  public static void main(String[] args) {
    try {
      PetDog myPet = new PetDog("Fang", "Chihuahua");
      PetDog yourPet = (PetDog)myPet.clone();
      yourPet.setName("Gnasher");                    // Change your dog's name
      yourPet.getFlea().setName("Atlas");            // Change your dog's flea's name
      System.out.println("\nYour pet details:\n"+yourPet);
      System.out.println("\nMy pet details:\n"+ myPet);

    } catch(CloneNotSupportedException e) {
      e.printStackTrace(System.err);
    }
  }
}
```

Don't worry about the try and catch blocks – these are necessary to deal with the exception that we mentioned earlier. You will learn all about exceptions in Chapter 7. Just concentrate on the code between the braces following try. If you run the example it will output the details on myPet and yourPet after the name for yourPet has been changed. Both names will be the same so the output will be:

```
C:\Java\3668\Ch06\TestFlea>java TestFlea
Your pet details:
This is a Dog
It's Gnasher the Chihuahua &
This is a Flea
It's Atlas the circus flea

My pet details:
This is a Dog
It's Fang the Chihuahua &
This is a Flea
It's Atlas the circus flea
```

Choosing a name for your pet's flea has changed the name for my pet's flea too. Unless you really want to share objects between the variables in two separate objects, you should implement the `clone()` method in your class to do the cloning the way you want. As an alternative to cloning (or in addition to) you could add a constructor to your class to create a new class object from an existing object. This creates a duplicate of the original object properly. You saw how you can do this in the previous chapter. If you implement your own `public` version of `clone()` to override the inherited version, you would typically code this method in the same way as you would the constructor to create a copy of an object. You could implement the `clone()` method in the `PetDog` class like this:

```
public Object clone() throws CloneNotSupportedException {
  PetDog pet = new PetDog(name, breed);
  pet.setName("Gnasher");
  pet.getFlea().setName("Atlas");

  return pet;
}
```

Here the method creates a new `PetDog` object using the name and breed of the current object. We then call the two objects' `setName()` methods to set the clones' names. If you compile and run the program, again with this change, altering the name of `myPet` will not affect `yourPet`. Of course, you could use the inherited `clone()` method to duplicate the current object, and then explicitly clone the `Flea` member to refer to an independent object:

```
// Override inherited clone() to make it public
public Object clone() throws CloneNotSupportedException {
  PetDog pet = (PetDog)super.clone();
  pet.petFlea = (Flea)petFlea.clone();

  return pet;
}
```

The new object created by the inherited `clone()` method is of type `PetDog`, but it is returned as a reference of type `Object`. In order to access the `thePet` member, we need a reference of type `PetDog` so the cast is essential. The same is true of our cloned `Flea` object. The effect of this version of the `clone()` method is the same as the previous version.

Casting Objects

You can cast an object to another class type, but only if the current object type and the new class type are in the same hierarchy of derived classes, and one is a superclass of the other. For example, earlier in this chapter we defined the classes `Animal`, `Dog`, `Spaniel`, `Cat` and `Duck`, and these classes are related in the hierarchy shown below:

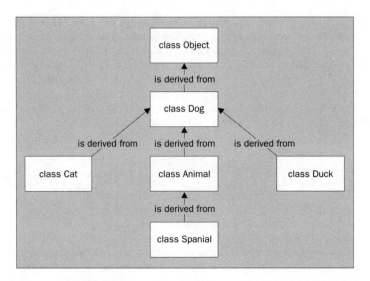

You can cast an object of a class upwards through its direct and indirect superclasses. For example, you could cast an object of type Spaniel directly to type Dog, type Animal or type Object. You could write:

```
Spaniel aPet = new Spaniel("Fang");
Animal theAnimal = (Animal)aPet;    // Cast the Spaniel to Animal
```

When you are assigning an object to a variable of a superclass type, you do not have to include the cast. You could write the assignment as:

```
Animal theAnimal = aPet;            // Cast the Spaniel to Animal
```

and it would work just as well. The compiler is always prepared to insert a cast to a superclass type when necessary.

When you cast an object to a superclass type, Java retains full knowledge of the actual class to which the object belongs. If this were not the case, polymorphism would not be possible. Since information about the original type of an object is retained, you can cast down a hierarchy as well. However, you must always write the cast explicitly since the compiler is not prepared to insert it, and the object must be a legitimate instance of the class you are casting to – that is, the class you are casting to must be the original class of the object, or must be a superclass of the object. For example, you could cast a reference stored in the variable theAnimal above to type Dog or type Spaniel, since the object was originally a Spaniel, but you could not cast it to Cat or Duck, since an object of type Spaniel does not have Cat or Duck as a superclass. To cast theAnimal to type Dog, you would write:

```
Dog aDog = (Dog)theAnimal;          // Cast from Animal to Dog
```

Now the variable aDog refers to an object of type Spaniel that also happens to be a Dog. Remember, you can only use the variable aDog to call the polymorphic methods from the class Spaniel that override methods that exist in Dog. You can't call methods that are not defined in the Dog class. If you want to call a method that is in the class Spaniel and not in the class Dog, you must first cast aDog to type Spaniel.

Although you cannot cast between unrelated objects, from Spaniel to Duck for instance, you can achieve a conversion by writing a suitable constructor but obviously, only where it makes sense to do so. You just write a constructor in the class to which you want to convert, and make it accept an object of the class you are converting from as an argument. If you really thought Spaniel to Duck was a reasonable conversion, you could add the constructor to the Duck class:

```
public Duck(Spaniel aSpaniel) {
    // Back legs off, and staple on a beak of your choice...
    super("Duck");            // Call the base constructor
    name = aSpaniel.getName();
    breed = "Barking Coot";   // Set the duck breed for a converted Spaniel
}
```

This assumes you have added a method, getName(), in the class Dog which will be inherited in the class Spaniel, and which returns the value of name for an object. This constructor accepts a Spaniel and turns out a Duck. This is quite different from a cast though. This creates a completely new object that is separate from the original, whereas a cast presents the same object as a different type.

When to Cast Objects

You will have cause to cast objects in both directions through a class hierarchy. For example, whenever you execute methods polymorphically, you will be storing objects in a variable of a base class type, and calling methods in a derived class. This will generally involve casting the derived class objects to the base class. Another reason you might want to cast up through a hierarchy is to pass an object of several possible subclasses to a method. By specifying a parameter as base class type, you have the flexibility to pass an object of any derived class to it. You could pass a Dog, Duck or Cat to a method as an argument for a parameter of type Animal, for instance.

The reason you might want to cast down through a class hierarchy is to execute a method unique to a particular class. If the Duck class has a method layEgg(), for example, you can't call this using a variable of type Animal, even though it references a Duck object. As we have already said, casting downwards through a class hierarchy always requires an explicit cast.

Try It Out – Casting Down to Lay an Egg

We'll amend the Duck class and use it along with the Animal class in an example. Add layEgg() to the Duck class as:

```
public class Duck extends Animal {
  public void layEgg() {
    System.out.println("Egg laid");
  }
    // Rest of the class as before...
}
```

If you now try to use this with the code:

```
public class LayEggs {
  public static void main(String[] args) {
```

```
        Duck aDuck = new Duck("Donald", "Eider");
        Animal aPet = aDuck;                  // Cast the Duck to Animal
        aPet.layEgg();                        // This won't compile!
    }
}
```

you will get a compiler message to the effect that layEgg() is not found in the class Animal.

Since you know this object is really a Duck, you can make it work by writing the call to layEgg() in the code above as:

```
    ((Duck)aPet).layEgg();                    // This works fine
```

The object pointed to by aPet is first cast to type Duck. The result of the cast is then used to call the method layEgg(). If the object were not of type Duck, the cast would cause an exception to be thrown.

> In general, you should avoid explicitly casting objects as much as possible, since it increases the potential for an invalid cast and can therefore make your programs unreliable. Most of the time you should find that if you design your classes carefully, you won't need explicit casts very often.

Identifying Objects

There are circumstances when you may not know exactly what sort of object you are dealing with. This can arise if a derived class object is passed to a method as an argument for a parameter of a base class type, for example, in the way we discussed in the previous section. In some situations you may need to cast it to its actual class type, perhaps to call a class specific method. If you try to make an illegal cast, an exception will be thrown, and your program will end, unless you have made provision for catching it. One way to obviate this situation is to test that the object is the type you expect before you make the cast.

We saw earlier in this chapter how we could use the getClass() method to obtain the Class object corresponding to the class type, and how we could compare it to a Class instance for the class we are looking for. You can also do this using the operator instanceof. For example, suppose you have a variable, pet, of type Animal, and you want to cast it to type Duck. You could code this as:

```
Duck aDuck;                       // Declare a duck

if(pet instanceof Duck) {
  aDuck = (Duck)pet;              // It is a duck so the cast is OK
  aDuck.layEgg();                 // and we can have an egg for tea
}
```

If pet does not refer to a Duck object, an attempt to cast the object referenced by pet to Duck would cause an exception to be thrown. This code fragment will only execute the cast and lay an egg if pet does point to a Duck object. The code fragment above could have been written much more concisely as:

```
if(pet instanceof Duck)
   ((Duck)pet).layEgg();          // It is a duck so we can have an egg for tea
```

So what is the difference between this and using `getClass()`? Well, it's quite subtle. The `instanceof` operator checks whether a cast of the object referenced by the left operand to the type specified by the right operand is legal. The result will be true if the object is the same type as the right operand, *or of any subclass type*. We can illustrate the difference by choosing a slightly different example. Suppose `pet` stores a reference to an object of type `Spaniel`. We want to call a method defined in the `Dog` class so we need to check that `pet` does really reference a `Dog` object. We can check for whether or not we have a `Dog` object with the statements:

```
if(pet instanceof Dog)
   System.out.println("We have a dog!");
else
   System.out.println("It's definitely not a dog!");
```

We will get confirmation that we have a `Dog` object here even though it is actually a `Spaniel` object. This is fine though for casting purposes. As long as the `Dog` class is in the class hierarchy for the object, the cast will work OK, so the operator is telling us what we need to know. However, suppose we write:

```
if(pet.getClass() == Dog.class)
   System.out.println("We have a dog!");
else
   System.out.println("It's definitely not a dog!");
```

Here the `if` expression will be `false` because the class type of the object is `Spaniel`, so its `Class` object is different from that of `Dog.class` – we would have to write `Spaniel.class` to get the value `true` from the `if` expression.

We can conclude from this that for casting purposes you should always use the `instanceof` operator to check the type of a reference. You only need to resort to checking the `Class` object corresponding to a reference when you need to confirm the exact type of the reference.

Designing Classes

A basic problem in object-oriented programming is deciding how the classes in your program should relate to one another. One possibility is to create a hierarchy of classes by deriving classes from a base class that you have defined, and adding methods and data members to specialize the subclasses. Our `Animal` class and the subclasses derived from it are an example of this. Another possibility is to define a set of classes which are not hierarchical, but which have data members that are themselves class objects. A `Zoo` class might well have objects of types derived from `Animal` as members, for instance. You can have class hierarchies that contain data members that are class objects – we already have this with our classes derived from `Animal` since they have members of type `String`. The examples so far have been relatively clear-cut as to which approach to choose, but it is not always so evident. Quite often you will have a choice between defining your classes as a hierarchy, and defining classes that have members that are class objects. Which is the best approach to take?

Like all questions of this kind, there are no clear-cut answers. If object-oriented programming was a process that we could specify by a fixed set of rules that you could just follow blindly, we could get the computer to do it. There are some guidelines though, and some contexts in which the answer may be more obvious.

Aside from the desirability of reflecting real-world relationships between types of objects, the need to use polymorphism is a primary reason for using subclasses (or interfaces as we shall see shortly). This is the essence of object-oriented programming. Having a range of related objects that can be treated equivalently can greatly simplify your programs. You have seen how having various kinds of animals specified by classes derived from a common base class `Animal` allows us to act on different types of animal as though they are the same, producing different results depending on what kind of animal is being dealt with, and all this automatically.

A Classy Example

Many situations involve making judgments about the design of your classes. The way to go may well boil down to a question of personal preference. Let's try to see how the options look in practice by considering a simple example. Suppose we want to define a class `PolyLine` to represent lines consisting of one or more connected segments, as illustrated in the diagram:

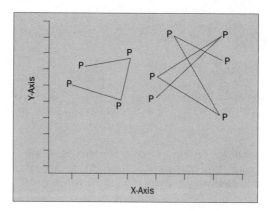

This shows two polylines, one defined by four points, the other defined by seven points.

It seems reasonable to represent points as objects of a class `Point`. Points are well-defined objects that will occur in the context of all kinds of geometric entities. We have seen a class for points earlier that we put in the package `Geometry`. Rather than repeat the whole thing, we will define the bare bones we need in this context:

```
public class Point {
  // Create a point from its coordinates
  public Point(double xVal, double yVal) {
    x = xVal;
    y = yVal;
  }

  // Create a point from another point
```

```
    public Point(Point point) {
        x = point.x;
        y = point.y;
    }

    // Convert a point to a string
    public String toString() {
        return x+","+y;
    }

    // Coordinates of the point
    protected double x;
    protected double y;
}
```

Both data members will be inherited in any subclass because they are specified as `protected`. They are also insulated from interference from outside the package containing the class. The `toString()` method will allow `Point` objects to be concatenated to a `String` object for automatic conversion – in an argument passed to the `println()` method for example.

The next question you might ask is, "Should I derive the class `PolyLine` from the class `Point`?" This has a fairly obvious answer. A polyline is clearly not a kind of point, so it is not logical to derive the class `PolyLine` from the `Point` class. This is an elementary demonstration of what is often referred to as the 'is a' test. If you can say that one kind of object 'is a' specialized form of another kind of object, you may have a good case for a derived class (but not always – there may be other reasons not to!). If not, you don't.

The complement to the 'is a' test is the **'has a'** test. If one object 'has a' component that is an object of another class, you have a case for a class member. A `House` object 'has a' door, so a `Door` variable is likely to be a member of the class `House`. Our `PolyLine` class will contain several points, which looks promising, but we should look a little more closely at how we might store them, as there are some options.

Designing the PolyLine Class

With the knowledge we have of Java, an array of `Point` objects looks like a good candidate to be a member of the class. There are disadvantages though. A common requirement with polylines is to be able to add a segment or two to an existing object. With an array storing the points, we will need to create a new array each time we add a segment, then copy all the points from the old array to the new one. This could be time consuming if we have a `PolyLine` object with a lot of segments.

We have another option. We could create a **linked list** of points. In its simplest form, a linked list of objects is an arrangement where each object in the list has a reference to the next object. As long as you have a variable containing the first `Point` object, you can access all the points in the list, as shown in the following diagram:

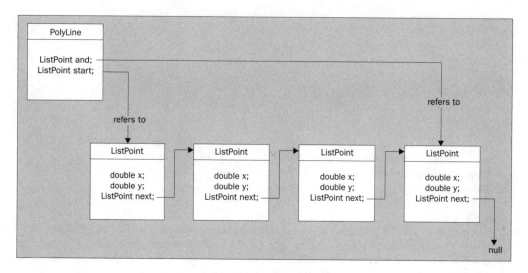

This illustrates the basic structure we might have for a linked list of points stored as a `PolyLine`. The points are stored as members of `ListPoint` objects. As well as constructors the `PolyLine` class will need a method to add points, but before we look into that, let's consider the `ListPoint` class in more detail.

There are at least three approaches you could take to define the `ListPoint` class, and there are arguments in favor of all three.

❑ You could define the `ListPoint` class with the x and y coordinates stored explicitly. The main argument against this would be that we have already encapsulated the properties of a point in the `Point` class, so why not use it.

❑ You could regard a `ListPoint` object as something that contains a reference to a `Point` object, plus members that refer to previous and following `ListPoint` objects in the list. This is not an unreasonable approach. It is easy to implement and not inconsistent with an intuitive idea of a `ListPoint`.

❑ You could view a `ListPoint` object as a specialized kind of `Point` so you would derive the `ListPoint` class from `Point`. Whether or not this is reasonable depends on whether you see this as valid. To my mind this is stretching the usual notion of a point somewhat – I would not use this.

The best option looks like the second approach. We could implement the `ListPoint` class with a data member of type `Point`, which defines a basic point with its coordinates. A `ListPoint` object would have an extra data member `next` of type `ListPoint` that is intended to contain a reference to the next object in the list. With this arrangement, you can find all the points in a `Polyline` object by starting with its `start` member that stores a reference to its first `ListPoint` object. This contains a reference to the next `ListPoint` object in its `next` member, which in turn contains a reference to the next, and so on through to the last `ListPoint` object. You will know it is the last one because its `next` member that usually points to the next `ListPoint` object will be `null`. Let's try it.

We can define the `ListPoint` class using the class `Point` with the code:

```
public class ListPoint {
  // Constructor
  public ListPoint(Point point) {
    this.point = point;           // Store point reference
    next = null;                  // Set next ListPoint as null
  }

  // Set the pointer to the next ListPoint
  public void setNext(ListPoint next) {
    this.next = next;             // Store the next ListPoint
  }

  // Get the next point in the list
  public ListPoint getNext() {
    return next;                  // Return the next ListPoint
  }

  // Return String representation
  public String toString() {
    return "(" + point + ")";
  }

    private ListPoint next;        // Refers to next ListPoint in the list
    private Point point;           // The point for this list point
}
```

How It Works

A `ListPoint` object is a means of creating a list of `Point` objects that originate elsewhere so we don't need to worry about duplicating `Point` objects stored in the list. We can just store the reference to the `Point` object passed to the constructor in the data member, `point`. The data member, `next`, should contain a reference to the next `ListPoint` in the list, and since that is not defined here, we set `next` to `null`.

The `setNext()` method will enable the `next` data member to be set for the existing last point in the list, when a new point is added to the list. A reference to the new `ListPoint` object will be passed as an argument to the method. The `getNext()` method enables the next point in the list to be determined, so this method is the means by which we can iterate through the entire list.

By implementing the `toString()` method for the class, we enable the automatic creation of a `String` representation for a `ListPoint` object when required. Here we differentiate the `String` representation of our `ListPoint` object by enclosing the `String` representation of `point` between parentheses.

We could now have a first stab at implementing the `PolyLine` class.

We can define the `PolyLine` class to use the `ListPoint` class as follows:

```
public class PolyLine {
  // Construct a polyline from an array of points
  public PolyLine(Point[] points) {
    if(points != null) {                         // Make sure there is an array
      // Create a one point list
      start = new ListPoint(points[0]);          // 1st point is the start
      end = start;                               // as well as the end

      // Now add the other points
      for(int i = 1; i < points.length; i++)
        addPoint(points[i]);
    }
  }

  // Add a Point object to the list
  public void addPoint(Point point) {
    ListPoint newEnd = new ListPoint(point);     // Create a new ListPoint
    if(start == null)
      start = newEnd;                            // Start is same as end
    else
      end.setNext(newEnd);        // Set next variable for old end as new end
      end = newEnd;                              // Store new point as end
  }

  // String representation of a polyline
  public String toString() {
    StringBuffer str = new StringBuffer("Polyline:");
    ListPoint nextPoint = start;                 // Set the 1st point as start
    while(nextPoint != null) {
      str.append(" "+ nextPoint);                // Output the current point
      nextPoint = nextPoint.getNext();           // Make the next point current
    }
    return str.toString();
  }

  private ListPoint start;                       // First ListPoint in the list
  private ListPoint end;                         // Last ListPoint in the list
}
```

You might want to be able to add a point to the list by specifying a coordinate pair. You could overload the `addPoint()` method to do this:

```
// Add a point to the list
public void addPoint(double x, double y) {
  addPoint(new Point(x, y));
}
```

We just create a new `Point` object in the expression that is the argument to the other version of `addPoint()`.

You might also want to create a `PolyLine` object from an array of coordinates. The constructor to do this would be:

```
// Construct a polyline from an array of coordinates
 public PolyLine(double[][] coords) {
   if(coords != null) {
     // Create a one point list
     start = new ListPoint(new Point(coords[0][0], coords[0][1]));
                                              // First is start
     end = start;                             // as well as end

     // Now add the other points
     for(int i = 1; i < coords.length ; i++)
       addPoint(coords[i][0], coords[i][1]);
   }
 }
```

How It Works

The `PolyLine` class has the data members `start` and `end` that we saw in the diagram. These will reference the first and last points of the list, or `null` if the list is empty. Storing the end point in the list is not essential since we could always find it by going through the list starting with start. However, having a reference to the last point saves a lot of time when we want to add a point to the list. The constructor accepts an array of `Point` objects and starts the process of assembling the object, by creating a list containing one `ListPoint` object produced from the first element in the array. It then uses the `addPoint()` method to add all the remaining points in the array to the list.

Adding a point to the list is deceptively simple. All the `addPoint()` method does is create a `ListPoint` object from the `Point` object passed as an argument, sets the `next` member of the old end point in the list to refer to the new point and finally stores a reference to the new end point in the member end.

The method `toString()` will return a string representing the `PolyLine` object as a list of point coordinates. Note how the `next` member of the `ListPoint` objects controls the loop that runs through the list. When the last `ListPoint` object is reached, the `next` member will be returned as `null`, and the `while` loop will end. We can now give the `PolyLine` class a whirl.

Try It Out – Using `PolyLine` Objects

We can create a simple example to illustrate how to use the `PolyLine` class:

```
public class TryPolyLine {
  public static void main(String[] args) {
    // Create an array of coordinate pairs
    double[][] coords = { {1., 1.}, {1., 2.}, { 2., 3.},
                          {-3., 5.}, {-5., 1.}, {0., 0.} };

    // Create a polyline from the coordinates and display it
    PolyLine polygon = new PolyLine(coords);
    System.out.println(polygon);
```

```
      // Add a point and display the polyline again
      polygon.addPoint(10., 10.);
      System.out.println(polygon);

      // Create Point objects from the coordinate array
      Point[] points = new Point[coords.length];
      for(int i = 0; i < points.length; i++)
      points[i] = new Point(coords[i][0],coords[i][1]);

      // Use the points to create a new polyline and display it
      PolyLine newPoly = new PolyLine(points);
      System.out.println(newPoly);
   }
}
```

Remember that all three classes, `Point`, `ListPoint`, and `PolyLine` need to be together in the same directory as this class. If you have keyed everything in correctly, the program will output three `PolyLine` objects.

Polyline: (1.0,1.0) (1.0,2.0) (2.0,3.0) (-3.0,5.0) (-5.0,1.0) (0.0,0.0)
Polyline: (1.0,1.0) (1.0,2.0) (2.0,3.0) (-3.0,5.0) (-5.0,1.0) (0.0,0.0)
                                     (10.0,10.0)
Polyline: (1.0,1.0) (1.0,2.0) (2.0,3.0) (-3.0,5.0) (-5.0,1.0) (0.0,0.0)

The first and the third lines of output are the same, with the coordinates from the `coords` array. The second has the extra point (10, 10) at the end.

The `PolyLine` class works well enough but it doesn't seem very satisfactory. Adding all the code to create and manage a list for what is essentially a geometric entity is not very object-oriented is it? Come to think of it, why are we making a list of points? Apart from the type of the data members of the `ListPoint` class, there's very little to do with `Point` objects in its definition, it's all to do with the linking mechanism. We might also have lots of other requirements for lists. If we were implementing an address book for instance, we would want a list of names. A cookery program would need a list of recipes. We might need lists for all kinds of things – maybe even a list of lists! Let's see if we can do better.

Let's put together a more general purpose linked list, and then use it to store polylines as before. You should save this in a new directory, as we will implement it as a whole new example.

A General-Purpose Linked List

The key to implementing a general-purpose linked list is the `Object` class that we discussed earlier in this chapter. Because the `Object` class is a superclass of every class, a variable of type `Object` can be used to store any kind of object. We could re-implement the `ListPoint` class in the form of a `ListItem` class. This will represent an element in a linked list that can reference any type of object:

```
class ListItem {
  // Constructor
  public ListItem(Object item) {
    this.item = item;            // Store the item
    next = null;                 // Set next as end point
```

```
    }

    // Return class name & object
    public String toString() {
      return "ListItem " + item ;
    }

    ListItem next;          // Refers to next item in the list
    Object item;            // The item for this ListItem
  }
```

It's basically similar to the `ListPoint` class except that we have omitted the methods to set and retrieve the next member reference. We will see why we don't need these in a moment. The `toString()` method assumes that the object referenced by item implements a `toString()` method. We won't use the `toString()` method here when we come to exercise the general linked list we are implementing, but it is a good idea to implement the `toString()` method for your classes anyway. If you do, class objects can always be output using the `println()` method which is very handy for debugging.

We can now use objects of this class in a definition of a class that will represent a linked list.

Defining a Linked List Class

The mechanics of creating and handling the linked list will be similar to what we had in the `PolyLine` class, but externally we need to deal in the objects that are stored in the list, not in terms of `ListItem` objects. In fact, we don't need to have the `ListItem` class separate from the `LinkedList` class. We can make it an inner class:

```
public class LinkedList {
  // Default constructor - creates an empty list
  public LinkedList() {}

  // Constructor to create a list containing one object
  public LinkedList(Object item) {
    if(item != null)
      current=end=start=new ListItem(item);    // item is the start and end
  }

  // Construct a linked list from an array of objects
  public LinkedList(Object[] items) {
    if(items != null) {
      // Add the items to the list

      for(int i = 0; i < items.length; i++)
        addItem(items[i]);
      current = start;
    }
  }

  // Add an item object to the list
  public void addItem(Object item) {
    ListItem newEnd = new ListItem(item); // Create a new ListItem
```

```
      if(start == null)                    // Is the list empty?
        start = end = newEnd;              // Yes, so new element is start and end
      else {                               // No, so append new element
        end.next = newEnd;                 // Set next variable for old end
        end = newEnd;                      // Store new item as end
      }
    }

    // Get the first object in the list
    public Object getFirst() {
      current = start;
      return start == null ? null : start.item;
    }

    // Get the next object in the list
    public Object getNext() {
      if(current != null)
        current = current.next;            // Get the reference to the next item
      return current == null ? null : current.item;
    }

    private ListItem start = null;         // First ListItem in the list
    private ListItem end = null;           // Last ListItem in the list
    private ListItem current = null;       // The current item for iterating
    private class ListItem {
      // Class definition as before
    }
  }
```

This will create a linked list containing any types of objects. The class has data members to track the first and last items in the list, plus the member `current`, which will be used to iterate through the list. We have three class constructors. The default constructor creates an empty list. There is a constructor to create a list with a single object, and another to create a list from an array of objects. Any list can also be extended by means of the `addItem()` method. Each of the constructors, apart from the default, sets the `current` member to the first item in the list, so if the list is not empty this will refer to a valid first item. You can see that since the `ListItem` class is a member of the `LinkedList` class, we can refer to its data members directly. This obviates the need for any methods in the `ListItem` class to get or set its fields. Since it is `private` it will not be accessible outside the `LinkedList` class so there is no risk associated with this – as long as we code the `LinkedList` class correctly of course.

The `addItem()` method works in much the same way as the `addPoint()` method did in the `PolyLine` class. It creates a new `ListItem` object, and updates the next member of the previous last item to refer to the new one. The complication is the possibility that the list might be empty. The check in the `if` takes care of this. We take special steps if `start` holds a `null` reference.

The `getFirst()` and `getNext()` methods are intended to be used together to access all the objects stored in the list. The `getFirst()` method returns the object stored in the first `ListItem` object in the list, and sets the `current` data member to refer to the first `ListItem` object. After calling the `getFirst()` method, successive calls to the `getNext()` method will return subsequent objects stored in the list. The method updates `current` to refer to the next `ListItem` object, each time it is called. When the end of the list is reached, `getNext()` returns `null`.

Try It Out – Using the General Linked List

We can now define the `PolyLine` class so that it uses a `LinkedList` object. All we need to do is to put a `LinkedList` variable as a class member that we initialize in the class constructors and implement all the other methods we had in the previous version of the class to use the `LinkedList` object:

```java
public class PolyLine {
  // Construct a polyline from an array of coordinate pairs
  public PolyLine(double[][] coords) {
    Point[] points = new Point[coords.length];   // Array to hold points

    // Create points from the coordinates
    for(int i = 0; i < coords.length ; i++)
      points[i] = new Point(coords[i][0], coords[i][1]);

    // Create the polyline from the array of points
    polyline = new LinkedList(points);
  }

  // Construct a polyline from an array of points
  public PolyLine(Point[] points) {
    polyline = new LinkedList(points);        // Create the polyline
  }

  // Add a Point object to the list
  public void addPoint(Point point) {
    polyline.addItem(point);                  // Add the point to the list
  }

  // Add a point from a coordinate pair to the list
  public void addPoint(double x, double y) {
    polyline.addItem(new Point(x, y));        // Add the point to the list
  }

  // String representation of a polyline
  public String toString() {
    StringBuffer str = new StringBuffer("Polyline:");
    Point point = (Point) polyline.getFirst();
                                              // Set the 1st point as start
    while(point != null) {
      str.append(" ("+ point+ ")");           // Append the current point
      point = (Point)polyline.getNext();      // Make the next point current
    }
    return str.toString();
  }

  private LinkedList polyline;                // The linked list of points
}
```

You can exercise this using the same code as last time – in the `TryPolyLine.java` file. Copy this file to the directory for this example.

How It Works

The `PolyLine` class implements all the methods that we had in the class before, so the `main()` method in the `TryPolyLine` class works just the same. Under the covers, the methods in the `PolyLine` class work a little differently. The work of creating the linked list is now in the constructor for the `LinkedList` class. All the `PolyLine` class constructors do is assemble a point array if necessary, and call the `LinkedList` constructor. Similarly, the `addPoint()` method creates a `Point` object from the coordinate pair it receives, and passes it to the `addItem()` method for the `LinkedList` object, `polyline`.

Note that the cast from `Point` to `Object` when the `addItem()` method is called is automatic. A cast from any class type to type `Object` is always automatic because the class is up the class hierarchy – remember that all classes have `Object` as a base. In the `toString()` method, we must insert an explicit cast to store the object returned by the `getFirst()` or the `getNext()` method. This cast is down the hierarchy so you must specify the cast explicitly.

You could use a variable of type `Object` to store the objects returned from `getFirst()` and `getNext()`, but this would not be a good idea. You would not need to insert the explicit cast, but you would lose a valuable check on the integrity of the program. You put objects of type `Point` into the list, so you would expect objects of type `Point` to be returned. An error in the program somewhere could result in an object of another type being inserted. If the object is not of type `Point` – due to the said program error for example – the cast to type `Point` will fail and you will get an exception. A variable of type `Object` can store anything. If you use this, and something other than a `Point` object is returned, it would not register at all.

Now that we have gone to the trouble of writing our own general linked list class, you may be wondering why someone hasn't done it already. Well, they have! The `java.util` package defines a `LinkedList` class that is much better than ours. Still, putting our own together was good experience, and I hope you found it educational, if not interesting. We will look at the `LinkedList` class in the `java.util` in Chapter 12.

Using the final Modifier

We have already used the keyword `final` to fix the value of a static data member of a class. You can also apply this keyword to the definition of a method, and to the definition of a class.

It may be that you want to prevent a subclass from overriding a method in your class. When this is the case, simply declare that method as `final`. Any attempt to override a `final` method in a subclass will result in the compiler flagging the new method as an error. For example, you could declare the method `addPoint()` as `final` within the class, `PolyLine`, by writing its definition in the class as:

```
public final void addPoint(Point point) {
    ListPoint newEnd = new ListPoint(point);   // Create a new ListPoint
    end.setNext(newEnd);       // Set next variable for old end as new end
    end = newEnd;              // Store new point as end
}
```

Any class derived from `PolyLine` would not be able to redefine this method. Obviously an `abstract` method cannot be declared as `final` – as it must be defined in a subclass.

If you declare a class as final, you prevent any subclasses from being derived from it. To declare the class PolyLine as final, you would define it as:

```
public final class PolyLine {
    // Definition as before...
}
```

If you now attempt to define a class based on PolyLine you will get an error message from the compiler. An abstract class cannot be declared as final since this would prevent the abstract methods in the class from ever being defined. Declaring a class as final is a drastic step that prevents the functionality of the class being extended by derivation, so you should be very sure that you want to do this.

Interfaces

In the classes that we derived from the class Animal, we had a common method, sound(), that was implemented individually in each of the subclasses. The method signature was the same in each class, and the method could be called polymorphically. The main point to defining the class Animal first, and then subsequently the classes Dog, and Cat, and so on from it, was to be able to get polymorphic behavior. When all you want is a set of one or more methods to be implemented in a number of different classes so that you can call them polymorphically, you can dispense with the base class altogether.

You can achieve the same end result much more simply by using a Java facility called an **interface**. The name indicates its primary use – specifying a set of methods that represent a particular class interface, which can then be implemented appropriately in a number of different classes. All of the classes will then share this common interface, and the methods in it can be called polymorphically. This is just one aspect of what you can do using an interface. We will start by examining what an interface is from the ground up, and then look at what we can do with it.

An **interface** is essentially a collection of related constants and/or abstract methods, and in most cases it will contain just methods. An interface doesn't define what a method does. It just defines its form – its name, its parameters, and its return type.

To make use of an interface, you **implement** the interface in a class – that is, you declare that the class implements the interface and you write the code for each of the methods declared in the interface as part of the class definition. When a class implements an interface, any constants that were defined in the interface definition are available directly in the class, just as though they were inherited from a base class. An interface can contain either constants, or abstract methods, or both.

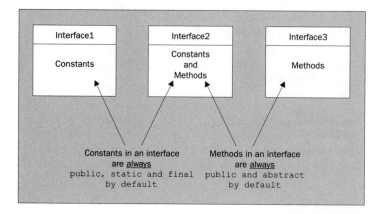

The methods in an interface are always `public` and `abstract`, so you do not need to specify them as such – it is considered to be bad programming practice to specify any attributes for them and you definitely cannot add any attributes other than the defaults, `public` and `abstract`. This implies that methods declared in an interface can never be `static` so an interface always declares instance methods. The constants in an interface are always `public`, `static` and `final`, so you do not need to specify the attributes for these either.

An interface is defined just like a class, but using the keyword `interface` rather than the keyword `class`. You store an interface definition in a `.java` file with the same name as the interface. The name that you give to an interface must be different from that of any other interface or class in the same package. Just as for classes, the members of the interface – the constants and/or method declarations – appear between braces. Let's start by looking at an interface that just defines constants.

Interfaces Containing Constants

Interfaces provide a very useful and easy to use mechanism for defining a set of constants and sharing them across several classes. Here is an interface containing only constants:

```
public interface ConversionFactors {
   double INCH_TO_MM = 25.4;
   double OUNCE_TO_GRAM = 28.349523125;
   double POUND_TO_GRAM = 453.5924;
   double HP_TO_WATT = 745.7;
   double WATT_TO_HP = 1.0/HP_TO_WATT;
}
```

You can save this in a file, `ConversionFactors.java`. Here we have five constants for conversions of various kinds – remember that constants defined in an interface are automatically `public`, `static`, and `final`. We have no choice about this – constants defined in an interface always have these attributes. Since they are static and final, you must always supply initializing values for constants defined in an interface. The names given to these use capital letters to indicate that they are `final` and cannot be altered – this is a common convention in Java. You can define the value of one constant in terms of a preceding constant, as in the definition of `WATT_TO_HP`. If you try to use a constant that is defined later in the interface – if, for example the definition for `WATT_TO_HP` appeared first – your code will not compile.

Since we have declared the interface as `public`, the constants are also available outside the package containing the `ConversionFactors` interface. You can access constants defined in an interface in the same way as for public and static fields in a class – by just qualifying the name with the name of the interface. For instance, you could write:

```
public MyClass {
   // This class can access any of the constants defined in ConversionFactors
   // by qualifying their names...
   public static double poundsToGrams(double pounds) {
      return pounds*ConversionFactors.POUND_TO_GRAM;
   }

   // Plus the rest of the class definition...
}
```

Since the `ConversionFactors` interface only includes constants, all a class has to do to gain access to them using their unqualified names is to declare that it implements the interface. For instance, here's a class that does that:

```
public MyOtherClass implements ConversionFactors {
   // This class can access any of the constants defined in ConversionFactors
   // using their unqualified names, and so can any subclasses of this class...
   public static double poundsToGrams(double pounds) {
      return pounds*POUND_TO_GRAM;
   }

   // Plus the rest of the class definition...
}
```

The constants defined in the `ConversionFactors` interface are now members of `MyOtherClass` and therefore will be inherited in any derived classes. Let's try a working class that implements `ConversionFactors`.

Try It Out – Implementing an Interface

Here's a simple class that implements the `ConversionFactors` interface:

```
public class TryConversions implements ConversionFactors {
   public static double poundsToGrams(double pounds) {
      return pounds*POUND_TO_GRAM;
   }

   public static double inchesToMillimeters(double inches) {
      return inches*INCH_TO_MM;
   }

   public static void main(String args[]) {
      int myWeightInPounds = 180;
      int myHeightInInches = 75;
      System.out.println("My weight in pounds: " +myWeightInPounds +
        " \t-in grams: "+ (int)poundsToGrams(myWeightInPounds));
```

```
     System.out.println("My height in inches: " +myHeightInInches +
       " \t-in millimeters: "+ (int)inchesToMillimeters(myHeightInInches));
   }
 }
```

Compile this with the interface definition in the same directory. When you execute it, you should see the output:

```
My weight in pounds: 180 -in grams: 81646
My height in inches: 75     -in millimeters: 1905
```

How It Works

The fact that we have only used static methods to access the constants from the interface is unimportant – it's just to keep the example simple. They are equally accessible from instance methods in a class.

The two conversion methods use the conversion factors defined in the `ConversionFactors` interface. You can see that we can use the unqualified names for the constants defined in the interface. You could delete the `implements ConversionFactors` bit from the first line, and confirm that it still works if you add the interface name as a qualifier to the references to `POUND_TO_GRAM` and `INCH_TO_MM`.

Interfaces Declaring Methods

You might also want to define an interface declaring the methods to be used for conversions:

```
public interface Conversions {
   double inchesToMillimeters (double inches);
   double ouncesToGrams(double ounces);
   double poundsToGrams(double pounds);
   double hpToWatts(double hp);
   double wattsToHP(double watts);
}
```

This interface declares five methods to perform conversions. Every method declared in the interface should have a definition within the class that implements it if you are going to create objects of the class. Since the methods in an interface are, by definition, `public`, you must use the `public` keyword when you define them in your class – otherwise your code will not compile. The implementation of an interface method in a class must not have an access specifier that is more restrictive than that implicit in the abstract method declaration, and you can't get less restrictive than `public`.

If we want to make use of this interface in the previous example as well as the `ConversionFactors` interface, we could redefine the `TryConversions` class as:

```
public class TryConversions implements ConversionFactors, Conversions {
   public double wattsToHP (double watts) {
     return watts*WATT_TO_HP;
   }
```

```
   public double hpToWatts (double hp) {
      return hp*HP_TO_WATT;
   }

   public double ouncesToGrams(double ounces) {
      return ounces*OUNCE_TO_GRAM;
   }

   public double poundsToGrams(double pounds) {
      return pounds*POUND_TO_GRAM;
   }

   public double inchesToMillimeters(double inches) {
      return inches*INCH_TO_MM;
   }

   public static void main(String args[]) {
      int myWeightInPounds = 180;
      int myHeightInInches = 75;

      TryConversions converter = new TryConversions();
      System.out.println("My weight in pounds: " +myWeightInPounds +
         " \t-in grams: "+ (int)converter.poundsToGrams(myWeightInPounds));
      System.out.println("My height in inches: " + myHeightInInches
                       + " \t-in millimeters: "
                       + (int)converter.inchesToMillimeters(myHeightInInches));
   }
}
```

Note how the methods we were using in the original definition of the class are now not declared as `static`. Since interface methods cannot be declared as `static`, we cannot make them static in the class that implements the interface. As the methods are now instance methods, we have to create a `TryConversions` object, `converter`, in order to call them.

You also may have noticed how we have implemented more than one interface in the class. A class can implement as many interfaces as you like. The names of all the interfaces that are implemented appear after the `implements` keyword separated by commas.

Of course, you don't *have to* implement every method in the interface, but there are some consequences if you don't.

A Partial Interface Implementation

You can omit the implementation of one or more of the methods from the interface in a class that implements the interface, but in this case the class inherits some abstract methods from the interface so we would need to declare the class itself as `abstract`:

```
public abstract class MyClass implements Conversions {
   // Implementation of two of the methods in the interface
   public double inchesToMillimeters(double inches) {
      return inches*INCH_TO_MM;
```

```
      }

      public double ouncesToGrams(double ounces) {
        return ounces*OUNCE_TO_GRAM;
      }

      // Definition of the rest of the class...
    }
```

You cannot create objects of type `MyClass`. To arrive at a useful class, you must define a subclass of `MyClass` that implements the remaining methods in the interface. The declaration of the class as `abstract` is mandatory when you don't implement all of the methods that are declared in an interface. The compiler will complain if you forget to do this.

Now we know how to write the code to implement an interface, we can tie up something we met earlier in this chapter. We mentioned that you need to implement the interface `Cloneable` to use the inherited method `clone()`. In fact this interface is empty with no methods or constants, so all you need to do to implement it in a class is to specify that the class in question implements. This means that you just need to write something like:

```
    public MyClass implements Cloneable {
        // Detail of the class...
    }
```

The sole purpose of the `Cloneable` interface is to act as a flag signalling that you are prepared to allow objects of your class to be cloned. Even though you have defined a public `clone()` method in your class, the compiler will not permit the `clone()` method to be called for objects of your class type unless you also specify that your class implements `Cloneable`.

Extending Interfaces

You can define one interface based on another by using the keyword `extends` to identify the base interface name. This is essentially the same form as we use to derive one class from another. The interface doing the extending acquires all the methods and constants from the interface it extends. For example, the interface `Conversions` would perhaps be more useful if it contained the constants that the interface `ConversionFactors` contains.

We could do this by defining the interface `Conversions` as:

```
    public interface Conversions extends ConversionFactors {
        double inchesToMillimeters (double inches);
        double ouncesToGrams(double ounces);
        double poundsToGrams(double pounds);
        double hpToWatts(double hp);
        double wattsToHP(double watts);
    }
```

Now the interface `Conversions` also contains the members of the interface `ConversionFactors`. Any class implementing the `Conversions` interface will have the constants from `ConversionFactors` available to implement the methods. Analogous to the idea of a superclass, the interface `ConversionFactors` is referred to as a **super-interface** of the interface `Conversions`.

Interfaces and Multiple Inheritance

Unlike a class, which can only extend one other class, an interface can extend any number of other interfaces. To define an interface that inherits the members of several other interfaces, you specify the names of the interfaces separated by commas following the keyword `extends`. For example:

```
public interface MyInterface extends HisInterface, HerInterface {
  // Interface members - constants and abstract methods...
}
```

Now `MyInterface` will inherit all the methods and constants that are members of `HisInterface` and `HerInterface`. This is described as **multiple inheritance**. In Java, classes do not support multiple inheritance, only interfaces do.

Some care is necessary when you use this capability. If two or more super-interfaces declare a method with the same signature – that is, with identical names and parameters – the method must have the same return type in all the interfaces that declare it. If they don't, the compiler will report an error. This is because it would be impossible for a class to implement both methods, as they have the same signature. If the method is declared identically in all the interfaces that declare it, then a single definition in the class will satisfy all the interfaces. As we said in the previous chapter, every method in a class must have a unique signature, and the return type is not part of it.

Using Interfaces

What you have seen up to now has primarily illustrated the mechanics of creating an interface and incorporating it into a class. The really interesting question is – what should you use interfaces for?

We have already illustrated one use for interfaces. An interface is a very handy means of packaging up constants. You can use an interface containing constants in any number of different classes that have access to the interface. All you need to do is make sure the class implements the interface and all the constants it contains are available. The constants are `static` and so will be shared among all objects of a class.

An interface that declares methods defines a standard set of operations. Different classes can add such a standard interface by implementing it. Thus objects of a number of different class types can share a common set of operations. Of course, a given operation in one class may be implemented quite differently in one class compared to another. But the way in which you invoke the operation is the same for objects of all class types that implement the interface. For this reason it is often said that an interface defines a **contract** for a set of operations.

We hinted at the third and perhaps most important use of interfaces at the beginning of this discussion. An interface defines a type, so you can expedite polymorphism across a set of classes that implement the same interface. This is an extremely useful and powerful facility. Let's have a look at how this works.

Interfaces and Polymorphism

You can't create objects of an interface type but you can create a variable of an interface type. For example:

```
Conversions converter = null;              // Variable of the Conversions
interface type
```

If we can't create objects of type `Conversions`, what good is it? Well, you use it to store a reference to an object of any class type that implements `Conversions`. This means that you can use this variable to call methods declared in the `Conversions` interface polymorphically. The `Conversions` is not a good example to show how this works. Let's consider a real world parallel that we can use to better demonstrate this idea, that of home audio/visual equipment and a remote control. I'm grateful to John Ganter who suggested this idea to me after reading a previous edition of this book.

You almost certainly have a TV, a hi-fi, a VCR, and maybe a DVD player, around your home, and each of them will have its own remote control. All the remote controls will probably have some common subset of buttons, power on/off, volume up, volume down, mute, and so on. Once you have more than four or so remotes cluttering the place up, you might consider one of these fancy universal remote control devices to replace them – sort of a single definition of a remote control, to suit all equipment.

A universal remote has a lot of similarities to an interface. By itself a universal remote does nothing. It defines a set of buttons for standard operations, but the operation of each button must be programmed specifically to suit each kind of device that you want to control. We can represent the TV, VCR, DVD, etc. by classes, each of which will make use of the same remote control interface – the set of buttons if you like, but each in a different way. Even though it uses the same button on the remote, Power On for the TV for instance is quite different from Power On for the VCR. Let's see how that might look in a concrete example.

Try It Out – Defining Interfaces

Here's how we might define an interface to model a simple universal remote:

```
public interface RemoteControl {
   boolean powerOnOff();              // Returns new state, on = true
   int volumeUp(int increment);       // Returns new volume level
   int volumeDown(int decrement);     // Returns new volume level
   void mute();                       // Mutes sound output
   int setChannel(int channel);       // Set the channel number and return it
   int channelUp();                   // Returns new channel number
   int channelDown();                 // Returns new channel number
}
```

The methods declared here in the `RemoteControl` interface should be self-explanatory. We have included just a few of the many possible remote operations here to conserve space in the book. You could add more if you want. You could have separate power on and off methods for instance, tone controls, and so on. There is no definition for any of these methods here. Methods declared in an interface are always `abstract` – by definition. There is also no access attribute for any of them. Methods declared in an interface are always `public` by default.

Now any class that requires the use of the functionality provided by a `RemoteControl` just has to declare that it implements the interface, and include the definitions for each of the methods in the interface. For example, here's the TV:

```
public class TV implements RemoteControl {
   public TV(String make, int screensize) {
      this.make = make;
      this.screensize = screensize;
```

```
      // In practice you would probably have more
      // arguments to set the max and min channel
      // and volume here plus other characteristics for a particular TV.
  }

  public boolean powerOnOff() {
    power = !power;
    System.out.println(make + " "+ screensize + " inch TV power "
                    + (power ? "on.":"off."));
    return power;
  }

  public int volumeUp(int increment) {
      if(!power)                  // If the power is off
        return 0;                 // Nothing works

    // Set volume - must not be greater than the maximum
    volume = volume+increment > MAX_VOLUME ? MAX_VOLUME : volume+increment;
    System.out.println(make + " "+ screensize + " inch TV volume level: "
                    + volume);
    return volume;
  }

  public int volumeDown(int decrement) {
    if(!power)                    // If the power is off
      return 0;                   // Nothing works

    // Set volume - must not be less than the minimum
    volume = volume-decrement < MIN_VOLUME ? MIN_VOLUME : volume-decrement;
    System.out.println(make + " "+ screensize + " inch TV volume level: "
                    + volume);
    return volume;
  }

  public void mute() {
    if(!power)                    // If the power is off
      return;                     // Nothing works

    volume = MIN_VOLUME;
    System.out.println(make + " "+ screensize + " inch TV volume level: "
                    + volume);
  }

  public int setChannel(int newChannel) {
    if(!power)                    // If the power is off
      return 0;                   // Nothing works

    // Channel must be from MIN_CHANNEL to MAX_CHANNEL
    if(newChannel>=MIN_CHANNEL && newChannel<=MAX_CHANNEL);
      channel = newChannel;
    System.out.println(make + " "+ screensize + " inch TV tuned to channel: "
                    + channel);
    return channel;
```

```
    }

    public int channelUp() {
      if(!power)                    // If the power is off
        return 0;                   // Nothing works

      // Wrap channel up to MIN_CHANNEL when MAX_CHANNEL is reached
      channel = channel<MAX_CHANNEL ? ++channel : MIN_CHANNEL;
      System.out.println(make + " "+ screensize + " inch TV tuned to channel: "
                         + channel);
      return channel;
    }

    public int channelDown() {
      if(!power)                    // If the power is off
        return 0;                   // Nothing works

      // Wrap channel down to MAX_CHANNEL when Min_CHANNEL is reached
      channel = channel>MIN_CHANNEL ? --channel : MAX_CHANNEL;
      System.out.println(make + " "+ screensize + " inch TV tuned to channel: "
                         + channel);
      return channel;
    }

    private String make = null;
    private int screensize = 0;
    private boolean power = false;

    private int MIN_VOLUME = 0;
    private int MAX_VOLUME = 100;
    private int volume = MIN_VOLUME;

    private int MIN_CHANNEL = 0;
    private int MAX_CHANNEL = 999;
    private int channel = 0;
}
```

This class implements all the methods declared in the `RemoteControl` interface, and each method
outputs a message to the command line so we'll know when it is called. Of course, if we missed out any
of the interface method definitions in the class, the class would be abstract and we would have to
declare it as such.

A VCR class might also implement `RemoteControl`:

```
public class VCR implements RemoteControl {
  public VCR(String make) {
    this.make = make;
  }

  public boolean powerOnOff() {
    power = !power;
    System.out.println(make + " VCR power "+ (power ? "on.":"off."));
```

```
      return power;
  }

  public int volumeUp(int increment) {
     if(!power)                    // If the power is off
       return 0;                   // Nothing works

    // Set volume - must not be greater than the maximum
    volume = volume+increment > MAX_VOLUME ? MAX_VOLUME : volume+increment;
    System.out.println(make + " VCR volume level: "+ volume);
    return volume;
  }

  public int volumeDown(int decrement) {
     if(!power)                    // If the power is off
       return 0;                   // Nothing works

    // Set volume - must not be less than the minimum
    volume = volume-decrement < MIN_VOLUME ? MIN_VOLUME : volume-decrement;
    System.out.println(make + " VCR volume level: "+ volume);
    return volume;
  }

  public void mute() {
     if(!power)                    // If the power is off
       return;                     // Nothing works

    volume = MIN_VOLUME;
    System.out.println(make + " VCR volume level: "+ volume);
  }

  public int setChannel(int newChannel) {
    if(!power)                     // If the power is off
      return 0;                    // Nothing works

    // Channel must be from MIN_CHANNEL to MAX_CHANNEL
    if(newChannel>=MIN_CHANNEL && newChannel<=MAX_CHANNEL)
      channel = newChannel;
    System.out.println(make + " VCR tuned to channel: "+ channel);
    return channel;
  }

  public int channelUp() {
    if(!power)                     // If the power is off
      return 0;                    // Nothing works

    // Wrap channel up to MIN_CHANNEL when MAX_CHANNEL is reached
    channel = channel<MAX_CHANNEL ? ++channel : MIN_CHANNEL;
    System.out.println(make + " VCR tuned to channel: "+ channel);
    return channel;
  }

  public int channelDown() {
```

```
      if(!power)                    // If the power is off
        return 0;                   // Nothing works

      // Wrap channel down to MAX_CHANNEL when Min_CHANNEL is reached
      channel = channel>MIN_CHANNEL ? --channel : MAX_CHANNEL;
      System.out.println(make + " VCR tuned to channel: "+ channel);
      return channel;
    }

    private String make = null;
    private boolean power = false;

    private int MIN_VOLUME = 0;
    private int MAX_VOLUME = 100;
    private int volume = MIN_VOLUME;

    private int MIN_CHANNEL = 0;
    private int MAX_CHANNEL = 99;
    private int channel = 0;
  }
```

Of course, we could continue, and define classes for other kinds of devices that used the remote, but these two will be sufficient to demonstrate the principle.

Let's see how we can use the RemoteControl interface and these two classes in a working example.

Try It Out – Polymorphism Using an Interface Type

We want to demonstrate polymorphic behavior with these classes. By introducing a bit of 'randomness' into our example, we can avoid having any prior knowledge of the objects involved. Here's the class to operate both TV and VCR objects via a variable of type RemoteControl:

```
public class TryRemoteControl {
  public static void main(String args[]) {
    RemoteControl remote = null;

    // We will create five objects to operate using our remote
    for(int i = 0 ; i<5 ; i++) {
      // Now create either a TV or a VCR at random
      if(Math.random()<0.5)
        // Random choice of TV make and screen size
        remote = new TV(Math.random()<0.5 ? "Sony" : "Hitachi",
                   Math.random()<0.5 ? 32 : 28);
      else // Random choice of VCR
        remote = new VCR(Math.random()<0.5 ? "Panasonic": "JVC");

      // Now operate it, whatever it is
      remote.powerOnOff();              // Switch it on
      remote.channelUp();               // Set the next channel up
      remote.volumeUp(10);              // Turn up the sound
    }
  }
}
```

This should be in the same directory as the other two class, and the interface. When you compile and run this, you should see output recording a random selection of five TV and VCR objects operated by our RemoteControl variable. I got:

```
Sony 28 inch TV power on.
Sony 28 inch TV tuned to channel: 1
Sony 28 inch TV volume level: 10
Panasonic VCR power on.
Panasonic VCR tuned to channel: 1
Panasonic VCR volume level: 10
Sony 32 inch TV power on.
Sony 32 inch TV tuned to channel: 1
Sony 32 inch TV volume level: 10
JVC VCR power on.
JVC VCR tuned to channel: 1
JVC VCR volume level: 10
Sony 28 inch TV power on.
Sony 28 inch TV tuned to channel: 1
Sony 28 inch TV volume level: 10
```

How It Works

The variable remote is of type RemoteControl so we can use it to store a reference to any class object that implements the RemoteControl interface. Within the for loop, we create either a TV or a VCR object at random. The TV or VCR object will be of a randomly chosen make, and any TV object will be either 28" or 32" – again chosen at random. The object that is created is then operated through remote by calling its powerOnOff(), channelUp(), and volumeUp() methods. Since the type of the object is determined at runtime, and at random, the output demonstrates we are clearly seeing polymorphism in action here through a variable of an interface type.

Using Multiple Interfaces

Of course, a RemoteControl object in the previous example can only be used to call the methods that are declared in the interface. If a class implements some other interface besides RemoteControl, then to call the methods declared in the second interface you would either need to use a variable of that interface type to store the object reference, or to cast the object reference to its actual class type. Suppose we have a class defined as:

```
public MyClass implements RemoteControl, AbsoluteControl {
    // Class definition including methods from both interfaces...
}
```

Since this class implements RemoteControl and AbsoluteControl, we can store an object of type MyClass in a variable of either interface type. For example:

```
AbsoluteControl ac = new MyClass();
```

Now we can use the variable ac to call methods declared in the AbsoluteControl interface. However, we cannot call the methods declared in the RemoteControl interface using ac, even though the object reference that it holds has these methods. One possibility is to cast the reference to the original class type, like this:

289

```
((MyClass)ac).powerOnOff();
```

Since we cast the reference to type `MyClass`, we can call any of the methods defined in that class. We can't get polymorphic behavior like this though. The compiler will determine the method that is called when the code is compiled. To call the methods in the `RemoteControl` interface polymorphically, you would have to have the reference stored as that type. Provided you know that the object is of a class type that implements the `RemoteControl` interface, you can get from the reference store in the variable `ac` to a reference of type `RemoteControl`. Like this for example:

```
if(ac instanceof RemoteControl)
  ((RemoteControl)ac).mute();
```

Even though the interfaces `RemoteControl` and `AbsoluteControl` are unrelated, you can cast the reference in `ac` to type `RemoteControl`. This is possible because the object that is referenced by `ac` is actually of type `MyClass`, which happens to implement both interfaces and therefore incorporates both interface types.

If you got a bit lost in this last section don't worry about it. You won't need this level of knowledge about interfaces very often.

Nesting Classes in an Interface Definition

You can put the definition of a class inside the definition of an interface. The class will be an inner class to the interface. An inner class to an interface will be `static` and `public` by default. The code structure would be like this:

```
interface Port {
  // Methods & Constants declared in the interface...

  class Info {
    // Definition of the class...
  }
}
```

This declares the interface, `Port`, with an inner class, `Info`. Objects of the inner class would be of type `Port.Info`. You might create one with a statement like this:

```
Port.Info info = new Port.Info();
```

The standard class library includes a number of interfaces with inner classes, including one with the name `Port` (in the `javax.sound.sampled` package) that has an inner class with the name `Info`, although the `Info` class does not have the default constructor that we have used in the illustration here. The circumstances where you might define a class as an inner class to an interface would be when objects of the inner class type have a strong logical association with the interface.

A class that implements the interface would have no direct connection with the inner class to the interface – it would just need to implement the methods declared by the interface, but it is highly likely it would make use of objects of the inner class type.

Interfaces and the Real World

An interface type is sometimes used to reference an object that encapsulates something that exists outside of Java, such as a particular physical device. This is done when the external device does not require methods implemented in Java code because all the function is provided externally. The interface method declarations just identify the mechanism for operating on the external object.

The example of the `Port` interface in the library is exactly that. A reference of type `Port` refers to an object that is a physical port on a sound card, such as that for the speaker or the microphone. The inner class, `Port.Info`, defines objects that encapsulate data to define a particular port. You can't create a `Port` object directly since there is no class of type `Port`. Indeed it doesn't necessarily make sense to do so since your system may not have any ports. Assuming your PC has sound ports you obtain a reference of type `Port` to an object that encapsulates a real port such as the microphone, by calling a static method defined in another class. The argument to the method would be a reference to an object of type `Port.Info` specifying the kind of port that you want. All of the methods defined in the `Port` interface would correspond to methods written in native machine code that would operate on the port. To call them you just use the `Port` reference that you have obtained.

Anonymous Classes

There are occasions where you need to define a class for which you will only ever want to define one object in your program, and the only use for the object is to pass it directly as an argument to a method. In this case, as long as your class extends an existing class, or implements an interface, you have the option of defining the class as an **anonymous class.** The definition for an anonymous class appears in the new expression, in the statement where you create and use the object of the class, so that there is no necessity to provide a name for the class.

We will illustrate how this is done using an example. Supposing we want to define an object of a class that implements the interface `ActionListener` for one time use. We could do this as follows:

```
pickButton.addActionListener(new ActionListener()
                          {
                            // Code to define the class
                            // that implements the ActionListener interface
                          }
                      );
```

The class definition appears in the new expression that creates the argument to the `addActionListener()` method. This method requires a reference of type `ActionListener` – in other words a reference to a class that implements the `ActionListener` interface. The parentheses following the name of the interface indicate we are creating an object reference of this type, and the details of the class definition appear between the parentheses. The anonymous class can include data members as well as methods, but obviously not constructors because the class has no name. Here all the methods declared in the `ActionListener` interface would need to be defined.

If the anonymous class extends an existing class, the syntax is much the same. In this case you are calling a constructor for the base class and, if this is not a default constructor, you can pass arguments to it by specifying them between the parentheses following the base class name. The definition of the anonymous class must appear between braces, just as in the previous example.

An anonymous class can be convenient where the class definition is short and simple. This technique should not be used extensively as it tends to make the code very difficult to understand.

Summary

You should now understand polymorphism, and how to apply it. You will find that this technique can be utilized to considerable advantage in the majority of your Java programs. It will certainly appear in many of the examples in the remaining chapters.

The important points we have covered in this chapter are:

❑   An **abstract method** is a method that has no body defined for it, and is declared using the keyword `abstract`.

❑   An **abstract class** is a class that contains one or more abstract methods. It must be defined with the attribute `abstract`.

❑   You can define one class based on another. This is called class derivation or inheritance. The base class is called a **superclass** and the derived class is called a **subclass**. A superclass can also be a subclass of another superclass.

❑   A subclass inherits certain members of its superclass. An inherited member of a class can be referenced and used as though it was declared as a normal member of the class.

❑   A subclass does not inherit the superclass constructors.

❑   The `private` members of a superclass are not inherited in a subclass. If the subclass is not in the same package as the superclass, then members of the superclass that do not have an access attribute are not inherited.

❑   The first statement in the body of a constructor for a subclass should call a constructor for the superclass. If it does not, the compiler will insert a call for the default constructor for the superclass.

❑   A subclass can re-implement, or overload, the methods inherited from its superclass. If two or more subclasses, with a common base class, re-implement a common set of methods, these methods can be selected for execution at run-time.

❑   A variable of a superclass can point to an object of any of its subclasses. Such a variable can then be used to execute the subclass methods inherited from the superclass.

❑   A subclass of an abstract class must also be declared as `abstract` if it does not provide definitions for all of the abstract methods inherited from its superclass.

❑   A class defined inside another class is called a nested class or inner class. An inner class may itself contain inner classes.

❑   An interface can contain constants, abstract methods, and inner classes.

❑   A class can implement one or more interfaces by declaring them in the class definition, and including the code to implement each of the interface methods.

❑   A class that does not define all the methods for an interface it implements must be declared as `abstract`.

❑   If several classes implement a common interface, the methods declared as members of the interface can be executed polymorphically.

Exercises

1. Define an abstract base class Shape that includes `protected` data members for the (x, y) position of a shape, a `public` method to move a shape, and a `public abstract` method `show()` to output a shape. Derive subclasses for lines, circles and rectangles. Also define the class PolyLine that you saw in this chapter with Shape as its base class. You can represent: a line as two points, a circle as a center and a radius, and a rectangle as two points on diagonally opposite corners. Implement the `toString()` method for each class. Test the classes by selecting ten random objects of the derived classes, then invoking the `show()` method for each. Use the `toString()` methods in the derived classes.

2. Define a class, ShapeList, that can store an arbitrary collection of any objects of subclasses of the Shape class.

3. Implement the classes for shapes using an interface for the common methods, rather than inheritance from the superclass, while still keeping Shape as a base class.

4. Extend the LinkedList class that we defined in this chapter so that it supports traversing the list backwards as well as forwards.

5. Add methods to the class LinkedList to insert and delete elements at the current position.

6. Implement a method in the LinkedList class to insert an object following an object passed as an argument. (Assume the objects stored in the list implement an `equals()` method that compares the This object with an object passed as an argument, and returns `true` if they are equal.)

Exceptions

Java uses exceptions as a way of signaling serious problems when you execute a program. The standard classes use them extensively. Since they arise in your Java programs when things go wrong, and if something can go wrong in your code, sooner or later it will, they are a very basic consideration when you are designing and writing your programs.

The reason we've been sidestepping the question of exceptions for the past six chapters is that you first needed to understand classes and inheritance before you could understand what an exception is, and appreciate what happens when an exception occurs. Now that you have a good grasp of these topics we can delve into how to use and deal with exceptions in a program.

In this chapter you will learn:

- ❑ What an exception is
- ❑ How you handle exceptions in your programs
- ❑ The standard exceptions in Java
- ❑ How to guarantee that a particular block of code in a method will always be executed
- ❑ How to define and use your own types of exceptions
- ❑ How to throw exceptions in your programs

The Idea Behind Exceptions

An exception usually signals an error, and is so-called because errors in your Java programs are bound to be the exception rather than the rule – by definition! An exception doesn't always indicate an error though – it can also signal some particularly unusual event in your program that deserves special attention.

If, in the midst of the code that deals with the normal operation of the program, you try to deal with the myriad, and often highly unusual, error conditions that might arise, your program structure will soon become very complicated and difficult to understand. One major benefit of having an error signaled by an exception is that it separates the code that deals with errors from the code that is executed when things are moving along smoothly. Another positive aspect of exceptions is that they provide a way of enforcing a response to particular errors – with many kinds of exceptions, you must include code in your program to deal with them, otherwise your code will not compile.

One important idea to grasp is that not all errors in your programs need to be signaled by exceptions. Exceptions should be reserved for the unusual or catastrophic situations that can arise. A user entering incorrect input to your program for instance is a normal event, and should be handled without recourse to exceptions. The reason for this is that dealing with exceptions involves quite a lot of processing overhead, so if your program is handling exceptions a lot of the time it will be a lot slower than it needs to be.

An **exception** in Java is an object that's created when an abnormal situation arises in your program. This exception object has data members that store information about the nature of the problem. The exception is said to be **thrown**, that is, the object identifying the exceptional circumstance is tossed, as an argument, to a specific piece of program code that has been written specifically to deal with that kind of problem. The code receiving the exception object as a parameter is said to **catch** it.

The situations that cause exceptions are quite diverse, but they fall into four broad categories:

Code or Data Errors	For example, you attempt an invalid cast of an object, you try to use an array index that's outside the limits for the array, or an integer arithmetic expression that has a zero divisor.
Standard Method Exceptions	For example, if you use the `substring()` method in the `String` class, it can throw a `StringIndexOutOfBoundsException` exception.
Throwing your own Exceptions	We'll see later in this chapter how you can throw a few of your own when you need to.
Java Errors	These can be due to errors in executing the Java Virtual Machine which runs your compiled program, but usually arise as a consequence of an error in your program.

Before we look at how you make provision in your programs for dealing with exceptions, we should understand what specific classes of exceptions could arise.

Types of Exceptions

An exception is always an object of some subclass of the standard class `Throwable`. This is true for exceptions that you define and throw yourself, as well as the standard exceptions that arise due to errors in your code. It's also true for exceptions that are thrown by methods in one or other of the standard packages.

Two direct subclasses of the class `Throwable` – the class `Error` and the class `Exception` – cover all the standard exceptions. Both these classes themselves have subclasses which identify specific exception conditions.

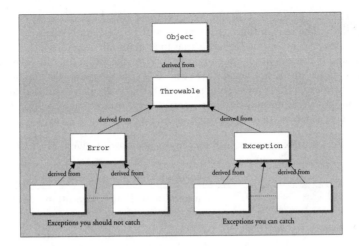

Error Exceptions

The exceptions that are defined by the class Error, and its subclasses, are characterized by the fact that they all represent conditions that you aren't expected to do anything about and, therefore, you aren't expected to catch them. There are three direct subclasses of Error – ThreadDeath, LinkageError, and VirtualMachineError. The first of these sounds the most serious, but in fact it isn't. A ThreadDeath exception is thrown whenever an executing thread is deliberately stopped, and in order for the thread to be destroyed properly you should not catch this exception. There are circumstances where you might want to – for clean-up operations for instance – in which case you must be sure to rethrow the exception to allow the thread to die. When a ThreadDeath exception is thrown and not caught, it's the thread that ends, not the program. We will deal with threads in detail in Chapter 11.

The LinkageError exception class has subclasses that record serious errors with the classes in your program. Incompatibilities between classes or attempting to create an object of a non-existent class type are the sorts of things that cause these exceptions to be thrown. The VirtualMachineError class has four subclasses that specify exceptions that will be thrown when a catastrophic failure of the Java Virtual Machine occurs. You aren't prohibited from trying to deal with these exceptions but, in general, there's little point in attempting to catch them. The exceptions that correspond to objects of classes derived from LinkageError and VirtualMachineError are all the result of catastrophic events or conditions. There is little or nothing you can do to recover from them during the execution of the program. In these sorts of situations, all you can usually do is read the error message generated by the exception, and then, particularly in the case of a LinkageError exception, try to figure out what might be wrong with your code to cause the exception to be thrown.

RuntimeException Exceptions

For almost all the exceptions that are represented by subclasses of the Exception class, you must include code in your programs to deal with them if your code may cause them to be thrown. If a method in your program has the potential to generate an exception of some such class, you must either handle the exception within the method, or register that your method may throw such an exception. If you don't, your program will not compile. We'll see in a moment how to handle exceptions and how to specify that a method can throw an exception.

One group of subclasses of Exception that are exempted from this are those derived from RuntimeException. The reason that RuntimeException exceptions are treated differently, and that the compiler allows you to ignore them, is that they generally arise because of serious errors in your code. In most situations there is little you can do to recover the situation. However, in some contexts for some of these exceptions, this is not always the case, and you may well want to include code to recognize them. There are quite a lot of subclasses of RuntimeException that are used to signal problems in various packages in the Java class library. Let's look at the exception classes that have RuntimeException as a base that are defined in the java.lang package.

The subclasses of RuntimeException defined in the standard package java.lang are:

Class Name	Exception Condition Represented
ArithmeticException	An invalid arithmetic condition has arisen such as an attempt to divide an integer value by zero.
IndexOutOfBoundsException	You've attempted to use an index that is outside the bounds of the object it is applied to. This may be an array, a String object, or a Vector object. The class Vector is defined in the standard package, java.util. We will be looking into the Vector class in Chapter 10.
NegativeArraySizeException	You tried to define an array with a negative dimension.
NullPointerException	You used an object variable containing null, when it should refer to an object for proper operation – for example, calling a method or accessing a data member.
ArrayStoreException	You've attempted to store an object in an array that isn't permitted for the array type.
ClassCastException	You've tried to cast an object to an invalid type – the object isn't of the class specified, nor is it a subclass, or a superclass, of the class specified.
IllegalArgumentException	You've passed an argument to a method which doesn't correspond with the parameter type.
SecurityException	Your program has performed an illegal operation that is a security violation. This might be trying to read a file on the local machine from an applet.
IllegalMonitor StateException	A thread has tried to wait on the monitor for an object that the thread doesn't own. (We'll look into threads in Chapter 11).
IllegalStateException	You tried to call a method at a time when it was not legal to do so.
Unsupported OperationException	Thrown if you request an operation to be carried out that is not supported.

In the normal course of events you shouldn't meet up with the last three of these. The `ArithmeticException` turns up quite easily in your programs, as does the `IndexOutOfBoundsException`. A mistake in a `for` loop limit will produce the latter. In fact there are two subclasses of `IndexOutOfBoundsException` that specify the type of exception thrown more precisely – `ArrayIndexOutOfBoundsException` and `StringIndexOutOfBoundsException`. A `NullPointerException` can also turn up relatively easily, as can `ArrayStoreException`, `ClassCastException`, and `IllegalArgumentException` surprisingly enough. The last three here arise when you are using a base class variable to call methods for derived class objects. Explicit attempts to perform an incorrect cast, or store a reference of an incorrect type or pass an argument of the wrong type to a method will all be picked up by the compiler. These exceptions can, therefore, only arise from using a variable of a base type to hold references to a derived class object

The `IllegalArgumentException` class is a base class for two further exception classes, `IllegalThreadStateException` and `NumberFormatException`. The former arises when you attempt an operation that is illegal in the current thread state. The `NumberFormatException` exception is thrown by the `valueOf()`, or `decode()` method in the classes representing integers – that is, the classes `Byte`, `Short`, `Integer`, and `Long`. The `parseXXX()` methods in these classes can also throw this exception. The exception is thrown if the `String` object passed as an argument to the conversion method is not a valid representation of an integer – if it contains invalid characters for instance. In this case a special return value cannot be used, so throwing an exception is a very convenient way to signal that the argument is invalid.

We will try out some of the `RuntimeException` exceptions later in the chapter as some of them are so easy to generate, but let's see what other sorts of exception classes have `Exception` as a base.

Other Subclasses of Exception

For all the other classes derived from the class `Exception`, the compiler will check that you've either handled the exception in a method where the exception may be thrown, or you've indicated that the method can throw such an exception. If you do neither your code won't compile. We'll look more at how we ensure the code does compile in the next two sections.

Apart from a few that have `RuntimeException` as a base, all exceptions thrown by methods in the Java class library are of a type that you must deal with. In Chapter 8 we will be looking at input and output where the code will be liberally sprinkled with provisions for exceptions being thrown.

> We'll see later in this chapter that when you want to define your own exceptions, you do this by subclassing the `Exception` class. Wherever your exception can be thrown by a method, the compiler will verify either that it is caught in the method, or that the method definition indicates that it can be thrown by the method, just as it does for the built-in exceptions.

Dealing with Exceptions

As we discussed in the previous sections, if your code can throw exceptions other than those of type `Error` or type `RuntimeException`, (you can take it that we generally include the subclasses when we talk about `Error` and `RuntimeException` exceptions) you must do something about it. Whenever you write code that can throw an exception, you have a choice. You can supply code within the method to deal with any exception that is thrown, or you can essentially ignore it by enabling the method containing the exception throwing code to pass it on to the code that called the method.

Let's first see how you can pass an exception on.

Specifying the Exceptions a Method Can Throw

Suppose you have a method which can throw an exception that is neither a subclass of `RuntimeException` nor of `Error`. This could be an `IOException` for example, which can be thrown if your method involves some file input or output operations. If the exception isn't caught and disposed of in the method, you must at least declare that the exception can be thrown. But how do you do that?

You do it simply by adding a `throws` clause in the definition of the method. Suppose we write a method that uses the methods from classes that support input/output that are defined in the package `java.io`. You'll see in the chapters devoted to I/O operations that some of these can throw exceptions represented by objects of classes `IOException` and `FileNotFoundException`. Neither of these are subclasses of `RuntimeException` or `Error`, and so the possibility of an exception being thrown needs to be declared. Since the method can't handle any exceptions it might throw, for the simple reason that we don't know how to do it yet, it must be defined as:

```
double myMethod() throws IOException, FileNotFoundException {
    // Detail of the method code...
}
```

As the fragment above illustrates, to declare that your method can throw exceptions you just put the `throws` keyword after the parameter list for the method. Then add the list of classes for the exceptions that might be thrown, separated by commas. This has a knock-on effect – if another method calls this method, it too must take account of the exceptions this method can throw. After all, calling a method that can throw an exception is clearly code where an exception may be thrown. The calling method definition must either deal with the exceptions, or declare that it can throw these exceptions as well. It's a simple choice. You either pass the buck, or decide that the buck stops here. The compiler checks for this and your code will not compile if you don't do one or the other. The reasons for this will become obvious when we look at the way a Java program behaves when it encounters an exception.

Handling Exceptions

If you want to deal with the exceptions where they occur, there are three kinds of code block that you can include in a method to handle them – try, `catch`, and `finally`:

❑ A `try` block encloses code that may give rise to one or more exceptions. Code that can throw an exception that you want to catch must be in a `try` block.

❑   A `catch` block encloses code that is intended to handle exceptions of a particular type that may be thrown in a `try` block.

❑   The code in a `finally` block is always executed before the method ends, regardless of whether any exceptions are thrown in the `try` block.

Let's dig into the detail of `try` and `catch` blocks first, then come back to the application of a `finally` block a little later.

The try Block

When you want to catch an exception, the code in the method that might cause the exception to be thrown must be enclosed in a `try` block. Code that can cause exceptions need not be in a `try` block but, in this case, the method containing the code won't be able to catch any exceptions that are thrown and it must declare that it can throw the types of exceptions that are not caught.

A `try` block is simply the keyword `try`, followed by braces enclosing the code that can throw the exception:

```
try {
   // Code that can throw one or more exceptions
}
```

Although we are discussing primarily exceptions that you must deal with here, a `try` block is also necessary if you want to catch exceptions of type `Error` or `RuntimeException`. When we come to a working example in a moment, we will use an exception type that you don't have to catch, simply because exceptions of this type are easy to generate.

The catch Block

You enclose the code to handle an exception of a given type in a `catch` block. The `catch` block must immediately follow the `try` block that contains the code that may throw that particular exception. A `catch` block consists of the keyword `catch` followed by a parameter between parentheses that identifies the type of exception that the block is to deal with. This is followed by the code to handle the exception enclosed between braces:

```
try {
   // Code that can throw one or more exceptions

} catch(ArithmeticException e) {
   // Code to handle the exception

}
```

This `catch` block only handles `ArithmeticException` exceptions. This implies this is the only kind of exception that can be thrown in the `try` block. If others can be thrown, this won't compile. We will come back to handling multiple exception types in a moment.

301

In general, the parameter for a catch block must be of type Throwable or one of the subclasses of the class Throwable. If the class that you specify as the parameter type has subclasses, the catch block will be expected to process exceptions of that class, plus all subclasses of the class. If you specified the parameter to a catch block as type RuntimeException for example, the code in the catch block would be invoked for exceptions defined by the class RuntimeException, or any of its subclasses.

We can see how this works with a simple example. It doesn't matter what the code does – the important thing is that it throws an exception we can catch.

Try It Out – Using a `try` and a `catch` Block

The following code is really just an exhaustive log of the program's execution:

```
public class TestTryCatch {
  public static void main(String[] args) {
    int i = 1;
    int j = 0;

    try {
      System.out.println("Try block entered " + "i = "+ i + " j = "+j);
      System.out.println(i/j);           // Divide by 0 - exception thrown
      System.out.println("Ending try block");

    } catch(ArithmeticException e) { // Catch the exception
      System.out.println("Arithmetic exception caught");
    }

    System.out.println("After try block");
    return;
  }
}
```

If you run the example, you should get the output:

```
Try block entered i = 1 j = 0
Arithmetic exception caught
After try block
```

How It Works

The variable j is initialized to 0, so that the divide operation in the try block will throw an ArithmeticException exception. We must use the variable j with the value 0 here because the Java compiler will not allow you to explicitly divide by zero – that is, the expression i/0 will not compile. The first line in the try block will enable us to track when the try block is entered, and the second line will throw an exception. The third line can only be executed if the exception isn't thrown – which can't occur in this example.

This shows that when the exception is thrown, control transfers immediately to the first statement in the catch block. It's the evaluation of the expression that is the argument to the println() method that throws the exception, so the println() method never gets called. After the catch block has been executed, execution then continues with the statement following the catch block. The statements in the try block following the point where the exception occurred aren't executed. You could try running the example again after changing the value of j to 1 so that no exception is thrown. The output in this case will be:

```
Try block entered i = 1 j = 1
1
Ending try block
After try block
```

From this you can see that the entire `try` block is executed. Execution then continues with the statement after the `catch` block. Because no arithmetic exception was thrown, the code in the `catch` block isn't executed.

> **You need to take care when adding `try` blocks to existing code. A `try` block is no different to any other block between braces when it comes to variable scope. Variables declared in a `try` block are only available until the closing brace for the block. It's easy to enclose the declaration of a variable in a `try` block, and, in doing so, inadvertently limit the scope of the variable and cause compiler errors.**

The `catch` block itself is a separate scope from the `try` block. If you want the catch block to output information about objects or values that are set in the `try` block, make sure the variables are declared in an outer scope.

try catch Bonding

The `try` and `catch` blocks are bonded together. You must not separate them by putting statements between the two blocks, or even by putting braces around the `try` keyword and the `try` block itself. If you have a loop block that is also a `try` block, the `catch` block that follows is also part of the loop. We can see this with a variation of the previous example.

Try It Out – A Loop Block That is a `try` Block

We can make j a loop control variable and count down so that eventually we get a zero divisor in the loop:

```java
public class TestLoopTryCatch {
  public static void main(String[] args) {
    int i = 12;

    for(int j=3 ;j>=-1 ; j--) {
      try {
        System.out.println("Try block entered " + "i = "+ i + " j = "+j);
        System.out.println(i/j);          // Divide by 0 - exception thrown
        System.out.println("Ending try block");

      } catch(ArithmeticException e) {     // Catch the exception
        System.out.println("Arithmetic exception caught");
      }
    }

    System.out.println("After try block");
    return;
  }
}
```

303

This will produce the output:

```
Try block entered i = 12 j = 3
4
Ending try block
Try block entered i = 12 j = 2
6
Ending try block
Try block entered i = 12 j = 1
12
Ending try block
Try block entered i = 12 j = 0
Arithmetic exception caught
Try block entered i = 12 j = -1
-12
Ending try block
After try block
```

How It Works

The `try` and `catch` blocks are all part of the loop since the `catch` is inextricably bound to the `try`. You can see this from the output. On the fourth iteration, we get an exception thrown because `j` is 0. However, after the `catch` block is executed, we still get one more iteration with `j` having the value –1.

Even though both the `try` and `catch` blocks are within the `for` loop, they have separate scopes. Variables declared within the `try` block cease to exist when an exception is thrown. You can demonstrate that this is so by declaring an arbitrary variable, `k` say, in the `try` block, and then adding a statement to output k in the `catch` block. Your code will not compile in this case.

Suppose you wanted the loop to end when an exception was thrown. You can easily arrange for this. Just put the whole loop in a `try` block, thus:

```
public static void main(String[] args) {
  int i = 12;
  try {
    System.out.println("Try block entered.");
    for(int j=3 ;j>=-1 ; j--) {
      System.out.println("Loop entered " + "i = "+ i + " j = "+j);
      System.out.println(i/j);          // Divide by 0 - exception thrown
    }
    System.out.println("Ending try block");

  } catch(ArithmeticException e) {     // Catch the exception
    System.out.println("Arithmetic exception caught");
  }

  System.out.println("After try block");
  return;
}
```

With this version of `main()`, the previous program will produce the output:

```
Try block entered.
Loop entered i = 12 j = 3
4
Loop entered i = 12 j = 2
6
Loop entered i = 12 j = 1
12
Loop entered i = 12 j = 0
Arithmetic exception caught
After try block
```

Now we no longer get the output for the last iteration because control passes to the catch block when the exception is thrown, and that is now outside the loop.

Multiple catch Blocks

If a try block can throw several different kinds of exception, you can put several catch blocks after the try block to handle them.

```
try {
  // Code that may throw exceptions

} catch(ArithmeticException e) {
  // Code for handling ArithmeticException exceptions
} catch(IndexOutOfBoundsException e) {
  // Code for handling IndexOutOfBoundsException exceptions
}
// Execution continues here...
```

Exceptions of type ArithmeticException will be caught by the first catch block, and exceptions of type IndexOutOfBounds Exception will be caught by the second. Of course, if an ArithmeticException exception is thrown, only the code in that catch block will be executed. When it is complete, execution continues with the statement following the last catch block.

When you need to catch exceptions of several different types for a try block, the order of the catch blocks can be important. When an exception is thrown, it will be caught by the first catch block that has a parameter type that is the same as that of the exception, *or a type that is a superclass of the type of the exception.* An extreme case would be if you specified the catch block parameter as type Exception. This will catch any exception that is of type Exception, or of a class type that is derived from Exception. This includes virtually all the exceptions you are likely to meet in the normal course of events.

This has implications for multiple catch blocks relating to exception class types in a hierarchy. The catch blocks must be in sequence with the most derived type first, and the most basic type last. Otherwise your code will not compile. The simple reason for this is that if a catch block for a given class type precedes a catch block for a type that is derived from the first, the second catch block can never be executed and the compiler will detect that this is the case.

Suppose you have a catch block for exceptions of type ArithmeticException, and another for exceptions of type Exception as a catch-all. If you write them in the following sequence, exceptions of type ArithmeticException could never reach the second catch block as they will always be caught by the first.

```
// Invalid catch block sequence - won't compile!
try {
  // try block code

} catch(Exception e) {
  // Generic handling of exceptions
} catch(ArithmeticException e) {
  // Specialized handling for these exceptions
}
```

Of course, this won't get past the compiler – it would be flagged as an error.

To summarize – if you have `catch` blocks for several exception types in the same class hierarchy, you must put the `catch` blocks in order, starting with the lowest subclass first, and then progressing to the highest superclass.

In principle, if you're only interested in generic exceptions, all the error handling code can be localized in one `catch` block for exceptions of the superclass type. However, in general it is more useful, and better practice, to have a `catch` block for each of the specific types of exceptions that a `try` block can throw.

The finally Block

The immediate nature of an exception being thrown means that execution of the `try` block code breaks off, regardless of the importance of the code that follows the point at which the exception was thrown. This introduces the possibility that the exception leaves things in an unsatisfactory state. You might have opened a file, for instance, and because an exception was thrown, the code to close the file is not executed.

The `finally` block provides the means for you to clean up at the end of executing a `try` block. You use a `finally` block when you need to be sure that some particular code is run before a method returns, no matter what exceptions are thrown within the previous `try` block. A `finally` block is always executed, regardless of what happens during the execution of the method. If a file needs to be closed, or a critical resource released, you can guarantee that it will be done if the code to do it is put in a `finally` block.

The `finally` block has a very simple structure:

```
finally {
  // Clean-up code to be executed last
}
```

Just like a `catch` block, a `finally` block is associated with a particular `try` block, and it must be located immediately following any `catch` blocks for the `try` block. If there are no `catch` blocks then you position the `finally` block immediately after the `try` block. If you don't do this, your program will not compile.

> The primary purpose for the `try` block is to identify code that may result in an exception being thrown. However, you can use it to contain code that doesn't throw exceptions for the convenience of using a `finally` block. This can be useful when the code in the `try` block has several possible exit points – `break` or `return` statements for example, but you always want to have a specific set of statements executed after the `try` block has been executed to make sure things are tidied up – such as closing any open files. You can put these in a `finally` block. Note: if a value is returned within a `finally` block, this return overrides any return executed in the `try` block.

Structuring a Method

We've looked at the blocks you can include in the body of a method, but it may not always be obvious how they are combined. The first thing to get straight is that a `try` block, plus any corresponding `catch` blocks, and the `finally` block all bunch together in that order:

```
try {
  // Code that may throw exceptions...

} catch(ExceptionType1 e) {
  // Code to handle exceptions of type ExceptionType1 or subclass
} catch(ExceptionType2 e) {
  // Code to handle exceptions of type ExceptionType2 or subclass
... // more catch blocks if necessary
} finally {
  // Code always to be executed after try block code

}
```

You can't have just a `try` block by itself. Each `try` block must always be followed by at least one block that is either a `catch` block or a `finally` block.

You must not include other code between a `try` block and its `catch` blocks, or between the `catch` blocks and the `finally` block. You can have other code that doesn't throw exceptions after the `finally` block, and you can have multiple `try` blocks in a method. In this case, your method might be structured as shown in the following diagram.

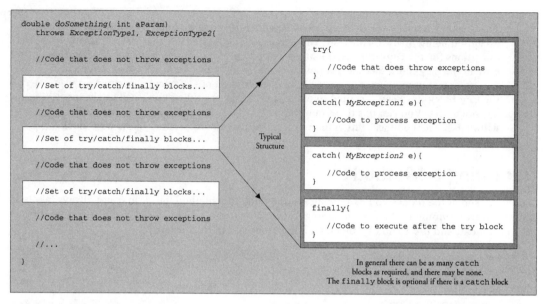

```
double doSomething( int aParam)
    throws ExceptionType1, ExceptionType2{

    //Code that does not throw exceptions

    //Set of try/catch/finally blocks...

    //Code that does not throw exceptions

    //Set of try/catch/finally blocks...

    //Code that does not throw exceptions

    //Set of try/catch/finally blocks...

    //Code that does not throw exceptions

    //...

}
```

Typical Structure

```
try{
    //Code that does throw exceptions
}

catch( MyException1 e){
    //Code to process exception
}

catch( MyException2 e){
    //Code to process exception
}

finally{
    //Code to execute after the try block
}
```

In general there can be as many `catch` blocks as required, and there may be none. The `finally` block is optional if there is a `catch` block

In many cases, a method will only need a single `try` block followed by all the `catch` blocks for the exceptions that need to be processed in the method, perhaps followed by a `finally` block. Java, however, gives you the flexibility to have as many `try` blocks as you want. This makes it possible for you to separate various operations in a method by putting each of them in their own `try` block – an exception thrown as a result of a problem with one operation does not prevent subsequent operations from being executed.

The `throws` clause that follows the parameter list for the method identifies exceptions that can be thrown in this method, but which aren't caught by any of the `catch` blocks within the method. We saw this earlier in this chapter. Exceptions that aren't caught can be thrown by code anywhere in the body of the method – in code not enclosed by a `try` block.

Execution Sequence

We saw how the sequence of execution proceeded with the simple case of a `try` block and a single `catch` block. We also need to understand the sequence in which code is executed when we have the `try-catch-finally` combinations of blocks, when different exceptions are thrown. This is easiest to comprehend by considering an example. We can use the following code to create a range of exceptions and conditions.

Try It Out – Execution Sequence of a `try` Block

It will be convenient, in this example, to use an input statement to pause the program. The method we will use can throw an exception of a type defined in the `java.io` package. We will start by importing the `java.io.IOException` class into the source file. We will give the class containing `main()` the name `TryBlockTest`, and we will define another method, `divide()`, in this class that will be called in `main()`. The overall structure of the `TryBlockTest` class source file will be:

```
import java.io.IOException;

public class TryBlockTest {
```

```
    public static void main(String[] args) {
      // Code for main()..
    }

    // Divide method
    public static int divide(int[] array, int index) {
      // Code for divide()...
    }
  }
```

The idea behind the divide() method is to pass it an array and an index as arguments. By choosing the
values in the array and the index value judiciously, we can get ArithmeticException and
ArrayIndexOutOfBoundsException exceptions thrown. We'll need a try block plus two catch blocks
for the exceptions, and we will throw in a finally block for good measure. Here's the code for divide():

```
    public static int divide(int[] array, int index) {
      try {
        System.out.println("\nFirst try block in divide() entered");
        array[index + 2] = array[index]/array[index + 1];
        System.out.println("Code at end of first try block in divide()");
        return array[index + 2];

      } catch(ArithmeticException e) {
        System.out.println("Arithmetic exception caught in divide()");
      } catch(ArrayIndexOutOfBoundsException e) {
        System.out.println("Index-out-of-bounds exception caught in divide()");
      } finally {
        System.out.println("finally block in divide()");
      }

      System.out.println("Executing code after try block in divide()");
      return array[index + 2];
    }
```

We can define the main() method with the following code:

```
    public static void main(String[] args) {
      int[] x = {10, 5, 0};                    // Array of three integers

      // This block only throws an exception if method divide() does
      try {
        System.out.println("First try block in main() entered");
        System.out.println("result = " + divide(x,0));  // No error
        x[1] = 0;                              // Will cause a divide by zero
        System.out.println("result = " + divide(x,0));  // Arithmetic error
        x[1] = 1;                              // Reset to prevent divide by zero
        System.out.println("result = " + divide(x,1));  // Index error

      } catch(ArithmeticException e) {
        System.out.println("Arithmetic exception caught in main()");
      } catch(ArrayIndexOutOfBoundsException e) {
        System.out.println("Index-out-of-bounds exception caught in main()");
```

```
      }

        System.out.println("Outside first try block in main()");
        System.out.println("\nPress Enter to exit");

        // This try block is just to pause the program before returning
        try {
          System.out.println("In second try block in main()");
          System.in.read();                 // Pauses waiting for input...
          return;

        } catch(IOException e) {            // The read() method can throw exceptions
          System.out.println("I/O exception caught in main()");
        } finally {                            // This will always be executed
          System.out.println("finally block for second try block in main()");
        }

        System.out.println("Code after second try block in main()");
    }
```

Because the read() method for the object in (this object represents the standard input stream, analogous to out) can throw an I/O exception, it must itself be called in a try block and have an associated catch block, unless we chose to add a throws clause to the header line of main().

If you run the example it will produce the output:

```
First try block in main()entered

First try block in divide() entered
Code at end of first try block in divide()
finally block in divide()
result = 2

First try block in divide() entered
Arithmetic exception caught in divide()
finally block in divide()
Executing code after try block in divide()
result = 2

First try block in divide() entered
Index-out-of-bounds exception caught in divide
finally block in divide()
Executing code after try block in divide()
Index-out-of-bounds exception caught in main()
Outside first try block in main()

Press Enter to exit
In second try block in main()

finally block for second try block in main()
```

How It Works

All the try, catch, and finally blocks in the example have output statements so we can trace the sequence of execution.

Within the divide() method the code in the try block can throw an arithmetic exception if the element array[index + 1] of the array passed to it is 0. It can also throw an ArrayIndexOutOfBounds exception in the try block if the index value passed to it is negative, or it results in index + 2 being beyond the array limits. Both these exceptions are caught by one or other of the catch blocks so they will not be apparent in the calling method main().

Note, however, that the last statement in divide() can also throw an index-out-of-bounds exception:

```
return array[index+2];
```

This statement is outside the try block so the exception will not be caught. The exception will therefore be thrown by the method when it is called in main(). However, we aren't obliged to declare that the divide() method throws this exception because the ArrayIndexOutOfBoundsException class is a subclass of RuntimeException, and is therefore exempted from the obligation to deal with it.

The main() method has two try blocks. The first try block encloses three calls to the divide() method. The first call will execute without error; the second call will cause an arithmetic exception in the method; and the third call will cause an index-out-of-bounds exception. There are two catch blocks for the first try block in main() to deal with these two potential exceptions.

The read() method in the second try block in main() can cause an I/O exception to be thrown. Since this is one of the exceptions that the compiler will check for, we must either put the statement that calls the read() method in a try block, and have a catch block to deal with the exception, or declare that main() throws the IOException exception. If we don't do one or the other, the program will not compile.

Using the read() method in this way has the effect of pausing the program until the *Enter* key is pressed. We'll be looking at read(), and other methods for I/O operations, in the next four chapters. The class IOException is in the package java.io, so we need the import statement for this class because we refer to it in the catch block. Remember that only classes defined in java.lang are included in your program automatically.

Normal Execution of a Method

The first line of output from the example, TryBlockTest, indicates that execution of the try block in main() has begun. The next block of four lines of output from the example is the result of a straightforward execution of the method divide(). No exceptions occur in divide(), so no catch blocks are executed.

The code at the end of the method divide(), following the catch blocks, isn't executed because the return statement in the try block ends the execution of the method. However, the finally block in divide() is executed before the return to the calling method occurs. If you comment out the return statement at the end of the divide() method's try block and run the example again, the code that follows the finally block will be executed.

The sequence of execution when no exceptions occur is shown in the diagram.

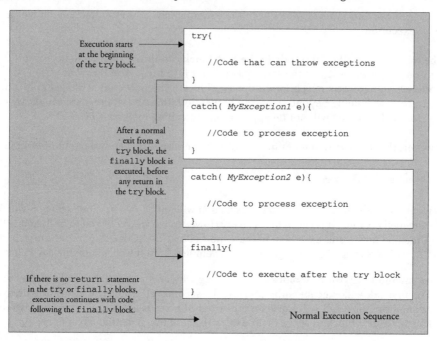

The previous diagram illustrates the normal sequence of execution in an arbitrary `try-catch-finally` set of blocks. If there's a `return` statement in the `try` block, this will be executed immediately after the `finally` block completes execution – so this prevents the execution of any code following the `finally` block. A `return` statement in a `finally` block will cause an immediate return to the calling point and the code following the `finally` block wouldn't be executed in this case.

Execution when an Exception is Thrown

The next block of five lines in the output correspond to an `ArithmeticException` being thrown and caught in the method `divide()`. The exception is thrown because the value of the second element in the array x is zero. When the exception occurs, execution of the code in the `try` block is stopped, and you can see that the code that follows the `catch` block for the exception in the `divide()` method is then executed. The `finally` block executes next, followed by the code after the `finally` block. The value in the last element of the array isn't changed from its previous value, because the exception occurs during the computation of the new value, before the result is stored.

The general sequence of execution in an arbitrary `try-catch-finally` set of blocks when an exception occurs is shown here.

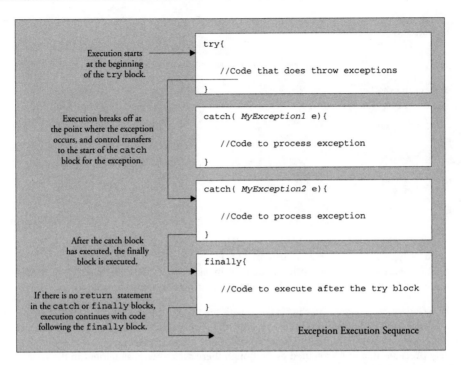

```
try{

    //Code that does throw exceptions

}
```
Execution starts at the beginning of the try block.

```
catch( MyException1 e){

    //Code to process exception

}
```
Execution breaks off at the point where the exception occurs, and control transfers to the start of the catch block for the exception.

```
catch( MyException2 e){

    //Code to process exception

}
```

```
finally{

    //Code to execute after the try block

}
```
After the catch block has executed, the finally block is executed.

If there is no return statement in the catch or finally blocks, execution continues with code following the finally block.

Exception Execution Sequence

Execution of the try block stops at the point where the exception occurs, and the code in the catch block for the exception is executed immediately. If there is a return statement in the catch block, this isn't executed until after the finally block has been executed. As discussed earlier, if a return statement that returns a value is executed within a finally block, that value will be returned, not the value from any previous return statement.

Execution when an Exception is not Caught

The next block of six lines in the output is a consequence of the third call to the method divide(). This causes an ArrayIndexOutOfBoundsException to be thrown in the try block, which is then caught. However, the code at the end of the method which is executed after the finally block, throws another exception of this type. This can't be caught in the method divide() because the statement causing it isn't in a try block. Since this exception isn't caught in the method divide(), the method terminates immediately and the same exception is thrown in main() at the point where the divide() method was called. This causes the code in the relevant catch block in main() to be executed in consequence.

An exception that isn't caught in a method is always propagated upwards to the calling method. It will continue to propagate up through each level of calling method until either it is caught, or the main() method is reached. If it isn't caught in main(), the program will terminate and a suitable message will be displayed. This situation is illustrated here.

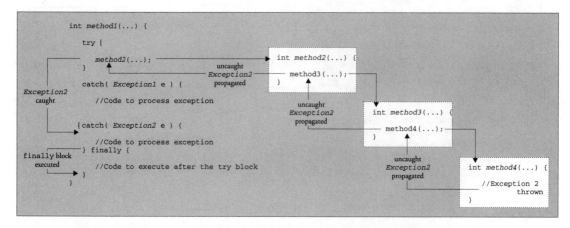

This shows `method1()` calling `method2()` which calls `method3()`, which calls `method4()` in which an exception of type `Exception2` is thrown. This exception isn't caught in `method4()` so execution of `method4()` ceases and the exception is thrown in `method3()`. It isn't caught, and continues to be rethrown until it reaches `method1()` where there's a `catch` block to handle it.

In our *Try It Out*, execution continues in `main()` with the output statements outside the first `try` block. The `read()` method pauses the program until you press the *Enter* key. No exception is thrown, and execution ends after the code in the `finally` block is executed. The `finally` block is tied to the `try` block that immediately precedes it, and is executed even though there's a `return` statement in the `try` block.

Nested try Blocks

We will not be going into these in detail, but you should note that you can have nested `try` blocks, as illustrated in this diagram.

```
try {

    try {

        //1st inner try block code...

    } catch( Exception1 ) {

        //...

    }

    //Outer try block code...

    try {

        //2nd inner try block code...

    } catch( Exception1 e ) {

        //try block code...

    }

} catch( Exception2 e ){

    //Outer catch block code...

}
```

Exceptions of type `Exception2` thrown anywhere in here that are not caught, will be caught by the `catch` block for the outer `try` block.

The `catch` blocks for the outer `try` block can catch any exceptions that are thrown, but not caught, by any code within the block, including code within inner `try-catch` blocks. In the example shown, the `catch` block for the outer `try` block will catch any exception of type `Exception2`. Such exceptions could originate anywhere within the outer `try` block. The illustration shows two levels of nesting, but you can specify more if you know what you're doing.

Rethrowing Exceptions

Even though you may need to recognize that an exception has occurred in a method by implementing a `catch` clause for it, this is not necessarily the end of the matter. In many situations, the calling program may need to know about it – perhaps because it will affect the continued operation of the program, or because the calling program may be able to compensate for the problem.

If you need to pass an exception that you have caught on to the calling program, you can rethrow it from within the `catch` block using a `throw` statement. For example:

```
try {
  // Code that originates an arithmetic exception

} catch(ArithmeticException e) {
  // Deal with the exception here
  throw e;              // Rethrow the exception to the calling program
}
```

The `throw` statement is the keyword `throw` followed by the exception object to be thrown. When we look at how to define our own exceptions later in this chapter, we'll be using exactly the same mechanism to throw them.

Exception Objects

Well, you now understand how to put `try` blocks together with `catch` blocks and `finally` blocks in your methods. You may be thinking, at this point, that it seems a lot of trouble to go to, just to display a message when an exception is thrown. You may be right, but whether you can do very much more depends on the nature and context of the problem. In many situations a message may be the best you can do, although you can produce messages that are a bit more informative than those we've used so far in our examples. For one thing we have totally ignored the exception object that is passed to the `catch` block.

The exception object that is passed to a `catch` block can provide additional information about the nature of the problem that originated it. To understand more about this, let's first look at the members of the base class for exceptions `Throwable`, because these will be inherited by all exception classes and are therefore contained in every exception object that is thrown.

The Class Throwable

The class Throwable is the class from which all Java exception classes are derived – that is, every exception object will contain the methods defined in this class. The class Throwable has two constructors, a default constructor, and a constructor that accepts an argument of type String. The String object that is passed to the constructor is used to provide a description of the nature of the problem causing the exception. Both constructors are public.

Objects of type Throwable contain two items of information about an exception:

❑   A message, that we have just referred to as being initialized by a constructor

❑   A record of the **execution stack** at the time the object was created

The execution stack keeps track of all the methods that are in execution at any given instant. It provides the means whereby executing a return gets back to the calling point for a method. The record of the execution stack that is stored in the exception object will consist of the line number in the source code where the exception originated followed by a trace of the method calls that immediately preceded the point at which the exception occurred. This is made up of the fully qualified name for each of the methods called, plus the line number in the source file where each method call occurred. The method calls are in sequence with the most recent method call appearing first. This will help you to understand how this point in the program was reached.

The Throwable class has the following public methods that enable you to access the message and the stack trace:

Method	Description
getMessage()	This returns the contents of the message, describing the current exception. This will typically be the fully qualified name of the exception class (it will be a subclass of Throwable), and a brief description of the exception.
printStackTrace()	This will output the message and the stack trace to the standard error output stream – which is the screen in the case of a console program.
printStackTrace (PrintStream s)	This is the same as the previous method except that you specify the output stream as an argument. Calling the previous method for an exception object, e, is equivalent to: e.printStackTrace(System.err);

There's another method, fillInStackTrace(), which will update the stack trace to the point at which this method is called. For example, if you put a call to this method in the catch block:

```
e.fillInStackTrace();
```

The line number recorded in the stack record for the method in which the exception occurred will be the line where fillInStackTrace() is called. The main use of this is when you want to rethrow an exception (so it will be caught by the calling method) and record the point at which it is rethrown. For example:

```
    e.fillInStackTrace();            // Record the throw point
    throw e;                         // Rethrow the exception
```

In practice, it's often more useful to throw an exception of your own. We'll see how to define your own exceptions in the next section, but first, let's exercise some of the methods defined in the `Throwable` class, and see the results.

Try It Out – Dishing the Dirt on Exceptions

The easiest way to try out some of the methods we've just discussed is to make some judicious additions to the catch blocks in the `divide()` method we have in the `TryBlockTest` class example:

```
public static int divide(int[] array, int index) {
  try {
    System.out.println("\nFirst try block in divide() entered");
    array[index + 2] = array[index]/array[index + 1];
    System.out.println("Code at end of first try block in divide()");
    return array[index + 2];

  } catch(ArithmeticException e) {
    System.err.println("Arithmetic exception caught in divide()\n" +
                       "\nMessage in exception object:\n\t" +
                       e.getMessage());
    System.err.println("\nStack trace output:\n");
    e.printStackTrace();
    System.err.println("\nEnd of stack trace output\n");
  } catch(ArrayIndexOutOfBoundsException e) {
    System.err.println("Index-out-of-bounds exception caught in divide()\n" +
                       "\nMessage in exception object:\n\t" + e.getMessage());
    System.err.println("\nStack trace output:\n");
    e.printStackTrace();
    System.out.println("\nEnd of stack trace output\n");
  } finally {
    System.err.println("finally clause in divide()");
  }
  System.out.println("Executing code after try block in divide()");
  return array[index + 2];
}
```

If you recompile the program and run it again, it will produce all the output, as before, but with extra information when exceptions are thrown in the `divide()` method. The new output generated for the `ArithmeticException` will be:

```
Message in exception object:
       / by zero

Stack trace output:

java.lang.ArithmeticException: / by zero
       at TryBlockTest.divide(TryBlockTest.java:54)
       at TryBlockTest.main(TryBlockTest.java:15)
```

317

```
        End of stack trace output
```

The additional output generated for the `ArrayIndexOutOfBoundsException` will be:

```
        Message in exception object:
                null

        Stack trace output:

        java.lang.ArrayIndexOutOfBoundsException
                at TryBlockTest.divide(TryBlockTest.java:54)
                at TryBlockTest.main(TryBlockTest.java:17)

        End of stack trace output
```

How It Works

The extra lines of code in each of the `catch` blocks in the `divide()` method output the message associated with the exception object e, by calling its `getMessage()` method. We could have just put e here which would invoke the `toString()` method for e and, in this case, the class name for e would precede the message. These are a couple of extra `println()` calls around the call to `printStackTrace()` to make it easier to find the stack trace in the output. These are called for the standard error stream object, `System.err`, for consistency with the stack trace output.

The first stack trace, for the arithmetic exception, indicates that the error originated at line 54 in the source file, `TryBlockText.java`, and the last method call was at line 15 in the same source file. The second stack trace provides similar information about the index-out-of-bounds exception, including the offending index value. As you can see, with the stack trace output, it's very easy to see where the error occurred, and how this point in the program was reached.

Standard Exceptions

The majority of predefined exception classes in Java don't add further information about the conditions that created the exception. The type alone serves to differentiate one exception from another in most cases. This general lack of additional information is because it can only be gleaned, in the majority of cases, by prior knowledge of the computation that is being carried out when the exception occurs, and the only person who is privy to that is you, since you're writing the program.

This should spark the glimmer of an idea. If you need more information about the circumstances surrounding an exception, you're going to have to obtain it, and, equally important, communicate it to the appropriate point in your program. This leads to the notion of defining your own exceptions.

Defining Your Own Exceptions

There are two basic reasons for defining your own exception classes:

❑   You want to add information when a standard exception occurs, and you can do this by rethrowing an object of your own exception class.

❑ You may have error conditions that arise in your code that warrant the distinction of a special exception class.

However, you should bear in mind that there's a lot of overhead in throwing exceptions, so it is not a valid substitute for 'normal' recovery code that you would expect to be executed frequently. If you have recovery code that will be executed often, then it doesn't belong in a `catch` block, rather in something like an `if-then-else` loop.

Let's see how to create our own exceptions.

Defining an Exception Class

Your exception classes must always have `Throwable` as a superclass, otherwise they will not define an exception. Although you can derive them from any of the standard exceptions, your best policy is to derive them from the `Exception` class. This will allow the compiler to keep track of where such exceptions are thrown in your program, and check that they are either caught or declared as thrown in a method. If you use `RuntimeException` or one of its subclasses, the compiler checking for `catch` blocks of your exception class will be suppressed.

Let's go through an example of how you define an exception class:

```
public class DreadfulProblemException extends Exception {
  // Constructors
  public DreadfulProblemException(){ }        // Default constructor

  public DreadfulProblemException(String s) {
    super(s);                          // Call the base class constructor
  }
}
```

This is the minimum you should supply. By convention, your exception should include a default constructor and a constructor that accepts a `String` object as an argument. The message stored in the superclass, `Exception` (in fact in `Throwable`, which is the superclass of `Exception`), will automatically be initialized with the name of your class, whichever constructor for your class objects is used. The `String` passed to the second constructor will be appended to the name of the class to form the message stored in the exception object.

Of course, you can add other constructors. In general, you'll want to do so, particularly when you're rethrowing your own exception after a standard exception has been thrown. In addition, you'll typically want to add instance variables to the class that store additional information about the problem, plus methods that will enable the code in a `catch` block to get at the data. Since your exception class is ultimately derived from `Throwable`, the stack trace information will be automatically available for your exceptions.

Throwing Your Own Exception

As we saw earlier, we throw an exception with a statement that consists of the keyword `throw`, followed by an exception object. This means you can throw your own exception with the statements:

```
DreadfulProblemException e = new DreadfulProblemException();
throw e;
```

The method will cease execution at this point – unless the code snippet above is in a `try` or a `catch` block with an associated `finally` clause; the contents of which will be executed before the method ends. The exception will be thrown in the calling program at the point where this method was called. The message in the exception object will only consist of the qualified name of our exception class.

If you wanted to add a specific message to the exception, you could define it as:

```
DreadfulProblemException e = new DreadfulProblemException("Uh-Oh, trouble.");
```

We're using a different constructor here. In this case the message stored in the superclass will be a string which consists of the class name with the string passed to the constructor appended to it. The `getMessage()` method inherited from `Throwable` will, therefore, return a `String` object containing the string:

```
"DreadfulProblemException: Uh-Oh, trouble."
```

You can also create an exception object and throw it in a single statement. For example:

```
throw new DreadfulProblemException("Terrible difficulties");
```

In all the examples, the stack trace record inherited from the superclass, `Throwable`, will be set up automatically.

An Exception Handling Strategy

You should think through what you want to achieve with the exception handling code in your program. There are no hard and fast rules. In some situations you may be able to correct a problem and enable your program to continue as though nothing happened. In other situations outputting the stack trace and a fast exit will be the best approach – a fast exit being achieved by calling the `exit()` method in the `System` class. Here we'll take a look at some of the things you need to weigh up when deciding how to handle exceptions.

Consider the last example where we handled arithmetic and index-out-of-bounds exceptions in the method, `divide()`. While this was a reasonable demonstration of the way the various blocks worked, it wasn't a satisfactory way of dealing with the exceptions in the program, for at least two reasons. First, it does not make sense to catch the arithmetic exceptions in the `divide()` method without passing them on to the calling method. After all, it was the calling method that set the data up, and only the calling program has the potential to recover the situation. Second, by handling the exceptions completely in the `divide()` method, we allow the calling program to continue execution, without any knowledge of the problem that arose. In a real situation this would undoubtedly create chaos, as further calculations would proceed with erroneous data.

We could have simply ignored the exceptions in the `divide()` method. This might not be a bad approach in this particular situation, but the first problem the calling program would have is determining the source of the exception. After all, such exceptions might also arise in the calling program itself. A second consideration could arise if the `divide()` method was more complicated. There could be several places where such exceptions might be thrown, and the calling method would have a hard time distinguishing them.

An Example of an Exception Class

Another possibility is to catch the exceptions in the method where they originate, then pass them on to the calling program. You can pass them on by throwing new exceptions that provide more **granularity** in identifying the problem (by having more than one exception type, or by providing additional data within the new exception type). For example, you could define more than one exception class of your own that represented an `ArithmeticException`, where each reflected the specifics of a particular situation. This situation is illustrated here.

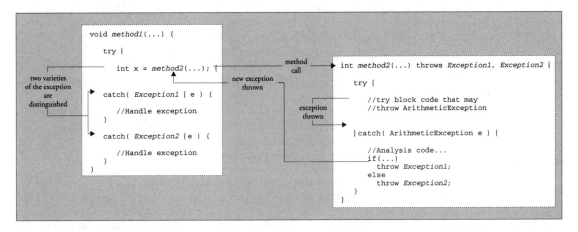

This shows how two different circumstances causing an `ArithmeticException` in `method2()`, are differentiated in the calling method, `method1()`. The method, `method2()`, can either throw an exception of type `Exception1`, or of type `Exception2`, depending on the analysis that is made in the `catch` block for the `ArithmeticException` type. The calling method has a separate `catch` block for each of the exceptions that may be thrown.

You could also define a new exception class that had instance variables to identify the problem more precisely. Let's suppose that in the last example, we wanted to provide more information to the calling program about the error that caused each exception in the `divide()` method. The primary exception can be either an `ArithmeticException` or an `ArrayIndexOutOfBoundsException`, but since we're dealing with a specific context for these errors we could give the calling program more information by throwing our own exceptions.

Let's take the `ArithmeticException` case as a model and define our own exception class to use in the program to help identify the reason for the error more precisely.

Try It Out – Define Your Own Exception Class

We can define the class which will correspond to an `ArithmeticException` in the method `divide()` as:

```
public class ZeroDivideException extends Exception {
  private int index = -1;        // Index of array element causing error

  // Default Constructor
  public ZeroDivideException(){ }

  // Standard constructor
  public ZeroDivideException(String s) {
    super(s);                              // Call the base constructor
  }

  public ZeroDivideException(int index) {
    super("/ by zero");                    // Call the base constructor
    this.index = index;                    // Set the index value
  }

  // Get the array index value for the error
  public int getIndex() {
    return index;                          // Return the index value
  }
}
```

How It Works

As we've derived the class from the class `Exception`, the compiler will check that the exceptions thrown are either caught, or identified as thrown in a method. Our class will inherit all the members of the class `Throwable` via the `Exception` class, so we'll get the stack trace record and the message for the exception maintained for free. It will also inherit the `toString()` method which is satisfactory in this context, but this could be overridden if desired.

We've added a data member, `index`, to store the index value of the zero divisor in the array passed to `divide()`. This will give the calling program a chance to fix this value if appropriate in the `catch` block for the exception. In this case the catch block would also need to include code that would enable the `divide()` method to be called again with the corrected array.

Let's now put it to work in our first `TryBlockTest` code example.

Try It Out – Using the Exception Class

We need to use the class in two contexts – in the method `divide()` when we catch a standard `ArithmeticException`, and in the calling method, `main()`, to catch the new exception. Let's modify `divide()` first:

```
public static int divide(int[] array, int index) throws ZeroDivideException {
  try {
    System.out.println("First try block in divide() entered");
    array[index + 2] = array[index]/array[index + 1];
```

```
     System.out.println("Code at end of first try block in divide()");
     return array[index + 2];

   } catch(ArithmeticException e) {
     System.out.println("Arithmetic exception caught in divide()");
     throw new ZeroDivideException(index + 1);  // Throw new exception
   } catch(ArrayIndexOutOfBoundsException e) {
     System.out.println(
               "Index-out-of-bounds index exception caught in divide()");
   }
   System.out.println("Executing code after try block in divide()");
   return array[index + 2];
 }
```

The first change is to add the `throws` clause to the method definition. Without this we'll get an error message from the compiler. The second change adds a statement to the `catch` block for `ArithmeticException` exceptions that throws a new exception.

This new exception needs to be caught in the calling method `main()`:

```
public static void main(String[] args) {
   int[] x = {10, 5, 0};                   // Array of three integers

   // This block only throws an exception if method divide() does
   try {
     System.out.println("First try block in main()entered");
     System.out.println("result = " + divide(x,0));  // No error
     x[1] = 0;                             // Will cause a divide by zero
     System.out.println("result = " + divide(x,0));  // Arithmetic error
     x[1] = 1;                             // Reset to prevent divide by zero
     System.out.println("result = " + divide(x,1));  // Index error

   } catch(ZeroDivideException e) {
     int index = e.getIndex();            // Get the index for the error
     if(index > 0) {                      // Verify it is valid and now fix the array
       x[index] = 1;                      // ...set the divisor to 1...
       x[index + 1] = x[index - 1];       // ...and set the result
       System.out.println("Zero divisor corrected to " + x[index]);
     }

   } catch(ArithmeticException e) {
     System.out.println("Arithmetic exception caught in main()");
   } catch(ArrayIndexOutOfBoundsException e) {
     System.out.println("Index-out-of-bounds exception caught in main()");
   }
   System.out.println("Outside first try block in main()");
 }
```

How It Works

All we need to add is the `catch` block for the new exception. We need to make sure that the index value for the divisor stored in the exception object is positive so that another exception is not thrown when we fix up the array. As we arbitrarily set the array element that contained the zero divisor to 1, it makes sense to set the array element holding the result to the same as the dividend. We can then let the method `main()` stagger on.

> A point to bear in mind is that the last two statements in the `try` block will not have been executed. After the `catch` block has been executed, the method continues with the code following the try-catch block set. In practice you would need to consider whether to ignore this. One possibility is to put the whole of the `try-catch` block code in `main()` in a loop that would normally only run one iteration, but where this could be altered to run additional iterations by setting a flag in the `catch` block.

This is a rather artificial example – so what sort of circumstances could justify this kind of fixing up of the data in a program? If the data originated through some kind of instrumentation measuring physical parameters such as temperatures or pressures, the data may contain spurious zero values from time to time. Rather than abandon the whole calculation you might well want to amend these as they occurred, and press on to process the rest of the data.

Summary

In this chapter you have learned what exceptions are and how to deal with them in your programs. You should make sure that you consider exception handling as an integral part of developing your Java programs. The robustness of your program code depends on how effectively you deal with exceptions that can be thrown within it.

The important concepts we have explored in this chapter are:

- ❑ Exceptions identify errors that arise in your program.

- ❑ Exceptions are objects of subclasses of the class `Throwable`.

- ❑ Java includes a set of standard exceptions that may be thrown automatically, as a result of errors in your code, or may be thrown by methods in the standard classes in Java.

- ❑ If a method throws exceptions that aren't caught, and aren't represented by subclasses of the class `Error`, or by subclasses of the class `RuntimeException`, then you must identify the exception classes in a `throws` clause in the method definition.

- ❑ If you want to handle an exception in a method, you must place the code that may generate the exception in a `try` block. A method may have several `try` blocks.

- ❑ Exception handling code is placed in a `catch` block that immediately follows the `try` block that contains the code that can throw the exception. A `try` block can have multiple `catch` blocks that deal with different types of exception.

❑ A `finally` block is used to contain code that must be executed after the execution of a `try` block, regardless of how the `try` block execution ends. A `finally` block will always be executed before execution of the method ends.

❑ You can throw an exception by using a `throw` statement. You can throw an exception anywhere in a method. You can also rethrow an existing exception in a `catch` block to pass it to the calling method.

❑ You can define your own exception classes that, in general, should be derived from the class `Exception`.

Exercises

1. Write a program that will generate exceptions of type `NullPointerException`, `NegativeArraySizeException`, and `IndexOutOfBoundsException`. Record the catching of each exception by displaying the message stored in the exception object, and the stack trace record.

2. Add an exception class to the last example that will differentiate between the index-out-of-bounds error possibilities, rethrow an appropriate object of this exception class in `divide()`, and handle the exception in `main()`.

3. Write a program that calls a method which throws an exception of type `ArithmeticException` at a random iteration in a `for` loop. Catch the exception in the method, and pass the iteration count when the exception occurred to the calling method, by using an object of an exception class you define.

4. Add a `finally` block to the method in the previous example to output the iteration count when the method exits.

Understanding Streams

This is the first of four chapters devoted to streams and file input/output. This chapter introduces **streams**, and deals with keyboard input, and output to the command line.

By the end of this chapter, you will have learned:

- ❏ What is a stream and what are the main classes that Java provides to support stream operations.
- ❏ What are stream readers and writers and what they are used for.
- ❏ How to read data from the keyboard.
- ❏ How to format data that you write to the command line.

Streams and the New I/O Capability

The package that supports stream input/output is `java.io`, and it is vast. It defines around fifty classes, many of which have a large number of methods. It is therefore quite impractical to go into them all in detail in a book of this kind. Refer to the java documentation for more information. Our strategy in this, and the following three chapters, will be to take a practical approach. The idea is to provide an overall grounding of the concepts involved, and to equip you with enough detailed knowledge to be able to do a number of specific, useful, and practical things in your programs. These are:

- ❏ To be able to read data of various kinds from the keyboard.
- ❏ To be able to create formatted output to the command line.
- ❏ To be able to read and write files containing basic data.
- ❏ To be able to read and write files containing objects.

To achieve this, we will give you an overview of what the important stream classes do, and how they interrelate, together with the classes that operate on streams. We will go into detail selectively, just exploring the classes and methods that we need to accomplish specific things. We will also be sticking to the latest and greatest I/O capability in the JDK 1.4, which makes it unnecessary to delve into a lot of the original stream classes.

Up to and including Java 1.3, the only way to read and write files was to use a **stream**. Java 1.4 introduced a new I/O capability in the `java.nio` and `java.nio.channels` packages for reading and writing files that contain data of the primitive Java types, including strings. This capability completely supersedes the stream I/O capability in this context. It is much more efficient, and in many ways easier to use, so we will limit our discussions of streams for handling files to the extent necessary to understand the new I/O capability. We will go into the new I/O capability in detail in the next two chapters.

Two areas where you must still use the facilities provided by the stream classes are reading from the keyboard, and writing to the command line. We will cover both of these in this chapter along with some general aspects of the stream classes and the relationships between them. The new I/O capability does not provide for objects to be written and read, so you still need to use streams for this. We will look into how we read and write objects to a file in Chapter 11 *Serializing Objects*.

Understanding Streams

A **stream** is an abstract representation of an input or output device that is a source of, or destination for, data. You can write data to a stream and read data from a stream. You can visualize a stream as a sequence of bytes that flows into or out of your program.

When you write data to a stream, the stream is called an **output stream**. The output stream can go to any device to which a sequence of bytes can be transferred, such as a file on a hard disk, or a phone line connecting your system to a remote system. An output stream can also go to your display screen, but only at the expense of limiting it to a fraction of its true capability. This is output to the command line. When you write to your display screen using a stream, it can only display characters, not graphical output. Graphical output requires more specialized support that we will discuss from Chapter 15 onwards. Note that while a printer can be considered notionally as a stream, printing in Java does not work this way. A printer in Java is treated as a graphical device, so sending output to the printer is very similar to displaying graphical output on your display screen. You will learn how printing works in Java in Chapter 20.

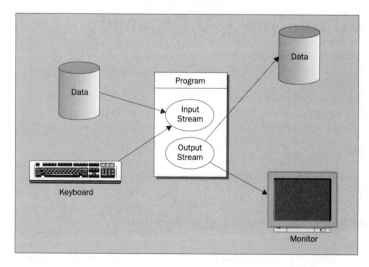

You read data from an **input stream**. In principle, this can be any source of serial data, but is typically a disk file, the keyboard, or a remote computer.

Under normal circumstances, file input and output for the machine on which your program is executing is only available to Java applications. It is not available to Java applets except to a strictly limited extent. If this were not so, a malicious Java applet embedded in a web page could trash your hard disk. An IOException will normally be thrown by any attempted operation on disk files on the local machine in a Java applet. The directory containing the .class file for the applet, and its subdirectories, are freely accessible to the applet. Also, the security features in Java can be used to control what an applet (and an application running under a Security Manager) can access so that an applet can only access files or other resources *for which it has explicit permission*.

The main reason for using a stream as the basis for input and output operations is to make your program code for these operations independent of the device involved. This has two advantages. First, you don't have to worry about the detailed mechanics of each device, which are taken care of behind the scenes. Second, your program will work for a variety of input/output devices without any changes to the code.

Stream input and output methods generally permit very small amounts of data, such as a single character or byte, to be written or read in a single operation. Transferring data to or from a stream like this may be extremely inefficient, so a stream is often equipped with a **buffer** in memory, in which case it is called a **buffered stream**. A buffer is simply a block of memory that is used to batch up the data that is transferred to or from an external device. Reading or writing a stream in reasonably large chunks will reduce the number of input/output operations necessary, and thus make the process more efficient.

When you write to a buffered output stream, the data is sent to the buffer, and not to the external device. The amount of data in the buffer is tracked automatically, and the data is usually sent to the device when the buffer is full. However, you will sometimes want the data in the buffer to be sent to the device before the buffer is full, and there are methods provided to do this. This operation is usually termed **flushing** the buffer.

Buffered input streams work in a similar way. Any read operation on a buffered input stream will read data from the buffer. A read operation for the device that is the source of data for the stream will only be read when the buffer is empty, and the program has requested data. When this occurs, a complete buffer-full of data will be read automatically from the device, if sufficient data is available.

Binary and Character Streams

The java.io package supports two types of streams, **binary streams,** which contain binary data, and **character streams,** which contain character data. Binary streams are sometimes referred to as **byte streams**. These two kinds of streams behave in different ways when you read and write data.

When you write data to a binary stream, the data is written to the stream as a series of bytes, exactly as it appears in memory. No transformation of the data takes place. Binary numerical values are just written as a series of bytes, four bytes for each value of type int, eight bytes for each value of type long, eight bytes for each value of type double, and so on. As we saw in Chapter 2, Java stores its characters internally as Unicode characters, which are 16-bit characters, so each Unicode character is written to a binary stream as two bytes, the high byte being written first.

Character streams are used for storing and retrieving text. You may also use character streams to read text files not written by a Java program. All binary numeric data has to be converted to a textual representation before being written to a character stream. This involves generating a character representation of the original binary data value. Reading numeric data from a stream that contains text involves much more work than reading binary data. When you read a value of type int from a binary stream, you know that it consists of four bytes. When you read an integer from a character stream, you have to determine how many characters make up the value. For each numerical value you read from a character stream, you have to be able to recognize where the value begins and ends, and then convert the **token** – the sequence of characters that represents the value – to its binary form. This is illustrated below:

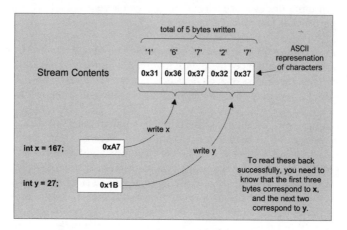

When you write strings to a stream as character data, by default, the Unicode characters are automatically converted to the local representation of the characters in the host machine, and these are then written to the stream. When you read a string, the default mechanism is to convert the data from the stream back to Unicode characters from the local machine representation. With character streams, your program reads and writes Unicode characters, but the stream will contain characters in the equivalent character encoding used by the local computer.

You don't have to accept the default conversion process for character streams. Java allows named mappings between Unicode characters and sets of bytes to be defined, called **charsets**, and you can select an available charset that should apply when data is transferred to, or from, a particular character stream. We won't be going into this in detail, but you can find more information on defining and using charsets in the SDK documentation for the Charset class.

The Classes for Input and Output

There are quite a number of stream classes, but as you will see, they form a reasonably logical structure. Once you see how they are related, you shouldn't have much trouble using them. We will work through the class hierarchy from the top down, so you will be able to see how the classes hang together, and how you can combine them in different ways to suit different situations.

The package java.io contains the classes that provide the foundation for Java's support for stream I/O:

Class	Description
InputStream	The base class for byte stream input operations.
OutputStream	The base class for byte stream output operations.

InputStream, and OutputStream are both **abstract** classes. As you are well aware by now, you cannot create instances of an abstract class – these classes only serve as a base from which to derive classes with more concrete input or output capabilities. However, both of the classes declare methods that define a basic set of operations for the streams they represent, so the fundamental characteristics of how a stream is accessed are set by these classes. Generally, the InputStream and OutputStream classes, and their subclasses, represent byte streams and provide the means of reading and writing binary data.

Basic Input Stream Operations

As we saw in the previous section, the InputStream class is abstract, so you cannot create objects of this class type. Nonetheless, input stream objects are often accessible via a reference of this type, so the methods identified in this class are what you get. The InputStream class includes three methods for reading data from a stream:

Method	Description
read()	This method is abstract in the InputStream class, so it has to be defined in a subclass. The method returns the next byte available from the stream as type int. If the end of the stream is reached, the method will return the value -1. An exception of type IOException will be thrown if an I/O error occurs.
read(byte[] array)	This method reads bytes from the stream into successive elements of array. The maximum of array.length bytes will be read. The method will not return until the input data is read, or the end of the stream is detected. The method returns the number of bytes read, or -1 if no bytes were read because the end of the stream was reached. If an I/O error occurs, an exception of type IOException will be thrown. If the argument to the method is null then a NullPointerException will be thrown. An input/output method that does not return until the operation is completed is referred to as a **blocking** method, and you say that the methods **blocks** until the operation is complete.
read(byte[] array, int offset, int length)	This works in essentially the same way as the previous method, except that up to length bytes are read into array starting with the element array[offset].

The data is read from the stream by these methods simply as bytes. No conversion is applied to the bytes read. If any conversion is required, for a stream containing bytes in the local character encoding for instance, you must provide a way to handle this. We will see how this might be done in a moment.

You can skip over bytes in an InputStream by calling its skip() method. You specify the number of bytes to be skipped as an argument of type long, and the actual number of bytes skipped is returned, also a value of type long. This method can throw an IOException if an error occurs.

You can close an InputStream by calling its close() method. Once you have closed an input stream, subsequent attempts to access or read from the stream will cause an IOException to be thrown.

The InputStream class has seven direct subclasses as shown in the diagram below.

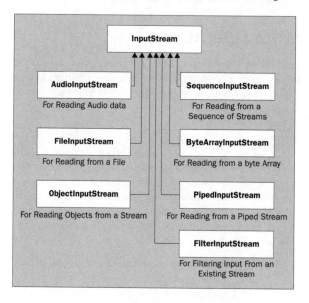

We will be using the FileInputStream class in Chapter 10 *Writing Files*, and the ObjectInputStream class in Chapter 11 *Reading Files*.

The FilterInputStream class has a further nine direct subclasses that provide more specialized ways of filtering or transforming data from an input stream. We will only be using the BufferedInputStream class, but here's the complete set with an indication of what each of them does:

BufferedInputStream	Buffers input from another stream in memory to make the read operations more efficient.
DataInputStream	Reads data of primitive types from a binary stream.
CheckedInputStream	Reads an input stream and maintains a checksum for the data that is read to verify its integrity.

`CipherInputStream`	Reads data from an encrypted input stream.
`DigestInputStream`	Reads data from an input stream and updates an associated message digest. A message digest is a mechanism for combining an arbitrary amount of data from a stream into a fixed length value that can be used to verify the integrity of the data.
`InflaterInputStream`	Reads data from a stream that has been compressed, such as a ZIP file for example.
`LineNumberInputStream`	Reads data from a stream and keeps track of the current line number. The line number starts at 0 and is incremented each time a newline character is read.
`ProgressMonitorInput Stream`	Reads data from an input stream and uses a progress-monitor to monitor reading the stream. If reading the stream takes a significant amount of time, a progress dialog will be displayed offering the option to cancel the operation. This is used in window-based applications for operations that are expected to be time consuming.
`PushbackInputStream`	Adds the capability to return the last byte that was read back to the input stream so you can read it again.

You can create a `BufferedInputStream` object from any other input stream, since the constructor accepts a reference of type `InputStream` as an argument. The `BufferedInputStream` class overrides the methods inherited from `InputStream`. For instance, in the following example:

```
BufferedInputStream keyboard = new BufferedInputStream(System.in);
```

the argument, `System.in`, is the static member of the `System` class that encapsulates input from the keyboard, and is of type `InputStream`. We will be looking into how we can best read input from the keyboard a little later in this chapter.

The effect of wrapping a stream in a `BufferedInputStream` object is to buffer the underlying stream in memory so that data can be read from the stream in large chunks – up to the size of the buffer provided. The data is then made available to the `read()` methods directly from memory, only executing a real read operation from the underlying stream when the buffer is empty. With a suitable choice of buffer size, the number of input operations that are needed will be substantially reduced, and the process will be a whole lot more efficient. The reason for this is that for most input streams, each read operation carries quite a bit of overhead, beyond the time required to actually transfer the data. In the case of a disk file for instance, the transfer of data from the disk to memory can only start once the read/write head has been positioned over the track that contains the data and the disk has rotated to the point where the read/write head is over the point in the track where the data starts. This delay before the transfer of data begins will typically be several milliseconds and will often be much longer than the time required to transfer the data. Thus by minimizing the number of separate read operations that are necessary you can substantially reduce to total time needed to read a significant amount of data.

The buffer size that you get by default when you call the constructor in the previous code fragment is 2048 bytes. This will be adequate for most situations where modest amounts of data are involved. The `BufferedInputStream` class also defines a constructor that accepts a second argument of type `int` that enables you to specify the size in bytes of the buffer to be used.

Deciding on a suitable size for a buffer is a matter of judgment. You need to think about how the buffer size will affect operations in your program. The total amount of data involved as well as the amount that you need to process at one time also come into it. For instance, you will usually want to choose a buffer size that is a multiple of the amount of data that your program will request in each read operation. Suppose you expect your program to read and process 600 bytes at a time for instance. In this case you should choose a buffer size that is a multiple of 600 bytes. The multiple, and therefore the total buffer size, is a balance between the amount of memory required for the buffer and its effect on the efficiency of your program. If you expect to be processing 100 sets of data, each of 600 bytes, you might settle on a buffer size of 6000 bytes as a reasonable choice. Each buffer-full would then consist of 10 sets of data, and there would only need to be ten physical read operations to refill the buffer.

Basic Output Stream Operations

The `OutputStream` class contains three `write()` methods for writing binary data to the stream. As can be expected, these mirror the `read()` methods of the `InputStream` class. This class is also abstract, so only subclasses can be instantiated. The principal direct subclasses of `OutputStream` are shown in the diagram below:

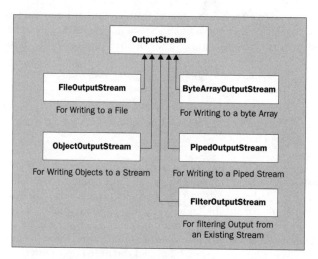

We will be using the `FileOutputStream` class that is derived from `OutputStream` when we write files in the next chapter, and will investigate the methods belonging to the `ObjectOutputStream` class in Chapter 12 *Serializing Objects*, when we learn how to write objects to a file.

Note that this is not the complete set of output stream classes. The `FilterOutputStream` has a further seven subclasses, including the `BufferedOutputStream` class that does for output streams what the `BufferedInputStream` class does for input streams. There is also the `PrintStream` class, which we will be looking at a little later in this chapter, since output to the command line is via a stream object of this type.

Stream Readers and Writers

Stream readers and **writers** are objects that can read and write byte streams as character streams. So a character stream is essentially a byte stream fronted by a reader or a writer. The base classes for stream readers and writers are:

Class	Description
Reader	The base class for reading a character stream.
Writer	The base class for writing a character stream.

Reader and Writer are both abstract classes. The Reader and Writer classes and their subclasses are not really streams themselves, but provide the methods you can use for reading and writing binary streams as character streams. Thus, a Reader or Writer object is typically created using an underlying InputStream or OutputStream object that encapsulates the connection to the external device, which is the ultimate source or destination of the data.

Using Readers

The Reader class has the direct subclasses shown in the diagram below:

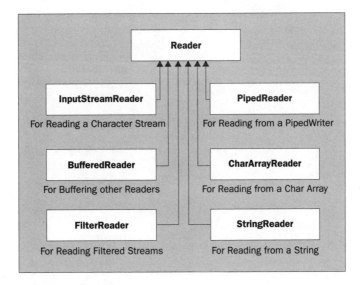

The concrete class that you would use to read a binary input stream as a character stream is InputStreamReader. You could create an InputStreamReader object like this:

```
InputStreamReader keyboard = new InputStreamReader(System.in);
```

The parameter to the InputStreamReader constructor is of type InputStream, so you can pass an object of any class derived from InputStream to it. The sample above creates an InputStreamReader object, keyboard, from the object System.in, the keyboard input stream.

The InputStreamReader class defines three varieties of read() method that will read one or more bytes from the underlying stream, and return them as Unicode characters, using the default conversion from the local character encoding. There are also two further constructors for InputStreamReader objects that will convert data from the stream using a charset that you specify.

Of course, it would be much more efficient if you buffered the stream using a BufferedReader object like this:

```
BufferedReader keyboard = new BufferedReader(new InputStreamReader(System.in));
```

Here, we wrap an InputStreamReader object around System.in, and then buffer it using a BufferedReader object. This will make the input operations much more efficient.

A CharArrayReader object is created from an array and enables you to read data from the array as though it is from a character input stream. A StringReader object class does essentially the same thing, but with a String object.

Using Writers

The main subclasses of the Writer class are as shown below:

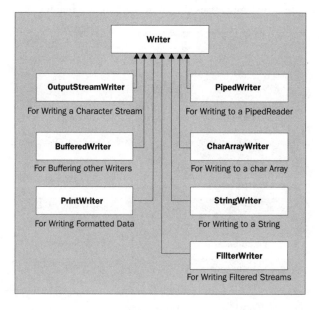

We will just look at a few details of the most commonly used of these classes.

The OutputStreamWriter class writes characters to an underlying binary stream. It also has a subclass, FileWriter that writes characters to a stream encapsulating a file. Both of these are largely superseded by the new I/O facilities that we will explore starting in the next chapter.

Note that the PrintWriter class has no particular relevance to printing, in spite of its name. The PrintWriter class defines methods for formatting binary data as characters, and writing it to a stream. It defines overloaded print() and println() methods that accept an argument of each of the basic data types, of type char[], of type String, and of type Object. The data that is written is a character representation of the argument. Numerical values and objects are converted to a string representation using the static valueOf() method in the String class. There are overloaded versions of this method for all of the primitive types plus type Object. In the case of an argument that is an Object reference, the valueOf() method just calls the toString() method for the object to produce the string to be written to the stream. The print() methods just write the string representation of the argument whereas the println() method appends \n to the output. You can create a PrintWriter object from a stream or from another Writer object.

An important point to note when using a PrintWriter object is that its methods do not throw I/O exceptions. To determine whether any I/O errors have occurred, you have to call the checkError() method for the PrintWriter object. This method will return true if an error occurred and false otherwise.

The StringWriter and CharArrayWriter classes are for writing character data to a StringBuffer object, or an array of type char[]. You would typically use these to perform data conversions so that the results are available to you from the underlying array, or string. For instance, you could combine the capabilities of a PrintWriter with a StringWriter to obtain a String object containing binary data converted to characters:

```
StringWriter strWriter = new StringWriter();
PrintWriter writer = new PrintWriter(strWriter);
```

Now you can use the methods for the writer object to write to the StringBuffer object underlying the StringWriter object:

```
double value = 2.71828;
writer.println(value);
```

You can get the result back as a StringBuffer object from the original StringWriter object:

```
StringBuffer str = strWriter.getBuffer();
```

Of course, the formatting done by a PrintWriter object does not help make the output line up in neat columns. If you want that to happen, you have to do it yourself. We'll take a look at how we might do this for command line output a little later in this chapter.

Let's now turn to keyboard input and command line output.

The Standard Streams

Your operating system will typically define three standard streams that are accessible through members of the System class in Java:

❑ A **standard input stream** that usually corresponds to the keyboard by default. This is encapsulated by the in member of the System class, and is of type InputStream.

❑ A **standard output stream** that corresponds to output on the command line. This is encapsulated by the out member of the System class, and is of type PrintStream.

❑ A **standard error output stream** for error messages that usually maps to the command line output by default. This is encapsulated by the err member of the System class, and is also of type PrintStream.

You can reassign any of these to another stream within a Java application. The System class provides the static methods setIn(), setOut(), and setErr() for this purpose. The setIn() method requires an argument of type InputStream that specifies the new source of standard input. The other two methods expect an argument of type PrintStream.

Since the standard input stream is of type InputStream, we are not exactly overwhelmed by the capabilities for reading data from the keyboard in Java. Basically, we can read a byte or an array of bytes using a read() method as standard, and that's it. If you want more than that, reading integers, or decimal values, or strings as keyboard input, you're on your own. Let's see what we can do to remedy that.

Getting Data From the Keyboard

To get sensible input from the keyboard, you have to be able to scan the stream of characters and recognize what they are. When you read a numerical value from the stream, you have to look for the digits and possibly the sign and decimal point, figure out where the number starts and ends in the stream, and finally convert it to the appropriate value. To write the code to do this from scratch would take quite a lot of work. Fortunately, we can get a lot of help from the StreamTokenizer class in the java.io package.

The term **token** refers to a data item, such as a number or a string that will, in general, consist of several consecutive characters of a particular kind from the stream. For example, a number is usually a sequence of characters that consists of digits, maybe a decimal point, and sometimes a sign in front. The class has the name StreamTokenizer because it can read characters from a stream, and parse it into a series of tokens that it recognizes.

You create a StreamTokenizer object from a stream reader object that reads data from the underlying input stream. Since we want to read the standard input stream, System.in, we shall use an InputStreamReader that converts the raw bytes from the stream from the local character encoding to Unicode characters before the StreamTokenizer object sees them. In the interests of efficiency we will also buffer the data from the InputStreamReader through a BufferedReader object that will buffer the data in memory. We will therefore create our StreamTokenizer object like this:

```
StreamTokenizer tokenizer = new StreamTokenizer(
                      new BufferedReader(
                        new InputStreamReader(System.in)));
```

The argument to the `StreamTokenizer` is the original standard input stream, `System.in`, inside an `InputStreamReader` object that converts the bytes to Unicode, inside a `BufferedReader` that supplies the stream of Unicode characters via a buffer in memory.

Before we can make use of our `StreamTokenizer` object for keyboard input, we need to understand a bit more about how it works.

Tokenizing a Stream

The `StreamTokenizer` class defines objects that can read an input stream and parse it into tokens. The input stream is read and treated as a series of separate bytes, and each byte is regarded as a character in the range `'u\0000'` to `'u\00FF'`. A `StreamTokenizer` object in its default state can recognize the following kinds of tokens:

Token	Description
Numbers	A sequence consisting of the digits 0 to 9, plus possibly a decimal point, and a + or - sign.
Strings	Any sequence of characters between a pair of single quotes or a pair of double quotes.
Words	Any sequence of letters or digits 0 to 9 beginning with a letter. A letter is defined as any of A to Z and a to z or \u00A0 to \u00FF. A word follows a whitespace character and is terminated by another whitespace character, or any character other than a letter or a digit.
Comments	Any sequence of characters beginning with a forward slash, /, and ending with the end-of-line character. Comments are ignored and not returned by the tokenizer.
Whitespace	All byte values from \u0000 to \u0020, which includes space, backspace, horizontal tab, vertical tab, line feed, form feed, and carriage return. Whitespace acts as a delimiter between tokens and is ignored (except within a quoted string).

To retrieve a token from the stream, you call the `nextToken()` method for the `StreamTokenizer` object:

```
int tokenType = 0;
try {
  while(tokenType = tokenizer.nextToken() != tokenizer.TT_EOF) {
      // Do something with the token...
  }

} catch (IOException e) {
  e.printStackTrace(System.err);
  System.exit(1);
}
```

The method can throw an IOException so the call is in a try block. The value returned depends on the token recognized, and from the value, you can determine where to find the token itself. In the fragment above we compare the value returned with the static constant TT_EOF that is defined in the StreamTokenizer class. This value is returned when the end of the stream has been reached. The token that was read from the stream is itself stored in one of two instance variables of the StreamTokenizer object. If the data item is a number, it is stored in a public data member, nval, which is of type double. If the data item is a quoted string or a word, a reference to a String object is stored in the public data member, sval, which of course is of type, String. The analysis that segments the stream into tokens is fairly simple, and the way in which an arbitrary stream is broken into tokens is illustrated below.

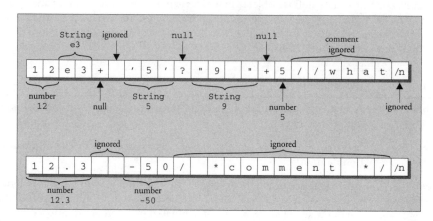

As we have said, the int value returned by the nextToken() method indicates what kind of data item was read. It can be any of the following constant values defined in the StreamTokenizer class:

Token Value	Description
TT_NUMBER	The token is a number that has been stored in the public field, nval, of type double, in the tokenizer object.
TT_WORD	The token is a word that has been stored in the public field, sval, of type String, in the tokenizer object.
TT_EOF	The end-of-the stream has been reached.
TT_EOL	An end of line character has been read. This is only set if the eolIsSignificant() method has been called with the argument, true. Otherwise end-of-line characters are treated as whitespace and ignored.

If a quoted string is read from the stream, the value that is returned by nextToken() will be the quote character used for the string as type int – either a single or a double quote. In this case, you retrieve the reference to the string that was read from the sval member of the tokenizer object. The value indicating what kind of token was read last is also available from a public data member, ttype, of the StreamTokenizer object, which is of type int.

Customizing a Stream Tokenizer

The default tokenizing mode can be modified by calling one or other of the following methods:

Method	Description
`resetSyntax()`	Resets the state of the tokenizer object so no characters have any special significance. This has the effect that all characters are regarded as ordinary, and will be read from the stream as single characters. The value of each character will be stored in the `ttype` field.
`ordinaryChar (int ch)`	Sets the character, `ch`, as an ordinary character. An ordinary character is a character that has no special significance. It will be read as a single character whose value will be stored in the `ttype` field. Calling this method will not alter the state of characters other than the argument value.
`ordinaryChars (int low, int hi)`	Causes all characters from `low` to `hi` inclusive to be treated as ordinary characters. Calling this method will not alter the state of characters other than those specified by the argument values.
`whitespaceChars (int low, int hi)`	Causes all characters from `low` to `hi` inclusive to be treated as whitespace characters. Unless they appear in a string, whitespace characters are treated as delimiters between tokens. Calling this method will not alter the state of characters other than those specified by the argument values.
`wordChars (int low, int hi)`	Specifies that the characters from `low` to `hi` inclusive are word characters. A word is at least one of these characters. Calling this method will not alter the state of characters other than those specified by the argument values.
`commentChar (int ch)`	Specifies that `ch` is a character that indicates the start of a comment. All characters to the end of the line following the character, `ch`, will be ignored. Calling this method will not alter the state of characters other than the argument value.
`quoteChar (int ch)`	Specifies that matching pairs of the character, `ch`, enclose a string. Calling this method will not alter the state of characters other than the argument value.
`slashStarComments (boolean flag)`	If the argument is `false`, this switches off recognizing comments between /* and */. A `true` argument switches it on again.
`slashSlashComments (boolean flag)`	If the argument is `false`, this switches off recognizing comments starting will a double slash. A `true` argument switches it on again.
`lowerCaseMode (boolean flag)`	An argument of `true` causes strings to be converted to lower case before being stored in `sval`. An argument of `false` switches off lower case mode.
`pushback()`	Calling this method causes the next call of the `nextToken()` method to return the `ttype` value that was set by the previous `nextToken()` call and to leave `sval` and `nval` unchanged.

If you want to alter a tokenizer, it is usually better to reset it by calling the `resetSyntax()` method, then call the other methods to set the tokenizer up the way that you want. If you adopt this approach, any special significance attached to particular characters will be apparent from your code. The `resetSyntax()` method makes all characters, including whitespace, and ordinary characters, so that no character has any special significance. In some situations you may need to set a tokenizer up dynamically to suit retrieving each specific kind of data that you want to extract from the stream. When you want to read the next character as a character, whatever it is, you just need to call `resetSyntax()` before calling `nextToken()`. The character will be returned by `nextToken()` and stored in the `ttype` field. To read anything else subsequently, you have to set the tokenizer up appropriately.

Let's see how we can use this class to read data items from the keyboard.

Try It Out – Creating a Formatted Input Class

One way of reading formatted input is to define our own class that uses a `StreamTokenizer` object to read from standard input. We can define a class, `FormattedInput`, which will define methods to return various types of data items entered via the keyboard:

```
import java.io.*;

public class FormattedInput {

  // Method to read an int value...

  // Method to read a double value...

  // Plus methods to read various other data types...

  // Helper method to read the next token
  private int readToken() {
    try {
      ttype = tokenizer.nextToken();
      return ttype;

    } catch (IOException e) {  // Error reading in nextToken()
      e.printStackTrace(System.err);
      System.exit(1);          // End the program
    }
    return 0;
  }

  // Object to tokenize input from the standard input stream
  private StreamTokenizer tokenizer = new StreamTokenizer(
                                  new BufferedReader(
                                    new InputStreamReader(System.in)));
  private int ttype;    // Stores the token type code
}
```

The default constructor will be quite satisfactory for this class, because the instance variable, `tokenizer`, is already initialized. The `readToken()` method is there for use in the methods that will read values of various types. It makes the `ttype` value returned by `nextToken()` available directly, and saves having to repeat the `try` and `catch` blocks in all the other methods.

All we need to add are the methods to read the data values that we want. Here is one way to read a value of type `int`:

```
// Method to read an int value
public int readInt() {
  for (int i = 0; i < 5; i++) {

    if (readToken() == tokenizer.TT_NUMBER) {
      return (int) tokenizer.nval;    // Value is numeric, so return as int
    } else {
      System.out.println("Incorrect input: " + tokenizer.sval
                      + " Re-enter an integer");
      continue;                       // Retry the read operation
    }

  }
  System.out.println("Five failures reading an int value"
                  + " - program terminated");
  System.exit(1);    // End the program
  return 0;
}
```

This method gives the user five chances to enter a valid input value before terminating the program. Terminating the program is likely to be inconvenient to say the least in many circumstances. If we make the method throw an exception in the case of failure here instead, and let the calling method decide what to do, this would be a much better way of signaling that the right kind of data could not be found.

We can define our own exception class for this. Let's define it as the type `InvalidUserInputException`:

```
public class InvalidUserInputException extends Exception {
  public InvalidUserInputException() {}

  public InvalidUserInputException(String message) {
    super(message);
  }
}
```

We haven't had to add anything to the base class capability. We just need the ability to pass our own message to the class. The significant thing we have added is our own exception type name.

Now we can change the code for the `readInt()` method so it works like this:

```
public int readInt() throws InvalidUserInputException {
  if (readToken() != tokenizer.TT_NUMBER) {
    throw new InvalidUserInputException(" readInt() failed. "
                                    + "Input data not numeric");
  }
  return (int) tokenizer.nval;
}
```

If you need a method to read an integer value and return it as one of the other integer types, byte, short, or long, you could implement it in the same way but just cast the value in nval to the appropriate type. You might want to add checks that the original value was an integer, and maybe that it was not out of range for the shorter integer types. For instance, to do this for type int, we could code it as:

```
public int readInt() throws InvalidUserInputException {
  if (readToken() != tokenizer.TT_NUMBER) {
    throw new InvalidUserInputException(" readInt() failed. "
                                        + "Input data not numeric");
  }

    if (tokenizer.nval > (double) Integer.MAX_VALUE
          || tokenizer.nval < (double) Integer.MIN_VALUE) {
    throw new InvalidUserInputException(" readInt() failed. "
                                        + "Input outside int range");
  }

    if (tokenizer.nval != (double) (int) tokenizer.nval) {
    throw new InvalidUserInputException(" readInt() failed. "
                                        + "Input not an integer");
  }
  return (int) tokenizer.nval;
}
```

The Integer class makes the maximum and minimum values of type int available in the public members MAX_VALUE and MIN_VALUE. Other classes corresponding to the basic numeric types provide similar fields. To determine whether the value in nval is really a whole number, we cast it to an integer, then cast it back to double and see whether it is the same value.

To implement readDouble(), the code is very simple. You don't need the cast for the value in nval since it is type double anyway:

```
public double readDouble() throws InvalidUserInputException {
  if (readToken() != tokenizer.TT_NUMBER) {
    throw new InvalidUserInputException(" readDouble() failed. "
                                        + "Input data not numeric");
  }
  return tokenizer.nval;
}
```

A readFloat() method would just need to cast nval to type float.

Reading a string is slightly more involved. You could allow input strings to be quoted, or unquoted as long as they were alphanumeric and did not contain whitespace characters. Here's how the method might be coded to allow that:

```
public String readString() throws InvalidUserInputException {
  if (readToken() == tokenizer.TT_WORD || ttype == '\"'
          || ttype == '\'') {
    return tokenizer.sval;
  } else {
```

```
                    throw new InvalidUserInputException(" readString() failed. "
                                                        + "Input data is not a string");
        }
    }
```

If either a word or a string is recognized, the token is stored as type `String` in the `sval` field of the `StreamTokenizer` object.

Let's see if it works.

Try It Out – Formatted Keyboard Input

We can try out our `FormattedInput` class in a simple program that iterates round a loop a few times to give you the opportunity to try out correct and incorrect input:

```
public class TestFormattedInput {
  public static void main(String[] args) {
    FormattedInput kb = new FormattedInput();
    for (int i = 0; i < 5; i++) {
      try {
        System.out.print("Enter an integer: ");
        System.out.println("Integer read: " + kb.readInt());
        System.out.print("Enter a double value: ");
        System.out.println("Double value read: " + kb.readDouble());
        System.out.print("Enter a string: ");
        System.out.println("String read: " + kb.readString());
      } catch (InvalidUserInputException e) {
        System.out.println("InvalidUserInputException thrown.\n"
                           + e.getMessage());
      }
    }
  }
}
```

It is best to run this example from the command line. Some Java IDEs are not terrific when it comes to keyboard input. If you try a few wrong values, you should see our exception being thrown.

How It Works

This just repeats requests for input of each of the three types of value we have provided methods for, over five iterations. Of course, after an exception of type `InvalidUserInputException` is thrown, the loop will go straight to the start of the next iteration – if there is one.

This code isn't foolproof. Bits of an incorrect entry can be left in the stream to confuse subsequent input and you can't enter floating-point values with exponents. However, it does work after a fashion and it's best not to look a gift horse in the mouth.

Writing to the Command Line

Up to now, we have made extensive use of the `println()` method from the `PrintStream` class in our examples to output formatted information to the screen. The `out` object in the expression, `System.out.println()`, is of type, `PrintStream`. This class outputs data of any of the basic types as a string. For example, an `int` value of `12345` becomes the string, `"12345"`, as generated by the `valueOf()` method from the `String` class. However, we also have the `PrintWriter` class that we discussed earlier to do the same thing since this class has all the methods that `PrintStream` provides.

The principle difference between the two classes is that with the `PrintWriter` class you can control whether or not the stream buffer is flushed when the `println()` method is called, whereas with the `PrintStream` class you cannot. The `PrintWriter` class will only flush the stream buffer when one of the `println()` methods is called if automatic flushing is enabled. A `PrintStream` object will flush the stream buffer whenever a newline character is written to the stream, regardless of whether it was written by a `print()` or a `println()` method.

Both the `PrintWriter` and `PrintStream` classes format basic data as characters. The functionality that is missing is the ability to specify a field width for each output value. However, it is quite easy to line your numeric output up in columns by defining your own subclass of either `PrintStream` or `PrintWriter`. The approach is similar with both so let's arbitrarily try the latter.

Try It Out – Creating a Formatted Output Class

There is more than one approach possible to producing output in a given field width. We will create a `FormattedWriter` class that defines objects that can write values of any of the basic types to a stream, with a given field width. The class will implement overloaded `print()` and `println()` methods for each of the primitive types.

We will define the class with a data member containing the width of the output field for data items. The basic class definition will be:

```java
import java.io.*;

public class FormattedWriter extends PrintWriter {
  public final static int LEFT_JUSTIFIED  = 1;
  public final static int RIGHT_JUSTIFIED = 2;
  private int justification = RIGHT_JUSTIFIED;

  private int width = 0;                     // Field width required for output

  // Constructor with a specified field width, autoflush, and justification
  public FormattedWriter(Writer output, boolean autoflush, int width,
                                        int justification) {
    super(output, autoflush);       // Call PrintWriter constructor
    if(width>0)
      this.width = width;               // Store the field width
    if(justification == LEFT_JUSTIFIED || justification == RIGHT_JUSTIFIED)
      this.justification = justification;
  }

  // Constructor with a specified field width
```

```
    public FormattedWriter(Writer output, int width) {
      this(output, false, width, RIGHT_JUSTIFIED);
    }

    // Constructor with a specified field width and justification
    public FormattedWriter(Writer output, int width, int justification) {
      this(output, false, width, justification);
    }

    // Constructor with a specified field width and autoflush option
    public FormattedWriter(Writer output, boolean autoflush, int width) {
      this(output, autoflush, width, RIGHT_JUSTIFIED);
    }

    // Lots of overloaded print() and println() methods
    // for basic data types...
  }
```

How It Works

There are four fields in our `FormatWriter` class. We have defined two static constants that identify whether the data is to be left or right justified in the output field. The justification member records this, and it has the value `RIGHT_JUSTIFIED` by default. The variable, `width`, of type, `int`, holds the output field width.

We have defined four constructors to provide flexibility in what you need to specify when you create an object of type `FormattedWriter`. As a minimum, two arguments are required, a reference of type `Writer` to an object encapsulating the output stream, and the field width. You can optionally specify the justification of the output in the field as one of the class constants we have defined for this purpose, and a `boolean` value that determines whether autoflushing of the stream is to be applied. All the constructors with fewer than four parameters call the constructor that has four by passing default values for the unspecified parameters. Note that we only set the width if the value supplied is positive, and we only set the justification if the argument is one or other of our constants. This ensures that our class object is always initialized correctly.

Since we derive our class from `PrintWriter`, we have all the facilities of the `PrintWriter` class available. At the moment, if you call `print()` or `println()` for a `FormatWriter` object, it will call the base class method, so the behavior will be exactly the same as a `PrintWriter` object. To change this, we will add our own `print()` and `println()` methods that override the base class methods. First, we will add a helper method.

Overriding print() and println()

We know that if `width` is non-zero, we want to output `width` characters for each value that we write to the stream. We need to figure out how many characters there are in each data value, subtract that from the total field width, and add that many blanks to the beginning or the end of the string representing the data value, depending on whether it is to be right or left justified. We can then write the resultant string of characters to the stream. If the character representation of the data exceeds the field width, we can output it as XXX...X with the number of X's corresponding to the specified `width`. This will show the user that the value can be displayed within the specified width.

The starting point for outputting a data value is to create a character representation for it. Once we have that, we need to extend it to the right to the required field width with spaces. We can implement a helper method, pad(), in our FormatWriter class that will accept a String object as an argument, and pad out the string appropriately before returning it:

```
// Helper method to form string
private String pad(String str) {
  if (width == 0) {
    return str;
  }

  int blanks = width - str.length();          // Number of blanks needed
  StringBuffer result = new StringBuffer();    // Will hold the output

  if(blanks<0) {                               // Data does not fit
    for(int i = 0 ; i<width ; i++)
      result.append('X');                      // so append X's
    return result.toString();                  // and return the result
  }

  if(blanks>0)                                 // If we need some blanks
    for(int i = 0 ; i<blanks ; i++)
      result.append(' ');                      // append them

  // Insert the value string at the beginning or the end
  result.insert(justification == LEFT_JUSTIFIED ? 0 : result.length(),
                                                        str);
  return result.toString();
}
```

We will only use this method inside the class, so we make it private. If the width is zero then we just return the original string. Otherwise, we assemble the string to be output in the StringBuffer object, result. If the string, str, has more characters than the field width, then we fill result with X's. Alternatively, you could mess up the nice neat columns here and output the whole string as-is instead.

If the length of str is less than the field width, we append the appropriate number of spaces to result. We then insert str at the beginning of result (index position 0), or the end (index position result.length()). Finally, we return a String object that we create from result by calling its toString() method.

We can now implement the print() methods and println() methods in our class very easily using the pad() method. Here's how the print() method for type long looks:

```
// Output type long formatted in a given width
public void print(long value) {
  super.print(pad(String.valueOf(value)));   // Pad to width and output
}
```

The print(long value) method calls the static valueOf() method in the String class to convert the value to a character string. The string is then passed to the pad() method to create a string of the required length, and this is passed to the print() method belonging to the superclass, PrintWriter.

The `print()` method for a `double` value will be almost identical – well the body of the method is identical:

```
// Output type double formatted in a given width
public void print(double value) {
  super.print(pad(String.valueOf(value)));   // Pad to width and output
}
```

The `print()` method for a `String` value is not a lot different:

```
// Output type String formatted in a given width
public void print(String str) {
  super.print(pad(str));   // Pad to width and output
}
```

You should now be able to implement all the other versions of `print()` similarly to these so add `print()` methods to the `FormattedWriter` class for types `int`, `boolean`, `char`, and `float`.

The `println()` methods that you also need to add are not very different. You just need to call the `println()` method for the base class in each case. For instance, we can implement the `println()` method for type `int` like this:

```
public void println(int value) {
  super.println(pad(String.valueOf(value)));   // Pad to width and output
}
```

Add the other println() methods for the remaining primitive types. You can block copy all the `print()` methods and then modify the copies as a shortcut to save typing. Make sure you change the method name and the `print()` call in the body in each case though.

If you want more flexibility with objects of the `FormattedWriter` class, you can add a `setWidth()` member to change the field width and perhaps a `getWidth()` member to find out what it is currently. The `setWidth()` method will be:

```
public void setWidth(int width) {
  if(width >= 0)
    this.width = width;
}
```

We test for a non-negative value before setting the width. Here we need to allow the possibility of resetting the width to zero, whereas in the constructor we only want to set width for a non-zero positive argument value. Now we can dynamically set the width for a `FormattedWriter` object, and all subsequent output using the object will be in a field of the width that we specify.

It's ready to roll, so let's give it a whirl.

Chapter 8

Try It Out – Outputting Data in Fixed Fields

Let's create a simple example that exercises our `FormatWriter` class by outputting integers, floating point values and strings:

```
import java.io.*;

public class TestFormattedWriter {
  public static void main(String[] args) {

    // Some arbitrary data to output
    int[] numbers = {
      1, 1, 2, 3, 5, 8, 13, 21, 34, 55, 89, 144, 233, 377
    };

    double[] values = {
      1.0, 1.0, 1.414, 1.732, 2.236, 2.828, 3.606, 4.582, 5.831,
      -123456789.23456
    };
    String[] strings = {
      "one", "one", "two", "three", "five", "eight", "thirteen"
    };

    // Create a formatted writer for a buffered output to the command line
    FormattedWriter out = new FormattedWriter(
                          new BufferedWriter(
                            new OutputStreamWriter(System.out)), 12,
                              FormattedWriter.RIGHT_JUSTIFIED);

    for (int i = 0; i < numbers.length; i++) {
      if (i % 6 == 0) {    // New line before each line of five values
        out.println();

      }
      out.print(numbers[i]);
    }

    out.setWidth(10);
    for (int i = 0; i < values.length; i++) {
      if (i % 5 == 0) {    // New line before each line of four values
        out.println();

      }
      out.print(values[i]);
    }

    for (int i = 0; i < strings.length; i++) {
      if (i % 4 == 0) {                // New line before each line of three
        out.println();

      }
      //out.print(strings[i], 14);    // Override width
```

350

```
        }
      }
    }
```

Of course, the file containing this class definition needs to be in the same directory as the definition for the FormattedWriter class. If you have typed in the FormattedWriter class and its multitude of methods correctly, this example should produce the output:

```
           1            1            2            3            5            8
          13           21           34           55           89          144
         233          377
         1.0          1.0        1.414        1.732        2.236
       2.828        3.606        4.582        5.831XXXXXXXXXX
             one          one          two        three
            five        eight     thirteen
```

How It Works

We first set up three arrays of different types containing interesting data to write to the command line. We then create a FormattedWriter object that will write data right-justified in a field width of 12 to a BufferedWriter object. The BufferedWriter buffers the OutputStreamWriter object that we wrap around System.out, the stream for output to the command line.

We then exercise our FormattedWriter object by writing each of the arrays to the stream differently. You can see the effect of exceeding the specified field width with the last value of type double. You might like to try this with the left-justified option specified in the constructor.

A FormattedWriter object can write to any type of Writer object so you are not limited to just command line output.

Summary

In this chapter, we have discussed the facilities for inputting and outputting basic types of data to a stream. The important points we have discussed include:

❑ A stream is an abstract representation of a source of serial input, or a destination for serial output.

❑ The classes supporting stream operations are contained in the package java.io.

❑ Two kinds of stream operations are supported, binary stream operations will result in streams that contain bytes, and character stream operations are for streams that contain characters in the local machine character encoding.

❑ No conversion occurs when characters are written to, or read from, a byte stream. Characters are converted from Unicode to the local machine representation of characters when a character stream is written.

❑ Byte streams are represented by sub classes of the classes InputStream and OutputStream.

❏ Character stream operations are provided by sub classes of the `Reader` and `Writer` classes.

❏ A nod is as good as a wink to a blind horse.

Exercises

1. Modify the `FormattedWriter` class to support centered output of the value in the output field.

2. Use a `StreamTokenizer` object to parse a string entered from the keyboard containing a series of data items separated by commas and output each of the items on a separate line.

3. Create a class defining an object that will parse each line of input from the keyboard that contains items separated by an arbitrary delimiter (for example, a colon, or a comma, or a forward slash, etc.) and return the items as an array of type `String[]`. For example, the input might be:

```
1/one/2/two
```

The output would be returned as an array of type `String[]` containing "1", "one", "2", "two".

Accessing Files and Directories

In this chapter, we will explore how we identify, access, and manipulate files and directories on your hard drive. This will include the ability to create new files and directories, but not to read or write files. We will get to that starting in the next chapter.

In this chapter you will learn:

❑ How you create `File` objects and use them to examine files and directories

❑ How you can use `File` class methods to examine the contents of the hard drives on your system

❑ How to create new files and directories on your hard drive

❑ How to create temporary files

❑ How you create `FileOutputStream` objects

Working with File Objects

It is easy to forget that a `File` object doesn't actually represent a file. You need to keep reminding yourself that a `File` object encapsulates a **pathname** or **reference** to what may or may not be a physical file or directory on your hard disk, not the physical file or directory itself. The fact that you create a `File` object does not determine that a file or directory actually exists. This is not as strange as it might seem at first sight. After all, you will often be defining a `File` object that encapsulates a path to a new file or directory that you intend to create.

As we will see, a `File` object serves two purposes:

❑ It enables you to check the pathname that it encapsulates against the physical file system and see whether it corresponds to a real file or directory.

❑ You can use it to create file stream objects.

The File class provides several methods for you to test the path that a File object encapsulates in various ways, as well as the physical file or directory it may represent. You can determine whether or not an object does represent a path to an existing file or directory, for example. If a File object does correspond to a real file, you have methods available that you can use to modify the file in a number of ways.

Creating File Objects

You have a choice of four constructors for creating File objects. The simplest accepts a String object as an argument that specifies a path for a file or a directory. For example, you could write the statement:

```
File myDir = new File("C:/j2sdk1.4.0/src/java/io");
```

This creates a File object encapsulating the path C:/j2sdk1.4.0/src/java/io. On my system, this happens to be the path to the directory, io, containing the classes in the java.io package. On the various flavors of the Microsoft Windows operating system, you can also use an escaped back slash separator, \\, when you define a path, instead of /, if you wish, but paths do tend to look rather busy if you do. For instance:

```
File myDir = new File("C:\\jdk1.4\\src\\java\\io");
```

It also requires more typing.

Note that the File class constructor here does not check the string that you pass as the argument in any way, so there is no guarantee that a File object encapsulates a valid representation of a path on your system at all. For instance, this will compile and execute perfectly well:

```
File junk = new File("dwe\n:;?cc/.*\naaf%)(");   // Not a valid path!
```

The argument to the constructor here does not define a valid file or directory path – at least not under any operating system that I am familiar with – but that statement compiles and executes. We can therefore deduce that you can pass *any* string as an argument to the File class constructor. It is up to you to ensure that it is valid for your system.

To specify a pathname to a file, you just need to make sure that the string that you pass as an argument to the constructor does refer to a file, and not a directory. For example, the statement:

```
File myFile = new File("C:/j2sdk1.4.0/src/java/io/File.java");
```

sets the object, myFile, to correspond to the source file for the definition of the class, File.

An important and easily overlooked characteristic of File objects is that they are **immutable**. Once you have created a File object you cannot change the path it encapsulates. We will see later that you can change the name of the physical file it references by using the rename() method belonging to the File object, but this will not change the File object itself. The File object will still encapsulate the original path so that once the file name has been changed the path encapsulated by the File object will no longer refer to an existing file. This can be confusing if you don't realize this is the case. Using this File object to test whether the file exists, for instance, will return false.

You can also create a `File` object that represents a pathname for a file by using a constructor that allows you to specify the directory that contains the file and the file name separately. The directory that contains the file is usually referred to as the **parent** directory. There are two constructors that allow you to do this, providing you with a choice as to how you specify the parent directory. In one, the first argument is a reference to a `File` object that encapsulates the path for the directory containing the file. In the other, the first argument specifies the parent directory path as a `String` object. The second argument in both cases is a `String` object identifying the file name.

For example, on my system, I can identify the Java source file for the `File` class with the statements:

```
File myDir = new File("C:/j2sdk1.4.0/src/java/io");  // Parent directory
File myFile = new File(myDir, "File.java");          // The path to the file
```

The first statement creates a `File` object that refers to the directory for the package `io`, and the second statement creates a `File` object that corresponds to the file, `File.java`, in that directory.

We could use the second of the two constructors to achieve the same result as the previous two statements:

```
File myFile = new File("C:/j2sdk1.4.0/src/java/io", "File.java");
```

Using a `File` object to specify the directory is much more useful than using a string directly. For instance, you can verify that the directory does really exist before attempting to access the file or files that you are interested in. You can also create the directory if necessary, as we shall see.

The fourth constructor allows you to define a `File` object from an object of type `URI` that encapsulates a Uniform Resource Identifier, commonly known as a **URI**. As you are undoubtedly aware, a URI is used to reference a resource on the World Wide Web and the most common form of URI is a URL – a Uniform Resource Locator. A URL usually consists of a protocol specification such as `HTTP`, a host machine identification such as `p2p.wrox.com`, plus a name that refers to a particular resource on that machine such as `java`, so for instance, `http://p2p.wrox.com/java` is a URL that references a page on a Wrox Press server that contains a list of forums related to Java books that are published by Wrox Press.

The URI class provides several constructors for creating URI objects but getting into the detail of these is too much of a diversion from our present topic – dealing with local files. However, the simplest constructor just accepts a reference to a `String` object and we could use this to create a `File` object like this:

```
File remoteFile = new File(new URL(http://p2p.wrox.com/java));
```

References to physical files inevitably tend to be system-dependent since each operating system will have its own conventions for specifying a path to a file. If you refer to a particular file in the directory `C:\My Java Stuff` under Windows, this path will not be recognized under Unix. However, Java provides capabilities that enable you to avoid system dependencies when you specify file paths, at least to some extent, so let's look at those in more detail.

Portable Path Considerations

The `File` class contains a static member, `separator`, of type `String` that defines the separator that is used between names in a path by your operating system. Under Unix, this will be defined as `"/"` and under MS Windows it will be `"\\"`. As we have seen, when you are specifying a path by a string under Windows, you can use either of these characters as a path name separator. Another static field, `separatorChar`, defines the same separator character as type `char` for convenience, so you can use whichever suits you. The `File` class also defines the system default character for separating one path from another as the static member `pathSeparator`, which is of type `String`, or `pathSeparatorChar`, which is of type `char`. The path separator is a semicolon under MS Windows and a colon under Unix.

Of course, the specific makeup of a path is system-dependent but we could have used the `separator` field in the `File` class to specify the path for `myFile` in a slightly more system-independent way, like this:

```
File myFile = new File("C:" + File.separator + "jdk1.4" + File.separator +
                       "src" + File.separator + "java" + File.separator +
                       "io", "File.java");
```

This defines the same path as the previous statement but without using an explicit separator character between the names in the path. While we have specified the pathname separator character in a portable fashion, the argument to the `File` class constructor is still specific to Windows because we have specified the drive letter as part of the path. To remove the Windows-specific element in the file path we would have to omit the drive letter from the path specification. In this case we would have a **relative path** specification.

Absolute and Relative Paths

In general, the pathname that you use to create a `File` object has two parts: an optional prefix, followed by a series of names separated by the system default separator character for pathnames. Under MS Windows the prefix for a path on a local drive will be a string defining the drive, such as `"C:\\"` or `"C:/"`. Under Unix the prefix will be a forward slash, `"/"`. A path that includes a prefix is an **absolute path** and since it includes a prefix it is not system-independent. A path without a prefix is a **relative path** and as long as it consists of one or more names separated by characters specified as `File.separator` or `File.separatorChar` it should be portable across different systems. The last name in a path can be a directory name or a filename. All other names must be directory names. If you use anything other than this – if you use any system-specific conventions to specify the path for instance – naturally you no longer have a system-independent path specification.

The pathnames we have used in the preceding code fragments have all been absolute paths, since we included the drive letter in the path for Windows, or a forward slash to identify the Unix root directory. If you omit this, you have a relative path, and the pathname string will be interpreted as a path *relative* to the current directory. This implies that you can reference a file that is in the same directory as your program by just the file name.

For example:

```
File myFile = new File("output.txt");
```

This statement creates a `File` object encapsulating the path to a file with the name `"output.txt"` in the current directory, whatever that happens to be. It corresponds to the directory that was current when program execution was initiated. We will see in a moment how we can obtain the absolute path from a `File` object, regardless of how the `File` object was created.

You could also refer to a file in a subdirectory of the current directory using a relative path:

```
File myFile = new File("dir" + separator + "output.txt");
```

Thus we can use a relative path specification to reference files in the current directory, or in any subdirectory of the current directory, and since a relative path does not involve the system-dependent prefix, this will work across different operating systems.

As we have seen, an absolute path in a Windows environment can have a prefix that is an explicit drive specification but you can also use the **UNC** (**U**niversal **N**aming **C**onvention) representation of a path that provides a machine-independent way of identifying paths to shared resources on a network. The UNC representation of a path always begins with two backslashes, followed by the machine name, followed by the share name. In general, a UNC path will be of the form:

```
\\servername\directory_path\filename
```

On a computer with the name `myPC`, with a shared directory `shared`, you could create a `File` object as follows:

```
File myFile = new File("\\\\myPC\\shared\\jdk1.4\\src\\java\\io",
                       "File.java");
```

If you are keen to practice your typing skills, you could also write this as:

```
File myFile = new File(File.separator + File.separator + "myPC" +
                       File.separator + "shared" + File.separator +
                       "jdk1.4" + File.separator + "src" + File.separator +
                       "java" + File.separator + "io", "File.java");
```

If you want to create a `File` object that refers to the root directory under Unix, you just use `"/"` as the path.

Accessing System Properties

While you can specify a relative path to a file is that not system-dependent, there may be circumstances where you want to specify a path that is independent of the current environment, but where the current directory, or even a subdirectory of the current directory, is not a convenient place to store a data file. In this case accessing one of the **system properties** can help. A system property specifies values for parameters related to the system environment in which your program is executing. Each system property is identified by a unique name, and has a value associated with the name that is defined as a string. There is a set of standard system properties that will always be available and you can access the values of any of these by passing the name of the property that you are interested in to the static `getProperty()` method that is defined in the `System` class.

For instance, the directory that is the default base for relative paths is defined by the property that has the name "user.dir", so we can access the path to this directory with the statement:

```
String currentDir = System.getProperty("user.dir");
```

We could then use this to specify explicitly where the file with the name "output.txt" is located:

```
File dataFile = new File(currentDir, "output.txt");
```

Of course, this is equivalent to just specifying the file name as the relative path, so we have not achieved anything new. However, there is another system property with the name "user.home" that has a value that defines a path to the user's home directory. We could therefore specify that the "output.txt" file is to be in this directory like this:

```
File dataFile = new File(System.getProperty("user.home"), "output.txt");
```

The location of the user's home directory is system-dependent, but wherever it is you can access it in this way without building system dependencies into your code.

Naturally, you could specify the second argument to the constructor here to include directories that are to be subdirectories of the home directory. For instance:

```
File dataFile = new File(System.getProperty("user.home"),
                         "dir" + File.separator + "output.txt");
```

On my system this defines the path:

```
C:\Documents and Settings\Ivor Horton\dir\output.txt
```

If you want to plug this code fragment into a main() method and see what path the resultant File object encapsulates, the following statement will output the absolute path for you.

```
System.out.println(dataFile.getAbsolutePath());
```

This uses the getAbsolutePath() method for the File object to obtain the absolute path as a reference to a String object. We will come back to this method in a moment.

If you would like to see what the full set of standard system properties are, you will find the complete list in the SDK documentation for the getProperties() method in the System class.

Testing and Checking File Objects

The File class provides more than 30 methods that you can apply to File objects, so we will look at the ones that will be most useful, grouped by the sorts of things that they do.

First of all, you can get information about a File object itself by using the following methods:

Method	Description
getName ()	Returns a String object containing the name of the file without the path – in other words the last name in the path stored in the object. For a File object representing a directory, just the directory name is returned.
getPath()	Returns a String object containing the path for the File object – including the file or directory name.
isAbsolute()	Returns true if the File object refers to an absolute path name, and false otherwise. Under Windows 95, 98, or NT, an absolute path name begins with either a drive letter followed by a colon then a backslash or a double backslash. Under Unix, an absolute path is specified from the root directory down.
getParent()	Returns a String object containing the name of the parent directory of the file or directory represented by the current File object. This will be the original path without the last name. The method returns null if there is no parent specified. This will be the case if the File object was created for a file in the current directory by just using a file name.
toString()	Returns a String representation of the current File object and is called automatically when a File object is concatenated with a String object. We have used this method implicitly in output statements. The string that is returned is the same as that returned by the getPath() method.
hashCode()	Returns a hash code value for the current File object. We will see more about what hash codes are used for in Chapter 10.
equals()	You use this method for comparing two File objects for equality. If the File object passed as an argument to the method has the same path as the current object, the method returns true. Otherwise, it returns false.

All of the above involve just the information encapsulated by the File object. The file or directory itself is not queried and may or may not exist. The methods in the File class that enable you to check out a file or directory are much more interesting and useful, so let's go directly to those next.

Querying Files and Directories

The following basic set of methods are provided for examining the file or directory that is identified by a `File` object:

Method	Description
exists()	Returns `true` if the file or directory referred to by the `File` object exists and `false` otherwise.
isDirectory()	Returns `true` if the `File` object refers to an existing directory and `false` otherwise.
isFile()	Returns `true` if the `File` object refers to an existing file and `false` otherwise.
isHidden()	Returns `true` if the `File` object refers to a file that is hidden and `false` otherwise. How a file is hidden is system-dependent. Under Unix a hidden file has a name that begins with a dot. Under Windows a file is hidden if it is marked as such within the file system.
canRead()	Returns `true` if you are permitted to read the file referred to by the `File` object, and `false` otherwise. This method can throw a `SecurityException` if read access to the file is not permitted.
canWrite()	Returns `true` if you are permitted to write to the file referred to by the `File` object and `false` otherwise. This method may also throw a `SecurityException` if you are not allowed to write to the file.
getAbsolutePath()	Returns the absolute path for the directory or file referenced by the current `File` object. If the object contains an absolute path, then the string returned by `getPath()` is returned. Otherwise, under MS Windows the path is resolved against the current directory for the drive identified by the pathname, or against the current user directory if no drive letter appears in the pathname, and against the current user directory under UNIX.
getAbsoluteFile()	Returns a `File` object containing the absolute path for the directory or file referenced by the current `File` object.

When you are working with a `File` object, you may not know whether it contains an absolute or a relative path. However, you may well want to get hold of its parent directory – to create another file for instance. For a `File` object created from a relative path, the `getParent()` method will return `null`. In this case you can use the `getAbsolutePath()` method to obtain the absolute path, or the `getAbsoluteFile()` method to ensure that you have a `File` object for which the `getParent()` method will return a string representing the complete path for the parent directory. For instance:

```
File dataFile = new File("output.txt");
```

Calling `getParent()` for `dataFile` here will return `null`. However, we can create a new `File` object encapsulating the absolute path:

```
dataFile = dataFile.getAbsoluteFile();
```

Now `dataFile` refers to a new object that encapsulates the absolute path to `"output.txt"`, so calling `getParent()` will return the path to the parent directory – which will correspond to the value of the `user.dir` system property in this case.

> Note that all operations involving the access of files on the local machine can throw a `SecurityException` if access is not authorized – in an applet for instance. This is the case with all of the methods here. However, for a `SecurityException` to be thrown, a security manager must exist on the local machine, but by default a Java application has no security manager. An applet, on the other hand, always has a security manager, by default. A detailed discussion of Java security is beyond the scope of this book. A comprehensive discussion of this topic is provided by the book "Professional Java Security" by Jess Garms and Daniel Somerfield, published by Wrox Press, ISBN 1861004257.

To see how some of these methods go together, we can try a simple example.

Try It Out – Testing for a File

Try the following source code. Don't forget the `import` statement for the `java.io` package, since the example won't compile without it. The source code is in a zip called `src.jar`, and can be found in the home directory for the JDK. If you haven't installed the Java source code on your system, you could try the example with the file that contains the source code for the example itself – `TryFile.java`:

> In all the examples in this chapter, you may need to specify substitute paths to suit your environment.

```java
import java.io.File;

public class TryFile {
  public static void main(String[] args) {

    // Create an object that is a directory
    File myDir = new File("C:/j2sdk1.4.0/src/java/io");
    System.out.println(myDir + (myDir.isDirectory() ? " is" : " is not")
                    + " a directory.");

    // Create an object that is a file
    File myFile = new File(myDir, "File.java");
    System.out.println(myFile + (myFile.exists() ? " does" : " does not")
                    + " exist");
    System.out.println(myFile + (myFile.isFile() ? " is" : " is not")
                    + " a file.");
```

```
            System.out.println(myFile + (myFile.isHidden() ? " is" : " is not")
                              + " hidden");
            System.out.println("You can" + (myFile.canRead() ? " " : "not ")
                              + "read " + myFile);
            System.out.println("You can" + (myFile.canWrite() ? " " : "not ")
                              + "write " + myFile);
            return;
        }
    }
```

On my machine, the above example produces the output:

```
C:\j2sdk1.4.0\src\java\io is a directory.
C:\j2sdk1.4.0\src\java\io\File.java does exist
C:\j2sdk1.4.0\src\java\io\File.java is a file.
C:\j2sdk1.4.0\src\java\io\File.java is not hidden
You can read C:\j2sdk1.4.0\src\java\io\File.java
You can write C:\j2sdk1.4.0\src\java\io\File.java
```

How It Works

This program first creates an object corresponding to the directory containing the `java.io` package. You will need to check the path to this directory on your own system and insert that as the argument to the constructor of the `File` object. The output statement then uses the conditional operator `?:` in conjunction with the `isDirectory()` method to display a message. If `isDirectory()` returns true, then `" is"` is selected. Otherwise, `" is not"` is selected. The program then creates another `File` object corresponding to the file `File.java` and displays further information about the file using the same sort of mechanism. Finally, the program uses the `canRead()` and `canWrite()` methods to determine whether read and write access to the file is permitted.

If you are using MS Windows, you might like to try out the separator \\ with this example and see if it makes a difference.

The following methods provide further information about the file or directory, if it exists:

Method	Description
list()	If the current `File` object represents a directory, a `String` array is returned containing the names of the members of the directory. If the directory is empty, the array will be empty. If the current file object is a file, `null` is returned. The method will throw an exception of type `SecurityException` if access to the directory is not authorized.
listFiles()	If the object for which this method is called is a directory, it returns an array of `File` objects corresponding to the files and directories in that directory. If the directory is empty, then the array that is returned will be empty. The method will return `null` if the object is not a directory, or if an I/O error occurs. The method will throw an exception of type `SecurityException` if access to the directory is not authorized.

Method	Description
length()	Returns a value of type long that is the length in bytes of the file represented by the current File object. If the pathname for the current object references a file that does not exist then the method will return zero. If the pathname refers to a directory, then the value returned is undefined.
lastModified()	Returns a value of type long that represents the time that the directory or file represented by the current File object was last modified. This time is the number of milliseconds since midnight on 1st January 1970 GMT. It returns zero if the file does not exist.

There is also a static method defined in the File class, listRoots(), which returns an array of File objects. Each element in the array that is returned corresponds to a root directory in the current file system. The path to every file in the system will begin with one or other of these roots. In the case of a Unix system for instance, the array returned will contain just one element corresponding to the single root on a Unix system, /. Under MS Windows, the array will contain an element for each logical drive that you have, including floppy drives, CD drives, and DVD drives. The following statements will list all the root directories on your system:

```
File[] roots = File.listRoots();
for(int i = 0 ; i<roots.length ; i++)
  System.out.println("Root directory " + i + ": " + roots[i]);
```

The for loop lists the elements of the array returned by the listRoots() method.

With a variation on the last example, we can try out some of these methods.

Try It Out – Getting More Information

We can arrange to list all the files in a directory and record when they were last modified with the following program:

```
import java.io.File;
import java.util.Date;    // For the Date class

public class TryFile2 {
  public static void main(String[] args) {

    // Create an object that is a directory
    File myDir = new File("C:/j2sdk1.4.0/src/java/io");
    System.out.println(myDir.getAbsolutePath()
                  + (myDir.isDirectory() ? " is " : " is not ")
                  + "a directory");
    System.out.println("The parent of " + myDir.getName() + " is "
                  + myDir.getParent());

    // Get the contents of the directory
    File[] contents = myDir.listFiles();
```

```
      // List the contents of the directory
      if (contents != null) {
        System.out.println("\nThe " + contents.length
                        + " items in the directory " + myDir.getName()
                        + " are:");
        for (int i = 0; i < contents.length; i++) {
          System.out
            .println(contents[i] + " is a "
                    + (contents[i].isDirectory() ? "directory" : "file")
                    + " last modified "
                    + new Date(contents[i].lastModified()));
        }
      } else {
        System.out.println(myDir.getName() + " is not a directory");
      }

      System.exit(0);
    }
  }
```

Again, you need to use a path that is appropriate for your system. You should not have any difficulty seeing how this works. The first part of the program creates a `File` object representing the same directory as in the previous example. The second part itemizes all the files and subdirectories in the directory. The output will look something like this,

```
C:\j2sdk1.4.0\src\java\io is a directory
The parent of io is C:\j2sdk1.4.0\src\java

The 78 items in the directory io are:
C:\j2sdk1.4.0\src\java\io\Bits.java is a file last modified Sat Oct 20 01:13:38
BST 2001
C:\j2sdk1.4.0\src\java\io\BufferedInputStream.java is a file last modified Sat Oct
20 01:13:38 BST 2001
C:\j2sdk1.4.0\src\java\io\BufferedOutputStream.java is a file last modified Sat
Oct 20 01:13:38 BST 2001
     .
     .
     .
```

and so on.

How It Works

You can see that the `getName()` method just returns the file name or the directory name, depending on what the `File` object represents.

The listFiles() method returns a File array, with each element of the array representing a member of the directory, which could be a subdirectory or a file. We store the reference to the array returned by the method in our array variable contents. After outputting a heading, we check that the array is not null. We then list the contents of the directory in the for loop. We use the isDirectory() method to determine whether each item is a file or a directory, and create the output accordingly. We could just as easily have used the isFile() method here. The lastModified() method returns a long value that represents the time when the file was last modified in milliseconds since midnight on January 1st 1970. To get this to a more readable form, we use the value to create a Date object, and the toString() method for the class returns what you see in the output. The Date class is defined in the java.util package. (See Chapter 13.) We have imported this into the program file but we could just as well use the fully qualified class name, java.util.Date, instead. If the contents array is null, we just output a message. You could easily add code to output the length of each file here, if you want.

Note that there is a standard system property with the name java.home that identifies the directory that is the root directory of the Java runtime environment. If you have installed the SDK (rather than just a JRE), this will be the jre subdirectory to the SDK subdirectory, which on my system is C:/SDK1.4. In this case the value of java.home will be "C:/sdk1.4/jre". You could therefore use this to refer to the file in the previous example in a system-independent way. If you create a File object from the value of the java.home property, calling its getParent() method will return the parent directory as a String object. This will be the SDK home directory so you could use this as the base directory to access the source files for the class libraries, like this:

```
File myDir = new File(new File(System.getProperty("java.home")).getParent(),
                      "src" + File.separator+"java" + File.separator+"io");
```

As long as the JRE in effect is the one installed as part of the SDK, we have a system-independent way of accessing the source files for the library classes.

Filtering a File List

The list() and listFiles() methods are overloaded with versions that accept an argument used to filter a file list. This enables you to get a list of those files with a given extension, or with names that start with a particular sequence of characters. For example, you could ask for all files starting with the letter 'T', which might return the two files we created above: "TryFile.java" and "TryFile2.java". The argument that you pass to the list() method must be a variable of type FilenameFilter whereas the listFiles() method is overloaded with versions to accept arguments of type FilenameFilter or FileFilter. Both FilenameFilter and FileFilter are interfaces that contain the abstract method accept(). The FilenameFilter interface is defined in the java.io package as:

```
public interface FilenameFilter {
  public abstract boolean accept(File directory, String filename);
}
```

The FileFilter interface, also defined in java.io, is very similar:

```
public interface FileFilter {
  public abstract boolean accept(File pathname);
}
```

The only distinction between these two is the parameter list for the method in the interfaces. The `accept()` method in the `FilenameFilter` class has two parameters for you to specify the directory plus the file name to identify a particular file, so this is clearly aimed at testing whether a given file should be included in a list of files. The `accept()` method for the `FileFilter` interface has just a single parameter of type `File`, this is used to filter files and directories.

The filtering of the list is achieved by the `list()` or `listFiles()` method by calling the method `accept()` for every item in the raw list. If the method returns `true`, the item stays in the list, and if it returns `false`, the item is not included. Obviously, these interfaces act as a vehicle to allow the mechanism to work, so you need to define your own class that implements the appropriate interface. If you are using the `list()` method, your class must implement the `FilenameFilter` interface. If you are using the `listFiles()` method, you can implement either interface. How you actually filter the filenames is entirely up to you. You can arrange to do whatever you like within the class that you define. We can see how this works by extending the previous example a little further.

Try It Out – Using the FilenameFilter Interface

We can define a class to specify a file filter as:

```
import java.io.File;
import java.io.FilenameFilter;
import java.util.Date;          // For the Date class

public class FileListFilter implements FilenameFilter {
  private String name;          // File name filter
  private String extension;     // File extension filter

  // Constructor
  public FileListFilter(String name, String extension) {
    this.name = name;
    this.extension = extension;
  }

  public boolean accept(File directory, String filename) {
    boolean fileOK = true;

    // If there is a name filter specified, check the file name
    if (name != null)
      fileOK &= filename.startsWith(name);

    // If there is an extension filter, check the file extension
    if (extension != null)
      fileOK &= filename.endsWith('.' + extension);

    return fileOK;
  }
}
```

This uses the methods `startsWith()` and `endsWith()`, which are defined in the `String` class that we discussed in Chapter 4. Save this source in the same directory as the previous example, as `FileListFilter.java`.

Now we need to modify our `TryFile2.java` code as follows:

```java
import java.io.File;
import java.io.FilenameFilter;
import java.util.Date;    // For the Date class

public class TryFile3 {
  public static void main(String[] args) {

    // Create an object that is a directory
    File myDir = new File("C:/j2sdk1.4.0/src/java/io");
    System.out.println(myDir.getAbsolutePath()
                    + (myDir.isDirectory() ? " is " : " is not ")
                    + "a directory");
    System.out.println("The parent of " + myDir.getName() + " is "
                    + myDir.getParent());

    // Define a filter for java source files beginning with F
    FilenameFilter select = new FileListFilter("F", "java");

    // Get the contents of the directory
    File[] contents = myDir.listFiles(select);

    // List the contents
    if (contents != null) {
      System.out.println("\nThe " + contents.length
                    + " matching items in the directory, "
                    + myDir.getName() + ", are:");
      for (int i = 0; i < contents.length; i++) {
        System.out
          .println(contents[i] + " is a "
                    + (contents[i].isDirectory() ? "directory" : "file")
                    + " last modified "
                    + new Date(contents[i].lastModified()));
      }
    } else {
      System.out.println(myDir.getName() + " is not a directory");
    }

    return;
  }
}
```

It is best to continue with our numbering convention and call the above script `TryFile3.java`. When you run this code, you should get something like the following:

```
C:\j2sdk1.4.0\src\java\io is a directory
The parent of io is C:\j2sdk1.4.0\src\java

The 15 matching items in the directory, io, are:
C:\j2sdk1.4.0\src\java\io\File.java is a file last modified Sat Oct 20 01:13:38
BST 2001
```

```
C:\j2sdk1.4.0\src\java\io\FileDescriptor.java is a file last modified Sat Oct 20
01:13:38 BST 2001
C:\j2sdk1.4.0\src\java\io\FileFilter.java is a file last modified Sat Oct 20
01:13:38 BST 2001
C:\j2sdk1.4.0\src\java\io\FileInputStream.java is a file last modified Sat Oct 20
01:13:38 BST 2001
    .
    .
    .
```

and so on.

How It Works

Our `FileListFilter` class has two instance variables – name and extension. The name variable stores the file name prefix, and extension selects file types to be included in a list. The constructor sets these variables, and the value of either can be omitted when the constructor is called, by specifying the appropriate argument as null. If you want a really fancy filter, you can have just one argument to the constructor and specify the filter as `*.java`, or `A*.java`, or even `A*.j*`. You would just need a bit more code in the constructor or possibly the `accept()` method to analyze the argument. Our implementation of the `accept()` method here only returns true if the file name that is passed to it by the `list()` method has initial characters that are identical to name and the file extension is the same as that stored in extension.

In the modified example, we construct an object of our filter class using the string "F" as the file name prefix and the string ".java" as the extension. This version of the example will now only list files with names beginning with F and with the extension .java.

Creating and Modifying Files and Directories

There are methods defined in the `File` class that you can use to change the physical file by making it read-only or renaming it. There are also methods that enable you to create files and directories, and to delete them. The methods that provide these capabilities are:

Method	Description
renameTo(File path)	The file represented by the current object will be renamed to the path represented by the `File` object passed as an argument to the method. Note that this does *not* change the current `File` object in your program – it alters the physical file. Thus, the file that the `File` object represents will no longer exist after executing this method, because the file will have a new name, and possibly will be located in a different directory. If the file's directory in the new path is different from the original, the file will be moved. The method will fail if the directory in the new path for the file does not exist, or if you don't have write access to it. If the operation is successful the method will return true. Otherwise, it will return false

Method	Description
`setReadOnly()`	Sets the file represented by the current object as read-only and returns `true` if the operation is successful.
`mkdir()`	Creates a directory with the path specified by the current `File` object. The method will fail if the parent directory of the directory to be created does not already exist. The method returns `true` if it is successful and `false` otherwise.
`mkdirs()`	Creates the directory represented by the current `File` object, including any parent directories that are required. It returns `true` if the new directory is created successfully, and `false` otherwise. Note that even if the method fails, some of the directories in the path may have been created.
`createNewFile()`	Creates a new empty file with the pathname defined by the current `File` object as long as the file does not already exist. The method returns `true` if the file was created successfully. Note that this method will only create a file in an existing directory – it will not create any directories specified by the path.
`createTempFile` `(String prefix,` `String suffix,` `File directory)`	This is a static method that creates a temporary file in the directory `directory`, with a name created using the first two arguments, and returns a `File` object corresponding to the file created. The string `prefix` represents the start of the file name and must be at least three characters long. The string `suffix` specifies the file extension. The file name will be formed from `prefix` followed by five or more generated characters, followed by `suffix`. If `suffix` is `null`, `.tmp` will be used. If `prefix` or `suffix` are too long for file names on the current system, they will be truncated, but neither will be truncated to less than three characters. If the `directory` argument is `null`, the system temporary directory will be used. If the file cannot be created, an `IOException` will be thrown. If `prefix` has less than three characters, an `IllegalArgumentException` will be thrown.
`createTempFile` `(String prefix,` `String suffix)`	Equivalent to `createTempFile(String prefix,` `String suffix,` `null)`.
`delete()`	This will delete the file or directory represented by the current `File` object and return `true` if the delete was successful. It won't delete directories that are not empty. To delete a directory, you must first delete the files it contains.
`deleteOnExit()`	Causes the file or directory represented by the current `File` object to be deleted when the program ends. This method does not return a value. The deletion will only be attempted if the JVM terminates normally. Once you call the method for a `File` object, the delete operation is irrevocable, so you will need to be cautious with this method.

371

Note that, in spite of the name, the files that you create by using the `createTempFile()` method are not necessarily temporary, as they will not be deleted automatically. You must use `delete()` or `deleteOnExit()` to ensure that files you no longer require are removed.

You can arrange for a temporary file to be deleted automatically at the end of the program by calling the `deleteOnExit()` method for the `File` object. For example, you might write:

```
File tempFile = File.createTempFile("list", null);
tempFile.deleteOnExit();
```

The first statement will create a temporary file with a name of the form `listxxxxx.tmp` in the default temporary directory. The `xxxxx` part of the name is generated automatically. Since we did not supply a `suffix`, the file extension will be `.tmp` by default. The second statement calls the `deleteOnExit()` method for `tempFile`, so we are assured that this file won't be left lying around after the program finishes. You can apply the `deleteOnExit()` method to any `File` object, not just those corresponding to temporary files, but do so with caution. As noted above, the delete is irrevocable once you have called the method!

We will be trying out some of these methods in examples later in this chapter. Now we understand how to define objects encapsulating a path in a Java program, we can move on to creating file stream objects. We will look at file output streams first.

Creating File Output Streams

You use a `FileOutputStream` object when you want to write to a physical file on a disk. The `FileOutputStream` class is derived from the `OutputStream` class and therefore inherits the methods of that class for writing to a file. However, we won't bother going into detail on these, or the versions in the `FileOutputStream` class that override them, as we will be using the new file channel capability to write to a file.

There are five constructors for `FileOutputStream` objects:

Constructor	Description
FileOutputStream (String filename)	Creates an output stream for the file `filename`. The existing contents of the file will be overwritten. If the file cannot be opened for any reason, an exception of type `FileNotFoundException` will be thrown.
FileOutputStream (String filename, boolean append)	Creates an output stream for the file `filename`. Data written to the file will be appended following the existing contents if `append` is `true`. If append is `false` any existing file contents will be overwritten. If the file cannot be opened for any reason, an exception of type `FileNotFoundException` will be thrown.

Constructor	Description
FileOutputStream (File file)	Creates a file output stream for the file represented by the object file. Any existing file contents will be overwritten. If the file cannot be opened, an exception of type FileNotFoundException will be thrown.
FileOutputStream (File file, boolean append)	Creates a file output stream for the file represented by the object file. Data written to the file will be appended following the existing contents if append is true. If append is false any existing file contents will be overwritten. If the file cannot be opened for writing for any reason, an exception of type FileNotFoundException will the thrown.
FileOutputStream (FileDescriptor desc)	Creates an output stream corresponding to the argument desc. A FileDescriptor object represents an existing connection to a file so, since the file must exist, this constructor does not throw an exception of type FileNotFoundException.

The first four constructors will also create the file if it does not already exist, but only if the parent directory exists, so it is a good idea to check this. All of these constructors can throw a SecurityException if writing to the file is not authorized on your system, although by default there is no security manager for an application in which case there are no restrictions on writing files. Once you have created a FileOutputStream object, the physical file is automatically opened, ready to be written. Once you have written the file, using a **channel** as we shall see in Chapter 10, you can close the file by calling the close() method for the FileOutputStream object. This also closes the file channel and releases all system resources associated with the stream.

To create a stream object of type FileOutputStream, you will typically create a File object first, and then pass that to a FileOutputStream constructor. This approach enables you to check the properties of the file using the File object before you try to create the stream and thus, avoid potential problems. Of course, you can create a FileOutputStream object directly from a String object that defines the path and file name, but it is generally much less convenient to do this. We will come back to the third possibility – creating a file stream object from a FileDescriptor object – in a moment.

In passing, here is how you would create a file output stream directly from the file name:

```
FileOutputStream outputFile = null;    // Place to store the stream reference
try {
  outputFile = new FileOutputStream("myFile.txt");
} catch(FileNotFoundException e) {
  e.printStackTrace(System.err);
}
```

If the file cannot be opened, the constructor will throw a `FileNotFoundException`, which won't be very convenient in most circumstances. We must put the call to the constructor in a `try` block and `catch` the exception if we want the code to compile, unless of course we arrange for the method containing the constructor call to pass on the exception with a `throws` clause. The exception will be thrown if the path refers to a directory rather than a file, or if the parent directory in the path does not exist. If the file does not exist, but the directory that is supposed to contain it does exist, the constructor will create a new file for you. Creating a `File` object first enables you to check the file out and deal with any potential problems. Let's look at ways in which you can apply this.

Ensuring a File Exists

Let's suppose that you want to append data to a file if it exists, and create a new file if it doesn't. Either way, you want to end up with a file output stream to work with. You will need to go through several checks to achieve this:

❑ Use the `File` object to verify that it actually represents a file rather than a directory. If it doesn't, you can't go any further so output an error message.

❑ Use the `File` object to decide whether the file exists. If it doesn't, ensure that you have a `File` object with an absolute path. You need this to obtain and check out the parent directory.

❑ Get the path for the parent directory and create another `File` object using this path. Use the new `File` object to check whether the parent directory exists. If it doesn't, create it using the `mkDirs()` method for the new `File` object.

Let's look at how that might be done in practice.

Try It Out – Ensure that a File Exists

You could guarantee a file is available with the following code:

```java
import java.io.File;
import java.io.FileOutputStream;
import java.io.FileNotFoundException;

public class GuaranteeAFile {
  public static void main(String[] args) {
    String filename = "C:/Beg Java Stuff/Bonzo/Beanbag/myFile.txt";
    File aFile = new File(filename);     // Create the File object

    // Verify the path is a file
    if (aFile.isDirectory()) {

      // Abort after a message
      // You could get input from the keyboard here and try again...
      System.out.println("The path " + aFile.getPath()
                         + " does not specify a file. Program aborted.");
      System.exit(1);
    }
```

```
      // If the file doesn't exist
      if (!aFile.isFile()) {
        // Check the parent directory...
        aFile = aFile.getAbsoluteFile();
        File parentDir = new File(aFile.getParent());
        if (!parentDir.exists()) {    // ... and create it if necessary
          parentDir.mkdirs();
        }
      }

      // Place to store the stream reference
      FileOutputStream outputFile = null;
      try {

        // Create the stream opened to append data
        outputFile = new FileOutputStream(aFile, true);
      } catch (FileNotFoundException e) {
        e.printStackTrace(System.err);
      }
      System.exit(0);
    }
}
```

After executing this code, you should find that the directories and the file have been created. You can try this out with paths with a variety of directory levels. Delete them all when you have done, though.

How It Works

We call isDirectory() in the if statement to see whether the path is just a directory. Instead of aborting at this point we could invite input of a new path from the keyboard, but I'll leave that for you to try. Next we check whether the file exists. If it doesn't we call getAbsoluteFile() to ensure that our File object has a parent path. If we don't do this and we have a file specified with a parent, in the current directory for instance, then getParent() will return null. Having established the File object with an absolute path, we create a File object for the directory containing the file. If this directory does not exist, calling mkdirs() will create all the directories required for the path so that we can then safely create the file stream. The FileOutputStream constructor can in theory throw a FileNotFoundException although not in our situation here. In any event, we must put the try and catch block in for the exception.

A further possibility is that you might start with two strings defining the directory path and the file name separately. You might then want to be sure that you had a valid directory before you created the file. You could do that like this:

```
String dirname = "C:/Beg Java Stuff";    // Directory name
String filename = "charData.txt";        // File name

File dir = new File(dirname);             // File object for directory
if (!dir.exists()) {      // If directory does not exist
  if (!dir.mkdirs()) {    // ...create it
    System.out.println("Cannot create directory: " + dirname);
    System.exit(1);
```

```
      }
   } else if (!dir.isDirectory()) {
      System.err.println(dirname + " is not a directory");
      System.exit(1);
   }

   // Now create the file...
```

If the directory doesn't exist, we call `mkdirs()` inside the nested `if` to create it. Since the method returns `false` if the directory was not created, this will check whether or not we have indeed managed to create the directory.

Avoiding Overwriting a File

In some situations, when the file does exist you may not want it to be overwritten. Here is one way you could avoid overwriting a file if it already exists:

```
String filename = "C:/Beg Java Stuff/myFile.txt";
File aFile = new File(filename);
FileOutputStream outputFile = null;   // Place to store the stream reference
if (aFile.isFile()) {
   System.out.println("myFile.txt already exists.");
} else {
   // Create the file stream
   try {
      // Create the stream opened to append data
      outputFile = new FileOutputStream(aFile);
      System.out.println("myFile.txt output stream created");
   } catch (FileNotFoundException e) {
      e.printStackTrace(System.err);
   }
}
```

Of course, if you want to be sure that the path will in fact result in a new file being created when it doesn't already exist, you would need to put in the code from the previous example that checks out the parent directory. The fragment above avoids overwriting the file but it is not terribly helpful. If the file exists, we create the same `FileOutputStream` object as before, but if it doesn't, we just toss out an error message. In practice, you are more likely to want the program to take some action so that the existing file is protected but the new file still gets written. One solution would be to rename the original file in some way if it exists, and then create the new one with the same name as the original. This takes a little work though.

Try It Out – Avoid Overwriting a File

Without worrying about plugging in the code that ensures that the file directory exists, here is how we could prevent an existing file from being overwritten.

```
import java.io.File;
import java.io.FileOutputStream;
```

```
import java.io.FileNotFoundException;

public class AvoidOverwritingFile {
  public static void main(String[] args) {
    String filepath = "C:/Beg Java Stuff/myFile.txt";
    File aFile = new File(filepath);
    FileOutputStream outputFile = null;      // Stores the stream reference
    if (aFile.isFile()) {
      File newFile = aFile;                  // Start with the original file

      // We will append "_old" to the file
      // name repeatedly until it is unique
      do {
        String name = newFile.getName();     // Get the name of the file
        int period =
          name.indexOf('.');                 // Find the separator for the extension
        newFile = new File(newFile.getParent(),
                          name.substring(0, period) + "_old"
                          + name.substring(period));
      } while (!aFile.renameTo(newFile));    // Stop when renaming works
    }

    // Now we can create the new file
    try {

      // Create the stream opened to append data
      outputFile = new FileOutputStream(aFile);
      System.out.println("myFile.txt output stream created");
    } catch (FileNotFoundException e) {
      e.printStackTrace(System.err);
    }
    System.exit(0);
  }
}
```

If you run this a few times, you should see some _old_old... files created.

How It Works

If the file exists, we execute the code in the if block. This stores the reference to the original File object in newFile as a starting point for the do-while loop that follows. Each iteration of the loop will append the string _old to the name of the file and create a new File object using this name in the original directory. The expression in the loop condition then tries to rename the original file using the new File object. If this fails, we go round the loop again and add a further occurrence of _old to the file name. Eventually we should succeed as long as we don't do it so often that we exceed the permitted file name length of the system. The getParent() method gives us the parent directory for the file and the getName() method returns the file name. We have to split the file name into the name part and the extension to append our _old string, and the charAt() method for the String object gives us the index position of the separating period. Of course, this code presumes the existence of a file extension since we define our original file name with one. It is quite possible to deal with files that don't have an extension but I'll leave that as a little digression for you.

FileDescriptor Objects

A `FileOutputStream` object has a method, `getFD()`, which returns an object of type `FileDescriptor` that represents the current connection to the physical file. You cannot create a `FileDescriptor` object yourself. You can only obtain a `FileDescriptor` object by calling the `getFD()` method for an object that represents a file stream. Once you have closed the stream, you can no longer obtain the `FileDescriptor` object for it since the connection to the file will have been terminated.

You can use a `FileDescriptor` object to create other stream objects when you want to have several connected to the same file concurrently. Since a `FileDescriptor` object represents an existing connection, you can only use it to create streams with read and/or write permissions that are consistent with the original stream. You can't use the `FileDescriptor` object from a `FileOutputStream` to create a `FileInputStream` for instance.

If you look at the documentation for the `FileDescriptor` class, you'll see that it also defines three public static data members: `in`, `out`, and `err`, which are themselves of type `FileDescriptor`. These correspond to the standard system input, the standard system output, and the standard error stream respectively, and they are there as a convenience for when you want to create byte or character stream objects corresponding to the standard streams.

> Don't confuse the data members of the **FileDescriptor** class with the data members of the same name defined by the **System** class in the **java.lang** package. The **in, out,** and **err** data members of the **System** class are of type **PrintStream**, so they have the **print()** and **println()** methods. The **FileDescriptor** data members do not.

Summary

In this chapter, we have discussed the facilities for inspecting physical files and directories, and for writing basic types of data to a file. The important points we have discussed include:

❑ An object of the class `File` can encapsulate a file or directory path. The path encapsulated by a `File` object does not necessarily correspond to a physical file or directory.

❑ You can use a `File` object to test whether the path it encapsulates refers to a physical file or directory. If it does not, there are methods available to create it together with any directories that are part of the path that may also be required.

❑ The `File` class defines static methods for creating temporary files.

❑ An object of type `FileDescriptor` can also identify a physical file.

❑ A `FileOutputStream` object can be created from a `File` object and the file will be opened for writing. If the file does not exist it will be created where possible.

❑ You can lead a horse to water but you can't make him drink.

Exercises

1. Modify the example that avoids overwriting a file to allow for file names that do not have extensions.

2. Filenames on many systems are not of unlimited length, so appending _old to file names may break down at some point. Modify the example that avoids overwriting a file to append a three-digit numerical value to the file name to differentiate it from the existing file instead of just adding _old. The program should check for the presence of three digits at the end of the name for the existing file and replace this with a value incremented by an amount to make it unique. (That is, increment the last three digits by 1 until a unique file name is created.)

3. Write a program that will list all the directories in a directory defined by a path supplied as a command line argument, or all the directories on a system if no command line argument is present. (Hint: The listRoots() method will give you the roots on a system and the listFiles() method will give you an array of File objects for the files and directories in any given directory – including a root.)

Writing Files

In this chapter, we will be looking at ways in which basic data can be written to a file using the new file I/O capability. The JDK 1.4 release introduced this new mechanism for file I/O that supersedes the read/write capability provided by readers and writers from the `java.io` package when applied to file streams. Since the new file I/O does everything that the old capability does, and does it better, we will focus just on that.

In this chapter you will learn:

- ❏ The principles of reading and writing files using the new I/O.
- ❏ How to obtain a file channel for a file.
- ❏ How to create a buffer and load it with data.
- ❏ What view buffers are and how you use them.
- ❏ How you use a channel object to write the contents of a buffer to a file.

File I/O Basics

If you are new to programming file operations, there are a couple of things that may not be apparent to you and can be a source of confusion so let's clarify them before we go any further.

Firstly, let's consider the nature of a file. Once you have written data to a file, you can regard it as just a linear sequence of bytes. The bytes in a file are referenced by their offset from the beginning, so the first byte is byte 0, the next byte is byte 1, the third byte is byte 2, and so on through to the end of the file. If there are n bytes in a file the last byte will be at offset n-1. There is no specific information in the file about how the data originated or what it represents unless you explicitly put it there. Even if there is, you need to know that it's there and read and interpret the data accordingly.

For instance if you write a series of 25 binary values of type int to a file, it will contain 100 bytes. There will be nothing in the file to indicate that the data consists of four byte integers so there is nothing to prevent you from reading the data back as 50 Unicode characters or 10 long values followed by a string, or any other arbitrary collection of data items that corresponds to 100 bytes. Of course, the result is unlikely to be very meaningful unless you interpret the data in the form in which it was written. This implies that to read data from a file correctly, you need to have prior knowledge of the structure and format of the data.

There are many ways in which the form of the data in the file may be recorded or implied. For instance, one way that the format of the data in a file can be communicated is to use an agreed file name extension for data of a particular kind, such as .java or .gif or .wav. Each type of file has a predefined structure so from the file extension you know how to interpret the data in the file. Another way is to use a generalized mechanism for communicating data and its structure such as XML. We will be looking into how we can work with XML in Java in Chapters 21 and 22.

You can access an existing file to read from or write to it in two different ways, described as **sequential access** or **random access**. The latter is sometimes referred to as **direct access**. Sequential access to a file is quite straightforward and works pretty much as you would expect. Sequential read access involves reading bytes from the file starting from the beginning with byte 0. Of course, if you are only interested in the file contents starting at byte 100, you can just read and ignore the first 100 bytes. Sequential write access involves writing bytes to the file either starting at the beginning if you are replacing the existing data or at the end if you are appending new data to the file.

The term **random access** is often misunderstood initially. Just like sequential access, random access is just a way of accessing data in a file and has nothing to do with how the data in the file is structured or how the physical file was originally written. You can access any file randomly for reading and/or writing. When you access a file randomly, you can read one or more bytes from the file starting at any point. For instance, you could read 20 bytes starting at the thirteenth byte in the file (which will be the byte at offset 12 of course), then read 50 bytes starting at the 101st byte or any other point that you choose. Similarly, you can update an existing file in random access mode by writing data starting at any point in the file. In random access mode, the choice of where to start reading or writing and how many bytes you read or write, is entirely up to you. You just need to know the offset for the byte where a read or write operation should start. Of course, for these to be sensible and successful operations, you have to have a clear idea of how the data in the file is structured.

> First a note of caution; before running any of the examples in this chapter, be sure to set up a separate directory for storing the files that you are using when you are testing programs. It's also not a bad idea to back up any files and directories on your system that you don't want to risk losing. But of course, you do back up your files regularly anyway – right?
>
> The old adage, 'If anything can go wrong, it will,' applies particularly in this context, as does the complementary principle, 'If anything can't go wrong, it will'. Remember also that the probability of something going wrong increases in proportion to the inconvenience it is likely to cause.

File Input and Output

The new file I/O capabilities introduced in Java 1.4 provide the potential for substantially improved performance at the cost of some slight increase in complexity over the I/O facilities of previous releases. There are three kinds of objects involved in reading and writing files using the new I/O capability:

❑ A **file stream object** that encapsulates the physical file that you are working with. We saw how to create `FileOutputStream` objects at the end of the previous chapter and you use these for files to which you want to write. In the next chapter we will be using `FileInputStream` objects for files that we want to read.

❑ One or more **buffer objects** in which you put the data to be written to a file, or from which you get the data that has been read. We will learn about buffer objects in the next section.

❑ A **channel object** that provides the connection to the file and does the reading or writing of the data using one or more buffer objects. We will see how to obtain a channel from a file stream object later in this chapter.

The way in which these types of object work together is illustrated in the diagram below:

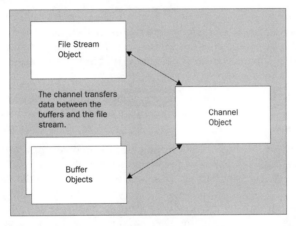

The process for writing and reading files is basically quite simple. To write to a file, you load data into one or more buffers that you have created, and then call a method for the channel object to write the data to the file that is encapsulated by the file stream. To read from a file, you call a method for the channel object to read data from the file into one or more buffers, and then retrieve the data from the buffers.

There are four classes defined in the `java.io` package that we will be using when we are working with files. As we have said, the `FileInputStream` and `FileOutputStream` classes define objects that provide access to a file for reading or writing respectively. You use an object of type `RandomAccessFile` when you want to access a file randomly, or when you want to use a single channel to both read from and write to a file. We will be exploring this, along with the `FileInputStream` class in the next chapter. You will see from the SDK documentation for the `FileInputStream`, `FileOutputStream`, and `RandomAccessFile` classes that they each provide methods for I/O operations. However, we will ignore these, as we will be using the services of a file channel to perform operations with objects of these stream classes. The only method from these classes that we will be using is the `close()` method, that closes the file and any associated channel.

Channels

Channels were introduced in the 1.4 release of Java to provide a faster capability for input and output operations with files, network sockets, and piped I/O operations between programs than the methods provided by the stream classes. We will only be discussing channels in the context of files. The channel mechanism can take advantage of buffering and other capabilities of the underlying operating system and therefore is considerably more efficient than using the operations provided directly within the file stream classes. As we said earlier, a channel transfers data between a file and one or more buffers. We will take a quick look at the overall relationship between the various classes that define channels and buffers, and then look into the details of how you use channels with file streams.

There are a considerable number of classes and interfaces defining both channels and buffers. They also have similar names such as `ByteBuffer` and `ByteChannel`. Of course, `File` and file stream objects are also involved in file I/O operations so you will be using at least four different types of objects working together when you read from or write to files. Just to clarify what they all do, here's a summary of the essential role of each of them in file operations:

❑ A `File` object encapsulates a path to a file or a directory, and such an object encapsulating a file path can be used to construct a file stream object.

❑ A `FileInputStream` object encapsulates a file that can be read by a channel. A `FileOutputstream` object encapsulates a file that can be written by a channel. As we will see in the next chapter, a `RandomAccessFile` object can encapsulate a file that can be both read and written by a channel.

❑ A buffer just holds data in memory. You load into a buffer what is to be written to a file using the buffer's `put()` methods. You use a buffer's `get()` methods to retrieve data that has been read from a file.

❑ You obtain a `FileChannel` object from a file stream object or a `RandomAccessFile` object. A `FileChannel` object can read and write a file using `read()` and `write()` methods with a buffer or buffers as the source or destination of the data.

The channel interfaces and classes that we will be using are in the `java.nio.channels` package. The classes that define buffers are defined in the `java.nio` package. In a program that reads or writes files we will therefore need `import` statements for class names from at least three packages, the two packages we have just introduced plus the `java.io` package.

Channel Operations

There are a series of channel interfaces, each of which declares a set of one or more related operations that a channel may perform. They all extend a common interface, `Channel`, which declares two methods:

❑ The `close()` method that closes a channel

❑ The `isOpen()` method that tests the state of the channel, returning `true` if it is open and `false` otherwise

Note that closing a channel does not necessarily close the file that the channel is attached to but closing a file also closes its channel. The channel interfaces are related as illustrated in the hierarchy shown below:

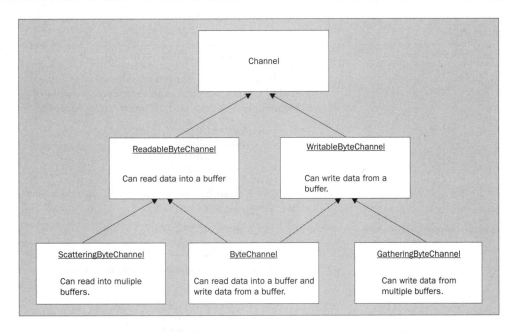

Each arrow points from a given interface to an interface that it implements. The `ByteChannel` interface simply combines the operations specified by the `ReadableByteChannel` and `WritableByteChannel` interface without declaring any additional methods. The `ScatteringByteChannel` interface extends the `ReadableByteChannel` interface by adding methods that allow data to be read and distributed amongst several separate buffers in a single operation. The `GatheringByteChannel` adds methods to those of the `WritableByteChannel` to permit writing from a number of separate buffers in a single operation.

The methods that each channel interface declares are as follows:

Interface	Method and Description
ReadableByteChannel	`int read(ByteBuffer input)`
	Reads bytes from a channel into the buffer specified by the argument and returns the number of bytes read, or −1 if the end of the stream is reached.
WritableByteChannel	`int write(ByteBuffer output)`
	Writes bytes from the buffer specified by the argument to the channel, and returns the number of bytes written.
ByteChannel	This interface just inherits methods from the `ReadableByteChannel` and `WritableByteChannel` interfaces. No additional methods are declared.

Table continued on following page

Interface	Method and Description
ScatteringByteChannel	`int read(ByteBuffer[] inputs)`
	Reads bytes from the channel into the array of buffers specified by the argument, and returns the number of bytes read, or -1 if the end of the stream is reached.

	`int read(ByteBuffer[] inputs,`
	`          int offset,`
	`          int length)`

	Reads bytes from the channel into length buffers from the array specified by the first argument starting with the buffer, `inputs[offset]`.
GatheringByteChannel	`int write(ByteBuffer[] outputs)`
	Writes bytes from the array of buffers specified by the argument to the channel, and returns the number of bytes written.

	`int write(ByteBuffer[] outputs,`
	`           int offset,`
	`           int length)`

	Writes bytes to the channel from length buffers from the array specified by the first argument, starting with the buffer, `outputs[offset]`.

All of these methods can throw exceptions of one kind or another and we will go into details on these when we come to apply them. Note that a channel only works with buffers of type `ByteBuffer`. There are other kinds of buffers as we shall see, but you can't use them directly with the `read()` and `write()` methods for a channel. We will see what determines the number of bytes read or written in an operation when we discuss buffers in detail.

File Channels

A `FileChannel` object defines a channel for a physical file, and provides an efficient mechanism for reading, writing, and manipulating the file. You can't create a `FileChannel` directly. You first have to create a file stream object for the file, then obtain a reference to the `FileChannel` object for the file by calling the `getChannel()` method for the file stream object. Here's how you would obtain the channel for a `FileOutputStream` object:

```
File aFile = new File("C:/Beg Java Stuff/myFile.text");
// Place to store an output stream reference
FileOutputStream outputFile = null;
try {
  // Create the stream opened to write
  outputFile = new FileOutputStream(aFile);
} catch (FileNotFoundException e) {
  e.printStackTrace(System.err);
```

```
    System.exit(1);
  }
  // Get the channel for the file
  FileChannel outputChannel = outputFile.getChannel();
```

The `FileChannel` class implements all of the channel interfaces that we discussed in the previous section, so any `FileChannel` object incorporates the methods we have seen for both reading and writing a file. However, a `FileChannel` object obtained from a `FileOutputStream` object will not be able to read from the file since the stream only permits output. Similarly, a `FileChannel` obtained from a `FileInputStream` object can only read from the file. If you try to perform a read operation on a file opened just for output, a `NonReadableChannelException` will be thrown. Attempting to write to a file opened for input will result in a `NonWritableChannelException` being thrown.

Once you have obtained a reference to a file channel, you are ready to read from or write to the file, but we need to learn a bit more about buffers before we can try that out.

Buffers

All the classes that define buffers have the abstract class `Buffer` as a base. The `Buffer` class therefore defines the fundamental characteristics common to all buffers. A particular buffer can store a sequence of elements of a given type, and an element can be of any primitive data type other than `boolean`. Thus, you can create buffers to store `byte` values, `char` values, `short` values, `int` values, `long` values, `float` values, or `double` values. The following classes in the `java.nio` package define these buffers:

Class	Description
ByteBuffer	A buffer that stores elements of type `byte`. You can also store the binary values of any of the other primitive types in this buffer, except for type `boolean`. Each binary value that you store will occupy a number of bytes in the buffer determined by the type – values of type `char` or `short` will occupy two bytes, `int` values will occupy four bytes, and so on. Only buffers of this type can be used in a file I/O operation.
CharBuffer	A buffer that only stores elements of type `char`.
ShortBuffer	A buffer that only stores elements of type `short`.
IntBuffer	A buffer that only stores elements of type `int`.
LongBuffer	A buffer that only stores elements of type `long`.
FloatBuffer	A buffer that only stores elements of type `float`.
DoubleBuffer	A buffer that only stores elements of type `double`.

We keep repeating *except for type boolean* every so often, so we had better address that. The various types of buffers only provide for the numerical data types and type `boolean` does not fit into this category. Of course, you may actually want to record some `boolean` values in a file. In this case, you have to devise a suitable alternative representation. You could use integer values 0 and 1, or perhaps strings "true" and "false", or even characters 't' and 'f'. You could even represent a `boolean` value as a single bit and pack eight of them at a time into a single byte, but this is only likely to be worthwhile if you have a lot of them. Which approach you choose will depend on what is most convenient in the context in which you are using them.

While we have seven different classes defining buffers, a channel only uses buffers of type `ByteBuffer` to read or write data. The other types of buffers in the table above are called **view buffers**, because they are usually created as views of an existing buffer of type `ByteBuffer`. We will see how and why a little later in this chapter.

Buffer Capacity

Each type of buffer stores **elements** of a specific kind – a `ByteBuffer` object holds bytes, a `LongBuffer` object holds integers of type `long`, and so on for the other buffer types. The **capacity** of a buffer is the maximum number of *elements* it can contain, not the number of *bytes* – unless, of course, it stores elements of type `byte`. The capacity of a buffer is fixed when you create it and cannot be changed subsequently. You can obtain the capacity for a buffer object as a value of type `int` by calling the `capacity()` method that it inherits from the `Buffer` class.

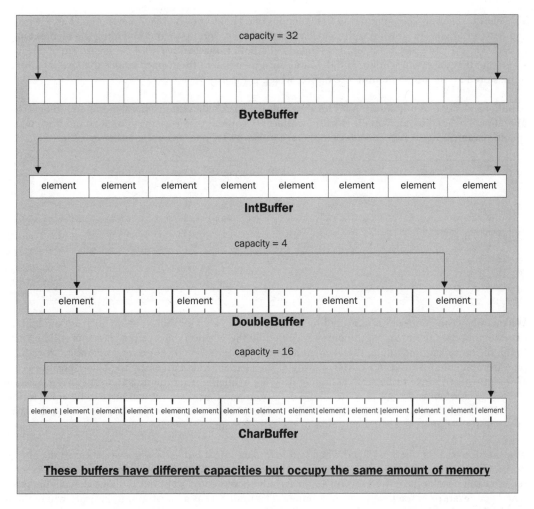

These buffers have different capacities but occupy the same amount of memory

Of course, for a buffer that stores bytes, the capacity will be the maximum number of bytes it can hold, but for a buffer of type `DoubleBuffer` for instance that stores `double` values, the capacity will be the maximum number of `double` values you can put in it. Elements in a buffer are indexed from zero so the index position for referencing elements in a buffer runs from 0 to *capacity-1*.

Buffer Position and Limit

A buffer also has a **limit** and a **position**, both of which affect read/write operations executed by a channel using the buffer.

The **position** is the index position of the next buffer element to be read or written. This sounds a little strange, but keep in mind that a buffer can be for file input or output. For example, with a buffer used for output, the position identifies the next element to be written to the file. For a buffer used for file input, the position identifies where the next element read from the file will be stored.

The **limit** is the index position of the first element that should <u>not</u> be read or written. Thus, elements can be read or written starting with the element at *position*, and up to and including the element at *limit-1*. Thus if you want to fill all the elements in a buffer, the *position* must be at zero since this is where the first data item will go, and the limit must be equal to the capacity since the last data item has to be stored at the last element in the buffer, which is *capacity-1*.

A buffer's position and limit are used for determining what elements are involved in a read or write operation executed by a channel. How they affect I/O operations is easier to understand if we take a specific example. Let's first consider an operation that writes data from the buffer to a file.

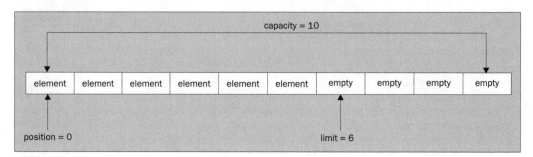

When a file write operation is executed by a channel using a given buffer, elements from the buffer will be written to the file starting at the index specified by the position. Successive elements will be written to the file up to, and including, the element at index position *limit-1*. For a read operation, data that is read from the file is stored in a buffer starting at the element index given by the buffer position. Elements will continue to be read, assuming they are available from the file, up to the index position *limit-1*. Thus when you want to write all the data from a buffer, the limit will have to be equal to the capacity. In this case the limit will be an index value that is one beyond the index value for the last element in the buffer, so *limit-1* will refer to the last element.

The position and limit are involved when you load data into a buffer or retrieve data from it. The position specifies where the next element should be inserted in a buffer or retrieved from it. As we shall see, you will usually have the position automatically incremented to point to the next available position when you insert or extract elements in a buffer. The limit acts as a constraint to indicate where the data in a buffer ends, a bit like an end-of-file marker. You cannot insert or extract elements beyond the position specified by the limit.

Since a buffer's position is an index, it must be greater than or equal to zero. You can also deduce that it must also be less than or equal to the limit. Clearly, the limit cannot be greater than the capacity of a buffer. Otherwise, we could be trying to write elements to positions beyond the end of the buffer. However, as we have seen, it can be equal to it. These relationships can be expressed as:

```
0 • position • limit • capacity
```

As a general rule, if your code attempts to do things directly or indirectly that result in these relationships being violated, an exception will be thrown.

When you create a new independent buffer, its capacity will be fixed at a value that you specify. It will also have a position of zero and its limit will be set to its capacity. When you create a view buffer from an existing `ByteBuffer`, the contents of the view buffer starts at the current position for the `ByteBuffer`. The capacity and limit for the view buffer will be set to the limit for the original buffer, divided by the number of bytes in an element in the view buffer. The limit and position for the view buffer will subsequently be independent of the limit and position for the original buffer.

Setting the Position and Limit

You can set the position and limit for a buffer explicitly by using the following methods defined in the `Buffer` class:

Method	Description
`position(int newPosition)`	Sets the position to the index value specified by the argument. The new position value must be greater than or equal to zero, and not greater than the current limit, otherwise an exception of type `IllegalArgumentException` will be thrown. If the buffer's mark is defined (we will come to the mark in the next section) and greater than the new position, it will be discarded.
`limit(int newLimit)`	Sets the limit to the index value specified by the argument. If the buffer's position is greater than the new limit it will be set to the new limit. If the buffer's mark is defined and exceeds the new limit it will be discarded. If the new limit value is negative or greater than the buffer's capacity, an exception of type `IllegalArgumentException` will be thrown.

Both of these methods return a reference of type `Buffer` for the object for which they were called. This enables you to chain them together in a single statement. For instance, given a buffer reference, `buf`, you could set both the position and the limit with the statement:

```
buf.limit(512).position(256);
```

This assumes the capacity of the buffer is at least 512 elements. If you are explicitly setting both the limit and the position you should always choose the sequence in which you set them to avoid setting a position that is greater than the limit. If the buffer's limit starts out less than the new position you want to set, attempting to set the position first will result in an `IllegalArgumentException` being thrown. Setting the limit first to a value less than the current position will have a similar effect. If you want to avoid checking the current limit and position when you want to reset both, you can always do it safely like this:

```
buf.position(0).limit(newLimit).position(newPosition);
```

Of course, the new position and limit values must be legal; otherwise an exception will still be thrown. In other words `newPosition` must be non-negative, and less than `newLimit`. To be 100% certain setting a new position and limit is going to work, you could code it something like this:

```
if(newPosition >= 0 && newLimit > newPosition)
  buf.position(0).limit(newLimit).position(newPosition);
else
  System.out.printn("Illegal position:limit settings."
                  + "Position: " + newPosition + " Limit: "+ newLimit);
```

You can determine whether there are any elements between the position and the limit in a buffer by calling the `hasRemaining()` method for the buffer:

```
if (buf.hasRemaining()) {    // If limit-position is >0
  System.out.println("We have space in the buffer!");
}
```

You can also find out how many elements can be accommodated using the `remaining()` method. For example:

```
System.out.println("The buffer can accommodate " + buf.remaining() +
                                           " more elements.");
```

Of course, the value returned by the `remaining()` method will be the same as the expression `buf.limit()-buf.position()`.

Creating Buffers

None of the classes that define buffers have constructors available. Instead, you use a static factory method to create a buffer. You will typically create a buffer object of type `ByteBuffer` by calling the static `allocate()` method for the class. You pass a value of type `int` as an argument to the method that defines the capacity of the buffer – the maximum number of elements the buffer must accommodate. For example:

```
// Buffer of 1024 bytes capacity
ByteBuffer buf =  ByteBuffer.allocate(1024);
```

When you create a new buffer using the `allocate()` method for the `Buffer` class, it will have a position of zero and its limit will be set to its capacity. This buffer will therefore have a position of 0, and a limit and capacity of 1024.

You can also create other types of buffers in the same way. For instance:

```
// Buffer stores 100 float values
FloatBuffer floatBuf =  FloatBuffer.allocate(100);
```

Since the elements are of type `float`, the data in this buffer will occupy 400 bytes. Its position will be 0, and its limit and capacity will be 100.

In practice, you are unlikely to want to create buffers other than `ByteBuffer` objects in this way, since you cannot use them directly for channel I/O operations. You will usually create a `ByteBuffer` first, and then create any view buffers that you need from this buffer.

View Buffers

You can use a `ByteBuffer` object to create a buffer of any of the other types we have introduced, that shares all or part of the memory that the original `ByteBuffer` uses to store data. Such a buffer is referred to as a **view buffer**, because it allows you to view the contents of the byte buffer as elements of another data type. Data is always transferred to or from a file as a series of bytes, but it will typically consist of data elements of a mix of types other than type `byte`. A view buffer therefore has two primary uses, for loading data items that are not of type `byte` into a byte buffer prior to writing it to a file, and accessing data that has been read from a file as elements that are other than type `byte`.

We could create a **view buffer** of type `IntBuffer` from a `ByteBuffer` object like this:

```
ByteBuffer buf = ByteBuffer.allocate(1024); // Buffer of 1024 bytes capacity
IntBuffer intBuf = buf.asIntBuffer();        // Now create a view buffer
```

The content of the view buffer, `intBuf`, that we create here will start at the byte buffer's current position, which in this case is zero since it is newly created. The remaining bytes in `buf` will effectively be shared with the view buffer. At least, the maximum number of them that is a multiple of 4 will be, since `intBuf` stores elements of type `int` that require 4 bytes each. The view buffer will have an initial position of 0, and a capacity and limit of 256. This is because 256 elements of type `int` completely fill the 1024 bytes remaining in `buf`. If we had allocated `buf` with 1023 bytes, then `intBuf` would have mapped to 1020 bytes of `buf`, and would have a capacity and limit of 255.

You could now use this view buffer to load the original buffer with values of type `int`. You could then use the original byte buffer to write the `int` values to a file. As we said at the outset, view buffers have a similar role when you are reading a file. You would have a primary buffer of type `ByteBuffer`, into which you read bytes from a file, and then you might access the contents of the `ByteBuffer` through a view buffer of type `DoubleBuffer` so you can retrieve the data read from the file as type `double`.

The `ByteBuffer` class defines the following methods for creating view buffers:

Method	Description
`asCharBuffer()`	Returns a reference to a view buffer of type `CharBuffer`.
`asShortBuffer()`	Returns a reference to a view buffer of type `ShortBuffer`.
`asIntBuffer()`	Returns a reference to a view buffer of type `IntBuffer`.
`asLongBuffer()`	Returns a reference to a view buffer of type `LongBuffer`.
`asFloatBuffer()`	Returns a reference to a view buffer of type `FloatBuffer`.
`asDoubleBuffer()`	Returns a reference to a view buffer of type `DoubleBuffer`.
`asReadOnlyBuffer()`	Returns a reference to a read-only view buffer of type `ByteBuffer`.

In each case, the view buffer's contents start at the current position of the original byte buffer. The position of the view buffer itself is initially set to zero, and its capacity and limit are set to the number of bytes remaining in the original byte buffer divided by the number of bytes in the type of element that the view buffer holds. The diagram below illustrates a view buffer of type `IntBuffer` that is created after the initial position of the byte buffer has been incremented by 2, possibly after inserting a `char` value into the byte buffer:

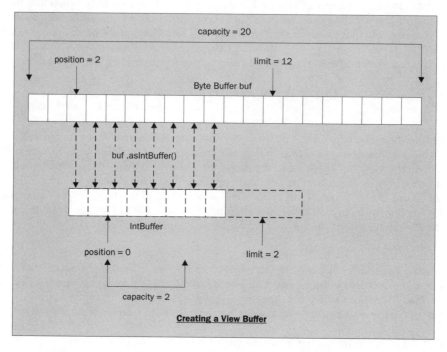

Creating a View Buffer

You can create as many view buffers from a buffer of type `ByteBuffer` as you want, and they can overlap or not as you require. A view buffer always maps to bytes in the byte buffer starting at the current position. You will frequently want to map several different view buffers to a single byte buffer each providing a view of a different segment of the byte buffer:

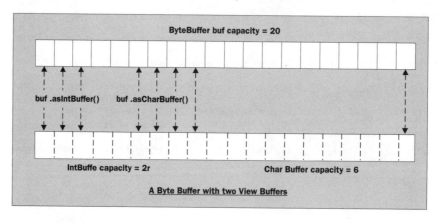

A Byte Buffer with two View Buffers

The diagram illustrates a byte buffer with a view buffer of type `IntBuffer` mapped to the first 8 bytes, and a view buffer of type `CharBuffer` mapped to the last 12 bytes. All you need to do to achieve this is to ensure the position of the byte buffer is set appropriately before you create each view buffer.

Duplicating and Slicing Buffers

You can duplicate any of the buffers we have discussed by calling the `duplicate()` method for a buffer. The method returns a reference to a buffer with the same type as the original, which shares the contents. The duplicate buffer initially has the same capacity, position, and limit as the original. However, although changes to the contents of the duplicate will be reflected in the original – and vice versa, each buffer's position and limit are independent of the other. One use for a duplicate buffer is when you want to access different parts of the buffer's contents concurrently. You can retrieve data from a duplicate buffer without affecting the original buffer in any way.

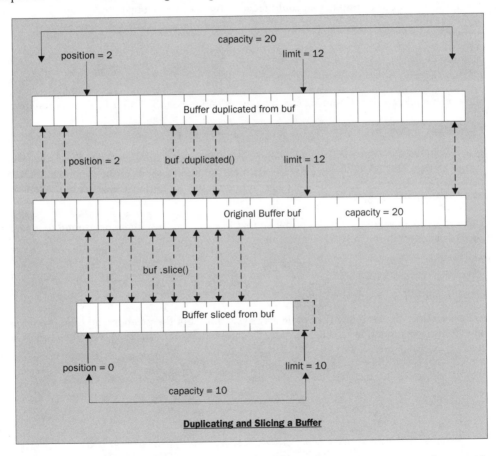

Duplicating and Slicing a Buffer

Thus a duplicate buffer is not really a new buffer in memory. It is just a new object that provides an alternative route to accessing the same block of memory that is being used to buffer the data. The `duplicate()` method returns a reference of a new object of the same type as the original, but has no independent data storage. It merely shares the memory that belongs to the original buffer object but with independent position and limit values.

You can also **slice** any of the buffers we have seen. Calling the `slice()` method for a buffer will return a reference to a new buffer object of the same type as the original that shares the elements remaining in the original buffer. In other words, it maps to a part of the original buffer starting at the element at its current position, up to and including the element at *limit-1*. Of course, if the position of the original buffer object is zero and the limit is equal to the capacity, the `slice()` method effectively produces the same result as the `duplicate()` method, that is the entire buffer will be shared. Slicing a buffer gives you access to the data in a given part of a buffer through two or more separate routes, each with its own independent position and limit.

Creating Buffers by Wrapping Arrays

You can also create a buffer by wrapping an existing array of the same type as the buffer elements by calling one of the static `wrap()` method in the `Buffer` class. This creates a buffer that already contains the data in the array. For example, you could create a `ByteBuffer` object by wrapping an array of type `byte[]`, like this:

```
String saying = "Handsome is as handsome does.";
byte[] array = saying.getBytes();    // Get string as byte array
ByteBuffer buf = ByteBuffer.wrap(array);
```

Of course, you could convert the string to a byte array and create the buffer in a single statement:

```
ByteBuffer buf = ByteBuffer.wrap(saying.getBytes());
```

In any event, the buffer object will not have memory of its own to store the data. The buffer will be backed by the byte array that we have used to define it so modifications to the elements in the buffer will alter the array, and vice versa. The capacity and limit for the buffer will be set to the length of the array and its position will be zero.

You can also wrap an array to create a buffer so that the position and limit correspond to a particular sequence of elements in the array. For example:

```
String saying = "Handsome is as handsome does.";
byte[] array = saying.getBytes();    // Get string as byte array
ByteBuffer buf = ByteBuffer.wrap(array, 9, 14);
```

This creates a buffer by wrapping the whole array as before, but the position and limit are set using the second and third argument, in effect specifying the subsection of the array that can be read or written.

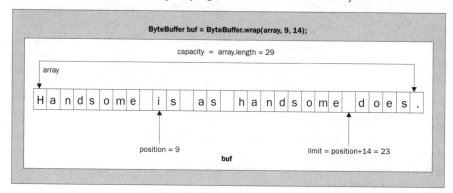

The buffer's capacity will be `array.length` and the position is set to the value of the second argument, 9. The third argument specifies the number of buffer elements that can be read or written so this value will be added to the position to define the limit. If either the second argument value or the sums of the second and third argument values do not represent legal index values for the array, then an exception of type `IndexOutOfBoundsException` will be thrown.

You can also wrap arrays of other basic types to create a buffer of the corresponding type. For example:

```
long[] numbers = { 1, 1, 2, 3, 5, 8, 13, 21, 34, 55, 89};
LongBuffer numBuf = LongBuffer.wrap(numbers);
```

The buffer of type `LongBuffer` that we create will have a capacity of `array.length`, which will be 11. The buffer position will be set to 0 and the limit will be set to the capacity. In a similar manner we can create buffers from arrays of any of the other basic types with the exception of type `boolean`.

If a buffer object has been created from an array, you can obtain a reference to the backing array that is storing the data in the buffer by calling `array()` for the buffer. For example, for the buffer created by the previous code fragment, we could obtain a reference to the original array like this:

```
long[] data = numBuf.array();
```

The variable data will now contain a reference to the original array, `numbers`, which we used to create `numBuf`. If the buffer had not been created from an array, the `array()` method will throw an exception of type `UnsupportedOperationException`.

If a buffer object is passed to a method as an argument, you might need to determine whether or not it has a backing array – before you can call its `array()` method for example, if you plan to alter the buffer's contents by changing the elements in the array. The `hasArray()` method for a buffer object will return `true` if the buffer was created from an array, and `false` otherwise. Typical usage of this method is something like this:

```
if(numBuf.hasArray()) {
  long[] data = numBuf.array();
  // Modify the data array directly to alter the buffer...

} else {
  // Modify the buffer using put() methods for the buffer object...
}
```

Obviously you would only take the trouble to do this if modifying the backing array was a whole lot more convenient or faster than using `put()` methods for the buffer. We will see how we use `put()` methods to modify a buffer's contents very soon.

You can create buffers of type `CharBuffer` by wrapping an object of type `String`, as well as an array of type `char[]`. For example:

```
String wisdom = "Many a mickle makes a muckle.";
CharBuffer charBuf = CharBuffer.wrap(wisdom);
```

Since a `String` object is immutable, the buffer that results from this is read-only. Attempting to transfer data into the buffer will result in an exception of type `ReadOnlyBufferException` being thrown.

Marking a Buffer

You use the **mark property** for a buffer to record a particular index position in the buffer, which you want to be able to return to later. You can set the mark to the current position by calling the buffer object's `mark()` method that is inherited from the `Buffer` class. For example:

```
buf.mark();
```

This method also returns a reference of type `Buffer` so you could chain it with the methods for setting the limit and position:

```
buf.limit(512).position(256).mark();
```

This will set the mark to 256, the same as the position.

After a series of operations that alter the position, you can reset the buffer's position to the mark that you have set by calling the `reset()` method that is inherited from the `Buffer` class:

```
buf.reset();
```

If you have not set the mark, or it has been discarded by an operation to set the limit or the position, the `reset()` method will throw an exception of type `InvalidMarkException`. The mark for a view buffer operates independently of the mark for the buffer from which it was created.

You probably won't need to mark a buffer most of the time. You would typically use it in a situation where you are scanning some part of a buffer to determine what kind of data it contains, after reading a file for instance. You could mark the point where you started the analysis, and then return to that point by calling `reset()` for the buffer when you have figured out how to deal with the data.

Buffer Data Transfers

Of course, before you can use a channel to write the contents of a buffer to a file, you need to load the buffer with the data. Methods for loading data into a buffer are referred to as **put methods**. Similarly, when a channel has read data from a file into a buffer, you are likely to want to retrieve the data from the buffer. In this case you use the buffer's **get methods**.

There are two kinds of operations that transfer data elements to or from a buffer. A **relative put or get operation** transfers one or more elements starting at the buffer's current position. In this case the position is automatically incremented by the number of elements transferred. In an **absolute put or get operation**, you explicitly specify an index for the position in the buffer where the data transfer is to begin. In this case the buffer's position will not be updated so it will remain at the index value it was before the operation was executed.

Transferring Data Into a Buffer

The `ByteBuffer` class and all the view buffer classes have two `put()` methods for transferring a single element of the buffer's type to the buffer. One is a relative `put()` method that transfers an element to a given index position in the buffer and the other is an absolute put method that places the element at an index position that you specify as an argument. They also have three relative put methods for bulk transfer of elements of the given type. Let's consider the `put()` methods for a `ByteBuffer` object as an example.

Method	Description
`put(byte b)`	Transfers the byte specified by the argument to the buffer at the current position, and increments the position by 1. An exception of type `BufferOverflowException` will be thrown if the buffer's position is not less than its limit.
`put(int index, byte b)`	Transfers the byte specified by the second argument to the buffer at the index position specified by the first argument. The buffer position is unchanged. An exception of type `IndexOutOfBoundsException` will be thrown if the index value is negative or greater than or equal to the buffer's limit.
`put(byte[]array)`	Transfers all the elements of array to this buffer starting at the current position. The position will be incremented by the length of the array. An exception of type `BufferOverflowException` will be thrown if there is insufficient space in the buffer to accommodate the contents of array.
`put(byte[]array, int offset, int length)`	Transfers elements `array[offset]` to `array[offset+length-1]` inclusive to the buffer. If there is insufficient space for them an exception of type `BufferOverflowException` will be thrown.
`put(ByteBuffer src)`	Transfers the bytes remaining in `src` to the buffer. This will be `src.remaining()` elements from the buffer `src` from its position index to `limit-1`. If there is insufficient space to accommodate these then an exception of type `BufferOverflowException` will be thrown. If `src` is identical to the current buffer – you are trying to transfer a buffer to itself in other words – an exception of type `IllegalArgumentException` will be thrown.

Each of these methods returns a reference to the buffer for which they were called. If the buffer is read-only, any of these methods will throw an exception of type `ReadOnlyBufferException`. We will see how a buffer can be read-only when we discuss *Using View Buffers* in more detail. Each `Buffer` class that stores elements of a given basic type – `CharBuffer`, `DoubleBuffer`, or whatever – will have `put()` methods analogous to these, but with arguments of a type appropriate to the type of element in the buffer.

The `ByteBuffer` class has some extra methods that enable you to transfer binary data of other primitive types to the buffer. For instance, you can transfer a value of type `double` to the buffer with either of the following methods:

Method	Description
`putDouble(double value)`	Transfers the `double` value specified by the argument to the buffer at the current position and increments the position by 8. If there are less than 8 bytes remaining in the buffer, an exception of type `BufferOverflowException` will be thrown.
`putDouble(int index,` `        double value)`	Transfers the `double` value specified by the second argument, to the buffer starting at the index position specified by the first argument. The buffer's position will be unchanged. If there are less than 8 bytes remaining in the buffer, an exception of type `BufferOverflowException` will be thrown. If index is negative or the buffer's limit is less than or equal to index+7, an exception of type `IndexOutOfBoundsException` will be thrown.

There are similar pairs of methods defined in the `ByteBuffer` class to transfer elements of other basic types. These are `putChar()`, `putShort()`, `putInt()`, `putLong()`, and `putFloat()`, each of which transfers a value of the corresponding type. Like the other `put()` methods we have seen, these all return a reference to the buffer for which they are called. This is to enable you to chain the calls for these methods together in a single statement if you wish. For instance:

```
ByteBuffer buf = ByteBuffer.allocate(50);
String text = "Value of e";
buf.put(text.getBytes()).putDouble(Math.E);
```

Here, we write the string to the buffer by converting it to bytes by calling its `getBytes()` method, and passing the result to the `put()` method for the buffer. The `put()` method returns a reference to the buffer, `buf`, so we use that to call the `putDouble()` method to write the 8 bytes for the `double` value, `Math.E`, to the buffer. The buffer will then contain a total of 18 bytes. Of course, `putDouble()` also returns a reference to `buf`, so we could chain further calls together in the same statement if we so wished.

Note that we are transferring the string characters to the buffer as bytes in the local character encoding, not as Unicode characters. To transfer them as the original Unicode characters, we could code the operations like this:

```
char[] array = text.toCharArray();      // Create char[] array from the string
// Now use a loop to transfer array elements one at a time
for (int i = 0 ; i< array.length ; i++) {
  buf.put(array[i]);
}
buf.putDouble(Math.E);                   // Transfer the binary double value
```

Using View Buffers

View buffers are intended to make it easier to transfer data elements of various basic types to or from a `ByteBuffer`. The only slightly tricky part is that you have to keep track of the position for the original `ByteBuffer` object yourself when you use a view buffer, since operations with the view buffer will not update the position for the backing byte buffer. We could do what the previous code fragment does using view buffers:

```
ByteBuffer buf = ByteBuffer.allocate(50);        // The original byte buffer
String text = "Value of e";

// Create view buffer
CharBuffer charBuf = buf.asCharBuffer();
// Transfer string via view buffer
charBuf.put(text);
// Update byte buffer position by the number of bytes we have transferred
buf.position(buf.position() + 2*charBuf.position());
// Transfer binary double value
buf.putDouble(Math.E);
```

Putting data into a view buffer with a relative `put` operation only updates the position of the view buffer. The position for the backing `ByteBuffer` is unchanged, so we must increment it to account for the number of bytes occupied by the Unicode characters we have written. Since we transfer the eight bytes for the constant `Math.E` directly using `buf`, the position will be incremented by 8 automatically.

Preparing a Buffer for Output to a File

We have seen that a buffer starts out with a position set to 0 – the first element position – and with its limit set to the capacity. Suppose we create a buffer with the statement:

```
ByteBuffer buf = ByteBuffer.allocate(80);
```

We can now create a view buffer that can store values of type `double` with the statement:

```
DoubleBuffer doubleBuf = buf.asCharBuffer();
```

The view buffer's initial state will be as shown below:

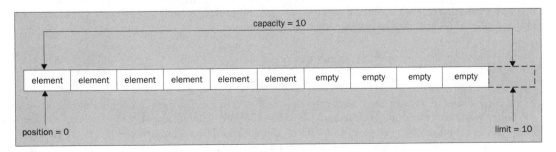

The limit is automatically set to the capacity, 10, so it points to one element beyond the last element. We could load six values of type `double` into this buffer with the following statements:

```
double[] data = { 1.0, 1.414, 1.732, 2.0, 2.236, 2.449 };
doubleBuf.put(data);             // Transfer the array elements to the buffer
```

This operation automatically increments the position for the buffer. Now the buffer will be as shown below:

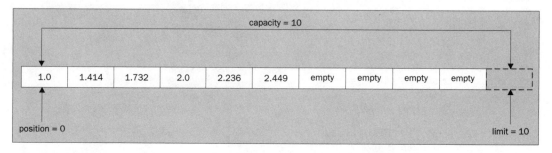

The position and limit values are now set to values ready for more data to be added to the buffer. The value of *position* points to the first empty element and *limit* points to one beyond the last empty element. Of course, the position for the backing `ByteBuffer` is still in its original state, but we can update that to correspond with the data we have loaded into the view buffer with the statement:

```
buf.setPosition(8*doubleBuf.getPosition());
```

If we now want to write the data we have in the buffer to a file, we must change the values for position and limit in the byte buffer to identify the elements that are to be written. A file write operation will write data elements starting from the element in the buffer at the index specified by *position*, and up to and including the element at the index *limit-1*. To write our data to the file, the limit for the byte buffer needs to be set to the current position, and the position needs to be set back to zero. We could do this explicitly using the methods we have seen. For instance:

```
// Limit to current position and position to 0
buf.limit(buf.position()).position(0);
```

This will first set the limit to the byte referenced by the current position, and then reset the position back to the first byte, byte 0. However, we don't need to specify the operation in such detail. The `Buffer` class conveniently defines a method, `flip()`, that does exactly this, so you would normally set up the buffer to be written to a file like this:

```
// Limit to current position and position to 0
buf.flip();
```

The `flip()` method returns the buffer reference as type `Buffer`, so you can chain this operation on the buffer with others in a single statement. So, after you have loaded your byte buffer with data, don't forget to flip it before you write it to a file. If you don't, your data will not be written to the file, but garbage may well be. If you loaded the data using a view buffer, you also have to remember to update the byte buffer's position before performing the flip.

While we are here, let's cover two other methods that modify the limit and/or the position for a buffer. The clear() method sets the limit to the capacity and the position to zero, so it restores these values to the state they had when the buffer was created. This does *not* reset the data in the buffer though. The contents are left unchanged. You call the clear() method when you want to reuse a buffer, either to load new data into it, or to read data into it from a channel. The rewind() method simply resets the position to zero, leaving the limit unchanged. This enables you to reread the data that is in the buffer. Both of these methods are defined in the base class, Buffer, and both return a reference to the buffer of type Buffer so you can chain these operations with others that are defined in the Buffer class.

Writing To a File

To start with, we will be using the simplest write() method for a file channel that writes the data contained in a single ByteBuffer object to a file. The number of bytes written to the file is determined by the buffer's position and limit when the write() method executes. Bytes will be written starting with the byte at the buffer's current position. The number of bytes written is *limit-position*, which is the number returned by the remaining() method for the buffer object. The write() method returns the number of bytes written as a value type int.

A channel write() operation can throw any of five different exceptions:

Exception	Description
NonWritableChannelException	Thrown if the channel was not opened for writing.
ClosedChannelException	Thrown if the channel is closed. Calling the close() method for the file channel will close the channel, as will calling the close() method for the file stream.
AsynchronousCloseException	Thrown if another thread closes the channel while the write operation is in progress.
ClosedByInterruptException	Thrown if another thread interrupts the current thread while the write operation is in progress.
IOException	Thrown if some other I/O error occurs.

The first of these is a subclass of RuntimeException, so you do not have to catch this exception. The other four are subclasses of IOException, which must be caught, so the write() method call must be in a try block. If you want to react specifically to one or other of these last four exceptions, you will need to add a catch block for that specific type. Otherwise you can just include a single catch block for type IOException to catch all four types of exception. For instance if you have set up a ByteBuffer, buf, ready to be written, you might code the write operation like this:

```
File aFile = new File("C:/Beg Java Stuff/myFile.text");
// Place to store an output stream reference
FileOutputStream outputFile = null;
```

```
try {
  // Create the stream opened to write
  outputFile = new FileOutputStream(aFile);
} catch (FileNotFoundException e) {
  e.printStackTrace(System.err);
}
// Get the channel for the file
FileChannel outputChannel = outputFile.getChannel();
```

```
try {
  outputChannel.write(buf);
} catch (IOException e) {
  e.printStackTrace(System.err);
}
```

A write() method for a channel will only return when the write operation is complete, but this does not guarantee that the data has actually been written to the file. Some of the data may still reside in the native I/O buffers. If the data you are writing is critical and you want to minimize the risk of losing it in the event of a system crash, you can force all outstanding output operations to a file that were previously executed by the channel to be completed by calling the force() method for the FileChannel object like this:

```
try {
  outputChannel.force();
} catch (IOException e) {
  e.printStackTrace(System.err);
}
```

The force() method will throw a ClosedChannelException if the channel is closed, or an IOException if some other I/O error occurs. Note that the force() method only guarantees that all data will be written for a local storage device.

Only one write operation can be in progress for a given file channel at any time. If you call write() while a write() operation initiated by another thread is in progress, your call to the write() method will block until the write that is in progress has been completed.

File Position

The position of a file is the index position of where the next byte is to be read or written. The first byte in a file is at position zero so the value for a file's position is the offset of the next byte from the beginning. Don't mix this up with a buffer's position that we discussed earlier – the two are quite independent, but of course, they are connected. When you write a buffer to a file using the write() method we discussed in the previous section, the byte in the buffer at the buffer's current position will be written to the file at its current position:

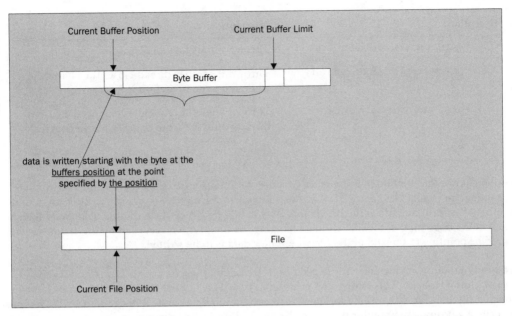

The file channel object maintains a record of the current position in the file. If the file stream was created to append to the file by using a FileOutputStream constructor with the append mode argument as true, then the file position recorded by the channel for the file will start out at the byte following the last byte. Otherwise, the initial file position will be the first byte of the file. The file position will generally be incremented by the number of bytes written each time you write to the file. There is one exception to this. The FileChannel class defines a special write() method that does the following:

Method	Description
write(ByteBuffer buf, long position)	This writes the buffer, buf, to the file at the position specified by the second argument, and not the file position recorded by the channel. Bytes from the buffer are written starting at the buffer's current position, and buf.remaining() bytes will be written. This does not update the channel's file position.

This method can throw any of the following exceptions:

Exception	Description
IllegalArgumentException	Thrown if you specify a negative value for the file position.
NonWritableChannelException	Thrown if the file was not opened for writing.

Table continued on following page

Exception	Description
ClosedChannelException	Thrown if the channel is closed.
AsynchronousCloseException	Thrown if another thread closes the channel while the write operation is in progress.
ClosedByInterruptException	Thrown if another thread interrupts the current thread while the write operation is in progress.
IOException	If any other I/O error occurs.

You might use this method in a sequence of writes to update a particular part of the file without disrupting the primary sequence of write operations. For example, you might record a count of the number of records in a file at the beginning. As you add new records to the file, you could update the count at the beginning of the file without changing the file position recorded by the channel, which would be pointing to the end of the file where new data is to be written.

You can find out what the current file position is by calling the position() method for the FileChannel object. This returns the position as type long rather than type int since it could conceivably be a large file with a lot more than two billion bytes in it. You can also set the file position by calling a position method for the FileChannel object, with an argument of type long specifying a new position. For instance, if we have a reference to a file channel stored in a variable outputChannel, we could alter the file position with the statements:

```
try {
  outputChannel.position(fileChannel.position() - 100);
} catch (IOException e) {
  e.printStackTrace(System.err);
}
```

This moves the current file position back by 100 bytes. This could be because we have written 100 bytes to the file and want to reset the position so we can rewrite it. The method must be in a try block because it can throw an exception of type IOException if an I/O error occurs.

You can set the file position beyond the end of the file. If you then write to the file, the bytes between the previous end of the file and the new position will contain junk values. If you try to read from a position beyond the end of the file, an end-of-file condition will be returned immediately.

When you are finished with writing a file you should close it by calling the close() method for the file stream object. This will close the file and the file channel. A FileChannel object defines its own close() method that will close the channel but not the file. It's time to start exercising your disk drive. Let's try an example.

Try It Out – Using a Channel to Write a String to a File

We will write the string "Garbage in, garbage out\n" to a file, charData.txt, that we will create in the directory Beg Java Stuff on drive C:. If you want to write to a different drive and/or directory, just change the program accordingly. Here is the code:

```java
import java.io.*;
import java.nio.*;
import java.nio.channels.FileChannel;

public class WriteAString {
  public static void main(String[] args) {
    String phrase = new String("Garbage in, garbage out\n");
    String dirname = "C:/Beg Java Stuff";    // Directory name
    String filename = "charData.txt";        // File name

    File dir = new File(dirname);            // File object for directory

    // Now check out the directory
    if (!dir.exists()){                      // If directory does not exist

      if (!dir.mkdir()){                     // ...create it

        System.out.println("Cannot create directory: " + dirname);
        System.exit(1);

      }
    } else if (!dir.isDirectory()) {
      System.err.println(dirname + " is not a directory");
      System.exit(1);

    }

    // Create the filestream
    File aFile = new File(dir, filename);
    FileOutputStream outputFile =
      null;                                  // Place to store the stream reference
    try {
      outputFile = new FileOutputStream(aFile, true);
      System.out.println("File stream created successfully.");
    } catch (FileNotFoundException e) {
      e.printStackTrace(System.err);
    }

    // Create the file output stream channel
    FileChannel outChannel = outputFile.getChannel();

    ByteBuffer buf = ByteBuffer.allocate(1024);
    System.out.println("New buffer:            position = " + buf.position()
                    + "\tLimit = " + buf.limit() + "\tcapacity = "
                    + buf.capacity());

    // Load the data into the buffer
    for (int i = 0; i < phrase.length(); i++) {
      buf.putChar(phrase.charAt(i));
    }

    System.out.println("Buffer after loading: position = " + buf.position()
                    + "\tLimit = " + buf.limit() + "\tcapacity = "
                    + buf.capacity());
```

```
      buf.flip();                  // Flip the buffer ready for file write
      System.out.println("Buffer after flip:    position = " + buf.position()
                       + "\tLimit = " + buf.limit() + "\tcapacity = "
                       + buf.capacity());

      // Write the file
      try {
        outChannel.write(buf);    // Write the buffer to the file channel
        outputFile.close();        // Close the output stream & the channel
        System.out.println("Buffer contents written to file.");
      } catch (IOException e) {
        e.printStackTrace(System.err);
      }
      System.exit(0);
    }
}
```

There is some command-line output from the program to trace what is going on. After you have compiled and run this program, you should see the output:

```
File stream created successfully.
New buffer:              position = 0    Limit = 1024    capacity = 1024
Buffer after loading: position = 48      Limit = 1024    capacity = 1024
Buffer after flip:       position = 0    Limit = 48      capacity = 1024
Buffer contents written to file.
```

You can inspect the contents of the file, charData.txt, using a plain text editor. They will look something like the following.

```
 G a r b a g e   i n ,   g a r b a g e   o u t
```

There are spaces between the characters, because we are writing Unicode characters to the file, and two bytes are written for each character in the original string. Your text editor may represent the first of each byte pair as something other than spaces, or possibly not at all, as they are bytes that contain zero. You might even find that your plain text editor will only display the first 'G'. If so, try to find another editor. If you run the example several times, the phrase will be appended to the file for each execution of the program.

> **Don't be too hasty deleting this or other files we will write later in this chapter, as we will reuse some of them in the next chapter when we start exploring how to read files.**

How It Works

We have defined three String objects:

- ❑ phrase – The string that we will write to the file
- ❑ dirname – The name of the directory we will create
- ❑ filename – The name of the file

In the `try` block, we first create a `File` object to represent the directory. If this directory does not exist, the `exists()` method will return `false` and the `mkdir()` method for `dir` will be called to create it. If the `exists()` method returns `true`, we must make sure that the `File` object represents a directory, and not a file.

Having established the directory one way or another, we create a `File` object, aFile, to represent the path to the file. We use this object to create a `FileOutputStream` object that will append data to the file. Omitting the second argument to the `FileOutputStream` constructor or specifying it as `false` would make the file stream overwrite any existing file contents. The file stream has to be created in a `try` block because the constructor can throw a `FileNotFoundException`. Once we have a `FileOutputStream` object, we call its `getChannel()` method to obtain a reference to the channel that we will use to write the file.

The next step is to create a `ByteBuffer` object and load it up with the characters from the string. We create a buffer with a capacity of 1024 bytes. This is so we can see clearly the difference between the capacity and the limit after flipping. We could have created a buffer exactly the size required with the statement:

```
ByteBuffer buf = ByteBuffer.allocate(2*phrase.length());
```

You can see how the position, limit, and capacity values change from the output. We use the `putChar()` method for the buffer object to transfer the characters one at a time in a loop and then output the information about the buffer status again. The limit is still as it was but the position has increased by the number of bytes written.

Finally, we write the contents of the buffer to the file. You can see here how flipping the buffer before the operation sets up the limit and position ready for writing the data to the file.

The `FileChannel` object has a method, `size()`, which will return the length of the file in bytes as a value of type, `long`. You could try this out by adding the following statement immediately after the statement that writes the buffer to the channel:

```
System.out.println("The file contains " + outChannel.size() + " bytes.");
```

You should see that 48 bytes are written to the file each time, since `phrase` contains 24 characters. The `size()` method returns the total number of bytes in the file so the number will grow by 48 each time you run the program.

Using a View Buffer

The code in the previous example is not the only way of writing the string to the buffer. We could have used a view buffer, like this:

```
ByteBuffer buf = ByteBuffer.allocate(1024);
CharBuffer charBuf = buf.asCharBuffer();
charBuf.put(phrase);                      // Transfer string to buffer
buf.limit(2*charBuf.position());          // Update byte buffer limit

// Create the file output stream channel
```

```
       FileChannel outChannel = outputFile.getChannel();

       // Write the file
       try {
         outChannel.write(buf);       // Write the buffer to the file channel
         outputFile.close();          // Close the output stream & the channel
       } catch(IOException e) {
         e.printStackTrace(System.err);
       }
```

Transferring the string via a view buffer of type CharBuffer is much simpler. The only fly in the ointment is that the backing ByteBuffer has no knowledge of this. The position for buf is still sitting firmly at zero with the limit as the capacity, so flipping it won't set it up ready to write to the channel. However, all we have to do is to set the limit corresponding to the number of bytes we transferred to the view buffer.

Of course, if we were writing the file for use by some other program, writing Unicode characters could be very inconvenient if the other program environment did not understand it. Let's see how we would write the data as bytes in the local character encoding.

Try It Out – Writing a String as Bytes

We will strip out the directory validation to keep the code shorter:

```
import java.io.*;
import java.nio.*;
import java.nio.channels.FileChannel;

public class WriteAStringAsBytes {
  public static void main(String[] args) {

    String phrase = new String("Garbage in, garbage out\n");
    String dirname = "C:/Beg Java Stuff";    // Directory name
    String filename = "byteData.txt";

    File aFile = new File(dirname, filename);

    // Create the file output stream
    FileOutputStream file = null;
    try {
      file = new FileOutputStream(aFile, true);
    } catch (FileNotFoundException e) {
      e.printStackTrace(System.err);
    }
    FileChannel outChannel = file.getChannel();
    ByteBuffer buf = ByteBuffer.allocate(phrase.length());
    byte[] bytes = phrase.getBytes();

    buf.put(bytes);
    buf.flip();

    try {
      outChannel.write(buf);
```

```
        file.close();    // Close the output stream & the channel
      } catch (IOException e) {
        e.printStackTrace(System.err);
      }
    }
  }
```

If you run this a couple of times and look into the `byteData.txt` file with your plain text editor, you should find:

```
Garbage in, garbage out
Garbage in, garbage out
```

There are no gaps between the letters this time because the Unicode character were converted to bytes in the default character encoding on your system by the `getBytes()` method for the string.

How It Works

We create the file stream and the channel essentially as in the previous example. This time the buffer is created with the precise amount of space we need. Since we will be writing each character as a single byte, the buffer capacity only needs to be the length of the string, `phrase`.

We convert the string to a byte array in the local character encoding using the `getBytes()` method defined in the `String` class. We transfer the contents of the array to the buffer using the relative `put()` method for the channel. After a quick flip of the buffer, we use the channel's `write()` method to write the buffer's contents to the file.

We could have written the conversion of the string to an array plus the sequence of operations with the buffer and the channel write operation much more economically, if less clearly, like this:

```
outChannel.write(buf.put(myStr.getBytes()).flip());
```

This makes use of the fact that the buffer methods we are using here return a reference to the buffer so we can chain them together.

Writing Varying Length Strings to a File

So far, the strings we have written to the file have all been of the same length. It is very often the case that you will want to write a series of strings of different lengths to a file. In this case, if you want to recover the strings from the file, you need to provide some information in the file that allows the beginning and/or end of each string to be determined. One possibility is to write the length of each string to the file immediately preceding the string itself.

To do this, we can get two view buffers from the byte buffer we will use to write the file, one of type `IntBuffer` and the other of type `CharBuffer`. Let's see how we can use that in another example that writes strings of various lengths to a file.

Try It Out – Writing Multiple Strings to a File

We will just write a series of useful proverbs to a file. Here's the code:

```
import java.io.*;
import java.nio.*;
import java.nio.channels.FileChannel;

public class WriteProverbs {
  public static void main(String[] args) {
    String dirName = "c:/Beg Java Stuff";    // Directory for the output file
    String fileName = "Proverbs.txt";        // Name of the output file
    String[] sayings = {
      "Indecision maximizes flexibility.",
      "Only the mediocre are always at their best.",
      "A little knowledge is a dangerous thing.",
      "Many a mickle makes a muckle.",
      "Who begins too much achieves little.",
      "Who knows most says least.",
      "A wise man sits on the hole in his carpet."
    };
    File aFile = new File(dirName, fileName);

    FileOutputStream outputFile = null;
    try {
      outputFile = new FileOutputStream(aFile, true);
    } catch (FileNotFoundException e) {
      e.printStackTrace(System.err);
      System.exit(1);
    }
    FileChannel outChannel = outputFile.getChannel();

    // Create a buffer to accommodate the longest string + its length value
    int maxLength = sayings[0].length();
    for (int i = 1; i < sayings.length; i++) {
      if (maxLength < sayings[i].length())
        maxLength = sayings[i].length ();
    }

    ByteBuffer buf = ByteBuffer.allocate(2 * maxLength + 4);

    // Write the file
    try {
      for (int i = 0; i < sayings.length; i++) {
        buf.putInt(sayings[i].length()).asCharBuffer().put(sayings[i]);
        buf.position(buf.position() + 2 * sayings[i].length()).flip();
        outChannel.write(buf);    // Write the buffer to the file channel
        buf.clear();
      }
      outputFile.close();         // Close the output stream & the channel
      System.out.println("Proverbs written to file.");
```

```
      } catch (IOException e) {
        e.printStackTrace(System.err);
        System.exit(1);
      }
    System.exit(0);
  }
}
```

When you execute this it should produce the rather terse output:

```
Proverbs written to file.
```

You can check the veracity of this assertion by inspecting the contents of the file with a plain text editor.

How It Works

The program writes the strings from the array, `sayings`, to the file.

We create a `String` array, `sayings[]`, that contains seven proverbs that are written to the stream in the `for` loop. We put the length of each proverb in the buffer using the `putInt()` method for the `ByteBuffer` object. We then use a view buffer of type `CharBuffer` to transfer the string to the buffer. The contents of the view buffer will start at the current position for the byte buffer. This corresponds to the byte immediately following the string length.

Transferring the string into the view buffer only causes the view buffer's position to be updated. The byte buffer's position is still pointing back at the byte following the string length where the first character of the string was written. We therefore have to increment the position for the byte buffer by twice the number of characters in the string before flipping it to make it ready to be written to the file.

The first time you run the program, the file doesn't exist, so it will be created. You can then look at the contents. If you run the program again, the same proverbs will be appended to the file, so there will be a second set. Alternatively, you could modify the `sayings[]` array to contain different proverbs the second time around. Each time the program runs, the data will be added at the end of the existing file.

After writing the contents of the byte buffer to the file, we call its `clear()` method to reset the position to zero and the limit back to the capacity. This makes it ready for transferring the data for the next proverb on the next iteration. Remember that it doesn't change the contents of the buffer though.

As we will write a program to read the `proverbs.txt` file back in the next chapter, you should leave it on your disk.

Direct and Indirect Buffers

When you allocate a byte buffer by calling the `allocate()` method for the `ByteBuffer` class, you get an **indirect buffer**. An indirect buffer is not used by the native I/O operations. Data to be written to a file has to be copied to an intermediate buffer in memory before the write operation can take place. Similarly, after a read operation the data is copied from the input buffer used by your operating system to the indirect buffer that you allocate.

Of course, with small buffers and limited amounts of data being read, using an indirect buffer doesn't add much overhead. With large buffers and lots of data, it can make a significant difference though. In this case, you can use the `allocateDirect()` method in the `ByteBuffer` class to allocate a **direct buffer**. The JVM will try to make sure that the native I/O operation makes use of the direct buffer, thus avoiding the overhead of the data copying process. The allocation and de-allocation of a direct buffer carries its own overhead, which may outweigh any advantages gained if the buffer size and data volumes are small.

You can test for a direct buffer by calling its `isDirect()` method. This will return `true` if it is a direct buffer and `false` otherwise.

You could try this out by making a small change to the previous example. Just replace the statement:

```
ByteBuffer buf = ByteBuffer.allocate(2 * maxLength + 4);
```

with the following two statements:

```
ByteBuffer buf = ByteBuffer.allocateDirect(2 * maxLength + 4);
System.out.println("Buffer is "+ (buf.isDirect()?"":"not")+"direct.");
```

This will output a line telling you whether the program is working with a direct buffer or not. It will produce the following output:

```
Buffer is direct.
Proverbs written to file.
```

Writing Numerical Data to a File

Let's see how we could set up our primes-generating program from Chapter 4 to write primes to a file instead of outputting them. We will base the new code on the `MorePrimes` version of the program. Ideally, we could add a command-line argument to specify how many primes we want. This is not too difficult. Here's how the code will start off:

```
public class PrimesToFile {
  public static void main(String[] args) {
    int primesRequired = 100;   // Default prime count
    if (args.length > 0) {
      try {
        primesRequired = Integer.valueOf(args[0]).intValue();
      } catch (NumberFormatException e) {
        System.out.println("Prime count value invalid. Using default of "
                           + primesRequired);
      }
      // Code to generate the primes...

      // Code to write the file...
    }
  }
}
```

Here, if we don't find a command-line argument that we can convert to an integer, we just use a default count of 100.

We can now generate the primes with code similar to that in Chapter 4 as follows:

```
long[] primes = new long[primesRequired];    // Array to store primes
primes[0] = 2;                               // Seed the first prime
primes[1] = 3;                               // and the second
// Count of primes found - up to now, which is also the array index
int count = 2;
// Next integer to be tested
long number = 5;

outer:
for (; count < primesRequired; number += 2) {

  // The maximum divisor we need to try is square root of number
  long limit = (long) Math.ceil(Math.sqrt((double) number));

  // Divide by all the primes we have up to limit
  for (int i = 1; i < count && primes[i] <= limit; i++)
    if (number % primes[i] == 0)             // Is it an exact divisor?
      continue outer;                        // yes, try the next number

  primes[count++] = number;                  // We got one!
}
```

Now all we need to do is add the code to write the primes to the file. Let's put this into a working example.

Try It Out – Writing Primes to a File

Here's the complete example with the additional code to write the file shown shaded:

```
import java.io.*;
import java.nio.*;
import java.nio.channels.FileChannel;

public class PrimesToFile {
  public static void main(String[] args) {
    int primesRequired = 100;   // Default count
    if (args.length > 0) {
      try {
        primesRequired = Integer.valueOf(args[0]).intValue();
      } catch (NumberFormatException e) {
        System.out.println("Prime count value invalid. Using default of "
                         + primesRequired);
      }
    }

    long[] primes = new long[primesRequired];    // Array to store primes
    primes[0] = 2;                               // Seed the first prime
    primes[1] = 3;                               // and the second
```

```
    // Count of primes found - up to now, which is also the array index
    int count = 2;
    // Next integer to be tested
    long number = 5;

    outer:
    for (; count < primesRequired; number += 2) {

      // The maximum divisor we need to try is square root of number
      long limit = (long) Math.ceil(Math.sqrt((double) number));

      // Divide by all the primes we have up to limit
      for (int i = 1; i < count && primes[i] <= limit; i++)
        if (number % primes[i] == 0)              // Is it an exact divisor?
          continue outer;                         // yes, try the next number

      primes[count++] = number;                   // We got one!
    }
```

```
    File aFile = new File("C:/Beg Java Stuff/primes.bin");
    FileOutputStream outputFile = null;
    try {
      outputFile = new FileOutputStream(aFile);    // Create the file stream
    } catch (FileNotFoundException e) {
      e.printStackTrace(System.err);
      System.exit(1);
    }
    FileChannel file =
      // Get the channel from the stream
      outputFile.getChannel();
    final int BUFFERSIZE = 100;                   // Byte buffer size
    ByteBuffer buf = ByteBuffer.allocate(BUFFERSIZE);
    LongBuffer longBuf = buf.asLongBuffer();      // View buffer for type long

    // Count of primes written to file
    int primesWritten = 0;

    while (primesWritten < primes.length) {
      longBuf.put(primes,                // Array to be written
                  primesWritten,         // Index of 1st element to be written
                  Math.min(longBuf.capacity(),
                      primes.length - primesWritten)); // Element count
      buf.limit(8 * longBuf.position());
      try {
        file.write(buf);
        primesWritten += longBuf.position();
      } catch (IOException e) {
        e.printStackTrace(System.err);
        System.exit(1);
      }
      longBuf.clear();
      buf.clear();
    }
```

```
    try {
      System.out.println("File written is " + file.size() + " bytes.");
      outputFile.close();    // Close the file and its channel
    } catch (IOException e) {
      e.printStackTrace(System.err);
      System.exit(1);
    }
    System.exit(0);
  }
}
```

This produces the output:

```
File written is 800 bytes.
```

This looks reasonable since we wrote 100 values of type `long` as binary data and they are 8 bytes each.

How It Works

We create a `FileOutputStream` object and obtain the channel in the way we have already seen. Since we did not specify we wanted to append to the file when we created the stream object, the file will be overwritten each time we run the program.

We create the `ByteBuffer` object with a capacity of 100 bytes. I chose this value so that it is not an exact multiple of 8 – the number of bytes occupied by each prime value. This makes the problem more interesting. You can change the buffer size by change the value set for `BUFFERSIZE`.

The primes will be transferred to the buffer through a view buffer of type `LongBuffer` that we obtain from the original buffer. Since the buffer is too small to hold all the primes, we have to load it and write the primes to the file in a loop.

The `primesWritten` variable counts how many primes we have written to the file so we can use this to control the `while` loop that writes the primes to the file. The loop continues as long as `primesWritten` is less than the number of elements in the `primes` array. The number of primes that the `LongBuffer` object can hold corresponds to `longBuf.capacity()`.We can transfer this number of primes to the buffer as long as there is that many left in the array still to be written to the file, so we do the transfer of a block of primes to the buffer like this:

```
      longBuf.put(primes, primesWritten,
              Math.min(longBuf.capacity(),
                      primes.length - primesWritten));
```

The first argument to the `put()` method is the array that is the source of the data and the second argument is the index position of the first element to be transferred. The third argument will be the capacity of the buffer as long as there are more than that number of primes still in the array. If there is less than this number on the last iteration, we will transfer `primes.length-primesWritten` values to the buffer.

Since we are using a relative put operation, loading the view buffer will change the position for that buffer to reflect the number of values transferred to it. However, the backing byte buffer that we use in the channel write operation will still have its limit and position unchanged. We therefore set the limit for the byte buffer with the statement:

```
buf.limit(8 * longBuf.position());
```

Since each prime occupies 8 bytes, multiplying the position value for the view buffer by 8 gives us the number of bytes occupied in the primary buffer. We then go ahead and write that buffer to the file and increment `primesWritten` by the position value for the view buffer, since this will be the number of primes that were written. Before the next iteration we call `clear()` for both buffers to reset their limits and positions to their original states – 0 and the capacity respectively. When we have written all the primes, the loop will end and we output the length of the file before closing it.

Since this file contains binary data, we will not want to view it except perhaps for debugging purposes.

Writing Mixed Data to a File

Sometimes, you may want to write more than one kind of data to a file. You may want to mix integers with floating-point values with text perhaps. One way to do this is to use multiple view buffers. We can illustrate the principle of how this works by outputting some text along with each binary prime value in the previous example. Rather than taking the easy route by just writing the same text for each prime value, let's add a character representation of the prime preceding each binary value. We'll add something like `prime = xxx` ahead of each binary value. The first point to keep in mind is that if we ever want to read the file successfully, we can't just dump strings of varying lengths in it. You would have no way to tell where the text ended and where the binary data began. We either have to fix the length of the string or provide data in the file that specifies the length of the string. We will therefore choose to write the data corresponding to each prime as three successive data items:

1. A count of the length of the string as binary value (it would sensibly be an integer type but we'll make it type `double` since we need the practice)

2. The string representation of the prime value: `prime = xxx`

3. The prime as a binary value of type `long`

The basic prime calculation will not change at all, so we only need to update the shaded code at the end in the previous example that writes the file.

The basic strategy we will adopt is to create a byte buffer, and then create a series of view buffers that map the three different kinds of data into it. A simple approach would be to write the data for one prime at a time, so let's try that first. Setting up the file stream and the channel will be more or less exactly the same:

```
File aFile = new File("C:/Beg Java Stuff/primes.txt");
FileOutputStream outputFile = null;
try {
  outputFile = new FileOutputStream(aFile);
```

```
    } catch (FileNotFoundException e) {
      e.printStackTrace(System.err);
      System.exit(1);
    }
    FileChannel file = outputFile.getChannel();
```

The file extension has been changed to .txt to differentiate it from the original binary file that we wrote. We will want to make use of both the binary file and this file when we are looking into file read operations.

The byte buffer has to be large enough to hold the double value that counts the characters in the string, the string itself, plus the long value for the prime. The original byte buffer with 100 bytes capacity will be plenty big enough so let's go with that:

```
    final int BUFFERSIZE = 100;    // Buffer size in bytes
    ByteBuffer buf = ByteBuffer.allocate(BUFFERSIZE);
```

We need to create three view buffers from the byte buffer, one that will hold the double value for the count, one for the string, and one for the binary prime value, but there is a problem.

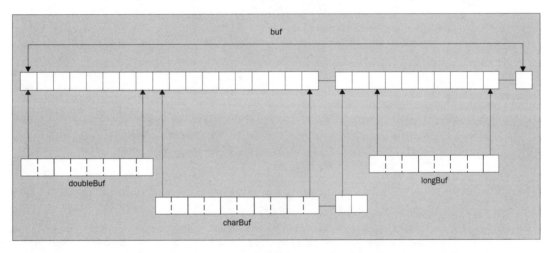

The length of the string will depend on the number of decimal digits in the prime value, so we don't know where it ends. This implies we can't map the last buffer to a fixed position. We are going to have to set this buffer up dynamically inside the file-writing loop after we figure out how long the string for the prime is. We can set up the first two view buffers outside the loop though:

```
    DoubleBuffer doubleBuf = buf.asDoubleBuffer();
    buf.position(8);
    CharBuffer charBuf = buf.asCharBuffer();
```

The first buffer that will hold the string length as type `double` will map to the beginning of the byte buffer, `buf`. The view buffer into which we will place the string needs to map to the position in `buf` immediately after the space required for the `double` value – 8 bytes from the beginning of `buf` in other words. Remember that the first element in a view buffer maps to the current position in the byte buffer. Thus, we can just set the position for `buf` to 8 before creating the view buffer, `charBuf`. All that's now needed is the loop to load up the first two view buffers, create the third view buffer and load it, and then write the file. Let's put the whole thing together as a working example.

Try It Out – Using Multiple View Buffers

The code for the loop is shaded in the following complete program:

```
import java.io.*;
import java.nio.*;
import java.nio.channels.FileChannel;

public class PrimesToFile2 {
  public static void main(String[] args) {
    int primesRequired = 100;    // Default count
    if (args.length > 0) {
      try {
        primesRequired = Integer.valueOf(args[0]).intValue();
      } catch (NumberFormatException e) {
        System.out.println("Prime count value invalid. Using default of "
                          + primesRequired);
      }
    }

    long[] primes = new long[primesRequired];    // Array to store primes
    primes[0] = 2;                               // Seed the first prime
    primes[1] = 3;                               // and the second
    // Count of primes found - up to now, which is also the array index
    int count = 2;
    long number = 5;                             // Next integer to be tested

    outer:
    for (; count < primesRequired; number += 2) {

      // The maximum divisor we need to try is square root of number
      long limit = (long) Math.ceil(Math.sqrt((double) number));

      // Divide by all the primes we have up to limit
      for (int i = 1; i < count && primes[i] <= limit; i++)
        if (number % primes[i] == 0)    // Is it an exact divisor?
          continue outer;               // yes, try the next number

      primes[count++] = number;         // We got one!
    }

    File aFile = new File("C:/Beg Java Stuff/primes.txt");
    FileOutputStream outputFile = null;
    try {
```

```
      outputFile = new FileOutputStream(aFile);
    } catch (FileNotFoundException e) {
      e.printStackTrace(System.err);
      System.exit(1);
    }
    FileChannel file = outputFile.getChannel();
    final int BUFFERSIZE = 100;    // Buffer size in bytes
    ByteBuffer buf = ByteBuffer.allocate(BUFFERSIZE);

    DoubleBuffer doubleBuf = buf.asDoubleBuffer();
    buf.position(8);
    CharBuffer charBuf = buf.asCharBuffer();
    LongBuffer longBuf = null;
    String primeStr = null;

    for (int i = 0; i < primes.length; i++) {
      primeStr = "prime = " + primes[i];          // Create the string
      doubleBuf.put(0,(double) primeStr.length());// Store the string length
      charBuf.put(primeStr);                       // Store the string
      buf.position(2 * charBuf.position() + 8);    // Position for 3rd buffer
      longBuf = buf.asLongBuffer();                // Create the buffer
      longBuf.put(primes[i]);               // Store the binary long value
      buf.position(buf.position() + 8);     // Set position after last value
      buf.flip();                           // and flip
      try {
        file.write(buf);                    // Write the buffer as before.
      } catch (IOException e) {
        e.printStackTrace(System.err);
        System.exit(1);
      }
      buf.clear();
      doubleBuf.clear();
      charBuf.clear();
    }
    try {
      System.out.println("File written is " + file.size() + " bytes.");
      outputFile.close();    // Close the file and its channel
    } catch (IOException e) {
      e.printStackTrace(System.err);
      System.exit(1);
    }
    System.exit(0);
  }
}
```

This should produce the output:

```
File written is 3742 bytes.
```

How It Works

We only need to discuss the loop. We first create the string because we need to know its length so we can put that in the buffer first. We insert the length as type `double` in the view buffer, `longBuf`. We can then put the string into `charBuf` as this buffer already maps to the elements 8 along from the start of `buf`. Next, we update the position in `buf` to the element following the string. This will allow us to map `longBuf` to the byte buffer correctly. After creating the third view buffer, `longBuf`, we load the prime value. We then update the position for `buf` to the byte following this value. This will be the position as previously set plus 8. Finally we flip `buf` to set the position and limit for writing, and then the channel writes to the file.

If you inspect the file with a plain text editor you should get an idea of what is in the file. You should be able to see the Unicode strings separated by the binary values we have written to the file.

This writes the file one prime at a time, so it's not going to be very efficient. It would be better to use a larger buffer and load it with multiple primes. Let's see how we can do that.

Try It Out – Multiple Records in a Buffer

We will be loading the byte buffer using three different view buffers repeatedly to put as many primes into the buffer as we can. The basic idea is illustrated below:

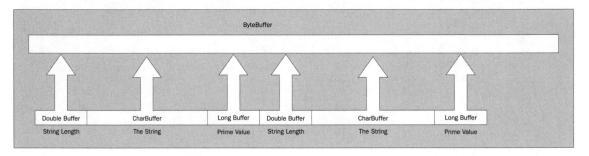

We will just show the new code that replaces the code in the previous example that allocates the buffers and writes the file:

```
import java.io.*;
import java.nio.*;
import java.nio.channels.FileChannel;

public class PrimesToFile3 {
  public static void main(String[] args) {

     // Code as in the previous example...

     final int BUFFERSIZE = 1024;    // Buffer size in bytes - bigger!
     ByteBuffer buf = ByteBuffer.allocate(BUFFERSIZE);
     String primeStr = null;
     int primesWritten = 0;
     while (primesWritten < primes.length) {
       while (primesWritten < primes.length) {
```

```
                  primeStr = "prime = " + primes[primesWritten];
                  if ((buf.position() + 2 * primeStr.length() + 16) > buf.limit()) {
                    break;
                  }
                  buf.asDoubleBuffer().put(0, (double) primeStr.length());
                  buf.position(buf.position() + 8);
                  buf.position(buf.position()
                                    + 2 * buf.asCharBuffer().put(primeStr).position());
                  buf.asLongBuffer().put(primes[primesWritten++]);
                  buf.position(buf.position() + 8);
                }
                buf.flip();
                try {
                  file.write(buf);
                } catch (IOException e) {
                  e.printStackTrace(System.err);
                  System.exit(1);
                }
                buf.clear();
              }
            try {
              System.out.println("File written is " + file.size() + " bytes.");
              outputFile.close();    // Close the file and its channel
            } catch (IOException e) {
              e.printStackTrace(System.err);
              System.exit(1);
            }
            System.exit(0);
          }
        }
```

You should get the same output as for the previous example here.

How It Works

To start with, we just create a byte buffer with a capacity of 1024 bytes. All the view buffers are created inside the inner while loop. Both loops end when primesWritten, which counts the number of primes written to the file, reaches the length of the primes array. The inner loop loads up the buffer and the outer loop writes the contents of the buffer to the file.

The first step in the inner loop is to create the prime string. This makes it possible to check whether there is enough free space in the byte buffer to accommodate the string plus the two binary values – the string length as type double and the prime itself of type long. If there isn't enough space, the break statement will be executed so the inner loop will end, and the channel will write the buffer contents to the file after flipping it. After the buffer has been written, the buffer's clear() method is called to reset the position to 0 and the limit to the capacity.

When there is space in the byte buffer, the inner loop loads the buffer starting with the statement:

```
          buf.asDoubleBuffer().put(0, (double)primeStr.length());
```

This creates a view buffer of type `DoubleBuffer` and calls its `put()` method to transfer the length of the string to the buffer. We don't save the view buffer reference because we will need a different one on the next iteration – one that maps to the position in the byte buffer following the data we are transferring for the current prime.

The next statement increments the position of the byte buffer, by the number of bytes in the string length value. We then execute the statement:

```
buf.position(buf.position()
              + 2 * buf.asCharBuffer().put(primeStr).position());
```

This statement is a little complicated so let's dissect it. The expression for the argument to the `position()` method within the parentheses executes first. This calculates the new position for `buf` as the current position, given by `buf.position()`, plus the value resulting from the expression:

```
2 * buf.asCharBuffer().put(primeStr).position()
```

The subexpression, `buf.asCharBuffer()`, creates a view buffer of type `CharBuffer`. The `put()` method for this is called to transfer `primeStr` to the buffer, and this returns a reference to the `CharBuffer` object. This is used to call its `position()` method that will return the position after transferring the string, so multiplying this by 2 gives the number of bytes occupied by the string in `buf`. Thus, the position for `buf` is updated to the point following the string.

The last step in the loop is to execute the statements:

```
buf.asLongBuffer().put(primes[primesWritten++]);
buf.position(buf.position() + 8);
```

The first statement here transfers the binary prime value to the buffer via a view buffer of type `LongBuffer` and increments the count of the number of primes written to the file. The second statement updates the position for `buf` to the next available byte. The inner `while` loop then continues with the next iteration to load the data for the next prime into the buffer. This will continue until there is insufficient space for another prime, whereupon the inner loop will end, and the buffer will be written to the file.

Gathering-Write Operations

We will look at one further file channel output capability before we try to read a file – the ability to transfer data to a file from several buffers in sequence in a single write operation. This is called a **gathering-write** operation. The advantage of this capability is that it avoids the necessity to copy information into a single buffer before writing it to a file. A gathering-write operation is one side of what are called **scatter-gather I/O operations**. We will look into the other side – the **scattering-read** operation – in the next chapter.

Just to remind you, a file channel has two methods that can perform a gathering-write operation:

Method	Description
`write(ByteBuffers[] buffers)`	Writes bytes from each of the buffers in the array `buffers`, to the file in sequence, starting at the channel's current file position.

`write(ByteBuffers[] buffers,`
    `int offset,`
    `int length)`
	Writes data to the file starting at the channel's current file position from `buffers[offset]` to `buffers[offset+length-1]` inclusive and in sequence.

Both these methods can throw the same five exceptions as the `write` method for a single `ByteBuffer` object. The second of these methods can also throw an `IndexOutOfBoundsException` if `offset` or `offset+length-1` is not a legal index value for the array `buffers`.

The data that is written from each buffer to the file is determined from that buffer's position and limit in the way we have seen. One obvious application of the gathering-write operation is when you are reading data from several different files into a number of buffers, and you want to merge the data into a single file. We can demonstrate how it works by using a variation on our primes writing program.

Try It Out – The Gathering Write

To simulate conditions where a gathering write could apply, we will set up the string length, the string itself, and the binary prime value in separate byte buffers. We will also write the prime string as bytes in the local encoding.

Here's the code:

```java
import java.io.*;
import java.nio.*;
import java.nio.channels.FileChannel;

public class GatheringWrite {
  public static void main(String[] args) {
    int primesRequired = 100;    // Default count
    if (args.length > 0) {
      try {
        primesRequired = Integer.valueOf(args[0]).intValue();
      } catch (NumberFormatException e) {
        System.out.println("Prime count value invalid. Using default of "
                            + primesRequired);
      }
    }

    long[] primes = new long[primesRequired];   // Array to store primes
    primes[0] = 2;                               // Seed the first prime
    primes[1] = 3;                               // and the second
    // Count of primes found – up to now, which is also the array index
    int count = 2;
```

```
long number = 5;                              // Next integer to be tested

outer:
for (; count < primesRequired; number += 2) {

  // The maximum divisor we need to try is square root of number
  long limit = (long) Math.ceil(Math.sqrt((double) number));

  // Divide by all the primes we have up to limit
  for (int i = 1; i < count && primes[i] <= limit; i++) {
    if (number % primes[i] == 0) {   // Is it an exact divisor?
      continue outer;                // yes, try the next number

    }
  }
  primes[count++] = number;          // We got one!
}

File aFile = new File("C:/Beg Java Stuff/primes.txt");
FileOutputStream outputFile = null;
try {
  outputFile = new FileOutputStream(aFile);
} catch (FileNotFoundException e) {
  e.printStackTrace(System.err);
  System.exit(1);
}
FileChannel file = outputFile.getChannel();
```

```
  // Array of buffer references
  ByteBuffer[] buffers = new ByteBuffer[3];
  buffers[0] = ByteBuffer.allocate(8);   // To hold a double value
  buffers[2] = ByteBuffer.allocate(8);   // To hold a long value

  String primeStr = null;
  for (int primesWritten = 0; primesWritten < primes.length;
       primesWritten++) {
    primeStr = "prime = " + primes[primesWritten];
    buffers[0].putDouble((double) primeStr.length()).flip();
    buffers[1] = ByteBuffer.allocate(primeStr.length());
    buffers[1].put(primeStr.getBytes()).flip();
    buffers[2].putLong(primes[primesWritten]).flip();
    try {
      file.write(buffers);
    } catch (IOException e) {
      e.printStackTrace(System.err);
      System.exit(1);
    }
    buffers[0].clear();
    buffers[2].clear();
  }
```

```
try {
  System.out.println("File written is " + file.size() + " bytes.");
```

```
        outputFile.close();    // Close the file and its channel
    } catch (IOException e) {
        e.printStackTrace(System.err);
        System.exit(1);
    }

    System.out.println("File closed");
    System.exit(0);
    }
}
```

When you execute this, it should produce the output:

```
File written is 2671 bytes.
File closed
```

The length of the file is considerably less than before, since we are writing the string as bytes rather than Unicode characters. The only part of the code that is different is shaded so we'll concentrate on that.

How It Works

We will be using three byte buffers: one for the string length, one for the string itself, and one for the binary prime value:

```
// Array of buffer references
ByteBuffer[] buffers = new ByteBuffer[3];
```

We therefore create a `ByteBuffer[]` array with three elements to hold references to these. The buffers holding the string length and the prime value are fixed in length so we are able to create those straight away to hold 8 bytes each:

```
buffers[0] = ByteBuffer.allocate(8);    // To hold a double value
buffers[2] = ByteBuffer.allocate(8);    // To hold a long value
```

We have to create dynamically, the buffer to hold the string, inside the `for` loop that iterates over all the prime values we have in the primes array.

After assembling the prime string, we transfer the length to the first buffer:

```
buffers[0].putDouble((double) primeStr.length()).flip();
```

Note that we flip the buffer in the same statement after the data value has been transferred, so it is set up ready to be written to the file.

Next, we create the buffer to accommodate the string, load the byte array equivalent of the string and flip the buffer:

```
buffers[1] = ByteBuffer.allocate(primeStr.length());
buffers[1].put(primeStr.getBytes()).flip();
```

All of the `put()` methods for the byte buffers we are using here automatically update the buffer position, so we can flip each buffer as soon as the data is loaded. An alternative to allocating this byte buffer directly to accommodate the byte array from the string, is to call the static `wrap()` method in the `ByteBuffer` class that wraps a byte array. We could achieve the same as the previous two statements with the single statement:

```
buffers[1] = ByteBuffer.wrap(primeStr.getBytes());
```

Since the `wrap()` method creates a buffer with a capacity the same as the length of the array, and with the position set to zero and the limit to the capacity, we don't need to flip the buffer – it is already in a state to be written.

The three buffers are ready so we write the array of buffers to the file like this:

```
try {
  file.write(buffers);
} catch (IOException e) {
  e.printStackTrace(System.err);
  System.exit(1);
}
```

Finally, we ready the first and third buffers for the next iteration by calling the `clear()` method for each of them:

```
buffers[0].clear();
buffers[2].clear();
```

Of course, the second buffer is recreated on each iteration, so there is no need to clear it. Surprisingly easy wasn't it?

Summary

In this chapter, we have discussed the facilities for checking out physical files and directories, and writing basic types of data to a file. The important points we have discussed include:

❑　An object of the class `File` can represent the path to a physical file.

❑　An object of type `FileDescriptor` can also represent a physical file.

❑　A `FileOutputStream` object can be created from a `File` object and the file will be opened for writing. If the file does not exist it will be created where possible.

❑　A `FileChannel` object for a file is returned by the `getChannel()` method for a file stream object.

❑　A buffer contains data to be written to a file, or data that has been read from a file. Only `ByteBuffer` objects can be used directly in file I/O operations.

❑　A buffer's position is the index position of the first element in the buffer to be written or read. A buffer's limit specifies the index position of the first element that is *not* to be written or read.

- A view buffer is a buffer that allows the data in a backing byte buffer to be viewed as being of a particular basic type.

- You insert data into a buffer using its `put()` methods and retrieve data from it using its `get()` methods. Relative `get()` and `put()` methods increment the buffer's position, whereas absolute `get()` and `put()` methods do not.

- You write the contents of a `ByteBuffer` object to a file using a `write()` method belonging to the `FileChannel` object for the file.

- The amount of data transferred between a buffer and a file in an I/O operation is determined by the buffer's position and limit. Data is read or written starting at the file's current position.

- You can lead a horse to water but you can't make him drink.

Exercises

1. Modify the example that writes proverbs to a file to separate the proverbs using a delimiter character. You will need to choose a delimiter character that will not appear in normal text.

2. Write a program that, using an integer array of date values containing month, day, and year as integers for some number of dates (10 say, so the `int` array will be two dimensional with 10 rows and 3 columns), will write a file with a string representation of each date written as Unicode characters. For example, the date values 3,2,1990 would be written to the file as 2nd March 1990. Make sure that the date strings can be read back, either by using a separator character of some kind to mark the end of each string, or write the length of each string before you write the string itself.

3. Extend the previous example to write a second file at the same time as the first, but containing the month, day, and year values as binary data. You should have both files open and be writing to both at the same time.

4. Write a program that, for a given `String` object defined in the code, will write strings to a file in the local character encoding (as bytes) corresponding to all possible permutations of the words in the string. For example, for the string, the fat cat, you would write the strings: the fat cat, the cat fat, cat the fat, cat fat the, fat the cat, fat cat the, to the file, although not necessarily in that sequence. (Don't use very long strings; with n words in the string, the number of permutations is $n!$).

Reading Files

In this chapter we will investigate how we can read files containing basic types of data. We will be exploring how to read files sequentially or at random, and how we can open a file for both read and write operations.

In this chapter you will learn:

❑   How to obtain a file channel for reading a file.

❑   How to use buffers in file channel read operations.

❑   How to read different types of data from a file.

❑   How to retrieve data from random positions in a file.

❑   How you can read and write the same file.

❑   How you can do direct data transfer between channels.

❑   What a memory-mapped file is and how you can access a memory-mapped file.

❑   What a file lock is and how you can lock all or part of a file.

File Read Operations

The process for reading a file parallels that of writing a file. You obtain a `FileChannel` object from a file from a file stream, and use the channel to read data from the file into one or more buffers. Initially we will be using a channel object from a `FileInputStream` object to read a file. Later when we want to read and write the same file we will be using a `FileChannel` object obtained from a `RandomAccessFile` object. Like the `FileOutputStream` class, the `FileInputStream` class defines its own methods for file input, as does the `RandomAccessFile` class. However, we will completely ignore these because the file channel methods for reading the file are much more efficient and will eventually obsolete the stream methods. In any event, if you are curious to see how the old stream input mechanism works you can find details of the methods that read from a file stream in the descriptions for the `FileInputStream` and `RandomAccessFile` classes in the documentation that accompanies the SDK.

The starting point for reading a file is to create a `FileInputStream` object. Creating `FileInputStream` objects is not very different from creating `FileOutputStream` objects so let's look into how we do that first.

> In our examples in this chapter we will be reading some of the files that we created in the last chapter so I hope that you kept them.

Creating File Input Streams

Since a `FileInputStream` object encapsulates a file that is essentially intended to be read and therefore must contain some data, a constructor for this class can only create an object for a file that already exists. There are three constructors for `FileInputStream` objects, each of which takes a single argument.

First of all you can create a `FileInputStream` object from a `String` object that specifies the file name. For example:

```
FileInputStream inputFile = null;    // Place to store the input stream reference
try {
  inputFile = new FileInputStream("C:/Beg Java Stuff/myFile.txt");

} catch(FileNotFoundException e) {
  e.printStackTrace(System.err);
  System.exit(1);
}
```

The `try` block is necessary here because this constructor will throw a `FileNotFoundException` if the file does not exist or the argument to the constructor specifies a directory rather than a file.

You could also use a `File` object to identify the file, like this:

```
File aFile = new File("C:/Beg Java Stuff/myFile.txt");
FileInputStream inputFile = null;    //Place to store the input stream reference
try {
  inputFile = new FileInputStream(aFile);

} catch(FileNotFoundException e) {
  e.printStackTrace(System.err);
  System.exit(1);
}
```

This constructor can also throw a `FileNotFoundException` so again we must create the `FileInputStream` object within a `try` block. Using a `File` object to create a `FileInputStream` object is the preferred approach because you can check that the file exists before creating the stream and thus avoid the possibility of throwing a `FileNotFoundException`.

The third possibility is to use a `FileDescriptor` object that you have obtained by calling the `getFD()` method for an existing `FileInputStream` object, or possibly a `RandomAccessFile` object. For example:

```
File aFile = new File("C:/Beg Java Stuff/myFile.text");
FileInputStream inputFile1 = null;      // Place to store an input stream reference
FileDescriptor fd = null;               // Place to store the file descriptor

try {
  // Create the stream opened to write
  inputFile1 = new FileInputStream(aFile);
  fd = inputFile1.getFD();              // Get the file descriptor for the file

} catch(IOException e) {                // For IOException or FileNotFoundException
  e.printStackTrace(System.err);
  System.exit(1);
}

// We can now create another input stream for the file from the file descriptor...
FileInputStream inputFile2 = new FileInputStream(fd);
```

The `getFD()` method can throw an exception of type `IOException` if an I/O error occurs. Since `IOException` is a superclass of `FileNotFoundException`, the `catch` block will catch either type of exception.

I'm sure that you noticed that the constructor call that creates `inputFile2` is not in a `try` block. This is not an oversight. When you create the `FileInputStream` object from a `FileDescriptor` object, the `FileNotFoundException` cannot be thrown since a `FileDescriptor` object always refers to an existing file. This is because a `FileDescriptor` object can only be obtained from a file stream object that already encapsulates a connection to a physical file so there can be no doubt that the file is real.

As with the `FileOutputStream` constructors, any of the `FileInputStream` constructors will throw a `SecurityException` if a security manager exists on the system and read access to the file is not permitted. Since this is a type of `RuntimeException` you don't have to catch it.

File Channel Read Operations

You obtain a reference to a `FileChannel` object that you can use to read a file by calling the `getChannel()` method of a `FileInputStream` object. Since a `FileInputStream` object opens a file as read-only, only channel read operations are legal. The channel returned by a `FileInputStream` object has three basic read operations available, each of which read starting at the byte indicated by the current position in the file. The file position will be incremented by the number of bytes read. The three `read()` methods for a `FileChannel` object are:

`read(ByteBuffer buf)`	Tries to read `buf.remaining()` bytes (equivalent to `limit-position` bytes) from the file into the buffer, `buf`, starting at the buffer's current position. The number of bytes read is returned as type `int`, or -1 if the channel reaches the end-of-file. The buffer position will be incremented by the number of bytes read and the buffer's limit will be left unchanged.
`read(ByteBuffer[] buffers)`	Tries to read bytes into each of the buffers in the `buffers` array in sequence. Bytes will be read into each buffer starting at the point defined by that buffer's position. The number of bytes read into each buffer is defined by the `remaining()` method for that buffer. The `read()` method returns the total number of bytes read as type `int`, or -1 if the channel reaches the end-of-file. Each buffer's position will be incremented by the number of bytes read into it. Each buffer's limit will be unchanged.

`read(ByteBuffer[] buffers,`
   `int offset,`
   `int length)`
	This operates in the same way as the previous method except that bytes are read starting with the buffer `buffers[offset]`, and up to and including the buffer `buffers[offset+length-1]`. This method will throw an exception of type `IndexOutOfBoundsException` if `offset` or `offset+length-1` are not valid index values for the array `buffers`.

As you can see, all three `read()` methods read data into one or more buffers of type `ByteBuffer`. Since you can only use `ByteBuffer` objects to receive the data read from the file, you can *only* read data from a file via a channel as a series of bytes. How you interpret these bytes afterwards though is up to you.

All three methods can throw exceptions of any of the following types: :

`NonReadableChannelException`	Thrown if the file was not opened for reading.
`ClosedChannelException`	Thrown if the channel is closed.
`AsynchronousCloseException`	Thrown if the channel is closed by another thread while the read operation is in progress.
`ClosedByInterruptException`	Thrown if another thread interrupts the current thread while the read operation is in progress.
`IOException`	Thrown if some other I/O error occurs.

The first of these is a subclass of `RuntimeException` so you are not obliged to catch this exception. If you don't need to identify the other exceptions individually, you can use a single `catch` block for exceptions of type `IOException` to catch any of them.

The `FileChannel` object keeps track of the file's current position, and this is initially set to zero, corresponding to the first byte available from the file. Each read operation increments the channel's file position by the number of bytes read, so the next read operation will start at that point, assuming you have not modified the file position by some other means. When you need to change the file position in the channel – to reread the file for instance – you just call the `position()` method for the `FileChannel` object, with the index position of the byte where you want the next read to start as the argument to the method. For example, with a reference to a `FileChannel` object stored in a variable `inChannel`, you could reset the file position back to the beginning of the file with the statements:

```
try {
  inChannel.position(0);    // Set file position to first byte

} catch(IOException e) {
  e.printStackTrace();
}
```

This method will throw a `ClosedChannelException` if the channel is closed, or an `IOException` if some other error occurs, so you need to put the call in a `try` block. It can also throw an `IllegalArgumentException` if the argument is negative. This is a subclass of `RuntimeException` You can legally specify a position beyond the end of the file, but a subsequent read operation will just return -1 indicating the end-of-file has been reached.

Calling the `position()` method with no argument specified returns the current file position. This version of the method can also throw exceptions of type `ClosedChannelException` and `IOException` so you must put the call in a `try` block or make the calling method declare the exceptions in a `throws` clause.

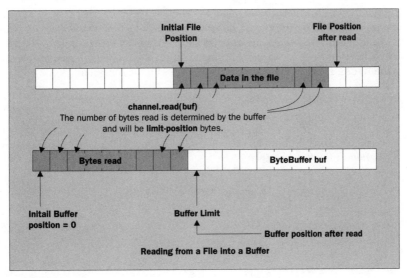

Reading from a File into a Buffer

The amount of data read from a file into a byte buffer is determined by the position and limit for the buffer when the read operation executes. Bytes are read into the buffer starting at the byte in the buffer given by its position, and assuming there are sufficient bytes available from the file, `limit-position` bytes will be stored in the buffer.

We will see some other channel `read()` methods later that we can use to read from a particular point in the file.

Reading a Text File

We can now attempt to read the very first file that we wrote in the previous chapter – `charData.txt`. We wrote this file as Unicode characters so we must take this into account when interpreting the contents of the file.

We can set up a `File` object encapsulating the file path to start with and create a `FileInputStream` object from that. We can then obtain a reference to the channel that we will use to read the file. We won't include all the checking here that you should apply to validate the file path, as you know how to do that:

```
File aFile = new File("C:/Beg Java Stuff/charData.txt");
FileInputStream inFile = null;

try {
  inFile = new FileInputStream(aFile);

} catch(FileNotFoundException e) {
  e.printStackTrace(System.err);
  System.exit(1);
}
FileChannel inChannel = inFile.getChannel();
```

Of course, we can only read the file as bytes into a byte buffer. We create that exactly as we saw previously when we were writing the file. We know that we wrote 48 bytes at a time to the file – we wrote the string `"Garbage in, garbage out \n"` that consists of 24 Unicode characters. However, we tried appending to the file an arbitrary number of times, so we should provide for reading as many Unicode characters as there are. We can set up the `ByteBuffer` with exactly the right size with the statement:

```
ByteBuffer buf = ByteBuffer.allocate(48);
```

The code that we use to read from the file needs to allow for an arbitrary number of 24-character strings in the file. Of course, it will also allow for the end-of-file being reached while reading the file. We can read from the file into the buffer like this:

```
try {
  while(inChannel.read(buf) != -1) {
    // Code to extract the data that was read into the buffer...
    buf.clear();                    // Clear the buffer for the next read
  }
  System.out.println("EOF reached.");

} catch(IOException e) {
  e.printStackTrace(System.err);
  System.exit(1);
}
```

The file is read in the expression used for the `while` loop condition. The `read()` method will return-1 when the end-of-file is reached so that will end the loop. Within the loop we have to extract the data from the buffer, do what we want with it, and then clear the buffer ready for the next read operation.

Getting Data from the Buffer

After the read operation, the buffer's position will point to the byte following the last byte that was read. Before we attempt to extract any data from the buffer we therefore need to flip the buffer to reset the position back to the beginning of the data and the limit to the byte following the last byte of data. One way to extract bytes from the buffer is to use the `ByteBuffer` object's `getChar()` method. This will retrieve a Unicode character from the buffer at the current position and increment the position by two. This could work like this:

```
buf.flip();
StringBuffer str = new StringBuffer(buf.remaining()/2);
while(buf.hasRemaining())
  str.append(buf.getChar());

System.out.println("String read: "+ str.toString());
```

This code should replace the comment in the previous fragment that appears at the beginning of the `while` loop. We first create a `StringBuffer` object in which we will assemble the string. This is the most efficient way to do this – using a `String` object would result in the creation of a new object each time we add a character to the string. The `remaining()` method for the buffer returns the number of bytes read after the buffer has been flipped, so we can just divide this by 2 to get the number of characters read. We extract characters one at a time from the buffer in the `while` loop and append them to the `StringBuffer` object. The `getChar()` method increments the buffer's position by 2 each time so eventually `hasRemaining()` will return `false`,when all the characters have been extracted, and the loop will end. We then just convert it to a string and output it on the command line.

This approach works OK but a better way is to use a view buffer of type `CharBuffer`. The `toString()` method for the `CharBuffer` object will give us the string that it contains directly. Indeed, we can boil the whole thing down to a single statement:

```
System.out.println("String read: " +
                    ((ByteBuffer)(buf.flip())).asCharBuffer().toString());
```

The `flip()` method returns a reference of type `Buffer` so we have to cast it to type `ByteBuffer` to make it possible to call the `asCharBuffer()` method for the buffer.

We can assemble these code fragments into a working example.

Try It Out – Reading Text from a File

Here's the code for the complete program:

```
import java.io.*;
import java.nio.ByteBuffer;
import java.nio.channels.FileChannel;
```

```
public class ReadAString {
  public static void main(String[] args) {
    File aFile = new File("C:/Beg Java Stuff/charData.txt");
    FileInputStream inFile = null;

    try {
      inFile = new FileInputStream(aFile);

    } catch(FileNotFoundException e) {
      e.printStackTrace(System.err);
      System.exit(1);
    }

    FileChannel inChannel = inFile.getChannel();
    ByteBuffer buf = ByteBuffer.allocate(48);
    try {
      while(inChannel.read(buf) != -1) {
        System.out.println("String read: " +
                          ((ByteBuffer)(buf.flip())).asCharBuffer().toString());
        buf.clear();                     // Clear the buffer for the next read
      }
      System.out.println("EOF reached.");
      inFile.close();                    // Close the file and the channel

    } catch(IOException e) {
      e.printStackTrace(System.err);
      System.exit(1);
    }
    System.exit(0);
  }
}
```

When you compile and run this, you should get output something like:

```
String read: "Garbage in, garbage out

String read: "Garbage in, garbage out

String read: "Garbage in, garbage out

EOF reached.
```

The gap between the lines of output is because each string ends with a '\n' character.

How It Works

There's nothing new here beyond what we have already discussed. If you want to output the length of the file, you could add a statement to call the size() method for the inChannel object:

```
System.out.println("File contains "+ inChannel.size() + " bytes.");
```

Immediately before the `while` loop would be a good place to put it, as the `size()` method can throw an `IOException`. You might also like to modify the code to output the buffer's position and limit before and after the read. This will show quite clearly how these change when the file is read.

Reading Binary Data

When you read binary data you still read bytes from the file, so the process is essentially the same as we used in the previous example. To read a binary file, we create a `FileInputStream` object and get the `FileChannel` object from it, then read the data into a byte buffer. We could set up a file channel to read our `primes.bin` file like this:

```
File aFile = new File("C:/Beg Java Stuff/primes.bin");
FileInputStream inFile = null;

try {
  inFile = new FileInputStream(aFile);

} catch(FileNotFoundException e) {
  e.printStackTrace(System.err);
  System.exit(1);
}
FileChannel inChannel = inFile.getChannel();
```

We have some options on the size of the byte buffer. The number of bytes in the buffer should be a multiple of eigth since a prime value is of type `long` but other than that we can make it whatever size we like. We could allocate a buffer to accommodate the number of primes that we want to output to the command line, six values say. This would make accessing the data very easy since we only need to set up a view buffer of type `LongBuffer` each time we read from the file. One thing against this is that reading such a small amount of data from the file in each read operation would not be a very efficient way to read the file. Before data transfer can start for a read operation there is a significant delay, usually of the order of several milliseconds, waiting for the disk to rotate until the data that we want to read is under the read heads. Therefore the more read operations you use to retrieve a given amount of data from the file the longer it takes. However, in the interests of understanding the mechanics of this let's see how it would work anyway. The buffer would be created like this:

```
final int PRIMECOUNT = 6;                    // Number of primes to read at a time
ByteBuffer buf = ByteBuffer.allocate(8*PRIMECOUNT);
```

We can then read the primes in a `while` loop inside a `try` block, like this:

```
long[] primes = new long[PRIMECOUNT];
try {
  primes = new long[(int)inChannel.size()/8];    // Array to hold 5 primes
  while(inChannel.read(buf) != -1) {
    // Access the primes via a view buffer of type LongBuffer...
    // Output the primes read...
    buf.clear();                     // Clear the buffer for the next read
  }
```

```
        System.out.println("EOF reached.");
        inFile.close();                           // Close the file and the channel

    } catch(IOException e) {
        e.printStackTrace(System.err);
        System.exit(1);
    }
```

We can create a view buffer of type `LongBuffer` that will help us get at the primes. We can obtain the view buffer by calling the `asLongBuffer()` method for the byte buffer, `buf`. The `LongBuffer` class offers you a choice of four `get()` methods for accessing long values in the buffer:

`get()`	Extracts a single value of type `long` from the buffer at the current position and returns it. The buffer position is then incremented by 1.
`get(int index)`	Extracts a single value of type `long` from the buffer position specified by the argument and returns it. The current buffer position is not altered.
`get(long[] values)`	Extracts `values.length` values of type `long` from the buffer starting at the current position and stores them in the array `values`. The current position is incremented by the number of values retrieved from the buffer. The method returns a reference to the buffer as type `LongBuffer`. If there are insufficient values available from the buffer to fill the array that you pass as the argument – in other words, `limit-position` is less than `values.length` – the method will throw an exception of type `BufferUnderflowException` and no values will be transferred to the array and the buffer's position will be unchanged.
`get(long[] values, int offset, int length)`	Extracts `length` values of type `long` from the buffer starting at the current position and stores them in the array `values`, starting at `values[offset]`. The current position is incremented by the number of values retrieved from the buffer. The method returns a reference to the buffer as type `LongBuffer`. If there are insufficient values available from the buffer – in other words, `limit-position` is less than `length` the method will throw an exception of type `BufferUnderflowException` no values will be transferred to the array, and the buffer's position will be unchanged.

The `BufferUnderflowException` class is a subclass of `RuntimeException` so you are not obliged to catch this exception, although it may be useful to do so if you want to avoid references to array elements that have not been loaded with data from the buffer.

With the buffer size we have chosen, perhaps the simplest way to access the primes in the buffer is like this:

```
LongBuffer longBuf = ((ByteBuffer)(buf.flip())).asLongBuffer();
System.out.println();                          // Newline for the buffer contents
while(longBuf.hasRemaining())                  // While there are values
  System.out.print(" " + longBuf.get());       // output them on the same line
```

If we wanted to collect the primes into an array, the form of `get()` method that transfers values to an array is more efficient than writing a loop to transfer them one at a time, but we have to be careful. Let's try it out in an example to see why.

Try It Out – Reading a Binary File

We will choose to read the primes six at a time into an array. Here's the program:

```java
import java.io.*;
import java.nio.ByteBuffer;
import java.nio.channels.FileChannel;

public class ReadPrimes {
  public static void main(String[] args) {
    File aFile = new File("C:/Beg Java Stuff/primes.bin");
    FileInputStream inFile = null;

    try {
      inFile = new FileInputStream(aFile);

    } catch(FileNotFoundException e) {
      e.printStackTrace(System.err);
      System.exit(1);
    }

    FileChannel inChannel = inFile.getChannel();
    final int PRIMECOUNT = 6;
    ByteBuffer buf = ByteBuffer.allocate(8*PRIMECOUNT);
    long[] primes = new long[PRIMECOUNT];
    try {
      while(inChannel.read(buf) != -1) {
        ((ByteBuffer)(buf.flip())).asLongBuffer().get(primes);

        System.out.println();
        for(int i = 0 ; i<primes.length ; i++)
          System.out.print("  " + primes[i]);

        buf.clear();                        // Clear the buffer for the next read
      }
      System.out.println("\nEOF reached.");
      inFile.close();                       // Close the file and the channel

    } catch(IOException e) {
      e.printStackTrace(System.err);
      System.exit(1);
    }
    System.exit(0);
  }
}
```

We get a whole lot of prime values, six to a line, then, when we almost have them all displayed, we suddenly get the output:

```
   . . .
   467  479  487  491  499  503Exception in thread "main" java.nio.BufferUnderflo
   wException
           at java.nio.LongBuffer.get(LongBuffer.java:609)
           at java.nio.LongBuffer.get(LongBuffer.java:633)
           at ReadPrimes.main(ReadPrimes.java:28)
```

How It Works

The reason is doesn't work very well is that the number of primes in the file is not divisible by the number of primes that we read into the view buffer. This is determined by the number of elements in the array primes. On the last iteration of the while loop that reads the file, there are insufficient values to fill the array so the get() method throws an exception of type BufferUnderflowException.

One way to deal with this is to catch the exception that is thrown. It's not a particularly good way because of the overhead in throwing and catching exceptions, but let's see how we could do it anyway. We could rewrite the while loop like this:

```
int primesRead = 0;
while(inChannel.read(buf) != -1) {
try {
  ((ByteBuffer)(buf.flip()))).asLongBuffer().get(primes);
  primesRead = primes.length;

} catch(BufferUnderflowException e) {
  LongBuffer longBuf = buf.asLongBuffer();
  primesRead = longBuf.remaining();
  longBuf.get(primes,0, primesRead);
}

System.out.println();
for(int i = 0 ; i< primesRead ; i++)
  System.out.print("   "+primes[i]);

  buf.clear();                    // Clear the buffer for the next read
}
```

When the exception is thrown on the last iteration, we catch it and read the remaining values in the view buffer using the alternate form of the get() method, where the second argument specifies the first array element to store a value in and the third argument specifies the number to be stored. To take account of the possibility that less than the whole array will contain primes when we output it, we set the number of primes that are read in the loop. Note that we must set the value of primesRead inside the catch block before we execute the get() method. Afterwards the number remaining will be zero.

Of course, although this works, it is a very poor way to deal with the problem. A better way is to avoid it altogether, like this:

```
int primesRead = 0;
while(inChannel.read(buf) != -1) {
```

```
  LongBuffer longBuf = ((ByteBuffer)(buf.flip())).asLongBuffer();
  primesRead = longBuf.remaining();
  longBuf.get(primes,0, longBuf.remaining());
  System.out.println();
  for(int i = 0 ; i< primesRead ; i++)
    System.out.print("  "+primes[i]);

  buf.clear();                      // Clear the buffer for the next read
}
```

The shaded lines reflect changes to the code in the original example. Now we always read the number of values available in `longBuf` so we can't cause the `BufferUnderflowException` to be thrown.

A further possibility is to use a buffer large enough to hold all the primes in the file. We can work this out from the value returned by the `size()` method for the channel – which is the length of the file in bytes. We could do that like this:

```
  final int PRIMECOUNT = (int)inChannel.size()/8;
```

Of course, you also must alter the `for` loop that outputs the primes so it doesn't attempt to put them all on the same line. There is a hazard with this though if you don't know how large the file is. Unless your PC is unusually replete with RAM, it could be inconvenient if the file contains the first billion primes. It might be as well to put an assertion to protect against an excess of primes:

```
  assert inChannel.size()<=100000;
  final int PRIMECOUNT = (int)inChannel.size()/8;
```

Now the program will not proceed if there are more than 100,000 primes in the file. Don't forget, to compile a program with assertions you must specify the `-source 1.4` options, and when you execute the program you need to specify the `-enableassertions` option.

Making the Output Pretty

One final point before we leave this example – the output is irritating. Why don't the columns line up? Well they should and could, but it's a bit more code that would clutter up the example. However, suppose we want to output the primes six to a line, left justified in a field width of 12. Here's one way we could do that:

```
  StringBuffer str = null;
  for(int i = 0 ; i< primesRead ; i++) {
    str = new StringBuffer("           ").append(primes[i]);
    System.out.print((i%6 == 0 ? "\n" : "") + str.substring(str.length()-12,
                     str.length()));
  }
```

This replaces the loop in the original code. On the first and every sixth prime output we start a new line by outputting "\n" as the first character in the argument to the `print()` method. We create a `StringBuffer` object, which contains 11 spaces, and append the `String` representation of the prime value to it. We then just output the string consisting of the last 12 characters in the `StringBuffer` object.

443

Reading Mixed Data

The `primes.txt` file that we created in the previous chapter contains data of three different types. We have the string length as a binary value of type `double` of all things, followed by the string itself describing the prime value, followed by the binary prime value as type `long`. Reading this file is a little trickier than it looks at first sight.

To start with we will set up the file input stream and obtain the channel for the file. Since, apart from the name of the file, this is exactly as in the previous example we won't repeat it here. Of course, the big problem is that we don't know ahead of time exactly how long the strings are. We have two strategies to deal with this:

❑   We can read the string length in the first read operation, then read the string and the binary prime value in the next. The only downside to this approach is that it's not a particularly efficient way to read the file as we will have read operations that each read a very small amount of data.

❑   We can set up a sizable byte buffer of an arbitrary capacity and just fill it with bytes from the file. We can then sort out what we have in the buffer. The problem with this approach is that the buffer's contents may well end part way through one of the data items from the file. We will have to do some work to detect this and figure out what to do next but this will be much more efficient than the first approach since we will vastly reduce the number of read operations that are necessary to read the entire file.

Let's try the first approach first as it's easier.

To read the string length we need a byte buffer with a capacity to hold a single value of type `double`:

```
ByteBuffer lengthBuf = ByteBuffer.allocate(8);
```

We can create a byte buffer to hold both the string and the binary prime value, but only after we know the length of the string. We will also need an array of type `byte[]` to hold the string characters – remember, we wrote the string as bytes, not Unicode characters. Some variables will come in handy:

```
int strLength = 0;        // Stores the string length
ByteBuffer buf = null;    // Stores a reference to the second byte buffer
byte[] strChars = null;   // Stores a reference to an array to hold the string
```

Since we need two read operations to get at all the data for a single prime, we will adopt a different strategy for reading the entire file. We will put both read operations in an indefinite loop and use a `break` statement to exit the loop when we hit the end-of-file (EOF). Here's how we can read the file:

```
while(true) {
  if(inChannel.read(lengthBuf) == -1)  // Read the string length, if its EOF
    break;                             // exit the loop

  lengthBuf.flip();
  strLength = (int)lengthBuf.getDouble(); // Extract length & convert to int
```

```
    buf = ByteBuffer.allocate(strLength+8);  // Buffer for string & prime

    if(inChannel.read(buf) == -1) {         // Read string & binary prime value
      assert false;                         // Should not get here!
      break;                                // Exit loop on EOF
    }

    buf.flip();
    strChars = new byte[strLength];         // Create the array for the string
    buf.get(strChars);                      // Extract string & binary prime value

    System.out.println("String length: " + strChars.length+ "  String: " +
                    new String(strChars) + "  Binary value: " + buf.getLong());

    lengthBuf.clear();                      // Clear the buffer for the next read
  }
```

After reading the string length into `lengthBuf` we can create the second buffer and allocate the array to store the string characters. We don't need any view buffers at all to get at the data from the file. The `getDouble()` method for `lengthBuf` provides us with the length of the string and we get the string and the binary prime value using the `get()` and `getLong()` methods for `buf`. Of course, if we find a string length value, there ought to be a string and a binary prime, so we have an assertion to signal something has gone wrong if this turns out not to be the case.

Let's see how it works out in practice.

Try It Out – Reading Mixed Data from a File

Here's the complete program code:

```
import java.io.FileInputStream;
import java.io.IOException;
import java.io.File;
import java.io.FileNotFoundException;

import java.nio.ByteBuffer;
import java.nio.channels.FileChannel;

public class ReadPrimesMixedData {
  public static void main(String[] args) {
    File aFile = new File("C:/Beg Java Stuff/primes.txt");
    FileInputStream inFile = null;

    try {
      inFile = new FileInputStream(aFile);

    } catch(FileNotFoundException e) {
      e.printStackTrace(System.err);
      System.exit(1);
    }

    FileChannel inChannel = inFile.getChannel();
```

```
    try {
      ByteBuffer lengthBuf = ByteBuffer.allocate(8);
      int strLength = 0;              // Stores the string length
      ByteBuffer buf = null;          // Stores a reference to the second byte buffer
      byte[] strChars = null;         // A reference to an array to hold the string

      while(true) {
        if(inChannel.read(lengthBuf) == -1)          // Read the string length,
          break;                                      // if its EOF exit the loop

        lengthBuf.flip();

        // Extract the length and convert to int
        strLength = (int)lengthBuf.getDouble();

        // Buffer for the string & the prime
        buf = ByteBuffer.allocate(strLength+8);

        if(inChannel.read(buf) == -1) {   // Read the string & binary prime value
          assert false;                   // Should not get here!
          break;                          // Exit loop on EOF
        }
        buf.flip();
        strChars = new byte[strLength];   // Create the array for the string
        buf.get(strChars);                // Extract string & binary prime value

        System.out.println("String length: " + strChars.length+ "  String: " +
                      new String(strChars) + "  Binary value: " +
                      buf.getLong());

        lengthBuf.clear();                    // Clear the buffer for the next read
      }

      System.out.println("\nEOF reached.");
      inFile.close();                   // Close the file and the channel

    } catch(IOException e) {
      e.printStackTrace(System.err);
      System.exit(1);
    }
    System.exit(0);
  }
}
```

Don't forget that you need to specify the -source 1.4 option when you compile code that includes assertions and the -enableassertions option when you execute it. You should get the output:

```
String length: 9  String: prime = 2  Binary value: 2
String length: 9  String: prime = 3  Binary value: 3
String length: 9  String: prime = 5  Binary value: 5
```

and so on down to the end:

```
String length: 11  String: prime = 523  Binary value: 523
String length: 11  String: prime = 541  Binary value: 541
```

EOF reached.

How It Works

We read the file with a relatively straightforward process. On each iteration of the loop that reads the file, we first read 8 bytes into `lengthBuf` since this will be the length of the following string as type `double`. Knowing the length of the string, we are able to create a second buffer, `buf`, to accommodate this plus the 8-byte long value that is the prime in binary. The loop continues until the read operation using `lengthBuf` reaches the end-of-file. If we reach EOF while reading data into `buf`, the program will assert.

Compacting a Buffer

The alternative approach to reading the file that we identified was to read bytes from the file into a large buffer for efficiency and then figure out what is in it. Processing the data will need to take account of the possibility that the last data item in the buffer may be incomplete – part of a `double` or `long` value or part of a string. The essence of this approach will therefore be as follows:

1. Read from the file into the buffer.

2. Extract the string length, the string, and the binary prime value from the buffer repeatedly until no more complete values are available.

3. Shift any bytes that are left over in the buffer back to the beginning of the buffer. These will be some part of a complete set of the string length, the string, and the binary prime value. Go back to point 1 to read more from the file.

The buffer classes provide a method, `compact()`, for performing the operation we need in point 3 here to shift bytes that are left over back to the beginning. An illustration of the action of the `compact()` method on a buffer is shown below.

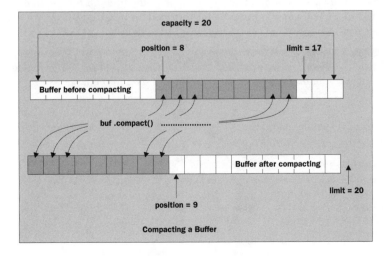

Compacting a Buffer

As you can see, everything remaining in the buffer, which will be elements from the buffer's position up to but not including the buffer's limit, is copied to the beginning of the buffer. The position is then set to the element following the last element copied and the limit is set to the capacity. This is precisely what you want when you have worked part way through the data in an input buffer and you want to add some more data from the file. Compacting the buffer sets the position and limit such that the buffer is ready to receive more data. The next read operation using the buffer will add data at the end of what was left in the buffer.

Any time we are processing an element from the buffer, accessing the string length, retrieving the string, or getting the binary value for a prime, we will need to check that there are at least the required number of bytes in the buffer. If there aren't, the buffer will need to be compacted, to shift what's left back to the start, and then replenished. Since we want to do this at three different points in the code, a method for this operation will come in handy:

```
private static int replenish(FileChannel channel, ByteBuffer buf)
   throws IOException {

  // Number of bytes left in file
  long bytesLeft = channel.size() - channel.position();

  if(bytesLeft == 0L)                         // If there are none
    return -1;                                // we have reached the end

  buf.compact().limit(buf.position()
              + (bytesLeft<buf.remaining() ? (int)bytesLeft : buf.remaining()));
  return channel.read(buf);
}
```

This method first checks that there really are some bytes left in the file with which to replenish the buffer. It then compacts the buffer and sets the limit for the buffer. The limit is automatically set to the capacity, but it is possible that the number of bytes left in the file is insufficient to fill the rest of the buffer. In this case the limit is set to accommodate the number of bytes available from the file. Note the throws clause. This indicates that the method can throw exceptions of type IOException. Exceptions of this type that are thrown are not handled by the code in the body of the method but are passed on to the calling method so we will need to put calls for this method in a try block. We can put the whole program together now.

Try It Out – Reading into a Large Buffer

Here are the changes to the original program code to read data into a large buffer:

```
import java.io.*;
import java.nio.ByteBuffer;
import java.nio.channels.FileChannel;

public class ReadPrimesMixedData {
  public static void main(String[] args) {

    // Create the file input stream and get the file channel as before...

    try {
```

```
        ByteBuffer buf = ByteBuffer.allocateDirect (1024);
        buf.position(buf.limit());        // Set the position for the loop operation
        int strLength = 0;                // Stores the string length
        byte[] strChars = null;           // Array for string

      while(true) {
        if(buf.remaining() < 8) {         // Verify enough bytes for string length
          if(replenish(inChannel, buf) == -1)  // If not, replenish the buffer
            break;                        // but exit loop on EOF
          else
            buf.flip();
        }
        strLength = (int)buf.getDouble();

        // Verify enough bytes for complete string
        if(buf.remaining()<strLength) {
          if(replenish(inChannel, buf) == -1) // If not, replenish the buffer
            assert false;                 // and we should never arrive here
          else
            buf.flip();
        }
        strChars = new byte[strLength];
        buf.get(strChars);

        if(buf.remaining()<8) {           // Verify enough bytes for prime value
          if(replenish(inChannel, buf) == -1)  // If not, replenish the buffer
            assert false;                 // and we should never arrive here
          else
            buf.flip();
        }

        System.out.println("String length: " + strChars.length + "  String: " +
                        new String(strChars) + "  Binary value: " +
                        buf.getLong());

      }
      System.out.println("\nEOF reached.");
      inFile.close();                     // Close the file and the channel

    } catch(IOException e) {
      e.printStackTrace(System.err);
      System.exit(1);
    }
    System.exit(0);
  }

  private static int replenish(FileChannel channel, ByteBuffer buf)
     throws IOException {

    // Number of bytes left in file
    long bytesLeft = channel.size() - channel.position();
    if(bytesLeft == 0L)                           // If there are none
      return -1;                                  // we have reached the end
```

```
      buf.compact().limit(buf.position() +
              (bytesLeft<buf.remaining() ? (int)bytesLeft : buf.remaining()));
      return channel.read(buf);
    }
  }
```

This should result in the same output as the previous example.

How It Works

All the work is done in the indefinite `while` loop. Before the loop executes we create a direct buffer with a capacity of 1024 bytes by calling the `allocateDirect()` method. A direct buffer will be faster if we are reading a lot of data from a file as the data are transferred directly from the file to our buffer. The code within the loop determines whether there are data in the buffer by calling the `remaining()` method for the buffer object. The default settings for the buffer, with the position at zero and the limit at the capacity, would suggest falsely that there are data in the buffer, so we set the position to the limit initially so that the `remaining()` method will return zero.

Within the loop we first check whether there are sufficient bytes for the double value specifying the string length. On the first iteration, this will definitely not be the case so the `replenish()` method will be called to compact the buffer and read data from the file. We then flip the buffer and get the length of the string. Of course, data in the file should be in groups of three items – string length, string, and binary prime value – so the end-of-file will be detected when trying to obtain the first of these. In this case we exit the loop by executing a `break` statement.

Next we get the string itself, after checking that there are sufficient bytes left in the buffer. We should never find EOF so we put an assertion rather than a break if EOF is detected. Finally we obtain the binary prime value in a similar way and output the group of three data items. The loop continues until all data have been read and processed and EOF is recognized when we are looking for a string length value.

Copying Files

You probably don't need a file copy program as your operating system is bound to provide a facility for this. However, it is a useful way of demonstrating how a file channel for any input file can transfer data directly to a file channel for an output file without involving explicit buffers.

A file channel defines two methods for direct data transfer: :

`transferTo(long position,`
`          long count,`
`          WritableByteChannel dst)`
	Attempts to transfer count bytes from this channel to the channel, dst. Bytes are read from this channel starting at the file position specified by position. The position of this channel is not altered by this operation but the position of dst will be incremented by the number of bytes written. Fewer than count bytes will be transferred if this channel's file has fewer than count bytes remaining, or if dst is non-blocking and has fewer than count bytes free in its system output buffer. The number of bytes transferred is returned as type int.

`transferFrom(ReadableByteChannel src,`
`            long position,`
`            long count)`
	Attempts to transfer count bytes to this channel from the channel src. Bytes are written to this channel starting at the file position specified by position. The position of this channel is not altered by the operation but the position of src will be incremented by the number of bytes read from it. If position is **greater** than the size of the file, then no bytes will be transferred. Fewer than count bytes will be transferred if the file corresponding to src has fewer than count bytes remaining in the file or if it is non-blocking and has fewer than count bytes free in its system input buffer. The number of bytes transferred is returned as type int.

A channel that was obtained from a `FileInputStream` object will only support the `transferTo()` method. Similarly, a channel that was obtained from a `FileOutputStream` object will only support the `transferFrom()` method. Both of these methods can throw any of the following flurry of exceptions:

`IllegalArgumentException`	Thrown if either count or position is negative.
`NonReadableChannelException`	Thrown if the operation attempts to read from a channel that was not opened for reading.
`NonWritableChannelException`	Thrown if the operation attempts to write to a channel that was not opened for writing.
`ClosedChannelException`	Thrown if either channel involved in the operation is closed.

Table continued on following page

AsynchronousCloseException	Thrown if either channel is closed by another thread while the operation is in progress.
ClosedByInterruptException	Thrown if another thread interrupts the current thread while the operation is in progress.
IOException	Thrown if some other I/O error occurs.

The value of these methods lies in the potential for using the I/O capabilities of the underlying operating system directly. Where this is possible, the operation is likely to be much faster than copying from one file to another in a loop using the read() and write() methods we have seen.

A file copy program is an obvious candidate for trying out these methods.

Try It Out – Direct Data Transfer between Channels

We will put together a program that will copy the file that is specified by a command line argument. We will copy the file to a backup file that we will create in the same directory as the original. We will create the name of the new file by appending "_backup" to the original file name as many times as necessary to form a unique file name. That operation is a good candidate for writing a helper method:

```
// Method to create a unique backup File object
public static File createBackupFile(File aFile) {
    aFile = aFile.getAbsoluteFile();              // Ensure we have an absolute path
    File parentDir = new File(aFile.getParent());    // Get the parent directory
    String name = aFile.getName();                  // Get the file name
    int period = name.indexOf('.');            // Find the extension separator
    if(period == -1)                            // If there isn't one
      period = name.length();                   // set it to the end of the string
    String nameAdd = "_backup";                 // String to be appended

    // Create a File object that is unique
    File backup = new File(name.substring(0,period) + nameAdd
                        + name.substring(period));
    while(backup.exists()) {                     // If the name already exists...
      name = backup.getName();                   // Get the current name of the file
      period += nameAdd.length();                // Increment separator index
      backup = new File(parentDir,name.substring(0,period) // add _backup again
                    + nameAdd + name.substring(period));
    }
    return backup;
  }
```

This method assumes the argument has already been validated as a real file. After making sure that aFile is not a relative path we extract the basic information we need to create the new file – the parent directory, the file name, and where the period separator is, if there is one. We then create a File object using the original file name with "_backup" appended. The while loop will execute as long as the name already exists as a file, and will append further instances of "_backup" until a unique file name is arrived at.

We can now write the method main() to use this method to create the destination file for the file copy operation:

```java
import java.io.*;
import java.nio.*;
import java.nio.channels.FileChannel;

public class FileCopy {
  public static void main(String[] args) {
    if(args.length==0) {
      System.out.println("No file to copy. Application usage is:\n"+
                          "java -classpath . FileCopy \"filepath\"" );
      System.exit(1);
    }
    File fromFile = new File(args[0]);

    if(!fromFile.exists()) {
      System.out.println("File to copy, "+fromFile.getAbsolutePath()
                    + ", does not exist.");
      System.exit(1);
    }

    File toFile = createBackupFile(fromFile);
    FileInputStream inFile = null;
    FileOutputStream outFile = null;
    try {
      inFile = new FileInputStream(fromFile);
      outFile = new FileOutputStream(toFile);

    } catch(FileNotFoundException e) {
      e.printStackTrace(System.err);
      assert false;
    }

    FileChannel inChannel = inFile.getChannel();
    FileChannel outChannel = outFile.getChannel();

    try {
      int bytesWritten = 0;
      long byteCount = inChannel.size();
      while(bytesWritten<byteCount)
        bytesWritten += inChannel.transferTo(bytesWritten,
                                        byteCount-bytesWritten,
                                        outChannel);

      System.out.println("File copy complete. " + byteCount
                    + " bytes copied to "
                    + toFile.getAbsolutePath());
      inFile.close();
      outFile.close();

    } catch(IOException e) {
      e.printStackTrace(System.err);
      System.exit(1);
    }
```

```
      System.exit(0);
   }


   // Code for createBackupFile() goes here...
 }
```

You could try this out by copying the source for the program using the command:

```
java FileCopy FileCopy.java
```

You should get output something like:

```
File copy complete. 3036 bytes copied to D:\Beg Java
1.4\Examples\FileCopy_backup.java
```

Of course, if the source file layout is different or you have a few more – or less – comments, the number of bytes copied will be different. Also the file path will be your path, not mine. In any event, you should be able to check that the new file's contents are identical to the original.

How It Works

We first obtain the command line argument and create a `File` object from it with the code:

```
    if(args.length==0) {
       System.out.println("No file to copy. Application usage is:\n"+
                          "java -classpath . FileCopy \"filepath\"" );
       System.exit(1);
    }
    File fromFile = new File(args[0]);
```

If there's no command line argument we supply a message explaining how to use the program.

Next we verify that this is a real file:

```
   if(!fromFile.exists()) {
      System.out.println("File to copy, "+fromFile.getAbsolutePath()
                      + ", does not exist.");
       System.exit(1);
   }
```

If it isn't, there's nothing we can do, so we bail out of the program.

Creating a `File` object for the backup file is a piece of cake:

```
      File toFile = createBackupFile(fromFile);
```

We saw how this method works earlier.

We now create a pair of file stream objects to work with:

```
FileInputStream inFile = null;
FileOutputStream outFile = null;
try {
   inFile = new FileInputStream(fromFile);
   outFile = new FileOutputStream(toFile);

} catch(FileNotFoundException e) {
   e.printStackTrace(System.err);
   assert false;
}
```

Since we checked the `File` objects, we know we won't see a `FileNotFoundException` being thrown but we still must provide for the possibility. Of course, the `FileInputStream` object corresponds to the file name entered on the command line. Creating the `FileOutputStream` object will result in a new empty file being created, ready for loading with the data from the input file.

Next we get the channel for each file from the file streams:

```
FileChannel inChannel = inFile.getChannel();
FileChannel outChannel = outFile.getChannel();
```

Once we have the channel objects we transfer the contents of the input file to the output file like this:

```
try {
   int bytesWritten = 0;
   long byteCount = inChannel.size();
   while(bytesWritten<byteCount)
     bytesWritten += inChannel.transferTo(bytesWritten,
                                   byteCount-bytesWritten,
                                   outChannel);

   System.out.println("File copy complete. " + byteCount
                   + " bytes copied to " + toFile.getAbsolutePath());
   inFile.close();
       outFile.close();

} catch(IOException e) {
   e.printStackTrace(System.err);
   System.exit(1);
}
```

The data is copied using the `transferTo()` method for `inChannel`. You could equally well use the `transferFrom()` method for `outChannel`. The chances are the `transferTo()` method will transfer all the data in one go. The `while` loop is there just in case it doesn't. The loop condition checks whether the number of bytes written is less than the number of bytes in the file. If it is, the loop executes another transfer operation for the number of bytes left in the file with the file position specified as the number of bytes written so far.

Random Access to a File

We can already read or write a file at random. The `FileChannel` class defines both a `read()` and a `write()` method that operate at a specified position in the file:

`read(ByteBuffer buf, long position)`	Reads bytes from the file into `buf` in the same way as we have seen previously except that bytes are read starting at the file position specified by the second argument. The channel's position is not altered by this operation. If position is greater than the number of bytes in the file then no bytes are read.
`write(ByteBuffer buf, long position)`	Writes bytes from `buf` to the file in the same way as we have seen previously except that bytes are written starting at the file position specified by the second argument. The channel's position is not altered by this operation. If `position` is less than the number of bytes in the file then bytes from that point will be overwritten. If `position` is greater than the number of bytes in the file then the file size will be increased to this point before bytes are written. In this case the bytes between the original end-of-file and where the new bytes are written will contain junk values.

These methods can throw the same exceptions as the corresponding method accepting a single argument, plus they may throw an exception of type `IllegalArgumentException` if a negative file position is specified.

Let's see how we can access a file randomly using the `read()` method above.

Try It Out – Reading a File Randomly

To show how easy it is to read from random positions in a file, we will write an example to extract a random selection of values from our `primes.bin` file. Here's the code:

```
import java.io.*;
import java.nio.*;
import java.nio.channels.FileChannel;

public class RandomFileRead {
  public static void main(String[] args) {
    File aFile = new File("C:/Beg Java Stuff/primes.bin");
    FileInputStream inFile = null;
    FileOutputStream outFile = null;

    try {
      inFile = new FileInputStream(aFile);

    } catch(FileNotFoundException e) {
      e.printStackTrace(System.err);
      System.exit(1);
    }
    FileChannel inChannel = inFile.getChannel();
```

```
      final int PRIMESREQUIRED = 10;
      ByteBuffer buf = ByteBuffer.allocate(8*PRIMESREQUIRED);

      long[] primes = new long[PRIMESREQUIRED];
      int index = 0;                               // Position for a prime in the file

      try {
        // Count of primes in the file
        final int PRIMECOUNT = (int)inChannel.size()/8;

        // Read the number of random primes required
        for(int i = 0 ; i<PRIMESREQUIRED ; i++) {
          index = 8*(int)(PRIMECOUNT*Math.random());
          inChannel.read(buf, index);              // Read the value
          buf.flip();
          primes[i] = buf.getLong();               // Save it in the array
          buf.clear();
        }

        // Output the selection of random primes 5 to a line in field width of 12
        StringBuffer str = null;
        for(int i = 0 ; i<PRIMESREQUIRED ; i++) {
          str = new StringBuffer("            ").append(primes[i]);
            System.out.print((i%5 == 0 ? "\n" : "")
                        + str.substring(str.length()-12, str.length()));
        }
        inFile.close();                            // Close the file and the channel

      } catch(IOException e) {
        e.printStackTrace(System.err);
        System.exit(1);
      }
        System.exit(0);
    }
  }
```

When I ran this, I got the output:

```
    359         107         383         109           7
    173         443         337          17         113
```

You should get something similar, but not the same since the random number generator is seeded using the current clock time.

How It Works

We access a random prime in the file by generating a random position in the file with the expression `8*(int)(PRIMECOUNT*Math.random())`. The value of `index` is a pseudo-random integer that can be from 0 to the number of primes in the file minus one, multiplied by 8 since each prime occupies eight bytes. Since `buf` has a capacity of 8 bytes, only one prime will be read each time. We store a randomly selected prime in each element of the primes array. Finally we output the primes five to a line in a field width of 12 characters.

The need to be able to access and update a file randomly arises quite often. Even with a simple personnel file for example you are likely to need the capability to update the address or the phone number for an individual. Assuming you have arranged for the address and phone number entries to be of a fixed length, you could update the data for any entry simply by overwriting it. If we want to read and write the same file we can just create two file streams and get two file channels for the file, one for input and one for output. Let's try that too.

Try It Out – Reading and Writing a File Randomly

We can modify the previous example so we overwrite each random prime that we retrieve with the value 99999L to make it stand out from the rest. This will mess up the primes.bin file but you can always run the program that created it again if you want to restore it. Here's the code:

```
import java.io.*;
import java.nio.*;
import java.nio.channels.FileChannel;

public class RandomReadWrite {
  public static void main(String[] args)
  {
    File aFile = new File("C:/Beg Java Stuff/primes.bin");
    FileInputStream inFile = null;
    FileOutputStream outFile = null;

    try {
      inFile = new FileInputStream(aFile);
      outFile = new FileOutputStream(aFile, true);

    } catch(FileNotFoundException e) {
      e.printStackTrace(System.err);
      System.exit(1);
    }
    FileChannel inChannel = inFile.getChannel();
    FileChannel outChannel = outFile.getChannel();

    final int PRIMESREQUIRED = 10;
    ByteBuffer buf = ByteBuffer.allocate(8*PRIMESREQUIRED);

    long[] primes = new long[PRIMESREQUIRED];
    int index = 0;                          // Position for a prime in the file
    final long REPLACEMENT = 99999L;        // Replacement for a selected prime

    try {
      final int PRIMECOUNT = (int)inChannel.size()/8;
      System.out.println("Prime count = "+PRIMECOUNT);
      for(int i = 0 ; i<PRIMESREQUIRED ; i++) {
        index = 8*(int)(PRIMECOUNT*Math.random());
        inChannel.read(buf, index);
        buf.flip();
        primes[i] = buf.getLong();
        buf.flip();
        buf.putLong(REPLACEMENT);
        buf.flip();
```

```
        outChannel.write(buf, index);
        buf.clear();
      }

      StringBuffer str = null;
    for(int i = 0 ; i<PRIMESREQUIRED ; i++) {
      str = new StringBuffer("            ").append(primes[i]);
        System.out.print((i%5 == 0 ? "\n" : "")
                     + str.substring(str.length()-12, str.length()));
    }
    inFile.close();                          // Close the file and the channel
    outFile.close();

  } catch(IOException e) {
    e.printStackTrace(System.err);
    System.exit(1);
  }
    System.exit(0);
  }
}
```

This will produce a set of ten random prime selections from the file. If you want to verify that we have indeed overwritten these values in the file you can run the `ReadPrimes` example that we wrote earlier in this chapter.

How It Works

All we had to do to write the file as well as read it was to create a `FileOutputStream` object for the file in addition to the `FileInputStream` object and access its file channel. We are then able to use one channel for writing to the file and the other for reading it. We can read and write sequentially or at random. The channel `read()` and `write()` methods we are using here explicitly specify the position where the data is to be read or written as an argument. In this case the file position recorded by the channel does not change. We could equally well change the file position for the channel before performing the read or write, like this:

```
for(int i = 0 ; i<PRIMESREQUIRED ; i++) {
  index = 8*(int)(PRIMECOUNT*Math.random());
  inChannel.position(index);                   // Set the file position
  inChannel.read(buf);                         // and read from the file
  buf.flip();
  primes[i] = buf.getLong();
  buf.flip();
  buf.putLong(REPLACEMENT);
  buf.flip();
  outChannel.position(index);                  // Set the file position
  outChannel.write(buf);                       // and write to the file
  buf.clear();
}
```

Now the file positions recorded by the channels are set explicitly and each channel's position is updated when it executes an I/O operation. Note that the position() method for a channel does not return a reference to the channel object so we cannot chain the position() and read() method calls together. You can only do this with buffer objects.

One problem with the example as it stands is that some of the selections could be 99999L, which is patently not prime. We could fix this by checking each value we store in the primes array:

```
for(int i = 0 ; i<PRIMESREQUIRED ; i++)
{
  while(true)
  {
    index = 8*(int)(PRIMECOUNT*Math.random());
    inChannel.position(index);                    // Set the file position
    inChannel.read(buf);                          // and read from the file
    buf.flip();
    primes[i] = buf.getLong();
    if(primes[i] != REPLACEMENT)
      break;
    else
      buf.clear();
  }
  buf.flip();
  buf.putLong(REPLACEMENT);
  buf.flip();
  outChannel.position(index);                     // Set the file position
  outChannel.write(buf);                          // and write to the file
  buf.clear();
}
```

The while loop now continues if the value read from the file is the same as REPLACEMENT, so another random file position will be selected. This continues until something other than the value of REPLACEMENT is found. Of course, if you run the example often enough, there won't be enough primes in the file to fill the array so the program will loop indefinitely looking for something other than REPLACEMENT. There are several ways you could deal with this. For instance, you could count how many iterations have occurred in the while loop and bail out if it reaches the number of primes in the file. You could also inspect the file first to see whether there are sufficient primes in the file to fill the array. If there are exactly 10 you can fill the array immediately. I'll leave it to you to fill in these details.

Read/Write Operations with a Single File Channel

If you want to be able to read and write a file using a single channel, you must use the channel provided by a RandomAccessFile object. A RandomAccessFile object is not related to the other file stream classes since its only base class is Object. Its original purpose was to provide random access to a file, which the other file stream classes could not, but as we have seen, this capability has been usurped by a channel anyway.

There are two constructors available for creating RandomAccessFile objects, and both require two arguments. For one constructor, the first argument is a File object that identifies the file path, and the second is a String object that specifies the access mode. The other constructor offer the alternative of using a String object as the first argument specifying the file path, with the second argument defining the access mode as before.

The access mode can be "r", which indicates that you just want to read the file, or it can be "rw", which indicates that you want to open the file to allow both read and write operations. If you specify the mode as anything else, the constructor will throw an IllegalArgumentException.

To create a RandomAccessFile object, you could write:

```
File myPrimes = new File("c:/Beg Java Stuff/primes.bin");
RandomAccessFile primesFile = null;
try {
  primesFile = new RandomAccessFile(myPrimes, "rw");

} catch(FileNotFoundException e) {
  e.printStackTrace(System.err);
  assert false;
}
```

This will create the random access file object, primesFile, corresponding to the physical file, primes.bin, and will open it for both reading and writing.

If the file does not exist when you specify "rw" as the mode, the file will be created automatically as long as the parent directory exists. Of course, there is the implicit assumption that you intend to write to the file before you try to read it. If you specify the mode as "r", the file must already exist. If it doesn't, the constructor will throw a FileNotFoundException. The same exception will be thrown if the file exists but cannot be opened for some reason. Like the file stream class constructors, a RandomAccessFile constructor can throw a SecurityException if a security manager exists and access to the file is denied.

You obtain the FileChannel object from a RandomAccessFile object in the same way as for the file stream objects we have been working with:

```
FileChannel ioChannel = primesFile.getChannel();
```

You can now use this channel to read and write the file sequentially or at random. It should be a trivial exercise for you to modify the previous example to use a channel from a RandomAccessFile object instead of the channels for the two file stream objects.

If you check the documentation for the RandomAccessFile class, you will find that it too records the file position and it describes it as a file-pointer. It also defines the getFilePointer() method for obtaining the current value of the file-pointer and the seek() method that alters it. The file-pointer for a RandomAccessFile object is identical to the file position recorded by its channel, and changes to one are immediately reflected in the other.

Memory-Mapped Files

A memory-mapped file is a file that has its contents mapped into an area of virtual memory in your computer so you can reference or update the data directly without performing any explicit file read or write operations on the physical file yourself. The memory that a file maps to may be paged in or out by the operating system, just like any other memory in your computer, so its immediate availability in real memory is not guaranteed. Because of the potentially immediate availability of the data it contains, a memory-mapped file is particularly useful when you need to access the file randomly. Your program code can reference data in the file as though it were resident in memory.

The `map()` method for a `FileChannel` object will return a reference to a buffer of type `MappedByteBuffer` that will map to a specified part of the channel's file: :

`map(int mode,`
`    long position,`
`    long size)`
	Maps a region of the channel's file to a buffer of type `MappedByteBuffer`. The file region that is mapped starts at `position` in the file and is of `length` size bytes. The first argument, `mode`, specifies how the buffer's memory may be accessed and can be any of the following three constant values, defined in the `FileChannel` class:
	
	`MAP_RO`. This is valid if the channel was opened for reading the file, in other words, if the channel was obtained from a `FileInputStream` object or a `RandomAccessFile` object. In this mode the buffer is read-only. If you try to modify the buffer's contents a `ReadOnlyBufferException` will be thrown.
	
	`MAP_RW`. This is valid if the channel was obtained from a `RandomAccessFile` object with "rw" as its access mode. You can access and change the contents of the buffer and any changes to the contents will eventually be propagated to the file.
	
	`MAP_COW`. The COW part of the name is for **C**opy **O**n **W**rite. This option for `mode` is also only valid if the channel was obtained from a `RandomAccessFile` object with `"rw"` as its access mode. You can access or change the buffer but changes will not be propagated to the file. Private copies of modified portions of the buffer will be created and used for subsequent buffer accesses.

Because the `MappedByteBuffer` class is a subclass of the `ByteBuffer` class, you have all the `ByteBuffer` methods available for a `MappedByteBuffer` object. This implies that you can create view buffers for a `MappedByteBuffer` object, for instance.

The `MappedByteBuffer` class defines three methods of its own to add to those inherited from the `ByteBuffer` class:

force()	If the buffer was mapped in MAP_RW mode this method forces any changes made to the buffer's contents to be written to the file and returns a reference to the buffer. For buffers created with MAP_RO or MAP_COW mode this method has no effect.
load()	Loads the contents of the buffer into memory and returns a reference to the buffer.
isLoaded()	Returns true if this buffer's contents is available in physical memory and false otherwise.

Using a memory-mapped file through a MappedByteBuffer is simplicity itself, so let's try it.

Try It Out – Using a Memory-Mapped File

We will access and modify the primes.bin file using a MappedByteBuffer. Here's the code:

```
import java.io.*;
import java.nio.*;
import java.nio.channels.FileChannel;

public class MemoryMappedFile {
  public static void main(String[] args) {
    File aFile = new File("C:/Beg Java Stuff/primes.bin");
    RandomAccessFile ioFile = null;

    try {
      ioFile = new RandomAccessFile(aFile,"rw");

    } catch(FileNotFoundException e) {
      e.printStackTrace(System.err);
      System.exit(1);
    }
    FileChannel ioChannel = ioFile.getChannel();


    final int PRIMESREQUIRED = 10;
    long[] primes = new long[PRIMESREQUIRED];

    int index = 0;                       // Position for a prime in the file
    final long REPLACEMENT = 999999L;    // Replacement for a selected prime

    try {
      final int PRIMECOUNT = (int)ioChannel.size()/8;
      MappedByteBuffer buf =
              ioChannel.map(ioChannel.MAP_RW, 0L, ioChannel.size()).load();

      for(int i = 0 ; i<PRIMESREQUIRED ; i++) {
        index = 8*(int)(PRIMECOUNT*Math.random());
        primes[i] = buf.getLong(index);
        buf.putLong(index, REPLACEMENT );
      }
```

```
        StringBuffer str = null;
        for(int i = 0 ; i<PRIMESREQUIRED ; i++) {
          str = new StringBuffer("        ").append(primes[i]);
            System.out.print((i%5 == 0 ? "\n" : "") + str.substring(str.length()-12,
                         str.length()));
        }
        ioFile.close();                      // Close the file and the channel

    } catch(IOException e) {
        e.printStackTrace(System.err);
        System.exit(1);
    }
        System.exit(0);
    }
}
```

This should output ten randomly selected primes but some or all of the selections may turn out to be 999999L, the value of REPLACEMENT.

How It Works

The statements of interest are those that are shaded. The others we have seen before. We create a RandomAccessFile object with "rw" access to the file:

```
    ioFile = new RandomAccessFile(aFile,"rw");
```

This statement executes in a try block since it can throw a FileNotFoundException. We get the file channel for ioFile with the statement:

```
    FileChannel ioChannel = ioFile.getChannel();
```

We then create and load a MappedByteBuffer object with the statement:

```
    MappedByteBuffer buf =
            ioChannel.map(ioChannel.MAP_RW, 0L, ioChannel.size()).load();
```

The buffer is created with the mode that permits the buffer to be accessed or modified and modifications will be written to the file. The buffer maps to the entire file since we specify the start file position as zero and the length mapped as the length of the file. The map() method returns a reference to the MappedByteBuffer object that is created and we use this to call its load() method to request that the contents of the file are loaded into memory immediately. The load() method also returns the same buffer reference that is stored in buf.

Note that it is not essential to call the load method before you access the data in the buffer. If the data is not available when you try to access it through the MappedByteBuffer object, it will be loaded for you. Try running the example with the call to load() removed. It should work the same as before.

Inside the for loop, we retrieve a value from the buffer at a random position, index:

```
    primes[i] = buf.getLong(index);
```

Note that we have not needed to execute any channel `read()` operations. The file contents are available directly through the buffer.

Next we change the value at the position we retrieved the value from to store in `primes[i]`:

```
buf.putLong(index, REPLACEMENT );
```

This will change the contents of the buffer and this change will subsequently be written to the file at some point. When this occurs depends on the underlying operating system.

Finally we output the contents of the `primes` array. We have been able to access and modify the contents of the file without having to execute any explicit I/O operations on the file. This is potentially much faster than using explicit read and write operations. How much faster depends on how your operating system handles memory-mapped files.

There is one risky aspect to memory-mapped files that we need to consider.

Locking a File

You need to take care that an external program does not modify a memory-mapped file, especially if the file could be truncated externally while you are accessing it. If you try to access a part of the file through a `MappedByteBuffer` that has become inaccessible because a segment has been chopped off the end of the file, then the results are somewhat unpredictable. You may get a junk value back that your program may not recognize as such, or an exception of some kind may be thrown. You can acquire a **lock** on the file to prevent this sort of problem. A file lock simply ensures your right of access to the file and may also inhibit the ability of others to access the file as long as your lock is in effect. This facility will only be available if the underlying operating system supports file locking.

A lock on a file is encapsulated by an object of the `FileLock` class that is defined in the `java.nio.channels` package. The `lock()` method for a `FileChannel` object tries to obtain an exclusive lock on the channel's file. Acquiring an **exclusive lock** on a file ensures that another program cannot access the file. Here's one way to obtain an exclusive lock on a file:

```
FileLock ioFileLock = null;
try {
  ioFileLock = ioChannel.lock();

} catch (IOException e) {
  e.printStackTrace(System.err);
  System.exit(1);
}
```

This method will attempt to acquire an exclusive lock on the channel's file so that no other program or thread can access the file while this channel holds the lock. If another program or thread already has a lock on the file, the `lock()` method will block until the lock on the file is released and can be acquired by this channel. The lock that is acquired is owned by the channel, `ioChannel`, and will be automatically released when the channel is closed. By saving the reference to the `FileLock` object, we can release the lock on the file when we are done by calling the `release()` method for the `FileLock` object. This invalidates the lock so file access is no longer restricted. You can call the `isValid()` method for a `FileLock` object to determine whether it is valid. A return value of true indicates a valid lock, otherwise false will be returned. Note that once created, a `FileLock` object is immutable. It also has no further effect on file access once it has been invalidated. If you want to lock the file a second time you must acquire a new lock.

Having your program hang until a lock is acquired is not an ideal situation. It is quite possible a file could be locked permanently – at least until the computer is rebooted – because of a programming error in another program, in which case your program will hang indefinitely. The `tryLock()` method for a channel offers an alternative way of requesting a lock that does not block. It either returns a reference to a valid `FileLock` object or returns `null` if the lock could not be acquired. This gives your program a chance to do something else or retire gracefully:

```
FileLock ioFileLock = null;
try {
  ioFileLock = ioChannel.tryLock();
  if(ioFileLock == null) {
    System.out.println("The file's locked - again!! Oh, I give up...");
    System.exit(1);
  }
} catch (IOException e) {
  e.printStackTrace(System.err);
  System.exit(1);
}
```

We will see in an example a better response to a lock than this, but you get the idea.

Locking Part of a File

There are overloaded versions of the `lock()` and `tryLock()` methods that allow you to specify just a part of the file you want to obtain a lock on:

`lock(long position, long size, boolean shared)`	Requests a lock on the region of this channel's file starting at `position` and of `length` size. If the last argument is `true`, the lock requested is a **shared lock**. If it is `false` the lock requested is an **exclusive lock**. If the lock cannot be obtained for any reason, the method will block until the lock can be obtained or the channel is closed by another thread.
`tryLock(long position, long size, boolean shared)`	This works in the same way as the method above, except that `null` will be returned if the requested lock cannot be acquired. This avoids the potential for hanging your program indefinitely.

The effect of a shared lock is to prevent an exclusive lock being acquired by another program that overlaps the region that is locked. However, a shared lock does permit another program to acquire a shared lock on a region of the file that may overlap the region to which the original shared lock applies. This implies that more than one program may be accessing and updating the same region of the file, so the effect of a shared lock is simply to ensure your code is not prevented from doing whatever it is doing by some other program with a shared lock on the file. Some operating systems do not support shared locks, in which case the request will always be treated as an exclusive lock.

Note that a single virtual machine does not allow overlapping locks so different threads running on the same VM cannot have overlapping locks on a file. However, the locks within two or more JVMs on the same computer can overlap. If another program changing the data in a file would cause a problem for you then the safe thing to do is to obtain an exclusive lock on the region of the file you are working with.

Practical File Locking Considerations

You can apply file locks in any context, not just with memory-mapped files. The fact that all or part of a file can be locked by a program means that you cannot ignore file locking when you are writing a real-world Java application that may execute in a context where file locking is supported. You need to include at least shared file locks for regions of a file that your program uses. In most instances, though, you will want to use exclusive locks since external changes to a file's contents are usually a problem if you are accessing the same data.

You don't need to obtain an exclusive lock on an entire file. Generally, if it is likely that other programs will be using the same file concurrently, it is not reasonable practice to lock everyone else out, unless it is absolutely necessary, such as a situation in which you may be performing a transacted operation that must either succeed or fail entirely. Circumstances where it would be necessary are when the correctness of your program result is dependent on the entire file's contents not changing. If you were computing a checksum for a file for instance, you need to lock the entire file. Any changes while your checksum calculation is in progress are likely to make it incorrect.

Most of the time it is quite sufficient to lock the portion of the file you are working with, and then release it once you have done with it. We can show the idea in the context of the program that lists the primes from the primes.bin file.

Try It Out – Using a File Lock

We will lock the region of the primes.bin file that we intend to read, and then release it after the read operation is complete. We will use the tryLock() method, since it does not block, and try to acquire the lock again if it fails to return a reference to a FileLock object. To do this sensibly we need to be able to pause the current thread rather than roaring round a tight loop frantically calling the tryLock() method. We will bring forward a capability from Chapter 15 to do this for us. We can pause the current thread by 200 milliseconds with the following code:

```
try {
  Thread.sleep(200);      // Wait for 200 milliseconds

} catch(InterruptedException e) {
  e.printStackTrace(System.err);
}
```

Chapter 11

The `static sleep()` method in the `Thread` class causes the current thread to sleep for the number of milliseconds specified by the argument. While our current thread is sleeping other threads can execute, so whoever has a lock on our file has a chance to release it.

Here's the code for the complete example:

```
import java.io.*;
import java.nio.*;
import java.nio.channels.*;                    // For FileChannel and FileLock

public class LockingPrimesRead {
  public static void main(String[] args)
    File aFile = new File("C:/Beg Java Stuff/primes.bin");
    FileInputStream inFile = null;

    try {
      inFile = new FileInputStream(aFile);

    } catch(FileNotFoundException e) {
      e.printStackTrace(System.err);
      System.exit(1);
    }
    FileChannel inChannel = inFile.getChannel();
    final int PRIMECOUNT = 6;
    ByteBuffer buf = ByteBuffer.allocate(8*PRIMECOUNT);
    long[] primes = new long[PRIMECOUNT];
    try {
      int primesRead = 0;
      FileLock inLock = null;
      while(true) {
        int tryLockCount = 0;

        // Get a lock on the file region we want to read
        while(true) {
          inLock = inChannel.tryLock(inChannel.position(),
                                     buf.remaining(),
                                     false);
          if(inLock == null) {
            if(++tryLockCount <100)
            {
              try {
                Thread.sleep(200);                 // Wait for 200 milliseconds

              } catch(InterruptedException e) {
                e.printStackTrace(System.err);
              }
              continue;                 // Continue with next loop iteration

            } else {
              System.out.println("Failed to acquire lock after "
                          + tryLockCount+" tries."+ " Terminating...");
              System.exit(1);
            } else {
```

468

```
                  System.out.println("\nAcquired file lock.");
                  break;
               }
            }
         }

         // Now read the file
         if(inChannel.read(buf) == -1)
           break;
         inLock.release();
         System.out.println("Released file lock.");

         LongBuffer longBuf = ((ByteBuffer)(buf.flip())).asLongBuffer();
         primesRead = longBuf.remaining();
           longBuf.get(primes,0, longBuf.remaining());
         StringBuffer str = null;
         for(int i = 0 ; i< primesRead ; i++) {
           if(i%6 == 0)
               System.out.println();
           str = new StringBuffer("            ").append(primes[i]);
           System.out.print(str.substring(str.length()-12));
         }
         buf.clear();                      // Clear the buffer for the next read
      }

      System.out.println("\nEOF reached.");
      inFile.close();                      // Close the file and the channel

   } catch(IOException e) {
      e.printStackTrace(System.err);
      System.exit(1);
   }
      System.exit(0);
   }
}
```

This will output primes from the file the same as the ReadPrimes example does, but interspersed with comments showing where we acquire and release the file lock.

How It Works

The overall while loop for reading the file is now indefinite since we need to obtain a file lock before reading the file. We attempt to acquire the file lock in the inner while loop with the statement:

```
inLock = inChannel.tryLock(inChannel.position(), buf.remaining(), false);
```

This requests an exclusive lock on buf.remaining() bytes in the file starting with the byte at the current file position. Acquiring a lock on just the part of the file that we want to read ensures that other programs are not prevented from accessing the rest of the file. We have to test the value returned by the tryLock() method for null to determine whether we have obtained a lock or not. The if statement that does this looks quite complex, but its overall operation is quite simple:

```
if(inLock == null)
  // Cause the thread to sleep for a while before retrying the lock...
else
  // We have the lock so break out of the loop...
```

If `inLock` is `null`, we try to acquire the lock again with the following code:

```
if(++tryLockCount <100) {
  try {
    Thread.sleep(200);                    // Wait for 200 milliseconds

  } catch(InterruptedException e) {
    e.printStackTrace(System.err);
  }
  continue;                               // Continue with next loop iteration
} else {
  System.out.println("Failed to acquire lock after "+tryLockCount+" tries."
                + " Terminating...");
  System.exit(1);
}
```

If we have tried fewer than 100 times to acquire the lock, we have another go after sending the current thread to sleep for 200 milliseconds. Once we have failed to acquire a lock 100 times, we abandon reading the file and exit the program.

Once we have acquired a lock, we read the file in the usual way and release the lock:

```
if(inChannel.read(buf) == -1)
  break;
inLock.release();
System.out.println("Released file lock.");
```

By releasing the lock immediately after reading the file, we ensure that the amount of time the file is blocked is a minimum. Of course, if the `read()` method returns -1 because EOF has been reached, we won't call the `release()` method for the `FileLock` object here because we exit the outer loop. However, after exiting the outer `while` loop we close the file stream and the channel, and closing the channel will release the lock.

Summary

In this chapter, we have discussed the various ways in which we can read basic types of data from a file. The important points we have discussed include:

❑ You can read a file using a `FileChannel` object obtained from a `FileInputStream` object or from a `RandomAccessFile` object.

❑ You can use a channel obtained from a `RandomAccessFile` object that was created with mode `"rw"` to both read and write the file.

❑ Data that are read from a file using a channel is stored in one or more buffers of type `ByteBuffer`.

❑ You can use view buffers to interpret the data read from a file as any basic type other than `boolean`.

❑ A memory-mapped file enables you to access data in the file as though it were resident in memory.

❑ Acquiring an **exclusive lock** on a file ensures that no other program can access the file while you hold the lock.

❑ Acquiring a **shared lock** on a file ensures your program has access to the file in circumstances where other programs may be accessing the same file.

❑ If you can't ride two horses at once, you shouldn't be in the circus.

Exercises

1. Write a program to read back and list the contents of the file written by the first exercise in the previous chapter.

2. Extend the `ReadPrimes` example that we produced in this chapter to optionally display the nth prime, when n is entered from the keyboard.

3. Extend the `ReadPrimes` program further to output a given number of primes, starting at a given number. For example, output 15 primes starting at the 30th. The existing capabilities should be retained.

4. Write a program that will output the contents of a file to the command line as groups of eight hexadecimal digits with five groups to a line, each group separated from the next by a space.

5. Write a program that will allow either one or more names and addresses to be entered from the keyboard and appended to a file, or the contents of the file to be read back and output to the command line.

6. Modify the previous example to store an index to the name and address file in a separate file. The index file should contain each person's second name, plus the position where the corresponding name and address can be found in the name and address file. Provide support for an optional command argument allowing a person's second name to be entered. When the command line argument is present, the program should then find the name and address and output it to the command line.

Serializing Objects

In this chapter, we will see how you can transfer objects to and from a stream. By the end of this chapter you will have learned:

- ❏ What serialization is and how you make a class serializable.
- ❏ How to write objects to a file.
- ❏ What transient fields in a class are.
- ❏ How to write basic types of data to an object file.
- ❏ How to implement the `Serializable` interface.
- ❏ How to read objects from a file.
- ❏ How to implement serialization for classes containing objects that are not serializable by default.

Storing Objects in a File

The process of storing and retrieving objects in an external file is called **serialization**. Note that an array of any type is an object for the purposes of serialization, even an array of values of a primitive type, such as type `int` or type `double`. Writing an object to a file is referred to as **serializing** the object, and reading an object from a file is called **deserializing** an object. Serialization is concerned with writing objects and the fields they contain to a stream, so this excludes `static` members of a class. Static fields will have whatever values are assigned by default in the class definition.

I think you will be surprised at how easy this is. Perhaps the most impressive aspect of the way serialization is implemented in Java is that you can generally read and write objects of almost any class type, including objects of classes that you have defined yourself, without adding any code to the classes involved to support this mechanism. For the most part, everything is taken care of automatically:

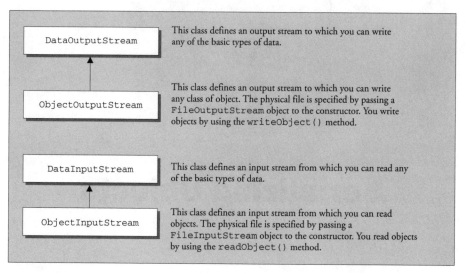

Two classes from the java.io package are used for serialization. An ObjectOutputStream object manages the writing of objects to a file, and reading the objects back is handled by an object of the class ObjectInputStream. As we saw in Chapter 8, these are derived from OutputStream and InputStream, respectively.

Writing an Object to a File

The constructor for the ObjectOutputStream class requires a reference to a FileOutputStream object as an argument that defines the stream for the file where you intend to store your objects. You could create an ObjectOutputStream object with the following statements:

```
File theFile = new File("MyFile");
// Check out the file...

// Create the object output stream for the file
ObjectOutputStream objectOut = null;
try {
  objectOut = new ObjectOutputStream(new FileOutputStream(theFile));

} catch(IOException e) {
  e.printStackTrace(System.err);
  System.exit(1);
}
```

We know from our earlier investigations into file input that the FileOutputStream constructor can throw a FileNotFoundException if the File object that you pass to the constructor represents a directory rather than a file, or if the file does not exist and cannot be created for some reason. In addition the ObjectOutputStream constructor will throw an IOException if an error occurs while the stream header is written to the file. Our catch block here will handle either of these exceptions.

While the previous code fragment will work perfectly well, it does not result in a stream that is particularly efficient since each output operation will write directly to the file. In practice you will probably want to buffer write operations on the file in memory, in which case you would create the `ObjectOutputStream` object like this:

```
objectOut = new ObjectOutputStream(
            new BufferedOutputStream(
                new FileOutputStream(theFile)));
```

The `BufferedOutputStream` constructor creates an object that buffers the `OutputStream` object that is passed to it, so here we get a buffered `FileOutputStream` object that we pass to the `ObjectOutputStream` constructor. With this arranged, each write operation to the `ObjectOutputStream` will write the `BufferedOutputStream` object. The `BufferedOutputStream` object will write the data to an internal buffer. Data from the buffer will be written to the file whenever the buffer is full, or when the stream is closed by calling its `close()` method or flushed by calling its `flush()` method. By default the buffer has a capacity of 512 bytes. If you want to use a buffer of a different size you can use the `BufferedOutputStream` constructor that accepts a second argument of type `int` that defines the size of the buffer in bytes.

To write an object to the file `MyFile`, you call the `writeObject()` method for `objectOut` with a reference to the object to be written as the argument. Since this method accepts a reference of type `Object` as an argument, you can pass a reference of any class type to the method. There are three basic conditions that have to be met for an object to be written to a stream:

❑   The class must be declared as `public`.

❑   The class must implement the `Serializable` interface.

❑   If the class has a direct or indirect base class that is not serializable, then that base class must have a default constructor – that is, a constructor that requires no arguments. The derived class must take care of transferring the base class data members to the stream.

Implementing the `Serializable` interface is a lot less difficult than it sounds, and we will see how in a moment. Later we will come back to the question of how to deal with a non-serializable base class.

If `myObject` is an instance of a public class that implements `Serializable`, then to write `myObject` to the stream that we defined above, you would use the statement:

```
try {
  objectOut.writeObject(myObject);

} catch(IOException e) {
  e.printStackTrace(System.err);
  System.exit(1);
}
```

The `writeObject()` method can throw any of the following three exceptions:

`InvalidClassException`	Thrown when there is something wrong with the class definition for the object being written. This might be because the class is not `public`, for instance.
`NotSerializableException`	Thrown if the object's class, or the class of a data member of the class, does not implement the `Serializable` interface.
`IOException`	Thrown when a file output error occurs.

The first two exception classes here are subclasses of `ObjectStreamException`, which is itself a subclass of `IOException`. Thus we can catch any of them with a `catch` block for `IOException`. Of course, if you want to take some specific action for any of these then you can catch them individually. Just be sure to put the `catch` blocks for the first two types of exception before the one for `IOException`.

The call to `writeObject()` takes care of writing everything to the stream that is necessary to reconstitute the object later in a read operation. This includes information about the class and all its superclasses, as well as the contents and types of the data members of the class. Remarkably, this works even when the data members are themselves class objects, as long as they are objects of `Serializable` classes. Our `writeObject()` call will cause the `writeObject()` method for each object that is a data member to be called, and this mechanism continues recursively until everything that makes up our object has been written to the stream. Each independent object that you write to the stream requires a separate call to the `writeObject()` method, but the objects that are members of an object are taken care of automatically. This is not completely foolproof in that the relationships between the class objects can affect this process, but for the most part this is all you need to do. We will be using serialization to write fairly complex objects to files in Chapter 20.

Writing Basic Data Types to an Object Stream

You can write data of any of the primitive types using the methods defined in the `ObjectOutputStream` class for this purpose. For writing individual items of data of various types, you have the following methods:

`writeByte(int b)`	`writeByte(byte b)`	`writeChar(int ch)`
`writeShort(int n)`	`writeInt(int n)`	`writeLong(long n)`
`writeFloat(float x)`	`writeDouble(double x)`	

None of them return a value and they can all throw an `IOException` since they are output operations.

You can write a string object to the file as a sequence of bytes using the `writeBytes()` method, passing a reference to a `String` as the argument to the method. Each character in the string is converted to a byte using the default charset. To write a string as a sequence of Unicode characters, you use the `writeChars()` method, again with a reference of type `String` as the argument. This writes each Unicode character in the string as two bytes. Note that these methods write just a sequence of bytes or characters. No information about the original `String` object is written so the fact that these characters belonged to a string is lost. If you want to write a `String` object to the file as an object, use the `writeObject()` method.

You have two methods that apply to arrays of bytes. These override the methods inherited from `InputStream`:

`Write(byte[] array)`	Writes the contents of `array` to the file as bytes.
`Write(byte[] array, int offset, int length)`	Writes `length` elements from `array` to the file starting with `array[offset]`.

In both cases just bytes are written to the stream as binary data, not the array object itself. An array of type `byte[]` will be written to the stream as an object by default, so you will only need to use these methods if you do not want an array of type `byte[]` written as an object.

You can mix writing data of the basic types and class objects to the stream. If you have a mixture of objects and data items of basic types that you want to store in a file, you can write them all to the same `ObjectOutputStream`. You just have to make sure that you read everything back in the sequence and form that it was written.

Implementing the Serializable Interface

A necessary condition for objects of a class to be serializable is that the class implements the `Serializable` interface but this may not be sufficient, as we shall see. In most instances, you need only declare that the class implements the `Serializable` interface to make the objects of that class type serializable. No other code is necessary. For example, the following declares a class that implements the interface.

```
public MyClass implements Serializable {
   // Definition of the class...
}
```

If your class is derived from another class that implements the `Serializable` interface, then your class also implements `Serializable` so you don't have to declare that this is the case. Let's try this out on a simple class to verify that it really works.

Try It Out – Writing Objects to a File

We will first define a serializable class that has some arbitrary fields with different data types:

```
import java.io.Serializable;

public class Junk implements Serializable {
  private static java.util.Random generator = new java.util.Random();
  private int answer;                          // The answer
  private double[] numbers;                     // Valuable data
  private String thought;                       // A unique thought

  public Junk(String thought) {
    this.thought = thought;
    answer = 42;                                // Answer always 42

    numbers = new double[3+generator.nextInt(4)]; // Array size 3 to 6
    for(int i = 0 ; i<numbers.length ; i++)    // Populate with
      numbers[i] = generator.nextDouble();      // random values
  }


  public String toString() {
    StringBuffer strBuf = new StringBuffer(thought);
    strBuf.append('\n').append(String.valueOf(answer));
    for(int i = 0 ; i<numbers.length ; i++)
      strBuf.append("\nnumbers[")
            .append(String.valueOf(i))
            .append("] = ")
            .append(numbers[i]);
    return strBuf.toString();
  }
}
```

An object of type `Junk` has three instance fields, a simple integer that is always 42, a `String` object, and an array of `double` values. The `toString()` method provides a `String` representation of a `Junk` object that we can output to the command line. The static field, `generator`, will not be written to the stream when an object of type `Junk` is serialized. The only provision we have made for serializing objects of type `Junk` is to declare that the class implements the `Serializable` interface.

We can write objects of this class type to a file with the following program:

```
import java.io.*;

public class SerializeObjects {
  public static void main(String[] args) {
    Junk obj1 = new Junk("A green twig is easily bent.");
    Junk obj2 = new Junk("A little knowledge is a dangerous thing.");
    Junk obj3 = new Junk("Flies light on lean horses.");
    ObjectOutputStream objectOut = null;
```

```
    try {
       // Create the object output stream
       objectOut = new ObjectOutputStream(
                   new BufferedOutputStream(
                   new FileOutputStream("C:/Beg Java Stuff/JunkObjects.bin")));

       // Write three objects to the file
       objectOut.writeObject(obj1);              // Write object
       objectOut.writeObject(obj2);              // Write object
       objectOut.writeObject(obj3);              // Write object
       System.out.println("\n\nobj1:\n" + obj1
                     +"\n\nobj2:\n" + obj2
                     +"\n\nobj3:\n" + obj3);

    } catch(IOException e) {
       e.printStackTrace(System.err);
       System.exit(1);
    }

    // Close the stream
    try {
       objectOut.close();                        // Close the output stream

    } catch(IOException e) {
       e.printStackTrace(System.err);
       System.exit(1);
    }
  }
}
```

When I ran this, I got the output:

```
obj1:
A green twig is easily bent.
42
numbers[0] = 0.20157825618636616
numbers[1] = 0.7123542196242817
numbers[2] = 0.8027761971323069

obj2:
A little knowledge is a dangerous thing.
42
numbers[0] = 0.929629487353265
numbers[1] = 0.5402881072148746
numbers[2] = 0.03259660544653753
numbers[3] = 0.94945294401263
numbers[4] = 0.17383591141346522

obj3:
Flies light on lean horses.
42
```

```
numbers[0]  =  0.6765377168813207
numbers[1]  =  0.3933764846876555
numbers[2]  =  0.7633265658906377
numbers[3]  =  0.31411955819992887
```

You should get something vaguely similar.

How It Works

We first create three objects of type `Junk` in the `main()` method. We then define a variable that will hold the stream reference. If we were to define this variable within the first `try` block, then it would not exist beyond the end of the `try` block so we could not refer to it after that point. Within the `try` block we create the `ObjectOutputStream` object that we will use to write objects to the file `C:/Beg Java Stuff/JunkObjects.bin`, via a buffered output stream. Each `Junk` object is written to the file by passing it to the `writeObject()` method for the `ObjectOutputStream` object. Each object will be written to the file including the values of its three instance fields, `answer`, `thought`, and `numbers`. The `String` object and the array are written to the file as objects. This is taken care of automatically and requires no special provision within our code. The static field, `generator`, is not written to the file.

Before we exit the program we close the stream by calling its `close()` method. We could put the call to `close()` within the first `try` block, but if an exception was thrown due to an I/O error the method would not get called. By putting it in a separate `try` block we ensure that we do call the `close()` method. The stream would be closed automatically when the program terminates but it is good practice to close any streams as soon as you are done with them. We will read the objects back from the file a little later in this chapter.

Conditions for Serialization

In general there can be a small fly in the ointment. For implementing the `Serializable` interface, to be sufficient to make objects of the class serializable, all the fields in the class must be serializable (or `transient` – which we will come to), and all superclasses of the class must also be serializable. This implies that the fields must be either of primitive types or of class types that are themselves serializable.

If a superclass of your class is not serializable, it still may be possible to make your class serializable. The conditions that must be met for this to be feasible are:

- ❏ Each superclass that is not serializable must have a public default constructor – a constructor with no parameters.

- ❏ Your class must be declared as implementing the `Serializable` interface.

- ❏ Your class must take responsibility for serializing and deserializing the fields for the superclasses that are not serializable.

This will usually be the case for your own classes, but there are one or two classes that come along with Java that do not implement the `Serializable` interface, and what's more, you can't make them serializable because they do not have a public default constructor. The `Graphics` class in the package `java.awt` is an example of such a class – we will see more of this class when we get into programming using windows. All is not lost however. There is an escape route. As long as you know how to reconstruct any fields that were not serializable when you read an object back from a stream, you can still serialize your objects by declaring the non-serializable fields as transient.

Transient Data Members of a Class

If your class has fields that are not serializable, or that you just don't want to have written to the stream, you can declare them as transient. For example:

```
public class MyClass implements Serializable {
  transient protected Graphics g;      // Transient class member

  // Rest of the class definition
}
```

Declaring a data member as transient will prevent the writeObject() method from attempting to write the data member to the stream. When the class object is read back, it will be created properly, including any members that you declared as transient. They just won't have their values set, because they were not written to the stream. Unless you arrange for something to be done about it, the transient fields will be null.

You may well want to declare some data members of a class as transient. You would do this when they have a value that is not meaningful long term or out of context – objects that represent the current time, or today's date, for instance. You must either provide code to explicitly reconstruct the members that you declare as transient when the object that contains them is read from the stream or accept the construction time defaults.

Reading an Object from a File

Reading objects back from a file is just as easy as writing them. First, you need to create an ObjectInputStream object for the file. To do this you just pass a reference to a FileInputStream object that encapsulates the file to the ObjectInputStream class constructor:

```
File theFile = new File("MyFile");
// Perhaps check out the file...

// Create the object output stream for the file
ObjectInputStream objectIn = null;
try {
  objectIn = new ObjectInputStream(new FileInputStream(theFile));

} catch(IOException e) {
  e.printStackTrace(System.err);
  System.exit(1);
}
```

The ObjectInputStream constructor will throw an exception of type StreamCorruptedException – a subclass of IOException – if the stream header is not correct, or of type IOException if an error occurs while reading the stream header. Of course, as we saw in the last chapter, the FileInputStream constructor can throw an exception of type FileNotFoundException.

Once you have created the ObjectInputStream object you call its readObject() method to read an object from the file:

```
Object myObject = null;
try {
  myObject = objectIn.readObject();

} catch(ClassNotFoundException e){
  e.printStackTrace(System.err);
  System.exit(1);

} catch(IOException e){
  e.printStackTrace(System.err);
  System.exit(1);
}
```

The readObject() method can throw the following exceptions.

ClassNotFoundException	Thrown if the class for an object read from the stream cannot be found.
InvalidClassException	Thrown if there is something wrong with the class for an object. This is commonly caused by changing the definition of a class for an object between writing and reading the file.
StreamCorruptedException	When objects are written to the stream, additional control data is written so that the object data can be validated when it is read back. This exception is thrown when the control information in the stream is inconsistent.
OptionalDataException	Thrown when basic types of data are read rather than an object. For instance, if you wrote a String object using the writeChars() method and then attempted to read it back using the readObject() method, this exception would be thrown.
IOException	Thrown if an error occurred reading the stream.

Clearly, if you do not have a full and accurate class definition for each type of object that you want to read from the stream, the stream object will not know how to create the object and the read will fail. The last four of the five possible exceptions are flavors of IOException, so you can use that as a catchall as we have in the code fragment above. However, ClassNotFoundException is derived from Exception, so you must put a separate catch block for this exception in your program. Otherwise it will not compile.

As the code fragment implies, the readObject() method will return a reference to the object as type Object, so you need to cast it to the appropriate class type in order to use it. Note that arrays are considered to be objects and are treated as such during serialization, so if you explicitly read an array from a file, you will have to cast it to the appropriate array type.

For example, if the object in the previous code fragment was of type MyClass, you could read it back from the file with the statements:

```
    MyClass theObject = null;     // Store the object here

  try {
    theObject = (MyClass)(objectIn.readObject());

  } catch(ClassNotFoundException e) {
    e.printStackTrace(System.err);
    System.exit(1);

  } catch(IOException e) {
    e.printStackTrace(System.err);
    System.exit(1);
  }
```

To deserialize the object, we call the method readObject() and cast the reference returned to the type MyClass.

Armed with the knowledge of how the readObject() method works, we can now read the file that we wrote in the previous example.

Try It Out – Deserializing Objects

We can read the file containing Junk objects with the following code:

```
import java.io.*;

class DeserializeObjects {
  public static void main(String args[]) {
    ObjectInputStream objectIn = null;  // Stores the stream reference
    int objectCount = 0;                // Number of objects read
    Junk object = null;                 // Stores an object reference
    try {
      objectIn = new ObjectInputStream(
                   new BufferedInputStream(
                   new FileInputStream("C:/Beg Java Stuff/JunkObjects.bin")));

      // Read from the stream until we hit the end
      while(true) {
        object = (Junk)objectIn.readObject();  // Read an object
        objectCount++;                         // Increment the count
        System.out.println(object);            // Output the object
      }

    } catch(ClassNotFoundException e) {
      e.printStackTrace(System.err);
      System.exit(1);

    } catch(EOFException e)          // This will execute when we reach EOF {
      System.out.println("EOF reached. "+ objectCount + " objects read.");

    } catch(IOException e)                // This is for other I/O errors  {
      e.printStackTrace(System.err);
      System.exit(1);
```

```
      }

      // Close the stream
      try {
        objectIn.close();                           // Close the input stream

      } catch(IOException e) {
        e.printStackTrace(System.err);
        System.exit(1);
      }
    }
  }
```

I got the output:

```
A green twig is easily bent.
42
numbers[0] = 0.20157825618636616
numbers[1] = 0.7123542196242817
numbers[2] = 0.8027761971323069
A little knowledge is a dangerous thing.
42
numbers[0] = 0.929629487353265
numbers[1] = 0.5402881072148746
numbers[2] = 0.03259660544653753
numbers[3] = 0.94945294401263
numbers[4] = 0.17383591141346522
Flies light on lean horses.
42
numbers[0] = 0.6765377168813207
numbers[1] = 0.3933764846876555
numbers[2] = 0.7633265658906377
numbers[3] = 0.31411955819992887
EOF reached. 3 objects read.
```

You should get output corresponding to the objects that were written to your file.

How It Works

We first define the objectIn variable that will store the reference to the stream. We will use the objectCount variable to accumulate a count of the total number of objects read from the stream. The object variable will store the reference to each object that we read. To make the program a little more general, we have implemented the read operation in a loop to show how you might read the file when you don't know how many objects there are in it. To read each object, we just call the readObject() method for the input stream and cast the reference returned to type Junk before storing it in object.

So we can see what we have read, the string representation of each object is displayed on the command line. The while loop will continue indefinitely reading objects from the stream. When the end of the file is reached, an exception of type EOFExcepion will be thrown so the loop will be terminated and the code in the catch block for this exception will execute. This outputs a message to the command line showing the number of objects that were read. As you can see, we get back all the objects that we wrote to the file originally.

Determining the Class of a Deserialized Object

Clearly, since the `readObject()` method returns the object that it reads from the stream as type `Object`, you need to know what the original type of the object was in order to be able to cast it to its actual type. For the most part, you will know what the class of the object is when you read it back. It is possible that in some circumstances you won't know exactly, but you have a rough idea, in which case you can test it. To bring the problem into sharper focus let's consider a hypothetical situation.

Suppose you have a file containing objects that represent employees. The basic characteristics of all employees are defined in a base class, `Person`, but various different types of employee are represented by subclasses of `Person`. You might have subclasses `Manager`, `Secretary`, `Admin`, and `ShopFloor` for instance. The file can contain any of the subclass types in any sequence. Of course, you can cast any object read from the file to type `Person` because that is the base class, but you want to know precisely what each object is so you can call some type specific methods. Since you know what the possible types are you can check the type of the object against each of these types and cast accordingly.

```
Person person = null;
try {
  person = (Person)objectIn.readObject();
  if(person instanceof Manager)
    processManager((Manager)person);
  else if(person instanceof Secretary)
    processSecretary((Secretary)person);
    // and so on…

} catch (IOException e){
}
```

Here we determine the specific class type of the object read from the file before calling a method that deals with that particular type of object. Don't forget though that the `instanceof` operator does not guarantee that the object being tested is actually of the type – `Manager` say. The object could also be of any type that is a subclass of `Manager`. In any event, the cast to type `Manager` will be perfectly legal.

Where you need to be absolutely certain of the type, you can use a different approach:

```
if(person.getClass().getName().equals(Manager))
  processManager((Manager)person);
else if(person.getClass().getName().equals(Secretary))
  processSecretary((Secretary)person);
// and so on…
```

This calls the `getClass()` method (inherited from `Object`) for the object read from the file and that returns a reference to the `Class` object representing the class of the object. Calling the `getName()` method for the `Class` object returns the fully qualified name of the class. This approach guarantees that the object is of the type for which we are testing, and is not a subclass of that type.

Another approach would be to just execute a cast to a particular type, and catch the `ClassCastException` that is thrown when the cast is invalid. This is fine if you do not expect the exception to be thrown under normal conditions, but if on a regular basis the object read from the stream might be other than the type to which you are casting, you will be better off with code that avoids the need to throw and catch the exception as this adds quite a lot of overhead.

Reading Basic Data from an Object Stream

The `ObjectInputStream` class defines methods for reading basic types of data back from an object stream. They are:

readBoolean()	readByte()	readChar()	readShort()
readInt()	readLong()	readFloat()	readDouble()

They each return a value of the corresponding type and they can all throw an `IOException` if an error occurs, or an `EOFException` if the end-of-file is reached.

Just to make sure that the process of serializing and deserializing objects is clear, we will use it in a simple example.

Using Object Serialization

Back in Chapter 6, we produced an example that created `PolyLine` objects containing `Point` objects in a generalized linked list. This is a good basis for demonstrating how effectively serialization takes care of handling objects that are members of objects. We can just modify the class `TryPolyLine` to use serialization.

Try It Out – Serializing a Linked List

The classes `PolyLine`, `Point`, and `LinkedList` and the inner class `ListItem` are exactly the same as in Chapter 6 except that we need to implement the `Serializable` interface in each of them.

The `PolyLine` definition needs to be amended to:

```
import java.io.Serializable;

public final class PolyLine implements Serializable  {
   // Class definition as before...
}
```

The `Point` definition needs a similar change:

```
import java.io.Serializable;

public class Point implements Serializable {
   // Class definition as before...
}
```

The `LinkedList` class and its inner class likewise:

```
import java.io.Serializable;

public class LinkedList implements Serializable {
   // Class definition as before...
```

```
    private class ListItem implements Serializable {
      // Inner class definition as before...
    }
}
```

Of course, each file must also have an import statement for the `java.io.Serializable` class as in the code above.

The modified version of the `TryPolyLine` class to write the `PolyLine` objects to a stream looks like this:

```
import java.io.*;

public class TryPolyLine {
  public static void main(String[] args) {
    // Create an array of coordinate pairs
    double[][] coords = { {1., 1.}, {1., 2.}, { 2., 3.},
                          {-3., 5.}, {-5., 1.}, {0., 0.} };

    // Create a polyline from the coordinates and display it
    PolyLine polygon = new PolyLine(coords);
    System.out.println(polygon);

    // Add a point and display the polyline again
    polygon.addPoint(10., 10.);
    System.out.println(polygon);

    // Create Point objects from the coordinate array
    Point[] points = new Point[coords.length];
    for(int i = 0; i < points.length; i++)
      points[i] = new Point(coords[i][0],coords[i][1]);

    // Use the points to create a new polyline and display it
    PolyLine newPoly = new PolyLine(points);
    System.out.println(newPoly);

    // Write both polyline objects to the file
    try {
      // Create the object output stream
      ObjectOutputStream objectOut =
                  new ObjectOutputStream(
                    new BufferedOutputStream(
                      new FileOutputStream("C:/Beg Java Stuff/Polygons.bin")));

      objectOut.writeObject(polygon);        // Write first object
      objectOut.writeObject(newPoly);        // Write second object
      objectOut.close();                     // Close the output stream

    } catch(IOException e) {
      e.printStackTrace(System.err);
      System.exit(1);
    }
```

```
      // Read the objects back from the file
      System.out.println("\nReading objects from the file: ");
      try {
        ObjectInputStream objectIn =
                     new ObjectInputStream(
                       new BufferedInputStream (
                         new FileInputStream("C:/Beg Java Stuff/Polygons.bin")));

        PolyLine theLine = (PolyLine)objectIn.readObject();
        System.out.println(theLine);          // Display the first object
        theLine = (PolyLine)objectIn.readObject();
        System.out.println(theLine);          // Display the second object
        objectIn.close();                      // Close the input stream

      } catch(ClassNotFoundException  e) {
        e.printStackTrace(System.err);
        System.exit(1);

      } catch(IOException e){
        e.printStackTrace(System.err);
        System.exit(1);
      }
    }
  }
```

This produces the output:

```
Polyline: (1.0,1.0) (1.0,2.0) (2.0,3.0) (-3.0,5.0) (-5.0,1.0) (0.0,0.0)
Polyline: (1.0,1.0) (1.0,2.0) (2.0,3.0) (-3.0,5.0) (-5.0,1.0) (0.0,0.0)
(10.0,10.0)
Polyline: (1.0,1.0) (1.0,2.0) (2.0,3.0) (-3.0,5.0) (-5.0,1.0) (0.0,0.0)

Reading objects from the file:
Polyline: (1.0,1.0) (1.0,2.0) (2.0,3.0) (-3.0,5.0) (-5.0,1.0) (0.0,0.0)
(10.0,10.0)
Polyline: (1.0,1.0) (1.0,2.0) (2.0,3.0) (-3.0,5.0) (-5.0,1.0) (0.0,0.0)
```

How It Works

We create two different PolyLine objects in the same manner as in the original example and we display them on standard output as before. We then create an ObjectOutputStream for the file, Polygons.bin, in the C:\Beg Java Stuff directory and write each of the PolyLine objects to the file using the writeObject() method. You should adjust the file name and directory to suit your environment if necessary. We then call the close() method to close the output stream. We don't need to explicitly write the LinkedList and Point objects to the stream. These are part of the PolyLine object so they are taken care of automatically. The same goes for when we read the PolyLine objects back. All the subsidiary objects are reconstructed automatically.

To read the file, we create an ObjectInputStream object for Polygons.bin. We then read the first object using the readObject() method and store the reference to it in the variable theObject. We then output the object, read, to the standard output stream. The same process is repeated for the second PolyLine object. It couldn't be simpler really, could it?

Serializing Classes Yourself

Earlier we identified situations where the default serialization we used in the example won't work – one occurs if your class has a superclass that is not serializable. As we said earlier, to make it possible to overcome this, the superclass must have a default constructor, and you must take care of serializing the fields inherited from the superclass yourself. If the superclass does not have a default constructor and you do not have access to the original definition of the superclass, you have a problem with no obvious solution.

Another situation is where your class has fields that don't travel well. If you use the `hashCode()` method that your classes will inherit from `Object`, then the `hashcode()` value for an object will be derived from its internal address, which will not be the same when you read the object from a file. You may have a class with vast numbers of fields with zero values, for instance, that you may not want to have written to the file. These are also cases where do-it-yourself serialization is needed.

To implement and control the serialization of a class yourself, you must implement two `private` methods in the class: one for input from an `ObjectInputStream` object, and the other for output to an `ObjectOutputStream` object. The `readObject()` and `writeObject()` methods for the stream will call these methods to perform I/O on the stream if you implement them.

Even though it isn't necessary in this class, we will take the `PolyLine` class as a demonstration vehicle for how this works. To do our own serialization, the class would be:

```
class PolyLine implements Serializable {
  // Class definition as before...

    // Serialized input method
    private void readObject(ObjectInputStream in) throws IOException {
      // Code to do the serialized input...
    }

    // Serialized output method
    private void writeObject(ObjectOutputStream out)
       throws IOException, ClassNotFoundException {
      // Code to do the serialized output...
    }
}
```

These two methods must have exactly the same signature in any class where they are required, and they must be declared as `private`.

In a typical situation, you will want to use the default serialization operations provided by the object stream and just add your own code to fix up the data members that you want to take care of – or have to in the case of a non-serialized base class. To get the default serialization done on input, you just call the `defaultReadObject()` method for the stream in your serialization method:

```
private void readObject(ObjectInputStream in) throws IOException {
  in.defaultReadObject();                    // Default serialized input
  // Your code to do serialized input...
}
```

You can get the default serialized output operation in a similar fashion by calling the `defaultWriteObject()` method for the stream object that is passed to your output method. Obviously, you must read back the data in exactly the same sequence as it was written, so the two methods will have essentially mirror operations on the same sequence of data items.

Serialization Problems and Complications

For most classes and applications, serialization will work in a straightforward fashion. There are situations that can cause confusion though. One such situation is when you want to write several versions of the same object to a file. You need to take care to ensure the result is what you want. Suppose you write an object to a file – a `PolyLine` object say. A little later in your code, you modify the `PolyLine` object in some way, by moving a point perhaps, and you now write the same object to the file again in its modified state. What happens? Does the file contain the two versions of the object? The answer – perhaps surprisingly – is no. Let's explore this in a little more detail.

Try It Out – Serializing Variations on an Object

Let's start by defining a very simple serializable class that we can use in our example:

```
import java.io.Serializable;

public class Data implements Serializable {
  private int value;

  public Data(int init) {
    value = init;
  }

  // Method to compare two Data objects
  public boolean equals(Object obj) {
    if(obj instanceof Data && ((Data)obj).value == value)
      return true;
    return false;
  }

  public void setValue(int val) {
    value = val;
  }

  public int getValue() {
    return value;
  }
}
```

Objects of type `Data` have a single field of type `int`. Two `Data` objects are equal if their `value` fields contain the same value. We can alter the `value` field for an object by calling its `setValue()` method so we can easily create variations on the same object. Now we can write an example that will write variations on a single instance of type `Data` to a file and then read them back:

```java
import java.io.*;

public class TestData {
  public static void main(String[] args) {
    Data data = new Data(1);
    try {
      // Create the object output stream
      ObjectOutputStream objectOut =
                new ObjectOutputStream(
                  new BufferedOutputStream(
                    new FileOutputStream("C:/Beg Java Stuff/dataObjects.bin")));

      // Write three variants of the object to the file
      objectOut.writeObject(data);                 // Write object
      System.out.println("1st Object written has value: "+data.getValue());
      data.setValue(2);                            // Modify the object
      objectOut.writeObject(data);                 // and write it again
      System.out.println("2nd Object written has value: "+data.getValue());
      data.setValue(3);                            // Modify the object again...
      objectOut.writeObject(data);                 // and write it once more
      System.out.println("3rd Object written has value: "+data.getValue());
      objectOut.close();                           // Close the output stream

    } catch(IOException e) {
      e.printStackTrace(System.err);
      System.exit(1);
    }

    // Read the three objects back from the file
    System.out.println("\nReading objects from the file: ");
    try {
      ObjectInputStream objectIn =
                new ObjectInputStream(
                  new BufferedInputStream(
                    new FileInputStream("C:/Beg Java Stuff/dataObjects.bin")));

      Data data1 = (Data)objectIn.readObject();
      Data data2 = (Data)objectIn.readObject();
      Data data3 = (Data)objectIn.readObject();
      System.out.println("1st object is " + (data1.equals(data2)? "" : "not ")
                  + "Equal to 2nd object.");
      System.out.println("2nd object is " + (data2.equals(data3)? "" : "not ")
                  + "Equal to 3rd object.");

      System.out.println("data1 = "+data1.getValue()  // Display object values
                  + "  data2 = " + data2.getValue()
                  + "  data3 = "+data3.getValue());
      objectIn.close();                            // Close the input stream

    } catch(ClassNotFoundException e) {
      e.printStackTrace(System.err);
      System.exit(1);
```

491

```
      } catch(IOException e) {
        e.printStackTrace(System.err);
        System.exit(1);
      }
    }
  }
```

This is a simple program that writes three objects to the file and records on the command line what objects were written. It then reads the objects back from the file and writes details of the objects that were read to the command line. When you run it you should see the output:

```
1st Object written has value: 1
2nd Object written has value: 2
3rd Object written has value: 3

Reading objects from the file:
1st object is Equal to 2nd object.
2nd object is Equal to 3rd object.
data1 = 1   data2 = 1   data3 = 1
```

All three objects that we read from the file are equal and identical to the first object that was written. This seems rather strange and unexpected so let's try to understand what is happening here.

How It Works

As you know, all variables of a class type store references, not objects, and you may have several different variables referring to the same object in your program. For this reason, the serialization output process keeps track of the objects that are written to the stream. Any attempt to write the same object to the stream will not result in duplicates of the object being written. Only a **handle**, which is a sort of reference, will be written to the stream and this will point to the first occurrence of the object in the stream.

Thus, in our example, the modified versions of the Data object will not be written to the file. The first write operation writes the original object referenced by Data to the stream. For the second and third write operations, the serialization process detects that we are writing an object that has previously been written to the file, and so only a handle that refers to the original unmodified version of the object will be written, and so the changes will be lost. This explains why, when we read the three objects back from the file, they all turn out to be identical. This is not what we intended in this case, so how can we get over this?

Resetting an Object Output Stream

The appropriate course of action in such situations is obviously going to be application dependent but in our example it is clear – we want each version of Data explicitly written to the file. You can make the ObjectOutputStream object forget the objects it has previously written to a stream by calling its reset() method:

```
objectOut.reset();      // Reset the stream
```

This clears the record that is kept within the stream object of what has been written and writes a 'reset marker' to the stream. When an `ObjectInputStream` object reads a 'reset marker' it too clears its record of what has been read, so that subsequent object read operations will be as if the stream started at that point. To make effective use of this, your code will clearly need to accommodate the possibility of multiple versions of the same object existing in the stream. It's your code, so you will know what you want to do. To make our example work as expected, we can reset the stream before each output operation after the first call to `writeObject()`, like this:

```
objectOut.writeObject(data);            // Write object
System.out.println("1st Object written has value: "+data.getValue());
data.setValue(2);                       // Modify the object
objectOut.reset();
objectOut.writeObject(data);            // and write it again
System.out.println("2nd Object written has value: "+data.getValue());
data.setValue(3);                       // Modify the object again...
objectOut.reset();
objectOut.writeObject(data);            // and write it once more
System.out.println("3rd Object written has value: "+data.getValue());
```

If you insert the calls to `reset()` in the original code and run the example again, you should get the output you were expecting.

A further complication arises with serialized objects when you change the definition of a class in some way. When an object is written to a file, part of the information identifying the class is a sort of hashcode, called a **version ID**, that is intended to ensure that the definition of the class used when you are reading an object from a file is the same as the class definition that was used when the object was written. Even cosmetic changes between writing and reading a stream, such as changing the name of a field, can alter the version ID, so in this case a read operation will fail with an `InvalidClassException` being thrown. In general, you need to make sure that the class definitions in a program reading a file are the same as those used when the file was written, although you can explicitly set the version number and deal with any changes yourself.

For more complex situations, it is possible to take complete control of the serialization process within your classes by implementing the `Externalizable` interface. This is important when the class definition for the object involves change over time. With careful programming you can accommodate modifications to classes without invalidating existing serialized objects. A detailed discussion of what is involved in this is outside the scope of this book.

Summary

In this chapter we have explored how we can write objects to a file and read them back. Making your class serializable makes it very easy to save your application data in a file. While what we have discussed is by no means exhaustive, you now know enough to deal with straightforward object serialization. The important points in this chapter are:

❑ To make objects of a class serializable the class must implement the `Serializable` interface.

❑ If a class has a superclass that does not implement the `Serializable` interface, then the superclass must have a public default constructor if it is to be possible to serialize the class.

- Objects are written to a file using an `ObjectOutputStream` object and read from a file using and `ObjectInputStream` object.

- Objects are written to a file by calling the `writeObject()` method for the `ObjectOutputStream` object corresponding to the file.

- Objects are read from a file by calling the `readObject()` method for the `ObjectInputStream` object corresponding to the file.

- When necessary, for instance if a superclass is not serializable, you can implement the `readObject()` and `writeObject()` methods for your classes.

- A good horse cannot be of a bad color.

Exercises

1. Define a `Person` class to encapsulate a person's name and address with the name and address being fields of type `Name` and `Address`. Write a program to allow names and addresses to be entered from the keyboard and stored as `Person` objects in a file. Once the file exists new entries should be appended to the file.

2. Extend the previous example to optionally list all the names and addresses contained within the file on the command line.

3. Extend the previous example to add an index based on the person's name for each person entered at the keyboard to locate the corresponding `Person` object in the object file. The index file will contain entries of type `IndexEntry` each of which encapsulates a name and a file position in the object file. The index file should be a separate file from the original file containing `Person` objects.

Note: You will probably find it easiest to delete the previous file before you run this example so that the object file can be reconstructed along with the index file. You can get and set the file position from the underlying file input stream object.

4. Use the index file to provide random direct access to the object file for querying random names entered from the keyboard. Entering a name from the keyboard should result in the address for the individual, or a message indicating the entry is not present in the file. The process will be to first search the index file for an object with a name field matching the keyboard entry. When an `IndexEntry` is found, you use the file position it contains to retrieve data from the file containing the `Person` objects.

Collection Classes

In this chapter we'll look at the collection classes that are defined in the `java.util` package. These provide you with a variety of ways for structuring and managing collections of objects in your programs. In particular the collection classes enable you to deal with situations where you don't know in advance how many objects you'll need to store, or where you need a bit more flexibility in the way in which you access an object from a collection than the indexing mechanism provided by an array.

In this chapter you will learn:

❑   What sets, lists, and maps are, and how they work

❑   What an `Iterator` object is used for

❑   Which container classes are available

❑   What a `Vector` is and how to use `Vector` objects in your programs

❑   How to manage `Vector` objects so that storing and retrieving elements is type safe

❑   What a `Stack` is and how you use it

❑   What `LinkedLists` are and how you use them

❑   How you store and retrieve objects in a hash table represented by a `HashMap` object

❑   How you can generate hash codes for your own class objects

Understanding the Collection Classes

The **collection classes** in `java.util` support various ways for you to store and manage objects of any kind in memory. They include a professional implementation of a linked list that we took so much trouble to develop for ourselves back in Chapter 6. If you want an array that automatically expands to accommodate however many objects you throw into it, or you need to be able to store and retrieve an object based on what it is, rather than using an index or a sequence number, then look no further. You get all this and more in the collection classes.

We'll be exploring the following capabilities provided by the package:

Class/Interface	Description
The `Iterator` interface	Declares methods for iterating through elements of a set, one at a time.
The `Vector` class	Supports an array-like structure for storing any type of object. The number of objects that you can store in a `Vector` object increases automatically as necessary.
The `Stack` class	Supports the storage of any type of object in a push down stack.
The `LinkedList` class	Supports the storage of any type of object in a doubly-linked list.
The `HashMap` class	Supports the storage of any type of object in a **hash table**, sometimes called a **map**.

We'll start by looking in general terms at various possible types of collections for objects.

Collections of Objects

Back in Chapter 6 we put together a basic class defining a linked list. An object of type `LinkedList` represented an example of a **collection** of objects that could be of any type. A **collection** is used as a generic term for any object that represents a set of objects grouped together by some means. A linked list is only one of a number of ways of grouping a number of objects together in a collection.

There are three main types of collections: **sets**, **sequences**, and **maps**. Let's first get an understanding of how these three types of collections work in principle, and then come back to look at the Java classes that implement versions of these. One point I would like to emphasize about the following discussion is that when we talk about a collection of objects, we mean a collection of references to objects. In Java collections only stores references – the objects themselves are external to the collection.

Sets

A **set** is probably the simplest kind of collection you can have. Here the objects are not usually ordered in any particular way at all and objects are simply added to the set without any control over where they go. It's a bit like putting things in your pocket – you just put things in and they rattle around inside your pocket in no particular order.

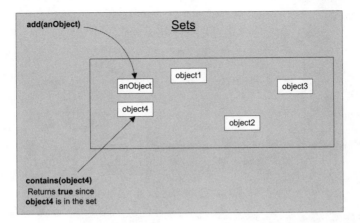

The principal access mechanism that you have for a set is simply to check whether a given object is a member of the set or not. For this reason, you cannot have duplicate objects in a set – each object in the set must be unique. Of course, you can also remove a given object from a set, but only if you know what the object is in the first place – in other words if you have a reference to the object in the set.

There are variations on the basic set that we have described here. For instance, sets can be ordered, so objects added to a set will be inserted into a sequence of objects ordered according to some criterion of comparison. Such sets require that the class that defines the objects to be stored implements suitable methods for comparing objects.

Sequences

A linked list is an example of a more general type of collection called a **sequence** or a **list**. A primary characteristic of a list is that the objects are stored in a linear fashion, not necessarily in any particular order, with a beginning and an end. This contrasts with a set where there is no order at all. An ordinary array is basically another example of a list, but is much more limited than a collection because it is fixed.

Collections generally have the ability to expand to accommodate as many elements as necessary. The Vector class, for example, is a collection class that provides similar functionality to an array, but which also has this ability to accommodate new elements as and when required.

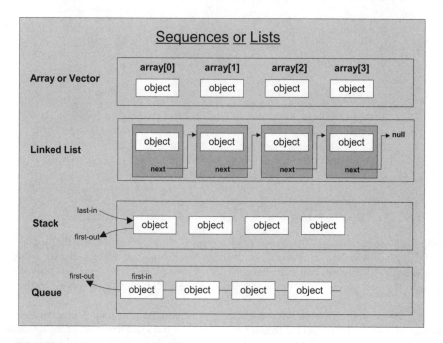

Because a list is linear, you will only be able to add a new object to the list at the beginning, or at the end, or inserted following a given object in sequence – after the fifth say. Generally, you can retrieve an object from a list in several ways. You can select the first or the last; you can get the object at a given position – as in indexing an array; or you can search for an object identical to a given object by checking all the objects in the sequence either backwards or forwards. You can also iterate through the list backwards or forwards accessing each object in sequence. We didn't implement all these capabilities in our linked list class in Chapter 6, but we could have done.

You can delete objects from a list in the same sorts of ways that you retrieve an object; that is, you can remove the first or the last, an object at a particular position in the sequence, or an object that is equal to a given object. Sequences or lists have the facility that they can store several copies of the same object at different places in the sequence. This is not true of all types of collections, as we will see.

A **stack**, which is a last-in first-out storage mechanism, is also considered to be a list, as is a **queue**, which is a first-in first-out mechanism. It is easy to see that a linked list can act as a stack, since using the methods to add and remove objects at the end of a list makes the list operate as a stack. Similarly, only adding objects by using the method to add an object to the end of a linked list, and only retrieving objects from the head of the list, makes it operate as a queue.

Maps

A **map** is rather different from a set or a sequence because the entries involve pairs of objects. A map is also referred to sometimes as a **dictionary** because of the way it works. Each object that is stored in a map has an associated **key** object, and both the object and its key are stored as a pair. The key determines where the object is stored in the map, and when you want to retrieve an object you must supply the appropriate key – so it acts as the equivalent of a word that you look up in a regular dictionary.

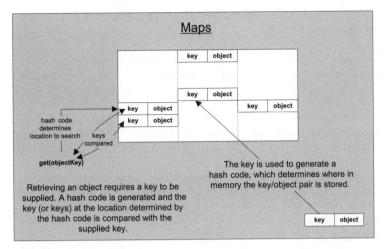

A key can be any kind of object that you want to use to reference the object stored. Because the key has to uniquely identify the object, all the keys in a map must be different. To put this in context let's take an example. Suppose you were creating a program to provide an address book. You might store all the details of each person – their name, address, phone number, or whatever – in a single object of type Entry perhaps, and store a reference to the object in a map. The key is the mechanism for retrieving objects, so assuming that all names are different, the name of the person would be a natural choice for the key. Thus the entries in the map in this case would be Name/Entry pairs. You would supply a Name object as the key, and get back the Entry object corresponding to the key. You might well have another map in this application where entries were keyed on the phone number. Then you could retrieve an entry corresponding to a given number. Of course, in practice, names are not unique – hence the invention of such delightful attachments to the person as social security numbers.

Hashing

Where a key/object pair is stored in a map is determined from the key by a process known as **hashing**. Hashing processes the key object to produce an integer value called a **hash code**. The hashCode() method that is defined in the Object class produces a hash code of type int for an object. The hash code is typically used as an offset from the start of the memory that has been allocated within the map, to determine the location where the key/object pair is to be stored. Ideally the hashing process should result in values that are uniformly distributed within a given range, and every key should produce a different hash code. In general, this may not be the case, but there are ways around this so it is not a problem. We will look at keys and hash codes in a little more detail when we discuss using maps later in this chapter.

Now let's look at how we can move through a collection.

Iterators

In the LinkedList class that we developed in Chapter 6 you might have thought that the mechanism for getting the objects from the list was a little cumbersome. It was necessary to obtain the first element by using one method, getFirst(), and successive elements by another method, getNext(). This makes the first element in a list a 'special case' so processing the elements has to take account of this and is a little more complicated than perhaps it needs to be.

A much better approach that can be used to process the elements from a collection sequentially involves something called an **iterator**.

> *It is worth noting at this point that Java also provides something called an enumerator. An enumerator provides essentially the same capability as an iterator, but it is recommended in the Java documentation that you should use an iterator in preference to an enumerator for collections.*

In general an iterator is an object that you can use to retrieve all the objects in a collection one by one. Someone dealing cards from a deck one by one is acting as an iterator for the card deck – without the shuffle, of course.

In Java, an iterator is an interface that can be implemented by a collection class. Any collection object can create an object of type Iterator that encapsulates references to all the objects in the original collection in some sequence, and that can be accessed using the Iterator interface methods. In other words an iterator provides an easy way to get at all the objects in a collection one at a time. The basic mechanism for using an iterator in Java is illustrated below.

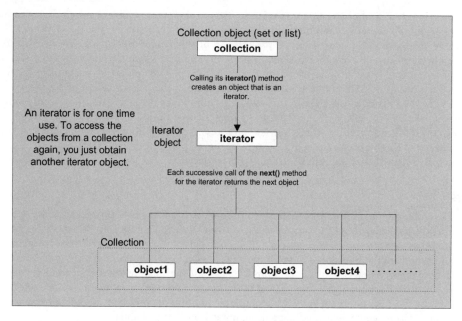

The Iterator interface in java.util declares just three methods:

Method	Description
next()	Returns an object as type Object starting with the first, and sets the Iterator object to return the next object on the next call of this method. If there is no object to be returned the method throws a NoSuchElementException exception.
hasNext()	Returns true if there is a next object to be retrieved by a call to next().

Method	Description
remove()	Removes the last object returned by next() from the collection that supplied the Iterator object. If next() has not been called or if you call remove() twice after calling next(), an IllegalStateException will be thrown. Not all iterators support this method, in which case an UnsupportedOperationException exception will be thrown if you call it.

Since calling the next() method for an object that implements Iterator returns successive objects from the collection, starting with the first, you can progress through all the objects in a collection very easily with a loop such as:

```
MyClass item;                            // Store an object from the collection
while(iter.hasNext()) {                  // Check that there's another
  item = (MyClass)iter.next();           // Retrieve next object
  // Do something with item...
}
```

This assumes iter is of type Iterator and stores a reference to an object obtained from whatever collection class we were using. As we shall see shortly, objects that are collections have a method, iterator(), that returns an iterator for the current contents of the collection. The loop continues as long as the hasNext() method returns true. Since the next() method returns the object as type Object, we will usually need to cast it to its actual type. Each time you need to go through the objects in a collection you obtain another iterator, as an iterator is a 'use once' object.

Only the Java collection classes that are sets or lists make iterators available directly. However, as we will see, a map provides methods to enable the keys or objects, or indeed the key/object pairs, to be viewed as a set, so an iterator can then be obtained to iterate over the objects in the set view of the map.

The iterator we have seen here is a one-way street – we can go through the objects in a collection one at a time, and that's it. This is fine for many purposes and is a lot safer than a hand coded loop, as there's no possibility of getting the boundary conditions wrong. However, if this is not enough, and there will be times when it isn't, there's another kind of iterator that is more flexible.

List Iterators

The ListIterator interface declares methods that you can use to traverse a collection of objects backwards or forwards. You don't have to elect for a particular direction either. You can change from forwards to backwards and *vice versa*, so an object can be retrieved more than once.

The ListIterator interface extends the Iterator interface so the iterator methods you have seen still apply. The methods defined in the ListIterator interface that you use to traverse the list of objects are:

Method	Description
next()	Retrieves the next object in sequence – the same as for the Iterator interface.
hasNext()	Returns true if there is an object that will be returned by next().
nextIndex()	Returns the index of the object that will be returned by the next call to next(), or returns the number of elements in the list if the ListIterator object is at the end of the list.
previous()	Returns the previous object in sequence in the list. You use this method to run backwards through the list.
hasPrevious()	Returns true if the next call to previous() will return an object.
previousIndex()	Returns the index of the object that will be returned by the next call to previous(), or returns -1 if the ListIterator object is at the beginning of the list.

You can alternate between calls to next() and previous() to go backwards and forwards through the list. Calling previous() immediately after calling next() will return the same element – and *vice versa*.

With a ListIterator you can add and replace objects, as well as remove them from the collection. ListIterator declares the following methods for this:

Method	Description
remove()	Removes the last object that was retrieved by next() or previous(). The UnsupportedOperation exception is thrown if the remove operation is not supported for this collection, and an IllegalStateException will be thrown if next() or previous() have not yet been called for the iterator.
add(Object obj)	Adds the argument immediately before the object that would be returned by the next call to next(), and after the object that would be returned by the next call to previous(). The call to next() after the add() operation will return the object that was added. The next call to previous() will not be affected. This method throws an UnsupportedOperationException if objects cannot be added, a ClassCastException if the class of the argument prevents it from being added, and IllegalOperationException if there is some other reason why the add cannot be done.

Method	Description
`set(Object obj)`	Replaces the last object retrieved by a call to `next()` or `previous()`. If neither `next()` nor `previous()` have been called, or `add()` or `remove()` have been called most recently, an `IllegalStateException` will be thrown. If the `set()` operation is not supported for this collection an `UnsupportedOperationException` will be thrown. If the class of the reference passed as an argument prevents the object being stored in the collection, a `ClassCastException` will be thrown. If some other characteristic of the argument prevents it being stored in the collection, an `IllegalArgumentException` will be thrown.

Now we know about iterators we need to find out a bit about the collection classes themselves in order to make use of them.

Collection Classes

You have a total of thirteen classes in `java.util` that you can use to manage collections of objects, and they support collections that are sets, lists, or maps, as follows:

	Class	Description
Sets:	HashSet	An implementation of a set that uses `HashMap` under the covers. Although a set is by definition unordered, there has to be *some* way to find an object reasonably efficiently. The use of a `HashMap` object to implement the set enables store and retrieve operations to be done in a constant time.
	TreeSet	An implementation of a set that orders the objects in the set in ascending sequence. This means that an iterator obtained from a `TreeSet` object will provide the objects in ascending sequence. The `TreeSet` classes use a `TreeMap` under the covers.
	LinkedHashSet	Implements a set using a hash table with all the entries linked in a doubly-linked list. This class can be used to make a copy of any set such that iteration ordering is preserved – something that does not apply to a `HashSet`.

Table continued on following page

	Class	Description
Lists:	Vector	Implements a list as an array that automatically increases in size to accommodate as many elements as you need. Objects are stored and retrieved using an index as in a normal array. You can also use an iterator to retrieve objects from a Vector. The Vector is the only container class that is synchronized – that is, it is well-behaved when concurrently accessed by two or more threads. We will discuss threads and synchronization in the next chapter.
	Stack	This class is derived from Vector and adds methods to implement a stack – a last-in first-out storage mechanism.
	LinkedList	Implements a linked list. The linked list defined by this class can also be used as a stack or a queue.
	ArrayList	Implements an array that can vary in size and can also be accessed as a linked list. This provides a similar function to the Vector class but is unsynchronized.
Maps:	Hashtable	Implements a map where all keys must be non-null. The class defining a key must implement the hashcode() method and the equals() method to work effectively. This class is a legacy of previous Java implementations and it is usually better to use the other classes that implement maps.
	HashMap	Implements a map that allows null objects to be stored and allows a key to be null (only one of course, since keys must be unique).
	LinkedHashMap	Inplements a map with all of its entries in a doubly-linked list. This class can be used to create a copy of a map of any type such that the order of the entries in the copy is the same as the original.
	WeakHashMap	Implements a map such that if a key to an object is no longer referenced ordinarily, the key/object pair will be discarded. This contrasts with HashMap where the presence of the key in the map maintains the life of the key/object pair, even though the program using the map no longer has a reference to the key, and therefore cannot retrieve the object.
	IdentityHashMap	Implements a map using a hash table where comparisons in searching the map for a key or a value compares references, not objects. This implies that two keys are equal only if they are the same key. The same applies to values.
	TreeMap	Implements a map such that the objects are arranged in ascending key order.

We can't go into all these classes in detail, but to introduce you to how these can be applied we will explore the three that you are likely to find most useful, `Vector`, `LinkedList`, and `HashMap`. Before we get into the specifics of using the container classes we need to look at the interfaces they implement, since these provide the means of applying them.

Collection Interfaces

The `java.util` package defines six collection interfaces that determine the methods that you use to work with each type of collection class. There are three basic collection interfaces, the `Set`, `List`, and `Map` interfaces, which relate to the fundamental organization of objects in a collection. These are implemented amongst the classes as follows:

Interface	Implemented by
Set	HashSet, TreeSet
List	Vector, Stack, ArrayList, LinkedList
Map	Hashtable, TreeMap, HashMap, WeakHashMap

The relationships between the interfaces that are implemented by the collection classes are shown in the following diagram.

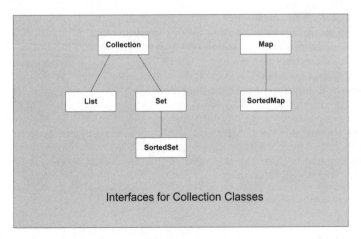

Interfaces for Collection Classes

The `Set` and `List` interfaces both extend a common interface, `Collection`. Note that the `Map` interface does not extend `Collection`. Don't confuse the `Collection` *interface* with the `Collections` *class* (with an 's') that we will see later. The two other interfaces for collections are `SortedSet` that extends the `Set` interface, and `SortedMap` that extends the `Map` interface. The `TreeSet` class implements the `SortedSet` interface, and the `SortedMap` interface is implemented by the `TreeMap` class.

It is important to keep in mind that any collection class object that implements the Collection interface can be referenced using a variable of type Collection. This means that any of the list or set collections can be referenced in this way; only the map class types are excluded (but not entirely, as you can obtain a list from a map and the classes implementing a map can provide a view of the values stored as a Collection reference). You will see that using a parameter of type Collection is a standard way of passing a list or set to a method.

These interfaces involve quite a number of methods, so rather than go through them in the abstract, let's see them at work in the context of specific classes. We will look at the Vector class first since it is close to the notion of an array that you are already familiar with.

Using Vectors

The Vector class defines a collection of elements of type Object that works rather like an array, but with the additional feature that it can grow itself automatically when you need more capacity. It implements the List interface so it can be used as a list. Because it stores elements of type Object, and Object is a superclass of every object, you can store any type of object in a Vector. This also means that potentially you can use a single Vector object to store objects that are instances of a variety of different classes. This is another advantage the Vector class has over arrays, but the circumstances where this is desirable are relatively rare.

This ability to store diverse objects has a downside. It implies that it's very easy for you to store objects in a Vector by mistake. You can set up a Vector in which you plan to store a particular kind of object, but there's nothing to prevent the storage of some other kind of object in the Vector, or to signal that this may cause problems. If you need to protect against this kind of error, you must program for it yourself. This isn't terribly difficult. As you'll see later in this chapter, all you need to do is package your Vector as a private member of a class that you define, and then supply methods to store objects in the Vector that will only accept the type that you want.

> **Like arrays, vectors only hold object references, not actual objects. To keep things simple we refer to a Vector as holding objects. We'll make the distinction only when it's important, but you should keep in mind that all the collection classes you're about to encounter hold object references.**

Creating a Vector

There are four constructors for a Vector. The default constructor creates an empty Vector object with the capacity to store up to a default number of objects, and the Vector object will increase in size each time you add an element when the Vector is full. The default capacity of a Vector object is ten objects, and the Vector object will double in size when you add an object when it is full. For example:

```
Vector transactions = new Vector();      // Create an empty Vector
```

If the default capacity isn't suitable for what you want to do, you can set the initial capacity of a `Vector` explicitly when you create it by using a different constructor. You just specify the capacity you require as an argument of type `int`. For example:

```
Vector transactions = new Vector(100);    // Vector to store 100 objects
```

The `Vector` object we're defining here will store 100 elements initially. It will also double in capacity each time you exceed the current capacity. The process of doubling the capacity of the `Vector` when more space is required can be quite inefficient. For example, if you end up storing 7000 objects in the `Vector` we've just defined, it will actually have space for 12800 objects. If each object reference requires 4 bytes, say, you'll be occupying more than 20 kilobytes of memory unnecessarily.

One way of avoiding this is to specify the amount by which the `Vector` should be incremented as well as the initial capacity when you create the `Vector` object. Both of these arguments to the constructor are of type `int`. For example:

```
Vector transactions = new Vector(100,10);
```

This `Vector` object has an initial capacity of 100, but the capacity will only be increased by 10 elements each time more space is required.

Why don't we increment the `Vector` object by 1 each time then? The reason is that the process of incrementing the capacity takes time because it involves copying the contents to a new area of memory. The bigger the vector is, the longer the copy takes, and that will affect your program's performance if it happens very often.

The last constructor creates a `Vector` object containing object references from another collection that is passed to the constructor as an argument of type `Collection`. Since all the set and list collection classes implement the `Collection` interface, the constructor argument can be of any set or list class type, including another `Vector`. The objects are stored in the `Vector` object that is created in the sequence in which they are returned from the iterator for the `Collection` object that is passed as the argument.

Let's see a vector working.

Try It Out – Using a Vector

We'll take a very simple example here, just storing a few strings in a vector:

```java
import java.util.*;

public class TrySimpleVector {
  public static void main(String[] args) {
    Vector names = new Vector();
    String[] firstnames = { "Jack", "Jill", "John",
                            "Joan", "Jeremiah", "Josephine"};

    for(int i = 0 ; i<firstnames.length ; i++)
      names.add(firstnames[i]);
```

```
        for(int i = 0 ; i<names.size() ; i++)
          System.out.println((String)names.get(i));
      }
    }
```

If you compile and run this, it will list the names that are defined in the program.

How It Works

We copy the references to the Vector object, names, in the first for loop. The add() method adds the object to the vector at the next available position. The second for loop retrieves the String references from the vector using the get() method. This returns the reference at the index position specified by the argument as type Object, so we have to cast it to the original type, String, in the println() call. The size() method returns the number of elements in the Vector, so this is the upper limit for the second for loop. Note that the Vector object doesn't care what type of objects are added – we could pass any type of reference to the add() method, even type Vector.

The Capacity and Size of a Vector

Although we said at the beginning that a Vector works like an array, this isn't strictly true. One significant difference is in the information you can get about the storage space it provides. An array has a single measure, its length, which is the count of the total number of elements it can reference. A vector has two measures relating to the space it provides – the **capacity** and the **size**.

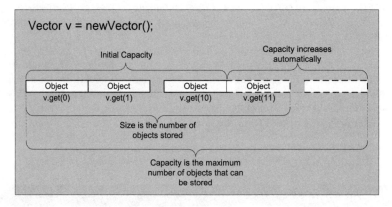

The **capacity** of a Vector is the maximum number of objects that it can hold at any given instant. Of course, the capacity can vary over time, because when you store an object in a Vector object that is full, its capacity will automatically increase. For example, the Vector object transactions that we defined in the last of the constructor examples earlier had an initial capacity of 100. After you've stored 101 objects in it, its capacity will be 110 objects. A vector will typically contain fewer objects than its capacity.

You can obtain the capacity of a Vector with the method capacity(), which returns it as a value of type int. For example:

```
int transMax = transactions.capacity();  // Get current capacity
```

If this statement follows the current definition we have for `transactions`, the variable `transMax` will have the value 100.

You can also ensure that a `Vector` has a sufficient capacity for your needs by calling its `ensureCapacity()` method. For example:

```
transactions.ensureCapacity(150);        // Set minimum capacity to 150
```

If the capacity of `transactions` is less than 150, the capacity will be increased to that value. If it's already 150 or greater, it will be unchanged by this statement. The argument you specify for `ensureCapacity()` is of type `int`. There's no return value.

Changing the Size

When you first create a `Vector` object, the elements don't reference anything. An element will be occupied once you've stored an `object` in it. The number of elements that are occupied by objects in a `Vector` is referred to as the **size** of the `Vector`. The size of a `Vector` clearly can't be greater than the capacity. As we have seen, you can obtain the size of a `Vector` object as a value of type `int` by calling the `size()` method for the object. For example, you could calculate the number of free entries in the `Vector` object `transactions` with the statement:

```
int freeCount = transactions.capacity() - transactions.size();
```

You usually increase the size value for a `Vector` indirectly by storing an object in it, but you can also change the size directly by calling a method. Using the method `setSize()`, you can increase and decrease the size. For example:

```
transactions.setSize(50);        // Set size to 50
```

The size of the `Vector` is set to the argument value (of type `int`). If the `Vector transactions` has less than fifty elements occupied, the additional elements up to fifty will be filled with `null` references. If it already contains more than fifty objects, all object references in excess of fifty will be discarded. The objects themselves may still be available if other references to them exist.

Looking back to the situation we discussed earlier, we saw how the effects of incrementing the capacity by doubling each time the current capacity was exceeded could waste memory. A `Vector` object provides you with a direct way of dealing with this – the `trimToSize()` method. This just changes the capacity to match the current size. For example:

```
transactions.trimToSize();        // Set capacity to size
```

If the size of the `Vector` is 50 when this statement executes, then the capacity will be too. Of course, you can still add more objects to the `Vector` as it will grow to accommodate them.

Storing Objects in a Vector

The simplest way to store an object in a `Vector` is to use the `add()` method as we did in the last example. To store a transaction in the `transactions` vector, you could write:

```
transactions.add(aTransaction);
```

This will add a reference to the object `aTransaction` to the `Vector` object called `transactions`. The new entry will be added at the end of the existing objects in the vector, and the size of the `Vector` will be increased by 1. All the objects that were already stored in the `Vector` remain at their previous index position.

You can also store an object at a particular index position in a `Vector` using another version of `add()` that has two parameters. The first argument is the index position and the second argument is the object to be stored. The index value must be less than or equal to the size of the `Vector`, which implies that either there is already an object reference at this position or it is the position at the end of the `Vector` that is next in line to receive one. The index value is the same as for an array – an offset from the first element – so you reference the first element using an index value of zero. For example, to insert the object `aTransaction` as the third entry of `transactions`, you would write:

```
transactions.add(2, aTransaction);
```

The index value is of type `int`, and represents the index value for the position of the new object. The new object, `aTransaction`, is inserted in front of the object that previously corresponded to the index value 2, so objects stored in elements with index values equal to or greater than 2 will be shuffled along, and their index values will increase by 1. If you specify an index value argument that is negative, or greater than or equal to the size of the `Vector`, the method will throw an `ArrayIndexOutOfBoundsException`.

To change an element in a vector you use the `set()` method. This accepts two arguments: the first argument is the index position where the object specified by the second argument is to be stored. To change the third element in the `Vector` object `transactions` to `theTransaction`, you would write:

```
transactions.set(2, theTransaction);
```

The method returns a reference of type `Object` to the object that was previously stored at this position. This gives you a chance to hang on to the displaced object if you want to keep it. If the first argument is negative, or is greater than or equal to the current size of the `Vector`, the method will throw an `ArrayIndexOutOfBoundsException`.

You can add all the objects from another collection to a vector, either appended at the end or inserted following a given index position. For instance, to append the contents of a `LinkedList` object, `myList`, to a `Vector` object, `transactions`, you would write:

```
transactions.addAll(myList);
```

The parameter to the method is of type `Collection`, so the objects in any list or set can be added. To insert the collection objects at a particular position, you specify the index position as the first argument. So to insert the objects in `myList` starting at index position i, you would write:

```
transactions.addAll(i, myList);
```

The object originally at position i, and objects originally to the right of position i, will all be shuffled to the right to make room for the new objects. If the index value passed as the first argument is negative, or is not less than the size of `transactions`, an `ArrayIndexOutOfBoundsException` object will be thrown. Adding a collection will increase the size of the vector by the number of objects added.

Retrieving Objects from a Vector

As we saw in the simple example earlier, if you have the index for an element, you can obtain the element at a particular position by using the `get()` method for the `Vector`. For the `transactions` vector you could write:

```
Transaction theTransaction = (Transaction)transactions.get(4);
```

This statement will retrieve the fifth element in the vector. Note that the explicit cast is essential here. If you don't cast the object returned to the type of the variable that you're using to store it, you'll get an error.

Of course, this is where an object of an incorrect type in the `Vector` will cause a problem. If the object returned here isn't of type `Transaction`, an exception will be thrown. Although you could always store it in a variable of type `Object`, you should always cast it to the original or most appropriate type. Note that the `get()` method will throw an exception of type `ArrayIndexOutOfBoundsException` if the argument is an illegal index value. The index must be non-negative and less than the size of the vector.

You can retrieve the first element in a `Vector` by using the `firstElement()` method, which returns the object stored as type `Object`. For example:

```
Transaction theTransaction = (Transaction)transactions.firstElement();
```

You can also retrieve the last element in a `Vector` by using the method `lastElement()` in a similar manner. However, a vector has a flavor of a list about it, and if you want to process the objects in your vector like a list, you can obtain an iterator.

Accessing Elements in a Vector through an Iterator

You can also obtain all the elements in a `Vector` object by using an `Iterator` object that you obtain from the `Vector` object. In most instances this will be the preferred way of accessing the elements in a `vector`. You obtain a reference to an iterator by calling the `iterator()` method for the `Vector` object:

```
Iterator theData = names.iterator();
```

The method `iterator()` returns an `Iterator` object that you can use to iterate through all the elements in the `Vector` object. You can now process them serially using the methods defined for `Iterator` class that we discussed earlier. For example, you could now output the elements from `names` in the last example we ran using the iterator:

```
while(theData.hasNext())
  System.out.println((String)theData.next());
```

This loop iterates through all the elements referenced by `theData` one at a time, and outputs each `String` object to the display. When we've retrieved the last element from the `Iterator`, the method `hasNext()` will return `false` and the loop will end.

You can also obtain a `ListIterator` reference from a vector by calling the `listIterator()` method:

```
ListIterator listIter = names.listIterator();
```

Now you can go backwards or forwards though the objects using the `ListIterator` methods that we saw earlier.

It is also possible to obtain a `ListIterator` object that encapsulates just a part of the vector, using a version of the `listIterator()` method that accepts an argument specifying the index position of the first vector element in the iterator:

```
ListIterator listIter = names.listIterator(2);
```

This statement will result in a list iterator that encapsulates the elements from `names` from the element at index position 2 to the end. The argument must not be negative and must be less than the size of `names`, otherwise an `IndexOutOfBoundsException` will be thrown. Take care not to mix the interface name with a capital L with the method name with a small l.

To cap that, you can retrieve an internal subset of the objects in a vector as a collection of type `List` using the `subList()` method:

```
List list = names.subList(2, 5);   //Extract elements 2 to 4 as a sublist
```

The first argument is the index position of the first element from the vector to be included in the list, and the second index is the element at the upper limit – *not* included in the list. Thus this statement extracts elements 2 to 4 inclusive. Both arguments to `subList()` must be positive, the first argument must be less than the size of the vector, and the second argument must not be greater than the size, otherwise an `IndexOutOfBoundsException` will be thrown.

There are lots of ways of using the `subList()` method in conjunction with other methods, for example:

```
ListIterator listIter = transactions.subList(5, 15).listIterator(2);
```

Here we obtain a list iterator for elements 2 to the end of the list returned by the `subList()` call, which will be elements 7 to 14 inclusive from the `transactions` vector.

Extracting All the Elements from a Vector

A `Vector` provides you with tremendous flexibility in use, particularly with the ability to automatically adjust its capacity. Of course, the flexibility you get through using a `Vector` comes at a price. There is always some overhead involved when you're retrieving elements. For this reason, there may be times when you want to get the elements contained in a `Vector` object back as a regular array. The method `toArray()` will do this for you. You would typically use the method `toArray()` to obtain the elements of a `Vector` object, `transactions`, as follows:

```
Object[] data = transactions.toArray();  // Extract the vector elements
```

The `toArray()` method returns an array of type `Object` containing all the elements from `transactions` in the correct sequence.

It may be inconvenient to have the elements returned as an array of type `Object`. You may need to cast each element to its proper type before using it, for instance. There is another version of `toArray()` that will return an array of the type that you specify as an argument. You might use this with the transactions `Vector` as follows:

```
Transaction[] data = new Transaction(transactions.size());
data = transactions.toArray(data);
```

We allocate sufficient space for the elements using the `size()` member of our `Vector` object. You could supply an array as an argument that has more elements than are necessary to store the contents of the `Vector`. In this case the extra elements will be set to `null`. You can also supply an array that is too small as the argument to `toArray()`. In this case a new array will be created of the type you specify for the argument, with sufficient space to hold all the objects from the vector.

Of course, the type of objects stored in the vector must be the same as, or a supertype of, the type of the array. If not, an exception of type `ArrayStoreException` will be thrown. The method will also throw an exception of type `NullPointerException` if you pass `null` as the argument.

Removing Objects from a Vector

You can remove the reference at a particular index position by calling the `remove()` method with the index position of the object as the argument. For example:

```
transactions.remove(3);
```

will remove the fourth reference from `transactions`. The references following this will now be at index positions that are one less than they were before, so that what was previously the fifth object reference will now be at index position 3. Of course, the index value that you specify must be legal for the `Vector` on which you're operating, meaning greater than or equal to 0 and less than its `size()`, otherwise an exception will be thrown. This version of the `remove()` method returns a reference to the object removed, so it provides a means for you to retain a reference to the object after you remove it from the vector:

```
Transaction aTransaction = (Transaction)transactions.remove(3);
```

Here we save a reference to the object that was removed in `aTransaction`. The cast is necessary because the reference is returned as type `Object`.

Sometimes you'll want to remove a particular reference, rather than the reference at a given index. If you know what the object is that you want to remove, you can use another version of the `remove()` method to delete it:

```
boolean deleted = transactions.remove(aTransaction);
```

This will search the vector `transactions` from the beginning to find the first reference to the object `aTransaction` and remove it. If the object is found and removed from the vector, the method returns `true`, otherwise it returns `false`.

Another way to remove a single element is to use the `removeElementAt()` method, which requires an argument specifying the index position for the element to be removed. This is clearly similar to the version of `remove()` that accepts an index as an argument, the difference being that here the return type is `void`.

There is also a `removeAll()` method that accepts an argument of type `Collection`, which removes elements from the collection passed to the method if they are present in the vector. The method returns `true` if the `Vector` object is changed by the operation, that is, at least one element was removed. You could use this in conjunction with the `subList()` method to remove a specific set of elements:

```
transactions.removeAll(transactions.subList(5,15));
```

This will remove elements 5 to 14 inclusive from the `Vector` object `transactions`, plus any duplicates of those objects that are in the vector.

The `retainAll()` method provides you with a backhanded removal mechanism. You pass a reference of type `Collection` as the argument to the method that contains the elements to be retained. Any elements not in the collection you pass to the method will be removed. For instance, you could keep the elements at index positions 5 to 15 and discard the rest with the statement:

```
transactions.retainAll(transactions.subList(5,15));
```

The method returns `true` if the `Vector` has been changed – in other words if at least one element has been removed as a result of the operation. The method will throw an exception of type `NullPointerException` if the argument is `null`.

If you want to discard all the elements in a `Vector`, you can use the `clear()` method to empty the `Vector` in one go:

```
transactions.clear();      // Dump the whole lot
```

With all these ways of removing elements from a `Vector`, there's a lot of potential for ending up with an empty `Vector`. It's often handy to know whether a `Vector` contains elements or not, particularly if there's been a lot of adding and deleting of elements. You can check whether or not a `Vector` contains elements by using the `isEmpty()` method. This returns `true` if a `Vector` object has zero `size`, and `false` otherwise.

Note that a `Vector` may contain only `null` references, but this doesn't mean the `size()` will be zero or that `isEmpty()` will return `true`. To empty a `Vector` object you must actually remove the elements, not just set the elements to `null`.

Searching a Vector

You can get the index position of an object stored in a `Vector` by passing the object as an argument to the method `indexOf()`. For example, the statement

```
int position = transactions.indexOf(aTransaction);
```

will search the `Vector` from the beginning for the object `aTransaction` using the `equals()` method for the argument, so your class needs to have a proper implementation of `equals()` for this to work. The variable `position` will contain either the index of the first reference to the object in `transactions`, or -1 if the object isn't found.

You have another version of the method `indexOf()` available that accepts a second argument that is the index position where the search for the object should begin. The main use for this arises when an object can be referenced more than once in a `Vector`. You can use the method in this situation to recover all occurrences of any particular object, as follows:

```
int position = -1;                                    // Search starting index
while(++position<transactions.size()) {               // Search with a valid index
  if(position = transactions.indexOf(aTransaction, position))<0) // Find next
    break;
  // Code to process the object in some way...
}
```

The `while` loop will continue as long as the method `indexOf()` returns a valid index value and the index doesn't get incremented beyond the end of the `Vector`.

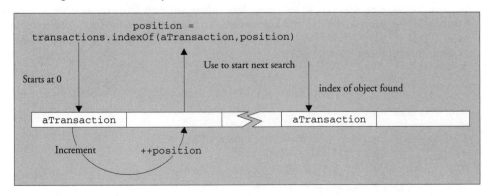

Each iteration will search `transactions` from the element given by the index stored in the variable `position`. The initial value of -1 is incremented in the `while` loop condition, so on the first iteration it is 0. On subsequent iterations where `indexOf()` finds an occurrence of `aTransaction`, the loop condition increments `position` to the next element ready for the next search. When no further references to the object can be found from the position specified by the second argument, the method `indexOf()` will return −1 and the loop will end by executing the break statement. If `aTransaction` happens to be found in the last element in the `Vector` at index position `size-1`, the value of position will be incremented to `size` by the loop condition expression, so the expression will be `false` and the loop will end.

Applying Vectors

Let's implement a simple example to see how using a `Vector` works out in practice. We will write a program to model a collection of people, where we can add the names of the persons that we want in the crowd from the keyboard. We'll first define a class to represent a person:

```
public class Person {
  // Constructor
  public Person(String firstName, String surname) {
    this.firstName = firstName;
    this.surname = surname;
  }

  public String toString() {
    return firstName + " " + surname;
  }

  private String firstName;       // First name of person
  private String surname;         // Second name of person
}
```

The only data members are the `String` members to store the first and second names for a person. By overriding the default implementation of the `toString()` method, provided by the `Object` class, we allow objects of the `Person` class to be used as arguments to the `println()` method for output, since as you are well aware by now, `toString()` will be automatically invoked in this case.

Now we can define a class that will represent a crowd. We could just create a `Vector` object in `main()` but this would mean any type of object could be stored. By defining our own class we can ensure that only `Person` objects can be stored in the `Vector` and in this way make our program less prone to errors.

The class definition representing a crowd is:

```
import java.util.*;
class Crowd {
  // Constructors
  public Crowd() {
    // Create default Vector object to hold people
    people = new Vector();
  }

  public Crowd(int numPersons) {
```

```
      // Create Vector object to hold people with given capacity
      people = new Vector(numPersons);
   }

   // Add a person to the crowd
   public boolean add(Person someone) {
      return people.add(someone);      // Use the Vector method to add
   }

   // Get the person at a given index
   Person get(int index) {
      return (Person)people.get(index);
   }

   // Get number of persons in crowd
   public int size() {
      return people.size();
   }

   // Get people store capacity
   public int capacity() {
      return people.capacity();
   }

   // Get an iterator for the crowd
   public Iterator iterator() {
      return people.iterator();
   }

   // Person store - only accessible through methods of this class
   private Vector people;
}
```

We've defined two constructors for the class for illustration purposes. One creates a Vector with a default capacity, and the other creates a Vector with the capacity given by the argument. Both constructors just call the appropriate Vector constructor. You could easily add the ability to provide the capacity increment with a third constructor, if you want.

By keeping the Vector member of the class private, we ensure the only way an object can be added to the Vector is by using the add() method in the class. Since this method only accepts an argument of type Person, we can be sure that it's impossible to store elements of any other type. Of course, if you wanted to allow other specific types to be stored, an object of type Child for example, you could arrange to derive the class Child from Person, so the add() method would allow an argument of type Child, since Person would be its superclass.

The remaining methods here are just to show how simple it is to implement the equivalent of the Vector methods for our class. In each case they use the Vector method to produce the required result. Now we are ready to put together a working example.

Try It Out – Creating the Crowd

We can now add a class containing a main() method to test these classes. We'll call it TryVector:

```
import java.util.*;
import java.io.*;

public class TryVector {
  public static void main(String[] args) {
    Person aPerson;                    // A person object
    Crowd filmCast = new Crowd();

    // Populate the crowd
    for( ; ; ) {                       // Indefinite loop
      aPerson = readPerson();          // Read in a film star
      if(aPerson == null)              // If null obtained...
        break;                         // We are done...
      filmCast.add(aPerson);           // Otherwise, add to the cast
    }

    int count = filmCast.size();
    System.out.println("You added " + count +
      (count == 1 ? " person":  " people") + " to the cast.\n");

    // Show who is in the cast using an iterator
    Iterator thisLot = filmCast.iterator();  // Obtain an iterator

    while(thisLot.hasNext())      // Output all elements
      System.out.println( thisLot.next() );
  }
}
```

Note the two `import` statements at the beginning. The first is needed for the `Iterator` in `main()`. The other is used for the `BufferedReader` and `InputStreamReader` objects in the `readPerson()` method. Let's now add this method to the `TryVector` class:

```
// Read a person from the keyboard
static public Person readPerson() {
  FormattedInput in = new FormattedInput();

  // Read in the first name and remove blanks front and back
  System.out.println(
                "\nEnter first name or ! to end:");
  String firstName = in.readString().trim();        // Read and trim a string

  if(firstName.charAt(0) == '!')                     // Check for ! entered
    return null;                                     // If so, we are done...

  // Read in the surname, also trimming blanks
  System.out.println("Enter surname:");
  String surname = in.readString().trim();           // Read and trim a string
  return new Person(firstName,surname);
}
```

Here we read the first name followed by the surname as two separate strings, and then create the `Person` object that is returned. If a `!` character was entered instead of a first name, `null` is returned by the `readPerson()` method signaling the end of the input. Since this method uses the `FormattedInput` class that we defined in Chapter 8, you need to copy the file containing the definition of this class to the same directory as the `TryVector` class. The `readString()` method that we defined in the `FormattedInput` class doesn't quite do what we want though. We could insist that the `!` character to end the input is entered between quotes. However, it's not a very natural way to enter the data. If we could get a single character that is not alphanumeric back as a string, then that would fix the problem for us. A small tweak of the `readString()` method in the `FormattedInput` class will accommodate that:

```
public String readString() {
   if(readToken()==tokenizer.TT_WORD || ttype == '\"' || ttype == '\'')
      return tokenizer.sval;
   else
      return String.valueOf((char)ttype);
}
```

You will recall that if you enter a string delimited by quotes, the quote character that you use is returned by the `nextToken()` method. If a character string is entered without quotes, then `TT_WORD` is returned. Thus the first `if` expression will be `true` if either of these is the case, so we return the string stored in `sval`. Of course, this will not include the double quote characters if they are present. Programming the method like this provides for quoted and unquoted strings, so we can enter names that contain spaces by putting them between quotes.

When a `!` is entered, it is returned by the `nextToken()` method, so in this case we return a string containing just this character to signal to the calling program that this is the end of the input. You could use any non-alphanumeric character for this. Note that `ttype` is of type `int` so we can't pass its value directly to the `valueOf()` method. If we did, we would get the string representation of its numerical value.

If you've swapped this version of the method into the `FormattedInput` class, and placed the source files for the other classes in the same directory, you should be ready to give it a whirl. With a modest film budget, I got the output (my input is in bold):

```
Enter first name or ! to end:
Roy
Enter surname:
Rogers

Enter first name or ! to end:
Marilyn
Enter surname:
Monroe

Enter first name or ! to end:
Robert
Enter surname:
"de Niro"
```

```
Enter first name or ! to end:
!
You added 3 people to the cast.

Roy Rogers
Marilyn Monroe
Robert de Niro
```

How It Works

Here we'll be assembling an all-star cast for a new blockbuster. The method `main()` creates a `Person` variable, which will be used as a temporary store for an actor or actress, and a `Crowd` object `filmCast`, to hold the entire cast.

The `for` loop uses the `readPerson()` method to obtain the necessary information from the keyboard and create a `Person` object. If ! or `"!"` is entered from the keyboard, `readPerson()` will return `null` and this will end the input process for cast members.

We then output the members of the cast by obtaining an `Iterator`. As you see, this makes the code for listing the members of the cast very simple. Instead of an iterator we could also have used the `get()` method that we implemented in `Crowd` to retrieve the actors:

```
for(int i = 0 ; i<filmCast.size() ; i++)
    System.out.println(filmCast.get());
```

Sorting

The output from the last example appears in the sequence in which you enter it. If we want to be socially correct, say, in the creation of a cast list, we should arrange them in alphabetical order. We could write our own method to sort `Person` objects in the `Crowd` object, but it will be a lot less trouble to take advantage of another feature of the `java.util` package, the `Collections` class – not to be confused with the `Collection` interface. The `Collections` class defines a variety of handy static methods that you can apply to collections, and one of them happens to be a `sort()` method.

The `sort()` method will only sort lists, that is, collections that implement the `List` interface. Obviously there also has to be some way for the `sort()` method to determine the order of objects from the list that it is sorting – in our case, `Person` objects. The most suitable way to do this for `Person` objects is to implement the `Comparable` interface for the class. The `Comparable` interface only declares one method, `compareTo()`. We saw this method in the `String` class so you know it returns –1, 0, or +1 depending on whether the current object is less than, equal to, or greater than the argument passed to the method. If the `Comparable` interface is implemented for the class, we just pass the collection object as an argument to the `sort()` method. The collection is sorted in place so there is no return value.

We can implement the `Comparable` interface very easily for our `Person` class, as follows:

```
public class Person implements Comparable {
    // Constructor
    public Person(String firstName, String surname) {
```

```
      this.firstName = firstName;
      this.surname = surname;
    }

    public String toString() {
      return firstName + " " + surname;
    }

    // Compare Person objects
    public int compareTo(Object person) {
      int result = surname.compareTo(((Person)person).surname);
      return result == 0 ? firstName.compareTo(((Person)person).firstName):result;
    }

    private String firstName;      // First name of person
    private String surname;        // Second name of person
  }
```

We use the compareTo() method for String objects to compare the surnames, and if they are equal the result is determined from the first names. We can't apply the sort() method from the Collections class to a Crowd object though – a Crowd is not a list since it doesn't implement the List interface. A Vector does though, so we can sort the people member of the Crowd class by adding a sort() method to the class:

```
class Crowd {
  // Sort the people
  public void sort() {
    Collections.sort(people);                    // Use the static sort method
  }

  // Rest of the class as before...
}
```

We can just pass our Vector object to the sort() method, and this will use the compareTo() method in the Person class to compare members of the list.

Let's see if it works for real.

Try It Out – Sorting the Stars

You can now add a statement to the main() method in TryVector, to sort the cast members:

```
public static void main(String[] args) {
  Person aPerson;                          // A person object
  Crowd filmCast = new Crowd();

  // Populate the cast
  for( ; ; ) {                             // Indefinite loop
    aPerson = readPerson();                // Read in a film star
    if(aPerson == null)                    // If null obtained...
```

```
        break;                          // We are done...
      filmCast.add(aPerson);            // Otherwise, add to the cast
    }


    int count = filmCast.size();
    System.out.println("You added "+count +
      (count == 1 ? " person":  " people")+ " to the cast.\n");

    filmCast.sort();                    // Sort the cast

    // Show who is in the cast using an iterator
    Iterator thisLot = filmCast.iterator();   // Obtain an iterator

    while(thisLot.hasNext())            // Output all elements
      System.out.println( thisLot.next() );
  }
```

If you run the example with these changes, the cast will be in alphabetical order in the output. Here's what I got:

```
Enter first name or ! to end:
Roy
Enter surname:
Rogers
Enter first name or ! to end:
Mae
Enter surname:
West

Enter first name or ! to end:
Charles
Enter surname:
Chaplin

Enter first name or ! to end:
!
You added 3 people to the cast.

Charles Chaplin
Roy Rogers
Mae West
```

How It Works

The sort() method for the Crowd object calls the sort() method defined in the Collections class, and this sorts the objects in the people vector in place. Like shelling peas!

Stack Storage

A stack is a storage mechanism that works on a last-in first-out basis, often abbreviated to LIFO. Don't confuse this with FIFO, which is first-in first-out, or FIFI, which is a name for a poodle. The operation of a stack is analogous to the plate stack you see in some self-service restaurants. The stack of plates is supported by a spring that allows the stack of plates to sink into a hole in the countertop so that only the top plate is accessible. The plates come out in the reverse order to the way they went in, so the cold plates are at the bottom, and the hot plates fresh from the dishwasher are at the top.

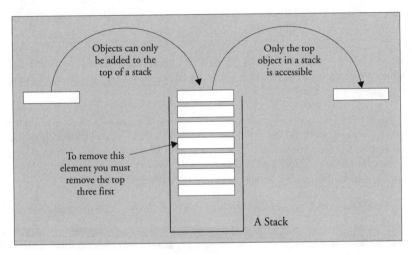

A stack in Java doesn't have a spring, but it does have all the facilities of a Vector object because the class Stack is derived from the class Vector. Of course, since we know the Vector class implements the List interface, a Stack object is also a List.

The Stack class adds five methods to those inherited from Vector, two of which provide you with the LIFO mechanism, and the other three give you extra capabilities. These methods are:

Method	Description
push (Object anObject)	Pushes a reference to the object passed as an argument to the method onto the top of the stack.
pop()	Pops the object reference off the top of the stack and returns it as type Object. This removes the reference from the stack. If the stack contains no references when you call this method the EmptyStackException will be thrown.
peek()	This method allows you to take a look at the object reference at the top of the stack without popping it off the stack. It returns the reference from the top of the stack as type Object without removing it. Like the previous method, this method can throw an EmptyStackException.

Table continued on following page

Method	Description
search (Object anObject)	This will return an int value which is the position on the stack of the reference to the object passed as an argument. The reference at the top of the stack is at position 1, the next reference is at position 2, and so on. Note that this is quite different from referencing elements in a Vector or an array, where indexes are an offset, so they start at 0. If the object isn't found on the stack, −1 is returned.
empty()	This method returns true if the stack is empty, and false otherwise.

The only constructor for a Stack object is the default constructor. This will call the default constructor for the base class, Vector, so you'll always get an initial capacity for 10 objects, but since it's basically a Vector, it will grow automatically in the same way.

One possible point of confusion is the relationship between the top of a Stack object, and the elements in the underlying Vector. Intuitively, you might think that the top of the stack is going to correspond to the first element in the Vector, with index 0. If so you would be totally *wrong*! The push() method for a Stack object is analogous to add() for a Vector, which adds an object to the end of the Vector. Thus the top of the Stack corresponds to the end of the Vector.

Let's try a Stack object out in an example so we get a feel for how the methods are used.

Try It Out – Dealing Cards

We can use a Stack along with another useful method from the Collections class to simulate dealing cards from a card deck. Let's start by defining a class to represent a card. Our Card class can use two integer data members – one to define the suit with values from 0 to 3 for clubs, diamonds, hearts, and spades, and the other with values from 1 to 13 to specify the face value of the card, 1 being an ace and 11 through 13 being jack, queen, and king. It will make the code clearer if we define some constants representing the suits and the court card values. Let's put that as a skeleton class definition:

```
class Card {
  // Suit values
  public static final int HEARTS = 0;

  public static final int CLUBS = 1;
  public static final int DIAMONDS = 2;
  public static final int SPADES = 3;

  // Card face values
  public static final int ACE = 1;
  public static final int JACK = 11;
  public static final int QUEEN = 12;
  public static final int KING = 13;
  private int suit;
  private int value;
}
```

We need a constructor that ensures that the suit and face value of a card are legal values. We can implement the constructor like this:

```
class Card {
  public Card(int value, int suit) throws IllegalArgumentException {
    if(value >= ACE && value <= KING)
      this.value = value;
    else
      throw new IllegalArgumentException("Invalid card value");
    if(suit >= HEARTS && suit <= SPADES)
      this.suit = suit;
    else
      throw new IllegalArgumentException("Invalid suit");
  }

  // Other members as before...
}
```

To deal with invalid arguments to the constructor, we just throw an exception of the standard type, IllegalArgumentException, that we create with a suitable message.

We will undoubtedly need to display a card so we will need a String representation of a Card object. The toString() method will do this for us:

```
class Card {
  public String toString() {
    String cardStr;
    switch(value) {
      case ACE: cardStr = "A";
            break;
      case JACK: cardStr = "J";
            break;
      case QUEEN: cardStr = "Q";
            break;
      case KING: cardStr = "K";
            break;
      default: cardStr = Integer.toString(value);
    }

    switch(suit) {
      case CLUBS: cardStr += "C";
            break;
      case DIAMONDS: cardStr += "D";
            break;
      case HEARTS: cardStr += "H";
            break;
      case SPADES: cardStr += "S";
            break;
      default:
        assert false;                    // We should never get to here
    }
```

```
      return cardStr;
    }

  // Other members as before...
}
```

Here we just use two `switch` statements to sort out the strings to represent the face value and the suit respectively from the values of the data members. In general, we might need to be able to compare cards, so we could also implement the `Comparable` interface:

```
class Card implements Comparable {
  // Compare two cards
  public int compareTo(Object card) {
    if(suit != ((Card)card).suit)                // First compare suits
      return suit < ((Card)card).suit ? -1: 1;   // Sequence is C<D<H<S
    else                                         // Suits are the same
      if(value == ((Card)card).value)            // So check face values
        return 0;                                // They are equal
      else
        return value < ((Card)card).value ? -1 : 1;
  }

  // Other members as before...
}
```

We could represent a hand of cards that is dealt from a deck as an object of type `Hand`. A `Hand` object will need to be able to accommodate an arbitrary number of cards as this will depend on what game the hand is intended for. We can define the `Hand` class using a `Stack` object to store the cards:

```
// Class defining a hand of cards
import java.util.*;

class Hand {
  public void add(Card card) {
    hand.push(card);
  }

  public String toString() {
    Iterator cards = hand.iterator();

    StringBuffer str = new StringBuffer();
    while(cards.hasNext())
      str.append(" "+ (Card)cards.next());
    return str.toString();
  }

  private Stack hand = new Stack();          // Stores the cards in the hand
}
```

The default constructor generated by the compiler will create a Hand object containing an empty Stack member, hand. The add() member will add the Card object passed as an argument by pushing it onto the hand. We also have implemented a toString() method here. We obtain an iterator to traverse the cards in the hand, and construct a string representation of the complete hand. Note that we should not use the pop() method here, because it removes an object from the stack, so using it here would remove all the cards from the hand.

We might well want to compare hands in general, but this is completely dependent on the context. The best approach to accommodate this when required would be to derive a game-specific class from Hand – a PokerHand class for instance – and make it implement its own version of the compareTo() method in the Comparable interface.

The last class we need will represent a deck of cards, and will also deal a hand:

```java
import java.util.*;
class CardDeck {
  // Create a deck of 52 cards
  public CardDeck() {
    for(int theSuit = Card.HEARTS; theSuit<= Card.SPADES; theSuit++)
      for(int theValue = Card.ACE; theValue <= Card.KING; theValue++)
        deck.push(new Card(theValue, theSuit));
  }

  // Deal a hand
  public Hand dealHand(int numCards) {
    Hand hand = new Hand();
    for(int i = 0; i<numCards; i++)
      hand.add((Card)deck.pop());
    return hand;
  }

  private Stack deck = new Stack();
}
```

The card deck is stored as a Stack object, deck. In the constructor, the nested for loops create the cards in the deck. For each suit in turn, we generate all the Card objects from ace to king and push them onto the Stack object, deck.

The dealHand() method creates a Hand object, and then pops numCards objects off the deck stack and adds each of them to hand. The Hand object is then returned. At the moment our deck is completely sequenced. We need a method to shuffle the deck:

```java
class CardDeck {
  // Shuffle the deck
  public void shuffle() {
    Collections.shuffle(deck);
  }

  // Rest of the class as before...
}
```

With the aid of another `static` method from the `Collections` class it couldn't be easier. The `shuffle()` method in `Collections` shuffles the contents of any collection that implements the `List` interface, so we end up with a shuffled deck of `Card` objects. For those interested in the details of shuffling, this `shuffle()` method randomly permutes the list by running backwards through its elements swapping the current element with a randomly chosen element between the first and the current element. The time taken to complete the operation is proportional to the number of elements in the list.

An overloaded version of the `shuffle()` method allows you to supply an object of type `Random` as the second argument that is used for selecting elements at random while shuffling.

The final piece is a class that defines `main()`:

```
class TryDeal {
  public static void main(String[] args) {
    CardDeck deck = new CardDeck();
    deck.shuffle();

    Hand myHand = deck.dealHand(5);
    Hand yourHand = deck.dealHand(5);
    System.out.println("\nMy hand is" + myHand);
    System.out.println("\nYour hand is" + yourHand);
  }
}
```

I got the output:

```
My hand is 3D KD 7D 8C 7S

Your hand is 9C 6D 6C 3C AS
```

You will almost certainly get something different.

How It Works

The code for `main()` first creates a `CardDeck` object and calls its `shuffle()` method to randomize the sequence of `Card` objects. It then creates two `Hand` objects of 5 cards by calling the `dealHand()` method. The output statements just display the hands that were dealt.

A `Stack` object is particularly suited to dealing cards, as we want to remove each card from the deck as it is dealt and this is done automatically by the `pop()` method that retrieves an object. When we need to go through the objects in a `Stack` collection without removing them, we can use an iterator as we did in the `toString()` method in the `Hand` class. Of course, since the `Stack` class is derived from `Vector`, all the `Vector` class methods are available too, when you need them.

I think you'll agree that using a stack is very simple. A stack is a powerful tool in many different contexts. A stack is often applied in applications that involve syntactical analysis, such as compilers and interpreters – including those for Java.

Linked Lists

The LinkedList collection class implements a generalized linked list. We have already seen quite a few of the methods that the class implements as the members of the List interface implemented in the Vector class. Nonetheless, let's quickly go through the methods that the LinkedList class implements. There are two constructors a default constructor that creates an empty list, and a constructor that accepts a Collection argument that will create a LinkedList object containing the objects from the collection that is passed to it.

To add objects to a list you have the add() and addAll() methods exactly as we discussed for a Vector object. You can also add an object at the beginning of a list using the addFirst() method, and you can add one at the end using addLast(). Both methods accept an argument of type Object and do not return a value. Of course, the addLast() method provides the same function as the add() method.

To retrieve an object at a particular index position in the list you can use the get() method, as in the Vector class. You can also obtain references to the first and last objects in the list by using the getFirst() and getLast() methods, respectively. To remove an object you can use the remove() method with an argument that is either an index value or a reference to the object that is to be removed. The removeFirst() and removeLast() methods do what you would expect.

Replacing an existing element in the list at a given index position is achieved by using the set() method. The first argument is the index value and the second argument is the new object at that position. The old object is returned and the method will throw an IndexOutOfBoundsException if the index value is not within the limits of the list. The size() method returns the number of elements in the list.

As with a Vector object, you can obtain an Iterator object by calling iterator(), and you can obtain a ListIterator object by calling listIterator(). You will recall that an Iterator object only allows you to go forward through the elements, whereas a ListIterator enables you to iterate backwards or forwards.

We could change the TryPolyLine example from Chapter 6 to use a LinkedList collection object rather than our homemade version.

Try It Out – Using a Genuine Linked List

We will put this example in a new directory, TryNewPolyLine. We can use the TryPolyLine class that contains main() and the Point class exactly as they are, so if you still have them, copy the source files to the new directory. We just need to change the PolyLine class definition:

```
import java.util.*;

public class PolyLine {
  // Construct a polyline from an array of points
  public PolyLine(Point[] points) {
    // Add the  points
    for(int i = 0; i < points.length; i++)
      polyline.add(points[i]);
  }
```

```
    // Construct a polyline from an array of coordinate
    public PolyLine(double[][] coords) {
      // Add the points
      for(int i = 0; i < coords.length; i++)
        polyline.add(new Point(coords[i][0], coords[i][1]));
    }

    // Add a Point object to the list
    public void addPoint(Point point) {
      polyline.add(point);     // Add the new point
    }

    // Add a point to the list
    public void addPoint(double x, double y) {
      polyline.add(new Point(x, y));
    }

    // String representation of a polyline
    public String toString() {
      StringBuffer str = new StringBuffer("Polyline:");
      Iterator points = polyline.iterator();            // Get an iterator

      while(points.hasNext())
        str.append(" "+ (Point)points.next());          // Append the current point

      return str.toString();
    }

    private LinkedList polyline = new LinkedList();      // Stores points for polyline
}
```

The class is a lot simpler because the LinkedList class provides all the mechanics of operating a linked list. Since the interface to the PolyLine class is the same as the previous version, the original version of main() will run unchanged and produce exactly the same output.

How It Works

The only interesting bit is the change to the PolyLine class. Point objects are now stored in the linked list implemented by the LinkedList object, polyline. We use the add() method to add points in the constructors and the addPoint() methods. The toString() method now uses an iterator to go through the points in the list. Using a collection class makes the PolyLine class very straightforward.

Using Maps

As we saw at the beginning of this chapter, a **map** is a way of storing data that minimizes the need for searching when you want to retrieve an object. Each object is associated with a key that is used to determine where to store the reference to the object, and both the key and the object are stored in the map. Given a key, you can always go more or less directly to the object that has been stored in the map based on the key. It's important to understand a bit more about how the storage mechanism works for a map, and in particular what the implications of using the default hashing process are. We will explore the use of maps primarily in the context of the HashMap class.

The Hashing Process

A map sets aside an array in which it will store key and object pairs. The index to this array is produced from the key object by using the hash code for the object to compute an offset into the array for storing key/object pairs. By default, this uses the `hashCode()` method for the object that's used as a key. This is inherited in all classes from `Object`.

Note that, while every key must be unique, each key doesn't have to result in a unique hash code. When two or more different keys produce the same hash value, it's called a **collision**. A `HashMap` object deals with collisions by storing all the key/object pairs that have the same hash value in a linked list. If this occurs very often, it is obviously going to slow up the process of storing and retrieving data. Retrieving an object that resulted in a collision when it was stored will be a two-stage process. The key will be hashed to find the location where the key/object pair should be. The linked-list will then have to be searched to sort out the particular key we are searching on from all the others that have the same hash value.

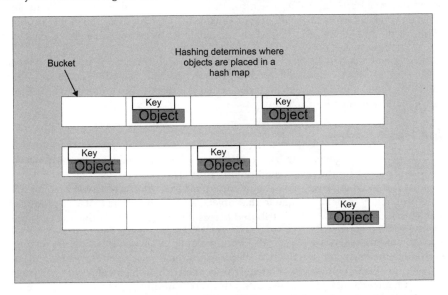

There is therefore a strong incentive to minimize collisions and the price of reducing the possibility of collisions in a hash table is having plenty of empty space in the table.

The class `Object` defines the method `hashCode()` so any object can be used as a key and it will hash by default. The method as it is implemented in `Object` in Java, however, isn't a panacea. Since it usually uses the memory address where an object is stored to produce the hash value, distinct objects will always produce different hash values. In one sense this is a plus, because the more likely it is that a unique hash value will be produced for each key, the more efficient the operation of the hash map is going to be. The downside is that different object instances that have identical data will produce different hash values, so you can't compare them.

This becomes a nuisance if you use the default `hashCode()` method in objects that you're using as keys. In this case, an object stored in a hash map can never be retrieved using a different key object instance, even though that key object may be identical in all other respects. Yet this is precisely what you'll want to do in many cases.

Consider an application such as a simple address book. You might store map entries keyed on the names of the people to whom the entries relate, and you would want to search the map based on a name that was entered from the keyboard. However, the object representing the newly entered name is inevitably going to be distinct from that used as a key for the entry. Using the former, you will not be able to find the entry corresponding to the name.

The solution to this problem is somehow to make a hash of the instance variables of the object. Then, by comparing the values of the data members of the new name object with those for the name objects used as keys in the hash map, you'll be able to make a match.

Using Your Own Class Objects as Keys

For objects of one of your own classes to be usable as keys in a hash table, you must override the `equals()` method of the `Object` class. In its default form, `equals()` accepts an object of the same class as an argument and returns a `boolean` value. The `equals()` method is used by methods in the `HashMap` class to determine when two keys are equal, so, in order to enable the changes discussed in the previous section, your version of this method should return `true` when two different objects contain identical data values.

You can also override the default `hashCode()` method, which returns the hash value for the object as type `int`. The `hashCode()` method is used to generate the `int` value that is the key. Your `hashCode()` method should produce hash codes that are reasonably uniform over the possible range of keys and generally unique for each key.

Generating Hash Codes

The various techniques for generating hash codes form a big topic, and we can only scratch the surface here. How you write the `hashCode()` method for your class is up to you, but it needs to meet certain requirements if it is to be effective. You should aim to return a number of type `int` for an object that has a strong probability of being unique to that object, and the numbers that you produce for several different objects should be as widely distributed across the range of `int` values as possible.

To achieve the uniqueness, you will typically want to combine the values of all the data members in an object to produce the hash code, so the first step is to produce an integer corresponding to each data member. You must then combine these integers to generate the return value that will be the hash code for the object. One technique you can use to do this is to multiply each of the integers corresponding to the data members by a different prime number and then sum the results. This should produce a reasonable distribution of values that have a good probability of being different for different objects. It doesn't matter which prime numbers you use as multipliers, as long as:

❑ They aren't so large as to cause the result to fall outside the range of type `int`

❑ You use a different one for each data member

So how do you get from a data member of a class to an integer? Generating an integer for data members of type `String` is easy: you just call the `hashCode()` method for the member. This has been implemented in the `String` class to produce good hash code values that will be the same for identical strings (take a look at the source code if you want to see how). You can use integer data members as they are, but floating point data members need a bit of judgment. If they have a small range in integer terms, you need to multiply them by a value that's going to result in a unique integer when they are cast to type `int`. If they have a very large range in integer terms you may need to scale them down.

Suppose you intended to use a `Person` object as a key in a hash table, and the class data members were `firstName` and `surname` of type `String`, and `age` of type `int`. You could implement the `hashCode()` method for the class as:

```
public int hashCode() {
    return 13*firstName.hashCode() + 17*surname.hashCode() + 19*age;
}
```

Wherever a data member is an object of another class rather than a variable of one of the basic types, you need to implement the `hashCode()` method for that class. You can then use that in the computation of the hash code for the key class.

Creating a HashMap

As we saw, all map classes implement the `Map` interface, so an object of any map class can be referenced using a variable of type `Map`. We will look in detail at the `HashMap` class since it is good for most purposes. There are four constructors you can use to create a `HashMap` object:

Constructor	Description
HashMap()	Creates a map with the capacity to store a default number of objects. The default capacity is 101 objects and the default load factor (more on the load factor below) is 0.75.
HashMap(int capacity)	Creates a map with the capacity to store the number of objects you specify in the argument and a default load factor of 0.75.
HashMap(int capacity, float loadFactor)	Creates a hash table with the capacity and load factor that you specify.
HashMap(Map map)	Creates a map with the capacity and load factor of the `Map` object passed as an argument.

To create a map using the default constructor, you can write something like this:

```
HashMap theMap = new HashMap();
```

The **capacity** for a map is simply the number of key/object pairs it can store. The capacity increases automatically as necessary, but this is a relatively time consuming operation. The capacity value of the map is combined with the hash code for the key that you specify to compute the index that determines where an object and its key are to be stored. To make this computation produce a good distribution of index values, you should ideally use prime numbers for the capacity of a hash table when you specify it yourself. For example:

```
HashMap myMap = new HashMap(151);
```

This map has a capacity for 151 objects and their keys, although the number of objects stored can never actually reach the capacity. There must always be spare capacity in a map for efficient operation. With too little spare capacity, there is an increased likelihood that keys will generate the same table index, so collisions become more likely.

The **load factor** is used to decide when to increase the size of the hash table. When the size of the table reaches a value which is the product of the load factor and the capacity, the capacity will be increased automatically to twice the old capacity plus 1 – the plus one ensuring it is at least odd, if not prime. The default load factor of 0.75 is a good compromise, but if you want to reduce it you could do so by using the third constructor:

```
HashMap aMap = new HashMap(151, 0.6f);   // 60% load factor
```

This map will work a bit more efficiently than the current default, but at the expense of having more unoccupied space. When 90 objects have been stored, the capacity will be increase to 303, (2*151+1).

Storing, Retrieving, and Removing Objects

Storing, retrieving, and removing objects in a HashMap is very simple. The four methods involved in this are:

Method	Description
put(Object key, Object value)	Stores the object value in the map using the key specified by the first argument. value will displace any existing object associated with key. The ejected object will be returned as type Object. If no object is stored at that map location or the key was used to store null as an object, null is returned.
putAll(Map map)	Transfers all the key/object pairs from map to the current map, replacing any objects that exist with the same keys.
get(Object key)	Returns the object stored with the same key as the argument. If no object was stored with this key or null was stored as the object, null is returned. Note that the object remains in the table.
remove(Object key)	Removes the entry associated with key if it exists, and returns the object as type Object. A null is returned if the entry does not exist, or if null was stored using key.

Any kind of object can be stored in a map, since all objects are stored as type Object. As with objects stored in a Vector, you can cast an object back to its original type when you retrieve it. The same caveats we saw for Vector objects, relating to the potential for storing objects of different types, apply to hash maps. If you want to limit the type of object that can be stored, you can use a HashMap object as a member of your own class, and implement its interface get(), put(), and putAll() methods yourself, to restrict what can be stored.

If you attempt to retrieve an object using get() and a null is returned, it is still possible that a null was stored as the object associated with the key that you supplied to the get() method. You can determine if this is the case by passing your key object to the containsKey() method for the map. This will return true if the key is stored in the map.

You should check that the value returned from the put() method is null. If you don't, you may unwittingly displace an object that was stored in the table earlier using the same key:

```
String myKey = "Goofy";
Integer theObject = new Integer(12345);

if(aMap.put(myKey, theObject) != null)
  System.out.println("Uh-oh, we bounced an object...");
```

Of course, you could throw your own exception here instead of displaying a message.

Note that the get() operation will return a reference to the object associated with the key, but it does not remove it from the table. To retrieve an object and delete the entry containing it from the table, you must use the remove() method. This accepts a key of type Object as an argument and returns the object corresponding to the key:

```
theObject = (Integer)aMap.remove(theKey);
```

As was noted in the table, if there's no stored object corresponding to theKey or null was stored as the object, null will be returned. Note how we have to explicitly cast the object returned from the hash map to the correct class.

Processing all the Elements in a Map

The Map interface provides three ways of obtaining a collection view of the contents of a map. You can obtain all the keys or all the key/object pairs from a Map object as an object of type Set. You can also get a Collection object that references all the objects in the map. Note that the Set or Collection object is essentially a view of the contents of a map, so changes to a HashMap object will be reflected in the associated Set or Collection, and vice versa. The three methods involved are:

Method	Description
keySet()	Returns a Set object referencing the keys from the map.
entrySet()	Returns a Set object referencing the key/object pairs – each pair being an object of type Map.Entry.
values()	Returns a Collection object referencing the objects stored in the map.

The type of the key/object pairs in the set returned by entrySet() looks a little unusual. The key/object pairs are of type Map.Entry because Entry is an interface declared within the Map interface.

Let's first see how we can use a set of keys. The method keySet() for the HashMap class returns a Set object referencing the set of keys that you can either use directly to access the keys or use indirectly to get at the objects stored in the map. For a HashMap object aMap, you could get the set of all the keys in the map with the statement:

```
Set keys = aMap.keySet();
```

Now you can get an iterator for this set of keys with the statement:

```
Iterator keyIter = keys.iterator();
```

You can use the `iterator()` method for the object `keys` to iterate over all the keys in the map. Of course, you can combine these two operations to get the iterator directly. For example:

```
Iterator keyIter = aMap.keySet().iterator();        // Get the iterator

while(keyIter.hasNext())                             // Iterate over the keys
    System.out.println((KeyType)keyIter.next());
```

This iterates over all the keys and outputs their `String` representation – `KeyType` in this fragment represents the class type of the keys.

The method `entrySet()` returns a `Set` object referencing the key/object pairs. In a similar way to the one that we used for the set of keys, you can obtain an iterator to make the `Map.Entry` objects available. Each `Map.Entry` object will contain the following methods to operate on it:

Method	Description
`getKey()`	Returns the key for the `Map.Entry` object as type `Object`.
`getValue()`	Returns the object for the `Map.Entry` object as type `Object`.
`setValue(Object new)`	Sets the object for this `Map.Entry` object to the argument and returns the original object. Remember that this alters the original map. This method throws: `UnsupportedOperationException` if `put()` is not supported by the underlying map. `ClassCastException` if the argument cannot be stored because of its type. `IllegalArgumentException` if the argument is otherwise invalid. `NullPointerException` if the map does not allow `null` objects to be stored. This last exception does not apply to `HashMap`.

A `Map.Entry` object will also need an `equals()` method for comparisons with another `Map.Entry` object passed as an argument and a `hashCode()` method to compute a hash code for the `Map.Entry` object. With a set of `Map.Entry` objects you can obviously access the keys and the corresponding objects by obtaining an iterator, and you can modify the object part of each key/object pair if you need to.

Finally the `values()` method for a `HashMap` object will return a `Collection` object that is a collection of all the objects in the map. This enables you to use the `iterator()` member to obtain an iterator for the collection of objects.

We have waded through a lot of the theory for `HashMap` objects; let's put together an example that applies it.

We can put together a very simple phone book that uses a map. We won't worry too much about error recovery so that we don't bulk up the code too much. We will reuse the `Person` class that we saw earlier, and the `FormattedInput` class with the modified version of the `readString()` method, plus the `InvalidUserInputException` class, so copy them to a new directory called `TryHashMap` or something similar. Besides the `Person` class we will need a `PhoneNumber` class, plus an `Entry` class that represents an entry in our phone book combining the name and number. We could add other stuff such as the address, but this is not necessary to show the principles. We will also define a `PhoneBook` class to represent the phone book.

Try It Out – Using a HashMap Map

We need to improve our old `Person` class to make `Person` objects usable as keys in the map that we will use – to store the phone book entries. We must add an `equals()` method and we'll override the default `hashCode()` method just to show how this can work. The extended version of the class will be as follows:

```
public class Person implements Comparable, Serializable {
  public boolean equals(Object person) {
    return compareTo(person) == 0;
  }

  public int hashCode() {
    return 7*firstName.hashCode()+13*surname.hashCode();
  }

  // The rest of the class as before...
}
```

Since the `String` class defines a good `hashCode()` method, we can easily produce a hash code for a `Person` object from the data members. To implement the `equals()` method we just call the method that we implemented for the `Comparable` interface. As it is likely to be required in this application, we have made the class serializable

There's another thing we could do that will be useful. We could add a `static` method to read data for a `Person` object from the keyboard:

```
import java.io.*;

public class Person implements Comparable, Serializable {
  // Read a person from the keyboard
  public static Person readPerson() {
    FormattedInput in = new FormattedInput();
    // Read in the first name and remove blanks front and back
    System.out.println("\nEnter first name:");
    String firstName = in.readString().trim();
    // Read in the surname, also trimming blanks
    System.out.println("Enter surname:");
```

```
      String surname = in. readString ().trim();
      return new Person(firstName,surname);
   }


   // Rest of the class as before...
}
```

You should have no trouble seeing how this works as it's almost identical to the readPerson() method we used previously.

We can make the PhoneNumber class very simple:

```
class PhoneNumber implements Serializable {
  public PhoneNumber(String areacode, String number) {
    this.areacode = areacode;
    this.number = number;

  }

  public String toString() {
    return areacode + ' ' + number;
  }

  private String areacode;
  private String number;
}
```

We could do a whole lot of validity checking of the number here, but it's not important for our example.

We could use a static method to read a number from the keyboard so let's add that too:

```
import java.io.*;

class PhoneNumber implements Serializable {
  // Read a phone number from the keyboard
  public static PhoneNumber readNumber() {
    FormattedInput in = new FormattedInput();

    int maxTries = 5;                              // Maximum number of errors
                                                   // in input
    String area = null;                            // Stores the area code
    String localcode = null;                       // Stores the local code

    for(;;) {                                      // Loop to allow retries
      try {
        // Read in the area code
        if(area == null) {                         // If there's no area code
          System.out.println("\nEnter the area code:");
          area = Integer.toString(in.readInt());   // read one from the k/b
        }
```

```
              // Read in the number
              if(localcode == null) {                      // If there's no local code
                 System.out.println("Enter the local code:");
                 localcode = Integer.toString(in.readInt());  // read one from the k/b
              }

              System.out.println("Enter the number:");
              String code = Integer.toString(in.readInt());  // Read last part of the
                                                              // number
              localcode += " " + code;                        // and append to local code
              return new PhoneNumber(area,localcode);

           } catch(InvalidUserInputException e) {
              if(--maxTries == 0) {                      //  If there were maxTries errors
                 System.out.println("Maximum number of errors exceeded. Terminating...");
                 System.exit(1);                         // then quit
              }
              System.err.println(e.getMessage()+"\nTry again");
              continue;                                   // otherwise try again
           }
        }
      }

      // Rest of the class as before...
   }
```

This is again similar to the `readPerson()` method except that we read the parts of the telephone number as integers and convert them to `String` objects. If you wanted to read them as `String` objects, then they would need to be entered between quotes if spaces are to be permitted. We allow for errors in the input here by reading the component parts of a number in a loop. If an invalid character is entered when reading a value, the `String` reference will be left as `null`. By testing for `area` and `localcode` being `null` before we read a value, we ensure that only the component that was in error needs to be reentered. If after five tries it's still not correct, we end the program.

An entry in the phone book will combine the name and the number, and would probably include other things such as the address. We can get by with the basics:

```
import java.io.*;

class BookEntry implements Serializable {
  public BookEntry(Person person, PhoneNumber number) {
    this.person = person;
    this.number = number;
  }

  public Person getPerson() {
    return person;
  }

  public PhoneNumber getNumber() {
    return number;
```

```
    }

    public String toString() {
      return person.toString() + '\n' + number.toString();
    }

    // Read an entry from the keyboard
    public static BookEntry readEntry() {
      return new BookEntry(Person.readPerson(), PhoneNumber.readNumber());
    }

    private Person person;
    private PhoneNumber number;
}
```

This is all pretty standard stuff. In the `static` method `readEntry()`, we just make use of the methods that read `Person` and `PhoneNumber` objects so this becomes very simple.

Now we come to the class that implements the phone book – called the `PhoneBook` class, of course:

```
import java.io.*;
import java.util.*;
```

```
class PhoneBook implements Serializable {
  public void addEntry(BookEntry entry) {
    phonebook.put(entry.getPerson(), entry);
  }

  public BookEntry getEntry(Person key) {
    return (BookEntry)phonebook.get(key);
  }

  public PhoneNumber getNumber(Person key) {
    return getEntry(key).getNumber();
  }

  private HashMap phonebook = new HashMap();
}
```

To store `BookEntry` objects we use a `HashMap` member, `phonebook`. We will use the `Person` object corresponding to an entry as the key, so the `addEntry()` method only has to retrieve the `Person` object from the `BookEntry` object that is passed to it, and use that as the first argument to the `put()` method for `phonebook`. Note that when we retrieve an entry, we must cast the object that is returned by the `get()` method to the `BookEntry` type, as `get()` returns type `Object`. All we need now is a class containing `main()` to test these classes:

```
class TryPhoneBook {
  public static void main(String[] args) {
    PhoneBook book = new PhoneBook();              // The phone book
    FormattedInput in = new FormattedInput();      // Keyboard input
    Person someone;
```

```
for(;;) {
    System.out.println("Enter 1 to enter a new phone book entry\n"+
                       "Enter 2 to find the number for a name\n"+
                       "Enter 9 to quit.");
    int what = 0;                              // Stores input selection
    try {
      what = in.readInt();

    } catch(InvalidUserInputException e) {
      System.out.println(e.getMessage()+"\nTry again.");
      continue;
    }

    switch(what) {
      case 1:
        book.addEntry(BookEntry.readEntry());
        break;
      case 2:
        someone = Person.readPerson();
        BookEntry entry = book.getEntry(someone);
        if(entry == null)
          System.out.println("The number for " + someone +
                             " was not found. ");
        else
          System.out.println("The number for " + someone +
                             " is " + book.getEntry(someone).getNumber());
        break;
      case 9:
        System.out.println("Ending program.");
        return;
      default:
        System.out.println("Invalid selection, try again.");
        break;
    }
  }
 }
}
```

This is what the example produces with my input:

```
Enter 1 to enter a new phone book entry
Enter 2 to find the number for a name
Enter 9 to quit.
1
Enter first name:
Slim
Enter surname:
Pickens
Enter the area code:
914
Enter the local code:
```

```
238
Enter the number:
6778
Enter 1 to enter a new phone book entry
Enter 2 to find the number for a name
Enter 9 to quit.
2

Enter first name:
Slim
Enter surname:
"Pickens"
The number for Slim Pickens is 914 238 6778
Enter 1 to enter a new phone book entry
Enter 2 to find the number for a name
Enter 9 to quit.
9
Ending program.
```

Of course, you can try it with several entries if you have the stamina.

How It Works

The main() method runs an ongoing loop that will continue until a 9 is entered. When a 1 is entered, the addEntry() method for the PhoneBook object is called with the expression BookEntry.readEntry() as the argument. The static method readEntry() calls the static methods in the Person class and the PhoneNumber class to read from the keyboard and create objects of these classes. The readEntry() method then passes these objects to the constructor for the BookEntry class, and the object that is created is returned. This object will be added to the HashMap member of the PhoneBook object.

If a 2 is entered, the getEntry() method is called. The argument expression calls the readPerson() member of the Person class to obtain the Person object corresponding to the name entered from the keyboard. This object is then used to retrieve an entry from the map in the PhoneBook object. Of course, if there is no such entry null will be returned, so we have to check for it and act accordingly.

Storing a Map in a File

This phone book is not particularly useful. The process of echoing what we just keyed in doesn't hold one's interest for long. What we need is a phone book that is held in a file. That's not difficult. We just need to add a constructor and another method to the PhoneBook class:

```
import java.util.*;
import java.io.*;
class PhoneBook implements Serializable {
  public PhoneBook() {
    if(filename.exists())
    try {
      ObjectInputStream in = new ObjectInputStream(
      new FileInputStream(filename));
```

```
        phonebook = (HashMap)in.readObject();
        in.close();

    } catch(ClassNotFoundException e) {
        System.out.println(e);

    } catch(IOException e) {
        System.out.println(e);
    }
}

public void save() {
    try {
        System.out.println("Saving phone book");
        ObjectOutputStream out = new ObjectOutputStream(
        new FileOutputStream(filename));
        out.writeObject(phonebook);
        System.out.println(" Done");
        out.close();

    } catch(IOException e) {
        System.out.println(e);
    }
}

private File filename = new File("Phonebook.bin");

// Other members of the class as before...
}
```

The new private data member, `filename`, defines the name of the file where the map holding the phone book entries is to be stored. Since we have only specified the file name and extension, the file will be assumed to be in the current directory. The `filename` object is used in the constructor that now reads the `HashMap` object from the file if it exists. If it doesn't exist it does nothing and the `PhoneBook` object will use the default empty `HashMap` object.

The `save()` method provides for storing the map away, so we will need to call this method before ending the program. To make it a little more interesting we could add a method to list all the entries in a phone book:

```
import java.util.*;
import java.io.*;
class PhoneBook implements Serializable {
    // List all entries in the book
    public void listEntries() {
        // Get the keys as a list
        LinkedList persons = new LinkedList(phonebook.keySet());
        Collections.sort(persons);                     // Sort the keys
        Iterator iter = persons.iterator();            // Get iterator for sorted keys

        while(iter.hasNext())
            System.out.println(phonebook.get((Person)iter.next()));
    }
```

```
    // Other members as before...
  }
```

If we want to list the entries in name sequence we have to do a little work. The keySet() method in HashMap returns a Set object for the keys, which are Person objects, but these will not be ordered in any way. By creating a LinkedList object from the set, we obtain a collection that we can sort using the sort() method from the Collections class. Finally we get an iterator to go through the HashMap using the keys in alphabetical order in the collection.

We can update main() to take advantage of the new features of the PhoneBook class:

```
class TryPhoneBook {
  public static void main(String[] args) {
    PhoneBook book = new PhoneBook();                   // The phone book
    FormattedInput in = new FormattedInput();           // Keyboard input
    Person someone;

    for(;;) {
      System.out.println("Enter 1 to enter a new phone book entry\n"+
                         "Enter 2 to find the number for a name\n"+
                         "Enter 3 to list all the entries\n" +
                         "Enter 9 to quit.");
      int what = 0;
      try {
        what = in.readInt();

      } catch(InvalidUserInputException e) {
        System.out.println(e.getMessage()+"\nTry again.");
        continue;
      }

      switch(what) {
        case 1:
          book.addEntry(BookEntry.readEntry());
          break;
        case 2:
          someone = Person.readPerson();
          BookEntry entry = book.getEntry(someone);
          if(entry == null)
            System.out.println("The number for " + someone +
                               " was not found. ");
          else
            System.out.println("The number for " + someone +
                               " is " + book.getEntry(someone).getNumber());
          break;
        case 3:
          book.listEntries();
          break;
        case 9:
          book.save();
          System.out.println("Ending program.");
```

```
            return;
         default:
            System.out.println("Invalid selection, try again.");
            break;
      }
    }
  }
}
```

How It Works

The first changes here are an updated prompt for input and a new case in the `switch` to list the entries in the phone book. The other change is to call the `save()` method to write the map that stores the phone book to a file before ending the program.

> Be aware of the default `hashCode()` method in the `Object` class when storing maps. The hash codes are generated from the address of the object, and getting a key object back from a file in exactly the same place in memory is about as likely as finding hairs on a frog. The result is that the hashcode generated from the key when it is read back will be different from when it was originally produced, so you will never find the entry in the map to which it corresponds.
>
> If we override the default `hashCode()` method then our hash codes are produced from the data members of the key objects, so they are always the same regardless of where the key objects are stored in memory.

The first time you run this version of `TryPhoneBook` it will create a new file and store the entire phone book in it. On subsequent occasions the `PhoneBook` constructor will read from the file, so all the previous entries are available.

In the next chapter we'll move on to look at some of the other components from the `java.util` package.

Summary

All of the classes in this chapter will be useful sooner or later when you're writing your own Java programs. We'll be applying many of them in examples throughout the remainder of the book.

The important elements we've covered are:

❑ You can use a `Vector` object as a kind of flexible array that expands automatically to accommodate any number of objects stored.

❑ The `Stack` class is derived from the `Vector` class and implements a pushdown stack.

❑ The `HashMap` class defines a hash map in which objects are stored based on an associated key.

❑ An Iterator is an interface for retrieving objects from a collection sequentially. An Iterator object allows you to access all the objects it contains serially – but only once. There's no way to go back to the beginning.

❑ The ListIterator interface provides methods for traversing the objects in a collection backwards or forwards.

❑ Objects stored in any type of collection can be accessed using Iterator objects.

❑ Objects stored in a Vector, a Stack, or a LinkedList can be accessed using ListIterator objects.

Exercises

1. Implement a version of the program to calculate prime numbers that we saw in Chapter 4 to use a Vector object instead of an array to store the primes. (Hint – remember the Integer class.)

2. Write a program to store a deck of 52 cards in a linked list in random sequence using a Random class object. You can represent a card as a two character string – "1C" for the ace of clubs, "JD" for the jack of diamonds, and so on. Output the cards from the stack as four hands of 13 cards.

3. Extend the program from the chapter that used a map to store names and telephone numbers such that you can enter a number to retrieve the name.

4. Implement a phone book so that just a surname can be used to search and have all the entries corresponding to the name display.

A Collection of Useful Classes

In this chapter we'll be looking at some more very useful classes in the java.util package but this time they are not collection classes – just a collection of classes. We will also be looking at the facilities provided by classes in the java.util.regex package that implements regular expressions in Java. Support for regular expressions is a very powerful and important addition to Java.

In this chapter you will learn:

❏   How to use the static methods in the Arrays class for filling, comparing, sorting, and searching arrays

❏   How to use the Observable class and the Observer interface to communicate between objects

❏   What facilities the Random class provides

❏   How to create and use Date and Calendar objects

❏   What regular expressions are and how you can create and use them

Utility Methods for Arrays

The Arrays class in java.util provides you with a set of static methods for operating on arrays. There are methods for sorting and searching arrays, as well as methods for comparing two arrays of elements of a basic type. You also have methods for filling arrays of elements with a given value. Let's look at the simplest method first, the fill() method for filling an array.

Filling an Array

The need to fill an array with a specific value arises quite often. The fill() method comes in a number of overloaded versions of the form:

```
fill(type [] array, type value)
```

Here type is a placeholder for the types supported by various versions of the method. The method stores value in each element of array. The return type is void so there is no return value. There are versions supporting type as any of the following:

boolean	byte	char	float	double
short	int	long	Object	

The version of `fill()` accepting an array argument of type `Object[]` will obviously process an array of any class type.

Here's how you could fill an array of integers with a particular value:

```
long[] values = new long[1000];
java.util.Arrays.fill(values, 888L);   // Every element as 888
```

It's a relatively common requirement to fill an array of type `char[]` with spaces. Here's how you might use the `fill()` method in a method to put a value in a fixed width field:

```
// Return a value right justified in a field
public static String fixedWidth(double value, int width) {
  String valStr = String.valueOf(value);
  assert width> valStr.length();

  char[] spaces = new char[width-valStr.length()];
  java.util.Arrays.fill(spaces, ' ');                    // Fill array with blanks

  return new StringBuffer().append(spaces).append(valStr).toString();
}
```

This converts the value passed as the first argument to a string and checks that the field width specified is greater than the length of this string. The assertion ensures that we don't attempt to create an array with a negative number of elements. We then create an array of type `char[]` that will provide the spaces to the left of the value string. We fill this using the `fill()` method from the `Arrays` class in the `java.util` package. We then assemble the field as a `StringBuffer` object by appending the array followed by the value string and convert the result to type `String` before returning it. Clearly you could easily create an overloaded version of this method to output values of any basic type in a fixed width field. You could even embellish it with an option for left or right justification in the field.

There is a further form of `fill()` method that accepts four arguments. This is of the form:

`fill(type[] array, int fromIndex, int toIndex, type value)`

This will fill part of `array` with `value`, starting at `array[fromIndex]` up to and including `array[toIndex-1]`. There are versions of this method for the same range of types at the previous set of `fill()` methods. This variety of `fill()` will throw an exception of type `IllegalArgumentException` if `fromIndex` is greater than `toIndex`. It will also throw an exception of type `ArrayIndexOutOfBoundsException` if `fromIndex` is negative or `toIndex` is greater than `array.length`.

We could have taken a different approach to the `fixedWidth()` method and used this version of `fill()` in the process:

```
public static String fixedWidth(long value, int width) {
  char[] valChars = String.valueOf(value).toCharArray();
  assert width> valChars.length;

  char[] field = new char[width];
  java.util.Arrays.fill(field, 0, width-valChars.length, ' ');  // Partial fill
  with spaces

  for(int i = 0 ; i<valChars.length ; i++)
    field[width-valChars.length+i] = valChars[i];          // Copy value characters

  return new String(field);
}
```

Here we assemble the whole field as a character array. We fill the elements of the `field` array that will not be occupied by characters for the value with spaces. We then copy the characters from the array `valChars` to the back of the field array. Finally we return a `String` object that we create from the field array.

Comparing Arrays

There are nine overloaded versions of the `equals()` method for comparing arrays, one for each of the types that apply to the `fill()` method. All versions of `equals()` are of the form:

equals(*type*[] array1, *type*[] array2)

The method returns `true` if `array1` is equal to `array2` and `false` otherwise. The two arrays are equal if they contain the same number of elements and the values of all corresponding elements in the two arrays are equal. If `array1` and `array2` are both `null`, they are also considered to be equal.

When floating point arrays are compared, `0.0` is considered to be equal to `-0.0`, and two elements that contain NaN are also considered to be equal. When arrays with elements of a class type are compared, the elements are compared by calling the `equals()` method for the class. If you have not implemented the `equals()` method in your own classes then the version inherited from the `Object` class will be used. This compares references, not objects, and so only returns `true` if both object references refer to the same object.

Here's how you can compare two arrays:

```
String[] numbers = {"one", "two", "three", "four" };
String[] values = {"one", "two", "three", "four" };
if(java.util.Arrays.equals(numbers, values))
  System.out.println("The arrays are equal");
else
  System.out.println("The arrays are not equal");
```

In this fragment both arrays are equal so the `equals()` method will return `true`.

Sorting Arrays

The static `sort()` method in the `Arrays` class will sort the elements of an array passed as an argument into ascending sequence. The method is overloaded for eight of the nine types (`boolean` is excluded) we saw for the `fill()` method for each of two versions of `sort()`:

```
sort(type[] array)
sort(type[] array, int fromIndex, int toIndex)
```

The first variety sorts the entire array into ascending sequence. The second variety sorts the elements from `array[fromIndex]` to `array[toIndex-1]` into ascending sequence. This will throw an exception of type `IllegalArgumentException` if `fromIndex` is greater than `toIndex`. It will also throw an exception of type `ArrayIndexOutOfBoundsException` if `fromIndex` is negative or `toIndex` is greater than `array.length`.

Obviously you can pass an array of elements of any class type to the versions of the `sort()` method that have the first parameter as type `Object[]`. If you are using either variety of the `sort()` method to sort objects then the class type of the objects must support the `Comparable` interface since the `sort()` method uses the `compareTo()` method to compare objects.

Here's how we can sort an array of strings:

```
String[] numbers = {"one", "two", "three", "four", "five",
                    "six", "seven", "eight"};
java.util.Arrays.sort(numbers);
```

After executing these statements the elements of the array `numbers` will contain:

```
"eight" "five" "four" "one" "seven" "six" "three" "two"
```

There are two further overloaded versions of `sort()` for sorting arrays of type `Object[]`. These are for sorting arrays where the order of elements is determined by using an external comparator object. The class type of the comparator object must implement the `Comparator` interface. One advantage of using an external comparator for sorting a set of objects is that you can have several comparators that can impose different orderings depending on the circumstances. For instance, in some cases you might want to sort a name file ordering by first name within second name. On other occasions you might want to sort by second name within first name. You can't do this using the `Comparable` interface implemented by the class. The `sort()` methods that make use of a comparator are:

```
sort(Object[] array, Comparator c)
sort(Object[] array, int fromIndex, int toIndex, Comparator c)
```

The `Comparator` interface declares two methods. The `equals()` method is used for comparing `Comparator` objects – the current `Comparator` object with another object of a type that also implements the `Comparator` interface. It returns a `boolean` value indicating whether the current object and the argument impose the same ordering on a set of objects. The `compare()` method in the `Comparator` interface is for comparing two objects identified by the two arguments of type `Object`. The method should return a negative integer, zero, or a positive integer when the first argument is less than, equal to, or greater than the second.

Searching Arrays

The `binarySearch()` method in the `Arrays` class will search the elements of a sorted array for a given value using the binary search algorithm. This only works if the elements of the array are in ascending sequence, so if they are not, you should call the `sort()` method to sort the array before calling the `binarySearch()` method. There are eight overloaded versions of the `binarySearch()` method of the form that we saw with the `fill()` method earlier. The `boolean` type is excluded from the nine types we saw, in this case as well.

```
binarySearch(type[] array, type value)
```

There is an additional version of the `binarySearch()` method for searching an array of type `Object[]` where you can supply a reference to a `Comparator` object as the fourth argument. All versions of the method return a value of type `int`, which is the index position in `array` where `value` was found. If the value is not in the array, a negative integer is returned that is produced by taking the value of the index position where the value would be if it was in the array, its sign reversing, and subtracting 1. For instance, suppose you have an array of integers containing the element values 2, 4, 6, 8, and 10:

```
int[] numbers = {2, 4, 6, 8, 10};
```

You could search for the value 7 with the statement:

```
int position = java.util.Arrays.binarySearch(numbers, 7);
```

The value of `position` will be -4, because if 7 was inserted in the array, it would be the fourth item in the array, or at index value 3 (remember that java arrays start at position zero). The return value is calculated as -3-1, which is -4. Thus if the value sought is not in the array then the return value is always negative.

Unless you are using a method that uses a comparator for searching arrays of objects, the class type of the array elements must implement the `Comparable` interface. Here's how we could search for a string in an array of strings:

```
String[] numbers ={"one", "two", "three", "four", "five", "six", "seven"};

java.util.Arrays.sort(numbers);
int position = java.util.Arrays.binarySearch(numbers, "three");
```

We have to sort the `numbers` array; otherwise the binary search won't work. After executing these statements the value of `position` will be 6.

Observable and Observer Objects

The class `Observable` provides you with an interesting mechanism for communicating a change in one class object to a number of other class objects. One use for this mechanism is in GUI programming where you often have one object representing all the data for the application – a text document, for instance, or a geometric model of a physical object– and several other objects that represent views of the data that are displayed in separate windows, where each shows a different representation or perhaps a subset of the data. This is referred to as the **document/view architecture** for an application, or sometimes the **model/view architecture**. This is a contraction of something referred to as the model/view/controller architecture and we will come back to this when we discuss creating Graphical User Interfaces (**GUI**). The document/view terminology is applied to any collection of application data – geometry, bitmaps, or whatever. It isn't restricted to what is normally understood by the term 'document'.

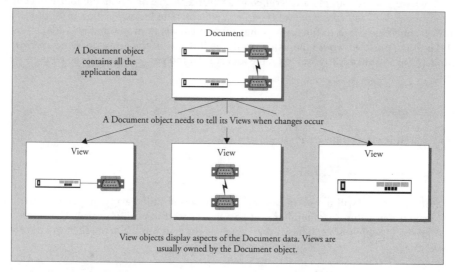

When the `Document` object changes, all the views need to be notified that a change has occurred, since they may well need to update what they display. The document is **observable** and all the views are **observers**. This is exactly what the `Observable` class is designed to achieve, when used in combination with an interface, `Observer`. A document can be considered to be an `Observable` object, and a view can be thought of as an `Observer` object. This enables the view to respond to changes in the document.

The document/view architecture portrays a many-to-many relationship. A document may have many observers, and a view may observe many documents.

Defining Classes of Observable Objects

You use the `Observable` class in the definition of a class of objects that may be observed. You simply derive the class for objects to be monitored, `Document` say, from the class `Observable`.

Any class that may need to be notified when a `Document` object has been changed must implement the interface `Observer`. This doesn't in itself cause the `Observer` objects to be notified when a change in an observed object occurs; it just establishes the potential for this to happen. You need to do something else to link the observers to the observable, which we'll come to in a moment.

The definition of the class for observed objects could be of the form:

```
public class Document extends Observable {
  // Details of the class definitions
}
```

The class `Document` here will inherit methods from the class `Observable` that operate the communications to the `Observer` objects.

A class for observers could be defined as:

```
public class View implements Observer {
  // Method for the interface
  public void update(Observable theObservableObject, Object arg) {
    // This method is called when the observed object changes
  }

  // Rest of the class definition...
}
```

To implement the `Observer` interface we need to define just one method, `update()`. This method is called automatically when an associated `Observable` object changes. The first argument that is passed to the `update()` method is a reference to the `Observable` object that changed and caused the method to be called. This enables the `View` object to access public methods in the associated `Observable` object, which would be used to access the data to be displayed, for example. The second argument passed to `update()` is used to convey additional information to the `Observer` object.

Observable Class Methods

The `Observable` class maintains an internal record of all the `Observer` objects related to the object to be observed. Your class, derived from `Observable`, will inherit the data members that deal with this. Your class of observable objects will also inherit nine methods from the class `Observable`. These are the following:

Method	Description
addObserver(Observer o)	Adds the object passed as an argument to the internal record of observers. Only `Observer` objects in the internal record will be notified when a change in the `Observable` object occurs.
deleteObserver (Observer o)	Deletes the object passed as an argument from the internal record of observers.
deleteObservers()	Deletes all observers from the internal record of observers.

Table continued on following page

Method	Description
`notifyObservers (Object arg)`	Calls the `update()` method for all of the `Observer` objects in the internal record if the current object has been set as changed. The current object is set as changed by calling the `setChanged()` method below. The current object and the argument passed to the `notifyObservers()` method will be passed to the `update()` method for each `Observer` object.
`notifyObservers()`	Calling this method is equivalent to the previous method with a `null` argument. (See `setChanged()` method below.)
`countObservers()`	The count of the number of `Observer` objects for the current object is returned as type `int`.
`setChanged()`	Sets the current object as changed. You must call this method before calling the `notifyObservers()` method. Note that this method is `protected`.
`hasChanged()`	Returns `true` if the object has been set as 'changed', and `false` otherwise.
`clearChanged()`	Resets the changed status of the current object to unchanged. Note that this method is also `protected`.

It's fairly easy to see how these methods are used to manage the relationship between an `Observable` object and its associated observers. To connect an observer to an `Observable` object, the `Observer` object must be registered with the `Observable` object by calling its `addObserver()` method. Once this is done the `Observer` will be notified automatically when changes to the `Observable` object occur. An observable object is responsible for adding `Observer` objects to its internal record through the `addObserver()` method. In practice, the `Observer` objects are typically created as objects that are dependent on the `Observable` object and then they are added to the record, so there's an implied ownership relationship.

This makes sense if you think about how the mechanism is often used in an application using the document/view architecture. A document has permanence since it represents the data for an application. A view is a transient presentation of some or all of the data in the document, so a `Document` object should naturally create and own its `View` objects. A view will be responsible for managing the interface to the application's user, but the update of the underlying data in the `Document` object would be carried out by methods in the `Document` object, which would then notify other `View` objects that a change has occurred.

Of course, you're in no way limited to using the `Observable` class and the `Observer` interface in the way in which we've described here. You can use them in any context where you want changes that occur in one class object to be communicated to others. We can exercise the process in a silly example.

Try It Out – Observing the Observable

We'll first define a class for an object that can exhibit change:

```java
import java.util.Observable;

public class JekyllAndHyde extends Observable {
  String name = "Dr. Jekyll";

  public void drinkPotion() {
    name = "Mr.Hyde";
    setChanged();
    notifyObservers();
  }

  public String getName() {
    return name;
  }
}
```

Now we can define the class of person who's looking out for this kind of thing:

```java
import java.util.Observer;
import java.util.Observable;

public class Person implements Observer {
  String name;              // Person's identity
  String says;              // What they say when startled

  // Constructor
  public Person(String name, String says) {
    this.name = name;
    this.says = says;
  }

  // Called when observing an object that changes
  public void update(Observable thing, Object o) {
    System.out.println("It's " + ((JekyllAndHyde)thing).getName() +
                       "\n" + name + ": " + says);
  }
}
```

We can gather a bunch of observers to watch Dr. Jekyll with the following class:

```java
// Try out observers
import java.util.Observer;

public class Horrific {
  public static void main(String[] args) {
    JekyllAndHyde man = new JekyllAndHyde();  // Create Dr. Jekyll

    Observer[] crowd =
    {
```

```
      new Person("Officer","What's all this then?"),
      new Person("Eileen Backwards", "Oh, no, it's horrible - those teeth!"),
      new Person("Phil McCavity", "I'm your local dentist - here's my card."),
      new Person("Slim Sagebrush", "What in tarnation's goin' on here?"),
      new Person("Freaky Weirdo", "Real cool, man. Where can I get that stuff?")
    };


    // Add the observers
    for(int i = 0; i < crowd.length; i++)
      man.addObserver(crowd[i]);

    man.drinkPotion();                    // Dr. Jekyll drinks up
  }
}
```

If you compile and run this, you should get the output:

```
It's Mr.Hyde
Freaky Weirdo: Real cool, man. Where can I get that stuff?
It's Mr.Hyde
Slim Sagebrush: What in tarnation's goin' on here?
It's Mr.Hyde
Phil McCavity: I'm your local dentist - here's my card.
It's Mr.Hyde
Eileen Backwards: Oh, no, it's horrible - those teeth!
It's Mr.Hyde
Officer: What's all this then?
```

How It Works

JekyllAndHyde is a very simple class with just two methods. The drinkPotion() method encourages Dr. Jekyll to do his stuff, and the getName() method enables anyone who is interested to find out who he is. The class extends the Observable class so we can add observers for an object of this class.

The revamped Person class implements the Observer interface, so an object of this class can observe an Observable object. When notified of a change in the object being observed, the update() method will be called. Here, it just outputs who the person is, and what they say.

In the Horrific class, after defining Dr. Jekyll in the variable man, we create an array, crowd, of type Observer to hold the observers – which are of type Person, of course. We can use an array of type Observer because the class Person implements the Observer interface. We pass two arguments to the Person class constructor: a name, and a string that is what the person will say when they see a change in Dr. Jekyll. We add each of the observers for the object man in the for loop.

Calling the drinkPotion() method for the object man results in the internal name being changed, the setChanged() method being called for the man object, and the notifyObservers() method that is inherited from the Observable class being called. This causes the update() method for each of the registered observers to be called, which generates the output. If you comment out the setChanged() call in the drinkPotion() method, and compile and run the program again, you'll get no output. Unless setChanged() is called, the observers aren't notified.

Now let's move on to look at the java.util.Random class.

Generating Random Numbers

We have already used the Random class a little, but let's investigate this in more detail. The class Random enables you to create multiple random number generators that are independent of one another. Each object of the class is a separate random number generator. Any Random object can generate pseudo-random numbers of types int, long, float, or double. These numbers are created using an algorithm that takes a 'seed' and 'grows' a sequence of numbers from it. Initializing the algorithm twice with the same seed would produce the same sequence because the algorithm is deterministic.

The integer values generated will be uniformly distributed over the complete range for the type, and the floating point values will be uniformly distributed over the range 0.0 to 1.0 for both types. You can also generate numbers of type double with a **Gaussian** (or normal) distribution that has a mean of 0.0 and a standard deviation of 1.0. This is the typical bell-shaped curve that represents the probability distribution for many random events.

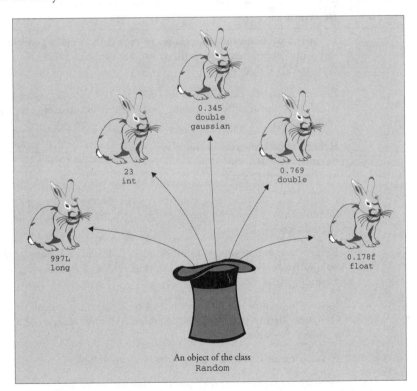

An object of the class
Random

There are two constructors for a Random object. The default constructor will create an object that uses the current time from your computer clock as the seed value for generating pseudo-random numbers. The other constructor accepts an argument of type long that will be used as the seed.

```
Random lottery = new Random();        // Sequence not repeatable
Random repeatable = new Random(997L);  // Repeatable sequence
```

If you use the default constructor, the sequence of numbers that is generated will be different each time a program is run, although beware of creating two generators in the same program with the default constructor. The time resolution used is one millisecond, so if you create two objects in successive statements they will usually generate the same sequence because the times used for the starting seed values will be identical. Random objects created using the same seed will always produce the same sequence, which can be very important when you are testing a program. Testing a program where the output is not repeatable can be a challenge! A major feature of random number generators created using a given seed in Java is that not only will they always produce the same sequence of pseudo-random numbers from a given seed, but they will also do so even on totally different computers.

Random Operations

The public methods provided by a Random object are:

Method	Description
nextInt()	Returns a pseudo-random number of type int. Values generated will be uniformly distributed across the complete range of values for a number of type int.
NextInt (int limit)	Returns a pseudo-random number of type int that is greater than or equal to 0, and less than limit – very useful for creating random array index values.
nextLong()	Returns a pseudo-random number of type long. Values generated will be uniformly distributed across the complete range of values for a number of type long.
nextFloat()	Returns a pseudo-random number of type float. Values generated will be uniformly distributed across the range 0.0f to 1.0, including 0.0f but excluding 1.0f.
nextDouble()	Returns a pseudo-random number of type double. Values generated will be uniformly distributed across the range 0.0 to 1.0, including 0.0 but excluding 1.0.
nextGaussian()	Returns a pseudo-random number of type double selected from a Gaussian distribution. Values generated will have a mean of 0.0 and a standard deviation of 1.0.
nextBoolean()	Returns true or false as pseudo-random values.
nextBytes (byte[] bytes)	Fills the array, bytes, with pseudo-random values.
setSeed (long seed)	Resets the random number generator to generate values using the value passed as an argument as a starting seed for the algorithm.

To produce a pseudo-random number of a particular type, you just call the appropriate method for a Random object. You can repeat the sequence of numbers generated by a Random object that you created with a seed value, by calling the setSeed() method with the same seed value as an argument.

We can give the Random class an outing with a simple program that simulates throwing a pair of dice. We'll assume you get six throws to try to get a double six.

Here's the program:

```
import java.util.Random;
import java.io.IOException;

public class Dice {
  public static void main(String[] args) {
    System.out.println("You have six throws of a pair of dice.\n" +
            "The objective is to get a double six. Here goes...\n");

    Random diceValues = new Random();       // Random number generator
    String[] theThrow = {"First ", "Second ", "Third ",
                    "Fourth ", "Fifth ", "Sixth "};
    int die1 = 0;                            // First die value
    int die2 = 0;                            // Second die value

    for(int i = 0; i < 6; i++)  {
      die1 = 1 + diceValues.nextInt(6);            // Number from 1 to 6
      die2 = 1 + diceValues.nextInt(6);            // Number from 1 to 6
      System.out.println(theThrow[i] + "throw: " + die1 + ", " + die2);

      if(die1 + die2 == 12) {                      // Is it double 6?
        System.out.println("    You win!!");       // Yes !!!
        return;
      }
    }
    System.out.println("Sorry, you lost...");
    return;
  }
}
```

If you compile this program you should get output that looks something like this:

```
You have six throws of a pair of dice.
The objective is to get a double six. Here goes...

First throw: 3, 2
Second throw: 1, 1
Third throw: 1, 2
Fourth throw: 5, 3
Fifth throw: 2, 2
Sixth throw: 6, 4
Sorry, you lost...
```

How It Works

We use one random number generator here that we create using the default constructor, so it will be seeded with the current time and will produce a different sequence of values each time the program is run. We simulate throwing the dice in the for loop. For each throw we need a random number between 1 and 6 for each die. The easiest way to produce this is to add one to the value returned by the nextInt() method when we pass 6 as the argument. If we wanted to make a meal of it we could obtain the same result by using the statement:

```
die1 = 1 + abs(diceValues.nextInt())%6;             // Number from 1 to 6
```

Remember that the pseudo-random integer values that we get from the nextInt() method will be uniformly distributed across the whole range of possible values for type int, positive and negative. That's why we need to use the abs() method from the Math class here to make sure we end up with a positive die value. The remainder after dividing the value resulting from abs(diceValues.nextInt()) by 6 will be between 0 and 5. Adding 1 to this produces the result we want.

> *Remember that the odds against a double six are 36:1, so you'll only succeed once on average out of every six times you run the example.*

Now we'll move on to look at dates and times.

Dates and Times

There are quite a few classes in the java.util package that are involved with dates and times, including the Date class, the Calendar class, and the GregorianCalendar class. In spite of the class name, a Date class object actually defines a particular instant in time to the nearest millisecond, measured from January 1, 1970, 00:00:00 GMT. Since it is relative to a particular instant in time, it also corresponds to a date. The Calendar class is the base class for GregorianCalendar, which represents the sort of day/month/year calendar everybody is used to, and also provides methods for obtaining day, month, and year information from a Date object. A Calendar object is always set to a particular date – a particular instant on a particular date to be precise– but you can change it by various means. From this standpoint a GregorianCalendar object is more like one of those desk calendars that just show one date, and you can flip over the days, months, or years to show another date.

There is also the TimeZone class that defines a time zone that can be used in conjunction with a calendar, and that you can use to specify the rules for clock changes due to daylight saving time. The ramifications of handling dates and times are immense so we will only be able to dabble here, but at least you will get the basic ideas. Let's take a look at Date objects first.

The Date Class

With the `Date` class you can create an object that represents a given date and time. You have two ways to do this using the following constructors:

Method	Description
`Date()`	Creates an object based on the current time from your computer clock to the nearest millisecond.
`Date(long time)`	Creates an object based on the time value in milliseconds since 00:00:00 GMT on January 1, 1970 that is passed as an argument.

With either constructor you create a `Date` object that represents a specific instant in time to the nearest millisecond. Carrying dates around as the number of milliseconds since the dawn of the year 1970 won't grab you as being incredibly user-friendly – but we'll come back to how we can interpret a `Date` object better in a moment. The `Date` class provides three methods for comparing `Date` objects:

Comparison Methods	Description
`after` `(Date earlier)`	Returns `true` if the current object represents a date that's later than the date represented by the argument `earlier`, and `false` otherwise.
`before` `(Date later)`	Returns `true` if the current object represents a date that's earlier than the date represented by the argument `later`, and `false` otherwise.
`equals` `(Object aDate)`	Returns `true` if the current object and the argument represent the same date and time, and `false` otherwise. This implies that they would both return the same value from `getTime()`.

The `equals()` method returns `true` if two different `Date` objects represent the same date and time. Since the `hashCode()` method is also implemented for the class, you have all you need to use `Date` objects as keys in a hash table.

Interpreting Date Objects

The `DateFormat` class is an abstract class that you can use to create meaningful `String` representations of `Date` objects. It isn't in the `java.util` package though – it's defined in the package `java.text`. There are four standard representations for the date and the time that are identified by constants defined in the `DateFormat` class. The effects of these will vary in different countries, because the representation for the date and the time will reflect the conventions of those countries. The constants in the `DateFormat` class defining the four formats are:

Date Format	Description
SHORT	A completely numeric representation for a date or a time, such as 2/2/97 or 4:15 am.
MEDIUM	A longer representation than SHORT, such as 5-Dec-97.
LONG	A longer representation than MEDIUM, such as December 5, 1997.
FULL	A comprehensive representation of the date or the time such as Friday, December 5, 1997 AD or 4:45:52 PST (Pacific Standard Time).

A Locale object identifies information that is specific to a country, a region, or a language. You can define a Locale object for a specific country, for a specific language, for a country and a language, or for a country and a language and a variant, the latter being a vendor or browser specific code such as WIN or MAC. When you are creating a Locale object you use ISO codes to specify the language and/or the country. The language codes are defined by ISO-639. Countries are specified by the country codes in the standard ISO-3166. You can find the country codes on the Internet at:

http://www.chemie.fu-berlin.de/diverse/doc/ISO_3166.html

or at:

http://www.din.de/gremien/nas/nabd/iso3166ma/codlstp1/en_listp1.html

You can find the language codes at:

http://www.ics.uci.edu/pub/ietf/http/related/iso639.txt

or at:

http://lcweb.loc.gov/standards/iso639-2/langhome.html

For some countries, the easiest way to specify the locale, if you don't have the ISO codes on the tip of your tongue, is to use the Locale objects defined within the Locale class. In Java 2 these are:

US	CANADA	CANADA_FRENCH	PRC
UK	GERMANY	FRANCE	ITALY
JAPAN	KOREA	CHINA	TAIWAN

Because the DateFormat class is abstract, you can't create objects of the class directly, but you can obtain DateFormat objects by using any of the following static methods, each of which returns a value of type DateFormat:

Static Method	Description
`getTimeInstance()`	Returns a time formatter for the default locale that uses the default style for the time.
`getTimeInstance (int timeStyle)`	Returns a time formatter for the default locale that uses the style for the time that is specified by the argument.
`getTimeInstance (int style, Locale aLocale)`	Returns a time formatter for the locale specified by the second argument that uses the style for the time that is specified by the first argument.
`getDateInstance()`	Returns a date formatter for the default locale that uses the default style for the date.
`getDateInstance (int dateStyle)`	Returns a date formatter for the default locale that uses the style for the date specified by the argument.
`getDateInstance (int dateStyle, Locale aLocale)`	Returns a date formatter for the locale specified by the second argument that uses the style for the date that is specified by the first argument.
`getInstance()`	Returns a default date and time formatter that uses the SHORT style for both the date and the time.
`getDateTimeInstance()`	Returns a date and time formatter for the default locale that uses the default style for both the date and the time.
`getDateTimeInstance (int dateStyle, int timeStyle)`	Returns a date and time formatter for the current locale that uses the styles for the date and the time specified by the arguments.
`getDateTimeInstance (int dateStyle, int timeStyle, Locale aLocale)`	Returns a date and time formatter for aLocale with the styles for the date and the time as specified by the first two arguments.

When you've obtained a `DateFormat` object for the country and the style that you want, and the sort of data you want to format – the date or the time or both – you're ready to produce a `String` from the `Date` object.

All you need to do is to pass the `Date` object to the `format()` method for the `DateFormat` object. For example:

```
Date today = new Date();    // Object for now - today's date
DateFormat fmt = getDateTimeInstance(Locale.FULL, Locale.US);
String formatted = fmt.format(today);
```

After executing these statements, the `String` variable, `formatted`, will contain a full representation of the date and the time when the `Date` object, `today`, was created.

We can try out some dates and formats in a simple example.

Try It Out – Producing Dates and Times

This example will show the four different date formats for four countries:

```
// Trying date formatting
import java.util.Locale;
import java.util.Date;
import java.text.DateFormat;

public class TryDateFormats {
  public static void main(String[] args) {
    Date today = new Date();
    Locale[] locales = {Locale.US, Locale.UK,
                        Locale.GERMANY, Locale.FRANCE};
    int[] styles = {DateFormat.FULL,DateFormat.LONG,
                    DateFormat.MEDIUM,DateFormat.SHORT};
    DateFormat fmt;
    String[] styleText = {"FULL", "LONG", "MEDIUM", "SHORT"};

    // Output the date for each locale in four styles
    for(int i = 0; i < locales.length; i++) {
      System.out.println("\nThe Date for " +
                         locales[i].getDisplayCountry() + ":");
      for(int j = 0; j < styles.length; j++) {
        fmt = DateFormat.getDateInstance(styles[j], locales[i]);
        System.out.println( "\tIn " + styleText[j] +
                            " is " + fmt.format(today));
      }
    }
  }
}
```

When I compiled and ran this it produced the following output:

```
The Date for United States:
        In FULL is Saturday, February 9, 2002
        In LONG is February 9, 2002
        In MEDIUM is Feb 9, 2002
        In SHORT is 2/9/02

The Date for United Kingdom:
        In FULL is 09 February 2002
        In LONG is 09 February 2002
        In MEDIUM is 09-Feb-2002
        In SHORT is 09/02/02

The Date for Germany:
        In FULL is Samstag, 9. Februar 2002
        In LONG is 9. Februar 2002
        In MEDIUM is 09.02.2002
        In SHORT is 09.02.02
```

```
The Date for France:
        In FULL is samedi 9 f vrier 2002
        In LONG is 9 f vrier 2002
        In MEDIUM is 9 f vr. 2002
        In SHORT is 09/02/02
```

How It Works

The program creates a `Date` object for the current date and time, and an array of `Locale` objects for four countries using values defined in the `Locale` class. It then creates an array of the four possible styles, and another array containing a `String` representation for each style that will be used in the output.

The output is produced in the nested `for` loops. The outer loop iterates over the countries, and the inner loop iterates over the four styles for each country. A `DateFormat` object is created for each combination of style and country, and the `format()` method for the `DateFormat` object is called to produce the formatted date string in the inner call to `println()`.

There are a couple of ways you could change the program. You could initialize the `locales []` array with the expression `DateFormat.getAvailableLocales()`. This will return an array of type `Locale` containing all of the supported locales, but be warned – there are a lot of them. You'll also find that the characters won't display for many countries because your machine doesn't support the country-specific character set. You could also use the method `getTimeInstance()` or `getDateTimeInstance()` instead of `getDateInstance()` to see what sort of output they generate.

Under the covers, a `DateFormat` object contains a `DateFormatSymbols` object that contains all the strings for the names of days of the week and other fixed information related to time and dates. This class is also in the `java.text` package. Normally you don't use the `DateFormatSymbols` class directly, but it can be useful when all you want are the days of the week.

Obtaining a Date Object from a String

The `parse()` method for a `DateFormat` object interprets a `String` object passed as an argument as a date and time, and returns a `Date` object corresponding to the date and the time. The `parse()` method will throw a `ParseException` if the `String` object can't be converted to a `Date` object, so you must call it within a `try` block.

The `String` argument to the `parse()` method must correspond to the country and style that you used when you obtained the `DateFormat` object. This makes it a bit tricky to use successfully. For example, the following code will parse the string properly:

```
Date aDate;
DateFormat fmt = DateFormat.getDateInstance(DateFormat.FULL, Locale.US);
try {
   aDate = fmt.parse("Saturday, July 4, 1998 ");
   System.out.println("The Date string is: " + fmt.format(aDate));

} catch(ParseException e) {
   System.out.println(e);
}
```

This works because the string is what would be produced by the locale and style. If you omit the day from the string, or you use the LONG style or a different locale, a `ParseException` will be thrown.

Gregorian Calendars

The Gregorian calendar is the calendar generally in use today in the western world, and is represented by an object of the GregorianCalendar class. A GregorianCalendar object encapsulates time zone information, as well as date and time data. There are no less than seven constructors for GregorianCalendar objects, from the default that creates a calendar with the current date and time in the default locale for your machine, through to a constructor where you can specify the year, month, day, hour, minute, and second. The default suits most situations.

You can create a calendar with a statement such as:

```
GregorianCalendar calendar = new GregorianCalendar();
```

This will be set to the current instant in time, and you can retrieve this as a Date object by calling the getTime() method for the calendar:

```
Date now = calendar.getTime();
```

You can create a GregorianCalendar object encapsulating a specific date and/or time with the following constructors:

```
GregorianCalendar(int year, int month, int day)
GregorianCalendar(int year, int month, int day, int hour, int minute)
GregorianCalendar(int year, int month, int day,
                  int hour, int minute, int second)
```

The day argument is the day within the month, so the value can be from 1 to 28, 29, 30, or 31, depending on the month and whether it's a leap year or not. The month value is zero-based so January is 0 and December is 11.

The GregorianCalendar class is derived from the abstract Calendar class from which it inherits a large number of methods and static constants for use with these methods. The constants includes month values with the names JANUARY to DECEMBER so you could create a calendar object with the statement:

```
GregorianCalendar calendar = new GregorianCalendar(1967, Calendar.MARCH, 10);
```

The time zone and locale will be the default for the computer on which this statement executes. If you want to specify a time zone there is a GregorianCalendar constructor that accepts an argument of type TimeZone. The TimeZone class is also defined in the java.util package. You can get the default TimeZone object by calling the static getDefault() method, but if you are going to the trouble of specifying a time zone, you probably want something other than the default. To create a particular time zone you need to know its ID. This is a string specifying a region or country plus a location. For instance, here are some examples of time zone IDs:

Europe/ Stockholm	Asia/Novosibirsk	Pacific/Guam	America/Chicago
Antarctica/ Palmer	Atlantic/ South_Georgia	Africa/Accra	Indian/Comoro

To obtain a reference to a `TimeZone` object corresponding to a given time zone ID, you pass the ID to the static `getTimeZone()` method. For instance, we could create a `Calendar` object for the Chicago time zone like this:

```
GregorianCalendar calendar =
        new GregorianCalendar(TimeZone.getTimeZone("America/Chicago"));
```

If you want to know what all the time zones IDs are, you could list them like this:

```
String[] ids = TimeZone.getAvailableIDs();
for(int i = 0 ; i<ids.length ; i++)
  System.out.println(ids[i]);
```

The calendar created from a `TimeZone` object will have the default locale. If you want to specify the locale explicitly, there's a constructor that accepts a `Locale` reference as the second argument. For example:

```
GregorianCalendar calendar =
        new GregorianCalendar(TimeZone.getTimeZone("America/Chicago"). Locale.US);
```

You can also create a `Calendar` object from a locale:

```
GregorianCalendar calendar =
        new GregorianCalendar(Locale.UK);
```

This will create a calendar set to the current time in the default time zone within the UK.

Setting the Date and Time

If you have a `Date` object available, there is a `setTime()` method that you can pass a `Date` object, to set a `GregorianCalendar` object to the time specified by the `Date` object:

```
calendar.setTime(date);
```

More typically you will want to set the date and/or time with explicit values such as day, month, and year, and there are several overloaded versions of the `set()` method for setting various components of the date and time. These are inherited in the `GregorianCalendar` class from its superclass, the `Calendar` class. You can set a `GregorianCalendar` object to a particular date like this:

```
GregorianCalendar calendar = new GregorianCalendar();
calendar.set(1995, 10, 29);  // Date set to 29th November 1999
```

The three arguments to the `set()` method here are the year, the month, and the day as type `int`. You need to take care with this method as it's easy to forget that the month is zero-based with January specified by 0. Note that the fields reflecting the time setting within the day will not be changed. They will remain at whatever they were. You can reset all fields for a `GregorianCalendar` object to zero by calling its `clear()` method, so calling `clear()` before you call `set()` here would ensure the time fields are all zero.

The other versions of the set() method are:

```
set(int year, int month, int day, int hour, int minute)
set(int year, int month, int day, int hour, int minute, int second)
set(int field, int value)
```

It's obvious what the first two of these do. In each case the fields not explicitly set will be left at their original values. The third version of set() sets a field specified by one of the integer constants defined in the Calendar class for this purpose:

Field	Value
AM_PM	Can have the values AM or PM, which correspond to values of 0 and 1.
DAY_OF_WEEK	Can have the values SUNDAY, MONDAY, etc., through to SATURDAY, which correspond to values of 1 to 7.
DAY_OF_YEAR	Can be set to a value from 1 to 366.
MONTH	Can be set to a value of JANUARY, FEBRUARY, etc., through to DECEMBER, corresponding to values of 0 to 11.
DAY_OF_MONTH or DATE	Can be set to a value from 1 to 31.
WEEK_OF_MONTH	Can be set to a value from 1 to 6.
WEEK_OF_YEAR	Can be set to a value from 1 to 54.
HOUR_OF_DAY	A value from 0 to 23.
HOUR	A value from 1 to 12 being the current hour in the am or pm.
MINUTE	The current minute in the current hour – a value from 0 to 59.
SECOND	The second in the current minute, 0 to 59.
MILLISECOND	The millisecond in the current second, 0 to 999.
YEAR	The current year, for example 1998.
ERA	Can be set to either GregorianCalendar.BC or GregorianCalendar.AD (both values being defined in the GregorianCalendar class).
ZONE_OFFSET	A millisecond value indicating the offset from GMT.
DST_OFFSET	A millisecond value indicating the offset for daylight saving in the current time zone.

With the exception of AD and BC as noted in the table, the constants for field values are also defined in the Calendar class. Thus you can set the day of the week with the statement:

```
calendar.set(Calendar.DAY_OF_WEEK, Calendar.TUESDAY);
```

Of course, since a variable of type `GregorianCalendar` also has all these constants you could use the variable name, `calendar`, instead of the class name as the qualifier for the name of the constants here.

Getting Date and Time Information

You can get information such as the day, the month, and the year from a `GregorianCalendar` object by using the `get()` method and specifying what you want as an argument. The possible arguments to the `get()` method are those defined in the table of constants above identifying calendar fields. All values returned are of type `int`. For example, you could get the day of the week with the statement:

```
int day = calendar.get(calendar.DAY_OF_WEEK);
```

You could now test this for a particular day using the constant defined in the class:

```
if(day == calendar.SATURDAY)
  // Go to game...
```

Since the values for `day` are integers, you could equally well use a `switch` statement:

```
switch(day) {
  case Calendar.MONDAY:
  // do the washing...
  break;
  case Calendar.MONDAY:
  // do something else...
  break;
  // etc...
}
```

Modifying Dates and Times

Of course, you might want to alter the current instant in the calendar, and for this you have the `add()` method. The first argument determines what units you are adding in, and you specify this argument using the same field designators as in the previous list. For example, you can add 14 to the year with the statement:

```
calendar.add(calendar.YEAR, 14);  // 14 years into the future
```

To go into the past, you just make the second argument negative:

```
calendar.add(calendar.MONTH, -6);  // Go back 6 months
```

You can increment or decrement a field of a calendar by 1 using the `roll()` method. This method modifies the field specified by the first argument by +1 or −1, depending on whether the second argument is `true` or `false`. For example, to decrement the current month in the object `calendar`, you would write:

```
calendar.roll(calendar.MONTH, false);   // Go back a month
```

The change can affect other fields. If the original month was January, rolling it back by one will make the date December of the previous year.

Of course, having modified a GregorianCalendar object, you can get the current instant back as a Date object using the getTime() method that we saw earlier. You can then use a DateFormat object to present this in a readable form.

Comparing Calendars

Checking the relationship between dates is a fairly fundamental requirement and you have three methods available for comparing Calendar objects:

Method	Description
before()	Returns true if the current object corresponds to a time before that of the Calendar object passed as an argument. Note that this implies a true return can occur if the date is the same but the time is different.
after()	Returns true if the current object corresponds to a time after that of the Calendar object passed as an argument.
equals()	Returns true if the current object corresponds to a time that is identical to that of the Calendar object passed as an argument.

These are very simple to use. To determine whether the object thisDate defines a time that precedes the time defined by the object today, you could write:

```
if(thisDate.before(today))
   // Do something
```

Alternatively you could write the same thing as:

```
if(today.after(thisDate))
   // Do something
```

It's time to look at how we can use calendars.

Try It Out – Using a Calendar

This example will deduce important information about when you were born. It uses the FormattedInput class to get input from the keyboard, so copy the class to the directory containing the source file for this example. Here's the code:

```
import java.util.GregorianCalendar;
import java.text.DateFormatSymbols;

class TryCalendar {
```

```
public static void main(String[] args) {
    FormattedInput in = new FormattedInput();

    // Get the date of birth from the keyboard
    System.out.println("Enter your birth date as dd mm yyyy: ");
    int day = in.readInt();
    int month = in.readInt();
    int year = in.readInt();

    // Create birth date calendar - month is 0 to 11
    GregorianCalendar birthdate = new GregorianCalendar(year, month-1,day);
    GregorianCalendar today = new GregorianCalendar();   // Today's date

    // Create this year's birthday
    GregorianCalendar birthday = new GregorianCalendar(
                            today.get(today.YEAR),
                            birthdate.get(birthdate.MONTH),
                            birthdate.get(birthdate.DATE));

    int age = today.get(today.YEAR) - birthdate.get(birthdate.YEAR);

    String[] weekdays = new DateFormatSymbols().getWeekdays(); // Get day names

    System.out.println("You were born on a " +
                    weekdays[birthdate.get(birthdate.DAY_OF_WEEK)]);
    System.out.println("This year you " +
                    (birthday.after(today)   ?"will be " : "are ") +
                    age + " years old.");
    System.out.println("This year your birthday "+
                    (today.before(birthday)? "will be": "was")+
                    " on a "+ weekdays[birthday.get(birthday.DAY_OF_WEEK)]);
    }
}
```

I got the output:

```
Enter your birth date as dd mm yyyy:
5 12 1964
You were born on a Saturday
This year you will be 34 years old.
This year your birthday will be on a Saturday
```

How It Works

We start by prompting for the day, month, and year for a date of birth to be entered through the keyboard as integers. We then create a `Calendar` object corresponding to this date. Note the adjustment of the month – the constructor expects January to be specified as `0`. We need a `Calendar` object for today's date so we use the default constructor for this. To compute the age this year, we just have to subtract the year of birth from this year, both of which we get from the `GregorianCalendar` objects.

To get at the strings for the days of the week, we create a `DateFormatSymbols` object and call its `getWeekdays()` method. This returns an array of eight `String` objects, the first of which is empty to make it easy to index using day numbers from 1 to 7. The second element in the array contains `"Sunday"`. You can also get the month names using the `getMonths()` method.

To display the day of the week for the date of birth we call the `get()` method for the `GregorianCalendar` object `birthdate`, and use the result to index the `weekdays[]` array. To determine the appropriate text in the next two output statements, we use the `after()` and `before()` methods for `Calendar` objects to compare today with the birthday date this year.

Regular Expressions

We have seen some elementary capability for searching strings when we discussed the `String` class back in Chapter 4. From Java 1.4, we have had much more sophisticated facilities for analyzing strings by searching for patterns known as **regular expressions**. Regular expressions are not unique to Java. Perl is perhaps better known for its support of regular expressions, many word processors, especially on Unix, and there are specific utilities for regular expressions too.

So what is a regular expression? A regular expression is simply a string that describes a pattern that is to be used to search for matches within some other string. It's not simply a passive sequence of characters to be matched, though. A regular expression is essentially a mini-program for a specialized kind of computer called a **state-machine**. This isn't a real machine but a piece of software specifically designed to interpret a regular expression and analyze a given string based on that.

The regular expression capability in Java is implemented through two classes in the `java.util.regex` package: the `Pattern` class that defines objects that encapsulate regular expressions, and the `Matcher` class that defines an object that encapsulates a state-machine that can search a particular string using a given `Pattern` object. The `java.util.regex` package also defines the `PatternSyntaxException` class that defines exception objects thrown when a syntax error is found when compiling a regular expression to create a `Pattern` object.

Using regular expressions in Java is basically very simple:

1. You create a `Pattern` object by passing a string containing a regular expression to the static `compile()` method in the `Pattern` class.

2. You then obtain a `Matcher` object, which can search a given string for the pattern, by calling the `matcher()` method for the `Pattern` object with the string that is to be searched as the argument.

3. You call the `find()` method (or some other methods as we shall see) for the `Matcher` object to search the string.

4. If the pattern is found, you query the matcher object to discover the whereabouts of the pattern in the string and other information relating to the match.

While this is a straightforward process that is easy to code, the hard work is in defining the pattern to achieve the result that you want. This is an extensive topic since in their full glory regular expressions are immensely powerful and can get very complicated. There are books devoted entirely to this so our aim will be to get enough of a bare bones understanding of how regular expressions work so you will be in a good position to look into the subject in more depth if you need to. Although regular expressions can look quite fearsome, don't be put off. They are always built step-by-step, so although the end result may look complicated and obscure, they are not at all difficult to put together. Regular expressions are a lot of fun and a sure way to impress your friends and maybe confound your enemies.

Defining Regular Expressions

You may not have heard of regular expressions before reading this book and therefore may think you have never used them. If so, you are almost certainly wrong. Whenever you search a directory for files of a particular type, "*.java" for instance, you are using a form of regular expression. However, to say that regular expressions can do much more than this is something of an understatement. To get an understanding of what we can do with regular expressions, we will start at the bottom with the simplest kind of operation and work our way up to some of the more complex problems they can solve.

Creating a Pattern

In its most elementary form, a regular expression just does a simple search for a substring. For example, if we want to search a string for the word *had*, the regular expression is exactly that. So the string defining this particular regular expression is "had". Let's use this as a vehicle for understanding the programming mechanism for using regular expressions. We can create a Pattern object for our expression "had" with the statement:

```
Pattern had = Pattern.compile("had");
```

The static compile() method in the Pattern class returns a reference to a Pattern object that contains the compiled regular expression. The method will throw an exception of type PatternSyntaxException if the regular expression passed as the argument is invalid. However, you don't have to catch this exception as it is a subclass of RuntimeException and therefore is unchecked. The compilation process stores the regular expression in a Pattern object in a form that is ready to be processed by a Matcher state-machine.

There's a further version of the compile() method that enables you to control more closely how the pattern will be applied when looking for a match. The second argument is a value of type int that specifies one or more of the following flags that are defined in the Pattern class:

CASE_INSENSITIVE	Matches ignoring case, but assumes only US-ASCII characters are being matched.
MULTILINE	Enables the beginning or end of lines to be matched anywhere. Without this flag only the beginning and end of the entire sequence will be matched.
UNICODE_CASE	When this is specified in addition to CASE_INSENSITIVE, case insensitive matching will be consistent with the Unicode standard.

DOTALL	Makes the expression . (which we will see shortly) match any character, including line terminators.
CANON_EQ	Matches taking account of canonical equivalence of combined characters. For instance, some characters that have diacritics may be represented as a single character or as a single character with a diacritic followed by a diacritic character. This flag will treat these as a match.
COMMENTS	Allows whitespace and comments in a pattern. Comments in a pattern start with # so from the first # to the end of the line will be ignored.
UNIX_LINES	Enables Unix lines mode where only '\n' is recognized as a line terminator.

All these flags are single bit values so you can combine them by ANDing them together or by simple addition. For instance, you can specify the CASE_INSENSITIVE and the UNICODE_CASE flags with the expression:

```
Pattern.CASE_INSENSITIVE & Pattern.UNICODE_CASE
```

Or you can write this as:

```
Pattern.CASE_INSENSITIVE + Pattern.UNICODE_CASE
```

If we wanted to match "had" ignoring case, we could create the pattern with the statement:

```
Pattern had = Pattern.compile("had", Pattern.CASE_INSENSITIVE);
```

In addition to the exception thrown by the first version of the compile() method, this version will throw an exception of type IllegalArgumentException if the second argument has bit values set that do not correspond to one of the flag constants defined in the Pattern class.

Creating a Matcher

Once we have a Pattern object, we can create a Matcher object that can search a particular string, like this:

```
String sentence = "Smith, where Jones had had 'had', had had 'had had'."
Matcher matchHad = had.matcher(sentence);
```

The first statement defines the string, sentence, that we want to search. To create the Matcher object, we call the matcher() method for the Pattern object with the string to be analyzed as the argument. This will return a Matcher object that can analyze the string that was passed to it. The parameter for the matcher() method is actually of type CharSequence. This is an interface that is implemented by both the String and StringBuffer classes so you can pass either type of reference to the method. The java.nio.CharBuffer class also implements CharSequence so you can pass the contents of a CharBuffer to the method too. This means that if you use a CharBuffer to hold character data you have read from a file, you can pass the data directly to the matcher() method to be searched.

An advantage of Java's implementation of regular expressions is that you can reuse a `Pattern` object to create `Matcher` objects to search for the pattern in a variety of strings. To use the same pattern to search another string, you just call the `matcher()` method for the `Pattern` object with the new string as the argument. You then have a new `Matcher` object that you can use to search the new string.

You can also change the string that a `Matcher` object is to search by calling its `reset()` method with a new string as the argument. For example:

```
matchHad.reset ("Had I known, I would not have eaten the haddock.");
```

This will replace the previous string, `sentence`, in the `Matcher` object so it is now capable of searching the new string. Like the `matcher()` method in the `Pattern` class, the parameter type for the `reset()` method is `CharSequence` so you can pass a reference of type `String`, `StringBuffer`, or `java.nio.CharBuffer` to it.

Searching a String

Now we have a `Matcher` object, we can use it to search the string. Calling the `find()` method for the `Matcher` object will search the string for the next occurrence of the pattern. If it is found, the method stores information about where it was found in the `Matcher` object and returns `true`. If it is not found it returns `false`. When the pattern has been found, calling the `start()` method for the `Matcher` object returns the index position in the string where the first character in the pattern was found. Calling the `end()` method returns the index position following the last character in the pattern. Both index values are returned as type `int`. You could therefore search for the first occurrence of the pattern like this:

```
if(m.find())
   System.out.println("Pattern found. Start: "+m.start()+" End: "+m.end());
else
   System.out.println("Pattern not found.");
```

Note that you must not call `start()` or `end()` for the `Matcher` object before you have succeeded in finding the pattern. Until a pattern has been matched, the `Matcher` object is in an undefined state and calling either of these methods will result in an exception of type `IllegalStateException` being thrown.

You will usually want to find all occurrences of a pattern in a string. When you call the `find()` method, searching starts at an index position in the string called the **append position** and stops either when the pattern is found and the value `true` is returned, or when the end of the string is reached, in which case the return value is `false`. The append position is initially zero, corresponding to the beginning of the string, but it gets updated if the pattern is found. Each time the pattern is found, the new append position will be the index position of the character immediately following the last character in the text that matched the pattern. The next call to `find()` will start searching at this new append position. Thus you can easily find all occurrences of the pattern by searching in a loop like this:

```
while(m.find())
   System.out.println(" Start: "+m.start()+" End: "+m.end());
```

At the end of this loop the append position will be at the index position of the character following the last occurrence of the pattern in the string. If you want to reset the append position back to zero, you just call an overloaded version of `reset()` for the `Matcher` object that has no arguments:

```
    m.reset();      //Reset this matcher
```

This resets the `Matcher` object to its original state before any search operations were carried out.

To make sure we understand the searching process, let's put it all together in an example.

Try It Out – Searching for a Substring

Here's a complete example to search a string for a pattern:

```
import java.util.regex.Matcher;
import java.util.regex.Pattern;
import java.util.Arrays;

class TryRegex {
  public static void main(String args[]) {
    //  A regex and a string in which to search are specified
    String regEx = "had";
    String str = "Smith , where Jones had had 'had', had had 'had had'.";

    // The matches in the output will be marked (fixed-width font required)
    char[]  marker = new char[str.length()];
    Arrays.fill(marker,' ');
    //   So we can later replace spaces with marker characters

    //   Obtain the required matcher
    Pattern pattern = Pattern.compile(regEx);
    Matcher m = pattern.matcher(str);

    // Find every match and mark it
    while( m.find() ){
      System.out.println("Pattern found at Start: "+m.start()+" End: "+m.end());
      Arrays.fill(marker,m.start(),m.end(),'^');
    }

    // Show the object string with matches marked under it
    System.out.println(str);
    System.out.println(new String(marker));
  }
}
```

This will produce the output:

```
Pattern found at Start: 19 End: 22
Pattern found at Start: 23 End: 26
Pattern found at Start: 28 End: 31
Pattern found at Start: 34 End: 37
Pattern found at Start: 38 End: 41
Pattern found at Start: 43 End: 46
Pattern found at Start: 47 End: 50
Smith, where Jones had had 'had', had had 'had had'.
                   ^^^ ^^^  ^^^   ^^^ ^^^  ^^^ ^^^
```

How It Works

We first define a string, regEx, containing the regular expression, and a string, str, that we will search. We also create an array of type char[] that we use to indicate where the pattern is found in the string. We fill the elements of this array with spaces initially using the static fill() method from the Arrays class that we discussed earlier. Later we will replace some of these spaces with '^' to indicate where the pattern has been found.

Once we have compiled the regular expression regEx into a Pattern object, pattern, we create a Matcher object, m, from pattern that applies to the string str. We then call the find() method for m in the while loop condition. This loop will continue as long as the find() method returns true. On each iteration we output the index values returned by the start() and end() methods that reflect the index position where the first character of the pattern was found and the index position following the last character. We also insert the '^' character in the marker array at the index positions where the pattern was found – again using the fill() method.

When the loop ends we have found all occurrences of the pattern in the string so we output the string str, with the contents of the marker array immediately below it on the next line. As long as we are using a fixed width font for output to the command line, the '^' characters will mark the positions where the pattern appears in the string.

We will reuse this example as we delve into further options for regular expressions by plugging in different definitions for regEx and the string that is searched, str. The output will be more economical if you delete or comment out the statement in the while loop that outputs the start and end index positions.

Matching an Entire String

There are occasions when you want to try to match a pattern against an entire string, in other words when you want to establish that the complete string that you are searching is a match for the pattern. Suppose you read an input value into your program as a string. This might be from the keyboard or possibly through a dialog box managing the data entry. You might want to be sure that the input string is an integer for example. If input should be of a particular form, you can use a regular expression to determine whether it is correct or not.

The matches() method for a Matcher object tries to match the entire input string with the pattern and returns true only if there is a match. We can illustrate how this works with the following code fragment:

```
String input = null;
// Read into input from some source...

Pattern yes = Pattern.compile("yes");
Matcher m = pattern.matcher(input);

if(m.matches())                              // Check if input matches "yes"
  System.out.println("Input is yes.");
else
  System.out.println("Input is not yes.");
```

Of course, this illustration is trivial, but later we will see how to define more sophisticated patterns that can check for a range of possible input forms.

Defining Sets of Characters

A regular expression can be made up of ordinary characters, which are upper and lower case letters and digits, plus sequences of meta-characters that have a special meaning. The pattern in the previous example was just the word "had", but what if we wanted to search a string for occurrences of "hid" or "hod" as well as "had", or even any three letter word beginning with 'h' and ending with 'd'?

You can deal with any of these possibilities with regular expressions. One option is to specify the middle character as a wildcard by using a period here, which is one example of a meta-character. This meta-character matches any character except end-of-line, so the regular expression "h.d", represents any sequence of three characters that start with 'h' and end with 'd'. Try changing the definitions of regEx and str in the previous example to:

```
String regEx = "h.d";
String str = "Ted and Ned Hodge hid their hod and huddled in the hedge.";
```

If you recompile and run the example again, the last two lines of output will be:

```
Ted and Ned Hodge hid their hod and huddled in the hedge.
                ^^^         ^^^       ^^^                ^^^
```

You can see that we didn't find "Hod" in Hodge because of the capital 'H' but we found all the other sequences beginning with 'h' and ending with 'd'.

Of course, the regular expression "h.d" would also have found "hzd" or "hNd" if they had been present, which is not what we want. We can limit the possibilities by replacing the period with just the collection of characters we are looking for between square brackets, like this:

```
String regEx = "h[aio]d";
```

The [aio] sequence of meta-characters defines what is called a **simple class** of characters consisting in this case of 'a', 'i', or 'o'. Here the term 'class' is used in the sense of a set of characters, not a class that defines a type. If you try this version of the regular expression in the previous example, the last two lines of output will be:

```
Ted and Ned Hodge hid their hod and huddled in the hedge.
                ^^^         ^^^
```

This now finds all sequences that begin with 'h' and end with 'd' and have a middle letter as 'a' or 'i' or 'o'.

There are a variety of ways in which you can define character classes in a regular expression. Here are some examples of the more useful forms:

`[aeiou]`	This is a simple class that any of the characters between the square brackets will match – in this example, any vowel. We used this form in the code fragment above to search for variations on "had".
`[^aeiou]`	This represents any character except those appearing to the right of the ^ character between the square brackets. Thus here we have specified any character that is not a vowel. Note this is any *character*, not any letter, so the expression "h[^aeiou]d" will look for "h!d" or "h9d" as well as "hxd" or "hWd". Of course, it will reject "had" or "hid" or any other form with a vowel as the middle letter.
`[a-e]`	This defines an inclusive range – any of the letters 'a' to 'e' in this case. You can also specify multiple ranges, for example: `[a-cs-zA-E]` This corresponds to any of the characters from 'a' to 'c', from 's' to 'z', or from 'A' to 'E'. If you want to specify that a position must contain a digit you could use `[0-9]`. To specify that a position can be a letter or a digit you could express it as `[a-zA-Z0-9]`.

Any of these can be used in combination with ordinary characters to form a regular expression. For example, suppose we wanted to search some text for any sequence beginning with 'b', 'c', or 'd', with 'a' as the middle letter, and ending with 'd' or 't'. The regular expression to do this could be defined as:

```
String regEx = "[b-d]a[dt]";
```

This will search for any occurrence of "bad", "cad", "dad", "bat", "cat", or "dat".

Logical Operators in Regular Expressions

You can use the `&&` operator to combine classes that define sets of characters. This is particularly useful when it is combined with the negation operator, ^, that appears in the second line of the table above. For instance, if you want to specify that any lower case consonant is acceptable, you could write it as:

```
"[b-df-hj-np-tv-z]"
```

However, it can much more conveniently be expressed as:

```
[a-z&&[^aeiou]]
```

This produces the intersection (in other words the characters common to both sets) of the set of characters 'a' through 'z' with the set that is not a lower case vowel. To put it another way, the lower case vowels are subtracted from the set 'a' through 'z' so we are left with just the consonants.

The | operator is a logical OR that you use to specify alternatives. A regular expression to find "hid", "had", or "hod" could be written as "hid|had|hod". You can try this in the previous example by changing the definition of regEx to:

```
          String regEx = "hid|had|hod";
```

Note that the | operation means either the whole expression to the left of the operator or the whole expression to the right, not just the characters on either side as alternatives.

You could also use the | operator to define an expression to find sequences beginning with an upper case or lower case 'h', followed by a vowel, and ending in 'd', like this:

```
    String regEx = "[h|H][aeiou]d";
```

With this as the regular expression in the example, the "Hod" in *Hodge* will be found as well as the other variations.

Predefined Character Sets

There are also a number of predefined character classes that provide you with a shorthand notation for commonly used sets of characters. Here are some that are particularly useful:

.	This represents any character, as we have already seen.
\d	This represents any digit and is therefore shorthand for [0-9].
\D	This represents any character that is not a digit. It is therefore equivalent to [^0-9].
\s	This represents any whitespace character.
\S	This represents any non-whitespace character and is therefore equivalent to [^\s].
\w	This represents a word character, which corresponds to an upper or lower case letter or a digit or an underscore. It is therefore equivalent to [a-zA-Z_0-9].
\W	This represents any character that is not a word character so it is equivalent to [^\w].

Note that when you are including any of the sequences that start with a backslash in a regular expression, you need to keep in mind that Java treats a backslash as the beginning of an escape sequence. You must therefore specify the backslash in the regular expression as \\. For instance, to find a sequence of three digits, the regular expression would be "\\d\\d\\d". This is peculiar to Java because of the significance of the backslash in Java strings, so it doesn't apply to other environments that support regular expressions, such as Perl.

Obviously you may well want to include a period, or any of the other meta-characters, as part of the character sequence you are looking for. To do this you can use an escape sequence starting with a backslash in the expression to define such characters. Since Java strings interpret a backslash as the start of a Java escape sequence, the backslash itself has to be represented as \\, the same as when using the predefined characters sets that begin with a backslash. Thus the regular expression to find the sequence "had." would be "had\\.".

Our earlier search with the expression "h.d" found embedded sequences such as "hud" in the word huddled. We could use the \s set that corresponds to any whitespace character to prevent this by defining regEx like this:

```
String regEx = "\\sh.d\\s";
```

This searches for a five-character sequence that starts and ends with any whitespace character. The output from the example will now be:

```
Ted and Ned Hodge hid their hod and huddled in the hedge.
                  ^^^^^        ^^^^^
```

You can see that the marker array shows the five-character sequences that were found. The embedded sequences are now no longer included, as they don't begin and end with a whitespace character.

To take another example, suppose we want to find *hedge* or *Hodge* as words in the sentence, bearing in mind that there's a period at the end. We could do this by defining the regular expression as:

```
String regEx = "\\s[h|H][e|o]dge[\\s|\\.]";
```

The first character is defined as any whitespace by \\s. The next character is defined as either 'h' or 'H' by [h|H]. This can be followed by either 'e' or 'o' specified by [e|o]. This is followed by plain text dge with either a whitespace character or a period at the end, specified by [\\s|\\.]. This doesn't cater for all possibilities. Sequences at the beginning of the string will not be found, for instance, nor will sequences followed by a comma. We'll see how to deal with these next.

Matching Boundaries

So far we have tried to find the occurrence of a pattern anywhere in a string. In many situations you will want to be more specific. You may want to look for a pattern that appears at the beginning of a line in a string but not anywhere else, or maybe just at the end of any line. As we saw in the previous example you may want to look for a word that is not embedded – you want to find the word "cat" but not the "cat" in "cattle" or in "Popacatapetl" for instance. The previous example worked for the string we were searching but would not produce the right result if the word we were looking for was followed by a comma or appeared at the end of the text. However, we have other options. There are a number of special sequences you can use in a regular expression when you want to match a particular boundary. For instance, these are especially useful:

^	Specifies the beginning of a line. For example, to find the word *Java* at the beginning of any line you could use the expression "^Java".
$	Specifies the end of a line. For example, to find the word *Java* at the end of any line you could use the expression "Java$". Of course, if you were expecting a period at the end of a line the expression would be "Java\\.$".
\b	Specifies a word boundary. To find words beginning with 'h' and ending with 'd' we could use the expression "\\bh.d\\b".
\B	A non-word boundary – the complement of \b above.

\A	Specifies the beginning of the string being searched. To find the word *The* at the very beginning of the string being searched you could use the expression "\\AThe\\b". The \\b at the end of the regular expression is necessary to avoid finding *Then* or *There* at the beginning of the input.
\z	Specifies the end of the string being searched. To find the word *hedge* followed by a period at the end of a string you could use the expression "\\bhedge\\.\\z".
\Z	The end of input except for the final terminator. A final terminator will be a newline character ('\n') if Pattern.UNIX_LINES is set. Otherwise it can also be a carriage return ('\r'), a carriage return followed by a newline, a next-line character ('\u0085'), a line separator ('\u2028'), or a paragraph separator ('\u2029').

While we have moved quite a way from the simple search for a fixed substring offered by the String class methods, we still can't search for sequences that may vary in length. If you wanted to find all the numerical values in a string, which might be sequences such as 1234 or 23.45 or 999.998 for instance, we don't yet have the ability to do that. Let's fix that now by taking a look at **quantifiers** in a regular expression, and what they can do for us.

Using Quantifiers

A quantifier following a subsequence of a pattern determines the possibilities for how that subsequence of a pattern can repeat. Let's take an example. Suppose we want to find any numerical values in a string. If we take the simplest case we can say an integer is an arbitrary sequence of one or more digits. The quantifier for one or more is the meta-character +. We have also seen that we can use \d as shorthand for any digit (remembering of course that it becomes \\d in a Java STRING literal), so we could express any sequence of digits as the regular expression:

    "\\d+"

Of course, a number may also include a decimal point and may be optionally followed by further digits. To indicate something can occur just once or not at all, as is the case with a decimal point, we can use the quantifier ?. We can write the pattern for a sequence of digits followed by a decimal point as:

    "\\d+\\.?"

To add the possibility of further digits we can append \\d+ to what we have so far to produce the expression:

    "\\d+\\.?\\d+"

This is a bit untidy. We can rewrite this as an integral part followed by an optional fractional part by putting parentheses around the bit for the fractional part and adding the ? operator:

    "\\d+(\\.\\d+)?"

However, this isn't quite right. We can have 2. as a valid numerical value | for instance so we want to specify zero or more appearances of digits in the fractional part. The * quantifier expresses that, so maybe we should use:

    "\\d+(\\.\\d*)?"

We are still missing something though. What about the value .25 or the value -3? The optional sign in front of a number is easy so let's deal with that first. To express the possibility that – or + can appear we can use [– | +], and since this either appears or it doesn't, we can extend it to [+ | –] ?. So to add the possibility of a sign we can write the expression as:

```
"[+|-]?\\d+(\\.\\d*)?"
```

We have to be careful how we allow for numbers beginning with a decimal point. We can't allow a sign followed by a decimal point or just a decimal point by itself to be interpreted as a number so we can't say a number starts with zero or more digits or that the leading digits are optional. We could define a separate expression for numbers without leading digits like this:

```
"[+|-]?\\.\\d+"
```

Here there is an optional sign followed by a decimal point and at least one digit. With the other expression there is also an optional sign so we can combine these into a single expression to recognize either form, like this:

```
"[+|-]?(\\d+(\\.\\d*)?)|(\\.\\d+)"
```

This regular expression identifies substrings with an optional plus or minus sign followed by either a substring defined by "\\d+(\\.\\d*)?" or a substring defined by "\\.\\d+". You might be tempted to use square brackets instead of parentheses here, but this would be quite wrong as square brackets define a set of characters, so any single character from the set is a match.

That was probably a bit more work than you anticipated but it's often the case that things that look simple at first sight can turn out to be a little tricky. Let's try that out in an example.

Try It Out – Finding Integers

This is similar to the code we have used in previous examples except that here we will just list each substring that is found to correspond to the pattern:

```java
import java.util.regex.Pattern;
import java.util.regex.Matcher;

public class FindingIntegers {
  public static void main(String args[]) {
    String regEx = "[+|-]?(\\d+(\\.\\d*)?)|(\\.\\d+)";
    String str = "256 is the square of 16 and -2.5 squared is 6.25 " +
                                   "and -.243 is less than 0.1234.";

    Pattern pattern = Pattern.compile(regEx);
    Matcher m = pattern.matcher(str);
    int i = 0;
    String subStr = null;
    while(m.find())
      System.out.println(m.group());            // Output the substring matched

  }
}
```

This will produce the output:

```
256
16
-2.5
6.25
.243
0.1234
```

How It Works

Well, we found all the numbers in the string so our regular expression works well, doesn't it? You can't do that with the methods in the `String` class. The only new code item here is the method, `group()`, that we call in the `while` loop for the `Matcher` object, m. This method returns a reference to a `String` object containing the subsequence corresponding to the last match of the entire pattern. Calling the `group()` method for the `Matcher` object, m, is equivalent to the expression `str.substring(m.start(), m.end())`.

Search and Replace Operations

You can implement a search and replace operation very easily using regular expressions. Whenever you call the `find()` method for a `Matcher` object, you can call the `appendReplacement()` method to replace the subsequence that was matched. You create a revised version of the original string in a new String Buffer object. There are two arguments to the `appendReplacement()` method. The first is a reference to the `StringBuffer` object that is to contain the new string, and the second is the replacement string for the matched text. We can see how this works by considering a specific example.

Suppose we define a string to be searched as:

```
String joke = "My dog hasn't got any nose.\n"
            +"How does your dog smell then?\n"
            +"My dog smells horrible.\n";
```

We now want to replace each occurrence of "dog" in the string by "goat". We first need a regular expression to find "dog":

```
String regEx = "dog";
```

We can compile this into a pattern and create a `Matcher` object for the string joke:

```
Pattern doggone = Pattern.compile(regEx);
Matcher m = doggone.matcher(joke);
```

We are going to assemble a new version of joke in a `StringBuffer` object that we can create like this:

```
StringBuffer newJoke = new StringBuffer();
```

This is an empty `StringBuffer` object ready to receive the revised text. We can now search for and replace instances of "dog" in `joke` by calling the `find()` method for `m`, and calling `appendReplacement()` each time it returns `true`:

```
while(m.find())
  m.appendReplacement(newJoke, "goat");
```

Each call of `appendReplacement()` copies characters from `joke` to `newJoke` starting at the character where the previous `find()` operation started and ending at the character preceding the first character matched: at `m.start()-1` in other words. The method will then append the string specified by the second argument to `newJoke`. This process is illustrated below.

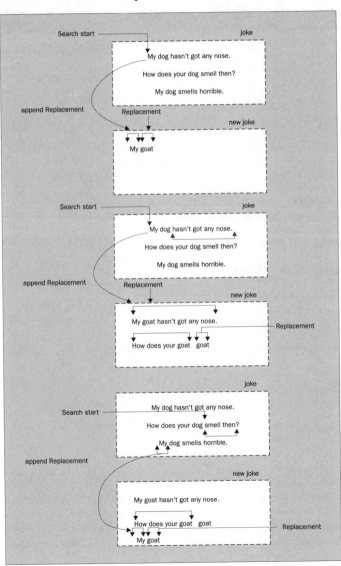

The find() method will return true three times, once for each occurrence of "dog" in joke. When the three steps shown in the diagram have been completed, the find() method returns false on the next loop iteration, terminating the loop. This leaves newJoke in the state shown in the last box above. All we now need to complete newJoke is a way to copy the text from joke that comes after the last subsequence that was found. The appendTail() method for the Matcher object does that:

```
m.appendTail(newJoke);
```

This will copy the text starting with the m.end() index position from the last successful match through to the end of the string. Thus this statement copies the segment " smells horrible." from joke to newJoke. We can put all that together and run it.

Try It Out – Search and Replace

Here's the code we have just discussed assembled into a complete program:

```
import java.util.regex.Pattern;
import java.util.regex.Matcher;

class SearchAndReplace {
  public static void main(String args[]) {
    String joke = "My dog hasn't got any nose.\n"
                 +"How does your dog smell then?\n"
                 +"My dog smells horrible.\n";
    String regEx = "dog";

    Pattern doggone = Pattern.compile(regEx);
    Matcher m = doggone.matcher(joke);

    StringBuffer newJoke = new StringBuffer();
    while(m.find())
      m.appendReplacement(newJoke, "goat");
    m.appendTail(newJoke);
    System.out.println(newJoke.toString());
  }
}
```

When you compile and execute this you should get the output:

```
My goat hasn't got any nose.
How does your goat smell then?
My goat smells horrible.
```

How It Works

Each time the find() method returns true in the while loop condition, we call the appendReplacement() method for the Matcher object, m. This copies characters from joke to newJoke, starting with the index position where the find() method started searching, and ending at the character preceding the first character in the match, which will be at m.start()-1. The method then appends the replacement string, "goat", to the contents of newJoke. Once the loop finishes, the appendTail() method copies characters from joke to newJoke, starting with the character following the last match at m.end(), through to the end of joke. Thus we end up with a new string similar to the original, but which has each instance of "dog" replaced by "goat".

The search and replace capability can be used to solve very simple problems. For example, if you want to make sure that any sequence of one or more whitespace characters is replaced by a single space, you can define the regular expression as `"\\s +"` and the replacement string as a single space `" "`. To eliminate all spaces at the beginning of each line, you can use the expression `"^\\s+"` and define the replacement string as empty, `""`.

Using Capturing Groups

Earlier we used the `group()` method for a `Matcher` object to retrieve the subsequence matched by the entire pattern defined by the regular expression. The entire pattern represents what is called a **capturing group** because the `Matcher` object captures the subsequence corresponding to the pattern match. Regular expressions can also define other capturing groups that correspond to parts of the pattern. Each pair of parentheses in a regular expression defines a separate capturing group in addition to the group that the whole expression defines. In the earlier example, we defined the regular expression by the statement:

```
String regEx = "[+|-]?(\\d+(\\.\\d*)?)|(\\.\\d+)";
```

This defines three capturing groups other than the whole expression: one for the subexpression `(\\d+(\\.\\d*)?)`, one for the subexpression `(\\.\\d*)`, and one for the subexpression `(\\.\\d+)`. The `Matcher` object stores the subsequence that matches the pattern defined by each capturing group, and what's more, you can retrieve them.

To retrieve the text matching a particular capturing group, you need a way to identify the capturing group that you are interested in. To this end, capturing groups are numbered. The capturing group for the whole regular expression is always number 0. Counting their opening parentheses from the left in the regular expression numbers the other groups. Thus the first opening parenthesis from the left corresponds to capturing group 1, the second opening parenthesis corresponds to capturing group 2, and so on for as many opening parentheses as there are in the whole expression. The diagram below illustrates how the groups are numbered in an arbitrary regular expression.

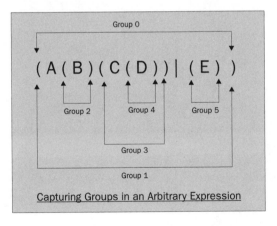

Capturing Groups in an Arbitrary Expression

As you see, it is easy to number the capturing groups as long as you can count left parentheses. Group 1 is the same as Group 0 because the whole regular expression is parenthesized. The other capturing groups in sequence are defined by `(B)`, `(C(D))`, `(D)`, and `(E)`.

To retrieve the text matching a particular capturing group after the `find()` method returns `true`, you call the `group()` method for the `Matcher` object with the group number as the argument. The `groupCount()` method for the `Matcher` object returns a value of type `int` that is the number of capturing groups within the pattern – that is, excluding group 0, which corresponds to the whole pattern. You therefore have all you need to access the text corresponding to any or all of the capturing groups in a regular expression.

Try It Out – Capturing Groups

Let's modify our earlier example to output the text matching each group:

```
import java.util.regex.Pattern;
import java.util.regex.Matcher;

public class TryCapturingGroups {
  public static void main(String args[]) {
    String regEx = "[+|-]?(\\d+(\\.\\d*)?)|(\\.\\d+)";
    String str = "256 is the square of 16 and -2.5 squared is 6.25 " +
                                      "and -.243 is less than 0.1234.";
    Pattern pattern = Pattern.compile(regEx);
    Matcher m = pattern.matcher(str);
    while(m.find())
      for(int i = 0; i<=m.groupCount() ; i++)
        System.out.println("Group " + i + ": " + m.group(i)); // Group i substring
  }
}
```

This produces the output:

```
Group 0: 256
Group 1: 256
Group 2: null
Group 3: null
Group 0: 16
Group 1: 16
Group 2: null
Group 3: null
Group 0: -2.5
Group 1: 2.5
Group 2: .5
Group 3: null
Group 0: 6.25
Group 1: 6.25
Group 2: .25
Group 3: null
Group 0: .243
Group 1: null
Group 2: null
Group 3: .243
Group 0: 0.1234
Group 1: 0.1234
Group 2: .1234
Group 3: null
```

How It Works

The regular expression here defines four capturing groups:

- ❏   Group 0: The whole expression.
- ❏   Group 1: The subexpression `(\\d+(\\.\\d*)?)`
- ❏   Group 2: The subexpression `(\\.\\d*)`
- ❏   Group 3: The subexpression `(\\.\\d+)`

After each successful call of the `find()` method for the `Matcher` object, m, we output the text captured by each group in turn by passing the index value for the group to the `group()` method. Note that because we want to output group 0 as well as the other groups, we start the loop index from 0 and allow it to equal the value returned by `groupCount()` so as to index over all the groups.

You can see from the output that group 1 corresponds to numbers beginning with a digit and group 3 corresponds to numbers starting with a decimal point, so either one or the other of these is always null. Group 2 corresponds to the sub-pattern within group 1 that matches the fractional part of a number that begins with a digit, so the text for this can only be non-null when the text for group 1 is non-null and the number has a decimal point.

Juggling Captured Text

Since we can get access to the text corresponding to each capturing group in a regular expression, we can move them around. The `appendReplacement()` method has special provision for recognizing references to capturing groups in the replacement text string. If $n, where n is an integer, appears in the replacement string, it will be interpreted as the text corresponding to group n. You can therefore replace the text matched to a complete pattern by any sequence of your choosing of the sub sequences corresponding to the capturing groups in the pattern. That's hard to describe in words, so let's demonstrate it with an example.

Try It Out – Rearranging Captured Group Text

I'm sure you remember that the `Math.pow()` method requires two arguments; the second argument is the power to which the first argument must be raised. Thus to calculate 16^3 you can write:

```
double result = Math.pow(16.0, 3.0);
```

Let's suppose we have written a Java program where we have mistakenly switched the two arguments so in trying to compute 16^3 we have written:

```
double result = Math.pow(3.0, 16.0);
```

Of course, this computes 3^{16}, which is not quite the same thing. Let's suppose further that this sort of error is strewn throughout the source code and in every case we have the arguments the wrong way round. We would need a month of Sundays to go through manually and switch the argument values so let's see if regular expressions can rescue the situation.

What we need to do is find each occurrence of `Math.pow()` and switch the arguments around. The intention here is to understand how we can switch things around so we will keep it simple and assume that the argument values to `Math.pow()` are always a numerical value or a variable name.

The key to the whole problem is to devise a regular expression with capturing groups for the bits we want to switch – the two arguments. Be warned – this is going to get a little messy; not difficult though – just messy.

We can define the first part of the regular expression that will find the sequence "Math.pow(". at any point where we want to allow an arbitrary number of whitespace characters we can use the sequence \\s*. You will recall that \\s in a Java string specifies the predefined character class \s which is whitespace. The * quantifier specifies zero or more of them. If we allow for whitespace between Math.pow and the opening parenthesis for the arguments, and some more whitespace after the opening parenthesis, the regular expression will be:

`"(Math.pow)\\s*\\(\\s*"`

We have to specify the opening parenthesis by `"\\("` since an opening parenthesis is a meta-character so we have to escape it.

This is followed by the first argument, which we said could be a number or a variable name. We created the expression to identify a number earlier. It was:

`"[+|-]?(\\d+(\\.\\d*)?)|(\\.\\d+)"`

To keep things simple we will assume that a variable name is just any sequence of letters, digits, or underscores that begins with a letter or an underscore, so we won't get involved with qualified names. We can match a variable name with the expression:

`"[a-zA-Z_]\\w*"`

We can therefore match either a variable name or a number with the pattern:

`"(([a-zA-Z_]\\w*)|([+|-]?(\\d+(\\.\\d*)?)|(\\.\\d+)))"`

This just ORs the two possibilities together and parenthesizes the whole thing so it will be a capturing group.

A comma that may be surrounded by zero or more whitespace characters on either side follows the first argument. We can match that with the pattern:

`\\s*,\\s*`

The pattern to match the second argument will be exactly the same as the first:

`"(([a-zA-Z_]\\w*)|([+|-]?(\\d+(\\.\\d*)?)|(\\.\\d+)))"`

Finally this must be followed by a closing parenthesis that may or may not be preceded by whitespace:

`\\s*\\)`

We can put all this together to define the entire regular expression as a `String` variable:

```
String regEx = "(Math.pow)"                                         // Math.pow
    + "\\s*\\(\\s*"                                                  // Opening (
    + "(([a-zA-Z_]\\w*)|([+|-]?(\\d+(\\.\\d*)?)|(\\.\\d+)))"         // First argument
    + "\\s*,\\s*"                                                    // Comma
    + "(([a-zA-Z_]\\w*)|([+|-]?(\\d+(\\.\\d*)?)|(\\.\\d+)))"         // Second argument
    + "\\s*\\)";                                                     // Closing (
```

Here we assemble the string literal for the regular expression by concatenating six separate string literals. Each of these corresponds to an easily identified part of the method call. If you count the left parentheses, excluding the escaped parenthesis of course, you can also see that capturing group 1 corresponds with the method name, group 2 is the first method argument, and group 8 is the second method argument.

We can put this in the example:

```java
import java.util.regex.Pattern;
import java.util.regex.Matcher;

public class TryCapturingGroups {
  public static void main(String args[]) {
    String regEx = "(Math.pow)"                                          // Math.pow
    + "\\s*\\(\\s*"                                                      // Opening (
    + "(([a-zA-Z_]\\w*)|([+|-]?(\\d+(\\.\\d*)?)|(\\.\\d+)))"             // First argument
    + "\\s*,\\s*"                                                        // Comma
    + "(([a-zA-Z_]\\w*)|([+|-]?(\\d+(\\.\\d*)?)|(\\.\\d+)))"             // Second argument
    + "\\s*\\)";                                                         // Closing (

    String oldCode =
        "double result = Math.pow( 3.0, 16.0);\n"
     + "double resultSquared = Math.pow(2 ,result );\n"
     + "double hypotenuse = Math.sqrt(Math.pow(2.0, 30.0)+Math.pow(2 , 40.0));\n";
    Pattern pattern = Pattern.compile(regEx);
    Matcher m = pattern.matcher(oldCode);

    StringBuffer newCode = new StringBuffer();
    while(m.find())
      m.appendReplacement(newCode, "$1\\($8,$2\\)");

    m.appendTail(newCode);

    System.out.println("Original Code:\n"+oldCode.toString());
    System.out.println("New Code:\n"+newCode.toString());
  }
}
```

You should get the output:

```
Original Code:
double result = Math.pow( 3.0, 16.0);
double resultSquared = Math.pow(2 ,result );
double hypotenuse = Math.sqrt(Math.pow(2.0, 30.0)+Math.pow(2 , 40.0));

New Code:
double result = Math.pow(16.0,3.0);
double resultSquared = Math.pow(result,2);
double hypotenuse = Math.sqrt(Math.pow(30.0,2.0)+Math.pow(40.0,2));
```

How It Works

We have defined the regular expression so that separate capturing groups identify the method name and both arguments. As we saw earlier, the method name corresponds to group 1, the first argument to group 2, and the second argument to group 8. We therefore define the replacement string to the `appendReplacement()` method as `"$1\\($8,$2\\)"`. The effect of this is to replace the text for each method call that is matched by the following, in sequence:

`$1`	The text matching capturing group 1, which will be the method name.
`\\(`	A left parenthesis.
`$8`	The text matching capturing group 8, which will be the second argument.
`,`	A comma.
`$2`	The text matching capturing group 2, which will be the first argument.
`\\)`	A right parenthesis.

The call to `appendTail()` is necessary to ensure that any text left at the end of `oldCode` following the last match for `regEx` gets copied to `newCode`.

In the process we have eliminated any superfluous whitespace that was laying around in the original text.

Summary

Regular expressions are a very powerful capability that we only touched on in this chapter.

The important elements we've covered are:

❑ The `java.util.Arrays` class provides static methods for sorting, searching, filling, and comparing arrays.

❑ Objects of type `Random` can generate pseudo-random numbers of type `int`, `long`, `float`, and `double`. The integers are uniformly distributed across the range of the type `int` or `long`. The floating point numbers are between 0.0 and 1.0. You can also generate numbers of type `double` with a Gaussian distribution with a mean of 0.0 and a standard deviation of 1.0, and random `boolean` values.

❑ Classes derived from the `Observable` class can signal changes to classes that implement the `Observer` interface. You define the `Observer` objects that are to be associated with an `Observable` class object by calling the `addObserver()` method. This is primarily intended to be used to implement the document/view architecture for applications in a GUI environment.

❑ You can create `Date` objects to represent a date and time that you specify in milliseconds since January 1, 1970, 00:00:00 GMT, or the current date and time from your computer clock.

❑ You can use a `DateFormat` object to format the date and time for a `Date` object as a string. The format will be determined by the style and the locale that you specify.

❏   A `GregorianCalendar` object represents a calendar set to an instant in time on a given date.

❏   A regular expression defines a pattern that is used for searching text.

❏   In Java a regular expression is compiled into a `Pattern` object that you can then use to obtain a `Matcher` object that will scan a given string looking for the pattern.

❏   The `appendReplacement()` method for a `Matcher` object enables you to make substitutions for patterns found in the input text.

❏   A capturing group in a regular expression records the text that matches a sub-pattern.

❏   By using capturing groups you can rearrange the sequence of substrings in a string matching a pattern.

Exercises

1. Define a static method to fill an array of type `char[]` with a given value passed as an argument to the method.

2. For the adventurous gambler – use a stack and a `Random` object in a program to simulate a game of Blackjack for one player using two decks of cards.

3. Write a program to display the sign of the Zodiac corresponding to a birth date entered through the keyboard.

4. Write a program using regular expressions to remove spaces from the beginning and end of each line in a file.

5. Write a program using a regular expression to reproduce a file with a sequential line number starting at "0001" inserted at the beginning of each line in the original file. You can use a copy of your Java source file as the input to test this.

6. Write a program using a regular expression to eliminate any line numbers that appear at the beginning of lines in a file. You can use the output from the previous exercise as a test for your program.

Threads

In this chapter we'll investigate the facilities Java has to enable you to overlap the execution of segments of a single program. As well as ensuring your programs run more efficiently, this capability is particularly useful when your program must, of necessity, do a number of things at the same time: for example, a server program on a network that needs to communicate with multiple clients.

In this chapter you will learn:

- ❏ What a thread is and how you can create threads in your programs.
- ❏ How to control interactions between threads.
- ❏ What synchronization means and how to apply it in your code.
- ❏ What deadlocks are, and how to avoid them.
- ❏ How to set thread priorities.
- ❏ How to get information about the threads in your programs.

Understanding Threads

Many programs, of any size, contain some code segments that are more or less independent of one another, and that may execute more efficiently if the code segments could be overlapped in time. Threads provide a way to do this. Of course, if like most people your computer only has one processor, you can't execute more than one computation at any instant, but you can overlap input/output operations with processing.

Another reason for using threads is to allow processes in a program that need to run continuously, such as a continuously running animation, to be overlapped with other activities in the same program. Java applets in a web page are executed under the control of your browser, and threads make it possible for multiple applets to be executing concurrently. In this case the threads serve to segment the activities running under the control of the browser so that they appear to run concurrently. If you only have one processor, this is an illusion created by your operating system since only one thread can actually be executing instructions at any given instant, but it's a very effective illusion. To produce animation, you typically put some code that draws a succession of still pictures in a loop that runs indefinitely.

The code to draw the picture generally runs under the control of a timer so that it executes at a fixed rate, for example, 20 times per second. Of course, nothing else can happen in the same thread while the loop is running. If you want to have another animation running, it must be in a separate thread. Then the multitasking capability of your operating system can allow the two threads to share the available processor time, thus allowing both animations to run.

Let's get an idea of the principles behind how threads operate. Consider a very simple program that consists of three activities:

❏ Reads a number of blocks of data from a file

❏ Performs some calculation on each block of data

❏ Writes the results of the calculation to another file

You could organize the program as a single sequence of activities. In this case the activities– read file, process, write file– run in sequence, and the sequence is repeated for each block to be read and processed. You could also organize the program so that reading a block from the file is one activity, performing the calculation is a second activity, and writing the results is a third activity. Both of these situations are illustrated below.

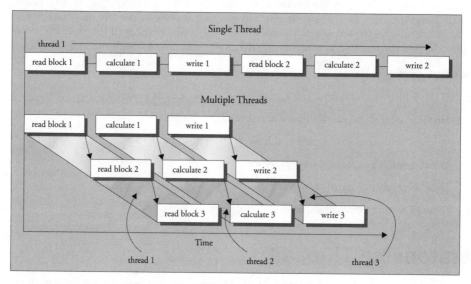

Once a block of data has been read, the computation process can start, and as soon as the computation has been completed, the results can be written out. With the program executing each step in sequence (that is, as a single thread), as shown in the top half of the diagram, the total time for execution will be the sum of the times for each of the individual activities. However, suppose we were able to execute each of the activities independently, as illustrated in the lower half of the diagram. In this case, reading the second block of data can start as soon as the first block has been read, and in theory we can have all three activities executing concurrently. This is possible even though you only have one processor, because the input and output operations are likely to require relatively little processor time while they are executing, so the processor can be doing other things while they are in progress. This can have the effect of reducing the total execution time for the program.

These three processes that we have identified that run more or less independently of one another – one to read the file, another to process the data, and a third to write the results – are called **threads**. Of course, the first example at the top of the diagram has just one thread that does everything in sequence. Every Java program has at least one thread. However, the three threads in the lower example aren't completely independent of one another. After all, if they were, you might as well make them independent programs. There are practical limitations too – the potential for overlapping these threads will be dependent on the capabilities of your computer, and of your operating system. However, if you can get some overlap in the execution of the threads, the program is going to run faster. There's no magic in using threads, though. Your computer has only a finite capacity for executing instructions, and if you have many threads running you may in fact increase the overall execution time because of the overhead implicit in managing the switching of control between threads.

An important consideration when you have a single program running as multiple threads is that the threads are unlikely to have identical execution times, and, if one thread is dependent on another, you can't afford to have one overtaking the other – otherwise you'll have chaos. Before you can start calculating in the example in the diagram, you need to be sure that the data block the calculation uses has been read, and before you can write the output, you need to know that the calculation is complete. This necessitates having some means for the threads to communicate with one another.

The way we have shown the threads executing in the previous diagram isn't the only way of organizing the program. You could have three threads, each of which reads the file, calculates the results, and writes the output, as shown here.

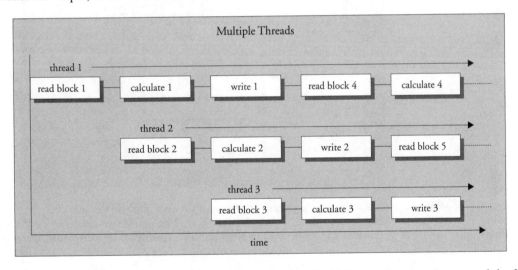

Now there's a different sort of contention between the threads. They are all competing to read the file and write the results, so there needs to be some way of preventing one thread from getting at the input file while another thread is already reading from it. The same goes for the output file. There's another aspect of this arrangement that is different from the previous version. If one thread, *thread1* say, reads a block, *block4* perhaps, that needs a lot of time to compute the results, another thread, *thread2* say, could conceivably read a following block, *block5* maybe, and calculate and write the results for *block5* before *thread1* has written the results for *block4*. If you don't want the results appearing in a different sequence from the input, you should do something about this. Before we delve into the intricacies of making sure our threads don't get knotted, let's first look at how we create a thread.

601

Creating Threads

Your program always has at least one thread: the one created when the program begins execution. With a program, this thread starts at the beginning of main(). With an applet, the browser is the main thread. That means that when your program creates a thread, it is in addition to the main thread of execution that created it. As you might have guessed, creating an additional thread involves using an object of a class, and the class you use is java.lang.Thread. Each additional thread that your program creates is represented by an object of the class Thread, or of a subclass of Thread. If your program is to have three additional threads, you will need to create three such objects.

To start the execution of a thread, you call the start() method for the Thread object. The code that executes in a new thread is always a method called run(), which is public, accepts no arguments, and doesn't return a value. Threads other than the main thread in a program always start in the run() method for the object that represents the thread. A program that creates three threads is illustrated diagrammatically here:

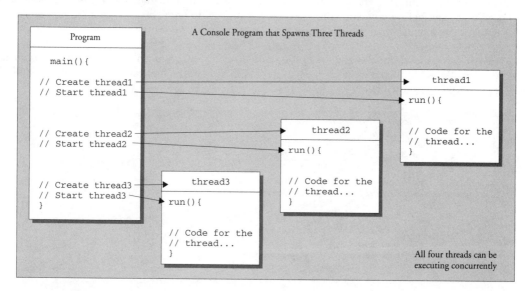

For a class representing a thread in your program to do anything, you must implement the run() method as the version defined in the Thread class does nothing. Your implementation of run() can call any other methods you want. Our illustration shows main() creating all three threads, but that doesn't have to be the case. Any thread can create more threads.

Now here comes the bite; you don't call the run() method to start a thread, you call the start() method for the object representing the thread and that causes the run() method to be called. When you want to stop the execution of a thread that is running, you call the stop() method for the Thread object.

The reason for this is somewhat complex but basically boils down to this: Threads are always owned and managed by the operating system and a new thread can only be created and started by the operating system. If you were to call the run() method yourself, it would simply operate like any other method, running in the same thread as the program that calls it.

When you call the `start()` method for a `Thread` object, you are calling a native code method that causes the operating system to initiate another thread from which the `run()` method for the `Thread` object executes.

In any case, it is not important to understand exactly how this works. Just remember: always start your thread by calling the `start()` method. If you try to call the `run()` method directly yourself, then you will not have created a new thread and your program will not work as you intended.

There are two ways in which you can define a class that is to represent a thread. One way is to define your class as a subclass of `Thread` and provide a definition of the method `run()` that overrides the inherited method. The other possibility is to define your class as implementing the interface `Runnable`, which declares the method `run()`, and then create a `Thread` object in your class when you need it. We will look at and explore the advantages of each approach in a little more detail.

Try It Out – Deriving a Subclass of Thread

We can see how this works by using an example. We'll define a single class, `TryThread`, which we'll derive from `Thread`. Execution starts in the method `main()`:

```java
import java.io.IOException;

public class TryThread extends Thread {
  private String firstName;            // Store for first name
  private String secondName;           // Store for second name
  private long aWhile;                 // Delay in milliseconds

  public TryThread(String firstName, String secondName, long delay) {
    this.firstName = firstName;        // Store the first name
    this.secondName = secondName;      // Store the second name
    aWhile = delay;                    // Store the delay
    setDaemon(true);                   // Thread is daemon
  }

  public static void main(String[] args) {
    // Create three threads
    Thread first = new TryThread("Hopalong ", "Cassidy ", 200L);
    Thread second = new TryThread("Marilyn ", "Monroe ", 300L);
    Thread third = new TryThread("Slim ", "Pickens ", 500L);

    System.out.println("Press Enter when you have had enough...\n");
    first.start();                     // Start the first thread
    second.start();                    // Start the second thread
    third.start();                     // Start the third thread

    try {
      System.in.read();                // Wait until Enter key pressed
      System.out.println("Enter pressed...\n");

    } catch (IOException e) {          // Handle IO exception
      System.out.println(e);           // Output the exception
    }
```

```
      System.out.println("Ending main()");
      return;
    }

    // Method where thread execution will start
    public void run() {
      try {
        while(true) {                              // Loop indefinitely...
          System.out.print(firstName);            // Output first name
          sleep(aWhile);                          // Wait aWhile msec.
          System.out.print(secondName + "\n"); // Output second name
        }
      } catch(InterruptedException e) {            // Handle thread interruption
        System.out.println(firstName + secondName + e);    // Output the exception
      }
    }
}
```

If you compile and run the code, you'll see something like this:

```
Press Enter when you have had enough...

Hopalong Marilyn Slim Cassidy
Hopalong Monroe
Marilyn Cassidy
Hopalong Pickens
Slim Monroe
Marilyn Cassidy
Hopalong Cassidy
Hopalong Monroe
Marilyn Pickens
Slim Cassidy
Hopalong Monroe
Marilyn Cassidy
Hopalong Cassidy
Hopalong Monroe
Marilyn Pickens
Slim Cassidy
Hopalong Cassidy
Hopalong Monroe
Marilyn
Enter pressed...

Ending main()
```

How It Works

There are three instance variables in our class `TryThread` and these are initialized in the constructor. The two `String` variables hold first and second names, and the variable `aWhile` stores a time period in milliseconds. The constructor for our class, `TryThread()`, will automatically call the default constructor, `Thread()`, for the base class.

Our class containing the method `main()` is derived from `Thread`, and implements `run()`, so objects of this class represent threads. The fact that each object of our class will have access to the method `main()` is irrelevant – the objects are perfectly good threads. Our method `main()` creates three such objects: `first`, `second`, and `third`.

Daemon and User Threads

The call to `setDaemon()`, with the argument `true` in the `TryThread` constructor, makes the thread that is created a **daemon thread**. A daemon thread is simply a background thread that is subordinate to the thread that creates it, so when the thread that created the daemon thread ends, the daemon thread dies with it. In our case, the method `main()` creates the daemon threads so that when `main()` returns, all the threads it has created will also end. If you run the example a few times pressing *Enter* at random, you should see that the daemon threads die after the `main()` method returns, because, from time to time, you will get some output from one or other thread after the last output from `main()`.

A thread that isn't a daemon thread is called a **user thread**. The diagram below shows two daemon threads and a user thread that are created by the main thread of a program.

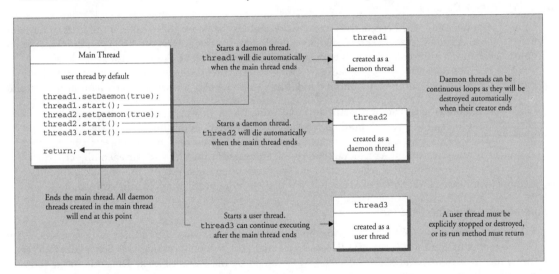

A user thread has a life of its own that is not dependent on the thread that creates it. It can continue execution after the thread that created it has ended. The default thread that contains `main()` is a user thread, as shown in the diagram, but `thread3` shown in the diagram could continue to execute after `main()` has returned. Threads that run for a finite time are typically user threads, but there's no reason why a daemon thread can't be finite. Threads that run indefinitely should usually be defined as daemon threads simply because you need a means of stopping them. A hypothetical example might help you to understand this so let's consider how a network server handling transactions of some kind might work in principle.

A network server might be managed overall by a user thread that starts one or more daemon threads to listen for requests. When the server starts up, the operator starts the management thread and this thread creates daemon threads to listen for requests. Each request recognized by one of these daemon threads might be handled by another thread that is created by the listening thread, so that each request will be handled independently. Where processing a transaction takes a finite time, and where it is important that the requests are completed before the system shuts down, the thread handling the request might be created as a user thread to ensure that it runs to completion, even if the listening thread that created it stops.

When the time comes to shut the system down, the operator doesn't have to worry about how many listening threads are running. When the main thread is shut down, all the listening threads will also shut down because they are daemon threads. Any outstanding threads dealing with specific transactions will then run to completion.

Note that you can only call `setDaemon()` for a thread before it starts; if you try to do so afterwards, the method will throw an `IllegalThreadStateException` exception. Also, a thread that is itself created by a daemon thread will be a daemon by default.

Creating Thread Objects

In the method `main()`, we create three `Thread` variables that store three different objects of our class `TryThread`. As you can see, each object has an individual name pair as the first two arguments to its constructor, and a different delay value passed as the third argument. All objects of the class `TryThread` are daemon threads because we call `setDaemon()` with the argument `true` in the constructor. Since the output can continue indefinitely, we display a message to explain how to stop it.

Once you've created a thread, it doesn't start executing by itself. You need to set it going. As we said earlier, you don't call the `run()` method for the `Thread` object to do this, you call its `start()` method. Thus we start the execution of each of the threads represented by the objects `first`, `second`, and `third` by calling the `start()` method that is inherited from `Thread` for each object. The `start()` method starts the object's `run()` method executing, then returns to the calling thread. Eventually all three threads are executing in parallel with the original application thread, `main()`.

Implementing the run() Method

The `run()` method contains the code for the thread execution. The code in this case is a single, infinite `while` loop which we put in a `try` block because the `sleep()` method that is called in the loop can throw the `InterruptedException` exception caught by the `catch` block. The code in the loop outputs the first name, calls the method `sleep()` inherited from `Thread`, and then outputs the second name. The `sleep()` method suspends execution of the thread for the number of milliseconds that you specify in the argument. This gives any other threads that have previously been started a chance to execute. This allows the output from the three threads to become a little jumbled.

Each time a thread calls the method `sleep()`, one of the other waiting threads jumps in. You can see the sequence in which the threads execute from the output. From the names in the output you can deduce that they execute in the sequence `first`, `second`, `third`, `first`, `first`, `second`, `second`, `first`, `first`, `third`, and so on. The actual sequence depends on your operating system scheduler so this is likely to vary from machine to machine. The execution of the `read()` method that is called in `main()` is blocked until you press *Enter*, but all the while the other threads continue executing. The output stops when you press *Enter* because this allows the main thread to continue and execute the `return`. Executing `return` ends the thread for `main()`, and since the other threads are daemon threads they also die when the thread that created them dies, although as you may have seen, they can run on a little after the last output from `main()`.

Stopping a Thread

If we did not create the threads in the last example as daemon threads, they would continue executing independently of main(). If you are prepared to terminate the program yourself (use *Ctrl+C* in a DOS session running Java) you can demonstrate this by commenting out the call to setDaemon() in the constructor. Pressing *Enter* will end main(), but the other threads will continue indefinitely.

A thread can signal another thread that it should stop executing by calling the interrupt() method for that Thread object. This in itself doesn't stop the thread, it just sets a flag in the thread that indicates an interruption has been requested. This flag must be checked in the run() method to have any effect. As it happens the sleep() method checks whether the thread has been interrupted, and throws an InterruptedException if it has been. You can see that in action by altering the previous example a little.

Try It Out – Interrupting a Thread

Make sure the call to the setDaemon() method is still commented out in the constructor, and modify the main() method as follows:

```
public static void main(String[] args) {
  // Create three threads
  Thread first = new TryThread("Hopalong ", "Cassidy ", 200L);
  Thread second = new TryThread("Marilyn ", "Monroe ", 300L);
  Thread third = new TryThread("Slim ", "Pickens ", 500L);

  System.out.println("Press Enter when you have had enough...\n");
  first.start();                       // Start the first thread
  second.start();                      // Start the second thread
  third.start();                       // Start the third thread
  try {
    System.in.read();                  // Wait until Enter key pressed
    System.out.println("Enter pressed...\n");

    // Interrupt the threads
    first.interrupt();
    second.interrupt();
    third.interrupt();

  } catch (IOException e) {            // Handle IO exception
    System.out.println(e);             // Output the exception
  }
  System.out.println("Ending main()");
  return;
}
```

Now the program will produce output that is something like:

```
Press Enter when you have had enough...

Slim Hopalong Marilyn Cassidy
Hopalong Monroe
Marilyn Cassidy
```

```
Hopalong Pickens
Slim Cassidy
Hopalong Monroe
Marilyn
Enter pressed...

Ending main()
Marilyn Monroe java.lang.InterruptedException: sleep interrupted
Slim Pickens java.lang.InterruptedException: sleep interrupted
Hopalong Cassidy java.lang.InterruptedException: sleep interrupted
```

How It Works

Since the method main() calls the interrupt() method for each of the threads after you press the *Enter* key, the sleep() method called in each thread registers the fact that the thread has been interrupted and throws an InterruptedException. This is caught by the catch block in the run() method and produces the new output you see. Because the catch block is outside the while loop, the run() method for each thread returns and each thread terminates.

You can check whether a thread has been interrupted by calling the isInterrupted() method for the thread. This returns true if interrupt() has been called for the thread in question. Since this is an instance method, you can use this to determine in one thread whether another thread has been interrupted. For example, in main() you could write:

```
if(first.isInterrupted())
    System.out.println("First thread has been interrupted.");
```

Note that this only determines whether the interrupted flag has been set by a call to interrupt() for the thread – it does not determine whether the thread is still running. A thread could have its interrupt flag set and continue executing – it is not obliged to terminate because interrupt() is called. To test whether a thread is still operating you can call its isAlive() method. This returns true if the thread has not terminated.

The instance method isInterrupted() has no effect on the interrupt flag in the thread – if it was set, it remains set. However, the static method interrupted() in the Thread class is different. It tests whether the currently executing thread has been interrupted and, if it has, it clears the interrupted flag in the current Thread object and returns true.

When an InterruptedException is thrown, the flag that registers the interrupt in the thread is cleared, so a subsequent call to isInterrupted() or interrupted() will return false.

Connecting Threads

If you need to wait in one thread until another thread dies, you can call the join() method for the thread that you expect isn't long for this world. Calling the join() method with no arguments will halt the current thread for as long as it takes the specified thread to die:

```
thread1.join();      // Suspend the current thread until thread1 dies
```

You can also pass a `long` value to the `join()` method to specify the number of milliseconds you're prepared to wait for the death of a thread:

```
thread1.join(1000); // Wait up to 1 second for thread1 to die
```

If this is not precise enough, there is a version of `join()` with two parameters. The first is a time in milliseconds and the second is a time in nanoseconds. The current thread will wait for the duration specified by the sum of the arguments. Of course, whether or not you get nanosecond resolution will depend on the capability of your hardware.

The `join()` method can throw an `InterruptedException` if the current thread is interrupted by another thread, so you should put a call to `join()` in a `try` block and catch the exception.

Thread Scheduling

The scheduling of threads depends to some extent on your operating system, but each thread will certainly get a chance to execute while the others are 'asleep', that is, when they've called their `sleep()` methods. If your operating system uses preemptive multitasking, as Windows 98 does, the program will work without the call to `sleep()` in the `run()` method (you should also remove the `try` and `catch` blocks, if you remove the `sleep()` call). However, if your operating system doesn't schedule in this way, without the `sleep()` call in `run()`, the `first` thread will hog the processor, and will continue indefinitely.

The diagram below illustrates how four threads might share the processor over time by calling the `sleep()` method to relinquish control.

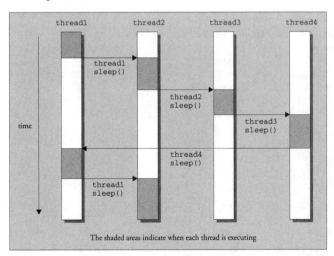

The shaded areas indicate when each thread is executing

Note that there's another method, `yield()`, defined in the `Thread` class, that gives other threads a chance to execute. You would use this when you just want to allow other threads a look-in if they are waiting, but you don't want to suspend execution of the current thread for a specific period of time. When you call the `sleep()` method for a thread, the thread will not continue for at least the time you have specified as an argument, even if no other threads are waiting. Calling `yield()` on the other hand will cause the current thread to resume immediately if no threads are waiting.

Implementing the Runnable Interface

As an alternative to defining a new subclass of Thread, we can implement the interface Runnable in a class. You'll find that this is generally much more convenient than deriving a class from Thread, because you can derive your class from a class other than Thread, and it can still represent a thread. Because Java only allows a single base class, if you derive your class from Thread, it can't inherit functionality from any other class. The interface Runnable only declares one method, run(), and this is the method that will be executed when the thread is started.

Try It Out – Using the Runnable Interface

To see how this works in practice, we can write another version of the previous example. We'll call this version of the program JumbleNames:

```java
import java.io.IOException;

public class JumbleNames implements Runnable {
  private String firstName;                    // Store for first name
  private String secondName;                   // Store for second name
  private long aWhile;                         // Delay in milliseconds

  // Constructor
  public JumbleNames(String firstName, String secondName, long delay) {
    this.firstName = firstName;                // Store the first name
    this.secondName = secondName;              // Store the second name
    aWhile = delay;                            // Store the delay
  }

  // Method where thread execution will start
  public void run() {
    try {
      while(true) {                            // Loop indefinitely...
        System.out.print(firstName);           // Output first name
        Thread.sleep(aWhile);                  // Wait aWhile msec.
        System.out.print(secondName+"\n");     // Output second name
      }
    } catch(InterruptedException e) {          // Handle thread interruption
      System.out.println(firstName + secondName + e);     // Output the exception
    }
  }

  public static void main(String[] args) {
    // Create three threads
    Thread first = new Thread(new JumbleNames("Hopalong ", "Cassidy ", 200L));
    Thread second = new Thread(new JumbleNames("Marilyn ", "Monroe ", 300L));
    Thread third = new Thread(new JumbleNames("Slim ", "Pickens ", 500L));

    // Set threads as daemon
    first.setDaemon(true);
    second.setDaemon(true);
    third.setDaemon(true);
```

```
        System.out.println("Press Enter when you have had enough...\n");
        first.start();                          // Start the first thread
        second.start();                         // Start the second thread
        third.start();                          // Start the third thread
        try {
          System.in.read();                     // Wait until Enter key pressed
          System.out.println("Enter pressed...\n");

        } catch (IOException e) {               // Handle IO exception
          System.out.println(e);                // Output the exception
        }
        System.out.println("Ending main()");
        return;
    }
}
```

How It Works

We have the same data members in this class as we had in the previous example. The constructor is almost the same as previously. We can't call setDaemon() in this class constructor because our class isn't derived from Thread. Instead, we need to do that in main() after we've created the objects representing the threads. The run() method implementation is also very similar. Our class doesn't have sleep() as a member, but because it's a public static member of the class Thread, we can call it in our run() method by using the class name.

In the method main(), we still create a Thread object for each thread of execution, but this time we use a constructor that accepts an object of type Runnable as an argument. We pass an object of our class JumbleNames to it. This is possible because our class implements Runnable.

Thread Names

Threads have a name, which in the case of the Thread constructor we're using in the example, will be a default name composed of the string "Thread*" with a sequence number appended. If you want to choose your own name for a thread, you can use a Thread constructor that accepts a String object specifying the name you want to assign to the thread. For example, we could have created the Thread object first with the statement:

```
Thread first = new Thread(new JumbleNames ("Hopalong ", "Cassidy ", 200L),
                          "firstThread");
```

This assigns the name "firstThread" to the thread. Note that this name is only used when displaying information about the thread. It has no relation to the identifier for the Thread object, and there's nothing, apart from common sense, to prevent several threads being given the same name.

You can obtain the name assigned to a thread by calling the getName() method for the Thread object. The name of the thread is returned as a String object. You can also change the name of a thread by calling the setName() method defined in the class Thread and passing a String object to it.

Once we've created the three Thread objects in the example, we call the setDaemon() method for each. The rest of main() is the same as in the original version of the previous example, and you should get similar output when you run this version of the program.

Managing Threads

In both the examples we've seen in this chapter, the threads are launched and then left to compete for computer resources. Because all three threads compete in an uncontrolled way for the processor, the output from the threads gets muddled. This isn't normally a desirable feature in a program. In most instances where you use threads, the way in which they execute will need to be managed so that they don't interfere with each other.

Of course, in our examples, the programs are deliberately constructed to release control of the processor part way through outputting a name. While this is very artificial, similar situations can arise in practice, particularly where threads are involved in a repetitive operation. It is important to appreciate that a thread can be interrupted while a source statement is executing. For instance, imagine that a bank teller is crediting a check to an account and at the same time the customer with that account is withdrawing some cash through an ATM machine. This might happen in the following way:

❏ The bank teller checks the balance of the customer's account, which is $500.

❏ The ATM machine asks for the account balance.

❏ The teller adds the value of the check, $100, to the account balance to give a figure of $600.

❏ The ATM machine takes $50 off the balance of $500, which gives a figure of $450, and spits out 5 $10 bills.

❏ The teller assigns the value of $600 to the account balance.

❏ The ATM machine assigns the value $450 to the account balance.

Here you can see the problem very well. Asking the account for its balance and assigning a new balance to the account are two different operations. As long as this is the case, we can never guarantee that this type of problem will not occur.

Where two or more threads share a common resource, such as a file or a block of memory, you'll need to take steps to ensure that one thread doesn't modify a resource while that resource is still being used by another thread. Having one thread update a record in a file while another thread is part way through retrieving the same record is a recipe for disaster. One way of managing this sort of situation is to use **synchronization** for the threads involved.

Synchronization

The objective of synchronization is to ensure that, when several threads want access to a single resource, only one thread can access it at any given time. There are two ways in which you can use synchronization to manage your threads of execution:

❏ You can manage code at the method level – this involves synchronizing methods.

❏ You can manage code at the block level – using synchronizing blocks.

We'll look at how we can use synchronized methods first.

Synchronized Methods

You can make a subset (or indeed all) of the methods for any class object mutually exclusive, so that only one of the methods can execute at any given time. You make methods mutually exclusive by declaring them in the class using the keyword synchronized. For example:

```
class MyClass {
  synchronized public void method1() {
    // Code for the method...
  }

  synchronized public void method2() {
    // Code for the method...
  }

  public void method3() {
    // Code for the method...
  }
}
```

Now, only one of the synchronized methods in a class object can execute at any one time. Only when the currently executing synchronized method for an object has ended can another synchronized method start for the same object. The idea here is that each synchronized method has guaranteed exclusive access to the object while it is executing, at least so far as the other synchronized methods for the class object are concerned.

The synchronization process makes use of an internal **lock** that every object has associated with it. The lock is a kind of flag that is set by a process, referred to as **locking** or a **lock action**, when a synchronized method starts execution. Each synchronized method for an object checks to see whether the lock has been set by another method. If it has, it will not start execution until the lock has been reset by an **unlock action**. Thus, only one synchronized method can be executing at one time, because that method will have set the lock that prevents any other synchronized method from starting.

> Note that there's no constraint here on simultaneously executing synchronized methods for two *different* objects of the same class. It's only concurrent access to any one object that is controlled.

Of the three methods in myClass, two are declared as synchronized, so for any object of the class, only one of these methods can execute at one time. The method that isn't declared as synchronized, method3(), can always be executed by a thread, regardless of whether a synchronized method is executing.

It's important to keep clear in your mind the distinction between an object that has instance methods that you declared as synchronized in the class definition and the threads of execution that might use them. A hypothetical relationship between three threads and two objects of the class myClass is illustrated in the following diagram:

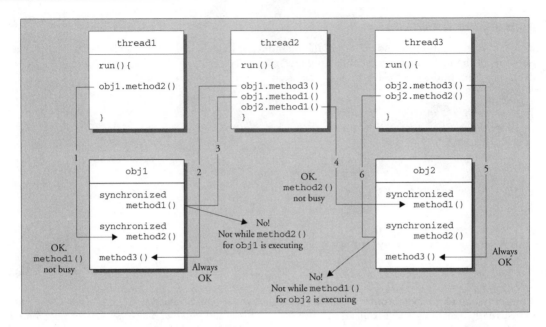

The numbers on the arrows in the diagram indicate the sequence of events. **No!** indicates that the thread waits until the method is unlocked so it can execute it. While method1() in obj2 is executing, method2() for the same object can't be executed. The synchronization of these two instance methods in an object provides a degree of protection for the object, in that only one synchronized method can mess with the data in the object at any given time.

However, each object is independent of any other object when it comes to synchronized instance methods. When a thread executes a synchronized method for an object, it is assured exclusive access to the object insofar as the synchronized methods in that object are concerned. Another thread, though, can still call the same method for a different object. While method1() is being executed for obj1, this doesn't prevent method1() for obj2 being executed by some other thread. Also, if there's a method in an object that has not been declared as synchronized – method3() in obj1 for example – any thread can call that at any time, regardless of the state of any synchronized methods in the object.

If you apply synchronization to static methods in a class, only one of those static methods in the class can be executing at any point in time, and this is per class synchronization and the class lock is independent of any locks for objects of the class.

An important point of principle that you need to understand is that the only method that is necessarily part of a thread in a class object that represents a thread is the run() method. Other methods for the same class object are only part of the thread if they are called directly or indirectly by the run() method. All the methods that are called directly or indirectly from the run() method for an object are all part of the same thread, but they clearly don't have to be methods for the same Thread object. Indeed they can be methods that belong to any other objects, including other Thread objects that have their own run() methods.

Using Synchronized Methods

To see how synchronization can be applied in practice, we'll construct a program that provides a simple model of a bank. Our bank is a very young business with only one customer account initially, but we'll have two clerks, each working flat out to process transactions for the account, one handling debits and the other handling credits. The objects in our program are illustrated here:

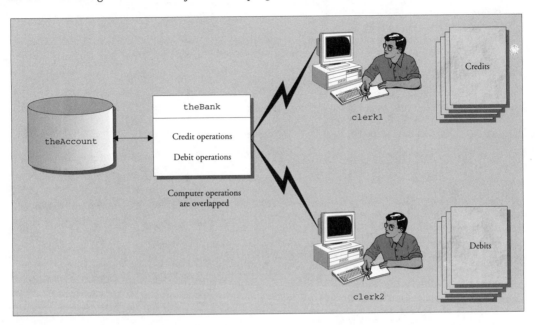

The bank in our model is actually a computer that performs operations on the account, and the account is stored separately. Each clerk can communicate directly with the bank. We'll be defining four classes that we will use in our program to model banking operations:

- ❑   A Bank class to represent the bank computer.

- ❑   An Account class to represent the account at the bank.

- ❑   A Transaction class to represent a transaction on the account – a debit or a credit for instance.

- ❑   A Clerk class to represent a bank clerk.

We will also define a class containing the method main() that will start the process off and determine how it all works.

> As we develop the code, we won't necessarily get it right first time, but we will improve as we find out more about how to program using threads. This will expose some of the sorts of errors and complications that can arise when you're programming using threads.

Try It Out – Defining a Bank Class

The bank computer is the agent that will perform the operations on an account so we will start with that. We can define the `Bank` class that will represent this as:

```
// Define the bank
class Bank {
  // Perform a transaction
  public void doTransaction(Transaction transaction) {
    int balance = transaction.getAccount().getBalance();    // Get current balance

    switch(transaction.getTransactionType()) {
      case Transaction.CREDIT:
        // Credits require a lot of checks...
        try {
          Thread.sleep(100);

        } catch(InterruptedException e) {
          System.out.println(e);
        }
        balance += transaction.getAmount();          // Increment the balance
        break;

      case Transaction.DEBIT:
        // Debits require even more checks...
        try {
          Thread.sleep(150);

        } catch(InterruptedException e) {
          System.out.println(e);
        }
        balance -= transaction.getAmount();          // Decrement the balance
        break;

      default:                                       // We should never get here
        System.out.println("Invalid transaction");
        System.exit(1);
    }
    transaction.getAccount().setBalance(balance);    // Restore the account balance
  }
}
```

How It Works

The `Bank` class is very simple. It keeps no records of anything locally as the accounts will be identified separately, and it only has one method that carries out a transaction. The `Transaction` object will provide all the information about what the transaction is, and to which account it applies. We have only provided for debit and credit operations on an account, but the switch could easily be extended to accommodate other types of transactions. Both of the transactions supported involve some delay while the standard nameless checks and verifications, that all banks have, are carried out. The delay is simulated by calling the `sleep()` method belonging to the `Thread` class.

Of course, during this time, other things in other threads may be going on. There are no instance variables to initialize in a `Bank` object so we don't need a constructor. Since our `Bank` object works using a `Transaction` object, let's define the class for that next.

Try It Out – Defining a Transaction on an Account

The `Transaction` class could represent any transaction on an account, but we are limiting ourselves to debits and credits. We can define the class as:

```
class Transaction {
  // Transaction types
  public static final int DEBIT = 0;
  public static final int CREDIT = 1;
  public static String[] types = {"Debit","Credit"};

  // Constructor
  public Transaction(Account account, int transactionType, int amount) {
    this.account = account;
    this.transactionType = transactionType;
    this.amount = amount;
  }

  public Account getAccount() {
    return account;
  }

  public int getTransactionType() {
    return transactionType;
  }

  public int getAmount() {
    return amount;
  }

  public String toString() {
    return types[transactionType] + " A//C: " + ": $" + amount;
  }

  private Account account;
  private int amount;
  private int transactionType;
}
```

How It Works

The type of transaction is specified by the `transactionType` field that must be one of the values defined for transaction types. We should build in checks in the constructor to ensure only valid transactions are created, but we'll forego this to keep the code volume down, and you certainly know how to do this sort of thing by now. A transaction records the amount for the transaction and a reference to the account to which it applies, so a `Transaction` object specifies a complete transaction. The methods are very straightforward, just accessor methods for the data members that are used by the `Bank` object, plus the `toString()` method in case we need it.

Try It Out – Defining a Bank Account

We can define an account as:

```
// Defines a customer account
public class Account {
  // Constructor
  public Account(int accountNumber, int balance) {
    this.accountNumber = accountNumber;          // Set the account number
    this.balance = balance;                      // Set the initial balance
  }

  // Return the current balance
  public int getBalance() {
    return balance;
  }

  // Set the current balance
  public void setBalance(int balance) {
    this.balance = balance;
  }

  public int getAccountNumber() {
    return accountNumber;
  }

  public String toString() {
    return "A//C No. "+accountNumber+" : $"+balance;
  }

  private int balance;                           // The current account balance
  private int accountNumber;                     // Identifies this account
}
```

How It Works

The Account class is also very simple. It just maintains a record of the amount in the account as a balance, and provides methods for retrieving and setting the current balance. Operations on the account are performed externally by the Bank object. We have a bit more than we need in the Account class at the moment, but the methods we don't use in the current example may be useful later.

Try It Out – Defining a Bank Clerk

A clerk is a slightly more complicated animal. He or she retains information about the bank and details of the current transaction and is responsible for initiating debits and credits on an account by communication with the central bank. Each clerk will work independently of the others so they will each be a separate thread:

```
public class Clerk implements Runnable {
  private Bank theBank;                // The employer - an electronic marvel
  private Transaction inTray;          // The in-tray holding a transaction
```

```
    // Constructor
    public Clerk(Bank theBank) {
      this.theBank = theBank;          // Who the clerk works for
      inTray = null;                   // No transaction initially
    }

    // Receive a transaction
    public void doTransaction(Transaction transaction) {
      inTray = transaction;
    }

    // The working clerk...
    public void run() {
      while(true) {
        while(inTray == null) {        // No transaction waiting?
          try {
            Thread.sleep(150);         // Then take a break...

          } catch(InterruptedException e) {
            System.out.println(e);
          }
        }

        theBank.doTransaction(inTray);
        inTray = null;                 // In-tray is empty
      }
    }

    // Busy check
    public boolean isBusy() {
      return inTray != null;           // A full in-tray means busy!
    }
  }
```

How It Works

A `Clerk` object is a thread since it implements the `Runnable` interface. Each clerk has an in-tray, capable of holding one transaction, and while the in-tray is not `null`, the clerk is clearly busy. A clerk needs to be aware of the `Bank` object that is employing him or her, so a reference is stored in `theBank` when a `Clerk` object is created. A transaction is placed in the in-tray for a clerk by calling his or her `doTransaction()` method. You can check whether a clerk is busy by calling the `isBusy()` member which will return `true` if a transaction is still in progress.

The real work is actually done in the `run()` method. If the in-tray is empty, indicated by a `null` value in `inTray`, then there's nothing to do, so after sleeping a while the loop goes around again for another look at the in-tray. When a transaction has been recorded, the method in `theBank` object is called to carry it out and the `inTray` is reset to `null`.

All we need now is the class to drive our model world, which we will call `BankOperation`. This class only requires the method `main()`, but there are quite a lot of things to do in this method so we'll put it together piece by piece.

Try It Out – Defining the Operation of the Bank

Apart from setting everything up, the `main()` method has to originate transactions on the accounts and pass them on to the clerks to be expedited. We will start with just one account and a couple of clerks. Here's the basic structure:

```
import java.util.Random;

public class BankOperation {
  public static void main(String[] args) {
    int initialBalance = 500;      // The initial account balance
    int totalCredits = 0;          // Total credits on the account
    int totalDebits =0;            // Total debits on the account
    int transactionCount = 20;     // Number of debits and credits

    // Create the account, the bank, and the clerks...

    // Create the threads for the clerks as daemon, and start them off

    // Generate the transactions of each type and pass to the clerks

    // Wait until both clerks are done

    // Now output the results
  }
}
```

The `import` for the `Random` class is there because we will need it in a moment. To create the `Bank` object, the clerks, and the account, we need to add the following code:

```
// Create the account, the bank, and the clerks...
Bank theBank = new Bank();                         // Create a bank
Clerk clerk1 = new Clerk(theBank);                 // Create the first clerk
Clerk clerk2 = new Clerk(theBank);                 // Create the second clerk
Account account = new Account(1, initialBalance);  // Create an account
```

The next step is to add the code to create the threads for the clerks and start them going:

```
// Create the threads for the clerks as daemon, and start them off
Thread clerk1Thread = new Thread(clerk1);
Thread clerk2Thread = new Thread(clerk2);
clerk1Thread.setDaemon(true);                      // Set first as daemon
clerk2Thread.setDaemon(true);                      // Set second as daemon
clerk1Thread.start();                              // Start the first
clerk2Thread.start();                              // Start the second
```

The code to generate the transactions looks a lot, but is quite repetitive:

```
// Generate transactions of each type and pass to the clerks
Random rand = new Random();                        // Random number generator
```

```
Transaction transaction;                              // Stores a transaction
int amount = 0;                                       // stores an amount of money
for(int i = 1; i <= transactionCount; i++) {
  amount = 50 + rand.nextInt(26);                     // Generate amount of $50 to $75
  transaction = new Transaction(account,              //   Account
                         Transaction.CREDIT,          //   Credit transaction
                         amount);                     //   of amount
  totalCredits += amount;                             // Keep total credit tally

  // Wait until the first clerk is free
  while(clerk1.isBusy()) {
    try {
      Thread.sleep(25);                               // Busy so try later

    } catch(InterruptedException e) {
      System.out.println(e);
    }
  }
  clerk1.doTransaction(transaction);                  // Now do the credit

  amount = 30 + rand.nextInt(31);                     // Generate amount of $30 to $60
  transaction = new Transaction(account,              //   Account
                         Transaction.DEBIT,           //   Debit transaction
                         amount);                     //   of amount
  totalDebits += amount;                              // Keep total debit tally
  // Wait until the second clerk is free
  while(clerk2.isBusy()) {
    try {
      Thread.sleep(25);                               // Busy so try later

    } catch(InterruptedException e) {
      System.out.println(e);
    }
  }
  clerk2.doTransaction(transaction);                  // Now do the debit
}
```

Once all the transactions have been processed, we can output the results. However, the clerks could still be busy after we exit from the loop, so we need to wait for both of them to be free before outputting the results. We can do this with a `while` loop:

```
// Wait until both clerks are done
while(clerk1.isBusy() || clerk2.isBusy()) {
  try {
    Thread.sleep(25);

  } catch(InterruptedException e) {
    System.out.println(e);
  }
}
```

Lastly, we output the results:

```
// Now output the results
System.out.println(
        "Original balance : $" + initialBalance+"\n" +
        "Total credits    : $" + totalCredits+"\n" +
        "Total debits     : $" + totalDebits+"\n" +
        "Final balance    : $" + account.getBalance() + "\n" +
        "Should be        : $" + (initialBalance + totalCredits - totalDebits));
```

How It Works

The variables in the `main()` method track the total debits and credits, and record the initial account balance. They are there to help us figure out what has happened after the transactions have been processed. The number of times we debit and then credit the account is stored in `transactionCount`, so the total number of transactions will be twice this value. We have added five further blocks of code to perform the functions indicated by the comments, so let's now go through each of them in turn.

The `Account` object is created with the account number as 1 and with the initial balance stored in `initialBalance`. We pass the bank object, `theBank`, to the constructor for each of the `Clerk` objects, so that they can record it.

The `Thread` constructor requires an object of type `Runnable`, so we can just pass the `Clerk` objects in the argument. There's no problem in doing this because the `Clerk` class implements the interface `Runnable`. You can always implicitly cast an object to a type that is any superclass of the object or any interface type that the object class implements.

All the transactions are generated in the `for` loop. The handling of debits is essentially the same as the handling of credits, so we'll only go through the code for the latter in detail. A random amount between $50 and $75 is generated for a credit transaction by using the `nextInt()` method for the `rand` object of type `Random` that we create. You'll recall that `nextInt()` returns an `int` value in the range 0 to one less than the value of the argument, so by passing 26 to the method, we get a value between 0 and 25 returned. We add 50 to this and, hey presto, we have a value between 50 and 75. We then use this amount to create a `Transaction` object that represents a credit for the account. To keep a check on the work done by the clerks, we add this credit to the total of all the credits generated that is stored in the variable `totalCredits`. This will allow us to verify whether or not the account has been updated properly.

Before we pass the transaction to `clerk1`, we must make sure that he or she isn't busy. Otherwise we would overwrite the clerk's in-tray. The `while` loop does this. As long as the `isBusy()` method returns `true`, we continue to call the `sleep()` method for a 25 millisecond delay, before we go round and check again. When `isBusy()` returns `false`, we call the `doTransaction()` method for the clerk with the reference to the `transaction` object as the argument. The `for` loop will run for 20 iterations, so we'll generate 20 random transactions of each type.

The third `while` loop works in the same way as the previous check for a busy clerk – the loop continues if either of the clerks is busy.

Lastly, we output the original account balance, the totals of credits and debits, and the final balance plus what it should be for comparison. That's all we need in the method `main()`, so we're ready to give it a whirl. Remember that all four classes need to be in the same directory.

Running the Example

Now, if you run the example, the final balance will be wrong. You should get results something like the following:

```
Original balance     : $500
Total credits         : $1252
Total debits          : $921
Final balance         : $89
Should be             : $831
```

Of course, your results won't be the same as this, but they should be just as wrong. The customer will not be happy. His account balance is seriously out – in the bank's favor, of course, as always. So how has this come about?

The problem is that both clerks are operating on the same account at the same time. Both clerks call the doTransaction() method for the Bank object, so this method is executed by both clerk threads. Separate calls on the same method are overlapping.

Try It Out – Synchronizing Methods

One way we can fix this is by simply declaring the method that operates on an account as synchronized. This will prevent one clerk getting at it while it is still in progress with the other clerk. To implement this you should amend the Bank class definition as follows:

```
// Define the bank
class Bank {
   // Perform a transaction
   synchronized public void doTransaction(Transaction transaction) {
      // Code exactly as before...
   }
}
```

How It Works

Declaring this method as synchronized will prevent a call to it from being executed while another is still in operation. If you run the example again with this change, the result will be something like:

```
Original balance     : $500
Total credits         : $1201
Total debits          : $931
Final balance         : $770
Should be             : $770
```

The amounts may be different because the transaction amounts are random, but your final balance should be the same as adding the credits to the original balance and subtracting the debits.

As we saw earlier, when you declare methods in a class as `synchronized`, it prevents concurrent execution of those methods within a single object, *including concurrent execution of the same method*. It is important not to let the fact that there is only one copy of a particular method confuse you. A given method can be potentially executing in any number of threads – as many threads as there are in the program in fact. If it was not synchronized, the `doTransaction()` method could be executed concurrently by any number of clerks.

Although this fixes the problem we had in that the account balance is now correct, the bank is still amazingly inefficient. Each clerk is kicking their heels while another clerk is carrying out a transaction. At any given time a maximum of one clerk is working. On this basis the bank could sack them all bar one and get the same throughput. We can do better, as we shall see.

Synchronizing Statement Blocks

In addition to being able to synchronize methods on a class object, you can also specify a statement or a block of code in your program as `synchronized`. This is more powerful, since you specify which particular object is to benefit from the synchronization of the statement or code block, not just the object that contains the code as in the case of a synchronized method. Here we can set a lock on any object for a given statement block. When the block that is synchronized on the given object is executing, no other code block or method that is synchronized on the same object can execute. To synchronize a statement, you just write:

```
synchronized(theObject)
    statement;              // Synchronized with respect to theObject
```

No other statements or statement blocks in the program that are synchronized on the object `theObject` can execute while this statement is executing. Naturally, this applies even when the statement is a call to a method, which may in turn call other methods. The statement here could equally well be a block of code between braces. This is powerful stuff. Now we can lock a particular object while the code block that is working is running.

To see precisely how you can use this in practice, let's create a modification of the last example. Let's up the sophistication of our banking operation to support multiple accounts. To extend our example to handle more than one account, we just need to make some changes to `main()`. We'll add one extra account to keep the output modest, but we'll modify the code to handle any number of accounts.

Try It Out – Handling Multiple Accounts

We can modify the code in `main()` that creates the account and sets the initial balance to create multiple accounts as follows:

```
public class BankOperation {
  public static void main(String[] args) {
      int[] initialBalance = {500, 800};            // The initial account balances
      int[] totalCredits = new int[initialBalance.length]; //Two different cr totals
      int[] totalDebits = new int[initialBalance.length];  //Two different db totals
      int transactionCount = 20;                    // Number of debits and of credits

      // Create the bank and the clerks...
      Bank theBank = new Bank();                    // Create a bank
```

```
    Clerk clerk1 = new Clerk(theBank );        // Create the first clerk
    Clerk clerk2 = new Clerk(theBank );        // Create the second clerk

    // Create the accounts, and initialize total credits and debits
    Account[] accounts = new Account[initialBalance.length];
    for(int i = 0; i < initialBalance.length; i++) {
      accounts[i] = new Account(i+1, initialBalance[i]); // Create accounts
      totalCredits[i] = totalDebits[i] = 0;
    }

    // Create the threads for the clerks as daemon, and start them off

    // Create transactions randomly distributed between the accounts

    // Wait until both clerks are done

    // Now output the results
  }
}
```

We now create an array of accounts in a loop, the number of accounts being determined by the number of initial balances in the `initialBalance` array. Account numbers are assigned successively starting from 1. The code for creating the bank and the clerks and for creating the threads and starting them is exactly the same as before. The shaded comments that follow the code indicate the other segments of code in `main()` that we need to modify.

The next piece we need to change is the creation and processing of the transactions:

```
// Create transactions randomly distributed between the accounts
Random rand = new Random();
Transaction transaction;                      // Stores a transaction
int amount = 0;                               // Stores an amount of money
int select = 0;                               // Selects an account
for(int i = 1; i <= transactionCount; i++) {
  // Choose an account at random for credit operation
  select = rand.nextInt(accounts.length);
  amount = 50 + rand.nextInt(26);             // Generate amount of $50 to $75
  transaction = new Transaction(accounts[select],      // Account
                              Transaction.CREDIT, // Credit transaction
                              amount);         //   of amount
  totalCredits[select] += amount;             // Keep total credit tally

  // Wait until the first clerk is free
  while(clerk1.isBusy()) {
    try {
      Thread.sleep(25);                        // Busy so try later
    }
    catch(InterruptedException e)
    {
      System.out.println(e);
    }
  }
```

```
    }
    clerk1.doTransaction(transaction);                   // Now do the credit

    // choose an account at random for debit operation
    select = rand.nextInt(accounts.length);
    amount = 30 + rand.nextInt(31);                       // Generate amount of $30 to $60
    transaction = new Transaction(accounts[select],   // Account
                                  Transaction.DEBIT,  // Debit transaction
                                  amount);            //   of amount
    totalDebits[select] += amount;                       // Keep total debit tally

    // Wait until the second clerk is free
    while(clerk2.isBusy()) {
      try {
        Thread.sleep(25);                              // Busy so try later

      } catch(InterruptedException e) {
        System.out.println(e);
      }
    }
    clerk2.doTransaction(transaction);                   // Now do the debit
  }
```

The last modification we must make to the method main() is for outputting the results. We now do this in a loop seeing as we have to process more than one account:

```
for(int i = 0; i < accounts.length; i++)
  System.out.println("Account Number:"+accounts[i].getAccountNumber()+"\n"+
    "Original balance   : $" + initialBalance[i] + "\n" +
    "Total credits      : $" + totalCredits[i] + "\n" +
    "Total debits       : $" + totalDebits[i] + "\n" +
    "Final balance      : $" + accounts[i].getBalance() + "\n" +
    "Should be          : $" + (initialBalance[i]
                              + totalCredits[i]
                              - totalDebits[i]) + "\n");
```

This is much the same as before except that we now extract values from the arrays we have created. If you run this version it will, of course, work perfectly. A typical set of results is:

```
Account Number:1
Original balance   : $500
Total credits      : $659
Total debits       : $614
Final balance      : $545
Should be          : $545

Account Number:2
Original balance   : $800
Total credits      : $607
Total debits       : $306
Final balance      : $1101
Should be          : $1101
```

How It Works

We now allocate arrays for the initial account balances, the totals of credits and debits for each account, and the totals for the accounts themselves. The number of initializing values in the initialBalance[] array will determine the number of elements in each of the arrays. In the for loop, we create each of the accounts with the appropriate initial balance, and initialize the totalCredits[] and totalDebits[] arrays to zero.

In the modified transactions loop, we select the account from the array for both the debit and the credit transactions by generating a random index value that we store in the variable select. The index select is also used to keep a tally of the total of the transactions of each type.

This is all well and good, but by declaring the methods in the class Bank as synchronized, we're limiting the program quite significantly. No operation of any kind can be carried out while any other operation is in progress. This is unnecessarily restrictive since there's no reason to prevent a transaction on one account while a transaction for a different account is in progress. What we really want to do is constrain the program to prevent overlapping of operations on the same account, and this is where declaring blocks of code to be synchronized on a particular object can help.

Let's consider the methods in the class Bank once more. What we really want is the code in the doTransaction() method to be synchronized so that simultaneous processing of the same account is prevented, not so that processing of different accounts is inhibited. What we need to do is synchronize the processing code for a transaction on the Account object that is involved.

Try It Out – Applying synchronized Statement Blocks

We can do this with the following changes:

```
class Bank {
  // Perform a transaction
  public void doTransaction(Transaction transaction) {
    switch(transaction.getTransactionType()) {
      case Transaction.CREDIT:
        synchronized(transaction.getAccount()) {
          // Get current balance
          int balance = transaction.getAccount().getBalance();

          // Credits require require a lot of checks...
          try {
            Thread.sleep(100);

          } catch(InterruptedException e) {
            System.out.println(e);
          }
          balance += transaction.getAmount();                // Increment the balance
          transaction.getAccount().setBalance(balance); // Restore account balance
          break;
        }

      case Transaction.DEBIT:
        synchronized(transaction.getAccount()) {
          // Get current balance
          int balance = transaction.getAccount().getBalance();
```

```
            // Debits require even more checks...
            try {
              Thread.sleep(150);

            } catch(InterruptedException e) {
              System.out.println(e);
            }
            balance -= transaction.getAmount();          // Increment the balance...
            transaction.getAccount().setBalance(balance);// Restore account balance
            break;
        }

        default:                                          // We should never get here
          System.out.println("Invalid transaction");
          System.exit(1);
      }
    }
  }
```

How It Works

The expression in parentheses following the keyword synchronized specifies the object for which the synchronization applies. Once one synchronized code block is entered with a given account object, no other code block or method can be entered that has been synchronized on the same object. For example, if the block performing credits is executing with a reference to the object accounts[1] returned by the getAccount() method for the transaction, the execution of the block carrying out debits cannot be executed for the same object, but it could be executed for a different account.

The object in a synchronized code block acts rather like a baton in a relay race that serves to synchronize the runners in the team. Only the runner with the baton is allowed to run. The next runner in the team can only run once they get hold of the baton. Of course, in any race there will be several different batons so you can have several sets of runners. In the same way, you can specify several different sets of synchronized code blocks in a class, each controlled by a different object. It is important to realize that code blocks that are synchronized with respect to a particular object don't have to be in the same class. They can be anywhere in your program where the appropriate object can be specified.

Note how we had to move the code to access and restore the account balance inside both synchronized blocks. If we hadn't done this, accessing or restoring the account balance could occur while a synchronized block was executing. This could obviously cause confusion since a balance could be restored by a debit transaction after the balance had been retrieved for a credit transaction. This would cause the effect of the debit to be wiped out.

If you want to verify that we really are overlapping these operations in this example, you can add output statements to the beginning and end of each method in the class Bank. Outputting the type of operation, the amount, and whether it is the start or end of the transaction will be sufficient to identify them. For example, you could modify the doTransaction() method in the Bank class to:

```
// Perform a transaction
public void doTransaction(Transaction transaction) {
```

```
switch(transaction.getTransactionType()) {
  case Transaction.CREDIT:
    synchronized(transaction.getAccount()) {
      System.out.println("Start credit of " +
              transaction.getAccount() + " amount: " +
              transaction.getAmount());

      // code to process credit...
      System.out.println("  End credit of " +
              transaction.getAccount() + " amount: " +
              transaction.getAmount());
    break;
    }

  case Transaction.DEBIT:
    synchronized(transaction.getAccount()) {
      System.out.println("Start debit of " +
              transaction.getAccount() + " amount: " +
              transaction.getAmount());
      // code to process debit...
      System.out.println("  End debit of " +
              transaction.getAccount() + " amount: " +
              transaction.getAmount());
    break;
    }

  default:                                          // We should never get here
    System.out.println("Invalid transaction");
    System.exit(1);
  }
}
```

This will produce quite a lot of output, but you can always comment it out when you don't need it. You should be able to see how a transaction for an account that is currently being worked on is always delayed until the previous operation on the account is completed. You will also see from the output that operations on different accounts do overlap. Here's a sample of what I got:

```
Start credit of A//C No. 2 : $800 amount: 74
  End credit of A//C No. 2 : $874 amount: 74
Start debit of A//C No. 2 : $874 amount: 52
Start credit of A//C No. 1 : $500 amount: 51
  End debit of A//C No. 2 : $822 amount: 52
  End credit of A//C No. 1 : $551 amount: 51
Start debit of A//C No. 2 : $822 amount: 38
  End debit of A//C No. 2 : $784 amount: 38
Start credit of A//C No. 2 : $784 amount: 74
  End credit of A//C No. 2 : $858 amount: 74
Start debit of A//C No. 1 : $551 amount: 58
Start credit of A//C No. 2 : $858 amount: 53
  End debit of A//C No. 1 : $493 amount: 58
...
```

You can see from the third and fourth lines here that a credit for account 1 starts before the preceding debit for account 2 is complete, so the operations are overlapped. If you want to force overlapping debits and credits on the same account, you can comment out the calculation of the value for `select` for the debit operation in the `for` loop in `main()`. This modification is shown shaded:

```
// Generate a random account index for debit operation
// select = rand.nextInt(accounts.length);
totalDebits[select] += amount;          // Keep total debit tally
```

This will make the debit transaction apply to the same account as the previous credit, so the transactions will always be contending for the same account.

Of course, this is not the only way of getting the operations to overlap. Another approach would be to equip accounts with methods to handle their own credit and debit transactions, and declare these as synchronized methods.

While testing that you have synchronization right is relatively easy in our example, in general it is extremely difficult to be sure you have tested a program that uses threads adequately. Getting the design right first is essential, and there is no substitute for careful design in programs that have multiple threads (or indeed any real time program that has interrupt handlers). You can never be sure that a real world program is 100% correct, only that it works correctly most of the time!

Deadlocks

Since you can synchronize code blocks for a particular object virtually anywhere in your program, there's potential for a particularly nasty kind of bug called a **deadlock**. This involves a mutual interdependence between two threads. One way this arises is when one thread executes some code synchronized on a given object, `theObject` say, and then needs to execute another method that contains code synchronized on another object, `theOtherObject` say. Before this occurs though, a second thread executes some code synchronized to `theOtherObject`, and needs to execute a method containing code synchronized to the first object, `theObject`. This situation is illustrated here:

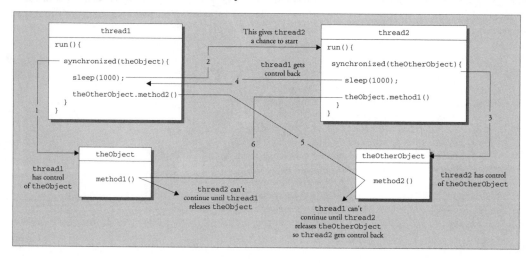

The sequence of events is as follows:

- ❑ thread1 starts first, and synchronizes on theObject. This prevents any methods for theObject being called by any other thread.

- ❑ thread1 then calls sleep() so thread2 can start.

- ❑ thread2 starts and synchronizes on theOtherObject. This prevents any methods for theOtherObject being called by any other thread.

- ❑ thread2 then calls sleep() allowing thread1 another go.

- ❑ thread1 wakes up and tries to call method2() for theOtherObject, but it can't until the code block in thread2 that is synchronized on theOtherObject completes execution.

- ❑ thread2 gets another go because thread1 can't proceed, and tries to call method1() for theObject. This can't proceed until the code block in thread1 that is synchronized on theObject completes execution.

Neither thread has any possibility of continuing – they are deadlocked. Finding and fixing this sort of problem can be very difficult, particularly if your program is complicated and has other threads that will continue to execute.

You can create a trivial deadlock in the last example by making the for loop in main() synchronized on one of the accounts. For example:

```
synchronized(accounts[1]) {
  for(int i = 1; i <= transactionCount; i++) {
    // code for generating transactions etc...
  }
}
```

A deadlock occurs as soon as a transaction for accounts[1] arises because the doTransaction() method in the theBank object that is called by a Clerk object to handle the transaction will be synchronized to the same object and can't execute until the loop ends. Of course, the loop can't continue until the method in the theBank object terminates so the program hangs.

In general, ensuring that your program has no potential deadlocks is extremely difficult. If you intend to do a significant amount of programming using threads, you will need to study the subject in much more depth than we can deal with here. A good book on the subject is *Concurrent Programming in Java: Design Principles and Patterns* written by Doug Lea (ISBN 0-201-69581-2).

Communicating between Threads

We've seen how we can lock methods or code blocks using synchronization to avoid the problems that uncontrolled thread execution can cause. While this gives us a degree of control, we're still introducing inefficiencies into the program. In the last example, there were several occasions where we used a loop to wait for a clerk thread to complete an operation before the current thread could sensibly continue. For example, we couldn't pass a transaction to a Clerk object while that object was still busy with the previous transaction. Our solution to this was to use a while loop to test the busy status of the Clerk object from time to time and call the sleep() method in between. But there's a much better way.

The Object class defines the methods wait(), notify(), and notifyAll(), which you can use to provide a more efficient way of dealing with this kind of situation. Since all classes are derived from Object, all classes inherit these methods. You can only call these methods from within a synchronized method, or from within a synchronized code block, and an exception of type IllegalMonitorStateException will be thrown if you call them from somewhere. The functions that these methods perform are:

Method	Description
wait()	There are three overloaded versions of this method.
	This version suspends the current thread until the notify() or notifyAll() method is called for the object to which the wait() method belongs. Note that when any version of wait() is called, the thread releases the synchronization lock it has on the object, so any other method or code block synchronized on the same object can execute. As well as enabling notify() or notifyAll() to be called by another thread, this also allows another thread to call wait() for the same object.
	Since all versions of the wait() method can throw an InterruptedException, you must call it in a try block with a catch block for this exception, or at least indicate that the method calling it throws this exception.
wait(long timeout)	This version suspends the current thread until the number of milliseconds specified by the argument has expired, or until the notify() or notifyAll() method for the object to which the wait() method belongs is called, if that occurs sooner.
wait(long timeout, int nanos)	This version works in the same way as the previous version, except the time interval is specified by two arguments, the first in milliseconds, and the second in nanoseconds.
notify()	This will restart a thread that has called the wait() method for the object to which the notify() method belongs. If several threads have called wait() for the object, you have no control over which thread is notified, in which case it is better to use notifyAll(). If no threads are waiting, the method does nothing.
notifyAll()	This will restart all threads that have called wait() for the object to which the notifyAll() method belongs.

The basic idea of the wait() and notify() methods is that they provide a way for methods or code blocks that are synchronized on a particular object to communicate. One block can call wait() to suspend its operation until some other method or code block synchronized on the same object changes it in some way, and calls notify() to signal that the change is complete. A thread will typically call wait() because some particular property of the object it is synchronized on is not set, or some condition is not fulfilled, and this is dependent on action by another thread. Perhaps the simplest situation is where a resource is busy because it is being modified by another thread, but you are by no means limited to that.

The major difference between calling `sleep()` and calling `wait()` is that `wait()` releases any objects on which the current thread has a lock, whereas `sleep()` does not. It is essential that `wait()` should work this way, otherwise there would be no way for another thread to change things so that the condition required by the current thread is met.

Thus the typical use of `wait()` is:

```
synchronized(anObject) {
  while(condition-not-met)
    anObject.wait();
  // Condition is met so continue...
}
```

Here the thread will suspend operation when the `wait()` method is called until some other thread synchronized on the same object calls `notify()` (or more typically `notifyAll()`). This allows the `while` loop to continue and check the condition again. Of course, it may still not be met, in which case the `wait()` method will be called again so another thread can operate on `anObject`. You can see from this that `wait()` is not just for getting access to an object. It is intended to allow other threads access until some condition has been met. You could even arrange that a thread would not continue until a given number of other threads had called `notify()` on the object to ensure that a minimum number of operations had been carried out.

It is generally better to use `notifyAll()` rather than `notify()` when you have more than two threads synchronized on an object. If you call `notify()` when there are two or more other threads suspended having called `wait()`, only one of the threads will be started, but you have no control over which it is. This opens the possibility that the thread that is started calls `wait()` again because the condition it requires is not fulfilled. This will leave all the threads waiting for each other, with no possibility of continuing.

Although the action of each of these methods is quite simple, applying them can become very complex. You have the potential for multiple threads to be interacting through several objects with `synchronized` methods and code blocks. We'll just explore the basics by seeing how we can use `wait()` and `notifyAll()` to get rid of a couple of the `while` loops we had in the last example.

Using wait() and notifyAll() in the Bank Program

In the `for` loop in `main()` that generates the transactions and passes them to the `Clerk` objects, we have two `while` loops that call the `isBusy()` method for a `Clerk` object. These were needed so that we didn't pass a transaction to a clerk while the clerk was still busy. By altering the `Clerk` class, so that it can use `wait()` and `notifyAll()`, we can eliminate the need for these.

Try It Out – Slimming Down the Transactions Loop

We want to make the `doTransaction()` method in the `Clerk` class conscious of the state of the `inTray` for the current object. If it is not `null`, we want the method to wait until it becomes so. To use `wait()` the block or method must be synchronized on an object – in this case the `Clerk` object since `inTray` is what we are interested in. We can do this by making the method synchronized:

```
public class Clerk implements Runnable {
  private Bank theBank;                  // The employer - an electronic marvel
```

```
      private Transaction inTray;           // The in-tray holding a transaction

      // Constructor
      public Clerk(Bank theBank) {
        this.theBank = theBank;             // Who the clerk works for
        inTray = null;                      // No transaction initially
      }

      // Receive a transaction
      synchronized public void doTransaction(Transaction transaction) {
        while(inTray != null) {
          try {
            wait();

          } catch(InterruptedException e) {
            System.out.println(e);
          }
        }
        inTray = transaction;
        notifyAll();
      }

      // Rest of the class as before...
    }
```

When `inTray` is `null`, the transaction is stored and the `notifyAll()` method is called to notify other threads waiting on a change to this `Clerk` object. If `inTray` is not `null`, this method waits until some other thread calls `notifyAll()` to signal a change to the `Clerk` object. We now need to consider where the `inTray` field is going to be modified elsewhere. The answer is in the `run()` method for the `Clerk` class, of course, so we need to change that too:

```
      synchronized public void run() {
        while(true) {
          while(inTray == null)             // No transaction waiting?
            try {
              wait();                        // Then take a break until there is

            } catch(InterruptedException e) {
              System.out.println(e);
            }

          theBank.doTransaction(inTray);
          inTray = null;                     // In-tray is empty
          notifyAll();                       // Notify other threads locked on this clerk
        }
      }

      // Rest of the class as before...
    }
```

Just to make it clear which methods are in what threads, the situation in our program is illustrated below.

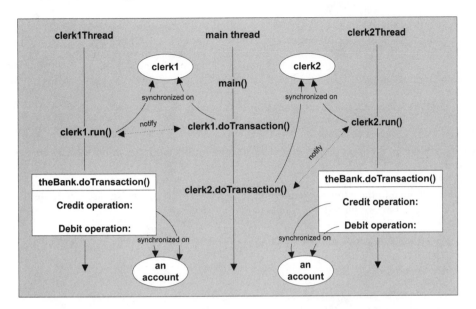

Here the run() method is synchronized on the Clerk object that contains it, and the method waits if inTray is null. Eventually the doTransaction() method for the current object should store a transaction in inTray, and then notify the thread that is waiting that it should continue.

It may seem odd having two methods in the same object synchronized on one and the same object that owns them, but remember that the run() and doTransaction() methods for a particular Clerk object are in separate threads.

The transaction processing method for the bank can be in both of the clerk threads, whereas the methods that hand over a transaction to a clerk are in the main thread. The diagram also shows which code is synchronized on what objects.

We can now modify the code in the for loop in main() to pass the transactions directly to the clerks. Except for deleting the two while loops that wait until the clerks are free, the code is exactly as before:

```
// Create transactions randomly distributed between the accounts
for(int i = 1; i <= transactionCount; i++) {
  // Generate a random account index for credit operation

  select = rand.nextInt(accounts.length);
  amount = 50 + rand.nextInt(26);                  // Generate amount of $50 to $75
  transaction = new Transaction(accounts[select],      // Account
                          Transaction.CREDIT, // Credit transaction
                          amount);             //  of amount
  totalCredits[select] += amount;                  // Keep total credit tally

  clerk1.doTransaction(transaction);               // Now do the credit

  // Generate a random account index for debit operation
  select = rand.nextInt(accounts.length);
```

```
    amount = 30 + rand.nextInt(31);              // Generate amount of $30 to $60
    transaction = new Transaction(accounts[select],    // Account
                                  Transaction.DEBIT,   // Debit transaction
                                  amount);             //  of amount
    totalDebits[select] += amount;               // Keep total debit tally

    clerk2.doTransaction(transaction);           // Now do the debit
  }
```

We have just deleted the loop blocks that were waiting until a clerk became free. This makes our code a lot shorter.

With a small change to the `isBusy()` method in the `Clerk` class, we can also eliminate the need for the `while` loop before we output the results in `main()`:

```
synchronized public void isBusy() {
  while(inTray != null) {            // Is this object busy?
    try {
      wait();                        // Yes, so wait for notify call

    } catch(InterruptedException e) {
      System.out.println(e);
    }
  return;                            // It is free now
  }
}
```

Now the `isBusy()` method will only return when the clerk object has no transaction waiting or in progress, so no return value is necessary. The `while` loop in `main()` before the final output statements can be replaced by:

```
// Wait until both clerks are done
clerk1.isBusy();
clerk2.isBusy();
```

How It Works

The `doTransaction()` method for a `Clerk` object calls the `wait()` method if the `inTray` field contains a reference to a transaction object, as this means the `Clerk` object is still processing a credit or a debit. This will result in the current thread (which is the main thread) being suspended until the `notifyAll()` method is called by this object's `run()` method to indicate a change to the clerk.

Because the `run()` method is also synchronized on the `Clerk` object, it too can call `wait()` in this case, if the `inTray` contains `null`, since this indicates that there is no transaction waiting for the clerk to expedite. A call to the `doTransaction()` method for the `Clerk` object will result in a transaction being stored in `inTray`, and the `notifyAll()` call will wake up the `run()` method to continue execution.

Because we've declared the `isBusy()` method as `synchronized`, we can call the `wait()` method to suspend the current thread if transactions are still being processed. Since we don't return from the method until the outstanding transaction is complete, we have no need of a `boolean` return value.

Thread Priorities

All threads have a priority that determines which thread is executed when several threads are waiting for their turn. This makes it possible to give one thread more access to processor resources than another. Let's consider an elementary example of how this could be used. Suppose you have one thread in a program that requires all the processor resources – some solid long running calculation– and some other threads that require relatively few resources. By making the thread that requires all the resources a low priority thread, you ensure that the other threads get executed promptly, while the processor bound thread can make use of the processor cycles that are left over after the others have had their turn.

The possible values for thread priority are defined in `static` data members of the class `Thread`. These members are of type `int`, and are declared as `final`. The maximum thread priority is defined by the member `MAX_PRIORITY`, which has the value 10. The minimum priority is `MIN_PRIORITY`, defined as 1. The value of the default priority that is assigned to the main thread in a program is `NORM_PRIORITY`, which is set to 5. When you create a thread, its priority will be the same as that of the thread that created it.

You can modify the priority of a thread by calling the `setPriority()` method for the `Thread` object. This method accepts an argument of type `int` that defines the new priority for the thread. An `IllegalArgumentException` will be thrown if you specify a priority that is less than `MIN_PRIORITY` or greater than `MAX_PRIORITY`.

If you're going to be messing about with the priorities of the threads in your program, you need to be able to find out the current priority for a thread. You can do this by calling the `getPriority()` method for the `Thread` object. This will return the current priority for the thread as a value of type `int`.

Using Thread Priorities

In the last example, you could set priorities for the threads by adding statements to `main()`:

```
clerk1Thread.setPriority(Thread.MIN_PRIORITY);    // Credits are a low priority
clerk2Thread.setPriority(Thread.MAX_PRIORITY);    // Debits are a high priority
```

You can put these statements following the call to the `start()` method for each of the `Thread` objects for the clerks. However, this can't have much effect in our program since one clerk can't get ahead of the other. This is because each clerk only queues one transaction and they are allocated alternately to each clerk.

In the interests of learning more about how thread priorities affect the execution of your program, let's change the example once more to enable a `Clerk` object to queue transactions. We can do this quite easily using a `LinkedList` object, which we discussed in Chapter 13. There are a couple of points to be aware of though.

The first point is that only the `Vector` class out of the collection classes is thread-safe – that is, safe for modification by more than one thread. For the others you must either only access them by methods and code blocks that are synchronized on the collection object, or wrap the collection class in a thread-safe wrapper. Let's change the example to incorporate the latter.

The second point is that whether thread priorities have any effect depends on your operating system. If it doesn't support thread priorities, then setting thread priorities in your Java code will have no effect. Let's run it anyway to see how it works.

Try It Out – Setting Thread Priorities

We can extend the `Clerk` class to handle a number of `Transaction` objects by giving the in-tray the capacity to store several transactions in a list, but not too many – we don't want to overwork the clerks. The `Collections` class provides methods for creating synchronized sets, lists, and maps from unsynchronized objects. The static `synchronizedList()` method in the `Collections` class accepts an argument that is a list and returns a `List` object that is synchronized. We can use this to make our `inTray` a synchronized list for storing transactions.

```java
import java.util.List;
import java.util.Collections;
import java.util.LinkedList;

public class Clerk implements Runnable {
  Bank theBank;
  // The in-tray holding transactions
  private List inTray = Collections.synchronizedList(new LinkedList());

  private int maxTransactions = 8;        // Maximum transactions in the in-tray

  // Constructor
  public Clerk(Bank theBank) {
    this.theBank = theBank;                     // Who the clerk works for
    //inTray      = null;                  //Commented out: don't need this now
  }
// Plus the rest of the class...
}
```

Note that we have deleted the statement from the constructor that originally set `inTray` to `null`. Now that we are working with a list, we must change the `doTransaction()` method in the `Clerk` class to store the transaction in the list as long as the tray is not full or, to say it another way, there are less than `maxTransactions` in the list. Here's the revised code to do this:

```java
synchronized public void doTransaction(Transaction transaction) {
  while(inTray.size() >= maxTransactions) {
    try {
      wait();

    } catch(InterruptedException e) {
      System.out.println(e);
    }
    inTray.add(transaction);
    notifyAll();
  }
}
```

The `size()` method for the list returns the number of objects it contains so checking this is trivial. We use the `add()` method to add a new `Transaction` object to the end of the list.

The `run()` method for a clerk retrieves objects from the in-tray so we must update that to deal with a list:

```
synchronized public void run() {
  while(true) {
    while(inTray.size() == 0) {     // No transaction waiting?
      try {
        wait();                     // Then take a break until there is

      } catch(InterruptedException e) {
        System.out.println(e);
      }
      theBank.doTransaction((Transaction)inTray.remove(0));
    notifyAll();                    // Notify other threads locked on this clerk
    }
  }
}
```

The remove() method in the List interface that we are using here removes the object at the index position in the list specified by the argument and returns a reference to it. Since we use 0 as the index we retrieve the first object in the list to pass to the doTransaction() method for the Bank object.

Since we now use a list to store transactions, the isBusy() method for a Clerk object also needs to be changed:

```
synchronized public void isBusy() {
  while(inTray.size() != 0) {             // Is this object busy?
    try {
      wait();                             // Yes, so wait for notify call

    } catch(InterruptedException e) {
      System.out.println(e);
    }
  }
  return;                                 // It is free now
}
```

Now the clerk is not busy if there are no transactions in the inTray list. Hence we test the value returned by size().

That's all we need to buffer transactions in the in-tray of each clerk. If you reactivate the output statements that we added to the method in the Bank class, you'll be able to see how the processing of transactions proceeds.

With the priorities set by the calls to setPriority() we saw earlier, the processing of credits should run ahead of the processing of debits, although the fact that the time to process a debit is longer than the time for a credit will also have a significant effect. To make the thread priority the determining factor, set the times in the calls to the sleep() method in the Bank class to the same value. You could then try changing the values for priorities around to see what happens to the sequence in which transactions are processed. Of course, if your operating system does not support priority scheduling, then it won't have any effect anyway.

How It Works

We've made the `inTray` object a synchronized `LinkedList`, by passing it to the static `synchronizedList()` method in the `Collections` class. This method returns a thread-safe `List` based on the original `LinkedList` object. We use the thread-safe `List` object to store up to `maxTransactions` transactions – eight in this case. The `doTransaction()` method for a `Clerk` object makes sure that a transaction is only added to the list if there are less than eight transactions queued.

The `doTransaction()` method for the `Bank` object always obtains the first object in the `List`, so the transactions will be processed in the sequence in which they were added to the `list`.

If your operating system supports priority scheduling, altering the thread priority values will change the pattern of servicing of the transactions.

Summary

In this chapter you have learned about threads and how you can create and manage them. We will be using threads from time to time in examples later in this book so be sure you don't move on from here without being comfortable with the basic ideas of how you create and start a thread.

The essential points that we have covered in this chapter are:

❑   Threads are subtasks in a program that can be in execution concurrently.

❑   A thread is represented by an object of the class `Thread`. Execution of a thread begins with the execution of the `run()` method defined in the class `Thread`.

❑   You define the code to be executed in a thread by implementing the `run()` method in a class derived from `Thread`, or in a class that implements the interface `Runnable`.

❑   A thread specified as **daemon** will cease execution when the thread that created it ends.

❑   A thread that isn't a daemon thread is called a **user thread**. A user thread will not be terminated automatically when the thread that created it ends.

❑   You start execution of a thread by calling the `start()` method for its `Thread` object. If you need to halt a thread before normal completion you can stop execution of a thread by calling the `interrupt()` method for its `Thread` object.

❑   Methods can be declared as `synchronized`. Only one `synchronized` instance method for an object can execute at any given time. Only one `synchronized static` method for a class can execute at one time.

❑   A code block can be declared as `synchronized` on an object. Only one synchronized code block for an object can execute at any given time.

❑   In a synchronized method or code block, you can call the `wait()` method inherited from the class `Object` to halt execution of a thread. Execution of the waiting thread will continue when the `notify()` or `notifyAll()` method inherited from `Object` is called by a thread synchronized on the same object.

❑   The notify() or notifyAll() method can only be called from a method or code block that is synchronized to the same object as the method or block that contains the wait() method that halted the thread.

❑   You can modify the relative priority of a thread by calling its setPriority() method. This only has an effect on execution in environments that support priority scheduling.

Exercises

1.   Modify the last example in the chapter so that each transaction is a debit or a credit at random.

2.   Modify the result of the previous exercise to incorporate an array of clerks, each running in their own thread, and each able to handle both debits and credits.

3.   Extend the result of the previous exercise to incorporate two supervisors for two teams of clerks, where the supervisors each run in their own thread. The supervisor threads should originate transactions and pass them to the clerks they supervise.

Creating Windows

Until now, the programs we have been creating have perhaps not been what you may instinctively think of as a program. We can't expect a user to know about classpaths and so on in order to run one of our programs. More traditionally, an application consists of one or more windows that the user can interact with. These windows, and the environment that the user interacts with, is known as the **Graphical User Interface (GUI)**.

In this chapter, we will investigate how to create a window for a Java application and we will take a first look at some of the components we can put together to create a graphical user interface in Java.

You will learn:

- ❑ How to create a resizable window.
- ❑ What components and containers are.
- ❑ How you can add components to a window.
- ❑ How to control the layout of components.
- ❑ How to create a menu bar and menus for a window.
- ❑ What a menu shortcut is and how you can add a shortcut for a menu item.
- ❑ What the restrictions on the capabilities of an applet are.
- ❑ How to convert an application into an applet.

Graphical User Interfaces in Java

There is a vast amount of functionality in the Java class libraries devoted to supporting graphical user interface (GUI) creation and management, far more than it is feasible to cover in a single book – even if it is big. Just the JFrame class, which we will be exploring in a moment, contains more than 200 methods when one includes those inherited from superclasses! We will therefore have to be selective in what we go into in detail, in terms of both the specific classes we discuss and their methods. We will however cover the basic operations that you need to understand to create your own applications and applets. With a good grasp of the basics, you should be able to explore other areas of the Java class library beyond those discussed without too much difficulty.

The fundamental elements that you need in order to create a GUI reside in two packages, java.awt and javax.swing. The java.awt package was the primary repository for classes you would use to create a GUI in Java 1.1 – 'awt' being an abbreviation for **A**bstract **W**indowing **T**oolkit, but many of the classes it defines have been superseded in Java 2 by javax.swing. Most of the classes in the javax.swing package define GUI elements, referred to as **Swing components,** that provide much-improved alternatives to components defined by classes in java.awt. We will be looking into the JButton class in the Swing set that defines a button, rather than the Button class in java.awt. However, the Swing component classes are generally derived from, and depend on, fundamental classes within java.awt, so you can't afford to ignore these.

The Swing classes are part of a more general set of GUI programming capabilities that are collectively referred to as the **Java Foundation Classes**, or **JFC** for short. JFC covers not only the Swing component classes, such as those defining buttons and menus, but also classes for 2D drawing from the java.awt.geom package, and classes that support drag-and-drop capability in the java.awt.dnd package. The JFC also includes an API defined in the javax.accessibility package that allows applications to be implemented that provide for users with disabilities.

The Swing component classes are more flexible than the component classes defined in the java.awt package because they are implemented entirely in Java. The java.awt components depend on native code to a great extent, and are, therefore, restricted to a 'lowest common denominator' set of interface capabilities. Because Swing components are pure Java, they are not restricted by the characteristics of the platform on which they run. Apart from the added function and flexibility of the Swing components, they also provide a feature called **pluggable look-and-feel** that makes it possible to change the appearance of a component. You can programmatically select the look-and-feel of a component from those implemented as standard, or you can create your own look-and-feel for components if you wish. The pluggable look-and-feel of the Swing components has been facilitated by designing the classes in a particular way, called the **Model View Control architecture**.

Model-View-Controller (MVC) Architecture

The design of the Swing component classes is loosely based on something called the **Model-View-Controller** architecture, or MVC. This is not of particular consequence in the context of applying the Swing classes, but it's important to be aware of it if you want to modify the pluggable look-and-feel of a component. MVC is not new, and did not originate with Java. In fact the idea of MVC emerged some time ago within the context of the Smalltalk programming language. MVC is an idealized way of modeling a component as three separate parts:

❑   The **model** that stores the data that defines the component.

❑   The **view** that creates the visual representation of the component from the data in the model.

❑   The **controller** that deals with user interaction with the component and modifies the model and/or the view in response to a user action as necessary.

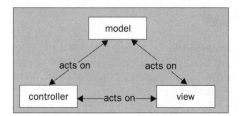

In object-oriented terms, each of the three logical parts for a component – the model, the view, and the controller – is ideally represented by a different class type. In practice this turns out to be difficult because of the dependencies between the view and the controller. Since the user interacts with the physical representation of the component, the controller operation is highly dependent on the implementation of the view. For this reason, the view and controller are typically represented by a single composite object that corresponds to a view with an integrated controller. In this case the MVC concept degenerates into the document/view architecture that we introduced when we discussed the `Observable` class and `Observer` interface. Sun call it the **Separable Model architecture**.

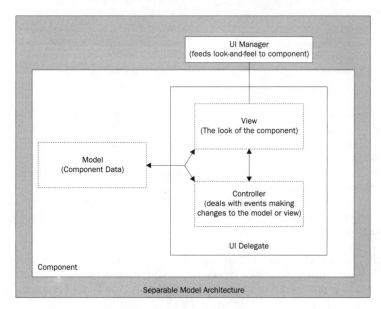

The way the Swing components provide for a pluggable look-and-feel is to make the visual appearance of a component and the interface to the user the responsibility of an independent object called the **UI delegate**. This is the view+controller part of the MVC model. Thus a different UI delegate can provide a component with a new look-and-feel.

The details of how you modify the look-and-feel of a component is beyond the scope of this book. It is, however, as well to be aware of the MVC architecture on which the Swing components are based since it appears quite often in the literature around Java, and should you want to change the look-and-feel of a component at some time.

Creating a Window

A basic window in Java is represented by an object of the class `Window` in the package `java.awt`. Objects of the class `Window` are hardly ever used directly since borders and a title bar are fairly basic prerequisites for a typical application window, and this class provides neither. The library class `JFrame`, defined in `javax.swing`, is a much more useful class for creating a window, since as well as a title bar and a border, it provides a wealth of other facilities. Its superclasses are shown below.

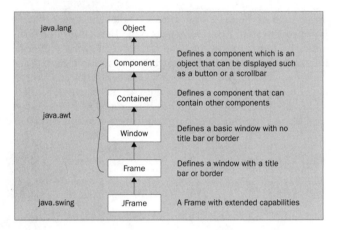

The `Component` class is the grandmother of all component classes – it defines the basic properties and methods shared by all components. We will see later that all the Swing components have the `Component` class as a base. The `Container` class adds the capability for a `Component` object to contain other components, which is a frequent requirement. Since `JFrame` has `Container` as a superclass, a `JFrame` object can contain other components. Beyond the obvious need for a window to be able to contain the components that represent the GUI, a menu bar should contain menus, for instance, which in turn will contain menu items: a toolbar will obviously contain toolbar buttons, and there are many other examples. For this reason the `Container` class is also a base for all the classes that define Swing components.

The `Window` class adds methods to the `Container` class that are specific to a window, such as the ability to handle events arising from user interaction with the window. The `Frame` class is the original class in `java.awt` that provided a proper window, with a title bar and a border, with which everyone is familiar. The `JFrame` class adds functionality to the `Frame` class to support much more sophisticated facilities for drawing and displaying other components. You can deduce from the hierarchy in the diagram how a `JFrame` object can easily end up with its 200+ methods as it has five superclasses from which it inherits members. We aren't going to trawl through all these classes and methods. We'll just look into the ones we need in context as we go along, and then see how they are applied for real. This will hopefully teach you the most important methods in this class.

You can display an application window simply by creating an object of type JFrame, calling a method for the object to set the size of the window, and then calling a method to display the window. Let's try that right away.

Try It Out – Framing a Window

Here's the code:

```
import javax.swing.JFrame;

public class TryWindow {
  // The window object
  static JFrame aWindow = new JFrame("This is the Window Title");

  public static void main(String[] args) {
    int windowWidth = 400;                          // Window width in pixels
    int windowHeight = 150;                         // Window height in pixels
    aWindow.setBounds(50, 100,                      // Set position
                      windowWidth, windowHeight);   // and size
    aWindow.setDefaultCloseOperation(JFrame.EXIT_ON_CLOSE);
    aWindow.setVisible(true);                       // Display the window
  }
}
```

Under Microsoft Windows, the program will display the window shown:

Try resizing the window by dragging a border or a corner with the mouse. You can also try minimizing the window by clicking on the icons to the right of the title bar. Everything should work OK so we are getting quite a lot for so few lines of code. You can close the application by clicking on the ☒ icon.

> This example will terminate OK if you have entered the code correctly, however errors could prevent this. If an application doesn't terminate properly for any reason you will have to get the operating system to end the task. Under MS Windows, switching to the DOS window and pressing *Ctrl+C* will do it.

How It Works

The import statement adds JFrame in the package javax.swing to our program. From now on most of our programs will be using the components defined in this package. The object of type JFrame is created and stored as the initial value for the static data member of the class TryWindow, so it will be created automatically when the TryWindow class is loaded. The argument to the constructor defines the title to be displayed in the application window.

The `main()` method calls three methods for the `aWindow` object. The method `setBounds()` defines the size and position of the window; the first pair of arguments correspond to the *x* and *y* coordinates of the top-left corner of our application window relative to the top-left corner of the display screen, and the second pair of arguments specify the width and height of the window in pixels. The screen coordinate system has the origin point, (0, 0), at the top-left corner of the screen, with the positive *x*-axis running left to right and the positive *y*-axis from top to bottom. The positive *y*-axis in screen coordinates is therefore in the opposite direction to that of the usual Cartesian coordinate system.

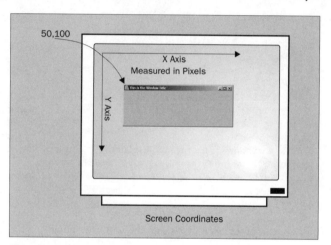

We have specified the top-left corner of our application window at position (50, 100) on the screen, which will be 50 pixels to the right and 100 pixels down. Since the window will be 400 pixels wide and 150 pixels high, the bottom right corner will be at position (450, 250). The actual physical width and height of the window as well as its position relative to the edge of the screen will depend on the size of your screen and the display resolution. For a given screen size, the higher the display resolution, the smaller the window will be and the closer it will be to the top left-hand corner, simply because the pixels on the screen will be closer together. We will see how we can get around this potential problem later in this chapter.

The `setDefaultCloseOperation()` method determines what happens when you close the window by clicking on either the ☒ icon or selecting Close from the menu that is displayed when you click on the ▩ in the top-left corner of the window. There are four possible argument values you can use here. The constant we have used at the argument to the method, `EXIT_ON_CLOSE`, is defined in the `JFrame` class. The effect of this is to close the window, dispose of the window resources and those of any components it contains, and finally to terminate the application. There are three other argument values you could use with the `setDefaultCloseOperation()` method that are defined in the `WindowConstants` interface. These values are:

Argument	Description
`DISPOSE_ON_CLOSE`	This causes the frame and any components it contains to be destroyed but doesn't terminate the application.
`DO_NOTHING_ON_CLOSE`	This makes the close operation for the frame window ineffective.

Argument	Description
HIDE_ON_CLOSE	This just hides the window by calling its setVisible() method with an argument of false. This is the default action if you don't call the setDefaultCloseOperation() method with a different argument value. When a window is hidden, you could always display the window again later by calling setVisible() with an argument of true.

Of course, you may want to take some action beyond the options we have discussed here when the user chooses to close the window. If the program involves entering a lot of data for instance, you may want to ensure that the user is prompted to save the data before the program ends. This involves handling an event associated with the close menu item or the close button, and we will be investigating this in the next chapter.

The method setVisible() with the argument set to true, displays our application window on top of any other windows currently visible on the screen. If you wanted to hide the window somewhere else in the program, you would call setVisible() with the argument set to false.

It's a very *nice* window, but not overly useful. All you can do with it is move, resize, and reshape it. You can drag the borders and maximize and minimize it. The close icon works because our program elected to dispose of the window and exit the program when the close operation is selected by setting the appropriate option through the setDefaultCloseOperation() method. If we omitted this method call, the window would close but the program would not terminate.

The setBounds() and setVisible() methods are members of the JFrame class inherited from the Component class, so these are available for any component. However, you don't normally set the size and position of other components, as we will see. The setDefaultCloseOperation() method is defined in the JFrame class so this method only applies to JFrame window objects.

Before we expand our JFrame example we need to look a little deeper into the make-up of the component classes.

Components and Containers

A component represents a graphical entity of one kind or another that can be displayed on the screen. A component is any object of a class that is a subclass of Component. As we have seen, a JFrame window is a component, but there are many others. Before getting into specifics, let's first get a feel for the general relationship between the groups of classes that represent components. Part of the class hierarchy with Component as a base is shown overleaf. The arrows in the diagram point towards the superclass.

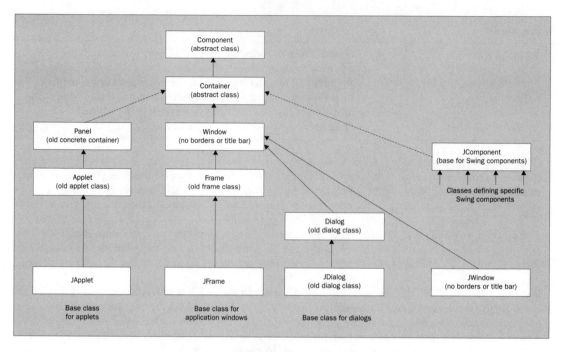

This shows some of the subclasses of Component – the ones that are important to us at the moment. We discussed the chain through to JFrame earlier, but the other branches are new. The classes that we will be using directly are all the most commonly derived classes.

Let's summarize how you would typically use the key classes in this hierarchy:

Class	Use
JFrame	This is used as the basic Java application window. An object of this class has a title bar and provision for adding a menu. You can also add other components to it. You will usually subclass this class to create a window class specific to your application. It is then possible to add GUI components or draw in this window if required, as we will see.
JDialog	You use this class to define a dialog window that is used for entering data into a program in various ways. You usually code the creation of a dialog in response to some menu item being selected.
JApplet	This is the base class for a Java 2 applet – a program designed to run embedded in a web page. All your Java 2 applets will have this class as a base. You can draw in a JApplet and also add menus and other components.
JComponent	The subclasses of JComponent define a range of standard components such as menus, buttons, checkboxes, and so on. You will use these classes to create the GUI for your application or applet.

All the classes derived from `Container` can contain other objects of any of the classes derived from `Component`, and are referred to generically as **containers**. Since the `Container` class is a sub class of the `Component` class, every container object is a `Component` too, so a container can contain other containers. The exception is the `Window` class and its subclasses, as objects of type `Window` (or of a subclass type) can't be contained in another container. If you try to do this, an exception will be thrown. The `JComponent` class is the base for all the Swing components used in a window as part of the GUI, so, since this class is derived from `Container`, all of the Swing components are also containers.

As you can see, the `JApplet` class, which is a base class for all Swing applets, is derived from `Component` via the `Container` class. An applet will, therefore, also inherit the methods from the `Container` and `Component` classes. It also inherits methods from the old `Applet` class, which it extends and improves upon. You should note that the `JApplet`, `JFrame`, and `JDialog` classes, and the `JComponent` class and its subclasses, are all in the package `javax.swing`. The `Applet` class is in `java.applet`, and all the others are in `java.awt`. The package `java.applet` is tiny – it only contains the one class plus three related interfaces, but we won't need to use it directly. We will always be using the `JApplet` class to define an applet, as it's significantly better than `Applet`.

Window and Frame Components

The basic difference between a `JFrame` object and a `Window` object is that a `JFrame` object represents the main window for an application, whereas a `Window` object does not – you always need a `JFrame` object before you can create a `Window` object.

Since the `JDialog` class is derived directly from the `Window` class, you can only create a `JDialog` object in an application in the context of a `JFrame` object. Apart from the default constructor, the constructors for the `JDialog` class generally require a `JFrame` object to be passed as an argument. This `JFrame` object is referred to as the **parent** of the `JDialog` object. A `JFrame` object has a border, is resizable, and has the ability to hold a built-in menu bar. Since a `JFrame` object is the top-level window in an application, its size and location are defined relative to the screen. A `JDialog` object with a `JFrame` object as a parent will be located relative to its parent.

Note that while we will discuss applets based on the `JApplet` class in this book, there is still a significant role for applets based on the more restricted capabilities of the `Applet` class. This is because as yet browsers do not support Java 2 applets by default. Both Netscape Navigator and Microsoft Internet Explorer require the Java Plug-In from Sun to be installed before a Java2 applet can be executed. You can download the Java Plug-In from the Sun Java web site at http://java.sun.com/products.

As we said, the `JApplet`, `JFrame`, and `JDialog` classes are all containers because they have `Container` as a base class and therefore, in principle, can contain any kind of component. They are also all components themselves since they are derived ultimately from the `Component` class. However, things are not quite as simple as that. You don't add the components for your application or applet GUI *directly* to the `JFrame` or `JApplet` object for your program. Let's look at how it actually works in practice.

Window Panes

When you want to add GUI components or draw in a window displayed from a `JFrame` object, you add the components to, or draw on, a **window pane** that is managed by the `JFrame` object. The same goes for an applet. Broadly speaking, window panes are container objects that represent an area of a window, and they come in several different types.

You will use a window pane called the **content pane** most of the time, but there are others. The relationship between the `contentPane` object, other window panes, and the application window itself is shown here.

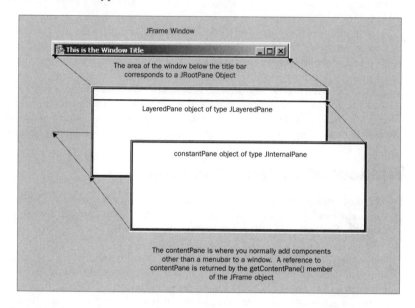

As you see, the area below the title bar in a `JFrame` window corresponds to a `JRootPane` object. This contains another pane, the `layeredPane` object in the illustration, which is of type `JLayeredPane`. This pane corresponds to the whole of the area occupied by the `JRootPane` object in the window and manages the menu bar if the window has one. The area in the `layeredPane` below the menu bar corresponds to the `contentPane` object, and it's here that you typically add GUI components. You also display text or do any drawing in the area covered by the content pane.

The `layeredPane` object has special properties for advanced applications that permit groups of components to be managed in separate layers that overlay one another within the pane. With this capability you can control how components are displayed relative to one another, because the layers are displayed in a particular order from back to front. The components in a layer at the front will appear on the screen in front of those in a layer that is towards the back.

There is also an additional pane not shown in the diagram. This is the `glassPane` object, and this also corresponds to the complete `JRootPane` area. The contents of the `glassPane` object displays on top of all the other panes, so this is used to display components that you always want to display on top of anything else displayed in the window – such as pop-up menus. You can also use the `glassPane` to display graphics that need to be updated relatively frequently – such as when you create an animation. When part of what is displayed is to be animated, a static background can be displayed independently via the `contentPane`. Since this doesn't need to be reprocessed each time the animated objects need to be redrawn, the whole process can be much more efficient.

The `JFrame` class defines methods to provide you with a reference to any of the panes:

Method	Description
getRootPane()	Returns the root pane as type JRootPane.
getLayeredPane()	Returns the layered pane as type JLayeredPane.
getContentPane()	Returns the content pane as type Container. This is the method you will use most frequently, since you normally add components to the content pane.
getGlassPane()	Returns the glass pane as type Component.

All the classes discussed here that represent panes are themselves Swing components, defined in the javax.swing package. A JApplet object has the same arrangement of panes as a JFrame object, so adding components to an applet, or drawing on it, works in exactly the same way. An applet defined as a JApplet object can also have a menu bar just like an application window.

All the panes, as well as the menu bar, are components, so before we start delving into how to add a menu bar or other components to a window, let's unearth a little more about the make-up of components in general.

Basics of Components

There's quite a lot of basic stuff that is common to all components that we have to examine before we can apply components properly. It also has applications in many different contexts. While this may seem like something of a catalog of classes and methods, without much in the way of practical application, please stay with it. We will be using most of these capabilities in a practical context later. To understand the fundamental things we can do with Swing components, we will examine what functionality they inherit from the Component and Container classes.

When a component is contained within another component, the outer object is referred to as the **parent**. You can find out what the parent of any given component is by calling its getParent() method. This method is inherited from the Component class and it returns the parent as type Container, since only a subclass of Container can hold other components. If there is no parent, as is the case with a JFrame component, this method will return null.

Component Attributes

The Component class defines attributes, which record the following information about an object:

❑ The **position** is stored as (x, y) coordinates. This fixes where the object is in relation to its container in the coordinate system of the container object.

❑ The **name** of the component is stored as a String object.

❑ The **size** is recorded as values for the width and the height of the object.

❑ The **foreground color** and **background color** that apply to the object. These color values are used when the object is displayed.

❑ The **font** used by the object when text is displayed.

❑ The **cursor** for the object – this defines the appearance of the cursor when it is over the object.

❑ Whether the object is **enabled** or not – when a component is enabled its enabled state is `true` and it has a normal appearance. When a component is disabled it is grayed out. Note that a disabled component can still originate events.

❑ Whether the object is **visible** on the screen or not – if an object is not marked as visible it is not drawn on the screen.

❑ Whether the object is **valid** or not – if an object is not valid, layout of the entities that make up the object has not been determined. This is the case before an object is made visible. You can make a `Container` object invalid by changing its contents. It will then need to be validated before it is displayed correctly.

You can only modify the characteristics of a `Component` object by calling its methods or affecting it indirectly in some way since none of the data members that store its characteristics are directly accessible – they are all `private`. For example, you can change the name of a `Component` object `myWindow` with the statement:

```
myWindow.setName("The Name");
```

If you subsequently want to retrieve the name of an object, you can use the `getName()` method which returns the name as a `String` object. For example:

```
String theName = myWindow.getName();
```

The `isVisible()`, `isEnabled()`, and `isValid()` methods return `true` if the object is visible, enabled, and valid respectively. You can set an object as visible or enabled by passing a value `true` as an argument to the methods `setVisible()` and `setEnabled()` respectively.

A common misconception with Swing components is that calling `setEnabled(false)` will inhibit events such as mouse clicks from the component. This is not the case. All it does is to set the internal enabled status to `false` and cause the component to be grayed out. To prevent events from a disabled component having an effect, you must call `isEnabled()` for the component in your event handling code to determine whether the component is enabled or not. You can then choose to do nothing when the `isEnabled()` method returns `false`.

Let's see how we can change the size and position of a `Component` object.

The Size and Position of a Component

Position is defined by *x* and *y* coordinates of type `int`, or by an object of type `Point`. A `Point` object has two public data members, x and y, corresponding to the *x* and *y* coordinate values. Size is defined by `width` and `height`, also values of type `int`, or by an object of type `Dimension`. The class `Dimension` has two public members of type `int`, namely `width` and `height`. The size and position of a component are often specified together by an object of type `Rectangle`. A `Rectangle` object has public data members, x and y, defining the top-left corner of the rectangle, with `width` and `height` members defining its size. All these data members are of type `int`.

Components have a 'preferred' size, which depends on the particular object. For example, the preferred size of a JButton object that defines a button is the size that accommodates the label for the button. Note that you will not normally adjust the size of a component unless you are placing it relative to your display screen, since the size will be managed automatically when it has a parent component. We will see the reason for this later in this chapter. A component also has a minimum size and if the space available to it is less than the minimum size, the component will not be displayed.

The methods to retrieve or alter the size and position are:

Method	Description
void setBounds(int x, int y, int width, int height)	Sets the position of the Component object to the coordinates (x, y), and the width and height of the object to the values defined by the third and fourth arguments.
void setBounds(Rectangle rect)	Sets the position and size of the Component object to be that of the Rectangle argument, rect.
Rectangle getBounds()	Returns the position and size of the object as an object of type Rectangle.
void setSize(Dimension d)	Sets the width and height of the Component object to the values stored in the members of the object d.
Dimension getSize()	Returns the current size of the Component object as a Dimension object.
setLocation(int x, int y)	Sets the position of the component to the point defined by (x, y).
setLocation(Point p)	Sets the position of the component to the point p.
Point getLocation()	Returns the position of the Component object as an object of type Point.

Another important method defined in the Component class is getToolkit(). This returns an object of type Toolkit that contains information about the environment in which your application is running, including the screen size in pixels. You can use the getToolkit() method to help set the size and position of a window on the screen. We can modify the previous example to demonstrate this.

Try It Out – Sizing Windows with Toolkit

We'll use the Toolkit object to display the window in the center of the screen with the width and height set as half of the screen width and height:

```
import javax.swing.JFrame;
import java.awt.Toolkit;
import java.awt.Dimension;

public class TryWindow {
```

```
      // The window object
      static JFrame aWindow = new JFrame("This is the Window Title");

      public static void main(String[] args) {
        Toolkit theKit = aWindow.getToolkit();          // Get the window toolkit
        Dimension wndSize = theKit.getScreenSize();   // Get screen size

        // Set the position to screen center & size to half screen size
        aWindow.setBounds(wndSize.width/4, wndSize.height/4,     // Position
                          wndSize.width/2, wndSize.height/2);   // Size
        aWindow.setDefaultCloseOperation(JFrame.EXIT_ON_CLOSE);
        aWindow.setVisible(true);                       // Display the window
      }
    }
```

If you try this example, you should see the application window centered on your display with a width and height of half that of the screen.

How It Works

The `Toolkit` object, `theKit`, is obtained by calling the `getToolkit()` method for the `JFrame` object, `aWindow`. This object represents the environment on your computer so it encapsulates all the properties and capabilities of that environment as far as Java is concerned, including the screen resolution and size.

> Note that you can't create a `Toolkit` object directly since `Toolkit` is an abstract class. There is only one `Toolkit` object in an application – the one that you get a reference for when you call `getToolkit()` for a component.

The `getScreenSize()` method that is a member of the `Toolkit` object returns an object of type `Dimension` containing data members `width` and `height`. These hold the number of pixels for the width and height of your display. We use these values to set the coordinates for the position of the window, and the width and height of the window through the `setBounds()` method.

This is not the only way of centering a window. A `java.awt.GraphicsEnvironment` object contains information about the graphics devices attached to a system, including the display – or displays-in systems with more than one. You can obtain a reference to a `GraphicsEnvironment` object that encapsulates information about the graphics devices on the local machine by calling the static `getLocalGraphicsEnvironment()` method, like this:

```
GraphicsEnvironment localGE = GraphicsEnvironment.getLocalGraphicsEnvironment();
```

You can now call this object's `getCenterPoint()` method to obtain a `Point` object containing the coordinates of the center of the screen:

```
Point center = localGE.getCenterPoint();
```

We could try this with a variation on the original version of TryWindow.

Here's the code:

```
import javax.swing.JFrame;
import java.awt.Point;
import java.awt.GraphicsEnvironment;

public class TryWindow
  // The window object
  static JFrame aWindow = new JFrame("This is the Window Title");

  public static void main(String[] args) {
    Point center =
            GraphicsEnvironment.getLocalGraphicsEnvironment().getCenterPoint();
    int windowWidth = 400;
    int windowHeight = 150;
    // set position and size
    aWindow.setBounds(center.x-windowWidth/2, center.y-windowHeight/2,
                      windowWidth, windowHeight);
    aWindow.setDefaultCloseOperation(JFrame.EXIT_ON_CLOSE);
    aWindow.setVisible(true);                      // Display the window
  }
}
```

When you execute this you should see the window displayed centered on your screen.

How It Works

This uses the coordinates of the point returned by the `getCenterPoint()` method to position the window. We calculate the position of the top-left corner of the application window by subtracting half the window width and half the height from the x and y coordinates of the screen center point, respectively.

Points and Rectangles

Let's digress briefly into more detail concerning the `Point` and `Rectangle` classes before continuing with the `Component` class methods, as they are going to come up quite often. Both these classes are defined in `java.awt`. You will find many of the methods provided by the `Point` and `Rectangle` classes very useful when drawing in a window. Entities displayed in a window will typically have `Rectangle` objects associated with them that define the areas within the window that they occupy. `Point` objects are used in the definition of other geometric entities such as lines and circles, and to specify their position in a window.

Note that neither `Point` nor `Rectangle` objects have any built-in representation on the screen. They aren't components; they are abstract geometric entities. If you want to display a rectangle you have to draw it. We will see how to do this in Chapter 13.

Point Objects

As we said, the `Point` class defines a point by two `public` data members of type `int`, x and y. Let's look at the methods that the class provides.

Try It Out – Playing with Point Objects

Try the following code:

```
import java.awt.Point;

public class PlayingPoints
  public static void main(String[] args) {
    Point aPoint = new Point();              // Initialize to 0,0
    Point bPoint = new Point(50,25);
    Point cPoint = new Point(bPoint);
    System.out.println("aPoint is located at: " + aPoint);
    aPoint.move(100,50);                     // Change to position 100,50

    bPoint.x = 110;
    bPoint.y = 70;

    aPoint.translate(10,20);                 // Move by 10 in x and 20 in y
    System.out.println("aPoint is now at: " + aPoint);

    if(aPoint.equals(bPoint))
      System.out.println("aPoint and bPoint are at the same location.");
  }
}
```

If you run the program you should see:

```
aPoint is located at: java.awt.Point[x=0,y=0]
aPoint is now at: java.awt.Point[x=110,y=70]
aPoint and bPoint are at the same location.
```

How It Works

You can see the three constructors that the `Point` class provides in action in the first few lines. We then manipulate the `Point` objects we've instantiated.

You can change a `Point` object to a new position with the `move()` method. Alternatively, you can use the `setLocation()` method to set the values of the x and y members. The `setLocation()` method does exactly the same as the `move()` method. It is included in the `Point` class for compatibility with the `setLocation()` method for a component. For the same reason, there is also a `getLocation()` method in the `Point` class that returns a copy of the current `Point` object. As the example shows, you can also translate a `Point` object by specified distances in the x and y directions using the `translate()` method.

Lastly, you can compare two `Point` objects using the `equals()` method. This compares the x and y coordinates of the two `Point` objects, and returns `true` if both are equal. The final output statement is executed because the `Point` objects are equal.

Note that this is not the only class that represents points. We will see other classes that define points when we discuss how to draw in a window.

Rectangle Objects

As discussed earlier, the `Rectangle` class defines four `public` data members, all of type `int`. The position of a `Rectangle` object is defined by the members x and y, and its size is defined by the members `width` and `height`. As they are all `public` class members, you can retrieve or modify any of these directly, but your code will be a little more readable if you use the methods provided.

There are no less than seven constructors that you can use:

Constructor	Description
`Rectangle()`	Creates a rectangle at (0, 0) with zero width and height.
`Rectangle(int x, int y, int width, int height)`	Creates a rectangle at (x, y) with the specified width and height.
`Rectangle(int width, int height)`	Creates a rectangle at (0, 0) with the specified width and height.
`Rectangle(Point p, Dimension d)`	Creates a rectangle at point p with the width and height specified by d.
`Rectangle(Point p)`	Creates a rectangle at point p with zero width and height.
`Rectangle(Dimension d)`	Creates a rectangle at (0, 0) with the width and height specified by d.
`Rectangle(Rectangle r)`	Creates a rectangle with the same position and dimensions as r.

You can retrieve or modify the position of a `Rectangle` object using the method `getLocation()` that returns a `Point` object, and `setLocation()` that comes in two versions, one of which requires *x* and *y* coordinates of the new position as arguments and the other, which requires a `Point` object. You can also apply the `translate()` method to a `Rectangle` object, in the same way as the `Point` object.

To retrieve or modify the size of a `Rectangle` object you use the methods `getSize()`, which returns a `Dimension` object, and `setSize()`, which requires either a `Dimension` object specifying the new size as an argument, or two arguments corresponding to the new width and height values as type `int`.

There are also several methods that
you can use to combine `Rectangle`
objects, and also to extend a
`Rectangle` object to enclose a point.
The effects of each of these methods
are shown in the following diagram.

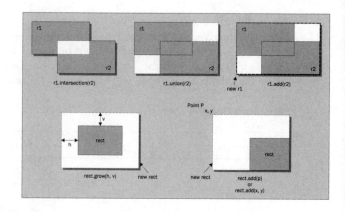

The rectangle that results from each operation is shown dashed. The methods illustrated in the diagram are:

Method	Description
`Rectangle intersection(` `Rectangle r)`	Returns a `Rectangle` object that is the intersection of the current object and the argument. If the two rectangles do not intersect, the `Rectangle` object returned is at position (0, 0) and the `width` and `height` members are zero so the rectangle is empty.
`Rectangle union(` `Rectangle r)`	Returns the smallest `Rectangle` object enclosing both the current `Rectangle` object and the `Rectangle` object r, passed as an argument.
`void add(Rectangle r)`	Expands the current `Rectangle` object to enclose the argument `Rectangle`.
`void add(Point p)`	Expands the current `Rectangle` object to enclose the `Point` object p. The result will be the smallest rectangle that encloses the original rectangle and the point.
`void add(int x, int y)`	Expands the current `Rectangle` object to enclose the point at (x, y).
`void grow(int h, int v)`	Enlarges the current `Rectangle` object by moving the boundary out from the center by h horizontally and v vertically.

You can also test and compare `Rectangle` objects in various ways with the following methods:

Method	Description
`boolean isEmpty()`	Returns `true` if the `width` and `height` members of the current `Rectangle` object are zero, and `false` otherwise.
`boolean equals(` `Object rect)`	Returns `true` if the `Rectangle` object passed as an argument is equal to the current `Rectangle` object, and returns `false` otherwise. The two rectangles will be equal if they are at the same position and have the same width and height. If the argument is not a `Rectangle` object, `false` is returned.
`boolean intersects(` `Rectangle rect)`	Returns `true` if the current `Rectangle` object intersects the `Rectangle` object passed as an argument, and `false` otherwise.
`boolean contains(` `Point p)`	Returns `true` if the current `Rectangle` object encloses the `Point` argument p, and `false` otherwise.
`boolean contains(` `int x, int y)`	Returns `true` if the current `Rectangle` object encloses the point (x, y), and `false` otherwise.

All of these will be useful when dealing with the contents of a Java window. You will then be dealing with points and rectangles describing the contents drawn in the window. For example, you might want to enable the user of your program to select some geometric shape from among those displayed on the screen, in order to work with it. You could use the `contains()` method to check whether the point corresponding to the current cursor position is within any of the `Rectangle` objects that enclose each of the circles, lines, or whatever is displayed in the window. Then you can decide which of the objects displayed on the screen the user wants to choose.

There are other classes defining rectangles that we shall meet when we start drawing in a window.

Visual Characteristics of a Component

Two things determine the visual appearance of a component: the representation of the component created by the Java code in the component class that is executed when the component is displayed, and whatever you draw on the component. You can draw on a `Component` object by implementing its `paint()` method. We used this method in Chapter 1 to output the text for our applet. The `paint()` method is called automatically when the component needs to be drawn.

The need to draw a component can arise quite often for a variety of reasons – for example, your program may request that the area that the component occupies should be redrawn, or the user may resize the window containing the component. Your implementation of this method must include code to generate whatever you want drawn within the `Component` object. Note that the component itself – the `JButton` or `JFrame` or whatever, will be drawn for you. You only need to override the `paint()` method for anything additional that you want to draw on it. We will be overriding the `paint()` method in Chapter 17 to draw in a window, so we will leave further discussion of it until then.

You can alter some aspects of the appearance of the basic component by calling methods for the object. The following methods have an effect on the appearance of a `Component` object:

Method	Description
void setBackground(Color aColor)	Sets the background color to `aColor`. The background color is the color used for the basic component, as created by the operating system.
Color getBackground()	Retrieves the current background color.
void setForeground(Color bColor)	Sets the foreground color to `bColor`. The foreground color is the color used for anything appearing on the basic component, such as the label on a button, for example.
Color getForeground()	Retrieves the current foreground color.
void setCursor(Cursor aCursor)	Sets the cursor for the component to `aCursor`. This sets the appearance of the cursor within the area occupied by the `Component` object.
void setFont(Font aFont)	Sets the font for the `Component` object.
Font getFont()	Returns the `Font` object used by the component.

To be able to make use of these properly, we need to understand what `Color` objects are, and we also need to know how to create `Cursor` and `Font` objects.

Defining Color

A screen color is represented by an object of class `Color`. You define a color value as a combination of the three primary colors: red, green, and blue. They are usually expressed in that sequence, and are often referred to as **RGB values**. There are other ways of specifying colors in Java, but we will confine ourselves to RGB. You can specify the intensity of each primary color to be a value between 0 and 255. If the intensities of all three are 0, you have the color black, and if all three are set to 255 you have white. If only one intensity value is positive and the others are zero, you will have a pure primary color; for example (0, 200, 0) will be a shade of green. We could define variables corresponding to these colors with the statements:

```
Color myBlack = new Color(0,0,0);          // Color black
Color myWhite = new Color(255,255,255);    // Color white
Color myGreen = new Color(0,200,0);        // A shade of green
```

The three arguments to the constructor correspond to the intensities of the red, green, and blue components of the color respectively. The `Color` class defines a number of standard color constants as `public final static` variables, whose RGB values are given in parentheses:

WHITE	(255, 255, 255)	RED	(255, 0, 0)	PINK	(255, 175, 175)
LIGHT_GRAY	(192, 192, 192)	ORANGE	(255, 200, 0)	MAGENTA	(255, 0, 255)
GRAY	(128, 128, 128)	YELLOW	(255, 255, 0)	CYAN	(0, 255, 255)
DARK_GRAY	(64, 64, 64)	GREEN	(0, 255, 0)	BLUE	(0, 0, 255)
BLACK	(0, 0, 0,)				

So if we want our window in the previous example to have a pink background, we could add the statement:

```
aWindow.setBackground(Color.PINK);
```

When you have created a `Color` object, you can brighten or darken the color it represents by calling its `brighter()` or `darker()` methods, which will increase or decrease the intensity of the color components by a predefined factor:

```
thisColor.brighter();          // Brighten the color
thatColor.darker();            // Darken the color
```

The intensities of the component colors will always remain between 0 and 255. When you call `brighter` and a color component is already at 255, it will remain at that value. The other component intensities will be increased if they are less than 255. In a similar way, the `darker()` method will not change a component intensity if it is zero. The factor used for darkening a color component is 0.7. To brighten a color component the intensity is increased by 1/0.7.

A fundamental point to remember here is that you can only obtain the colors available within the computer and the operating system environment on which your Java program is running. If you only have a limited range of colors, the `brighter()` and `darker()` methods may appear to have no effect. Although you can create `Color` objects that are supposed to represent all kinds of colors, if your computer only supports sixteen colors you will always end up with one of your sixteen. If your machine supports 24-bit color and this is supported in your system environment, then everything should be fine and dandy.

You can obtain any of the component intensities by calling `getRed()`, `getGreen()`, or `getBlue()` for a `Color` object. A color can also be obtained as a value of type `int` that is a composite of the red, green, and blue components of the color represented by a `Color` object using the `getRGB()` method. You can also create a `Color` object from a single RGB value of type `int`.

To compare two `Color` objects you can use the `equals()` method. For example to compare two color objects `colorA` and `colorB`, you could write:

```
if(colorA.equals(colorB))
   // Do something...
```

The `equals()` method will return `true` if all three components of the two `Color` objects are equal. You could also use the `getRGB()` method to do the same thing:

```
if(colorA.getRGB() == colorB.getRGB())
   // Do something....
```

This compares the two integer RGB values for equality.

System Colors

The package java.awt defines the class SystemColor as a subclass of the Color class. The SystemColor class encapsulates the standard system colors used for displaying various components. The class contains definitions for 24 public final static variables of type SystemColor that specify the standard system colors used by the operating system for a range of GUI components. For example, the system colors for a window are referenced by:

WINDOW	Defines the background color for a window.
WINDOW_TEXT	Defines the text color for a window.
WINDOW_BORDER	Defines the border color for a window.

You can find the others covering colors used for menus, captions, controls, and so on, if you need them, by looking at the documentation for the SystemColor class.

If you want to compare a SystemColor value with a Color object you have created, then you must use the getRGB() method in the comparison. This is because the SystemColor class stores the colors internally in a way that makes use of the fields it inherits from the Color class differently from a normal Color object. For example, to see whether colorA corresponds to the system background color for a window you would write:

```
if(colorA.getRGB() == SystemColor.WINDOW.getRGB())
   // colorA is the window background color...
```

Creating Cursors

An object of the Cursor class represents a mouse cursor. The Cursor class contains a range of final static constants that specify standard cursor types. You use these to select or create a particular cursor. The standard cursor types are:

DEFAULT_CURSOR	N_RESIZE_CURSOR	NE_RESIZE_CURSOR
CROSSHAIR_CURSOR	S_RESIZE_CURSOR	NW_RESIZE_CURSOR
WAIT_CURSOR	E_RESIZE_CURSOR	SE_RESIZE_CURSOR
TEXT_CURSOR	W_RESIZE_CURSOR	SW_RESIZE_CURSOR
HAND_CURSOR	MOVE_CURSOR	

The resize cursors are the ones you see when resizing a window by dragging its boundaries. Note that these are not like the Color constants, which are Color objects – these constants are of type int, not type Cursor, and are intended to be used as arguments to a constructor.

To create a `Cursor` object representing a text cursor you could write:

```
Cursor myCursor = new Cursor(Cursor.TEXT_CURSOR);
```

Alternatively you can retrieve a cursor of the predefined type using a `static` class method:

```
Cursor myCursor = Cursor.getPredefinedCursor(Cursor.TEXT_CURSOR);
```

This method is particularly useful when you don't want to store the `Cursor` object, but just want to pass it to a method, such as `setCursor()` for a `Component` object.

If you want to see what the standard cursors look like, you could add a cursor to the previous example, along with the pink background:

Try It Out – Color and Cursors

We will change the background color of the content pane for the application window and try out a different cursor. Make the following changes to `TryWindow.java`; we will use the code we created earlier that utilizes the toolkit:

```
import javax.swing.JFrame;
import java.awt.Toolkit;
import java.awt.Dimension;
import java.awt.Color;
import java.awt.Cursor;

public class TryWindow
{
  // The window object
  static JFrame aWindow = new JFrame("This is the Window Title");

  public static void main(String[] args)
  {
    Toolkit theKit = aWindow.getToolkit();      // Get the window toolkit
    Dimension wndSize = theKit.getScreenSize(); // Get screen size

    // Set the position to screen center & size to half screen size
    aWindow.setBounds(wndSize.width/4, wndSize.height/4,    // Position
                  wndSize.width/2, wndSize.height/2);   // Size
    aWindow.setDefaultCloseOperation(JFrame.EXIT_ON_CLOSE);
    aWindow.setCursor(Cursor.getPredefinedCursor(Cursor.CROSSHAIR_CURSOR));
    aWindow.getContentPane().setBackground(Color.PINK);
    aWindow.setVisible(true);                            // Display the window
  }
}
```

You can try all the cursors by plugging in each of the standard cursor names in turn. You could also try out a few variations on the background color.

Selecting Fonts

An object of type Font represents a font. The Font class is actually quite complicated, so we'll only scratch the surface enough for our needs here. The Font class differentiates between a **character**, the letter uppercase 'Q' say, and a **glyph**, which is the shape defining its appearance when it is displayed or printed. In general a given character in one font will have a different glyph in a different font. For fonts corresponding to many languages, German, French, or Finnish for example, a character may involve more than one glyph to display it. This is typically the case for characters that involve **diacritic marks**, which are additional graphics attached to a character. The letter ä for instance combines the normal letter 'a' with an umlaut, the two dots over it, so it may be represented by two glyphs, one for the appearance of the letter and the other for the appearance of the umlaut. A Font object contains a table that maps the Unicode value for each character to the glyph code or codes that create the visual representation of the character.

To create a Font object you must supply the font name, the style of the font, and the point size. For example, consider the following statement:

```
Font myFont = new Font("Serif", Font.ITALIC, 12);
```

This defines a 12-point Times Roman italic font. The other options you could use for the style are PLAIN and BOLD. The name we have given to the font here, "Serif", is a **logical font name**. Other logical font names we could have used are "Dialog", "DialogInput", "Monospaced", "SansSerif" or "Symbol". Instead of a logical font name, we can supply a font face name – the name of a particular font such as "Times New Roman" or "Palatino".

It is important to keep in mind that fonts are for presenting characters visually, on the screen or on a printer for instance. Although Java has a built-in capability to represent characters by Unicode codes, it doesn't have any fonts because it doesn't display or print characters itself. The responsibility for this rests entirely with your operating system. Although your Java programs can store strings of Japanese or Tibetan characters, if your operating system doesn't have fonts for these characters you can't display or print them. Therefore to display or print text in the way that you want, you need to know what font face names are available in the system on which your code is running. We will come back to this in a moment.

You can specify combined styles by adding them together. If we want myFont to be BOLD and ITALIC we would have written the statement as:

```
Font myFont = new Font("Serif", Font.ITALIC + Font.BOLD, 12);
```

You retrieve the style and size of an existing Font object by calling its methods getStyle() and getSize(), both of which return a value of type int. You can also check the individual font style for a Font object with the methods isPlain(), isBold(), and isItalic(). Each of these methods returns a boolean value indicating whether the Font object has that style.

Before you create a font using a particular font face name, you need to know that the font is available on the system where your code is executing. For this you need to use a method, getAllFonts(), in the GraphicsEnvironment class defined in the java.awt package. We met this class earlier when we were centering a window. We could do this as follows:

```
GraphicsEnvironment e = GraphicsEnvironment.getLocalGraphicsEnvironment();
Font[] fonts = e.getAllFonts();      // Get the fonts
```

We get a reference to the `GraphicsEnvironment` object for the current machine by calling the static method `getLocalGraphicsEnvironment()` as illustrated. We then use this to call its `getAllFonts()` method. The `getAllFonts()` method returns an array of `Font` objects consisting of those available on the current system. You can then check this list for the font you want to use. Each of the `Font` instances in the array will be of a 1 point size, and since 1 point is approximately 1/72 of an inch or 0.353mm, you will typically want to change this unless your screen and eyesight are really exceptional. To change the size and/or style of a font you call its `deriveFont()` method. This method comes in three versions, all of which return a new `Font` object with the specified size and/or style:

`deriveFont()` Method	Description
deriveFont(int Style)	Creates a new `Font` object with the style specified – one of PLAIN, BOLD, ITALIC or BOLD+ITALIC.
deriveFont(float size)	Creates a new `Font` object with the size specified.
deriveFont(int Style, float size)	Creates a new `Font` object with the style and size specified.

To use the last font from the array of `Font` objects to create an equivalent 12-point font you could write:

```
Font newFont = fonts[fonts.length-1].deriveFont(12.0f);
```

If you look in the documentation for the `Font` class, you will see that there is a fourth version of `deriveFont()` that involves an `AffineTransform`, but we'll leave `AffineTransform` objects until Chapter 18.

Getting a `Font` object for every font in the system can be a time-consuming process if you have many fonts installed. A much faster alternative is to get the font names, and then use one of these to create the `Font` object that you require. You can get the face names for all the fonts in a system like this:

```
GraphicsEnvironment e = GraphicsEnvironment.getLocalGraphicsEnvironment();
String[] fontnames = e.getAvailableFontFamilyNames();
```

The array `fontnames` will contain the names of all the font faces available, and you can use one or more of these to create the `Font` objects you need.

Try It Out – Getting the List of Fonts

This program will output your screen size and resolution, as well as the list of font family names installed on your machine:

```
import java.awt.*;

public class SysInfo
  public static void main(String[] args) {
```

```
    Toolkit theKit = Toolkit.getDefaultToolkit();

    System.out.println("\nScreen Resolution: "
                    + theKit.getScreenResolution() + " dots per inch");

    Dimension screenDim = theKit.getScreenSize();
    System.out.println("Screen Size: "
                    + screenDim.width + " by "
                    + screenDim.height + " pixels");

    GraphicsEnvironment e = GraphicsEnvironment.getLocalGraphicsEnvironment();
    String[] fontnames = e.getAvailableFontFamilyNames();
    System.out.println("\nFonts available on this platform: ");
    for (int i = 0; i < fontnames.length; i++)
      System.out.println(fontnames[i]);

    return;
    }
  }
```

On my system I get the following output:

Screen Resolution: 120 dots per inch
Screen Size: 1280 by 1024 pixels

Fonts available on this platform:
Abadi MT Condensed Light
Albertus
Albertus Extra Bold
Albertus Medium
Algerian
Alien
Allegro BT
AmerType Md BT
Andes
Angerthas
Antique Olive
Antique Olive Compact
Architect
Arial
Arial Alternative
Arial Alternative Symbol
Arial Black
Arial MT Black

...plus many more.

How It Works

We first get a `Toolkit` object by calling the `static` method `getDefaultToolkit()` – this is the key to the other information. The `getScreenResolution()` returns the number of pixels per inch as a value of type `int`. The `getScreenSize()` method returns a `Dimension` object which specifies the width and height of the screen in pixels.

We use the `getAllFonts()` method discussed previously to get a `String` array containing the names of the fonts which we output to the screen.

Font Metrics

Every component has a method `getFontMetrics()` that you can use to retrieve **font metrics** – the wealth of dimensional data about a font. You pass a `Font` object as an argument to the method, and it returns an object of type `FontMetrics` that you can use to obtain data relating to the particular font. For example, if `aWindow` is a `Frame` object and `myFont` is a `Font` object, you could obtain a `FontMetrics` object corresponding to the font with the statement:

```
FontMetrics metrics = aWindow.getFontMetrics(myFont);
```

You could use the `getFont()` method for a component to explore the characteristics of the font that the component contains. For example:

```
FontMetrics metrics = aWindow.getFontMetrics(aWindow.getFont());
```

You can now call any of the following `FontMetrics` methods for the object to get at the basic dimensions of the font:

Method	Description
int getAscent()	Returns the **ascent** of the font, which is the distance from the base line to the top of the majority of the characters in the font. The **base line** is the line on which the characters rest. Depending on the font, some characters can extend beyond the ascent.
int getMaxAscent()	Returns the maximum ascent for the font. No character will exceed this ascent.
int getDescent()	Returns the **descent** of the font, which is the distance from the base line to the bottom of most of the font characters that extend below the base line. Depending on the font, some characters may extend beyond the descent for the font.
int getMaxDescent()	Returns the maximum descent of the characters in the font. No character will exceed this descent.
int getLeading()	Returns the **leading** for the font, which is the line spacing for the font – that is the spacing between the bottom of one line of text and the top of the next. The term originated when type was actually made of lead, and there was a strip of lead between one line of type and the next when a page was typeset.
int getHeight()	Returns the height of the font, which is defined as the sum of the ascent, the descent, and the leading.

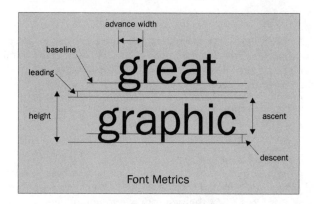

The diagram shows how the dimensions relate to the font. The **advance width** for a character is the distance from the reference point of the character to the reference point of the next character. The **reference point** for a character is on the base line at the left edge of the character. Each character will have its own advance width which you can obtain by calling a FontMetrics method charWidth(). For example, to obtain the advance width for the character 'x' the following statement could be used:

```
int widthX = metrics.charWidth('X');
```

You can also obtain the advance widths for all the characters in the font as an array of type int with the method getWidths():

```
int[] widths = metrics.getWidths();
```

The numerical value for the character is used to index the array, so you can get the advance width for the character 'x' with the expression widths['X']. If you just want the maximum advance width for the characters in the font, you can call the method getMaxAdvance(). Lastly, you can get the total advance width for a String object by passing the object to the method stringWidth(). The advance width is returned as a value of type int.

Although you now know a great deal about how to create and manipulate fonts, we haven't actually created and used one. We will remedy this after we have got a feel for what Swing components can do and learned a little about using containers.

Swing Components

Swing components all have the JComponent class as a base which itself extends the Component class to add the following capability:

❑ Supports pluggable look-and-feel for components, allowing you to change the look and feel programmatically, or implement your own look-and-feel for all components displayed.

❑ Support for tooltips – a **tooltip** being a message describing the purpose of a component when the mouse cursor lingers over it. Tooltips are defined by the JTooltip class.

❑ Support for automatic scrolling in a list, a table, or a tree when a component is dragged with the mouse.

❑ Special debugging support for graphics, providing component rendering in slow motion so you can see what is happening.

❑ Component classes can be easily extended to create your own custom components.

All the Swing component classes are defined in the `javax.swing` package and have class names that begin with J. There are quite a few Swing components, so we'll get an overview of what's available and how the classes relate to one another and then go into the detail of particular components when we use them in examples.

Buttons

The Swing button classes define various kinds of buttons operated by clicking with a mouse. The button classes have `AbstractButton` as a base, as shown below.

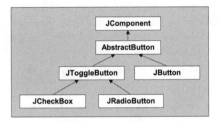

The `JButton` class defines a regular pushbutton that you would use as a dialog button or in a toolbar.

 This is an example of a `JButton` object. This component has a border of type `BevelBorder` added to it.

The `JToolBar` class is used in conjunction with the `JButton` class to create a toolbar containing buttons. A toolbar is dockable without any additional programming effort on your part, as we will see.

`JToggleButton` defines a two-state button, pressed or not, and there are two more specialized versions defined by `JCheckBox` and `JRadioButton`. Radio buttons defined as `JRadioButton` objects generally operate in a group so that only one button can be in the pressed state at any one time. This grouping is established by adding the `JRadioButton` object to a `ButtonGroup` object that takes care of the state of the buttons in the group.

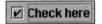 This is an example of a `JCheckBox` object. Clicking on the checkbox changes its state from checked to unchecked or vice versa.

All the buttons can be displayed with a text label, an icon, or both.

Menus

The Swing components include support for pop-up or context menus as well as menu bars. The classes defining elements of a menu are shown overleaf.

671

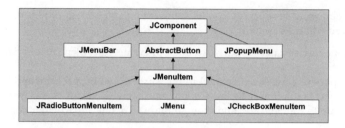

The JMenuBar class defines a **menu bar** usually found at the top of an application window. A JMenu object represents a top-level menu item on a menu bar that pops up a list of menu items when it is clicked. The items in a menu are defined by the JMenuItem class. The JPopupMenu class defines a context menu that is typically implemented to appear at the current cursor position when the right mouse button is clicked. A JCheckBoxMenuItem component is a menu item with a checkbox that is ticked when the item is selected. The JRadioButtonMenuItem class defines a menu item that is part of a group where only one item can be selected at any time. The group is created by adding JRadioButtonMenuItem objects to a ButtonGroup object. We will be implementing a menu in an application and an applet later in this chapter.

Text Components

The capability of the Swing text components is very wide indeed.

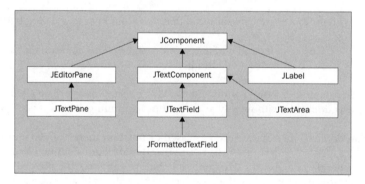

The most elementary text component is a JLabel object:

I am a label   A JLabel component is passive and does not react to input events so you can't edit it.

A JTextField component looks similar to a label in that it displays a single line of text, but in this case it is editable.

10-Feb-2002   JFormattedTextField component is a JTextField component that can control and format the data that is displayed or entered. It can supply automatic formatting in many instances. Here it has automatically displayed a Date object as a date.

The `JTextArea` defines a component that allows editing of multi-line text.

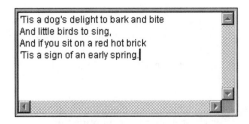

This is an example of a `JTextArea` component. The scrollbars are supplied automatically and you can also display multiple rows and columns.

The `JEditPane` and `JTextPane` components are a different order of complexity from the others and enable you to implement sophisticated editing facilities relatively easily. The `JEditPane` supports editing of plain text, text in HTML, and RTF (Rich Text Format). The `JTextPane` class extends `JEditPane` and allows you to embed images or other components within the text managed by the component.

Other Swing Components

Other Swing components you will use regularly include the `JPanel` component. The `JPanel` class defines something like a physical panel that you can use to group a set of components. For instance, you might use two `JPanel` objects to support two separate groups of `JButton` components in the content pane of an application window.

The `JList` and `JTable` components are also very useful.

This is a `JList` component that implements a list of items. This component has a border of type `EtchedBorder` added to it. You can select entries from the list.

First Name	Second Name
Marilyn	Monroe
Slim	Pickens
Clint	Eastwood

This is a `JTable` component that implements a table of items from which you can select a row, or a column, or a single element. A `JTable` component automatically takes care of reordering the columns when a column is dragged to a new position using the mouse.

Any component can have a border added, and the `javax.swing.borders` package contains eight classes representing different kinds of borders you can use for a component.

We have not introduced all the Swing component classes by any means, and you will be meeting a few more as you progress through the rest of the book.

673

Using Containers

A container is any component with the `Container` class as a base; so all the Swing components are containers. The `Container` class is the direct base class for the `Window` class and it provides the ability to contain other components. Since the `Container` class is an `abstract` class, you cannot create instances of `Container`. Instead it is objects of the subclasses such as `Window`, `JFrame`, or `JDialog` that inherit the ability to contain other components.

> Note that a container cannot contain an object of the class `Window`, or an object of any of the classes derived from `Window`. An object of any other class that is derived from `Component` can be contained.

The components within a container are displayed within the area occupied by the container on the display screen. A dialog box, for example, might contain a `JList` object offering some choices: `JCheckbox` objects offering other options and `JButton` objects representing buttons enabling the user to end the dialog or enter the selections – all these components would appear within the boundaries of the dialog box. Of course, for the contained components to be visible the container must itself be displayed, as the container effectively 'owns' its components. The container also controls how its embedded components are laid out by means of a **layout manager**.

Before we look at what a layout manager is, and how the layout of the components in a container is determined, let's look into the basic methods defined in the `Container` class, and therefore available to all containers.

You can find out about the components in a container object by using the following methods defined in the `Container` class:

Method	Description
`int getComponentCount()`	Returns a count of the number of components contained by the current component.
`Component getComponent (int index)`	Returns the component identified by the `index` value. The `index` value is an array index so it must be between 0 and one less than the number of components contained, otherwise an `ArrayIndexOutOfBoundsException` will be thrown.
`Component[] getComponents()`	Returns an array of all the components in the current container.

If we have a `Container` object, `content`, perhaps the content pane of a `JFrame` window, we could iterate through the components in the `Container` with the following statements:

```
Component aComponent = null;                        // Stores a Component
int numComponents = content.getComponentCount();   // Get the count

for(int i = 0; i < numComponents; i++)
  aComponent = content.getComponent(i);             // Get each component
  // Do something with it...
}
```

This retrieves the components in `content` one at a time in the `for` loop. Alternatively we could retrieve them all at once:

```
Component[] theComponents = content.getComponents(); // Get all components

for(int i = 0; i < theComponents.length; i++) {
  // Do something with theComponents[i]...
}
```

Adding Components to a Container

The components stored in a container are recorded in an array within the `Container` object. The array is increased in size when necessary to accommodate as many components as are present. To add a component to a container you use the method `add()`. The `Container` class defines the following four overloaded versions of the `add()` method:

add() Method	Description
Component add(Component c)	Add the component c to the end of the list of components stored in the container. The return value is c.
Component add(Component c, int index)	Adds the component c to the list of components in the container at the position specified by index. If index is -1, the component is added to the end of the list. If the value of index is not -1 it must be less than the number of components in the container, and greater than or equal to 0. The return value is c.
void add(Component c, Object constraints)	Add the component c to the end of the list of components stored in the container. The position of the component relative to the container is subject to the constraints defined by the second parameter. We will see what constraints are in the next section.
void add(Component c, Object constraints, int index)	Adds the component c to the list of components in the container at the position specified by index, and position subject to constraints. If index is -1, the component is added to the end of the list. If the value of index is not -1 it must be less than the number of components in the container, and greater than or equal to 0.

Note that adding a component does not displace any components already in the container. When you add a component at a given position, other components are moved in the sequence to make room for the new one. However, a component can only be in one container at a time. Adding a component to a container that is already in another container will remove it from the original container.

In order to try adding components to a container we need to understand what the constraints are that appear in some of the add() methods, and look at how the layout of components in a container is controlled.

Container Layout Managers

An object called a **layout manager** determines the way that components are arranged in a container. All containers will have a default layout manager but you can choose a different layout manager when necessary. There are many layout manager classes provided in the java.awt and javax.swing packages, so we will introduce those that you are most likely to need. It is possible to create your own layout manager classes, but creating layout managers is beyond the scope of this book. The layout manager for a container determines the position and size of all the components in the container: you should not change the size and position of such components yourself. Just let the layout manager take care of it.

Since the classes that define layout managers all implement the LayoutManager interface, you can use a variable of type LayoutManager to store any of them if necessary. We will look at six layout manager classes in a little more detail. The names of these classes and the basic arrangements that they provide are as follows:

Layout Manager	Description
FlowLayout	Places components in successive rows in a container, fitting as many on each row as possible, and starting on the next row as soon as a row is full. This works in much the same way as your text processor placing words on a line. Its primary use is for arranging buttons although you can use it with other components. It is the default layout manager for JPanel objects.
BorderLayout	Places components against any of the four borders of the container and in the center. The component in the center fills the available space. This layout manager is the default for the contentPane in a JFrame, JDialog, or JApplet object.
CardLayout	Places components in a container one on top of the other – like a deck of cards. Only the 'top' component is visible at any one time.
GridLayout	Places components in the container in a rectangular grid with the number of rows and columns that you specify.
GridBagLayout	This also places the components into an arrangement of rows and columns but the rows and columns can vary in length. This is a complicated layout manager with a lot of flexibility in how you control where components are placed in a container.

Layout Manager	Description
BoxLayout	This arranges components either in a row or in a column. In either case the components are clipped to fit if necessary, rather than wrapping to the next row or column. The BoxLayout manager is the default for the Box container class.
SpringLayout	Allows components to have their position defined by 'springs' or 'struts' fixed to an edge of the container or another component in the container.

The BoxLayout, SpringLayout, and Box classes are defined in the javax.swing package. The other layout manager classes in the list above are defined in java.awt.

One question to ask is why do we need layout managers at all? Why don't we just place components at some given position in a container? The basic reason is to ensure that the GUI elements for your Java program are displayed properly in every possible Java environment. Layout managers automatically adjust components to fit the space available. If you fix the size and position of each of the components, they could run into one another and overlap if the screen area available to your program is reduced.

To set the layout manager of a container, you can call the setLayout() method for the container. For example, you could change the layout manager for the container object aWindow of type JFrame to flow layout with the statements:

```
FlowLayout flow = new FlowLayout();
aWindow.getContentPane().setLayout(flow);
```

Remember that we can't add components directly to a JFrame object – we must add them to the content pane for the window. The same goes for JDialog and JApplet objects.

With some containers you can set the layout manager in the constructor for that container, as we shall see in later examples. Let's look at how the layout managers work, and how to use them in practice.

The Flow Layout Manager

The flow layout manager places components in a row, and when the row is full, it automatically spills components onto the next row. The default positioning of the row of components is centered in the container. There are actually three possible row-positioning options that you specify by constants defined in the class. These are FlowLayout.LEFT, FlowLayout.RIGHT, and FlowLayout.CENTER – this last option being the default.

The flow layout manager is very easy to use, so let's jump straight in and see it working in an example.

Try It Out – Using a Flow Layout Manager

As we said earlier, this layout manager is used primarily to arrange a few components whose relative position is unimportant. Let's implement a TryFlowLayout program based on the TryWindow example:

```
import javax.swing.JFrame;
import javax.swing.JButton;

import java.awt.Toolkit;
import java.awt.Dimension;
import java.awt.Container;
import java.awt.FlowLayout;

public class TryFlowLayout {
  // The window object
  static JFrame aWindow = new JFrame("This is a Flow Layout");

  public static void main(String[] args) {
    Toolkit theKit = aWindow.getToolkit();          // Get the window toolkit
    Dimension wndSize = theKit.getScreenSize();      // Get screen size
    // Set the position to screen center & size to half screen size
    aWindow.setBounds(wndSize.width/4, wndSize.height/4,    // Position
                      wndSize.width/2, wndSize.height/2);   // Size
    aWindow.setDefaultCloseOperation(JFrame.EXIT_ON_CLOSE);

    FlowLayout flow = new FlowLayout();              // Create a layout manager
    Container content = aWindow.getContentPane();    // Get the content pane
    content.setLayout(flow);                         // Set the container layout mgr

    // Now add six button components
    for(int i = 1; i <= 6; i++)
      content.add(new JButton("Press " + i));        // Add a Button to content pane

    aWindow.setVisible(true);                        // Display the window
  }
}
```

Since it is based on the TryWindow class, only the new code is highlighted. The new code is quite simple. We create a FlowLayout object and make this the layout manager for aWindow by calling setLayout(). We then add six JButton components of a default size to aWindow in the loop.

If you compile and run the program you should get a window similar to the following:

The Button objects are positioned by the layout manager flow. As you can see, they have been added to the first row in the window, and the row is centered. You can confirm that the row is centered and see how the layout manger automatically spills the components on to the next row once a row is full by reducing the size of the window.

Here the second row is clearly centered. Each button component has been set to its preferred size, which comfortably accommodates the text for the label. The centering is determined by the alignment constraint for the layout manager, which defaults to CENTER.

It can also be set to RIGHT or LEFT by using a different constructor. For example, you could have created the layout manager with the statement:

```
FlowLayout flow = new FlowLayout(FlowLayout.LEFT);
```

The flow layout manager then left-aligns each row of components in the container. If you run the program with this definition and resize the window, it will look like:

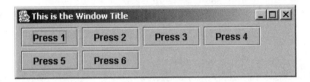

Now the buttons are left aligned. Two of the buttons have spilled from the first row to the second because there is insufficient space across the width of the window to accommodate them all.

The flow layout manager in the previous examples applies a default gap of 5 pixels between components in a row, and between one row and the next. You can choose values for the horizontal and vertical gaps by using yet another FlowLayout constructor. You can set the horizontal gap to 20 pixels and the vertical gap to 30 pixels with the statement:

```
FlowLayout flow = new FlowLayout(FlowLayout.LEFT, 20, 30);
```

If you run the program with this definition of the layout manager, when you resize the window you will see the components distributed with the spacing specified.

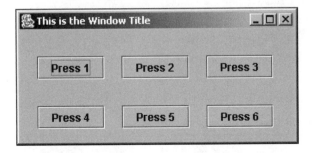

You can also set the gaps between components and rows explicitly by calling the setHgap() or the setVgap() method. To set the horizontal gap to 35 pixels, you would write:

```
flow.setHgap(35);                           // Set the horizontal gap
```

Don't be misled by this. You can't get differential spacing between components by setting the gap before adding each component to a container. The last values for the gaps between components that you set for a layout manager will apply to all the components in a container. The methods getHgap() and getVgap() will return the current setting for the horizontal or vertical gap as a value of type int.

The initial size at which the application window is displayed is determined by the values we pass to the setBounds() method for the JFrame object. If you want the window to assume a size that just accommodates the components it contains, you can call the pack() method for the JFrame object. Add the following line immediately before the call to setVisible():

```
aWindow.pack();
```

If you recompile and run the example again, the application window should fit the components.
As we've said, you add components to an applet created as a JApplet object in the same way as for a JFrame application window. We can verify this by adding some buttons to an example of an applet. We can try out a Font object and add a border to the buttons to brighten them up a bit at the same time.

Try It Out – Adding Buttons to an Applet

We can define the class for our applet as follows:

```
import javax.swing.JButton;
import javax.swing.JApplet;

import java.awt.Font;
import java.awt.Container;
import java.awt.FlowLayout;

import javax.swing.border.BevelBorder;

public class TryApplet extends JApplet {
  public void init() {
    Container content = getContentPane();                    // Get content pane
    content.setLayout(new FlowLayout(FlowLayout.RIGHT)); // Set layout

    JButton button;                                          // Stores a button
    Font[] fonts = { new Font("Arial", Font.ITALIC, 10), // Two fonts
                     new Font("Playbill", Font.PLAIN, 14)
                   };

    BevelBorder edge = new BevelBorder(BevelBorder.RAISED); // Bevelled border

    // Add the buttons using alternate fonts
    for(int i = 1; i <= 6; i++) {
      content.add(button = new JButton("Press " + i));  // Add the button
```

```
            button.setFont(fonts[i%2]);              // One of our own fonts
            button.setBorder(edge);                  // Set the button border
        }
    }
}
```

Of course, to run the applet we will need an .html file containing the following:

```
<APPLET CODE="TryApplet.class" WIDTH=300 HEIGHT=200>
</APPLET>
```

This specifies the width and height of the applet – you can use your own values here if you wish. You can save the file as TryApplet.html.

Once you have compiled the applet source code using javac, you can execute it with the appletviewer program by entering the following command from the folder the .html file and class are in:

```
appletviewer TryApplet.html
```

You should see the AppletViewer window displaying our applet.

The arrangement of the buttons is now right justified in the flow layout. We have the button labels alternating between the two fonts that we created. The buttons also look more like buttons with a beveled edge.

How It Works

As we saw in Chapter 1, an applet is executed rather differently from a Java program and it is not really an independent program at all. The browser (or appletviewer in this case) initiates and controls the execution of the applet. An applet does not require a main() method. To execute the applet, the browser first creates an instance of our applet class, TryApplet, and then calls the init() method for it. This method is inherited from the Applet class (the base for JApplet) and you typically override this method to provide your own initialization.

We need the import statement for java.awt in addition to that for javax.swing because our code refers to the Font, Container, and FlowLayout classes.

Before creating the buttons, we create a BevelBorder object that we will use to specify the border for each button. In the loop that adds the buttons to the content pane for the applet, we select one or other of the Font objects we have created depending on whether the loop index is even or odd, and then set edge as the border by calling the setBorder() member. This would be the same for any component. Note how the size of each button is automatically adjusted to accommodate the button label. Of course, the font selection depends on the two fonts being available on your system, so if you don't have the ones that appear in the code, change it to suit what you have.

The buttons look much better with raised edges. If you wanted them to appear sunken, you would specify `BevelBorder.LOWERED` as the constructor argument. You might like to try out a `SoftBevelBorder` too. All you need to do is use the class name, `SoftBevelBorder`, when creating the border.

Using a Border Layout Manager

The border layout manager is intended to place up to five components in a container. Possible positions for these components are on any of the four borders of the container and in the center. Only one component can be at each position. If you add a component at a position that is already occupied, the previous component will be displaced. A border is selected by specifying a constraint that can be NORTH, SOUTH, EAST, WEST, or CENTER. These are all `final static` constants defined in the `BorderLayout.class`.

You can't specify the constraints in the `BorderLayout` constructor since a different constraint has to be applied to each component. You specify the position of each component in a container when you add it using the `add()` method. We can modify the earlier application example to add five buttons to the content pane of the application window in a border layout:

Try It Out – Testing the BorderLayout Manager

Make the following changes to `TryFlowLayout.java` to try out the border layout manager and exercise another border class:

```
import javax.swing.JFrame;
import javax.swing.JButton;

import java.awt.Toolkit;
import java.awt.Dimension;
import java.awt.Container;
import java.awt.BorderLayout;

import javax.swing.border.EtchedBorder;

public class TryBorderLayout {
  // The window object
  static JFrame aWindow = new JFrame("This is a Border Layout");

  public static void main(String[] args) {
    Toolkit theKit = aWindow.getToolkit();        // Get the window toolkit
    Dimension wndSize = theKit.getScreenSize();  // Get screen size

    // Set the position to screen center & size to half screen size
    aWindow.setBounds(wndSize.width/4, wndSize.height/4,    // Position
                      wndSize.width/2, wndSize.height/2);  // Size
    aWindow.setDefaultCloseOperation(JFrame.EXIT_ON_CLOSE);

    BorderLayout border = new BorderLayout();        // Create a layout manager
    Container content = aWindow.getContentPane();    // Get the content pane
    content.setLayout(border);                       // Set the container layout mgr
    EtchedBorder edge = new EtchedBorder(EtchedBorder.RAISED);  // Button border
```

```
      // Now add five JButton components and set their borders
      JButton button;
      content.add(button = new JButton("EAST"), BorderLayout.EAST);
      button.setBorder(edge);
      content.add(button = new JButton("WEST"), BorderLayout.WEST);
      button.setBorder(edge);
      content.add(button = new JButton("NORTH"), BorderLayout.NORTH);
      button.setBorder(edge);
      content.add(button = new JButton("SOUTH"), BorderLayout.SOUTH);
      button.setBorder(edge);
      content.add(button = new JButton("CENTER"), BorderLayout.CENTER);
      button.setBorder(edge);

      aWindow.setVisible(true);                          // Display the window
    }
  }
```

If you compile and execute the example, you will see the window shown below.

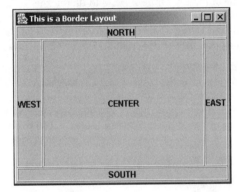

You can see here how a raised `EtchedBorder` edge to the buttons looks.

How It Works

Components laid out with a border layout manager are extended to fill the space available in the container. The "NORTH" and "SOUTH" buttons are the full width of the window and the "EAST" and "WEST" buttons occupy the height remaining unoccupied once the "NORTH" and "SOUTH" buttons are in place. It always works like this, regardless of the sequence in which you add the buttons – the "NORTH" and "SOUTH" components occupy the full width of the container and the "CENTER" component takes up the remaining space. If there are no "NORTH" and "SOUTH" components, the "EAST" and "WEST" components will extend to the full height of the container.

The width of the "EAST" and "WEST" buttons is determined by the space required to display the button labels. Similarly, the "NORTH" and "SOUTH" buttons are determined by the height of the characters in the labels.

You can alter the spacing between components by passing arguments to the `BorderLayout` constructor – the default gaps are zero. For example, you could set the horizontal gap to 20 pixels and the vertical gap to 30 pixels with the statement:

683

```
content.setLayout(new BorderLayout(20, 30));
```

Like the flow layout manager, you can also set the gaps individually by calling the methods setHgap() and setVgap() for the BorderLayout object. For example:

```
BorderLayout border = new BorderLayout();    // Construct the object
content.setLayout(border);                    // Set the layout
border.setHgap(20);                           // Set horizontal gap
```

This sets the horizontal gap between the components to 20 pixels and leaves the vertical gap at the default value of zero. You can also retrieve the current values for the gaps with the getHgap() and getVgap() methods.

Using a Card Layout Manager

The card layout manager generates a stack of components, one on top of the other. The first component that you add to the container will be at the top of the stack, and therefore visible, and the last one will be at the bottom. You can create a CardLayout object with the default constructor, CardLayout(), or you can specify horizontal and vertical gaps as arguments to the constructor. The gaps in this case are between the edge of the component and the boundary of the container. We can see how this works in an applet:

Try It Out – Dealing Components

Because of the way a card layout works, we need a way to interact with the applet to switch from one component to the next. We will implement this by enabling mouse events to be processed, but we won't explain the code that does this in detail here. We will leave that to the next chapter.

Try the following code:

```
import javax.swing.JApplet;
import javax.swing.JButton;

import java.awt.Container;
import java.awt.CardLayout;

import java.awt.event.ActionEvent;                    // Classes to handle events
import java.awt.event.ActionListener;

public class TryCardLayout extends JApplet implements ActionListener {
  CardLayout card = new CardLayout(50,50);             // Create layout

  public void init() {
    Container content = getContentPane();
    content.setLayout(card);                           // Set card as the layout mgr
    JButton button;                                    // Stores a button
    for(int i = 1; i <= 6; i++) {
      content.add(button = new JButton("Press " + i), "Card" + i); // Add a button
      button.addActionListener(this);                  // Add listener for button
    }
  }
```

```
    // Handle button events
    public void actionPerformed(ActionEvent e) {
        card.next(getContentPane());                    // Switch to the next card
    }
}
```

If you run the program the applet should be as shown below. Click on the button – and the next button will be displayed.

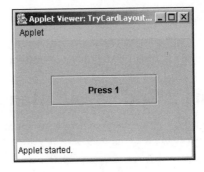

How It Works

The CardLayout object, card, is created with horizontal and vertical gaps of fifty pixels. In the init() method for our applet, we set card as the layout manager and add six buttons to the content pane. Note that we have two arguments to the add() method. Using card layout requires that you identify each component by some Object. In this case we pass a String object as the second argument to the add() method. We use an arbitrary string for each consisting of the string "Card" with the sequence number of the button appended to it.

Within the loop we call the addActionListener() method for each button to identify our applet object as the object that will handle events generated for the button (such as clicking on it with the mouse). When you click on a button, the actionPerformed() method for the applet object will be called. This just calls the next() method for the layout object to move the next component in sequence to the top. We will look at event handling in more detail in the next chapter.

The argument to the next() method identifies the container as the TryCardLayout object that is created when the applet starts. The CardLayout class has other methods that you can use for selecting from the stack of components:

Method	Description
void previous(Container parent)	Selects the previous component in the container, parent.
void first(Container parent)	Selects the first component in the container, parent.
void last(Container parent)	Selects the last component in the container, parent.
void show(Container parent, String name)	Selects the component in the container, parent, associated with the String object, name. This must be one of the String objects specified when you called the add() method to add components.

Using the `next()` or `previous()` methods you can cycle through the components repeatedly, since the next component after the last is the first, and the component before the first is the last.

The `String` object that we supplied when adding the buttons identifies each button and can be used to switch to any of them. For instance, you could switch to the button associated with "Card4" before the applet is displayed by adding the following statement after the loop that adds the buttons:

```
card.show(content, "Card4");     // Switch to button "Card4"
```

This calls the `show()` method for the layout manager. The first argument is the container and the second argument is the object identifying the component to be at the top.

Using a Grid Layout Manager

A grid layout manager arranges components in a rectangular grid within the container. There are three constructors for creating `GridLayout` objects:

Constructor	Description
`GridLayout()`	Creates a grid layout manager that will arrange components in a single row (that is, a single column per component) with no gaps between components.
`GridLayout(int rows, int cols)`	Creates a grid layout manager that arranges components in a grid with `rows` number of rows and `cols` number of columns, and with no gaps between components.
`GridLayout(int rows, int cols, int hgap, int vgap)`	Creates a grid layout manager that arranges components in a grid with `rows` number of rows and `cols` number of columns, and with horizontal and vertical gaps between components of `hgap` and `vgap` pixels, respectively.

In the second and third constructors shown above, you can specify either the number of rows, or the number of columns as zero (but not both). If you specify the number of rows as zero, the layout manager will provide as many rows in the grid as are necessary to accommodate the number of components you add to the container. Similarly, setting the number of columns as zero indicates an arbitrary number of columns. If you fix both the rows and the columns, and add more components to the container than the grid will accommodate, the number of columns will be increased appropriately.

We can try out a grid layout manager in a variation of a previous application:

Try It Out – Gridlocking Buttons

Make the highlighted changes to `TryWindow.java`.

```
import javax.swing.JFrame;
import java.awt.*;
import javax.swing.border.EtchedBorder;
```

```java
public class TryGridLayout {
  // The window object
  static JFrame aWindow = new JFrame("This is a Grid Layout");

  public static void main(String[] args) {
    Toolkit theKit = aWindow.getToolkit();            // Get the window toolkit
    Dimension wndSize = theKit.getScreenSize();       // Get screen size

    // Set the position to screen center & size to half screen size
    aWindow.setBounds(wndSize.width/4, wndSize.height/4,    // Position
                      wndSize.width/2, wndSize.height/2);   // Size
    aWindow.setDefaultCloseOperation(JFrame.EXIT_ON_CLOSE);
    GridLayout grid = new GridLayout(3,4,30,20);      // Create a layout manager
    Container content = aWindow.getContentPane();     // Get the content pane
    content. setLayout(grid);                         // Set the container layout mgr

    EtchedBorder edge = new EtchedBorder(EtchedBorder.RAISED);  // Button border

    // Now add ten Button components
    JButton button;                                   // Stores a button
    for(int i = 1; i <= 10; i++) {
      content.add(button = new JButton("Press " + i));   // Add a Button
      button.setBorder(edge);                            // Set the border
    }

    aWindow.setVisible(true);                         // Display the window
  }
}
```

We create a grid layout manager, grid, for three rows and four columns, and with horizontal and vertical gaps between components of 30 and 20 pixels respectively. With ten buttons in the container, the application window will be as shown below.

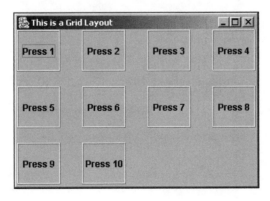

Using a BoxLayout Manager

The BoxLayout class defines a layout manager that arranges components in either a single row or a single column. You specify whether you want a row-wise or a columnar arrangement when creating the BoxLayout object. The BoxLayout constructor requires two arguments. The first is a reference to the container to which the layout manager applies, and the second is a constant value that can be either BoxLayout.X_AXIS for a row arrangement, or BoxLayout.Y_AXIS for a column arrangement.

Components are added from left to right in a row, or from top to bottom in a column. Components in the row or column do not spill onto the next row or column when the row is full. When this occurs, the layout manager will reduce the size of components or even clip them if necessary and keep them all in a single row or column. With a row of components, the box layout manager will try to make all the components the same height, and try to set a column of components to the same width.

The container class, Box, is particularly convenient when you need to use a box layout since it has a BoxLayout manager built in. It also has some added facilities providing more flexibility in the arrangement of components than other containers, such as JPanel objects, provide. The Box constructor accepts a single argument that specifies the orientation as either BoxLayout.X_AXIS or BoxLayout.Y_AXIS. The class also has two static methods, createHorizontalBox() and createVerticalBox(), that each return a reference to a Box container with the orientation implied.

As we said earlier a container can contain another container, so you can easily place a Box container inside another Box container to get any arrangement of rows and columns that you want. Let's try that out.

Try It Out – Boxes Containing Boxes

We will create an application that has a window containing a column of radio buttons on the left, a column of checkboxes on the right, and a row of buttons across the bottom. Here's the code:

```
import javax.swing.*;

import java.awt.Toolkit;
import java.awt.Dimension;
import java.awt.Container;
import java.awt.BorderLayout;

import javax.swing.border.Border;

public class TryBoxLayout {
  // The window object
  static JFrame aWindow = new JFrame("This is a Box Layout");

  public static void main(String[] args) {
    Toolkit theKit = aWindow.getToolkit();        // Get the window toolkit
    Dimension wndSize = theKit.getScreenSize();  // Get screen size

    // Set the position to screen center & size to half screen size
    aWindow.setBounds(wndSize.width/4, wndSize.height/4,    // Position
                      wndSize.width/2, wndSize.height/2);  // Size
    aWindow.setDefaultCloseOperation(JFrame.EXIT_ON_CLOSE);
```

```java
    // Create left column of radio buttons
    Box left = Box.createVerticalBox();
    ButtonGroup radioGroup = new ButtonGroup();            // Create button group
    JRadioButton rbutton;                                  // Stores a button
    radioGroup.add(rbutton = new JRadioButton("Red"));     // Add to group
    left.add(rbutton);                                     // Add to Box
    radioGroup.add(rbutton = new JRadioButton("Green"));
    left.add(rbutton);
    radioGroup.add(rbutton = new JRadioButton("Blue"));
    left.add(rbutton);
    radioGroup.add(rbutton = new JRadioButton("Yellow"));
    left.add(rbutton);

    // Create right columns of checkboxes
    Box right = Box.createVerticalBox();
    right.add(new JCheckBox("Dashed"));
    right.add(new JCheckBox("Thick"));
    right.add(new JCheckBox("Rounded"));

    // Create top row to hold left and right
    Box top = Box.createHorizontalBox();
    top.add(left);
    top.add(right);
    // Create bottom row of buttons
    JPanel bottomPanel = new JPanel();
    Border edge = BorderFactory.createRaisedBevelBorder();  // Button border
    JButton button;
    Dimension size = new Dimension(80,20);
    bottomPanel.add(button = new JButton("Defaults"));
    button.setBorder(edge);
    button.setPreferredSize(size);
    bottomPanel.add(button = new JButton("OK"));
    button.setBorder(edge);
    button.setPreferredSize(size);
    bottomPanel.add(button = new JButton("Cancel"));
    button.setBorder(edge);
    button.setPreferredSize(size);

    // Add top and bottom panel to content pane
    Container content = aWindow.getContentPane();          // Get content pane
    content.setLayout(new BorderLayout());                 // Set border layout manager
    content.add(top, BorderLayout.CENTER);
    content.add(bottomPanel, BorderLayout.SOUTH);

    aWindow.setVisible(true);                              // Display the window
  }
}
```

When you run this example and try out the radio buttons and checkboxes, it should produce a window something like that shown overleaf.

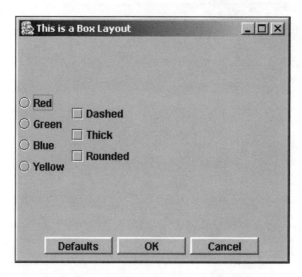

It's not an ideal arrangement, but we will improve on it.

How It Works

The shaded code is of interest – the rest we have seen before. The first block creates the left column of radio buttons providing a color choice. A Box object with a vertical orientation is used to contain the radio buttons. If you tried the radio buttons you will have found that only one of them can ever be selected. This is the effect of the ButtonGroup object that is used – to ensure radio buttons operate properly, you must add them to a ButtonGroup object.

The ButtonGroup object ensures that only one of the radio buttons it contains can be selected at any one time. Note that a ButtonGroup object is not a component – it's just a logical grouping of radio buttons – so you can't add it to a container. We must still independently add the buttons to the Box container that manages their physical arrangement. The Box object for the right-hand group of JCheckBox objects works in the same way as that for the radio buttons.

Both the Box objects holding the columns are added to another Box object that implements a horizontal arrangement to position them side-by-side. Note how the vertical Box objects adjust their width to match that of the largest component in the column. That's why the two columns are bunched towards the left side. We will see how to improve on this in a moment.

We use a JPanel object to hold the buttons. This has a flow layout manager by default, which suits us here. Calling the setPreferredSize() method for each button sets the preferred width and height to that specified by the Dimension object, size. This ensures that, space permitting, each button will be 80 pixels wide and 20 pixels high.

We have introduced another way of obtaining a border for a component here. The BorderFactory class (defined in the javax.swing package) contains static methods that return standard borders of various kinds. The createBevelBorder() method returns a reference to a BevelBorder object as type Border – Border being an interface that all border objects implement. We use this border for each of the buttons. We will try some more of the methods in the BorderFactory class later.

To improve the layout of the application window, we can make use of some additional facilities provided by a `Box` container.

Struts and Glue

The `Box` class contains static methods to create an invisible component called a **strut**. A vertical strut has a given height in pixels and zero width. A horizontal strut has a given width in pixels and zero height. The purpose of these struts is to enable you to insert space between your components, either vertically or horizontally. By placing a horizontal strut between two components in a horizontally arranged `Box` container, you fix the distance between the components. By adding a horizontal strut to a vertically arranged `Box` container, you can force a minimum width on the container. You can use a vertical strut in a horizontal box to force a minimum height.

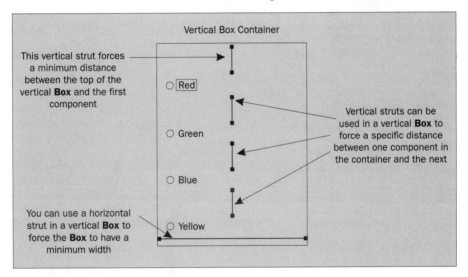

Note that although vertical struts have zero width, they have no maximum width so they can expand horizontally to have a width that takes up any excess space. Similarly, the height of a horizontal strut will expand when there is excess vertical space available.

A vertical strut is returned as an object of type `Component` by the static `createVerticalStrut()` method in the `Box` class . The argument specifies the height of the strut in pixels. To create a horizontal strut, you use the `createHorizontalStrut()` method.

We can space out our radio buttons by inserting struts between them:

```
// Create left column of radio buttons
Box left = Box.createVerticalBox();
left.add(Box.createVerticalStrut(30));                   // Starting space
ButtonGroup radioGroup = new ButtonGroup();              // Create button group
JRadioButton rbutton;                                    // Stores a button
radioGroup.add(rbutton = new JRadioButton("Red"));       // Add to group
left.add(rbutton);                                       // Add to Box
left.add(Box.createVerticalStrut(30));                   // Space between
radioGroup.add(rbutton = new JRadioButton("Green"));
```

```
        left.add(rbutton);
        left.add(Box.createVerticalStrut(30));                  // Space between
        radioGroup.add(rbutton = new JRadioButton("Blue"));
        left.add(rbutton);
        left.add(Box.createVerticalStrut(30));                  // Space between
        radioGroup.add(rbutton = new JRadioButton("Yellow"));
        left.add(rbutton);
```

The extra statements add a 30 pixel vertical strut at the start of the columns, and a further strut of the same size between each radio button and the next. We can do the same for the checkboxes:

```
        // Create right columns of checkboxes
        Box right = Box.createVerticalBox();
        right.add(Box.createVerticalStrut(30));                  // Starting space
        right.add(new JCheckBox("Dashed"));
        right.add(Box.createVerticalStrut(30));                  // Space between
        right.add(new JCheckBox("Thick"));
        right.add(Box.createVerticalStrut(30));                  // Space between
        right.add(new JCheckBox("Rounded"));
```

If you run the example with these changes the window will look like this:

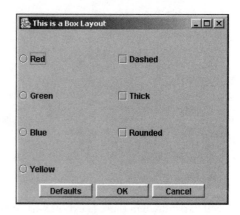

It's better, but far from perfect. The columns are now equally spaced in the window because the vertical struts have assumed a width to take up the excess horizontal space that is available. The distribution of surplus space vertically is different in the two columns because the number of components is different. We can control where surplus space goes in a Box object with **glue**. Glue is an invisible component that has the sole function of taking up surplus space in a Box container.

While the name gives the impression that it binds components together, it, in fact, provides an elastic connector between two components that can expand or contract as necessary, so it acts more like a spring. Glue components can be placed between the actual components in the Box and at either or both ends. Any surplus space that arises after the actual components have been accommodated is distributed between the glue components added. If you wanted all the surplus space to be at the beginning of a Box container, for instance, you should first add a single glue component in the container.

You create a component that represents glue by calling the `createGlue()` method for a `Box` object. You then add the glue component to the `Box` container in the same way as any other component wherever you want surplus space to be taken up. You can add glue at several positions in a row or column, and spare space will be distributed between the glue components. We can add glue after the last component in each column to make all the spare space appear at the end of each column of buttons. For the radio buttons we can add the statement,

```
// Statements adding radio buttons to left Box object
left.add(Box.createGlue());                        // Glue at the end
```

and similarly for the right box. The glue component at the end of each column of buttons will take up all the surplus space in each vertical `Box` container. This will make the buttons line up at the top. Running the program with added glue will result in the following application window.

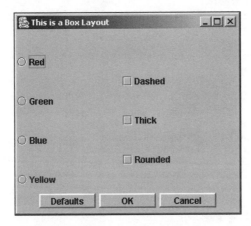

It's better now, but let's put together a final version of the example with some additional embroidery.

Try It Out – Embroidering Boxes

We will use some `JPanel` objects with a new kind of border to contain the vertical `Box` containers.

```
import javax.swing.*;
import java.awt.*;
import javax.swing.border.*;

public class TryBoxLayout {
  // The window object
  static JFrame aWindow = new JFrame("This is a Box Layout");

  public static void main(String[] args) {
    // Set up the window as before...

    // Create left column of radio buttons with struts and glue as above...
    // Create a panel with a titled border to hold the left Box container
    JPanel leftPanel = new JPanel(new BorderLayout());
    leftPanel.setBorder(new TitledBorder(
```

```
                                      new EtchedBorder(),    // Border to use
                                      "Line Color"));        // Border title
        leftPanel.add(left, BorderLayout.CENTER);

        // Create right columns of checkboxes with struts and glue as above...
        // Create a panel with a titled border to hold the right Box container
        JPanel rightPanel = new JPanel(new BorderLayout());
        rightPanel.setBorder(new TitledBorder(
                                      new EtchedBorder(),    // Border to use
                                      "Line Properties"));   // Border title
        rightPanel.add(right, BorderLayout.CENTER);

        // Create top row to hold left and right
        Box top = Box.createHorizontalBox();
        top.add(leftPanel);
        top.add(Box.createHorizontalStrut(5));       // Space between vertical boxes
        top.add(rightPanel);

        // Create bottom row of buttons
        JPanel bottomPanel = new JPanel();
        bottomPanel.setBorder(new CompoundBorder(
             BorderFactory.createLineBorder(Color.black, 1),        // Outer border
             BorderFactory.createBevelBorder(BevelBorder.RAISED))); // Inner border

        // Create and add the buttons as before...
        Container content = aWindow.getContentPane();  // Set the container layout mgr
        BoxLayout box = new BoxLayout(content, BoxLayout.Y_AXIS);
                                                        // Vertical for content pane
        content.setLayout(box);           // Set box layout manager
        content.add(top);
        content.add(bottomPanel);
        aWindow.setVisible(true);                       // Display the window
    }
}
```

The example will now display the window shown below.

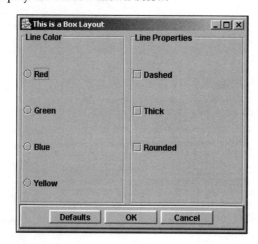

How It Works

Both vertical boxes are now contained in a `JPanel` container. Since `JPanel` objects are Swing components, we can add a border, and this time we add a `TitledBorder` border that we create directly using the constructor. A `TitledBorder` is a border specified by the first argument to the constructor, plus a title that is a `String` specified by the second argument to the constructor. We use a border of type `EtchedBorder` here, but you can use any type of border.

We introduce space between the two vertically aligned `Box` containers by adding a horizontal strut to the `Box` container that contains them. If you wanted space at each side of the window, you could add struts to the container before and after the components.

The last improvement is to the panel holding the buttons along the bottom of the window. We now have a border that is composed of two types, one inside the other: a `LineBorder` and a `BevelBorder`. A `CompoundBorder` object defines a border that is a composite of two border objects, the first argument to the constructor being the outer border and the second being the inner border. The `LineBorder` class defines a border consisting of a single line of the color specified by its first constructor argument and a thickness in pixels specified by the second. There is a static method defined for the class, `createBlackLineBorder()` that creates a black line border that is one pixel wide, so we could have used that here.

Using a GridBagLayout Manager

The `GridBagLayout` manager is much more flexible than the other layout managers we have seen and, consequently, rather more complicated to use. The basic mechanism arranges components in an arbitrary rectangular grid, but the rows and columns of the grid are not necessarily the same height or width. A component is placed at a given cell position in the grid specified by the coordinates of the cell, where the cell at the top-left corner is at position (0, 0). A component can occupy more than one cell in a row and/or column in the grid, but it always occupies a rectangular group of cells.

Each component in a `GridBagLayout` has its own set of constraints. These are defined by an object of type `GridBagConstraints` that you associate with each component, before adding the component to the container. The location of each component, its relative size, and the area it occupies in the grid, are all determined by its associated `GridBagConstraints` object.

A `GridBagConstraints` object has no less than eleven public instance variables that may be set to define the constraints for a component. Since they also interact with each other there's more entertainment here than with a Rubik's cube. Let's first get a rough idea of what these instance variables in a `GridBagConstraints` object do:

Instance Variable	Description
`gridx` and `gridy`	Determines the position of the component in the container as coordinate positions of cells in the grid, where (0, 0) is the top-left position in the grid.
`gridwidth` and `gridheight`	Determines the size of the area occupied by the component in the container.

Table continued on following page

Instance Variable	Description
`weightx` and `weighty`	Determines how free space is distributed between components in the container.
`anchor`	Determines where a component is positioned within the area allocated to it in the container.
`ipadx` and `ipady`	Determines by how much the component size is to be increased above its minimum size.
`fill`	Determines how the component is to be enlarged to fill the space allocated to it.
`insets`	Specifies the free space that is to be provided around the component within the space allocated to it in the container.

That seems straightforward enough. We can now explore the possible values we can set for these and then try them out.

GridBagConstraints Instance Variables

A component will occupy at least one grid position, or **cell**, in a container that uses a `GridBagLayout` object, but it can occupy any rectangular array of cells. The total number of rows and columns, and thus the cell size, in the grid for a container is variable, and determined by the constraints for all of the components in the container. Each component will have a position in the grid plus an area it is allocated defined by a number of horizontal and vertical grid positions.

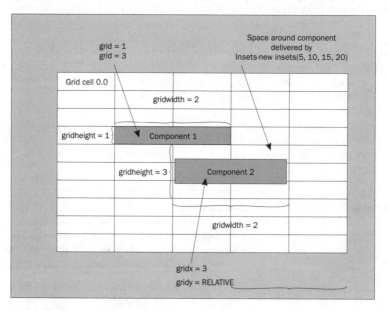

The top-left cell in a layout is at position (0, 0). You specify the position of a component by defining where the top-left cell that it occupies is, relative to either the grid origin, or relative to the last component that was added to the container. You specify the position of the top-left cell that a component occupies in the grid by setting values of type `int` for the `gridx` and `gridy` members of the `GridBagConstraints` object. The default value for `gridx` is `GridBagConstraints.RELATIVE` – a constant that places the top-left grid position for the component in the column immediately to the right of the previous component. The same value is the default for `gridy`, which places the next component immediately below the previous one.

You specify the number of cells occupied by a component horizontally and vertically by setting values for the `gridwidth` and `gridheight` instance variables for the `GridBagConstraints` object. The default value for both of these is 1. There are two constants you can use as values for these variables. With a value of `GridBagConstraints.REMAINDER`, the component will be the last one in the row or column. If you specify the value as `GridBagConstraints.RELATIVE`, the component will be the penultimate one in the row or column.

If the preferred size of the component is less than the display area, you can control how the size of the component is adjusted to fit the display area by setting the `fill` and `insets` instance variables for the `GridBagConstraints` object.

Variable	Description
`fill`	The value for this variable is of type `int`, and it determines how the size of the component is adjusted in relation to the array of cells it occupies. The default value of `GridBagConstraints.NONE` means that the component is not resized.
	A value of `GridBagConstraints.HORIZONTAL` adjusts the width of the component to fill the display area.
	A value of `GridBagConstraints.VERTICAL` adjusts the height of the component to fill the display area.
	A value of `GridBagConstraints.BOTH` adjusts the height and the width to completely fill the display area.
`insets`	This variable stores a reference to an object of type `Insets`. An `Insets` object defines the space allowed between the edges of the components and boundaries of the display area it occupies. Four parameter values to the class constructor define the top, left-side, bottom and right-side padding from the edges of the component. The default value is `Insets(0, 0, 0, 0)`.

If you don't intend to expand a component to fill its display area, you may still want to enlarge the component from its minimum size. You can adjust the dimensions of the component by setting the following `GridBagConstraints` instance variables:

Variable	Description
ipadx	An int value that defines the number of pixels by which the top and bottom edges of the component are to be expanded. The default value is 0.
ipady	An int value that defines the number of pixels by which the left and right edges of the component are to be expanded. The default value is 0.

If the component is still smaller than its display area in the container, you can specify where it should be placed in relation to its display area by setting a value for the anchor instance variable of the GridBagConstraints object. Possible values are NORTH, NORTHEAST, EAST, SOUTHEAST, SOUTH, SOUTHWEST, WEST, NORTHWEST, and CENTER, all of which are defined in the GridBagConstraints class.

The last GridBagConstraints instance variables to consider are weightx and weighty which are of type double. These determine how space in the container is distributed between components in the horizontal and vertical directions. You should always set a value for these, otherwise the default of 0 will cause the components to be bunched together adjacent to one another in the center of the container. The absolute values for weightx and weighty are not important. It is the relative values that matter. If you set all the values the same (but not zero), the space for each component will be distributed uniformly. Space is distributed in the proportions defined by the values.

For example, if three components in a row have weightx values of 1.0, 2.0, and 3.0, the first will get 1/6 of the total in the *x* direction, the second will get 1/3, and the third will get half. The proportion of the available space that a component gets in the *x* direction is the weightx value for the component divided by the sum of the weightx values in the row. This also applies to the weighty values for allocating space in the *y* direction.

We'll start with a simple example of placing two buttons in a window, and introduce another way of obtaining a standard border for a component.

Try It Out – Applying the GridBagConstraints Object

Make the following changes to the previous program and try out the GridBagLayout manager.

```
import javax.swing.*;
import java.awt.*;
import javax.swing.border.Border;

public class TryGridBagLayout {
  // The window object
  static JFrame aWindow = new JFrame("This is a Gridbag Layout");

  public static void main(String[] args) {
    Toolkit theKit = aWindow.getToolkit();          // Get the window toolkit
    Dimension wndSize = theKit.getScreenSize();   // Get screen size

    // Set the position to screen center & size to half screen size
    aWindow.setBounds(wndSize.width/4, wndSize.height/4,    // Position
                      wndSize.width/2, wndSize.height/2);   // Size
```

```
            aWindow.setDefaultCloseOperation(JFrame.EXIT_ON_CLOSE);

            GridBagLayout gridbag = new GridBagLayout();       // Create a layout manager
            GridBagConstraints constraints = new GridBagConstraints();
            aWindow.getContentPane().setLayout(gridbag);       // Set the container layout mgr

            // Set constraints and add first button
            constraints.weightx = constraints.weighty = 10.0;
            constraints.fill = constraints.BOTH;               // Fill the space
            addButton("Press", constraints, gridbag);          // Add the button

            // Set constraints and add second button
            constraints.gridwidth = constraints.REMAINDER;     // Rest of the row
            addButton("GO", constraints, gridbag);             // Create and add button

            aWindow.setVisible(true);                                  // Display the window
        }

    static void addButton(String label,
                        GridBagConstraints constraints,
                        GridBagLayout layout) {
        // Create a Border object using a BorderFactory method
        Border edge = BorderFactory.createRaisedBevelBorder();

        JButton button = new JButton(label);             // Create a button
        button.setBorder(edge);                          // Add its border
        layout.setConstraints(button, constraints);      // Set the constraints
        aWindow.getContentPane().add(button);            // Add button to content pane
    }
}
```

The program window will look like that shown below:

As you see, the left button is slightly wider than the right button. This is because the length of the button label affects the size of the button.

How It Works

Because the process will be the same for every button added, we have implemented the helper function `addButton()`. This creates a `Button` object, associates the `GridBagConstraints` object with it in the `GridBagLayout` object, and then adds it to the content pane of the frame window.

After creating the layout manager and `GridBagConstraints` objects we set the values for `weightx` and `weighty` to 10.0. A value of 1.0 would have the same effect. We set the `fill` constraint to `BOTH` to make the component fill the space it occupies. Note that when the `setConstraints()` method is called to associate the `GridBagConstraints` object with the button object, a copy of the constraints object is stored in the layout – not the object we created. This allows us to change the constraints object and use it for the second button without affecting the constraints for the first.

The buttons are more or less equal in size in the *x* direction (they would be exactly the same size if the labels were the same length) because the `weightx` and `weighty` values are the same for both. Both buttons fill the space available to them because the `fill` constraint is set to `BOTH`. If `fill` was set to `HORIZONTAL`, for example, the buttons would be the full width of the grid positions they occupy, but just high enough to accommodate the label, since they would have no preferred size in the *y* direction.

If we alter the constraints for the second button to:

```
// Set constraints and add second button
constraints.weightx = 5.0;                        // Weight half of first
constraints.insets = new Insets(10, 30, 10, 20);  // Left 30 & right 20
constraints.gridwidth = constraints.RELATIVE;     // Rest of the row
addButton("GO", constraints, gridbag);            // Add button to content pane
```

the application window will be as shown:

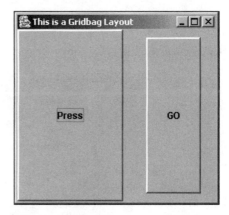

Now the second button occupies one third of the space in the *x* direction – that is a proportion of $5/(5+10)$ of the total – and the first button occupies two thirds. Note that the buttons still occupy one grid cell each – the default values for `gridwidth` and `gridheight` of 1 apply – but the `weightx` constraint values have altered the relative sizes of the cells for the two buttons in the *x* direction.

The second button is also within the space allocated – ten pixels at the top and bottom, thirty pixels on the left and twenty on the right (set with the `insets` constraint). You can see that for a given window size here, the size of a grid position depends on the number of objects. The more components there are, the less space they will each be allocated.

Suppose we wanted to add a third button, the same width as the **Press** button, and immediately below it. We could do that by adding the following code immediately after that for the second button:

```
// Set constraints and add third button
constraints.insets = new Insets(0,0,0,0);        // No insets
constraints.gridx = 0;                           // Begin new row
constraints.gridwidth = 1;                       // Width as "Press"
addButton("Push", constraints, gridbag);         // Add button to content pane
```

We reset the `gridx` constraint to zero to put the button at the start of the next row. It has a default `gridwidth` of 1 cell, like the others. The window would now look like:

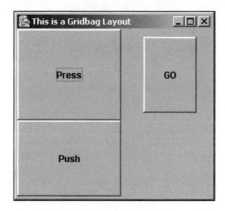

Having seen how it looks now, clearly it would be better if the **GO** button were the height of **Press** and **Push** combined. To arrange them like this, we need to make the height of the **GO** button twice that of the other two buttons. The height of the **Press** button is 1 by default, so by making the height of the **GO** button 2, and resetting the `gridheight` constraint of the **Push** button to 1, we should get the desired result. Modify the code for the second and third buttons to:

```
// Set constraints and add second button
constraints.weightx = 5.0;                          // Weight half of first
constraints.gridwidth = constraints.REMAINDER;      // Rest of the row
constraints.insets = new Insets(10, 30, 10, 20);    // Left 30 & right 20
constraints.gridheight = 2;                         // Height 2x "Press"
addButton("GO", constraints, gridbag);              // Add button to content pane

// Set constraints and add third button
constraints.gridx = 0;                              // Begin new row
constraints.gridwidth = 1;                          // Width as "Press"
constraints.gridheight = 1;                         // Height as "Press"
constraints.insets = new Insets(0, 0, 0, 0);        // No insets
addButton("Push", constraints, gridbag);            // Add button to content pane
```

With these code changes, the window will be:

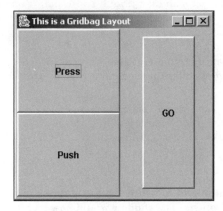

We could also see the effect of padding the components out from their preferred size by altering the button constraints a little:

```
// Create constraints and add first button
constraints.weightx = constraints.weighty = 10.0;
constraints.fill = constraints.NONE;
constraints.ipadx = 30;                          // Pad 30 in x
constraints.ipady = 10;                          // Pad 10 in y
addButton("Press", constraints, gridbag);        // Add button to content pane

// Set constraints and add second button
constraints.weightx = 5.0;                       // Weight half of first
constraints.fill = constraints.BOTH;             // Expand to fill space
constraints.ipadx = constraints.ipady = 0;       // No padding
constraints.gridwidth = constraints.REMAINDER;   // Rest of the row
constraints.gridheight = 2;                      // Height 2x "Press"
constraints.insets = new Insets(10, 30, 10, 20); // Left 30 & right 20
addButton("GO", constraints, gridbag);           // Add button to content pane

// Set constraints and add third button
constraints.gridx = 0;                           // Begin new row
constraints.fill = constraints.NONE;
constraints.ipadx = 30;                          // Pad component in x
constraints.ipady = 10;                          // Pad component in y
constraints.gridwidth = 1;                       // Width as "Press"
constraints.gridheight = 1;                      // Height as "Press"
constraints.insets = new Insets(0, 0, 0, 0);     // No insets
addButton("Push", constraints, gridbag);         // Add button to content pane
```

With the constraints for the buttons as before, the window will look like:

Both the Push and the Press button occupy the same space in the container, but, because `fill` is set to NONE, they are not expanded to fill the space in either direction. The `ipadx` and `ipady` constraints specify by how much the buttons are to be expanded from their preferred size – by thirty pixels on the left and right, and ten pixels on the top and bottom. The overall arrangement remains the same.

You need to experiment with using `GridBagLayout` and `GridBagConstraints` to get a good feel for how the layout manager works because you are likely to find yourself using it quite often.

Using a SpringLayout Manager

You can set the layout manager for the content pane of a `JFrame` object, `aWindow`, to be a `SpringLayout` manager like this:

```
SpringLayout layout = new SpringLayout();        // Create a layout manager
Container content = aWindow.getContentPane();    // Get the content pane
content.setLayout(layout);
```

The layout manager defined by the `SpringLayout` class determines the position and size of each component in the container according to a set of constraints that are defined by `Spring` objects. Every component within a container using a `SpringLayout` manager has an object associated with it of type `SpringLayout.constraints` that can define constraints on the position of each of the four edges of the component. Before you can access the `SpringLayout.constraints` object for an object, you must first add the object to the container. For example:

```
JButton button = new JButton("Press Me");
content.add(button);
```

Now we can call the `getConstraint()` method for the `SpringLayout` object to obtain the object encapsulating the constraints:

```
SpringLayout.Constraints buttonConstr = layout.getConstraints(button);
```

To constrain the location and size of the `button` object, we will call methods of the `buttonConstr` object to set individual constraints.

Understanding Constraints

The top, bottom, left, and right edges of a component are referred to by their compass points, north, south, west, and east. When you need to refer to a particular edge in your code – for setting a constraint for instance, you use constants that are defined in the `SpringLayout` class, NORTH, SOUTH, WEST, and EAST respectively.

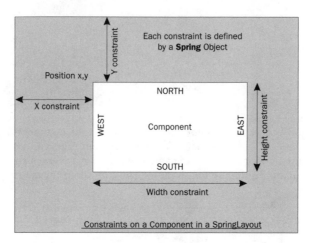

Constraints on a Component in a SpringLayout

As the diagram shows, the position of a component is determined by a horizontal constraint on the x-coordinate of the component and a vertical constraint on the y-coordinate. These obviously also determine the location of the WEST and NORTH edges of the component, since the position determines where the top-left corner is located. The width and height are determined by horizontal constraints that relate the position of the EAST and SOUTH edges to the positions of the WEST and NORTH edges respectively. Thus the constraints on the positions of the EAST and SOUTH edges are determined by constraints that are derived from the others, as follows:

```
EAST-constraint = X-constraint + width-constraint
SOUTH-constraint = Y-constraint + height-constraint
```

You can set the X, Y, width, and height constraints independently as we shall see in a moment, and you can also set a constraint explicitly for any edge. If you set a constraint on the SOUTH or EAST edges of a component, the Y or X constraint will be adjusted if necessary to ensure the relationships above still hold.

Defining Constraints

The `Spring` class in the `javax.swing` package defines an object that represents a constraint. A `Spring` object is defined by three integer values that relate to the notional length of the spring: the minimum value, the preferred value, and the maximum value. A `Spring` object will also have an actual value that lies between the minimum and the maximum, and that will determine the location of the edge to which it applies. You can create a `Spring` object like this:

```
Spring spring = Spring.constant(10, 30, 50);     // min=10, pref=30, max=50
```

The static `constant()` method creates a `Spring` object from the three arguments that are the minimum, preferred, and maximum values for the object. If all three values are equal, the object is called a strut because its value is fixed at the common value you set for all three. There's an overloaded version of the `constant()` method for creating struts:

```
Spring strut = Spring.constant(40); // min, pref, and max all set to 40
```

The `Spring` class also defines static methods that operate on `Spring` objects:

`sum(Spring spr1, Spring spr2)`	Returns a reference to a new `Spring` object that has minimum, preferred, and maximum values that are the sum of the corresponding values of the arguments.
`minus (Spring spr)`	Returns a reference to a new `Spring` object with minimum, preferred, and maximum values that are the same magnitude as those of the argument but with opposite signs.
`max(Spring spr1, Spring spr2)`	Returns a reference to a new `Spring` object that has minimum, preferred, and maximum values that are the maximum of the corresponding values of the arguments.

Setting Constraints for a Component

The `setX()` and `setY()` methods for a `SpringLayout.Constraints` object set the constraints for the `WEST` and `NORTH` edges of the component respectively. For example:

```
Spring xSpring = Spring.constant(5,10,20);    // Spring we'll use for X
Spring ySpring = Spring.constant(3,5,8);      // Spring we'll use for Y
buttonConstr.setX(xSpring);                   // Set the WEST edge constraint
buttonConstr.setY(xSpring);                   // Set the NORTH edge constraint
```

The `setX()` method defines a constraint between the `WEST` edge of the container, and the `WEST` edge of the component. Similarly, the `setY()` method defines a constraint between the `NORTH` edge of the container and the `NORTH` edge of the component. This fixes the location of the component in relation to the origin of the container.

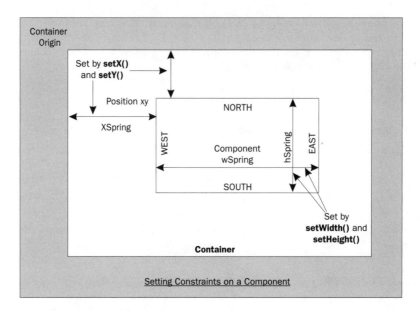

Setting Constraints on a Component

To set the width and height of the component, you call the setWidth() and setHeight() methods for its SpringLayout.Constraints object:

```
Spring wSpring = Spring.constant(30,50,70);    // Spring we'll use for width
Spring hSpring = Spring.constant(15);          // Strut we'll use for height
buttonConstr.setWidth(wSpring);                // Set component width constraint
buttonConstr.setHeight(hSpring);               // Set component height constraint
```

The width constraint is applied between the WEST and EAST edges and the height constraint applies between the component's NORTH and SOUTH edges. Since we have specified a strut for the height, there is no leeway on this constraint; its value is fixed at 15.

If you want to explicitly set an edge constraint for a component, you call the setConstraint() method for the component's SpringLayout.Constraints object:

```
layout.getConstraints(newButton)
      .setConstraint(StringLayout.EAST, Spring.sum(xSpring, wSpring));
```

This statement ties the EAST edge of the newButton component to the WEST edge of the container by a Spring object that is the sum of xSpring and wSpring.

You can also set constraints between pairs of vertical or horizontal edges where one edge can belong to a different component from the other. For instance, we could add another button to the container like this:

```
JButton newButton = new JButton("Push");
content.add(newButton);
```

We can now constrain its WEST and NORTH edges by tying the edges to the EAST and SOUTH edges of button. We use the putConstraint() method for the SpringLayout object to do this:

```
SpringLayout.Constraints newButtonConstr = layout.getConstraints(newButton);
layout.putConstraint(SpringLayout.WEST,
                     newButton,
                     xSpring,
                     SpringLayout.EAST,
                     button);
```

The first two arguments to the `putConstraint()` method for the layout object are the edge specification and a reference to the dependent component respectively. The third argument is a `Spring` object defining the constraint. The fourth and fifth arguments specify the edge and a reference to the component to which the dependent component is anchored. Obviously, since constraints can only be horizontal or vertical, both edges should have the same orientation. There is an overloaded version of the `putConstraint()` method where the third argument is a value of type `int` that defines a fixed distance between the edges.

Let's look at a simple example using a `SpringLayout` object as the layout manager.

Try It Out – Using a SpringLayout Manager

Here's the code for an example that displays six buttons in a window.

```
import javax.swing.JButton;
import javax.swing.JFrame;
import javax.swing.SpringLayout;
import javax.swing.Spring;

import java.awt.Container;
import java.awt.Dimension;
import java.awt.Toolkit;

public class TrySpringLayout {
  // The window object
  static JFrame aWindow = new JFrame("This is a Spring Layout");

  public static void main(String[] args) {
    Toolkit theKit = aWindow.getToolkit();          // Get the window toolkit
    Dimension wndSize = theKit.getScreenSize();      // Get screen size

    // Set the position to screen center & size to half screen size
    aWindow.setBounds(wndSize.width/4, wndSize.height/4,    // Position
                      wndSize.width/2, wndSize.height/2);   // Size
    aWindow.setDefaultCloseOperation(JFrame.EXIT_ON_CLOSE);

    SpringLayout layout = new SpringLayout();        // Create a layout manager
    Container content = aWindow.getContentPane();    // Get the content pane
    content.setLayout(layout);                       // Set the container layout mgr

    JButton[] buttons = new JButton[6];              // Array to store buttons
    for(int i = 0; i < buttons.length; i++) {
      buttons[i] = new JButton("Press " + (i+1));
      content.add(buttons[i]);        // Add a Button to content pane
```

```
    }

    Spring xSpring = Spring.constant(5,15,25);     // x constraint for 1st button
    Spring ySpring = Spring.constant(10,30, 50);   // y constraint for first button
    Spring wSpring = Spring.constant(30,80,130);   // Width constraint for buttons

    // Connect x,y for first button to left and top of container by springs
    SpringLayout.Constraints buttonConstr = layout.getConstraints(buttons[0]);
    buttonConstr.setX(xSpring);
    buttonConstr.setY(ySpring);

    // Set width and height of buttons and hook buttons together
    for(int i = 0 ; i< buttons.length ; i++) {
      buttonConstr = layout.getConstraints(buttons[i]);
      buttonConstr.setHeight(ySpring);        // Set the button height constraint
      buttonConstr.setWidth(wSpring);         // and its width constraint

      // For buttons after the first tie W and N edges to E and N of predecessor
      if(i>0) {
        layout.putConstraint(SpringLayout.WEST, buttons[i],
                          xSpring,SpringLayout.EAST, buttons[i-1]);
        layout.putConstraint(SpringLayout.NORTH, buttons[i],
                          ySpring,SpringLayout.SOUTH, buttons[i-1]);
      }
    }
    aWindow.setVisible(true);                       // Display the window
  }
}
```

When you compile and run this you should get a window with the buttons laid out as shown below.

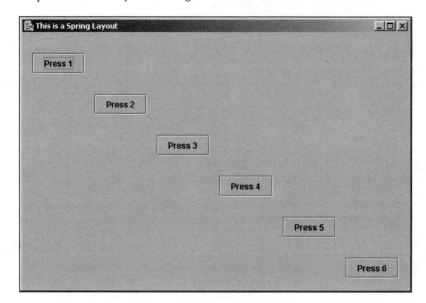

How It Works

After adding six buttons to the content pane of the window, we define two `Spring` objects that we will use to position the first button:

```
Spring xSpring = Spring.constant(5,15,25);     // x constraint for 1st button
Spring ySpring = Spring.constant(10,30, 50);   // y constraint for first button
```

We also define a spring we will use to determine the width of each button:

```
Spring wSpring = Spring.constant(30,80,130);   // Width constraint for buttons
```

We then set the location of the first button relative to the container:

```
// Connect x,y for first button to left and top of container by springs
SpringLayout.Constraints buttonConstr = layout.getConstraints(buttons[0]);
buttonConstr.setX(xSpring);
buttonConstr.setY(ySpring);
```

This fixes the first button. We can define the positions of each the remaining buttons relative to its predecessor. We do this by adding constraints between the NORTH and WEST edges of each button and the SOUTH and EAST edges of its predecessor. This is done in the `for` loop after setting the width and height constraints for each button :

```
// Set width and height of buttons and hook buttons together
for(int i = 0 ; i< buttons.length ; i++) {
  buttonConstr = layout.getConstraints(buttons[i]);
  buttonConstr.setHeight(ySpring);         // Set the button height constraint
  buttonConstr.setWidth(wSpring);          // and its width constraint

  // For buttons after the first tie W and N edges to E and N of predecessor
  if(i>0) {
    layout.putConstraint(SpringLayout.WEST,buttons[i],
                         xSpring,SpringLayout.EAST, buttons[i-1]);
    layout.putConstraint(SpringLayout.NORTH,buttons[i],
                         ySpring,SpringLayout.SOUTH, buttons[i-1]);
  } // end if
} // end for
```

This places each component after the first relative to the bottom right corner of its predecessor so the buttons are laid out in a cascade fashion.

Relating the Container Size to the Components

Of course, the size of the application window in our example is independent of the components within it. If you resize the window the springs have no effect. If you call `pack()` for the `aWindow` object before calling its `setVisible()` method, the window will shrink to a width and height just accommodating the title bar so you won't see any of the components. This is because `SpringLayout` does not adjust the size of the container by default so the effect of `pack()` is as though the content pane was empty.

We can do much better than this. We can set constraints on the edges of the container using springs that will control its size. We can therefore place constraints on the height and width of the container in terms of the springs that we used to determine the size and locations of the components. This will have the effect of relating all the springs that determine the size and position of the buttons to the size of the application window. Try adding the following code to the example immediately preceding the call to setVisible() for the window object:

```
SpringLayout.Constraints constr = layout.getConstraints(content);
constr.setConstraint(SpringLayout.EAST,
                Spring.sum(buttonConstr.getConstraint(SpringLayout.EAST),
                        Spring.constant(15)));
constr.setConstraint(SpringLayout.SOUTH,
                Spring.sum(buttonConstr.getConstraint(SpringLayout.SOUTH),
                        Spring.constant(10)));
aWindow.pack();
```

This sets the constraint on the EAST edge of a container that is the Spring constraining the EAST edge of the last button plus a strut 15 units long. This positions the right edge of the container 15 units to the right of the right edge of the last button. The bottom edge of the container is similarly connected by a fixed link, 10 units long, to the bottom edge of the last button. If you recompile with these additions and run the example again, you should find that not only is the initial size of the window set to accommodate all the buttons, but also when you resize the window the size and positions of the buttons adapt accordingly. Isn't that nice?

The SpringLayout manager is extremely flexible and can do much of what the other layout mangers can do if you choose the constraints on the components appropriately. It's well worth experimenting to see the effect of various configurations of springs on your application.

Adding a Menu to a Window

As we have already discussed, a JMenuBar object represents the menu bar that is placed at the top of a window. You can add JMenu or JMenuItem objects to a JMenuBar object and these will be displayed on the menu bar. A JMenu object is a menu item with a label that can display a pull-down menu when clicked. A JMenuItem object represents a simple menu item with a label that results in some program action when clicked – such as opening a dialog. A JMenuItem can have an icon in addition to, or instead of, a String label. Each item on the pull-down menu for an object of type JMenu, can be an object of either type JMenu, JMenuItem, JCheckBoxMenuItem, or JRadioButtonMenuItem.

A JCheckBoxMenuItem is a simple menu item with a checkbox associated with it. The checkbox can be checked and unchecked and typically indicates that that menu item was selected last time the pull-down menu was displayed. You can also add separators in a pull-down menu. These are simply bars to separate one group of menu items from another. A JRadioButtonMenuItem is a menu item much like a radio button in that it is intended to be one of a group of like menu items added to a ButtonGroup object. Both JCheckBoxMenuItem and JRadioButtonMenuItem objects can have icons.

Creating JMenu and JMenuItem

To create a `JMenu` object you call a `JMenu` class constructor and pass a `String` object to it that contains the label for the menu. For example, to create a File menu you would write:

```
JMenu fileMenu = new JMenu("File");
```

Creating a `JMenuItem` object is much the same:

```
JMenuItem openMenu = new JMenuItem("Open");
```

If you create a `JCheckboxMenuItem` object by passing just a `String` argument to the constructor, the object will represent an item that is initially unchecked. For example, you could create an unchecked item with the following statement:

```
JCheckboxMenuItem circleItem = new JCheckboxMenuItem("Circle");
```

Another constructor for this class allows you to set the check mark by specifying a second argument of type `boolean`. For example:

```
JCheckboxMenuItem lineItem = new JCheckboxMenuItem("Line", true);
```

This creates an item with the label, `Line`, which will be checked initially. You can, of course, also use this constructor to explicitly specify that you want an item to be unchecked by setting the second argument to `false`.

A `JRadioButtonMenuItem` object is created in essentially the same way:

```
JRadioButtonMenuItem item = new JRadioButtonMenuItem("Curve", true);
```

This creates a radio button menu item that is selected.

If you want to use a menu bar in your application window, you must create your window as a `JFrame` object, since the `JFrame` class incorporates the capability to manage a menu bar. You can also add a menu bar to `JDialog` and `JApplet` objects. Let's see how we can create a menu on a menu bar.

Creating a Menu

To create a window with a menu bar, we will define our own window class as a subclass of `JFrame`. This will be a much more convenient way to manage all the details of the window compared to using a `JFrame` object directly as we have been doing up to now. By extending the `JFrame` class, we can add our own members that will customize a `JFrame` window to our particular needs. We can also override the methods defined in the `JFrame` class to modify their behavior, if necessary.

We will be adding functionality to this example over several chapters, so create a directory for it with the name `Sketcher`. This program will be a window-based sketching program that will enable you to create sketches using lines, circles, curves, and rectangles, and to annotate them with text. By building an example in this way, you will gradually create a much larger Java program than the examples seen so far, and you will also gain experience of combining many of the capabilities of `javax.swing` and other standard packages in a practical situation.

Try It Out – Building a Menu

To start with, we will have two class files in the Sketcher program. The file `Sketcher.java` will contain the method `main()` where execution of the application will start, and the file `SketchFrame.java` will contain the class defining the application window.

We will define a preliminary version of our window class as:

```java
// Frame for the Sketcher application
import javax.swing.*;

public class SketchFrame extends JFrame {
  // Constructor
  public SketchFrame(String title) {
    setTitle(title);                             // Set the window title
    setDefaultCloseOperation(EXIT_ON_CLOSE);

    setJMenuBar(menuBar);                        // Add the menu bar to the window

    JMenu fileMenu = new JMenu("File");          // Create File menu
    JMenu elementMenu = new JMenu("Elements");   // Create Elements menu

    menuBar.add(fileMenu);                       // Add the file menu
    menuBar.add(elementMenu);                    // Add the element menu
  }

  private JMenuBar menuBar = new JMenuBar();     // Window menu bar
}
```

After you have entered this code into a new file, save the file in the `Sketcher` directory as `SketchFrame.java`.

Next, you can enter the code for the `Sketcher` class in a separate file:

```java
// Sketching application
import java.awt.Toolkit;
import java.awt.Dimension;

public class Sketcher {
  static SketchFrame window;                     // The application window

  public static void main(String[] args) {
    window = new SketchFrame("Sketcher");        // Create the app window
    Toolkit theKit = window.getToolkit();        // Get the window toolkit
```

```
        Dimension wndSize = theKit.getScreenSize();  // Get screen size

        // Set the position to screen center & size to half screen size
        window.setBounds(wndSize.width/4, wndSize.height/4,       // Position
                         wndSize.width/2, wndSize.height/2);      // Size

        window.setVisible(true);
    }
}
```

Save this file as `Sketcher.java` in the `Sketcher` directory. If you compile and run `Sketcher` you should see the window shown.

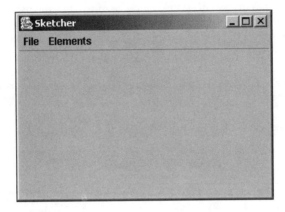

How It Works

The `Sketcher` class has a `SketchFrame` variable as a data member, which we will use to store the application window object. We must declare this variable as `static` as there will be no instances of the `Sketcher` class around. The variable, `window`, is initialized in the method `main()` that is called when program execution begins. Once the `window` object exists, we set the size of the window based on the screen size in pixels, which we obtain using the `Toolkit` object. This is exactly the same process that we saw earlier in this chapter. Finally in the method `main()`, we call the `setVisible()` method for the window object with the argument `true` to display the application window.

In the constructor for the `SketchFrame` class, we could pass the title for the window to the superclass constructor to create the window with the title bar directly. However, later when we have developed the application a bit more we will want to add to the title, so we call the `setTitle()` member to set the window title here. Next we call the `setJMenuBar()` method that is inherited from the `JFrame` class, to specify `menuBar` as the menu bar for the window. To define the two menus that are to appear on the menu bar, we create one `JMenu` object with the label `"File"` and another with the label `"Elements"` – these labels will be displayed on the menu bar. We add the `fileMenu` and `elementMenu` objects to the menu bar by calling the `add()` method for the `menuBar` object.

The instance variable that we have defined in the `SketchFrame` class represents the menu bar. Both the menu items on the menu bar are of type `JMenu`, so we need to add pull-down menus to each of them. The File menu will provide the file input, output, and print options, and we will eventually use the Elements menu to choose the kind of geometric figure we want to draw. Developing the menu further, we can now add the menu items.

Adding Items to a Pull-Down Menu

Both the items on the menu bar need a pull-down menu – they can't do anything by themselves because they are of type JMenu. You use a version of the add() method defined in the JMenu class to add items to a pull-down menu.

The simplest version creates a menu item with the label that you pass as an argument. For example:

```
JMenuItem newMenu = fileMenu.add("New");                    // Add the menu item "New"
```

This will create a JMenuItem object with the label "New", add it to the menu for the fileMenu item, and return a reference to it. You will need the reference to react to the user clicking the item.

You can also create the JMenuItem object explicitly and use the second version of the add() method to add it:

```
JMenuItem newMenu = new JMenuItem("New");          // Create the item
fileMenu.add(newMenu);                             // and add it to the menu
```

You can operate on menu items by using the following methods defined in the JMenuItem class:

Method	Description
void setEnabled(boolean b)	If b has the value true the menu item is enabled. If b has the value false the menu item is disabled. The default state is enabled.
void setText(String label)	Sets the menu item label to the string stored in the label.
String getText()	Returns the current menu item label.

Since the JMenu class is a subclass of JMenuItem, these methods also apply to JMenu objects. To add a separator to a pull-down menu you call the addSeparator() method for the JMenu object.

Let's now create the pull-down menus for the **File** and **Element** menus on the menu bar in the Sketcher application, and try out some of the menu items.

Try It Out – Adding Pull-Down Menus

We can change the definition of our SketchFrame class to do this:

```
// Frame for the Sketcher application
import javax.swing.*;

public class SketchFrame extends JFrame {
  // Constructor
  public SketchFrame(String title) {
    setTitle(title);                              // Set the window title
    setDefaultCloseOperation(EXIT_ON_CLOSE);
```

```
      setJMenuBar(menuBar);                          // Add the menu bar to the window

      JMenu fileMenu = new JMenu("File");            // Create File menu
      JMenu elementMenu = new JMenu("Elements");     // Create Elements menu

      // Construct the file pull down menu
      newItem = fileMenu.add("New");                 // Add New item
      openItem = fileMenu.add("Open");               // Add Open item
      closeItem = fileMenu.add("Close");             // Add Close item
      fileMenu.addSeparator();                       // Add separator
      saveItem = fileMenu.add("Save");               // Add Save item
      saveAsItem = fileMenu.add("Save As...");       // Add Save As item
      fileMenu.addSeparator();                       // Add separator
      printItem = fileMenu.add("Print");             // Add Print item

      // Construct the Element pull-down menu
      elementMenu.add(lineItem = new JRadioButtonMenuItem("Line", true));
      elementMenu.add(rectangleItem = new JRadioButtonMenuItem("Rectangle", false));
      elementMenu.add(circleItem = new JRadioButtonMenuItem("Circle", false));
      elementMenu.add(curveItem = new JRadioButtonMenuItem("Curve", false));
      ButtonGroup types = new ButtonGroup();
      types.add(lineItem);
      types.add(rectangleItem);
      types.add(circleItem);
      types.add(curveItem);

      elementMenu.addSeparator();

      elementMenu.add(redItem = new JCheckBoxMenuItem("Red", false));
      elementMenu.add(yellowItem = new JCheckBoxMenuItem("Yellow", false));
      elementMenu.add(greenItem = new JCheckBoxMenuItem("Green", false));
      elementMenu.add(blueItem = new JCheckBoxMenuItem("Blue", true));

      menuBar.add(fileMenu);                          // Add the file menu
      menuBar.add(elementMenu);                       // Add the element menu
    }

    private JMenuBar menuBar = new JMenuBar();        // Window menu bar

    // File menu items
    private JMenuItem newItem,    openItem,    closeItem,
                      saveItem, saveAsItem, printItem;

    // Element menu items
    private JRadioButtonMenuItem lineItem, rectangleItem, circleItem,  // Types
                                 curveItem, textItem;
    private JCheckBoxMenuItem    redItem,    yellowItem,               // Colors
                                 greenItem, blueItem ;
}
```

If you recompile Sketcher once more, you can run the application again to try out the menus. If you extend the File menu, you will see that it has the menu items that we have added.

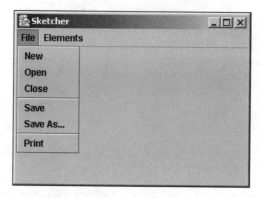

Now if you extend the Elements menu it should appear as shown with the Line and Blue items checked.

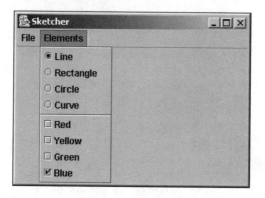

How It Works

We have defined the variables storing references to the menu items for the drop-down menus as private members of the class. For the File menu items they are of type JMenuItem. In the Element menu the items select a type of shape to be drawn, and, as these are clearly mutually exclusive, we are using type JRadioButtonMenuItem for them. We could use the same type for the element color items, but in order to try it out we are using the JCheckBoxMenuItem type.

To create the items in the File menu, we pass the String for the label for each to the add() method and leave it to the JMenu object to create the JMenuItem object.

The first group of Elements menu items are JRadioButtonMenuItem objects and we create each of these in the argument to the add() method. To ensure only one is checked at a time, we also add them to a ButtonGroup object. The color menu items are of type JCheckBoxMenuItem so the current selection is indicated by a check mark on the menu. We will make Line the default element type and Blue the default color, so we set both of these as checked by specifying true as the second argument to the constructor.

The other items will be unchecked initially because we have specified the second argument as false. We could have omitted the second argument to leave these items unchecked by default. It then means that you need to remember the default in order to determine what is happening. It is much better to set the checks explicitly.

You can see the effect of the `addSeparator()` method from the `JMenu` class. It produces the horizontal bar separating the items for element type from those for color. If you select any of the unchecked element type items on the Elements pull-down menu, they will be checked automatically, and only one can appear checked. More than one of the color items can be checked at the moment, but we will add some code in the next chapter to make sure only one of these items is checked at any given time.

We could try putting the color selection item in an additional pull-down menu. We could do this by changing the code that follows the statement adding the separator in the Elements menu as follows:

```
elementMenu.addSeparator();
```

```
JMenu colorMenu = new JMenu("Color");            // Color submenu
elementMenu.add(colorMenu);                      // Add the submenu
colorMenu.add(redItem = new JCheckBoxMenuItem("Red", false));
colorMenu.add(yellowItem = new JCheckBoxMenuItem("Yellow", false));
colorMenu.add(greenItem = new JCheckBoxMenuItem("Green", false));
colorMenu.add(blueItem = new JCheckBoxMenuItem("Blue", true));
```

Now we add a `JMenu` object, `colorMenu`, to the pull-down menu for Elements. This has its own pull-down menu consisting of the color menu items. The Color item will be displayed on the Elements menu with an arrow to show a further pull-down menu is associated with it. If you run the application again and extend the pull-down menus, the window should be as shown.

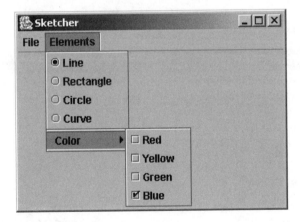

Whether you choose this menu structure or the previous one is a matter of taste. It might even be better to have a separate item on the menu bar but we'll leave it at that for now. We will see in the next chapter that the programming necessary to deal with menu selections by the user is the same in either case.

Adding an Shortcut for a Menu Item

A **shortcut** is a unique key combination used to select a menu on the menu bar direct from the keyboard. A typical shortcut under Windows would be the *Alt* key plus a letter from the menu item label, so the shortcut for the File menu item might be *Alt+F*. When you enter this key combination the menu is displayed. We can add shortcuts for the File and Elements menu items by adding the following statements after we add the menu items to the menu bar:

```
    fileMenu.setMnemonic('F');                // Create shortcut
    elementMenu.setMnemonic('E');             // Create shortcut
```

The setMnemonic() method is inherited from the AbstractButton class, so all subclasses of this class inherit this method. The argument is a character in the String that is the label for the item that is to be the shortcut character – under Windows the File menu would then pop up if you key *Alt+F*. The effect of setMnemonic() is to implement the shortcut and underline the shortcut character letter in the menu label.

An **accelerator** is a key combination that you can enter to select an item from a menu. Under Windows, the *Ctrl* key is frequently used in combination with a letter as an accelerator for a menu item, so *Ctrl+L* might be the combination for the Line item in the Elements menu. For menu items you call the setAccelerator() method to define an accelerator. For example, for the Line menu item you could write:

```
    lineItem.setAccelerator(KeyStroke.getKeyStroke('L', Event.CTRL_MASK ));
```

The KeyStroke class defines a keystroke combination. The static method, getKeyStroke() returns the KeyStroke object corresponding to the arguments. The first argument is the character and the second argument specifies the modifier key. The Event class (in java.awt) defines Event.SHIFT_MASK, Event.ALT_MASK, and what we used here, Event.CTRL_MASK. If you want to combine the *Alt* and *Ctrl* keys for instance, you can add them – Event.ALT_MASK + Event.CTRL_MASK.

Let's see how this works in practice.

Try It Out – Adding Menu Shortcuts

We can add some shortcuts to Sketcher by amending the statements that add the items to the File menu in the SketchFrame class constructor:

```
    // Frame for the Sketcher application
    import javax.swing.*;
    import java.awt.Event;

    public class SketchFrame extends JFrame {
      // Constructor
      public SketchFrame(String title) {
        setTitle(title);                         // Call the base constructor
        setDefaultCloseOperation(EXIT_ON_CLOSE);
        setJMenuBar(menuBar);                    // Add the menu bar to the window

        JMenu fileMenu = new JMenu("File");      // Create File menu
        JMenu elementMenu = new JMenu("Elements"); // Create Elements menu
        fileMenu.setMnemonic('F');               // Create shortcut
        elementMenu.setMnemonic('E');            // Create shortcut

        // Construct the file pull down menu as before...

        // Add File menu accelerators
        newItem.setAccelerator(KeyStroke.getKeyStroke('N',Event.CTRL_MASK ));
```

```
            openItem.setAccelerator(KeyStroke.getKeyStroke('O',Event.CTRL_MASK ));
            saveItem.setAccelerator(KeyStroke.getKeyStroke('S',Event.CTRL_MASK ));
            printItem.setAccelerator(KeyStroke.getKeyStroke('P',Event.CTRL_MASK ));

            // Construct the Element pull down menu as before...

            // Add element type accelerators
            lineItem.setAccelerator(KeyStroke.getKeyStroke('L',Event.CTRL_MASK ));
            rectangleItem.setAccelerator(KeyStroke.getKeyStroke('E',Event.CTRL_MASK ));
            circleItem.setAccelerator(KeyStroke.getKeyStroke('I',Event.CTRL_MASK ));
            curveItem.setAccelerator(KeyStroke.getKeyStroke('V',Event.CTRL_MASK ));

            elementMenu.addSeparator();

            // Create the color submenu as before...

            // Add element color accelerators
            redItem.setAccelerator(KeyStroke.getKeyStroke('R',Event.CTRL_MASK ));
            yellowItem.setAccelerator(KeyStroke.getKeyStroke('Y',Event.CTRL_MASK ));
            greenItem.setAccelerator(KeyStroke.getKeyStroke('G',Event.CTRL_MASK ));
            blueItem.setAccelerator(KeyStroke.getKeyStroke('B',Event.CTRL_MASK ));

            menuBar.add(fileMenu);                    // Add the file menu
            menuBar.add(elementMenu);                 // Add the element menu
        }

    // File menu items and the rest of the class as before...
    }
```

If you save `SketchFrame.java` after you have made the changes, you can recompile Sketcher and run it again. The file menu will now appear as show below:

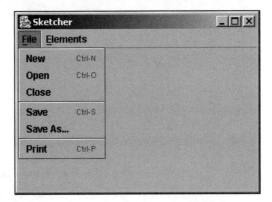

How It Works

We use the `setMnemonic()` method to set the shortcuts for the menu bar items and the `setAccelerator()` method to add accelerators to the submenu items. You must make sure that you do not use duplicate key combinations, and the more menu items you have accelerators for, the trickier this gets. The File menu here defines the standard Windows accelerators. You can see that the `setAccelerator()` method adds the shortcut key combination to the item label.

The menus don't actually work at the moment but at least they look good! We will start adding the code to implement menu operations in the next chapter.

More on Applets

Applets are a peculiar kind of program as they are executed in the context of a web browser. This places some rather severe restrictions on what you can do in an applet, to protect the environment in which they execute. Without these restrictions they would be a very direct means for someone to interfere with your system – in short, a virus delivery vehicle.

System security in Java programs is managed by a **security manager.** This is simply an object that provides methods for setting and checking security controls that determine what is and what is not allowed for a Java program. What an applet can and cannot do is determined by both the security manager that the browser running the applet has installed, and the security policy that is in effect for the system.

Unless permitted explicitly by the security policy in effect, the main default limitations on an applet are:

❑ An applet cannot have any access to files on the local computer.

❑ An applet cannot invoke any other program on the local computer.

❑ An applet cannot communicate with any computer other than the computer from which the HTML page containing the applet was downloaded.

Obviously there will be circumstances where these restrictions are too stringent. In this case you can set up a security policy that allows certain operations for specific trusted programs, applets, or sites, by authorizing them explicitly in a **policy file**. A policy file is an ASCII text file that defines what is permitted for a particular code source. We won't be going into details on this, but if you need to set up a policy file for your system, it is easiest to use the `policytool` program supplied with the JDK.

Because they are normally shipped over the Internet as part of an HTML page, applets should be compact. This doesn't mean that they are inevitably simple or unsophisticated. Because they can access the host computer from which they originated, they can provide a powerful means of enabling access to files on that host, but they are usually relatively small to allow them to be easily downloaded.

The `JApplet` class includes the following methods, which are all called automatically by the browser or applet viewer controlling the applet:

Method	Description
`void init()`	You implement this method to do any initialization that is necessary for the applet. This method is called once by the browser when the applet starts execution.
`void start()`	You implement this method to start the processing for the applet. For example, if your applet displays an animated image, you would start a thread for the animation in this method.
	This method is called by the browser immediately after `init()`. It is also called if the user returns to the current `.html` page after leaving it.

Method	Description
void stop()	This method is called by the browser when the user moves off the page containing the applet. You implement this to stop any operations that you started in the start() method.
void destroy()	This method is called after the stop() method when the browser is shut down. In this method you can release any resources your applet uses that are managed by the local operating system. This includes such things as resources used to display a window.

These are the basic methods you need to implement in the typical applet. We really need some graphics knowledge to go further with implementing an applet, so we will return to the practical application of these methods in Chapter 13.

Converting an Application to an Applet

Subject to the restrictions described in the previous section, you can convert an application to an applet relatively easily. You just need to be clear about how each part of program executes. You know that an application is normally started in the method main(). The method main() is not called for an applet but the method init() is, so one thing you should do is add an init() method to the application class. The other obvious difference is that an applet always extends the JApplet class.

We can demonstrate how to convert an application so that it also works as an applet, by changing the definition of the Sketcher class. This doesn't make a very sensible applet, but you can see the principles at work.

Try It Out – Running Sketcher as an Applet

You need to modify the contents of Sketcher.java so that it contains the following:

```
// Sketching application
import java.awt.Dimension;
import java.awt.Toolkit;
import javax.swing.JApplet;

public class Sketcher extends JApplet {
  public static void main(String[] args) {
    theApp = new Sketcher();          // Create the application object
    theApp.init();                    // ...and initialize it
  }

  public void init() {
    window = new SketchFrame("Sketcher");          // Create the app window
    Toolkit theKit = window.getToolkit();          // Get the window toolkit
    Dimension wndSize = theKit.getScreenSize();    // Get screen size

    // Set the position to screen center & size to half screen size
    window.setBounds(wndSize.width/4, wndSize.height/4,          // Position
                     wndSize.width/2, wndSize.height/2);         // Size
```

```
      window.setVisible(true);
  }

  private static SketchFrame window;          // The application window
  private static Sketcher theApp;             // The application object
}
```

To run Sketcher as an applet, you should add an `.html` file to the `Sketcher` directory with the contents:

```
<APPLET CODE="Sketcher.class" WIDTH=300 HEIGHT=200>
</APPLET>
```

If you recompile the revised version of the `Sketcher` class, you can run it as before, or using `AppletViewer`.

How It Works

The class now extends the class `JApplet`, and an `import` statement has been added for the `javax.swing` package.

The `init()` method now does most of what the method `main()` did before. The method `main()` now creates an instance of the `Sketcher` class and stores it in the `static` data member `theApp`. The method `main()` then calls the `init()` method for the new `Sketcher` object. The `window` variable no longer needs to be declared as `static` since it is always created in the `init()` method.

The class member, `theApp`, must be declared as `static` for the case when the program is run as an application. When an application starts execution, no `Sketcher` object exists, so the data member, `theApp`, does not exist either. If `theApp` is not declared as `static`, you can only create the `Sketcher` object as a local variable in `main()`.

Even if Sketcher is running as an applet, the application window appears as a detached window from the **AppletViewer** window, and it is still positioned relative to the screen.

Of course, when we come to implement the **File** menu, it will no longer be legal to derive the `Sketcher` class from the `JApplet` class since it will contravene the rule that an applet must not access the files on the local machine. It is also not recommended to create frame windows from within an untrusted applet, so you will get a warning from the `appletviewer` about this.

All you need to do to revert back to just being an application is to remove the `import` statement for `javax.swing` and remove `extends JApplet` from the `Sketcher` class header line. Everything else can stay as it is.

Summary

In this chapter you have learned how to create an application window, and how to use containers in the creation of the GUI for a program. We discussed the following important points:

- ❏ The package `javax.swing` provides classes for creating a graphical user interface (GUI).

- ❏ A component is an object that is used to form part of the GUI for a program. All components have the class `Component` as a superclass.

- ❏ A container is a component that can contain other components. A container object is created with a class that is a subclass of `Container`. The classes `JPanel`, `JApplet`, `JWindow`, `JFrame`, and `JDialog` are containers.

- ❏ The class `JApplet` is the base class for an applet. The `JFrame` class is a base class for an application window with a title bar, borders, and a menu.

- ❏ The arrangement of components in a container is controlled by a layout manager.

- ❏ The default layout manager for the content pane of `JFrame`, `JApplet`, and `JDialog` objects is `BorderLayout`.

- ❏ The `GridBagLayout` provides the most flexible control of the positioning of components in a container. The position of a component in a `GridBagLayout` is controlled by a `GridBagConstraints` object.

- ❏ A `Box` container can be used to arrange components or containers in rows and columns. You can use multiple nested `Box` containers in combination to create more complex arrangements quite easily, that otherwise might require `GridBagLayout` to be used.

- ❏ A layout manager of type `SpringLayout` arranges components by applying constraints in the form of `Spring` objects to their edges.

- ❏ A menu bar is represented by a `JMenuBar` object. Menu items can be objects of type `JMenu`, `JMenuItem`, `JCheckBoxMenuItem`, or `JRadioButtonMenuItem`.

- ❏ You associate a pull-down menu with an item of type `JMenu`.

- ❏ You can create a shortcut for a menu by calling its `setMnemonic()` method, and you can create an accelerator key combination for a menu item by calling its `setAccelerator()` method.

In the next chapter we will move on to look at events – that is, how we associate program actions with menu items and components within a window, and how to close a window when the close icon is clicked.

Exercises

1. Create an application, with a square window in the center of the screen that is half the height of the screen by deriving your own window class from `JFrame`.

2. Add six buttons to the application in the previous example in a vertical column on the left side of the application window.

3. Add a menu bar containing the items File, Edit, Window, and Help.

4. Add a pull-down menu for Edit containing the two groups of items of your own choice with a separator between them.

5. Add another item to the Edit pull-down menu which itself has a pull-down menu, and provide accelerators for the items in the menu.

6. Here's an exercise to tickle the brain cells – use a `SpringLayout` to obtain the button arrangement shown below in an application window.

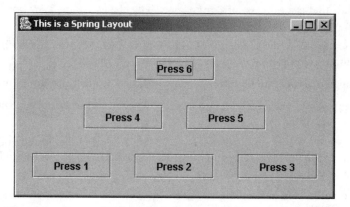

Handling Events

In this chapter you will learn how a window-based Java application is structured, and how to respond to user actions in an application or an applet. This is the fundamental mechanism you will be using in virtually all of your graphical Java programs. Once you understand how user actions are handled in Java, you will be equipped to implement the application-specific code that is necessary to make your program do what you want.

In this chapter you will learn:

❑   What an event is.

❑   What an event-driven program is and how it is structured.

❑   How events are handled in Java.

❑   How events are categorized in Java.

❑   How components handle events.

❑   What an event listener is, and how you create one.

❑   What an adapter class is and how you can use it to make programming the handling of events easier.

❑   What actions are and how you use them.

❑   How to create a toolbar.

Window-based Java Programs

Before we get into the programming specifics of window-based programs, we need to understand a little of how such programs are structured, and how they work. There are fundamental differences between the console programs that we have been producing up to now, and a window-based Java program. With a console program, you start the program, and the program code determines the sequences of events. Generally everything is predetermined. You enter data when required and the program will output data when it wants. At any given time, the specific program code to be executed next is generally known.

A window-based application, or an applet come to that, is quite different. The operation of the program is driven by what you do with the GUI. Selecting menu items or buttons using the mouse, or through the keyboard, causes particular actions within the program. At any given moment you have a whole range of possible interactions available to you, each of which will result in a different program action. Until you do something, the specific program code that is to be executed next is not known.

Event-driven Programs

Your actions when you're using the GUI for a window-based program or an applet – clicking a menu item or a button, moving the mouse and so on – are first identified by the operating system. For each action, the operating system determines which of the programs currently running on your computer should know about it, and passes the action on to that program. When you click a mouse button, it's the operating system that registers this and notes the position of the mouse cursor on the screen. It then decides which application controls the window where the cursor was when you pressed the button, and communicates the mouse button-press to that program. The signals that a program receives from the operating system as a result of your actions are called **events**.

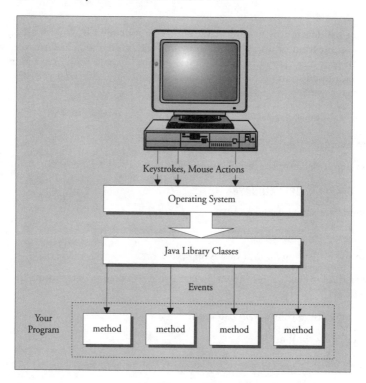

A program is not obliged to respond to any particular event. If you just move the mouse, for instance, the program need not invoke any code to react to that. If it doesn't, the event is quietly disposed of. Each event that the program does recognize is associated with one or more methods, and when the event occurs – when you click a menu item, for example – the appropriate methods will be called automatically. A window-based program is called an **event-driven program**, because the sequence of events created as a result of your interaction with the GUI drives and determines what happens in the program.

Events are not limited to window-based applications – they are a quite general concept. Most programs that control or monitor things are event-driven. Any occurrence external to a program such as a switch closing, or a preset temperature being reached, can be registered as an event. In Java you can even create events within your program to signal some other part of the code that something noteworthy has happened. However, we're going to concentrate on the kinds of events that occur when you interact as a user with a program.

The Event-handling Process

To manage the user's interaction with the components that make up the GUI for a program, we must understand how events are handled in Java. To get an idea of how this works, let's consider a specific example. Don't worry too much about the class names and other details here. Just try to get a feel for how things connect together.

Suppose the user clicks a button in the GUI for your program. The button is the **source** of this event. The event generated as a result of the mouse click is associated with the JButton object in your program that represents the button on the screen. An event always has a source object – in this case the JButton object. When the button is clicked, it will create a new object that represents and identifies this event – in this case an object of type ActionEvent. This object will contain information about the event and its source. Any event that is passed to a Java program will be represented by a particular event object – and this object will be passed as an argument to the method that is to handle the event.

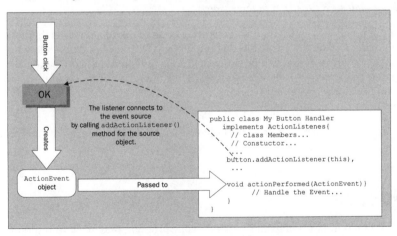

The event object corresponding to the button click will be passed to any **listener** object that has previously registered an interest in this kind of event – a listener object being simply an object that listens for particular events. A listener is also called a **target** for an event. Here, 'passing the event to the listener' just means the event source calling a particular method in the listener object and passing the event object to it as an argument. A listener object can listen for events for a particular object – just a single button for instance, or it can listen for events for several different objects – a group of menu items for example. Which approach you take depends on the context, and which is most convenient from a programming point of view. Your programs will often involve both.

So how do you define a listener? You can make the objects of any class listener objects by making the class implement a **listener interface**. There are quite a variety of listener interfaces, to cater for different kinds of events. In the case of our button click, the `ActionListener` interface needs to be implemented to receive the event from the button. The code that is to receive this event object and respond to the event is implemented in a method declared in the listener interface. In our example, the `actionPerformed()` method in the `ActionListener` interface is called when the event occurs, and the event object is passed as an argument. Each kind of listener interface defines particular methods for receiving the events that that listener has been designed to deal with.

Simply implementing a listener interface isn't sufficient to link the listener object to an event source. You still have to connect the listener to the source, or sources, of the events that you want it to deal with. You register a listener object with a source by calling a particular method in the source object. In this case, we call the `addActionListener()` method for the `JButton` object, and pass the listener object as an argument to the method.

This mechanism for handling events using listeners is very flexible, and very efficient, particularly for GUI events. Any number of listeners can receive a particular event. However, a particular event is only passed to the listeners that have registered to receive it, so only interested parties are involved in responding to each event. Since being a listener just requires a suitable interface to be implemented, you can receive and handle events virtually anywhere you like. The way in which events are handled in Java, using listener objects, is referred to as the **delegation event model**. This is because the responsibility for responding to events that originate with a component, such as a button or a menu item, is not handled by the objects that originated the events themselves – but is delegated to separate listener objects.

> *Not all event handling necessarily requires a separate listener. A component can handle its own events, as we shall see a little later in this chapter.*

A very important point to keep in mind when writing code to handle events is that all such code executes in the same thread, the event-dispatching thread. This implies that while your event-handling code is executing, no other events can be processed. The code to handle the next event will only start executing when the current event-handler finishes. Thus the responsiveness of your program to the user is dependent on how long your event-handling code takes to execute. For snappy performance, your event handlers must take as little time as possible to execute.

Let's now get down to looking at the specifics of what kinds of events we can expect, and the range of listener interfaces that process them.

Event Classes

There are many different kinds of events to which your program may need to respond – from menus, buttons, from the mouse, from the keyboard, and a number of others. In order to have a structured approach to handling events, these are broken down into subsets. At the topmost level, there are two broad categories of events in Java:

❑   **Low-level Events** – these are events that arise from the keyboard or from the mouse, or events associated with operations on a window such as reducing it to an icon or closing it. The meaning of a low-level event is something like 'the mouse was moved', 'this window has been closed' or 'this key was pressed.

❑ **Semantic Events** – these are specific component-related events such as pressing a button by clicking it to cause some program action, or adjusting a scrollbar. They originate, and you interpret them, in the context of the GUI you have created for your program. The meaning of a semantic event is typically along the lines of: 'the OK button was pressed', or 'the Save menu item was selected'. Each kind of component, a button, or a menu item for example, can generate a particular kind of semantic event.

These two categories can seem to be a bit confusing as they overlap in a way. If you click a button, you create a semantic event as well as a low level event. The click produces a low-level event object in the form of 'the mouse was clicked' as well as a semantic event 'the button was pushed'. In fact it produces more than one mouse event, as we shall see. Whether your program handles the low-level events or the semantic event, or possibly both kinds of event, depends on what you want to do.

Most of the events relating to the GUI for a program are represented by classes defined in the package java.awt.event. This package also defines the listener interfaces for the various kinds of events that it defines. The package javax.swing.event defines classes for events that are specific to Swing components.

Low-level Event Classes

There are four kinds of low-level events that you can elect to handle in your programs. They are represented by the following classes in the java.awt.event package:

Event	Description
FocusEvent	Objects of this class represent events that originate when a component gains or loses the keyboard focus. Only the component that has the focus can receive input from the keyboard, so it will usually be highlighted or have the cursor displayed.
MouseEvent	Objects of this class represent events that result from user actions with the mouse such as moving the mouse or pressing a mouse button.
KeyEvent	Objects of this class represent events that arise from pressing keys on the keyboard.
WindowEvent	Objects of this class represent events that relate to a window, such as activating or deactivating a window, reducing a window to its icon, or closing a window. These events relate to objects of the Window class or any subclass of Window.

The MouseEvent class has two subclasses that identify more specialized mouse events. One is the MenuDragMouseEvent class that defines event objects signaling when the mouse has been dragged over a menu item. The other is the MouseWheelEvent class that defines event objects indicating when the mouse wheel is rotated.

Just so that you know, this isn't an exhaustive list of all of the low-level event classes. It's a list of the ones you need to know about. For example, there's the **PaintEvent** class that is concerned with the internals of how components get painted on the screen. There's also another low-level event class, **ContainerEvent**, which defines events relating to a container such as adding or removing components. You can ignore this class as these events are handled automatically.

Each of these classes defines methods that enable you to analyze the event. For a MouseEvent object, for example, you can get the coordinates of the cursor when the event occurred. These low-level event classes also inherit methods from their superclasses, and are related in the manner shown in the diagram:

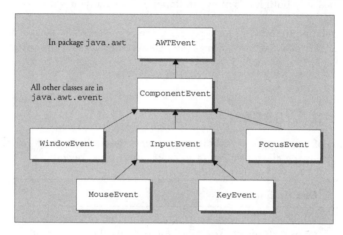

The class AWTEvent is itself a subclass of java.util.EventObject. The EventObject class implements the Serializable interface, so all objects of the event classes in the diagram are serializable. It also defines a method, getSource(), which returns the object that is the source of an event as type Object. All the event classes shown inherit this method.

The class AWTEvent defines constants, which are public final values identifying the various kinds of events. These constants are named for the sake of consistency as the event name in capital letters, followed by _MASK. The constants identifying the low-level events that you are most likely to be interested in are:

MOUSE_EVENT_MASK	MOUSE_MOTION_EVENT_MASK	MOUSE_WHEEL_EVENT_MASK
KEY_EVENT_MASK	ADJUSTMENT_EVENT_MASK	TEXT_EVENT_MASK
WINDOW_EVENT_MASK	WINDOW_FOCUS_EVENT_MASK	WINDOW_STATUS_EVENT_MASK
ITEM_EVENT_MASK	FOCUS_EVENT_MASK	

Each of these constants is a value of type long with a single bit being set to 1 and all the remaining set to 0. Because they are defined this way you can combine them using a bitwise OR operator and you can separate a particular constant out from a combination by using a bitwise AND.

The list of event masks above is not exhaustive. There are masks for component events represented by objects of the class `ComponentEvent`, and for container events. These events occur when a component is moved or resized, or a component is added to a container, for example. There is also a mask for events associated with components that receive text input. You won't normally need to get involved in these events so we won't be discussing them further.

You use the identifiers for event masks to enable a particular group of events in a component object. You call the `enableEvents()` method for the component, and pass the variable for the events you want enabled as an argument. However, you *only* do this when you aren't using a listener. Registering a listener automatically enables the events that the listener wants to hear, so you don't need to call the `enableEvents()` method. The circumstance when you might do this is when you want an object to handle some of its own events although you can achieve the same result using a listener.

Making a Window Handle its own Events

Using listeners is the preferred way of handling events since it is easier than enabling events directly for an object, and the code is clearer. Nonetheless, we should take a look at how you deal with events after calling `enableEvents()`. An example of where you might want to call `enableEvents()` exists in our `SketchFrame` class in the Sketcher program.

As you may recall from the previous chapter, we used the `setDefaultCloseOperation()` method to determine what happened when you close the window by clicking on the ☒ icon. Although the `EXIT_ON_CLOSE` argument value that we used disposed of the frame and closed the application, it didn't provide any opportunity to do any checking or clean-up before causing the program to exit. We can respond to the close icon being clicked in the program ourselves, rather than letting the `JFrame` facilities handle the associated event within the window object itself. This will eventually enable us to prompt the user to save any data that has been created, and then shut down the application ourselves when a close event occurs, so let's give it a try.

Try It Out – Closing a Window

We need to modify the `SketchFrame` class definition from the previous chapter as follows:

```
// Frame for the Sketcher application
import javax.swing.*;
import java.awt.Event;
import java.awt.AWTEvent;

import java.awt.event.WindowEvent;

public class SketchFrame extends JFrame {
  // Constructor
  public SketchFrame(String title) {
    setTitle(title);                            // Set the window title
    //   setDefaultCloseOperation(EXIT_ON_CLOSE);

    // rest of code as before
```

```
        menuBar.add(fileMenu);                          // Add the file menu
        menuBar.add(elementMenu);                        // Add the element menu
        enableEvents(AWTEvent.WINDOW_EVENT_MASK);        // Enable window events
    }

    // Handle window events
    protected void processWindowEvent(WindowEvent e) {
        if (e.getID() == WindowEvent.WINDOW_CLOSING) {
            dispose();                          // Release resources
            System.exit(0);                     // Exit the program
        }
        super.processWindowEvent(e);            // Pass on the event
    }

    private JMenuBar menuBar = new JMenuBar();           // Window menu bar

    // File menu items
    private JMenuItem newItem,   openItem,   closeItem,
                      saveItem, saveAsItem, printItem;

    // Element menu items
    private JRadioButtonMenuItem lineItem, rectangleItem, circleItem,   // Types
                                 curveItem, textItem;
    private JCheckBoxMenuItem    redItem,   yellowItem,                  // Colors
                                 greenItem, blueItem ;
}
```

We add the call to enableEvents() as the last in the constructor. Note that we have commented out
the statement that sets EXIT_ON_CLOSE as the close option for the window. You could delete the
statement if you want. When you compile SketchFrame and run Sketcher, you'll be able to close
the window as before, and the program will shut down gracefully. However, this time it's our method
that's doing it.

How It Works

The import statement makes the java.awt.event package and its various event classes available to
the class file. We call enableEvents() in the constructor with WINDOW_EVENT_MASK as the
argument to enable window events. This enables all the window events represented by the
WindowEvent class. An object of this class can represent one of a number of different window events
that are each identified by an **event ID**, which is a constant defined within the class. The event IDs for
the WindowEvent class are:

Event ID	Description
WINDOW_OPENED	The event that occurs the first time a window is made visible.
WINDOW_CLOSING	The event that occurs as a result of the close icon being selected or Close being selected from the window's system menu.

Event ID	Description
WINDOW_CLOSED	The event that occurs when the window has been closed.
WINDOW_ACTIVATED	The event that occurs when the window is activated – obtains the focus in other words. When another GUI component has the focus, you could make the window obtain the focus by clicking on it for instance.
WINDOW_DEACTIVATED	The event that occurs when the window is deactivated – loses the focus in other words. Clicking on another window would cause this event, for example.
WINDOW_GAINED_FOCUS	The event that occurs when the window gains the focus. This implies that the window or one of its components will receive keyboard events.
WINDOW_LOST_FOCUS	The event that occurs when the window loses the focus. This implies that keyboard events will not be delivered to the window or any of its components.
WINDOW_ICONIFIED	The event that occurs when the window is minimized and reduced to an icon.
WINDOW_DEICONIFIED	The event that occurs when the window is restored from an icon.
WINDOW_STATE_CHANGED	This event occurs when the window state changes – when it is maximized or minimized for instance.

If any of these events occur, the processWindowEvent() method that we have added to the class will be called. Our version of the method overrides the base class method from java.awt.Window that is responsible for passing the event to any listeners that have been registered. The argument of type WindowEvent that is passed to the method will contain the event ID that identifies the particular event that occurred. To obtain the ID of the event, we call the getID() method for the event object, and compare that with the ID identifying the WINDOW_CLOSING event. If the event is WINDOW_CLOSING, we call the dispose() method for the window to close the window and release the system resources it is using. We then call the exit() method defined in the class System to close the application.

> *The getID() method is defined in the class AWTEvent which is a superclass of all the low-level event classes we have discussed, so all event objects of these types have this method.*

In our SketchFrame class, the dispose() method is inherited originally from the Window class via the base class, JFrame. This method releases all the resources for the window object including those for all components owned by the object. Calling the dispose() method doesn't affect the window object itself in our program. It just tells the operating system that the resources used to display the window and the components it contains on the screen are no longer required. The window object is still around together with its components, so you could call its methods or even open it again.

> Note that we call the `processWindowEvent()` method in the superclass if it is not
> the closing event. This is very important as it allows the event to be passed on to any
> listeners that have been registered for these events. If we don't call
> `processWindowEvent()` for the superclass, any events that we do not handle will
> be lost, because the base class method is normally responsible for passing the event to
> the listeners that have been registered to receive it.

If we had not commented out the call to the `setDefaultCloseOperation()` method, our
`processWindowEvent()` method would still have been called when the close icon was clicked. In
this case we did not need to call `dispose()` and `exit()` ourselves. It would have been taken care of
automatically after our `processWindowEvent()` method had finished executing. This would be
preferable as it means there would be less code in our program, and the code to handle the default close
action is there in the `JFrame` class anyway.

Enabling Other Low-level Events

The `enableEvents()` method is inherited from the `Component` class. This means that any
component can elect to handle its own events. You just call the `enableEvents()` method for the
component and pass an argument defining the events you want the component to handle. If you want to
enable more than one type of event for a component, you just combine the event masks from
`AWTEvent` that we saw earlier by linking them with a bitwise OR. To make our window handle mouse
events as well as window events, you could write:

```
enableEvents(AWTEvent.WINDOW_EVENT_MASK | AWTEvent.MOUSE_EVENT_MASK);
```

Of course, you must now also implement `processMouseEvent()` for the class. Like the
`processWindowEvent()` method, this method is `protected` and has `void` as a return type. It passes
the event as an argument of type `MouseEvent`. There are two other methods specific to the `Window`
class that handle events:

Event Handling Methods	Description
`processWindowFocusEvent( WindowEvent e)`	This method is called for any window focus events that arise as long as such events are enabled for the window.
`processWindowStateEvent( WindowEvent e)`	This method will be called for events arising as a result of the window changing state.

These methods and the `processWindowEvent()` method are only available for objects of type
`Window`, or for a subclass of `Window`, so don't try to enable window events on other components.

The other event-handling methods that you can override to handle component events are:

Event Handling Methods	Description
`processEvent(AWTEvent e)`	This method is called first for any events that are enabled for the component. If you implement this method, and fail to call the base class method, none of the methods for specific groups of events will be called.
`processFocusEvent(FocusEvent e)`	This method will be called for focus events, if they are enabled for the component.
`processKeyEvent(KeyEvent e)`	This method will be called for key events, if they are enabled for the component.
`processMouseEvent(MouseEvent e)`	This method will be called for mouse button events, if they are enabled for the component.
`processMouseMotionEvent( MouseEvent e)`	This method will be called for mouse move and drag events, if they are enabled for the component.
`processMouseWheelEvent( MouseWheelEvent e)`	This method will be called for mouse wheel rotation events, if they are enabled for the component.

All the event-handling methods for a component are `protected` methods that have a return type of `void`. The default behavior implemented by these methods is to dispatch the events to any listeners registered for the component. If you don't call the base class method when you override these methods after your code has executed, this behavior will be lost.

> Although it was very convenient to handle the window closing event in the `SketchFrame` class by implementing `processWindowEvent()`, as a general rule you should use listeners to handle events. Using listeners is the recommended approach to handling events in the majority of circumstances, since separating the event handling from the object that originated the event results in a simpler code structure that is easier to understand, and is less error prone. We will change this in the Sketcher code a little later in this chapter.

Low-level Event Listeners

To create a class that defines an event listener, your class must implement a listener interface. All event listener interfaces extend the interface `java.util.EventListener`. This interface doesn't declare any methods though – it's just used to identify an interface as being an event listener interface. It also allows a variable of type `EventListener` to be used for storing a reference to any kind of event listener object.

There are a very large number of event listener interfaces. We'll look at just eight at this point that are concerned with low-level events. These declare the following methods:

The `WindowListener` **interface**

Defines methods to respond to events reflecting changes in the state of a window.

Defined Methods	Description
`windowOpened(WindowEvent e)`	Called the first time the window is opened.
`windowClosing(WindowEvent e)`	Called when the system menu Close item or the window close icon is selected.
`windowClosed(WindowEvent e)`	Called when the window has been closed.
`windowActivated(WindowEvent e)`	Called when the window is activated – by clicking on it, for example.
`windowDeactivated(WindowEvent e)`	Called when a window is deactivated – by clicking on another window, for example.
`windowIconified(WindowEvent e)`	Called when a window is minimized and reduced to an icon.
`windowDeiconified(WindowEvent e)`	Called when a window is restored from an icon.

The `WindowFocusListener` **interface**

Defines methods to respond to a window gaining or losing the focus. When a window has the focus, one of its child components can receive input from the keyboard. When it loses the focus, keyboard input via a child component of the window is not possible.

Defined Methods	Description
`windowGainedFocus(WindowEvent e)`	Called when the window gains the focus such that the window or one of its components will receive keyboard events.
`windowLostFocus( WindowEvent e)`	Called when the window loses the focus. After this event, neither the window nor any of its components will receive keyboard events.

The `WindowStateListener` **interface**

Defines a method to respond to any change in the state of a window.

Defined Methods	Description
`windowStateChanged( Window Event e)`	Called when the window state changes – when it is maximized or iconified for example.

The *MouseListener* **interface**

Defines methods to respond to events arising when the mouse cursor is moved into or out of the area occupied by a component or one of the mouse buttons is pressed, released, or clicked.

Defined Methods	Description
mouseClicked(MouseEvent e)	Called when a mouse button is clicked on a component – that is, when the button is pressed and released.
mousePressed(MouseEvent e)	Called when a mouse button is pressed on a component.
mouseReleased(MouseEvent e)	Called when a mouse button is released on a component.
mouseEntered(MouseEvent e)	Called when the mouse enters the area occupied by a component.
mouseExited(MouseEvent e)	Called when the mouse exits the area occupied by a component.

The *MouseMotionListener* **interface**

Defines methods that are called when the mouse is moved or dragged with a button pressed.

Defined Methods	Description
mouseMoved(MouseEvent e)	Called when the mouse is moved within a component.
mouseDragged(MouseEvent e)	Called when the mouse is moved within a component while a mouse button is held down.

The *MouseWheelListener* **interface**

Defines a method to respond to the mouse wheel being rotated. This is frequently used to scroll information that is displayed, but you can use it in any way that you want.

Defined Methods	Description
mouseWheelMoved(MouseWheelEvent e)	Called when the mouse wheel is rotated.

The `KeyListener` **interface**

Defines methods to respond to events arising when a key on the keyboard is pressed or released.

Defined Methods	Description
`keyTyped(KeyEvent e)`	Called when a key on the keyboard is pressed then released.
`keyPressed(KeyEvent e)`	Called when a key on the keyboard is pressed.
`keyReleased(KeyEvent e)`	Called when a key on the keyboard is released.

The `FocusListener` **interface**

Defines methods to respond to a component gaining or losing the focus. You might implement these methods to change the appearance of the component to reflect whether or not it has the focus.

Defined Methods	Description
`focusGained(FocusEvent e)`	Called when a component gains the keyboard focus.
`focusLost(FocusEvent e)`	Called when a component loses the keyboard focus.

There is a further listener interface, `MouseInputListener`, which is defined in the `javax.swing.event` package. This listener implements both the `MouseListener` and `MouseMotionListener` interfaces so it declares methods for all possible mouse events in a single interface.

The `WindowListener`, `WindowFocusListener`, and `WindowStateListener` interfaces between them define methods corresponding to each of the event IDs defined in the `WindowEvent` class that we saw earlier. If you deduced from this that the methods in the other listener interfaces correspond to event IDs for the other event classes, well, you're right. All the IDs for mouse events are defined in the `MouseEvent` class. These are:

MOUSE_CLICKED	MOUSE_PRESSED	MOUSE_DRAGGED
MOUSE_ENTERED	MOUSE_EXITED	MOUSE_RELEASED
MOUSE_MOVED	MOUSE_WHEEL	

The `MOUSE_MOVED` event corresponds to just moving the mouse. The `MOUSE_DRAGGED` event arises when you move the mouse while keeping a button pressed.

The event IDs defined in the `KeyEvent` class are:

KEY_TYPED	KEY_PRESSED	KEY_RELEASED

Those defined in the `FocusEvent` class are:

```
FOCUS_GAINED                    FOCUS_LOST
```

To implement a listener for a particular event type you just need to implement the methods declared in the corresponding interface. We could handle some of the window events for our `SketchFrame` class by making the application class the listener for window events.

Try It Out – Implementing a Low-level Event Listener

First, delete the call to the `enableEvents()` method in the `SketchFrame()` constructor. Then delete the definition of the `processWindowEvent()` method from the class definition.

Now we can modify the `Sketcher` class so that it is a listener for window events:

```java
// Sketching application
import java.awt.Dimension;
import java.awt.Toolkit;
import java.awt.event.WindowListener;
import java.awt.event.WindowEvent;

public class Sketcher implements WindowListener {
  public static void main(String[] args) {
    theApp = new Sketcher();                // Create the application object
    theApp.init();                          // ...and initialize it
  }

  // Initialization of the application
  public void init() {
    window = new SketchFrame("Sketcher");       // Create the app window
    Toolkit theKit = window.getToolkit();       // Get the window toolkit
    Dimension wndSize = theKit.getScreenSize(); // Get screen size

    // Set the position to screen center & size to half screen size
    window.setBounds(wndSize.width/4, wndSize.height/4,      // Position
                     wndSize.width/2, wndSize.height/2);     // Size

    window.addWindowListener(this);             // theApp as window listener
    window.setVisible(true);                    // Display the window
  }

  // Handler for window closing event
  public void windowClosing(WindowEvent e) {
    window.dispose();                         // Release the window resources
    System.exit(0);                           // End the application
  }

  // Listener interface functions we must implement - but don't need
  public void windowOpened(WindowEvent e) {}
  public void windowClosed(WindowEvent e) {}
  public void windowIconified(WindowEvent e) {}
  public void windowDeiconified(WindowEvent e) {}
```

741

```
      public void windowActivated(WindowEvent e) {}
      public void windowDeactivated(WindowEvent e) {}

      private static SketchFrame window;           // The application window
      private static Sketcher theApp;              // The application object
   }
```

If you run the Sketcher program again, you will see it works just as before, but now the Sketcher class object is handling the close operation.

How It Works

The import statements for the package java.awt.event that we have added to the source file ARE essential here because we need access to the WindowListener interface. The Sketcher class implements the WindowListener interface, so an object of type Sketcher can handle window events. The method main() now creates a Sketcher object and calls the init() method that we have added to the class definition to initialize it. The init() method does what main() did in the previous version of Sketcher. It also calls the addWindowListener() method for the window object. The argument to addWindowListener() is the listener object that is to receive window events. Here it is the variable this – which refers to the application object. If we had other listener objects that we wanted to register to receive this event, we would just need to add more calls to the addWindowListener() method – one call for each listener.

To implement the WindowListener interface in the Sketcher class, we must implement all seven methods that are declared in the interface. If we don't do this, the class would be abstract and we could not create an object of type Sketcher. Only the windowClosing() method has any code here – all the rest are empty because we don't need to use them. The windowClosing() method does the same as the processWindowEvent() method that we implemented for the previous version of the SketchFrame class, but here we don't need to check the object passed to it as this method is only called for a WINDOW_CLOSING event. We don't need to pass the event on either: this is only necessary when you handle events in the manner we discussed earlier. Here, if there were other listeners around for our window events they would automatically receive the event.

We have included the code that calls dispose() and exit() here, but if we have set the default close operation in SketchFrame to EXIT_ON_CLOSE, we could omit these too. We really only need to put our application clean-up code in the windowClosing() method, and this will just be prompting the user to save any application data. We will get to that eventually.

Having to implement six methods that we don't need is rather tedious. But we have a way to get around this though – by using what is called an **adapter class**, to define a listener.

Using Adapter Classes

An **adapter class** is a term for a class that implements a listener interface with methods that have no content, so they do nothing. The idea of this is to enable you to derive your own listener class from any of the adapter classes that are provided, and then implement just the methods that you are interested in. The other empty methods will be inherited from the adapter class so you don't have to worry about them.

There's an adapter class defined in the javax.swing.event package that defines the methods for the MouseInputListener interface. There are five further adapter classes defined in the java.awt.event package that cover the methods in the other low-level listener interfaces we have seen:

FocusAdapter	WindowAdapter	KeyAdapter
MouseAdapter	MouseMotionAdapter	MouseInputAdapter

The `WindowAdapter` class implements all of the methods defined in the `WindowListener`, `WindowFocusListener`, and `WindowStateListener` interfaces. The other five each implement the methods in the corresponding listener interface.

To handle the window closing event for the Sketcher application, we could derive our own class from the `WindowAdapter` class and just implement the `windowClosing()` method. If we also make it an inner class for the class `Sketcher`, it will automatically have access to the members of the `Sketcher` object, regardless of their access specifiers.

Try It Out – Implementing an Adapter Class

The version of the `Sketcher` class to implement this will be as follows, with changes to the previous version highlighted:

```java
// Sketching application
import java.awt.Dimension;
import java.awt.Toolkit;

import java.awt.event.WindowEvent;
import java.awt.event.WindowAdapter;

public class Sketcher {
  public static void main(String[] args) {
    theApp = new Sketcher();              // Create the application object
    theApp.init();                        // ...and initialize it
  }

  // Initialization of the application
  public void init() {
    window = new SketchFrame("Sketcher");
    Toolkit theKit = window.getToolkit();          // Get the window toolkit
    Dimension wndSize = theKit.getScreenSize();    // Get screen size

    // Set the position to screen center & size to 2/3 screen size
    window.setBounds(wndSize.width/6, wndSize.height/6,      // Position
                     2*wndSize.width/3, 2*wndSize.height/3);  // Size

    window.addWindowListener(new WindowHandler());  // Add window listener
    window.setVisible(true);                        // Display the window
  }

  // Handler class for window events
  class WindowHandler extends WindowAdapter {
    // Handler for window closing event
    public void windowClosing(WindowEvent e) {
      window.dispose();                     // Release the window resources
      System.exit(0);                       // End the application
    }
```

```
        }
    private static SketchFrame window;              // The application window
    private static Sketcher theApp;                 // The application object
}
```

How It Works

As the `Sketcher` class is no longer the listener for `window`, it doesn't need to implement the `WindowListener` interface. The `WindowHandler` class is the listener class for window events. Because the `WindowHandler` class is an inner class to the `Sketcher` class, it has access to all the members of the class, so calling the `dispose()` method for the `window` object is still quite straightforward – we just access the `window` member of the top-level class.

The `WindowAdapter` object that is the listener for the `window` object is created in the argument to the `addWindowListener()` method for `window`. We don't need an explicit variable to contain it. It will be stored in a data member of the `Window` class object. This data member is inherited from the `Window` superclass for our `SketchFrame` class.

> **An easy mistake to make when you're using adapter classes is to misspell the name of the method that you are using to implement the event – typically by using the wrong case for a letter. In this case, you won't be overriding the adapter class method at all; you will be adding a new method. Your code will compile perfectly well but your program will not handle any events. They will all be passed to the method in the adapter class with the name your method should have had – which does nothing of course. This can be a bit mystifying until you realize where the problem is.**

We haven't finished with low-level events yet by any means and we'll return to handling more low-level events in the next chapter when we begin to add drawing code to the Sketcher program. In the meantime, let's start looking at how we can manage semantic events.

Semantic Events

As we saw earlier, semantic events relate to operations on the components in the GUI for your program. If you select a menu item or click on a button for example, a semantic event is generated. There are three classes that represent the basic semantic events you will be dealing with most of the time, and they are derived from the `AWTEvent` class, as shown in the diagram.

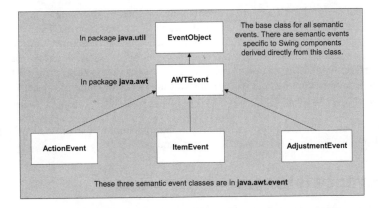

An `ActionEvent` is generated when you perform an action on a component such as clicking on a menu item or a button. An `ItemEvent` occurs when a component is selected or deselected and an `AdjustmentEvent` is produced when an adjustable object, such as a scrollbar, is adjusted.

Different kinds of components can produce different kinds of semantic events. The components that can originate these events are:

Event Type	Produced by Objects of Type
ActionEvent	Buttons: JButton, JToggleButton, JCheckBox Menus: JMenuItem, JMenu, JCheckBoxMenuItem, JRadioButtonMenuItem Text: JTextField
ItemEvent	Buttons: JButton, JToggleButton, JCheckBox Menus: JMenuItem, JMenu, JCheckBoxMenuItem, JRadioButtonMenuItem
AdjustmentEvent	JScrollbar

These three types of event are also generated by the old AWT components but we won't go into these here as we are concentrating on the Swing components. Of course, any class you derive from these component classes to define your own customized components can be the source of the event that the base class generates. If you define your own class for buttons, `MyFancyButton` say, your class will have `JButton` as a base class, inherit all of the methods from the `JButton` class, and objects of your class will originate events of type `ActionEvent` and `ItemEvent`.

There are quite a large number of semantic events that are specific to Swing components. Classes that have `AbstractButton` as a base, which includes menu items and buttons, can generate `ChangeEvent` events that signal some change in the state of a component. Components corresponding to the `JMenuItem` class and classes derived from `JMenuItem` can generate `MenuDragMouseEvent` and `MenuKeyEvent` events. An `AncestorEvent` is an event that is communicated to a child component from a parent component. We will look at the detail of some of these additional events when we need to handle them to apply the components in question.

As with low-level events, the most convenient way to handle semantic events is to use listeners, so we'll delve into the listener interfaces for semantic events next.

Semantic Event Listeners

We have a listener interface defined for each of the three semantic event types that we have introduced so far, and they each declare a single method:

Listener Interface	Method
`ActionListener`	`void actionPerformed(ActionEvent e)`
`ItemListener`	`void itemStateChanged(ItemEvent e)`
`AdjustmentListener`	`void adjustmentValueChanged(` `   AdjustmentEvent e)`

Since each of these semantic event listener interfaces declares only one method, there is no need for corresponding adapter classes. The adapter classes for the low-level events were only there because of the number of methods involved in each listener interface. To define your semantic event listener objects, you just define a class that implements the appropriate listener interface. We can try that out by implementing a simple applet now, and then see how we can deal with semantic events in a more complicated context by adding to the Sketcher program later.

Semantic Event Handling in Applets

Event handling in an applet is exactly the same as in an application, but we ought to see it for ourselves. Let's see how we would handle events for buttons in an applet. We can create an applet that uses some buttons that have listeners. To make this example a bit more gripping, we'll throw in the possibility of monetary gain.

That's interesting to almost everybody. Let's suppose we want to have an applet to create random numbers for a lottery. The requirement is to generate six different random numbers between 1 and 49. It would also be nice to be able to change a single number if you don't like it, so we'll add that capability as well. Since your local lottery may not be like this, we will implement the applet to make it easy for you to adapt the applet to fit your requirements.

By displaying the six selected numbers on buttons, we can provide for changing one of the choices by processing the action event for that button. Thus, clicking a button will provide another number. We'll also add a couple of control buttons, one to make a new selection for a complete set of lottery numbers, and another just for fun to change the button color. Here's how the applet will look when running under appletviewer:

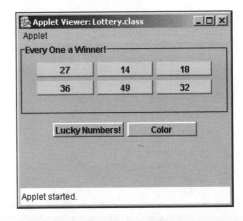

Try It Out – A Lottery Applet

We can outline the broad structure of the applet's code as follows:

```
// Applet to generate lottery entries
import javax.swing.*;
import java.awt.*;
import java.util.Random;                // For random number generator
import java.awt.event.ActionListener;
import java.awt.event.ActionEvent;

public class Lottery extends JApplet {
  // Initialize the applet
  public void init() {
    // Set up the lucky numbers buttons...

    // Set up the control buttons...
  }

  // Custom button showing lottery selection
  // Each button listens for its own events
  class Selection extends JButton implements ActionListener {
    // Constructor
    public Selection(int value) {
      // Create the button showing the value...
    }

    // Handle selection button event
    public void actionPerformed(ActionEvent e) {
      // Change the current selection value to a new selection value
    }
    // Details of the rest of the selection class definition...
  }

  // Class defining a handler for a control button
  class HandleControlButton implements ActionListener {
    // Constructor...
```

```
    // Handle button click
    public void actionPerformed(ActionEvent e) {
      // Handle button click for a particular button...
    }

    // Rest of the inner class definition...
  }

  final static int numberCount = 6;              // Number of lucky numbers
  final static int minValue = 1;                 // Minimum in range
  final static int maxValue = 49;                // Maximum in range
  static int[] values = new int[maxValue-minValue+1]; // Array of possible values
  static {                                       // Initialize array
    for(int i = 0 ; i<values.length ; i++)
      values[i] = i + minValue;
  }

  // An array of custom buttons for the selected numbers
  private Selection[] luckyNumbers = new Selection[numberCount];

  private static Random choice = new Random();   // Random number generator
}
```

How It Works

The applet class is called `Lottery` and it contains two inner classes, `Selection` and `HandleControlButton`. The `Selection` class provides a custom button that will show a number as its label, the number being passed to the constructor as an argument. We can make an object of the `Selection` class listen for its own action events. As we said at the outset, an event for a selection button will change the label of the button to a different value so of course we'll need to make sure this doesn't duplicate any of the values for the other buttons.

The two control buttons will use separate listeners to handle their action events and the response to an event will be quite different for each of them. One control button will create a new set of lucky numbers while the other control button will just change the color of the buttons.

The `numberCount` member of the `Lottery` class sets the number of values that is created. The `minValue` and `maxValue` members specify the range of possible values. The possible values for selections are stored in the `values` array, and this is set up in the static initialization block. The `Lottery` class has an array of `Selection` objects as a data member – we can have arrays of components just like arrays of any other kind of object. Since the `Selection` buttons will all be the same, it's very convenient to create them as an array, and having an array of components will enable us to set them up in a loop. We also have a `Random` object as a member as we will need to generate some random integers.

We can now set about filling in the sections of the program that we roughed out previously.

Filling in the Details

To generate `maxCount` random values from the elements in the `values` array is quite independent of everything else here, so we'll define a static method in the `Lottery` class to do this.

```
public class Lottery extends JApplet {
  // Generate numberCount random selections from the values array
  static int[] getNumbers() {
    int[] numbers = new int[numberCount];   // Store for the numbers to be returned
    int candidate = 0;                       // Stores a candidate selection
    for(int i = 0; i < numberCount; i++) {  // Loop to find the selections

      search:
      // Loop to find a new selection different from any found so far
      for(;;) {
        candidate = values[choice.nextInt(values.length)];
        for(int j = 0 ; j<i ; j++)           // Check against existing selections
          if(candidate==numbers[j])          // If it is the same
            continue search;                 // get another random selection

        numbers[i] = candidate;              // Store the selection in numbers array
        break;                               // and go to find the next
      }
    }
    return numbers;                          // Return the selections
  }

  // Plus the rest of the class definition...
}
```

The getNumbers() method returns a reference to an int array containing the selections – which must all be different, of course. We start the process by creating an array to hold the selections, and a variable, candidate to hold a potential selection from the values array. We generate a new selection for each iteration of the outer for loop. The process is quite simple. In the indefinite for loop with the label, search, we choose a random value from the values array using our random number generator, and then check its value against any selections already stored in the numbers array. If it is the same as any of them, the labeled continue will go to the next iteration of the indefinite for loop. This will continue until a selection is found that is different from the others. In this way we ensure that we end up with a set of selections that are all different.

Let's implement the init() method for the Lottery class next, as this sets up the Selection buttons and the rest of the applet.

Try It Out – Setting Up the Lucky Number Buttons

In the class outline we identified two tasks for the init() method. The first was setting up the lucky number buttons to be contained in the luckyNumbers array.

Here's the code to do that:

```
// Initialize the applet
public void init() {
  // Set up the selection buttons
  Container content = getContentPane();
  content.setLayout(new GridLayout(0,1));  // Set the layout for the applet

  // Set up the panel to hold the lucky number buttons
```

```
    JPanel buttonPane = new JPanel();   // Add the pane containing numbers

    // Let's have a fancy panel border
    buttonPane.setBorder(BorderFactory.createTitledBorder(
                      BorderFactory.createEtchedBorder(Color.cyan,
                                                       Color.blue),
                                            "Every One a Winner!"));

    int[] choices = getNumbers();              // Get initial set of numbers
    for(int i = 0; i<numberCount; i++) {
     luckyNumbers[i] = new Selection(choices[i]);
     buttonPane.add(luckyNumbers[i]);
    }
    content.add(buttonPane);

    // Set up the control buttons...
  }
```

How It Works

The first step is to define the layout manager for the applet. To make the layout easier, we will use one panel to hold the selection buttons and another to hold the control buttons. We can position these panels one above the other by specifying the layout manager for the content pane of the applet as a grid layout with one column. The top panel will contain the lucky number buttons and the bottom panel will contain the control buttons.

The `buttonPane` panel that holds the lucky number buttons is of type `JPanel`, so it has a `FlowLayout` object as its layout manager by default. A flow layout manager allows components to assume their 'natural' or 'preferred size', so we will set the preferred size for the buttons in the `Selection` class constructor. We decorate the panel with a border by calling its `setBorder()` method. The argument is returned by the static `createTitledBorder()` method from the `BorderFactory` class. The first argument passed to `createTitledBorder()` is the border to be used, and the second is the title.

We use an etched border that is returned by another static method in the `BorderFactory` class. The two arguments to this method are the highlight and shadow colors to be used for the border. A big advantage of using the `BorderFactory` methods rather than creating border objects from the border class constructors directly is that border objects will be shared where possible, so you can use a particular border in various places in your code and only one object will be created.

The buttons to display the chosen numbers will be of type `Selection`, and we will get to the detail of this inner class in a moment. We call our static method `getNumbers()` to obtain the first set of random values for the buttons. We then create and store each button in the `luckyNumbers` array and add it to the panel in the `for` loop. Since these buttons are going to listen for their own events, we don't need to worry about setting separate action listeners for them. The last step here is to add the `buttonPane` panel to the `content` pane for the applet.

We should now add the code for the control buttons to the `init()` method.

Try It Out – Setting up the Control Buttons

The listeners for each of the control buttons will be of the same class type, so the listener object will need some way to determine which button originated a particular event. One way to do this is to use constants as IDs to identify the control buttons, and pass the appropriate ID to the class constructor for the listener object.

We could define the constants PICK_LUCKY_NUMBERS and COLOR as fields in the Lottery class for this purpose. The COLOR control button will also reference a couple of Color variables, startColor and flipColor. You can add the following statements to the Lottery class after the definition of the luckyNumbers array:

```
// An array of custom buttons for the selected numbers
private Selection[] luckyNumbers = new Selection[numberCount];

final public static int PICK_LUCKY_NUMBERS = 1;              // Select button ID
final public static int COLOR = 2;                          // Color button ID

// swap colors
Color flipColor = new Color(Color.yellow.getRGB()^Color.red.getRGB());

Color startColor = new Color(Color.yellow.getRGB());        // start color
```

The code to add the other panel and the control buttons is as follows:

```
// Initialize the applet
public void init() {
    // Setting up the selections buttons as previously...

    // Add the pane containing control buttons
    JPanel controlPane = new JPanel(new FlowLayout(FlowLayout.CENTER, 5, 10));

    // Add the two control buttons
    JButton button;                                 // A button variable
    Dimension buttonSize = new Dimension(100,20);   // Button size

    controlPane.add(button = new JButton("Lucky Numbers!"));
    button.setBorder(BorderFactory.createRaisedBevelBorder());
    button.addActionListener(new HandleControlButton(PICK_LUCKY_NUMBERS));
    button.setPreferredSize(buttonSize);

    controlPane.add(button = new JButton("Color"));
    button.setBorder(BorderFactory.createRaisedBevelBorder());
    button.addActionListener(new HandleControlButton(COLOR));
    button.setPreferredSize(buttonSize);

    content.add(controlPane);
}
```

How It Works

We create another `JPanel` object to hold the control buttons and just to show that we can, we pass a layout manager object to the constructor. It's a `FlowLayout` manager again, but this time we explicitly specify that the components are to be centered and the horizontal and vertical gaps are to be 5 and 10 pixels respectively.

We declare the `button` variable to use as a temporary store for the reference to each button while we set it up. We also define a `Dimension` object that we will use to set a common preferred size for the buttons. The buttons are `JButton` components, not custom components, so we must set each of them up here with a listener and a border. We add a raised bevel border to each button to make them look like buttons – again using a `BorderFactory` method.

The listener for each button is an object of the inner class `HandleControlButton`, and we pass the appropriate button ID to the constructor for reasons that will be apparent when we define that class. To set the preferred size for each button object, we call its `setPreferredSize()` method. The argument is a `Dimension` object that specifies the width and height. Finally, after adding the two buttons to `controlPane`, we add that to the content pane for the applet.

The inner class `HandleControlButton` defines the listener object for each control button, so let's implement that next.

Try It Out – Defining the Control Button Handler Class

We have already determined that the class constructor will accept an argument that identifies the particular button for which it is listening. This is to enable the `actionPerformed()` method in the listener class to choose the course of action appropriate to the button. Here's the inner class definition to do that:

```
class HandleControlButton implements ActionListener {
  private int buttonID;

  // Constructor
  public HandleControlButton(int buttonID) {
    this.buttonID = buttonID;                    // Store the button ID
  }

  // Handle button click
  public void actionPerformed(ActionEvent e) {
    switch(buttonID) {
      case PICK_LUCKY_NUMBERS:
        int[] numbers = getNumbers();            // Get maxCount random numbers
        for(int i = 0; i < numberCount; i++)
          luckyNumbers[i].setValue(numbers[i]);  // Set the button values
        break;
      case COLOR:
        Color color = new Color(
              flipColor.getRGB()^luckyNumbers[0].getBackground().getRGB());
        for(int i = 0; i < numberCount; i++)
          luckyNumbers[i].setBackground(color);  // Set the button colors
        break;
```

```
      }
    }
  }
```

How It Works

The constructor stores its argument value in the data member, `buttonID`, so each listener object will have the ID for the button available. This is used in the `actionPerformed()` method to select the appropriate code to execute for a particular button. Each case in the `switch` statement corresponds to a different button. You could extend this to enable the class to handle as many different buttons as you want by adding case statements. Because of the way we have implemented the method, each button must have a unique ID associated with it. Of course, this isn't the only way to do this, as we'll see in a moment.

For the `PICK_LUCKY_NUMBERS` button, we just call the `getNumbers()` method to produce a set of numbers, and then call the `setValue()` method for each selection button and pass a number to it. We will implement the `setValue()` method when we define the selection class in detail, in a moment.

For the `COLOR` button, we create a new color by exclusive ORing (that is, XOR) the `RGB` value of `flipColor` with the current button color. You will recall from our discussion of the `^` operator (in Chapter 2) that you can use it to exchange two values, and that is what we are doing here. `flipColor` was defined as the two colors, `Color.yellow` and `Color.red`, exclusive ORed together. Exclusive ORing this with either color will produce the other so we flip from one color to the other automatically for each button by exclusive ORing the background and `flipColor`. We must get the `RGB` value for each color and operate on those – you can't apply the `^` operator to the objects. We then turn the resulting `RGB` value back into a `Color` object.

Let's now add the inner class, `Selection`, which defines the lucky number buttons.

Try It Out – Defining the Selection Buttons

Each button will need to store the value shown on the label, so the class will need a data member for this purpose. The class will also need a constructor, the `setValue()` method to set the value for the button to a new value, and a method to compare the current value for a button to a given value. We need to be able to set the value for a button for two reasons – we call it when we set up all six selections in the listener for the control button, and we want to reset the value for a button to change it individually.

The method to compare the value set for a button to a given integer will enable us to exclude a number that was already assigned to a button in the process of generating the button values. We'll also need to implement the `actionPerformed()` method to handle the action events for the button, as the buttons are going to handle their own events. Here's the basic code for the class definition:

```
class Selection extends JButton implements ActionListener {
  // Constructor
  public Selection(int value) {
    super(Integer.toString(value));       // Call base constructor and set the label
    this.value = value;                    // Save the value
    setBackground(startColor);
    setBorder(BorderFactory.createRaisedBevelBorder());    // Add button border
    setPreferredSize(new Dimension(80,20));
    addActionListener(this);               // Button listens for itself
```

```
    }

    // Handle selection button event
    public void actionPerformed(ActionEvent e) {
      // Change this selection to a new selection
      int candidate = 0;
      for(;;) {                                   // Loop to find a different selection
        candidate = values[choice.nextInt(values.length)];
        if(isCurrentSelection(candidate))         // If it is not different
          continue;                               // find another
        setValue(candidate);                      // We have one so set the button value
        return;
      }
    }
    // Set the value for the selection
    public void setValue(int value) {
      setText(Integer.toString(value));           // Set value as the button label
      this.value = value;                         // Save the value
    }

    // Check the value for the selection
    boolean hasValue(int possible) {
      return value==possible;                     // Return true if equals current value
    }

    // Check the current choices
    boolean isCurrentSelection(int possible) {
      for(int i = 0; i < numberCount; i++)        // For each button
        if(luckyNumbers[i].hasValue(possible))    // check against possible
          return true;                            // Return true for any =
      return false;                               // Otherwise return false
    }

    private int value;                            // Value for the selection button
  }
```

How It Works

The constructor calls the base class constructor to set the initial label for the button. It also stores the value of type int that is passed as an argument. The setValue() method just updates the value for a selection button with the value passed as an argument and changes the button label by calling the setText() method which is inherited from the base class, JButton. The hasValue() method returns true if the argument value passed to it is equal to the current value stored in the data member value, and false otherwise.

The actionPerformed() method has a little more meat to it but the technique is similar to that in the getNumbers() method. To change the selection, we must create a new random value for the button from the numbers values array, but excluding all the numbers currently assigned to the six buttons. To do this we just check each candidate against the six existing selections by calling the isCurrentSelection(), and continue choosing a new candidate until we find one that's different.

In the `isCurrentSelection()` method, we just work through the array of `Selection` objects, `luckyNumbers`, comparing each value with the `possible` argument using the `hasValue()` method. If any button has the same value as `possible`, the method returns `true`, otherwise it returns `false`.

We're ready to start generating lottery entries. If you compile the `Lottery.java` file you can run the applet using `AppletViewer`. You will need an HTML file of course. The following contents for the file will do the job:

```
<APPLET CODE="Lottery.class" WIDTH=300 HEIGHT=200>
</APPLET>
```

You can adjust the width and height values to suit your monitor resolution if necessary.

The applet should produce a selection each time you click the left control button. Clicking on any of the selection buttons will generate an action event that will cause a new value to be created for the button. This enables you to replace any selection that you know to be unlucky with an alternative.

Undoubtedly, anyone who profits from using this applet will have immense feelings of gratitude and indebtedness towards the author, who will not be offended in the slightest by any offers of a portion of that success, however large!

Alternative Event Handling Approaches

As we indicated in the discussion, there are various approaches to implementing listeners. Let's look at a couple of other ways in which we could have dealt with the control button events.

Instead of passing a constant to the listener class constructor to identify which button was selected, we could have used the fact that the event object has a method, `getSource()`, that returns a reference to the object that is the source of the event. To make use of this, a reference to both button objects would need to be available to the `actionPerformed()` method. We could easily arrange for this to be the case by adding a couple of fields to the `Lottery` class:

```
JButton pickButton = new JButton("Lucky Numbers!");
JButton colorButton = new JButton("Color");
```

The inner class could then be defined as:

```
class HandleControlButton implements ActionListener {
  // Handle button click
  public void actionPerformed(ActionEvent e) {
    Object source = e.getSource();              // Get source object reference

    if(source == pickButton) {                  // Is it the pick button?
        int[] numbers = getNumbers();           // Get maxCount random numbers
        for(int i = 0; i < numberCount; i++)
          luckyNumbers[i].setValue(numbers[i]); // Set the button values

    } else if(source == colorButton) {          // Is it the color button?
      Color color = new Color(
```

```
                        flipColor.getRGB()^luckyNumbers[0].getBackground().getRGB());
        for(int i = 0; i < numberCount; i++)
          luckyNumbers[i].setBackground(color);   // Set the button colors
      }
    }
  }
```

We no longer need to define a constructor, as the default will do. The `actionPerformed()` method now decides what to do by comparing the reference returned by the `getSource()` method for the event object with the two button references. With the previous version of the listener class, we stored the ID as a data member, so a separate listener object was needed for each button. In this case there are no data members in the listener class, so we can use one listener object for both buttons.

The code to add these buttons in the `init()` method would then be:

```
// Add the two control buttons
Dimension buttonSize = new Dimension(100,20);
pickButton.setPreferredSize(buttonSize);
pickButton.setBorder(BorderFactory.createRaisedBevelBorder());

colorButton.setPreferredSize(buttonSize);
colorButton.setBorder(BorderFactory.createRaisedBevelBorder());

HandleControlButton controlHandler = new HandleControlButton();
pickButton.addActionListener(controlHandler);
colorButton.addActionListener(controlHandler);

controlPane.add(pickButton);
controlPane.add(colorButton);
content.add(controlPane);
```

The only fundamental difference here is that we use one listener object for both buttons.
There is another possible way to implement listeners for these buttons. We could define a separate class for each listener – this would not be unreasonable as the actions to be performed in response to the semantic events for each button are quite different. We could use anonymous classes in this case – as we discussed back in Chapter 6. We could do this by adding the listeners for the button objects in the `init()` method like this:

```
// Add the two control buttons
Dimension buttonSize = new Dimension(100,20);
pickButton.setPreferredSize(buttonSize);
pickButton.setBorder(BorderFactory.createRaisedBevelBorder());

colorButton.setPreferredSize(buttonSize);
colorButton.setBorder(BorderFactory.createRaisedBevelBorder());

pickButton.addActionListener(
   new ActionListener() {
     public void actionPerformed(ActionEvent e) {
       int[] numbers = getNumbers();
```

```
          for(int i = 0; i < numberCount; i++)
            luckyNumbers[i].setValue(numbers[i]);
      }
    });

    colorButton.addActionListener(
      new ActionListener() {
        public void actionPerformed(ActionEvent e) {
          Color color = new Color(flipColor.getRGB()^luckyNumbers[0]
                                    .getBackground().getRGB());
          for(int i = 0; i < numberCount; i++)
            luckyNumbers[i].setBackground(color);
        }
      });
```

```
  controlPane.add(pickButton);
  controlPane.add(colorButton);
  content.add(controlPane);
```

Now the two listeners are defined by anonymous classes, and the implementation of the `actionPerformed()` method in each just takes care of the particular button for which it is listening. This is a very common technique when the action to be performed in response to an event is simple.

Handling Low-level and Semantic Events

We said earlier in this chapter that a component generates both low-level and semantic events, and you could handle both if you want. We can demonstrate this quite easily with a small extension to the Lottery applet. Suppose we want to change the cursor to a hand cursor when it is over one of the selection buttons. This would be a good cue that you can select these buttons individually. We can do this by adding a mouse listener for each button.

Try It Out – A Mouse Listener for the Selection Buttons

There are many ways in which you could define the listener class. We'll define it as a separate class, called `MouseHandler`:

```
// Mouse event handler for a selection button
import java.awt.Cursor;
import java.awt.event.MouseEvent;
import java.awt.event.MouseAdapter;

class MouseHandler extends MouseAdapter {
  Cursor handCursor = new Cursor(Cursor.HAND_CURSOR);
  Cursor defaultCursor = new Cursor(Cursor.DEFAULT_CURSOR);

  // Handle mouse entering the selection button
  public void mouseEntered(MouseEvent e) {
    e.getComponent().setCursor(handCursor);     // Switch to hand cursor
  }
```

```
   // Handle mouse exiting the selection button
   public void mouseExited(MouseEvent e) {
     e.getComponent().setCursor(defaultCursor); // Change to default cursor
   }
 }
```

All we need to do to expedite this is to add a mouse listener for each of the six selection buttons. We only need one listener object and after creating this we only need to change the loop in the `init()` method for the applet to add the listener:

```
int[] choices = getNumbers();              // Get initial set of numbers
MouseHandler mouseHandler = new MouseHandler();     // Create the listener
for(int i = 0 ; i<numberCount ; i++) {
  luckyNumbers[i] = new Selection(choices[i]);
  luckyNumbers[i].addMouseListener(mouseHandler);
  buttonPane.add(luckyNumbers[i]);
}
```

How It Works

The `mouseEntered()` method will be called when the mouse enters the area of the component with which the listener is registered, and we can then change the cursor for the component to a hand cursor. When the cursor is moved out of the area occupied by the component, the `mouseExited()` method is called, and we restore the default cursor.

There are just two extra statements in `init()` that create the listener object and then add it for each selection button within the loop. If you recompile the applet and run it again, a hand cursor should appear whenever the mouse is over the selection buttons. Of course, you are not limited to just changing the cursor in the event handle. You could highlight the button by changing its color for instance. You could apply the same technique for any kind of component where the mouse is the source of actions for it.

Semantic Event Listeners in an Application

An obvious candidate for implementing semantic event listeners is in the Sketcher program, to support the operation of the menu bar in the class `SketchFrame`. When we click on an item in one of the pull-down menus, a semantic event will be generated that we can listen for and then use to determine the appropriate program action.

Listening to Menu Items

We will start with the Elements menu. This is concerned with identifying the type of graphic element to be drawn next, and the color in which it will be drawn. We won't be drawing them for a while, but we can put in the infrastructure to set the type and color for an element without worrying about how it will actually be created and drawn.

To identify the type of element, we can define constants that will act as IDs for the four types of element we have provided for in the menu so far. This will help us with the operation of the listeners for the menu item as well as provide a way to identify a particular type of element. Since we will accumulate quite a number of application wide constants, it will be convenient to define them in an interface that can be implemented by any class that refers to any of the constants. Here's the initial definition including constants to define line, rectangle, circle and curve elements:

```
// Defines application wide constants
public interface Constants {
  // Element type definitions
  int LINE      = 101;
  int RECTANGLE = 102;
  int CIRCLE    = 103;
  int CURVE     = 104;

  // Initial conditions
  int DEFAULT_ELEMENT_TYPE = LINE;
}
```

Save this in the same directory as the rest of the Sketcher program as Constants.java. Each element type ID is an integer constant with a unique value and we can obviously extend the variety of element types if necessary. We have defined a constant, DEFAULT_ELEMENT_TYPE, representing the initial element type to apply when the application starts. We should do the same thing for the Color submenu and supply a constant that specifies the initial element color:

```
// Defines application wide constants
import java.awt.Color;

public interface Constants {
  // Element type definitions
  int LINE      = 101;
  int RECTANGLE = 102;
  int CIRCLE    = 103;
  int CURVE     = 104;

  // Initial conditions
  int DEFAULT_ELEMENT_TYPE = LINE;
  Color DEFAULT_ELEMENT_COLOR = Color.BLUE;
}
```

We have defined the DEFAULT_ELEMENT_COLOR as type Color, so we have added an import statement for java.awt to get the definition for the Color class. When we want to change the default start-up color or element type, we just need to change the values of the constants in the Constants interface. This will automatically take care of setting things up – as long as we implement the program code appropriately.

We can add fields to the SketchFrame class to store the current element type and color, since these are application-wide values, and are not specific to a view:

```
    private Color elementColor = DEFAULT_ELEMENT_COLOR;        // Current element color
    private int elementType = DEFAULT_ELEMENT_TYPE;            // Current element type
```

We can now use these to ensure that the menu items are checked appropriately when the application starts. We also want the constants from the Constants interface available, so make the following changes to the SketchFrame class definition:

```java
import javax.swing.*;
import java.awt.Event;
import java.awt.Color;

public class SketchFrame extends JFrame implements Constants {
  // Constructor
  public SketchFrame(String title) {
    setTitle(title);                                 // Set the window title
    setJMenuBar(menuBar);                            // Add the menu bar to the window
    setDefaultCloseOperation(EXIT_ON_CLOSE);

    // Code to create the File menu...

    // Construct the Element pull down menu
    elementMenu.add(lineItem = new JRadioButtonMenuItem(
                                "Line", elementType==LINE));
    elementMenu.add(rectangleItem = new JRadioButtonMenuItem(
                                "Rectangle", elementType==RECTANGLE));
    elementMenu.add(circleItem = new JRadioButtonMenuItem(
                                "Circle", elementType==CIRCLE));
    elementMenu.add(curveItem = new JRadioButtonMenuItem(
                                "Curve", elementType==CURVE));
    ButtonGroup types = new ButtonGroup();

    // ...plus the rest of the code for the element types as before...

    elementMenu.addSeparator();

    elementMenu.add(colorMenu);                      // Add the sub-menu
    colorMenu.add(redItem = new JCheckBoxMenuItem(
                        "Red", elementColor.equals(Color.RED)));
    colorMenu.add(yellowItem = new JCheckBoxMenuItem(
                        "Yellow", elementColor.equals(Color.YELLOW)));
    colorMenu.add(greenItem = new JCheckBoxMenuItem(
                        "Green", elementColor.equals(Color.GREEN)));
    colorMenu.add(blueItem = new JCheckBoxMenuItem(
                        "Blue", elementColor.equals(Color.BLUE)));

    // Add element color accelerators
    // ... plus the rest of the constructor as before...
  }

  // ...plus the rest of the class and include the two new data members...
  private Color elementColor = DEFAULT_ELEMENT_COLOR;      // Current element color
  private int elementType = DEFAULT_ELEMENT_TYPE;          // Current element type
}
```

When we construct the element objects, we use the `elementType` and `elementColor` members to set the state of each menu item. Only the element type menu item corresponding to the default type set in `elementType` will be checked because that's the only comparison that will produce a true result as an argument to the `JRadioButtonMenuItem` constructor. The mechanism is the same for the color menu items, but note that we use the `equals()` method defined in the `Color` class for a valid comparison. We might just get away with using `==` since we are only using constant `Color` values defined in the class, but as soon as we use a color that is not one of these, this would no longer work. Of course, we have to use `==` for the element type items because the IDs are of type `int`.

Having got that sorted out, we can have a go at implementing the listeners for the **Elements** menu, starting with the type menu items.

Try It Out – Handling Events for the Element Type Menu

We will add an inner class that will define listeners for the menu items specifying the element type. This class will implement the `ActionListener` interface because we want to respond to actions on these menu items. Add the following definition as an *inner* class to `SketchFrame`:

```
// Handles element type menu items
class TypeListener implements ActionListener {
  // Constructor
  TypeListener(int type) {
    this.type = type;
  }

  // Sets the element type
  public void actionPerformed(ActionEvent e) {
    elementType = type;
  }

  private int type;                        // Store the type for the menu
}
```

Now we can use objects of this class as listeners for the menu items. Add the following code to the `SketchFrame` constructor, after the code that sets up the type menu items for the **Elements** menu just before the last two lines of the constructor:

```
// Add type menu item listeners
lineItem.addActionListener(new TypeListener(LINE));
rectangleItem.addActionListener(new TypeListener(RECTANGLE));
circleItem.addActionListener(new TypeListener(CIRCLE));
curveItem.addActionListener(new TypeListener(CURVE));

  menuBar.add(fileMenu);                   // Add the file menu
  menuBar.add(elementMenu);                // Add the element menu
}
```

It will also be necessary to add the following two `import` statements to the `SketchFrame` class.

```
import java.awt.event.ActionListener;
import java.awt.event.ActionEvent;
```

Recompile Sketcher and see how it looks.

761

How It Works

It won't look any different as the listeners just set the current element type in the SketchFrame object. The listener class is remarkably simple. Each listener object stores the type corresponding to the menu item that is passed as the constructor argument. When an event occurs, the actionPerformed() method just stores the type in the listener object in the elementType member of the SketchFrame object.

Now we can do the same for the color menu items.

Try It Out – Implementing Color Menu Item Listeners

We will define another class that is an inner class to SketchFrame that defines listeners for the Color menu items:

```
// Handles color menu items
class ColorListener implements ActionListener {
  public ColorListener(Color color) {
    this.color = color;
  }

  public void actionPerformed(ActionEvent e) {
    elementColor = color;
  }

  private Color color;
}
```

We just need to create listener objects and add them to the menu items. Add the following code at the end of the SketchFrame constructor after the code that sets up the Color submenu:

```
// Add color menu item listeners
redItem.addActionListener(new ColorListener(Color.RED));
yellowItem.addActionListener(new ColorListener(Color.YELLOW));
greenItem.addActionListener(new ColorListener(Color.GREEN));
blueItem.addActionListener(new ColorListener(Color.BLUE));

menuBar.add(fileMenu);           // Add the file menu
menuBar.add(elementMenu);        // Add the element menu
}
```

This adds a listener object for each menu item in the Color menu.

How It Works

The ColorListener class works in the same way as the TypeListener class. Each class object stores an identifier for the menu item for which it is listening – in this case a Color object corresponding to the color the menu item sets up. The actionPerformed() method just stores the Color object from the listener object in the elementColor member of the SketchFrame object.

Of course, the menu doesn't quite work as it should. The menu item check marks are not being set correctly, as you can see below. We want an exclusive check, as with the radio buttons; more than one color at a time doesn't make sense:

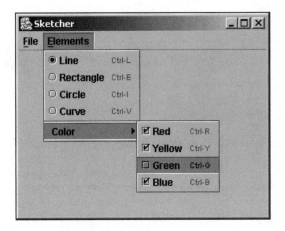

Fixing the Color Menu Checks

One way to deal with the problem is to make the listener object for a color menu item set the checks for all the menu items. You could code this in the `ColorListener` class as:

```
class ColorListener implements ActionListener {
  public void actionPerformed(ActionEvent e) {
    elementColor = color;

    // Set the checks for all menu items
    redItem.setState(color.equals(Color.RED));
    greenItem.setState(color.equals(Color.GREEN));
    blueItem.setState(color.equals(Color.BLUE));
    yellowItem.setState(color.equals(Color.YELLOW));
  }
  // Rest of the class as before...
}
```

This calls the `setState()` method for each menu item. If the argument is `true` the checkmark is set, and if it is `false`, it isn't. Clearly this will only set the checkmark for the item that corresponds to the color referenced by `color`. This is quite straightforward but there is a better way.

A `ButtonGroup` object works with `JCheckBoxMenuItem` objects because they have `AbstractButton` as a base class. Therefore we could add these menu items to their own button group in the `SketchFrame` constructor, and it will all be taken care of for us. The `ButtonGroup` object tracks the state of all of the buttons in the group. When any button is turned on, all the others are turned off, so only one button in the group can be on at one time. So add the following code – it could go anywhere after the items have been created but place it following the code that adds the items to the Color menu for consistency with the element type code.

```
ButtonGroup colors = new ButtonGroup();        // Color menu items button group
colors.add(redItem);
colors.add(yellowItem);
```

```
            colors.add(greenItem);
            colors.add(blueItem);
```

Now our Color menu checks are set automatically so we can forget about them.

Using Actions

One difficulty with the code that we have added to support the menus is that it is very menu specific. What I mean by this is that if we are going to do a proper job on the Sketcher application, we will undoubtedly want it to have a toolbar. The toolbar will surely have a whole bunch of buttons that perform exactly the same actions as the menu items we have just implemented, so we will be in the business of doing the same thing over again in the toolbar context. Of course, the only reason I brought it up, as I'm sure you anticipated, is that there is another way of working with menus, and that is to use an **action** object.

An action object is a bit of a strange beast, and it can be quite hard to understand at first so we will take it slowly. First of all let's look at what we mean by an 'action' here, as it is a precise term in this context. An action is an object of any class that implements the `Action` interface. This interface declares methods that operate on an action object, for example storing properties relating to the action, enabling it and disabling it. The `Action` interface happens to extend the `ActionListener` interface so an `action` object is a listener as well as an action. Now that we know an `Action` object can get and set properties, and is also a listener, how does that help us in implementing the Sketcher GUI?

The answer is in the last capability of an `Action` object. Some Swing components, such as those of type `JMenu` and `JToolBar`, have an `add()` method that accepts an argument of type `Action`. When you add an `Action` object to these using the `add()` method, the method creates a component from the `Action` object that is *automatically of the right type*. If you add an `Action` object to a `JMenu` object, a `JMenuItem` will be created and returned by the `add()` method. On the other hand, when you add exactly the same `Action` object to a `JToolBar` object, an object of type `JButton` will be created and returned. This means that you can add the very same `Action` object to both a menu and a toolbar, and since the `Action` object is its own listener you automatically get both supporting the same action. Clever, eh?

First, we should look at the `Action` interface.

The Action Interface

In general, properties are items of information that relate to a particular object and are stored as part of the object. Properties are often stored in a map, where a key identifies a particular property, and the value corresponding to that property can be stored in association with the key. The `Properties` class that is defined in the `java.util` package does exactly that. The `Action` interface has provision for storing seven basic standard properties that relate to an `Action` object:

❑ A **name** – a `String` object that is used as the label for a menu item or a toolbar button.

❑ A **small icon** – an `Icon` object to be displayed on a toolbar button.

❑ A **short description** of the action – a `String` object to be used as a tooltip.

❑ An **accelerator key** for the action – defined by a `KeyStroke` object.

❑   A **long description** of the action –a `String` object that is intended to be used as context sensitive help.

❑   A **mnemonic key** for the action – this is a key code of type `int`.

❑   An **action command key** – defined by an entry in a `KeyMap` object associated with a component.

Just so you are aware of them I have included the complete set here, but we will concentrate on just using the first three. We haven't met `Icon` objects before, but we will get to them a little later in this chapter.

You are not obliged to provide for all of these properties in your action classes, but the interface provides the framework for it. These properties are stored internally in a map collection in your action class, so the `Action` interface defines constants that you use as keys for each of the standard properties. These constants are all of type `String`, and the ones we are interested in are NAME, SMALL_ICON, and SHORT_DESCRIPTION. The others are ACCELERATOR_KEY, LONG_DESCRIPTION, MNEMONIC_KEY, and ACTION_COMMAND_KEY. There is another constant of type `String` defined in the interface with the name DEFAULT. This is for you to use to store a default property for the action.

The `Action` interface also declares the following methods:

Method	Description
`void putValue(String key,` `    Object value)`	Stores the `value` with the key `key` in the map supported by the action class. To store the name of an action within a class method you might write: `putValue(NAME, theName);` This uses the standard key, NAME to store the object `theName`.

`Object getValue(String key)`	This retrieves the object from the map corresponding to the key `key`. To retrieve a small icon within an action class method you might write:
	
	`Icon lineIcon =`
	`(Icon)getValue(SMALL_ICON);`

`boolean isEnabled()`	Returns `true` if the action object is enabled and `false` otherwise.
`void setEnabled(boolean state)`	Sets the action object as enabled if the argument state is `true` and disabled if it is `false`. This operates on both the toolbar button and the menu item if they have been created using the same object.

Table continued on following page

Method	Description
void addPropertyChangeListener (PropertyChangeListener listener)	This adds the listener passed as an argument that listens for changes to properties such as the enabled state of the object. This is used by a container for an action object to track property changes.
void removePropertyChangeListener(PropertyChangeListener listener)	This removes the listener passed as an argument. This is also for use by a `Container` object. Of course, since the `Action` interface extends the `ActionListener` interface, it also incorporates the `ActionPerformed()` method that you are already familiar with.

So far, all we seem to have with this interface is a license to do a lot of work in implementing it but it's not as bad as that. The `javax.swing` package defines a class, `AbstractAction`, that already implements the `Action` interface. If you extend this class to create your own action class, you get a basic infrastructure for free. Let's try it out in the context of Sketcher.

Using Actions as Menu Items

This will involve major surgery on our `SketchFrame` class. Although we'll be throwing away all those fancy varieties of menu items we spent so much time putting together, at least you know how they work now, and we'll end up with much less code after re-engineering the class, as you'll see. As the saying goes, you've got to crack a few eggs to make a soufflé.

We'll go back nearly to square one and reconstruct the class definition. First we will delete a lot of code from the existing class definition. Comments show where we will add code to re-implement the menus using actions. Get your definition of `SketchFrame` to the following state:

```
// Frame for the Sketcher application
import javax.swing.*;
import java.awt.*;
import java.awt.event.*;

public class SketchFrame extends JFrame implements Constants {
  // Constructor
  public SketchFrame(String title) {
    setTitle(title);                           // Set the window title
    setJMenuBar(menuBar);                      // Add the menu bar to the window
    setDefaultCloseOperation(EXIT_ON_CLOSE);   // Default is exit the application

    JMenu fileMenu = new JMenu("File");        // Create File menu
    JMenu elementMenu = new JMenu("Elements"); // Create Elements menu
    fileMenu.setMnemonic('F');                 // Create shortcut
    elementMenu.setMnemonic('E');              // Create shortcut

    // We will construct the file pull down menu here using actions...
```

```
    // We will add the types menu items here using actions...

    elementMenu.addSeparator();

    JMenu colorMenu = new JMenu("Color");          // Color sub-menu
    elementMenu.add(colorMenu);                     // Add the sub-menu

    // We will add the color menu items here using actions...

    menuBar.add(fileMenu);                          // Add the file menu
    menuBar.add(elementMenu);                       // Add the element menu
  }

  // We will add inner classes defining action objects here...

  // We will add action objects as members here...

  private JMenuBar menuBar = new JMenuBar();        // Window menu bar
  private Color elementColor = DEFAULT_ELEMENT_COLOR;  // Current element color
  private int elementType = DEFAULT_ELEMENT_TYPE;   // Current element type
}
```

Note that we have put the statement to set the default close operation as EXIT_ON_CLOSE back in so we won't need to call dispose() and exit() in the window event handler. The old inner classes have been deleted, as well as the fields storing references to menu items. All the code to create the menu items has been wiped as well, along with the code that added the listeners. We are ready to begin reconstruction. We can rebuild it, stronger, faster, better!

Defining Action Classes

We will need three inner classes defining actions, one for the File menu items, another for the element type menu items, and the third for element colors. We will derive all these from the AbstractAction class that already implements the Action interface. The AbstractAction class has three constructors:

Method	Description
AbstractAction()	Defines an object with a default name and icon.
AbstractAction(String name)	Defines an object with the name specified by the argument and a default icon.
AbstractAction(String name, Icon icon)	Defines an object with the name and icon specified by the arguments.

The AbstractAction class definition already provides the mechanism for storing action properties. For the last two constructors, the argument values that are passed will be stored using the standard keys that we described earlier. For the moment, we will only take advantage of the second constructor, and leave icons till a little later.

We can define the FileAction inner class as follows:

```
class FileAction extends AbstractAction {
  // Constructor
  FileAction(String name) {
    super(name);
  }

 // Constructor
  FileAction(String name, KeyStroke keystroke) {
    this(name);
    if(keystroke != null)
      putValue(ACCELERATOR_KEY, keystroke);
  }

  // Event handler
  public void actionPerformed(ActionEvent e) {
    // We will add action code here eventually...
  }
}
```

We have two constructors. The first just stores the name for the action by calling the base class constructor. The second stores the name by calling the first constructor and then stores the accelerator keystroke using the appropriate key if the argument is not null. Calling the other constructor rather than the base class constructor is better here, in case we add code to the other constructor later on (as we shall!).

Since our class is an action listener, we can implement the actionPerformed() method in it. We don't yet know what we are going to do with the File menu item actions, so we will leave it open for now and let the actionPerformed() method do nothing. Add this inner class to SketchFrame where the comment indicates.

The SketchFrame class will need a data member of type FileAction for each menu item we intend to add, so add the following statement to the SketchFrame class definition:

```
// File actions
private FileAction newAction, openAction, closeAction,
                   saveAction, saveAsAction, printAction;
```

We can define an inner class for the element type menus next:

```
class TypeAction extends AbstractAction {
  TypeAction(String name, int typeID) {
    super(name);
    this.typeID = typeID;
  }

  public void actionPerformed(ActionEvent e) {
    elementType = typeID;
  }

  private int typeID;
}
```

Add this definition to the `SketchFrame` class following the previous inner class. The only extra code here compared to the previous action class is that we retain the `typeID` concept to identify the element type. This makes the listener operation simple and fast. Because each object corresponds to a particular element type, there is no need for any testing of the event – we just store the current `typeID` as the new element type in the `SketchFrame` class object. We won't be adding accelerator key combinations for type menu items so we don't need to provide for them in the class.

Add the following statement to the `SketchFrame` class for the members that will store references to the `TypeAction` objects:

```
// Element type actions
private TypeAction lineAction, rectangleAction, circleAction, curveAction;
```

The third inner class is just as simple:

```
// Handles color menu items
class ColorAction  extends AbstractAction {
  public ColorAction(String name, Color color) {
    super(name);
    this.color = color;
  }

  public void actionPerformed(ActionEvent e) {
    elementColor = color;
    // This is temporary - just to show it works
    getContentPane().setBackground(color);
  }

  private Color color;
}
```

We also use the same idea that we used in the listener class for the color menu items in the previous implementation of `SketchFrame`. Here we have a statement in the `actionPerformed()` method that sets the background color of the content pane to the element color. When you click on a color menu item, the background color of the content pane will change so you will be able to see that it works. We'll remove this code later.

Add the following statement to the `SketchFrame` class for the color action members:

```
// Element color actions
private ColorAction redAction, yellowAction,
                    greenAction, blueAction;
```

We can try these action classes out now.

Try It Out – Actions in Action

All we need to do to create the menu items is use the `add()` method to add a suitable `Action` object to a menu. This all happens in the `SketchFrame` constructor – with the aid of a helper method that will economize on the number of lines of code:

```
public SketchFrame(String title) {
  setTitle(title);                             // Set the window title
  setJMenuBar(menuBar);                        // Add the menu bar to the window
  setDefaultCloseOperation(EXIT_ON_CLOSE);     // Default is exit the application

  JMenu fileMenu = new JMenu("File");          // Create File menu
  JMenu elementMenu = new JMenu("Elements");   // Create Elements menu
  fileMenu.setMnemonic('F');                   // Create shortcut
  elementMenu.setMnemonic('E');                // Create shortcut

  // Create the action items for the file menu
  newAction = new FileAction("New", KeyStroke.getKeyStroke('N',Event.CTRL_MASK ));
  openAction = new FileAction("Open", KeyStroke.getKeyStroke('O',Event.CTRL_MASK ));
  closeAction = new FileAction("Close");
  saveAction = new FileAction("Save", KeyStroke.getKeyStroke('S',Event.CTRL_MASK ));
  saveAsAction = new FileAction("Save As...");
  printAction = new FileAction("Print",
                         KeyStroke.getKeyStroke('P',Event.CTRL_MASK ));

  // Construct the file pull down menu
  addMenuItem(fileMenu, newAction);
  addMenuItem(fileMenu, openAction);
  addMenuItem(fileMenu, closeAction);
  fileMenu.addSeparator();                                     // Add separator
  addMenuItem(fileMenu, saveAction);
  addMenuItem(fileMenu, saveAsAction);
  fileMenu.addSeparator();                                     // Add separator
  addMenuItem(fileMenu, printAction);

  // Construct the Element pull down menu
  addMenuItem(elementMenu, lineAction = new TypeAction("Line", LINE));
  addMenuItem(elementMenu, rectangleAction = new TypeAction("Rectangle",
                                                  RECTANGLE));
  addMenuItem(elementMenu, circleAction = new TypeAction("Circle", CIRCLE));
  addMenuItem(elementMenu, curveAction = new TypeAction("Curve", CURVE));

  elementMenu.addSeparator();

  JMenu colorMenu = new JMenu("Color");        // Color sub-menu
  elementMenu.add(colorMenu);                  // Add the sub-menu

  addMenuItem(colorMenu, redAction = new ColorAction("Red", Color.RED));
  addMenuItem(colorMenu, yellowAction = new ColorAction("Yellow", Color.YELLOW));
  addMenuItem(colorMenu, greenAction = new ColorAction("Green", Color.GREEN));
  addMenuItem(colorMenu, blueAction = new ColorAction("Blue", Color.BLUE));

  menuBar.add(fileMenu);                        // Add the file menu
  menuBar.add(elementMenu);                     // Add the element menu
}
```

We have added four blocks of code. The first two are for the file menu, one creating the action object and the other calling a helper method, addMenuItem(), to create the menu items. The other two are for the element type and color menus. We create the action items for these menus in the arguments to the helper method calls. It's convenient to do this, as the constructor calls are relatively simple.

The helper method will add an item specified by its second argument to the menu specified by the first. By declaring the second argument as type Action, we can pass a reference to an object of any class type that implements the Action interface, so this includes any of our action classes. Here's the code:

```
private JMenuItem addMenuItem(JMenu menu, Action action) {
  JMenuItem item = menu.add(action);                      // Add the menu item

  KeyStroke keystroke = (KeyStroke)action.getValue(action.ACCELERATOR_KEY);
  if(keystroke != null)
    item.setAccelerator(keystroke);
  return item;                                            // Return the menu item
}
```

As you can see, the method takes care of adding the accelerator key for the menu item if one has been defined for the Action object. If there isn't one, the getValue() method will return null, so it's easy to check. We don't need access to the menu item that is created in the method at the moment since it is added to the menu. However, it is no problem to return the reference from the method and it could be useful if we wanted to add code to do something with the menu item at some point.

If you compile and run Sketcher, you will get a window that looks like this:

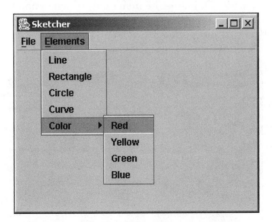

How It Works

We create an Action object for each item in the file menu. We then call our private addMenuItem() method for each item in turn to create the menu items corresponding to the Action objects, and add them to the file menu. The addMenuItem() method automatically adds an accelerator key for a menu item if it exists in the Action object. We declare the addMenuItem() method as private because it has no role outside of the SketchFrame class and therefore should not be accessible.

The items for the other menus are created in the same way using the `addMenuItem()` method. We create the `Action` objects in the expressions for the arguments to the method, as they are relatively simple expressions. Because we store the references to the `Action` objects, they will be available later when we want to create toolbar buttons corresponding to the menu items. Note that we have omitted the accelerators for the Elements menu items here on the grounds that they were not exactly standard or convenient.

You may be wondering at this point why we have to set the accelerator key for a menu item explicitly, and why an accelerator key stored within an `Action` object is not added to the menu item automatically. There's a very good reason for not having the `add()` method automatically set an accelerator key from an `Action` object. Pressing an accelerator key combination would be the equivalent of clicking any item created from a corresponding `Action` object. This could be a toolbar button and a menu item. Thus if the accelerator keys were automatically set for both components, you would get events from both components when you press the accelerator key combination – not exactly what you would want as each action would then be carried out twice!

If you try out the color menus you should see the background color change. If it doesn't there's something wrong somewhere.

Now we have the menus set up using action objects, we are ready to tackle adding a toolbar to our application.

Adding a Toolbar

A toolbar is a bar, usually positioned below the menu bar, which contains a row of buttons that typically provides a more direct route to menu options. We could add a toolbar to the Sketcher program for the menu items that are likely to be most popular. Just so that you know where we are heading, the kind of toolbar we will end up with ultimately is shown below.

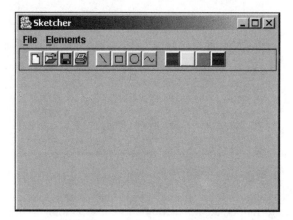

The four buttons in the first group are for the most used functions in the file menu. The other two groups of four buttons select the element type and element color respectively. So how are we going to put this toolbar together?

Adding the toolbar itself couldn't be easier. A toolbar is a Swing component defined by the `JToolBar` class. You can add a member to the `SketchFrame` class for a toolbar by adding the following field to the class definition:

```
private JToolBar toolBar = new JToolBar();        // Window toolbar
```

You can position this following the declaration of the `menuBar` member. It simply creates a `JToolBar` object as a member of the class. To add it to the frame window, you need to add the following statement after the existing code in the `SketchFrame` constructor:

```
getContentPane().add(toolBar, BorderLayout.NORTH);
```

This adds the (empty) toolbar to the top of the content pane for the frame window. The content pane has the `BorderLayout` manager as the default, which is very convenient. A `JToolBar` object should be added to a `Container` using the `BorderLayout` manager since it is normally positioned at one of the four sides of a component. An empty toolbar is not much use though, so let's see how to add buttons.

Adding Buttons to a Toolbar

The `JToolBar` class inherits the `add()` methods from the `Container` class, so you could create `JButton` objects and add them to the toolbar. However, since a toolbar almost always has buttons corresponding to menu functions, a much better way is to use the `add()` method defined in the `JToolBar` class to add an `Action` object to the toolbar. We can use this to add any of the `Action` objects that we created for our menus, and have the toolbar button events taken care of without any further work.

For example, we could add a button for the `openAction` object corresponding to the **Open** menu item in the **File** menu with the statement:

```
toolBar.add(openAction);          // Add a toolbar button
```

That's all you need basically. The `add()` method will create a `JButton` object based on the `Action` object passed as the argument. A reference to the `JButton` object is returned in case you want to store it to manipulate it in some way – adding a border for instance. Let's see how that looks.

Try It Out – Adding a Toolbar Button

Assuming you have added the declaration for the `toolBar` object to the `SketchFrame` class, you just need to add a couple of statements preceding the last statement in the constructor to add the toolbar to the content pane:

```
public SketchFrame(String title) {
  // Constructor code as before...

  JButton button = toolBar.add(openAction);                       // Add toolbar button
  button.setBorder(BorderFactory.createRaisedBevelBorder()); // Add button border
  getContentPane().add(toolBar, BorderLayout.NORTH);              // Add the toolbar
}
```

If you recompile Sketcher and run it, the window should look like that shown below.

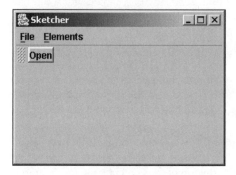

How It Works

There's not much to say about this. The `add()` method for the `toolBar` object created a `button` based on the `openAction` object that we passed as an argument. We store the reference returned in `button` so that we can add a border to the button.

A feature that comes for free with a `JToolBar` object is that it is automatically dockable, and can float as an independent window. You can drag the toolbar using the mouse by clicking the cursor in the gray area to the left of the button, and it will turn into a free-floating window.

You can also drag the toolbar to any of the four sides of the content pane to dock it again. You must drag with the cursor in the gray area of the toolbar to dock it. Dragging with the cursor in the toolbar title area just moves the window. It's not always convenient to have the toolbar floating or docked against borders other than its normal position. You can inhibit the ability to drag the toolbar around by calling the `setFloatable()` method for the `JToolBar` object, passing a boolean argument of `false`. Let's do this for Sketcher, so add the following statement to the `SketchFrame` constructor before the statement that adds the toolbar to the content pane:

```
    toolBar.setFloatable(false);      // Inhibit toolbar floating
    getContentPane().add(toolBar, BorderLayout.NORTH);
  }
```

A `true` argument to the method will allow the toolbar to float, so you can switch this on and off in your program as you wish. You can also test whether the toolbar can float by calling the `isFloatable()` method for the `JToolBar` object. This will return `true` if the toolbar is floatable, and `false` otherwise. If you recompile `SketchFrame` and run Sketcher again you will see that the gray bit at the left hand end of the toolbar is no longer there, and you cannot drag the toolbar around.

The button that has been created uses the name from the `Action` object as its label by default. We really want toolbar buttons with icons, so that's got to be the next step.

Adding Icons

A reference to an icon is generally stored in a variable of type `Icon`. `Icon` is an interface that declares methods to obtain the height and width of an icon in pixels – these are the `getHeight()` and `getWidth()` methods respectively, and to paint the icon image on a component – the `paint()` method. One class that implements the `Icon` interface is `ImageIcon` and it is this class that you use to create an icon object in your program from a file containing the icon image. The class provides several constructors that create an `ImageIcon` object and the one we will use accepts a `String` argument that specifies the file where the icon image is to be found. The `String` object can be just a file name, in which case the file should be in the current directory – the one that contains the `.class` files for the application or applet. You can also supply a string that specifies the path and file name where the file containing the image is to be found. The `ImageIcon` constructors accept icon files in **PNG** (Portable Network Graphics format, which have `.png` extensions), **GIF** (**G**raphics **I**nterchange **F**ormat, or `.gif` files), or **JPEG** (**J**oint **P**hotographic **E**xperts **G**roup format, `.jpg` files) formats, but we will assume GIF files in our code.

We will put the icons for Sketcher in a subdirectory of the Sketcher directory called `Images`, so create a subdirectory to your Sketcher application directory with this name. To create an icon for the `openAction` object from an image in a file `open.gif` in the `Images` directory, we could write:

```
openAction.putValue(Action.SMALL_ICON, new ImageIcon ("Images/open.gif"));
```

This stores the `ImageIcon` object in our `Action` object associated with the `SMALL_ICON` key. The `add()` method for the toolbar object will then look for the icon for the toolbar button it creates using this key. Let's see if it works.

> You will need to create the GIF files containing the icons. Any graphics editor that can save files in the GIF format will do, Paint Shop Pro, Microsoft Paint, or gimp, for instance. I created my icons as 16x16 pixels since it is a fairly standard size for toolbar buttons. Make sure the file for the `openAction` object is called `open.gif`, and stored in the `Images` subdirectory. We will need GIF files for other buttons too, and they will each have a file name that is the same as the label on the corresponding menu item.
>
> If you want to put them together in one go, for the file menu toolbar button you will need `save.gif`, `new.gif` and `print.gif`, for the element types you will need `line.gif`, `rectangle.gif`, `circle.gif`, and `curve.gif`, and for the colors you will need `red.gif`, `yellow.gif`, `green.gif` and `blue.gif`. GIF files for all these icons are available along with the Sketcher source code at the Wrox web site: http://www.wrox.com/Consumer/Store/Download.asp .

Try It Out – A Button with an Icon

You can add the statement to create the icon for the Action object just before we create the toolbar button:

```
public SketchFrame(String title) {
  // Constructor code as before...

    openAction.putValue(Action.SMALL_ICON, new ImageIcon ("Images/open.gif"));
    JButton button = toolBar.add(openAction);                    // Add toolbar button
    button.setBorder(BorderFactory.createRaisedBevelBorder());// Add button border

    toolBar.setFloatable(false);                              // Inhibit toolbar floating
    getContentPane().add(toolBar, BorderLayout.NORTH);        // Add the toolbar
}
```

In fact you could put the statement anywhere after the openAction object is created, but here will be convenient. If you recompile Sketcher and run it again, you should see the window below.

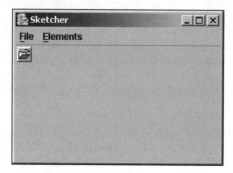

How It Works

The ImageIcon object that we store in our openAction object is automatically used by the add() method for the toolBar object to add the icon to the button. Fortunately we don't get the label on the toolbar button as well as the icon since the label is automatically inhibited by the presence of an icon. If you look at the corresponding menu item though, we get both the label and the icon. This might not be what you want so we will return to this point a little later in this chapter.

It would be better if we altered the inner classes that define the Action objects to add icons automatically when a suitable .gif file is available. Let's try that now.

Try It Out – Adding All the Toolbar Buttons

We can modify the constructor for each inner class to add the corresponding icon. Here's how we can implement this in the FileAction class:

```
FileAction(String name) {
  super(name);
  String iconFileName = "Images/" + name + ".gif";
  if(new File(iconFileName).exists())
    putValue(SMALL_ICON, new ImageIcon(iconFileName));
}
```

Because we refer to the `File` class here, we need to add an import statement for `java.io.File` to the beginning of the `SketchFrame.java` source file. This code assumes all icon files follow the convention that their name is the same as the `String` associated with the NAME key. If you want to have any file name, you could pass the `String` defining the file name to the constructor. If the icon file is not available then nothing happens, so the code will work whether or not an icon is defined. We only need to add the code to this constructor since the other constructors in the `FileAction` class call this one.

The code that you add to the constructors for the `TypeAction` and `ColorAction` inner classes is exactly the same as here, so go ahead and copy it across.

We can reduce the code we need in the SketchFrame constructor a little by defining a helper method in the `SketchFrame` class to create toolbar buttons as follows:

```
private JButton addToolBarButton(Action action) {
    JButton button = toolBar.add(action);                    // Add toolbar button
    button.setBorder(BorderFactory.createRaisedBevelBorder());// Add button border
    return button;
}
```

The argument is the `Action` object for the toolbar button that is to be added, and the code is essentially the same as the specific code we had in the `SketchFrame` constructor to create the button for the `openAction` object. We can remove that from the `SketchFrame` constructor and replace it by the following code to create all the buttons that we need:

```
public SketchFrame(String title) {
    // Constructor code as before...

    // Add file buttons
    toolBar.addSeparator();                                  // Space at the start
    addToolBarButton(newAction);
    addToolBarButton(openAction);
    addToolBarButton(saveAction);
    addToolBarButton(printAction);

    // Add element type buttons
    toolBar.addSeparator();
    addToolBarButton(lineAction);
    addToolBarButton(rectangleAction);
    addToolBarButton(circleAction);
    addToolBarButton(curveAction);

    // Add element color buttons
    toolBar.addSeparator();
    addToolBarButton(redAction);
    addToolBarButton(yellowAction);
    addToolBarButton(greenAction);
    addToolBarButton(blueAction);
    toolBar.addSeparator();                                  // Space at the end
```

```
toolBar.setBorder(BorderFactory.createCompoundBorder(        // Toolbar border
                 BorderFactory.createLineBorder(Color.darkGray),
                 BorderFactory.createEmptyBorder(2,2,4,2)));
```

```
  toolBar.setFloatable(false);                          // Inhibit toolbar floating
  getContentPane().add(toolBar, BorderLayout.NORTH); // Add the toolbar
}
```

Now you should get the window with the toolbar that we showed at the beginning, with a nice neat toolbar. You can see the color buttons in action since they will change the background color.

How It Works

The extra code in the inner class constructors stores an icon in each object if there is a GIF file with the appropriate name in the `Images` subdirectory. We create each of the toolbar buttons by calling our `addToolBarButton()` helper method with an `Action` item corresponding to a menu item. The helper method passes the `Action` object to the `add()` method for the `JToolBar` object to create a `JButton` object. It also adds a border to the button. The `addToolBarButton()` method returns a reference to the button object in case we need it.

We have added a further statement to add a border to the toolbar. We use the `createCompoundBorder()` method to create a border with an outer border that is a single line, and an inner border that is empty but inserts space around the inside of the outer border as specified by the arguments. The arguments to `createEmptyBorder()` are the width in pixels of the border in the sequence top, left, bottom and right.

Fixing the Menus

Things are perhaps still not quite as we would have them. If you take a look at the menus you will see what I mean.

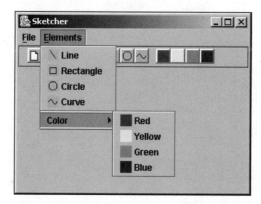

All of the menu items now have icons too. While this is a helpful cue to what the toolbar icons are, maybe you would rather not have them as they look a little cluttered. We could get rid of the icons very easily by modifying the menu items that are created by the `add()` method for the `JMenu` objects in the `addMenuItem()` method. The `JMenuItem` class has a `setIcon()` method that accepts a reference of type `Icon` to set an icon for a menu item. If we want to remove the icon, we just pass `null` to it.

We just need to add one statement to `addMenuItem()` method in the `SketchFrame` class to remove the icons for all the menu items, like this:

```
private JMenuItem addMenuItem(JMenu menu, Action action) {
  JMenuItem item = menu.add(action);                      // Add the menu item

  KeyStroke keystroke = (KeyStroke)action.getValue(action.ACCELERATOR_KEY);
  if(keystroke != null)
    item.setAccelerator(keystroke);
  item.setIcon(null);                                     // Remove the icon
  return item;                                            // Return the menu item
}
```

When you run Sketcher with this modification to `SketchFrame`, you should see the menu items without icons.

How It Works

When we construct each of the menu items using our helper method `addMenuItem()` we remove the icon from the `JMenuItem` that is created by passing `null` to its `setIcon()` method. Thus none of the menu item objects has an icon associated with it. Of course, the toolbar buttons are unaffected and retain the icons defined by the `Action` objects they are created from.

Adding Tooltips

I'm sure you have seen tooltips in operation. These are the little text prompts that appear automatically when you let the mouse cursor linger over certain GUI elements on the screen for a second or two. They disappear automatically when you move the cursor. I think you will be surprised at how easy it is to implement support for tooltips in Java.

The secret is in the `Action` objects that we are using. `Action` objects have a built-in capability to store tooltip text because it is already provided for with the `SHORT_DESCRIPTION` key that is defined in the interface. All we have to do is store the tooltip text in our inner classes that are derived from `AbstractAction`. The tooltip will then be automatically available on the toolbar buttons that we create. Let's work through our `Action` classes and provide for tooltip text.

We can provide for tooltip text in each of our inner classes by adding constructors with an extra parameter for it. We need two additional constructors in the `FileAction` class, one for when the Action item has an accelerator key, and the other for when it doesn't. The definition of the first new `FileAction` class constructor will be:

```
FileAction(String name, KeyStroke keystroke, String tooltip) {
  this(name, keystroke);                        // Call the other constructor
  if(tooltip != null)                           // If there is tooltip text
    putValue(SHORT_DESCRIPTION, tooltip);       // ...squirrel it away
}
```

This just calls the constructor that accepts arguments defining the name and the keystroke. It then stores the tooltip string using the SHORT_DESCRIPTION key, as long as it isn't null. Although you wouldn't expect a null to be passed for the tooltip text reference, it's best not to assume it as this could crash the program. If it is null we do nothing.

The other constructor will take care of a tooltip for an Action item without an accelerator keystroke:

```
FileAction(String name, String tooltip) {
  this(name);                             // Call the other constructor
  if(tooltip != null)                     // If there is tooltip text
    putValue(SHORT_DESCRIPTION, tooltip); // ...squirrel it away
}
```

Of course, we must now change the code in the SketchFrame constructor that creates FileAction items so that we incorporate the tooltip argument:

```
      // Create the action items for the file menu
newAction = new FileAction("New", KeyStroke.getKeyStroke('N',Event.CTRL_MASK ),
                      "Create new sketch");
openAction = new FileAction("Open", KeyStroke.getKeyStroke('O',Event.CTRL_MASK),
                      "Open existing sketch");
closeAction = new FileAction("Close", "Close sketch");
saveAction = new FileAction("Save", KeyStroke.getKeyStroke('S',Event.CTRL_MASK),
                      "Save sketch");
saveAsAction = new FileAction("Save As...", "Save as new file");
printAction = new FileAction("Print", KeyStroke.getKeyStroke('P',Event.CTRL_MASK),
                      "Print sketch");
```

We can do exactly the same with the TypeAction class – just add the following constructor definition:

```
TypeAction(String name, int typeID, String tooltip) {
  this(name, typeID);
  if(tooltip != null)                             // If there is a tooltip
    putValue(SHORT_DESCRIPTION, tooltip);         // ...squirrel it away
}
```

We must then modify the code in the SketchFrame constructor to pass a tooltip string when we create a TypeAction object:

```
      // Construct the Element pull down menu
addMenuItem(elementMenu, lineAction = new TypeAction("Line", LINE, "Draw lines"));
addMenuItem(elementMenu, rectangleAction = new TypeAction("Rectangle",RECTANGLE,
                                        "Draw rectangles"));
addMenuItem(elementMenu, circleAction = new TypeAction("Circle", CIRCLE,
                                        "Draw circles"));
addMenuItem(elementMenu, curveAction = new TypeAction("Curve", CURVE,
                                        "Draw curves"));
```

And a constructor that does exactly the same needs to be added to the ColorAction class:

```
public ColorAction(String name, Color color, String tooltip) {
  this(name, color);
```

```
   if(tooltip != null)                                // If there is a tooltip
      putValue(SHORT_DESCRIPTION, tooltip);           // ...squirrel it away
 }
```

The corresponding changes in the `SketchFrame` constructor are:

```
JMenu colorMenu = new JMenu("Color");               // Color sub-menu
elementMenu.add(colorMenu);                          // Add the sub-menu
addMenuItem(colorMenu, redAction = new ColorAction
                            ("Red", Color.RED, "Draw in red"));
addMenuItem(colorMenu, yellowAction = new ColorAction
                            ("Yellow", Color.YELLOW, "Draw in yellow"));
addMenuItem(colorMenu, greenAction = new ColorAction
                            ("Green", Color.GREEN, "Draw in green"));
addMenuItem(colorMenu, blueAction = new ColorAction
                            ("Blue", Color.BLUE, "Draw in blue"));
```

Of course, if you want to put your own tooltip text for any of these, you can. You should keep it short since it is displayed on the fly. We can try our tooltips out now we have the last piece in place. Just recompile the `SketchFrame` class and run Sketcher again. You should be able to see the tooltip when you let the cursor linger over a button.

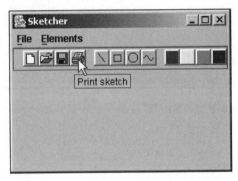

How It Works

`Action` objects act as a repository for the tooltip text for a toolbar button. If an `Action` object contains a tooltip property, a toolbar button that you create from it will automatically have the tooltip operational. Try lingering the cursor over a menu item. Since the menu items are also created from `Action` items, tooltips are available for them, too.

Disabling Actions

You won't want to have all of the menu items and toolbar buttons enabled all of the time. For instance, while there is no sketch active, the Save and Print menu items should not be operational, and neither should the corresponding buttons. The `Action` objects provide a single point of control for enabling or disabling menu items and the corresponding toolbar buttons. To disable an action, you call the `setEnabled()` method for the `Action` object with an argument of `false`. You can restore the enabled state by calling the method with a `true` argument. The `isEnabled()` method for an `Action` object returns `true` if the action is enabled, and `false` otherwise.

Let's see toolbar button inaction in action in Sketcher.

Try It Out – Disabling Actions

We will disable the actions corresponding to the Save, Close and Print actions. Add the following statements to the end of the SketchFrame constructor:

```
// Disable actions
saveAction.setEnabled(false);
closeAction.setEnabled(false);
printAction.setEnabled(false);
```

That's all that's necessary. If you run the modified version of Sketcher, menu items and toolbar buttons corresponding to the Action objects we have disabled will be grayed out and non-operational.

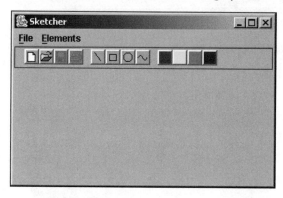

If you extend the File menu, you will see that the corresponding menu items are grayed out, too.

How It Works

The state of both the JMenuItem and JButton objects created from an Action object is determined by the state of the Action object. Disabling the Action object disables any menus or toolbar buttons created from it. If you want a demonstration that they really are disabled, try disabling a couple of the color actions.

Summary

In this chapter you have learned how to handle events in your applications and in your applets. Events are fundamental to all window-based applications, as well as most applets, so you will be applying the techniques from this chapter throughout the rest of the book.

The most important points we have discussed in this chapter are:

❑ A user interaction generates an event in the context of a component.

❑ There are two categories of events associated with a component: **low-level events** from the mouse, keyboard or window system events such as opening or closing a window, and **semantic events** which represent component actions such as pressing a button or selecting a menu item.

❑ Both low-level and semantic events can arise simultaneously.

❑ An event for a component can be handled by the component object itself, or by a separate object that implements a listener interface corresponding to the event type.

❑ A component that is to handle its own events does so by calling its `enableEvents()` method and implementing the class method to process the kind of event that has been enabled.

❑ A listener object that is registered with a component will receive notification of the events originating with the component that correspond to the type(s) of events the listener can handle.

❑ A listener interface for low-level events requires several event-handling methods to be implemented.

❑ A listener interface for semantic events declares a single event handling method.

❑ An adapter class defines a set of empty methods for one or more low-level event interfaces. You can create your own class defining a low-level event listener by deriving your class from an adapter class, and then implementing the event handling methods in which you are interested.

❑ Events in applications and in applets are handled in exactly the same way.

❑ An `Action` object is an object of a class that implements the `Action` interface. `Action` objects can be used to create menu items and associated toolbar buttons.

❑ An `Action` object is automatically the listener for the menu item and toolbar button that are created from it.

Exercises

1. Modify Sketcher to add an Exit action for the File menu and the toolbar.

2. Modify the lottery applet to present the six numbers selected in ascending sequence.

3. Replace the action listener for the selection buttons in the Lottery applet with a mouse listener, and use the `mousePressed()` method to update the selection with a new value.

4. Modify the Lottery applet to implement the mouse listener for a selection button as an inner class to the `Lottery` class.

5. Modify the Lottery applet to implement the control buttons on a toolbar based on `Action` objects.

6. Change the Lottery applet to handle the `MOUSE_ENTERED` and `MOUSE_EXITED` events within the toolbar buttons you added in the previous exercise.

7. Add tooltips to the lucky number buttons and the toolbar buttons in the Lottery applet. (You can make the tooltip the same for each of the lucky number buttons.)

Drawing in a Window

In this chapter we will look at how you can draw using the Java 2D facilities that are part of JFC. We will see how to draw in an applet and in an application. We will investigate how we can combine the event-handling capability that we learned about in the previous chapter with the drawing facilities we'll explore in this chapter, so that we can implement an interactive Graphical User Interface for creating a sketch.

By the end of this chapter you will have learned:

- ❑ What components are available for creating a GUI.

- ❑ How coordinates are defined for drawing on a component.

- ❑ How you implement drawing on a component.

- ❑ How to structure the components in a window for drawing.

- ❑ What kinds of shapes you can draw on a component.

- ❑ How you implement mouse listener methods to enable interactive drawing operations.

Using the Model/View Architecture

We need to develop an idea of how we're going to manage the data for a sketch in the Sketcher program before we start drawing a sketch, because this will affect where and how we handle events. We already have a class that defines an application window, SketchFrame, but this class would not be a very sensible place to store the underlying data that defines a sketch. For one thing, we'll want to save a sketch in a file, and serialization is the easiest way to do that. If we're going to use serialization to store a sketch, we won't want all the stuff in the implementation of the SketchFrame class muddled up with the data relating to the sketch we have created.

For another, it will make the program easier to implement if we separate out the basic data defining a sketch from the definition of the GUI. This will be along the lines of the MVC architecture that we first mentioned in Chapter 15, a variant of which is used in the definition of Swing components.

Ideally, we should manage the sketch data in a class designed specifically for that purpose – this class will be the **model** for a sketch.

A class representing a **view** of the data in the model class will display the sketch and handle user interactions – so this class will combine viewing functions and a sketch controller. The general GUI creation and operations not specific to a view will be dealt with in the SketchFrame class. This is not the only way of implementing the things we want in the Sketcher program, but it's quite a good way.

Our model object will contain a mixture of text and graphics that will go to make up a sketch. We'll call our model class SketchModel and we'll call the class representing a view of the model SketchView, although we won't be adding the view to the program until the next chapter. The following diagram illustrates the relationships between the classes we will have in Sketcher.

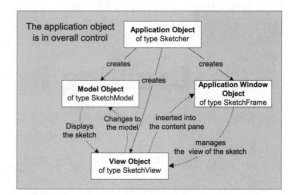

The application object will have overall responsibility for managing links between the other objects involved in the program. Any object that has access to the application object will be able to communicate with any other object as long as the application class has methods to make each of the objects available. Thus the application object will act as the communication channel between objects.

Note that SketchFrame is not the view class – it just defines the application window and the GUI components associated with that. When we create a SketchView object in the next chapter, we'll arrange to insert the SketchView object into the content pane of the SketchFrame object, and manage it using the layout manager for the content pane. By defining the view class separately from the application class, we separate the view of a sketch from the menus and other components we use to interact with the program. One benefit of this is that the area in which we display the document has its own coordinate system, independent of that of the application window.

To implement the foundations for the model/view design in Sketcher we need to define classes for the model and the view, at least in outline. The class to contain the data defining a sketch we can define in skeleton form as:

```
import java.util.Observable;

class SketchModel extends Observable {
  // Detail of the rest of class to be filled in later...
}
```

We obviously have a bit more work to do on this class, so we will add to this as we go along. Since it extends the Observable class, we will be able to register the view class with it as an observer, and automatically notify the view of any changes. This facility will come into its own when we have multiple views. We can define the view class as a component by deriving it from JComponent. This will build in all the methods for operating as a component and we can override any of these as necessary. The view class also needs to implement the Observer interface so that we can register it with the model. Here's the outline:

```java
import javax.swing.JComponent;
import java.util.Observer;
import java.util.Observable;

class SketchView extends JComponent implements Observer {
  public SketchView(Sketcher theApp) {
    this.theApp = theApp;
  }

  // Method called by Observable object when it changes
  public void update(Observable o, Object rectangle) {
    // Code to respond to changes in the model...
  }

  private Sketcher theApp;               // The application object
}
```

The view is definitely going to need access to the model in order to display it, but rather than store a reference to the model, the constructor has a parameter to enable the application object to be passed to it. By storing the application object in the view, rather than a reference to the model, and adding a method to the application object to return a reference to the model, we make the view object independent of the model object. If a completely different object represents the model because, for example, a new file is loaded, we don't need to change the view object. As long as the view object is registered as an observer for the new model, the view will automatically redraw the new sketch when it is notified by the model that it has changed.

To integrate a model and its view into the Sketcher application, we just need to add some code to the Sketcher class:

```java
import java.awt.*;
import java.awt.event.*;
import java.util.Observer;
import java.util.Observable;

public class Sketcher {
  public static void main(String[] args) {
    theApp = new Sketcher();                 // Create the application object
    theApp.init();                           // ... and initialize it
  }

  public void init() {
    window = new SketchFrame("Sketcher", this);   // Create the app window
    Toolkit theKit = window.getToolkit();         // Get the window toolkit
    Dimension wndSize = theKit.getScreenSize();   // Get screen size

    // Set the position to screen center & size to 2/3 screen size
    window.setBounds(wndSize.width/6, wndSize.height/6,       // Position
                2*wndSize.width/3, 2*wndSize.height/3);   // Size

    window.addWindowListener(new WindowHandler()); // Add window listener

    sketch = new SketchModel();                   // Create the model
```

```
      view = new SketchView(this);              // Create the view
      sketch.addObserver((Observer)view);       // Register the view with the model
      window.getContentPane().add(view, BorderLayout.CENTER);
      window.setVisible(true);
    }

    // Return a reference to the application window
    public SketchFrame getWindow() {
      return window;
    }

    // Return a reference to the model
    public SketchModel getModel() {
      return sketch;
    }

    // Return a reference to the view
    public SketchView getView() {
      return view;
    }

    // Handler class for window events
    class WindowHandler extends WindowAdapter {
      // Handler for window closing event
      public void windowClosing(WindowEvent e) {
        // Code to be added here later...
      }
    }

    private SketchModel sketch;        // The data model for the sketch
    private SketchView view;           // The view of the sketch
    private static SketchFrame window; // The application window
    private static Sketcher theApp;    // The application object
  }
```

There is no code in the `windowClosing()` method at present, so this assumes we have restored
EXIT_ON_CLOSE as the default closing action in the `SketchFrame` class. We will be adding code to
the `windowClosing()` method when we get to save sketches on disk. The `SketchFrame` constructor
needs to be modified as follows:

```
    public SketchFrame(String title, Sketcher theApp) {
      setTitle(title);                              // Set the window title
      this.theApp = theApp;
      setJMenuBar(menuBar);                         // Add the menu bar to the window
      setDefaultCloseOperation(EXIT_ON_CLOSE);      // Default is exit the application

      // Rest of the constructor as before...
    }
```

You need to add the `theApp` variable to the `SketchFrame` class:

```
private Sketcher theApp;
```

There are new methods in the Sketcher class that return a reference to the application window, the model, and the view, so any of these are accessible from anywhere that a reference to the application object is available.

After creating the model and view objects, we register the view as an observer for the model to enable the model to notify the view when it changes. We then add the `view` to the content pane of the `window` object, which is the main application window. Since it is added in the center using the `BorderLayout` manager for the content pane, it will occupy all the remaining space in the pane.

Now that we know roughly the direction in which we are heading, let's move on down the road.

Coordinate Systems in Components

In Chapter 15, we saw how your computer screen has a coordinate system that is used to define the position and size of a window. We also saw how we can add components to a container with their position established by a layout manager. This coordinate system is analogous to the screen coordinate system. The origin is at the top-left corner of the container, with the positive *x*-axis running horizontally from left to right, and the positive *y*-axis running from top to bottom. The positions of buttons in a `JWindow` or a `JFrame` object are specified as a pair of (x, y) pixel coordinates, relative to the origin at the top-left corner of the container object on the screen. Below you can see the coordinate system for the Sketcher application window.

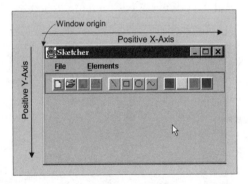

Of course, the layered pane for the window object will have its own coordinate system with the origin in the top-left corner of the pane, and this is used to position the menu and the content pane. The content pane will have its own coordinate system too that will be used to position the components it contains.

It's not just containers and windows that have their own coordinate system: each `JButton` object also has its own system, as do `JToolBar` objects. In fact, *every* component has its own coordinate system.

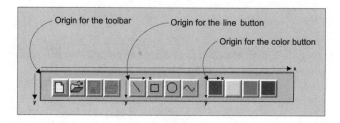

It's clear that a container needs a coordinate system for specifying the positions of the components it contains. You also need a coordinate system to draw on a component – to draw a line for instance you need to be able to specify where it begins and ends in relation to the component – and while the coordinate system here is similar to that used for positioning components in a container, it's not exactly the same. It's more complicated when you are drawing – but for very good reasons. Let's see how the coordinate system for drawing works.

Drawing on a Component

Before we get into the specifics of how you draw on a component, let's understand the principle ideas behind it. When you draw on a component using the Java 2D capabilities, there are two coordinate systems involved. When you draw something – a line or a curve for instance – you specify the line or the curve in a device-independent logical coordinate system called the **user coordinate system** for the component, or **user space**. By default this coordinate system has the same orientation as the system that we discussed for positioning components in containers. The origin is at the top-left corner; the positive *x*-axis runs from left to right, and the positive *y*-axis from top to bottom. Coordinates are usually specified as floating point values, although integers can also be used.

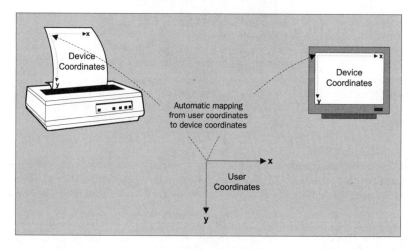

A particular graphical output device will have its own **device coordinate system, or device space.** This has the same orientation as the default user coordinate system, but the coordinate units depend on the characteristics of the device. Your display, for instance, will have a different device coordinate system for each configuration of the screen resolution, so the coordinate system when your display is set to 1024x768 resolution will be different from the coordinate system for 800x600 pixels.

*Incidentally, the drawing process is often referred to as **rendering**, since graphical output devices are generally raster devices and the drawing elements such as lines, rectangles, text, and so on need to be rendered into a rasterized representation before they can be output to the device.*

Having a device-independent coordinate system for drawing means that you can use essentially the same code for outputting graphics to a variety of different devices – to your display screen, for example, or to your printer – even though these devices themselves have quite different coordinate systems with different resolutions. The fact that your screen might have 90 pixels per inch while your printer may have 600 dots per inch is automatically taken care of. Java 2D will deal with converting your user coordinates to the device coordinate system that is specific to the output device you are using.

With the default mapping from user coordinates to device coordinates, the units for user coordinates are assumed to be 1/72 of an inch. Since for most screen devices the pixels are approximately 1/72 inch apart, the conversion amounts to an identity transformation. If you want to use user coordinates that are in some other units, you have to provide for this yourself. We will look into the mechanism that you would use to do this when we discuss transformations in the next chapter.

Graphics Contexts

The user coordinate system for drawing on a component using Java 2D is encapsulated in an object of type `Graphics2D`, which is usually referred to as a **graphics context**. It provides all the tools you need to draw whatever you want on the surface of the component. A graphics context enables you to draw lines, curves, shapes, filled shapes, as well as images, and gives you a great deal of control over the drawing process.

The `Graphics2D` class is derived from the `Graphics` class that defined device contexts in earlier versions of Java, so if you feel the need to use the old drawing methods, they are all inherited in the `Graphics2D` class. We will be concentrating on the new more powerful and flexible facilities provided by `Graphics2D` but, as you will see, references to graphics contexts are usually passed around as type `Graphics` so you need to be aware of it. Note that both the `Graphics` and `Graphics2D` classes are abstract classes, so you can't create objects of either type directly. An object representing a graphics context is entirely dependent on the component to which it relates, so a graphics context is always obtained for use with a particular component.

The `Graphics2D` object for a component takes care of mapping user coordinates to device coordinates, so it contains information about the device that is the destination for output as well as the user coordinates for the component. The information required for converting user coordinates to device coordinates is encapsulated in three different kinds of object:

❑ A `GraphicsEnvironment` object encapsulates all the graphics devices (as `GraphicsDevice` objects) and fonts (as `Font` objects) that are available on your computer.

❑ A `GraphicsDevice` object encapsulates information about a particular device such as a screen or a printer, and stores it in one or more `GraphicsConfiguration` objects.

❑ A `GraphicsConfiguration` object defines the characteristics of a particular device such as a screen or a printer. Your display screen will typically have several `GraphicsConfiguration` objects associated with it, each corresponding to a particular combination of screen resolution and number of displayable colors.

The graphics context also maintains other information necessary for drawing operations such as the drawing color, the line style and the specification of the fill color and pattern for filled shapes. We will see how to work with these attributes in examples later in this chapter.

Since a graphics context defines the drawing context for a specific component, before you can draw on a component you must have a reference to its graphics context object. For the most part, you will draw on a component by implementing the paint() method that is called whenever the component needs to be reconstructed. An object representing the graphics context for the component is passed as an argument to the paint() method, and you use this to do the drawing. The graphics context includes all the methods that you use to draw on a component and we will be looking into many of these in this chapter.
The paint() method is not the only way of drawing on a component. You can obtain a graphics context for a component at any time just by calling its getGraphics() method.

There are occasions when you want to get a component redrawn while avoiding a direct call of the paint() method. In such cases you should call repaint() for the component. There are five versions of this method that you can use; we'll look at four:

repaint() Method	Description
repaint()	Causes the entire component to be repainted by calling its paint() method after all of the currently outstanding events have been processed.
repaint(long msec)	Requests that the entire component is repainted within msec milliseconds.
repaint(int msec, int x, int y, int width, int height)	Adds the region specified by the arguments to the **dirty region** list if the component is visible. The dirty region list is simply a list of areas of the component that need to be repainted. The component will be repainted by calling its paint() method when all currently outstanding events have been processed or within msec milliseconds. The region is the rectangle at position (x, y) with the width and height as specified by the last two arguments.
repaint(Rectangle rect)	Adds the rectangle specified by rect to the dirty region list if the component is visible.

You will find that the first and the last methods are the ones you use most of the time.

That's enough theory for now. Time to get a bit of practice.

Let's get an idea of how we can draw on a component by drawing on the SketchView object that we added to Sketcher. All we need to do is implement the paint() method in the SketchView class.

Try It Out – Drawing in a View

Add the following implementation of the method to the SketchView class:

```
import javax.swing.JComponent;
import java.util.Observer;
```

```
import java.util.Observable;
import java.awt.*;                                       // For Graphics

class SketchView extends JComponent implements Observer {
  public void paint(Graphics g) {
    // Temporary code
    Graphics2D g2D = (Graphics2D)g;                       // Get a Java 2D device context

    g2D.setPaint(Color.RED);                              // Draw in red
    g2D.draw3DRect(50, 50, 150, 100, true);              // Draw a raised 3D rectangle
    g2D.drawString("A nice 3D rectangle", 60, 100);      // Draw some text
  }

    // Rest of the class as before...
}
```

If you recompile the file SketchFrame.java and run Sketcher, you can see what the paint()
method produces. You should see the window shown here.

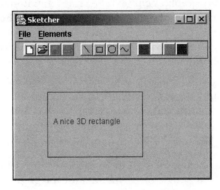

OK, it's not your traditional meaning of 3D. In this case, the edges of the rectangle are highlighted so
that that they appear to be beveled and lift from the top left hand corner (or the coordinate origin).

How It Works

The graphics context is passed as the argument to the paint() method as type Graphics (the base
class for Graphics2D) so to use the methods defined in the Graphics2D class we must first cast it to
that type. The paint() method has a parameter type of Graphics for compatibility reasons.

Once we have cast the graphics context, we then set the color in which we will draw by calling the
setPaint() method for the Graphics2D object and passing the drawing color as an argument. All
subsequent drawing operations will now be in Color.RED. We can change this again later with another
call to setPaint() when we want to draw in a different color.

Next we call the draw3DRect() method defined in the Graphics2D class that draws a 3D rectangle.
The first two arguments are integers specifying the x and y coordinates of the top-left corner of the
rectangle to be drawn, relative to the user space origin of the component – in this case the top-left
corner of the view object in the content pane. The third and fourth arguments are the width and height
of the rectangle respectively, also in user coordinates.

The drawString() method draws the string specified as the first argument at the position determined by the second and third argument – these are the *x* and *y* coordinates in user coordinates of the bottom-left corner of the first letter of the string. The string will be drawn by obtaining the glyphs for the current Font object in the device context corresponding to the characters in the string. As we said when we discussed Font objects, the glyphs for a font define the physical appearance of the characters.

However, there's more to drawing than is apparent from this example. The graphics context has information about the line style to be drawn, as well as the color, the font to be used for text, and more besides. Let's dig a little deeper into what is going on.

The Drawing Process

A Graphics2D object maintains a whole heap of information that determines how things are drawn. Most of this information is contained in six attributes within a Graphics2D object:

❑ The **paint** attribute determines the drawing color for lines. It also defines the color and pattern to be used for filling shapes. The paint attribute is set by calling the setPaint(Paint paint) method for the graphics context. Paint is an interface that is implemented by the Color class that defines a color. It is also implemented by the GradientPaint and TexturePaint classes that are a color pattern and a texture respectively. You can therefore pass references of any of these types to the setPaint() method. The default paint attribute is the color of the component.

❑ The **stroke** attribute defines a **pen** that determines the line style, such as solid, dashed or dotted lines, and the line thickness. It also determines the shape of the ends of lines. The stroke attribute is set by calling the setStroke(Stroke s) method for a graphics context. The default stroke attribute defines a square pen that draws a solid line with a thickness of 1 user coordinate unit. The ends of the line are square and joins are mitered.

❑ The **font** attribute determines the font to be used when drawing text. The font attribute is set by calling the setFont(Font font) method for the graphics context. The default font is the font set for the component.

❑ The **transform** attribute defines the transformations to be applied during the rendering process. What you draw can be translated, rotated and scaled as determined by the transforms currently in effect. There are several methods for applying transforms to what is drawn, as we will see. The default transform is the identity transform, which leaves things unchanged.

❑ The **clip** attribute defines the boundary of an area on a component. Rendering operations are restricted so that drawing only takes place within the area enclosed by the clip boundary. The clip attribute is set by calling one of the two setClip() methods for a graphics context. The default clip attribute is the whole component area.

❑ The **composite** attribute determines how overlapping shapes are drawn on a component. You can alter the transparency of the fill color of a shape so an underlying shape shows through. You set the composite attribute by calling the setComposite(Composite comp) method for the graphics context. The default composite attribute causes a new shape to be drawn over whatever is already there, taking account of the transparency of any of the colors used.

All of the objects representing attributes are stored as references within a `Graphics2D` object. Therefore, you must always call a `setXXX()` method to alter an attribute in a graphics context, not try to modify an external object directly. If you alter an object externally that has been used to set an attribute, the results are unpredictable.

You can also affect how the rendering process deals with 'jaggies' when drawing lines. The process to eliminate 'jaggies' on sloping lines is called **antialiasing***, and you can change the antialiasing that is applied by calling one of the two* `setRenderingHints()` *methods for a graphics context. We will not be going into this aspect of drawing further though.*

There's a huge amount of detail on attributes under the covers. Rather than going into all that here, we'll explore how to apply new attributes to a graphics context piecemeal where it is relevant to the various examples we will create.

Rendering Operations

The following basic methods are available to a `Graphics2D` object for rendering various kinds of entity:

Method	Description
`draw(Shape shape)`	Renders a shape using the current attributes for the graphics context. We will be discussing what a shape is next.
`fill(Shape shape)`	Fills a shape using the current attributes for the graphics context. We will see how to do this later in this chapter.
`drawString(String text)`	Renders a text string using the current attributes for the graphics context. We will be applying this further in the next chapter.
`drawImage()`	Renders an image using the current attributes for the graphics context. This is quite a complicated operation so we won't be getting very far into this.

Let's see what shapes are available. They'll help make Sketcher a lot more useful.

Shapes

Classes that define geometric shapes are contained in the `java.awt.geom` package, so to use them in a class we will need an `import` statement for this package at the beginning of the class file. You can add one to `SketchView.java` right now if you like. While the classes that define shapes are in `java.awt.geom`, the `Shape` interface is defined in `java.awt`, so you will usually need to import class names from both packages into your source file.

Any class that implements the `Shape` interface defines a shape – visually it will be some composite of straight lines and curves. Straight lines, rectangles, ellipses and curves are all shapes.

A graphic context knows how to draw Shape objects. To draw a shape on a component, you just need to pass the object defining the shape to the draw() method for the Graphics2D object for the component. To look at this in detail, we'll split the shapes into three groups, straight lines and rectangles, arcs and ellipses, and freeform curves. First though, we must take a look at how points are defined.

Classes Defining Points

There are two classes in the java.awt.geom package that define points, Point2D.Float and Point2D.Double. From the class names you can see that these are both inner classes to the class Point2D, which also happens to be an abstract base class for both too. The Point2D.Float class defines a point from a pair of (x,y) coordinates of type float, whereas the Point2D.Double class defines a point as a coordinate pair of type double. The Point class in the java.awt package also defines a point, but in terms of a coordinate pair of type int. This class also has Point2D as a base.

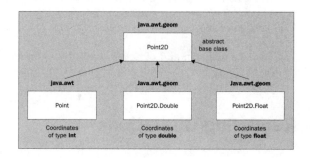

The Point class actually predates the Point2D class, but the class was redefined to make it a subclass of Point2D when Point2D was introduced, hence the somewhat unusual class hierarchy with only two of the subclasses as inner classes. The merit of this arrangement is that all of the subclasses inherit the methods defined in the Point2D class, so operations on each of the three kinds of point are the same.

The three subclasses of Point2D define a default constructor that defines the point 0,0, and a constructor that accept a pair of coordinates of the type appropriate to the class type.

The operations that each of the three concrete point classes inherit are:

1. **Accessing coordinate values:**
The getX() and getY() methods return the x and y coordinates of a point as type double, regardless of how the coordinates are stored. These are abstract methods in the Point2D class so they are defined in each of the subclasses. Although you get coordinates as double values from all three concrete classes via these methods you can always access the coordinates with their original type directly since the coordinates are stored in public fields with the same names, x and y, in each case.

2. **Calculating the distance between two points:**
You have no less that three overloaded versions of the distance() method for calculating the distance between two points, and returning it as type double:

`distance(double x1, double y1,` `         double x2, double y2)`	This is a static version of the method that calculates the distance between the points x1,y1 and x2,y2.
`distance(double xNext,` `double yNext)`	Calculates the distance from the current point (the object for which the method is called) and the point xNext,yNext.
`distance(Point2D nextPoint)`	Calculates the distance from the current point to the point, `nextPoint`. The argument can be any of the subclass types, `Point`, `Point2D.Float` or `Point2D.Double`.

Here's how you might calculate the distance between two points:

```
Point2D.Double p1 = new Point2D.Double(2.5, 3.5);
Point p2 = new Point(20, 30);
double lineLength = p1.distance(p2);
```

You could also have calculated this distance without creating the points by using the static method:

```
double lineLength = Point2D.distance(2.5, 3.5, 20, 30);
```

Corresponding to each of the three `distance()` methods there is a convenience method, `distanceSq()`, with the same parameter list that returns the square of the distance as type `double`.

3. **Comparing points:**

The `equals()` method compares the current point with the point object referenced by the argument and returns true if they are `equal` and `false` otherwise.

4. **Setting a new location for a point:**

The inherited `setLocation()` method comes in two versions. One accepts an argument that is a reference of type `Point2D`, and sets the coordinate values of the current point to those of the point passed as an argument. The other accepts two arguments of type double that are the x and y coordinates of the new location. The `Point` class also defines a version of `setLocation()` that accepts two arguments of type int to define the new coordinates.

Lines and Rectangles

The `java.awt.geom` package contains the following classes for shapes that are straight lines and rectangles:

Class	Description
Line2D	This is an abstract base class defining a line between two points. There are two concrete subclasses – `Line2D.Float` and `Line2D.Double` that define lines in terms of user coordinates of type `float` and `double` respectively. You can see from their names that the subclasses are nested classes to the abstract base class, `Line2D`.
Rectangle2D	This is the abstract base class for the `Rectangle2D.Double` and `Rectangle2D.Float` classes that define rectangles. A rectangle is defined by the coordinates of the position of its top-left corner plus its width and height. The `Rectangle2D` class is also the abstract base class for the `Rectangle` class in the `java.awt` package, which stores the position coordinates and the height and width as values of type `int`.
RoundRectangle2D	This is the abstract base class for `RoundRectangle2D.Double` and `RoundRectangle2D.Float` classes that define rectangles with rounded corners. The rounded corners are specified by a width and height.

As with the classes defining points, the `Rectangle` class that is defined in the `java.awt` package predates the `Rectangle2D` class, but the definition of the `Rectangle` class was changed to make `Rectangle2D` a base for compatibility reasons. Note that there is no equivalent to the `Rectangle` class for lines defined by integer coordinates. If you are browsing the documentation, you may notice there is a `Line` interface, but this is nothing to do with geometry.

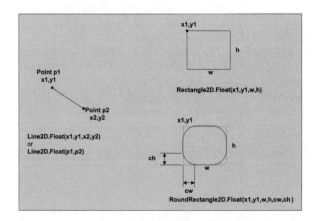

You can define a line by supplying two Point2D objects to a constructor, or two pairs of (x, y) coordinates. For example, here's how you define a line by two coordinate pairs:

```
Line2D.float line = new Line2D.Float(5.0f, 100.0f, 50.0f, 150.0f);
```

This draws a line from the point (5.0, 100.0) to the point (50.0, 150.0). You could also create the same line using Point2D.Float objects:

```
Point2D.Float p1 = new Point2D.Float(5.0f, 100.0f);
Point2D.Float p2 = new Point2D.Float(50.0f, 150.0f);
Line2D.float line = new Line2D.Float(p1, p2);
```

You draw a line using the draw() method for a Graphics2D object, for example:

```
g2D.draw(line);          // Draw the line
```

To create a rectangle, you specify the coordinates of its top-left corner, and the width and height:

```
float width = 120.0f;
float height = 90.0f;
Rectangle2D.Float rectangle = new Rectangle2D.Float(50.0f, 150.0f, width, height);
```

The default constructor creates a rectangle at the origin with a zero width and height. You can set the position, width, and height of a rectangle by calling its setRect() method. There are three versions of this method. One of them accepts arguments for the coordinates of the top-left corner and the width and height as float values, exactly as in the constructor. Another accepts the same arguments but of type double. The third accepts an argument of type Rectangle2D so you can pass either type of Rectangle2D to it.

A Rectangle2D object has getX() and getY() methods for retrieving the coordinates of the top-left corner, and getWidth() and getHeight() methods that return the width and height.

A round rectangle is a rectangle with rounded corners. The corners are defined by a width and a height and are essentially a quarter segment of an ellipse (we will get to ellipses later). Of course, if the corner width and height are equal then the corner will be a quarter of a circle.

You can define a round rectangle using coordinates of type double with the statements:

```
Point2D.Double position = new Point2D.Double(10, 10);
double width = 200.0;
double height = 100;
double cornerWidth = 15.0;
double cornerHeight = 10.0;
RoundRectangle2D.Double roundRect = new RoundRectangle2D.Double(
                      position.x, position.y,       // Position of top-left
                      width, height,                 // Rectangle width & height
                      cornerWidth, cornerHeight);    // Corner width & height
```

The only difference between this and defining an ordinary rectangle is the addition of the width and height to be applied for the corner rounding.

Combining Rectangles

You can combine two rectangles to produce a new rectangle that is either the **union** of the two original rectangles or the **intersection**. Let's take a couple of specifics to see how this works. We can create two rectangles with the statements:

```
float width = 120.0f;
float height = 90.0f;
Rectangle2D.Float rect1 = new Rectangle2D.Float(50.0f, 150.0f, width, height);
Rectangle2D.Float rect2 = new Rectangle2D.Float(80.0f, 180.0f, width, height);
```

We can obtain the intersection of the two rectangles with the statement:

```
Rectangle2D.Float rect3 = rect1.createIntersection(rect2);
```

The effect is illustrated in the diagram below by the shaded rectangle. Of course, the result is the same if we call the method for rect2 with rect1 as the argument. If the rectangles don't overlap the rectangle that is returned will be the rectangle from the bottom right of one rectangle to the top right of the other that does not overlap either.

The following statement produces the union of the two rectangles:

```
Rectangle2D.Float rect3 = rect1.createUnion(rect2);
```

The result is shown in the diagram by the rectangle with the heavy boundary that encloses the other two.

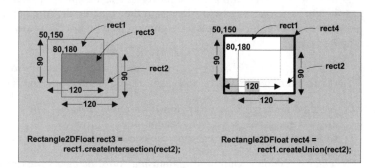

Testing Rectangles

Perhaps the simplest test you can apply is for an empty rectangle. The isEmpty() method that is implemented in all the rectangle classes returns true if the Rectangle2D object is empty – which is when either the width or the height (or both) are zero.

You can also test whether a point lies inside any type of rectangle object by calling its contains() method. There are contains() methods for all the rectangle classes that accept a Point2D argument or a pair of (x, y) coordinates of a type matching that of the rectangle class: they return true if the point lies within the rectangle. Each shape class defines a getBounds2D() method that returns a Rectangle2D object that encloses the shape.

This method is frequently used in association with the contains() method to test efficiently whether the cursor lies within a particular shape. Testing whether the cursor is within the enclosing rectangle will be a lot faster in general than testing whether it is within the precise boundary of the shape, and is good enough for many purposes – when selecting a particular shape on the screen to manipulate it in some way for instance.

There are also versions of the contains() method to test whether a given rectangle lies within the area occupied by a rectangle object – this obviously enables you to test whether a shape lies within another shape. The given rectangle can be passed to the contains() method as the coordinates of its top-left corner and its height and width as type double, or as a Rectangle2D reference. The method returns true if the rectangle object completely contains the given rectangle.

Let's try drawing a few simple lines and rectangles by inserting some code in the paint() method for the view in Sketcher.

Try It Out – Drawing Lines and Rectangles

Begin by adding an import statement to SketchView.java for the java.awt.geom package:

```
import java.awt.geom.*;
```

Now replace the previous code in the paint() method in the SketchView class with the following:

```
public void paint(Graphics g) {
  // Temporary code
  Graphics2D g2D = (Graphics2D)g;                    // Get a Java 2D device context

  g2D.setPaint(Color.RED);                           // Draw in red

  // Position width and height of first rectangle
  Point2D.Float p1 = new Point2D.Float(50.0f, 10.0f);
  float width1 = 60;
  float height1 = 80;

  // Create and draw the first rectangle
  Rectangle2D.Float rect = new Rectangle2D.Float(p1.x, p1.y, width1, height1);
  g2D.draw(rect);

  // Position width and height of second rectangle
  Point2D.Float p2 = new Point2D.Float(150.0f, 100.0f);
  float width2 = width1 + 30;
  float height2 = height1 + 40;

  // Create and draw the second rectangle
  g2D.draw(new Rectangle2D.Float(
                   (float)(p2.getX()), (float)(p2.getY()), width2, height2));
  g2D.setPaint(Color.BLUE);                          // Draw in blue

  // Draw lines to join corresponding corners of the rectangles
  Line2D.Float line = new Line2D.Float(p1,p2);
```

```
        g2D.draw(line);

        p1.setLocation(p1.x + width1, p1.y);
        p2.setLocation(p2.x + width2, p2.y);
        g2D.draw(new Line2D.Float(p1,p2));

        p1.setLocation(p1.x, p1.y + height1);
        p2.setLocation(p2.x, p2.y + height2);
        g2D.draw(new Line2D.Float(p1,p2));

        p1.setLocation(p1.x - width1, p1.y);
        p2.setLocation(p2.x - width2, p2.y);
        g2D.draw(new Line2D.Float(p1, p2));

        p1.setLocation(p1.x, p1.y - height1);
        p2.setLocation(p2.x, p2.y - height2);
        g2D.draw(new Line2D.Float(p1, p2));

        g2D.drawString("Lines and rectangles", 60, 250); // Draw some text
    }
```

If you type this in correctly and recompile SketchView class, the Sketcher window will look like:

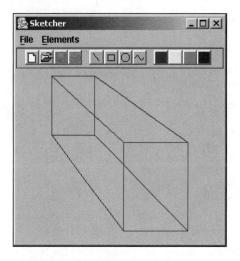

How It Works

After casting the graphics context object that is passed to the paint() method to type Graphics2D we set the drawing color to red. All subsequent drawing that we do will be in red until we change the color with another call to setPaint(). We define a Point2D.Float object to represent the position of the first rectangle, and we define variables to hold the width and height of the rectangle. We use these to create the rectangle by passing them as arguments to the constructor that we have seen before, and display the rectangle by passing the rect object to the draw() method for the graphics context, g2D. The second rectangle is defined by essentially the same process, except that this time we create the Rectangle2D.Float object in the argument expression for the draw() method.

Note that we have to cast the values returned by the `getX()` and `getY()` members of the `Point2D` object as they are returned as type `double`. It is generally more convenient to reference the `x` and `y` fields directly as we do in the rest of the code.

We change the drawing color to blue so that you can see quite clearly the lines we are drawing. We use the `setLocation()` method for the point objects to move the point on each rectangle to successive corners, and draw a line at each position. The caption also appears in blue since that is the color in effect when we call the `drawString()` method to output the text string.

Arcs and Ellipses

There are shape classes defining both arcs and ellipses. The abstract class representing a generic ellipse is:

Class	Description
Ellipse2D	This is the abstract base class for the `Ellipse2D.Double` and `Ellipse2D.Float` classes that define ellipses. An ellipse is defined by the top-left corner, width and height of the rectangle that encloses it.

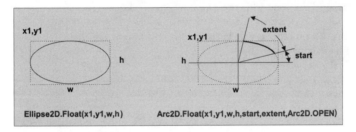

The class representing an elliptic arc is:

Class	Description
Arc2D	This is the abstract base class for the `Arc2D.Double` and `Arc2D.Float` classes that define arcs as a portion of an ellipse. The full ellipse is defined by the position of the top-left corner and the width and height of the rectangle that encloses it. The arc length is defined by a start angle measured in degrees anticlockwise relative to the horizontal axis of the full ellipse, plus an angular extent measured anti-clockwise from the start angle in degrees. An arc can be OPEN, which means the ends are not connected; CHORD, which means the ends are connected by a straight line, or PIE which means the ends are connected by straight lines to the center of the whole ellipse. These constants are defined in `Arc2D`.

Arcs and ellipses are closely related since an arc is just a segment of an ellipse. To define an ellipse you supply the data necessary to define the enclosing rectangle – the coordinates of the top-left corner, the width, and the height. To define an arc you supply the data to define the ellipse, plus additional data that defines the segment that you want. The seventh argument to the arc constructor determines the type, whether OPEN, CHORD, or PIE.

You could define an ellipse with the statements:

```
Point2D.Double position = new Point2D.Double(10,10);
double width = 200.0;
double height = 100;
Ellipse2D.Double ellipse = new Ellipse2D.Double(
                        position.x, position.y, // Top-left corner
                        width, height);         // width & height of rectangle
```

You could define an arc that is a segment of the previous ellipse with the statement:

```
Arc2D.Double arc = new Arc2D.Double(
                        position.x, position.y, // Top-left corner
                        width, height,          // width & height of rectangle
                        0.0, 90.0,              // Start and extent angles
                        Arc2D.OPEN);            // Arc is open
```

This defines the upper-right quarter segment of the whole ellipse as an open arc. The angles are measured anticlockwise from the horizontal in degrees. As we saw earlier the first angular argument is where the arc starts, and the second is the angular extent of the arc.

Of course, a circle is just an ellipse where the width and height are the same, so the following statement defines a circle with a diameter of 150:

```
double diameter = 150.0;
Ellipse2D.Double circle = new Ellipse2D.Double(
                        position.x, position.y, // Top-left corner
                        diameter, diameter);    // width & height of rectangle
```

This presumes the point `position` is defined somewhere. You will often want to define a circle by its center and radius – adjusting the arguments to the constructor a little does this easily:

```
Point2D.Double center = new Point2D.Double(200, 200);
double radius = 150;
Ellipse2D.Double newCircle = new Ellipse2D.Double(
            center.x-radius, center.y-radius,    // Top-left corner
            2*radius, 2*radius);                 // width & height of rectangle
```

The fields storing the coordinates of the top-left corner of the enclosing rectangle and the width and height are public members of `Ellipse2D` and `Arc2D` objects. They are `x`, `y`, `width` and `height` respectively. An `Arc2D` object also has public members, `start` and `extent`, that store the angles.

Try It Out – Drawing Arcs and Ellipses

Let's modify the `paint()` method in `SketchView.java` once again to draw some arcs and ellipses.

```
    public void paint(Graphics g) {
        // Temporary code
        Graphics2D g2D = (Graphics2D)g;                 // Get a Java 2D device context
```

```
Point2D.Double position = new Point2D.Double(50,10);   // Initial position
double width = 150;                                    // Width of ellipse
double height = 100;                                   // Height of ellipse
double start = 30;                                     // Start angle for arc
double extent = 120;                                   // Extent of arc
double diameter = 40;                                  // Diameter of circle

// Define open arc as an upper segment of an ellipse
Arc2D.Double top = new Arc2D.Double(position.x, position.y,
                              width, height,
                              start, extent,
                              Arc2D.OPEN);

// Define open arc as lower segment of ellipse shifted up relative to 1st
Arc2D.Double bottom = new Arc2D.Double(
                         position.x, position.y - height + diameter,
                         width, height,
                         start + 180, extent,
                         Arc2D.OPEN);

// Create a circle centered between the two arcs
Ellipse2D.Double circle1 = new Ellipse2D.Double(
                         position.x + width/2 - diameter/2,position.y,
                         diameter, diameter);

// Create a second circle concentric with the first and half the diameter
Ellipse2D.Double circle2 = new Ellipse2D.Double(
                   position.x + width/2 - diameter/4, position.y + diameter/4,
                   diameter/2, diameter/2);

// Draw all the shapes
g2D.setPaint(Color.BLACK);                         // Draw in black
g2D.draw(top);
g2D.draw(bottom);

g2D.setPaint(Color.BLUE);                          // Draw in blue
g2D.draw(circle1);
g2D.draw(circle2);
g2D.drawString("Arcs and ellipses", 80, 100);      // Draw some text
}
```

Running Sketcher with this version of the paint() method in SketchView will produce the window shown here.

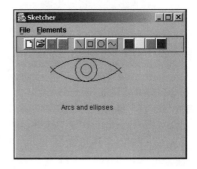

How It Works

This time we create all the shapes first and then draw them. The two arcs are segments of ellipses of the same height and width. The lower segment is shifted up with respect to the first so that they intersect, and the distance between the top of the rectangle for the first and the bottom of the rectangle for the second is `diameter`, which is the diameter of the first circle we create.

Both circles are created centered between the two arcs and are concentric. Finally we draw all the shapes – the arcs in black and the circles in blue.

Next time we change the code in Sketcher, we will be building the application as it should be, so remove the temporary code from the `paint()` method and the code that sets the background color in the `ColorAction` inner class to the `SketchFrame` class.

Curves

There are two classes that define arbitrary curves, one defining a quadratic or second order curve and the other defining a cubic curve. The cubic curve just happens to be a Bézier curve (so called because it was developed by a Frenchman, Monsieur P. Bézier, and first applied in the context of defining contours for programming numerically-controlled machine tools). The classes defining these curves are:

Class	Description
QuadCurve2D	This is the abstract base class for the `QuadCurve2D.Double` and `QuadCurve2D.Float` classes that define a quadratic curve segment. The curve is defined by its end points plus a control point that defines the tangent at each end. The tangents are the lines from the end points to the control point.
CubicCurve2D	This is the abstract base class for the `CubicCurve2D.Double` and `CubicCurve2D.Float` classes that define a cubic curve segment. The curve is defined by its end points plus two control points that define the tangent at each end. The tangents are the lines from the end points to the corresponding control point.

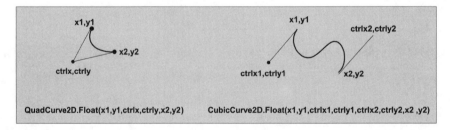

In general, there are many other methods for modeling arbitrary curves, but the two defined in Java have the merit that they are both easy to understand, and the effect on the curve segment when the control point is moved is quite intuitive.

An object of each curve type defines a curve segment between two points. The control points – one for a QuadCurve2D curve and two for a CubicCurve2D curve – control the direction and magnitude of the tangents at the end points. A QuadCurve2D curve constructor has six parameters corresponding to the coordinates of the starting point for the segment, the coordinates of the control point and the coordinates of the end point. We can define a QuadCurve2D curve from a point start to a point end, plus a control point, control, with the statements:

```
Point2D.Double startQ = new Point2D.Double(50, 150);
Point2D.Double endQ = new Point2D.Double(150, 150);
Point2D.Double control = new Point2D.Double(80,100);

QuadCurve2D.Double quadCurve
        = new QuadCurve2D.Double(startQ.x, startQ.y,      // Segment start point
                                 control.x, control.y,    // Control point
                                 endQ.x, endQ.y);         // Segment end point
```

The QuadCurve2D subclasses have public members storing the end points and the control point so you can access them directly. The coordinates of the start and end points are stored in the fields, x1, y1, x2, and y2. The coordinates of the control point are stored in ctrlx and ctrly.

Defining a cubic curve segment is very similar – you just have two control points, one for each end of the segment. The arguments are the (x, y) coordinates of the start point, the control point for the start of the segment, the control point for the end of the segment and finally the end point. We could define a cubic curve with the statements:

```
Point2D.Double startC = new Point2D.Double(50, 300);
Point2D.Double endC = new Point2D.Double(150, 300);
Point2D.Double controlStart = new Point2D.Double(80, 250);
Point2D.Double controlEnd = new Point2D.Double(160, 250);

CubicCurve2D.Double cubicCurve = new CubicCurve2D.Double(
                startC.x, startC.y,                    // Segment start point
                controlStart.x, controlStart.y,        // Control point for start
                controlEnd.x, controlEnd.y,            // Control point for end
                endC.x, endC.y);                       // Segment end point
```

The cubic curve classes also have public members for all the points: x1, y1, x2 and y2 for the end points, and ctrlx1, ctrly1, ctrlx2 and ctrly2 for the corresponding control points.

We can understand these better if we try them out. This time let's do it with an applet.

Try It Out – Drawing Curves

We can define an applet to display the curves we used as examples above:

```
import javax.swing.JApplet;
import javax.swing.JComponent;

import java.awt.Color;
import java.awt.Graphics2D;
```

```java
import java.awt.Container;
import java.awt.Graphics;

import java.awt.geom.Point2D;
import java.awt.geom.CubicCurve2D;
import java.awt.geom.QuadCurve2D;

public class CurveApplet extends JApplet {
  // Initialize the applet
  public void init() {
    pane = new CurvePane();                        // Create pane containing curves
    Container content = getContentPane();          // Get the content pane

    // Add the pane displaying the curves to the content pane for the applet
    content.add(pane);                   // BorderLayout.CENTER is default position
  }

  // Class defining a pane on which to draw
  class CurvePane extends JComponent {
    // Constructor
    public CurvePane() {
      quadCurve = new QuadCurve2D.Double(          // Create quadratic curve
                    startQ.x, startQ.y,            // Segment start point
                    control.x, control.y,          // Control point
                    endQ.x, endQ.y);               // Segment end point

      cubicCurve = new CubicCurve2D.Double(        // Create cubic curve
                    startC.x, startC.y,            // Segment start point
                    controlStart.x, controlStart.y, // Control point for start
                    controlEnd.x, controlEnd.y,    // Control point for end
                       endC.x, endC.y);            // Segment end point
    }

    public void paint(Graphics g) {
      Graphics2D g2D = (Graphics2D)g;              // Get a 2D device context

      // Draw the curves
      g2D.setPaint(Color.BLUE);
      g2D.draw(quadCurve);
      g2D.draw(cubicCurve);
    }
  }
}
// Points for quadratic curve
Point2D.Double startQ = new Point2D.Double(50, 75);     // Start point
Point2D.Double endQ = new Point2D.Double(150, 75);      // End point
Point2D.Double control = new Point2D.Double(80, 25);    // Control point

// Points for cubic curve
Point2D.Double startC = new Point2D.Double(50, 150);        // Start point
Point2D.Double endC = new Point2D.Double(150, 150);         // End point
Point2D.Double controlStart = new Point2D.Double(80, 100);  // 1st control point
Point2D.Double controlEnd = new Point2D.Double(160, 100);   // 2nd control point
```

```
    QuadCurve2D.Double quadCurve;                    // Quadratic curve
    CubicCurve2D.Double cubicCurve;                  // Cubic curve
    CurvePane pane = new CurvePane();                // Pane to contain curves
}
```

You will need an HTML file to run the applet. The contents can be something like:

```
<applet code="CurveApplet.class" width=300 height=300></applet>
```

This will display the applet in `appletviewer`. If you want to display it in your browser, you need to convert the HTML using the `HTMLConverter` program. If you don't already have it you can download it from the `http://java.sun.com` web site.

If you run the applet using `appletviewer`, you will get a window looking like that here.

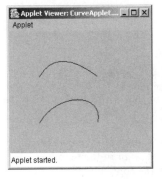

How It Works

We need an object of our own class type so that we can implement the `paint()` method for it. We define the inner class `CurvePane` for this purpose with `JComponent` as the base class so it is a Swing component. We create an object of this class (which is a member of the `CurveApplet` class) and add it to the content pane for the applet using its inherited `add()` method. The layout manager for the content pane is `BorderLayout`, and the default positioning is `BorderLayout.CENTER` so the `CurvePane` object fills the content pane.

The points defining the quadratic and cubic curves are defined as fields in the `CurveApplet` class and these are referenced in the `paint()` method for the `CurvePane` class to create the objects representing curves. These points are used in the `CurvePane` class constructor to create the curves. We draw the curves by calling the `draw()` method for the `Graphics2D` object and passing a reference to a curve object as the argument.

It's hard to see how the control points affect the shape of the curve, so let's add some code to draw the control points.

Try It Out – Displaying the Control Points

We will mark the position of each control point by drawing a small circle around it. We can define a marker using an inner class of `CurveApplet` that we can define as:

```
// Inner class defining a control point marker
class Marker {
```

```
public Marker(Point2D.Double control)  {
  center = control;                    // Save control point as circle center

  // Create circle around control point
  circle = new Ellipse2D.Double(control.x-radius, control.y-radius,
                           2.0*radius, 2.0*radius);
}

  // Draw the marker
  public void draw(Graphics2D g2D) {
    g2D.draw(circle);
  }

  // Get center of marker - the control point position
  Point2D.Double getCenter() {
    return center;
}

Ellipse2D.Double circle;             // Circle around control point
Point2D.Double center;               // Circle center - the control point
static final double radius = 3;      // Radius of circle
}
```

The argument to the constructor is the control point that is to be marked. The constructor stores this control point in the member, center, and creates an Ellipse2D.Double object that is the circle to mark the control point. The class also has a method, draw(), to draw the marker using the Graphics2D object reference that is passed to it. The getCenter() method returns the center of the marker as a Point2D.Double reference. We will use this method when we draw tangent lines from the end points of a curve to the corresponding control points.

We will add fields to the CurveApplet class to define the markers for the control points. These definitions should follow the members that defines the points:

```
// Markers for control points
Marker ctrlQuad = new Marker(control);
Marker ctrlCubic1 = new Marker(controlStart);
Marker ctrlCubic2 = new Marker(controlEnd);
```

We can now add code to the paint() method for the CurvePane class to draw the markers and the tangents from the endpoints of the curve segments:

```
public void paint(Graphics g) {
  // Code to draw curves as before...

  // Create and draw the markers showing the control points
  g2D.setPaint(Color.RED);                    // Set the color
  ctrlQuad.draw(g2D);
  ctrlCubic1.draw(g2D);
  ctrlCubic2.draw(g2D);
```

```
        // Draw tangents from the curve end points to the control marker centers
        Line2D.Double tangent = new Line2D.Double(startQ, ctrlQuad.getCenter());
        g2D.draw(tangent);
        tangent = new Line2D.Double(endQ, ctrlQuad.getCenter());
        g2D.draw(tangent);

        tangent = new Line2D.Double(startC, ctrlCubic1.getCenter());
        g2D.draw(tangent);
        tangent = new Line2D.Double(endC, ctrlCubic2.getCenter());
        g2D.draw(tangent);
    }
```

If you recompile the applet with these changes, when you execute it again you should see the window shown here.

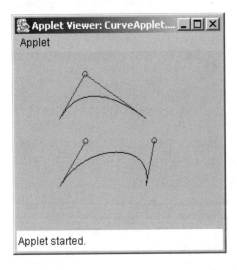

How It Works

In the `Marker` class constructor, the top-left corner of the rectangle enclosing the circle for a control point is obtained by subtracting the radius from the *x* and *y* coordinates of the control point. We then create an `Ellipse2D.Double` object with the width and height as twice the value of `radius` – which is the diameter of the circle.

In the `paint()` method we call the `draw()` method for each of the `Marker` objects to draw a red circle around each control point. The tangents are just lines from the endpoints of each curve segment to the centers of the corresponding `Marker` objects.

It would be good to see what happens to a curve segment when you move the control points around. Then we could really see how the control points affect the shape of the curve. That's not as difficult to implement as it might sound, so let's give it a try.

Try It Out – Moving the Control Points

We will arrange to allow a control point to be moved by positioning the cursor on it, pressing a mouse button and dragging it around. Releasing the mouse button will stop the process for that control point, so you will then be free to manipulate another one. To do this we will add another inner class to `CurveApplet` that will handle mouse events:

```
class MouseHandler extends MouseInputAdapter {
  public void mousePressed(MouseEvent e) {
    // Check if the cursor is inside any marker
    if(ctrlQuad.contains(e.getX(), e.getY()))
      selected = ctrlQuad;
    else if(ctrlCubic1.contains(e.getX(), e.getY()))
      selected = ctrlCubic1;
    else if(ctrlCubic2.contains(e.getX(), e.getY()))
      selected = ctrlCubic2;
  }

  public void mouseReleased(MouseEvent e) {
    selected = null;                         // Deselect any selected marker
  }

  public void mouseDragged(MouseEvent e) {
    if(selected != null) {                   // If a marker is selected
      // Set the marker to current cursor position
      selected.setLocation(e.getX(), e.getY());
      pane.repaint();                        // Redraw pane contents
    }
  }

  Marker selected = null;                    // Stores reference to selected marker
}
```

We need to add two import statements to the beginning of the source file, one because we reference the MouseInputAdapter class, and the other because we refer to the MouseEvent class:

```
import javax.swing.event.MouseInputAdapter;
import java.awt.event.MouseEvent;
```

The mousePressed() method calls a method contains() that should test whether the point defined by the arguments is inside the marker. We can implement this in the Marker class like this:

```
// Test if a point x,y is inside the marker
public boolean contains(double x, double y) {
  return circle.contains(x,y);
}
```

This just calls the contains() method for the circle object that is the marker. This will return true if the point (x, y) is inside.

The mouseDragged() method calls a method setLocation() for the selected Marker object, so we need to implement this in the Marker class, too:

```
// Sets a new control point location
public void setLocation(double x, double y) {
  center.x = x;                  // Update control point
  center.y = y;                  // coordinates
  circle.x = x-radius;           // Change circle position
}
```

```
      circle.y = y-radius;                    // correspondingly
   }
```

After updating the coordinates of the point, center, we also update the position of circle by setting its data member directly. We can do this because x and y are public members of the Ellipse2D.Double class.

We can create a MouseHandler object in the init() method for the applet and set it as the listener for mouse events for the pane object:

```
public void init() {
    pane = new CurvePane();                    // Create pane containing curves
    Container content = getContentPane();      // Get the content pane

    // Add the pane displaying the curves to the content pane for the applet
    content.add(pane);                         // BorderLayout.CENTER is default position

    MouseHandler handler = new MouseHandler();  // Create the listener
    pane.addMouseListener(handler);             // Monitor mouse button presses
    pane.addMouseMotionListener(handler);       // as well as movement
}
```

Of course, to make the effect of moving the control points apparent, we must update the curve objects before we draw them. We can add the following code to the paint() method to do this:

```
public void paint(Graphics g) {
    Graphics2D g2D = (Graphics2D)g;              // Get a 2D device context

    // Update the curves with the current control point positions
    quadCurve.ctrlx = ctrlQuad.getCenter().x;
    quadCurve.ctrly = ctrlQuad.getCenter().y;
    cubicCurve.ctrlx1 = ctrlCubic1.getCenter().x;
    cubicCurve.ctrly1 = ctrlCubic1.getCenter().y;
    cubicCurve.ctrlx2 = ctrlCubic2.getCenter().x;
    cubicCurve.ctrly2 = ctrlCubic2.getCenter().y;

    // Rest of the method as before...
```

We can update the data members that store the control point coordinates for the curves directly because they are public members of each curve class. We get the coordinates of the new positions for the control points from their markers by calling the getCenter() method for each, and then accessing the appropriate data member of the Point2D.Double object that is returned.

813

If you recompile the applet with these changes and run it again you should get something like the window here.

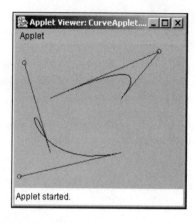

You should be able to drag the control points around with the mouse. If it is a bit difficult to select the control points, just make the value of `radius` a bit larger. Note how the angle of the tangent as well as its length affects the shape of the curve.

How It Works

In the `MouseHandler` class, the `mousePressed()` method will be called when you press a mouse button. In this method we check whether the current cursor position is within any of the markers enclosing the control points. We do this by calling the `contains()` method for each marker object and passing the coordinates of the cursor position to it. The `getX()` and `getY()` methods for the `MouseEvent` object supply the coordinates of the current cursor position. If one of the markers does enclose the cursor, we store a reference to the `Marker` object in the `selected` member of the `MouseHandler` class for use by the `mouseDragged()` method.

In the `mouseDragged()` method, we set the location for the `Marker` object referenced by `selected` to the current cursor position and call `repaint()` for the pane object. The `repaint()` method causes the `paint()` method to be called for the component, so everything will be redrawn, taking account of the modified control point position.

Releasing the mouse button will cause the `mouseReleased()` method to be called. In here we just set the `selected` field back to `null` so no `Marker` object is selected. Remarkably easy, wasn't it?

Complex Paths

You can define a more complex shape as an object of type `GeneralPath`. A `GeneralPath` object can be a composite of lines, `Quad2D` curves, and `Cubic2D` curves, or even other `GeneralPath` objects.

The process for determining whether a point is inside or outside a `GeneralPath` object is specified by the **winding rule** for the object. There are two winding rules that you can specify by constants defined in the class:

Winding Rule	Description
WIND_EVEN_ODD	In this case, a point is interior to a `GeneralPath` object if the boundary is crossed an odd number of times by a line from a point exterior to the `GeneralPath` to the point in question. You can use this winding rule for any kind of shape, including shapes with holes.
WIND_NON_ZERO	In this case, whether a point is inside or outside a path is determined by considering how the path crosses a line drawn from the point in question to infinity taking account of the direction in which the path is drawn. Looking along the line from the point, the point is interior to the `GeneralPath` object if the difference between the number of times the line is crossed by a boundary from left to right, and the number of times from right to left is non-zero. You can use this rule for general paths without holes – in other words, shapes that are bounded by a single contiguous path. This rule does not work for shapes bounded by more than one contiguous path – with holes in other words – since the result will vary depending on the direction in which each path is drawn. However, it does work for a closed re-entrant path – a path that intersects itself.

These winding rules are illustrated below:

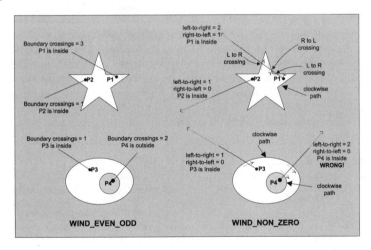

The safe option is WIND_EVEN_ODD.

There are four constructors for `GeneralPath` objects:

Constructor	Description
`GeneralPath()`	Defines a general path with a default winding rule of WIND_NON_ZERO.
`GeneralPath(int rule)`	Creates an object with the winding rule specified by the argument. This can be WIND_NON_ZERO or WIND_EVEN_ODD.
`GeneralPath(int rule, int capacity)`	Creates an object with the winding rule specified by the first argument and the number of path segments specified by the second argument. In any event, the capacity is increased when necessary.
`GeneralPath(Shape shape)`	Creates an object from the object passed as an argument.

We can create a `GeneralPath` object with the statement:

```
GeneralPath p = new GeneralPath(GeneralPath.WIND_EVEN_ODD);
```

A `GeneralPath` object embodies the notion of a current point of type `Point2D` from which the next path segment will be drawn. You set the initial current point by passing a pair of (x, y) coordinates as values of type `float` to the `moveTo()` method for the object. For example:

```
p.moveTo(10.0f,10.0f);          // Set the current point to 10,10
```

A segment is added to the general path, starting at the current point, and the end of each segment that you add becomes the new current point that is used to start the next segment. Of course, if you want disconnected segments in a path, you can call `moveTo()` to move the current point to wherever you want before you add a new segment. If you need to get the current position at any time, you can call the `getCurrentPoint()` method for a `GeneralPath` object and get the current point as type `Point2D`.

You can use the following methods to add segments to a `GeneralPath` object:

Methods to Add Segments	Description
`lineTo(float x, float y)`	Draws a line from the current point to the point (x, y).
`quadTo(float ctrlx, float ctrly, float x2, float y2)`	Draws a quadratic curve segment from the current point to the point $(x2, y2)$ with $(ctrlx, ctrly)$ as the control point.
`curveTo(float ctrlx1, float ctrly1, float ctrlx2, float ctrly2, float x2, float y2)`	Draws a Bezier curve segment from the current point with control point $(ctrlx1, ctrly1)$ to $(x2, y2)$ with $(ctrlx2, ctrly2)$ as the control point.

Each of these methods updates the current point to be the end of the segment that is added. A path can consist of several subpaths since a new subpath is started by a moveTo() call. The closePath() method closes the current subpath by connecting the current point after the last segment to the point defined by the previous moveTo() call.

Let's illustrate how this works with a simple example. We could create a triangle with the following statements:

```
GeneralPath p = new GeneralPath(GeneralPath.WIND_EVEN_ODD);
p.moveTo(50.0f, 50.0f);              // Start point for path
p.lineTo(150.0f, 50.0f);             // Line from 50,50 to 150,50
p.lineTo(150.0f, 250.0f);            // Line from 150,50 to 150,250
p.closePath();                       // Line from 150,250 back to
start
```

The first line segment starts at the current position set by the moveTo() call. Each subsequent segment begins at the endpoint of the previous segment. The closePath() call joins the latest endpoint to the point set by the previous moveTo() – which in this case is the beginning of the path. The process is much the same using quadTo() or curveTo() calls and of course you can intermix them in any sequence you like.

Once you have created a path for a GeneralPath object by calling its methods to add segments to the path, you can remove them all by calling its reset() method. This empties the path.
The GeneralPath class implements the Shape interface, so a Graphics2D object knows how to draw a path. You just pass a reference to the draw() method for the graphics context. To draw the path, p, that we defined above in the graphics context g2D, you would write:

```
g2D.draw(p);    // Draw path p
```

Let's try an example.

Try It Out – Reaching for the Stars

You won't usually want to construct a GeneralPath object as we did above. You will probably want to create a particular shape, a triangle or a star say, and then draw it at various points on a component. You might think you can do this by subclassing GeneralPath, but unfortunately GeneralPath is declared as final so subclassing is not allowed. However, you can always add a GeneralPath object as a member of your class. Let's draw some stars using our own Star class. We will use a GeneralPath object to create the star shown in the diagram.

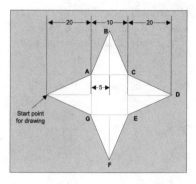

Here's the code for a class defining the star:

```
import java.awt.geom.Point2D;
import java.awt.geom.GeneralPath;
import java.awt.Shape;

class Star {
  public Star(float x, float y) {
    start = new Point2D.Float(x, y);                              // store start point
    createStar();
  }

  // Create the path from start
  void createStar() {
    Point2D.Float point = start;
    p = new GeneralPath(GeneralPath.WIND_NON_ZERO);
    p.moveTo(point.x, point.y);
    p.lineTo(point.x + 20.0f, point.y - 5.0f);                    // Line from start to A
    point = (Point2D.Float)p.getCurrentPoint();
    p.lineTo(point.x + 5.0f, point.y - 20.0f);                    // Line from A to B
    point = (Point2D.Float)p.getCurrentPoint();
    p.lineTo(point.x + 5.0f, point.y + 20.0f);                    // Line from B to C
    point = (Point2D.Float)p.getCurrentPoint();
    p.lineTo(point.x + 20.0f, point.y + 5.0f);                    // Line from C to D
    point = (Point2D.Float)p.getCurrentPoint();
    p.lineTo(point.x - 20.0f, point.y + 5.0f);                    // Line from D to E
    point = (Point2D.Float)p.getCurrentPoint();
    p.lineTo(point.x - 5.0f, point.y + 20.0f);                    // Line from E to F
    point = (Point2D.Float)p.getCurrentPoint();
    p.lineTo(point.x - 5.0f, point.y - 20.0f);                    // Line from F to g
    p.closePath();                                                // Line from G to start
  }

  Shape atLocation(float x, float y) {
    start.setLocation(x, y);                                      // Store new start
    p.reset();                                                    // Erase current path
    createStar();                                                 // create new path
    return p;                                                     // Return the path
  }
```

```
    // Make the path available
    Shape getShape() {
      return p;
    }

    private Point2D.Float start;                    // Start point for star
    private GeneralPath p;                          // Star path
}
```

We can draw stars on an applet:

```
import javax.swing.JApplet;
import javax.swing.JComponent;
import java.awt.Graphics;
import java.awt.Graphics2D;

public class StarApplet extends JApplet {
  // Initialize the applet
  public void init() {
    getContentPane().add(pane);      // BorderLayout.CENTER is default position
  }

  // Class defining a pane on which to draw
  class StarPane extends JComponent {
    public void paint(Graphics g) {
      Graphics2D g2D = (Graphics2D)g;
      Star star = new Star(0,0);                     // Create a star
      float delta = 60f;                             // Increment between stars
      float starty = 0f;                             // Starting y position

      // Draw 3 rows of 4 stars
      for(int yCount = 0; yCount < 3; yCount++) {
        starty += delta;                             // Increment row position
        float startx = 0f;                           // Start x position in a row

        // Draw a row of 4 stars
        for(int xCount = 0; xCount<4; xCount++) {
          g2D.draw(star.atLocation(startx += delta, starty));
        }
      }
    }
  }

  StarPane pane = new StarPane();                    // Pane containing stars
}
```

The HTML file for this applet could contain:

```
<applet code="StarApplet.class" width=360 height=240></applet>
```

This is large enough to accommodate our stars. If you compile and run the applet, you should see the AppletViewer window shown here.

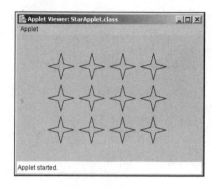

How It Works

The Star class has a GeneralPath object, p, as a member. The constructor sets the coordinates of the start point from the arguments, and calls the createStar() method that creates the path for the star. The first line is drawn relative to the start point that is set by the call to moveTo() for p. For each subsequent line, we retrieve the current position by calling getCurrentPoint() for p and drawing the line relative to that. The last line to complete the star is drawn by calling closePath().

We always need a Shape reference to draw a Star object, so we have included a getShape() method in the class that simply returns a reference to the current GeneralPath object as type Shape. The atLocation() method recreates the path at the new position specified by the arguments and returns a reference to it.

The StarApplet class draws stars on a component defined by the inner class StarPane. We draw the stars using the paint() method for the StarPane object, which is a member of the StarApplet class. Each star is drawn in the nested loop with the position specified by (x, y). The y coordinate defines the vertical position of a row, so this is incremented by delta on each iteration of the outer loop. The coordinate x is the position of a star within a row so this is incremented by delta on each iteration of the inner loop.

Filling Shapes

Once you know how to create and draw a shape, filling it is easy. You just call the fill() method for the Graphics2D object and pass a reference of type Shape to it. This works for any shape but for sensible results the boundary should be closed.

Let's try it out by modifying the applet example that displayed stars.

Try It Out – Filling Stars

To fill the stars we just need to call the fill() method for each star in the paint() method of the StarPane object. Modify the paint() method as follows:

```
public void paint(Graphics g) {
  Graphics2D g2D = (Graphics2D)g;
  Star star = new Star(0,0);                    // Create a star
```

```
   float delta = 60;                          // Increment between stars
   float starty = 0;                          // Starting y position

   // Draw 3 rows of 4 stars
   for(int yCount = 0 ; yCount<3; yCount++) {
     starty += delta;                         // Increment row position
     float startx = 0;                        // Start x position in a row

     // Draw a row of 4 stars
     for(int xCount = 0 ; xCount<4; xCount++) {
       g2D.setPaint(Color.BLUE);              // Drawing color blue
       g2D.draw(star.atLocation(startx += delta, starty));
       g2D.setPaint(Color.GREEN);             // Color for fill is green
       g2D.fill(star.getShape());             // Fill the star
     }
   }
 }
```

We also need an import statement for the `Color` class name:

```
import java.awt.Color;
```

Now the applet window will look something like that
shown here – but in color of course.

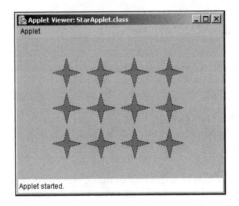

How It Works

We set the color for drawing and filling the stars separately, simply to show that we can get both. The
stars are displayed in green with a blue boundary. You can fill a shape without drawing it – just call the
`fill()` method. You could amend the example to do this by modifying the inner loop to:

```
   for(int xCount = 0 ; xCount<4; xCount++) {
     g2D.setPaint(Color.GREEN);                          // Color for fill is green
     g2D.fill(star.atLocation(startx += delta, starty)); // Fill the star
   }
```

Now all we will get is the green fill for each shape – no outline.

Gradient Fill

You are not limited to filling a shape with a uniform color. You can create a GradientPaint object that represents a graduation in shade from one color to another and pass that to the setPaint() method for the graphics context. There are four GradientPaint class constructors:

Constructor	Description
GradientPaint (Point2D p1, Color c1, Point2D p2, Color c2)	Defines a gradient from point p1 with the color c1 to the point p2 with the color c2. The color varies linearly from color c1 at point p1 to color c2 at point p2. By default the gradient is **acyclic**, which means the color variation only applies between the two points. Beyond either end of the line the color is the same as the nearest end point.
GradientPaint (float x1, float y1, Color c1, float x2, float y2, Color c2)	The same as the previous constructor but with the points specified by their coordinates.

GradientPaint
(Point2D p1, Color c1,
  Point2D p2, Color c2,
  boolean cyclic)
	With the last argument specified as false, this is identical to the first constructor. If you specify cyclic as true, the color gradation repeats cyclically off either end of the line – that is you get repetitions of the color gradient in both directions.

GradientPaint
(float x1, float y1,
  Color c1, float x2, float y2,
  Color c2, boolean cyclic)
	This is the same as the previous constructor except for the explicit point coordinates.

Points off the line defining the color gradient will have the same color as the normal (that is, right-angle) projection of the point onto the line.

This stuff is easier to demonstrate than to describe, so here's the output from the example we're about to code:

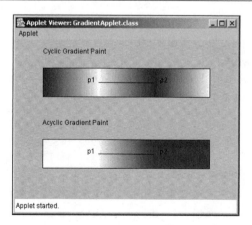

Try It Out – Color Gradients

We create an example similar to our star applet that will draw rectangles with `GradientPaint` fills. Here's the complete code:

```java
import javax.swing.JComponent;
import javax.swing.JApplet;

import java.awt.*;
import java.awt.geom.*;

public class GradientApplet extends JApplet {
  // Initialize the applet
  public void init() {
    getContentPane().add(pane);          // BorderLayout.CENTER is default position
  }

  // Class defining a pane on which to draw
  class GradientPane extends JComponent {
    public void paint(Graphics g) {
      Graphics2D g2D = (Graphics2D)g;

      Point2D.Float p1 = new Point2D.Float(150.f, 75.f);    // Gradient line start
      Point2D.Float p2 = new Point2D.Float(250.f, 75.f);    // Gradient line end
      float width = 300;
      float height = 50;
      GradientPaint g1 = new GradientPaint(p1, Color.WHITE,
                                           p2, Color.DARK_GRAY,
                                           true);            // Cyclic gradient
      Rectangle2D.Float rect1 = new Rectangle2D.Float(
                              p1.x-100, p1.y-25, width,height);
      g2D.setPaint(g1);                             // Gradient color fill
      g2D.fill(rect1);                              // Fill the rectangle
      g2D.setPaint(Color.BLACK);                    // Outline in black
      g2D.draw(rect1);                              // Fill the rectangle
      g2D.draw(new Line2D.Float(p1, p2));
      g2D.drawString("Cyclic Gradient Paint", p1.x-100, p1.y-50);
      g2D.drawString("p1", p1.x-20, p1.y);
      g2D.drawString("p2", p2.x+10, p2.y);

      p1.setLocation(150, 200);
      p2.setLocation(250, 200);
      GradientPaint g2 = new GradientPaint(p1, Color.WHITE,
                                           p2, Color.DARK_GRAY,
                                           false);           // Acyclic gradient
      rect1.setRect(p1.x-100, p1.y-25, width, height);
      g2D.setPaint(g2);                             // Gradient color fill
      g2D.fill(rect1);                              // Fill the rectangle
      g2D.setPaint(Color.BLACK);                    // Outline in black
      g2D.draw(rect1);                              // Fill the rectangle
      g2D.draw(new Line2D.Float(p1, p2));
      g2D.drawString("Acyclic Gradient Paint", p1.x-100, p1.y-50);
```

```
        g2D.drawString("p1", p1.x-20, p1.y);
        g2D.drawString("p2", p2.x+10, p2.y);
      }
    }

    GradientPane pane = new GradientPane();   // Pane containing filled rectangles
  }
```

If you run this applet with the following HTML, you should get the window shown above.

```
    <applet code="GradientApplet.class" width=400 height=280></applet>
```

Note that to get a uniform color gradation, your monitor needs to be set up for at least 16 bit (65536 colors) colors, preferably 24 bits (16.7 million colors).

How It Works

To import the individual class names that are used in this example needs nine import statements so here we just import all the class names in each of the three packages. As a rule, it is better practice to only import the class names that you use in your code, but we will use the * form to import all the names in a package when this reduces the number of import statements significantly.

The applet displays two rectangles, and they are annotated to indicate which is which. The applet also displays the gradient lines, which lie in the middle of the rectangles. You can see the cyclic and acyclic gradients quite clearly. You can also see how points off the gradient line have the same color as the normal projection onto the line.

The first block of shaded code in the paint() method creates the upper rectangle where the GradientPaint object that is used is g1. This is created as a cyclic gradient between the points p1 and p2 varying from white to dark gray. These shades have been chosen because the book is in black and white, but you can try any color combination you like. To set the color gradient for the fill, we call setPaint() for the Graphics2D object and pass g1 to it. Any shapes drawn and/or filled subsequent to this call will use the gradient color, but here we just fill the rectangle, rect1.

To make the outline and the annotation clearer, we set the current color back to black before calling the draw() method to draw the outline of the rectangle, and the drawString() method to annotate it.

The code for the lower rectangle is essentially the same as that for the first. The only important difference is that we specify the last argument to the constructor as false to get an acyclic gradient. This causes the colors of the ends of the gradient line to be the same as the end points. We could have omitted the Boolean parameter here, and got an acyclic gradient by default.

The applet shows how points off the gradient line have the same color as the normal projection onto the line. This is always the case regardless of the orientation of the gradient line. Try changing the definition of g1 for the upper rectangle to:

```
    GradientPaint g1 = new GradientPaint(p1.x, p1.y - 20, Color.WHITE,
                                         p2.x, p2.y + 20, Color.DARK_GRAY,
                                         true);              // Cyclic gradient
```

You will also need to draw the gradient line in its new orientation:

```
g2D.draw(rect1);                                             // Fill the rectangle

//g2D.draw(new Line2D.Float(p1, p2));
g2D.draw(new Line2D.Float(p1.x, p1.y - 20, p2.x, p2.y + 20));
```

The annotation for the end points will also have to be moved:

```
g2D.drawString("p1",p1.x - 20,p1.y - 20);
g2D.drawString("p2",p2.x + 10,p2.y + 20);
```

If you run the applet with these changes, you can see how the gradient is tilted, and how the colors of a point off the gradient line matches that of the point that is the orthogonal projection onto it.

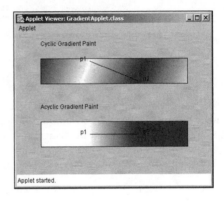

Managing Shapes

When we create shapes in Sketcher, we'll have no idea of the sequence of shape types that will occur. This is determined totally by the person using the program to produce a sketch. We'll therefore need to be able to draw shapes and perform other operations on them without knowing what they are – and polymorphism can help here.

We don't want to use the shape classes defined in java.awt.geom directly as we will want to add our own attributes such as color or line style, and store them as part of the object. We could consider using the shape classes as base classes for our shapes, but we couldn't use the GeneralPath class in this scheme of things because, as we have already seen, it's final and we might not want this restriction. We could consider defining an interface that all our shape classes would implement. However, there will be some methods that have a common implementation in all our shape classes so we would need to repeat this code in every class.

Taking all of this into account, the easiest approach might be to define a common base class for our shape classes, and include a member in each class to store a shape object of one kind or another. We'll then be able to include a polymorphic method to return a reference to a shape as type Shape for use with the draw() method of a Graphics2D object.

We can start by defining a base class, `Element`, from which we'll derive the classes defining specific types of shapes. The `Element` class will have data members that are common to all types of shapes, and we can put the methods that we want to execute polymorphically in this class too. All we need to do is make sure that each shape class that is derived from the `Element` class has its own implementation of these methods.

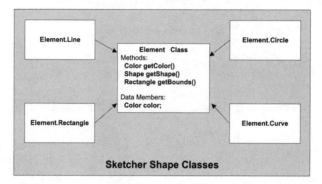

The diagram shows the initial members that we will declare in the `Element` base class. The only data member for now is the `color` member to store the color of a shape. The `getShape()` and `getBounds()` methods will be `abstract` here since the `Element` class is not intended to define a shape, but we will be able to implement the `getColor()` method in this class. The other methods will be implemented by the subclasses of `Element`.

Initially, we'll define the five classes shown in the diagram that represent shapes, with the `Element` class as a base. They provide objects that represent straight lines, rectangles, circles, freehand curves and blocks of text. These classes will all inherit the data members that we define for the `Element` class. As you can see from the names of our shape classes, they are all nested classes to the class `Element`. The `Element` class will serve as the base class, as well as house our shape classes. This will avoid any possible confusion with other classes that might have names such as `Line` or `Circle` for instance. Since there will be no `Element` objects around, we will declare our shape classes as static members of the `Element` class.

We can now define the base class, `Element`. Note that this won't be the final version, as we'll be adding more functionality in later chapters. Here's the code that needs to go in `Element.java` in the Sketcher directory:

```
import java.awt.Color;
import java.awt.Shape;

public abstract class Element {
  public Element(Color color) {
    this.color = color;
  }

  public Color getColor() {
    return color;
  }

  public abstract Shape getShape();
```

```
        public abstract java.awt.Rectangle getBounds();

        protected Color color;                           // Color of a shape
    }
```

We have defined a constructor to initialize the data member, and the `getColor()` method. The other methods are `abstract`, so they must be implemented by the subclasses.

Note that the return type for the abstract `getBounds()` method is fully qualified using the package name. This is to prevent confusion with our own `Rectangle` class that we will add later on in this chapter.

Storing Shapes in the Document

Even though we haven't defined the classes for the shapes that Sketcher will create, we can implement the mechanism for storing them in the `SketchModel` class. We'll be storing all of them as objects of type `Element`. We can use a `LinkedList` collection class object to hold an arbitrary number of `Element` objects, since a `LinkedList` can store any kind of object. It also has the advantage that deleting a shape from the list is fast.

We can add a member to the `SketchModel` class that we added earlier to the Sketcher program to store elements:

```
import java.util.Observable;
import java.util.LinkedList;

class SketchModel extends Observable {
    protected LinkedList elementList = new LinkedList();
}
```

We will want methods to add and delete `Element` objects from the linked list, and a method to return an iterator for the list, so we should add those to the class too:

```
import java.util.Observable;
import java.util.LinkedList;
import java.util.Iterator;

class SketchModel extends Observable {
    public boolean remove(Element element) {
        boolean removed = elementList.remove(element);
        if(removed) {
            setChanged();
            notifyObservers(element.getBounds());
        }

        return removed;
    }

    public void add(Element element) {
        elementList.add(element);
        setChanged();
```

```
      notifyObservers(element.getBounds());
    }

    public Iterator getIterator() {
      return elementList.listIterator();
    }

    protected LinkedList elementList = new LinkedList();
}
```

All three methods make use of methods defined in the `LinkedList` class so they are very simple. The `add()` and `remove()` functions have a parameter type of `Element` so only our shapes can be added to the linked list or removed from it. When we add or remove an element, the model is changed and therefore we call the `setChanged()` method inherited from `Observable` to record the change, and the `notifyObservers()` method to communicate this to any observers that have been registered with the model. We pass the `Rectangle` object returned by `getBounds()` for the shape to `notifyObservers()`. Each of the shape classes defined in `java.awt.geom` implements the `getBounds()` method to return the rectangle that bounds the shape. We will be able to use this in the view to specify the area that needs to be redrawn.

In the `remove()` method, it is possible that the element was not removed – because it was not there for instance – so we test the `boolean` value returned by the `remove()` method for the `LinkedList` object. We also return this value, as the caller may want to know if an element was removed or not.

Next, even though we haven't defined any of our specific shape classes, we can still make provision for displaying them in the view class.

Drawing Shapes

We will draw the shapes in the `paint()` method for the `SketchView` class, so remove the old code from the `paint()` method now. We can replace it for drawing our own shapes like this:

```
import javax.swing.JComponent;
import java.util.*;
import java.awt.*;

class SketchView extends JComponent implements Observer {
  public SketchView(Sketcher theApp) {
    this.theApp = theApp;
  }

  // Method called by Observable object when it changes
  public void update(Observable o, Object rectangle) {
    // Code to respond to changes in the model...
  }

  public void paint(Graphics g) {
    Graphics2D g2D = (Graphics2D)g;                    // Get a 2D device context
    Iterator elements = theApp.getModel().getIterator();
```

```
    Element element;                        // Stores an element

    while(elements.hasNext()) {             // Go through the list
      element = (Element)elements.next();   // Get the next element
      g2D.setPaint(element.getColor());     // Set the element color
      g2D.draw(element.getShape());         // Draw its shape
    }
  }

  // Method called by Observable object when it changes
  public void update(Observable o, Object rectangle) {
    // Code to respond to changes in the model...
  }

    private Sketcher theApp;                // The application object
  }
```

The getModel() method that we implemented in the Sketcher class returns a reference to the SketchModel object, and this is used to call the getIterator() method which will return an iterator for the list of elements. Using a standard while loop, we iterate through all the elements in the list. For each element, we obtain its color and pass that to the setPaint() method for the graphics context. We then pass the Shape reference returned by the getShape() method to the draw() method for g2D. This will draw the shape in the color passed previously to the setPaint() method. In this way we can draw all the elements stored in the model.

It's time we put in place the mechanism for creating Sketcher shapes.

Drawing Using the Mouse

We've drawn shapes so far using data internal to the program. In our Sketcher program we want to be able to draw a shape using the mouse in the view, and then store the finished shape in the model. We want the process to be as natural as possible, so we'll implement a mechanism that allows you to draw by pressing the left mouse button (more accurately, button 1) and dragging the cursor to draw the selected type of shape. So for a line, the point where you depress the mouse button will be the start point for the line, and the point where you release the button will be the end point.

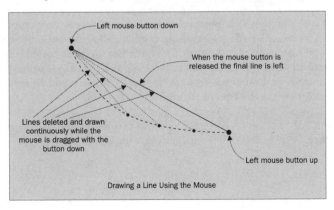

Left mouse button down

When the mouse button is released the final line is left

Lines deleted and drawn continuously while the mouse is dragged with the button down

Left mouse button up

Drawing a Line Using the Mouse

829

As you drag the mouse with the button down, we'll display the line as it looks at that point. Thus the line will be displayed dynamically all the time the mouse cursor is being dragged and the left button remains pressed. This process is called **rubber-banding**.

We can use essentially the same process of pressing the mouse button and dragging the cursor for all four of our shapes. Thus two points will define each shape – the cursor position where the mouse button is pressed, and the cursor position where the mouse button is released, (plus the color for the shape, of course). This implies that our shape constructors will all have three parameters, the two points and the color. Let's look at how we handle mouse events to make this work.

Handling Mouse Events

Because all the drawing operations for a sketch will be accomplished using the mouse, we must implement the process for creating elements within the methods that will handle the mouse events. The mouse events we're interested in will originate in the SketchView object because that's where we'll be drawing shapes. We will make the view responsible for handling all its own events, which will include events that occur in the drawing process as well as interactions with existing shapes.

Drawing a shape, such as a line, interactively will involve us in handling three different kinds of mouse event. Let's summarize what they are, and what we need to do when they occur:

Event	Action
Left Button (Button 1) pressed	Save the cursor position somewhere as the starting point for the line. We'll store this in a data member of the inner class to SketchView that we'll create to define listeners for mouse events.
Mouse dragged	Save the current cursor position somewhere as the end point for the line. Erase any previously drawn temporary line, and create a new temporary line from the starting point that was saved initially. Draw the new temporary line.
Left Button (Button 1) released	If there's a reference to a temporary line stored, add it to the sketch model, and redraw it.

You'll remember from the previous chapter that there are two mouse listener interfaces: MouseListener which has methods for handling events that occur when the mouse buttons are pressed or released and MouseMotionListener which has methods for handling events that arise when the mouse is moved. You will also recall that the MouseInputAdapter class implements both, and since we need to implement methods from both interfaces, we'll add an inner class to the SketchView class that extends the MouseInputAdapter class.

Since there's quite a lot of code involved in this, we will first define the bare bones of the class to handle mouse events, and then build in the detail until it does what we want.

Add the following class outline as an inner class to `SketchView`:

```java
import javax.swing.JComponent;
import java.util.*;                  // For Observable, Observer, Iterator
import java.awt.*;                   // For Graphics, Graphics2D, Point
import java.awt.event.MouseEvent;
import javax.swing.event.MouseInputAdapter;

class SketchView extends JComponent implements Observer {
  // Rest of the class as before

  class MouseHandler extends MouseInputAdapter {
    public void mousePressed(MouseEvent e)  {
      // Code to handle mouse button press...
    }

    public void mouseDragged(MouseEvent e) {
      // Code to handle the mouse being dragged...
    }

    public void mouseReleased(MouseEvent e) {
      // Code to handle the mouse button being release...
    }

    private Point start;                   // Stores cursor position on press
    private Point last;                    // Stores cursor position on drag
    private Element tempElement;           // Stores a temporary element
  }
}
```

We have implemented the three methods that we will need to create an element. The
`mousePressed()` method will store the position of the cursor in the `start` member of the
`MouseHandler` class, so it will be available to the `mouseDragged()` method that will be called
repeatedly when you drag the mouse cursor with the button pressed. The `mouseDragged()` method
will create an element using the current cursor position and the position saved in `start`, and store a
reference to it in the `tempElement` member of the class. The `last` member will be used to store the
cursor position when `mouseDragged()` is called. Both `start` and `last` are of type `Point` since this
is the type that we will get for the cursor position, but remember that `Point` is a subclass of `Point2D`,
so you can always cast a `Point` reference to `Point2D` when necessary. The process ends when you
release the mouse button, causing the `mouseReleased()` method to be called.

An object of type `MouseHandler` will be the listener for mouse events for the view object, so we
should put this in place in the `SketchView` constructor. Add the following code at the end of the
existing code:

```java
public SketchView(Sketcher theApp) {
  this.theApp = theApp;
  MouseHandler handler = new MouseHandler();           // create the mouse listener
  addMouseListener(handler);                           // Listen for button events
```

```
            addMouseMotionListener(handler);                      // Listen for motion events
    }
```

We call the `addMouseListener()` and `addMotionListener()` methods and pass the same listener object because our listener class deals with both. Both these methods are inherited from the `Component` class that also defines an `addMouseWheelListener()` method for when you want to handle mouse wheel events.

Let's go for the detail of the `MouseHandler` class now, starting with the `mousePressed()` method.

Handling Mouse Button Press Events

The first thing we will need to do is find out which button is pressed. It is generally a good idea to make mouse button operations specific to a particular button. That way you avoid potential confusion when you extend the code to support more functionality. This is very easy to do. The `getButton()` method for the `MouseEvent` object that is passed to a handler method returns a value of type `int` that indicates which of the three supported buttons changed state. It can return one of four constant values that are defined in the `MouseEvent` class, BUTTON1, BUTTON2, BUTTON3, or NOBUTTON, the last constant being the return value when no button has changed state in the current mouse event. On a two-button mouse or a wheel mouse, button 1 for a right-handed user is the left button and button 2 is the right button. Of course, these are reversed if you have a left-handed mouse setup. Button 3 is the middle button when there is one. We can detect when button1 is pressed by using the following code in the `mousePressed()` method:

```
public void mousePressed(MouseEvent e) {
    if(e.getButton() == MouseEvent.BUTTON1)
        // Code to handle button 1 press...
}
```

A `MouseEvent` object records the current cursor position, and you can get a `Point` reference to it by calling the `getPoint()` method. For example:

```
public void mousePressed(MouseEvent e) {
    start = e.getPoint();                       // Save the cursor position in start
    if(e.getButton() == MouseEvent.BUTTON1) {
        // Rest of the code to handle button 1 press...
    }
}
```

This saves the current cursor position in the `start` field of our `MouseHandler` object. We save it before the `if` statement as we are likely to want the current cursor position available whichever button was pressed.

As well as saving the cursor position, our implementation of `mousePressed()` must set things up to enable the `mouseDragged()` method to create an element and display it. One thing the `mouseDragged()` method needs to know is whether button 1 is down or not. The `getButton()` method won't do this in this case since it records which button changed state in the event, not which button is down, and the button state won't change as a consequence of a mouse dragged event. We can store the state of button one when the `mousePressed()` method is called, though. Then it will be available to the `mouseDragged()` method. First, we need to add a suitable field to the `MouseHandler` class:

```
        private boolean button1Down = false;          // Flag for button 1 state
```

Now we can store the state when the `mousePressed()` method executes:

```
    public void mousePressed(MouseEvent e) {
       start = e.getPoint();                     // Save the cursor position in start
       if(button1Down = (e.getButton() == MouseEvent.BUTTON1)) {
          // Rest of the code to handle button 1 press...
       }
    }
```

The `mouseDragged()` method is going to be called very frequently, and to implement rubber-banding of the element each time, the redrawing of the element needs to be very fast. We don't want to have the whole view redrawn each time, as this will carry a lot of overhead. We need a different approach.

Using XOR Mode

One way to do this is to draw in **XOR mode**. You set XOR mode by calling the `setXORMode()` method for a graphics context, and passing a color to it – usually the background color. In this mode the pixels are not written directly to the screen. The color in which you are drawing is combined with the color of the pixel currently displayed together with a third color that you specify, by exclusive ORing them together, and the resultant pixel color is written to the screen. The third color is usually set to be the background color, so the color of the pixel that is written is the result of the following operation:

```
    resultant_Color = foreground_color^background_color^current_color
```

The effect of this is to flip between the drawing color and the background color. The first time you draw a shape, the result will be in the color you are drawing with, except for overlaps with other shapes, since they won't be in the background color. When you draw the same shape a second time the result will be the background color so the shape will disappear. Drawing a third time will make it reappear. We saw how this works back in Chapter 2 when we were discussing the bitwise exclusive OR operation.

Based on what we have said, we can implement the `mousePressed()` method for the `MouseHander` class like this:

```
    public void mousePressed(MouseEvent e) {
      start = e.getPoint();                      // Save the cursor position in start
      if(button1Down = (e.getButton() == MouseEvent.BUTTON1)) {
        g2D = (Graphics2D)getGraphics();                    // Get graphics context
        g2D.setXORMode(getBackground());                    // Set XOR mode
        g2D.setPaint(theApp.getWindow().getElementColor());  // Set color
      }
    }
```

If button 1 was pressed, we obtain a graphics context for the view, so we must add another member to the `MouseHandler` class to store this:

```
        private Graphics2D g2D = null;                    // Temporary graphics context
```

We use the object, g2D, to set XOR mode, as we will use this mode in the mouseDragged() method to erase a previously drawn shape without reconstructing the whole sketch. The last thing that is done here is to retrieve the current drawing color that is recorded in the SketchFrame object. You will remember that this is set when you select a menu item or a toolbar button. We use theApp object stored in the view to get the SketchFrame object, and then call its getElementColor() member to retrieve the color. This method doesn't exist in SketchFrame, but it's not difficult. Add the following method to the SketchFrame class definition:

```
public Color getElementColor() {
  return elementColor;
}
```

With the button press code in place, we can have a go at implementing mouseDragged().

Handling Mouse Dragging Events

We can obtain the cursor position in the mouseDragged() method in the same way as for the mousePressed()method, which is by calling getPoint() for the event object, so we could write:

```
last = e.getPoint();                    // Get cursor position
```

But then we only want to handle drag events for button 1, so we will make this conditional upon the button1Down field having the value true. When mouseDragged() is called for the first time, we won't have created an element, so we can just create one from the points stored in start and last, and then draw it using the graphics context saved by the mousePressed() method. The mouseDragged() method will be called lots of times while you drag the mouse though, and for every occasion other than the first, we must take care to redraw the old element before creating the new one. Since we are in XOR mode, drawing the element a second time will draw it in the background color, so it will disappear. Here's how we can do all that:

```
public void mouseDragged(MouseEvent e) {
  last = e.getPoint();                          // Save cursor position

  if(button1Down) {
    if(tempElement == null) {                   // Is there an element?
      tempElement = createElement(start, last); // No, so create one
    } else {
      g2D.draw(tempElement.getShape());         // Yes - draw to erase it
      tempElement.modify(start, last);          // Now modify it
    }
    g2D.draw(tempElement.getShape());           // and draw it
  }
}
```

If button 1 is pressed, button1Down will be true so we are interested. We first check for an existing element by comparing the reference in tempElement with null. If there isn't one we create an element of the current type by calling a method, createElement(), that we will add to the SketchView class in a moment. We save a reference to the element that is created in the tempElement member of the listener object.

If `tempElement` is not `null` then an element already exists so we modify the existing element to incorporate the latest cursor position by calling a method `modify()` for the element object. We will need to add an implementation of this method for each element type. Finally we draw the latest version of the element referenced by `tempElement`. Since we expect to call the `modify()` method for an element polymorphically, we should add it to the base class, `Element`. It will be abstract in the `Element` class so add the following declaration to the class definition:

```
public abstract void modify(Point start, Point last);
```

Since we reference the `Point` class here we need an `import` statement for it in the `Element.java` file:

```
import java.awt.Point;
```

We can implement `createElement()` as a `private` member of the `MouseHandler` class, since it's not needed anywhere else. The parameters for the method are just two points that will be used to define each element. Here's the code:

```
private Element createElement(Point start, Point end) {
  switch(theApp.getWindow().getElementType()) {
    case LINE:
      return new Element.Line(start, end,
                           theApp.getWindow().getElementColor());
    case RECTANGLE:
      return new Element.Rectangle(start, end,
                               theApp.getWindow().getElementColor());

    case CIRCLE:
      return new Element.Circle(start, end,
                             theApp.getWindow().getElementColor());
    case CURVE:
    return new Element.Curve(start, end,
                          theApp.getWindow().getElementColor());
    default:
      assert false;                       // We should never get to here
  }
  return null;
}
```

Since we refer to the constants identifying element types here, we must make the `SketchView` class implement the `Constants` interface, so modify the class to do that now. The first line of the definition will be:

```
class SketchView extends JComponent
               implements Observer, Constants
```

The `createElement()` method returns a reference to a shape as type `Element`. We determine the type of shape to create by retrieving the element type ID stored in the `SketchFrame` class by the menu item listeners that we put together in the previous chapter. The `getElementType()` method isn't there in the `SketchFrame` class yet, but you can add it now as:

```
public int getElementType() {
  return elementType;
}
```

The switch statement in createElement() selects the constructor to be called, and as you see, they are all essentially of the same form. If we fall through the switch with an ID that we haven't provided for, we return null. Of course, none of these shape class constructors exists in Sketcher yet. So if you want to try compiling the code we have so far, you will need to comment out each of the return statements. The constructor calls imply that all our shape classes are inner classes to the Element class. We will see how to implement these very soon. But first, let's add the next piece of mouse event handling we need – handling button release events.

Handling Button Release Events

When the mouse button is released, we will have created an element. In this case all we need to do is to add the element referred to by the tempElement member of the MouseHandler class to the SketchModel object that represents the sketch. One thing we need to consider though. Someone might click the mouse button without dragging it. In this case there won't be an element to store, so we just clean up the data members of the MouseHandler object.

```
public void mouseReleased(MouseEvent e) {
  if(button1Down = (e.getButton()==MouseEvent.BUTTON1)) {
    button1Down = false;                    // Reset the button 1 flag
    if(tempElement != null) {
      theApp.getModel().add(tempElement);   // Add element to the model
      tempElement = null;                   // No temporary now stored
    }
    if(g2D != null) {                       // If there's a graphics context
      g2D.dispose();                        // ...release the resource
      g2D = null;                           // Set field to null
    }
    start = last = null;                    // Remove the points
  }
}
```

When the button1 is released it will change state so we can use the getButton() method here. Of course, once button 1 is released we need to reset our flag, button1Down. If there is a reference stored in tempElement we add it to the model by calling the add() method that we defined for it and set tempElement back to null. It is important to set tempElement back to null here. Failing to do that would result in the old element reference being added to the model when you click the mouse button.

When we add the new element to the model, the view will be notified as an observer, so the update() method in the view will be called. We can implement the update() method in the SketchView class like this:

```
public void update(Observable o, Object rectangle) {
  if(rectangle == null)
    repaint();
  else
```

```
    repaint((Rectangle)rectangle);
  }
```

If `rectangle` is not `null`, then we have a reference to a `Rectangle` object that was provided by the `notifyObservers()` method call in the `add()` method for the `SketchModel` object. This rectangle is the area occupied by the new element, so we pass this to the `repaint()` method for the view to add just this area to the area to be redrawn on the next call of the `paint()` method. If `rectangle` is `null`, we call the version of `repaint()` that has no parameter to redraw the whole view.

Another important operation here is calling the `dispose()` method for the g2D object. Every graphics context makes use of finite system resources. If you use a lot of graphics context objects and you don't release the resources they use, your program will consume more and more resources. Under Windows for instance you may eventually run out, your computer will stop working, and you'll have to reboot. When you call `dispose()` for a graphics context object it can merely no longer be used, so we set g2D back to `null` to be on the safe side.

> A reminder about a potential error in using adapter classes – be sure to spell the method names correctly. If you don't, your method won't get called, but the base class member will. The base class method does nothing so your code won't work as you expect. There will be no warning or error messages about this because your code will be perfectly legal – though quite wrong. You will simply have added an additional and quite useless method to those defined in the adapter class.

We have implemented all three methods that we need to draw shapes. We could try it out if only we had a shape to draw.

Defining Our Own Shape Classes

All the classes that define shapes in Sketcher will be static nested classes of the `Element` class. As we have already said, as well as being a convenient way to keep our shape class definitions together, this will also avoid possible conflict with classes such as the `Rectangle` class in the Java class library.

We can start with the simplest – a class representing a line.

Defining Lines

A line will be defined by two points and its color. We can define the `Line` class as a nested class in the base class `Element`, as follows:

```
import java.awt.Color;
import java.awt.Shape;
import java.awt.Point;
import java.awt.geom.*;                        // For classes defining shapes

public abstract class Element {
  // Code defining the base class...
```

```
     // Nested class defining a line
     public static class Line extends Element {
       public Line(Point start, Point end, Color color) {
         super(color);
         line = new Line2D.Double(start, end);
       }

       public Shape getShape() {
         return line;
       }

       public java.awt.Rectangle getBounds() {
         return line.getBounds();
       }

       public void modify(Point start, Point last) {
         line.x2 = last.x;
         line.y2 = last.y;
       }

       private Line2D.Double line;
     }
   }
```

We have to specify the Line class as static to avoid a dependency on an Element object being available. The Element class is abstract so there's no possibility of creating objects of this type. The constructor has three parameters, the two end points of the line as type Point and the color. Point arguments to the constructor can be of type Point2D or type Point as Point2D is a superclass of Point. After passing the color to the base class constructor, we create the line as a Line2D.Double object. Since this implements the Shape interface, we can return it as type Shape from the getShape() method.

The getBounds() method couldn't be simpler. We just return the Rectangle object produced by the getBounds() method for the object, line. However, note how we have fully qualified the return type. This is because we will be adding a Rectangle class as a nested class to the Element class. When we do, the compiler will interpret the type Rectangle here as our rectangle class, and not the one defined in the java.awt package. You can always use a fully qualified class name when conflicts like this arise.

Try It Out – Drawing Lines

If you have saved the Element class definition as Element.java in the same directory as the rest of the Sketcher classes, all you need to do is make sure all the constructor calls other than Element.Line are commented out in the createElement() member of the MouseHandler class, that is an inner class to SketchView. The code for the method should look like this:

```
       private Element createElement(Point start, Point end) {
         switch(theApp.getWindow().getElementType()) {
           case LINE:
             return new Element.Line(start, end,
                                 theApp.getWindow().getElementColor());
```

```
               case RECTANGLE:
//                   return new Element.Rectangle(start, end,
//                                      theApp.getWindow().getElementColor());

               case CIRCLE:
//                   return new Element.Circle(start, end,
//                                      theApp.getWindow().getElementColor());

               case CURVE:
//                   return new Element.Curve(start, end,
//                                      theApp.getWindow().getElementColor());
               default:
                   assert false;                        // We should never get to here
           }
           return null;
       }
```

If you compile and run Sketcher you should be able to draw a figure like that shown below.

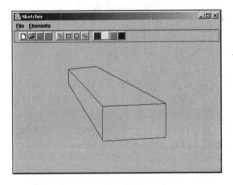

You can only draw lines at this point though. Trying to draw anything else will result in an assertion because we will fall through the cases in the createElement() method until we hit the default case.

How It Works

As you drag the mouse Element.Line objects are being repeatedly created and drawn to produce the rubber banding effect. Each line is from the point where you pressed the mouse button to the current cursor position. Try drawing different colors. It should all work. If it doesn't, maybe you forgot to remove the getContentPane().setBackground(color) call that we put temporarily in ColorActions actionPerformed() method in SketchFrame.

If you are typing in the code as you go (and I hope that you are!), you may have made a few mistakes, as there's been such a lot of code added to Sketcher. In this case don't look back at the code in the book first to find out why. Before you do that, try using the Java debugger that comes with the JDK, or even just instrumenting the methods that might be the problem with println() calls of your own so you can trace what's going on. It's good practice for when you are writing your own code.

Defining Rectangles

The interactive mechanism for drawing a rectangle is similar to that for a line. When you are drawing a rectangle, the point where the mouse is pressed will define one corner of the rectangle, and as you drag the mouse the cursor position will define an opposite corner, as illustrated below.

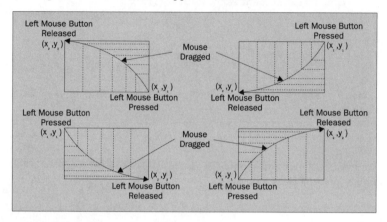

Releasing the mouse button will establish the final rectangle shape to be stored in the model. As you can see, the cursor position when you press the mouse button can be any corner of the rectangle. This is fine from a usability standpoint, but our code needs to take account of the fact that a `Rectangle2D` object is always defined by the top-left corner, plus a width and a height.

The diagram shows the four possible orientations of the mouse path as it is dragged in relation to the rectangle drawn. The top-left corner will have coordinates that are the minimum x and the minimum y from the points at the ends of the diagonal. The width will be the absolute value of the difference between the x coordinates for the two ends, and the height will be the absolute value of the difference between the y coordinates. From that we can define our class.

Try It Out – The Element.Rectangle Class

Here's the definition of the class for a rectangle object:

```
class Element {
  // Code for the base class definition...

  // Nested class defining a line...
```

```
  // Nested class defining a rectangle
  public static class Rectangle extends Element {
    public Rectangle(Point start, Point end, Color color) {
      super(color);
      rectangle = new Rectangle2D.Double(
        Math.min(start.x, end.x), Math.min(start.y, end.y),    // Top-left corner
        Math.abs(start.x - end.x), Math.abs(start.y - end.y)); // Width & height
    }
```

```
      public Shape getShape() {
        return rectangle;
      }
      public java.awt.Rectangle getBounds() {
        return rectangle.getBounds();
      }

      public void modify(Point start, Point last) {
        rectangle.x = Math.min(start.x, last.x);
        rectangle.y = Math.min(start.y, last.y);
        rectangle.width = Math.abs(start.x - last.x);
        rectangle.height = Math.abs(start.y - last.y);
      }

      private Rectangle2D.Double rectangle;
    }
}
```

If you uncomment the line in the `createElement()` method that creates rectangles and recompile, you will be ready to draw rectangles as well as lines.

You only need to recompile `Element.java` and `SketchView.java`. The rest of Sketcher is still the same. If you run it again, you should be able to draw rectangles and lines – in various colors, too.

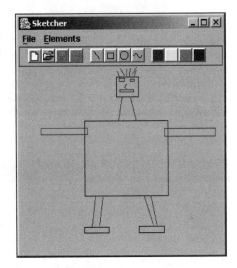

How It Works

The code works in essentially the same way as for lines. You can drag the mouse in any direction to create a rectangle. The constructor sorts out the correct coordinates for the top-left corner. This is because the rectangle is being defined from its diagonal, so the rectangle is always defined from the point where the mouse button was pressed to the current cursor position. Because its top left corner always defines the position of a `Rectangle2D` object, we can no longer tell from this object which diagonal was used to define it.

Defining Circles

The most natural mechanism for drawing a circle is to make the point where the mouse button is pressed the center, and the point where the mouse button is released the end of the radius – that is, on the circumference. We'll need to do a little calculation for this.

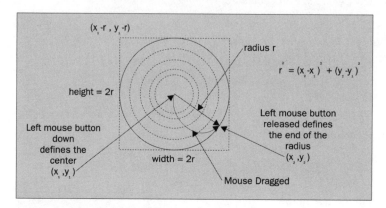

The diagram illustrates the drawing mechanism. Circles will be drawn dynamically as the mouse is dragged, with the cursor position being on the circumference of the circle. Pythagoras' theorem, as shown in the diagram, provides the formula that you might use to calculate the radius from the point at the center and the point on the circumference. However, Java makes this easy. Remember the distance() method defined in Point2D class? That does exactly what is shown here so we will be able to use that to obtain the radius directly. When we have that we can then calculate the top-left point by subtracting the radius from the coordinates of the center. We will create a circle shape as a particular case of an Ellipse2D object and so the height and width of the enclosing rectangle will be just twice the radius.

Try It Out – Adding Circles

Here's how this is applied in the definition of the Element.Circle class:

```
class Element {
  // Code defining the base class...

  // Nested class defining a line...

  // Nested class defining a rectangle...

  // Nested class defining a circle
  public static class Circle extends Element {
    public Circle(Point center, Point circum, Color color) {
      super(color);

      // Radius is distance from center to circumference
      double radius = center.distance(circum);
      circle = new Ellipse2D.Double(center.x - radius, center.y - radius,
                                    2.*radius, 2.*radius );
    }
```

```
        public Shape getShape() {
          return circle;
        }

        public java.awt.Rectangle getBounds() {
          return circle.getBounds();
        }

        public void modify(Point center, Point circum) {
          double radius = center.distance(circum);
          circle.x = center.x - (int)radius;
          circle.y = center.y - (int)radius;
          circle.width = circle.height = 2*radius;
        }

        private Ellipse2D.Double circle;
      }
    }
```

If we amend the createElement() method in the MouseHandler class by uncommenting the line that creates Element.Circle objects, we will be ready to draw circles. You are now equipped to produce artwork such as that shown here.

How It Works

The circle is generated with the button down point as the center and the cursor position while dragging is on the circumference. The distance() method defined in the Point2D class is used to calculate the radius, and then this value is used to calculate the coordinates of the top-left corner of the enclosing rectangle. The circle is stored as an Ellipse2D.Double object with a width and height as twice the radius.

Drawing Curves

Curves are a bit trickier to deal with than the other shapes. We want to be able to create a freehand curve by dragging the mouse, so that as the cursor moves the curve extends. This will need to be reflected in how we define the Element.Curve class. Let's first consider how the process of drawing a curve is going to work, and define the Element.Curve class based on that.

The `QuadCurve2D` and `CubicCurve2D` classes don't really suit our purpose here. A curve is going to be represented by a series of connected line segments, but we don't know ahead of time how many there are going to be – as long as the mouse is being dragged we'll collect more points. This gives us a hint as to the approach we could adopt for creating a curve.

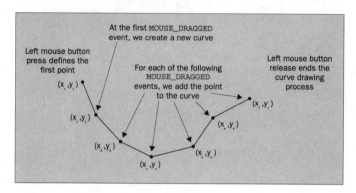

This looks like a job for a `GeneralPath` object. It can handle any number of segments and we can add to it. If we construct an initial curve as soon as we have two points – which is when we receive the first MOUSE_DRAGGED event – we can extend the curve by calling the `modify()` method to add another segment for each of the subsequent MOUSE_DRAGGED events.

Try It Out – The Element.Curve Class

This means that the outline of the `Curve` class is going to be:

```
class Element {
  // Code defining the base class...

  // Nested class defining a line...

  // Nested class defining a rectangle...

  // Nested class defining a circle...

  // Nested class defining a curve
  public static class Curve extends Element {
    public Curve(Point start, Point next, Color color) {
      super(color);
      curve = new GeneralPath();
      curve.moveTo(start.x, start.y);

      curve.lineTo(next.x, next.y);
    }

    // Add another segment
    public void modify(Point start, Point next) {
      curve.lineTo(next.x,
                   next.y);
```

```
      }

      public Shape getShape()  {
        return curve;
      }

      public java.awt.Rectangle getBounds() {
        return curve.getBounds();
      }

      private GeneralPath curve;
    }
  }
```

The Curve class constructor creates a GeneralPath object and adds a single line segment to it by moving the current point to start by calling moveTo(), and then calling its lineTo() method with next as the argument. Additional segments are added by the modify() method. This calls lineTo() for the GeneralPath member of the class with the new point as the argument. This will add a line from the end of the last segment that was added to the new point.

Try It Out – Drawing Curves

Of course, we need to uncomment the line creating an Element.Curve object in the createElement() method. Then we are ready to roll again. If we recompile Sketcher we will be able to give freehand curves a whirl, and produce elegant sketches such as that here.

How It Works

Drawing curves works in essentially the same way as drawing the other elements. The use of XOR mode is superfluous with drawing a curve since we only extend it, but it would be quite a bit of work to treat it as a special case. This would only be justified if drawing curves was too slow and produced excessive flicker.

You may be wondering if you can change from XOR mode back to the normal mode of drawing in a graphics context. Certainly you can: just call the setPaintMode() method for the graphics context object to get back to the normal drawing mode.

There's some fabricated text in the last screenshot. In the next chapter we'll add a rather more sophisticated facility for adding text to a sketch. Don't draw too many masterpieces yet. We won't be able to preserve them for the nation and posterity by saving them in a file until the chapter after the next.

Summary

In this chapter you have learned how to draw on components and how you can use mouse listeners to implement a drawing interface. The important points we have covered in this chapter are:

❑   A `Graphics2D` component represents the drawing surface of the component.

❑   You draw on a component by calling methods for its `Graphics2D` object.

❑   The user coordinate system for drawing on a component has the origin in the top-left corner of the component by default with the positive x-axis from left to right, and the positive y-axis from top to bottom. This is automatically mapped to the device coordinate system, which is in the same orientation.

❑   You normally draw on a component by implementing its `paint()` method. The `paint()` method is passed a `Graphics2D` object that is the graphics context for the component but as type `Graphics`. You must cast the `Graphics` object to type `Graphics2D` to be able to access the `Graphics2D` class methods. The `paint()` method is called whenever the component needs to be redrawn.

❑   You can't create a `Graphics2D` object. If you want to draw on a component outside of the `paint()` method, you can obtain a `Graphics2D` object for the component by calling its `getGraphics()` method.

❑   There is more than one drawing mode that you can use. The default mode is **paint mode**, where drawing overwrites the background pixels with pixels of the current color. Another mode is **XOR mode** where the current color is combined with the background color. This is typically used to alternate between the current color and a color passed to the `setXORMode()` method.

❑   The `Graphics2D` class defines methods for drawing outline shapes as well as filled shapes.

❑   The `java.awt.geom` package defines classes that represent 2D shapes.

Exercises

1.   Add the code to the Sketcher program to support drawing an ellipse.

2.   Modify the Sketcher program to include a button for switching fill mode on and off.

3.   Extend the classes defining rectangles, circles and ellipses to support filled shapes.

4.   Extend the curve class to support filled shapes.

5. (Harder – for curve enthusiasts!) Implement an applet to display a curve as multiple CubicCurve2D objects from points on the curve entered by clicking the mouse. The applet should have two buttons – one to clear the window and allow points on the curve to be entered, and the other to display the curve. Devise your own scheme for default control points.

6. (Also harder!) Modify the previous example to ensure that the curve is continuous – this implies that the control points either side of an interior point, and the interior point itself, should be on a straight line. Allow control points to be dragged with the mouse, but still maintaining the continuity of the curve.

Extending the GUI

In this chapter we will investigate how we can improve the GUI for Sketcher. After adding a status bar, we will investigate how to create dialogs, and how we can use them to communicate with the user and to manage input. Another GUI capability we will be exploring is pop-up menus, and we will be using these to enhance the Sketcher application. All of this will give you a lot more practice in implementing event listeners and more besides.

In this chapter you will learn:

❏   How to create a status bar

❏   How to create a dialog

❏   What a modal dialog is and how it differs from a non-modal dialog

❏   How to create a message box dialog

❏   How you can use components in a dialog to receive input

❏   What a pop-up menu is

❏   What context menus are and how you can implement them

Creating a Status Bar

One limitation of the Sketcher program as it stands is that you have no direct feedback on what current element type and color have been selected. As a gentle start to this chapter, let's fix that now. A window status bar is a common and very convenient way of displaying the status of various application parameters, each in its own pane.

We can make up our own class, StatusBar for instance, that will define a status bar. Ideally we would design a class for a generic status bar and customize it for Sketcher, but we will take the simple approach of designing a class that is specific to Sketcher. The JPanel class would be a good base for our StatusBar class since it represents a panel, and we can add objects representing status bar panes to it. We can use the JLabel class as a base for defining status bar panes and add sunken borders to them for a distinct appearance.

Let's start with a status bar at the bottom of Sketcher with two panes to show the current element type and color. Then we will know exactly what we are about to draw. We can start by defining the StatusBar class that will represent the status bar in the application window, and we'll define the StatusPane class as an inner class to StatusBar.

Try It Out – Defining a Status Bar Class

Here's an initial stab at the definition for the StatusBar class:

```
// Class defining a status bar
import javax.swing.*;
import javax.swing.border.BevelBorder;
import java.awt.*;

class StatusBar extends JPanel implements Constants {
  // Constructor
  public StatusBar() {
    setLayout(new FlowLayout(FlowLayout.LEFT, 10, 3));
    setBackground(Color.LIGHT_GRAY);
    setBorder(BorderFactory.createLineBorder(Color.DARK_GRAY));
    setColorPane(DEFAULT_ELEMENT_COLOR);
    setTypePane(DEFAULT_ELEMENT_TYPE);
    add(colorPane);                        // Add color pane to status bar
    add(typePane);                         // Add type pane to status bar
  }

  // Set color pane label
  public void setColorPane(Color color) {
  // Code to set the color pane text...
  }

  // Set type pane label
  public void setTypePane (int elementType) {
  // Code to set the type pane text....
  }

  // Panes in the status bar
  private StatusPane colorPane = new StatusPane("BLUE");
  private StatusPane typePane = new StatusPane("LINE");

  // Class defining a status bar pane
  class StatusPane extends Jlabel {
    public StatusPane(String text) {
      setBackground(Color.LIGHT_GRAY);          // Set background color
      setForeground(Color.BLACK);
```

```
      setFont(paneFont);                    // Set the fixed font
      setHorizontalAlignment(CENTER);       // Center the pane text
      setBorder(BorderFactory.createBevelBorder(BevelBorder.LOWERED));
      setPreferredSize(new Dimension(100,20));
      setText(text);                        // Set the text in the pane
    }

    // Font for pane text
    private Font paneFont = new Font("Serif", Font.PLAIN, 10);
  }
}
```

How It Works

Since the `StatusBar` class implements our `Constants` interface, all the variables that represent possible element types and colors are available. This outline version of `StatusBar` has two data members of type `StatusPane`, which will be the panes showing the current color and element type. The initial information to be displayed by a `StatusPane` object is passed to the constructor as a `String` object.

In the `StatusBar` constructor, we update the information to be displayed in each pane by calling the `setColorPane()` and `setTypePane()` methods. These ensure that initially the `StatusPane` objects display the default color and type that we've defined for the application. One or other of these methods will be called whenever it is necessary to update the status bar. We'll complete the definitions for `setColorPane()` and `setTypePane()` when we've been through the detail of the `StatusPane` class.

The `StatusBar` panel has a `FlowLayout` manager that is set in the constructor. The panes in the status bar need only display a small amount of text, so we've derived the `StatusPane` class from the `JLabel` class – so a pane for the status bar will be a specialized kind of `JLabel`. This means that we can call the `setText()` method that is inherited from `JLabel` to set the text for our `StatusPane` objects. The `StatusPane` objects will be left-justified when they are added to the status bar, as a result of the first argument to the `setLayout()` method call in the `StatusBar` constructor. The layout manager will leave a ten-pixel horizontal gap between successive panes in the status bar, and a three-pixel vertical gap between rows of components. The border for the status bar is a single dark gray line that we add using the `BorderFactory` method.

The only data member in the `StatusPane` class is the `Font` object, `font`. We've defined the font to be used for pane text as a standard 10-point Serif. In the constructor we set the background color to light gray, the foreground color to dark gray, and we set the standard font. We also set the alignment of the text as centered by calling the inherited method `setHorizontalAlignment()`, and passing the value `CENTER` to it – this is defined in the base class, `JLabel`.

If we can maintain a fixed width for each pane, it will prevent the size of the pane jumping around when we change the text. So we've set the `setPreferredSize()` at the minimum necessary for accommodating our longest text field. Lastly, in the `StatusPane` constructor we set the text for the pane by calling the inherited `setText()` method.

Try It Out – Updating the Panes

We can code the `setColorPane()` method as:

```java
// Set color pane label
public void setColorPane(Color color) {
  String text = null;                          // Text for the color pane
  if(color.equals(Color.RED))
    text = "RED";

  else if(color.equals(Color.YELLOW))
    text = "YELLOW";
  else if(color.equals(Color.GREEN))
    text = "GREEN";
  else if(color.equals(Color.BLUE))
    text = "BLUE";
  else
    text = "CUSTOM COLOR";
  colorPane.setForeground(color);
  colorPane.setText(text);                     // Set the pane text
}
```

In the code for the `setTypePane()` method we can use `switch` rather than `if` statements to test the parameter value because it is of type `int`:

```java
// Set type pane label
public void setTypePane(int elementType) {
  String text = null;                          // Text for the type pane
  switch(elementType) {
    case LINE:
      text = "LINE";
      break;
    case RECTANGLE:
      text = "RECTANGLE";
      break;
    case CIRCLE:
      text = "CIRCLE";
      break;
    case CURVE:
      text = "CURVE";
      break;
    default:
      assert false;
  }
  typePane.setText(text);                       // Set the pane text
}
```

How It Works

This code is quite simple. The text to be displayed in the color pane is selected in the series of `if-else` statements. They each compare the color passed as an argument with the standard colors we use in Sketcher and set the `text` variable accordingly. The last `else` should never be reached at the moment, but it will be obvious if it is. This provides the possibility of adding more flexibility in the drawing color later on. Note that we also set the foreground color to the currently selected element color, so the text will be drawn in the color to which it refers.

The type pane uses a `switch` as it is more convenient but the basic process is the same as for the color pane. If something goes wrong somewhere that results in an invalid element type, the program will assert through the default case.

All we need now is to implement the status bar in the `SketchFrame` class. For this we must add a data member to the class that defines the status bar, add the status bar to the content pane of the window in the class constructor, and extend the `actionPerformed()` methods in the `TypeAction` and `ColorAction` classes to update the status bar when the element type or color is altered.

Try It Out – The Status Bar in Action

You can add the following statement to the `SketchFrame` class to define the status bar as a data member, following the members defining the menu bar and toolbar:

```
private StatusBar statusBar = new StatusBar();     // Window status bar
```

We create `statusBar` as a data member so that it can be accessed throughout the class definition, including from within the `Action` classes. You need to add one statement to the end of the `SketchFrame` class constructor:

```
public SketchFrame(String title, Sketcher theApp) {
  // Constructor code as before...
    getContentPane().add(statusBar, BorderLayout.SOUTH);       // Add the statusbar
  }
```

This adds the status bar to the bottom of the application window. To update the status bar when the element type changes, you can add one statement to the `actionPerformed()` method in the inner class, `TypeAction`:

```
public void actionPerformed(ActionEvent e) {
  elementType = typeID;
  statusBar.setTypePane(typeID);
  }
```

The type pane is updated by calling the `setTypePane()` method for the status bar and passing the current element type to it as an argument. We can add a similar statement to the `actionPerformed()` method to update the color pane:

```
public void actionPerformed(ActionEvent e) {
  elementColor = color;
  statusBar.setColorPane(color);
  }
```

If you now recompile and run Sketcher again, you'll see the status bar in the application.

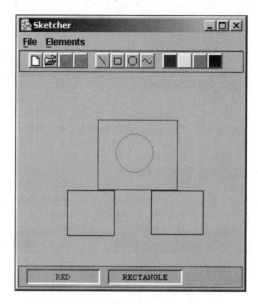

As you change the element type and color, the status bar will be updated automatically.

Using Dialogs

A dialog is a window that is displayed within the context of another window – its parent. You use dialogs to manage input that can't be handled conveniently through interaction with the view: selecting from a range of options for instance, or enabling data to be entered from the keyboard. You can also use dialogs for information messages or warnings. The JDialog class in the javax.swing package defines dialogs, and a JDialog object is a specialized sort of Window. A JDialog object will typically contain one or more components for displaying information or allowing data to be entered, plus buttons for selection of dialog options (including closing the dialog), so there's quite a bit of work involved in putting one together. However, for many of the typical dialogs you will want to use, the JOptionPane class provides an easy shortcut to creating dialogs. Below is a dialog that we'll create later in this chapter using just one statement.

We'll use this dialog to provide a response to clicking on a Help/About menu item that we will add to Sketcher in a moment. First though, we need to understand a little more about how dialogs work.

Modal and Non-modal Dialogs

There are two different kinds of dialog that you can create, and they have distinct operating characteristics. You have a choice of creating either a **modal dialog** or a **non-modal dialog**. When you display a modal dialog – by selecting a menu item or clicking a button, it inhibits the operation of any other windows in the application until you close the dialog. The dialog opposite that displays a message is a modal dialog. The dialog window retains the focus as long as it is displayed and operation of the application cannot continue until you click the OK button. Modal dialogs that manage input will normally have at least two buttons, an OK button that you use to accept whatever input has been entered and then close the dialog, and a Cancel button to just close the dialog and abort the entry of the data. Dialogs that manage input are almost always modal dialogs, simply because you won't generally want to allow other interactions to be triggered until your user's input is complete.

A non-modal dialog can be left on the screen for as long as you want, since it doesn't block interaction with other windows in the application. You can also switch the focus back and forth between using a non-modal dialog and using any other application windows that are on the screen.

Whether you create a modal or a non-modal dialog is determined either by an argument to a dialog class constructor, or by which constructor you choose, since some of them create non-modal dialogs by default. The default, no-argument JDialog constructor creates a non-modal dialog with an empty title bar. Since you have no provision for specifying a parent window for the dialog, a shared hidden frame will be used as the parent in this case. You have a choice of five constructors for creating a JDialog object where the parent can be a window of type Frame or JFrame:

Constructor	Description		
	title bar	parent window	Mode
JDialog(Frame parent)	(empty)	parent	non-modal
JDialog(Frame parent, String title)	title	parent	non-modal
JDialog(Frame parent, boolean modal)	(empty)	parent	modal (when modal arg is true) non-modal (when modal arg is false)
JDialog(Frame parent, String title, boolean modal)	title	parent	modal (when modal arg is true) non-modal (when modal arg is false)
JDialog(Frame parent, String title, boolean modal, GraphicsConfiguration gc)	title	parent	modal (when modal arg is true) non-modal (when modal arg is false)

Clearly since the first parameter is of type `Frame`, you can supply a reference of type `Frame` or type `JFrame`. There are a further five constructors for creating `JDialog` objects with a `Dialog` or `JDialog` object as the parent. The only difference between these and the ones in the table overleaf is that the type of the first parameter is `Dialog` rather than `Frame`. Any of these constructors can throw an exception of type `HeadlessException` if the system on which the code is executing does not have a display attached.

After you've created a `JDialog` object using any of the constructors, you can change the kind of dialog window it will produce from modal to non-modal, or vice versa, by calling the `setModal()` method for the object. If you specify the argument to the method as `true`, the dialog will be modal, and a `false` argument will make it non-modal. You can also check whether a `JDialog` object is modal or not. The `isModal()` method for the object will return `true` if it represents a modal dialog, and `false` otherwise.

All `JDialog` objects are initially invisible, so to display them you must call the `setVisible()` method for the `JDialog` object with the argument `true`. This method is inherited from the `Component` class via the `Container` and `Window` classes. If you call `setVisible()` with the argument `false`, the dialog window is removed from the screen. Once you've displayed a modal dialog window, the user can't interact with any of the other application windows until you call `setVisible()` for the dialog object with the argument `false`, so you typically do this in the event handler which is called to close the dialog. Note that the `setVisible()` method only affects the visibility of the dialog. You still have a perfectly good `JDialog` object so that when you want to display the dialog again, you just call its `setVisible()` method with an argument set to `true`. Of course, if you call `dispose()` for the `JDialog` object, or set the default close operation to `DISPOSE_ON_CLOSE`, then you won't be able to use the `JDialog` object again.

To set or change the title bar for a dialog, you just pass a `String` object to the `setTitle()` method for the `JDialog` object. If you want to know what the current title for a dialog is, you can call the `getTitle()` method which will return a `String` object containing the title bar string.

Dialog windows are resizable by default, so you can normally change the size of a dialog window by dragging its boundaries. If you don't want to allow a dialog window to be resized, you can inhibit this by calling the `setResizable()` for the `JDialog` object with the argument as `false`. An argument value of `true` re-enables the resizing capability.

A Simple Modal Dialog

The simplest kind of dialog is one that just displays some information. We could see how this works by adding a Help menu with an About menu item, and then displaying an About dialog to provide information about the application.

Let's derive our own dialog class from `JDialog` so we can create an About dialog.

Try It Out – Defining the AboutDialog Class

The constructor for our `AboutDialog` class will need to accept three arguments – the parent `Frame` object, which will be the application window in Sketcher, a `String` object defining what should appear on the title bar and a `String` object for the message we want to display. We'll only need one button in the dialog window, an OK button to close the dialog. We can make the whole thing self-contained by making the `AboutDialog` class the action listener for the button, and since it's only relevant in the context of the `SketchFrame` class, we can define it as an inner class.

```
public class SketchFrame extends Jframe implements Constants {
  // SketchFrame class as before...

    // Class defining a general purpose message box
    class AboutDialog extends JDialog implements ActionListener   {
      public AboutDialog(Frame parent, String title, String message)  {
        super(parent, title, true);
        // If there was a parent, set dialog position inside
        if(parent != null) {
          Dimension parentSize = parent.getSize();      // Parent size
          Point p = parent.getLocation();               // Parent position
          setLocation(p.x+parentSize.width/4,p.y+parentSize.height/4);
        }

        // Create the message pane
        JPanel messagePane = new JPanel();
        messagePane.add(new JLabel(message));
        getContentPane().add(messagePane);

        // Create the button pane
        JPanel buttonPane = new JPanel();
        JButton button = new JButton("OK");             // Create OK button
        buttonPane.add(button);                          // add to content pane
        button.addActionListener(this);
        getContentPane().add(buttonPane, BorderLayout.SOUTH);
        setDefaultCloseOperation(DISPOSE_ON_CLOSE);
        pack();                                          // Size window for components
        setVisible(true);
      }

    // OK button action
    public void actionPerformed(ActionEvent e)   {
      setVisible(false);                                // Set dialog invisible
      dispose();                                        // Release the dialog resources
    }
  }
}
```

How It Works

The constructor first calls the base JDialog class constructor to create a modal dialog with the title bar given by the title argument. It then defines the position of the dialog relative to the position of the frame.

When we create an instance of the **AboutDialog** class in the Sketcher program a little later in this chapter, we'll specify the **SketchFrame** object as the parent for the dialog. The parent relationship between the application window and the dialog implies a lifetime dependency. When the **SketchFrame** object is destroyed, the **AboutDialog** object will be too, because it is a child of the **SketchFrame** object. This doesn't just apply to **JDialog** objects – any **Window** object can have another **Window** object as a parent.

By default the `AboutDialog` window will be positioned relative to the top-left corner of the screen. To position the dialog appropriately, we set the coordinates of the top-left corner of the dialog as one quarter of the distance across the width of the application window, and one quarter of the distance down from the top-left corner of the application window.

You add the components you want to display in a dialog to the content pane for the `JDialog` object. The content pane has a `BorderLayout` manager by default, just like the content pane for the application window, and this is quite convenient for our dialog layout. The dialog contains two `JPanel` objects that are created in the constructor, one to hold a `JLabel` object for the message that is passed to the constructor, and the other to hold the **OK** button that will close the dialog. The `messagePane` object is added so that it fills the center of the dialog window. The `buttonPane` position is specified as `BorderLayout.SOUTH`, so it will be at the bottom of the dialog window. Both `JPanel` objects have a `FlowLayout` manager by default.

We want the `AboutDialog` object to be the listener for the **OK** button so we pass the `this` variable as the argument to the `addActionListener()` method call for the button.

The `pack()` method is inherited from the `Window` class. This method packs the components in the window, setting the window to an optimal size for the components it contains. Note that if you don't call `pack()` here, the size for your dialog will not be set and you won't be able to see it.

The `actionPerformed()` method will be called when the **OK** button is selected. This just disposes of the dialog by calling the `dispose()` method for the `AboutDialog` object so the dialog window will disappear from the screen and the resources it was using will be released.

To add a **Help** menu with an **About** item to our Sketcher application, we need to insert some code into the `SketchFrame` class constructor.

Try It Out – Creating an About Menu Item

You shouldn't have any trouble with this. We can make the `SketchFrame` object the listener for the **About** menu item so add `ActionListener` to the list of interfaces implemented by `SketchFrame`:

```
public class SketchFrame extends JFrame implements Constants, ActionListener {
```

The changes to the constructor to add the **Help** menu will be:

```
public SketchFrame(String title , Sketcher theApp) {
    setTitle(title);                          // Set the window title
    this.theApp = theApp;
    setJMenuBar(menuBar);                     // Add the menu bar to the window
    setDefaultCloseOperation(EXIT_ON_CLOSE);  // Default is exit the application

    JMenu fileMenu = new JMenu("File");       // Create File menu
    JMenu elementMenu = new JMenu("Elements"); // Create Elements menu

    JMenu helpMenu = new JMenu("Help");       // Create Help menu
    fileMenu.setMnemonic('F');                // Create shortcut
    elementMenu.setMnemonic('E');             // Create shortcut
    helpMenu.setMnemonic('H');                // Create shortcut
```

```
// All the stuff for the previous menus and the toolbar, as before...
```

```
// Add the About item to the Help menu
aboutItem = new JMenuItem("About");        // Create the item
aboutItem.addActionListener(this);         // Listener is the frame
helpMenu.add(aboutItem);                   // Add item to menu
menuBar.add(helpMenu);                     // Add the Help menu
}
```

Add `aboutMenu` as a private member of the `SketchFrame` class:

```
// Sundry menu items
private JMenuItem aboutItem;
```

Lastly, we need to implement the method in the `SketchFrame` class to handle the About menu item's events:

```
// Handle About menu action events
public void actionPerformed(ActionEvent e)  {
  if(e.getSource() == aboutItem)
  {
    // Create about dialog with the app window as parent
    AboutDialog aboutDlg = new AboutDialog(this, "About Sketcher",
                            "Sketcher Copyright Ivor Horton 2001");
  }
}
```

You can now recompile `SketchFrame.java` to try out our smart new dialog.

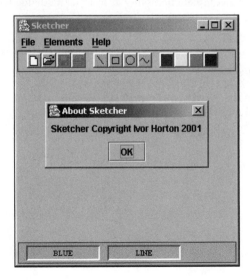

The dialog pops up when you select the About item in the Help menu. Until you select the OK button in the About Sketcher dialog, you can't interact with the application window at all since we created this as a modal dialog. By changing the last argument in the call to the superclass constructor in the AboutDialog constructor, you can make it non-modal and see how that works. This kind of dialog is usually modal though.

If you resize the application window before you display the About dialog, you'll see that its position of the dialog relative to the application window is adjusted accordingly.

How It Works

This is stuff that should be very familiar by now. We create a JMenu object for the Help item on the menu bar, and add a shortcut for it by calling its setMnemonic() member. We create a JMenuItem object which is the About menu item and call its addActionListener() method to make the SketchFrame object the listener for the item. After adding the menu item to the Help menu, we add the helpMenu object to the menubar object.

We create an AboutDialog object in the actionPerformed() method for the SketchFrame object, as this will be called when the About menu item is clicked. Before we display the dialog, we verify that the source of the event is the menu item, aboutItem. This is not important now, but we will add other menu items later, and we will want to handle their events using the same actionPerformed() method. The dialog object is self-contained and disposes of itself when the OK button is clicked. The dialog that we want to display here will always display the same message, so there's no real point in creating and destroying it each time we want to display it. You could arrange for the dialog box object to be created once, and the reference stored as a member of the SketchFrame class. Then you make it visible in the actionPerformed() method for the menu item and make it invisible in the actionPerformed() method responding to the dialog OK button event.

This is all very well, but it was a lot of work just to get a dialog with a message displayed. Deriving a class from JDialog gives you complete flexibility as to how the dialog works, but we didn't really need it in this case. Didn't we say there was an easier way?

Instant Dialogs

The JOptionPane class in the javax.swing package defines a number of static methods that will create and display standard modal dialogs for you. The simplest dialog you can create this way is a message dialog rather like our About message dialog. The following methods produce message dialogs:

Dial-a-Dialog Methods	Description
showMessageDialog (Component parent, Object message)	This method displays a modal dialog with the default title "Message". The first argument is the parent for the dialog. The Frame object containing the component will be used to position the dialog. If the first argument is null, a default Frame object will be created and that will be used to position the dialog centrally on the screen. The second argument specifies what is to be displayed in addition to the default OK button. This can be a String object specifying the message or an Icon object defining an icon to be displayed. It can also be a Component, in which case the component will be displayed. If some other type of object is passed as the second argument, its toString() method will be called, and the String object that is returned will be displayed. You will usually get a default icon for an information message along with your message. You can pass multiple items to be displayed by passing an array of type Object[] for the second argument. Each array element will be processed as above according to its type and they will be arranged in a vertical stack. Clever, eh?

showMessageDialog
(Component parent,
   Object message,
   String title,
   int messageType)
	This displays a dialog as above, but with the title specified by the third argument. The fourth argument, messageType, can be:
	
	ERROR_MESSAGE
	INFORMATION_MESSAGE
	WARNING_MESSAGE
	QUESTION_MESSAGE
	PLAIN_MESSAGE
	
	These determine the style of the message constrained by the current look and feel. This will usually include a default icon, such as a question mark for QUESTION_MESSAGE.

showMessageDialog
(Component parent,
   Object message,
   String title,
   int messageType,
   Icon icon)
	This displays a dialog as above except that the icon will be what you pass as the fifth argument. Specifying a null argument for the icon will produce a dialog the same as the previous version of the method.

We could have used one of these for the About dialog instead of all that messing about with inner classes. Let's see how.

Try It Out – An Easy About Dialog

Delete the inner class, AboutDialog, from SketchFrame – we won't need that any longer. Change the implementation of the actionPerformed() method in the SketchFrame class to:

```
       public void actionPerformed(ActionEvent e) {
         if(e.getSource() == aboutItem) {
           // Create about dialog with the menu item as parent
           JOptionPane.showMessageDialog(this,                       // Parent
                           "Sketcher Copyright Ivor Horton 2001",    // Message
                           "About Sketcher",                          // Title
                           JOptionPane.INFORMATION_MESSAGE);          // Message type
         }
       }
```

Compile `SketchFrame` again and run Sketcher. When you click on the **Help/About** menu item, you should get something like the following:

The pretty little icon comes for free.

How It Works

All the work is done by the static `showMessageDialog()` method in the `JOptionPane` class. What you get is controlled by the arguments that you supply, and the Swing look-and-feel in use. By default this will correspond to what is usual for your system. On a PC running Windows, we get the icon you see because we specified the message type as `INFORMATION_MESSAGE`. You can try plugging in the other message types to see what you get.

Input Dialogs

`JOptionPane` also has four static methods that you can use to create standard modal input dialogs:

`showInputDialog(Object message)`

This method displays a default modal input dialog with a text field for input. The message you pass as the argument is set as the caption for the input field and the default also supplies an **OK** button, a **Cancel** button and **Input** as a title. For example, if you pass the message "Enter Input:" as the argument in the following statement,

```
    String input = JOptionPane.showInputDialog("Enter Input:");
```

the dialog shown will be displayed:

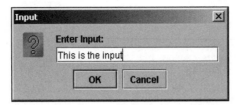

When you click on the OK button, whatever you entered in the text field will be returned and stored in input – "This is the input" in this case. If you click on the Cancel button, null will be returned. Note that this is not the same as no input. If you click on OK without entering anything in the text field, a reference to an empty String object will be returned.

```
showInputDialog(Component parent, Object message)
```

This produces the same dialog as the previous method, but with the component you specify as the first argument as the parent of the dialog.

```
showInputDialog(Component parent, Object message,
                String title, int messageType)
```

In this case the title of the dialog is supplied by the third argument, and the style of the message is determined by the fourth argument. The values for the fourth argument can be any of those discussed earlier in the context of message dialogs. For instance, you could display the dialog shown with the following statement:

```
String input = JOptionPane.showInputDialog(null, "Enter Input:",
                              "Dialog for Input", JOptionPane.WARNING_MESSAGE);
```

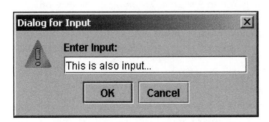

The data that you enter in the text field is returned by the showInputDialog() method when the OK button is pressed as before.

```
showInputDialog(Component parent, Object message,
                String title, int messageType,
                Icon icon, Object[] selections,
                object initialSelection)
```

This version of the method provides a list of choices in a drop-down list box. The items from which to choose are passed as the sixth argument as an array and they can be of any class type. The initial selection to be displayed when the dialog is first displayed is specified by the seventh argument. Whatever is chosen when the OK button is clicked will be returned as type Object, and, if the Cancel button is clicked, null will be returned. You can specify your own icon to replace the default icon by passing a reference of type Icon as the fifth argument. The following statements display the dialog shown:

```
String[] choices = {"Money", "Health", "Happiness", "This", "That", "The Other"};
String input = (String)JOptionPane.showInputDialog(null, "Choose now...",
                            "The Choice of a Lifetime",
                            JOptionPane.QUESTION_MESSAGE,
                            null,            // Use default icon
                            choices,         // Array of choices
                            choices[1]);     // Initial choice
```

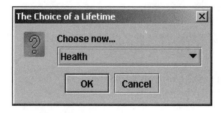

Note that you have to cast the reference returned by this version of the showInputDialog() method to the type of choice value you have used. Here we are using type String, but the selections could be type Icon, or whatever you want.

Using a Dialog to Create Text Elements

It would be good if our Sketcher program also provided a means of adding text to a picture – after all, you might want to put your name to a sketch. A dialog is the obvious way to provide the mechanism for entering the text when we create text elements. We can use one of the showInputDialog() methods for this, but first we need to add a Text menu item to the Elements menu, and we will need a class to represent text elements, the Element.Text class of course, with Element as a base class. Let's start with the Element.Text class.

Text is a little tricky. For one thing we can't treat it just like another element. There is no object that implements the Shape interface that represents a text string so, unless we want to define one, we can't use the draw() method for a graphics context to display text. We have to use the drawString() method. We'll also have to figure out the bounding rectangle for the text on screen for ourselves. With Shape objects you could rely on the getBounds() method supplied by the 2D shape classes in java.awt.geom, but with text you're on your own.

Ideally we want to avoid treating text elements as a special case. Having many tests for types while we're drawing a sketch in the paint() method for the view generates considerable processing overhead that we would be better off without. One way around this is to make every element draw itself. We could implement a polymorphic method in each element class, draw() say, and pass a Graphics2D object to it. Each shape or text element could then figure out how to draw itself. The paint() method in the view class would not need to worry about what type of element was being drawn at all.

Let's see how that works out. We can start by adding an abstract method, `draw()` to the `Element` class definition:

```
public abstract class Element {
  public Element(Color color) {
    this.color = color;
  }

  public   Color getColor() {
    return color;
  }

  public abstract java.awt.Rectangle getBounds();
  public abstract void modify(Point start, Point last);
  public abstract void draw(Graphics2D g2D);

  protected Color color;                    // Color of a shape

  // Plus definitions for our shape classes...
}
```

Note that we have deleted the `getShape()` method as we won't be needing it further. You can remove it from all the nested classes of the `Element` class. The `draw()` method now needs to be implemented in each of the nested classes to the `Element` class, but because each of the current classes has a `Shape` member, it will be essentially the same in each. The version for the `Element.Line` class will be:

```
public void draw(Graphics2D g2D) {
  g2D.setPaint(color);                  // Set the line color
  g2D.draw(line);                       // Draw the line
}
```

This just sets the color and passes the `Shape` object that is a member of the class to the `draw()` method for the `Graphics2D` object. To implement the `draw()` method for the other element classes, just replace the argument to the `g2D.draw()` method call, with the name of the `Shape` member of the class, and update the comments. You also need to make the `Graphics2D` class accessible so add an `import` statement for it to `Element.java`:

```
import java.awt.Graphics2D;
```

You can now change the implementation of the `paint()` method in the `SketchView` class to:

```
public void paint(Graphics g) {
  Graphics2D g2D = (Graphics2D)g;                       // Get a 2D device context
  Iterator elements = theApp.getModel().getIterator();
  while(elements.hasNext())                             // Go through the list
    ((Element)elements.next()).draw(g2D);               // Get the next element to draw
                                                        // itself
}
```

Chapter 19

It's now quite a lot shorter as the element sets its own color in the graphics context and we don't need to store the reference to the element within the loop. We are ready to get back to the `Element.Text` class.

We must not forget to update the `mouseDragged()` method in the `MouseHandler` class in `SketchView` to use the new mechanism for drawing elements:

```
public void mouseDragged(MouseEvent e) {
  last = e.getPoint();                              // Save cursor position
  if(button1Down)          {
    if(tempElement == null)                         // Is there an element?
      tempElement = createElement(start, last);     // No, so create one
    else  {
      tempElement.draw(g2D);                        // Yes - draw to erase it
      tempElement.modify(start, last);              // Now modify it
    }
    tempElement.draw(g2D);                          // and draw it
  }
}
```

We can define the `Element.Text` class quite easily now. We will need five arguments for the constructor though – the font to be used for the string, the string to be displayed, the position where it is to be displayed, its color, and its bounding rectangle. To get a bounding rectangle for a string, we need access to a graphics context, so it will be easier to create the bounding rectangle before we create a text element.

Here's the class definition:

```
class Element {
  // Code that defines the base class...
  // Definitions for the other shape classes...

  // Class defining text element
  public static class Text extends Element  {
    public Text(Font font, String text, Point position, Color color,
                                    java.awt.Rectangle bounds) {
      super(color);
      this.font = font;
      this.position = position;
      this.text = text;
      this.bounds = bounds;
      this.bounds.setLocation(position.x, position.y - (int)bounds.getHeight());
    }

    public java.awt.Rectangle getBounds() {
      return bounds;
    }

    public void draw(Graphics2D g2D)  {
      g2D.setPaint(color);
      Font oldFont = g2D.getFont();                 // Save the old font
      g2D.setFont(font);                            // Set the new font
      g2D.drawString(text, position.x, position.y);
```

```
        g2D.setFont(oldFont);                       // Restore the old font
    }

    public void modify(Point start, Point last) {
        // No code is required here, but we must supply a definition
    }

    private Font font;                              // The font to be used
    private String text;                            // Text to be displayed
    private Point position;                         // Position of the text
  java.awt.Rectangle bounds;                        // The bounding rectangle
  }
}
```

How It Works

In the constructor we pass the color to the superclass constructor, and store the other argument values in data members of the `Element.Text` class. When we create the bounding rectangle to pass to the constructor, the default reference point for the top-left corner of the rectangle will be (0, 0). This is not what we want for our text object so we have to modify it.

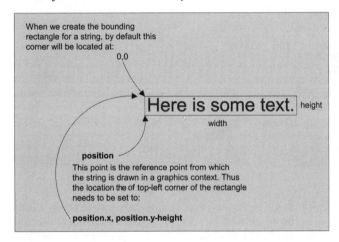

In the constructor, we adjust the coordinates of the top-left corner of the bounding rectangle relative to the point, `position`, where the string will be drawn. Remember that the point coordinates passed to the `drawString()` method correspond to the bottom-left corner of the first character in the string.

The code to draw text is not difficult – it's just different from drawing shapes. It amounts to calling `setPaint()` to set the text color, setting the font in the graphics context by calling its `setFont()` method and finally calling `drawString()` to display the text.

To work with text, we could do with a menu item and a toolbar button to set the element type to text, so let's deal with that next.

Try It Out – Adding the Text Menu Item

We'll add a `textAction` member to the `SketchFrame` class, so amend the declaration for the `TypeAction` members to:

```
private TypeAction lineAction, rectangleAction, circleAction,
                   curveAction, textAction;
```

You will need an icon in the `Images` directory that is a subdirectory to the Sketcher directory if you want to create a toolbar button for text. I just created an icon with 'T' on it, ![T icon], but you can create something fancier if you have a mind to. The file containing the icon should have the name `Text.gif`, because that's what the `TypeAction` object will assume.

To add the menu item, you need to add a statement to the `SketchFrame` constructor following the statements that create the other items in the element menu:

```
// Construct the Element pull-down menu
// Code to add the other Element menu items as before...
addMenuItem(elementMenu, textAction = new TypeAction("Text", TEXT, "Draw text"));
```

This assumes we have defined the value of `TEXT` in the `Constants` interface, so add that and a default font for use with text elements now:

```
public interface Constants {
   // Element type definitions
   int LINE      = 101;
   int RECTANGLE = 102;
   int CIRCLE    = 103;
   int CURVE     = 104;
   int TEXT      = 105;

   // Initial conditions
   int DEFAULT_ELEMENT_TYPE = LINE;
   Color DEFAULT_ELEMENT_COLOR = Color.BLUE;
   Font DEFAULT_FONT = new Font("Times New Roman",Font.PLAIN, 12);
}
```

If you don't have the Times New Roman font on your machine, choose a font that you do have. We will need a data member in the application window object to hold a reference to the current font. It will start out as the default font, but we will be adding the means to alter this later. Add the following data member after the others in `SketchFrame`:

```
private Color elementColor = DEFAULT_ELEMENT_COLOR;    // Current element color
private int elementType = DEFAULT_ELEMENT_TYPE;        // Current element type
private Font font = DEFAULT_FONT;                       // Current font
```

Of course, we also need a method to retrieve it from the application window object:

```
public Font getCurrentFont() {
   return font;
}
```

Now the view will be able to get the current font when necessary, via the application object.

If you want the toolbar button as well, you will need to add one statement to the `SketchFrame` constructor following the others that add element type selection buttons:

```
// Add element type buttons
toolBar.addSeparator();
addToolBarButton(lineAction);
addToolBarButton(rectangleAction);
addToolBarButton(circleAction);
addToolBarButton(curveAction);
addToolBarButton(textAction);
```

The action events for the menu item and toolbar button for text are taken care of and the final piece is dealing with mouse events when we create a text element.

Text elements are going to be different to shapes in how they are created. To create a text element we need to know what the text is, its color, its font, and where it is to be placed. We will also have to construct its bounding rectangle. This sounds as though it might be easier than geometric elements, but there are complications.

Try It Out – Creating Text Elements

We start the process of creating geometric elements in `SketchView`'s `MouseHandler` class, but we can't simply start with the `mousePressed()` method, as would at first seem logical. The problem is the sequence of events. We want to display a dialog to manage the text entry, but if we display a dialog in the `mousePressed()` method, the `mouseReleased()` event will get lost, unless you're happy to hold down the mouse button while typing into the text field with the other hand! A simple solution is to separate the creation of text elements altogether, and create them in the `mouseClicked()` method. This method is called after the mouse button is released, so all the other events will have occurred and been dealt with.

We can implement this method in the inner class, `MouseHandler`, to create a text element along the following lines:

```
public void mouseClicked(MouseEvent e) {
  if((e.getButton()== MouseEvent.BUTTON1) &&
     (theApp.getWindow().getElementType() == TEXT)) {

    start = e.getPoint();                // Save cursor position - start of text
    String text = JOptionPane.showInputDialog(
             (Component)e.getSource(),      // Used to get the frame
             "Enter Text:",                 // The message
             "Dialog for Text Element",     // Dialog title
             JOptionPane.PLAIN_MESSAGE);    // No icon

    if(text != null && text.length()!=0)  {   // If we have text
                                              // create the element

       // Code to create the Element.Text element
       // and add it to the sketch model...
    }
  }
}
```

We will need to import `JOptionPane` from `javax.swing` into `SketchView.java` so add the import:

```
import javax.swing.JOptionPane;
```

We only want to do something here if it was mouse button 1 that was clicked and the current element type is TEXT. In this case we save the cursor position and pop a dialog to permit the text string to be entered. If there was one that is not an empty string, we go ahead and create a text element and add it to the sketch model.

We still have to add the code for creating a text element. The tricky part is figuring out what the rectangle bounding the text is. The `Font` class defines a `getStringBounds()` method that returns a rectangle bounding a string in a given context in which the string is drawn. Unfortunately, as the documentation for this method says, it does not always return a rectangle enclosing all of the text. To get a rectangle that completely encloses the text in every case we must create a `TextLayout` object for the text and call its `getBounds()` method.

This `TextLayout` class is defined in the `java.awt.font` package so we will need an import statement for that in the `SketchView.java` file:

```
import java.awt.font.TextLayout;
```

A `TextLayout` object encapsulates the graphical representation of a given text string on a particular graphics device so, as well as the text and the font, a `TextLayout` class constructor needs information on the dimensions of the font in the context of the graphical device. The `FontRenderContext` class in the `java.awt.font` package defines an object encapsulating the information necessary to display text in a given graphics context. You can obtain a `FontRenderContext` object from a `Graphics2D` object, g2D, like this:

```
FontRenderContext frc = g2D.getFontRenderContext();
```

All we need now is a `Graphics2D` object. We can get that using the `getGraphics()` method that our `SketchView` object inherits from the `JComponent` class:

```
Graphics2D g2D = (Graphics2D)getGraphics();
```

We have all the pieces we need to create the bounding rectangle for the text, and hence the `Element.Text` object. Here's the code that goes in the `if` statement that will create the text element and add it to the model:

```
if(text != null)  {                              // If we have text
                                                 // create the element
   g2D = (Graphics2D)getGraphics();
   Font font = theApp.getWindow().getCurrentFont();
   tempElement = new Element.Text(
           font,                                 // The font
           text,                                 // The text
           start,                                // Position of the  text
```

```
                theApp.getWindow().getElementColor(),  // The text color
          new java.awt.font.TextLayout(text, font,   // The bounding rectangle
                    g2D.getFontRenderContext()).getBounds().getBounds()
                                     );

    if(tempElement != null) {                        // If we created one
      theApp.getModel().add(tempElement);            // add it to the model
      tempElement = null;                            // and reset the field
    }
    g2D.dispose();                                   // Release context resources
    g2D = null;
    start = null;
  }
```

The bounding rectangle for the text is produced by the rather fearsome looking expression for the last argument to the `Element.Text` constructor. It's much easier than it looks so let's take it apart.

The `TextLayout` constructor we are using requires three arguments, the text string, the font, and a `FontRenderContext` object for the context in which the text is to be displayed. We call the `getBounds()` method for the `TextLayout` object, which returns a reference to a rectangle of type `Rectangle2D`. Since we want a rectangle of type `Rectangle` to pass to our `Element.Text` constructor, we call the `getBounds()` method for the `Rectangle2D` object, hence the repetition in the code.

Once the element has been created, we just add it to the model, and clean up the variables that we were using.

We must now make sure that the other mouse event handlers do nothing when the current element is TEXT. We don't want the XOR mode set when we are just creating text elements for instance. A simple additional condition that tests the current element type will take care of it in the `mousePressed()` method:

```
    public void mousePressed(MouseEvent e) {
      // Code to handle mouse button press...
      if((button1Down = (e.getButton()==MouseEvent.BUTTON1)) &&
         (theApp.getWindow().getElementType() != TEXT)) {
        start = e.getPoint();                    // Save the cursor position in start
        g2D = (Graphics2D)getGraphics();                 // Get graphics context
        g2D.setXORMode(getBackground());                 // Set XOR mode
        g2D.setPaint(theApp.getWindow().getElementColor());   // Set color
      }
    }
```

The `if` expression will only be `true` if button 1 was pressed and the current element type is not TEXT. We can update the `mouseDragged()` method in a similar way:

```
    public void mouseDragged(MouseEvent e) {
      last = e.getPoint();                             // Save cursor position

      if(button1Down && (theApp.getWindow().getElementType() != TEXT)) {
        if(tempElement == null)                         // Is there an element?
          tempElement = createElement(start, last);     // No, so create one
```

```
        else {
          g2D.draw(tempElement.getShape());        // Yes - draw to erase it
          tempElement.modify(start, last);         // Now modify it
        }
        g2D.draw(tempElement.getShape());          // and draw it
      }
    }
```

We have also updated the statements that draw an element to call the new method in the element classes. The change to the mouseReleased() method is exactly the same as for mousePressed() so let's go ahead and modify the if condition. The only other change we need to make is to make the status bar respond to the TEXT element type being set. To do this we just need to make a small addition to the definition of the setTypePane() method in the StatusBar class:

```
public void setTypePane(int elementType) {
  String text;              // Text for the type pane
  switch(elementType) {
    // case label as before...

    case TEXT:
      text = "TEXT";
      break;
    default:
      assert false;
  }
  typePane.setText(text);   // Set the pane text
}
```

How It Works

The mouseClicked() handler responds to mouse button 1 being clicked when the element type is TEXT. This method will be called after the mouseReleased() method. Within the if statement that determines this, we create a dialog to receive the text input by calling the static showInputDialog() in the JOptionPane class. If you selected the **Cancel** button in the dialog, text will be null so in this case we do nothing. If text is not null, we create an Element.Text object at the current cursor position containing the text string that was entered in the dialog. We then add this to the model, as long as it's not null. It is important to remember to reset the start and tempElement members back to null, so as not to confuse subsequent event handling operations.

Incidentally, although there isn't a method to detect double-clicks on the mouse button, it's easy to implement. The getClickCount() method for the MouseEvent object that is passed to mouseClicked() returns the click count. To respond to a double-click you would write:

```
if(e.getClickCount() == 2) {
  //Response to double-click...
}
```

The other event handling methods behave as before so far as the geometric elements are concerned, and do nothing if the element type is TEXT. We can try it out.

Testing the TextDialog Class

All you need to do now is recompile Sketcher and run it again. Note that you may need to tweak the import statements in the various classes we have been adding to in order to allow it to compile as we have added many lines of code. To open the text dialog, select the new toolbar button or the menu item and click in the view where you want the text to appear.

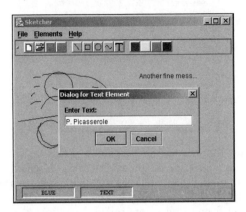

You just type the text that you want and click on the OK button. The text will be displayed starting at the point in the view where you clicked the mouse button. You can draw text in any of the colors – just like the geometric elements.

A Font Selection Dialog

We don't really want to be stuck with 12 point Times New Roman. We need to be free to be creative! A font dialog that pops up in response to a click on a suitable menu item should enable us to change the font for text elements to any of those available on the system. It should also give us a chance to see how we can get at and process the fonts that are available. We can also learn more about how to add components in a dialog. Let's first establish what our font dialog will do.

We want to be able to choose the font name from those available on the system, the style of the font, whether plain, bold, or italic, as well as the point size. It would also be nice to see what a font looks like before we decide to use it. The dialog will therefore need to obtain a list of the fonts available and display them in a component. It will also need a component to allow the point size to be selected, and some means for choosing the style.

This is not going to be a wimpy dialog like those we have seen so far. This is going to be a real Java programmer's dialog. We can drag in a diversity of components here, just for the experience. We will build it step-by-step, as it will be quite a lot of code. Just so you know where we're headed, the finished dialog is shown overleaf:

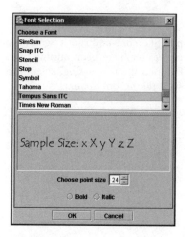

The component for choosing the font is a Swing component of type JList that can display a list of any type of component. Below that is a panel holding a JLabel object, which displays a sample of the current font. The list of font names and the panel below are displayed in a split pane defined by the JSplitPane class. Here the pane is split vertically but it can also hold two panels side by side. The point size is displayed in another Swing component called a combobox, which is an object of type JComboBox. The font style options are radio buttons so only one can be selected at any time. Finally, we have two buttons to close the dialog.

We can start by defining the FontDialog class with its data members and its constructor, and then build on that.

Try It Out – A FontDialog Class

The major work will be in the dialog class constructor. That will set up all the GUI elements as well as the necessary listeners to respond to operations with the dialog. The dialog object will need to know that the SketchFrame object that represents the Sketcher application window is the parent, so we will pass a SketchFrame reference to the constructor.

Here's the code for the outline of the class:

```
// Class to define a dialog to choose a font
import java.awt.*;
import javax.swing.*;
import javax.swing.event.*;
import javax.swing.border.*;
import java.awt.event.*;

class FontDialog extends JDialog implements Constants {
  // Constructor
  public FontDialog(SketchFrame window) {
    // Code to initialize the data members...
    // Code to create buttons and the button panel...
    // Code to create the data input panel...
    // Code to create the font choice and add it to the input panel...
    // Code to create the font size choice
```

```
        //   and add it to the input panel...
        // Code to create the font style checkboxes
        //   and add them to the input panel...
        // ...and then some!
    }
    private Font font;                  // Currently selected font
    private int fontStyle;              // Font style - Plain,Bold,Italic
    private int fontSize;               // Font point size
}
```

We will be adding a few more data members shortly, but at least we know we will need these. The code to initialize the data members within the `FontDialog` constructor of the font dialog is easy. We will initialize the `font` member and the associated `fontStyle` and `fontSize` members from the current font in the application window:

```
public FontDialog(SketchFrame window) {
    // Call the base constructor to create a modal dialog
    super(window, "Font Selection", true);

    font = window.getCurrentFont();     // Get the current font
    fontStyle = font.getStyle();        // ...style
    fontSize = font.getSize();          // ...and size

    // Plus the code for the rest of the constructor...
}
```

We call the base class constructor and pass the window object to it as parent. The second argument is the title for the dialog and the third argument determines that it is modal. The `getCurrentFont()` method returns the font stored in the window object, and we use this to initialize the `fontStyle` and `fontSize` members, so the first time we open the dialog this will be the default setting.

Creating the Buttons

Next we can add the code to the constructor that will create the button panel with the **OK** and **Cancel** buttons. We will place this at the bottom of the content pane for the dialog using the default `BorderLayout` manager:

```
public FontDialog(SketchFrame window) {
    // Initialization as before...

    // Create the dialog button panel
    JPanel buttonPane = new JPanel();                    // Create a panel to hold buttons

    // Create and add the buttons to the buttonPane
    buttonPane.add(ok = createButton("OK"));             // Add the OK button
    buttonPane.add(cancel = createButton("Cancel"));     // Add the Cancel button
    getContentPane().add(buttonPane, BorderLayout.SOUTH);// Add pane to content pane

    // Plus the code for the rest of the constructor...
}
```

The `buttonPane` object will have a `FlowLayout` manager by default, so this will take care of positioning the buttons. We add the button pane to the dialog content pane using `BorderLayout.SOUTH` to place it at the bottom of the window. Because creating each button involves several steps, we are using a helper method `createButton()` that only requires the button label as an argument. Note that we store each button reference in a variable, so we will need to add these as members of the `FontDialog` class:

```
private JButton ok;                      // OK button
private JButton cancel;                  // Cancel button
```

We will use these references in the listeners for the button, as we will see in a moment.

We can code the `createButton()` method as a member of the `FontDialog` class as follows:

```
JButton createButton(String label) {
  JButton button = new JButton(label);                 // Create the button
  button.setPreferredSize(new Dimension(80,20));       // Set the size
  button.addActionListener(this);                      // Listener is the dialog
  return button;                                       // Return the button
}
```

We set the preferred size of the button here to ensure the buttons are all the same size. Without this call, each button would be sized to fit its label so it would look a bit untidy. The listener is the `FontDialog` class, so the `FontDialog` must implement the `ActionListener` interface, which implies an `actionPerformed()` method:

```
class FontDialog extends JDialog
               implements Constants, ActionListener {       // For buttons etc.
  // Constructor definition...
  // createButton() definition...

  public void actionPerformed(ActionEvent e) {
    Object source = e.getSource();                      // Get the source of the event
    if(source == ok) {                                  // Is it the OK button?
      ((SketchFrame)getOwner()).setCurrentFont(font);   // Set the selected font
      setVisible(false);                                // Hide the dialog
    }
    else if(source == cancel)                           // If it is the Cancel button
      setVisible(false);                                // just hide the dialog
  }
  // Plus the rest of the class definition...
}
```

The `getSource()` member of the `ActionEvent` object, e, returns a reference to the object that originated the event, so we can use this to determine which button the method is being called for. We just compare the `source` object (which is holding the reference to the object to which the event applies) to each button object in turn. If it is the **OK** button, we call the `setCurrentFont()` method in the `SketchFrame` object that is the parent for this dialog to set the font. If it is the **Cancel** button we just hide the dialog so Sketcher can continue. Of course we must add the definition of `setCurrentFont()` to the `SketchFrame` class. The code for this will be:

```
  public void setCurrentFont(Font font) {
    this.font = font;
  }
```

Let's now get back to the `FontDialog` constructor.

Adding the Data Pane

We can now add a panel to contain the components that will receive input. We will have a `JList` object for the font names, a `JComboBox` object for the point size of the font and three `JRadioButton` objects for selecting the font style. We will add the code to create the panel first:

```
public FontDialog(SketchFrame window) {
  // Initialization as before...
  // Button panel code as before...

  // Code to create the data input panel
  JPanel dataPane = new JPanel();                      // Create the data entry panel
  dataPane.setBorder(BorderFactory.createCompoundBorder(   // Create pane border
                 BorderFactory.createLineBorder(Color.BLACK),
                 BorderFactory.createEmptyBorder(5, 5, 5, 5)));
  GridBagLayout gbLayout = new GridBagLayout();        // Create the layout
  dataPane.setLayout(gbLayout);                        // Set the pane layout
  GridBagConstraints constraints = new GridBagConstraints();

  // Plus the code for the rest of the constructor...
}
```

Here we use a `GridBagLayout` manager so we can set constraints for each component that we add to the `dataPane` container. We also set a black line border for `dataPane` with an inset empty border five pixels wide. This uses the `BorderFactory` static methods that you have seen before.

The first component we will add to `dataPane` is a label prompting for the font selection:

```
public FontDialog(SketchFrame window) {
  // Initialization as before...
  // Button panel code as before...
  // Set up the data input panel to hold all input components as before...

  // Code to create the font choice and add it to the input panel
  JLabel label = new JLabel("Choose a Font");
  constraints.fill = GridBagConstraints.HORIZONTAL;
  constraints.gridwidth = GridBagConstraints.REMAINDER;
  gbLayout.setConstraints(label, constraints);
  dataPane.add(label);

  // Plus the code for the rest of the constructor...
}
```

With the `fill` constraint set as `HORIZONTAL`, the components in a row will fill the width of the `dataPane` container, but without affecting the height. With the width constraint set to `REMAINDER`, the `label` component will fill the width of the row.

Implementing the Font List

The next component we will add is the `JList` object that displays the list of fonts, but we won't add this directly to the `dataPane`. The list of fonts will have to be obtained using the `GraphicsEnvironment` object that encapsulates information about the system in which the application is running. You will remember that we must call a `static` method in the `GraphicsEnvironment` class to get the object. Here's the code to create the list of font names:

```
public FontDialog(SketchFrame window) {
  // Initialization as before...

  // Button panel code as before...
  // Set up the data input panel to hold all input components as before...
  // Add the font choice prompt label as before...

  // Code to set up font list choice component
  GraphicsEnvironment e = GraphicsEnvironment.getLocalGraphicsEnvironment();
  String[] fontNames = e.getAvailableFontFamilyNames();   // Get the font names

  fontList = new JList(fontNames);                         // Create list of font names
  fontList.setValueIsAdjusting(true);                      // single event selection
  fontList.setSelectionMode(ListSelectionModel.SINGLE_SELECTION); // Choose 1 font
  fontList.setSelectedValue(font.getFamily(),true);
  fontList.addListSelectionListener(this);
  JScrollPane chooseFont = new JScrollPane(fontList); // Scrollable list
  chooseFont.setMinimumSize(new Dimension(300,100));
  chooseFont.setWheelScrollingEnabled(true);               // Enable mouse wheel scroll

  // Plus the code for the rest of the constructor...
}
```

We obtain the list of font family names for the system on which Sketcher is running, by calling the `getAvailableFontFamilyNames()` method for the `GraphicsEnvironment` object. The `fontList` variable will need to be accessible in the method handling events for the list, so this will be another data member of the class:

```
  private JList fontList;                 // Font list
```

The `fontNames` array holds `String` objects, but you can create a `JList` object for any kind of object, images for example. You can also create a `JList` object by passing a `Vector` that contains the objects you want in the list to the constructor. It is possible to allow multiple entries from a list to be selected, in which case the selection process may cause multiple events – when you drag the cursor over several list items for example. You can ensure that there is only one event for a selection, even though multiple items are selected, by calling the `setValueIsAdjusting()` method with the argument `true`. Calling `setSelectionMode()` with the argument `SINGLE_SELECTION` ensures that only one font name can be selected. You have two possible multiple selections you can enable.

Passing the value `SINGLE_INTERVAL_SELECTION` to the method allows a series of consecutive items to be selected. Passing `MULTIPLE_SELECTION_INTERVAL` provides you with total flexibility and allows any number of items anywhere to be selected. The initial selection in the list is set by the `setSelectedValue()` call. We pass the family name for the current font as the argument specifying the initial selection. There is a complementary method, `getSelectedValue()`, that we will be using in the event handler.

There's a special kind of listener for JList selection events that implements the ListSelectionListener interface. Since we set the FontDialog object as the listener for the list in the call to the addListSelectionListener() method, we had better make sure the FontDialog class implements the interface:

```
class FontDialog extends JDialog
              implements Constants, ActionListener,      // For buttons etc.
                         ListSelectionListener {         // For list box
```

There's only one method in the ListSelectionListener interface, and we can implement it like this:

```
// List selection listener method
public void valueChanged(ListSelectionEvent e) {
  if(!e.getValueIsAdjusting()) {
    font = new Font((String)fontList.getSelectedValue(), fontStyle, fontSize);
    fontDisplay.setFont(font);
    fontDisplay.repaint();
  }
}
```

This method is called when you select an item in the list. We have only one list so we don't need to check which object was the source of the event. If we needed to, we could call the getSource() method for the event object that is passed to valueChanged(), and compare it with the references to the JList objects.

The ListSelectionEvent object that is passed to the valueChanged() method contains records of the index positions of the list items that changed. You can obtain these as a range by calling getFirstIndex() for the event object for the first in the range, and getLastIndex() for the last. We don't need to worry about this because we have disallowed multiple selections and we just want the newly selected item in the list.

We have to be careful though. Since we start out with an item already selected, selecting another font name from the list will cause two events – one for deselecting the original font name, and the other for selecting the new name. We make sure we only deal with the last event by calling the getValueIsAdjusting() method for the event object in the if expression. This returns false when all changes due to a selection are complete, and true if things are still changing. Once we are sure nothing further is changing, we retrieve the selected font name from the list by calling its getSelectedValue() method. The item is returned as type Object so we have to cast it to type String before using it. We create a new Font object using the selected family name and the current values for fontStyle and fontSize. We store the new font in the data member font, and also call the setFont() member of a data member fontDisplay that we haven't added yet. This will be a JLabel object displaying a sample of the current font. After we've set the new font, we call repaint() for the label, fontDisplay, to get it redrawn.

If we allowed multiple selections on the list with the SINGLE_SELECTION_INTERVAL method, we could use the getFirstIndex() and getLastIndex() methods to get the range of index values for the item that may have changed. If on the other hand you employ the MULTIPLE_SELECTION_INTERVAL option, you would need to figure out which items in the range were actually selected. You could do this by calling the getSelectedIndices() method or the getSelectedValues() method for the list object. The first of these returns an int array of index values for selected items, and the second returns an array of type Object containing references to the selected items.

A JList object doesn't support scrolling directly, but it is scrolling 'aware'. To get a scrollable list, one with scrollbars, you just need to pass the JList object to the JScrollPane constructor, as we do in the FontDialog constructor. This creates a pane with scrollbars – either vertical, horizontal, or both, as necessary. We set a minimum size for the JScrollPane object to limit how small it can be made in the split pane into which we will insert it in a moment. Note how easy it is to get the mouse wheel supported for scrolling here. We just call the setWheelScrollingEnabled() method for the scroll pane with the argument as true and it's done.

Displaying the Selected Font

We will display the selected font in a JLabel object that we place in another JPanel pane. Adding the following code to the constructor will do this:

```
public FontDialog(SketchFrame window) {
  // Initialization as before...
  // Button panel code as before...
  // Set up the data input panel to hold all input components as before...
  // Add the font choice prompt label as before...
  // Set up font list choice component as before...

  // Panel to display font sample
  JPanel display = new JPanel();
  fontDisplay = new JLabel("Sample Size: x X y Y z Z");
  fontDisplay.setPreferredSize(new Dimension(300,100));
  display.add(fontDisplay);

  // Plus the code for the rest of the constructor...
}
```

We create the JPanel object, display, and add the JLabel object, fontDisplay, to it. Remember, we update this object in the valueChanged() handler for selections from the list of font names. We will also be updating it when the font size or style is changed. The fontDisplay object just represents some sample text. You can choose something different if you like.

Just for the experience, let's use a split pane to hold the scroll pane containing the list, chooseFont, and the display panel.

Using a Split Pane

A JSplitPane object represents a pane with a movable horizontal or vertical split, so that it can hold two components. The split pane divider can be adjusted by dragging it with the mouse. Here's the code to do that:

```
public FontDialog(SketchFrame window) {
   // Initialization as before...
   // Button panel code as before...
   // Set up the data input panel to hold all input components as before...
   // Add the font choice prompt label as before...
   // Set up font list choice component as before...
   // Panel to display font sample as before...

   //Create a split pane with font choice at the top
   // and font display at the bottom
   JSplitPane splitPane = new JSplitPane(JSplitPane.VERTICAL_SPLIT,
                                         true,
                                         chooseFont,
                                         display);
   gbLayout.setConstraints(splitPane, constraints);   // Split pane constraints
   dataPane.add(splitPane);                           // Add to the data pane

   // Plus the code for the rest of the constructor...
}
```

The constructor does it all. The first argument specifies that the pane supports two components, one above the other. You can probably guess that for side-by-side components you would specify JSplitPane.HORIZONTAL_SPLIT. If the second constructor argument is true, the components are redrawn continuously as the divider is dragged. If it is false the components are not redrawn until you stop dragging the divider.

The third argument is the component to go at the top, or to the left for HORIZONTAL_SPLIT, and the fourth argument is the component to go at the bottom, or to the right, as the case may be.

We don't need to do it here, but you can change the components in a split pane. You have methods setLeftComponent(), setRightComponent(), setTopComponent(), and setBottomComponent() to do this. You just pass a reference to a component to whichever method you want to use. There are also corresponding get methods to retrieve the components in a split pane. You can even change the orientation by calling the setOrientation() method and passing JSplitPane.HORIZONTAL_SPLIT, or JSplitPane.VERTICAL_SPLIT to it.

There is a facility to provide a widget on the divider to collapse and restore either pane. We don't need it, but if you want to try this here, you can add a statement after the JSplitPane constructor call:

```
splitPane.setOneTouchExpandable(true);
```

Passing false to this method will remove the widget.

Once we have created the splitPane object we add it to the dataPane panel with constraints that make it fill the full width of the container.

Next we can add the font size selection mechanism.

Using a Spinner

We could use another list for this, but to broaden our horizons we will use another Swing component, a JSpinner object. The JSpinner class is defined in the javax.Swing package. A JSpinner object displays a sequence of numbers or objects so the user can select any one from the set. The spinner displays up and down arrows at the side of the spinner for stepping through the list. You can also use the keyboard up/down arrow keys for this.

The sequence of choices in a spinner is managed by a SpinnerModel object. There are three concrete spinner model classes, depending on what sort of items you are choosing from:

Class	Description
SpinnerNumberModel	A model for a sequence of numbers. Numbers are stored internally and returned as type Number, which is the superclass of the classes encapsulating the primitive numerical types – Integer, Long, Double etc. Number is also the superclass of other classes such as BigDecimal, but only the classes corresponding to the primitive types are supported.
SpinnerListModel	A model for a sequence defined by an array or a List object. You could use this to use a sequence of strings as the choices in the spinner.
SpinnerDateModel	A model for a sequence of dates specified as Date objects.

We won't be able to go through all the detail on these, so let's just take a JSpinner object using a SpinnerNumberModel to contain the sequence as that fits with selecting a font size.

We will be using a fixed range of point sizes to choose from, so let's add some constants to our Constants interface to define this:

```
int pointSizeMin = 8;    // Minimum font point size
int pointSizeMax = 24;   // Maximum font point size
int pointSizeStep = 2;   // Point size step
```

Thus our smallest point size is eight, the largest is 24, and the step from 8 onwards is 2.

We create a JSpinner object by passing a SpinnerModel reference to it. For instance:

```
JSpinner spinner = new JSpinner(spinnerModel);
```

In our case the spinner model will be of type SpinnerNumberModel, and the constructor we will use expects four arguments, a current value that will be the one displayed initially, a minimum value, a maximum, and the step size. Here's how we can create that for our dialog:

```
public FontDialog(SketchFrame window) {
    // Initialization as before...
    // Button panel code as before...
    // Set up the data input panel to hold all input components as before...
    // Add the font choice prompt label as before...
```

```
// Set up font list choice component as before...
// Panel to display font sample as before...
// Create a split pane with font choice at the top as before...

// Set up the size choice using a spinner
JPanel sizePane = new JPanel();                    // Pane for size choices
label = new JLabel("Choose point size");           // Prompt for point size
sizePane.add(label);                               // Add the prompt

chooseSize = new JSpinner(new SpinnerNumberModel(fontSize,
                          pointSizeMin, pointSizeMax, pointSizeStep));
chooseSize.addChangeListener(this);  sizePane.add(chooseSize);

  // Add spinner to pane
gbLayout.setConstraints(sizePane, constraints);    // Set pane constraints
dataPane.add(sizePane);                            // Add the pane

// Plus the code for the rest of the constructor...
}
```

We again create a panel to contain the spinner and its associated prompt as it makes the layout easier. The default FlowLayout in the panel is fine for what we want. We had better add a couple more members to the FontDialog class to store the references to the chooseSize and fontDisplay objects:

```
private JSpinner chooseSize;                        // Font size options
private JLabel fontDisplay;                         // Font sample
```

A spinner generates ChangeEvent events when an item is selected that are sent to listeners of type ChangeListener. The listener for our spinner is the FontDialog object so we need to specify that it implements the ChangeListener interface:

```
class FontDialog extends JDialog
              implements Constants, ListSelectionListener,
                         ActionListener, ChangeListener {
```

The ChangeListener interface defines one method, stateChanged(), which has a parameter of type ChangeEvent. You obtain a reference to the source of the event by calling getSource() for the event object. You then need to cast the reference to the type of the source, in our case, JSpinner. For example:

```
public void stateChanged(ChangeEvent e) {
  JSpinner source = (JSpinner)e.getSource();
}
```

Of course, we want the value that is now selected in the spinner and the getValue() method will return a reference to this as type Object. Since we are using a SpinnerNumberModel object as the spinner model, the object encapsulating the value will actually be of type Number so we will have to cast the reference returned by getValue() to this type. We can get a little closer to want we what by amending our stateChanged() method to:

```
    public void stateChanged(ChangeEvent e) {
      Number value = (Number)((JSpinner)e.getSource()).getValue();
    }
```

We are not really interested in a `Number` object though. What we want is the integer value so we can store it in the `fontSize` member of the dialog and then derive a new font. The `intValue()` method for the `Number` object will produce that. We can therefore arrive at the final version of `setChanged()` that does what we want:

```
    public void stateChanged(ChangeEvent e) {
      fontSize = ((Number)(((JSpinner)e.getSource()).getValue())).intValue();
      font = font.deriveFont((float)fontSize);
      fontDisplay.setFont(font);
      fontDisplay.repaint();
    }
```

That first statement looks quite daunting but since we put it together a step at a time, you should see that it isn't really difficult – just a lot of parentheses to keep in sync.

Using Radio Buttons to Select the Font Style

We will create two `JRadioButton` objects for selecting the font style. One will select bold or not, and the other will select italic or not. A plain font is simply not bold or italic. You could use `JCheckBox` objects here if you prefer – they would work just as well. Here's the code:

```
public FontDialog(SketchFrame window) {
    // Initialization as before...
    // Button panel code as before...
    // Set up the data input panel to hold all input components as before...
    // Add the font choice prompt label as before...
    // Set up font list choice component as before...
    // Panel to display font sample as before...
    // Create a split pane with font choice at the top as before...
    // Set up the size choice using a spinner as before...

    // Set up style options using radio buttons
    JRadioButton bold = new JRadioButton("Bold", (fontStyle & Font.BOLD) > 0);
    JRadioButton italic = new JRadioButton("Italic", (fontStyle & Font.ITALIC) > 0);
    bold.addItemListener(new StyleListener(Font.BOLD));         // Add button listeners
    italic.addItemListener(new StyleListener(Font.ITALIC));
    JPanel stylePane = new JPanel();                            // Create style pane
    stylePane.add(bold);                                        // Add buttons
    stylePane.add(italic);                                      // to style pane...
    gbLayout.setConstraints(stylePane, constraints);           // Set pane constraints
    dataPane.add(stylePane);                                    // Add the pane

    getContentPane().add(dataPane, BorderLayout.CENTER);
    pack();
    setVisible(false);
}
```

1 1 1 1

It looks like a lot of code but it's repetitive as we have two radio buttons. The second argument to the JRadioButton constructor sets the state of the button. If the existing style of the current font is BOLD and/or *ITALIC*, the initial states of the buttons will be set accordingly. We add a listener of type StyleListener for each button and we will add this as an inner class to FontDialog in a moment. Note that we pass the style constant that corresponds to the set state of the button to the constructor for the listener.

The stylePane object presents the buttons using the default FlowLayout manager, and this pane is added as the last row to dataPane. The final step is to add the dataPane object as the central pane in the content pane for the dialog. The call to pack() lays out the dialog components with their preferred sizes if possible, and the setVisible() call with the argument false means that the dialog is initially hidden. Since this is a complex dialog we won't want to create a new object each time we want to display the font dialog. We will just call the setVisible() method for the dialog object with the argument true.

Listening for Radio Buttons

The inner class, StyleListener, in the FontDialog class will work on principles that you have seen before. A radio button (or a checkbox) generates ItemEvent events and the listener class must implement the ItemListener interface:

```
class StyleListener implements ItemListener {
  public StyleListener(int style) {
    this.style = style;
  }

  public void itemStateChanged(ItemEvent e) {
    if(e.getStateChange()==ItemEvent.SELECTED)   // If style was selected
      fontStyle |= style;                        // turn it on in the font style
    else
      fontStyle &= ~style;                       // otherwise turn it off
    font = font.deriveFont(fontStyle);           // Get a new font
    fontDisplay.setFont(font);                   // Change the label font
    fontDisplay.repaint();                       // repaint
  }
    private int style;                           // Style for this listener
}
```

The constructor accepts an argument that is the style for the button, so the value of the member, style, will be the value we want to set in the fontStyle member that we use to create a new Font object,– either Font.BOLD or Font.ITALIC. Since the listener for a particular button already contains the corresponding style, the itemStateChanged() method that is called when an item event occurs just switches the value of style in the fontStyle member of FontDialog either on or off, dependent on whether the radio button was selected or deselected. It then derives a font with the new style, sets it in the fontDisplay label and repaints it.

We have now completed the FontDialog class. If you have been creating the code yourself, now would be a good time to try compiling the class. All we need now is some code in the SketchFrame class to make use of it.

Try It Out – Using the Font Dialog

To get the font dialog operational in Sketcher, we need to add a new menu, **Options**, to the menu bar with a **Choose font...** menu item, and we need to install a listener for it. To keeps things ship-shape it would be best to add the fragments of code in the `SketchFrame` constructor in the places where we do similar things.

Create the **Options** menu with the following constructor code:

```
JMenu fileMenu = new JMenu("File");              // Create File menu
JMenu elementMenu = new JMenu("Elements");       // Create Elements menu
JMenu optionsMenu = new JMenu("Options");        // Create options menu
JMenu helpMenu = new JMenu("Help");              // Create Help menu

fileMenu.setMnemonic('F');                       // Create shortcut
elementMenu.setMnemonic('E');                    // Create shortcut
optionsMenu.setMnemonic('O');                    // Create shortcut
helpMenu.setMnemonic('H');                       // Create shortcut
```

You can add the menu item like this, somewhere in the constructor:

```
// Add the font choice item to the options menu
fontItem = new JMenuItem("Choose font...");
fontItem.addActionListener(this);
optionsMenu.add(fontItem);
```

We can add a declaration for the `fontItem` member of the `SketchFrame` class by adding it to the existing declaration for the `aboutItem`, which is probably somewhere near the bottom in your file. It may take some hunting with the amount of code we have got in this class now:

```
private JMenuItem aboutItem, fontItem;
```

You need to add the **Options** menu to the menu bar before the **Help** menu to be consistent with convention:

```
menuBar.add(fileMenu);                           // Add the file menu
menuBar.add(elementMenu);                        // Add the element menu
menuBar.add(optionsMenu);                        // Add the options menu
```

You can create a `FontDialog` object by adding a statement to the end of the `SketchFrame` constructor:

```
fontDlg = new FontDialog(this);
```

We can reuse the `FontDialog` object as often as we want. All we need to do to display it is to call its `setVisible()` method. Of course, we will need to declare `fontDlg` as a member of the `SketchFrame` class:

```
private FontDialog fontDlg;                      // The font dialog
```

To support the new menu item, you need to modify the `actionPerformed()` method in the `SketchFrame` class to handle its events:

```
public void actionPerformed(ActionEvent e) {
  if(e.getSource() == aboutItem) {

    // Create about dialog with the menu item as parent
    JOptionPane.showMessageDialog(this,                          // Parent
                      "Sketcher Copyright Ivor Horton 2000",// Message
                      "About Sketcher",                     // Title
                      JOptionPane.INFORMATION_MESSAGE);     // Message type
  } else if(e.getSource() == fontItem) {      // Set the dialog window position
    Rectangle bounds = getBounds();
    fontDlg.setLocation(bounds.x + bounds.width/3, bounds.y + bounds.height/3);

    fontDlg.setVisible(true);             // Show the dialog
  }
}
```

All the new `else: if` block does, is make the dialog visible after setting its location in relation to the application window. If you recompile Sketcher you will be able to play with fonts to your heart's content.

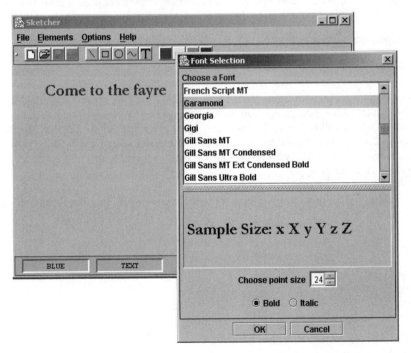

How It Works

This last piece is relatively trivial. The additional menu is added to the menubar just like the other menus. The menu item is a `JMenuItem` object rather than an `Action` object and the `actionPerformed()` method is called when the **Choose font...** menu item is clicked. This sets the top-left corner of the dialog window one third of the way in from the top and left sides of the application window. It then calls `setVisible()` for the dialog object to display it.

Pop-up Menus

The `javax.swing` package defines a class, `JPopupMenu`, that represents a menu that you can pop up at any position within a component, but conventionally you display it at the current mouse cursor position when a particular mouse button is pressed. There are two constructors in the `PopupMenu` class: one to which you pass a `String` object that defines a name for the menu, and a default constructor that defines a menu without a name. If you specify a name for a pop-up menu with a statement such as,

```
generalPopup = new PopupMenu("General");
```

the name is primarily for identification purposes and is not always displayed when the menu is popped up: it depends on your environment. Under Windows for instance it doesn't appear. This is different from a menu on a menu bar where the string you pass to the constructor is what appears on the menu bar.

Let's add a pop-up menu to the `SketchFrame` class by adding a data member of type `JPopupMenu`:

```
private JPopupMenu popup = new JPopupMenu("General");        // Window pop-up
```

To populate a pop-up menu with menu items, you add `JMenuItem` objects or `Action` objects by passing each of them to the `add()` method for the `JPopupMenu` object. You can also pass a `String` object to `add()`, which will create a `JMenuItem` object and add it to the pop-up. A reference to the menu item object is always returned by the various overloaded `add()` methods. Handling the events for the menu items is an identical process to that for regular menu items, and `Action` objects handle their own events as we have seen.

We will now add menu items to the pop-up we created above by adding the following code to the class constructor:

```
// Create pop-up menu
popup.add(lineAction);
popup.add(rectangleAction);
popup.add(circleAction);
popup.add(curveAction);
popup.add(textAction);

popup.addSeparator();
popup.add(redAction);
popup.add(yellowAction);
popup.add(greenAction);
popup.add(blueAction);
```

This adds the element menu items to the pop-up. We could also add the font choice menu item but you can't add a `JMenuItem` object to two different menus. You could either create an `Action` object that would pop up the font dialog, or you could add a different menu item to the pop-up that did the same thing when it was clicked.

Displaying a Pop-up Menu

You can display a pop-up within the coordinate system of any component, by calling the `show()` method for the `JPopupMenu` object. The method requires three arguments to be specified, a reference to the component that is the context for the pop-up, and the *x* and *y* coordinates where the menu is to be displayed, relative to the origin of the parent. For example:

```
generalPopup.show(view, xCoord, yCoord);
```

This displays the pop-up at position (xCoord, yCoord) in the coordinate system for the component, `view`.

A pop-up menu is usually implemented as a **context menu**. The principal idea of a context menu is that it's not just a single menu: it displays a different set of menu items depending on the context – that is, what is under the mouse cursor when the button is pressed. The mouse button that you press to display a context menu is sometimes called a **pop-up trigger**, simply because pressing it triggers the display of the pop-up. On systems that support the notion of a pop-up trigger, the pop-up trigger is fixed, but it can be different between systems. It is usually the right mouse button on a two- or three-button mouse, and on systems with a one-button mouse, you typically have to hold down a modifier key while pressing the mouse button.

The `MouseEvent` class has a special method, `isPopupTrigger()`, that returns `true` when the event should display a pop-up menu. This method will only return `true` in the `mousePressed()` or `mouseReleased()` methods. It will always return `false` in methods corresponding to other mouse events. This method helps to get over the problem of different mouse buttons being used on different systems to display a popup. If you use this method to decide when to display a popup, you've got them covered – well, almost. You would typically use this with the following code to display a pop-up.

```
public void mouseReleased(MouseEvent e) {
  if(e.isPopupTrigger())
    // Code to display the pop-up menu...
}
```

We have shown conceptual code for the `mouseReleased()` method here. This would be fine for Windows but unfortunately it may not work on some other systems – Solaris for instance. This is because in some operating system environments the `isPopupTrigger()` only returns `true` when the button is pressed, not when it is released. The pop up trigger is not just a particular button – it is a mouse-pressed or mouse-released event with a particular button. This implies that if you want your code to work on a variety of systems using the 'standard' mouse button to trigger the pop-up in every case, you must implement the code to call `isPopupTrigger()` and pop the menu in both the `mousePressed()` and `mouseReleased()` methods. The method will only return `true` in one or the other. Of course, you could always circumvent this by ignoring convention and pop the menu for a specific button press with code like this:

```
    if((e.getButton() == e.BUTTON3)
      // Code to display the pop-up menu...
```

Now the pop-up would only operate with button 3, regardless of the convention for the underlying operating system, but the user may not be particularly happy about having to use a different popup trigger for your Java program compared to other applications on the same system.

We will try a pop-up menu in Sketcher assuming Windows is the applicable environment. You should be able to change it to suit your environment if it is different, or even add the same code for both MOUSE_PRESSED and MOUSE_RELEASED events if you wish.

Try It Out – Displaying a Pop-up Menu

In Sketcher, the pop-up menu would sensibly operate in the area where the sketch is displayed – in other words triggering the pop-up menu has to happen in the view. Assuming you have already added the code that we discussed in the previous section to SketchFrame, we just need to add a method to SketchFrame to make the pop-up available to the view:

```
// Retrieve the pop-up menu
public JPopupMenu getPopup() {
  return popup;
}
```

Now a SketchView object can get a reference to the pop-up in the SketchFrame object by using the application object to get to this method.

We will implement the pop-up triggering in the mouseReleased() method consistent with Windows, but remember, all you need to do to make your code general is to put it in the mousePressed() method too. Here's how mouseReleased() should be in the MouseHandler inner class to SketchView:

```
public void mouseReleased(MouseEvent e) {
    if(e.isPopupTrigger()) {
      start = e.getPoint();
      theApp.getWindow().getPopup().show((Component)e.getSource(),
                                         start.x, start.y);
      start = null;
    } else if((e.getButton()==MouseEvent.BUTTON1) &&
              (theApp.getWindow().getElementType() != TEXT)) {
      button1Down = false;                  // Reset the button 1 flag
      if(tempElement != null) {
        theApp.getModel().add(tempElement);  // Add element to the model
        tempElement = null;                  // No temporary now stored
      }
      if(g2D != null)  {                     // If there's a graphics context
        g2D.dispose();                       // ...release the resource
        g2D = null;                          // Set field to null
      }
      start = last = null;                   // Remove the points
    }
  }
```

We get hold of a reference to the pop-up menu object by calling getPopup() for the object reference returned by the application object's getWindow() method. The component where the pop-up is to appear is identified in the first argument to the show() method for the pop-up by calling getSource() for the MouseEvent object, e. This will return a reference to the view, as type Object, so we need to cast this to the Component type since that is what the show() method for the pop-up expects. The position, which we store temporarily in start, is just the current cursor position when the mouse button is released. We could use the position stored in start by the mousePressed() method, but if the user drags the cursor before releasing the button, the menu will appear at a different position from where the button is released.

If you recompile Sketcher and run it again, you should get the pop-up menu appearing in response to a right button click, or whatever button triggers a context menu on your system.

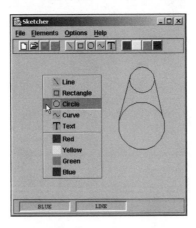

Note how we get the Icons and the label for each of the menu items. This is because we have defined both in the Action objects that we used to generate the menu.

How It Works

The isPopupTrigger() method for the MouseEvent object returns true when the button corresponding to a context menu is pressed or released. In this case we call the show() method for the pop-up menu object that we created in the SketchFrame object. When you click on a menu item in the pop-up, or click elsewhere, the pop-up menu is automatically hidden. Now any element type or color is a couple of clicks away.

This is just a pop-up menu, not a context menu. A context menu should be different depending on what's under the cursor. We will now look more closely at how we could implement a proper context menu capability in Sketcher.

Implementing a Context Menu

As a context menu displays a different menu depending on the context, it follows that the program needs to know what is under the cursor at the time the right mouse button is pressed. Let's take the specific instance of the view in Sketcher where we are listening for mouse events. We could define two contexts for the cursor in the view – one when an already-drawn element is under the cursor, and another when there is no element under the cursor. In the first context, we could display a special pop-up menu that is particularly applicable to an element – with menu items to delete the element, or move it, for example. In the second context we could display the pop-up menu that we created in the previous example. Our context menu when a drawn element is under the cursor is going to look like that shown below.

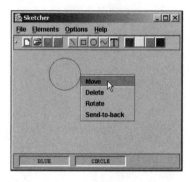

For the context menu to be really useful, the user will need to know which element is under the cursor before they pop up the context menu, otherwise they can't be sure to which element the pop-up menu operations will apply. Deleting the wrong element could be irritating.

What we need is some visual feedback to show when an element is under the cursor – highlighting the element under the cursor by changing its color, for instance.

Try It Out – Highlighting an Element

To highlight an element, we will draw it in magenta rather than its normal color. Every element will need a `boolean` variable to indicate whether it is highlighted or not. This variable will be used to determine which color should be used in the `draw()` method. We can add this variable as a data member of the `Element` class:

```
protected boolean highlighted = false;          // Highlight flag
```

You can add this line immediately following the statement for the other data members in the `Element` class definition. The variable `highlighted` will be inherited by all of the sub classes of `Element`.

We can also add the method to set the `highlighted` flag to the `Element` class:

```
// Set or reset highlight color
public void setHighlighted(boolean highlighted) {
  this.highlighted = highlighted;
}
```

This method will also be inherited by all of the sub classes of `Element`.

To implement the basis for getting highlighting to work, you need to change one line in the `draw()` method for each of the sub classes of `Element` – that is, `Element.Line`, `Element.Circle`, `Element.Curve`, `Element.Rectangle`, and `Element.Text`. The line to change is the one that sets the drawing color – it's the first line in each of the `draw()` methods. You should change it to:

```
g2D.setPaint(highlighted ? Color.MAGENTA : color);
```

Now each element can potentially be highlighted.

How It Works

The `setHighlighted()` method accepts a `boolean` value as an argument and stores it in the data member, `highlighted`. When you want an element to be highlighted, you just call this method with the argument as `true`. To switch highlighting off for an element, you call this method with the argument `false`.

Previously, the `setPaint()` statement just set the color stored in the data member, `color`, as the drawing color. Now, if `highlighted` is `true`, the color will be set to magenta, and if `highlighted` is `false`, the color stored in the data member, `color`, will be used.

To make use of highlighting to provide the visual feedback necessary for a user-friendly implementation of the context menu, we need to determine at all times what is under the cursor. This means we must track and analyze all mouse moves *all the time*!

Tracking Mouse Moves

Whenever the mouse is moved, the `mouseMoved()` method in the `MouseMotionListener` interface is called. We can therefore track mouse moves by implementing this method in the `MouseHandler` class that is an inner class to the `SketchView` class. Before we get into that, we need to decide what we mean by an element being under the cursor, and more crucially, how we are going to find out to which element, if any, this applies.

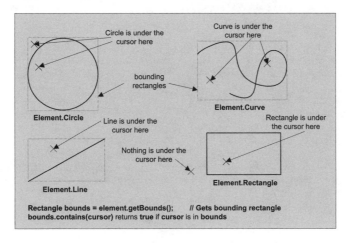

It's not going to be too difficult. We can arbitrarily decide that an element is under the cursor when the cursor position is inside the bounding rectangle for an element. This is not too precise a method, but it has the great attraction that it is extremely simple. Precise hit-testing on an element would carry considerably more processing overhead. Electing to add any greater complexity will not help us to understand the principles here, so we will stick with the simple approach.

So what is going to be the methodology for finding the element under the cursor? Brute force basically: whenever the mouse is moved, we can just search through the bounding rectangles for each of the elements in the document until we find one that encloses the current cursor position. We will then arrange for the first element that we find to be highlighted. If we get right through all the elements in the document without finding a bounding rectangle that encloses the cursor, then there isn't an element under the cursor.

To record a reference to the element that is under the cursor, we will add a data member of type `Element` to the `SketchView` class. If there isn't an element under the cursor, we will make sure that this data member is `null`.

Try It Out – Referring to Elements

Add the following statement after the statement declaring the `theApp` data member in the `SketchView` class definition:

```
private Element highlightElement;              // Highlighted element
```

The `mouseMoved()` method is going to be called very frequently, so we need to make sure it executes as quickly as possible. This means that for any given set of conditions, we execute the minimum amount of code. Here's the implementation of the `mouseMoved()` method in the `MouseHandler` class in `SketchView`:

```
// Handle mouse moves
public void mouseMoved(MouseEvent e) {
  Point currentCursor = e.getPoint();  // Get current cursor position
  Iterator elements = theApp.getModel().getIterator();
  Element element = null;                           // Stores an element

  while(elements.hasNext())  {                      // Go through the list
    element = (Element)elements.next();             // Get the next element
    if(element.getBounds().contains(currentCursor)) { // Under the cursor?
      if(element==highlightElement)             // If it's already highlighted
        return;                                 // we are done
      g2D = (Graphics2D)getGraphics();          // Get graphics context
      if(highlightElement!=null)    {           // If an element is highlighted
        highlightElement.setHighlighted(false);// un-highlight it and
        highlightElement.draw(g2D);             // draw it normal color
      }
      element.setHighlighted(true);             // Set highlight for new element
      highlightElement = element;               // Store new highlighted element
      element.draw(g2D);                        // Draw it highlighted
      g2D.dispose();                    // Release graphic context resources
      g2D = null;
```

```
      return;
    }
  }

  // Here there is no element under the cursor so...
  if(highlightElement!=null)    {              // If an element is highlighted
    g2D = (Graphics2D)getGraphics();           // Get graphics context
    highlightElement.setHighlighted(false);    // ...turn off highlighting
    highlightElement.draw(g2D);                // Redraw the element
    highlightElement = null;                   // No element highlighted
    g2D.dispose();                             // Release graphic context resources
    g2D = null;
  }
}
```

To check that highlighting works, recompile Sketcher and run it again. If you draw a few elements, you should see them change color as the cursor moves over them.

How It Works

This method is a fair amount of code so let's work through it step by step. The first statement saves the current cursor position in the local variable, currentCursor. The next two statements obtain a Graphics2D object and declare a variable, element, which we will use to store each element that we retrieve from the model. The variable, g2D will be passed to the draw() method for any element that we need to redraw highlighted or un-highlighted as the case may be.

We use an iterator we get from the model to go through the elements – you have seen how this works previously. In the loop, we obtain the bounding rectangle for each element by calling its getBounds() method, and then call the contains() method for the rectangle that is returned. This will return true if the rectangle encloses the point, currentCursor, that is passed as an argument. When we find an element under the cursor, it is quite possible that the element is already highlighted because the element was found last time the mouseMoved() method was called. This will occur when you move the cursor within the rectangle bounding an element. In this case we don't need to do anything, so we return from the method.

If the element found is not the same as last time, we obtain a graphics context for the view since we definitely need it to draw the new element we have found under the cursor in the highlight color. We then check that the variable highlightElement is not null – it will be null if the cursor just entered the rectangle for an element and previously none was highlighted. If highlightElement is not null we must un-highlight the old element before we highlight the new one. To do this we call its setHighlighted() method with the argument false, and call its draw() method. We don't need to involve the paint() method for the view here since we are not adding or removing elements – we are simply redrawing an element that is already displayed. To highlight the new element, we call its setHighlighted() method with the argument true, store a reference to the element in highlightElement and call its draw() method to get it drawn in the highlight color. We then release the graphics context resources by calling the dispose() method for g2D, set the variable back to null and return.

The next block of code in the method is executed if we exit the while loop because no element is under the cursor. In this case we must check if there was an element highlighted last time around. If there was, we un-highlight it, redraw it in its normal color and reset highlightElement to null.

Defining the Other Context Menu

The context menu when the cursor is over an element should be implemented in the view. We already have the menu defined in `SketchFrame` for when the cursor is not over an element. All we need is the context menu for when it is – plus the code to decide which menu to display when `isPopupTrigger()` returns `true` for a mouse event.

You already know that we will have four menu items in the element context menu:

❑ **Move** – to move the element under the cursor to a new position. This will work by dragging it with the left mouse button down (button 1).

❑ **Delete** – this will delete the element under the cursor.

❑ **Rotate** – this will allow you to rotate the element under the cursor about the top-left corner of its bounding rectangle by dragging it with the left mouse button down.

❑ **Send-to-back** – this is to overcome the problem of an element not being accessible, never highlighted that is, because it is masked by the bounding rectangle of another element.

Since we highlight an element by searching the list from the beginning, an element towards the end may never be highlighted if the rectangle for an earlier element completely encloses it. Moving the earlier element that is hogging the highlighting to the end of the list will allow the formerly masked element to be highlighted.

Try It Out – Creating Context Menus

We will add the necessary data members to the `SketchView` class to store the element pop-up reference, and the `JMenuItem` objects that will be the pop-up menu items:

```
private JPopupMenu elementPopup = new JPopupMenu("Element");
private JMenuItem moveItem, deleteItem,rotateItem, sendToBackItem;
```

We must add import statements for `JPopupMenu` and `JMenuItem`:

```
import javax.swing.JPopupMenu;
import javax.swing.JMenuItem;
```

We will create the `elementPopup` context menu in the `SketchView` constructor:

```
public SketchView(Sketcher theApp) {
    this.theApp = theApp;
    MouseHandler handler = new MouseHandler();      // create the mouse listener
    addMouseListener(handler);                       // Listen for button events
    addMouseMotionListener(handler);                 // Listen for motion events

    // Add the pop-up menu items
    moveItem = elementPopup.add("Move");
    deleteItem = elementPopup.add("Delete");
    rotateItem = elementPopup.add("Rotate");
    sendToBackItem = elementPopup.add("Send-to-back");
```

```
      // Add the menu item listeners
      moveItem.addActionListener(this);
      deleteItem.addActionListener(this);
      rotateItem.addActionListener(this);
      sendToBackItem.addActionListener(this);
  }
```

We add the menu items using the add() method that accepts a String argument, and returns a reference to the JMenuItem object that it creates. We then use these references to add the view object as the listener for all the menu items in the pop-up.

We must make sure the SketchView class declares that it implements the ActionListener interface:

```
class SketchView extends JComponent
                  implements Observer, Constants, ActionListener {
```

We can add the actionPerformed() method to SketchView that will handle action events from the menu items.

> As with the new data members above, be careful to add this to the **SketchView** class and not inside the inner **MouseHandler** class by mistake!

```
  public void actionPerformed(ActionEvent e ) {
    Object source = e.getSource();
    if(source == moveItem) {
      // Process a move...

    } else if(source == deleteItem) {
      // Process a delete...

    } else if(source == rotateItem) {
      // Process a rotate

    } else if(source == sendToBackItem) {
      // Process a send-to-back...
    }
  }
```

Of course, we will need two more import statements in the SketchView.java file:

```
  import java.awt.event.ActionEvent;
  import java.awt.event.ActionListener;
```

To pop the menu we need to modify the code in the mouseReleased() method of the MouseHandler inner class a little:

```
        public void mouseReleased(MouseEvent e) {
          if(e.isPopupTrigger()) {
            start = e.getPoint();

            if(highlightElement == null)
              theApp.getWindow().getPopup().show((Component)e.getSource(),
                                                  start.x, start.y);
            else
              elementPopup.show((Component)e.getSource(), start.x, start.y);

            start = null;
          }
          // Plus the rest of the code as before...
        }
```

This just adds an if-else to display the element dialog when there is an element highlighted. If you recompile Sketcher you should get a different context menu depending on whether an element is under the cursor or not.

How It Works

The mouseReleased() method in the MouseHandler inner class now pops one or other of the two pop-ups we have, depending on whether the reference in highlightElement is null or not. You can select items from the general pop-up to set the color or the element type, but the element pop-up menu does nothing at present. It just needs a few lines of code somewhere to do moves and rotations and stuff. Don't worry – it'll be like falling off a log – but not so painful.

Deleting Elements

Let's take the easiest one first – deleting an element. All that's involved here is calling remove() for the model object from the actionPerformed() method in SketchView. Let's give it a try.

Try It Out – Deleting Elements

The code we need to add to actionPerformed() in the SketchView class looks like this:

```
        public void actionPerformed(ActionEvent e) {
          Object source = e.getSource();
          if(source == moveItem) {
            // Process a move...

          } else if(source == deleteItem) {
            if(highlightElement != null) {                  // If there's an element
              theApp.getModel().remove(highlightElement);   // then remove it
              highlightElement = null;                      // Remove the reference
            }
          } else if(source == rotateItem) {
            // Process a rotate
          } else if(source == sendToBackItem) {

            // Process a send-to-back...
          }
        }
```

This is a cheap operation requiring only six lines. Recompile, create a few elements, and then watch them disappear with a right button click.

How It Works

After verifying that `highlightElement` is not `null`, we call the `remove()` method that we added in the `SketchModel` class way back. This will delete the element from the list, so when the view is repainted it will no longer be displayed. The repaint occurs automatically because the `update()` method for the view – the method we implemented for the `Observer` interface – will be called because the model has changed. Of course, we must remember to set `highlightElement` to `null` too, otherwise it could get drawn by a mouse handler even though it is no longer in the model.

Let's do another easy one – Send-to-Back.

Implementing the Send-to-Back Operation

The send-to-back operation is really an extension of the delete operation. We can move an element from wherever it is in the list by deleting it, then adding it again at the end of the list.

Try It Out – The Send-to-Back Operation

The `actionPerformed()` method in the `SketchView` class has the job of removing the highlighted element from wherever it is in the model, and then adding it back at the end:

```
public void actionPerformed(ActionEvent e) {
  Object source = e.getSource();
  if(source == moveItem) {
    // (Process a move...)

  } else if(source == deleteItem) {
    // Code as inserted here earlier

  } else if(source == rotateItem) {
    // (Process a rotate)

  } else if(source == sendToBackItem) {
    if(highlightElement != null) {
      theApp.getModel().remove(highlightElement);
      theApp.getModel().add(highlightElement);
      highlightElement.setHighlighted(false);
      highlightElement = null;
      repaint();
    }
  }
}
```

A little harder this time – eight lines of code. You can try this by drawing a few concentric circles, with the outermost drawn first. An outer circle will prevent an inner circle from being highlighted, but applying **Send-to-back** to the outer circle will make the inner circle accessible.

899

How It Works

This uses the `remove()` method in `SketchModel` to remove the highlighted element, and then calls the `add()` method to put it back – it will automatically be added to the end of the elements in the list. We switch off the highlighting of the element to indicate that it's gone to the back of the queue, and reset `highlightElement` back to `null`.

We have run out of easy ones. We must now deal with a not quite so easy one – the move operation. To handle this we must look into a new topic – transforming the user coordinate system. If you are not of a mathematical bent, some of what we will discuss here can sound complicated. Even if your math may be very rusty, you should not have too many problems. Like a lot of things it's the unfamiliarity of the jargon that makes it seem more difficult than it is.

Transforming the User Coordinate System

We said when we started learning how to draw on a component that the drawing operations are specified in a user-coordinate system, and the user coordinates are converted to a device coordinate system. The conversion of coordinates from user system to device system is taken care of by the methods in the graphics context object that we use to do the drawing, and they do this by applying a **transformation** to the user coordinates. The term 'transformation' refers to the computational operations that result in the conversion.

By default, the origin, the (0, 0) point, in the user coordinate system corresponds to the (0, 0) point in the device coordinates system. The axes are also coincident too, with positive *x* heading from left to right, and positive *y* from top to bottom. However you can move the origin of the user coordinate system relative to its default position. Such a move is called a **translation**.

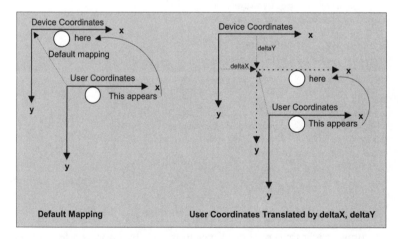

A fixed value, `deltaX` say, is added to each *x* coordinate, and another value, `deltaY` say, is added to every *y* coordinate and the effect of this is to move the origin of the user coordinate system relative to the device coordinate system: everything will be shifted to the right and down compared to where it would have been without the translation. Of course, the `deltaX` and `deltaY` values can be negative, in which case it would shift things to the left and up.

A translation is one kind of **affine transformation**. Affine is a funny word. Some say it goes back to Laurel and Hardy where Ollie says, "This is affine mess you've got us into", but I don't subscribe to that. An affine transformation is actually a linear transformation that leaves straight lines still straight and parallel lines still parallel. As well as translations, there are other kinds of affine transformation that you can define:

❑ **Rotation** – the user coordinates system is rotated through a given angle about its origin.

❑ **Scale** – the x and y coordinates are each multiplied by a scaling factor, and the multipliers for x and y can be different. This enables you to enlarge or reduce something in size. If the scale factor for one coordinate axis is negative, then objects will be reflected in the other axis. Setting the scale factor for x coordinates to –1, for example, will make all positive coordinates negative and vice versa so everything is reflected in the y axis.

❑ **Shear** – this is perhaps a less familiar operation. It adds a value to each x coordinate that depends on the y coordinate, and adds a value to each y coordinate that depends on the x coordinate. You supply two values to specify a shear, sX and sY say, and they change the coordinates in the following way:

Each x coordinate becomes $(x + sX * y)$
Each y coordinate becomes $(y + sY * x)$

The effect of this can be visualized most easily if you first imagine a rectangle that is drawn normally. A shearing transform can squash it by tilting the sides – rather like when you flatten a carton – but keep opposite sides straight and parallel.

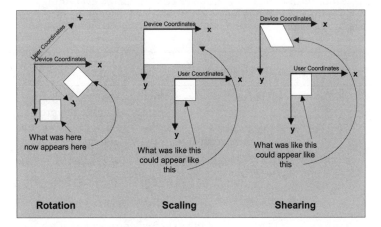

The illustration shows:

❑ A rotation of -π/4 radians, which is –45 degrees. Rotation angles are expressed in radians and a positive angle rotates everything from the positive x-axis towards the positive y-axis – therefore clockwise. The rotation in the illustration is negative and therefore counterclockwise.

❑ A scaling transformation corresponding to an x scale of 2.5 and a y scale of 1.5.

❑ A shearing operation where only the x coordinates have a shear factor. The factor for the y coordinates is 0 so they are unaffected and the transformed shape is the same height as the original.

The AffineTransform Class

In Java, the `AffineTransform` class in the `java.awt.geom` package represents an affine transformation. Every `Graphics2D` graphics context has one. The default `AffineTransform` object in a graphics context is the **identity transform**, which leaves user coordinates unchanged. It is applied to the user coordinate system anyway for everything you draw, but all the coordinates are unaltered by default. You can retrieve a copy of the current transform for a graphics context object by calling its `getTransform()` method. For example:

```
AffineTransform at = g2D.getTransform();    // Get current transform
```

While this retrieves a copy of the current transform for a graphics context, you can also set it with another transform object:

```
g2D.setTransform(at);
```

You can retrieve the transform currently in effect with `getTransform()`, set it to some other operation before you draw some shapes, and then restore the original transform later with `setTransform()` when you're finished. The fact that `getTransform()` returns a reference to a copy rather than a reference to the original transform object is important. It means you can alter the existing transform and then restore the copy later.

Although the default transform object for a graphics context leaves everything unchanged, you could set it to do something by calling one of its member functions. All of these have a return type of `void` so none of them return anything:

Transform Default	Description

setToTranslation (double deltaX, double deltaY)	This method makes the transform a translation of `deltaX` in *x* and `deltaY` in *y*. This replaces whatever the previous transform was for the graphics context. You could apply this to the transform for a graphics context with the statements:
	
	`// Save current transform and set a new one`
	`AffineTransform at = g2D.getTransform();`
	`at.setToTranslation(5.0, 10.0);`
	
	The effect of the new transform will be to shift everything that is drawn in the graphics context, `g2D`, 5.0 to the right, and down by 10.0. This will apply to everything that is drawn in `g2D` subsequent to the statement that sets the new transform.

Transform Default	Description
setToRotation (double angle)	You call this method for a transform object to make it a rotation of angle radians about the origin. This replaces the previous transform. To rotate the axes 30 degrees clockwise, you could write: `g2D.getTransform().setToRotation(30*Math.PI/180);` This statement gets the current transform object for g2D and sets it to be the rotation specified by the expression 30*Math.PI/180. Since π radians is 180 degrees, this expression produces the equivalent to 30 degrees in radians.

setToRotation (double angle, double deltaX, double deltaY)	This method defines a rotation of angle radians about the point deltaX,deltaY. It is equivalent to three successive transform operations – a translation by deltaX, deltaY, then a rotation through angle radians about the new position of the origin and then a translation back by -deltaX,-deltaY to restore the previous origin point.
	
	You could use this to draw a shape rotated about the shape's reference point. For example, if the reference point for a shape was at shapeX,shapeY, you could draw the shape rotated through π/3 radians with the following:
	
	`g2D.getTransform().setToRotation(Math.PI/3,`
	`                                 shapeX, shapeY);`
	`// Draw the shape...`
	
	The coordinate system has been rotated about the point shapeX,shapeY, and will remain so until you change the transformation in effect. You would probably want to restore the original transform after drawing the shape rotated.

setToScale (double scaleX, double scaleY)	This method sets the transform object to scale the x coordinates by scaleX, and the y coordinates by scaleY. To draw everything half scale you could set the transformation with the statement: `g2D.getTransform().setToScale(0.5, 0.5);`
setToShear (double shearX, double shearY)	The x coordinates are converted to x+shearX*y, and the y coordinates are converted to y+shearY*x.

All of these methods that we have discussed here replace the transform in an AffineTransform object. We can modify the existing transform object in a graphics context, too.

Modifying the Transformation for a Graphics Context

Modifying the current transform for a `Graphics2D` object involves calling a method for the `Graphics2D` object. The effect in each case is to *add* whatever transform you are applying to whatever the transform did before. You can add each of the four kinds of transforms that we discussed before using the following methods defined in the `Graphics2D` class:

```
translate(double deltaX, double deltaY)
translate(int deltaX, int deltaY)
rotate(double angle)
rotate(double angle, double deltaX, double deltaY)
scale(double scaleX, double scaleY)
shear(double shearX, double shearY)
```

Each of these adds or **concatenates** the transform specified to the existing transform object for a `Graphics2D` object. Therefore you can cause a translation of the coordinate system followed by a rotation about the new origin position with the statements:

```
g2D.translate(5, 10);        // Translate the origin
g2D.rotate(Math.PI/3);       // Clockwise rotation 60 degrees
g2D.draw(line);              // Draw in translate and rotated space
```

Of course, you can apply more than two transforms to the user coordinate system – as many as you like. However, it is important to note that the order in which you apply the transforms matters. To see why, look at the example below.

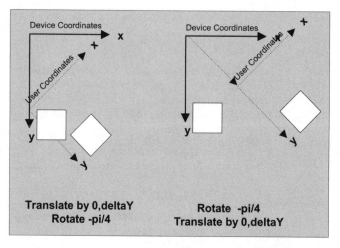

This shows just two transforms in effect, but it should be clear that the sequence in which they are applied makes a big difference. This is because the second transform is always applied relative to the new position of the coordinate system after the first transform has been applied. If you need more convincing that the order in which you apply transforms matters, you can apply some transforms to yourself. Stand with your back to any wall in the room. Now apply a translation – take three steps forward. Next apply a rotation – turn through 45 degrees clockwise. Make a mental note of where you are. If you now go back and stand with your back to the wall in the original position and first turn through 45 degrees before you take the three steps forward, you will clearly be in quite a different place in the room from the first time around.

Next on our affine tour – how we can create completely new `AffineTransform` objects.

Creating AffineTransform Objects

Of course, there are constructors for `AffineTransform` objects: the default 'identity' constructor and a number of other constructors, but we don't have space to go into them here. The easiest way to create transform objects is to call a `static` member of the `AffineTransform` class. There are four static methods corresponding to the four kinds of transform that we discussed earlier:

```
getTranslateInstance(double deltaX, double deltaY)
getRotateInstance(double angle)
getScaleInstance(double scaleX, double scaleY)
getShearInstance(double shearX, double shearY)
```

Each of these returns an `AffineTransform` object containing the transform that you specify by the arguments. To create a transform to rotate the user space by 90 degrees, you could write:

```
AffineTransform at = AffineTransform.getRotateInstance(Math.PI/2);
```

Once you have an `AffineTransform` object, you can apply it to a graphics context by passing it as an argument to the `setTransform()` method. It has another use too: you can use it to transform a `Shape` object. The `createTransformedShape()` method for the `AffineTransform` object does this. Suppose we define a `Rectangle` object with the statement:

```
Rectangle rect = new Rectangle(10, 10, 100, 50);
```

We now have a rectangle that is 100 wide by 50 high, at position 10,10. We can create a transform object with the statement:

```
AffineTransform at = getTranslateInstance(25, 30);
```

This is a translation in x of 25, and a translation in y of 30. We can create a new `Shape` from our rectangle with the statement:

```
Shape transRect = at.createTransformedShape(rect);
```

Our new `transRect` object will look the same as the original rectangle but translated by 25 in x and 30 in y, so its top-left corner will now be at (35, 40).

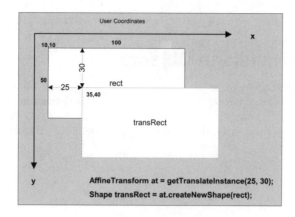

However, even though it will still look like a rectangle it will not be a `Rectangle` object. The `createTransformedShape()` method always returns a `GeneralPath` object since it has to work with any transform. This is because some transformations will deform a shape – applying a shear to a rectangle results in a shape that is no longer a rectangle. The method also has to apply any transform to any `Shape` object, and returning a `GeneralPath` shape makes this possible.

Let's try some of this out. A good place to do this is with our shape classes. At the moment we draw each shape or text element in the place where the cursor happens to be. Let's use a translation to change how this works. We will redefine each nested class to `Element` so that it translates the user coordinate system to where the shape should be, and then draws itself at the origin (0, 0). You could try to do this yourself before reading on. You just need to apply some of the transform methods we have been discussing.

Try It Out – Translation

To make this work we will need to save the position for each element that is passed to the constructor – this is the start point recorded in the `mousePressed()` method – and use this to create a translate transform in the `draw()` method for the element. Since we are going to store the position of every class object that has `Element` as a base, we might as well store the location in a data member of the base class. We can redefine the base class, `Element`, to do this:

```
public abstract class Element {
  public Element(Color color) {
    this.color = color;
  }

  public Color getColor(){
    return color;
  }

  // Set or reset highlight color
  public void setHighlighted(boolean highlighted) {
    this.highlighted = highlighted;
  }

  public Point getPosition() {
    return position;
```

```
   }

   public abstract java.awt.Rectangle getBounds();
   public abstract void modify(Point start, Point last);
   public abstract void draw(Graphics2D g2D);

   protected Color color;                      // Color of a shape
   protected boolean highlighted = false;      // Highlight flag
   final static Point origin = new Point();    // Point 0,0
   protected Point position;                   // Element position


   // Definitions for our shape classes...
 }
```

You might consider passing the start point to the `Element` constructor, but this wouldn't always work. This is because we need to figure out what the reference point is in some cases – for rectangles, for example. The position of a rectangle will be the top left corner, which is not necessarily the start point. We have included a method to retrieve the position of an element, as we are sure to need it. We also have added another member, `origin`, which is the point (0, 0). This will be useful in all the derived classes, as we will now draw every element at that point. Since we only need one, it is `static`, and since we won't want to change it, it is `final`.

Let's start with the nested class, `Line`.

Translating Lines

We need to update the constructor first of all:

```
   public Line(Point start, Point end, Color color) {
     super(color);
     position = start;
     line = new Line2D.Double(origin, new Point(end.x - position.x,
                                                 end.y - position.y));
   }
```

We've saved the point start in `position`, and created the `Line2D.Double` shape as the origin. Of course, we have to adjust the coordinates of the end point so that it is relative to (0, 0).

We can now implement the `draw()` method to use a transform to move the coordinate system to where the line should be drawn. We can economize on the code in the element classes a little by thinking about this because a lot of the code is essentially the same. Here's how we would implement the method for the `Element.Line` class directly:

```
   public void draw(Graphics2D g2D) {
     g2D.setPaint(highlighted ? Color.MAGENTA : color);  // Set the line color
     AffineTransform old = g2D.getTransform();            // Save the current transform
     g2D.translate(position.x, position.y);               // Translate to position
     g2D.draw(line);                                      // Draw the line
     g2D.setTransform(old);                               // Restore original transform
   }
```

Before you do this, let's cover what this does. To draw the line in the right place, we just have to apply a translation to the coordinate system before the draw() operation. Saving a copy of the old transform is most important, as that enables us to restore the original scheme after we've drawn the line. If we don't do this, subsequent draw operations in the same graphics context will have more and more translations applied cumulatively, so objects get further and further away from where they should be. Only one line of code here involves the element itself, however:

```
g2D.draw(line);                              // Draw the line
```

All the rest will be common to most of the types of shapes – text being the exception. We could add an overloaded draw() method to the base class, Element, that we can define like this:

```
protected void draw(Graphics2D g2D, Shape element) {
  g2D.setPaint(highlighted ? Color.MAGENTA : color);   // Set the element color
  AffineTransform old = g2D.getTransform();       // Save the current transform
  g2D.translate(position.x, position.y);          // Translate to position
  g2D.draw(element);                              // Draw the element
  g2D.setTransform(old);                          // Restore original transform
}
```

You may need to add an import for java.awt.geom.AffineTransform. This will draw any Shape object after applying a translation to the point, position. We can now call this method from the draw() method in the Element.Line class:

```
public void draw(Graphics2D g2D) {
  draw(g2D, line);                         // Call base draw method
}
```

You can now go ahead and implement the draw() method in exactly the same way for all the nested classes to Element, with the exception of the Element.Text class. Just pass the underlying Shape reference for each class as the second argument to the overloaded draw() method. We can't use the base class helper method in the Element.Text because text is not a Shape object. We will come back to the class defining text as a special case.

We must think about the bounding rectangle for a line now. We don't want the bounding rectangle for a line to be at (0, 0). We want it to be defined in terms of the coordinate system before it is translated. This is because when we use it for highlighting, no transforms are in effect. For that to work the bounding rectangle must be in the same reference frame.

This means that we must apply the translation to the bounding rectangle that corresponds to the Line2D.Double shape. A base class helper method will come in handy here too:

```
protected java.awt.Rectangle getBounds(java.awt.Rectangle bounds) {
  AffineTransform at = AffineTransform.getTranslateInstance(position.x,
                                                            position.y);
  return at.createTransformedShape(bounds).getBounds();
}
```

Just add this method to the code for the Element class.

We first create an `AffineTransform` object that applies a translation to the point, `position`. Then we apply the `createTransformedShape()` method to the rectangle that is passed as the argument – which will be the bounding rectangle for a shape at $(0, 0)$ – to get a corresponding shape translated to its proper position. Even though we get a `GeneralPath` object back, we can get a rectangle from that quite easily by calling its `getBounds()` method. Thus our helper method accepts a reference to an object of type `java.awt.Rectangle`, and returns a reference to the rectangle that results from translating this to the point, `position`. This is precisely what we want to do with the bounding rectangles we get with our shapes defined at the origin. We can now use this to implement the `getBounds()` method for the `Element.Line` class:

```
public java.awt.Rectangle getBounds() {
   return getBounds(line.getBounds());
}
```

We just pass the reference to the `line` member of the class as the argument to the base class version of `getBounds()`, and return the rectangle that is returned by that method. The `getBounds()` methods for the nested classes `Rectangle`, `Circle`, and `Curve` will be essentially the same – just change the argument to the base class `getBounds()` call to the `Shape` reference corresponding to each class. To implement the `getBounds()` method for the `Text` class, just pass the `bounds` member of that class as the argument to the base class `getBounds()` method.

We must also update the `modify()` method, and this is going to be specific to each class. To adjust the end point of a line so that it is relative to the start point at the origin, we must change the method in the `Element.Line` class as follows:

```
public void modify(Point start, Point last) {
   line.x2 = last.x - position.x;
   line.y2 = last.y - position.y;
}
```

That's the `Element.Line` class complete. We can apply the same thing to all the other classes in the `Element` class.

Translating Rectangles

Here's the changes to `Element.Rectangle` constructor:

```
public Rectangle(Point start, Point end, Color color) {
   super(color);
   position = new Point(Math.min(start.x, end.x),
                        Math.min(start.y, end.y));
   rectangle = new Rectangle2D.Double(origin.x,
                                      origin.y,
                                      Math.abs(start.x - end.x),    // Width
                                      Math.abs(start.y - end.y));   // & height
}
```

The expressions for the coordinates for the point, `position`, ensure that we do set it as the location of the top-left corner. The rectangle object is defined with its top-left corner at the origin, and its width and height as before. We have to adjust the `modify()` method to adjust the location stored in position, and leave the rectangle defined at the origin:

```
public void modify(Point start, Point last) {
    position.x = Math.min(start.x, last.x);
    position.y = Math.min(start.y, last.y);
    rectangle.width = Math.abs(start.x - last.x);
    rectangle.height = Math.abs(start.y - last.y);
}
```

You should already have added the revised version of the `draw()` and `getBounds()` methods for an `Element.Rectangle` object essentially the same as that for lines.

Translating Circles

The `Element.Circle` class constructor is also very easy:

```
public Circle(Point center, Point circum, Color color) {
    super(color);

    // Radius is distance from center to circumference
    double radius = center.distance(circum);
    position = new Point(center.x - (int)radius,
                         center.y - (int)radius);

    circle = new Ellipse2D.Double(origin.x, origin.y,     // Position - top-left
                            2.*radius, 2.*radius );  // Width & height
}
```

The radius is calculated as before, and we make the top-left corner of the `Ellipse2D.Double` object the origin point. Thus `position` is calculated as for the top-left corner in the previous version of the constructor. We can adjust the `modify()` method to record the new coordinates of `position`:

```
public void modify(Point center, Point circum) {
    double radius = center.distance(circum);
    position.x = center.x - (int)radius;
    position.y = center.y - (int)radius;
    circle.width = circle.height = 2*radius;
}
```

The `draw()` and `getBounds()` methods are already done, so it's curves next.

Translating Curves

The `Element.Curve` class is just as simple:

```
public Curve(Point start, Point next, Color color) {
    super(color);
```

```
        curve = new GeneralPath();
        position = start;
        curve.moveTo(origin.x, origin.y);
        curve.lineTo(next.x - position.x,
                     next.y - position.y);
    }
```

We store the start point in `position`, and create the curve starting at $(0, 0)$. The end point has to be adjusted so that it is defined relative to $(0, 0)$. Adding a new segment in the `modify()` method also has to be changed to take account of the new origin for the curve relative to the start point:

```
    public void modify(Point start, Point next) {
        curve.lineTo(next.x - start.x,
                     next.y - start.y);
    }
```

We just subtract the coordinates of the original start point that we saved in `position` from the point, `next`. The methods for drawing the curve and getting the bounding rectangle have already been updated, so the last piece is the `Element.Text` class.

Translating Text

The first step is to remove the declaration for the member, `position`, from this class, as we will now be using the member of the same name that is inherited from the base class.

The only changes we need to make to the constructor are as follows:

```
    public Text(Font font, String text, Point position,
                Color color, java.awt.Rectangle bounds) {
        super(color);
        this.font = font;
        this.position = position;
        this.position.y -= (int)bounds.getHeight();
        this.text = text;
        this.bounds = new java.awt.Rectangle(origin.x, origin.y,
                                             bounds.width, bounds.height);
    }
```

The bounding rectangle for the text object now has its top left corner at the origin. The point `position` that defines where the text is to be drawn is set to correspond to the top-left corner of the rectangle bounding the text, to be consistent with the way it is defined for the other elements. We will need to take account of this in our implementation of the `draw()` method because the `drawString()` method expects the position for the text to be the bottom-left corner:

```
    public void draw(Graphics2D g2D) {
        g2D.setPaint(highlighted ? Color.MAGENTA : color);
        Font oldFont = g2D.getFont();              // Save the old font
        g2D.setFont(font);                         // Set the new font
```

```
      AffineTransform old = g2D.getTransform();      // Save the current transform
      g2D.translate(position.x, position.y);         // Translate to position
      g2D.drawString(text, origin.x, origin.y+(int)bounds.getHeight());
      g2D.setTransform(old);                         // Restore original transform

    g2D.setFont(oldFont);                            // Restore the old font
  }
```

The transformation applied in the `draw()` method here is essentially the same as for the other classes. We now add the height of the bounding rectangle to the *y* coordinate of position in the argument to `drawString()`. This specifies the bottom-left corner of the first text character.

You can now recompile Sketcher for another trial. If you have done everything right it should still work as before.

How It Works

All the classes defining elements create the elements at the origin, and store their location in a member, `position`, that is inherited from the base class, `Element`. The draw methods all apply a transform to move the coordinate system to the point stored in `position` before drawing the element. The `draw()` methods then restore the original transform to leave the graphics context unchanged. Each of the `getBounds()` methods returns a bounding rectangle in the original untransformed coordinate system, because that is the context in which we shall be using it. We are now ready to try moving elements around.

Moving an Element

Now we can implement the **Move** operation that we provided for in the context menu. Taking the trouble to define all the elements relative to the origin and using a transform to position them correctly, really pays off when you want to apply other transformations to the elements. We can add a `move()` method to the base class, `Element`, that will move any element, and it is just two lines of code:

```
public void move(int deltax, int deltay) {
  position.x += deltax;
  position.y += deltay;
}
```

Let's review the process that we will implement to make a move. From a user point of view, to move an element you just click on the **Move** menu item, then drag the highlighted element to where you want it to be with button 1 held down.

In programming terms a move will be initiated in the `actionPerformed()` method in `SketchView` that responds to a menu selection. When the **Move** menu item is clicked, we will set the operating mode to what we will define as `MOVE` mode, so that we can detect this in the mouse handler methods that will expedite a move. The **Rotate** menu will work in exactly the same way, setting a `ROTATE` mode. To accommodate this we will add a member, `mode`, of type `int`, to store the current operating mode. By default, it will be `NORMAL`.

Add the following declaration to `SketchView`:

```
private int mode = NORMAL;
```

We will add the definitions of these operating modes to the `Constants` interface by adding the following statements:

```
// Operating modes
int NORMAL = 0;
int MOVE   = 1;
int ROTATE = 2;
```

When we set the operating mode to other than `NORMAL`, the methods dealing with mouse events will need to know to which element the mode applies, so we will add another member to `SketchView` to record this:

```
private Element selectedElement;
```

Now we can implement `actionPerformed()` in the `SketchView` class as:

```
public void actionPerformed(ActionEvent e) {
  Object source = e.getSource();
  if(source == moveItem) {
    mode = MOVE;
    selectedElement = highlightElement;

  } else if(source == deleteItem) {
    if(highlightElement != null)    {          // If there's an element
      theApp.getModel().remove(highlightElement);   // then remove it
      highlightElement = null;                 // Remove the reference
    }
  } else if(source == rotateItem) {
    mode = ROTATE;
    selectedElement = highlightElement;

  } else if(source == sendToBackItem) {
    if(highlightElement != null) {
      theApp.getModel().remove(highlightElement);
      theApp.getModel().add(highlightElement);
      highlightElement.setHighlighted(false);
      highlightElement = null;
    ...
```

All the moving of the highlighted element will be managed in the `mouseDragged()` method in the `MouseHandler` inner class to `SketchView`.

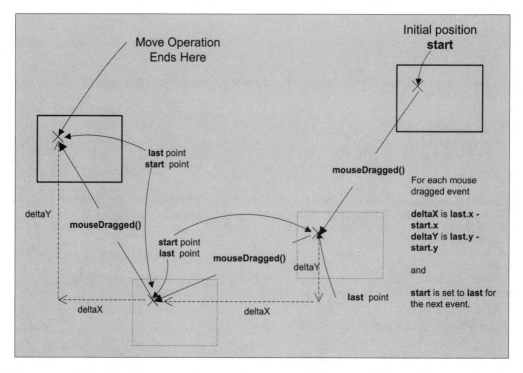

Each move will be from the previous cursor position stored in start, to the current cursor position when the MOUSE_DRAGGED event occurred. The current cursor position will be obtained by calling the getPoint() method for the event object passed to the mouseDragged() method. Once each mouse move has been processed, the current cursor position will then be stored in the variable start, ready for the next event. For each MOUSE_DRAGGED event, we will move the element the distance between successive cursor positions.

Try It Out – Moving Elements

Since the element classes are equipped to move, and we have kitted out SketchView to handle the menu item action, we just need to add the code to the methods in MouseHandler. The mousePressed() method records the start point for a move, and it also sets up the XOR mode for drawing. That's precisely what we will need to move or rotate elements, so we do not need to alter it at all.

We have to test for the setting of mode in the mouseDragged() method though, and, in principle, execute different code depending on what it is. We have three possibilities: NORMAL, where we do as we did before; MOVE, where we will execute a move operation; and ROTATE, which we will come to later. Here's the new version of mouseDragged() to accommodate moving elements:

```
public void mouseDragged(MouseEvent e) {
    last = e.getPoint();                              // Save cursor position

    if(button1Down && (theApp.getWindow().getElementType() != TEXT)
                 && (mode == NORMAL)) {
        if(tempElement == null) {                     // Is there an element?
```

```
      tempElement = createElement(start, last);      // No, so create one
    } else {
      tempElement.draw(g2D);                          // Yes - draw to erase it
      tempElement.modify(start, last);                // Modify it
    }
    tempElement.draw(g2D);                            // and draw it

  } else if(button1Down && mode == MOVE && selectedElement != null) {
    selectedElement.draw(g2D);                        // Draw to erase the element
    selectedElement.move(last.x-start.x, last.y-start.y);  // Move it
    selectedElement.draw(g2D);                        // Draw in its new position
    start = last;                                     // Make start current point
  }
}
```

Now we only execute the previous code in NORMAL mode. For MOVE mode, if button 1 is down and there is an element selected to move, we move it by erasing it at the current position, moving the element by calling its move() method, and drawing it at the new position. The current last will be start for the next MOUSE_DRAGGED event.

The final alterations to our code occur in the mouseReleased() method:

```
public void mouseReleased(MouseEvent e) {
  if(e.isPopupTrigger()) {
    start = e.getPoint();

    if(highlightElement==null)
      theApp.getWindow().getPopup().show((Component)e.getSource(),
                                         start.x, start.y);
    else
      elementPopup.show((Component)e.getSource(), start.x, start.y);

  } else if((e.getButton()==MouseEvent.BUTTON1) &&
            (theApp.getWindow().getElementType() != TEXT) && mode == NORMAL) {
    button1Down = false;                              // Reset the button 1 flag
    if(tempElement != null) {
      theApp.getModel().add(tempElement);   // Add element to the model
      tempElement = null;                             // No temporary element now stored
    }
  } else if((e.getButton()==MouseEvent.BUTTON1) &&
            (mode == MOVE || mode == ROTATE)) {
    button1Down = false;                              // Reset the button 1 flag
    if(selectedElement != null)
      repaint();
    mode = NORMAL;
  }

  if(g2D != null) {
    g2D.dispose();                                    // Release graphic context resource
    g2D = null;                                       // Set it to null
  }
```

```
        start = last = null;                    // Remove the points
        selectedElement = tempElement = null;   // Reset elements
    }
```

The last block of code is not entirely new – some of it has been relocated from earlier in the code for the previous version. We have an extra condition in the original `if` expression to check for NORMAL mode. The next `if` tests for MOVE mode or ROTATE mode because in either case we will have changed an element by dragging it around, and will therefore want to redraw the view. This is the one place where we must do this explicitly because the model is not aware of these changes. If `selectedElement` is not `null`, we call `repaint()` for the view to get it redrawn and we restore NORMAL mode. Outside of all the `if`s we reset everything back to `null`.

If you recompile Sketcher and rerun it, you can now produce sketches like that below:

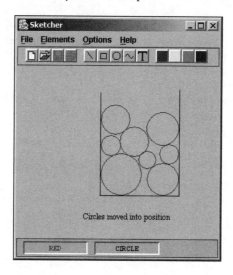

How It Works

Using a transform to position each element means that a move consists of just altering the `position` member of an element. The move operation depends on setting a MOVE mode for the mouse event handling methods to respond to. A move for each element is the same: drawing the element in XOR mode in its original position to erase it, moving it, and then drawing it again in the new position. You may see pixels left behind as you move elements, particularly text.

This is due to rounding in the floating-point operations mapping user coordinates to device coordinates. They all disappear when the move is complete and the whole picture is redrawn.

Now we have made Move work, Rotate will be a piece of cake.

Rotating Elements

Clearly we are going to make use of another transform to implement this. We know how to create a rotate | transform, so all we need to figure out is the mechanics of how the user accomplishes the rotation of an element.

916

The first step is already in place – the `actionPerformed()` method in `SketchView` already sets ROTATE mode in response to the **Rotate** menu action. The user will then drag the element to the angle required with the mouse, while holding button 1 down. We need to work out the rotation angle for each MOUSE_DRAGGED event. The diagram below shows what happens when the mouse is dragged for a rotation.

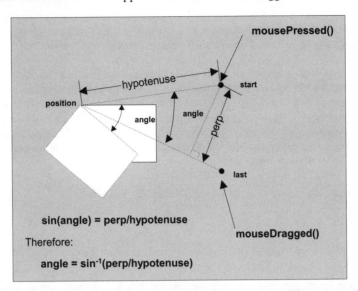

The angle in the diagram is exaggerated so we can see what is going on. The `mousePressed()` method is called when the button is first pressed at some arbitrary position and the cursor position is recorded in `start`. When the `mouseDragged()` method is called, we record the cursor position in `last`, and we now need to calculate `angle`. We must apply a little high school math to get this, which you can ignore if you are rusty with trigonometry.

We can get the length of the perpendicular from the point `start` to the line extending from `position` to `last` with a static method in the `Line2D` class:

```
double perp = Line2D.ptLineDist(position.x, position.y,
                                last.x, last.y,
                                start.x, start.y);
```

The `ptLineDist()` method calculates the perpendicular distance of the point specified by the last two arguments, to the line specified by the first four arguments – the first pair of arguments being the coordinates of the beginning of the line, and the second pair being the coordinates of the end point.

We know how to get the distance from `position` to `start`. We just apply the `distance()` method that is defined in the `Point` class:

```
double hypotenuse = position.distance(start);
```

From the diagram you can see that we can calculate `angle` as:

```
sin-1(perp/hypotenuse)
```

This comes from the definition of what the sine of an angle is. The `Math` class provides a method to calculate `sin-1` values (also called arcsine values), so we can calculate `angle` as:

```
double angle = Math.asin(perp/hypotenuse);
```

The `asin()` method returns an angle in radians between $-\pi/2$ and $\pi/2$, which is fine for us. We are unlikely to create an angle outside this range for a `mouseDragged()` event.

Of course, we need to know which way the rotation is going, clockwise or counterclockwise. Another static method in the `Line2D` class can help out here. The `relativeCCW()` method determines where a point lies with respect to a line. If you have to rotate the line clockwise to reach the point, the method returns -1, and if you have to rotate the line counterclockwise it returns $+1$. We can use this to test whether the point, `last`, is clockwise or counterclockwise with respect to the line from `position` to `start`. Since angles rotating the coordinate system clockwise are positive, we can calculate a suitably signed value for `angle` with the statement:

```
double angle = -Line2D.relativeCCW(position.x, position.y,
                                   start.x, start.y,
                                   last.x, last.y)*Math.asin(perp/hypotenuse);
```

The minus sign is necessary because the method returns -1 when `last` is clockwise with respect to the line from `position` to `start`. That's all the math we need. Let's do it.

Try It Out – Rotating Elements

To deal with `ROTATE` mode in the `mouseDragged()` method, we can add an extra `else if` clause after the one we added for `MOVE`:

```
    } else if(button1Down && mode == ROTATE && selectedElement != null) {
      selectedElement.draw(g2D);                      // Draw to erase the element
      selectedElement.rotate(getAngle(selectedElement.getPosition(),
                                                        start, last));
      selectedElement.draw(g2D);              // Draw in its new position
      start = last;                           // Make start current point
    }
```

After drawing the element to erase it, we call its `rotate()` method to rotate it and then redraw it in the new position. We will add the definition for the `rotate()` method to the `Element` class in a moment. The argument to the `rotate()` method is the angle in radians through which the element is to be rotated, and that is returned by a helper method, `getAngle()`. We can add that to the `MouseHandler` class as:

```
    // Helper method for calculating getAngle()
    double getAngle(Point position, Point start, Point last) {
      // Get perpendicular distance from last to the line from position to start
      double perp = Line2D.ptLineDist(position.x, position.y,
                                       last.x, last.y, start.x, start.y);
      // Get the distance from position to start
      double hypotenuse = position.distance(start);
```

```
    if(hypotenuse == 0.0)              // Make sure it's
      hypotenuse = 1.0;                // non-zero

    // Angle is the arc sine of perp/hypotenuse. Clockwise is positive angle
    return -Line2D.relativeCCW(position.x, position.y,
                               start.x, start.y,
                               last.x, last.y)*Math.asin(perp/hypotenuse);
  }
```

This is basically just an assembly of the code fragments calculating the angle in the last section. We will need an import statement for `Line2D` for `SketchView`:

```
import java.awt.geom.Line2D;
```

We completed the `mouseReleased()` method when we dealt with MOVE mode so there's nothing further to add there.

Now we must empower our element classes to rotate themselves. We will add a data member to the base class to store the rotation angle, and a method to rotate the element:

```
public abstract class Element {
  public Element(Color color) {
  this.color = color; }

  public   Color getColor()    {
  return color;   }

  // Set or reset highlight color
  public void setHighlighted(boolean highlighted) {
    this.highlighted = highlighted;
  }

  public Point getPosition() {
    return position;
  }

  protected void draw(Graphics2D g2D, Shape element) {
    g2D.setPaint(highlighted ? Color.MAGENTA : color);  // Set the element color
    AffineTransform old = g2D.getTransform();           // Save the current transform
    g2D.translate(position.x, position.y);              // Translate to position
    g2D.rotate(angle);                                  // Rotate about position
    g2D.draw(element);                                  // Draw the element
    g2D.setTransform(old);                              // Restore original transform
  }

  protected java.awt.Rectangle getBounds(java.awt.Rectangle bounds) {
    AffineTransform at = AffineTransform.getTranslateInstance(
                                              position.x, position.y);
    at.rotate(angle);
    return  at.createTransformedShape(bounds).getBounds();
  }
```

```
public void move(int deltax, int deltay) {
  position.x += deltax;
  position.y += deltay;
}

public void rotate(double angle) {
this.angle += angle;   }

public abstract Rectangle getBounds();
public abstract void draw(Graphics2D g2D);
public abstract void modify(Point start, Point last);

protected Color color;                       // Color of a shape
protected boolean highlighted = false;       // Highlight flag
final static Point origin = new Point();     // Point 0,0
protected Point position;                    // Element position
protected double angle = 0.0;                // Rotation angle

// inner shape classes declared here
}
```

All the `rotate()` method does is add the angle passed to it to the current value of `angle`. The value of `angle` is assumed to be in radians. Naturally, when we create an element the angle will be zero. We have modified the `draw()` method in the base class to apply a rotation through `angle` radians about the point `position`. It is important that we apply the rotation after the translation, otherwise the translation would be applied in the rotated coordinate system, which would give quite a different result from what we require. Since we now have the possibility of rotated shapes, the `getBounds()` method also has to take account of this, so we apply a rotation here, too. We mustn't forget that the `draw()` method in the `Element.Text` class is a special case. We need to add a line to this method to apply the rotation:

```
public void draw(Graphics2D g2D) {
      g2D.setPaint(highlighted ? Color.MAGENTA : color);
      Font oldFont = g2D.getFont();                  // Save the old font
      g2D.setFont(font);                             // Set the new font

      AffineTransform old = g2D.getTransform();      // Save the current
                                                     // transform
      g2D.translate(position.x, position.y);         // Translate to position
      g2D.rotate(angle);                             // Rotate about position
      g2D.drawString(text, origin.x, origin.y+(int)bounds.getHeight());
      g2D.setTransform(old);                         // Restore original
                                                     // transform

      g2D.setFont(oldFont);                          // Restore the old font
  }
```

Recompile all the stuff we have changed and try out the new context menus. Having a rotate capability adds flexibility and with the move operation giving you much more precision in positioning elements relative to one another, this should enable a massive leap forward in the quality of your artwork.

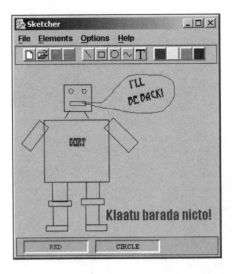

How It Works

Rotating elements just involves adding an extra transform before each element is drawn. Because we draw each element at the origin, rotating an element becomes relatively simple.

Choosing Custom Colors

We made provision in the status bar for showing a custom color. It would be a shame not to make use of this, so let's add a dialog to enable any color to be chosen. This is going to be a lot easier than you imagine.

To keep it simple, we will implement this as a facility on the general pop-up menu, although in practice you would probably want it accessible from the main menu and the toolbar. We will add a member to the `SketchFrame` class for the menu item:

```
private JMenuItem customColorItem;
```

We just need to add this to the pop-up and to add an action listener for it. This requires two statements in the `SketchFrame` constructor:

```
customColorItem = popup.add("Custom Color...");    // Add the item
customColorItem.addActionListener(this);           // and add its listener
```

You can add these statements following the others that set up the pop-up menu. Selecting this menu item will now cause the `actionPerformed()` method in the `SketchFrame` class to be called so we will implement the custom color choice in there. Let's try it out.

Try It Out – Choosing a Custom Color

We will use the facilities provided by the `JColorChooser` class that does precisely what we want. Here's how we will use it in the `actionPerformed()` method:

```
        // Handle About menu action events
        public void actionPerformed(ActionEvent e)   {
          if(e.getSource() == aboutItem) {
            // Create about dialog with the menu item as parent
            JOptionPane.showMessageDialog(this,                            // Parent
                            "Sketcher Copyright Ivor Horton 2001", // Message
                            "About Sketcher",                      // Title
                            JOptionPane.INFORMATION_MESSAGE);      // Message type

          } else if(e.getSource() == fontItem) {        // Set the dialog window position
            Rectangle bounds = getBounds();
            fontDlg.setLocation(bounds.x + bounds.width/3, bounds.y + bounds.height/3);
            fontDlg.setVisible(true);             // Show the dialog

          } else if(e.getSource() == customColorItem) {
            Color color = JColorChooser.showDialog(this, "Select Custom Color",
                                                      elementColor);

            if(color != null) {
              elementColor = color;
              statusBar.setColorPane(color);
            }
          }
        }
      }
```

With the JColorChooser class imported, recompile and rerun Sketcher and select the **Custom Color...** menu item from the general pop-up. You will see the dialog below.

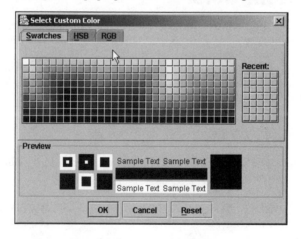

How It Works

The JColorChooser class defines a complete color choosing facility that you can use in your own dialog, or create a complete modal dialog by calling the static method showDialog() as we have done here. The arguments to showDialog() are a reference to the parent component for the dialog, the title for the dialog, and the initial color selection. You can choose a color using any of the three tabs that provide different mechanisms for defining the color that you want. When you click on OK, the color that you chose is returned as type Color. Exiting the dialog by any other means than selecting the OK button returns null. We just store the color returned in elementColor, and set it in the status bar pane.

Summary

In this chapter you have learned how to use dialogs to manage data input. You have also learned how to implement context menus, which can bring a professional feel to the GUI in your applications. You have applied scrollbars to varying data values as well as scrolling a window, so you should be in a position to use them in whatever context you need.

The important points we have covered in this chapter are:

- ❏ A modal dialog blocks input from other windows in the same application as long as it is displayed.

- ❏ A non-modal dialog does not block input to other windows. You can switch the focus between a non-modal dialog and other windows in the application whenever necessary.

- ❏ The JOptionPane class provides static methods for creating simple dialogs.

- ❏ A pop-up menu is a menu that can be displayed at any point within the coordinate system of a component.

- ❏ A context menu is a pop-up menu that is specific to what lies at the point where the menu is displayed – so the contents of the menu depend on the context.

- ❏ A context menu is displayed as a result of a pop-up trigger, which is usually a right mouse button click.

- ❏ The AffineTransform class defines an affine transformation that can be applied to a graphics context and to a Shape object.

- ❏ A Graphic2D object always contains an AffineTransform object, and the default transform leaves coordinates unchanged.

- ❏ The transform for a graphics context is applied immediately before user coordinates for a shape are converted to device coordinates.

- ❏ There are four kinds of transform you can create: translations, rotations, scaling, and shearing.

- ❏ You can combine any number of transformations in a single AffineTransform object.

Exercises

1. Implement a dialog initiated from a toolbar button to select the current element color.

2. Add a menu item to the Element context menu that will display information about the element at the cursor in a dialog – what it is and its basic defining data.

3. Display a special context menu when the cursor is over a TEXT object that provides a menu option to edit the text through a dialog.

4. Change the implementations of the element classes to make use of the combined translate and rotate operation.

5. Add a toolbar button to switch highlighting on and off. The same button should turn it on when it is off and vice versa, so you need to change the button label appropriately.

6. Add a Scale menu item to the element context menu that will allow an element to be scaled by dragging the mouse cursor.

7. Implement a main menu item and a toolbar button for choosing a custom color.

Filing and Printing Documents

In this chapter we will explore serializing and printing documents in an application, and adding these as the finishing touches to our Sketcher program. These capabilities are not available to an untrusted applet for security reasons, so everything we will cover here only applies to applications and trusted applets. Although we have already covered serialization in Chapter 11, you will find that there is quite a difference between understanding how the basic methods for object input and output work, and applying them in a practical context.

In this chapter you will learn:

- ❏ How to use the `JFileChooser` class
- ❏ How to save a sketch in a file as objects
- ❏ How to implement the **Save As** menu mechanism
- ❏ How to open a sketch stored in a file and integrate it into the application
- ❏ How to create a new sketch and integrate it into the application
- ❏ How to ensure that the current sketch is saved before the application is closed or a new sketch is loaded
- ❏ How printing in Java works
- ❏ How to print in landscape orientation rather than portrait orientation
- ❏ How to implement multipage printing
- ❏ How to output components to your printer

Serializing the Sketch

Our Sketcher program can only be considered to be a practical application if we can save sketches in a file and retrieve them later – in other words we need to implement serialization for a `SketchModel` object and use that to make the File menu work. Ideally, we want to be able to write the model for a sketch to a file and be able to read it back at a later date and reconstruct exactly the same model object. This naturally leads us to choose serialization as the way to do this, because the primary purpose of serialization is the accurate storage and retrieval of objects.

We've seen how to serialize objects, back in Chapter 11. All we need to do to serialize a sketch document in our Sketcher program is to apply what we learned there. Of course, there are quite a few classes involved in a sketch document but it will be remarkably easy, considering the potential complexity of a sketch – I promise!

Of course, saving a sketch on disk and reading it back from a file will be significantly more work than implementing serialization for the document. The logic of opening and saving files so as not to lose anything accidentally can get rather convoluted. Before we get into that, there is a more fundamental point we should address – our sketch doesn't have a name. We should at least make provision for assigning a file name to a sketch, and maybe display the name in the title bar of the application window.

Try It Out – Assigning a Document Name

Since the sketch is going to have a name, because we intend to store it somewhere, let's define a default directory to hold sketches. Add the following lines to the end of the `Constants` interface (`Constants.java`):

```
File DEFAULT_DIRECTORY = new File("C:/Sketches");
String DEFAULT_FILENAME = "Sketch.ske";
```

If you want to store your sketches in a different directory you can set the definition of `DEFAULT_DIRECTORY` to suit your needs. The file extension, `.ske`, to identify sketches is also arbitrary. You can change this if you would prefer to use a different extension. Since we reference the `File` class here, we must add an `import` statement to the `Constants` source file to get at it:

```
import java.io.File;
```

We can now add the following data members to the `SketchFrame` class definition:

```
private String frameTitle;                      // Frame title
private String filename = DEFAULT_FILENAME;     // Current model file name
private File modelFile;                         // File for the current sketch
```

The `frameTitle` member specifies the basic title for the Sketcher application window. We will append the file name for the sketch to it. The `modelFile` member will hold a reference to the `File` object identifying the file containing the current sketch, once the sketch has been saved. At this point you can update the import statements for the `SketchFrame` class to import all the classes from the `java.io` package as we will be using quite a few more of them in this chapter:

```
import java.io.*;
```

We can arrange for the `frameTitle` to be initialized and the default file name to be appended to the basic window title in the `SketchFrame` constructor. We can also make sure that `DEFAULT_DIRECTORY` exists and is valid. The following code will do this:

```
public SketchFrame(String title, Sketcher theApp) {
  //setTitle(title);                    // comment out this line
  // Code as before...

  frameTitle = title + ": ";
  setTitle(frameTitle + filename);

  if(!DEFAULT_DIRECTORY.exists())
    if(!DEFAULT_DIRECTORY.mkdirs())
      JOptionPane.showMessageDialog(this,
                                "Error creating default directory",
                                "Directory Creation Error",
                                JOptionPane.ERROR_MESSAGE);
}
```

Since we will be implementing the event handling for the File menu, you can remove or comment out the statements from the constructor that disable the actions for this:

```
// Disable actions
//saveAction.setEnabled(false);
//closeAction.setEnabled(false);
//printAction.setEnabled(false);
```

If you recompile Sketcher and run it, you should now see the default file name for a sketch displayed in the title bar.

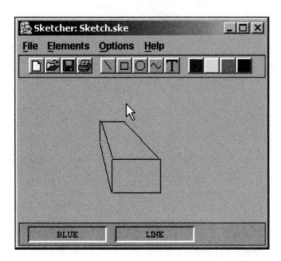

We now have a name assigned to the document, but there's another point to consider if we're preparing to store a sketch. When we close the application, we should have a means of checking whether the document needs to be saved. Otherwise it will be all too easy to close Sketcher and lose the brilliant sketch that we have just spent three hours crafting. Checking whether the sketch needs to be saved isn't difficult. We just need to record the fact that the document has changed.

Try It Out – Recording Changes to a Sketch

To provide the means of recording whether a sketch has been changed or not we can add a `boolean` data member to the `SketchFrame` class that we will set to `true` when the `SketchModel` object changes, and `false` when it is unchanged – as is the case when it has just been loaded or saved in a file. Add the following data member definition to the class:

```
private boolean sketchChanged = false;          // Model changed flag
```

This is sometimes referred to as the 'dirty' flag for the model, because it records when something has been done to sully the pristine state of the model data. The flag is `false` by default because the sketch is empty and therefore unchanged by definition. Any change that the user makes to the model should result in the flag being set to `true`, and when the model is written to a file, the flag should be reset to `false`. This will avoid unnecessary save operations while the sketch in memory remains unchanged.

We already have in place the means to signal changes to a sketch, since the `SketchModel` class has `Observable` as a base class. An `Observable` object can automatically notify any registered `Observer` objects when a change takes place. All we need to do is to make the `SketchFrame` class implement the `Observer` interface, and register the application window as an observer of the sketch object.

```
public class SketchFrame extends JFrame
                      implements Constants, ActionListener, Observer {
  // Method called by SketchModel object when it changes
  public void update(Observable o, Object obj) {
    sketchChanged = true;
  }
  // Rest of the class as before...
}
```

The `Observer` interface and the `Observable` class are defined in the `java.util` package, so we must import them into the `SketchFrame.java` file with the statements:

```
import java.util.Observer;
import java.util.Observable;
```

We can register the application window as an observer for the `SketchModel` object by adding one statement to the `init()` method in the `Sketcher` class:

```
sketch.addObserver(window);               // Register window as observer
```

The `window` field in the `Sketcher` object stores a reference to the application window. Whenever an element is added to the sketch, or deleted from it, the application window object will be notified. We can now press ahead with serializing the document.

Implementing the Serializable Interface

As I hope you still remember, the fundamental step in making objects serializable is to implement the `Serializable` interface in every class that defines objects we want written to a file. We need a methodical approach here, so how about top-down – starting with the `SketchModel` class.

Try It Out – Serializing SketchModel Objects

This is where we get a great deal from astonishingly little effort. To implement serialization for the `SketchModel` class you must first modify the class definition header to:

```
class SketchModel extends Observable implements Serializable {
```

The `Serializable` interface is defined in the package `java.io` so we need to add an `import` statement to the beginning of the `SketchModel.java` file:

```
import java.io.Serializable;
```

The `Serializable` interface declares no methods – so that's it!

Is that enough to serialize a sketch? Not quite. For a class to be serializable, all its data members must be serializable or declared as `transient`. If this is not the case then an exception of type `NotSerializableException` will be thrown. To avoid this we must trawl through the data elements of the `SketchModel` class, and if any of these are our own classes we must make sure they either implement the `Serializable` interface, or are declared as `transient`.

We also must not assume that objects of a standard class type are serializable, because some most definitely are not. It's a fairly quick fishing trip though, because our `SketchModel` class only has one data member – the linked list of elements that make up the sketch. If the `SketchModel` object is to be serializable we simply need to make sure the `elementList` member is serializable.

Serializing the List of Elements

Looking through the javadocs we can see that the `LinkedList` class is serializable, so all we need to worry about are the list elements themselves. We can make the base class for our shape class, `Element`, serializable by declaring that it implements the interface:

```
public abstract class Element implements Serializable {
```

Don't forget that we now need an `import` statement for the `Serializable` interface in `Element.java`. Since we will be using several classes from the `java.io` package, let's save a few lines and import all the names into `Element.java`:

```
import java.io.*;
```

The data members of the `Element` class that are object references are of type `Color` or of type `Point`, and since both of these classes are serializable, as you can verify from the SDK documentation, our `Element` class is serializable. Now we need to look at the subclasses of `Element`.

Subclasses of `Element` will inherit the implementation of the `Serializable` interface but there is a tiny snag. At the time of writing, *none* of the `Shape` classes in the `java.awt.geom` package are serializable, and we have been using them all over the place.

We are not completely scuppered though. Remember that you can always implement the `readObject()` and `writeObject()` methods in a class and then implement your own serialization. We can take the data that we need to recreate the required `Shape` object and serialize that in our implementation of the `writeObject()` method. We will then be able to reconstruct the object from the data in the `readObject()` method. Let's start with our `Element.Line` class.

Serializing Lines

Just to remind you of one of the things we discussed back in the I/O chapters, the `writeObject()` method that serializes objects must have the form:

```
private void writeObject(ObjectOutputStream out) throws IOException {
  // Code to serialize the object...
}
```

Our `Element.Line` objects are always drawn from (0, 0) so there's no sense in saving the start point in a line – it's always the same. We just need to serialize the end point, so add the following to the `Element.Line` class:

```
private void writeObject(ObjectOutputStream out) throws IOException {
  out.writeDouble(line.x2);
  out.writeDouble(line.y2);
}
```

We don't need to worry about exceptions that might be thrown by the `writeDouble()` method at this point. These will be passed on to the method that calls `writeObject()`. The coordinates are public members of the `Line2D.Double` object so we can reference them directly to write them to the stream. The rest of the data relating to a line is stored in the base class, `Element`, and as we said earlier they are all taken care of. The base class members will be serialized automatically when an `Element.Line` object is written to a file. We just need the means to read it back.

To recap what you already know, the `readObject()` method to deserialize an object is also of a standard form:

```
private void readObject(ObjectInputStream in)
        throws IOException, ClassNotFoundException {
  // Code to deserialize an object...
}
```

For the `Line` class, the implementation will read the coordinates of the end point of the line and reconstitute `line` – the `Line2D.Double` member of the class. Adding the following method to the `Element.Line` class will do that:

```
private void readObject(java.io.ObjectInputStream in)
        throws IOException, ClassNotFoundException {
```

```
      double x2 = in.readDouble();
      double y2 = in.readDouble();
      line = new Line2D.Double(0,0,x2,y2);
   }
```

That's lines serialized. Looks as though it's going to be easy. We can do rectangles next.

Serializing Rectangles

A rectangle is always drawn with its top left corner at the origin, so we only need to write the width and height to the file:

```
   private void writeObject(ObjectOutputStream out) throws IOException {
      out.writeDouble(rectangle.width);
      out.writeDouble(rectangle.height);
   }
```

The width and height members of the Rectangle2D.Double object are public, so we can access them directly to write them to the stream.

Deserializing an Element.Rectangle object is almost identical to the way we desirialized a line:

```
   private void readObject(ObjectInputStream in)
            throws IOException, ClassNotFoundException {
      double width = in.readDouble();
      double height = in.readDouble();
      rectangle = new Rectangle2D.Double(0,0,width,height);
   }
```

An Element.Circle object is actually going to be easier.

Serializing Circles

A circle is drawn as an ellipse with the top left corner of the bounding rectangle at the origin. The only item of data we will need to reconstruct a circle is the diameter:

```
   private void writeObject(ObjectOutputStream out) throws IOException {
      out.writeDouble(circle.width);
   }
```

The diameter is recorded in the width member (and also in the height member) of the Ellipse2D.Double object. We just write it to the file.

We can read a circle back with the following code:

```
   private void readObject(ObjectInputStream in)
            throws IOException, ClassNotFoundException {
      double width = in.readDouble();
      circle = new Ellipse2D.Double(0,0,width,width);
   }
```

This reconstitutes the circle using the diameter that was written to the file.

Serializing Curves

Curves are a little trickier. One complication is that we create a curve as a GeneralPath object, and we have no idea how many segments make up the curve. We can obtain a special Iterator object of type PathIterator for a GeneralPath object that will make available to us all the information necessary to create the GeneralPath object. PathIterator is an interface that declares methods for retrieving details of the segments that make up a GeneralPath object, so a reference to an object of type PathIterator encapsulates all the data defining that path.

The getPathIterator() method in the GeneralPath class returns a reference of type PathIterator. The argument to getPathIterator() is an AffineTransform object that is applied to the path. This is based on the assumption that a single GeneralPath object may be used to create a number of different appearances on the screen.

You might have a GeneralPath object that defines a complicated object, a boat for example. You could draw several boats on the screen simply by applying a transform before you draw each boat to set its position and orientation and use the same GeneralPath object for all. This avoids the overhead of creating multiple instances of what are essentially identical objects. That's why the getIterator() method enables you to obtain an iterator for a particular transformed instance of a GeneralPath object. However, we want an iterator for the unmodified path to get the basic data that we need, so we pass a default AffineTranform object, which does nothing.

The PathIterator interface declares four methods:

Method	Description
currentSegment(double[] coords) currentSegment(float[] coords)	Returns the current segment. See the text following this table for a detailed description.
getWindingRule()	Returns a value of type int defining the winding rule. The value can be WIND_EVEN_ODD or WIND_NON_ZERO.
next()	Moves the iterator to the next segment as long as there is another segment.
isDone()	Returns true if the iteration is complete, and false otherwise.

The array argument, coords, that you pass to either version of the currentSegment() method is used to store data relating to the current segment, and should have six elements to record the coordinates of one, two, or three points, depending on the current segment type.

The method returns an int value that indicates the type of the segment, and can be one of the following values:

Segment Type	Description
SEG_MOVETO	The segment corresponds to a `moveTo()` operation. The coordinates of the point moved to are returned as the first two elements of the array, `coords`.
SEG_LINETO	The segment corresponds to a `lineTo()` operation. The coordinates of the end point of the line are returned as the first two elements of the array, `coords`.
SEG_QUADTO	The segment corresponds to a `quadTo()` operation. The coordinates of the control point for the quadratic segment are returned as the first two elements of the array, `coords`, and the end point is returned as the third and fourth elements.
SEG_CUBICTO	The segment corresponds to a `curveTo()` operation. The array `coords` will contain coordinates of the first control point, the second control point, and the end point of the cubic curve segment.
SEG_CLOSE	The segment corresponds to a `closePath()` operation. The segment closes the path by connecting the current point to the first point in the path. No values are returned in the `coords` array.

We have all the tools we need to get the data on every segment in the path. We just need to get a `PathIterator` reference and use the `next()` method to go through it. Our case is simple: we only have a single `moveTo()` segment – always to (0, 0) – followed by one or more `lineTo()` segments. We will still test the return type, though, to show how it's done, and in case there are errors. We're going to end up with an array of coordinates with an unpredictable number of elements: it sounds like a case for a `Vector`, particularly since `Vector` objects are serializable.

A `Vector` object only stores object references, not the `float` values that we have, so we'll have to convert our coordinate values to objects of type `Float` before storing them. The first segment is a special case. It is always a move to (0, 0), whereas all the others will be lines. Thus the procedure will be to get the first segment and discard it after verifying it is a move, and then get the remaining segments in a loop. Here's the code:

```
private void writeObject(ObjectOutputStream out) throws IOException {
  PathIterator iterator = curve.getPathIterator(new AffineTransform());
  Vector coords = new Vector();
  int maxCoordCount = 6;
  float[] temp = new float[maxCoordCount];   // Stores segment data

  int result = iterator.currentSegment(temp);  // Get first segment
  assert(result == iterator.SEG_MOVETO);
  iterator.next();                             // Next segment
  while(!iterator.isDone()) {                  // While we have segments
    result = iterator.currentSegment(temp);       // Get the segment data
    assert(result == iterator.SEG_LINETO);

    coords.add(new Float(temp[0]));            // Add x coordinate to Vector
    coords.add(new Float(temp[1]));             // Add y coordinate
```

```
        iterator.next();                    // Go to next segment
    }

    out.writeObject(coords);                // Save the Vector
}
```

We obtain a `java.awt.geom.PathIterator` object for the `Element.Curve` object that we will use to extract the segment data for the curve. We will have to import this class into `Element.java`. We create a `Vector` object in which we will store the coordinate data as objects and we will serialize this vector in the serialization of the curve. We also create a `float[]` array to hold the numerical coordinate values for a segment. All six elements are used when the segment is a cubic Bezier curve. In our case fewer are used but we must still supply an array with six elements as an argument to the `currentSegment()` method because that's what the method expects to receive.

After verifying that the first segment is a move-to segment, we use the path iterator to extract the segment data that defines the curve. We use the `Float` class constructor to create `Float` objects to store in the `Vector` object `coords`. The assertion is there to make sure that the curve consists only of line segments after the initial move-to.

We will need an import statement for `Vector` to make the class accessible in the `Element.java` source file:

```
import java.util.Vector;
```

It's worth considering how we might handle a `GeneralPath` object that consisted of a variety of different segments in arbitrary sequence. For the case where the path consisted of a set of line, quad, or cubic segments, you could get away with using a `Vector` object to store the coordinates for each segment, and then store these objects in another `Vector`. You could deduce the type of segment from the number of coordinates you have stored in each `Vector` object for a segment since line, cubic, and quad segments each require a difference number of points. In the general case you would need to define classes to represent the segments of various types, plus moves, of course. If these had a common base class, then you could store all the objects for a path in a `Vector` as base class references. Of course, you would need to make sure your segment classes were serializable too.

To deserialize a curve, we just have to read the `Vector` object from the file, and recreate the `GeneralPath` object for the `Element.Curve` class:

```
private void readObject(ObjectInputStream in)
            throws IOException, ClassNotFoundException {
  Vector coords = (Vector)in.readObject();     // Read the coordinates Vector
  curve = new GeneralPath();                    // Create a path
  curve.moveTo(0,0);                            // Move to the origin
  float x, y;                                   // Stores coordinates

  for(int i = 0 ; i<coords.size() ; i += 2 ) { // For each pair of elements
    x = ((Float)coords.get(i)).floatValue();    // Get x value
    y = ((Float)coords.get(i+1)).floatValue(); // Get y value
    curve.lineTo(x,y);                          // Create a line segment
  }
}
```

This should be very easy to follow now. We read the data we wrote to the stream – the `Vector` of `Float` objects. The first segment is always a move to the origin. All the succeeding segments are lines specified by pairs of elements from the `Vector`. The `floatValue()` method for the `Float` objects that are stored in the `Vector` object returns the numerical coordinate values. We use these to create the line segments.

Serializing Text

`Element.Text` is the last element type we have to deal with. Fortunately, `Font`, `String`, and `java.awt.Rectangle` objects are all serializable already, which means that `Element.Text` is serializable by default and we have nothing further to do. We can now start implementing the listener operations for the File menu.

Supporting the File Menu

To support the menu items in the File menu, we must add some code to the `actionPerformed()` method in the `FileAction` class. We can try to put a skeleton together but a problem presents itself immediately: the ultimate source of an event will be either a toolbar button (a `JButton` object) or a menu item (a `JMenuItem` object) that was created from a `FileAction` object. How do we figure out what the action was that originated the event? We only have one definition of the `actionPerformed()` method shared amongst all `FileAction` class objects so we need a way to determine which particular `FileAction` object caused the event. That way we can decide what we should do in response to the event.

Each `FileAction` object stores a `String` that was passed to the constructor as the name argument, and was then passed on to the base class constructor. If only we had thought of saving it, we could compare the name for the current object with the name for each of the `FileAction` objects in the `SketchFrame` class. Then we could tell which object the `actionPerformed()` method was called for.

All is not lost though. We can call the `getValue()` method for the `ActionEvent` object to retrieve the name for the action object that caused the event. We can then compare that with the name for each of the `FileAction` objects that we store as members of the `SketchFrame` class. We can therefore implement the `actionPerformed()` member of the `FileAction` class like this:

```
public void actionPerformed(ActionEvent e) {
   String name = (String)getValue(NAME);
   if(name.equals(saveAction.getValue(NAME))) {
     // Code to handle file Save operation...
   } else if(name.equals(saveAsAction.getValue(NAME))) {
     // Code to handle file Save As operation...
   } else if(name.equals(openAction.getValue(NAME))) {
     // Code to handle file Open operation...
   } else if(name.equals(newAction.getValue(NAME))) {
     // Code to handle file New operation...
   } if(name.equals(printAction.getValue(NAME))) {
     // Code to handle Print operation..
   }
}
```

Calling `getValue()` with the argument as the `NAME` key that is defined in the `Action` interface returns the `String` object that was stored for the `FileAction` object when it was created. If the name for the current object matches that of a particular `FileAction` object, then that must be the action to which the event applies, so we know what to do. We have one `if` or `else-if` block for each action, and we will code these one by one.

Many of these operations will involve dialogs. We need to get at the file system and display the list of directories and files to choose from, for an Open operation for instance. It sounds like a lot of work, and it certainly would be, if it weren't for a neat facility provided by the `JFileChooser` class.

Using a File Chooser

The `JFileChooser` class in the `javax.swing` package provides an easy to use mechanism for creating file dialogs for opening and saving files. You can use a single object of this class to create all the file dialogs you need, so add a member to the `SketchFrame` class to store a reference to a `JFileChooser` object that we will create in the constructor:

```
private JFileChooser files;                    // File chooser dialog
```

There are several `JFileChooser` constructors but we will discuss just a couple of them here. The default constructor creates an object with the current directory as the default directory but that won't quite do for our purposes. What we want is for the default directory to be the `DEFAULT_DIRECTORY`, which we defined in the `Constants` interface, so we'll use the constructor that accepts a `File` object specifying a default directory to create a `JFileChooser` object in the `SketchFrame` constructor. Add the following statement to the constructor following the statements that we added earlier that ensured `DEFAULT_DIRECTORY` actually existed on the hard drive:

```
files = new JFileChooser(DEFAULT_DIRECTORY);
```

Any dialogs created by the `files` object will have `DEFAULT_DIRECTORY` as the default directory that is displayed. We can now use the `files` object to implement the event handling for the File menu. There are a considerable number of methods in the `JFileChooser` class, so rather than trying to summarize them all, which would take many pages of text and be incredibly boring, let's try out the ones that we can apply to Sketcher to support the File menu.

File Save Operations

In most cases we will want to display a modal file save dialog when the Save menu item or toolbar button is selected. As luck would have it, the `JFileChooser` class has a method `showSaveDialog()` that does precisely what we want. All we have to do is pass it a reference to the `Component` object that will be the parent for the dialog to be displayed. The method returns a value indicating how the dialog was closed. We could display a save dialog in a `FileAction()` method with the statement:

```
int result = files.showSaveDialog(SketchFrame.this);
```

This will automatically create a File Save dialog with the `SketchFrame` object as parent, and **Save** and **Cancel** buttons. The `SketchFrame.this` notation is used to refer to the `this` pointer for the `SketchFrame` object from within a method of an inner class object of type `FileAction`. The file chooser dialog will be displayed centered in the parent component – our `SketchFrame` object here. If you specify the parent component as `null`, the dialog will be centered on the screen. This also applies to all the other methods we will discuss that display file chooser dialogs.

When you need a file open dialog, you can call the `showOpenDialog()` member of a `JFileChooser` object. Don't be fooled here though. A save dialog and an open dialog are essentially the same. They only differ in minor details – the title bar and one of the button labels. The sole purpose of both dialogs is simply to select a file – for whatever purpose. If you wanted to be perverse, you could pop up a save dialog to open a file and vice versa!

You also have the ability to display a customized dialog from a `JFileChooser` object. Although it's not strictly necessary for us here – we could make do with the standard file dialogs – we will adopt a custom approach, as it will give us some experience of using a few more `JFileChooser` methods.

You can display a dialog by calling the `showDialog()` method for the `JFileChooser` object supplying two arguments. The first is the parent component for the dialog window, and the second is the approve button text – the approve button being the button that you click on to expedite the operation rather than cancel it. You could display a dialog with a Save button with the statement:

```
int result = files.showDialog(SketchFrame.this, "Save");
```

If you pass `null` as the second argument here, the button text will be whatever was set previously – possibly the default.

Before you display a custom dialog, though, you would normally do a bit more customizing of what is to be displayed. We will be using the following `JFileChooser` methods to customize our dialogs:

Method	Description
`setDialogTitle()`	The `String` object passed as an argument is set as the dialog title bar text.
`setApproveButtonText()`	The `String` object passed as an argument is set as the approve button label.
`setApproveButtonToolTipText()`	The `String` object passed as an argument is set as the approve button tooltip.
`setApproveButtonMnemonic()`	The character passed as an argument is set as the approve button mnemonic defining a shortcut. The shortcut will appear as part of the tooltip.

A file chooser can be set to select files, directories, or both. You can determine which of these is allowed by calling the `setFileSelectionMode()` method. The argument must be one of the constants `FILES_ONLY`, `DIRECTORIES_ONLY`, and `FILES_AND_DIRECTORIES` as defined in the `JFileChooser` class, `FILES_ONLY` being the default. You also have the `getFileSelectionMode()` method to enable you to determine what selection mode is set. To allow multiple selections to be made from the list in the file dialog, you call the `setMultiSelectionEnabled()` method for your `JFileChooser` object with the argument `true`.

If you want the dialog to have a particular file selected when it opens, you can pass a `File` object specifying that file to the `setSelectedFile()` method for the `JFileChooser` object. This will pre-select the file in the file list for the dialog if the file already exists, and insert the name in the file name field if it doesn't. The file list is created when the `JFileChooser` object is created but naturally files may be added or deleted over time and when this occurs you will need to reconstruct the file list. Calling the `rescanCurrentDirectory()` method before you display the dialog will do this for you. You can change the current directory at any time by passing a `File` object specifying the directory to the `setCurrentDirectory()` method.

That's enough detail for now. Let's put our customizing code together.

Try It Out – Creating a Customized File Dialog

We will first add a method to the `SketchFrame` class to create our customized file dialog and return the `File` object corresponding to the file selected, or `null` if a file was not selected:

```
// Display a custom file save dialog
private File showDialog(String dialogTitle,
                        String approveButtonText,
                        String approveButtonTooltip,
                        char approveButtonMnemonic,
                        File file) {                    // Current file - if any

  files.setDialogTitle(dialogTitle);
  files.setApproveButtonText(approveButtonText);
  files.setApproveButtonToolTipText(approveButtonTooltip);
  files.setApproveButtonMnemonic(approveButtonMnemonic);
  files.setFileSelectionMode(files.FILES_ONLY);
  files.rescanCurrentDirectory();
  files.setSelectedFile(file);
  int result = files.showDialog(SketchFrame.this, null);  // Show the dialog
  return (result == files.APPROVE_OPTION) ? files.getSelectedFile() : null;
}
```

This method accepts five arguments that are used to customize the dialog – the dialog title, the button label, the button tooltip, the shortcut character for the button, and the `File` object representing the file for the current sketch. Each of the options is set using one of the methods for the `JFileChooser` object that we discussed earlier. The last argument is used to select a file in the file list initially. If it is `null`, no file will be selected from the file list.

Note that we reconstruct the file list for the dialog by calling the `rescanCurrentDirectory()` method. This is to ensure that we always display an up-to-date list of files. If we didn't do this, the dialog would always display the list of files that were there when we created the `JFileChooser` object. Any changes to the contents of the directory since then would not be taken into account.

The return value from the showDialog() member of the JFileChooser object files determines whether the approve button was selected or not. If it was, we return the File object from the file chooser that represents the selected file, otherwise we return null. A method calling our showDialog() method can determine whether or not a file was chosen by testing the return value for null.

We can now use this method when we implement handling of a <u>S</u>ave menu item action event. A save operation is a little more complicated than you might imagine at first sight, so let's consider it in a little more detail.

Implementing the Save Operation

First of all, what happens in a save operation should depend on whether the current file has been saved before. If it has, the user won't want to see a dialog every time. Once it has been saved the first time, the user will want it written away without displaying the dialog. We can use the modelFile member of the SketchFrame class to determine whether we need to display a dialog or not. We added this earlier to hold a reference to the File object for the sketch. Before a sketch has been saved this will be null, and if it is not null we don't want to show the dialog. When the sketch has been saved, we will store a reference to the File object in modelFile so this will generally hold a reference to the file holding the last version of the sketch that was saved.

Secondly, if the sketch is unchanged – indicated by the sketchChanged member being false – either because it is new and therefore empty or because it hasn't been altered since it was last saved, we really don't need to save it at all.

We can package up these checks for when we need to save and when we display the dialog in another method in the SketchFrame class. We'll call it saveOperation(), and make it a private member of the SketchFrame class:

```
// Save the sketch if it is necessary
private void saveOperation() {
  if(!sketchChanged)
    return;

  File file = modelFile;
  if(file == null) {
    file = showDialog("Save Sketch",
                      "Save",
                      "Save the sketch",
                      's',
                      new File(files.getCurrentDirectory(), filename));
    if(file == null ||  (file.exists() &&     // Check for existence
       JOptionPane.NO_OPTION ==               // Overwrite warning
         JOptionPane.showConfirmDialog(SketchFrame.this,
                                 file.getName()+" exists. Overwrite?",
                                 "Confirm Save As",
                                 JOptionPane.YES_NO_OPTION,
                                 JOptionPane.WARNING_MESSAGE)))
            return;                            // No selected file
  }
  saveSketch(file);
}
```

We first check the sketchChanged flag. If the flag is false, either the sketch is empty, or it hasn't been changed since the last save. Either way there's no point in writing it to disk, so we return immediately. We then initialize the local variable, file, with the reference stored in modelFile. If modelFile was not null, then we skip the entire if and just call the saveSketch() method to write the file to modelFile – we will get to the detail of the saveSketch() method in a moment.

The condition tested in the next if looks rather complicated but this is primarily due to the plethora of arguments in the showConfirmDialog() call and we can break the condition down into its component parts quite easily. There are two logical expressions separated by || so if either is true then we execute a return. The first expression just checks for file being null so if this is the case we return immediately. If the first expression is false, file is not null and the second expression will be evaluated.

This will be true if file references a file that does exist AND the value returned from the showConfirmDialog() method is JOptionPane.NO_OPTION. The dialog just warns of the overwrite potential so if JOptionPane.NO_OPTION is returned then the user has elected not to overwrite the file. Remember that with the || operator, if the left operand is true then the right operand will not be evaluated. Similarly, with the && operator, if the left operand is false then the right operand will not be evaluated. This means that the showConfirmDialog() method will only be executed if file is not null – so the left expression for the || is false – and file references a file that does exist – so the left operand for the && is true. If we don't execute the return, then we fall through the if to call our helper method saveSketch() with file as the argument.

Writing a Sketch to a File

Writing a sketch to a file just means making use of what we learned about writing objects to a file. We have already ensured that a SketchModel object is serializable, so we can write the sketch to an ObjectOutputStream with the following method in SketchFrame:

```
// Write a sketch to outFile
private void saveSketch(File outFile) {
  try {
    ObjectOutputStream out =  new ObjectOutputStream(
                         new BufferedOutputStream(
                         new FileOutputStream(outFile)));
    out.writeObject(theApp.getModel());        // Write the sketch to the
                                               // stream
    out.close();                               // Flush & close it
  } catch(IOException e) {
    System.err.println(e);
    JOptionPane.showMessageDialog(SketchFrame.this,
                         "Error writing a sketch file.",
                         "File Output Error",
                         JOptionPane.ERROR_MESSAGE);
    return;                                    // Serious error - return
  }
  if(outFile != modelFile) {                   // If we are saving to a new file
                                               // we must update the window
    modelFile = outFile;                       // Save file reference
    filename = modelFile.getName();            // Update the file name
    setTitle(frameTitle + modelFile.getPath()); // Change the window title
```

```
    }
    sketchChanged = false;                           // Set as unchanged
}
```

The `saveSketch()` method writes the current `SketchModel` object to the object output stream that we create from the `File` object that is passed to it. If an error occurs, an exception of type `IOException` will be thrown, in which case we write the exception to the standard error output stream, and pop up a dialog indicating that an error has occurred. We assume the user might want to retry the operation so we just return rather than terminate the application.

If the write operation succeeds, then we need to consider whether the data members in the window object relating to the file need to be updated. This will be the case when the `File` object passed to the `saveSketch()` method is not the same as the reference in `modelFile`. If this is so, we update the `modelFile` and `filename` members of the window object, and set the window title to reflect the new file name and path. In any event, the `sketchChanged` flag is reset to `false`, as the sketch is now safely stored away in the file.

We can now put together the code to handle the <u>S</u>ave menu item event.

Try It Out – Saving a Sketch

The code to handle the <u>S</u>ave menu item event will go in the `actionPerformed()` method of the inner class `FileAction`. We have done all the work, so it amounts to just one statement:

```java
public void actionPerformed(ActionEvent e) {
  String name = (String)getValue(NAME);
  if(name.equals(saveAction.getValue(NAME))) {
    saveOperation();
  }
  // Plus the rest of the code for the method...
}
```

You can recompile Sketcher and run it again. The <u>S</u>ave menu item and toolbar button should now be working. When you select either of them, you should get the dialog displayed below. This version has the look-and-feel of Windows of course. If you are using a different operating system it won't be exactly the same.

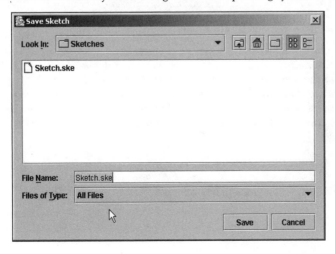

All the buttons in the dialog are fully operational. Go ahead and try them out, and then save the sketch using the default name. Next time you save the sketch the dialog won't appear. Be sure to check out the button tooltips. You should see the shortcut key combination as well as our tooltip text.

If you create a few sketch files, you should also get a warning if you attempt to overwrite an existing sketch file with a new one.

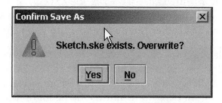

You can now save any sketch in a file – regardless of its complexity – with protection against accidentally overwriting existing files. I hope you agree that the save operation was remarkably easy to implement.

How It Works

This just calls our `saveOperation()` method in the `SketchFrame` object associated with the `FileAction` object containing the `actionPerformed()` method. This carries out the save as we have discussed.

Creating a File Filter

One customizing option we haven't used but you might like to try is to supply a file filter for our sketch files. The default filter in a `JFileChooser` object accepts any file or directory, but you can add filters of your own, and these implements two abstract methods declared in the `FileFilter` class:

Method	Description
`accept(File file)`	Returns `true` if the file represented by the object file is accepted by the file filter, and `false` otherwise.
`getDescription()`	Returns a `String` object describing the filter – for example, `"Sketch files"`.

The `FileFilter` class is defined in the `javax.swing.filechooser` package. Note that there is a `FileFilter` *interface* defined in the `java.io` package that declares just one method, `accept()`, which is the same as the method in the `FileFilter` class. This interface is for use with the `listFiles()` method that is defined in the `File` class, not for `JFileChooser` objects, so make sure you don't confuse them. The filter object that you use with a file chooser must have the `FileFilter` *class* as a superclass, and your filter class must define the `getDescription()` method as well as the `accept()` method.

We can define our own file filter class for Sketcher as:

```
import javax.swing.filechooser.FileFilter;
import java.io.File;

public class ExtensionFilter extends FileFilter {
```

```
   public ExtensionFilter(String ext, String descr) {
     extension = ext.toLowerCase();                    // Store the extension as
                                                        // lower case
     description = descr;                               // Store the description
   }

   public boolean accept(File file) {
    return(file.isDirectory()||file.getName()
             .toLowerCase().endsWith(extension));
   }

   public String getDescription() {
     return description;
   }

   private String description;                          // Filter description
   private String extension;                            // File extension
 }
```

To create a filter for files with the extension `.ske` we could write:

```
ExtensionFilter sketchFilter = new ExtensionFilter(".ske",
                                       "Sketch files (*.ske)");
```

If you add the `ExtensionFilter.java` source file to the Sketcher program directory, we could try this out by adding a little code to the `showDialog()` member of the `SketchFrame` class.

Try It Out – Using a File Filter

We only need to add three lines of code:

```
   private File showDialog(String dialogTitle,
                           String approveButtonText,
                           String approveButtonTooltip,
                           char approveButtonMnemonic,
                           File file) {              // Current file - if any


     files.setDialogTitle(dialogTitle);
     files.setApproveButtonText(approveButtonText);
     files.setApproveButtonToolTipText(approveButtonTooltip);
     files.setApproveButtonMnemonic(approveButtonMnemonic);
     files.setFileSelectionMode(files.FILES_ONLY);
     files.rescanCurrentDirectory();
     files.setSelectedFile(file);

     ExtensionFilter sketchFilter = new ExtensionFilter(".ske",
                                        "Sketch files (*.ske)");
     files.addChoosableFileFilter(sketchFilter);      // Add the filter
     files.setFileFilter(sketchFilter);               // and select it

     int result = files.showDialog(SketchFrame.this, null);
```

```
                return(result == files.APPROVE_OPTION) ? files.getSelectedFile() : null;
            }
```

Now when you display a file save dialog, it will use the Sketcher file filter by default, and will only display directories or files with the extension .ske. The user can override this by selecting the All Files option in the dialog, whereupon all files in the current directory will be displayed.

How It Works

The file filter, sketchFilter, that we create is added to the list of available filters in the JFileChooser object by passing a reference to the addChoosableFileFilter() method. We then set this filter as the one in effect by calling the setFileFilter() method. The JFileChooser object will check each file in the file list by passing a File object to the accept() method for our file filter object. This will only return true for directories or files with the extension .ske. The description of the filter is obtained by the JFileChooser object calling the getDescription() method in the Sketcher FileFilter class and displaying it in the dialog.

Of course, the available list of file filters will include the 'accept all' filter that is there by default. You might want to suppress this in some situations and there is a method defined in the JFileChooser class to do this:

```
    files.setAcceptAllFileFilter(false);      // Remove 'all files' filter
```

Of course, passing an argument of true to this method will restore the filter to the list. You can also discover whether the all files filter is used by calling the isAcceptAllFileFilterUsed() method, which will return true if it is and false otherwise.

You can also remove specific FileFilter objects from the list maintained by the JFileChooser object. Just pass a FileFilter reference to the removeChoosableFileFilter() method for your file chooser, for example:

```
    files.removeChoosableFileFilter(sketchFilter);      // removes our filter
```

This would remove the filter we have defined for Sketcher files.

File Save As Operations

For save as... operations, we will always display a save dialog, regardless of whether the file has been saved before and ignoring the state of the dirty flag. Apart from that and some cosmetic differences in the dialog itself, the operation is identical to the **Save** menu item event handling. With the showDialog() method available in the SketchFrame class, the implementation becomes almost trivial.

Try It Out – File Save As Operations

The code in the else if block in actionPerformed() for this operation will be:

```
            else if(name.equals(saveAsAction.getValue(NAME))) {
                File file = showDialog("Save Sketch As",
                                       "Save",
```

```
                              "Save the sketch",
                              's',
                              modelFile == null ? new File(
                                          files.getCurrentDirectory(),
                                          filename):modelFile);
      if(file != null) {
          if(file.exists() && !file.equals(modelFile))
              if(JOptionPane.NO_OPTION ==                  // Overwrite warning
                  JOptionPane.showConfirmDialog(SketchFrame.this,
                                      file.getName()+" exists. Overwrite?",
                                      "Confirm Save As",
                                      JOptionPane.YES_NO_OPTION,
                                      JOptionPane.WARNING_MESSAGE))
              return;                                       // No file selected
          saveSketch(file);
      }
      return;
  }
```

Recompile with these additions and you will have a working **Save As...** option on the File menu, with a file filter in action too!

How It Works

Most of this is under the Save menu operation. We have a fancy expression as the last argument to the `showDialog()` method. This is because the **Save As...** operation could be with a sketch that has been saved previously, or with a sketch that has never been saved. The expression passes `modelFile` as the argument if it is not `null`, and creates a new `File` object as the argument from the current directory and file name if it is. If we get a non-null `File` object back from the `showDialog()` method, then we check for a potential overwrite of an existing file. This will be the case if the selected file exists and is also different from `modelFile`. In this instance we display a YES/NO dialog warning of this just to ensure that overwriting the existing file is intended. If the user closes the dialog by selecting the No button, we just return, otherwise we save the current sketch in the file.

Since we have sketches written to disk, let's now look at how we can implement the operation for the Open menu item so we can try reading them back.

File Open Operations

Supporting the file/open operation is in some ways a little more complicated than save. We have to consider the currently displayed sketch first of all. Opening a new sketch will replace it, so does it need to be saved before the file open operation? If it does, we must deal with that before we can read a new sketch from the file. Fortunately, most of this is already done by our `saveOperation()` method. We just need to add a prompt for the save operation when necessary. We could put this in a `checkForSave()` method that we can implement in the `SketchFrame` class as:

```
// Prompt for save operation when necessary
public void checkForSave() {
  if(sketchChanged)
    if(JOptionPane.YES_OPTION ==
```

```
                JOptionPane.showConfirmDialog(SketchFrame.this,
                            "Current file has changed. Save current file?",
                            "Confirm Save Current File",
                            JOptionPane.YES_NO_OPTION,
                            JOptionPane.WARNING_MESSAGE))
            saveOperation();
    }
```

This will be useful outside the SketchFrame class a little later on, so we have declared it as a public class member. If the sketchChanged flag is true, we pop up a confirm dialog to verify that the sketch needs to be saved. If it does, we call the saveOperation() method to do just that.

When we get to the point of reading a sketch from the file, some further slight complications arise. We must replace the existing SketchModel object and its view in the application with a new SketchModel object and its view.

With those few thoughts, we are now ready to make it happen.

Try It Out – Implementing the Open Menu Item Operation

The file open process will be similar to a save operation, but instead of writing the file, it will read it. We'll add a helper method openSketch() to SketchFrame that, given a File object, will do the reading. Using this method, the code to handle the **Open** menu item event will be:

```
    } else if(name.equals(openAction.getValue(NAME))) {
        checkForSave();

        // Now open a sketch file
        File file = showDialog(
                        "Open Sketch File",          // Dialog window title
                        "Open",                       // Button lable
                        "Read a sketch from file",    // Button tooltip text
                        'o',                          // Shortcut character
                        null);                        // No file selected
        if(file != null)                              // If a file was selected
            openSketch(file);                         // then read it
    }
```

We can implement the openSketch() method in the SketchFrame class as:

```
    // Method for opening file
    public void openSketch(File inFile) {
        try {
            ObjectInputStream in = new ObjectInputStream(new BufferedInputStream(
                                    new FileInputStream(inFile)));
            theApp.insertModel((SketchModel)in.readObject());
            in.close();
            modelFile = inFile;
            filename = modelFile.getName();                 // Update the file name
            setTitle(frameTitle+modelFile.getPath());       // Change the window title
            sketchChanged = false;                          // Status is unchanged
```

```
    } catch(Exception e) {
    System.out.println(e);
    JOptionPane.showMessageDialog(SketchFrame.this,
                              "Error reading a sketch file.",
                              "File Input Error",
                              JOptionPane.ERROR_MESSAGE);
    }
}
```

The SketchModel object that is read from the file is passed to a new method in the Sketcher class insertModel(). This method has to replace the current sketch with the new one that is passed as the argument. We can implement the method like this:

```
public void insertModel(SketchModel newSketch) {
    sketch = newSketch;                        // Store the new sketch
    sketch.addObserver((Observer)view);        // Add the view as observer
    sketch.addObserver((Observer)window);      // Add the app window as
                                               // observer

    view.repaint();                            // Repaint the view
}
```

After we have loaded the new model, we update the window title bar and record the status as unchanged in the SketchFrame object. If you compile Sketcher once more, you can give the file open operation a workout.

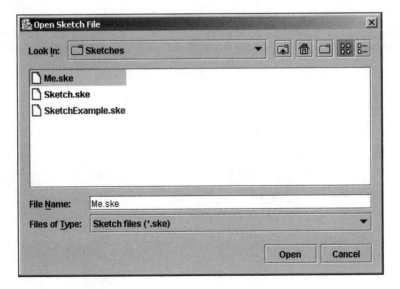

Don't forget to try out the tooltip for the **O**pen button. You should see the shortcut key combination *Alt+O* appended to the tooltip text.

How It Works

After dealing with saving the current sketch in the `actionPerformed()` member of the `FileAction` class, we use our `showDialog()` method that we defined in the `SketchFrame` class to display a file open dialog. Our `showDialog()` method is all-purpose – we can put any kind of label on the button or title in the title bar so we can use it to display any of the dialogs we need for file operations.

If a `File` object was selected in the dialog, we pass this to the `openSketch()` member of `SketchFrame` to read a new sketch from the file. The `openSketch()` method creates an `ObjectInputStream` object from the `File` object passed as an argument, and reads a `SketchModel` object from the stream by calling the `readObject()` method. The object returned by the `readObject()` method has to be cast to the appropriate type – `SketchModel` in our case. We pass this `SketchModel` object to the `insertModel()` method for the application object. This replaces the current sketch reference in the `sketch` member of the application object with a reference to the new sketch, and then sets the view and the application window as observers. Calling `repaint()` for the view object displays the new sketch, since the `paint()` method for the view object obtains a reference to the current model by calling the `getModel()` member of the application object, which will return the reference to the new model.

Starting a New Sketch

The File | New menu item simply starts a new sketch. This is quite similar to the open operation except that we must create an empty sketch rather than read a new one from disk. The processes of checking for the need to save the current sketch and inserting the new `SketchModel` object into the application will be the same.

Try It Out – Implementing the New Operation

We need to place the code to do this in the `else-if` block corresponding to the `newAction` object event. This is in the code in the `actionPerformed()` method in the `FileAction` class:

```
else if(name.equals(newAction.getValue(NAME))) {
    checkForSave();
    theApp.insertModel(new SketchModel());      // Insert new empty sketch
    modelFile = null;                            // No file for it
    filename = DEFAULT_FILENAME;                 // Default name
    setTitle(frameTitle + files.getCurrentDirectory() +
            "\\" + filename);
    sketchChanged = false;                       // Not changed yet
}
```

Now you can create a new sketch.

How It Works

All the saving of the existing sketch is dealt with by our `checkForSave()` method. The new part is the last five lines of code. We call the `SketchModel` constructor to create a new empty sketch, and pass it to the `insertModel()` method for the application object. This will insert the new sketch into the application and get the view object to display it. We then update the data members of the window that record information about the file for the current sketch and its status. We also set the `sketchChanged` flag to `false` as it's an empty sketch.

Preventing Data Loss on Close

At the moment we're still not calling `checkForSave()` when we close the application with the window icon. This means we could lose hours of work in an instant. But it's very simple. We just need to get the event handler for the window closing event to call the `checkForSave()` method for the window object.

To implement this we can use the `WindowListener` for the application window that we have already added in the `Sketcher` class. This listener receives notification of events associated with opening and closing the window as well as minimizing and maximizing it. We just need to add some code to the body of the `windowClosing()` method for the listener. We require one extra line in the `Sketcher` class definition:

```
// Handler class for window events
class WindowHandler extends WindowAdapter {
   // Handler for window closing event
   public void windowClosing(WindowEvent e) {
      window.checkForSave();
   }
}
```

The `WindowHandler` class is a subclass of the `WindowAdapter` class. In the subclass you just define the methods you are interested in to override the empty versions in the adapter class. The `WindowListener` interface declares the following seven methods corresponding to various window events:

Method	Description
`windowActivated(WindowEvent e)`	Called when the window receives the focus and becomes the currently active window.
`windowDeactivated(WindowEvent e)`	Called when the window ceases to be the currently active window.
`windowIconified(WindowEvent e)`	Called when the window is minimized.
`windowDeiconified(WindowEvent e)`	Called when the window returns to its normal state from a minimized state.
`windowOpened(WindowEvent e)`	Called the first time a window is made visible.
`windowClosed(WindowEvent e)`	Called when a window has been closed by calling its `dispose()` method.
`windowClosing(WindowEvent e)`	Called when the user selects the close icon or the Close item from the system menu for the window.

Clearly, using the `WindowAdapter` class as a base saves a lot of time and effort. Without it we would have to define all seven of the methods declared in the interface in our class. Because our anonymous class is an inner class its methods can access the fields of the `Sketcher` class, so the `windowClosing()` method we have defined can call our `checkForSave()` method for the `window` member of the `Sketcher` class object.

Now if you close the application window without having saved your sketch, you will be prompted to save it.

How It Works

This makes use of the code that we implemented for the save operation, packaged in the `checkForSave()` method. This does everything necessary to enable the sketch to be saved before the application window is closed. Defining methods judiciously makes for economical coding.

This still leaves us with the now redundant File | Close button to tidy up. As it's not really any different from the File | New function, let's change it to an application `Exit` button and reposition it at the bottom of the File menu. First, delete the statements that create the `closeAction` object and add it to the File menu. Next we can insert statements for an `else if` block corresponding to the `closeAction` object event in the `actionPerformed()` method for the `FileAction` inner class to `SketchFrame` that will provide the close action functionality – checking to see whether the file should be saved before exiting the program:

```
else if(name.equals(closeAction.getValue(NAME))) {
   checkForSave();
   System.exit(0);
}
```

Then we can redo the menu layout in the File menu constructor and add the mnemonic key *Ctrl-X* for E<u>x</u>it:

```
fileMenu.addSeparator();                                    // Add separator
addMenuItem(fileMenu, printAction);
fileMenu.addSeparator();                                    // Add separator
addMenuItem(fileMenu, closeAction = new FileAction("Exit",
         KeyStroke.getKeyStroke('X',Event.CTRL_MASK ),
         "Exit Sketcher"));
// We will add the types menu items here using actions...
```

All but one of our File actions are now operable. To complete the set we just need to get print up and running.

Printing in Java

Printing is always a messy business – inevitably so, because you have to worry about tedious details such as the size of a page, the margin sizes, and how many pages you're going to need for your output. As you might expect, the process for printing an image is different from printing text and you may also have the added complication of several printers with different capabilities being available, so with certain types of documents you need to select an appropriate printer. The way through this is to take it one step at a time. Let's understand the general principles first.

There are five packages dedicated to supporting printing capabilities in Java. These are:

Package	Description
`javax.print`	Defines classes and interfaces that enable you to determine what printers are available and what their capabilities are. It also enables you to identify types of documents to be printed.
`javax.print.attribute`	Defines classes and interfaces supporting the definition of sets of printing attributes. For example, you can define a set of attributes required by a particular document when it is printed, such as color output and two-sided printing, for instance.
`javax.print.attribute.standard`	Defines classes that identify a set of standard printing attributes.
`javax.print.event`	Defines classes that identify events that can occur while printing and interfaces that identify listeners for printing events.
`java.awt.print`	Defines classes and attributes for expediting the printing of 2D graphics and text.

The first four of these packages make up what is called the **Print Service API** that was added to Java in SDK 1.4. This allows printing on all Java platforms and has facilities for discovering and using multiple printers with varying capabilities. Since in all probability you have just a single printer available, we will concentrate in the first instance on understanding the classes and interfaces defined in the `java.awt.print` package that carry out print operations on a given printer, and stray into classes and interfaces from the other packages when necessary.

There are four classes in the `java.awt.print` package and we will be using all of them eventually:

`PrinterJob`	An object of this class type controls printing to a particular print service (such as a printer or fax capability).
`PageFormat`	An object of this class type defines the size and orientation of a page that is to be printed.
`Paper`	An object of this class type defines the size and printable area of a sheet of paper.
`Book`	An object of this class type defines a multipage document where pages may have different formats and require different rendering processes.

The `PrinterJob` class here drives the printing process. Don't confuse this with the `PrintJob` class in the `java.awt` package – this is involved in the old printing process introduced in Java 1.1 and the `PrinterJob` class now supersedes this. A `PrinterJob` class object provides the interface to a printer in your environment, and you use `PrinterJob` class methods to set up and initiate the printing process for a particular document. You start printing off one or more pages in a document by calling the `print()` method for the `PrinterJob` object.

953

A `PageFormat` object encapsulates information about a page, such as its dimensions, margin sizes, and orientation. An object of type `Paper` describes the characteristics of a physical sheet of paper that will be part of a `PageFormat` object. A `Book` object encapsulates a document consisting of a collection of pages that are typically processed in an individual way. We will be getting into the detail of how you work with these a little later in this chapter.

There are three interfaces in the `java.awt.print` package:

`Printable`	Implemented by a class to print a single page.
`Pageable`	Implemented by a class to print a multipage document where each page may be printed by a different `Printable` object.
`Printer Graphics`	Declares a method for obtaining a reference to the `PrinterJob` object for use in a method that is printing a page.

When you print a page, an object of a class that implements the `Printable` interface determines what is actually printed. Such an object is referred to as a **page painter**.

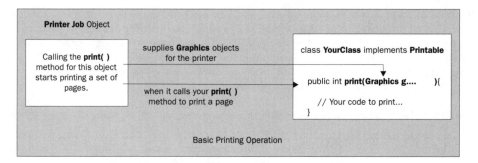

The `Printable` interface only defines one method, `print()`, which is called by a `PrinterJob` object when a page should be printed. Therefore the `print()` method does the printing of a page. Note that we have mentioned two `print()` methods one defined in the `PrinterJob` class that you call to starting the printing process, and another declared in the `Printable` interface that you implement in your class that is to do the printing legwork for a single page.

The printing operation you must code when you implement the `print()` method declared in the `Printable` interface works through a graphics context object that provides the means for writing data to your printer. The first argument that is passed to your `print()` method when it is called by a `PrinterJob` object is a reference of type `Graphics` that represents the graphics context for the printer. The object that it references is actually of type `Graphics2D`, which parallels the process you are already familiar with for drawing on a component. Just as with writing to the display, you use the methods defined in the `Graphics` and `Graphics2D` classes to print what you want, and the basic mechanism for printing 2D graphics or text on a page is identical to drawing on a component. The `Graphics` object for a printer also happens to implement the `PrinterGraphics` interface (not to be confused with the `PrintGraphics` interface in the `java.awt` package!) that declares just one method, `getPrinterJob()`. You call this method to obtain a reference to the object that is managing the print process. You would do this if you need to call `PrinterJob` methods to extract information about the print job, such as the job name or the user name.

A class that implements the `Pageable` interface defines an object that represents a set of pages to be printed rather than a single page. You would implement this interface for more complicated printing situations where a different page painter may print each page using an individual `PageFormat` object. It's the job of the `Pageable` object to supply information to the `PrinterJob` object about which page painter and `PageFormat` object should be used to print each page. The `Pageable` interface declares three methods:

`getNumberOfPages()`	Returns the number of pages to be printed as type `int`, or the constant value `Pageable.UNKNOWN_NUMBER_OF_PAGES` if the number of pages is not known.
`getPageFormat(int pageIndex)`	Returns the `PageFormat` object describing the size and orientation of the page specified by the argument. An exception of type `IndexOutOfBoundsException` will be thrown if the page does not exist.
`getPrintable(int pageIndex)`	Returns a reference to the `Printable` object responsible for printing the page specified by the argument. An exception of type `IndexOutOfBoundsException` will be thrown if the page does not exist.

A `Book` object also encapsulates a document that consists of a number of pages, each of which may be processed individually for printing. The difference between this and an object of a class that implements `Pageable` is that you can add individual pages to a `Book` object programmatically, whereas a class implementing `Pageable` encapsulates all the pages. We will look at how both of these options work later in this chapter.

Creating and Using PrinterJob Objects

Because the `PrinterJob` class encapsulates and manages the printing process for a given printer that is external to the JVM, you can't create an object of type `PrinterJob` directly using a constructor. You can obtain a reference to a `PrinterJob` object for the default printer on a system by calling the static method `getPrinterJob()` that is defined in the `PrinterJob` class:

```
PrinterJob printJob = PrinterJob.getPrinterJob(); // For the default printer
```

The object `printJob` provides the interface to the default printer, and controls each print job that you send to it.

A printer is encapsulated by a `PrintService` object, and you can obtain a reference of type `PrintService` to the object encapsulating the printer that will be used by a `PrinterJob` object by calling its `getPrintService()` method:

```
PrintService printer = printJob().getPrintService();
```

You can query the object that is returned for information about the capabilities of the printer and the kinds of documents it can print but we won't divert down that track for the moment. One point you should keep in mind is that sometimes there may not be a printer available on the machine on which your code is running. In this case the getPrintService() method will return null, so it's a good idea to call the method and test the reference returned, even if you don't want to obtain details of the printer.

If there are multiple print services available, such as several printers or perhaps a fax capability, you can obtain an array of PrintService references for them by calling the static lookupPrintServices() method in the PrinterJob class. For example:

```
PrintServices[] printers = PrinterJob.lookupPrintServices();
```

The printers array will have one element for each print service that is available. If there are no print services available, the array will have zero length. If you want to select a specific printer for the PrinterJob object to work with, you just pass the array element corresponding to the print service of your choice to the setPrintService() method for the PrinterJob object. For example:

```
if(printers.length>0)
   printJob.setPrintService(printers[0]);
```

The if statement checks that there are some print services before we attempt to set the print service. Without this we could get an IndexOutOfBoundsException exception if the printers array has no elements.

Displaying a Print Dialog

When you want to provide the user with control over the printing process, you can display a print dialog by calling the printDialog() method. This displays the modal dialog that applies to your particular print facility. There are two versions of the printDialog() method for a PrinterJob object. The version without arguments will display the native dialog if the PrinterJob object is printing on a native printer, so we'll look at that first, and return to the other version later.

If the dialog is closed using the button that indicates printing should proceed, the printDialog() method will return true, otherwise it will return false. The method will throw an exception of type HeadlessException if there is no display attached to the system. Thus to initiate printing you can call the printDialog() method and, if it returns true, call the print() method for the PrinterJob object. Note that the print() method will throw an exception of type PrinterException if an error in the printing system causes the operation to be aborted.

Of course, the PrinterJob object can have no prior knowledge of what you want to print so you have to call a method to tell the PrinterJob object where the printed pages are coming from before you initiate printing. The simplest way to do this is to call the setPrintable() method, and pass a reference to an object of a class that implements the Printable interface as the argument.

In Sketcher, the obvious candidate to print a sketch is the SketchView object (a reference to which is stored in the view member of the application object). Thus we could allow sketches to be printed by making the SketchView class implement the Printable interface. That done, we could then set the source of the printed output just by passing a reference to the view to the setPrintable() method for a PrinterJob object. You might consider the SketchModel object to be a candidate to do the printing, but printing is not really related to a sketch, any more than plotting or displaying on the screen is. The model is the input to the printing process, not the owner of it. It is generally better to keep the model dedicated to encapsulating the data that represents the sketch.

Starting the Printing Process

Let's use what we now know about printing to add some code to the `actionPerformed()` method in the `FileAction` class. This will handle the event for the `printAction` object in the `SketchFrame` class:

```
if(name.equals(printAction.getValue(NAME))) {
    // Get a printing object
    PrinterJob printJob = PrinterJob.getPrinterJob();
    PrintService printer = printJob.getPrintService();
    if(printer == null) {
      JOptionPane.showMessageDialog(SketchFrame.this,
                                "No default printer available.",
                                "Printer Error",
                                JOptionPane.ERROR_MESSAGE);
      return;
    }
    // The view is the page source
    printJob.setPrintable(theApp.getView());

    if(printJob.printDialog()) {                 // Display print dialog
                                                 // If true is returned...
      try {
        printJob.print();                        // then print
      } catch(PrinterException pe) {
        System.out.println(pe);
        JOptionPane.showMessageDialog(SketchFrame.this,
                                "Error printing a sketch.",
                                "Printer Error",
                                JOptionPane.ERROR_MESSAGE);
      }
    }
}
```

The code here obtains a `PrinterJob` object and, after verifying that we do have a printer to print on, sets the view as the printable source. The expression for the second `if` will display a print dialog, and if the return value from the `printDialog()` method call is `true`, we call the `print()` method for the `printJob` object to start the printing process. This is one of two overloaded `print()` methods defined in the `PrinterJob` class. We will look into the other one when we try out the alternative `printDialog()` method.

You will need to add three more `import` statements to the `SketchFrame.java` file:

```
import javax.print.PrintService;
import java.awt.print.PrinterJob;
import java.awt.print.PrinterException;
```

The `SketchFrame` class still won't compile at the moment, as we haven't made the `SketchView` class implement the `Printable` interface yet.

Printing Pages

The class object that you pass to the `setPrintable()` method is responsible for all the detail of the printing process. This class must implement the `Printable` interface, which implies defining the `print()` method in the same class. We can make the `SketchView` class implement the `Printable` interface like this:

```
import javax.swing.*;              // For various Swing components
import java.awt.*;
import java.util.*;                // For Observer, Observer, Iterator
import java.awt.event.*;           // For events
import javax.swing.event.MouseInputAdapter;
import java.awt.geom.Line2D;
import java.awt.print.*;

class SketchView extends JComponent
              implements Observer, Constants, ActionListener,
                         Printable {
  public int print(Graphics g,            // Graphics context for printing
                   PageFormat pageFormat,  // The page format
                   int pageIndex)          // Index number of current page
              throws PrinterException {
    // Code to do the printing
  }
  // Rest of the class definition as before...
}
```

The `import` statements here have been changed to import all the names in a package where this significantly reduces the number of lines required. The `PrinterJob` object will call the `print()` method here for each page to be printed. This process starts when you call the `print()` method for the `PrinterJob` object that has overall control of the printing process. You can see that our `print()` method can throw an exception of type `PrinterException`. If you identify a problem within your `print()` method code, the way to signal the problem to the `PrinterJob` object is to throw an exception of this type.

One point to keep in mind – you should not assume that the `PrinterJob` object will call the `print()` method for your `Printable` object just once per page. In general the `print()` method is likely to be called several times for each page as the output destined for the printer is buffered within the Java printing system and the buffer will not necessarily be large enough to hold a complete page. You don't need to worry about this unduly. Just don't build any assumptions into your code about how often `print()` is called for a given page.

Of course, our `PrinterJob` object in the `actionPerformed()` method code has no way of knowing how many pages need to be printed. When we call the `PrinterJob` object's `print()` method, it will continue calling the `SketchView` object's `print()` method until the value returned indicates there are no more pages to be printed. You can return one of two values from the `print()` method in the `Printable` interface – `PAGE_EXISTS` to indicate you have rendered a page, or `NO_SUCH_PAGE` if there are no more pages to be printed. Both of these constants are defined in the `Printable` interface. The `PrinterJob` object will continue calling `print()` until the `NO_SUCH_PAGE` value is returned.

You can see that there are three arguments passed to the `print()` method in the `Printable` interface. The first is the graphics context that you must use to write to the printer. The reference passed to the method is actually of type `Graphics2D`, so you will typically cast it to this type before using it – just as we did within the `paint()` method for a component to draw on the screen. In the `print()` method in our view class, we could draw the sketch on the printer with the statements:

```
public int print(Graphics g,          // Graphics context for printing
                 PageFormat pageFormat,  // The page format
                 int pageIndex)        // Index number of current page
                 throws PrinterException {
   Graphics2D g2D = (Graphics2D) g;
   paint(g2D);
   return PAGE_EXISTS;
}
```

This will work after a fashion, but we have more work to do before we can try this out. At the moment, it will print the same page over and over, indefinitely, so let's take care of that as a matter of urgency!

It's the third argument that carries an index value for the page. The first page in a print job will have index value 0, the second will have index value 1, and so on for as long as there are more pages to be printed. If we intend to print our sketch on a single page, we can stop the printing process by checking the page index:

```
public int print(Graphics g,          // Graphics context for printing
                 PageFormat pageFormat,  // The page format
                 int pageIndex)        // Index number of current page
                 throws PrinterException {
   if(pageIndex>0)
     return NO_SUCH_PAGE;
   Graphics2D g2D = (Graphics2D) g;
   paint(g2D);                         // Draw the sketch
   return PAGE_EXISTS;
}
```

We only want to print one page, so if the value passed as the third parameter is greater than 0, we return NO_SUCH_PAGE to stop the printing process.

While at least we won't now print endlessly, we still won't get an output formatted the way we want it. We must look into how we can use the information provided by the second argument that is passed to the `print()` method, the `PageFormat` object, to position the output properly.

The PageFormat Class

The `PageFormat` reference that is passed to the `print()` method for a page provides details of the page size, the position and size of the printable area on the page, and the orientation – portrait or landscape.

Perhaps the most important pieces of information you can get are where the top left corner of the **printable area** (or **imageable area** to use the terminology of the method names) is on the page, and its width and height, since this is the area you have available for printing your output. The printable area on a page is simply the area within the current margins defined for your printer. The position of the printable area is returned by the methods getImageableX() and getImageableY(). These return the *x* and *y* coordinates of the upper left corner of the printable area in user coordinates of type double for the printing context, which happen to be in units of 1/72 of an inch, which corresponds to a point – as in point size for a font. The width and height of the printable area are returned in the same units by the getImageableWidth() and getImageableHeight() methods.

The origin of the page coordinate system, the point (0,0), corresponds initially to the top left corner of the paper. If you want the output to be placed in the printable area on the page, the first step will be to move the origin of the graphics context that you will use for writing to the printer to the position of the top left corner of the printable area.

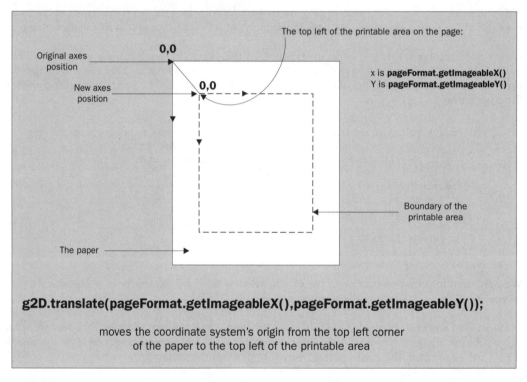

g2D.translate(pageFormat.getImageableX(),pageFormat.getImageableY());

moves the coordinate system's origin from the top left corner
of the paper to the top left of the printable area

We know how to do this – it's exactly what we have been doing in the draw() method for each of our element classes. We call the translate() method for the graphics context. Here's how this would work for the print() method in the SketchView class:

```
public int print(Graphics g,              // Graphics context for printing
                 PageFormat pageFormat,    // The page format
                 int pageIndex)            // Index number of current page
                 throws PrinterException {
    if(pageIndex>0)
```

```
        return NO_SUCH_PAGE;
      Graphics2D g2D = (Graphics2D) g;

      // Move origin to page printing area corner
      g2D.translate(pageFormat.getImageableX(), pageFormat.getImageableY());

      paint(g2D);                              // Draw the sketch
      return PAGE_EXISTS;
    }
```

The `translate()` method call moves the user coordinate system so that the (0,0) point is positioned at the top left corner on the printable area on the page.

Let's see if that works in practice.

Try It Out – Printing a Sketch

You should have added the code we saw earlier to the `actionPerformed()` method to handle the **Print** menu item event, and the code to `SketchView` to implement the `Printable` interface that we have evolved. Don't forget the import statement for `java.awt.print`. If you compile and run Sketcher, you should be able to print a sketch.

On my system, when I select the toolbar button to print, I get the dialog shown below.

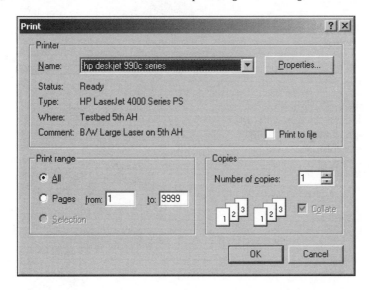

This is the standard dialog for my printer under Windows. In your environment you will get a dialog for your default printer. The reason the dialog indicates that there are 9999 pages to be printed is that we haven't said how many, so the maximum is being assumed.

How It Works

The code in the `actionPerformed()` method displays the print dialog by calling the `printDialog()` method for the `PrinterJob` object that we obtain. Clicking on the **OK** button causes the `print()` method for the `PrinterJob` object to be called. This in turn causes the `print()` method in the `SketchView` class to be called once for each page to be printed, and one more time to end the process.

In the `print()` method in `SketchView`, we adjust the origin of the user coordinate system for the graphics context so that its position is at the top left corner of the printable area on the page. Only one page is printed because we return `NO_SUCH_PAGE` when the page index value that is passed to the `print()` method is greater than 0. Incidentally, if you want to see how many times the `print()` method gets called for a page, just add a statement at the beginning of the method to output some trace information to the console.

I used the print facility to print the sketch shown here, and frankly, I was disappointed.

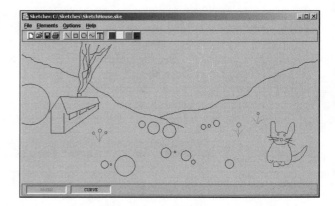

The picture that I get printed on the paper is shown here. There's only one flower in view, and that interesting cross between a rabbit and a cat is completely missing.

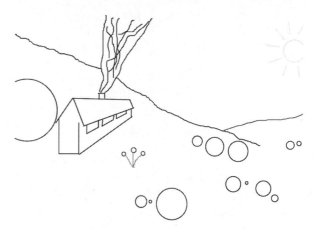

The boulder on the left only appears in part. I know it's not all on the screen, but it's all in the model, so I was hoping to see the picture in its full glory. If you think about it, it's very optimistic to believe that we could automatically get the whole sketch printed. First of all, neither the PrinterJob object nor the view object has any idea how big the sketch is. That's a fairly fundamental piece of data if you want a complete sketch printed. Another consideration is that the left extremity of the boulder on the left of the sketch is to the left of the y axis, but I'd rather like to see it in the picture. It would be nice if we could take account of that too. Let's see how we might do it.

Note that material change to the Element subclasses will cause problems. Sketches serialized before the changes will not deserialize after.

Printing the Whole Sketch

A starting point is to figure out the extent of the sketch. Ideally we need a rectangle that encloses all the elements in the sketch. It's really surprisingly easy to get that. Every element has a getBounds() method that returns a Rectangle object enclosing the element. As we saw in Chapter 15, the Rectangle class also defines a member add() method. It combines a Rectangle object passed as an argument with the Rectangle object for which it is called, and returns the smallest Rectangle object that will enclose both: this is referred to as the **union** of the two rectangles. With these two bits of information and an iterator from element list in the SketchModel object, we can get the rectangle enclosing the entire sketch by implementing the following method in the SketchModel class:

```
// Get the rectangle enclosing an entire sketch
Rectangle getModelExtent() {
  Iterator elements = getIterator();
  Rectangle rect = new Rectangle();          // An empty rectangle
  Element element;                            // Stores an element
  while(elements.hasNext()) {                 // Go through the list
    element = (Element)elements.next();       // Get the next element
    rect.add(element.getBounds());            // Expand union
  }
  if(rect.width == 0)                         // Make sure width
    rect.width = 1;                           // is non-zero
  if(rect.height == 0)                        // and the height
    rect.height = 1;
  return rect;
}
```

Don't forget to add an import for the Rectangle class to the SketchModel source file:

```
import java.awt.Rectangle;
```

Using the iterator for the element list, we expand the bounding rectangle for every element so we end up with a rectangle that bounds everything in the sketch. A zero width or height for the rectangle is unlikely, but we want to be sure it can't happen because we will use these values as divisors later.

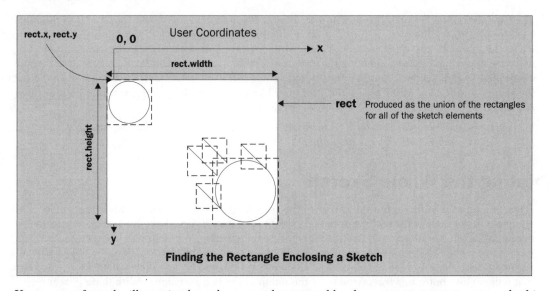

Finding the Rectangle Enclosing a Sketch

You can see from the illustration how the rectangle returned by the getModelExtent() method is simply the rectangle that encloses all the bounding rectangles for the individual elements. If you visualize the origin of the user coordinate system being placed at the top left corner of the printable area on the page, you can appreciate that a section of the sketch in the illustration will be hanging out to the left outside the printable area. This can arise quite easily in Sketcher, when you are drawing a circle with the center close to either of the axes, for instance, or if you move a shape so this is the case. We can avoid missing part of the sketch from the printed output by first translating the origin of the coordinate system to the top left corner of rect, and then translating the origin at this position to the top left corner of the printable area on the page.

The following code in the print() method in the SketchView class will do this:

```
public int print(Graphics g,              // Graphics context for printing
                 PageFormat pageFormat,    // The page format
                 int pageIndex)            // Index number of current page
          throws PrinterException {
  if(pageIndex>0)
    return NO_SUCH_PAGE;
  Graphics2D g2D = (Graphics2D) g;

  // Get sketch bounds
  Rectangle rect = theApp.getModel().getModelExtent();

  // Move origin to page printing area corner
  g2D.translate(pageFormat.getImageableX(), pageFormat.getImageableY());

  // Move origin to rect top left
  g2D.translate(-rect.x, -rect.y);

  paint(g2D);                                // Draw the sketch
  return PAGE_EXISTS;
}
```

We get the rectangle bounding the sketch by calling the `getModelExtent()` method that we put together just now. We then use `rect` in the second statement that calls `translate()` for the `Graphics2D` object to position the top left corner of `rect` at the origin. We could have combined these two translations into one, but we will keep them separate, first to make it easier to see what is going on, and second because we will be adding some other transformations later in between these translations. There is a potentially puzzling aspect to the second translation – why are the arguments to the `translate()` method negative?

To understand this, it is important to be clear about what we are doing. It's easy to get confused by this so we'll take it step by step. First of all, remember that the paper is a physical entity with given dimensions and its coordinate system just defines where each point will end up on the paper when you print something. Of course, we can move the coordinate system about in relation to the paper, and we can scale or even rotate it to get something printed where we want.

Now consider our sketch. The point (`rect.x`, `rect.y`) is the top left corner of the rectangle bounding our sketch, the area we want to transfer to the page, and this point is fixed – we can't change it to make it the origin for instance. With the current paper coordinates at the top left of the printable area, it might print something like that shown here:

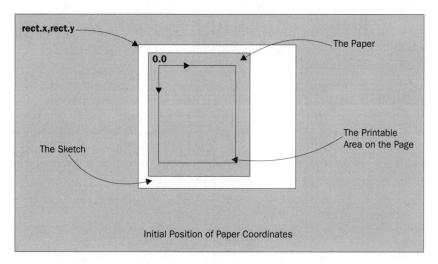

When we print our sketch we really want the point (`rect.x`, `rect.y`) to end up at the top left corner of the printable area on the page. In other words, we have to move the origin of the coordinate system for the paper so that the point (`rect.x`, `rect.y`) in the new coordinate system is the top left corner of the printable area. To do this we must move the origin to the new position shown.

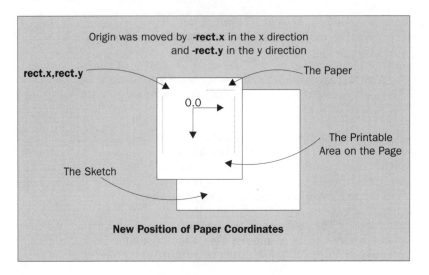

Thus a translation of the origin to the point ($-$rect.x, $-$rect.y) does the trick.

We have the sketch in the right place on the page, but it won't necessarily fit into the space available on the paper. We must scale the sketch so that it doesn't hang out beyond the right side or below the bottom of the printable page area.

Scaling the Sketch to Fit

We saw earlier that we can get the width and height of the printable area on a page by calling the getImageableWidth() and getImageableHeight() methods for the PageFormat object that is passed to the print() method. We also have the width and height of the rectangle that encloses the entire sketch. This gives the information that we need to scale the sketch to fit on the page. There are a couple of tricky aspects that we need to think about though.

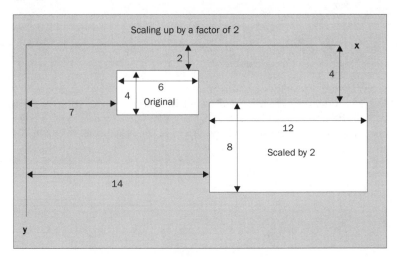

Firstly, note that when you scale a coordinate system, a unit of length along each of the axes changes in size, so things move relative to the origin as well as relative to one another. When you scale up with a factor greater than 1, everything moves away from the origin. The illustration above shows the effect of scaling a rectangle up by a factor of 2. The dimensions of the rectangle are doubled, but so is the distance of the new rectangle from each of the axes.

The reverse happens with scale factors less than 1. We want to make sure that we scale the sketch to fit the page while keeping its top left corner at the top left of the printable area. This means that we can't just apply the scaling factor necessary to make the sketch fit the page in the new coordinate system we showed in the previous illustration. If we were to scale with this coordinate system, the sketch will move in relation to the origin, away from it if we are scaling up as is the case in the illustration, or towards it if we are scaling down. As a consequence, the top left corner of the sketch would no longer be at the top left of the printable area. Thus we must apply the scaling operation to make the sketch fit on the page *after* we have translated the paper origin to the top left corner of the printable area, but *before* we translate this origin point to make the top left corner of the sketch appear at the top left corner of the printable area. This will ensure that the sketch is scaled to fit the page and the top left of the sketch will stay at the top left corner of the printable area on the page and not will move to some other point.

Secondly, we want to make sure that we scale x and y by the same factor. If we apply different scales to the x and y axes in the user coordinate system, the relative proportions of a sketch will not be maintained and our circles will become ellipses and squares will become rectangles.

We can calculate the scale factors we need to apply to get the sketch to fit within the printable area of the page with the following statements:

```
// Calculate the x and y scales to fit the sketch to the page
double scaleX = pageFormat.getImageableWidth()/rect.width;
double scaleY = pageFormat.getImageableHeight()/rect.height;
```

We are using variables of type `double` for the scale factors here because the `getImageableWidth()` and `getImageableHeight()` methods return values of type `double`. The scale factor for the x axis needs to be such that when we multiply the width of the sketch, `rect.width`, by the scale factor, the result is the width of the printable area on the page returned by `getImageableWidth()`, and similarly for scaling the y axis. Since we want to apply the same scale to both axes, we should calculate the minimum of the scale factors `scaleX` and `scaleY`. If we then apply this minimum to both axes, the sketch will fit within the width and height of the page and still be in proportion.

Try It Out – Printing the Whole Sketch

We just need to add some code to the `print()` method in `SketchView` to calculate the required scale factor, and then use the `scale()` method for the `Graphics2D` object to apply the scaling transformation:

```
public int print(Graphics g,              // Graphics context for printing
                 PageFormat pageFormat,    // The page format
                 int pageIndex)            // Index number of current page
                 throws PrinterException {
  if(pageIndex>0)
    return NO_SUCH_PAGE;
  Graphics2D g2D = (Graphics2D) g;
```

```
                   // Get sketch bounds
                   Rectangle rect = theApp.getModel().getModelExtent();

                   // Calculate the scale to fit sketch to page
                   double scaleX = pageFormat.getImageableWidth()/rect.width;
                   double scaleY = pageFormat.getImageableHeight()/rect.height;

                   // Get minimum scale factor
                   double scale = Math.min(scaleX, scaleY);

                   // Move origin to page printing area corner
                   g2D.translate(pageFormat.getImageableX(), pageFormat.getImageableY());

                   g2D.scale(scale, scale);                // Apply scale factor

                   g2D.translate(-rect.x, -rect.y);        // Move origin to rect top left

                   paint(g2D);                             // Draw the sketch
                   return PAGE_EXISTS;
                 }
```

If you compile and run Sketcher with these changes, you should now be able to print each sketch within a page.

How It Works

We calculate the scaling factors for each axis as the ratio of the dimension of the printable area on the page to the corresponding dimension of the rectangle enclosing the sketch. We then take the minimum of these two scale factors as the scale to be applied to both axes. As long as the scale transformation is applied after the translation of the coordinate system to the top left corner of the printable page area, one or other dimension of the sketch will fit exactly within the printable area of the page.

The output is now fine, but if the width of the sketch is greater than the height, we waste a lot of space on the page. Ideally in this situation we would want to print with a landscape orientation rather than the default portrait orientation. Let's see what possibilities we have for that.

Printing in Landscape Orientation

We can easily determine when a landscape orientation would be preferable by comparing the width of a sketch with its height. If the width is larger than the height, a landscape orientation will make better use of the space on the paper and we will get a larger scale picture.

You can set the orientation in a PageFormat object by calling its setOrientation() method. You can pass one of three possible argument values, which are defined within the PageFormat class:

Argument Value	Description
PORTRAIT 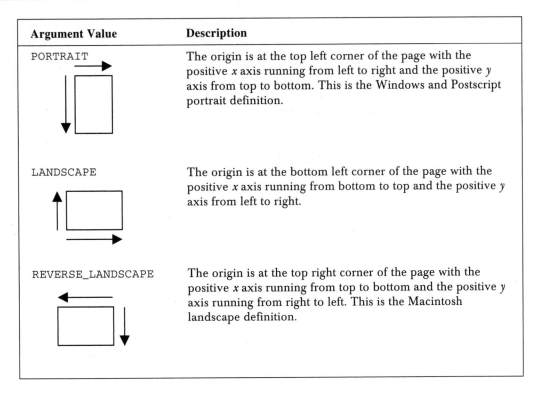	The origin is at the top left corner of the page with the positive x axis running from left to right and the positive y axis from top to bottom. This is the Windows and Postscript portrait definition.
LANDSCAPE	The origin is at the bottom left corner of the page with the positive x axis running from bottom to top and the positive y axis from left to right.
REVERSE_LANDSCAPE	The origin is at the top right corner of the page with the positive x axis running from top to bottom and the positive y axis running from right to left. This is the Macintosh landscape definition.

In each case the long side of the paper is in the same orientation as the y axis, but note that a Macintosh landscape specification has the origin at the top right corner of the page rather than the top left or bottom left.

Let's incorporate LANDSCAPE into the print() method in SketchView:

```
public int print(Graphics g,                    // Graphics context for printing
                 PageFormat pageFormat,          // The page format
                 int pageIndex)                  // Index number of current page
          throws PrinterException {
  if(pageIndex>0)
    return NO_SUCH_PAGE;
  Graphics2D g2D = (Graphics2D) g;

  // Get sketch bounds
  Rectangle rect = theApp.getModel().getModelExtent();

  // If the width is more than the height, set landscape
  if(rect.width>rect.height) {
    pageFormat.setOrientation(pageFormat.LANDSCAPE);
  }

  // Rest of the code as before...
}
```

Having set the orientation for the `PageFormat` object, the methods returning the coordinates for the position of the printable area and the width and height all return values consistent with the orientation. Thus the width of the printable area will be greater than the height if the orientation has been set to `LANDSCAPE`. Everything looks fine until we try it out. If you recompile with this modification to `SketchView`, the sketch is printed landscape, but the output is clipped so that a portion of the sketch to the right of the page in landscape orientation is missing. Indeed it looks very much as though the width of the printable area in landscape orientation is the same as that for portrait orientation.

That's exactly true, and this is a clue to what's wrong. We have modified the `PageFormat` object to landscape orientation, but the `Graphics2D` object that was passed to our `print()` method was produced based on the `PageFormat` object in its original state – portrait orientation. If we had known ahead of time back in the `actionPerformed()` method in the `FileAction` inner class to `SketchFrame`, we could have set up the `PageFormat` object for the print job before our `print()` method ever gets called. This could be done by modifying the code that initiates printing in the `actionPerformed()` method like this:

```
// Get a printing object
PrinterJob printJob = PrinterJob.getPrinterJob();
PrintService printer = printJob.getPrintService();
if(printer == null) {
  JOptionPane.showMessageDialog(SketchFrame.this,
                          "No default printer available.",
                          "Printer Error",
                          JOptionPane.ERROR_MESSAGE);
    return;
}
PageFormat pageFormat = printJob.defaultPage();
SketchView theView = theApp.getView();
Rectangle rect = theView.getModelExtent();          // Get sketch bounds

// If the sketch width is greater than the height, print landscape
if(rect.width>rect.height)
    pageFormat.setOrientation(pageFormat.LANDSCAPE);

printJob.setPrintable(theView, pageFormat);
```

Calling the `defaultPage()` method for a `PrinterJob` object returns a reference to the default page for the current printer. You can then change that to suit the conditions that you want to apply in the printing operation and pass the reference to an overloaded version of the `setPrintable()` method. The call to `setPrintable()` here makes the `printJob` object print using the `theView` object as the `Printable`, object, using the `PageFormat` object specified by the second argument. With this code we would not need to worry about the orientation in the `print()` method for the `Printable` object. It is taken care of before `print()` ever gets called.

However, while the code above provides a good solution it is interesting to look into how we can change the clip rectangle; let's see how we can make our `print()` method accommodate landscape orientation. To make the printing work properly we need to reset the clip rectangle in the `Graphics2D` object to reflect the landscape orientation of the paper. It actually isn't that difficult. We can amend `print()` like this:

```
public int print(Graphics g,                    // Graphics context for printing
                 PageFormat pageFormat,          // The page format
                 int pageIndex)                  // Index number of current page
                 throws PrinterException {
  if(pageIndex>0)
    return NO_SUCH_PAGE;
  Graphics2D g2D = (Graphics2D) g;

  // Get sketch bounds
  Rectangle rect = theApp.getModel().getModelExtent();

  // If the width is more than the height, set landscape
  if(rect.width>rect.height) {
    pageFormat.setOrientation(pageFormat.LANDSCAPE);

    // Now set the clip rectangle to the printable page area
    g2D.setClip((int)pageFormat.getImageableX(),       // x coordinate
                (int)pageFormat.getImageableY(),       // x coordinate
                (int)pageFormat.getImageableWidth(),   // width
                (int)pageFormat.getImageableHeight()); // height
  }
  // Rest of the code as before...
}
```

The new rectangle defining the boundaries for clipping the output is exactly the printable area on the page. We have to cast the coordinates and the width and height from `double` to `int` because that type is required for the arguments to the `setClip()` method. If you recompile and try printing a sketch that is wider than it is long, it should come out perfectly in landscape orientation.

User Page Setup

Of course, there are many situations where the best orientation from a paper usage point of view may not be what the user wants. Instead of automatically setting landscape or portrait based on the dimensions of a sketch, you could just provide the user with a dialog to select the page setup parameters. The `PrinterJob` class makes this very easy since it provides a method to display the dialog and set the user selections in a `PageFormat` object. To make use of this we could change the printing code in the `SketchFrame` class like this:

```
PrinterJob printJob = PrinterJob.getPrinterJob(); // Get a printing object
PageFormat pageFormat = printJob.defaultPage();   // Get the page format
pageFormat = printJob.pageDialog(pageFormat);     // Show page setup dialog

// Print using the user page format settings
printJob.setPrintable(theApp.getView(),pageFormat);
```

The `defaultPage()` method returns a reference to a `PageFormat` object that is initialized to the default size and orientation for the current printer. We pass this reference to the `pageDialog()` method, and this displays the dialog shown using the values from the `PageFormat` object.

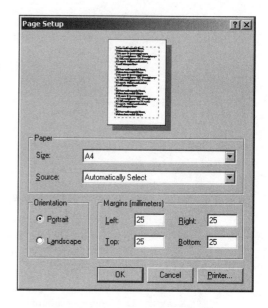

As you can see, with my printer I can select the paper size and the source tray. I can also set the margin sizes as well as select portrait or landscape orientation. When the dialog is closed normally with the OK button, the method returns a new `PageFormat` object that incorporates the values set by the user in the dialog. If the `Cancel` button is used to close the dialog, the original reference that was passed as an argument is returned. The overloaded `setPrintable()` method with two parameters will use the `PageFormat` object passed as the second argument when the `print()` method for the object referenced by the first argument is called.

Of course, the `print()` method in `SketchView` should just use whatever `PageFormat` object is handed to it. This will be set with the options that the user chose in the dialog and the `Graphics` object will be created consistent with that. This corresponds with the version of the `print()` method that we used in the example *'Printing the Whole Sketch'*.

Using the Java Print Dialog

The overloaded version of the `printDialog()` method that we sidestepped earlier generates a Java based print dialog rather than using the native dialog. This method requires a single argument of type `PrintRequestAttributeSet`. This interface type is defined in the `javax.print.attribute` package, which declares methods for adding attributes relating to a print request to a set of such attributes. These attributes specify things such as the number of copies to be printed, the orientation of the image on the paper, or the media or media tray to be selected for the print job. The `HashPrintRequestAttributeSet` class that is defined in the same package implements this interface and encapsulates a set of print request attributes stored as a hash map. It will be useful if we can define a set of attributes that have some persistence in Sketcher so they can be carried forward from one print request to the next. We can add an initially empty set of print request attributes to the `SketchFrame` class like this:

```
    private HashPrintRequestAttributeSet requestAttr =
                        new  HashPrintRequestAttributeSet();
```

There are other `HashPrintRequestAttributeSet` class constructors that will create non-empty attribute sets but this will suffice for our needs. You will need an import statement for the class in the `SketchFrame.java` file:

```
import javax.print.attribute.HashPrintRequestAttributeSet;
```

Now we have a print request attribute set object, we can modify the `actionPerformed()` method in the `FileAction` inner class to use the Java print dialog:

```
// Get a printing object
PrinterJob printJob = PrinterJob.getPrinterJob();
PrintService printer = printJob.getPrintService();
if(printer == null) {
  JOptionPane.showMessageDialog(SketchFrame.this,
                        "No default printer available.",
                        "Printer Error",
                        JOptionPane.ERROR_MESSAGE);
  return;
}

// The view is the page source
printJob.setPrintable(theApp.getView());

HashPrintRequestAttributeSet printAttr = new HashPrintRequestAttributeSet();
if(printJob.printDialog(printAttr)) {      // Display print dialog
                                           // If true is returned...
  try {
    printJob.print(printAttr);             // then print
  } catch(PrinterException pe) {
    System.out.println(pe);
    JOptionPane.showMessageDialog(SketchFrame.this,
                        "Error printing a sketch.",
                        "Printer Error",
                        JOptionPane.ERROR_MESSAGE);
  }
}
```

Note that we also use an overloaded version of the `print()` method for the `PrinterJob` object to which we pass the print request attribute set. Thus the print operation will use whatever attributes were set or modified in the print dialog displayed by the `printDialog()` method. If you run Sketcher with these changes you should see a dialog with three tabs similar to that shown below when you print a sketch:

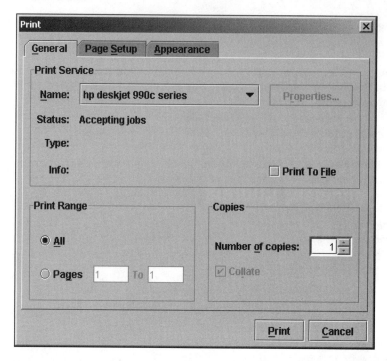

Now we have the ability to set attributes on any of the tabs in the dialog and the attributes will be stored in the `PrintAttr` member of the `SketchFrame` class that we passed to the `printDialog()` method. Since we also pass this reference to the `print()` method for the `PrinterJob` object, the print request will be executed using these attributes. This is accomplished by passing a `PageFormat` object to our `Printable` object that prints a page that has its size, orientation, and other attributes set from the print request attributes defined by `PrintAttr`. Note that although you can set print attributes in the dialog, they may be overridden by your code that does the printing. For instance, you render the sketch in color by setting the color for each element before you draw it, so selecting monochrome for the color appearance tab will have no effect. Similarly, the code determines whether to use portrait or landscape orientation, so the selection in the dialog for this will be overridden too.

Setting Print Request Attributes Programmatically

Print request attributes are specifications of the kinds of options displayed in the dialog we just saw. They specify things like the number of copies, whether printing is in color or monochrome, the page margin sizes, and so on. Each print request attribute is identified by a class that implements the `PrintRequestAttribute` interface, and the `javax.print.attributes.standard` package defines a series of classes for standard print request attributes, as well as classes for other types of print attributes. There are a large number of standard classes for print request attributes and we don't have the space to go into the details of them all here so we will just pick one to show how you can query and set them.

All the classes that implement the `PrintRequestAttribute` interface are identified in the interface documentation. We will use the `Copies` class in the `javax.print.attributes.standard` package that specifies the number of printed copies to be produced.

We will be adding an instance of the `Copies` class to our `PrintAttr` object to specify the number of copies to be printed and this will be displayed by the print dialog. We can create an object specifying the number of copies to be produced like this:

```
HashPrintRequestAttributeSet printAttr = new HashPrintRequestAttributeSet();
Copies twoCopies = new Copies(2);
if (printer.isAttributeCategorySupported(twoCopies.getCategory()))
   printAttr.add(twoCopies);

   if(printJob.printDialog(printAttr)) {      // Display print dialog
```

The argument to the constructor specifies the number of copies to be produced. Our object specifies just two copies but you can go for more if you have the paper, the time, and the inclination.

Before we add this object to the print request attribute set though, we verify that the printer does actually support the production of multiple copies. Obviously it only makes sense to set an attribute for a printer that has the appropriate capability – you won't be able to print in color on a monochrome printer for instance. We can call the `isAttributeCategorySupported()` method for the `PrintService` object that we obtained from the `PrinterJob` object to do this.

The `isAttributeCategorySupported()` method requires an argument of type `Class` to identify the attribute category that we are querying, and we obtain this by calling the `getCategory()` method for our `Copies` object. If the attribute is supported, we add the `twoCopies` object to the set encapsulated by `printAttr` by calling its `add()` method.

You can add the three lines of code to the `actionPerformed()` method in the `FileAction` inner class and add an import statement for the `Copies` class to `SketchFrame.java`:

```
import javax.print.attribute.standard.Copies;
```

If you recompile and run Sketcher once more, the print dialog should come up with two copies set initially.

Of course, setting thing like margin sizes and page orientation once and for all may not be satisfactory in many cases. It is easy to envisage situations where you may want to print some pages in a document in portrait orientation while others, perhaps containing illustrations, are printed landscape. Let's see how we can handle that in Java.

Multipage Document Printing

If you need to print a document that contains multiple pages in a print job, you can do it in the implementation of the `print()` method declared in the `Printable` interface. The `PrinterJob` object will continue to call this method until the value `NO_SUCH_PAGE` is returned. However, this won't be convenient in every case. In a more complicated application than Sketcher, as well as having different page orientations, you may want to have different class objects printing different kinds of pages – rendering the same data as graphical or textual output for instance. You can't do this conveniently with just one class implementing the `Printable` interface. You also need something more flexible than just passing a class object that does printing to the `PrinterJob` object by calling its `setPrintable()` method.

The solution is to implement the `Pageable` interface in a class, and call the `setPageable()` method for the `PrinterJob` object instead of `setPrintable()`. The essential difference between the `Printable` and `Pageable` interfaces is that a `Printable` object encapsulates a single page to be printed whereas a `Pageable` object encapsulates multiple pages. Each of the pages to be printed by a `Pageable` object is encapsulated by a `Printable` object though.

Implementing the Pageable Interface

A class that implements the `Pageable` interface defines a set of pages to be printed. A `Pageable` object must be able to supply the `PrinterJob` object a count of the number of pages for a job, a reference of type `Printable` for the object that is to print each page, plus a `PageFormat` object defining the format of each page. The `PrinterJob` acquires this information by calling the three methods declared in the `Pageable` interface:

Method	Description
`getNumberOfPages()`	Must return an `int` value specifying the number of pages to be printed. If the number of pages cannot be determined then the value UNKNOWN_NUMBER_OF_PAGES can be returned. This value is defined in the `Pageable` interface.
`getPageFormat(int pageIndex)`	This method must return a `PageFormat` object for the page specified by the page index that is passed to it.
`getPrintable(int pageIndex)`	This method must return a reference of type `Printable` to the object responsible for printing the page specified by the page index that is passed to it.

At the start of a print job the `PrinterJob` object will call the `getNumberOfPages()` method to determine how many pages are to be printed. If you return the value UNKNOWN_NUMBER_OF_PAGES then the process relies on a `Printable` object returning NO_SUCH_PAGE at some point to stop printing. It is therefore a good idea to supply the number of pages when it can be determined.

For each page index, the `PrinterJob` object will call the `getPageFormat()` method to obtain the `PageFormat` object to be used, and call the `getPrintable()` method to obtain a reference to the object that will do the printing. Of course, just because you *can* supply a different `Printable` object for each page doesn't mean that you *must*. You could use as many or as few as you need for your application. Remember that the `print()` method for a `Printable` object may be called more than once by the `PrinterJob` object to print a particular page and the page should be rendered each time, so you must not code the method in a way that presumes otherwise.

Creating PageFormat Objects

As we saw earlier, you can get the default `PageFormat` object for the print service you are using by calling the `defaultPage()` method for the `PrinterJob` object. The default `PageFormat` class constructor can also be used to create an object that is portrait oriented but in this case you have no guarantee that it is compatible with the current print service. A `PageFormat` object encapsulates information about the size of the paper and the margins, in effect, so the object produced by the default constructor is unlikely to correspond with your printer setup. If you want to go this route, you can pass a reference to a `PageFormat` object to the `validatePage()` method for a `PrinterJob()` object. For example:

```
// Object for current printer
PrinterJob printJob = PrinterJob.getPrinterJob();

// Validated page
PageFormat pageFormat = printJob.validatePage(new PageFormat());
```

Note that the `validatePage()` method does not return the same reference that is passed as an argument. The method clones the object that was passed to it and returns a reference to the clone, which will have been modified if necessary to suit the current printer. Since it does not modify the object in place, you always need to store the reference that is returned.

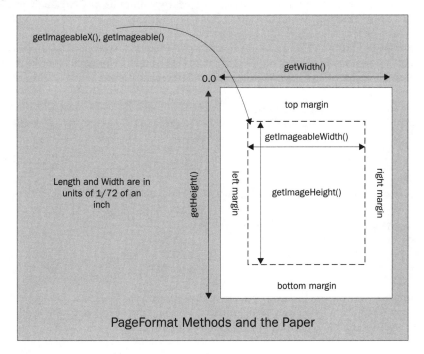

PageFormat Methods and the Paper

Once you have a `PageFormat` object, you can modify the orientation of the page by calling its `setOrientation()` method as we have seen. The `PageFormat` class defines several methods to retrieve information about the paper – we have seen that we can get the position and size of the printable area on the page for instance by calling the `getImageableX()`, `getImageableY()`, `getImageableWidth()`, and `getImageableHeight()` methods. You also have `getWidth()` and `getHeight()` methods in the `PageFormat` class that return the overall width and height of the page. These are all actually properties of the paper itself, which is represented by an object of the `Paper` class. You can also work with the `Paper` object for a `PageFormat` object directly.

Dealing with Paper

The `Paper` class encapsulates the size of the paper and the size and position of the printable area on the page. The default constructor for the `Paper` class creates an American letter sized sheet with one inch margins – the printable area being the area inside the margins. You can change the size of the paper by calling the `setSize()` method for the `Paper` object as we'll see in a moment.

Rather than creating an independent `Paper` object, you will normally retrieve a reference to the `Paper` object for a `PageFormat` object by calling its `getPaper()` method. If you then want to change the size of the paper or the printable area – the page margins in other words – you call the `setSize()` or the `setImageableArea()` method for the `Paper` object. You can restore the paper details by passing an object of type `Paper` back to the `PageFormat` object by calling its `setPaper()` method with a reference to a `Paper` object as the argument.

The `setSize()` method for a `Paper` object has two parameters of type `double` that are the width and height of the paper in units of 1/72 of an inch. If you use A4 paper, you could specify the size of the paper for a `PageFormat` object with the following statements:

```
Paper paper = pageFormat.getPaper();
final double MM_TO_PAPER_UNITS = 1.0/25.4*72.0;   // 25.4 mm to an inch
double widthA4 = 210*MM_TO_PAPER_UNITS;
double heightA4 = 297*MM_TO_PAPER_UNITS;
paper.setSize(widthA4, heightA4);
```

If you use letter size paper that is 8.5 by 11 inches, it's somewhat simpler:

```
Paper paper = pageFormat.getPaper();
double widthLetterSize = 72.0*8.5;
double heightLetterSize = 72.0*11.0;
paper.setSize(widthLetterSize, heightLetterSize);
```

The `setImageableArea()` method expects four arguments of type `double` to be supplied. The first two are the coordinates of the top left corner of the printable area and the next two are the width and the height. All these values are in units of 1/72 of an inch. To set 20 mm margins on your A4 sheet you could write:

```
double marginSize = 20.0* MM_TO_PAPER_UNITS;          // 20 mm wide
paper.setImageableArea(marginSize, marginSize,        // Top left
                       widthA4-2.0*marginSize,        // Width
                       heightA4-2.0*marginSize);      // Height
```

If you are printing on letter size paper, a one-inch margin might be more appropriate so you would write:

```
double marginSize = 72.0;                          // 1 inch wide
paper.setImageableArea(marginSize, marginSize,     // Top left
                  widthLetterSize-2.0*marginSize,  // Width
                  heightLetterSize-2.0*marginSize); // Height
```

Of course, there's no reason why a class that implements `Pageable` cannot also implement `Printable`, so we could do this in Sketcher, just to get a feel for the `Pageable` interface in action.

Try It Out – Using the Pageable Interface

We will just print two pages in a print job in Sketcher, a cover page with a title for the sketch, plus the sketch itself, which may be portrait or landscape of course. We could produce both pages in `SketchView`, but to make it more interesting, let's define a separate class to represent a `Printable` object for the cover page:

```
import java.awt.*;
import java.awt.geom.*;
import java.awt.print.*;

class SketchCoverPage implements Printable {
  public SketchCoverPage(Sketcher theApp) {
    this.theApp = theApp;
  }

  // Print the cover page
  public int print(Graphics g,
              PageFormat pageFormat,
              int pageIndex)
              throws PrinterException {
    // If it's page 0 print the cover page...
  }

  private Sketcher theApp;
}
```

The sole reason for having the `Sketcher` field in the class is so we can get at the name of the sketch to print on the cover page. Since the need has come up, we should add a `getSketchName()` method to the `SketchFrame` class that will supply a reference to the `String` object containing the file name:

```
public String getSketchName() {
  return filename;
}
```

We can use this in the implementation of the `print()` method in the `SketchCoverPage` class. The method needs to recognize when it is being called to print the first page – that is when the page index is zero – and then print the cover page. You could do whatever you like here to produce a fancy cover page, but we'll just put the code to draw a line border inset from the page, and put the sketch file name in the middle in a box. Here's how we would do that:

```
public int print(Graphics g,
                 PageFormat pageFormat,
                 int pageIndex)
        throws PrinterException {
  if(pageIndex>0)
    return NO_SUCH_PAGE;

  Graphics2D g2D = (Graphics2D) g;
  float x = (float)pageFormat.getImageableX();
  float y = (float)pageFormat.getImageableY();

  GeneralPath path = new GeneralPath();
  path.moveTo(x+1, y+1);
  path.lineTo(x+(float)pageFormat.getImageableWidth()-1, y+1);
  path.lineTo(x+(float)pageFormat.getImageableWidth()-1,
              y+(float)pageFormat.getImageableHeight()-1);
  path.lineTo(x+1, y+(float)pageFormat.getImageableHeight()-1);
  path.closePath();

  g2D.setPaint(Color.red);
  g2D.draw(path);

  // Get a 12 pt bold version of the default font
  Font font = g2D.getFont().deriveFont(12.f).deriveFont(Font.BOLD);

  g2D.setFont(font);                         // Set the new font
  String sketchName = theApp.getWindow().getSketchName();
  Rectangle2D textRect = new java.awt.font.TextLayout(sketchName, font,
                         g2D.getFontRenderContext()).getBounds();
  double centerX = pageFormat.getWidth()/2;
  double centerY = pageFormat.getHeight()/2;
  Rectangle2D.Double surround = new Rectangle2D.Double(
                                  centerX-textRect.getWidth(),
                                  centerY-textRect.getHeight(),
                                  2*textRect.getWidth(),
                                  2*textRect.getHeight());
  g2D.draw(surround);

  // Draw text in the middle of the printable area
  g2D.setPaint(Color.blue);
  g2D.drawString(sketchName, (float)(centerX-textRect.getWidth()/2),
                             (float)(centerY+textRect.getHeight()/2));
  return PAGE_EXISTS;
}
```

To center the file name on the page we need to know the width and height of the text string when it is printed. The getStringBounds() method in the Font class returns the rectangle bounding the string. The second argument is a reference to an object of type FontRenderContext that is returned by the method we have called here for g2D. A FontRenderContext object contains all the information the getStringBounds() method needs to figure out the rectangle bounding the text when it is printed. This includes information about the size of the font as well as the resolution of the output device – the printer in our case.

Let's now implement the `Pageable` interface in the `SketchView` class. We must add three methods to the class `getNumberOfPages()` that returns the number of pages to be printed, `getPrintable()` that returns a reference to the `Printable` object that will print a page with a given index, and `getPageFormat()` that returns a reference to a `PageFormat` object corresponding to a particular page.

```java
import javax.swing.*;
import java.awt.*;
import java.util.*;                // For Observer
import java.awt.event.*;           // For events
import javax.swing.event.*;        // For mouse input adapter
import java.awt.geom.*;
import java.awt.print.*;

class SketchView extends      JComponent
                 implements Observer,
                            Constants,
                            ActionListener,
                            Printable,
                            Pageable {
  // Always two pages
  public int getNumberOfPages() {
    return 2;
  }

  // Return the Printable object that will render the page
  public Printable getPrintable(int pageIndex) {
    if(pageIndex == 0)                          // For the first page
      return new SketchCoverPage(theApp);       // return the cover page
    else
      return this;
  }

  public PageFormat getPageFormat(int pageIndex) {
    // Code to define the PageFormat object for the page...
  }

  public int print(Graphics g,
                   PageFormat pageFormat,
                   int pageIndex)
            throws PrinterException {
    // Revised printing code...
  }
  // Plus the rest of the class as before...
}
```

The first two methods are already implemented here. We will always print two pages, the first page being printed by a `SketchCoverPage` object and the second page by the view object. Since we are providing custom `PageFormat` objects for each page, we will need to amend the `print()` method in `SketchView` to just use the `PageFormat` object it gets. First, let's see how we can produce the `PageFormat` object for a page. To make use of some of the methods we have discussed, we will double the size of the margins for the cover page but leave the margins for the other page at their default sizes. We will also sort out whether the second page should be printed in portrait or landscape orientation. Here's the code to do that:

```
public PageFormat getPageFormat(int pageIndex) {
  // Get the default page format and its Paper object
  PageFormat pageFormat = PrinterJob.getPrinterJob().defaultPage();
  Paper paper = pageFormat.getPaper();

  if(pageIndex==0) {                        // If it's the cover page...
                                            // ...make the margins twice the size
    double leftMargin = paper.getImageableX();          // Top left corner
                                                        // is indented
    double topMargin = paper.getImageableY();           // by the left and
                                                        // top margins

    // Get right and bottom margins
    double rightMargin =
                paper.getWidth()-paper.getImageableWidth()-leftMargin;
    double bottomMargin =
                paper.getHeight()-paper.getImageableHeight()-topMargin;

    // Double the margin sizes
    leftMargin *= 2.0;
    rightMargin *= 2.0;
    topMargin *= 2.0;
    bottomMargin *= 2.0;

    // Set new printable area
    paper.setImageableArea(leftMargin, topMargin,
                    paper.getWidth()-leftMargin-rightMargin,
                    paper.getHeight()-topMargin-bottomMargin);

    // Restore the paper
    pageFormat.setPaper(paper);

  } else {                                  // We are printing a sketch so decide
                                            // on portrait or landscape
    Rectangle rect = theApp.getModel().getModelExtent();    // Get sketch
                                                            // bounds

    // If the width is more than the height, set landscape
    if(rect.width>rect.height) {
      pageFormat.setOrientation(pageFormat.LANDSCAPE);
    }
  }
  return pageFormat;                        // Return the page format
}
```

Since we are going to deal with the cover page as a special page, we don't really have to adjust the paper margins here – we could just adjust the position of the text when we print the cover page. However, this way the page format is determined independently of the print operation, which is a more sensible approach, and you get to see how margins can be set.

We now want to change the `print()` method implementation in `SketchView` just to draw the page with the `PageFormat` object it is given. Here's the modified `print()` method. Although we have seen all this code previously, you should check it carefully as some of the original code we have been adding as we went along has now been removed:

```
public int print(Graphics g,
                 PageFormat pageFormat,
                 int pageIndex)
                 throws PrinterException {
  if(pageIndex != 1)                        // Cover page is page 0, this is page 1
    return NO_SUCH_PAGE;

  Graphics2D g2D = (Graphics2D) g;

  // Get sketch bounds
  Rectangle rect = theApp.getModel().getModelExtent();   // Get sketch bounds

  // Calculate the scale to fit sketch to page
  double scaleX = pageFormat.getImageableWidth()/rect.width;
  double scaleY = pageFormat.getImageableHeight()/rect.height;

  double scale = Math.min(scaleX,scaleY);      // Get minimum scale factor

  // Move origin to page printing area corner
  g2D.translate(pageFormat.getImageableX(), pageFormat.getImageableY());
  g2D.scale(scale,scale);                         // Apply scale factor
  g2D.translate(-rect.x, -rect.y);                // Move top left to the origin

  paint(g2D);                                     // Draw the sketch
  return PAGE_EXISTS;
}
```

It works much as before – the code dealing with the page orientation has been removed, and we only print when the page index is 1. The orientation of the page is taken care of automatically because the `PageFormat` object is set up before this method is called. The `Graphics` object that is passed to `print()` will reflect the orientation specified in the `PageFormat` object.

The last thing we need to do is alter the code in the `actionPerformed()` method for the inner class `FileAction` in `SketchFrame`. We must replace the `setPrintable()` method call with a `setPageable()` call:

```
if(name.equals(printAction.getValue(NAME))) {
  // Get a printing object
  PrinterJob printJob = PrinterJob.getPrinterJob();
  PrintService printer = printJob.getPrintService();
    if(printer == null) {     JOptionPane.showMessageDialog(SketchFrame.this,
                              "No default printer available.",
                              "Printer Error",
                              JOptionPane.ERROR_MESSAGE);

    return;
  }
```

```
      printJob.setPageable(theApp.getView());    // The view is the page source
      if(printJob.printDialog()) {               // Display print dialog
                                                 // If true is returned...
        try {
          printJob.print();                      // then print
        } catch(PrinterException pe) {
          System.out.println(pe);
          JOptionPane.showMessageDialog(SketchFrame.this,
                                        "Error printing a sketch.",
                                        "Printer Error",
                                        JOptionPane.ERROR_MESSAGE);
        }
      }
```

This code is the earlier version that uses the `printDialog()` method without an argument to show the effect in this context. If you comment out the most recent code, you can try both versions by juggling the commented out code. On my system, the print dialog now shows the correct number of pages to be printed, courtesy of the `Pageable` interface implementation that we added to Sketcher.

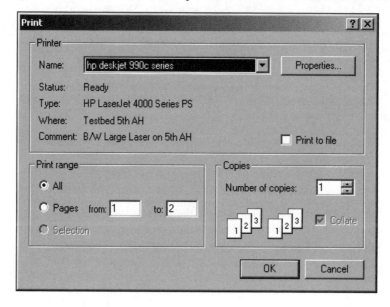

How It Works

The `PrinterJob` object now calls methods in the `Pageable` interface that we have implemented for the view. The number of pages in the document is now determined by our `getNumberOfPages()` method, and the `PageFormat` and `Printable` objects are now obtained individually for each page.

If you switch the code back to using the `printDialog()` and `print()` methods with an argument of type `PrintRequestAttributeSet`, the print operation will run in the same way. The print attributes passed to the `print()` method will not override those specified in the `PageFormat` object returned by the `getPageFormat()` method for the `Pageable` object. If the attribute set passed to the print method includes attributes not determined by the `Pageable` object – such as a `Copies` attribute object – these will have an effect on the printing process.

Printing Using a Book

A `Book` object is a repository for a collection of pages where the pages may be printed using different formats. The page painter for a page in a book is represented by a `Printable` object and each `Printable` object within a book can print one or possibly several pages with a given format.

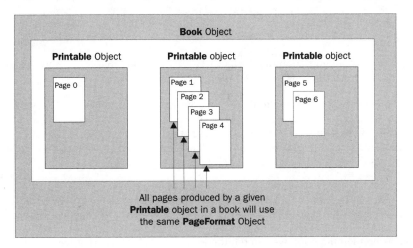

Because the `Book` class implements the `Pageable` interface, you print a book in the same way as you print a `Pageable` object. Once you have assembled all the pages you want in a `Book` object, you just pass a reference to it to the `setPageable()` method for your `PrinterJob` object. Let's take it from the top.

The `Book` class only has a default constructor, and that creates an empty book. Thus, we create a book like this:

```
Book sketchBook = new Book();
```

You add a page to a book by calling the `append()` method for the `Book` object. There are two overloaded versions of `append()`: one to add a `Printable` object that represents a single page, and the other to add a `Printable` object that represents several pages. In the latter case, all the pages are printed using the same `PageFormat` object.

The first version of `append()` accepts two arguments: a reference to the `Printable` object and a reference to an associated `PageFormat` object. We could add the cover page of a sketch just as in the previous example to the `sketchBook` object like this:

```
PageFormat pageFormat = PrinterJob.getPrinterJob().defaultPage();
Paper paper = pageFormat.getPaper();

double leftMargin = paper.getImageableX();    // Top left corner is indented
double topMargin = paper.getImageableY();       // by the left and top margins
double rightMargin = paper.getWidth()-paper.getImageableWidth()-leftMargin;
double bottomMargin = paper.getHeight()-paper.getImageableHeight()-topMargin;
leftMargin *= 2.0;                                // Double the left margin...
```

```
rightMargin *= 2.0;                          // ...and the right...
topMargin *= 2.0;                            // ...and the top...
bottomMargin *= 2.0;                         // ...and the bottom

paper.setImageableArea(leftMargin, topMargin,  // Set new printable area
                  paper.getWidth()-leftMargin-rightMargin,
                  paper.getHeight()-topMargin-bottomMargin);
pageFormat.setPaper(paper);                  // Restore the paper
sketchBook.append(new SketchCoverPage(theApp), pageFormat);
```

Apart from the last statement that appends the `Printable` object that represents the page painter, all this code is the same as in the previous example.

To add the second page of the sketch to the `Book` object, we could write:

```
pageFormat = PrinterJob.getPrinterJob().defaultPage(); // Get another default page
Rectangle rect = getModelExtent();               // Get sketch bounds

if(rect.width>rect.height)                       // If width is more
                                                 // than the height
   pageFormat.setOrientation(pageFormat.LANDSCAPE); // ... set landscape
sketchBook.append(theApp.getView(), pageFormat); // Append the page
```

Now we have assembled the book we can tell the `PrinterJob` object that we want to print the book:

```
printJob.setPageable(sketchBook);            // The book is the
                                             // source of pages
```

Now all we need to do is call the `print()` method for the `PrinterJob` object to start printing. To expedite printing, the `PrinterJob` will communicate with the `Book` object to get the number of pages to be printed and to get the page painter and page format appropriate to print each page. The total number of pages is returned by the `getNumberOfPages()` method for the `Book` object. A reference to the `Printable` object for a given page index is returned by the `getPrintable()` method for the `Book` object and the `PageFormat` object for a given page index is returned by the `getPageFormat()` method. Obviously, in the case of Sketcher, using a `Book` object doesn't offer much advantage over the `Pageable` object that we used in the previous example. In situations where you have more complex documents with a lot of pages with diverse formats it can make things much easier.

You use the other version of `append()` for a `Book` object to add a given number of pages to a book that will be produced by a single `Printable` object, and where all the pages have the same format. Here's an example:

```
Book book = new Book();
book.append(painter, pageFormat, pageCount);
```

Here the `painter` argument is a reference of type `Printable` that will print `pageCount` pages all with the same format, `pageFormat`. A typical instance where you might use this might be a long text document. The document could consist of many pages but they all are printed with the same page format. The view object for the document would typically provide a method to figure out the number of pages that are necessary to output the document.

Printing Swing Components

Printing components is easier than you might think. Swing components are particularly easy to print because they already know how to draw themselves. You should not call a Swing component's paint() method when you want to print it though. Rendering of Swing components is buffered by default to improve the efficiency of displaying them but printing one by calling its paint() method adds a lot of unnecessary overhead to the printing operation. Instead you should call the print() method that is defined in the JComponent class. This will render the component directly to the graphics context that is passed as an argument, so there is no buffering of the output. The method automatically prints any child components that the component contains, so you only need to call print() directly for a top-level component.

The print() method for a Swing component that has JComponent as a base calls three protected methods to actually carry out the printing:

printComponent(Graphics g)	Prints the component.
printBorder(Graphics g)	Prints the component border.
printChildren(Graphics g)	Prints components that are children of the component.

If you want to customize how a Swing component is printed you can subclass the component and override any or all of these. This doesn't apply to a JFrame component though. The JFrame class is a subclass of Frame and does not have JComponent as a superclass. However, you can still call the print() method for a JFrame component to print it. In this case it's inherited from the Container class.

Let's implement a capability to print the Sketcher application window to see how this can be done.

Try It Out – Printing the Sketcher Window

First we will add a menu item to the File menu in Sketcher to print the window. We will define this using an instance the FileAction class:

```
saveAsAction = new FileAction("Save As...", "Save as new file");
printAction = new FileAction("Print",
      KeyStroke.getKeyStroke('P',Event.CTRL_MASK), "Print sketch");
printWindowAction = new FileAction("Print window",
      KeyStroke.getKeyStroke('W',Event.CTRL_MASK), "Print current window");

addMenuItem(fileMenu, newAction);
addMenuItem(fileMenu, openAction);
fileMenu.addSeparator();                                // Add separator

addMenuItem(fileMenu, saveAction);
addMenuItem(fileMenu, saveAsAction);
fileMenu.addSeparator();                                // Add separator
addMenuItem(fileMenu, printAction);
addMenuItem(fileMenu, printWindowAction);
// Rest of the code as before...
```

987

We need to add the `printWindowAction` member to the class so change the declaration for the file action members of the `SketchFrame` class to:

```
private FileAction newAction, openAction, closeAction, saveAction,
                   saveAsAction, printAction, printWindowAction;
```

Because our new menu item is a `FileAction` object, events originating from it will invoke the handler that we defined in the `FileAction` inner class. We need to add some code to the `actionPerformed()` method in the inner class to deal with them. Add the following code after the `if` that handles the `printAction` events:

```
} else if(name.equals(printWindowAction.getValue(NAME))) {
  PrinterJob printJob = PrinterJob.getPrinterJob(); // Get a print job
  PrintService printer = printJob.getPrintService();
  PrintRequestAttributeSet printAttr =
                    new HashPrintRequestAttributeSet();
  if(printer == null) {
    JOptionPane.showMessageDialog(SketchFrame.this,
                          "No default printer available.",
                          "Printer Error",
                          JOptionPane.ERROR_MESSAGE);
    return;
  }
  PageFormat pageFormat = printJob.defaultPage();  // and default format

  // The app window is the page source
  printJob.setPrintable(theApp.getWindow(),pageFormat);

  if(printJob.printDialog(printAttr)) {         // Display print dialog
                                                // If true is returned...
    try {
      printJob.print(printAttr);                     // ...then print
    } catch(PrinterException pe) {
      JOptionPane.showMessageDialog(SketchFrame.this,
                            "Error printing the window.",
                            "Printer Error",
                            JOptionPane.ERROR_MESSAGE);
    }
  }
}
```

The application window, which is the `SketchFrame` object, `window`, is responsible for printing the window because it is obviously best placed to do this, so we must make the `SketchFrame` class implement the `Printable` interface. Change the first line of the class definition to:

```
public class SketchFrame extends JFrame
                implements Constants, ActionListener, Observer, Printable
```

Now we can add the definition of the `print()` method to the class:

```
// Print the window
public int print(Graphics g,
                 PageFormat pageFormat,
                 int pageIndex)
           throws PrinterException {

  if(pageIndex>0)    // Only one page page 0 to be printed
    return NO_SUCH_PAGE;

  // Scale the component to fit
  Graphics2D g2D = (Graphics2D) g;

  // Calculate the scale factor to fit the window to the page
  double scaleX = pageFormat.getImageableWidth()/getWidth();
  double scaleY = pageFormat.getImageableHeight()/getHeight();

  double scale = Math.min(scaleX,scaleY);   // Get minimum scale factor

  // Move paper origin to page printing area corner
  g2D.translate(pageFormat.getImageableX(), pageFormat.getImageableY());
  g2D.scale(scale,scale);                    // Apply the scale factor

  print(g2D);                                // Draw the component
  return PAGE_EXISTS;
}
```

Make sure you have the necessary additional imports:

```
import javax.print.PrintService;
import javax.print.attribute.PrintRequestAttributeSet;
import javax.print.attribute.HashPrintRequestAttributeSet;
```

If you recompile and run Sketcher once more, the File | Print window menu item should be operational.

How It Works

The menu operation and the printing mechanism are as we have already discussed. The SketchFrame object is the page painter for the window so the print() method is where it all happens. After checking the page index value and casting the Graphics reference passed to the method to Graphics2D, we calculate the scaling factor to fit the window to the page. The getWidth() and getHeight() methods inherited in our SketchFrame class return the width and height of the window respectively. We then apply the scale just as we did for printing a sketch. The coordinates of the top left corner of the window are at (0,0) so we can just print it once we have applied the scaling factor. Calling the inherited print() method with g2D as the argument does this.

I'm sure you will have noticed that the output has deficiencies. The title bar and window boundary are missing. Of course, a JFrame object is a top-level window, and since it is derived from the Frame class it is a heavyweight component with its appearance determined by its peer, which is outside the Java code. The print() method for the JFrame object that we call to print the window does not include the peer created elements of the window. The printAll() method does though. Modify the code in the print() method to call printAll() rather than print(), like this :

```
    printAll(g2D);                              // Draw the component
    return PAGE_EXISTS;
```

Now you should get the whole application window printed.

Summary

In this chapter you have added full support for the File menu to the Sketcher application, for both sketch storage and retrieval, and for printing. You should find that the techniques that you have used here are readily applicable in other Java applications. The approach to saving and restoring a model object is not usually dependent on the kind of data it contains. Of course, if your application is a word processor, you will have a little more work to do taking care that the number of lines printed on each page is a whole number of lines. In other words you will have to make sure you avoid having the top half of a line of text on one page, and the bottom half on the next. There are other Java classes to help with that, however, and we don't really have the space to discuss them here – but look them up – the javax.swing.text package is a veritable gold mine for text handling!

If you have been following all the way with Sketcher, you now have an application that consists of well over a thousand lines of code, so you should be pretty pleased with yourself.

The important points we have covered in this chapter are:

❑ You can implement writing your model object to a file and reading it back by making it serializable.

❑ The JFileChooser class provides a generalized way for displaying a dialog to enable a file to be chosen.

❑ A printing operation is initiated by creating a PrinterJob object. This object encapsulates the interface to your printer and is used to manage the printing process.

❑ A PrintService object encapsulates a printer.

❑ A PageFormat object defines the format for a page, and methods for this object can provide information on the paper size and orientation and the printable area on the page.

❑ An object of type Paper defines a page.

❑ You can display a print dialog by calling the printDialog() method for a PrinterJob object. The no argument version of printDialog() will display the native print dialog, whereas the version accepting a single argument of type PrintRequestAttributeSet displays a Java print dialog.

❑ Printing a page is always done by an object of a class that implements the Printable interface.

❑ You print a page by calling methods for the Graphics object passed to the print() method in the Printable interface by the PrinterJob object.

❑ You can manage multipage print jobs by implementing the Pageable interface in a class. This will enable different types of class object to be used to print different pages.

❑ A Book object can encapsulate a series of pages to be printed. Each Printable object that is appended to a book prints one or more pages in a given format.

Exercises

1. At the moment in Sketcher, you can close a file selection dialog with the approve button without a file being selected. Modify Sketcher so that the dialog will continue to be displayed until you select a file or close the dialog with the Cancel button.

2. Modify the Sketcher program to print the title at the top of the page on which the sketch is printed.

3. Modify the printing of a sketch so that a solid black boundary line is drawn around the sketch on the page.

4. Modify Sketcher to print a single sketch laid out on four pages. The sketch should be enlarged to provide the best fit on the four pages without distorting circles – that is, the same scale should be applied to the x and y axes.

5. Use a Book object to print a cover page plus the sketch spread over four pages as in the previous exercise.

Java and XML

Release 1.4 of the SDK introduced capabilities for processing **Extensible Markup Language** (XML) documents as part of the standard set of class libraries. These are collectively referred to as JAXP, the Java API for XML. In this chapter and the next we will be exploring not only how we can read XML documents, but also how we can create and modify them. This chapter provides a brief outline of XML and some related topics, plus a practical introduction to reading XML documents from within your Java programs using one of the two available mechanisms for this. In the next chapter we will discuss the second approach to reading XML documents, as well as how we can modify them and create new ones. Inevitably, we can only skim the surface in a lot of areas since XML itself is a huge topic. However, you should find enough in this chapter and the next to give you a good feel for what XML is about, and how you can handle XML documents in Java.

In this chapter you will learn:

- ❏ What a well-formed XML document is
- ❏ What constitutes a valid XML document
- ❏ What the components in an XML document are, and how they are used
- ❏ What a DTD is and how it is defined
- ❏ What namespaces are and why you use them
- ❏ What the SAX and DOM APIs are, and how they different.
- ❏ How you read documents using SAX

XML

XML, or the e**X**tensible **M**arkup **L**anguage to give it its full title, is a system and hardware independent language for expressing data and its structure within an **XML document**. An **XML document** is a Unicode text file that contains the data together with **markup** that defines the structure of the data. Because an XML document is a text file, you can create XML using any plain text editor, although an editor designed for creating and editing XML will obviously make things easier. The precise definition of XML is in the hands of the World Wide Web Consortium (W3C), and if you want to consult the XML 1.0 specification, you can find it at http://www.w3.org/XML.

The term 'markup' derives from a time when the paper draft of a document to be printed was *marked up* by hand to indicate to the typesetter how the printed form of the document should look. Indeed the ancestry of XML can be traced back to a system that was originally developed by IBM in the 1960s to automate and standardize markup for system reference manuals for IBM hardware and software products. XML markup looks similar to HTML in that it consists of tags and attributes added to the text in a file. However, the superficial appearance is where the similarity between XML and HTML ends. XML and HTML are profoundly different in purpose and capability.

Firstly, although an XML document can be created, read, and understood by a person, XML is primarily for communicating data from one computer to another. XML documents will therefore more typically be generated and processed by computer programs. An XML document defines the structure of the data it contains so a program that receives it can properly interpret it. Thus XML is a tool for transferring information and its organization between computer programs. The purpose of HTML on the other hand is solely the description of how data should look when it is displayed or printed. The only structuring information that generally appears in an HTML document relates to the appearance of the data as a visible image. The purpose of HTML is data presentation.

Secondly, HTML provides you with a set of tags that is essentially fixed and geared to the presentation of data. XML is a language in which you can define new sets of tags and attributes to suit different kinds of data – indeed to suit any kind of data including *your* particular data. Because XML is extensible, it is often described as a **meta-language** – a language for defining new languages in other words. The first step in using XML to exchange data is to define the language that you intend to use for that purpose - in XML.

Of course, if I invent a set of XML markup to describe data of a particular kind, you will need to know the rules for creating XML documents of this type if you want to create, receive, or modify them. As we shall see, the definition of the markup that has been used within an XML document can be included as part of the document. It also can be provided as a separate entity, in a file identified by a URI for instance, that can be referenced within any document of that type. The use of XML has already been standardized for very diverse types of data. There are XML languages for describing the structures of chemical compounds and, musical scores, as well as plain old text such as in this book.

The Java API for **XML** **P**rocessing (**JAXP**) provides you with the means for reading, creating, and modifying XML documents from within your Java programs. In order to understand and use this API there are two basic topics you need to be reasonably familiar with:

❑ What an XML document is for and what it consists of.

❑ What a DTD is and how it relates to an XML document.

You also need to be aware of what an XML namespace is, if only because JAXP has methods relating to handling these. You can find more information on JAXP at http://sun.java.com/xml/jaxp/.

Just in case you are new to XML, we will briefly explore the basic characteristics of XML and DTDs before we start applying the classes and methods provided by JAXP to process XML documents. We will also briefly explore what XML namespaces are for. If you are already comfortable with these topics you can skip most of this chapter and pick up where we start talking about SAX. Let's start by looking into the general organization of an XML document.

XML Document Structure

An XML document basically consists of two parts, a **prolog** and a **document body**:

- ❑ The **prolog** provides information necessary for the interpretation of the contents of the document body. It contains two optional components, and since you can omit both, the prolog itself is optional. The two components of the prolog, in the sequence in which they must appear, are:

- ❑ An **XML declaration** that defines the version of XML that applies to the document, and may also specify the particular Unicode character encoding used in the document and whether the document is standalone or not. Either the character encoding or the standalone specification can be omitted from the XML declaration but if they do appear they must be in the given sequence.

- ❑ A **document type declaration** specifying an external **Document Type Definition** (DTD) that identifies markup declarations for the elements used in the body of the document, or explicit markup declarations, or both.

- ❑ The **document body** contains the data. It comprises one or more **elements** where each element is defined by a begin tag and an end tag. The elements in the document body define the structure of the data. There is always a single **root element** that contains all the other elements. All of the data within the document is contained within the elements in the document body.

Processing instructions (**PI**) for the document may also appear at the end of the prolog and at the end of the document body. Processing instructions are instructions intended for an application that will process the document in some way. You can include comments that provide explanations or other information for human readers of the XML document as part of the prolog and as part of the document body.

When an XML document is said to be **well-formed**, it just means that it conforms to the rules for writing XML, as defined by the XML specification. Essentially an XML document is well-formed if its prolog and body are consistent with the rules for creating these. In a well-formed document there must be only one root element and all elements must be properly nested. We will summarize more specifically what is required to make a document well-formed a little later in this chapter, after we have looked into the rules for writing XML.

An **XML processor** is a software module that is used by an application to read an XML document and gain access to the data and its structure. An XML processor also determines whether an XML document is well-formed or not. Processing instructions are passed through to an application without any checking or analysis by the XML processor. The XML specification describes how an XML processor should behave when reading XML documents, including what information should be made available to an application for various types of document content.

Here's an example of a well-formed XML document:

```
<proverb>Too many cooks spoil the broth.</proverb>
```

The document just consists of a root element that defines a proverb. There is no prolog and, formally, you don't have to supply one, but it would be much better if the document did include at least the XML version that is applicable, like this:

```
<?xml version="1.0"?>
<proverb>Too many cooks spoil the broth.</proverb>
```

The first line is the prolog and it consists of just an XML declaration, which specifies that the document is consistent with XML version 1.0. The XML declaration must start with <?xml with no spaces within this five character sequence. We could also include an encoding declaration following the version specification in the prolog. For example:

```
<?xml version="1.0" encoding="UTF-8"?>
<proverb>Too many cooks spoil the broth.</proverb>
```

The first line states that as well as being XML version 1.0, the document uses the "UTF-8" Unicode encoding. If you omit the encoding specification, "UTF-8" or "UTF-16" will be assumed, and since "UTF-8" includes ASCII as a subset, you don't need to specify an encoding if all you are using is ASCII text. The version and the character encoding specifications must appear in the order shown. If you reverse them you have broken the rules so the document would no longer be well-formed.

If we want to specify that the document is not dependent on any external definitions of markup, we can add a standalone specification to the prolog like this:

```
<?xml version="1.0" encoding="UTF-8" standalone="yes"?>
<proverb>Too many cooks spoil the broth.</proverb>
```

Specifying the value for standalone as "yes" indicates to an XML processor that the document is self-contained. A value of "no" would indicate that the document is dependent on an external definition of the markup used.

Valid XML Documents

A **valid** XML document is a well-formed document that has an associated **D**ocument **T**ype **D**efinition or **DTD** (we will learn more about DTDs later in this chapter). In a valid document the DTD must be consistent with the rules for creating a DTD and the document body must be consistent with the DTD. A DTD essentially defines a markup language for a given type of document and is identified in the `DOCTYPE` declaration in the document prolog. It specifies how all the elements that may be used in the document can be structured, and the elements in the body of the document must be consistent with it.

The previous example is well-formed, but not valid, since it does not have an associated DTD that defines the `<proverb>` element. Note that there is nothing *wrong* with an XML document that is not valid. It may not be ideal, but it is a perfectly legal XML document. Valid in this context is a technical term that only means that a document does not have a DTD.

An XML processor may be **validating** or **non-validating**. A validating XML processor will check that an XML document has a DTD and that its contents are correctly specified. It will also verify that the document is consistent with the rules expressed in the DTD and report any errors that it finds. A non-validating XML processor will not check that the document body is consistent with the DTD. As we shall see, you can usually choose whether the XML processor that you use to read a document is validating or non-validating simply by switching the validating feature on or off.

Here's a variation on the example from the previous section with a document type declaration added:

```
<?xml version="1.0" encoding="UTF-8" standalone="no"?>
<!DOCTYPE proverb SYSTEM "proverb.dtd">
<proverb>Too many cooks spoil the broth.</proverb>
```

A document type declaration always starts with `<!DOCTYPE` so it is easily recognized. The name that appears in the `DOCTYPE` declaration, in this case `proverb`, must always match that of the root element for the document. We have specified the value for `standalone` as "no", but it would still be correct if we left it out because the default value for `standalone` is "no" if there are external markup declarations in the document. The `DOCTYPE` declaration indicates that the markup used in this document can be found in the DTD at the URI `proverb.dtd`. We will see a lot more about the `DOCTYPE` declaration later in this chapter.

Having an external DTD for documents of a given type does not eliminate all the problems that may arise when exchanging data. Obviously confusion may arise when several people independently create DTDs for the same type of document. My DTD for documents containing sketches created by Sketcher is unlikely to be the same as yours. Other people with sketching applications may be inventing their versions of a DTD for representing a sketch so the potential for conflicting definitions for markup is considerable. To obviate the difficulties that this sort of thing would cause, standard markup languages are being developed in XML that can be used universally for documents of common types. For instance, the Mathematical Markup Language (MATHML) is a language defined in XML for mathematical documents and the Synchronized Multimedia Integration Language (SMIL) is a language for creating documents that contain multimedia presentations. There is also the Scalable Vector Graphics (SVG) language for representing 2D graphics such as design drawings or even sketches created by Sketcher.

Let's understand a bit more about what XML markup consists of.

Elements in an XML Document

XML markup divides the contents of a document up into **elements** by enclosing segments of the data between tags. As we said, there will always be one root element that contains all the other elements in a document. In the example above, the following is an element:

```
<proverb>Every dog has his day.</proverb>
```

In this case this is the only element and is therefore the root element. A **start tag**, <proverb>, indicates the beginning of an element, and an **end tag**, </proverb>, marks its end. The name of the element, proverb in this case, always appears in both the start and end tags. The text between the start and end tags for an element is referred to as **element content** and in general may consist of just data, which is referred to as **character data**, other elements, which is described as **markup**, or a combination of character data and markup, or it may be empty. The latter is referred to as an **empty element**.

When an element contains plain text, then the content is described as **parsed character data** (PCDATA). This means that the XML processor will parse it – it will analyze it in other words – looking to see if it can be broken down further. In fact PCDATA allows for a mixture of ordinary data and other elements, referred to as **mixed content**, so a parser will be looking for the characters that delimit the start and end of markup tags. Consequently, ordinary text must not contain characters that might cause it to be recognized as a tag. Thus you can't include < or & characters explicitly as part of the text within an element, for instance. Since it could be a little inconvenient to completely prohibit such characters within ordinary text, you can include them using **predefined** entities when you need to. XML recognizes the following predefined entities that represent characters that would otherwise be recognized as part of markup:

&	&	'	'	"	"
<	<	>	>		

Here's an element that makes use of a predefined entity:

```
<text> This is parsed character data within a &lt;text&gt;
element&apos;</text>
```

The content of this element is the string:

This is parsed character data within a <text> element.

Here's an example of an XML document containing several elements:

```
<?xml version="1.0"?>
<address>
  <buildingnumber>29</buildingnumber>
  <street> South Lasalle Street</street>
  <city>Chicago</city>
  <state>Illinois</state>
  <zip>60603</zip>
</address>
```

This document evidently defines an address. Each tag pair identifies and categorizes the information between the tags. The data between `<address>` and `</address>` is an address and this is a composite of five further elements that each contain character data that forms part of the address. We can easily identify what each of the components of the address is from the elements that enclose each sub-unit of the data.

Rules for Tags

The tags that delimit an element have a precise form. Each element start tag must begin with < and end with > and each element end tag must start with </ and end with >. The tag name – also known as the **element type name** – identifies the element and differentiates it from the others. Note that the element name must immediately follow the opening < in the case of a start tag and the </ in the case of an end tag. If you insert a space here it is incorrect and will be flagged as an error by an XML processor.

Since the `<address>` element contains all of the other elements that appear in the document, this is the root element. When one element encloses another, it must always do so completely if the document is to be well-formed. Unlike HTML where a somewhat cavalier use of the language is usually tolerated, XML elements must *never* overlap. For instance, you can't have:

```
<address><zip>60603</address></zip>
```

An element that is enclosed by another element is referred to as the **child** of the enclosing element, and the enclosing element is referred to as the **parent** of the child element. In our example, the `<address>` element is the parent of the other four because it directly encloses each of them and the enclosed elements are child elements of the `<address>` element. In a well-formed document each begin tag must always be matched by a corresponding end tag, and vice versa. If this isn't the case, the document is not well-formed.

Don't forget that there must be only one root element that encloses all the other elements in a document. This implies that you cannot have an element of the same type as the root element as a child of any element in the document.

Empty Elements

We already know that an element that contains nothing at all, just a start tag immediately followed by an end tag, is called an **empty element**. For instance:

```
<commercial></commercial>
```

You have an alternative way to represent empty elements. Instead of writing a start and end tag with nothing between them, you can write an empty element as a single tag with a forward slash immediately following the tag name:

```
<commercial/>
```

This is equivalent to a start tag followed by an end tag. There must be no spaces between the opening < and the element name, or between the / and the > marking the end of the tag.

You may be thinking at this point that an empty element is of rather limited use, whichever way you write it. Although by definition an empty element has no content, it can and often does contain additional information that is provided within **attributes** that appear within the tag. We shall see how we add attributes to an element a little later in this chapter. Additionally, an empty element can be used as a marker or flag to indicate something about the data within its parent. For example, you might use an empty element as part of the content for an `<address>` element to indicate that the address corresponds to a commercial property. Absence of the `<commercial/>` element would indicate a private residence.

Document Comments

When you create an XML document using an editor, it is often useful to add explanatory text to the document. You include comments in an XML document like this:

```
<!-- Prepared on 14th January 2002 -->
```

Comments can go just about anywhere in the prolog or the document body, but not inside a start tag or an end tag, or within an empty element tag. You can spread a comment over several lines if you wish, like this:

```
<!--
   Eeyore, who is a friend of mine,
    has lost his tail.
-->
```

For compatibility with SGML from which XML is derived, the text within a comment should not contain a sequence of two or more hyphens and it also must not end with a hyphen. A comment that ends with `--->` is not well-formed and will be rejected by an XML processor. While an XML processor of necessity scans comments in order to distinguish them from markup and document data they are not part of the character data within a document. XML processors need not make comments available to an application, although some may do so.

Element Names

If we're going to be creating elements then we're going to have to give them names, and XML is very generous in the names we're allowed to use. For example, there aren't any reserved words to avoid in XML, as there are in most programming languages, so we do have a lot of flexibility in this regard. However, there are certain rules, which you must follow. The names you choose for elements must begin with a letter or an underscore and can include digits, periods, and hyphens. Here are some examples of valid element names:

```
net_price   Gross-Weight   _sample   clause_3.2   pastParticiple
```

In theory you can use colons within a name but since colons have a special purpose in the context of names, as we shall see later, you should not do so. Since XML documents use the Unicode character set, any national language alphabets defined within that set may be used for names. HTML users need to remember that tag names in XML are case sensitive, so `<Address>` is not the same as `<address>`.

Note also that names starting with upper or lowercase x, followed by m followed by l, are reserved, so you must not define names beginning `xml` or `XmL` or any of the other six possible sequences.

Defining General Entities

There is a frequent requirement to repeat a given block of parsed character data in the body of a document. An obvious example of this is some kind of copyright notice that you may want to insert in various places. You can define a named block of parsed text like this:

```
<!ENTITY copyright "© 2002 Wrox Press">
```

This is an example of declaration of a **general entity**. You can put declarations of general entities within a DOCTYPE declaration in the document prolog or within an external DTD. We will describe how a little later in this chapter. The block of text that appears between the double quotes in the entity declaration is identified by the name copyright. You could equally well use single quotes as delimiters for the string. Wherever you want to insert this text in the document, you just need to insert the name delimited by an & at the beginning and ; at the end, thus:

```
&copyright;
```

This is called an entity reference. This is exactly the same notation as the predefined entities representing markup characters that we saw earlier. It will cause the equivalent text to be inserted at this point when the document is parsed. Of course, since a general entity is parsed text, you need to take care that the document is still well-formed and valid after the substitution has been made.

An entity declaration can include entity references. For instance, we could declare the copyright entity like this:

```
<!ENTITY copyright "© 2002 Wrox Press &documentDate;">
```

The text contains a reference to a documentDate entity. Entity references may only appear in a document after their corresponding entity declarations so the declaration for the documentDate entity must precede the declaration for the copyright entity:

```
<!ENTITY documentDate "24th January 2002">
<!ENTITY copyright "© 2002 Wrox Press &documentDate;">
```

Entity declarations can contain nested entity references to any depth so the declaration for the documentDate entity could contain other entity references. Substitutions for entity references will be made recursively by the XML processor until all references have been resolved. An entity declaration must not directly or indirectly contain a reference to itself though.

You can also use general entities that are defined externally. You use the SYSTEM keyword followed by the URL for where the text is stored in place of the text in the ENTITY declaration. For instance:

```
<!ENTITY usefulstuff SYSTEM "http://www.some-server.com/inserts/stuff.txt">
```

The reference &usefulstuff; represents the contents of the file stuff.txt.

CDATA Sections

It is possible to embed **unparsed character data** (**CDATA**) anywhere in a document where character data can occur. You do this by placing the unparsed character data in a CDATA section, which begins with < ! [CDATA[and ends with]] >. The data is described as unparsed because the XML processor will not analyze it in any way, but will make it available to an application. The data within a CDATA section can be anything at all it can even be binary data. A CDATA section can be used for including markup in a document that you don't want to have parsed. For instance:

```
<explanation> A typical circle element is written as:
<![CDATA[
  <circle radius="15">
    <position x="30" y="50"/>
  </circle>
]]>
</explanation>
```

The lines shown shaded are within a CDATA section, and although they look suspiciously like markup, an XML processor looking for markup will not scan them. We have used some of the reserved characters in here without escaping them, but since the data in a CDATA section is not parsed, they will not be identified as markup.

Element Attributes

You can put additional information within an element in the form of one or more **attributes**. An attribute is identified by an attribute name, and the value is specified as a string between single or double quotes. For example:

```
<elementname attributename="Attribute value"> ... </elementname>
```

As we said earlier, empty elements frequently have attributes. Here's an example of an empty element with three attributes:

```
<color red="255" green="128" blue="64"></color>
```

This would normally be written in the shorthand form, like this:

```
<color red="255" green="128" blue="64" />
```

You could also use single quotes to delimit an attribute value if you wish.

The names of the three attributes here are red, green, and blue, which identify the primary components of the color, and the values between 0 and 255 represent the contribution of each primary color to the result. Attribute names are defined using the same rule as element names. The attributes in an element follow the element name in the start tag (or the only tag in the case of an empty element) and are separated from it by at least one space. If a tag has multiple attributes, they must be separated by spaces. You can also put spaces either side of the = sign but it is clearer without, especially where there are several attributes. HTML fans should note that a comma separator between attributes is not allowed in XML and will be reported as an error.

A string that is an attribute value must not contain a delimiting character explicitly within the string, but you can put a double quote as part of the value string if you use single quotes as delimiters, and vice-versa. For instance, you could write the following:

```
<textstuff answer="it's mine" explanation='He said"It is mine"'/>
```

The value for the `answer` attribute uses double quotes as delimiters so it can contain a single quote explicitly. Similarly, the value for the second attribute uses single quotes so the string can contain a double quote. Of course, someone is bound to want both a single quote and a double quote as part of the value string. Easy, just use an escape sequence for the one that is a delimiter. For instance, we could rewrite the previous example as:

```
<textstuff answer='it&apos;s mine' explanation="He said&quot;It's mine&quot;"/>
```

In general it's easiest to stick to a particular choice of delimiter for strings and always escape occurrences of the delimiter within a string.

In our Sketcher program, we can create circles that are specified by a radius and a position. We can easily define a circle in XML – in fact there are many ways in which we could do this. Here's one example:

```
<circle radius="15">
  <position x="30" y="50"/>
</circle>
```

The `radius` attribute for the `<circle>` tag specifies the radius, and its position is specified by an empty `<position/>` tag with the x and y coordinates of the circles position specified by attributes x and y. A reasonable question to ask is whether this the best way of representing a circle. We should explore our options in this context a little further.

Attributes versus Elements

Obviously we could define a circle without using attributes, maybe like this:

```
<circle>
  <radius>15</radius>
  <position>
    <x-coordinate>30</x-coordinate>
    <y-coordinate>50</y-coordinate>
  </position>
</circle>
```

This is the opposite extreme. There are no attributes here, only elements. Where the content of an element is one or more other elements – as in the case of the `<circle>` and `<position>` elements here – it is described as **element content**. A document design where all the data is part of element content and no attributes are involved is described as **element-normal**.

Of course, it is also possible to represent the data defining a circle just using attributes within a single element:

```
<circle positionx=30 positiony=50 radius=15/>
```

Now we have just one element defining a circle with all the data defined by attribute values. Where all the data in a document is defined as attribute values it is described as **attribute-normal**.

An element can also contain a mixture of text and markup – so called **mixed content** – so we have a further way in which we could define a circle in XML, like this:

```
<circle>
  <position>
    <x-coordinate>30</x-coordinate>
    <y-coordinate>50</y-coordinate>
  </position>
  15
</circle>
```

Now the value for the radius just appears as text as part of the content of the `<circle>` element along with the position element. The disadvantage of this arrangement is that it's not obvious what the text is so some information about the structure has been lost compared to the previous example.

So which is the better approach, to go for attributes or elements? Well, it can be either, or both, if you see what I mean. It depends on what the structure of the data is, how the XML is generated, and how it will be used. One overriding consideration is that an attribute is a single value. It has no inner structure so anything that does have substructure must be expressed using elements. Where data is essentially hierarchical, representing family trees in XML for instance, you will want to use nested elements to reflect the structure of the data. Where the data is serial or tabular, temperature and rainfall or other weather data over time for instance, you may well use attributes within a series of elements within the root element.

If you are generating an XML document interactively using an editor, then readability is an important consideration since poor readability will encourage errors. You will lean towards whatever makes the editing easier – and for the most part elements are easier to find and edit than attributes. Attribute values should be short for readability so this limits the sort of data that you can express as an attribute. You probably would not want to see the soliloquy from Shakespeare's Hamlet appearing as an attribute value for instance. That said, if the XML is computer generated and is not primarily intended for human viewing, the choice is down to the most efficient way to handle the data in the computer. Attributes and their values are readily identified in a program so documents are likely to make use of attributes wherever the structure of the data does not require otherwise. We will see how this works out in practice when we get to use the Java API for processing XML.

Whitespace and Readability

The indentation shown in the examples so far have been included just to provide you with visual cues to the structure of the data. It is not required, and an XML processor will ignore the whitespace between elements. When you are creating XML in an editor, you can use whitespace generally between elements to present the XML document visually so that it is easier for a human reader to understand. Whitespace can consist of spaces, tabs, carriage returns, and line feed characters. You can see that a circle expressed without whitespace, as shown below, would be significantly less readable:

```
<circle><position><x-coordinate>30</x-coordinate><y-coordinate>50</y-
coordinate></position>15</circle>
```

Having said that, we don't have complete freedom of where we can put whitespace within a tag, as we have already seen. The tag name must immediately follow the opening < or </ in a tag and there can be no space within an opening </ delimiter, or a closing /> delimiter in the case of an empty element. You must also separate an attribute from the tag name or from another attribute with at least one space. Beyond that you can put additional spaces within a tag wherever you like.

Data Structure in XML

The ability to nest elements is fundamental to defining the structure of the data in a document. We can easily represent the structure of the data in our XML fragment defining an address, as shown below.

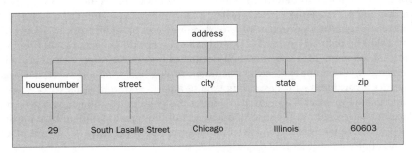

The structure follows directly from the nesting of the elements. The <address> element contains all of the others directly, so the nested elements are drawn as subsidiary or child elements of the <address> element. The items that appear within the tree structure – the elements and the data items – are referred to as **nodes**.

The diagram below shows the structure of the first circle definition in XML that we created in the previous section. Even though there's an extra level of elements in this diagram, there are strong similarities to the structure above.

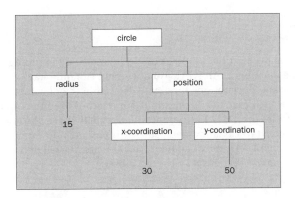

We can see that both structures have a single root element, <address> in the first example and <circle> in the second. We can also see that each element contains either other elements or some data that is a segment of the document content. In both diagrams all the document content lies at the bottom. Nodes at the extremities of a tree are referred to as **leaf nodes**.

1005

In fact an XML document *always* has a structure similar to this. Each element in a document can contain other elements, or text, or elements and text, or it can be empty.

Document Type Definitions

We have seen several small examples of XML and in each case it was fairly obvious what the content was meant to represent, but where are the rules that ensure such data is represented consistently and correctly in different documents? Do the <radius> and <position> elements have to be in that sequence in a <circle> element and could we omit one or other of them?

Clearly there has to be a way to determine what is correct and what is incorrect for any particular element in a document. As we mentioned earlier, a **D**ocument **T**ype **D**efinition (**DTD**) defines how valid elements are constructed for a particular type of document, so the XML for purchase order documents in a company could be defined by one DTD, and sales invoice documents by another. The document type definition for a document is specified in a **document type declaration** – commonly known as a DOCTYPE declaration – that appears in the document prolog following any XML declaration. A DTD essentially defines a **vocabulary** for describing data of a particular kind – the set of elements that you use to identify the data in other words. It also defines the possible relationships between these elements – how they can be nested. The contents of a document of the type indentified by a particular DTD must be defined and structured according to rules that make up the DTD. Any document of a given type can be checked for validity against its DTD.

A DTD can be an integral part of a document but it is usually, and more usefully, defined separately. Including a DTD in an XML document makes the document self-contained, but it does increase its bulk. It also means that the DTD has to appear within each document of the same type. A separate DTD that is external to a document avoids this and provides a single reference point for all documents of a particular type. An external DTD also makes maintenance of the DTD for a document type easier as it only needs to be changed in one place for all documents that make use of it. Let's look at how we identify the DTD for a document and then investigate some of the ways in which elements and their attributes can be defined in a DTD.

Declaring a DTD

You use a document type declaration (a DOCTYPE declaration) in the prolog of an XML document to specify the DTD for the document. An XML 1.0 document can only have one DOCTYPE declaration. You can include the markup declarations for elements used in the document explicitly within the DOCTYPE statement, in which case the declarations are referred to as the **internal subset**. You can also specify a URI that identifies the DTD for the document, usually in the form of a URL. In this case the set of declarations is referred to as the **external subset**. If you include explicit declarations as well as a URI referencing an external DTD, the document has both an internal and an external subset. Here is an example of an XML document that has an external subset:

```
<?xml version="1.0"?>
<!DOCTYPE address SYSTEM "http://docserver/dtds/AddressDoc.dtd">
<address>
  <buildingnumber> 29 </buildingnumber>
  <street> South Lasalle Street</street>
  <city>Chicago</city>
```

```
        <state>Illinois</state>
        <zip>60603</zip>
    </address>
```

The name following the DOCTYPE keyword must always match the root element name in the document so the DOCTYPE declaration here indicates that the root element in the document has the name address. The declaration also indicates that the DTD in which this and the other elements in the document are declared is an external DTD located at the URI following the SYSTEM keyword. This URI, which is invariably a URL, is called the **system ID** for the DTD.

In principle you can also specify an external DTD by a **public ID** using the keyword PUBLIC in place of the SYSTEM. A public ID is just a unique public name that identifies the DTD – a URN in other words. As you probably know, the idea behind URNs is to get over the problem of changes to URLs. Public IDs are intended for DTDs that are available as public standards for documents of particular types such as SVG. However, there is a slight snag. Since there is no mechanism defined for resolving public IDs to find the corresponding URL, if you specify a public ID you still have to supply a system ID with a URL so the XML processor can find it, so you won't see public IDs in use much.

If the file containing the DTD is stored on the local machine, you can specify its location relative to the directory containing the XML document. For example, the following DOCTYPE declaration implies the DTD is in the same directory as the document itself:

```
<!DOCTYPE address SYSTEM "AddressDoc.dtd">
```

The AddressDoc.dtd file includes definitions for the elements that may be included in a document containing an address. In general a relative URL is assumed to be relative to the location of the document containing the reference.

Defining a DTD

In looking at the details of how we put a DTD together we will use examples where the DTD is an internal subset, but the declarations in an external DTD are exactly the same. Here's an example of a document with an integral DTD:

```
<?xml version="1.0"?>
<!DOCTYPE proverb [   <!ELEMENT proverb (#PCDATA)>   ]>
<proverb>A little knowledge is a dangerous thing.</proverb>
```

All the internal definitions for elements used within the document appear between the square brackets in the DOCTYPE declaration. In this case there is just one element declared, the root element, and the element content is PCDATA – parsed character data.

We could define an external DTD in a file with the name proverbDoc.dtd in the same directory as the document. The file would contain just a single line:

```
<!ELEMENT proverb (#PCDATA)>
```

The XML document would then be:

```
<?xml version="1.0"?>
<!DOCTYPE proverb SYSTEM "proverbDoc.dtd">
<proverb>A little knowledge is a dangerous thing.</proverb>
```

The DTD is referenced by a relative URI that is relative to the directory containing the document.

When you want to have both an internal and an external subset you just put both in the DOCTYPE declaration with the external DTD reference appearing first. Entities from both are available for use in the document but where there is any conflict between them the entities defined in the internal subset take precedence over those declared in the external subset.

The syntax for defining elements and their attributes is rather different from the syntax for XML markup. It also can get quite complex so we won't be able to go into it comprehensively here. However, we do need to have a fair idea of how a DTD is put together in order to understand the operation of the Java API for XML, so let's look at some of the ways in which we can define elements in a DTD.

Defining Elements in DTDs

The DTD will define each type of element that can appear in the document using an ELEMENT type declaration. For example, the <address> element could be defined like this:

```
<!ELEMENT address (buildingnumber, street, city, state, zip)>
```

This defines the element with the name address. The information between the parentheses specifies what can appear within an <address> element. The definition states that an <address> element contains exactly one each of the elements <buildingnumber>, <street>, <city>, <state>, and <zip> in that sequence. This is an example of **element content** since only elements are allowed within an <address> element. Note the space that appears between the element name and the parentheses enclosing the content definition. This is required, and a parser will flag the absence of at least one space here as an error. The ELEMENT identifier must be in capital letters and must immediately follow the opening "<!".

The definition of the <address> above makes no provision for anything other than the five elements shown, and in that sequence. Any whitespace that you put between these elements in a document is therefore not part of the content and will be ignored by a parser, and therefore it is known as **ignorable whitespace**. That said, you can still find out if there is whitespace there when the document is parsed, as we shall see.

We can define the <buildingnumber> element like this:

```
<!ELEMENT buildingnumber (#PCDATA)>
```

This states that the element can only contain parsed character data, specified by #PCDATA. This is just ordinary text, and since it will be parsed, it cannot contain markup. The # character preceding the word PCDATA is necessary just to ensure it cannot be confused with an element or attribute name – it has no other significance. Since element and attribute names must start with a letter or an underscore, the # prefix to PCDATA ensures that it cannot be interpreted as such.

The PCDATA specification does provide for markup – child elements – to be mixed in with ordinary text. In this case you must specify the names of the elements that can occur mixed in with the text. If you wanted to allow a `<suite>` element specifying a suite number to appear alongside the text within a `<buildingnumber>` element you could express it like this:

```
<!ELEMENT buildingnumber (#PCDATA|suite)*>
```

This indicates that the content for a `<buildingnumber>` element is parsed character data and the text can be combined with `<suite>` elements. The | operator here has the same meaning as the | operator we met in the context of regular expressions in Chapter 13. It means one or other of the two operands but not both. The * following the parentheses is required here, and has the same meaning as the * operator that we also met in the context of regular expressions. It means that the operand to the left can appear zero or more times.

If you want to allow several element types to be optionally mixed in with the text, you separate them by |. Note that it is not possible to control the sequence in which mixed content appears.

The other elements used to define an address are similar, so we could define the whole document with its DTD like this:

```
<?xml version="1.0"?>
<!DOCTYPE address
[
    <!ELEMENT address (buildingnumber, street, city, state, zip)>
    <!ELEMENT buildingnumber (#PCDATA)>
    <!ELEMENT street (#PCDATA)>
    <!ELEMENT city (#PCDATA)>
    <!ELEMENT state (#PCDATA)>
    <!ELEMENT zip (#PCDATA)>
]>
<address>
  <buildingnumber> 29 </buildingnumber>
  <street> South Lasalle Street</street>
  <city>Chicago</city>
  <state>Illinois</state>
  <zip>60603</zip>
</address>
```

One point to note is that we have no way to constrain the text in an element definition. It would be nice to be able to specify that the building number had to be numeric, for example, but the DTD grammar and syntax provide no way to do this. This is a serious limitation of DTDs and one of the driving forces behind the development of an alternative, XML Schemas. Schemas are beyond the scope of this book but if you want to know more you should get hold of a copy of *Pro XML Schemas* by Jon Duckett, Oliver Griffin, et al, Wrox Press Ltd., (ISBN 1-861005-47-4)

If we were to create the DTD for an address document as a separate file, the file contents would just consist of the element definitions:

```
<!ELEMENT address (buildingnumber, street, city, state, zip)>
<!ELEMENT buildingnumber (#PCDATA)>
```

```
<!ELEMENT street (#PCDATA)>
<!ELEMENT city (#PCDATA)>
<!ELEMENT state (#PCDATA)>
<!ELEMENT zip (#PCDATA)>
```

The DOCTYPE declaration identifies the DTD for a particular document so it is not part of the DTD. If the DTD above were stored in the AddressDoc.dtd file in the same directory as the document, the DOCTYPE declaration in the document would be:

```
<?xml version="1.0"?>
<!DOCTYPE address SYSTEM "AddressDoc.dtd">
<address>
  <buildingnumber> 29 </buildingnumber>
  <street> South Lasalle Street</street>
  <city>Chicago</city>
  <state>Illinois</state>
  <zip>60603</zip>
</address>
```

Of course, the DTD file would also include definitions for element attributes, if there were any. These will be useful later, so save the DTD as AddressDoc.dtd, and the XML file above (as Address.xml perhaps), in your Beg Java Stuff directory.

One further possibility we need to consider is that in many situations it is desirable to allow some child elements to be omitted. For instance, <buildingnumber> may not be included in some cases. The <zip> element, while highly desirable, might also be left out in practice. We can indicate that an element is optional by using the **cardinality operator**, ?. This operator expresses the same idea as the equivalent regular expression operator – that a child element may or may not appear. The DTD would then look like this:

```
<!DOCTYPE address
[
    <!ELEMENT address (buildingnumber?, street, city, state, zip?)>
    <!ELEMENT buildingnumber (#PCDATA)>
    <!ELEMENT street (#PCDATA)>
    <!ELEMENT city (#PCDATA)>
    <!ELEMENT state (#PCDATA)>
    <!ELEMENT zip (#PCDATA)>
]>
```

The ? operator following an element indicates that the element may be omitted or may appear just once. This is just one of three cardinality operators that you use to specify how many times a particular child element can appear as part of the content for the parent. The other two cardinality operators are *, which we have already seen, and +. In each case the operator follows the operand to which it applies. We now have four operators that we can use in element declarations and they are each similar in action to their equivalent in the regular expression context:

+	This operator indicates that there can be one or more occurrences of its operand. In other words there *must* be at least one occurrence, but there may be more.
*	This operator indicates that there can be zero or more occurrences of its operand. In other words, there can be none or any number of occurrences of the operand to which it applies.
?	This indicates that its operand may appear once or not at all.
|	This operator indicates that there can be an occurrence of either its left operand or its right operand, but not both.

We might want to allow a building number or a building name in an address, in which case the DTD could be written:

```
<!DOCTYPE address
[
  <!ELEMENT address ((buildingnumber | buildingname), street, city, state, zip?)>
  <!ELEMENT buildingnumber (#PCDATA)>
  <!ELEMENT buildingname (#PCDATA)>
  <!ELEMENT street (#PCDATA)>
  <!ELEMENT city (#PCDATA)>
  <!ELEMENT state (#PCDATA)>
  <!ELEMENT zip (#PCDATA)>
]>
```

The DTD now states that either `<buildingnumber>` or `<buildingname>` must appear as the first element in `<address>`. But we might want to allow neither, in which case we would write the third line as:

```
  <!ELEMENT address ((buildingnumber | buildingname)?, street, city, state, zip?)>
```

The ? operator applies to the parenthesized expression (buildingnumber | buildingname), so it now states that either `<buildingnumber>` or `<buildingname>` may or may not appear, so we allow one, or the other, or none.

Of course, you can use the | operator repeatedly to express a choice between any number of elements, or indeed, subexpressions between parentheses. For example, given that you have defined elements Linux, Solaris, and Windows, you might define the element operatingsystem as:

```
  <!ELEMENT operatingsystem (Linux | Solaris | Windows)>
```

If you wanted to allow an arbitrary operating system to be identified as a further alternative, you could write:

```
  <!ELEMENT operatingsystem (AnyOS | Linux | Solaris | Windows)>
  <!ELEMENT AnyOS (#PCDATA)>
```

You can combine the operators we have seen to produce definitions for content of almost unlimited complexity. For example:

1011

```
<!ELEMENT breakfast ((tea|coffee), orangejuice?,
                    ((egg+, (bacon|sausage)) | cereal) , toast)>
```

This states that `<breakfast>` content is either a `<tea>` or `<coffee>` element, followed by an optional `<orangejuice>` element, followed by either one or more `<egg>` elements and a `<bacon>` or `<sausage>` element, or a `<cereal>` element, with a mandatory `<toast>` element bringing up the rear. However, while you can produce mind-boggling productions for defining elements it is wise to keep things as simple as possible.

After all this complexity, we mustn't forget that an element may also be empty, in which case it can be defined like this:

```
<!ELEMENT position EMPTY>
```

This states that the `<position>` element has no content. Elements can also have attributes so let's take a quick look at how they can be defined in a DTD.

Defining Element Attributes

You use an `ATTLIST` declaration in a DTD to define the attributes for a particular element. As you know, attributes are name-value pairs associated with a particular element and values are typically, but not exclusively, text. Where the value for an attribute is text, it is enclosed between quotation marks, so it is always unparsed character data. Attribute values that consist of text are therefore specified just as `CDATA`. No preceding # character is necessary in this context since there is no possibility of confusion.

We could declare the elements for a document containing circles as follows:

```
<?xml version="1.0"?>
```

```
<!DOCTYPE circle
[
    <!ELEMENT circle (position)>
    <!ATTLIST circle
            radius CDATA #REQUIRED
    >

    <!ELEMENT position EMPTY>
    <!ATTLIST position
            x CDATA #REQUIRED
            y CDATA #REQUIRED
    >
]>
```

```
<circle radius="15">
  <position x="30" y="50"/>
</circle>
```

Three items define each attribute – the attribute name, the type of value (CDATA), and whether or not the attribute is mandatory. This third item may also define a default value for the attribute, in which case this value will be assumed if the attribute is omitted. The #REQUIRED specification against an attribute name indicates that it must appear in the corresponding element. You specify the attribute as #IMPLIED if it need not be included. In this case the XML processor will not supply a default value for the attribute. An application is expected to have a default value of its own for the attribute value that is implied by the attribute's omission.

Save this XML in your /Beg Java Stuff directory with a suitable name such as "circle with DTD.xml" it will come in handy later.

You specify a default value for an attribute between double quotes. For example:

```
<!ATTLIST circle
        radius CDATA "1"
>
```

This indicates that the value of radius will be 1 if the attribute is not specified for a <circle> element.

You can also insist that a value for an attribute must be one of a fixed set. For instance, suppose we had a color attribute for our circle that could only be red, blue, or green. We could define it like this:

```
<!ATTLIST circle
        color (red|blue|green) #IMPLIED
>
```

The value for the color attribute in a <circle> element must be one of the options between the parentheses. In this case the attribute can be omitted because it is specified as #IMPLIED, and an application processing it will supply a default value. To make the inclusion of the attribute mandatory, we would define it as:

```
<!ATTLIST circle
        color (red|blue|green) #REQUIRED
>
```

An important aspect of defining possible attribute values by an enumeration like this is that an XML editor can help the author of a document by prompting with the list of possible attribute values from the DTD when the element is being created.

An attribute that is declared as #FIXED must always have the default value. For example:

```
<!ATTLIST circle
        color (red|blue|green) #REQUIRED
        line_thickness medium #FIXED
>
```

Here the XML processor will only supply an application with the value medium for the thickness attribute. If you were to specify this attribute for the <circle> element in the body of the document you can only use the default value, otherwise it is an error.

Defining Parameter Entities

You will often need to repeat a block of information in different places in a DTD. A **parameter entity** identifies a block of parsed text by a name that you can use to insert the text at various places within a DTD. Note that parameter entities are only for use within a DTD. You cannot use parameter entity references in the body of a document. You declare general entities in the DTD when you want to repeat text within the document body.

The form for a parameter entity is very similar to what we saw for general entities except that a % character appears between ENTITY and the entity name separated from both by a space. For example, it is quite likely that you would want to repeat the x and y attributes that we defined in the <position> element in the previous section in other elements. We could define a parameter entity for these attributes and then use that wherever these attributes should appear in an element declaration. Here's the parameter entity declaration:

```
<!ENTITY % coordinates "x CDATA #REQUIRED y CDATA #REQUIRED">
```

Now we can use the entity name to insert the x and y attribute definitions in an attribute declaration:

```
<!ATTLIST position %coordinates; >
```

A parameter entity declaration must precede its use in a DTD.

The substitution string in a parameter entity declaration is parsed, and can include parameter and general entity references. As with general entities, a parameter entity can also be defined by a reference to a URI containing the substitution string.

Other Types of Attribute Value

There are a further eight possibilities for specifying the type of the attribute value. We won't go into detail on these but, so you can recognize them, they are:

ENTITY	An entity defined in the DTD. An entity here is a name identifying an unparsed entity defined elsewhere in the DTD by an ENTITY tag. The entity may or may not contain text. An entity could represent something very simple such as <, which refers to a single character, or it could represent something more substantial such as an image.
ENTITIES	A list of entities defined in the DTD separated by spaces.
ID	An ID is a unique name identifying an element in a document. This is to enable internal references to a particular element from elsewhere in the document.
IDREF	A reference to an element elsewhere in a document via its ID.
IDREFS	A list of references to IDs separated by spaces.
NMTOKEN	A name conforming to the XML definition of a name. This just says that the value of the attribute will be consistent with the XML rules for a name.
NMTOKENS	A list of name tokens separated by spaces.

NOTATION	A name identifying a notation – which is typically a format specification for an entity such a JPEG or Postscript file. The notation will be identified elsewhere in the DTD using a NOTATION tag that may also identify an application capable of processing an entity in the given format.

A DTD for Sketcher

With what we know of XML and DTDs, we can have a stab at putting together a DTD for storing Sketcher files as XML. As we said before, an XML language has already been defined for representing and communicating two-dimensional graphics. This is called Scalable Vector Graphics, and you can find it at http://www.w3.org/TR/SVG/. While this would be the choice for transferring 2D graphics as XML documents in a real-world context, our objective is to exercise our knowledge of XML and DTDs, so we will reinvent our own version of this wheel even though it will have fewer spokes and may wobble a bit.

First, let's consider what our general approach is going to be. Since our objective is to define a DTD that will enable us to exercise the Java API for XML with Sketcher, we will define the language to make it an easy fit to Sketcher, rather than worry about the niceties of the best way to represent each geometric element. Since Sketcher itself was a vehicle for trying out various capabilities of the Java class libraries, it evolved in a somewhat topsy-like fashion with the result that the classes defining geometric entities are not necessarily ideal. However, we will just map these directly in XML in order to avoid the mathematical jiggery-pokery that would be necessary if we adopted a more formal representation of geometry in XML.

A sketch is a very simple document. It's basically a sequence of lines, circles, rectangles, curves, and text. We can therefore define the root element, <sketch>, in the DTD as:

```
<!ELEMENT sketch (line|circle|rectangle|curve|text)*>
```

This just says that a sketch consists of zero or more of any of the elements between the parentheses. We now need to define each of these elements.

A line is easy. It is defined by its location, which is its start point, and an end point. It also has an orientation – its rotation angle – and a color. We could define a <line> element like this:

```
<!ELEMENT line (color, position, endpoint)>
  <!ATTLIST line
         angle CDATA                    #REQUIRED
  >
```

A line is fully defined by two points, but our Line class includes a rotation field so we have included that too. Of course, a position is also a point so it would be possible to use a <point> element for this, but differentiating the position for a geometric element will make it a bit easier for a human reader to read an XML document containing a sketch.

We could define color by a color attribute to the <line> element with a set of alternative values, but to allow the flexibility for lines of any color, it would be better to define a <color> element with three attributes for RGB values. In this case we can define the <color> element as:

```
<!ELEMENT color EMPTY>
  <!ATTLIST color
            R CDATA                        #REQUIRED
            G CDATA                        #REQUIRED
            B CDATA                        #REQUIRED
  >
```

We must now define the `<position>` and `<endpoint>` elements. These are both points defined by an (x,y) coordinate pair so you would sensibly define them consistently. Empty elements with attributes are the most economical way here and we can use a parameter entity for the attributes:

```
<!ENTITY % coordinates "x CDATA #REQUIRED y CDATA #REQUIRED">
<!ELEMENT position EMPTY>
  <!ATTLIST position %coordinates;>
<!ELEMENT endpoint EMPTY>
  <!ATTLIST endpoint %coordinates;>
```

A rectangle will be defined very similarly to a line since it is defined by its position, which corresponds to the top left corner, plus the coordinates of the bottom right corner. It also has a color and a rotation angle. Here's how this will look in the DTD:

```
<!ELEMENT rectangle (color, position, bottomright)>
  <!ATTLIST rectangle
            angle CDATA                    #REQUIRED
  >
<!ELEMENT bottomright EMPTY>
  <!ATTLIST bottomright %coordinates;>
```

We don't need to define the `<color>` and `<position>` elements since we have already defined these earlier for the `<line>` element.

The `<circle>` element is no more difficult. Its position is the center, and it has a radius and a color. It also has a rotation angle. We can define it like this:

```
<!ELEMENT circle (color, position)>
  <!ATTLIST circle
            radius CDATA                   #REQUIRED
            angle CDATA                    #REQUIRED
  >
```

The `<curve>` element is a little more complicated because it is defined by an arbitrary number of points, but it is still quite easy:

```
<!ELEMENT curve (color, position, point+)>
  <!ATTLIST curve  angle CDATA  #REQUIRED>
<!ELEMENT point EMPTY>
  <!ATTLIST point %coordinates;>
```

The start point of the curve is defined by the `<position>` element and it includes at least one `<point>` element, which is specified by the + operator.

Lastly we have the element that defines a text element in Sketcher terms. We need to allow for the font name and its style and point size, a rotation angle for the text, and a color – plus the text itself, of course, and its position. A `Text` element is also a little different from the other elements, as its bounding rectangle is required to construct it, so we must also include that. We have some choices as to how we define this element. We could use mixed element content in a `<text>` element, combining the text string with `<font>` and `<position>` elements, for instance.

The disadvantage of this is that we cannot limit the number of occurrences of the child elements and how they are intermixed with the text. We can make the definition more precisely controlled by enclosing the text in its own element. Then we can define the `<text>` element as having element content – like this:

```
<!ELEMENT text (color, position, font, string)>
    <!ATTLIST text  angle CDATA  #REQUIRED>

<!ELEMENT font EMPTY>
    <!ATTLIST font
            fontname   CDATA                  #REQUIRED
            fontstyle (plain|bold|italic) #REQUIRED
            pointsize CDATA                  #REQUIRED
    >
<!ELEMENT string (#PCDATA|bounds)*>

<!ELEMENT bounds EMPTY>
    <!ATTLIST point
            width CDATA   #REQUIRED
            height CDATA  #REQUIRED
    >
```

The `<string>` element content will be a `<bounds>` element defining the height and width of the bounding rectangle plus the text to be displayed. The `<font>` element provides the name, style, and size of the font as attribute values and since nothing is required beyond that it is an empty element. Children of the `<text>` element that we have already defined specify the color and position of the text.

That's all we need. The complete DTD for Sketcher documents will be:

```
<!ELEMENT sketch (line|circle|rectangle|curve|text)*>

<!ELEMENT color EMPTY>
    <!ATTLIST color
            R CDATA                  #REQUIRED
            G CDATA                  #REQUIRED
            B CDATA                  #REQUIRED
    >

<!ENTITY % coordinates "x CDATA #REQUIRED y CDATA #REQUIRED">

<!ELEMENT position EMPTY>
    <!ATTLIST position %coordinates;>

<!ELEMENT endpoint EMPTY>
```

```
        <!ATTLIST endpoint %coordinates;>

<!ELEMENT line (color, position, endpoint)>
    <!ATTLIST line
            angle CDATA                     #REQUIRED
    >

<!ELEMENT rectangle (color, position, bottomright)>
    <!ATTLIST rectangle
            angle CDATA                     #REQUIRED
    >

<!ELEMENT bottomright EMPTY>
    <!ATTLIST bottomright %coordinates;>

<!ELEMENT circle (color, position)>
    <!ATTLIST circle
            radius CDATA                    #REQUIRED
            angle CDATA                     #REQUIRED
    >

<!ELEMENT curve (color, position, point+)>
    <!ATTLIST curve  angle CDATA  #REQUIRED>

<!ELEMENT point EMPTY>
    <!ATTLIST point %coordinates;>

<!ELEMENT text (color, position, font, string)>
    <!ATTLIST text  angle CDATA  #REQUIRED>

<!ELEMENT font EMPTY>
    <!ATTLIST font
            fontname  CDATA                             #REQUIRED
            fontstyle (plain|bold|italic|bold-italic) #REQUIRED
            pointsize CDATA                             #REQUIRED
    >

<!ELEMENT string (#PCDATA|bounds)*>

<!ELEMENT bounds EMPTY>
    <!ATTLIST bounds
            width    CDATA                  #REQUIRED
            height   CDATA                  #REQUIRED
    >
```

We can use this DTD to represent any sketch in XML. Stash it away in your `Beg Java Stuff` directory as `sketcher.dtd`. We will try it out later.

Rules for a Well-Formed Document

Now that we know a bit more about XML elements and what goes into a DTD, we can formulate what you must do to ensure your XML document is well-formed. The rules for a document to be well-formed are quite simple:

1. If the XML declaration appears in the prolog, it must include the XML version. Other specifications in the XML document must be in the prescribed sequence – character encoding then standalone specification.

2. If the document type declaration appears in the prolog the DOCTYPE name must match that of the root element and the markup declarations in the DTD must be according to the rules for writing markup declarations.

3. The body of the document must contain at least one element, the root element, which contains all the other elements, and an instance of the root element must not appear in the content of another element. All elements must be properly nested.

4. Elements in the body of the document must be consistent with the markup declarations identified by the DOCTYPE declaration.

The rules for writing an XML document are absolutely strict. Break one rule and your document is not well-formed and will not be processed. This strict application of the rules is essential because we are communicating data and its structure. If any laxity were permitted it would open the door to uncertainty about how the data should be interpreted. HTML used to be quite different from XML in this respect. Until recently, the rules for writing HTML were only loosely applied by HTML readers such as web browsers.

For instance, even though a paragraph in HTML should be defined using a begin tag, <p>, and an end tag, </p>, you can usually get away with omitting the end tag, and you can use both capital and lower-case p, and indeed close a capital-case P paragraph with a lower-case p, and vice versa. You can often have overlapping tags in HTML and get away with that too. While it is not to be recommended, a loose application of the rules for HTML is not so harmful since HTML is only concerned with data presentation. The worst that can happen is that the data does not display quite as you intended.

Recently, the W3C has released a number of specifications that make HTML an XML language, and we can expect compliance within the next few years. The enduring problem is, of course, that the Internet has many years of material that is still very useful but that will never be well-formed XML, so browsers may never be fully XML compliant.

XML Namespaces

This is the last topic we need a little insight into before we get back into Java programming. Even though they are very simple, XML namespaces can be very confusing. The confusion arises because it is so easy to make assumptions about what they imply when you first meet them. Let's look briefly at why we have XML namespaces in the first place and then see what an XML namespace actually is.

We saw earlier that an XML document can only have one DOCTYPE declaration. This can identify an external DTD by a URI or include explicit markup declarations, or it may do both. What happens if we want to combine two or more XML documents that each have their own DTD into a single document? The short answer is we can't – not easily anyway. Since the DTD for each document will have been defined without regard for the other, element name collisions are a real possibility. It may be impossible to differentiate between different elements that share a common name and in this case major revisions of the documents' contents as well as a new DTD will be necessary to deal with this. It won't be easy.

XML namespaces are intended to help deal with this problem. They enable names used in markup to be qualified so that you can make duplicate names used in different markup unique by putting them in separate namespaces. An XML namespace is just a collection of element and attribute names that is identified by a URI. Each name in an XML namespace is qualified by the URI that identifies the namespace. Thus different XML namespaces may contain common names without causing confusion since each name is notionally qualified by the unique URI for the namespace that contains it.

I say 'notionally qualified' because you don't actually qualify names using the URI directly. You use another name called a **namespace prefix** whose value is the URI for the namespace. For example, I could have a namespace that is identified by the URI http://www.wrox.com/Toys and a namespace prefix, toys, that contains a declaration for the name rubber_duck. I could have a second namespace with the URI http://www.wrox.com/BathAccessories and the namespace prefix BathAccessories that also defines the name rubber_duck.

The rubber_duck name from the first namespace is referred to as Toys:rubber_duck and that from the second namespace is BathAccessories:rubber_duck so there is no possibility of confusing them. The colon is used in the qualified name to separate the namespace prefix from the local name, which is why we said earlier you should avoid the use of colons in ordinary XML names.

Let's come back to the confusing aspects of namespaces for a moment. There is a temptation to imagine that the URI that identifies an XML namespace also identifies a document somewhere that specifies the names that are in the namespace. This is not required by the namespace specification. The URI is just a unique identifier for the namespace and a unique qualifier for a set of names. It does not necessarily have any other purpose, or even have to refer to a real document. It only needs to be unique. The definition of how names within a given namespace relate to one another and the rules for markup that uses them is an entirely separate question. This may be provided by a DTD or some other mechanism such as an XML Schema.

Namespace Declarations

A namespace is associated with a particular element in a document, which of course can be, but does not have to be, the root element. A typical namespace declaration in an XML document looks like this:

```
<sketcher:sketch xmlns:sketcher="http://www.wrox.com/dtds/sketches">
```

A namespace declaration uses a special reserved attribute name, xmlns, within an element and in this instance the namespace applies to the <sketch> element. The name sketcher that is separated from xmlns by a colon is the namespace prefix and it has the value http://www.wrox.com/dtds/sketches. You can use the namespace prefix to qualify names within the namespace, and since this maps to the URI, the URI is effectively the qualifier for the name. The URL that I've given here is hypothetical – it doesn't actually exist, but it could. The sole purpose of the URI identifying the namespace is to ensure that names within the namespace are unique so it doesn't matter whether it exists or not. You can add as many namespace declarations within an element as you want and each namespace declared in an element is available within that element and its content.

With the namespace declared with the sketcher prefix, we can use the <circle> element that is defined in the sketcher namespace like this:

```
<sketcher:sketch xmlns:sketcher="http://www.wrox.com/dtds/sketches">
  <sketcher:circle radius="15" angle="0">
    <sketcher:color R="150" G="250" B="100"/>
    <sketcher:position x="30" y="50"/>
  </sketcher:circle>
</sketcher:sketch>
```

Each reference to the element name is qualified by the namespace prefix sketcher. A reference in the same document to a <circle> element that is defined within another namespace can be qualified by the prefix specified in the declaration for that namespace. By qualifying each element name by its namespace prefix, we avoid any possibility of ambiguity.

A namespace has **scope** – a region of an XML document over which the namespace declaration is visible. The scope of a namespace is the content of the element within which it is declared, plus all direct or indirect child elements. The namespace declaration above applies to the <sketch> element and all the elements within it. If you declare a namespace in the root element for a document, its scope is the entire document.

You can declare a namespace without specifying a prefix. This namespace then becomes the default namespace in effect for this element and its content, and unqualified element names are assumed to belong to this namespace. Here is an example:

```
<sketch xmlns="http://www.wrox.com/dtds/sketches">
```

There is no namespace prefix specified so the colon following xmlns is omitted. This namespace becomes the default, so we can use element and attribute names from this namespace without qualification and they are all implicitly within the default namespace. For instance:

```
<sketch xmlns="http://www.wrox.com/dtds/sketches">
  <circle radius="15" angle="0">
    <color R="150" G="250" B="100"/>
    <position x="30" y="50"/>
  </circle>
</sketch>
```

This markup is a lot less cluttered than the earlier version that used qualified names, which makes it much easier to read. It is therefore advantageous to declare the namespace that you use most extensively in a document as the default.

You can declare several namespaces within a single element. Here's an example of a default namespace in use with another namespace:

```
<sketch xmlns="http://www.wrox.com/dtds/sketches"
        xmlns:print="http://www.wrox.com/dtds/printed">
  <circle radius="15" angle="0">
    <color R="150" G="250" B="100"/>
    <position x="30" y="50"/>
  </circle>
  <print:circle print:lineweight="3" print:linestyle="dashed"/>
</sketch>
```

Here the namespace with the prefix `print` contains names for elements relating to hardcopy presentation of sketch elements. The `<circle>` element in the `print` namespace is qualified by the namespace prefix so it is distinguished from the element with the same name in the default namespace.

XML Namespaces and DTDs

For a document to be valid you must still have a DTD and the document must be consistent with it. The way in which a DTD is defined has no specific provision for namespaces. The DTD for a document that uses namespaces must therefore define the elements and attributes using qualified names and must also make provision for the `xmlns` attribute with or without its prefix in the markup declaration for any element in which it can appear. Because the markup declarations in a DTD have no specific provision for accommodating namespaces, a DTD is a less than ideal vehicle for defining the rules for markup when namespaces are used. The XML Schema specification provides a much better solution, and overcomes a number of other problems associated with DTDs.

However, the XML Schema specification has been finalized and approved relatively recently – in the first half of 2001. Consequently the present JAXP implementation distributed as part of SDK 1.4 has no specific provision for schemas so we won't go into them here.

Working with XML Documents

Right at the beginning of this chapter we introduced the notion of an XML processor as a module that is used by an application to read XML documents. An XML processor parses the contents of a document and makes the elements together with their attributes and content available to the application, so it is also referred to as an **XML parser**. In case you haven't met the term before a **parser** is just a program module that breaks text in a given language down into its component parts. A natural language processor would have a parser that identifies the grammatical segments in each sentence. A compiler has a parser that identifies variables, constants, operators, etc. in a program statement. An application accesses the content of a document through an API provided by an XML parser and the parser does the job of figuring out what the document consists of.

Java supports two complementary APIs for processing an XML document:

❑ **SAX**, which is the **S**imple **A**PI for **X**ML parsing.

❑ **DOM**, which is the **D**ocument **O**bject **M**odel for XML.

The support in SDK 1.4 is for DOM level 2 version 1 and for SAX version 2. SDK 1.4 also supports **XSLT** version 1.0 where **XSL** is the e**X**tensible **S**tylesheet **L**anguage and **T** is **T**ransformations – a language for transforming one XML document into another, or into some other textual representation such as HTML. However, we will concentrate on the basic application of DOM and SAX. XSLT is such an extensive topic that there are several books devoted entirely to it.

For more information on XSLT please refer to XSLT Programmer's Reference 2nd Edition, *by Michael H. Kay, Wrox Press Ltd., (ISBN 1-861005-06-7).*

Before we get into detail on these APIs, let's look at the broad differences between SAX and DOM, and get an idea of the circumstances in which you might choose to use one rather than the other.

SAX Processing

SAX uses an **event-based** process for reading an XML document that is implemented through a callback mechanism. This is very similar to the way in which we handle GUI events in Java. As the parser reads a document, each parsing event, such as recognizing the start or end of an element, results in a call to a particular method that is associated with that event. Such a method is often referred to as a **handler**. It is up to you to implement these methods to respond appropriately to the event. Each of your methods then has the opportunity to react to the event that will result in it being called in any way that you wish. Below you can see the events that would arise from the XML document example that we saw earlier.

SAX Processing of XML

Each type of event results in a different method in your program being called. There are, for instance, different events for registering the beginning and end of a document. You can also see that the start and end of each element result in two further kinds of events, and another type of event occurs for each segment of document data. Thus this particular document will involve five different methods in your program being called – some of them more than once, of course, so there is one method for each type of event.

Because of the way SAX works, your application inevitably receives the document a piece at a time, with no representation of the whole document. This means that if you need to have the whole document available to your program with its elements and content properly structured you have to assemble it yourself from the information supplied to your callback methods.

Of course, it also means that you don't have to keep the entire document in memory if you don't need it, so if you are just looking for particular information from a document, all <phonenumber> elements for instance, you can just save those as you receive them through the callback mechanism, and discard the rest. As a consequence, SAX is a particularly fast and memory efficient way of selectively processing the contents of an XML document.

First of all, SAX itself is not an XML document parser; it is a public domain definition of an interface to an XML parser, where the parser is an external program. The public domain part of the SAX API is in three packages that are shipped as part of the SDK:

❑   org.xml.sax – this defines the Java interfaces specifying the SAX API and the InputSource class that encapsulates a source of an XML document to be parsed.

❑   org.xml.sax.helpers – this defines a number of helper classes for interfacing to a SAX parser.

❑   org.xml.sax.ext – this defines interfaces representing optional extensions to SAX2 to obtain information about a DTD, or to obtain information about comments and CDATA sections in a document.

In addition to these, the javax.xml.parsers package provides factory classes that you use to gain access to a parser and the javax.xml.transform package defines interfaces and classes for XSLT 1.0 processing of an XML document.

In Java terms there are several interfaces involved. The XMLReader interface that is defined in the org.xml.sax package specifies the methods that the SAX parser will call as it recognizes elements, attributes, and other components of an XML document. You must provide a class that implements these methods and responds to the method calls in the way that you want.

DOM Processing

DOM works quite differently to SAX. When an XML document is parsed, the whole document tree is assembled in memory and returned to your application as an object of type Document that encapsulates it, as illustrated below.

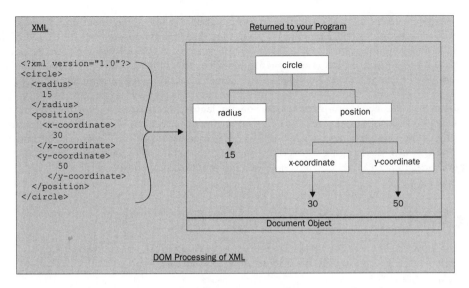

DOM Processing of XML

Once you have the `Document` object available you can call the object's methods to navigate through the elements in the document tree starting with the root element. With DOM, the entire document is available to you for you to process as often and in as many ways as you want. This is a major advantage over SAX processing. The downside to this is the amount of memory occupied by the document – there is no choice, you get it all no matter how big it is. With some documents the amount of memory required may be prohibitively large.

DOM has one other unique advantage over SAX. It allows you to modify existing documents or create new ones. If you want to create an XML document programmatically and then transfer it to an external destination such as a file or another computer, DOM is the API for this since SAX has no direct provision for creating or modifying XML documents. We will go into detail on how we can use a DOM parser in the next chapter.

Accessing Parsers

The `javax.xml.parsers` package defines four classes supporting the processing of XML documents:

`SAXParserFactory`	Enables you to create a configurable factory object that you can use to create a `SAXParser` object encapsulating a SAX-based parser.
`SAXParser`	Defines an object that wraps a SAX-based parser.
`DocumentBuilderFactory`	Enables you to create a configurable factory object that you can use to create a `DocumentBuilder` object encapsulating a DOM-based parser.
`DocumentBuilder`	Defines an object that wraps a DOM-based parser.

All four classes are abstract. This is because JAXP is designed to allow different parsers and their factory classes to be plugged in. Both DOM and SAX parsers are developed independently of the Java SDK so it is important to be able to integrate new parsers as they come along. As we will see, the Crimson parser that is currently distributed with the SDK is controlled and developed by the Apache Project, but you may want to take advantage of the new features provided by the Xerces parser from the same organization.

These abstract classes act as wrappers for the specific factory and parser objects that you need to use for a particular parser and insulate your code from a particular parser implementation. An instance of a factory object that can create an instance of a parser is created at runtime, so your program can use a different parser without changing or even recompiling your code. Now that you have a rough idea of the general principles, let's get down to specifics and practicalities, starting with SAX.

Using SAX

To process an XML document with SAX, you first have to establish contact with the parser that you want to use. The first step towards this is to create a SAXParserFactory object like this:

```
SAXParserFactory spf = SAXParserFactory.newInstance();
```

The SAXParserFactory class is defined in the javax.xml.parsers package along with the SAXParser class that encapsulates a parser. The SAXParserFactory class is abstract but the static newInstance() method will return a reference to an object of a class type that is a concrete implementation of SAXParserFactory. This will be the factory object for creating a particular parser object, normally the default parser that comes with the SDK. To use a different parser, you would need to obtain a reference to a factory object for that parser. We will see how you can arrange to do this a little later in this chapter.

The SAXParserFactory object has methods for determining whether the parser that it will attempt to create will be namespace aware, or will validate the XML as it is parsed:

isNamespaceAware()	Returns true if the parser to be created is namespace aware, and false otherwise.
isValidating()	Returns true if the parser to be created will validate the XML during parsing, and false otherwise.

You can set the factory object to produce namespace aware parsers by calling its setNamespaceAware() method with an argument value of true. An argument of false sets the factory object to produce parsers that are not namespace aware. A parser that is namespace aware recognizes the structure of names in a namespace – with a colon separating the namespace prefix from the name. A namespace aware parser will report the URI and local name separately for each element and attribute. A parser that is not namespace aware will only report an element or attribute name as a single name even when it contains a colon. In other words, a parser that is not namespace aware will treat a colon as just another character that is part of a name.

Similarly, calling the `setValidating()` method with an argument of `true` will cause the factory object to produce parsers that will validate the XML as a document is parsed. A validating parser will verify that the document body has a DTD and that the document content is consistent with the DTD and any internal subset that is included in the `DOCTYPE` declaration. Of course, if you configure the factory object to create a parser that is either namespace aware or validating, the parser you intend to use must include the capability, otherwise a request to create a parser will fail.

We can now use our `SAXParserFactory` object to create a `SAXParser` object as follows:

```
SAXParser parser = null;
try {
 parser = spf.newSAXParser();
}catch(SAXException e){
  e.printStackTrace(System.err);
  System.exit(1);
} catch(ParserConfigurationException e) {
  e.printStackTrace(System.err);
  System.exit(1);
}
```

The `SAXParser` object that is created here will encapsulate the default parser. The `newSAXParser()` method for the factory object can throw the two exceptions we are catching here. A `ParserConfigurationException` will be thrown if a parser cannot be created consistent with the configuration determined by the `SAXParserFactory` object and a `SAXException` will be thrown if any other error occurs. For instance, if you call the `setValidating()` option and the parser does not have the capability for validating documents, this exception would be thrown. This should not arise with the parser supplied by default, though, since it supports both of these features.

The `ParserConfigurationException` class is defined in the `javax.xml.parsers` package, but the `SAXException` class is in the `org.xml.sax` package so we need a separate import statement for that. Now let's see what the default parser is by putting the code fragments we have looked at so far together in a working example.

Try It Out – Accessing a SAX Parser

Here's the code to create a `SAXParser` object and output some details about it to the command line:

```
import javax.xml.parsers.SAXParserFactory;
import javax.xml.parsers.SAXParser;
import javax.xml.parsers.ParserConfigurationException;
import org.xml.sax.SAXException;
public class TrySAX {
  public static void main(String args[]) {
    // Create factory object
    SAXParserFactory spf = SAXParserFactory.newInstance();
    System.out.println("Parser will "+(spf.isNamespaceAware()?"":"not ") +
                  "be namespace aware");
    System.out.println("Parser will "+(spf.isValidating()?"":"not ") +
                  "validate XML");

    SAXParser parser = null;                       // Stores parser reference
    try {
     parser = spf.newSAXParser();                  // Create parser object
```

```
      }catch(ParserConfigurationException e){// Thrown if a parser cannot be created
                                             // that is consistent with the
      e.printStackTrace(System.err);        // configuration in spf
      System.exit(1);
    } catch(SAXException e) {                // Thrown for any other error
      e.printStackTrace(System.err);
      System.exit(1);
    }

    System.out.println("Parser object is: "+ parser);
  }
}
```

When I ran this I got the output:

```
Parser will not be namespace aware
Parser will not validate XML
Parser object is: org.apache.xerces.jaxp.SAXParserImpl@fd13b5
```

How It Works

The output shows that the default configuration for the SAX parser produced by our
SAXParserFactory object, spf, will be neither namespace aware nor validating. The parser supplied
with the SDK is one that was first developed by Sun and was subsequently donated to the XML Apache
Project. It is referred to by the name **Crimson**. You can find information on the advantages and
limitations of this particular SAX parser on the http://xml.apache.org web site.

The code to create the parser works as we have already discussed. Once we have an instance of the
factory method we use that to create an object encapsulating the parser. Although the reference is
returned as type SAXParser, the object is of type SAXParserImpl, which is a concrete
implementation of the abstract SAXParser class for a particular parser.

The Crimson parser is capable of validating XML and can be namespace aware. All we need to do is to
specify which of these options we require by calling the appropriate method. We can set the parser
configuration for the factory object, spf, so that we get a validating and namespace aware parser by
adding two lines to the program:

```
      // Create factory object
      SAXParserFactory spf = SAXParserFactory.newInstance();
      spf.setNamespaceAware(true);
      spf.setValidating(true);
```

If you compile and run the code again, you should get output something like:

```
Parser will be namespace aware
Parser will validate XML
Parser object is: org.apache.xerces.jaxp.SAXParserImpl@13582d
```

We arrive at a SAXParser instance without tripping any exceptions and we clearly now have a
namespace aware and validating parser.

Using a Different Parser

You might like to try a different parser at this point. There are SAX parsers available from a number of sources but the Xerces parser produced by the XML Apache Project is easy and free to obtain, and a snap to set up. As well as supporting SAX version 2 (SAX2), it also supports DOM level 2 (DOM2). You can download the latest version, currently Xerces 2, from the download page on their web site at http://xml.apache.org. The binaries are distributed in a .zip file that you can unzip to a suitable location on your hard drive – the archive unzips to create its own directory structure. You will find everything you need in there, including documentation.

The simplest way to try out an alternative parser without making it a permanent selection over the default is to include the path to the .jar file that contains the parser implementation in the -classpath option on the command line. For instance, if you have downloaded the Xerces 2 parser from the Apache web site and extracted the file from the zip directly to your C:\ drive, you can run the example with the Xerces parser like this:

```
java -classpath .;C:\xerces-2_0_0\xercesImpl.jar -enableassertions TrySAX
```

Don't forget the period in the classpath definition that specifies the current directory. Without it the TrySAX.class file will not be found. If you omit the -classpath option, the program will revert to using the default parser. Of course, you can use this technique to select a particular parser when you have several installed on your PC. Just add the path to the directory that contains the JAR for the parser to the classpath.

If you want to make the choice of the Xerces parser more permanent, you can copy the xercesImpl.jar file to the ext directory for the JRE. This will be the jdk1.4\jre\lib\ext directory. A JAR containing a parser in the ext directory will always be found before the default parser.

Updating the Default Parser

The Crimson parser that comes with the JDK is developed independently by the Apache Project so it is quite possible there could be newer releases of this that you might want to instal if only to fix any bugs that might have appeared. You can override the default parser by placing a .jar archive containing the Crimson release you want to use in the directory jdk1.4\jre\lib\endorsed. Indeed you can use this directory to override any of the externally developed packages that are distributed with the SDK.

Parser Features and Properties

Specific parsers such as Xerces define their own features and properties that control and report on the processing of XML documents. A **feature** is an option that is either on or off, so it is set as a boolean value, either true or false. Namespace awareness and validating capability are both features of a parser. A **property** is an option with a value that is an object, usually a String object. Some properties have values that you set to influence the parser's operation while the values for other properties are set by the parser for you to retrieve to provide information about the parsing process.

You will find details of the features and properties supported by the Xerces 2 parser in the documentation that appears in the /doc directory that was created when you unzipped the Xerces archive.

Features of a Parser

As we have seen, namespace awareness and whether a parser is validating or not are both features, and these can be set by calling either setNamespaceAware() or setValidating() for the SAXParserFactory object, but a parser will typically have a number of other features. You can set other features for a parser by calling the setFeature() method for the SAXParserFactory object before you create the SAXParser instance. The first argument is a String that identifies a particular feature and the second argument is a boolean value that you specify as true or false to set the feature on or off. Of course, all features that you want must be set before you create the parser object. You will find details of the features that a SAX parser may have at http:/www.saxproject.org.

Here's how we might set the parser configuration to use string interning so that fast comparisons for string equality can be used by the parser:

```
try {
  spf.setFeature("http://xml.org/sax/features/string-interning", true);
} catch(ParserConfigurationException e) { // Serious parser configuration error
  e.printStackTrace();
  System.exit(1);

} catch(SAXNotRecognizedException e) {    // Feature name not recognized
  e.printStackTrace();
  System.exit(1);

} catch(SAXNotSupportedException e) {     // Feature recognized but not supported
{
  e.printStackTrace();
  System.exit(1);
}
```

The SAXNotRecognizedException and SAXNotSupportedException classes are subclasses of SAXException defined in the org.xml.sax package. You could therefore catch either of these with a single catch block for an exception object of type SAXException. With explicit catch blocks as we have here, you would need an import statement for each of the class names.

There is no set collection of features for a SAX2 parser so a parser may implement any number of arbitrary features. While it is not mandatory, there are a standard set of features that most, if not all, SAX2 parsers are likely to support. They all have names of the form http://xml.org/sax/features/name, and you can find details of these on the official web site for SAX noted earlier.

If you need to check whether a particular feature is set – you might want to check the default status for instance –, you just call the getFeature() method for the SAXParserFactory object with a reference to a string containing the URI for the feature. The method returns a boolean value indicating the status of the feature. Note that it can throw the same exceptions as the setFeature() method so you have to put the call in a try block.

Properties of a Parser

You can set the properties for a parser by calling the setProperty() method for the SAXParser object once you have created it. The first argument is the name of the property as type String and the second argument is the value for the property. The property value can be of any class type as the parameter type is Object but it is usually of type String. The setProperty() method will throw a SAXNotRecognizedException if the property name is not recognized or SAXNotSupportedException if the property name is recognized but not supported. Both of these exception classes are defined in the org.xml.sax package.

You can also retrieve the values for some properties during parsing to obtain additional information about the most recent parsing event. You use the parser's getProperty() method in this case. The argument to the method is the name of the property and the method returns a reference to the property's value.

As with features, there is no defined set of parser properties so you need to consult the parser documentation for information on these. At the time of writing there are four standard properties for a SAX parser, but since these involve the more advanced features of SAX parser operation, they are beyond the scope of this book.

Parsing Documents with SAX

To parse a document using the XMLParser object you simply call its parse() method. You have to supply two arguments to the parse() method. The first identifies the XML document and the second is a reference of type DefaultHandler to a handler object that you will have created to process the contents of the document. The DefaultHandler object must contain a specific set of public methods that the XMLParser object expects to be able to call for each event, where each type of event corresponds to a particular syntactic element it finds in the document.

The DefaultHandler class that is defined in the org.xml.sax.helpers package already contains do-nothing definitions of all the callback methods that the XMLParser object expects to be able to call. Thus all you have to do is to define a class that extends the DefaultHandler class, and then override the methods in the DefaultHandler class for the events that you are interested in. But let's not gallop too far ahead. We need to look into the versions of the parse() method that we have available before we get into handling parsing events.

The XMLParser class defines ten overloaded versions of the parse() method but we are only interested in five of them. The other five use a now deprecated handler type, HandlerBase, that was applicable to SAX1, so we shall ignore those and just look at the versions that relate to SAX2. All versions of the method have a return type of void, and the five varieties of the parse() method that we will consider are:

`parse(File aFile,` `        DefaultHandler handler)`	Parses the document in the file specified by `aFile` using `handler` as the object containing the callback methods called by the parser. This will throw an exception of type `IOException` if an I/O error occurs and of type `IllegalArgumentException` if `aFile` is null.
`parse(String uri,` `        DefaultHandler handler)`	Parses the document specified by `uri` using `handler` as the object defining the callback methods. This will throw an exception of type `SAXException` if `uri` is null and an exception of type `IOException` if an I/O error occurs.
`parse(InputStream input,` `        DefaultHandler handler)`	Parses `input` as the source of the XML with `handler` as the event handler. This will throw an exception of type `IOException` if an I/O error occurs, and of type `IllegalArgumentException` if `input` is null.

`parse(InputStream input,`
`        DefaultHandler handler,`
`        String systemID)`
	Parses `input` as above, but uses `systemID` to resolve any relative URIs.

`parse(InputSource source,` `        DefaultHandler handler)`	Parses the document specified by `source` using handler as the object providing the callback methods to be called by the parser.

The `InputSource` class is defined in the `org.xml.sax` package. It defines an object that wraps a variety of sources for an XML document that you can use to pass a document reference to a parser. You can create an `InputSource` object from an `InputStream` object, a `Reader` object encapsulating a character stream, or a `String` specifying a URI – either a public name or a URL. If you specify the document source as a URL, it must be fully qualified.

Implementing a SAX Handler

As we have already seen, the `DefaultHandler` class in the `org.xml.sax.helpers` package provides a default do-nothing implementation of each of the callback methods a SAX parser may call when parsing a document. These methods are declared in four interfaces that are implemented by the `DefaultHandler` class:

❑ The `ContentHandler` interface declares methods that will be called to identify the content of a document to an application. You will usually want to implement all the methods defined in this interface in your subclass of `DefaultHandler`.

❑ The `EntityResolver` interface declares one method, `resolveEntity()`, that is called by a parser to pass a public and/or system ID to your application to allow external entities in the document to be resolved.

❑ The `DTDHandler` interface declares two methods that will be called to notify your application of DTD-related events.

❑ The `ErrorHandler` interface defines three methods that will be called when the parser has identified an error of some kind in the document.

All four interfaces are defined in the `org.xml.sax` package. Of course you can define a handler class that implements these interfaces, but you will probably find it easier to extend the `DefaultHandler` class.

The basic methods that you must implement to deal with parsing events related to document content are those declared by the `ContentHandler` interface so let's concentrate on those first. All the methods have a `void` return type, and they are as follows

`startDocument()`	Called when the start of a document is recognized.
`endDocument()`	Called when the end of a document is recognized.

`startElement(String uri,`
    `String localName,`
    `String qName,`
    `Attributes attr)`
	Called when the start of an element is recognized. Up to three names may be provided for the element:
	
	`uri` is the namespace URI for the element name. This will be an empty string if there is no uri or if namespace processing is not being done.
	
	`localName` is the unqualified local name for the element. This will be an empty string if namespace processing is not being done. In this case the element name is reported via the qName parameter.
	
	`qName` is the qualified name for the element. This will be just the name if the parser is not namespace aware. (A colon, if it appears, is then just an ordinary character.)
	
	The `attr` reference encapsulates the attributes for the element that have explicit values.

`endElement(String uri,`
`         String localName,`
`         String qName)`
	:Called when the end of an element is recognized. The references passed to the method are as described for the `startElement()` method.

`characters(char[] ch,`
`         int start,`
`         int length)`
	Called for each segment of character data that is recognized. Note that a contiguous segment of text within an element can be returned as several chunks by the parser via several calls to this method. The characters that are available are from `ch[start]` to `ch[start+length-1]`. and you must not try to access the array outside these limits.

`ignorableWhitespace(char[] ch,`
`         int start,`
`         int length)`
	Called for each segment of ignorable whitespace that is recognized within the content of an element. Note that a contiguous segment of ignorable whitespace within an element can be returned as several chunks by the parser via several calls to this method. The whitespace characters are that available are from `ch[start]` to `ch[start+length-1]`. and you must not try to access the array outside these limits.

`startPrefixMapping(String prefix,` `         String uri)`	Called when the start of a prefix URI namespace mapping is identified. Most of the time you can disregard this method as a parser will automatically replace prefixes for elements and attribute names by default.
`endPrefixMapping(String prefix)`	Called when the end of a prefix URI namespace mapping is identified. Most of the time you can disregard this method for the reason noted above.
`processingInstruction(String target,` `         String data)`	Called for each processing instruction recognized.
`skippedEntity(String name)`	Called for each entity that the parser skips.

setDocumentLocator(Locator locator)	Called by the parser to pass a `Locator` object to your code that you can use to determine the location in the document of any SAX document event. The `Locator` object can provide the public identifier, the system ID, the line number, and the column number in the document for any event. Just implement this method if you want to receive this information for each event.

Your implementations of these methods can throw an exception of type SAXException if an error occurs.

The DefaultHandler class is just like the adapter classes we have used for defining GUI event handlers. All we have to do to implement our own handler is extend the DefaultHandler class, and define our own implementations for the methods we are interested in. The same caveat applies here that applied with adapter classes – you must take care that the signatures of your methods are correct. Otherwise you are simply adding a new method rather than overriding one of the inherited methods. In this case your program will then do nothing for the given event since the original do-nothing version of the method will execute rather than your version. Let's try implementing a handler class.

Try It Out – Handling Parsing Events

Let's first define a handler class to deal with document parsing events. We will just implement a few of the methods from the ContentHandler interface – only those that apply to a simple document – and we will not worry about errors for the moment. Here's the code:

```
import org.xml.sax.helpers.DefaultHandler;
import org.xml.sax.Attributes;

public class MySAXHandler extends DefaultHandler {
  public void startDocument() {
     System.out.println("Start document: ");
  }
    public void endDocument()  {
     System.out.println("End document: ");
  }

  public void startElement(String uri, String localName,
                        String qname, Attributes attr) {
     System.out.println("Start element: local name: " + localName + " qname: "
                                         + qname + " uri: "+uri);
  }

  public void endElement(String uri, String localName, String qname) {
     System.out.println("End element: local name: " + localName + " qname: "
                                         + qname + " uri: "+uri);
  }

  public void characters(char[] ch, int start, int length) {
     System.out.println("Characters: " + new String(ch, start, length));
```

```
    }

  public void ignorableWhitespace(char[] ch, int start, int length) {
    System.out.println("Ignorable whitespace: " + new String(ch, start, length));
  }
}
```

Each handler method just outputs information about the event to the command line. Now we can define a program to use a handler of this class type to parse an XML document. We will make the example read the name of the XML file from the command line. Here's the code:

```
import javax.xml.parsers.SAXParserFactory;
import javax.xml.parsers.SAXParser;
import javax.xml.parsers.ParserConfigurationException;
import org.xml.sax.SAXException;
import java.io.File;
import java.io.IOException;

public class TrySAXHandler {
  public static void main(String args[]) {
    if(args.length == 0) {
      System.out.println("No file to process. Usage is:"
                                      +"\njava TrySax \"filename\" ");
      return;
    }
    File xmlFile = new File(args[0]);
    process(xmlFile);
  }

  private static void process(File file) {
    SAXParserFactory spf = SAXParserFactory.newInstance();
    SAXParser parser = null;
    spf.setNamespaceAware(true);
    spf.setValidating(true);
    System.out.println("Parser will "+(spf.isNamespaceAware()?"":"not ")
                                      + "be namespace aware");
    System.out.println("Parser will "+(spf.isValidating()?"":"not ")
                                      + "validate XML");
    try {
     parser = spf.newSAXParser();
     System.out.println("Parser object is: "+ parser);

    } catch(SAXException e) {
      e.printStackTrace(System.err);
      System.exit(1);

    } catch(ParserConfigurationException e) {
      e.printStackTrace(System.err);
      System.exit(1);
    }

    System.out.println("\nStarting parsing of "+file+"\n");
```

```
        MySAXHandler handler = new MySAXHandler();
        try {
            parser.parse(file, handler);
        } catch(IOException e) {
          e.printStackTrace(System.err);

        } catch(SAXException e) {
          e.printStackTrace(System.err);
        }
      }
    }
  }
```

I created the `circle.xml` file with the content:

```
<?xml version="1.0"?>
<circle>
  <radius>15</radius>
  <position>
    <x-coordinate>30</x-coordinate>
    <y-coordinate>50</y-coordinate>
  </position>
</circle>
```

I saved this in my `D:\Beg Java Stuff` directory but you can put it wherever you want and adjust the command line argument accordingly. The command to execute `TrySAXHandler` with this file is:

```
java TrySAXHandler "D:/Beg Java Stuff/circle.xml"
```

On my PC the program produced the output:

```
Parser will be namespace aware
Parser will validate XML
Parser object is: org.apache.xerces.jaxp.SAXParserImpl@c9ba38

Starting parsing of circle.xml

Start document:
Start element: local name: circle qname: circle uri:
Characters:

Start element: local name: radius qname: radius uri:
Characters: 15
End element: local name: radius qname: radius uri:
Characters:

Start element: local name: position qname: position uri:
Characters:

Start element: local name: x-coordinate qname: x-coordinate uri:
Characters: 30
```

```
End element: local name: x-coordinate qname: x-coordinate uri:
Characters:

Start element: local name: y-coordinate qname: y-coordinate uri:
Characters: 50
End element: local name: y-coordinate qname: y-coordinate uri:
Characters:

End element: local name: position qname: position uri:
Characters:

End element: local name: circle qname: circle uri:
End document:
```

How It Works

Much of the code in the `TrySAXHandler` class is the same as in the previous example. The `main()` method first checks for a command line argument. If there isn't one we issue a message and end the program. You might want to add some code following the command line argument check to make sure the file does exist. We saw how to do this way back in the chapters on file I/O.

We then call the static `process()` method with a reference to the `File` object for the XML document as the argument. This method creates the `XMLParser` object in the way we have seen previously then creates a handler object of type `MySAXHandler` for use by the parser. The parsing process is started by calling the `parse()` method for the parser object, `parser`, with the `file` reference as the first argument and the `handler` reference as the second argument. This identifies the object whose methods will be called for parsing events.

We have overridden six of the do-nothing methods inherited from `DefaultHandler` in the `MySAXHandler` class and you can see from the output which ones get called. All they do is output a message along with the information that is passed as arguments. You can see from the output that there is no URI for a namespace in the document so the qname is identical to `localname`.

Note how we form a `String` object in the `characters()` method from the specified sequence of elements in the ch array. We must only access the `length` elements from this array that start with the element ch(start).

The output also shows that the `characters()` method is sometimes called with just whitespace passed to the method in the ch array. This whitespace is ignorable whitespace that appears between the elements but the parser is not recognizing it as such. This is because there is no DTD to define how elements are to be constructed in this document so the parser has no way to know what can be ignored.

You can see that the output shows string values for both a `local` name and a qname. This is because we have the namespace awareness feature switched on. If you comment out the statement that calls `setNamespaceAware()` and recompile and re-execute the example, you will see that we only get a qname reported. Both the `local` name and URI outputs will be empty.

Processing a Document with a DTD

We can run the example again with the `Address.xml` file in the `Beg Java Stuff` directory to see how using a DTD affects processing. This should have the contents:

```
<?xml version="1.0"?>
<!DOCTYPE address SYSTEM "AddressDoc.dtd">
<address>
  <buildingnumber> 29 </buildingnumber>
  <street> South Lasalle Street</street>
  <city>Chicago</city>
  <state>Illinois</state>
  <zip>60603</zip>
</address>
```

The `AddressDoc.dtd` file in the same directory as `Address.xml` should contain:

```
<!ELEMENT address (buildingnumber, street, city, state, zip)>
  <!ELEMENT buildingnumber (#PCDATA)>
  <!ELEMENT street (#PCDATA)>
  <!ELEMENT city (#PCDATA)>
  <!ELEMENT state (#PCDATA)>
  <!ELEMENT zip (#PCDATA)>
```

If the path to the file contains spaces you will need to specify the path between double quotes in the command line argument. I got the output:

```
Parser will be namespace aware
Parser will validate XML
Parser object is: org.apache.xerces.jaxp.SAXParserImpl@c9ba38

Starting parsing of Address.xml

Start document:
Start element: local name: address qname: address uri:
Ignorable whitespace:

Start element: local name: buildingnumber qname: buildingnumber uri:
Characters:  29
End element: local name: buildingnumber qname: buildingnumber uri:
Ignorable whitespace:

Start element: local name: street qname: street uri:
Characters:  South Lasalle Street
End element: local name: street qname: street uri:
Ignorable whitespace:

Start element: local name: city qname: city uri:
Characters: Chicago
End element: local name: city qname: city uri:
Ignorable whitespace:

Start element: local name: state qname: state uri:
Characters: Illinois
End element: local name: state qname: state uri:
Ignorable whitespace:
```

1039

```
Start element: local name: zip qname: zip uri:
Characters: 60603
End element: local name: zip qname: zip uri:
Ignorable whitespace:

End element: local name: address qname: address uri:
End document:
```

We can see that with a DTD, the ignorable whitespace is recognized as such, and is passed to our `ignorableWhitespace()` method. Although the parser is validating the XML, we can't be confident that the document is valid. If any errors are found, the default do-nothing error-handling methods inherited from the `DefaultHandler` class will be called. We can fix this quite easily by modifying our `MySAXHandler` class, but let's first look at processing some other XML document flavors.

Processing a Document with Namespaces

We can convert our `Address.xml` file to use a namespace by modifying the root element like this:

```
<address xmlns="C:/Beg Java Stuff/AddressNamespace">
```

With this change to the XML file, the URI for the default namespace is
C:/Beg Java Stuff/AddressNamespace. This doesn't really exist, but it doesn't need to. It's just a unique qualifier for the names within the namespace.

We will also need to use a different DTD that takes account of the use of a namespace so we must modify the `DOCTYPE` declaration in the document:

```
<!DOCTYPE address SYSTEM "AddressNamespaceDoc.dtd">
```

You can now save the revised XML document with the name `AddressNamespace.xml`.

We must also create the new DTD. This is the same as the previous one with the addition of a declaration for the `xmlns` attribute for the `<address>` element:

```
<!ATTLIST address xmlns CDATA #IMPLIED>
```

If you run the previous example with this version of the XML document, you should see the URI in the output. Since the namespace is the default, there is no prefix name so the values for the `localname` and `qname` parameters to the `startElement()` and `endElement()` methods are the same.

Using Qualified Names

We can change the document to make explicit use of the namespace prefix like this:

```
<?xml version="1.0"?>
<!DOCTYPE addresses:address SYSTEM "AddressNamespaceDoc.dtd">
<addresses:address  xmlns:addresses="D:/Beg Java Stuff/AddressNamespace">
  <addresses:buildingnumber> 29 </addresses:buildingnumber>
  <addresses:street> South Lasalle Street</addresses:street>
```

```
       <addresses:city>Chicago</addresses:city>
       <addresses:state>Illinois</addresses:state>
       <addresses:zip>60603</addresses:zip>
    </addresses:address>
```

Unfortunately we also have to update the DTD. Otherwise if the qualified names are not declared in the DTD they will be regarded as errors. We need to change the DTD to:

```
    <!ELEMENT addresses:address (addresses:buildingnumber, addresses:street,
                         addresses:city, addresses:state, addresses:zip)>
    <!ATTLIST addresses:address xmlns:addresses CDATA #IMPLIED>
    <!ELEMENT addresses:buildingnumber (#PCDATA)>
    <!ELEMENT addresses:street (#PCDATA)>
    <!ELEMENT addresses:city (#PCDATA)>
    <!ELEMENT addresses:state (#PCDATA)>
    <!ELEMENT addresses:zip (#PCDATA)>
```

The namespace prefix is `addresses`, and the URI is the local file path. Each element name is qualified by the namespace prefix. We can usefully add implementations for two further callback methods in our `TrySAXHandler` class:

```
    public void startPrefixMapping(String prefix, String uri) {
      System.out.println("Start \"" + prefix + "\" namespace scope. URI: " + uri);
    }
    public void endPrefixMapping(String prefix) {
      System.out.println("End \"" + prefix + "\" namespace scope.");
    }
```

The parser won't call these methods by default. We have to switch the `http://xml.org/sax/features/namespace-prefixes` feature on to get this to happen. We can add a call to the `setFeature()` method for the parser factory object to do this in the `process()` method, immediately before we create the parser object in the `try` block:

```
    spf.setFeature("http://xml.org/sax/features/namespace-prefixes",true);
    parser = spf.newSAXParser();
```

We place it here, rather than following the call to `setValidating()`, because the method can throw an exception of type `ParserConfigurationException` and it needs to be in a `try` block. Now the parser will call the `startPrefixMapping()` method at the beginning of each namespace scope, and the `endPrefixMapping()` method at the end. If you parse this document, you will see that the qname values are the local name qualified by the namespace prefix. You should also see that the start and end of the namespace scope are recorded.

Handling other Parsing Events

We have only considered events arising from the recognition of document content, those declared in the `ContentHandler` interface. In fact the `DefaultHandler` class defines do-nothing methods declared in the other three interfaces that we saw earlier. For instance, when a parsing error occurs a parser calls a method to report the error. There are three methods for error reporting that are declared in the `ErrorHandler` interface and are implemented by the `DefaultHandler` class:

`warning(SAXParseException spe)`	Called to notify you ofconditions that are not errors or fatal errors. The exception object, `spe`, that is passed to the method contains information to enable you to locate the error in the original document.
`error(SAXParseException spe)`	Called to notify you that an error has been identified. An error is anything in a document that violates the XML 1.0 specification but is recoverable and allows the parser to continue processing the document normally.
`fatalError(SAXParseException spe)`	A fatal error is a non-recoverable error. After a fatal error the parser will not continue normal processing of the document.

Each of these methods is declared to throw an exception of type `SAXException` but you don't have to implement them so that they do this. With the `warning()` and `error()` methods you will probably want to output an error message and return to the parser so it can continue processing. Of course, if your `fatalError()` method is called, processing of the document will not continue anyway, so it would be appropriate to throw an exception in this case.

Obviously your implementation of any of these methods will want to make use of the information from the `SAXParseException` object that is passed to the method. This object has four methods that you can call to obtain additional information that will help you locate the error:

`getLineNumber()`	Returns the line number of the end of the document text where the error occurred as type `int`. If this information is not available, −1 is returned.
`getColumnNumber()`	Returns the line number within the document that contains the end of the text where the error occurred as type `int`. If this information is not available, −1 is returned. The first column in a line is column 1.
`getPublicID()`	Returns the public identifier of the entity where the error occurred as type `String`, or `null` if no public identifier is available.
`getSystemID()`	Returns the system identifier of the entity where the error occurred as type `String`, or `null` if no system identifier is available.

A simple implementation of the `warning()` method could be like this:

```
public void warning(SAXParseException spe) {
   System.out.println("Warning at line "+spe.getLineNumber());
   System.out.println(spe.getMessage());
}
```

This outputs a message indicating the document line number where the error occurred. It also outputs the string returned by the getMessage() method inherited from the base class, SAXException. This will usually indicate the nature of the error that was detected.

You could implement the error() callback method similarly but you might want to implement fatalError() so that it throws an exception. For example:

```
public void fatalError(SAXParseException spe) throws SAXException {
    System.out.println("Fatal error at line "+spe.getLineNumber());
    System.out.println(spe.getMessage());
    throw spe;
}
```

Here we just rethrow the SAXParseException after outputting an error message indicating the line number that caused the error. The SAXParseException class is a subclass of SAXException so we can rethrow spe as the superclass type.

You could try these out with the previous example by adding these methods to the MySAXHandler class. You could introduce a few errors into the XML file to get these methods called. Try deleting the DOCTYPE declaration or deleting the forward slash on an element end tag or even just deleting one character in an element name.

Summary

In this chapter we have discussed the fundamental characteristics of XML and how Java supports the analysis and synthesis of XML documents. The key points we have covered include the following:

❑ XML is a language for describing data that is to be communicated from one computer to another. Data is described in the form of text that contains the data plus markup that defines the structure of the data.

❑ XML is also a meta-language because you can use XML to create new languages for defining and structuring data.

❑ Markup consists of XML elements that may also include attributes, where an attribute is a name/value pair.

❑ The structure and meaning of a particular type of document can be defined within a Document Type Definition (DTD).

❑ A DTD can be defined in an external file or it can be part of a document.

❑ A DTD is identified by a DOCTYPE declaration in a document.

❑ An XML namespace defines a set of names qualified by a prefix that corresponds to a URI.

❑ The SAX API defines a simple event-driven mechanism for analyzing XML documents.

❑ A SAX parser is a program that parses an XML document and identifies each element in a document by calling a particular method in your program. The methods that are called are those defined by the SAX API.

Exercises

1. Write a program using SAX that will count the number of occurrences of each element type in an XML document and display them. The document file to be processed should be identified by the first command line argument.

2. Modify the program resulting from the previous exercise so that it will accept optional additional command line arguments that are the names of elements. When there are two or more command line arguments, the program should only count and report on the elements identified by the second and subsequent command line arguments.

Creating and Modifying XML Documents

In this chapter we will concentrate on understanding what we can do with the DOM API. As we outlined in the previous chapter, DOM uses a mechanism that is completely different to SAX. As well as providing an alternative mechanism for parsing XML documents, DOM also adds the capability for you to modify them and create new ones.

In this chapter you will learn:

❑   What a document object model is

❑   How you create a DOM parser

❑   How you access the contents of a document using DOM

❑   How you create and update a new XML document

❑   How to modify Sketcher to read and write sketches as XML documents

The Document Object Model (DOM)

As we saw in the previous chapter, a DOM parser presents you with an object encapsulating the entire XML structure. You can then call methods belonging to this object to navigate through the document tree and process the elements and attributes in the document in whatever way you want. This is quite different to SAX as we have already noted, but nonetheless there is quite a close relationship between DOM and SAX.

The mechanism for getting access to a DOM parser is very similar to what we used to obtain a SAX parser. You start with a factory object that you obtain like this:

```
DocumentBuilderFactory builderFactory = DocumentBuilderFactory.newInstance();
```

The `newInstance()` method is a `static` method in the factory class for creating factory objects. As with SAX, this approach of dynamically creating a factory object that you then use to create a parser allows you the change to parser you are using without modifying or recompiling your code. You use the factory object to create a `DocumentBuilder` object that encapsulates a DOM parser:

```
DocumentBuilder builder = null;
try {
  builder = builderFactory.newDocumentBuilder();
} catch(ParserConfigurationException e) {
  e.printStackTrace();
}
```

As we shall see, when a DOM parser reads an XML document, it makes it available in its entirety as an object of type `Document`. The name of the class that encapsulates a DOM parser has obviously been chosen to indicate that it can also build new `Document` objects. A DOM parser can throw exceptions of type `SAXException` and parsing errors are handled in essentially the same way in DOM and SAX2. The `DocumentBuilderFactory`, `DocumentBuilder`, and `ParserConfigurationException` classes are all defined in the `javax.xml.parsers` package. Let's jump straight in and try this out for real.

Try It Out – Creating an XML Document Builder

Here's the code to create a document builder object:

```
import javax.xml.parsers.DocumentBuilderFactory;
import javax.xml.parsers.DocumentBuilder;
import javax.xml.parsers.ParserConfigurationException;
import org.xml.sax.SAXException;

public class TryDOM {
  public static void main(String args[]) {
    DocumentBuilderFactory builderFactory = DocumentBuilderFactory.newInstance();
    DocumentBuilder builder = null;
    try {
      builder = builderFactory.newDocumentBuilder();
    }
    catch(ParserConfigurationException e) {
      e.printStackTrace();
      System.exit(1);
    }
    System.out.println("Builder Factory = " + builderFactory +"\nBuilder = "
                                            + builder);
  }
}
```

I got the output:

```
Builder Factory = org.apache.xerces.jaxp.DocumentBuilderFactoryImpl@430b5c
Builder = org.apache.xerces.jaxp.DocumentBuilderImpl@9ed927
```

1048

How It Works

The static `newInstance()` method in the `DocumentBuilderFactory` class returns a reference to a factory object. We call the `newDocumentBuilder()` method for the factory object to obtain a reference to a `DocumentBuilder` object that encapsulates a DOM parser. This will be the default parser. If we want the parser to validate the XML or provide other capabilities, we need to set the parser features before we create the `DocumentBuilder` object by calling methods for the `DocumentBuilderFactory` object.

You can see that we get a version of the Crimson parser as a DOM parser. Many DOM parsers are built on top of SAX parsers and this is the case with both the Crimson and Xerces parsers.

Setting DOM Parser Features

The idea of a feature for a DOM parser is the same as with SAX – a parser option that can be either on or off. The `DocumentBuilderFactory` object has the following methods for setting DOM parser features:

`setNamespaceAware(boolean aware)`	Calling this method with a `true` argument sets the parser to be namespace aware. The default setting is `false`.
`setValidating(boolean validating)`	Calling this method with a `true` argument sets the parser to validate the XML in a document as it is parsed. The default setting is `false`.
`setIgnoringElementContentWhitespace(` `boolean ignore)`	Calling this method with a `true` argument sets the parser to remove ignorable whitespace in element content so the `Document` object produced by a parser will not contain ignorable whitespace. The default setting is `false`.
`setIgnoringComments(boolean ignore)`	Calling this method with a `true` argument sets the parser to remove comments as the document is parsed. The default setting is `false`.
`setExpandEntityReferences(` `boolean expand)`	Calling this method with a `true` argument sets the parser to expand entity references. The default setting is `true`.
`setCoalescing(boolean coalesce)`	Calling this method with a `true` argument sets the parser to convert `CDATA` sections to text and append it to any adjacent text. The default setting is `false`.

As you see, by default the parser that is produced is neither namespace aware nor validating. We should at least set these two features before creating our parser. This is quite simple:

```
DocumentBuilderFactory builderFactory = DocumentBuilderFactory.newInstance();
builderFactory.setNamespaceAware(true);
builderFactory.setValidating(true);
```

If you add the shaded statements to the example, the `newDocumentBuilder()` method for the factory object should now return a validating and namespace aware parser. With a validating parser, we should define an `ErrorHandler` object that will deal with parsing errors. You identify the `ErrorHandler` object to the parser by calling the `setErrorHandler()` method for the `DocumentBuilder` object:

```
builder.setErrorHandler(handler);
```

Here `handler` refers to an object that implements the three methods declared in the `org.xml.sax.ErrorHandler` interface. We discussed these in the previous chapter in the context of SAX parser error handling, and the same applies here. If you do create a validating parser, you should implement and register an `ErrorHandler` object. Otherwise the parser may not work properly.

The factory object has methods to check the status of parser features corresponding to each of the `setXXX()` methods above. The checking methods all have corresponding names of the form `isXXX()`, so to check whether a parser will be namespace aware, you call the `isNamespaceAware()` method. Each method returns `true` if the parser to be created will have the feature set, and `false` otherwise.

Parsing a Document

Once you have created a `DocumentBuilder` object, you just call its `parse()` method with a document source as an argument to parse a document. The `parse()` method will return a reference of type `Document` to a object that encapsulates the entire XML document. The `Document` interface is defined in the `org.w3c.dom` package.

There are five overloaded versions of the `parse()` method that provide various options for you to identify the source of the XML document. They all return a reference to a `Document` object:

`parse(File file)`	Parses the document in the file identified by `file`.
`parse(String uri)`	Parses the document at the URI, `uri`.
`parse(InputSource source)`	Parses the document from `source`.
`parse(InputStream stream)`	Parses the document read from the input stream, `stream`.
`parse(InputStream stream, String systemID)`	Parses the document read from the input stream, `stream`. The second argument, `systemID`, is used to resolve relative URIs.

All five versions of the parse method can throw three types of exception. An exception of type `IllegalArgumentException` will be thrown if you pass `null` to the method for the parameter that identifies the document source. The method will throw an exception of type `IOException` if any I/O error occurs, and of type `SAXException` in the event of a parsing error. Both these last exceptions must be caught. Note that it is a `SAXException` that can be thrown here. Exceptions of type `DOMException` only arise when you are navigating the tree for a `Document` object.

You could `parse()` a document using the `DocumentBuilder` object, `builder`, like this:

```
File xmlFile = new File("D:/Beg Java Stuff/Address.xml");
Document xmlDoc = null;
  try {
    xmlDoc = builder.parse(xmlFile);
  }
    catch(SAXException e) {
    e.printStackTrace();
    System.exit(1);
  }
    catch(IOException e) {
    e.printStackTrace();
    System.exit(1);
  }
```

This code fragment requires imports for the `File` and `IOException` classes in the `java.io` package as well as the `org.w3c.dom.Document` class name. We can now call methods for the `xmlDoc` object to navigate through the elements in the document tree structure. Let's look at what the possibilities are.

Navigating a Document Object Tree

The `Node` interface that is defined in the `org.w3c.dom` package is fundamental to all objects that encapsulate components of an XML document, and this includes the `Document` object itself. The subinterfaces of `Node` that identify components of a document are:

`Element`	Represents an XML element.
`Attr`	Represents an attribute for an element.
`Text`	Represents text that is part of element content. This interface is a subinterface of `CharacterData`, which in turn is a subinterface of `Node`. References of type `Text` will therefore have methods from all three interfaces.
`CDATASection`	Represents a CDATA section – unparsed character data.
`Comment`	Represents a document comment. This interface also extends the `CharacterData` interface.
`DocumentType`	Represents the contents of a `DOCTYPE` declaration.
`Entity`	Represents an entity that may be parsed or unparsed.
`EntityReference`	Represents a reference to an entity.
`Notation`	Represents a notation declared in the DTD for a document. A notation is a definition of an unparsed entity type.
`ProcessingInstruction`	Represents a processing instruction for an application.

Each of these interfaces declares its own set of methods and inherits the method declared in the `Node` interface. Every XML document will be modeled as a hierarchy of nodes that will be accessible as one or other of the interface types in the table above. At the top of the node hierarchy for a document will be the `Document` node that is returned by the `parse()` method. Each type of node may or may not have child nodes in the document hierarchy, and those that do can only have certain types of child node. The types of nodes in a document that can have children are as follows:

Node Type	Possible Children
`Document`	`Element` (only 1), `DocumentType` (only 1), `Comment`, `ProcessingInstruction`
`Element`	`Element`, `Text`, `Comment`, `CDATASection`, `EntityReference`, `ProcessingInstruction`
`Attr`	`Text`, `EntityReference`
`Entity`	`Element`, `Text`, `Comment`, `CDATASection`, `EntityReference`, `ProcessingInstruction`
`EntityReference`	`Element`, `Text`, `Comment`, `CDATASection`, `EntityReference`, `ProcessingInstruction`

Of course, what each node may have as children follows from the XML specification, not just the DOM specification. There is one other type of node that extends the `Node` interface – `DocumentFragment`. This is not formally part of a document in the sense that a node of this type is a programming convenience. It is used to house a fragment of a document – a sub-tree of elements – for use when moving fragments of a document around, for instance, so it provides a similar function to a `Document` node but with less overhead. A `DocumentFragment` node can have the same range of child nodes as an `Element` node.

The starting point for exploring the entire document tree is the root element for the document. We can obtain a reference to an object that encapsulates the root element by calling the `getDocumentElement()` method for the `Document` object:

```
Element root = xmlDoc.getDocumentElement();
```

This method returns the root element for the document as type `Element`. You can also get the node corresponding to the `DOCTYPE` declaration as type `DocumentType` like this:

```
DocumentType doctype = xmlDoc.getDoctype();
```

The next step is to obtain the child nodes for the root element. We can use the `getChildNodes()` method that is defined in the `Node` interface for this. This method returns a `NodeList` reference that encapsulates all the child elements for that element. You can call this method for any node that has children, including the `Document` node if you wish. We can therefore obtain the child elements for the root element with the following statement:

```
NodeList children = root.getChildNodes();
```

A `NodeList` reference encapsulates an ordered collection of `Node` references, each of which may be one or other of the possible node types for the current node. So with an `Element` node, any of the `Node` references in the list that is returned can be of type `Element`, `Text`, `Comment`, `CDATASection`, `EntityReference`, or `ProcessingInstruction`. Note that if there are no child nodes, the `getChildNodes()` method will return a `NodeList` reference that is empty, not `null`. You call the `getChildNodes()` method to obtain a list of child nodes for any node type that can have them.

The `NodeList` interface declares just two methods:

`getLength()`	Returns the number of nodes in the list as type `int`.
`item(int index)`	Returns a reference of type `Node` to the object at position `index` in the list.

We can use these methods to iterate through the child elements of the root element, perhaps like this:

```
Node[] nodes = new Node[children.getLength()];
for(int i = 0 ; i<nodes.getLength() ; i++)
  nodes[i] = children.item(i);
```

Of course, we will normally be interested in the specific types of nodes that are returned so we will want to extract them as specific types or at least determine what they are before processing them. This is not difficult. You can test the type of any node using the `instanceof` operator. Here's one way we could extract just the child nodes that are of type `Element`:

```
java.util.Vector elements = new java.util.Vector();
Node node = null;
for(int i = 0 ; i<nodes.getLength() ; i++) {
  node = children.item(i);
if(node instanceof Element)
    elements.add(node);
}
```

A simple loop like this is not a very practical approach to navigating a document. In general we have no idea of the level to which elements are nested in a document and this loop only examines one level. We need an approach that will allow any level of nesting. This is a job for recursion. Let's put together a working example to illustrate this.

Try It Out – Listing a Document

We can extend the previous example to list the nodes in a document. We will add a `static` method to the `TryDOM` class to list child elements recursively. We will output details of each node followed by its children. Here's the code:

```
import javax.xml.parsers.*;
import org.xml.sax.*;
import org.w3c.dom.*;

import java.io.File;
```

```
import java.io.IOException;

public class TryDOM implements ErrorHandler {
  public static void main(String args[]) {
    if(args.length == 0) {
      System.out.println("No file to process."+
                             "Usage is:\njava TryDOM \"filename\"");

      System.exit(1);
    }
    File xmlFile = new File(args[0]);
    DocumentBuilderFactory builderFactory = DocumentBuilderFactory.newInstance();
    builderFactory.setNamespaceAware(true);          // Set namespace aware
    builderFactory.setValidating(true);              // and validating parser feaures

    DocumentBuilder builder = null;
    try {
      builder = builderFactory.newDocumentBuilder();  // Create the parser
      builder.setErrorHandler(new TryDOM()); //Error handler is instance of TryDOM

    } catch(ParserConfigurationException e) {
      e.printStackTrace();
      System.exit(1);
    }
    Document xmlDoc = null;

    try {
      xmlDoc = builder.parse(xmlFile);

    } catch(SAXException e) {
      e.printStackTrace();

    } catch(IOException e) {
      e.printStackTrace();
    }
    DocumentType doctype = xmlDoc.getDoctype();        // Get the DOCTYPE node
    System.out.println("DOCTYPE node:\n" + doctype);   // and output it
    System.out.println("\nDocument body contents are:");
    listNodes(xmlDoc.getDocumentElement(),"");            // Root element & children
  }

  // output a node and all its child nodes
  static void listNodes(Node node, String indent) {
    String nodeName = node.getNodeName();
    System.out.println(indent+nodeName+" Node, type is "
                                        +node.getClass().getName()+":");
    System.out.println(indent+" "+node);

    NodeList list = node.getChildNodes();        // Get the list of child nodes
    if(list.getLength() > 0) {                   // As long as there are some...
      System.out.println(indent+"Child Nodes of "+nodeName+" are:");
      for(int i = 0 ; i<list.getLength() ; i++) //...list them & their children...
        listNodes(list.item(i),indent+" ");      // by calling listNodes() for each
```

```
      }
   }

   public void fatalError(SAXParseException spe) throws SAXException {
      System.out.println("Fatal error at line "+spe.getLineNumber());
      System.out.println(spe.getMessage());
      throw spe;
   }

   public void warning(SAXParseException spe) {
      System.out.println("Warning at line "+spe.getLineNumber());
      System.out.println(spe.getMessage());
   }

   public void error(SAXParseException spe) {
      System.out.println("Error at line "+spe.getLineNumber());
      System.out.println(spe.getMessage());
   }
}
```

I have removed the statement outputting details of the parser to reduce the output a little. Run this with the version of `Address.xml` that includes a `DOCTYPE` declaration. The program produces quite a lot of output starting with:

```
DOCTYPE node:
org.apache.crimson.tree.Doctype@decdec

Document body contents are:
address Node, type is org.apache.crimson.tree.ElementNode2:
 <address>
  <buildingnumber> 29 </buildingnumber>
  <street> South Lasalle Street</street>
  <city>Chicago</city>
  <state>Illinois</state>
  <zip>60603</zip>
 /address>
Child Nodes of address are:
 #text Node, type is org.apache.crimson.tree.TextNode:


 buildingnumber Node, type is org.apache.crimson.tree.ElementNode2:
   <buildingnumber> 29 </buildingnumber>
 Child Nodes of buildingnumber are:
   #text Node, type is org.apache.crimson.tree.TextNode:
     29
 #text Node, type is org.apache.crimson.tree.TextNode:
```

and so on down to the last few lines:

```
 zip Node, type is org.apache.crimson.tree.ElementNode2:
   <zip>60603</zip>
```

1055

```
Child Nodes of zip are:
  #text Node, type is org.apache.crimson.tree.TextNode:
    60603
#text Node, type is org.apache.crimson.tree.TextNode:
```

How It Works

Since we have set the parser configuration in the factory object to include validating the XML, we have to provide an `org.xml.sax.ErrorHandler` object for the parser. The `TryDOM` class implements the `warning()`, `error()`, and `fatalError()` methods declared by the `ErrorHandler` interface so an instance of this class takes care of it.

We call the `getDoctype()` method for the `Document` object to obtain the node corresponding to the `DOCTYPE` declaration:

```
DocumentType doctype = xmlDoc.getDoctype();      // Get the DOCTYPE node
System.out.println("DOCTYPE node:\n" + doctype);  // and output it
```

You can see from the output that we only get the class name with a hash code for the object appended. We will see how we can get more detail a little later.

After outputting a header line showing where the document body starts, we output the contents starting with the root element. The `listNodes()` method does all the work. We pass a reference to the root element that we obtain from the `Document` object with the statement:

```
listNodes(xmlDoc.getDocumentElement(),"");        // Root element & children
```

The first argument to `listNodes()` is the node to be listed and the second argument is the current indent for output. On each recursive call of the method, we will append a couple of spaces. This will result in each nested level of nodes being indented in the output by two spaces relative to the parent node output.

The first step in the `listNodes()` method is to get the name of the current node by calling its `getNodeName()` method:

```
String nodeName = node.getNodeName();        // Get name of this node
```

We then output the name of the current node followed by its class name with the statement:

```
System.out.println(indent + nodeName + " Node, type is "
                   + node.getClass().getName()+":");
```

The `indent` parameter defines the indentation for the current node. Calling `getClass()` for the node object returns a `Class` object encapsulating its class type. We then call the `getName()` method for the `Class` object to obtain the class type name for the node.

The next statement outputs the node itself:

```
System.out.println(indent+" "+node);
```

This will automatically output the string produced by the `toString()` method for the node. Take a look at the output that corresponds to this as it is quite revealing. The node corresponding to the root element is first, and for this we get the entire document contents generated by the `toString()` method:

```
<address>
  <buildingnumber> 29 </buildingnumber>
  <street> South Lasalle Street</street>
  <city>Chicago</city>
  <state>Illinois</state>
  <zip>60603</zip>
</address>
```

On the basis of this, when you create a new `Document` object and want to write it as a document to a file, you might be tempted to use the `toString()` method for the root element to provide all the text for the document body. This would be unwise. It would work for this particular parser but you cannot be sure that another parser will do the same. There is no prescribed string returned by `toString()` so what you get will depend entirely on the parser and maybe on the particular release of the parser. When you want to write a document to a file, extract the data from the `Document` object and assemble the text yourself.

The remainder of the `listNodes()` code iterates through the child nodes of the current node if it has any:

```
NodeList list = node.getChildNodes();        // Get the list of child nodes
if(list.getLength() > 0) {                   // As long as there are some...
  System.out.println(indent+"Child Nodes of "+nodeName+" are:");
    for(int i = 0 ; i<list.getLength() ; i++) //...list them & their children...
      listNodes(list.item(i),indent+" ");    // by calling listNodes() for each
```

The `for` loop simply iterates through the list of child nodes obtained by calling the `getChildNodes()` method. Each child is passed as an argument to the `listNodes()` method, which will list the node and iterate through its children. In this way the method will work through all the nodes in the document. You can see that we append an extra couple of spaces to `indent` in the second argument to the `listNodes()` call for a child node. The `indent` parameter in the next level down will reference a string that is two spaces longer. This ensures that the output for the next level of nodes will be indented relative to the current node.

You can see from the output that the output produced by the `toString()` method for each node by the Crimson parser encompasses its child nodes too. Of course, we get all of them explicitly as nodes in their own right, so there is a lot of duplication in the output. You may have noticed that the output is strange in some ways. We seem to have picked up some extra `#text` nodes from somewhere that seem to contain just whitespace. Each block of text or whitespace is returned as a node with the name `#text`, and that includes ignorable whitespace here. The newline characters at the end of each line in the original document, for instance, will contribute text nodes that are ignorable whitespace.

If you don't want to see it, getting rid of the ignorable whitespace is very simple. We just need to set another parser feature in the factory object:

```
builderFactory.setNamespaceAware(true);              // Set namespace aware
builderFactory.setValidating(true);                  // and validating parser features
builderFactory.setIgnoringElementContentWhitespace(true);
```

Calling this method will result in a parser that will not report ignorable whitespace as a node, so you won't see it in the Document object. If you run the example again with this change, the #text nodes arising from ignorable whitespace will no longer be there. Of course, this is not necessarily a plus since now the output produced by the toString() method is not as readable as it was before because everything appears on a single line.

Node Types

We saw earlier that the subinterfaces of Node identify nodes of different types. Type Element corresponds to an element and type Text identifies element content that is text. We also saw how we could determine the type of a given Node reference using the instanceof operator. There's another way of figuring out what a Node reference is that is often more convenient. The getNodeType() method in the Node interface returns a value of type int that identifies the type of node. It can be any of the following constant values that are defined in the Node interface:

DOCUMENT_NODE	DOCUMENT_TYPE_NODE
ELEMENT_NODE	ATTRIBUTE_NODE
TEXT_NODE	CDATA_SECTION_NODE
DOCUMENT_FRAGMENT_NODE	COMMENT_NODE
ENTITY_NODE	ENTITY_REFERENCE_NODE
NOTATION_NODE	PROCESSING_INSTRUCTION_NODE

In the main it is obvious what type each of these represents. The DOCUMENT_FRAGMENT_NODE represents a collection of elements that form part of a document. The advantage of having the type of node as an integer is that we can sort out what type a given Node reference is by using a switch statement:

```
switch(node.getNodeType()) {
  case Node.DOCUMENT_NODE:
    // Code to process a document node
    break;
  case Node.DOCUMENT_TYPE_NODE:
    // Code to process a DOCTYPE node
    break;
  case Node.DOCUMENT_NODE:
    // Code to process a document node
    break;
  case Node.ELEMENT_NODE:
    // Code to process an element node
    break;
  // ... and so on for the rest of the type values...
  default:
    assert false;
}
```

We can include code to process any given node type following the corresponding case label.

There is also an alternative to using `getChildNodes()` for working through the children of a node. Calling the `getFirstChild()` method for a `Node` object returns a reference to its first child node, and the `getNextSibling()` method returns the next sibling node – the next node on the same level in other words. Both of these methods return `null` if the child requested does not exist. You can use these in combination to iterate through all the child nodes of a given node. We can illustrate how this works by writing a new version of our `listNodes()` method:

```
static void listNodes(Node node, String indent) {
  String nodeName = node.getNodeName();
  System.out.println(indent+nodeName+" Node, type is "
                                    +node.getClass().getName()+":");
  System.out.println(indent+" "+node);
  Node childNode = node.getFirstChild();        // Get first child
  while(childNode != null) {                     // While we have a child...
    listNodes(childNode, indent+"  ");           // ...list it, then...
    childNode = childNode.getNextSibling();      // ...get next child
  }
}
```

As long as `childNode` is not `null` the `while` loop will continue to execute. Within the loop we call `listNodes()` for the current child then store a reference to the next sibling node in `childNode`. Eventually `getNextSibling()` will return `null` when there are no more child nodes and the loop will end. You can plug this code back into the example if you want to see it in action.

Accessing Attributes

You will usually want to access the attributes for an element, but only if it has some. You can test whether an element has attributes by calling its `hasAttributes()` method. This will return `true` if the element has attributes and `false` otherwise, so you might use it like this:

```
if(node instanceof Element && node.has Attributes()) {
    // Process the element with its attributes

} else {
    // Process the element without attributes
}
```

The `getAttributes()` method for an element returns a `NamedNodeMap` reference that contains the attributes, the `NamedNodeMap` interface being defined in the `org.w3c.dom` package. In general, a `NamedNodeMap` object is a collection of `Node` references that can be accessed by name, or serially by iterating through the collection. Since the nodes are attributes in this instance, the nodes will actually be of type `Attr`.

The `NamedNodeMap` interface declares the following methods for retrieving nodes from the collection:

`item(int index)`	Returns the `Node` reference at index position `index`.
`getLength()`	Returns the number of `Node` references in the collection as type `int`.
`getNamedItem(String name)`	Returns the `Node` reference with the node name `name`.
`getNamedItemNS(String uri, String localName)`	Returns the `Node` reference with the name `localName` in the namespace at `uri`.

Obviously the last two methods apply when you know what attributes to expect. We can apply the first two methods to iterate through the collection of attributes in a `NamedNodeMap`:

```
if(node instanceof Element && node.hasAttributes()) {
  NamedNodeMap attrs = node.getAttributes();
  for(int i = 0 ; i<attrs.getLength() ; i++) {
      Attr attribute = (Attr)attrs.item(i); // Process the attribute...
  }

} else {   // Process the element without attributes
}
```

We now are in a position to obtain each of the attributes for an element as a reference of type `Attr`. To get at the attribute name and value we call the `getName()` and `getValue()` methods declared in the `Attr` interface respectively, both of which return a value of type `String`.

Try It Out – Listing Elements with Attributes

We can modify the `listNodes()` method in the previous example to include attributes with the elements. Here's the revised version:

```
static void listNodes(Node node) {
    String nodeName = node.getNodeName();
    System.out.println(indent+nodeName+" Node, type is "
                                        +node.getClass().getName()+":");
    System.out.println(indent+" "+node);

    if(node instanceof Element && node.hasAttributes()) {
      System.out.println(indent+"Element Attributes are:");
      NamedNodeMap attrs = node.getAttributes();//...get the attributes
      for(int i = 0 ; i<attrs.getLength() ; i++) {
        Attr attribute = (Attr)attrs.item(i);        // Get an attribute
        System.out.println(indent+attribute.getName()+"="+attribute.getValue());
      }
    }

    NodeList list = node.getChildNodes();       // Get the list of child nodes
    if(list.getLength() > 0) {                   // As long as there are some...
      System.out.println(indent+"Child Nodes of "+nodeName+" are:");
      for(int i = 0 ; i<list.getLength() ; i++)// ...list them & their children...
        listNodes(list.item(i),indent+"  ");    // by calling listNodes()
```

```
        }
    }
```

Don't forget to update the import statements in the example. The complete set will now be:

```
import javax.xml.parsers.DocumentBuilderFactory;
import javax.xml.parsers.DocumentBuilder;
import javax.xml.parsers.ParserConfigurationException;
import org.xml.sax.SAXException;
import org.xml.sax.SAXParseException;
import org.xml.sax.ErrorHandler;
import org.w3c.dom.Document;
import org.w3c.dom.DocumentType;
import org.w3c.dom.NodeList;
import org.w3c.dom.Node;
import org.w3c.dom.Element;
import org.w3c.dom.Attr;
import org.w3c.dom.NamedNodeMap;
import java.io.File;
import java.io.IOException;
```

You can recompile the code with these changes and run the example with the `circle with DTD.xml` file that we created back when we were discussing DTDs. You might want to comment out the call to `setIgnoringElementContentWhitespace()` to get the ignorable whitespace back in the output.

How It Works

All the new code to handle attributes is in the `listNodes()` method. After verifying that the current node is an `Element` node and does have attributes, we get the collection of attributes as a `NamedNodeMap` object. We then iterate through the collection extracting each node in turn. Nodes are indexed from zero and we obtain the number of nodes in the collection by calling its `getLength()` method. Since an attribute node is returned by the `item()` method as type `Node`, we have to cast the return value to type `Attr` to call the methods in this interface. We output the attribute and its value, making use of the `getName()` and `getValue()` methods for the `Attr` object in the process of assembling the output string.

The `Attr` interface also declares a `getSpecified()` method that returns `true` if the attribute value was explicitly set in the document rather than being a default value from the DTD. It also declares a `getOwnerElement()` method that returns an `Element` reference to the element to which this attribute applies.

You can see from the output that the `toString()` method for the root element node results in a string containing the entire document body, including the attributes.

Accessing the DOCTYPE Declaration

A node of type `DocumentType` encapsulates a `DOCTYPE` declaration and we have already obtained this in the example by calling the `getDoctype()` method for the `Document` object. The output we have obtained up to now is a little spartan so now we will remedy that. A `DOCTYPE` declaration is a little complicated as it may have an internal set of definitions, an external subset specified by a system ID, an external subset specified by public ID, or all three. We need to use the methods declared in the `DocumentType` interface to figure out what we have in any particular instance.

`getName()`	Returns the name of the DTD as a `String` object. This must be the same as the root node name if the document is to be valid.
`getSystemID()`	Returns a reference to a `String` object that contains the URI that is the system ID for the external subset.
`getPublicID()`	Returns a reference to a `String` object that contains the URI that is the public ID for the external subset.
`getInternalSubset()`	Returns a reference to a `String` object that contains the declarations in the internal subset. If there is no internal subset, the method returns `null`.
`getEntities()`	Returns a reference to a `NamedNodeMap` object that contains the general entities declared in the DTD. This will include general entities declared in both the internal and external subset but it does not include parameter entities. A general entity is an entity that is used within the document body. A parameter entity can only be used within the DTD.
`getNotations()`	Returns a reference to a `NamedNodeMap` object that contains the notations declared in the DTD. Notations are format declarations for external content such as images.

All these are quite straightforward. Let's see how we can use some of these to include DOCTYPE declarations in the output from the previous example.

Try It Out – Accessing Document Type Nodes

We identify the `DocumentType` node in our `main()` method but to avoid bulking `main()` up any further let's package the processing of a `DocumentType` node in another method, `getDoctypeString()`. This method will accept a `DocumentType` reference as an argument and return a complete DOCTYPE declaration as a `String` object. Here's the code for that:

```java
private static String getDoctypeString(DocumentType doctype) {
    // Create the opening string for the DOCTYPE declaration with its name
    String str = doctype.getName();
    StringBuffer doctypeStr = new StringBuffer("<!DOCTYPE ").append(str);

    // Check for a system ID or a public ID
    final char QUOTE = '\"';
    if((str = doctype.getSystemId()) != null)
      doctypeStr.append(" SYSTEM ").append(QUOTE).append(str).append(QUOTE);
    else if((str = doctype.getPublicId()) != null) // Check for a public ID
      doctypeStr.append(" PUBLIC ").append(QUOTE).append(str).append(QUOTE);

    // Check for an internal subset
    if((str = doctype.getInternalSubset()) != null)
      doctypeStr.append('[').append(str).append(']');

    return doctypeStr.append('>').toString();  // Append '>', return the string
  }
```

Now we can amend `main()` to call this method:

```
DocumentType doctype = xmlDoc.getDoctype();                    // Get DOCTYPE node
System.out.println("DOCTYPE node:\n" + getDoctypeString(doctype));  // & output it
```

Here we are replacing the output statement we had previously with this one that calls our new method.

You can try this out with the `circle with DTD.xml` file or maybe some other XML files with DTD declarations. At the time of writing, the version of Crimson that is distributed with SDK 1.4 does not return the internal subset when the `getInternalSubset()` method is called. If you want to see this output, try installing the Xerces parser. With Xerces 1.4.2 I got the output:

```
DOCTYPE node:
<!DOCTYPE circle[
<!ELEMENT circle (position)>
<!ELEMENT position EMPTY>
<!ATTLIST circle
 radius CDATA #REQUIRED
 >
<!ATTLIST position
 x CDATA #REQUIRED
  y CDATA #REQUIRED
  >
]>

Document body contents are:
circle Node, type is org.apache.xerces.dom.DeferredElementImpl:
 [circle: null]
Element Attributes are:
radius=15
Child Nodes of circle are:
#text Node, type is org.apache.xerces.dom.DeferredTextImpl:
[#text:
]
position Node, type is org.apache.xerces.dom.DeferredElementImpl:
[position: null]
Element Attributes are:
x=30
y=50
#text Node, type is org.apache.xerces.dom.DeferredTextImpl:
[#text:
]
```

You can see that the output from the `toString()` method for a node is rather different here from that produced by the Crimson parser.

How It Works

All the work is done in the `getDoctypeString()` method. It starts out by forming a basic string in a `StringBuffer` object:

```
        String str = doctype.getName();
        StringBuffer doctypeStr = new StringBuffer("<!DOCTYPE ").append(str);
```

This will produce a string of the form "`<!DOCTYPE rootname`". We can now append any further bits of the declaration to this string and close it off with a '`>`' character at the end.

We have defined the char constant, `QUOTE`, to make the code a little easier to read. We use this when we check for a system ID or a public ID:

```
        if((str = doctype.getSystemId()) != null)
          doctypeStr.append(" SYSTEM ").append(QUOTE).append(str).append(QUOTE);
        else if((str = doctype.getPublicId()) != null)  // Check for a public ID
          doctypeStr.append(" PUBLIC ").append(QUOTE).append(str).append(QUOTE);
```

This reuses the `str` variable to store the reference returned by the `getSystemID()` method. If this is not `null`, we append the `SYSTEM` keyword followed by the system ID itself, inserting the necessary spaces and double quotes at the appropriate points. Otherwise we look for a public ID and if it exists we append that to the string in a similar fashion.

Next we check for an internal subset of definitions:

```
        if((str = doctype.getInternalSubset()) != null)
          doctypeStr.append('[').append(str).append(']');
```

If there is an internal subset string we append that too, topped and tailed with square brackets. The final step is to append a closing '`>`' character and create a `String` object from the `StringBuffer` object before returning it.

```
        return doctypeStr.append('>').toString();   // Append '>' and return the string
```

I'll bet that was a whole lot easier than you expected. We will now put DOM into reverse and look into how we can synthesize XML documents.

Creating XML Documents

You can create an XML document in a file programmatically by a two-step process. You can first create a `Document` object that encapsulates what you want in your XML document. Then you can use the `Document` object to create the hierarchy of elements that has to be written to the file. We will first look at how we create a suitable `Document` object.

The simplest way to create a `Document` object programmatically is to call the `newDocument()` method for a `DocumentBuilder` object and it will return a reference to a new empty `Document` object:

```
        Document newDoc = builder.newDocument();
```

This is rather limited, especially since there's no way with DOM2 to modify the `DocumentType` node to reflect a suitable `DOCTYPE` declaration.

There's an alternative approach that provides a bit more flexibility but it is not quite so direct. You first call the `getDOMImplementation()` method for the `DocumentBuilder` object:

```
DOMImplementation domImpl = builder.getDOMImplementation();
```

This returns a reference of type `DOMImplementation` to an object that encapsulates the underlying DOM implementation. This interface type is defined in the `org.w3c.dom` package.

There are three methods you can call for a `DOMImplementation` object:

`createDocument(`
 	
`String namespaceURI,`
 	
`String qualifiedName,`
 	
`DocumentType doctype)`
	Creates a `Document` object with the root element having the name `qualifiedName` that is defined in the namespace specified by `namespaceURI`. The third argument specifies the `DOCTYPE` node to be added to the document. If you don't want to declare a `DOCTYPE`, then `doctype` can be specified as `null`.
	
	This method will throw an exception of type `DOMException` if the second argument is incorrect in some way.

`createDocumentType(`
 	
`String qualifiedName,`
 	
`String publicID,`
 	
`String systemID)`
	Creates a node of type `DocumentType` that represents a `DOCTYPE` declaration. The first argument is the qualified name of the root element, the second argument is the public ID of the external subset of the DTD, and the third argument is its system ID. This method will also throw an exception of type `DOMException` if the first argument contains an illegal character or is not of the correct form.

`hasFeature(String feature,`
 	
`String version)`
	Returns `true` if the DOM implementation has the feature with the name `feature`. The second argument specifies the DOM version number of the feature and can be either `"1.0"` or `"2.0"` with DOM level 2.

You can see from the first two methods here that there is a big advantage to using a `DOMImplementation` object to create a document. First of all, you can create a `DocumentType` object by calling the `createDocumentType()` method:

```
DocumentType doctype = null;
try {
  doctype = domImpl.createDocumentType("sketch", null, "sketcher.dtd");

} catch(DOMException e) {
  // Handle the exception
}
```

This code fragment creates a `DocumentType` node for an external `DOCTYPE` declaration with the name sketch, with the system ID sketcher.dtd. There is no public ID in this case since we specified the second argument as `null`. You can now use the `DocumentType` object in the creation of a document:

1065

```
Document newDoc = null;
try {
  doctype = domImpl.createDocumentType("sketch", null, "sketcher.dtd");
  newDoc = domImpl.createDocument(null, "sketch", doctype);
}
catch(DOMException e) {
  // Handle the exception
}
```

The DOMException object that may be thrown by either of these two methods has a public field with the name code that is of type int. This stores an error code identifying the type of error that caused the exception so you can check the value of code to determine the cause of the error. This exception can be thrown by a number of different methods that you use to create nodes in a document so the values that code can have is not limited to the two methods we have just used. There are fifteen possible values for code that are defined in the DOMException class but obviously you would only check for those that apply to the code in the try block where the exception may arise.

The possible values for code in a DOMException object thrown by the createDocument() method are:

INVALID_CHARACTER_ERR	The second argument specifying the root element name contains an invalid character.
NAMESPACE_ERR	The qualified name of the root element is malformed in some way, or the first argument specifying the namespace URI is null but the root element name has a prefix, or the qualified name of the root element has a prefix.
WRONG_DOCUMENT_ERR	The document does not support the DocumentType node specified.

The createDocumentType() method can also throw an exception of type DOMException with code set to either of the first two values above.

We therefore might code the catch block in the previous fragment like this:

```
catch(DOMException e) {
  switch(e.code) {
    case DOMException.INVALID_CHARACTER_ERR:
      System.err.println("Qualified name contains an invalid character");
      break;
    case DOMException.NAMESPACE_ERR:
      System.err.println("Qualified name is malformed or invalid");
      break;
    case DOMException.WRONG_DOCUMENT_ERR:
      System.err.println("Document does not support this doctype");
      break;
    default:
      assert false;
    System.err.println(e.getMessage());
  }
}
```

Of course, you can also output the stack trace, return from the method, or even end the program here if you want.

Adding to a Document

The Document interface declares methods for adding nodes to a Document object. You can create nodes encapsulating elements, attributes, text, entity references, comments, CDATA sections, and processing instructions so you can assemble a Document object representing a complete XML document. The methods declared by the Document interface are:

`createElement(String name)`	Returns a reference to an `Element` object encapsulating an element with `name` as the tag name. The method will throw an exception of type `DOMException` with `INVALID_CHARACTER_ERR` set if `name` contains an invalid character.

`createElementNS(`
 	
  `String nsURI,`
 	
  `String qualifiedName)`
	Returns a reference to an `Element` object encapsulating an element with `qualifiedName` as the tag name in the namespace `nsURI`. The method will throw an exception of type `DOMException` with `INVALID_CHARACTER_ERR` set if `qualifiedName` contains an invalid character or `NAMESPACE_ERR` if it has a prefix `"xml"` and `nsURI` is not `http://www.w3.org/XML/1998/namespace`.

`createAttribute(String name)`	Returns a reference to an `Attr` object encapsulating an attribute with `name` as the attribute name and its value as `" "`. The method will throw an exception of type `DOMException` with `INVALID_CHARACTER_ERR` set if `name` contains an invalid character.

`createAttribute(`
 	
  `String nsURI,`
 	
  `String qualifiedName)`
	Returns a reference to an `Attr` object encapsulating an attribute with `qualifiedName` as the attribute name in the namespace `nsURI` and its value as `" "`. The method will throw an exception of type `DOMException` with `INVALID_CHARACTER_ERR` set if the name contains an invalid character or `NAMESPACE_ERR` if the name conflicts with the namespace.

`createTextNode(String text)`	Returns a reference to a `Text` node containing the string `text`.
`createComment(String comment)`	Returns a reference to a `Comment` node containing the string `comment`.

`createCDATASection(String data)`	Returns a reference to a `CDATASection` node with the value `data`. Throws a `DOMException` if you try to create this node if the `Document` object encapsulates an HTML document.

`createEntityReference(`
 	
  `String name)`
	Returns a reference to an `EntityReference` node with the name specified. Throws a `DOMException` with the code `INVALID_CHARACTER_ERR` if name contains invalid characters and `NOT_SUPPORTED_ERR` if the `Document` object is an HTML document.

`createProcessingInstruction(`
 	
  `String target,`
 	
  `String name)`
	Returns a reference to a `ProcessingInstruction` node with the specified name and target. Throws a `DOMException` with the code `INVALID_CHARACTER_ERR` if `target` contains illegal characters and `NOT_SUPPORTED_ERR` if the `Document` object is an HTML document.

`createDocumentFragment()`	Creates an empty `DocumentFragment` object. You can insert a `DocumentFragment` object into a `Document` object using methods that the `Document` interface (and the `DocumentFragment` interface) inherits from the `Node` interface. You can use the same methods to insert nodes into a `DocumentFragment` object.

The references to HTML in the table above arise because a `Document` object can be used to encapsulate an HTML document. Our interest is purely XML so we won't be discussing this aspect further.

Of course, having a collection of nodes within a document does not define any structure. In order to establish the structure of a document you have to associate each attribute node that you have created with the appropriate element, and you must also make sure that each element other than the root is a child of some element. Along with all the other types of node, the `Element` interface inherits two methods from the `Node` interface that enable you to make one node a child of another:

`appendChild(` `Node child)`	Appends the node `child` to the end of the list of existing child nodes. This method throws a `DOMException` with the code `HIERARCHY_REQUEST_ERR` if the current node does not allow children, the code `WRONG_DOCUMENT_ERR` if child belongs to another document, or the code `NO_MODIFICATION_ALLOWED_ERR` if the current node is read-only.

`insertBefore(`
 	
  `Node child,`
 	
  `Node existing)`
	Insert `child` as a child node immediately before `existing` in the current list of child nodes. This method can throw `DOMException` with the same error codes as above, plus `NOT_FOUND_ERR` if `existing` is not a child of the current node.

The `Element` interface also declares four methods for adding attributes:

`setAttributeNode(`
 	
  `Attr attr)`
	Adds the node `attr` to the element. If an attribute node with the same name already exists, it will be replaced by `attr`. The method returns either a reference to an existing `Attr` node that has been replaced or `null`. The method can throw a `DOMException` with the following codes:
	
	`WRONG_DOCUMENT_ERR` if `attr` belongs to another document,
	
	`NO_MODIFICATION_ALLOWED_ERR` if the element is read-only,
	
	`INUSE_ATTRIBUTE_ERR` if `attr` already belongs to another element.

`setAttributeNodeNS(`
 	
  `Attr attr)`
	As above but applies to an element defined within a namespace.

`setAttribute(`
 	
  `String name,`
 	
  `String value)`
	Add a new attribute node with the specified `name` and `value`. If the attribute has already been added, its value is changed to `value`. The method can throw `DOMException` with the codes:
	
	`INVALID_CHARACTER_ERR` if `name` contains an illegal character,
	
	`NO_MODIFICATION_ALLOWED_ERR` if the element is read-only.

`setAttributeNS(`
 	
  `String nsURI,`
 	
  `String qualifiedName,`
 	
  `String value)`
	As above but with the attribute within the namespace `nsURI`. In addition this method can throw a `DOMException` with the code `NAMESPACE_ERR` if `qualifiedName` is invalid or not within the namespace.

Since we know enough about constructing a `Document` object to have a stab at putting together an object encapsulating a real XML document, let's have a stab at it.

Storing a Sketch as XML

We have already defined a DTD in the previous chapter that is suitable for defining a sketch. We can see how we can put together the code to store a sketch as an XML document instead of as a serialized object. Obviously we'll use the DTD we already have, and we can create a `Document` object with a `DocumentType` node via a `DOMImplementation` object from a `DocumentBuilder` object. We can do this with two statements in a `try` block:

```
Document doc = null;
try {
  DOMImplementation domImpl = DocumentBuilderFactory.newInstance()
```

```
                                                        .newDocumentBuilder()
                                                        .getDOMImplementation();
    doc = domImpl.createDocument(null, "sketch",
                    domImpl.createDocumentType("sketcher", null, "sketcher.dtd"));

} catch(ParserConfigurationException e) {
    e.printStackTrace(System.err);
    // Display the error and terminate the current activity...

} catch(DOMException e) {
    e.printStackTrace(System.err);
    // Determine the kind of error from the error code,
    // display the error, and terminate the current activity...
}
```

They are rather long statements since they accomplish in a single statement what we previously did in several steps. However, they are quite simple. The first statement creates a `DocumentBuilderFactory` object from which a `DocumentBuilder` object is created from which a reference `DOMImplementation` object is obtained and stored in `domImpl`. This is used in the next statement to create the `Document` object for a sketch and its `DocumentType` object defining the `DOCTYPE` declaration for `sketcher.dtd`. Eventually we will add this code to the `SketchModel` class but let's leave that to one side for the moment while we look at how we can fill out the detail of the `Document` object from the objects representing elements in a sketch.

A sketch in XML is a simple two-level structure. The root node in an XML representation of a sketch will be a `<sketch>` element, so to define the structure we only need to add an `Element` node to the content for the root node for each element in the sketch. A good way to implement this would be to add a method to each of the sketch `Element` classes that adds its own `org.w3c.dom.Element` node to the `Document` object. This will make each object representing a sketch element able to create its own XML representation.

The Sketcher classes we have to modify are the inner classes to the `Element` class, plus the `Element` class itself. The inner classes are `Element.Line`, `Element.Rectangle`, `Element.Circle`, `Element.Curve`, and `Element.Text`. The nodes that have to be added for each kind of geometric element derive directly from the declaration in the DTD, so it will help if you have this to hand while we go through these classes. If you typed it in when we discussed it in the last chapter, maybe you can print a copy.

Adding Element Nodes

Polymorphism is going to be a big help in this so let's first define an abstract method in the `Element` base class to add an element node to a document. We can add the declaration immediately after the declaration for the abstract `draw()` method, like this:

```
public abstract void draw(Graphics2D g2D);
public abstract void addElementNode(Document document);
```

Each of the inner classes will need to implement this method since they are derived from the `Element` class.

We will need a couple of `import` statement at the beginning of our `Element.java` file in Sketcher:

```
import org.w3c.dom.Document;
import org.w3c.dom.Attr;
```

Note that we definitely *don't* want to use the * notation to import all of the names from this package. If we do, we will get our sketcher Element class confused with the Element interface in the org.w3c.dom package. We are going to have to use qualified names wherever there is a potential clash.

The XML elements that we will create for geometric elements in a sketch will all need <position> and <color> elements as children. If we define methods in the base class Element, to create these, they will be inherited in each of the subclasses of Element Here's how we can define a method in the Element class to create a <color> element:

```
protected org.w3c.dom.Element createColorElement(Document doc) {
    org.w3c.dom.Element colorElement = doc.createElement("color");

    Attr attr = doc.createAttribute("R");
    attr.setValue(String.valueOf(color.getRed()));
    colorElement.setAttributeNode(attr);

    attr = doc.createAttribute("G");
    attr.setValue(String.valueOf(color.getGreen()));
    colorElement.setAttributeNode(attr);

    attr = doc.createAttribute("B");
    attr.setValue(String.valueOf(color.getBlue()));
    colorElement.setAttributeNode(attr);
    return colorElement;
}
```

The method for creating the node for a position element will use essentially the same process, but we have several nodes that represent points that are the same apart from their names. We can share the code by putting it into a method that we call with the appropriate type name:

```
protected org.w3c.dom.Element createPointTypeElement(Document doc,
                                          String name,
                                          String xValue,
                                          String yValue) {
    org.w3c.dom.Element element = doc.createElement(name);

    Attr attr = doc.createAttribute("x");        // Create attribute x
    attr.setValue(xValue);                       // and set its value
    element.setAttributeNode(attr);              // Insert the x attribute

    attr = doc.createAttribute("y");             // Create attribute y
    attr.setValue(yValue);                       // and set its value
    element.setAttributeNode(attr);              // Insert the y attribute
    return element;
}
```

This will create an element with the name specified by the second argument so we can use this in a method in the Element class to create a node for a <position> element:

```
    protected org.w3c.dom.Element createPositionElement(Document doc) {
      return createPointTypeElement(doc, "position",
                                    String.valueOf(position.getX()),
                                    String.valueOf(position.getY()));
    }
```

We will be able to create <endpoint>, <bottomright>, or <point> nodes in the same way in methods in the subclasses of Element.

Adding a Line Node

The method to add a <line> node to the Document object will create a <line> element with an angle attribute, and then add three child elements: <color>, <position>, and <endpoint>. You can add the following implementation of the addElementNode() method to the Element.Line class:

```
public void addElementNode(Document doc) {
  org.w3c.dom.Element lineElement = doc.createElement("line");

  // Create the angle attribute and attach it to the <line> node
  Attr attr = doc.createAttribute("angle");
  attr.setValue(String.valueOf(angle));
  lineElement.setAttributeNode(attr);

  // Append the <color>, <position>, and <endpoint> nodes as children
  lineElement.appendChild(createColorElement(doc));
  lineElement.appendChild(createPositionElement(doc));
  lineElement.appendChild(createEndpointElement(doc));

  // Append the <line> node to the document root node
  doc.getDocumentElement().appendChild(lineElement);
}
```

When we have a <Line> element in a sketch, calling this method with a reference to a Document object as an argument will add a child node corresponding to the <line> element. To complete this we must add the createEndpointElement() to the Element.Line class:

```
private org.w3c.dom.Element createEndpointElement(Document doc) {
  return createPointTypeElement(doc, "endpoint",
                                String.valueOf(line.x2+position.x),
                                String.valueOf(line.y2+position.y));
}
```

This calls the createPointTypeElement() method that is inherited from the base class. Since the position of a line is recorded in the base class and the end point of the line is relative to that point, we must add the coordinates of position in the base class to the coordinates of the end point of the line to get the original end point coordinates back.

Adding a Rectangle Node

The code to add a <rectangle> node to the Document object will be almost the same as adding a <line> node:

```
public void addElementNode(Document doc) {
  org.w3c.dom.Element rectElement = doc.createElement("rectangle");

  // Create the angle attribute and attach it to the <rectangle> node
  Attr attr = doc.createAttribute("angle");
  attr.setValue(String.valueOf(angle));
  rectElement.setAttributeNode(attr);

  // Append the <color>, <position>, and <bottomright> nodes as children
  rectElement.appendChild(createColorElement(doc));
  rectElement.appendChild(createPositionElement(doc));
  rectElement.appendChild(createBottomrightElement(doc));

  doc.getDocumentElement().appendChild(rectElement);
}
```

We also must define the `createBottomrightElement()` method in the `Element.Rectangle` class:

```
private org.w3c.dom.Element createBottomrightElement(Document doc) {
  return createPointTypeElement(doc, "bottomright",
                        String.valueOf(rectangle.width+position.x),
                        String.valueOf(rectangle.height+position.y));
}
```

A rectangle is defined relative to the origin so we have to adjust the coordinates of the bottom right corner by adding the corresponding `position` coordinates.

Adding a Circle Node

Creating the node for a `<circle>` element is not very different:

```
public void addElementNode(Document doc) {
  org.w3c.dom.Element circleElement = doc.createElement("circle");

  // Create the radius attribute and attach it to the <circle> node
  Attr attr = doc.createAttribute("radius");
  attr.setValue(String.valueOf(circle.width/2.0));
  circleElement.setAttributeNode(attr);

  // Create the angle attribute and attach it to the <circle> node
  attr = doc.createAttribute("angle");
  attr.setValue(String.valueOf(angle));
  circleElement.setAttributeNode(attr);

  // Append the <color> and <position> nodes as children
  circleElement.appendChild(createColorElement(doc));
  circleElement.appendChild(createPositionElement(doc));

  doc.getDocumentElement().appendChild(circleElement);
}
```

1073

There's nothing new here. We can use either the `width` or the `height` member of the `Ellipse2D.Double` class object to get the diameter of the circle. We divide the `width` field for the circle object by `2.0` to get the radius.

Adding a Curve Node

Creating a `<curve>` node is a bit more long-winded as a `GeneralPath` object represents a curve, and we have to extract the arbitrary number of defining points from it. The code that does this is more or less what we used in the `writeObject()` method for a curve so it is nothing new:

```java
public void addElementNode(Document doc) {
  org.w3c.dom.Element curveElement = doc.createElement("curve");

  // Create the angle attribute and attach it to the <curve> node
  Attr attr = doc.createAttribute("angle");
  attr.setValue(String.valueOf(angle));
  curveElement.setAttributeNode(attr);

  // Append the <color> and <position> nodes as children
  curveElement.appendChild(createColorElement(doc));
  curveElement.appendChild(createPositionElement(doc));

  // Get the defining points via a path iterator
  PathIterator iterator = curve.getPathIterator(new AffineTransform());
  int maxCoordCount = 6;                     // Maximum coordinates for a segment
  float[] temp = new float[maxCoordCount];        // Stores segment data

  int result = iterator.currentSegment(temp);     // Get first segment
  assert result == iterator.SEG_MOVETO;           // ... should be move to

  iterator.next();                                // Next segment
  while(!iterator.isDone())    {                   // While we have segments
    result = iterator.currentSegment(temp);       // Get the segment data
    assert result == iterator.SEG_LINETO;         // Should all be lines

    // Create a <point> node and add it to the list of children
    curveElement.appendChild(createPointTypeElement(doc, "point",
                       String.valueOf(temp[0]+position.x),
                       String.valueOf(temp[1]+position.y));
    iterator.next();                              // Go to next segment
  }

  doc.getDocumentElement().appendChild(curveElement);
}
```

We add one `<point>` node as a child of the `Element` node for a curve for each defining point after the first. Since the defining points for the `GeneralPath` object were created relative to the origin, we have to add the corresponding coordinates of position to the coordinates of each defining point.

Adding a Text Node

A text node is a little different and involves quite a lot of code. As well as the usual <color> and <position> child nodes, we also have to append a <font> node to define the font and a <string> node. The <font> node has three attributes that define the font name, the font style, and the point size. The <string> node has the text well as a <bounds> element that has two attributes defining the width and height of the text. Here's the code:

```java
public void addElementNode(Document doc) {
    org.w3c.dom.Element textElement = doc.createElement("text");

    // Create the angle attribute and attach it to the <text> node
    Attr attr = doc.createAttribute("angle");
    attr.setValue(String.valueOf(angle));
    textElement.setAttributeNode(attr);

    // Append the <color> and <position> nodes as children
    textElement.appendChild(createColorElement(doc));
    textElement.appendChild(createPositionElement(doc));

    // Create and apppend the <font> node
    org.w3c.dom.Element fontElement = doc.createElement("font");
    attr = doc.createAttribute("fontname");
    attr.setValue(font.getName());
    fontElement.setAttributeNode(attr);

    attr = doc.createAttribute("fontstyle");
    String style = null;
    int styleCode = font.getStyle();
    if(styleCode == Font.PLAIN)
      style = "plain";
    else if(styleCode == Font.BOLD)
      style = "bold";
    else if(styleCode == Font.ITALIC)
      style = "italic";
    else if(styleCode == Font.ITALIC+Font.BOLD)
        style = "bold-italic";
    assert style != null;
    attr.setValue(style);
    fontElement.setAttributeNode(attr);

    attr = doc.createAttribute("pointsize");
    attr.setValue(String.valueOf(font.getSize()));
    fontElement.setAttributeNode(attr);
    textElement.appendChild(fontElement);

    // Create the <string> node
    org.w3c.dom.Element string = doc.createElement("string");

    // Create the <bounds> node and its attributes
    org.w3c.dom.Element bounds = doc.createElement("bounds");
    attr = doc.createAttribute("width");
```

```
        attr.setValue(String.valueOf(this.bounds.width));
        bounds.setAttributeNode(attr);
        attr = doc.createAttribute("height");
        attr.setValue(String.valueOf(this.bounds.height));
        bounds.setAttributeNode(attr);
        string.appendChild(bounds);          // Set <bounds> element as <string> content

        string.appendChild(doc.createTextNode(text));
        textElement.appendChild(string);// Set <text> as <string> content
        doc.getDocumentElement().appendChild(textElement);
    }
```

Since the font style can be "plain", "bold", "bold-italic", or just "italic", we have a series of
if statement to determine the value for the attribute. The style is stored in a Font object as an integer
with different values for plain, bold, and italic. The values corresponding to bold and italic can be
combined, in which case the style is "bold-italic".

All the element objects in a sketch can now add their own node to a Document object. We should now
be able to make a SketchModel object use this capability to create a document that encapsulates the
entire sketch.

Creating a Document Object for a Complete Sketch

We can add a createDocument() method to the SketchModel class to create a Document object
and populate it with the nodes for the elements in the current sketch model. Creating the Document
object will use the code fragment we saw earlier. You need to add some import statements at the
beginning of the SketchModel.java source file for the new interfaces and classes we will be using:

```
import javax.swing.JOptionPane;
import javax.xml.parsers.*;
import org.w3c.dom.Document;
import org.w3c.dom.DOMImplementation;
import org.w3c.dom.DOMException;
```

Here's the method definition you can add to the class:

```
// Creates a DOM Document object encapsulating the current sketch
public Document createDocument() {
  Document doc = null;
  try {
    DOMImplementation domImpl = DocumentBuilderFactory.newInstance()
                                                 .newDocumentBuilder()
                                                 .getDOMImplementation();
    doc = domImpl.createDocument(null, "sketch",
                domImpl.createDocumentType("sketcher", null, "sketcher.dtd"));

  } catch(ParserConfigurationException e) {
    JOptionPane.showInternalMessageDialog(null,
                "Parser configuration error while creating document",
                "DOM Parser Error",
                JOptionPane.ERROR_MESSAGE);
```

```
        System.err.println(e.getMessage());
        e.printStackTrace(System.err);
        return null;

    } catch(DOMException e) {
      JOptionPane.showInternalMessageDialog(null,
                "DOM exception thrown while creating document",
                "DOM Error",
                JOptionPane.ERROR_MESSAGE);
        System.err.println(e.getMessage());
        e.printStackTrace(System.err);
        return null;
    }

    // Each element in the sketch can create its own node in the document
    Iterator iter = getIterator();                      // Iterator for sketch elements
    while(iter.hasNext())                               // For each element...
        ((Element)iter.next()).addElementNode(doc);     // ...add its node.
    return doc;
}
```

Now notice that this requires the DTD file for sketcher in the same folder as a saved sketch. In our case, we've made the default c:\sketches so a copy will need to be present there.

We now pop up a dialog and return null if something goes wrong when we are creating the Document object. In case of an exception of type DOMException being thrown, you could add a switch statement to analyze the value in the code member of the exception and provide a more specific message in the dialog.

The SketchModel object can now create a DOM Document object encapsulating the entire sketch. All we now need is some code to use this to write an XML file.

Saving a Sketch as XML

Of course, we could modify Sketcher so that it could save sketches either as objects or as XML, but to keep things simple we will add menu items to the File menu to export or import a sketch as XML. In broad terms, here's what we have to do to the SketchFrame class to save a sketch as an XML file:

❑   Add Import XML and Export XML menu items.

❑   Add XML ImportAction and XMLExportAction inner classes defining the Action types for the new menu items, either to save the current sketch as an XML file or to replace the current sketch by a new sketch created from an XML file.

❑   Implement the process of creating an XML document as text from the Document object created by the createDocument() method that we added to the SketchModel class.

❑   Implement writing the text for the XML document to a file.

By adding new `Action` classes for our two new menu items, we avoid cluttering up the existing `FileAction` class any further. Clearly, a lot of the work will be in the implementation of the new `Action` classes, so let's start with the easy bit – adding the new menu items to the File menu. First, we can add two new fields for the menu items by changing the existing definition in the `SketchFrame` class:

```
private FileAction newAction,  openAction,   closeAction,
                   saveAction, saveAsAction, printAction;
private XMLExportAction exportAction;   // Stores action for XML export menu item
private XMLImportAction importAction;   // Stores action for XML import menu item
```

These store the references to the `Action` objects for the new menu items.

We can add the menu items in the `SketchFrame` constructor, immediately following the menu separator definition that comes after the `saveAsAction` menu item:

```
addMenuItem(fileMenu, saveAction);
addMenuItem(fileMenu, saveAsAction);
fileMenu.addSeparator();                                  // Add separator
addMenuItem(fileMenu,
        exportAction = new XMLExportAction("Export XML",
                                    "Export sketch as an XML file"));
addMenuItem(fileMenu,
        importAction = new XMLImportAction("Import XML",
                                    "Import sketch from an XML file"));
fileMenu.addSeparator();                                  // Add separator
```

Now we can add code in the `SketchFrame` class for the two inner classes. We can define the `ExportAction` class within the `SketchFrame` class like this:

```
    class XMLExportAction extends AbstractAction {
      public XMLExportAction(String name, String tooltip) {
        super(name);
        if(tooltip != null)                        // If there is tooltip text
          putValue(SHORT_DESCRIPTION, tooltip);    // ...squirrel it away
      }

      public void actionPerformed(ActionEvent e) {
        JFileChooser chooser = new JFileChooser(DEFAULT_DIRECTORY);
        chooser.setDialogTitle("Export Sketch as XML");
        chooser.setApproveButtonText("Export");
        ExtensionFilter xmlFiles = new ExtensionFilter(".xml",
                                          "XML Sketch files (*.xml)");
        chooser.addChoosableFileFilter(xmlFiles);            // Add the filter
        chooser.setFileFilter(xmlFiles);                     // and select it
        int result = chooser.showDialog(SketchFrame.this, null); // Show dialog
        File file = null;
        if(chooser.showDialog(SketchFrame.this, null) == chooser.APPROVE_OPTION){
          file = chooser.getSelectedFile();
          if(file.exists()) {                           // Check file exists
            if(JOptionPane.NO_OPTION ==                 // Overwrite warning
```

```
                JOptionPane.showConfirmDialog(SketchFrame.this,
                            file.getName()+" exists. Overwrite?",
                            "Confirm Save As",
                            JOptionPane.YES_NO_OPTION,
                            JOptionPane.WARNING_MESSAGE))
          return;                                    // No overwrite
        }
        saveXMLSketch(file);
    }
  }
}
```

This is very similar to code that appears in the `FileAction` class. The constructor only provides for what we use – a menu item name plus a tooltip. If you want to have the option for an icon for use on a toolbar button, you can add that in the same way as for the `FileAction` constructors. The `actionPerformed()` method pops up a `CFFileChooser` dialog to enable the destination file for the XML to be selected. The chosen file is passed to a new method that we will put together, `saveXMLSketch()`, which will handle writing the XML document to the file.

We can define the `XMLImportAction` inner class like this:

```
class XMLImportAction extends AbstractAction {
  public XMLImportAction(String name, String tooltip) {
    super(name);
    if(tooltip != null)                        // If there is tooltip text
      putValue(SHORT_DESCRIPTION, tooltip);    // ...squirrel it away
  }

  public void actionPerformed(ActionEvent e) {
    JFileChooser chooser = new JFileChooser(DEFAULT_DIRECTORY);
    chooser.setDialogTitle("Import Sketch from XML");
    chooser.setApproveButtonText("Import");
    ExtensionFilter xmlFiles = new ExtensionFilter(".xml",
                                        "XML Sketch files (*.xml)");
    chooser.addChoosableFileFilter(xmlFiles);        // Add the filter
    chooser.setFileFilter(xmlFiles);                 // and select it
    int result = chooser.showDialog(SketchFrame.this, null);  // Show dialog
    if(chooser.showDialog(SketchFrame.this, null) == chooser.APPROVE_OPTION)
      openXMLSketch(chooser.getSelectedFile());
  }
}
```

This is more of the same but in the opposite direction as Stanley might have said. Once the name of the file to be imported has been identified in the `JFileChooser` dialog, we call `openXMLSketch()` to read the XML from the file and create the corresponding sketch.

Now we can go on to the slightly more difficult bits. We will start by looking at how we can write an XML document to a file, since we can't test the process for reading a sketch as XML until we have written some.

Writing the XML File

Before we start, let's add a few constants to our `Constants` interface in the Sketcher code:

```
String QUOTE_ENTITY = "&quot;";
char QUOTE = '\"';
char NEWLINE = '\n';
char TAG_START = '<';
char TAG_END = '>';
String EMPTY_TAG_END = "/>";
String END_TAG_START = "</";
```

We will standardize on using a double quote as a string delimiter in the XML that we will generate. We will therefore substitute the `QUOTE_ENTITY` constant for any double quotes that appear in the text for a Sketcher `Text` element. The other constants will come in useful when we are assembling XML markup.

We will make the `saveXMLSketch()` method a member of the `SketchFrame` class. This method will obtain a `FileChannel` object for the `File` object that is passed as an argument. The `FileChannel` object can then be used to write the XML to the file. Here's how we can define this method:

```
private void saveXMLSketch(File outFile) {
  FileOutputStream outputFile = null;       // Stores an output stream reference
  try {
    outputFile = new FileOutputStream(outFile);   · // Output stream for the file
    FileChannel outChannel = outputFile.getChannel(); // Channel for file stream
    writeXMLFile(theApp.getModel().createDocument(), outChannel);

  } catch(FileNotFoundException e) {
    e.printStackTrace(System.err);
    JOptionPane.showMessageDialog(SketchFrame.this,
                 "Sketch file " + outFile.getAbsolutePath() + " not found.",
                 "File Output Error",
                 JOptionPane.ERROR_MESSAGE);
    return;                                 // Serious error - return
  }
}
```

This calls another method that we have yet to write. The `writeXMLFile()` method will assemble the XML from the `Document` object passed as the first argument, and write that to the `FileChannel` referenced by the second argument.

We don't really expect to end up in the `catch` block. If we do, something is seriously wrong somewhere. Don't forget to import the `FileChannel` class name. The `import` statement you must add to `SketchFrame` is:

```
import java.nio.channels.FileChannel;
```

The DOM `Document` object provides no convenient way to get a complete XML document as a string or series of strings. The `toString()` method for a `Node` object looked hopeful in this respect – at least for the Crimson parser, but we saw that what the `toString()` method produced depended on the parser so we can't rely on that. The only way is for us to slog it out for ourselves. Our `writeXMLFile()` method will have to navigate the `Document` object and its nodes in order to create all the well-formed and valid XML that has to be written to the file to form a complete XML document.

Creating an XML document won't be difficult. We already know how to navigate a `Document` object and write the nodes to the command line. We did that in an example a few pages back. We will need to make sure the code we use here writes everything we need to produce well-formed XML but it will be essentially the same as what we have seen. The only difference here is that we are writing to a file channel rather than the command line but that should not be any trouble since we know how to do that, too. If we take a little care in the appearance of the XML, we should be able to end up with an XML file defining a sketch that is reasonably readable.

Since we want to be able to look at the XML file for a sketch in an editor, we will write is as the 8-bit Unicode subset `UTF-8`. With all that knowledge and experience, we can implement `writeXMLFile()` in the `SketchFrame` class like this:

```
private void writeXMLFile(org.w3c.dom.Document doc, FileChannel channel) {
  StringBuffer xmlDoc = new StringBuffer(
                          "<?xml version=\"1.0\" encoding=\"UTF-8\"?>");
  xmlDoc.append(NEWLINE).append(getDoctypeString(doc.getDoctype()));
  xmlDoc.append(getDocumentNode(doc.getDocumentElement(), ""));

  try {
    channel.write(ByteBuffer.wrap(xmlDoc.toString().getBytes("UTF-8")));

  } catch(UnsupportedEncodingException e) {
    System.out.println(e.getMessage());

  } catch(IOException e) {
    JOptionPane.showMessageDialog(SketchFrame.this,
                                "Error writing XML to channel.",
                                  "File Output Error",
                                  JOptionPane.ERROR_MESSAGE);
    e.printStackTrace(System.err);
    return;
  }
}
```

Initially we create a `StringBuffer` object that will eventually contain the entire XML document. It starts out initialized with the XML declaration and we append the text corresponding to the `DOCTYPE` declaration. We use the `getDoctypeString()` method to generate this and this method will be virtually identical to the method of the same name from the example earlier in this chapter, as we shall see in a moment. This method accepts an argument of type `DocumentType`, assembles a complete `DOCTYPE` delcaration from that, and returns it as type `String`. This is appended to `xmlDoc` following a newline character that will start the declaration on a new line.

We introduce another new method in the code for the `writeXMLFile()` method in the statement:

```
xmlDoc.append(getDocumentNode(doc.getDocumentElement(), ""));
```

This is for good reason. We will need a recursive method to navigate the nodes in the `Document` object that represent the body of the document and create the XML for that. The string that is returned will be the entire document body, so once we have appended this to `xmlDoc` we have the complete document. We will implement the `getDocumentNode()` method shortly.

The other statement deserving some explanation is the one in the `try` block that writes the complete document to the file:

```
channel.write(ByteBuffer.wrap(xmlDoc.toString().getBytes("UTF-8")));
```

Starting from the inside, and working outwards: Calling the `toString()` method for `xmlDoc` returns the contents as type `String`. We then call the `getBytes()` method for the `String` object to obtain an array of type `byte[]` containing the contents of the `String` object encoded as UTF-8. We then call the static `wrap()` method in the `ByteBuffer` class (that will need importing) to create a `ByteBuffer` object that wraps the array. The buffer that is returned has its limit and position set ready for the buffer contents to be written to a file. We can therefore pass this `ByteBuffer` object directly to the `write()` method for the `FileChannel` object to write the contents of the buffer, which will be the entire XML document, to the file. How's that for a powerful statement.

The code for the `getDoctypeString()` method will be:

```
private String getDoctypeString(org.w3c.dom.DocumentType doctype) {
    // Create the opening string for the DOCTYPE declaration with its name
    String str = doctype.getName();
    StringBuffer doctypeStr = new StringBuffer("<!DOCTYPE ").append(str);

    // Check for a system ID
    if((str = doctype.getSystemId()) != null)
      doctypeStr.append(" SYSTEM ").append(QUOTE).append(str).append(QUOTE);

    // Check for a public ID
    if((str = doctype.getPublicId()) != null)
      doctypeStr.append(" PUBLIC ").append(QUOTE).append(str).append(QUOTE);

    // Check for an internal subset
    if((str = doctype.getInternalSubset()) != null)
      doctypeStr.append('[').append(str).append(']');

    return doctypeStr.append(TAG_END).toString();  // Append '>' & return string
}
```

This is almost identical to the method as implemented in our previous example.

Creating XML for the Document Body

The recursive `getDocumentNode()` method to assemble the XML for the document body is a little more work than the others but it will work much like the method we wrote earlier to list nodes in a document. The method will find out the specific type of the current node then append the appropriate XML string to a `StringBuffer` object. If the current node has child nodes, the method will call itself to deal with each of these nodes. We can implement the `writeDocumentNode()` method like this:

```
private String getDocumentNode(Node node, String indent) {
  StringBuffer nodeStr = new StringBuffer().append(NEWLINE).append(indent);
  String nodeName = node.getNodeName();        // Get name of this node

  switch(node.getNodeType()) {
    case Node.ELEMENT_NODE:
    nodeStr.append(TAG_START);
    nodeStr.append(nodeName);
    if(node.hasAttributes()) {                   // If the element has attributes...
      org.w3c.dom.NamedNodeMap attrs = node.getAttributes();   // ...get them
      for(int i = 0 ; i<attrs.getLength() ; i++) {
        org.w3c.dom.Attr attribute = (org.w3c.dom.Attr)attrs.item(i);
        // Append " name="value" to the element string
        nodeStr.append(' ').append(attribute.getName()).append('=')
                .append(QUOTE).append(attribute.getValue()).append(QUOTE);

      }
    }
    if(!node.hasChildNodes()) {             // Check for no children for this element
      nodeStr.append(EMPTY_TAG_END);        // There are none-close as empty element
      return nodeStr.toString();            // and return the completed element

    } else {                                // It has children
      nodeStr.append(TAG_END);              // so close start-tag
      NodeList list = node.getChildNodes();      // Get the list of child nodes
      assert list.getLength()>0;                 // There must be at least one

      // Append child nodes and their children...
      for(int i = 0 ; i<list.getLength() ; i++)
        nodeStr.append(getDocumentNode(list.item(i), indent+" "));
    }
    nodeStr.append(NEWLINE).append(indent).append(END_TAG_START)
                          .append(nodeName).append(TAG_END);

    break;

    case Node.TEXT_NODE:
    nodeStr.append(replaceQuotes(((org.w3c.dom.Text)node).getData()));
    break;

    default:
    assert false;
  }
  return nodeStr.toString();
}
```

We start out by creating the `StringBuffer` object and appending a newline and the indent to it to make each element start on a new line. This should result in a document we can read comfortably in a text editor.

After saving the name of the current node in `nodeName`, we determine what kind of node we are dealing with in the `switch` statement. We could have used the `instanceof` operator and `if` statements to do this but here there's a chance to try out the alternative approach that we discussed earlier. We only identify two cases in the switch, corresponding to the constants `Node.ELEMENT_NODE` and `Node.TEXT_NODE`. This is because our DTD for Sketcher doesn't provide for any others so we don't expect to find them.

For a node that is an element we begin appending the start tag for the element, including the element name. We then check for the presence of attributes for this element. If there are some, we get them as a `NamedNodeMap` object in the same manner as our earlier example. We then just iterate through the collection of attributes and build the text that corresponds to each, appending the text to the `StringBuffer` object `nodeStr`.

Once we have finished with the attributes for the current node, we determine whether it has child nodes. If it has no child nodes, it has no content, so we can complete the tag for the current node making it an empty element. Since the element is now complete we can return it as a `String`. If the current element has child nodes we obtain those in a `NodeList` object. We then iterate through the nodes in the `NodeList` and call `getDocumentNode()` for each with an extra space appended to `indent`. The `String` that is returned for each call is appended to `nodeStr`. When all the child nodes have been processed we are done so we can exit the switch and return the contents of `nodeStr` as a `String`.

The other possibility is that the current node is text. This will arise from an `Element.Text` object in the sketch. It is also possible that this text may contain double quotes – the delimiter that we are using for strings in our XML. We therefore call `replaceQuotes()` to replace all occurrence of `QUOTE` in the text with the `QUOTE_ENTITY` constant that we defined in our `Constants` interface, before appending the string to `nodeStr`.

We can implement the `replaceQuotes()` method in `SketchFrame` as:

```
public String replaceQuotes(String str) {
  StringBuffer buf = new StringBuffer();
  for(int i = 0 ; i<str.length() ; i++)
    if(str.charAt(i)==QUOTE)
      buf.append(QUOTE_ENTITY);
    else
      buf.append(str.charAt(i));

  return buf.toString();
}
```

This just tests each character in the original string. If it's a delimiter for an attribute value, it's replaced by the entity reference `&quot;` in the output string `buf`.

Well, we are done – almost. We must not forget the extra `import` statements we need in the `SketchFrame.java` file:

```
import java.nio.ByteBuffer;
import java.nio.channels.FileChannel;
import org.w3c.dom.Node;
import org.w3c.dom.NodeList;
```

These cover the new classes that we used in our new code for I/O and for DOM without using fully qualified names.

Try It Out – Writing a Sketch as XML

Recompile sketcher with the new code. Once you have fixed any errors you can run Sketcher and export your sketch as XML. You can then inspect the file in your editor. You can also process the file with our `TryDOM` and `TrySAX` programs to check that the XML is valid.

How It Works

We have been through the detailed mechanics of this. The `SketchModel` object creates a `Document` object that is populated by nodes encapsulating the sketch elements. Each node is created by the corresponding sketch element. We then navigate through the nodes in the document to create the XML for each node.

We can now have a go at importing an XML sketch.

Reading an XML Representation of a Sketch

The Import XML operation will also be implemented in the `SketchFrame` class. We have already added the menu item and the `XMLImportAction` class that is used to create it. We just need to implement the `openXMLSketch()` method that is called by the `actionPerformed()` method in the `XMLImportAction` class.

Assuming our XML representation of a sketch is well-formed and valid, creating a `Document` object encapsulating a sketch will be a piece of cake. We will just get a DOM parser to do it – and it will verify that the document is well-formed and valid along the way. We will need an `ErrorHandler` object to deal with parsing errors, so let's add an inner class to our `SketchFrame` class for that:

```
class DOMErrorHandler implements org.xml.sax.ErrorHandler {
  public void fatalError(org.xml.sax.SAXParseException spe)
     throws org.xml.sax.SAXException {
    JOptionPane.showMessageDialog(SketchFrame.this,
                          "Fatal error at line "+spe.getLineNumber()
                      + "\n"+spe.getMessage(),
                          "DOM Parser Error",
                          JOptionPane.ERROR_MESSAGE);
    throw spe;
  }

  public void warning(org.xml.sax.SAXParseException spe) {
    JOptionPane.showMessageDialog(SketchFrame.this,
                          "Warning at line "+spe.getLineNumber()
                      + "\n"+spe.getMessage(),
                          "DOM Parser Error",
```

```
                                         JOptionPane.ERROR_MESSAGE);
    }

    public void error(org.xml.sax.SAXParseException spe) {
      JOptionPane.showMessageDialog(SketchFrame.this,
                                    "Error at line "+spe.getLineNumber()
                                  + "\n"+spe.getMessage(),
                                    "DOM Parser Error",
                                    JOptionPane.ERROR_MESSAGE);

    }
  }
```

This implements the three methods declared in the `ErrorHandler` interface. In contrast to our previous example using a DOM error handler, rather than writing error information to the command line, here we display it in a suitable dialog.

Here's how we can implement the `openXMLSketch()` method in the `SketchFrame` class:

```
private void openXMLSketch(File xmlFile) {
  DocumentBuilderFactory builderFactory = DocumentBuilderFactory.newInstance();
  builderFactory.setValidating(true);           // Add validating parser feature
  builderFactory.setIgnoringElementContentWhitespace(true);

  try {
    DocumentBuilder builder = builderFactory.newDocumentBuilder();
    builder.setErrorHandler(new DOMErrorHandler());
    checkForSave();
    theApp.insertModel(createSketchModel(builder.parse(xmlFile)));
    filename = xmlFile.getName();             // Update the file name
    setTitle(frameTitle+xmlFile.getPath());   // Change the window title
    sketchChanged = false;                     // Status is unchanged

  } catch(ParserConfigurationException e) {
    JOptionPane.showMessageDialog(SketchFrame.this,
                                  e.getMessage(),
                                  "DOM Parser Factory Error",
                                  JOptionPane.ERROR_MESSAGE);
    e.printStackTrace(System.err);

  } catch(org.xml.sax.SAXException e) {
    JOptionPane.showMessageDialog(SketchFrame.this,
                                  e.getMessage(),
                                  "DOM Parser Error",
                                  JOptionPane.ERROR_MESSAGE);
    e.printStackTrace(System.err);

  } catch(IOException e) {
    JOptionPane.showMessageDialog(SketchFrame.this,
                                  e.getMessage(),
                                  "I/O Error",
```

```
                                              JOptionPane.ERROR_MESSAGE);
      e.printStackTrace();
    }
  }
}
```

Most of the code here is devoted to catching exceptions that we hope will not get thrown. We set up the parser factory object to produce a validating parser that will ignore surplus whitespace. The latter feature will avoid extraneous nodes in the `Document` object that will be created by the parser from the XML file.

After storing a reference to the DOM parser that is created in `builder`, we create a `DOMErrorHandler` object and set that as the handler for any parsing errors that arise. If the parser finds any errors, we will see a dialog displayed indicating what the error is. We use the `builder` object to parse the XML file that is identified by the `File` object, `xmlFile` and pass the `Document` object that is returned by the `parse()` method to the `createSketchModel()` method that we will be adding to the `SketchFrame` class next. This method has the job of creating a new `SketchModel` object from the `Document` object.

Let's see how we can create a new `SketchModel` object encapsulating a new sketch by analyzing the `Document` object.

Creating the Model

We know that a sketch in XML is a two-level structure. There is a root element, `<sketch>`, that contains one XML element for each of the elements in the original sketch. Therefore to recreate the sketch, we just need to extract the children of the root node in the `Document` object and then figure out what kind of sketch element each child represents. Whatever it is, we want to create a sketch element object of that type and add it to a model. The simplest way to create sketch element objects from a given document node is to add a constructor to each of the classes that define sketch elements. We will add these constructors after we have defined the `createSketchModel()` method in the `SketchFrame` class. Here's the code for that:

```
private SketchModel createSketchModel(org.w3c.dom.Document doc) {
  SketchModel model = new SketchModel();                      // The new model object

  // Get the first child of the root node
  org.w3c.dom.Node node = doc.getDocumentElement().getFirstChild();

  // Starting with the first child, check out each child in turn
  while (node != null) {
    assert node instanceof org.w3c.dom.Element;               // Should all be Elements

    String name = ((org.w3c.dom.Element)node).getTagName();   // Get the name

    if(name.equals("line"))                                   // Check for a line
      model.add(new Element.Line((org.w3c.dom.Element)node));

    else if(name.equals("rectangle"))                         // Check for a rectangle
      model.add(new Element.Rectangle((org.w3c.dom.Element)node));

    else if(name.equals("circle"))                            // Check for a circle
```

1087

```
        model.add(new Element.Circle((org.w3c.dom.Element)node));

    else if(name.equals("curve"))                          // Check for a curve
        model.add(new Element.Curve((org.w3c.dom.Element)node));

    else if(name.equals("text"))                           // Check for a text
        model.add(new Element.Text((org.w3c.dom.Element)node));

    node = node.getNextSibling();                          // Next child node
  }
    return model;
}
```

This works in a straightforward fashion. We get the first child node of the root node by calling `getDocumentElement()` for the document object to obtain a reference to the `org.w3c.dom.Element` object that encapsulates the root node, then call its `getFirstChild()` method to obtain a reference of type `Node` to its first child. All the children of the root element should be `Element` nodes, and the assertion verifies this.

We determine what kind of element each child node is by checking its name. We call a sketch `Element` constructor corresponding to the node name to create the sketch element to be added to the model. Each of these constructors creates an object from the `org.w3c.dom.Element` object reference that is passed as the argument. We just have to implement these constructors in the subclasses of `Element` and we are done.

Creating Sketch Elements from XML Elements

Every element has to have the `color` field in the base class set to a color determined from a `<color>` element in the document. We can therefore usefully add a base class method to take care of this. Add the following to the `Element` class definition:

```
protected void setElementColor(org.w3c.dom.Element colorElement) {
    color = new Color(Integer.parseInt(colorElement.getAttribute("R")),
                      Integer.parseInt(colorElement.getAttribute("G")),
                      Integer.parseInt(colorElement.getAttribute("B")));
}
```

The method expects to receive a reference to an `org.w3c.dom.Element` object as an argument that contains the RGB values for the color. We extract the value of each of the attributes in the `colorElement` object by calling its `getAttribute()` method with the attribute name as the argument. We pass each of the values obtained to the `Color` constructor and we store the reference to this object in `color`. Because the attribute values are strings, we have to convert them to numerical values using the static `parseInt()` method that is defined in the `Integer` class.

The same applies to the position field in the `Element` class, so we will define a method in the `Element` class to initialize it from an `org.w3c.dom.Element` object:

```
protected void setElementPosition(org.w3c.dom.Element posElement) {
    position = new Point();
    position.setLocation(Double.parseDouble(posElement.getAttribute("x")),
                         Double.parseDouble(posElement.getAttribute("y")));
}
```

This uses essentially the same mechanism as the previous method. Here the attributes strings represent `double` values so we use the static `parseDouble()` method from the `Double` class to convert them to the numeric equivalent.

Every sketcher element has a color, a position, and an angle that are stored in base class fields so we can create a base class constructor to initialize these from the document node for the element:

```
protected Element(org.w3c.dom.Element xmlElement) {
  // Get the <color> element
  org.w3c.dom.NodeList list = xmlElement.getElementsByTagName("color");
  setElementColor((org.w3c.dom.Element)list.item(0));        // Set the color

  list = xmlElement.getElementsByTagName("position");        // Get <position>
  setElementPosition((org.w3c.dom.Element)list.item(0));     // Set the position

  angle = Double.parseDouble(xmlElement.getAttribute("angle")); // Set the angle
}
```

We have declared this constructor as `protected` to prevent the possibility of it being called externally. Every one of our new constructors in the inner classes to `Element` will call this constructor first. An important point to remember is that if a constructor for a derived class object does not call a base class constructor as the first statement in the body of the constructor, the compiler will insert a call to the no-arg constructor for the base class. This means that a base class always has to have a no-arg constructor if the derived class constructors do not call a base class constructor with arguments.

We first extract the child element for the current element with the name `"color"` by calling the `getElementsByTagName()` method for `xmlElement`. This method, declared in the `org.w3c.dom.Element` interface, returns a `NodeList` object containing all the child nodes with the given name. If you pass the string `"*"` as the argument to this method, it will return all child `org.w3c.dom.Element` objects in the node list. There's another method, `getElementsByTagNameNS()`, that is declared in the `Element` interface that does the same for documents using namespaces. The first argument in this case is the namespace URI and the second argument is the element name. The strings to either or both arguments can be `"*"`, in which case all namespaces and/or names will be matched.

We pass the reference to the element with the name `"color"` to the `setElementColor()` method that is inherited from the base class. This sets the value of the `color` field in the base class.

Next we initialize the `position` field in the `Element` class by calling the `setElementPosition()` method. The process is much the same as for the `color` field. Lastly we set the `angle` field by converting the string that is the value for the angle attribute for the current node to type `double`.

Now we are ready to add the new constructors to the subclasses to create sketch elements from XML elements.

Creating a Line Element

We can construct an `Element.Line` object by first calling the base class constructor we have just defined to set the `color`, `position`, and `angle` fields, and then setting the `line` field in the derived class. Here's the code for the constructor:

```
    // Content is <color>, <position>, <endpoint> elements. Attribute is angle.
  public Line(org.w3c.dom.Element xmlElement) {
    super(xmlElement);

    org.w3c.dom.NodeList list = xmlElement.getElementsByTagName("endpoint");
    org.w3c.dom.Element endpoint = (org.w3c.dom.Element)list.item(0);
    line = new Line2D.Double(origin.x, origin.y,
              Double.parseDouble(endpoint.getAttribute("x"))-position.getX(),
              Double.parseDouble(endpoint.getAttribute("y"))-position.getY());
  }
```

To save having to refer back to the DTD, the first comment in the constructor outlines the XML corresponding to the element. We first call the base class constructor and then extract the child element that is the <endpoint> element. You will doubtless recall that all our sketch elements are defined at the origin. This makes moving an element very easy and allows all elements to be moved in the same way – by modifying the position field. We therefore create the Line2D.Double object as a line starting at the origin. The coordinates of its end point are the values stored in the <endpoint> child element minus the corresponding coordinates of position that were set in the base class constructor.

Creating a Rectangle Element

This constructor will be almost identical to the previous constructor for a line:

```
    // Rectangle has angle attribute. Content is <color>,<position>,<bottomright>
  public Rectangle(org.w3c.dom.Element xmlElement) {
    super(xmlElement);

    org.w3c.dom.NodeList list = xmlElement.getElementsByTagName("bottomright");
    org.w3c.dom.Element bottomright = (org.w3c.dom.Element)list.item(0);
    rectangle = new Rectangle2D.Double(origin.x, origin.y,
          Double.parseDouble(bottomright.getAttribute("x"))-position.getX(),
          Double.parseDouble(bottomright.getAttribute("y"))-position.getY());
  }
```

Spot the differences! This code is so similar to that of the Line constructor that I don't think it requires further explanation.

Creating a Circle Element

Here's the code for the Circle constructor:

```
    // Circle has radius, angle attributes. Content is <color>, <position>
  public Circle(org.w3c.dom.Element xmlElement) {
    super(xmlElement);

    double radius = Double.parseDouble(xmlElement.getAttribute("radius"));
    circle = new Ellipse2D.Double(origin.x, origin.y,     // Position - top-left
                          2.*radius, 2.*radius );  // Width & height
  }
```

Compared to the previous two constructors the only change is the last bit where we use the `radius` attribute value to define the `Ellipse2D.Double` object representing the circle.

Creating a Curve Element

Before you nod off, this one's a little more challenging as there may be an arbitrary number of child nodes:

```
// Curve has angle attribute. Content is <color>, <position>, <point>+
public Curve(org.w3c.dom.Element xmlElement) {
  super(xmlElement);

  curve = new GeneralPath();
  curve.moveTo(origin.x, origin.y);
  org.w3c.dom.NodeList nodes = xmlElement.getElementsByTagName("point");
  for(int i = 0 ; i<nodes.getLength() ; i++)
    curve.lineTo(
                 (float)(Double.parseDouble(
        ((org.w3c.dom.Element)nodes.item(i)).getAttribute("x")) - position.x),
                 (float)(Double.parseDouble(
        ((org.w3c.dom.Element)nodes.item(i)).getAttribute("y")) - position.y));
}
```

Having said that, the first part calls the base class constructor the same as ever. It's more interesting when we get the list of `Element` nodes with the name `"point"` by calling `getElementsByTagName()` for the `xmlElement` object. These are the nodes holding the coordinates of the points that define the curve. It is important to us here that the method returns the nodes in the `NodeList` object in the sequence in which they were originally added to the XML document. If it didn't, we would have no way to reconstruct the curve. With the data encapsulated in the nodes from the `NodeList` object that is returned, we can reconstruct the `GeneralPath` object that describes the curve. The first point on the curve is always the origin, so the first definition in the path is defined by calling its `moveTo()` method to move to the origin.

Each of the `<point>` nodes contains a point on the path in absolute coordinates. Since we want the curve to be defined relative to the origin, we subtract the coordinates of the start point, `position`, from the corresponding coordinates stored in each node. We use the resulting coordinates to define the end on each line segment by passing them to the `lineTo()` method for the path object.

Creating a Text Element

Recreating an `Element.Text` object from a `<text>` element is the messiest of all. It certainly involves the most code. It's not difficult though. There are just a lot of bits and pieces to take care of.

```
// Text has angle attribute. Content is <color>, <position>, <font>, <string>
// <font> has attributes fontname, fontstyle, pointsize
// fontstyle is "plain", "bold", "italic", or "bold-italic"
// <string> content is text plus <bounds>
public Text(org.w3c.dom.Element xmlElement) {
  super(xmlElement);

  // Get the font details
  org.w3c.dom.NodeList list = xmlElement.getElementsByTagName("font");
```

1091

```
      org.w3c.dom.Element fontElement = (org.w3c.dom.Element)list.item(0);
      String styleStr = fontElement.getAttribute("fontstyle");
      int style = 0;
      if(styleStr.equals("plain"))
        style = Font.PLAIN;
      else if(styleStr.equals("bold"))
        style = Font.BOLD;
      else if(styleStr.equals("italic"))
        style = Font.ITALIC;
      else if(styleStr.equals("bold-italic"))
        style = Font.BOLD + Font.ITALIC;
      else
        assert false;

      font = new Font(fontElement.getAttribute("fontname"), style,
                    Integer.parseInt(fontElement.getAttribute("pointsize")));

      // Get string bounds
      list = xmlElement.getElementsByTagName("bounds");
      org.w3c.dom.Element boundsElement = (org.w3c.dom.Element)list.item(0);

      this.bounds = new java.awt.Rectangle(origin.x, origin.y,
                      Integer.parseInt(boundsElement.getAttribute("width")),
                      Integer.parseInt(boundsElement.getAttribute("height")));

      // Get the string
      list = xmlElement.getElementsByTagName("string");
      org.w3c.dom.Element string = (org.w3c.dom.Element)list.item(0);
      list = string.getChildNodes();

      StringBuffer textStr = new StringBuffer();
      for(int i = 0 ; i<list.getLength() ; i++)
        if(list.item(i).getNodeType()==org.w3c.dom.Node.TEXT_NODE)
          textStr.append(((org.w3c.dom.Text)list.item(i)).getData());

      text = textStr.toString().trim();
  }
```

The attributes of the <string> element define the font. Only the fontstyle attribute needs some analysis since we have to represent the style by an integer constant. This means testing for the possible values for the string and setting the appropriate integer value in style. Of course, we could have stored the style as a numeric value, but that would have been meaningless to a human reader. Making the attribute value a descriptor string makes it completely clear. After obtaining the style code we have an assertion to make sure it actually happened. Of course, since the XML was created by Sketcher, the only reasons why this would assert is if there is an error in the code somewhere, or the XML was written by a different version of Sketcher, or the XML was generated by hand. Of course, errors in the XML due to inconsistencies with the DTD would be caught by the parser and signaled by one or other of our ErrorHandler methods.

Text content for an element can appear distributed among several child <Text> nodes. We accommodate this possibilty by concatenating the data from all the child <Text> nodes that we find, and then trimming any leading and trailing white space from the string before storing it in text.

That's all the code we need. You now need to make sure all the imports are in place for the source files we have modified. In addition to what was already there, the `Element.java` file needs:

```
import org.w3c.dom.Document;
import org.w3c.dom.Attr;
```

The `SketchFrame.java` file needs the following `import` statements added to the original set:

```
import java.nio.ByteBuffer;
import java.nio.channels.FileChannel;
import org.w3c.dom.Node;
import org.w3c.dom.NodeList;
import javax.xml.parsers.DocumentBuilderFactory;
import javax.xml.parsers.DocumentBuilder;
import javax.xml.parsers.ParserConfigurationException;
```

You should also have added the following imports to the `SketchModel.java` file:

```
import javax.swing.JOptionPane;
import javax.xml.parsers.DocumentBuilderFactory;
import javax.xml.parsers.DocumentBuilder;
import javax.xml.parsers.ParserConfigurationException;
import org.w3c.dom.Document;
import org.w3c.dom.DOMImplementation;
import org.w3c.dom.DOMException;
```

If everything compiles, you are ready to try exporting and importing sketches.

Try It Out– Sketches in XML

You can try various combinations of elements to see how they look in XML. Be sure to copy the `sketcher.dtd` file to the directory in which you are storing exported sketches. If you don't, you won't be able to import them since the DTD will not be found. Don't forget you can look at the XML using any text editor and in most browsers. I created the sketch below.

When I exported this I got an XML file with the contents:

```
<?xml version="1.0" encoding="UTF-8"?>
<!DOCTYPE sketch SYSTEM "sketcher.dtd">
<sketch>
 <circle radius="15.0" angle="0.0">
  <color B="255" G="0" R="0"/>
  <position x="153.0" y="109.0"/>
 </circle>
 <circle radius="18.027756377319946" angle="0.0">
  <color B="255" G="0" R="0"/>
  <position x="217.0" y="123.0"/>
 </circle>
 <circle radius="134.61797799699713" angle="0.0">
  <color B="255" G="0" R="0"/>
  <position x="78.0" y="48.0"/>
 </circle>
 <line angle="0.0">
  <color B="0" G="0" R="255"/>
  <position x="191.0" y="158.0"/>
  <endpoint x="162.0" y="194.0"/>
 </line>
 <line angle="0.0">
  <color B="0" G="0" R="255"/>
  <position x="162.0" y="193.0"/>
  <endpoint x="197.0" y="198.0"/>
 </line>
 <line angle="0.0">
  <color B="0" G="255" R="0"/>
  <position x="185.0" y="94.0"/>
  <endpoint x="137.0" y="104.0"/>
 </line>
 <line angle="0.0">
  <color B="0" G="255" R="0"/>
  <position x="246.0" y="110.0"/>
  <endpoint x="285.0" y="166.0"/>
 </line>
 <curve angle="0.0">
  <color B="0" G="0" R="255"/>
  <position x="132.0" y="224.0"/>
  <point x="132.0" y="223.0"/>
  <point x="133.0" y="222.0"/>
  <point x="134.0" y="222.0"/>
  <point x="137.0" y="222.0"/>
  <!-- points cut here for the sake of brevity -->
  <point x="211.0" y="245.0"/>
  <point x="212.0" y="245.0"/>
  <point x="213.0" y="245.0"/>
  <point x="214.0" y="245.0"/>
 </curve>
```

```
<text angle="0.3183694064160789">
 <color B="0" G="255" R="0"/>
 <position x="42.0" y="283.0"/>
 <font fontname="Comic Sans MS" fontstyle="bold-italic" pointsize="18"/>
 <string>
  <bounds width="271" height="21"/>
  The Complete Set! &quot;Try it out&quot;
 </string>
</text>
</sketch>
```

This file is also available as sketchexample.xml in the code download for this book from the Wrox Press web site, http://www.wrox.com. You could try importing it into Sketcher and see if you get the same sketch.

Summary

In this chapter we have discussed how we can use a DOM parser to analyze XML and how JAXP supports the synthesis and modification of XML documents using DOM. The key points we have covered include the following:

❑ An object of type DocumentBuilder encapsulates a DOM parser.

❑ You create an object encapsulating a DOM parser by using a DocumentBuilderFactory object that you obtain by calling the static newInstance() method that is defined in the DocumentFactoryBuilder class.

❑ You can parse an XML document by passing the document as an argument to the parse() method for a DocumentBuilder object.

❑ A DOM parser creates a Document object that encapsulates an entire XML document as a tree of Node objects.

❑ The DOM API defines the methods that a Document object has that enable you to analyze an XML document by navigating through the nodes in the Document object.

❑ The DOM API also defines methods for creating a new XML document encapsulated by a Document object.

❑ When you want to create a new XML document that includes a DTD you should use the createDocument() method for a DOMImplementation object rather than the newDocument() method for a DocumentBuilder object.

Exercises

1. Write a program using DOM that will count the number of occurrences of each element type in an XML document and display them. The document file should be identified by the first command line argument. The program should also accept optional additional command line arguments that are the names of elements. When there are two or more command line arguments, the program should only count and report on the elements identified by the second and subsequent command line arguments.

2. Implement the XML Import capability in Sketcher using SAX rather than DOM.

Keywords

The following keywords are reserved in Java, so you must not use them as names in your programs:

abstract	int
assert	interface
boolean	long
break	native
byte	new
case	package
catch	private
char	protected
class	public
const	return
continue	short
default	static
do	strictfp
double	super
else	switch

extends	synchronized
final	this
finally	throw
float	throws
for	transient
goto	try
if	void
implements	volatile
import	while
instanceof	

You should also not attempt to use the boolean values true and false, or null as names in your programs.

Computer Arithmetic

In the chapters of this book, we have deliberately kept discussion of arithmetic to a minimum. However, it is important overall and fundamental to understanding how some operators work, so I have included a summary of the subject in this appendix. If you feel confident about your math knowledge, this will all be old hat to you and you need read no further. If you find the math parts tough, then this section should show you how easy it really is.

Binary Numbers

First let's consider what we mean when we write a common everyday number such as 321 or 747. Put more precisely we mean:

321 is:
3 x 10 x 10 + 2 x 10 + 1

and 747 is:
7 x 10 x 10 + 4 x 10 + 7

Because it is built around powers of ten, we call this the decimal system (derived from the Latin *decimalis* meaning *of tithes*, which was a tax of 10% – ah, those were the days...).

Representing numbers in this way is very handy for people with ten fingers and ten toes, or creatures with ten of any kind of appendage for that matter. However, your PC is quite unhandy in this context, being built mainly of switches that are either on or off. This is OK for counting up to two, but not spectacular at counting to ten. For this reason your computer represents numbers to base 2 rather than base 10. This is called the **binary** system of counting, analogous to the **bi**cycle (two wheels). With the decimal system, to base 10, the digits used can be from 0 to 9. In the binary system, to base 2, the digits can only be 0 or 1, ideal when you only have on/off switches to represent them. Each digit in the binary system is called a **bit**, being an abbreviation for **b**inary dig**it**. In an exact analogy to our usual base 10 counting, the binary number 1101 is therefore:

1 x 2 x 2 x 2 + 1 x 2 x 2 + 0 x 2 + 1

which amounts to 13 in the decimal system. In the following figure you can see the decimal equivalents of 8-bit binary numbers illustrated.

Binary	Decimal	Binary	Decimal
0000 0000	0	1000 0000	128
0000 0001	1	1000 0001	129
0000 0010	2	1000 0010	130
...	...	...	...
0001 0000	16	1001 0000	144
0001 0001	17	1001 0001	145
...	...	...	...
0111 1100	124	1111 1100	252
0111 1101	125	1111 1101	253
0111 1110	126	1111 1110	254
0111 1111	127	1111 1111	255

Note that using just 7 bits we can represent all the decimal numbers from 0 to 127, which is a total of 2^7, or128 numbers, and using all 8 bits we get 256, or 2^8 numbers. In general, if we have n bits we can represent 2^n positive integers with values from 0 to 2^n-1.

Hexadecimal Numbers

When we get to larger binary numbers, for example:

1111 0101 1011 1001 1110 0001

the notation starts to be a little cumbersome, particularly when you consider that if you apply the same method to work out what this in decimal, it's only 16,103,905, a miserable 8 decimal digits. You can sit more angels on a pinhead than that. Well, as it happens, we have an excellent alternative.

Arithmetic to base 16 is a very convenient option. Each digit can have values from 0 to 15 (the digits from 10 to 15 being represented by the letters A to F as shown in the next figure) and values from 0 to 15 correspond quite nicely with the range of values that four binary digits can represent.

Hexadecimal	Decimal	Binary
0	0	0000
1	1	0001
2	2	0010
...	...	...
9	9	1001
A	10	1010
B	11	1011
C	12	1100
D	13	1101
E	14	1110
F	15	1111

Since a hexadecimal digit corresponds exactly to 4 binary bits, we can represent the binary number above as a hexadecimal number just by taking successive groups of four binary digits starting from the right, and writing the equivalent base 16 digit for each group. The binary number:

1111 0101 1011 1001 1110 0001

will therefore come out as:

F5B9E1

We have six hexadecimal digits corresponding to the six groups of four binary digits. Just to show it all works out with no cheating, we can convert this number directly from hexadecimal to decimal, by again using the analogy with the meaning of a decimal number, as follows:

F5B9E1 is:
15 x 16 x 16 x 16 x 16 x 16 + 5 x 16 x 16 x 16 x 16 + 11 x 16 x 16 x 16 + 9 x 16 x 16 + 14 x16 + 1

This in turn turns out to be:

15,728,640 + 327,680+ 45,056 + 2304 + 224 + 1

which fortunately totals to the same number we got when we converted the equivalent binary number to a decimal value.

Negative Binary Numbers

There is another aspect to binary arithmetic that you need to understand – negative numbers. So far we have assumed everything is positive – the optimist's view if you will – our glass is still half full. But we can't avoid the negative side of life forever – the pessimist's perspective that our glass is already half empty. How do we indicate a negative number? Well, we only have binary digits at our disposal and indeed they contain the solution.

For numbers that we want to have the possibility of negative values (referred to as **signed** numbers) we must first decide on a fixed length (in other words, the number of binary digits) and then designate the leftmost binary digit as a sign bit. We have to fix the length in order to avoid any confusion about which bit is the sign bit as opposed to bits that are digits. A single bit is quite capable of representing the sign of a number because a number can be either positive – corresponding to a sign bit being 0, or negative – indicated by the sign bit being 1.

Of course, we can have some numbers with 8 bits, and some with 16 bits, or whatever, as long as we know what the length is in each case. If the sign bit is 0 the number is positive, and if it is 1 it is negative. This would seem to solve our problem, but not quite. If we add -8 in binary to +12 we would really like to get the answer +4. If we do that simplistically, just putting the sign bit of the positive value to 1 to make it negative, and then doing the arithmetic with conventional carries, it doesn't quite work:

12 in binary is	0000 1100
-8 in binary we suppose is	1000 1000

since +8 is 0000 1000. If we now add these together we get:

$$1001\ 0100$$

This seems to be -20, which is not what we wanted at all. It's definitely not +4, which we know is 0000 0100. Ah, I hear you say, you can't treat a sign just like another digit. But that is just what we do have to do when dealing with computers because, dumb things that they are, they have trouble coping with anything else. So we really need a different representation for negative numbers. Well, we could try subtracting +12 from +4 since the result should be -8:

+4 is	0000 0100
Take away +12	0000 1100
and we get	1111 1000

For each digit from the fourth from the right onwards we had to borrow 1 to do the sum, analogously to our usual decimal method for subtraction. This supposedly is -8, and even though it doesn't look like it, it is. Just try adding it to +12 or +15 in binary and you will see that it works. So what is it? It turns out that the answer is what is called the **two's complement** representation of negative binary numbers.

Now here we are going to demand a little faith on your part and avoid getting into explanations of why it works. We will just show you how the 2's complement form of a negative number can be constructed from a positive value, and that it does work so you can prove it to yourself. Let's return to our previous example where we need the 2's complement representation of -8. We start with +8 in binary:

0000 1000

We now flip each digit – if it is one make it zero, and vice versa:

1111 0111

This is called the 1's complement form, and if we now add 1 to this we will get the 2's complement form:

	1111 0111
Add one to this	0000 0001
and we get:	1111 1000

Now this looks pretty similar to our representation of -8 we got from subtracting +12 from +4. So just to be sure, let's try the original sum of adding -8 to +12:

+12 is	0000 1100
Our version of -8 is	1111 1000
and we get:	0000 0100

So the answer is 4 – magic! It works! The carry propagates through all the leftmost 1's, setting them back to zero. One fell off the end, but we shouldn't worry about that. It's probably the one we borrowed from off the end in the subtraction sum we did to get -8. In fact what is happening is that we are making the assumption that the sign bit, 1 or 0, repeats forever to the left. Try a few examples of your own, you will find it always works quite automatically. The really great thing is, it makes arithmetic very easy (and fast) for your computer.

Floating Point Numbers

We often have to deal with very large numbers: the number of protons in the universe, for example, which needs around 79 decimal digits. Clearly there are lots of situations where we need more than the 10 decimal digits we get from a 4 byte binary number. Equally, there are lots of very small numbers. The amount of time in minutes it takes the typical car salesman to accept your offer on his 1982 Ford LTD (and only covered 380,000 miles...). A mechanism for handling both these kinds of numbers is – as you will have guessed from the title of this section – **floating-point** numbers.

A floating-point representation of a number is a decimal point followed by a fixed number of digits, multiplied by a power of 10 to get the number you want. It's easier to demonstrate than explain, so let's take some examples. The number 365 in normal decimal notation would be written in floating point form as:

```
0.365E03
```

where the E stands for "**exponent**" and is the power of ten that the 0.365 (the mantissa) is multiplied by, to get the required value. That is:

```
0.365 x 10 x 10 x 10
```

which is clearly 365.

Now let's look at a smallish number:

```
.365E-04
```

This is evaluated as .365 x 10^{-4}, which is .0000365 – exactly the time in minutes required by the car salesman to accept your cash.

The number of digits in the mantissa of a floating-point number depends on the type of the floating-point number that you are using. The Java type **float** provides the equivalent of approximately 7 decimal digits, and the type **double** provides around 17 decimal digits. The number of digits is approximate because the mantissa is binary, not decimal, and there's not an exact mapping between binary and decimal digits.

Suppose we have a large number such as 2,134,311,179. How does this look as a floating-point number? Well, as type **float** it looks like:

```
0.2134311E10
```

It's not quite the same. We have lost three low order digits so we have approximated our original value as 2,134,311,000. This is a small price to pay for being able to handle such a vast range of numbers, typically from 10^{-38} to 10^{+38} either positive or negative, as well having an extended representation that goes from a minute 10^{-308} to a mighty 10^{+308}. As you can see, they are called floating-point numbers for the fairly obvious reason that the decimal point "floats" depending on the exponent value.

Aside from the fixed precision limitation in terms of accuracy, there is another aspect you may need to be conscious of. You need to take great care when adding or subtracting numbers of significantly different magnitudes. A simple example will demonstrate the kind of problem that can arise. We can first consider adding .365E-3 to .365E+7. We can write this as a decimal sum:

```
.000365 + 3,650,000
```

This produces the result:

```
3,650,000.000365
```

Which when converted back to floating point becomes:

```
.3650000E+7
```

So we might as well not have bothered. The problem lies directly with the fact that we only carry 7 digits precision. The 7 digits of the larger number are not affected by any of the digits of the smaller number because they are all further to the left. Funnily enough, you must also take care when the numbers are very nearly equal. If you compute the difference between such numbers you may end up with a result that only has one or two digits precision. It is quite easy in such circumstances to end up computing with numbers that are total garbage.

Index of Data types, Keywords and Operators

This is not a comprehensive list of Data types, Keywords and Operators. For the 'Guide to the Index' please refer to Main Index.

Data types

byte, 40, 41, 43
char, 62
double, 44
float, 44
int, 40, 41
long, 40, 41, 42
short, 40, 41, 43

Keywords

abstract, 252
assert, 114
catch, 301
class, 21, 176, 278
extends, 236, 241, 282
final, 176, 180, 276, 277
for, 99
implements, 257
import, 209
interface, 278
native, 231
new, 188
package, 206
private, 24, 213, 244
protected, 213, 245
public, 31, 206, 209, 213, 244, 280
return, 178
static, 31, 176, 180, 184, 226
super, 239, 242, 244

synchronized, 613, 628
this, 182
throw, 315
throws, 300
try, 301
void, 31, 177

Operators

+ (addition), 138
+= (add=), 138
add= (+=), 57
AND (&), 64, 86
assignment (=), 67
complement (~), 64
conditional AND (&&), 86
conditional OR (||), 88
decrement (–), 51, 55
divide= (/=), 57
increment (++), 51, 55
modulus (%), 51, 55
modulus= (%=), 57
multiply= (*=), 57
NOT (!), 89
OR (|), 64, 88
shift left (<<), 68
shift right (>>), 68
shift right fill (>>>), 68
subtract= (-=), 57
XOR (^), 64

Index of Classes, Exceptions, Interfaces and Methods

This is not a comprehensive list of Classes, Exceptions, Interfaces and Methods. For the 'Guide to the Index' please refer to Main Index.

Classes

Methods

Main Index

A Guide to the Indexes

Two separate indexes precede this main index. These are indexed listings of 'Data types, Keywords and Operators' and 'Classes, Exceptions, Interfaces and Methods'. The same information is available in this main index under the individual known names of the methods, classes, keywords, etc. Reversed entries for these are also included e.g. methods listed under the appropriate class.

The ~ character is used to reduce the need to duplicate almost identical entries (e.g. canRead()/~Write () methods means canRead() method/canWrite() method).

The use of XYZ indicates that numerous options exist. The page locators apply to all options (e.g. MAP_XYZ constants includes MAP_COW, MAP_RO and MAP_RW).

1135

Notes